Route 1
Mack, Colorado
A History of the Communities of Mack and New Liberty

Printed and bound in the United States of America

Front endleaf: Threshing scene on the Charles Kiefer farm at Mack in the fall of 1910. *(Photo courtesy of Agnes R. Kiefer)*
Back endleaf: "Horse on the Mountain" scene on the Bookcliffs east of New Liberty. *(Photo by Phyllis Likes)*

Several pictures were used from the book, *"Uintah Railway — The Gilsonite Route,"* by permission of the author Henry J. Bender, Jr. on 14 October 1995, in person in Grand Junction, Colorado.

Publisher's Cataloging-in-Publication

Names: Likes, Homer C., author | Phyllis Maluy Likes, author.
Title: Route 1, Mack, Colorado: a history of the communities of Mack and New Liberty
Description: Second edition. Includes index. | Lilburn, GA : Likes Publishing, 2025. |
Identifiers: LCCN: 2025904809 | ISBN 9798889020820 (hardcover) | ISBN 9798889020837 (ebook)
Subjects: LCSH: Mack (Colorado)—History. | New Liberty (Colorado)—History. | Uintah Railway—History. | Highline Canal (Colorado)—History. | Colorado—Biography.
BISAC: HISTORY / United States / State & Local / West (AK, CA, CO, HI, ID, MT, NV, UT, WY). | HISTORY / United States / 20th Century. | Classification: F782.M5L5 2025 | DDC 978.81703—dc21

ROUTE 1
MACK, COLORADO

A History of the Communities of Mack and New Liberty

BY
HOMER C. LIKES
AND
PHYLLIS C. MALUY LIKES

Likes Publishing
Orem, Utah
1997

We dedicate this history to our parents

Clyde and Retta Appier Likes
Clem and Mary Darrow Maluy

for making the sacrifices and meeting the challenges which made it possible for us to have a good place to grow up and to associate with friends we will never forget. May this story be of special interest to their posterity for many generations to come.

Homer C. and Phyllis C. Maluy Likes

About the Authors

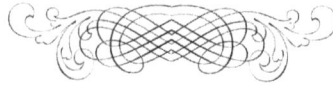

Homer C. and **Phyllis C. Maluy Likes** are children of two of the original homestead families in New Liberty, Colorado.

Homer's parents Clyde William and Retta May Appier Likes acquired sixty acres of land at the March 1918 homestead drawing. The family arrived in Grand Valley August 1918, six weeks after Homer was born. They moved onto the homestead in May 1919.

Phyllis' parents Clem and Mary Darrow Maluy were also awarded a homestead at the drawing. They built a small house on the property, then later built their permanent home there. Clem's father Patrick Maluy also acquired a homestead, which he later sold to his son William "Bill" Maluy.

Homer grew up in New Liberty and graduated from New Liberty School. He attended Fruita Union High School for one year. After entering the Civilian Conservation Corps (CCC) in 1937 he was assigned to Glenwood Springs for eight months. During World War II he worked for Lockheed Aircraft Factory in Burbank, California, then served in the CB's (Naval Construction Battalions) in the Pacific Islands for the remainder of the war.

Phyllis was born in 1930 and spent all of her growing-up years in New Liberty. She graduated from New Liberty School and attended Fruita Union High School. In 1946 she married Homer and moved to the Likes homestead.

Homer and Phyllis bought the Likes farm in 1948. Their two children, Dennis and Retta-Marie were born while living there and both attended New Liberty School. The family moved from New Liberty in January 1958 to Moab, Utah.

Homer pursued his love for mechanics and worked for mining companies. He then worked as a heavy-duty diesel mechanic for construction companies in Moab, Price, and Springville, Utah. He retired in 1981.

While in Moab, Phyllis decided to go back to school. She took a stenographer course on a government MDTA grant at Moab High School. She then attended the College of Eastern Utah in Price. After moving to Orem in 1966, she attended two semesters at Brigham Young University and then worked nine years as a bookkeeper.

Homer and Phyllis have been interested in genealogy for many years, and have done extensive research on both their family lines. Phyllis has been a professional researcher twelve years. Both Homer and Phyllis have served 28 years as family history consultants at the Utah Valley Regional Family History Center in the library on Brigham Young University campus.

Homer and Phyllis have never forgotten their beloved roots. They decided to write an accurate history of New Liberty and its people to show their love and appreciation for their heritage. In 1982, they started researching available records, interviewing people and gathering pictures. In 1991, they decided that New Liberty and Mack were too intertwined to have a history about one without the other. They doubled their efforts, and included Mack in the research and history.

This book is a culmination of 15 years of hard work, joyous research, and pleasant contact with many family, friends, and old acquaintances. It is a work of love and devotion sure to be enjoyed by all who read it.

Homer and Phyllis live in Orem, Utah surrounded by their family. As of this printing they have 14 grandchildren and 14 great-grandchildren.

— Retta-Marie Likes Brandow

A Tribute
to the Pioneers of Mack and New Liberty

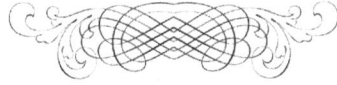

A pioneer prepares the way for other generations by forging onward and pressing forward. The pioneers of Mack and New Liberty represented many countries, states, personalities, and the character it took to accomplish feats.

Nine countries, other than the United States, represented their birth places. They are: Canada, Denmark, Germany, Greece, Ireland, Mexico, Netherlands, Norway, and Sweden. Think of the challenges these people faced to cross the ocean by ship, or a thousand or more miles of country without roads by foot or horse and wagon to a strange and new country. Most knew no English, and some didn't know their destination once they arrived in America. It would be interesting to know why and how their paths led to western Colorado.

There were 34 United States states or territories represented by their birth places: Arkansas, California, Colorado, Delaware, Florida, Illinois, Indiana, Indian Territory, Iowa, Kansas, Kentucky, Maryland, Massachusetts, Michigan, Minnesota, Mississippi, Missouri, Nebraska, Nevada, New Jersey, New Mexico, North Carolina, Ohio, Oklahoma, Oklahoma Territory, Pennsylvania, South Carolina, South Dakota, Tennessee, Texas, Utah, West Virginia, Wisconsin, and Wyoming. Two main interests brought most of them to western Colorado; the Uintah Railway and homesteading. Both interests represented the beginning of endeavors to be accomplished with ingenuity, diligence, and sacrifice.

The main thing these pioneers accomplished was to take all these different personalities, attributes, and aspirations and meld them into two large and wonderful communities full of harmony, love, and cooperation. The security and strength derived from these efforts were felt by all. When we mention personalities, it is said that "it takes all kinds." We believe there was a great diversity of personalities, talents, and strengths, creating a well-balanced unit. We all learned to be tolerant, patient, compassionate, and to laugh at ourselves and others with learning and respect. What a legend! What a heritage! What an example!

Boyd K. Packer said, "Character is being able to carry out a worthy decision after the emotions of making that decision has been made." Our pioneers had the character to first make the decision to come to western Colorado, then face the challenges they met while establishing these communities. They had character and built on that character — for us. We are now the pioneers. Let us build on our heritage for our progeny.

They, the Builders of the Nation

They, the builders of the Nation,
Blazing trails along the way;
Stepping stones for generations
Were their deeds of every day.
Building new and firm foundations,
Pushing on the wild frontier,
Forging onward, ever onward,
Blessed, honored Pioneer!

Service ever was their watch-cry;
Love became their guiding star;
Courage, their unfailing beacon,
Radiating near and far.
Ev'ry day some burden lifted,
Ev'ry day some heart to cheer,
Ev'ry day some hope the brighter,
Blessed, honored Pioneer!

— *Ida R. Alldredge*

We are so thankful for the example, heritage, and opportunities provided us by our pioneering parents, neighbors, and friends. They are everlasting!

— Homer and Phyllis Likes

Table of Contents

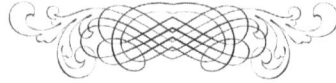

Preface

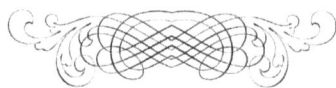

Homer and Phyllis Maluy Likes, authors and compilers of this history, are the "we" in the following preface. We are children of pioneer families who were among the first settlers in the New Liberty community. We began gathering pictures and family information for this history as early as 1982. As we have compiled the following history, it has been particularly gratifying to learn more about our neighbors and friends among whom we lived for so many years.

We have been actively researching and compiling family histories for over 35 years. Since 1969 we have served as Family History Consultants at the Utah Valley Regional Family History Center located in the Harold B. Lee Library on Brigham Young University campus. From that experience we have developed a great love for history, and have learned many methods of finding and compiling information.

In late 1990, a committee in Fruita began to formulate a plan for a Mack/New Liberty reunion to be held in August of 1991. People were encouraged to write family biographies and send them to be published in *The Fruita Times*. That seemed to fit in very well with our desire to write a history of these two communities. As many of you know, the reunion was a rousing success. We had a wonderful time running around trying to get to say a few words to everyone!

We sent and received many letters across the country, and we made many phone calls to various families. We have read, enjoyed, and used the family biographies and pictures submitted to *The Fruita Times* and those sent to us.

At first the idea of combining a history of Mack with that of New Liberty didn't appeal to us. After a time, however, it seemed the natural thing to do, as the two communities interacted a great deal. As you will see, this history covers Mack and the rural area served by Rural Route

#1 from the Mack Post Office, consisting of the Mack Mesa and New Liberty. Thus, our title, "Route 1 Mack, Colorado."

A history of New Liberty, or the "Lower Valley," would not be complete without some background on the Grand Valley Irrigation Project known as the "Highline Canal." It was built and operated for many years under the authority of the United States Bureau of Reclamation. We included some of that history, both in writing and pictures. Enough land records for New Liberty and Mack Mesa were found to identify those who filed on the various plots originally, and to whom they later belonged. We express special gratitude to Bill Klapwyk, Project Manager of the Grand Valley Water User's Association, for allowing us to review and copy parts of the project history, photograph collection, land records, etc., at the Water Users' Office.

We have relied on memory as little as possible by documenting information when documentation was available. We know that each person remembers incidents in history in a different way. We are grateful to all who have contributed in any way to help us compile the information presented in these pages. We are also grateful to those who allowed us to copy a large number of fantastic family photos; many of which are included herein.

We spent countless hours at the Mesa County Public Library in Grand Junction researching obituaries (they have an excellent obituary card index), cemetery indexes, old newspapers, including *The Daily Sentinel*, *The Grand Junction News*, and some items from *The Fruita Times*. We have used information from obituaries going back to as early as 1898. Having *The Daily Sentinel* and other newspapers available on microfilm has provided a tremendous boost in gathering information for this history. We are so grateful for all the modern conveniences available to us!

We were able to search many of the microfilm copies of *The Daily Sentinel* through the Inter-Library Loan system of the Harold B. Lee Library at Brigham Young University near our home. *The Daily Sentinel* research covered the years 1903 through 1905, and 1917 through 1949. A few items were found in later papers. We also searched a couple of Utah newspapers at BYU for some specific items — *The Vernal Express* of Vernal, Utah and *The San Juan Record* of Monticello, Utah.

We researched the 1900, 1910, and 1920 census records for the Mack, Loma, and Fruita districts, plus a few other areas. This research revealed a surprising amount of information about some families. Census records are readily available at our local Family History Center at BYU.

We copied marriage and land records at the County Recorder's office in the Mesa County Court house. We also copied records at Mesa County School District #51 headquarters. Officials there were very helpful in providing information concerning school history.

We are very grateful to May Sanders for compiling and preserving the early school board records for districts #37 and #44, which were placed at our disposal. Those records provided a wealth of information about the Mack and New Liberty Schools. We also had access to the books of the Sorosis Club minutes.

All of the original pioneers are gone, as are many of their descendants. We are happy to bring their lives to light through this history so generations present and future can enjoy and learn from their great examples. In these pages we will attempt to tell at least part of the story of the people of the communities of Mack and New Liberty. We will share some of their hopes, their triumphs, their heartbreaks — to help you appreciate and know them better.

It is our sincere hope that whoever reads this history will enjoy it at least half as much as we have enjoyed compiling it. We have come to better know and appreciate the many people among whom we lived and with whom we associated for so many years. That alone is considerable reward for the time, effort, and expense we have invested in this work.

We sincerely thank those who have helped with the editing: our daughter, Retta-Marie Likes Brandow, our son Dennis Likes, our grandson Jared Likes, and our granddaughter Shauntai Brandow. Our thanks, also, to professional editors Richard Scholle and Shea Cutler.

We would like to sincerely thank Eugene Thomas, Editor and Publisher of *The Fruita Times* at Fruita, Colorado. Gene has shown an intense interest in this project from the start. Gene also comes from pioneer stock, and his expertise, opinions, and contributions, personally and through *The Fruita Times*, have been a great help.

We also give thanks to our son, Dennis Likes our "Resident Computer Engineer," who helped set up much of our equipment and offered abundant advice. Finally, to our grandson, Jared Likes, our "Computer Expert," whose expertise has contributed immensely in scanning and inserting pictures, page layout, editing, computer programs, and technical support in keeping the equipment functioning.

PART ONE

MACK AND NEW LIBERTY HISTORIES

A people who take no pride in the noble achievements of remote ancestors will never achieve anything worthy to be remembered with pride by remote descendants.

—Macaulav

MESA COUNTY, COLORADO

Map courtesy of Carl Landini and the Consolidated Farm Service Agency, 754 Campus Dr., Grand Junction, Colorado

Chapter One

The Beginning

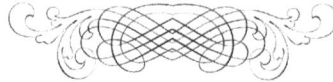

The Grand Valley

According to an article written by William L. Chenowith in *The Historian*, October 1995, "Grand Valley" was named in 1876 by Henry Gannett, a pioneer map maker of the Rocky Mountain region.

The Grand Valley begins near the top of the Continental Divide in a myriad of canyons and valleys which gradually become wider and deeper as they carry the waters of the Grand River and it's tributaries in a westerly direction toward the Pacific Ocean. Near the vicinity of Grand Junction, Colorado, and further west, the river flows through a broad valley several miles wide and extends westward into Utah and beyond, much of it suitable for irrigated farms.

Before white settlers arrived, the valley and surrounding mountains were peopled by members of the Ute Indian Tribe. In 1881 the Utes agreed to vacate the area and allow the white settlers to take over. Many settlers came into the valley almost immediately thereafter and began to establish homes and farms.

Rainfall in the valley is insufficient for growing crops, but the pioneers knew that by diverting water from the Grand River to irrigate the land, it would be possible to overcome that problem.

In 1882 construction began on a thirty-mile-long canal with the settlers furnishing most of the labor and the Travelers' Insurance Company providing financial assistance.

At a point in DeBeque Canyon the water was diverted from the Grand River at water level with nothing more than a simple check built into the stream to direct the water into the canal. The name "Grand River" was officially changed to "Colorado River" 25 July 1921, by an act of Congress.

That early irrigation venture proved unprofitable for the insurance company; they eventually sold to the settlers at a loss. The project proved very successful under local management and served as a model for further irrigation development in the valley. That project eventually became known as "Grand Valley Irrigation Company."

Between 1894 and 1898, the Grand Valley Canal was extended as far west as Mack. The portion bringing irrigation water to Loma and Mack areas became known as the "Kiefer Extension," pioneered by the Kiefer brothers, Joe, Frank and Ben.

Leo Kiefer, nephew of Kiefer brothers, standing at the Kiefer Ditch where it crosses Highway 6 & 50 in the early 1970s. *(Kiefer Collection)*

The Uintah Railway

The Uintah Railway played a major roll in the development of Mack. It is not our intent to write a lengthy and detailed history of the Uintah Railway, since an excellent history was written by Henry E. Bender of San Jose, California, in 1970 as a thesis. That history, *Uintah Railway, The Gilsonite Route,* has become very popular among present and former residents of Mack, Colorado, and vicinity. We recommend it as excellent reading. In 1995 a second edition of Bender's history was published and was soon sold out. We have uncovered some interesting items pertaining to the Uintah Railway not included in Bender's history, and we have decided to include these as part of our history.

In the "Out and About" section of the Sunday, 12 October 1995 issue of the Grand Junction *Daily Sentinel* appeared an article written by columnist Dave Fishell. The article may have been prompted by the second edition of the *Uintah Railway.* We quote in part from the article, as it provides an excellent overview of the comings and goings of the Uintah:

Where busy little Colorado and Utah mining/railroad centers once stood, today you're lucky to see a few crumbling foundations.

Of the miles of twisting, sweeping narrow-gauge tracks that once crossed the Bookcliffs, only a few tire-eating spikes and mounds of the old rail bed remain.

And at Mack, once active with two rail lines and tourists seeking rest in the small, yet elegant hotel, only a handful of the historic structures still stand.

For almost four decades, the far end of Grand Valley was home to one of the most unusual railroads that ever chugged across the rugged West. Built for the sole purpose of hauling a black, lightweight substance called gilsonite, the Uintah Railway covered isolated desert and steep cliffs even the mighty Denver and Rio Grande feared to tackle.

After the first mines opened, huge sacks of gilsonite were hauled by wagon over a skinny, dangerous route across the Bookcliffs and down to a Rio Grande loading area near Fruita

However, the costs of operating the wagons across such difficult terrain were tremendous. Soon, gilsonite company officials were trying to entice the Denver & Rio Grande to build a [branch] line northwest out of the Grand Valley, up and over the Bookcliffs to the mining settlements of Dragon and [later] Watson.

Afraid of owning a railroad that only had one source of business, and, no doubt afraid of the mighty cliffs as well, the Rio Grande said no.

Only one option was left for the gilsonite operators ... build a railroad of their own. In 1902 a tiny company town named after an early-day mining company officer [John M. Mack] was surveyed just a few miles east of the Utah border and right next to the existing Rio Grande main line. And for the next 37 years, Mack would not only be the base for the Uintah Railway, but for hundreds of employees who worked the mines, hauled the loads and kept up the railroad as well ...

Horse-drawn freight wagons prepare to leave Dragon for Vernal about 1903.
(*McCoy collection*)

The Rainbow Mine (above and below) was located four miles southwest of Watson, the last town on the line. A 4.1-mile railway branch called Rainbow Junction was built about two-thirds of a mile from Watson to accommodate this mine. The town of Rainbow, with two rows of small houses, was built to house the miners. Rainbow was to become the main supplier of gilsonite for the Uintah. *(McCoy Collection)*

Uintah Railway Office Staff (above) in front of the office at Mack in the 1920s. Standing left to right: Accountant W. R. Lockett, Claim Agent Frank A. Kennedy, Engineer and Purchasing Agent F. G. Morss, Chief Dispatcher J. L. Booth, Superintendent Walter L. Rader, Assistant Dispatcher H. M. Phillips, and General Manager L. C. Sprague. Seated on bench: Eunice Newton, Hotel Superintendent Maud Levi, Freida Grieser, and Assistant Secretary & Treasurer Fred Baird. Eight railroaders, plus a little one, (below) gathered by one of the Uintah Railway engines. Picture was taken about 1910. (*Above: Baird Family Collection, courtesy of Esther Baird Sproule; below: McCoy Collection*)

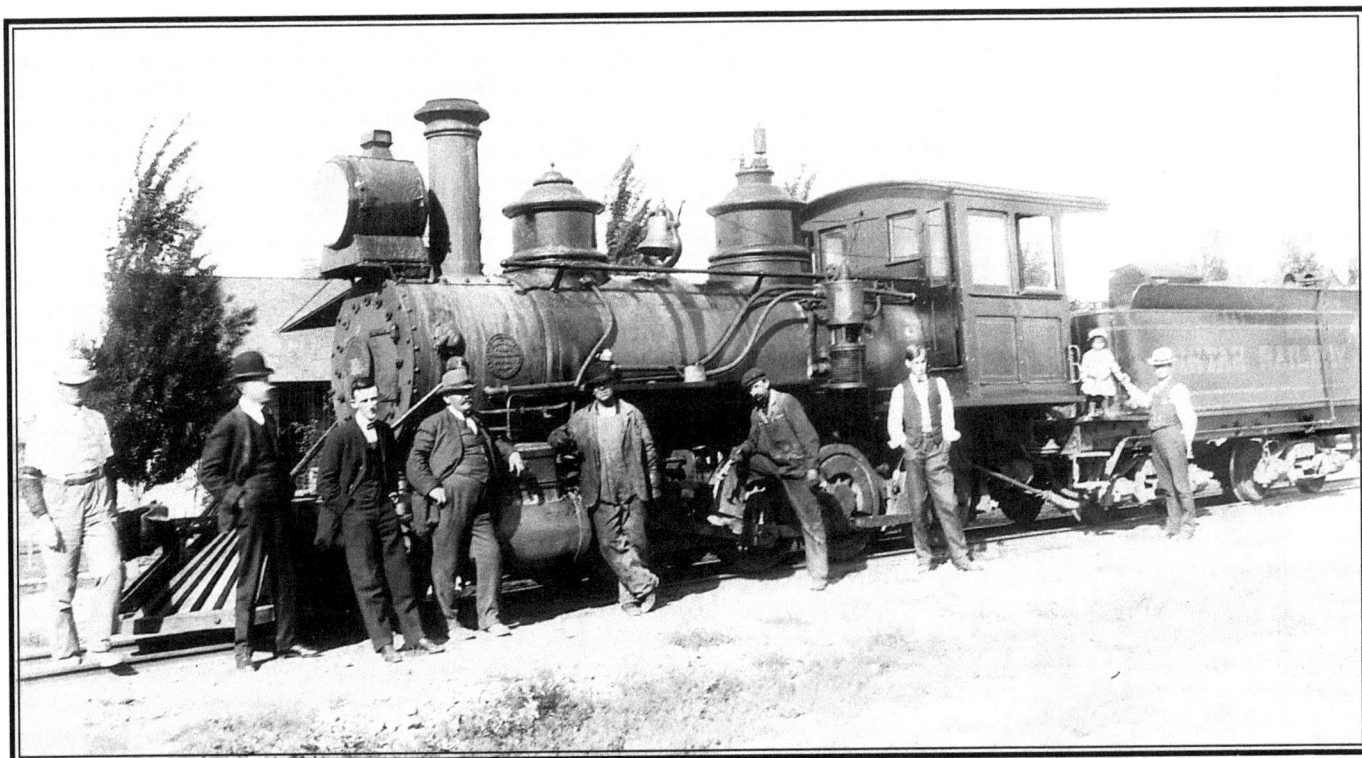

4

Above: Engine #11 at the Mack Depot with water car, gondola, and passenger/mail cars. The Mack Hotel is in the background. Passengers are standing in front of the depot. Below: Repairmen at the Atchee roundhouse posing with Engine Number Ten. The engine is also displayed with the Lyman story submerged in mud under the destroyed trestle at Mile Post 2, west of Mack. (*Both photos are courtesy of the McCoy Collection*)

In 1903, following the announcement of the opening of the gilsonite fields and the expected transporting of the product to the Grand Valley, the town of Grand Junction began looking forward to reaping the many benefits of the new business. Articles in the Grand Junction newspapers of that period reflected a fair amount of speculation going on at the time. Following is an article that appeared in *The Daily Sentinel* of 18 June 1903:

Work on the new road from Fruita to the asphaltum beds west of that place is progressing quite rapidly, and in a short time 200 teams and over 500 men will be working at the mines and hauling to the railroad. It has not been fully decided whether the gilsonite will be hauled to Fruita or to Crevasse, a side track seven miles west of that place [Fruita], but as soon as the road can be finished, work will begin in earnest.

At present there are 150 men and 50 teams employed. A road suitable for traction engines will be built part of the way and these machines will be used over the heaviest grades, and trains of several wagons will be hauled.

The work is being done by a big St. Louis and Salt Lake concern that has a contract for paving the streets of St. Louis†. The contract calls for the work to be finished by June of next year, in time for the opening of the World's Fair. All the supplies for the mines are being purchased in Fruita. After the St. Louis contract is finished the company will continue shipping to the other large cities of the country and expects to put a great deal of money into circulation in the lower valley. The beds are practically inexhaustible. Young Joseph Leiter, the famous Chicago 'Wheat King,' is an interested party.

The Daily Sentinel news article of 23 July 1903 told a different story:

A gentleman up from Fruita today states that he was told yesterday upon almost unmistakable authority that the Rio Grande would have six hundred teams at Crevasse shortly to begin the construction of a road into the asphaltum fields, ninety miles from that point ...

The following day, 24 July 1903, came this message via *The Daily Sentinel*:

Work on Crevasse Branch to begin at once ... Last Saturday this paper made the very important announcement that the Rio Grande [rail]road would construct a branch road from Crevasse to the asphaltum fields in the Uintah reservation ... Grand Junction wants to be up and doing to secure in advance the trade of that section, which will be brought to it's very doors by the building of that road ...

Through 1904 and 1905 *The Daily Sentinel* was silent regarding the construction of the new road, however, the *Grand Junction News* of 8 October 1904 had this to say:

The Uintah Railroad, which is being constructed along the Book Cliffs from Mack, Colorado, a station on the Rio Grande Railroad, to tap the extensive gilsonite deposits of the White River country, will have for it's terminus at the present a station called Dragon at the head of Evacuation Creek. Dragon is fifty-five miles southeast of Vernal and a first class wagon road will be constructed between these two points.

Within the past few days amended articles of incorporation of the Uintah Railway Company have been filed with the County Clerk, which broadens the scope and territory of this line which was at first simply intended to tap the great gilsonite beds in the Uintah Indian Reservation. But it's scope of usefulness will now have to be enlarged and it will become an important feeder to the Rio Grande system, and incidentally open up a vast territory, which is now partially settled, to the merchants of Grand Junction.

The purpose of the amended articles of incorporation is to extend this railroad to Vernal and Fort Duchesne and thus give these towns immediate railway connection and rapid transit for their people and products for which they must find a market. Only fifty miles more of this road to reach Vernal and Fort Duchesne, and then the traffic which has been going on between Price, Utah, and these points over 150 miles of stage road, will be transferred to the Uintah Railroad. Steps have already been taken to change the mail route to go via this road.

†The gilsonite was being used to pave the streets.

It is needless to say that this tapping of the rich and practically virgin territory with the railroad will mean much in Grand Junction. A large amount of this trade must necessarily come to our young city, if our merchants are wise enough to prepare to meet the people in the spirit of fairness and cordiality. Only a few months ago our Chamber of Commerce was speculating upon the feasibility of an extended line of railway to the north and reaching the new Moffat road on it's way westward. Now behold the railroad is already built and what are we going to do with it. Make the very best we can of it, the Sun hopes ...

The Uintah had the distinction of being the "steepest and crookedest" railroad built anywhere without utilizing the aid of cogs for traction, as used on other mountain railroads. However, special engines were required to provide the necessary power and traction for the steep grades and sharp curves.

Maintenance of the roadbed was not without problems; occasionally deep snow, snow slides, landslides and flash floods would shut the trains down for varied periods of time. A few miles above Atchee was one slide area that was particularly troublesome. Several times through the years the earth moved in that spot and caused delays in traffic. In 1929 a major slide on that site caused a shut-down that lasted for over seven weeks.

In addition to its primary purpose of hauling gilsonite, the Uintah was also to serve as means of transportation for passengers and mail, and freight service for farmers and stockmen. Post offices and hotels were established at Mack, Carbonera, Atchee, Watson, and the end of the line at Dragon. As was mentioned previously, a horse-drawn stage service from Dragon to Vernal provided transportation for freight, mail and passengers, thus establishing an important link to the Uintah Basin. For a time gasoline-powered vehicles were used on the route in an attempt to speed up the operation, but because of regular break-downs, much was left to be desired.

The Uintah was also used in many ways to accommodate people's needs: for business, touring, or transportation to shop and visit family and friends in Grand Valley; for U. S. Mail; and as freight service for farmers and stockmen. Above, the Uintah used the tracks for a special employee excursion on the 4th of July. (*McCoy Collection*)

(Above) Looking toward Atchee is a view of four levels of tracks showing the "steepness and crookedness" of the railway. Also, the old wagon road, that gilsonite was hauled on by horse and wagon to Fruita or Crevasse, is still visible in the bottom of the canyon. (Below) A train with two cars on a 7.5% grade near Shale siding. (*McCoy Collection*)

(Above) a train on 5% grade above Deer Run Siding (M.P. 36). Notice the two engines; since it is quite a long, heavy load, one engine is at the center of the train. (Below) a two-engine train heading into Moro Castle on 7.5% grade. Calls to the memory "she'll be coming around the mountain when she comes!" *(McCoy Collection)*

Snow was always a problem and a threat. (Above) a locomotive, pushing the snow plow, is headed back home to Atchee after clearing the tracks. (Below) the locomotive and plow on the siding at the top of Baxter Pass. (*McCoy Collection*)

Dragon-Green River-Vernal Stage Line

The Dragon-Green River-Vernal Stage Line began at Dragon and crossed the White River, the badlands or "Devil's Playground," and finally crossed the Green River on a ferry before reaching Vernal. A picture of a stage coach in the mud along the Green River (above) and a picture of the Green River ferry (below) are both taken at Alhandra. *(McCoy Collection)*

An interesting story was discovered during the course of our research that will help illustrate a type of service provided by the Uintah. In August 1907 The Latter-day Saints (Mormons) had completed a new tabernacle at Vernal, Utah†, and Joseph F. Smith, then the presiding authority, was scheduled to dedicate the new building. To get President Smith and his party to Vernal from Salt Lake City without having to travel the west to east distance by horse and buggy, the party rode the D&RG RR to Mack, then the Uintah to Dragon, finally, from there to Vernal by stage.

In November 1911, the rail line was completed from Dragon farther north and west to Watson, Utah, where another post office and hotel were established. As noted in a previous article, a proposal to extend the railroad as far as Vernal was carefully considered, but the idea was eventually abandoned.

The Uintah Railway prospered for many years, but in the late 1930s began to experience financial problems which led to the company filing for permission to abandon in August 1938.

In *The Daily Sentinel* of 17 May 1939 appeared the following nostalgic review of the "Last Train Ride," written by Preston Walker, Editor of *The Daily Sentinel* ... We have included it here in it's entirety, as it tells the story so well.

> The iron horses are idle, ghost towns dot the once-prosperous rail line, and Indians jog down mountain trails on their horses, once more unmolested by the steam monster that belches smoke and fire. The Uintah Railway is no more.
>
> Tuesday [16 May 1939] a mixed train pulled out of Mack on it's last run over one of the most unique rail lines in the world. Chugging, tugging and pulling over the famous Baxter pass, the train visited each small town on the route, picking up furniture and residents. Returning to Mack yesterday evening, it left behind ghost towns and the many memories of faithful and hazardous service.

†This tabernacle will be dedicated as a temple November 2-4, 1997. This is the first existing building to be converted for us as a temple.

> Boiler fires were out, employees of 25 years must seek new jobs; livestock cars, ore cars, coal cars, tank cars and box cars stand idly on the tracks. Behind, connected now with the outside world by only horse trails, are the towns of Dragon, Watson, roadside stations along the line, and the once prosperous terminal of Atchee, now all but deserted.
>
> So ends the pioneering railroad saga that extended over more than a quarter of a century. Next chapter will be the sale of all the holdings of the railroad. This is expected within a few weeks. In all probability the track will be torn up and the rolling stock sold for salvage.
>
> When yesterday's 'last train' rolled out of Mack, there were some 20 persons aboard, mainly those interested in railroading or those interested in making the last trip on the scenic road, built in 1905 and operating since that time.
>
> One could not help but wonder what the feelings of the rail employees were as the train left. Also we wondered what an Indian brave and his squaw thought as we passed them on the road. Did they know this was the train's last trip? Did they think back to the time the iron monster continued to push their ancestors westward? Did they think (as we thought) 'we are still here, the train is gone.'
>
> Engineer Roy Eno, for 20 years an employee of the Uintah, guided the train on it's last run. At every stop, Engineer Eno, as he has done regularly for more than a decade, stepped from his cab and carefully oiled the intricate parts of the Mallay No. 50, one of the few engines of it's type in the world.
>
> Engineer Eno had little to say regarding this last run, but there was no difficulty in ascertaining that not only to him, but all members of the train crew, the day was a sad one. Not because it meant their jobs, but because yesterday's run meant the end of a great railroad and industrial story — a story of the true west.
>
> Pulling out of Mack on schedule, the train of one coach, a box car, and two flat cars, climbed to the top of Baxter pass. It is six miles from Atchee to the top of the pass and in that six miles the train climbs over 2,000 feet with many of the grades 7 1/2 percent and the curves more than 60 degrees.
>
> At Wendella, on the western side of the pass, water cars, the last to be carried westward, were filled and taken to Dragon and

SPECIAL

Service on All Freight and Passenger Business Between
Mack, Colo., and Watson, Utah, at All Times, Via

The Uintah Railway

Mack, Colorado

TRAIN SCHEDULES IN EFFECT

Passenger and freight service Mondays, Wednesdays and
Fridays out of Mack. Tuesdays, Thursdays and Saturdays out
of Watson.

Train leaves Mack at 11:30 a. m.; arrives
at Watson 5:30 p. m.

Train leaves Watson at 9:15 a. m.; arrives
at Mack at 3:15 p. m.

For Further Information Phone Fruita 05J2

This ad appeared in *The Daily Sentinel* on 5 Mar 1937. Since service had been on a daily basis for
years, it is apparent they were already cutting back.

13

Watson to furnish the last water supply for those two cities.

Stopping and turning at Watson, end of the line, the train took on a carload of furniture consigned to Grand Junction. While waiting at this last point, passengers learned that what few residents were left planned on being gone within a few days. Most had resided at this western terminal for 15 to 20 years.

As the train pulled out of this point, headed for Mack, the Watson telegraph operator stepped on the rear platform, his telegraph key in his hand, his office closed for good.

Stopping on the return trip at each town and station, baggage was taken on, passengers hunted seats and left behind them towns boarded up, post offices empty for all time to come. We think the general feeling on the train was 'we have just completed one more funeral.'

As the little train roared along the main highway some three miles west of Mack, many persons stopped along the road to take pictures of the last run. All of Mack was gathered as the train pulled into its home station, where it will stay.

Crew members of the last run, all veterans, were Roy Eno, engineer; George Lehman, fireman; and John Beaslin, conductor, J. [sic] V. Earp , superintendent, also made the trip and did much toward making this run an interesting and delightful one so far as the passengers were concerned.

The Uintah Railway has been the only road of it's kind in the world. During the first years of operation, Shay engines, built in the Atchee shops, were used. These remarkable engines have a gear drive on one side only, but were able to climb the stiff grades.

Later it was discovered that bigger engines would be needed, and as a result the Baldwin Manufacturing company sent engineers here to develop a new type narrow gauge engine that would negotiate the sharp curves and at the same time pull more of a load. As a result the Mallay engines were purchased at the cost of $52,000 each. It was one of these that pulled yesterday's train.

These engines hinge in the middle, one set of drivers at many times going in the opposite direction from the other. Also, the water tanks are on the sides, insuring more weight on the drive wheels and therefore more traction. Also increasing traction is a sand hopper on the front of the locomotive. Sand is blown under

the wheels on sharp, steep grades and curves to keep the eight-foot drivers from slipping. The only other engines of this type in the world are several in operation at a South American mine.

Many memories are recalled during the history of the Uintah. Engineer Baxter, for whom Baxter Pass is named, surveyed the rail line and accomplished what was known throughout the world as an outstanding feat ... Charles D. Vail, now head of the state highway department, was civil engineer on the line for a time ... Jack Dempsey, long before he gained fame, but at the time he started boxing, was a section hand during its construction ... And so on down the line.

And so we say 'adios' to what now will be western history. Time marches on, and perhaps some day a highway will run over this beautiful pass, but we will shed a tear for the passing of a great project, leaving in it's wake towns and people that will soon be only memories ... "

Mrs. J. L. Booth wrote an account of the "Last Trip" in the Mack news items. She included, in addition to those named in Walker's story, the names of other people who also made the last run. They were: Mrs. George Komatas and children, Mrs. Scop Keffalos and Miss Mildred Hogsett (teacher at the Mack school). Mrs. Booth also mentioned that General Manager McClain and Superintendent E. V. Earp would be detained for a time "until the company's property is disposed of."

And families who lived in Mack had begun to move to new locations:

The J. L. Booth family have moved to their farm east of Mack ... Mr. and Mrs. Glen Griffin and daughter, Jane, will depart next week for San Diego, California; Mr. and Mrs. E. C. Dunlap and son, Harold, will move to Grand Junction. The H. G. Spencer family and Mr. and Mrs. George Lehman have taken up residence in Grand Junction ... etc.

Arthur T. Herr and Meyer Goldstein of Denver bought the salvage rights to the entire system and they, in turn, contracted the actual dismantling to Moore Construction Company of Price, Utah. Moore Construction hired several of the former Uintah employees to assist with the wrecking job, providing employment for them for most of another year.

During 1939 the equipment and rails were sold to various mining and transportation interests; the homes and warehouses were sold to individuals and were torn down or moved away. The cross ties from the roadbed became building material for many farm buildings in the area; one could buy cross ties "by the mile." The ties can still be seen in use as fence posts, cribbing, bridge timbers, etc.

Notice of final dissolution of the company was filed 1 November 1939. However, news of the loading out of locomotives and other equipment continued on into the early part of 1940.

The final note appeared in the Mack news items written by Mrs. W. J. Cox on 28 April 1940:

"The Uintah is dismantling it's last locomotive ... The boiler will be shipped to Denver and the remainder will be cut up for scrap."

(Above) Engine #21 during the scrapping operations in 1939. (Below) business car B-1, also used as a tourist coach, is shown on blocks in the bone yard. It belonged to the D&RG RR before the Uintah Railway obtained it. *(McCoy Collection)*

The demise of the railroad was a sad time for many people whose homes and means of income had been tied to the railroad operation for many years. Carbonera, Atchee, Dragon and Watson became "ghost towns." One must look carefully these days to see any remains of these former thriving mining/railroad towns where many people once lived and worked. At Atchee one can see remnants of the shop building and some evidences of the dwellings and other buildings. The shop building played a very important part in the Uintah operation. There they built special cars, and modified and maintained the locomotives and all the rolling equipment.

At present a sign posted at the town site of Atchee directs visitors to stay on the road or risk being prosecuted for trespassing! The latest insulting deed — the county road is closed illegally by locked gate at some distance on either side of Baxter Pass. Quite different from the days when Tom Kelley and later, the Youngs, were in residence! Citizens could and should eliminate that problem!

Mack, the end of the wrecking job — virtually all the rails and equipment belonging to the Uintah Railway are gone. *(Photo courtesy of the Booth family collection; Uintah Railway book by permission of Henry E. Bender Jr.)*

For a few years after the railroad was abandoned the trestle across the wash immediately west of Atchee was used by auto traffic, but it became unsafe and was bypassed. Until recently shreds of the old trestle were still hanging. In many areas the roadbed once used by the railroad is barely evident. But of course, most of that grade was soon widened and made into a road for auto traffic. After more than fifty-five years, one can still see remnants of cross-ties, cinders, an occasional spike, bolt, or tie-plate in areas where the roadbed is not used for autos.

For a time, gilsonite was trucked over the widened railroad grade to Mack. **Cecil Monger,** of Mack, managed the trucking operation for awhile. During that time one driver lost his truck when it left the grade a short distance below the south summit of Baxter Pass. As far as we know, the remains of that truck are still lying in the brush below.

It appears an attempt to revive the hauling of gilsonite over Baxter Pass was made in 1946. *The Daily Sentinel* published an article 17 April 1946 noting that:

Trucks owned by V. L. Covington began hauling Gilsonite over Baxter Pass to Mack. The road required much work to become passable, still needs a lot of work. Covington expects to use five or more trucks on the haul.

In the 1950s a pipeline was constructed to provide a totally different means of shipping the gilsonite from the mines to a new refinery just west of Fruita. The gilsonite was mined hydraulically (with high-pressure water jets), and after passing through a pulverizing process it was pumped in slurry form through a pipeline to the summit of Baxter Pass, and from there it flowed by gravity the remainder of the distance through the pipeline to the refinery. There the gilsonite was refined into coke, gasoline, diesel fuel, and other petroleum products. The refinery was a thriving business for several years, but it eventually evolved into another type of operation. Gilsonite is still being mined, but transportation is nothing like it used to be and the ore is not shipped to Mack or Fruita.

GHOST TOWNS ON THE OLD UINTAH RAILWAY LINE

On the following pages are pictures of thriving towns and stations along the Uintah Railway that became ghost towns within a short time after the closing of the railway in 1939.

Opposite page: (Bottom) Lake McAndrews was on the west side of Baxter Pass, and was the source of ice for the Uintah Railway system and Mack. Shown is a passenger train, section houses (Paul & Betty Garber lived in one when first married), and storage ice house on the lake. The ice house was later moved to Mack. *(McCoy Collection)*

Atchee (above) is located 28.3 miles northwest of Mack and was the maintenance headquarters for the Uintah Railway. This was taken in 1905 before the store, hotel, schoolhouse, more homes and car shop were built. Shown is the water tank, company houses, and engine house where they repaired and remodeled the locomotives. (McCoy Collection) (Middle) Atchee many years later, the schoolhouse is directly above the row of trees. *(Used from the Historian issued with the Fruita Times)*

Carbonera town and coal mine, 20 miles northwest of Mack, supplied coal for Mack and everyone and everything on the Uintah Line. This picture was taken in 1936 or 1937. (Carbonera in Spanish means coal mine.) *(McCoy Collection)*

Watson was the end of the Uintah line, 62.7 miles northwest of Mack, and located in Utah. The big dark building with the large canopy is the warehouse. All freight for Vernal was unloaded from the Uintah box cars at this warehouse and transferred to horse drawn freight wagons. Just behind the warehouse is the hotel. Notice the laundry hanging on the clotheslines, and the saddled horse standing on the point of the mountain on the right. *(McCoy Collection)*

Dragon was 1.3 miles from the Dragon mine and 53.3 miles northwest of Mack, located just inside the Utah State line. The Uintah Railway depot is to the left and the freight warehouse toward the right, with stables and freight wagons behind it. Lumber for the hotel is in the foreground. *(McCoy Collection)*

18

Chapter Two

Mack

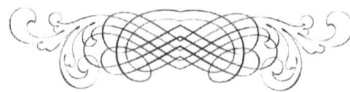

(Above) A panorama of Mack taken by Judge Kennedy about 1910 from the hill south of town. Notice the curvature of the earth. L-R: Train cars, water tower, Hughes' home in front, company houses, Uintah Office, Uintah Hotel, Mack Mercantile with the first schoolhouse behind it.

(Below) A panorama of Mack taken by Judge Kennedy about 1908 from the water tank west of town. L-R: Unknown house, four company houses, (the Homer Marshall Phillips family lived in the first house on the left and the Fred Cole family lived in the corner house on the fight); Uintah Office Building; Uintah Hotel; between the Uintah Railway and the D&RG Railroad tracks is the depot; and far right, Hughes' home, where Leo Kiefer was born in 1908. The "wye" of the railroad tracks is in the foreground, notice a plume of smoke on the horizon from an approaching train. *(Photos courtesy of Agnes Kiefer)*

In 1904, the Barber Asphalt Company founded the town of Mack as the headquarters for the Uintah Railway. Located a little over a mile east of a siding on the Rio Grande Railroad called Crevass, Mack became the transfer point of gilsonite from the Uintah to the Rio Grande. Local men transferred the 200-pound sacks of ore from the Uintah cars to the Denver & Rio Grande cars. A "Transfer Gang" of brawny individuals worked for the entire life of the railroad to accomplish that task. Besides several men who lived in Mack, a few of the New Liberty settlers worked occasionally on that job: Charles Cavendish, Clarence Deacon, John Morrow, Bob Sanders, Ted Wassenberg, Tony Overbye and Dean Waters. Thus, the Uintah had the work force they needed and the settlers had a much needed pay check to supplement their farm income.

Mack eventually became home to a population of approximately 200, with a post office, grocery stores, lumber store, and other places of business. The Uintah Hotel at Mack became a popular stopover for travelers on both the Uintah and the Rio Grande Railroads, and also for motorists who later were brave enough to venture across the *barren waste* on the *Pikes Peak Coast to Coast Highway* which ran through Mack.

No domestic water supply was available locally to supply Mack with water so the Uintah Railway used tank cars to haul water from Columbine (on the north slope of Baxter Pass) to Mack. At Mack they

This panorama of Mack taken from the south in 1906 by Judge Kennedy. From the left: Water tank warehouse (that was moved over by the Mack Mercantile building and used as the first Mack Schoolhouse), unknown house, Uintah company houses, Uintah Office, D&RGW Railroad Depot, Uintah Hotel, Mack Mercantile. *(Photo courtesy of Erma Slaugh Armstrong)*

pumped the water from the tank cars into a high, elevated wooden tank. The height of the tank made it possible to provide enough gravity force so water under pressure flowed through a piping system to homes, offices and stores. A building at the base of the water tower housed a boiler and steam engine that powered the pump and a generator to provide electricity for the town. Sometime in the 1920s the wooden tank collapsed, endangering the life of **Jack Eagan**, the power plant operator at the time. A new steel water tank and pump house north of the highway soon replaced the wooden one.

The wooden water tower was located west and a little south from the hotel. We expected to find the story of the collapse of the tower as we reviewed *The Daily Sentinel* through the years, but we missed it, or there was no story published. Perhaps if we had a more definite date of its collapse, there would have been more of a chance to find a story. Betty Booth Garber tells us that she and Hazel Eagan witnessed the collapse from the doorway of the Eagan home. It appears likely the event occurred around 1926 or 1927.

Mack became a trade center for the homesteaders who settled to the north. They could send or receive shipments of freight and parcel post, and buy groceries, hardware and other supplies. Farmers were also able to exchange some of their produce for cash or groceries, and dry goods to supplement their home needs.

Mack is still on the map but has little resemblance to the time before 1939 when the railroad closed down. Part of the Uintah Hotel is still standing and is readily recognizable by those who remember its heyday. The grounds surrounding the hotel are nothing like they were in the 20s and 30s, when **Chris Pappas** was the caretaker. A few businesses and dwellings are still in town, plus a post office built in more recent years, which is its third location.

(Above) The Mack Uintah Hotel soon after it was built by the Uintah Railway Company, probably spring of 1906. The hotel cost $17,000 to build and $4,500 to furnish, and was the pride of the Uintah Railway and Mack. Travelers from across the nation stayed at the hotel. *(Photo courtesy of James McCoy)*

(Below) A closeup of the Uintah Hotel in 1906. The family, father, mother, and five children, standing out in front of the hotel is probably the manager and his family. It must be Sunday as everyone is dressed up. It is such a peaceful setting with the couple strolling down the sidewalk. There was undoubtedly people and activity around the depot and hotel most of the time. Notice the wire mesh for the vines to grow on in front of the hotel. The depot has a train parked in front. The light post below looks like an Indian head with a hat on it. *(Photo courtesy Erma Slaugh Armstrong)*

(Above) Looking east the Mack Hotel was caught in a beautiful winter wonderland scene in the late 20's. The Mack Mercantile can be seen at the end of the sidewalk. (*Uintah Railway Book, page 118, by permission of Henry Bender Jr.*)

(Below) The Mack Hotel in the 30's in early spring. The white posts and boards in the front is a turnstile. A turnstile is a post with revolving horizontal bars placed in an entrance to allow the passage of persons one at a time. *(Photo courtesy of Betty Booth Garber.)*

The dining room and lounge are an example of the hotel's warm and inviting western-style decor. The hotel was known for its good food, especially the Sunday chicken dinner, plus their clean and comfortable rooms. *(Both photos courtesy of Jim McCoy)* *(The Chicken Dinner Ad was taken from the April 8, 1922 issue of The Daily Sentinel)*

(Right) The Uintah Railway Office after a snow storm. The Uintah Office was built in 1904/5 and was used as such until the Uintah Railway closed down in 1939. *(Kennedy photo, Booth/Garber Collection)*

(Middle) The Leonard Slaugh family bought the Uintah Office in 1940 and lived there until 1952. The photo was taken during that time. Frank A. "Judge" Kennedy rented an upstairs apartment from the Slaughs. On 13 Jan 1944 he died from asphyxiation when he somehow started a fire in his bedding. Judge Kennedy worked as superintendent, claims agent, and auditor for the Uintah Railway before it closed down in 1939. He was also a professional photographer, and took hundreds of pictures of the railway and Mack. Many of his pictures are included in this book. *(Photo courtesy Erma Slaugh Armstrong)*

(Left) The Uintah Office burned down the afternoon of 1 April 1960, apparently from a defective flue as the fire started in the roof. It had been used as a rock shop and storage of household goods. The loss was estimated at $50,000, and there was no insurance. An era was gone up in smoke, and a great loss was felt by the town folk. *(Photo courtesy Uintah Railway Book, page 195, by permission of author, Henry A. Bender, Jr.)*

The Mack D&RGW Railroad Depot, in front of the Uintah Office and Hotel panorama taken in 1908. View shows the south side of the depot that faced the D&RGW Railroad tracks where freight was loaded and passengers boarded. Photo taken from the Hughes home. *(Photo by Judge F. A. Kennedy, courtesy of James the McCoy)*

(Center Left) A unique motor car #31 is parked in front of the depot at Mack on the Uintah Railway tracks. Behind the depot a freight train is parked on the D&RG RR tracks. (Left) The Mack Depot at a quiet time in the late 30s. The lone person standing beside the depot is unidentified. (Center Right) People pictured are being light-hearted while waiting for the train at the Mack Depot. A woman and a man have exchanged bonnet and hat for a funny flair as F. A. Kennedy took the picture. The depot was one of the main places of interest in the small town; people from across the nation would stop there for different reasons. *(All three photos by Judge F. A. Kennedy, courtesy of James the McCoy)*

(Above) Uintah Railway crew transferring sacks of gilsonite, weighing up to 225 pounds each, from the Uintah Railway flat cars to the D&RG Railroad boxcars at the Mack Station. Looking east, visible in the upper left is the wooden water tank referred to on page 19. Also visible at the top of the picture is the Mack Depot.

(Below) Looking north is the depot in 1937, before the closing of the Uintah Railway. The trees in the background are on the south side of the hotel. The Uintah Railway track ended just to the right of the passenger/mail car in the background. *(Both photos courtesy the Uintah Railway book by permission of author, Henry E. Bender, Jr.)*

(Above) This photo shows the Mack Mercantile and the Independent Lumber Co. combined with W. H. Cox standing in front. The *Mack Mercantile* was built about 1904 by Carl Osborn, a Fruita grocer, who hired Charlie Kiefer to manage it. Charlie managed it until 1905, when he went to Indiana. Osborn contacted him in 1908 and asked him to again take over management of the store. By 1910 W. H. Cox was the manager, and he managed it sporadically until 1916. We have no records showing when Carl Osborn sold it, but on 24 September 1925, W. H. Cox purchased the store from W. E. Roberson and E. L. Smith. On 10 August 1928, Cox made a deal with Biggs and Kurtz Co. to trade the store for some orchard land on the Redlands. On February 1932, Cox bought the store back. In October 1936 he disposed of all his stock in the Mack Mercantile, and on 24 July 1937, closed the store for good. *The Independent Lumber Company:* Apparently the store opened in 1918 and occupied the same property as the Mack Mercantile Company. Sometime in the late 1920s a new building was built across the tracks to the south to house the Independent Lumber Company. Mack items in *The Daily Sentinel* of 14 February 1923 noted that Clem Miller succeeded R. J. Mulvaney as the local manager of the Independent Lumber Co. of Mack. Miller moved to DeBeque and Mack Talley managed the place until the business was moved to Fruita in the 1930s. *(Photo courtesy of Betty Booth Garber)*

(Above) Pack burros in front of Mack Mercantile, in 1905. *(Photo courtesy of Erma Slaugh Armstrong)*

(Right) Pack burros about 1908 in back of Mack Mercantile; the person in the center is Charlie Kiefer, store manager. *(Photo courtesy of Agnes Kiefer)*

Mack Cafe was owned by Cecil Monger about 1950. The picture was taken from Marshall Eddings yard, across the highway. Some owners of the cafe include George Rittenhouse (he probably built it in the early 20s); Herman Rowe; Fred A. Cole; Saul Pacheco; Nelson Monger; and Cecil Monger. *(Photo courtesy Nancy Eddings Wiswell)*

Frank Overbye's Garage in Mack 21 February 1945. Standing in front is Tony Overbye (Frank's father), Caroline Overbye (Frank's daughter on her birthday), Frank Overbye, and an unidentified person. *(Photo courtesy of Helen Overbye Peterson)*

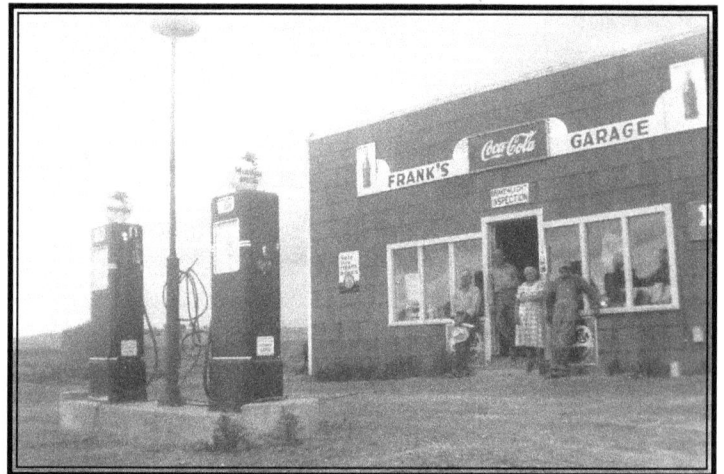

Frank Overbye's Garage in Mack in 1947. There has been a lot of improvement. Standing in front and to the right is Frank's mother and father, Tony & Cora Overbye, Frank is standing in the doorway, the other person is unidentified. *(Photo courtesy of Frank Overbye)*

Cutting ice on Lake McAndrews over Baxter Pass. The stores and hotel depended on this ice supply year-round for their ice boxes (refrigerators) and to freeze ice cream in the hand-turned ice cream freezers. The ice was hauled to Mack in Uintah Railway ice-freight cars, and stored in an ice house, probably packed in sawdust. It's amazing how well this worked. It was a tradition to have home made ice cream on the 4th of July in our childhood days. What a treat that was! *(Photo courtesy of Helen Overbye Peterson)*

(Above) "The Last Chance Service Station" in 1939 located on the west end of Mack on Highway 6 & 50. Ada Bush is standing in the doorway. Some of the owners include C. P. Simpson (possibly built the store in 1919); Ed Daily; Charlie Smith (twice); Reetis Bush; Alvin Koch; and the Clements. *(Photo courtesy of Evelyn Bush Welch)*

(Below) The Desert Gateway Store located on the east end of Mack on highway 6 & 50, possibly in the 1940s or 50s. Some of the owners include Chester Wright who built it in the 20s; Alice Hitner; Ira Carpenter; Ray Muth; Delbert Hahn; Raymond Wilson (twice); Gary Mead; Perry Bowers; Dave Lynch; and the present owners, T. J. and Barbara Smith. *(8 Aug 1991 issue of the* Fruita Times, *photo from Fern Muth)*

(Above) Mack Ladies' Guild about 1912 or 1913. Left to right: Dora Lyman (husband killed on Uintah Railway), Kate Baird, Harriet Golden, Jennie Cox (husband manager of Mack Mercantile), Mrs. Pease, Eleanor Halpin, Mrs. Stamm, Marian Pease, ?, Mrs. W. D. Halpin, May Kiefer, Bessie Cox Brown (Mack school teacher), and Mrs. H. C. Olsen. (Photo courtesy of *Agnes Kiefer*)

(Below left) A nice quiet, fall afternoon to sit and visit on the bench in front of the Uintah Hotel about 1910. *(Esther Baird Sproule Collection)* (Below right) Summer of 1935. Left to right: Effie Simpson, Jo Bowen, Sara Boyden and G. Boyden. *(Photo courtesy of JoAnn Bowen Montague)*

(Upper) In front of J.C.Penneys in Grand Junction, 1930.. L-R: ?, Simpson; LaVon Goech, teacher at Atchee; Gene Leighty, teacher at Atchee; ?; ?; Julia and Roy McCoy; girl in front ? *(Photo courtesy of Jim McCoy)* (Above) Chris Pappas was the caretaker of the Mack Hotel grounds. Picture taken in back of the hotel about 1926. *(Maybelle Cox Collection)*

(Upper) Birdie Lopholm and Sarah Boyden, Postmistress at Mack, standing in front of the Colorado/Utah State Line Monument the day of the celebration of the opening of the highway from Mack to Cisco, Utah, 25 September 1931. *(Photo courtesy of Odis Simpson)* (Above) Frank Weber former owner of Mack grocery store, Clarence Stites, former Mack Grade School Principal and Teacher, and Ora Cotner former owner of Mack Garage. Photo taken in Salem, Oregon in August 1956. *(Photo courtesy of Shirley Cotner Barshaw)*

(Right) An outing on Douglas Pass of some Mack residents. L-R: Lee and Olive Starbuck, Charlotte "Lottie" Booth and, daughter, Charlotte, Everett, JoAnn and Jo Bowen, James Booth and Mrs. Schultz. *(Photo courtesy of JoAnn Bowen Montague)*

(Above) Elva Baird's 12th birthday, 7 July 1928. Front row only identified, left to right: Elva Baird, Louise ?, Helen Baird, Esther Baird, Jodell Simpson, and Mary Simpson. *(Photo courtesy of Esther Baird Sproule)*

(Above right) Elmer and Lola Rector Dunlap in front of the Rector home in Mack in the early 30s.

(Center right) Woody's Gang! About 1928. Left to Right: Glen Stewart, Keith Wright, ? Robbins, Doug Booth, Clyde Wright, Ray Wagaman.

(Below) Zona Wright and Opal Wells. Two beauties in the rumble seat! *(Photos courtesy of Betty Booth Garber)*

(Below right) Jiggs Hoffman was once a very familiar face in Mack as he made his daily visits in his horse-drawn buggy. *(Photo courtesy of JoAnn Bowen Montague)*

(Above) Easter Sunday, 1935, Mack, Colorado. Back row, left to right: Patty Maluy, Mary Ellen Wassenburg, Charlotte Booth, and June Spencer. Front row: Wilma Maluy, Shirley Spencer, and Norma Maluy. *(Photo courtesy of June Spencer Barnes)*

(Above) Betty Booth and Dick Wagaman at the time of their graduation from Fruita Union High School in 1931, standing in front of the Uintah Hotel at Mack. They went through all 12 years of grade and high school together. *(Photo courtesy of Betty Booth Garber)*

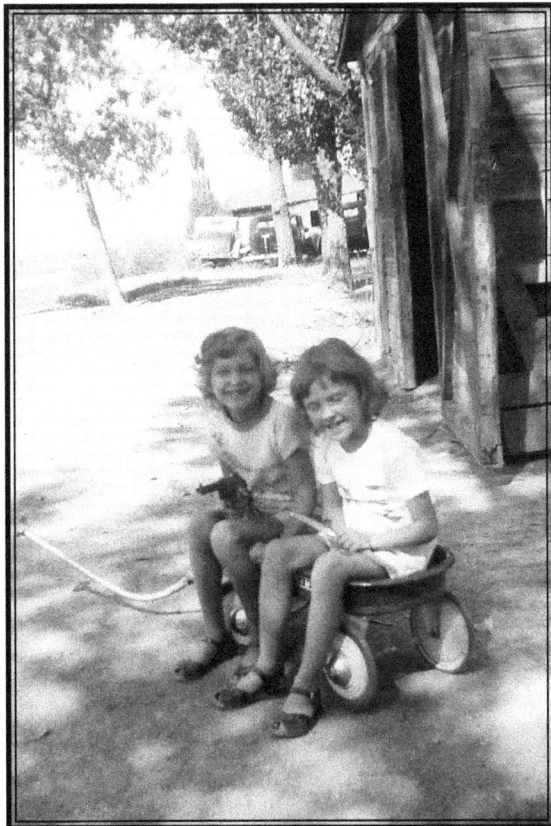

(Left) In 1952 at Mack, Colorado, Janice Monger and Nancy Eddings. Janice says, "Stick 'em up." *(Photo courtesy of Nancy Eddings Wiswell)*

(Right) A couple more beauties at Mack, Colorado! Lola Rector and Betty Booth in matching coveralls in front of the Booth home. *(Photo courtesy of Helen Overbye Peterson)*

The Mack Post Office

The Mesa County Colorado Post Office list, compiled in 1985 by Charles Teed of the Grand Junction Stamp Club, gave the beginning date of the Mack Post Office as 21 April 1904. The Mesa County Genealogical Society recently published the list in September 1995.

We have no information on the Mack Post Office between that date and 26 December 1917. We wonder if Uintah office workers took care of the mail, in addition to other duties.

Wednesday, 26 December 1917, the Civil Service Commission advertised in *The Daily Sentinel* for applications to fill the position of postmaster at the Mack Post Office to be in by 26 June 1918. Compensation of $552 per year was offered.

A history of the Mack Post Office published in the *Fruita Times,* 15 August 1991, named William Chapman as the first postmaster. Because of *The Daily Sentinel*

ad mentioned above, Clarinda Wesner (see Wesner history) may have been the person who filled the position in 1918. We have also learned that Blanche Baird was the postmaster at least during 1920.

The first post office was located in the Uintah Railway office. In 1924, Sara Boyden, the newly appointed postmaster, moved the post office into her home on the south side of the Rio Grande tracks.

Sara Boyden officially retired 31 January 1940. Mrs. Charles Kiefer then filled the position as postmaster. Because of ill health, she had to resign after serving for only a short time. After Mrs. Kiefer's resignation, Clyde "Cherp" Phillips filled the position on a temporary status. He served until Alta Smith became the postmaster on 17 August 1940.

Alta located the post office in a building next to the "Last Chance" store at the west end of town, near the school. The Charley Smith family operated the store.

Later, following the death of Charley Smith, the post office was detached from the store building and moved a short distance northeast and attached to Alta's home. It remained there as long as Alta was

(Left) The Mack Post Office between 1924 and 1940 when it was located at the Boyden residence on the south side of the Rio Grand tracks. *(Photo courtesy of JoAnn Bowen Montague)*

(Right) Alta Smith, postmaster, Shirley Smith, sister-in-law of Charley Smith, and Delores Smith, daughter of Alta and Charley Smith, in front of the Smith's Store, the Mack Post Office, and Alex Wilkinson's Garage in about 1940. Alta served as postmaster from 1940 to 1971 and Delores was postmaster from 1971 to 1987. *(Photo taken from the Fruita Times, issue 15 August 1991. It was submitted by Delores Smith Likes)*

(Above left) Alta Smith is shown in front of the Mack Post Office during her second decade as postmaster on 17 February 1958. She served from 1940 to 1971. The sign above says "POST OFFICE, Mack, Colo., Elevation 4531." (Above right) Alta is shown sorting mail in the post office. It looks a lot like Christmas, but it is the same day, taken 17 February 1958. This shows how busy and important the post office is to the people of Mack and New Liberty. *(Photo courtesy of Delores Smith Likes)*

postmaster, and for a time afterward.

When Alta Smith was appointed postmaster in 1940, the mail came to Mack from Grand Junction on the D&RG Railroad, and a two-wheel cart was used to take the mail from the depot to the post office in the morning, and back to the depot in the evening.

In 1942, John Hayden, who operated the Uintah Stage Line from Grand Junction to Mack, was awarded a contract to carry the mail, and in 1951 Red Hiatt got the contract to carry the mail on a star route† from Grand Junction, via Fruita and Loma, to Mack. Later contractors included Marvin Ottman and Jack Murphy. The mail is still brought to the Lower Valley by a contract carrier.

The Uintah Railway began closing down in 1937, and the Atchee Post Office, with Ruby Luton as postmaster, was closed and the Atchee mail was handled at the Mack Post Office. In 1954, the Westwater, Utah Post Office, where Velda Bittle was postmaster, was also closed and the Westwater mail came through the Mack Post Office.

Alta retired as postmaster in August of 1971. Her daughter, Delores Smith Likes, was named officer in charge at the post office on 1 September 1971, and was appointed postmaster 11 December 1971.

The post office remained on the Smith property until 1984, when a new 1,944 square foot post office building was built on Hotel Circle, south of U.S. Highway 6 & 50 in Mack. At the time the new building was occupied, with Delores as postmaster, there were 72 boxes rented in the post office and 67 patrons on the rural route.

Delores was postmaster until she retired on 3 September 1987.

Upon Delores's retirement, Jim Salas was named officer in charge, then he was appointed postmaster. He has continued to serve since that time.

The Mack Post Office is an impressive structure, neatly kept, with a large paved parking lot.

†A postal route between postal stations, specifically between one city or town and another over which mail is transported in bulk by a private carrier under contract.

(Above) The new Mack Post Office, 1 November 1984. The post office was moved to this new building, having been located in an attachment to the home of Alta Smith since 1940. (Below left) Delores Smith Likes is shown in the Mack Post Office during her tenure as postmaster. She was in the office from 1971 to 1987. *(Both photos courtesy of Delores Smith Likes)*

(Below right) Fifty-one years of Mack post office administration are represented by these two former postmasters, Alta Smith and Delores Smith Likes, and the present postmaster, Jim Salas. Jim has served as postmaster since Delores retired in 1987. *(Photo taken by Gene Thomas, used in the Fruita Times, 15 August 1991 issue)*

Rural Route I

In July of 1924 *The Daily Sentinel* reported that settlers in the new area (New Liberty/Mack Mesa) were seeking to interest the postal authorities in establishing a rural mail route to the north and west of Mack. They decided that a route 21.3 miles in length would serve 82 families in that area. New roads and bridges had recently been constructed to serve the community.

Upon completion of his survey, also in July 1924, Postal Inspector Martin G. Wenger recommended that a rural route be established. In October 1924, the Civil Service Commission advertised for interested persons to submit applications for the position of rural mail carrier on the new mail route. Examinations were held in Grand Junction 22 November 1924 to decide who would qualify for the job. Only those persons living in the area covered by the new route would be eligible to apply.

In December 1924 Byron Boyden, husband of the postmaster, began serving as a temporary rural carrier on the new route.

Before the rural service was available, the farmers of New Liberty and Mack Mesa had to travel to Mack to pick up their mail.

Everett Bowen was selected as rural carrier from among six applicants. We are unable to name the other five. The Mack News Items in *The Daily Sentinel* of 16 February 1925 announced his appointment:

W. E. Bowen has received his appointment as rural mail carrier out of Mack, and will take over the route on March 2. Until then Mr. Boyden and Mr. Nelson, his assistant, will have charge of the route.

(Upper) W. E. Bowen with the first car he used on the Mack mail route. With him is his daughter, JoAnn, now Mrs. Hal Montague. *(Fruita Times, 2 August 1962)* (Above) Mr. Bowen in front of Mack Post Office. (Right) Alta Smith, postmistress, and Mr. Bowen, mail carrier, in front of Mack Post Office. The Mack School can be seen in the background. Both photos were taken in 1958. *(Photos courtesy of Delores Smith Likes)*

William Everett Bowen began his career as mail carrier on "Route #1, Mack, Colorado," on 2 March 1925. He continued in that position for 37½ years, and retired on 31 July 1962.

Following is an extraction from an article in the *Fruita Times,* 2 August 1962, written by Alta Smith, honoring W. E. Bowen on his retirement:

...It [Rural Route I] was established as a tri-weekly route and there were around 82 families receiving mail three times a week. It was soon changed to a daily route. There was no bridge over Badger wash and the route could not be approved until this bridge was built in the late fall of 1924.

Bowen carried the mail in a Model T Ford and quite often had to resort to a team and buggy, even a few times he had to carry it on horseback. The 21½ miles made a good day's ride as the roads were not good and there were lots of mud holes to get thru. Mack wash, north of town, had to be forded and on the highway west of town there was a cement slab for a crossing. On one trip the water came up so fast at the wash it caught the car and the engine was flooded with sand, dirt and water, which ruined his practically new car. The wages were $73.60 per month. As more families moved into the valley the route grew until at one time there were about 100 families being served. ... Since the farms and ranches have consolidated, families have moved out. Both New Liberty and Mack schools have been closed and now there are about 52 families living on the route. The roads have been improved, as 14 miles are paved and the rest has a good coat of gravel.

Bowen will miss the many friends made through his daily contact with people of the lower valley, and they will no doubt miss the many acts of kindness he performed beyond the call of duty. He was never too rushed to stop a few minutes and visit with his patrons, whether they were the men, the women, or the small bashful children who watched daily for his coming. Mrs. Bowen remarked, "Oh, the goodies Ev brought home from those wonderful people on his route."

Milton Alstatt carried the mail as substitute carrier until Laurene Wells received the appointment as regular carrier. Laurene was also appointed carrier at the Loma Post Office when Tom Saunders retired from that position.

In 1975, Laurene was appointed postmaster at Loma and Milton Alstatt was appointed carrier on the Mack and Loma rural routes, where he served 35 years until retiring in 1980.

When Milton retired, Burke Swisher was appointed carrier on the Mack and Loma routes and still held that position as of 1991.

In 1991, previous to the New Liberty/Mack reunion, JoAnn Bowen Montague sent a letter to the editor of the *Fruita Times.* Let us reminisce

Everett Bowen at retirement in 1962. *(Photo courtesy of JoAnn Bowen Montague)*

Milton Alstatt served as mail carrier for New Liberty and Loma. *(Photo courtesy of Lona Alstatt)*

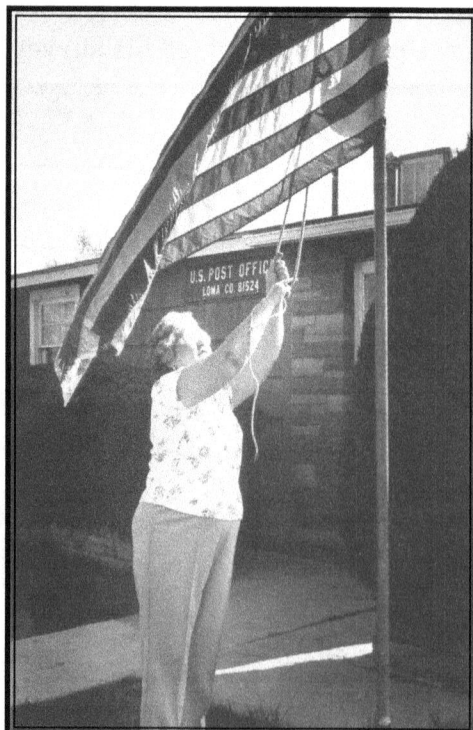

Laurene Wells raising the United States flag at the Loma post office. *(Photo courtesy of Laurene Wells)*

Friends and neighbors present at Everett Bowen's retirement party in July 1962. Front row, L-R: Everett Bowen, Jo Bowen, Mrs. Smith Kilby, Estellene Thomas, Mildred Brayton and Laura Berry. Second row: Bill Knapp, May Sanders, Holly Kelley, Al Alstatt, Rev. Clyde Likes, Elsie Arpke, Anna Shires and Lois Pollock. Third row: Della Swyhart, Edna Smith, Anna Alstatt, Margaret Morrow, Hazel Daily, Laura Weir, Charlotte Booth and Lois Saunders. Back row: Maxwell Sanders, Guy Gerry, Floyd Thomas, Al Daily, Jim Booth, Bill Pollock, Chester Wright and Helen MacTaggart. *(Photo courtesy of JoAnn Bowen Montague)*

with her as we review her letter:

I'm sending you a copy, not too legible, of a map [on the following page] made 66 years ago by Byron Boyden and my father, Everett Bowen, which outlined the mail route from Mack north over the red mesa and then northwest through the community of New Liberty. I have marked in red[†], as was done on the original, the exact route, which I can still remember with much nostalgia.

First, he left the Post Office and drove to the Hollingers' house (surely many of our generation recall sledding down that hill in winter), where he turned east and left mail at Bill and Helen Cox's. I remember Helen Cox with great fondness; she gave my father all her 'coffee coupons' during WWII, for which he was ever grateful. Later the Coxes moved closer to the Davidsons. I read with great interest Deyon's [Davidson Boughton] article, but was surprised she never mentioned the wonderful cherry orchards her folks had — I've had lots of cherry pies from that orchard!

Apparently in 1925 there were no other stops on that route, at least, if there were, they weren't marked. No Cutlers, Deacons, Dilles, Carrolls or Lofgrens or Watters, or other names I've long since forgotten.[†] Our house was the next marked on the route. From there he left mail for the Fishers (the Grimsbys were not there at that time) and went on to the Clem Maluy home, turning north at "Shires' Corner." The school was marked, I suppose, to drop mail at the "teacherage," which, at different times, included such individuals as Grace Curtis and her sister, Florence Chilson; Faust M. Yates and his wife, (I remember he played the fiddle at the Mack dances); Inez Porter at one time; and, again, many others whose names escape me. From there the Likes's was the next mail box, with the Snavelys, Morrows and Alstatts all having to walk some distance to get their mail. Arpkes moved into the area much later. He stopped at Bob and Fern Cox's house, and then the Price's and the Williams', the Dean's on the back road, and the Summers' at the corner. The McCampbell's was the next stop; Wiant's was somewhat off the road. The Boydens lived out there at that time, across

† We have marked the route with a heavy black line with arrows showing the direction of travel.

†The author is wondering about the Kilbys, Herrons, Barrs, Earps, Schunters, Pollocks, Pachecos and several others who should have been on the route at that time.

from the Sumnicht's and next to the Burkett's. Turning here, the Weir's and Gerry's were the next to receive mail; then he went down the hill, stopping at the Bill Maluy's. I didn't remember that Bill lived there, but it couldn't have been anyone else. [Patrick Maluy lived there at that time, then Bill Maluy and family in 1927].

Another turn and the Phillips's mail was dropped off, as well as the Harrison's. Around the hill and the Thomas' were next. After that the Daily's, although I wonder when the Knapps moved there. And finally he went back to the post office, the entire trip taking about three hours.

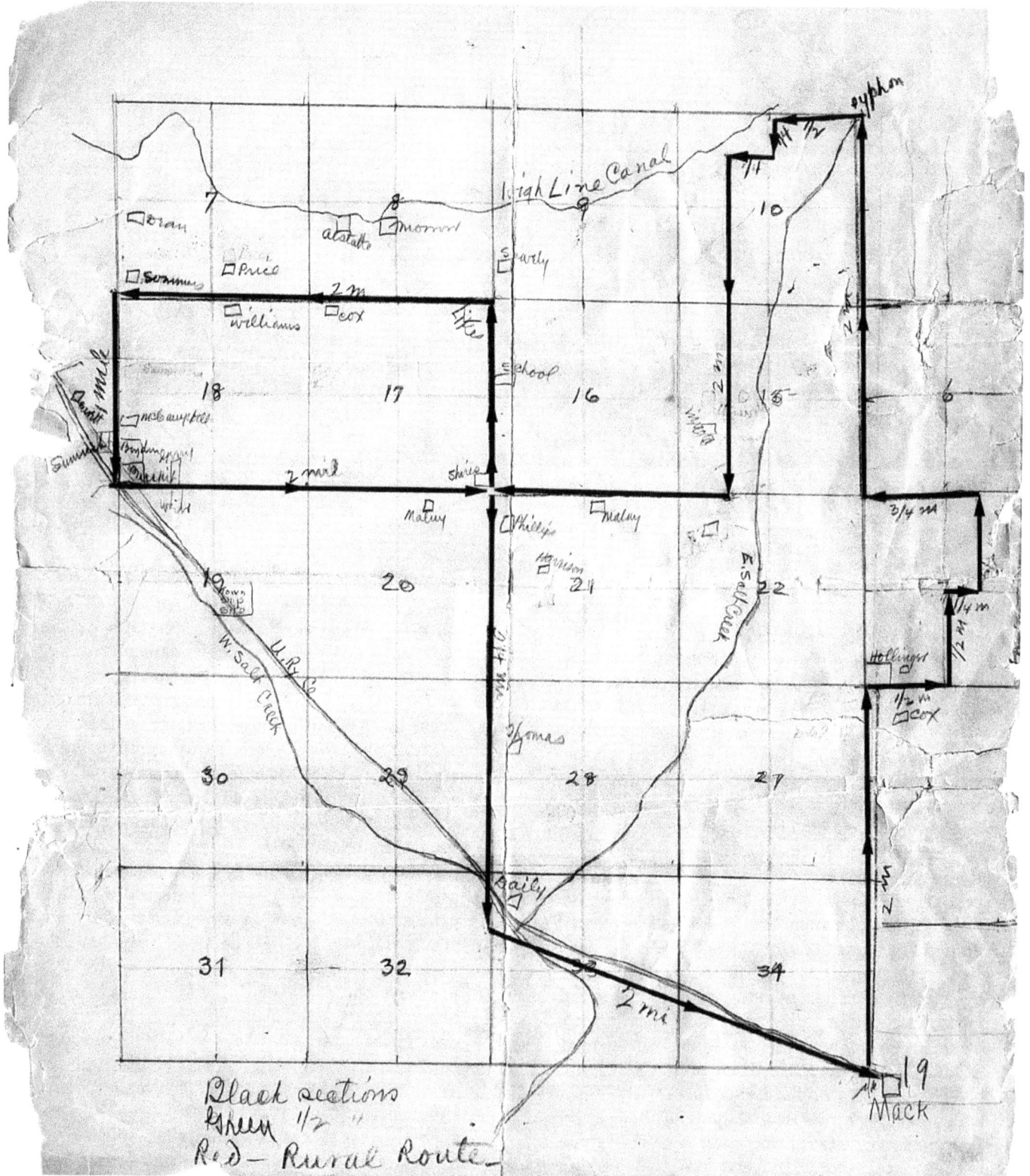

Original map of Rural Route #1 drawn by Everett Bowen and Byron Boyden in 1925 to outline the route and delivery stops and to figure the length of the route by miles. The map became 72 years old in February 1997. We have added a thick black line with arrows pointing in the direction of travel in place of Bowen's red line. *(Map courtesy of JoAnn Bowen Montague)*

Mack School

Mack School began in 1906 with eight to 11 pupils in a one-room building. The building was formerly used by the Uintah Railroad as a warehouse and situated between the Rio Grande and Uintah Railroad tracks, probably southwest of the hotel.

The first teacher at Mack School is said to have been Miss Bessie Cox, daughter of Samuel and Mary Cox. Many of us knew Bessie as the sister of Bob, Bill, and Ira Cox. Records show that Miss Cox became Mrs. Haywood Brown on 18

1903: Miss Bessie Cox is the teacher at the Hunter School. Included among the students are her brothers Robert, William, & Ira, and sister Ethel. (*Picture copied from the 75th Anniversary Edition 15 October 1959 of the Fruita Times.*)

June 1906. So — was the first teacher **Miss** Bessie Cox or **Mrs.** Bessie Brown?

The second year, 1907-1908, Catherine Dillard of Grand Junction, was the teacher. During the summer of 1907 the building was moved from what must have been a noisy and dirty location by the tracks to a new location just north of Mack Mercantile. A snapshot submitted by Betty Booth Garber and printed in the *Fruita Times* of 2 May 1991, shows the school building quite clearly as it appeared, perhaps in the early 1920s (See page 28).

Sources we have investigated give conflicting information on Mack School. The following

information is the most consistent. The dates, names, etc., are extracted from school board records compiled by May Sanders. Some items are hard to interpret. Since all the pupils are not listed, perhaps the intent was to include only the names of new students each year. However, a few names appear in more than one year:

1908/09 — teacher $60 per year, Ethel MacTaggert; 13 pupils: Ira Cox, Arthur Gibson, Irma Gibson, Clarence Swanson, Karl Goeglien, Earl Goeglien, Bertha Goeglien, Gail Gillespie, Marvel Gillespie, Francis Gillespie, Eleanor Halpin, Marvin Pease, Florence Tyler.

1909/10 — teacher, Ethel MacTaggert; pupils: Marion Pease, Claude May, Howard Tyler, Ralph Tyler, Homer Tyler, Earl Cox, Leonard Cox, Willie Jones, Heber Jones, Charlie Jones.

1910/11 — Teacher, Ethel MacTaggert; pupils: Bertha Marshall, Lucille Marshall, Marguerite Marshall, Rose Padia, Willie Padia, Claude Padia, Viva Pulliam, Harry Pulliam, Bafino Gaurrez.

1911/12 — Teacher: $75 per year, Jessie Lacey; 11 pupils: Gladys Anderson, Viola Anderson, Robert Stewart.

1912/13 — Teacher, Edna Penfield; pupils: Nina Miller, Arthur Wattman, Lietta King.

1913/14 — Teacher, Harriett Weir; pupils: Josie Cox, Leonard Cox, Earl Cox, Marguerite Marshall, Bertha Marshall, Lucille Marshall, Cleone Fitzpatrick, Lila Haight. (A notation says: Marshalls moved to Oregon; Fitzpatricks to Atchee)

1914/15 — Teacher, $80 per year, Ida Davis; 13 pupils: Victor Albo, Cantwell Brown, John Kiefer, Jack Wilderman, Alice Anderson, Evelyn Seeds.

1915/16 — Teacher: Ida Davis; pupils: Leo Kiefer, Matt Crews, Tom Hebson, Russell Rector,

(Above) Mack School students about 1917. Front row: (left to right) Joe Hebson, Lloyd Divine, Genevieve Miller, Catherine Halpin and Dorothy Devine. Back row: Teacher, Miss Faye Wagner, Leo Kiefer, Bessie Devine, Francis Calton, John Kiefer (partially hidden), Ruby Wagner, Alice Anderson, and Zelma Devine. *(Photo courtesy of Agnes Kiefer)*

(Right) Mack School students and teacher gathered for this picture in February 1919. Front row: (Left to right) Jack Eagan, Irene Hutton, Earl "Dick" Wagaman, Opal Wesner, Hazel Wagaman, Kenneth Goings, George Baird, Gordon Booth, Henry Simpson, and Joe Hutton. Second row: William Simpson, Orval Wagaman, Agnes Kiefer, Etta Simpson, Eula Rader, and Nellie Hutton. Third row: Odis Simpson and dog "Troubles", Leo Kiefer, Roy Wagaman, John Simpson, John Kiefer, and Paul Wagaman. Back row: Alice Rader, and Miss Phyllis Gex, teacher. *(Photo courtesy of Agnes Kiefer and Odis Simpson)*

The school building in each photo is the old Mack School building that stood north of the Mack Mercantile. It was rented from the Uintah Railway paying one dollar per year for rent. The building was replaced not too many years after these photos by a larger frame structure located north of the highway and farther west.

Lester Rector, Winnie Rector, Richard Talley.

1916/17 — Teacher, Faye Wagner; 15 pupils: Genevieve Miller, Joe Hebson, David Grouseman, Lloyd Devine, Zelma Devine, Dorothy Devine, Bessie Devine, Lawrence Weaver, Laura Weaver, Ralph Waynich.

1917/18 — Teacher, Faye Wagner; 24 pupils: Francis Galton, Jack Lyman, Louis Malito, Joe Malito, Katherine Malito, Janeva Malito, Orval Wagaman, Paul Wagaman, Roy Wagaman, Hazel Wagaman, Agnes Kiefer, Opal Wesner, Ruth Poole.

1918/19 — Teacher, Phyllis Gex (pronounced "Jay"); no other record. However, a picture of teacher and students of Mack School, 1919, was submitted by Dick Wagaman and published in the *Fruita Times* 14 February 1991. Dick Wagaman provided the following names of students: Jack Eagen, Irene Hutton, Earl "Dick" Wagaman, Opal Wesner, Hazel Wagaman, Kenneth Goings, George Baird, Gordon Booth, Henry Simpson, Joe Hutton, William Simpson, Orval Wagaman, Agnes Kiefer, Etta Simpson, Eula Rader, Nellie Hutton, Odis Simpson, Leo Kiefer, Roy Wagaman, John Simpson, John Kiefer, Paul Wagaman, Alice Rader.

1919/20 — The following taken from Educational Directories, not from May Sanders' records, gives the School Board of Directors as: President, C. C. Kiefer; Secretary, Robert Cox; and Treasurer, F. A. Kennedy. The teacher was Margaret Weimer, with Lillian Roberson as Assistant. *The Daily Sentinel* noted that "there were 30 pupils, nearly double the enrollment of last year."

The first motion picture was shown in Mack 22 July 1920, probably by F. A. "Judge" Kennedy, and probably in the Mack School building.

There must have been an addition to the school during the summer of 1920, as there are two teachers in the following lists, and the lists apparently include all students.

1920/21 -- The School Board, President, Donald MacTaggert; Secretary, Charles C. Kiefer; Treasurer, John E. Wesner. Teacher of the upper grades, $115 per year, Maud Levi; pupils: Jack Eagen, Mary Erne, Raymond Fisher, Lee and Amon Jones, Elizabeth Johnson, Rose Perry, Willie Simpson, Etta Simpson, Ray Stuart, Helen and Margaret Trevarthen, Eula Rader, Lizzie Winkle, Etta Davenport, Margaret Groves, Donald Kiefer. (In the 1921 school census the Perry children's name was spelled **Perri**)

Teacher of the lower grades, Margaret Weimer; pupils: Billie [Betty] Booth, Dorothy Dean, Lulu Dean, Desta Mulvaney; Hazel Eagen; Mary Smith; Flora Perry; Mary Perry; Gertrude Wesner; Bernadine Calderwood, Willie Huffman. (Lillian Roberson taught four months, Alta Platt after January)

1921/22, School Board: President, J. E. Wesner; Secretary, A. W. Alstatt; Treasurer, Donald MacTaggert. Teachers: Margaret Weimer & Maude Levi;. Pupils: Eleanor Barr, Elmer Snow, Clifford Snow, Mable Snow, Fred Baird, George Baird, Betty Booth, Gordon Booth, Kenneth Goings, Arlin Jones, Marlin Jones, Eldon Levi, Henry Simpson, Palmer Simpson, Martin Saunders, Madonna Weimer, Margaret McCampbell, Melba McCampbell, Paul Wagaman, Hazel Wagaman, Earl Wagaman, Orval Wagaman, Jerome Kiefer. (The McCampbell girls are in a 1922 New Liberty School picture; they must have moved during the school year.)

On 30 March 1922 the community held a meeting to consider a school bond consisting of $7,500 for Mack and $3,500 for New Liberty —it was defeated. They somehow resolved the problem with the bond, because on 19 July they held another meeting to decide the location of a new Mack School. Apparently they also needed to vote on an expected cost of $7,500. Construction began in the fall of 1922 locating the new school building at the west end of town.

Citizens of the two communities met 27 June 1922 at New Liberty to divide the Mack/New Liberty School District.

Records show the School Board members for District #44 (Mack district) in 1922-23 to be President, Dick Stewart; Secretary, F. B. Baird; and Treasurer, Donald MacTaggert. Teachers were: Upper Grades, Julia A. Knight; Lower Grades, Margaret Robbins.

(Left) The program at which this picture was taken took place at Mack School during the school year of 1917-18. Back row from left: ?, Matt Crews, ?, and teacher, Faye Wagner. Middle row: John Kiefer, Agnes Kiefer, Genevieve Miller, and Leo Kiefer. Front row: Francis Calton, ?, Opal Wesner, Jewel Miller,?, Catherine Halpin, Jerome Kiefer and Joe Hebson. (Agnes Kiefer Collection)

(Below) Eighth grade class about 1924 in front of the new schoolhouse. Back Row: George Baird, Howard Gosnell, Gordon Booth, Hazel Wagaman, and Jerome Kiefer. Front Row: Etta Simpson, Opal Wesner, Agnes Kiefer, and Mary Trevarthan. Gordon Booth and Hazel Wagaman were in the 7th grade. (Photo courtesy Betty Booth Garber)

(Above) 1933-34 student body at Mack school: Back row, L-R Eloise Harris, Clara Holt, Lela Velasquez, Mr. Dugger Saunders (5-6-7-8th grades), Miss Mildred Hogsett (later Kelley, 1-2-3-4th grades), Mae Wagaman, Miriam Sowers, Cleofus Velasquez, Middle row: Charity Sparks, (?) Zaldain, Cecilia Anne Kiefer, Charlotte Booth, Helen Keffalos, Delores Collins, Lois Harris, Margaret Herron, Blanche Smith, Margaret Kiefer, June Spencer, Mary Ellen Walsenburgh, Corinne Daily, (?) Zaldain, Mary Velasquez, Shirley Spencer, Dorothy Keffalos, Madeline Kirby. Boys in front: Just above front row Phillip Goodwin, Silo Romero, Mike Velasquez, Wilbur Smith, Fred Holt, Myron Goodwin, George Keffalos, Blaine Barr, Gordon Robertson (and Tag), James Holt, Robert Holt, Tom Barr, Fred Herron, Ernest Robertson, David Holt, Edward Collins, and just behind him, Pete Zaldain. *(Photo courtesy of C. Anne Kiefer Schmalz and Helen Keffalos Dodson)*

(Above) 1928-29 student body: The ones identified are, Front Row: Charlie Overbye, Fred Herron, ?, Margaret Kiefer, Clyde Wright, Bob MacTaggart, ?, ?; 2nd Row: 2nd Mae Wagaman; 3rd Doug Booth, end of row, Leon Daily with Edmond Daily behind him; 3rd Row: 2nd Jessie MacTaggart; 4th Row: 2nd Josie MacTaggart, 3rd Ray Wagaman; Back row: 2nd Dalton Barr, 4th Woodrow Booth, end of row, Keith Wright. *(C. Anne Kiefer Schmalz Collection)*

46

The Mack news items in *The Daily Sentinel* of 10 April 1923 noted that the new school building was almost complete. Pupils in the first four grades moved into their new quarters that week and the upper grades were scheduled to make the move the following week. The school building featured two large rooms on the south side with seating capacity for 40 pupils. An assembly hall was located near the front of the building in which was provided a booth for motion picture projection equipment. A teacherage was built some time later.

Mack Items for 24 December 1926, F. B. Baird, Correspondent

The largest crowd ever assembled at Mack met at the school auditorium Wednesday evening to enjoy the Christmas program and community Christmas tree. The back of the stage of the auditorium was transformed into a beautiful winter scene, in front of which, during the first part of the evening, fairies, brownies and all sorts of animated toys danced and played in their busy preparations for Christmas. The last half of the program was a two-act play in which Mr. and Mrs. Pat Finnegan, otherwise Fred Baird Jr., and Opal Wells, imbued in the spirit of Christmas, make it possible for all members of the Finnegan's flat to enjoy a happy Christmas. Between the two parts of the program, Betty Booth, with the assistance of Helen Overbye and Hazel Eagen at the piano, gave a most delightful pianologue. Not forgetting that the protection of our country makes it possible for us to enjoy Christmas in any way we please, the children gave a most beautiful and impressive patriotic selection. At the close of the program Santa appeared and distributed candy and nuts and a gift to every child in the community, the people of the community having provided the money to purchase them.

Following are names of some teachers who do not appear above; we cannot place them in proper order. However, we do know that Patrick Allen Daily was one of the first teachers in the new school building. Florence Simon and Miss Francis taught in 1926-27, Ruth Smith, Miss Palmer, Miss Lockett, Mildred Hogsett (1932-1941), Miss Beahm (1938, Enid Starr, Pauline Geering, Faust M. Yates, Dugger Saunders,

Walter Poirier, Mrs. Chapman, Margaret Kiefer, Alma Finch, John Lemke and Mr. & Mrs. Stites (1946). Mack School was closed in 1953 and the pupils bused to New Liberty and Loma.

Deyon Davidson Boughton shared the following story about her own experiences at Mack School:

I'm sure I was as ready as any five year old, but I was surprised when mother said it was time for my first day at school. The year was 1935 and Mildred Hogsett was teacher for the four grades in the "little room." I wanted one of the desks by the windows but they were not for first graders. Big desks with the hinged top were for big kids; little kids lined up on the other side of the room at metal-framed, wood-topped desks with a shelf underneath the top. Some desks had a shelf under the seat where papers and books were neatly stored when they weren't spilling out on the floor.

The room had a U.S. flag and presidential portraits of Washington and Lincoln on either side of the official school room clock. Palmer Method posters marched ABCs above the blackboard. Coats and overshoes waited in cloak rooms just inside the front door and under the rope that tolled the bell, handy when a big boy made a quick swing as he went out the door. Outside were a rickety merry-go-round and swings. A large open area provided room to play Pump-Pump-Pull Away, Red Rover, Mother May I, Tag, plus a vast variety of group games. The school room was heated by a coal furnace that pumped warm air into the large floor grate in the corner. On wintry days that was a popular standing spot.

The toilets were located a long walk from the school building. There was a common sink in the hallway, to remedy hands that didn't pass hygiene inspection or needed redemption from the paste pot, and a bubble drinking fountain. How often I received a drenching; how quickly I turned from the wet faced, wet haired victim into an evil person who pushed Richard into the bubble fountain resulting in his broken tooth. I cried for a couple of reasons. First, I really didn't want to hurt anybody, and second for being wrong when I merely did unto my tormentor what had been done unto me zillions of times.

With four grades together it is hard for me to keep people sorted as to grade or age. Big kids helped little kids and we were all one "little room" community. Donna and Bruce McTaggert, Milton and Gale Cox, Maurine and Emmett Collins, Shirley and Wilbur Smith, and Freddy Herron were near my age and were from Red Mesa. Ben Rowe from north of Hollinger Hill and Mary Catherine Daily from west of Mack, both lived nearer New Liberty, but attended Mack School. Crystel Ann Komatas was spastic and held her own pretty well, especially with her wits. Most of the time we were considerate of her. There were Vangie and George Pappas, Katherine and George Komatas, Vesta, Erma, and Ralph Slaugh, Richard Smith, Charity and Clinton Sparks, Linden Goodwin, Theresa and Silo Romero. I know I've missed some classmates and I apologize; at the same time I remember fondly other people in that far away place, the "big room."

The auditorium stage opened into the "little room" and special events took us through that door and before an audience of anxious parents. We practiced and were getting ready to perform a Christmas play. I was excited but going home my head started to ache and every bump of the bus made it hurt more. I was crying as I started walking up the lane to the house and because I was hot, I sat down in a snow bank. I must have dozed a few minutes because when I got back on my feet, Mom was coming down the lane to meet me ... Several kids had recently come down with Scarletina, but I had a case of Scarlet Fever. It was a snowy evening when Dr. Herman Graves came from Grand Junction, drove up the slick lane, and gave me a shot in my hip that settled the fever. I slept for several days and couldn't move for several more; I had jaundice, mumps, and measles. I missed six weeks of school.

There is a reason for that tale. When I went back to school, I could keep up with my classmates because Mother tutored me. Education had moved along and I had a lot of catching up to do.

In the corner of the class room was a big sand box. A little community scene was constructed using miniatures. It was interesting and I thought I had things that might fit in so I brought them to school. I learned a surprising lesson. My little trinkets were made in China. "We hated China — they were wicked" and I had to fight to keep my trinkets from being broken up or thrown out. Objects made in Japan were OK.

A very few years later, on a Sunday when listening to my favorite Green Hornet, The Shadow and other mystery programs on the radio, we heard a frightening announcement. "The Japs bombed Pearl Harbor." Next day, the "big room" teacher, Mr. Lemke, brought a radio and we listened as President Roosevelt spoke of "a day of infamy." We hated Japan, but China was OK. I remembered when we hated China, and I was bewildered. I learned an informal lesson that governments are not much different than school rooms. You never know who is mad at who or why or whether they will make up or not.

My folks made arrangements for me to eat a hot lunch at Fred Coles' Mack Cafe. Those who worked there were nice and it gave me a chance to play the punch board for candy. Remember the little rolled up pieces of paper that you punched out with a tiny key and perhaps you won a bar of candy and maybe more. One time I won about ten bars of candy and left them at Coles to eat one (or two) at a time for the next few days.

I never did get to use a big desk in the "little room." The two room school was growing and the stage converted to fourth and fifth grade classes with teacher Bernice Beahm. By now the school had a "teacherage." Mr. and Mrs. Claycomb lived in the big suite and Miss Beahm in the smaller. At that time an unmarried school marm was not expected to date, and when it was discovered that over Christmas vacation Miss Beahm had become Mrs. Gardner, she had to move on.

The library Bookmobile arrived regularly and presented authors who opened new worlds. An assortment of rhythm instruments, bells, tambourines, cymbals, etc. were found in a drawer under a closet in the hall, and music became part of our education.

Separation of church and state is a democratic doctrine. With the variety of religious convictions, there is justification for strict adherence. The Christmas carols we sang as a classroom and as a school are very special in my memory. I am sorry it is no longer part of education, but then neither is the Palmer Method of legible penmanship.

(Above) The Mack School eighth grade graduating class of 1938. Left to right: Delbert Slaugh, Jay Rowe, Blanche Smith, Ernest Robertson, Charlotte Booth, June Spencer, Ed Collins and Helen McDowell. Four of the class members — Slaugh, Rowe, Smith, and Collins, went on to graduate from Fruita Union High School with the class of 1942. Smith and Collins (cousins) were classmates for all 12 years of school. Slaugh lost his life in World War II. *(Photo lent to the Fruita Times by Blanche Smith Hutchison and printed in the 4 September 1992 issue. We have copied it from that issue.)*

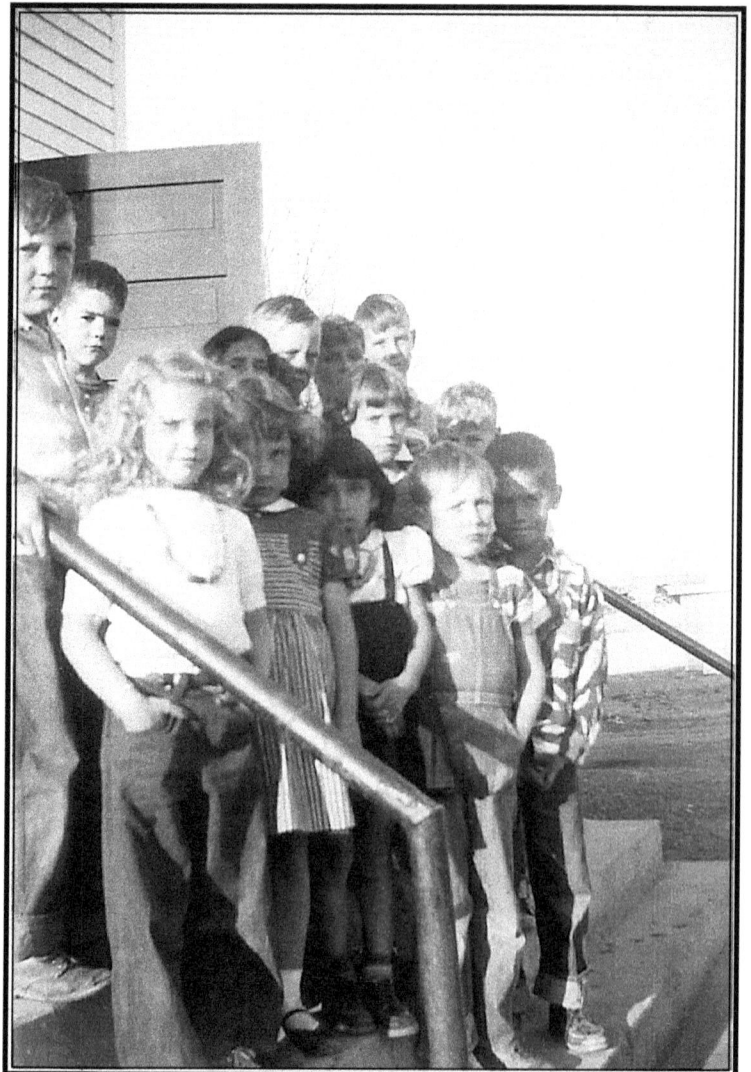

(Right) Mack school first, second, and third grades on 7 May 1952, Nancy Eddings seventh birthday. Not all are identified. Gene Wilkinson, Doug Green, Lorene Ortega, Bobby Rich, Janice Monger, Nancy Lee Eddings, Florence Ortega, and Larry Overbye. *(Photo courtesy of Nancy Lee Eddings Wiswell)*

49

The Colorado Young Citizens League introduced us to democracy as we elected class officers and practiced Robert's Rules of Order. CYCL was lost as a teaching tool when years later Senator McCarthy felt the initials could be misinterpreted as Young Communist League. We were about as far from Communism as we could get. As the Depression shifted into World War II and on into the Cold War, new social fears manifested themselves.

As sixth graders, we entered the "big room." Miss Hogsett, our primary teacher, returned as Mrs. Kelly to teach for a while, but Mr. Lemke soon came on the scene. During this time we came very close to the reality of dying when Frank Davies Jr. was killed in a hiking accident. We attended the funeral as a class.

Seventh grade produced an interesting educational contraption — an ornate world globe with planets extended around it. By moving a handle one could watch sky positions. The world was truly round and large maps revealed countries we were hearing about: Germany, Japan, Hawaii.

The outside world was becoming a part of our lives, lives that too soon would be touched by war. The CCC (Civilian Conservation Corps) camp south of Fruita provided housing and food for unemployed men during the depression and a POW camp during the war; which our CYCL let us tour. Patriotism sharpened as we saved pennies to buy War Bonds, collected scrap metal, and quit buying toothpaste in tubes. A shortage of sugar for candy- making was about the harshest reality we had to face. There were occasional practice blackouts when we turned off lights, put heavy blankets over the windows, and tried to imagine enemy planes flying overhead ready to shoot on sight.

I finished the eighth grade pretty much as I started the first. I had measles twice and missed several days during those crucial final tests. Mrs. Finch was our 8th grade teacher and when I walked down the aisle to pick up my graduation certificate, it was blank. She was sure that I couldn't possibly enter high school if I didn't go back on Saturday and take tests. I dutifully went back and took the dreaded tests while one of her daughters sat backwards on a chair and spat on the floor. Mrs. Finch asked what I expected to do as a vocation, I said I thought I would make vacation a vocation. She gave me a certificate that declared that I had satisfactorily completed eight years of elementary school and that high school was ready for me.

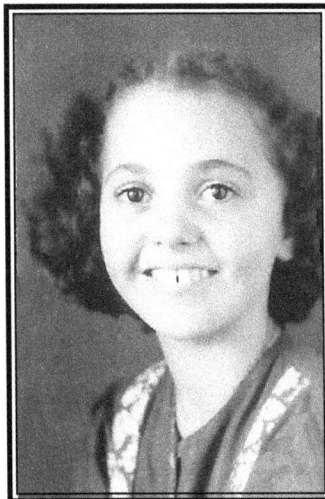

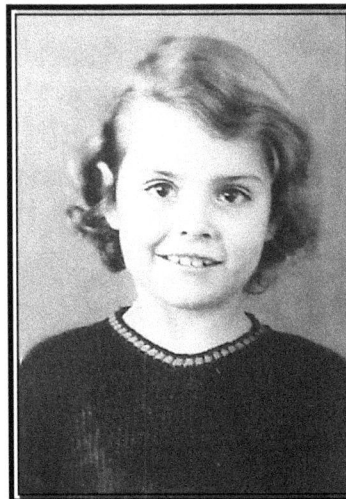

(Upper) Teachers at Mack School—Miss Mildred Hogsett became Mrs. Kelly and Miss Bernice Beahm became Mrs. Gardner. (Lower) Milton Cox, Mary Catherine Daily, and Deyon Davidson, classmates. Photos taken in 1938. *(Photos courtesy of Deyon Davidson Boughton)*

50

(Left) The "new" Mack schoolhouse, from the east, in 1923. The building was the pride of the community and used for many activities. The first movies in the valley were shown here by F. A. Kennedy. *(Photo courtesy of Frank and Velma Overbye)*

(Below) The Mack schoolhouse in its prime. Photo taken from the south during recess on a sunny spring day in the early 1940s. The students are unidentified. *(Photo courtesy of Erma Slaugh Armstrong)*

(Right) The Mack schoolhouse after it was closed in 1953, having been in service for 30 years. The teacherage can be seen in the background. It later became the home of Charles Ashburn and family. *(Photo courtesy of Frank and Velma Overbye, taken from their car window)*

The Mack Schoolhouse was used for a variety of community activities. The above poster was created by Jim McCoy for a benefit dance to be held at the schoolhouse to raise money for the Fruita Union High School band. Jim was a member of the band. The poster was written in reds and blues on a cardboard taken from the back of a tablet. *(Poster courtesy of Jim McCoy)*

Highline Hustlers Club

Following is a history of the Highline Hustlers Club as told to Deyon Davidson Boughton by her mother, Garnet Rachel Davidson. The club was evidently organized in the mid-1920s.

The ladies of Mack Mesa and the High Line community did their own thing ...

Monday—Washing Day
Tuesday—Ironing Day
Wednesday—Cleaning Day
Thursday—Club Day
Friday—Baking Day
Saturday—Shopping Day
Sunday—Praying Day

The creed of the depression-era housewife, as depicted by Capper's Weekly, was pictorial patterns painstakingly embroidered on bleached feed sacks, which were used for drying dishes.

It could also be said that every day was egg-gathering day, milking day, cream-skimming day; and that every spring included planting, every summer was filled with weeding and irrigating, every fall had its harvesting and canning, and every winter its sewing and patching days.

Those were cold days, those were hot days, those were long days, and those were the days that without the social contact of a club, life could have been very dull.

Club members would go to visit, gossip, entertain, play games, compare lives, have Home Demonstrations; they would go to have lots of fun. Lyda said, "They would surely have to hustle." Thus was born the Highline Hustlers Club. Charter members were:

Blanch Hollinger (first president)
Helen MacTaggert (first secretary)
Minnie Barr
Lois Collins Saunders
Emma Davidson
Garnet Davidson (first bride)
Lyda Hatcher
Lillian Herron
Mrs. Oscar Mayne
Iona Mayne

(Above) The Highline Hustler Club's building acquired from the Highline Canal Work Camp #7, and moved to Q & 11 8/10 Rd. Photo taken by Phyllis Likes on its present location at 831 N 1st St. in Grand Junction, Colorado.

(Above) The "Hi diddle diddle, the cat and the fiddle" bedspread embroidered by the Highline Hustlers Club women. Embroidered in red with red material surrounding each block, it is quite striking. Picture taken by Phyllis Likes at the Cross Orchards Living History Site where it is located.

(Below) Closeups of three blocks in the bedspread, the center one shows the name of the club and the year it was done. *(Courtesy of Cross Orchards Living History Site, Museum of Western Colorado)*

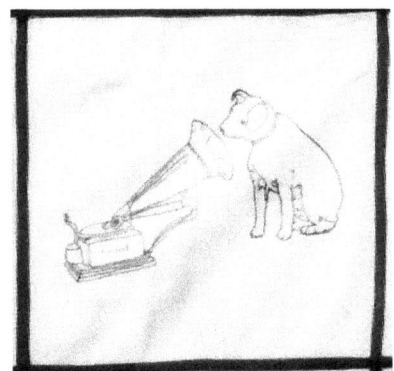

Caroline Peach
Edna Smith.

Jennie Brewster and Helen Cox soon arrived, joining a club with only two requirements. "Live in the general area, and — tell your age."

As people would come and go, club attendance averaged thirteen, and they snickered as they called themselves "the dirty dozen."

In 1925, a load of coal from the Farmers Mine could not get to Red Mesa without going down into Loma, through Mack, then back north. Visiting neighbors waded the wash on foot. Determined Hustlers, assisted by equally determined spouses, brought pressure on the county to build a bridge across the wash. Once accomplished it united the two farming communities of Red Mesa and Loma.

In spare moments, the Hustlers created a "Hi diddle diddle, the cat and the fiddle" bedspread. Embroidered on white squares with Turkey Red cotton floss, many secrets, dreams, and jokes were depicted. Emblazoned on the top was the year, 1928. That labor of love and laughter hangs in the Museum of Western Colorado in Grand Junction.

In 1929, Highline Canal Work Camp #7 was being dismantled. Darie Hendersen, manager, told the Hustlers they could have the building if they would get it moved. Rog Long donated property, and the three-room structure, moved by teams of horses, became a fixture in Red Mesa/Loma. The recent addressing system would locate it at Q and 11 8/10 Rd.

Costs of operation were financed by chili suppers, box socials, pie auctions, amateur hours, and dances with music provided by neighborhood musicians. Quince Long called the squares, Charley Hatcher, the Virginia Reel. "Circle and dance with the girl across the hall!" Who would get whom? That was when a wallflower might slip in leaving the belle-of-the-ball to find a chair.

When everyone was plumb tuckered out, musicians played "Be It Ever So Humble, There's No Place Like Home." Dancers found their partners, families gathered up sleeping children, and the dance was over. There were no strangers at those very popular country dances.

The clubhouse was used to house transient workers and as a dining center for harvest crews working neighboring farms.

During the 1940s "Uncle Sam" provided a community hall in Loma, which detracted from entertainment at the Highline Hustlers Club House. The building sat relatively unused for several years before Chalmers Creamery moved it to 831 N. 1st St. in Grand Junction, where it still stands. The land was deeded back to Mr. Long.

Throughout World War II, the Hustlers made quilts, folded bandages; and, dutifully patriotic, bought Victory Bonds. (They also elected two club family members, Oscar Mayne and Roe Saunders, to terms as county commissioners.)

Hustlers' Bonds lay in the Hatcher safety deposit box for many years. When the government asked that old bonds be cashed or replaced with new series bonds, the Highline Hustlers Club faced a decision: What to do with the money? There wasn't much, but there was some. A few of the younger members wanted to go to Disneyland but older members recalled the hard work and opted for a good cause.

About that time, the son of one of the charter members was hurt in an accident and needed financial assistance. Remaining charter members were pleased to help.

Through depression and war years, more than a third of a century, the Highline Hustlers Club was a driving force for fun and community concerns. Charter members moved away and passed away leaving the fun and work in the capable hands of a new generation of Hustlers ...

The Loma Community Hall has been listed in the National Register of Historic Places. It was built by the Works Progress Administration for the Federal Resettlement Administration. Saturday-night dances there were attended by people from all over Mesa County. It is still in use by the community. *(The Fruita Times, 5 January 1996)*

Uintah Country Club

The Uintah Club was organized at Mack in 1922 to provide social activities for local citizens. For the year of 1923 the officers elected were:

Miss Margaret McIlvaney,[†] president
Dick Stewart, vice president
Harry Lofquist, secretary- treasurer
Mrs. F. G. Morse, dramatic director
Ray McBeth, social director
Byron Boyden, physical director

The club held occasional dances and dinners and other types of entertainment for the benefit of the community. There was a small charge at these functions to raise funds for things like the school children's special needs, a tennis court, and eventually, a golf course.

Mack items in *The Daily Sentinel* of 14 February 1923 noted:

The new school building is coming along fine and it is expected to be ready for occupancy by the middle of March ... The Uintah Country Club hosted a dance at the hotel Monday evening with nearly 100 percent membership attendance. A splendid orchestra from Grand Junction furnished the music and everybody had a fine time. The eighth grade students of the Mack School sold pop and homemade candy, the proceeds of which will be used to purchase their class pins ... The Uintah Country Club is now a year old and is a very healthy and lively club.

Interest in the dances hosted by the Uintah Club continued for many years, as evidenced by an article in the Mack news items of 15 April 1926:

"A large crowd of dance lovers from Atchee came down to Mack on a special train Saturday evening to attend the dance at the school auditorium."

An item of interest appeared in Mack news items of 14 February 1924 noting that the new golf course was in use. On 18 February there was a story about a Mack woman, Mrs. P. E. Trim, wife of a Uintah Agent. She was accidentally struck on the head by a golf club swung by her husband, knocking her unconscious. Mrs. Trim was rushed to St. Mary's Hospital where it was learned her skull had not been fractured. She soon regained consciousness, and after several days in residence recovered enough to be allowed to return home. Surely you have heard of "hazards" built into golf courses, but isn't that a bit much?

Jim McCoy sent us an article from the *Colorado West*, Montrose, Colorado, paper, dated 17 June 1973 that told of

Golfers at the Uintah Country Club's Mack Golf Course in about the mid 1920s. The only one identified is Fred Baird, the third from the right. *(Photo courtesy of Esther Baird Sproule)*

† There is some confusion with the name "McIlvaney:" there is also a "Mulvaney." Possibly they are one and the same.

the 10th anniversary tournament held at the Mack Golf Course in 1933. This article tells about the establishment of the golf course in 1923, which attracted golfers from Grand Junction and Fruita and other points up the valley, as well as the enthusiasts from Mack, and the demise of the course in 1938. The following are excerpts from that article:

Mack's famous golf course
By Reford Theobold
Sentinel correspondent

In case one doesn't recall the chain of events, this was 1923 when Mack was in its prime. The town had four general stores, including the Mack Mercantile, a huge store in its day. Three filling stations and two train depots lined the streets of Mack, along with a hotel, post office, pool hall, restaurant, garage, and lumber yard. Nearby, Loma was another teeming community with such businesses as a canning factory to its credit.

With all this progress surrounding the town of Mack, postmaster, Byron Boyden, sensed the need for a golf course. So the former Chicagoan set about to create what would be the first golf course in Mesa County, and perhaps the entire Western Slope.

Boyden was not a professional golfer, but he did play the game a lot. Thus, he was the natural choice to lay out and manage the project. He later became the "pro" at the Mack Golf Course.

After 10 years of careful care, the Mack course was in its best condition. The well-trimmed prairie fairways were short, however, and the sand greens were usually quite hilly.

The course demanded pinpoint accuracy, rather than the ability to hit the long ball. Because the course was nothing but sand, both fairway and green, it would have challenged the ability of the best of modern golfers, even sand-trap expert Chi Chi Rodriguez.

The tournament consisted of two rounds, or 18 holes.

On the day of the tournament, the players had arranged to have a professional photographer on the scene to record the moment for posterity. After all, this was the biggest turnout the tourney had ever had, and there was something special about the number 10.

The 32 entries had just completed the first nine holes, and were waiting near the first tee for the man with the camera. Two hours after the scheduled time, the photographer arrived. All but one of the golfers, however, had returned to the course to finish the tournament. Thus, with only

Golfers at the Mack Golf Course on 12 November 1933, the same time the 10th Anniversary Tournament was taking place. This is the picture mentioned in the story above; the women golfers, some spectators and Byron Boyden. L-R: ?, Edmund Daily, Ray Wagaman, Mr. Sowers, ?, Mr. MacClain, Walter Rader, ?, Mrs. Sowers, ?, Mrs. Warner, Byron Boyden, Mrs. Walter Rader, Mrs. Laird, Mr. Laird, Sarah Boyden, ?, ?, Miss Cumming, Ann Wagaman, Jodell Simpson, Hazel Wagaman, Vic Earp, JoAnn Bowen and Mary Simpson *(Photo courtesy of JoAnn Bowen Montague)*

Lee Warner 32-33 65
Jack Evans 36-31 67
W.Bunce 34 36 70
R.Pixler 37-33 70
J.McClain 37-37 74
O.Wageman 38-36 74
R.Hogan 38-36 74
H.Nolan 38-36 74
W.Patten 39-36 75
C.Timmen 40-36 76
S.Reynolds 40-37 77
K.Jorgaman 41-37 78
S.Kilby 42-36 78
C.Palmer 43-34 77
B.Boyden 39-40 79
S.McMullin 41-38 79
C.Osborn 43-37 80
P.Greibel 39-41 80
V.Garms 41-40 81
H.Phillips 41-41 82
G.Conroy 43-40 83
H.Spencer 42-43 85
Dr.Hammond 42-43 85
E.Daily 41-40 81
T.James 41-46 87
O.Simpson 44-44 88
G.Gerporth 44-44 88
H.Litsey 46-43 89
T.Schmalbert 42-42 90
V.Earp 44-51 95
H.Vorbeck 49-55 104
D.Jones 52-53 105
H.Cunningham 55-57 112

The list of participants and their scores for the 10th Anniversary Tournament at the Mack Golf Course on 12 November 1933. *(Taken from the* Colorado West, *Montrose Colorado, newspaper, courtesy of Jim McCoy)*

"Captain" John Cooley, the same Cooley who ran the Mack Hotel, was responsible for giving Warner his start.

Lee Warner had never played golf when Cooley gave him some clubs shortly before the 10th annual tournament. Warner said, "I took to it like a duck to water."

Warner then entered the tournament, his first, and beat some of the best golfers in the county.

Time was not on Mack's side, however. Seeing the idea and its accompanying success, other towns began to build courses. Both Fruita and Grand Junction had courses of their own by the time of the 10th Annual Mack Tournament.

The county tournament was held in three parts in those days; one at Mack, one at Fruita and the last at Grand Junction.

In 1929, Fruita's course boasted of 125 members. Located south of the Colorado River on the west side of town, this was the most scenic. It was built among the pinions and included many natural hazards.

In fact, all the courses in the area were improving with each one. The first Grand Junction course used cotton seed hulls on the greens. Still, the course at Mack was dying a slow death.

Five years after the 10th tourney, Mack hosted its final meet. Only one golfer entered the event, as opposed to the 32 in 1933.

The lone golfer? Byron Boyden, of course.

A tournament was held each year at Mack through 1938, when the 15th and final one was held, and the only golfer to show up was Byron Boyden. That pretty much marked the end of the Mack Golf Course. With courses constructed at Grand Junction and Fruita, interest in the Mack Golf Course faded.

Byron Boyden there to represent the players, the picture was taken. The people in the photo commemorating the event are only a few women golfers who happened to be playing that day, and some spectators, along with Boyden.

In an effort to make up for the situation, the list of participants and their respective scores were posted at the left of the picture. Most of them were well-known people from the Fruita and Grand Junction areas, including the founder of the now defunct Evans Hardware who grabbed second place. Number three finisher W. F. Bunce who was the blacksmith in Fruita. Roy Pixler made his mark in the world in Montrose, where he had the Coors distributorship.

Robert Hogan became a salesman for C. D. Smith. His wife, Lucy, was clerk of district court for 20 years, and an experienced law clerk. Nolan, his first name unknown, was the pro at the new Grand Junction golf course. Phillip Griebel, for whom Fruita Junior High's Greibel Field is named, was a school teacher...

With the lead well in hand, Lee Warner tapped the golf ball into the final hole to capture the 10th annual Mack Golf Tournament.

Superintendent of the railroad,

Byron Boyden sitting forlornly as the only contestant at the 15th Anniversary Tournament held at the Mack Golf Course in the fall of 1938. *(Taken from the* Montrose West, *Montrose, Colorado, newspaper, courtesy of Jim McCoy.)*

Chapter Three

The Challenges and Blessings of 1918

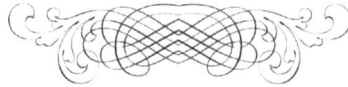

World War I

During the settling of the lower valley, World War I was raging across the ocean in Europe. The *Daily Sentinel* published stories each day about the wins and losses on the battle fronts, and an occasional bit of news about some local young man's achievement or movement from one unit to another or to some other area. Young men on both sides of the battle lines were being exposed to the terrible dangers and deprivations of war. Many thousands of them lost their lives, including some who were near and dear to families in the lower valley. Remember, this was the "WAR TO END ALL WARS!"

All men under 35 years of age were required to register for the draft in September 1918, be they single or married, even married men with children. Consequently, the names of many settlers of New Liberty and residents of Mack appeared in the lists published by the classification board in October 1918. Following is part of that list including only those whose names you may recognize from the New Liberty/Mack areas:

Albert W. Alstatt
Fred J. Baird
Clyde L. Balkwill
Samuel J. Barr
James L. Booth
William E. Bowen
William J. Carr
Thomas B. Carroll
Charles W. Cavendish
Chris Christopherson
Florian D. Christopherson

Earl O. Cox
Robert M. Cox
William J. Cox
Matthew D. Crews
Arthur H. Cutler
Robert P. Demaree
Roy E. Eno
Thomas W. Kelley

Clyde W. Likes
Quince Long
Roger H. Long
Hiram M. Long
John B. Morrow
Robert M. Phillips
James F. Wagaman
John E. Wesner

Not many in the above list were called to serve. William J. Cox is the only one we are aware of who went further than a training base.

The Daily Sentinel of Monday evening, 11 November 1918, headlined the news that people all over the world had been hoping and praying for:

World War Ends !!!

Troops from Fort Duschene in Utah being transferred from the Uintah Railway to the D&RG RR at the Mack Depot, 15 September 1911. *(Agnes Kiefer Collection)*

WORLD WAR ENDS

German Envoys Signed the Armistice Terms at Midnight and the Fighting Ceased At Six O'clock This Morning

President Addresses a Joint Session of Congress Giving Terms of Surrender

THE PAPER ALL THE PEOPLE READ.

want ads from day to day, put in the Sentinel always pay.

THE DAILY SENTINEL

VOL XXV   GRAND JUNCTION COLORADO MONDAY EVENING NOVEMBER 11 1918   No 301

WOODROW WILSON

The facts which have today a ruling classed in stern success and known of every aspect of the whole continent of the part to the great success of peace... of Germany, Belgium and Italy.

HELP NEEDED AT HOSPITAL VERY BADLY

MARSHAL FOCH IS IN PARIS

(By Associated Press.)

A GREAT EXTRA WIRE SERVICE

MUST ESTABLISH A JUST DEMOCRACY THROUGHOUT WORLD

Everything for which America fought has been accomplished, says President Wilson— Lend Helping Hand to Defeated Enemy

(By Associated Press.)

Washington, Nov. 11.—President Wilson issued a formal proclamation at 10 o'clock this morning announcing that an armistice with Germany had been signed. The proclamation is as follows:

"My Fellow Countrymen: An armistice was signed this morning. Everything for which America has fought has been accomplished. It will be our fortunate duty to assist, by example, by sober friendly council and by material aid, in establishing a just democracy throughout the world.—Woodrow Wilson."

LIGHT WINDOWS

IMMEDIATE EVACUATION OF AND FULL INDEMNITY TO OCCUPIED TERRITORIES WERE PROVIDED FOR IN PEACE TERMS

Germans Must Cease Operations on Both Land and Sea Within Six Hours; Immediately Evacuate France, Belgium, Alsace-Lorraine and Luxemburg; Surrender All Allied Soldiers and Civilians Now Held Prisoners; Surrender Vast Quantities of War Materials and a Large Part of High Seas Fleet Together With One Hundred and Sixty Submarines; Retire With All Armies to Right Bank of the Rhine and Comply With Other Stringent Conditions.

WORLD IS DELIRIOUS WITH JOY AT NEWS OF WAR'S END

Even People of Berlin Are Marching Through The Streets Singing The Marseillaise, Cheering For Allied Governments and Venting Vengeance Upon Former Rulers; Allied Nations Wild With Joy At Delivery From Four Years of Devastating Warfare; Joint Session of Congress This Afternoon That President Might Make Known To The World the Terms With Which The Huns Have Complied.

[By Associated Press.]

Washington, Nov. 11.—The terms of the armistice with Germany were read to congress by President Wilson at 1 o'clock this afternoon.

NEW GERMAN GOVERNMENT SIGNS PEACE TERM

THE DAILY SENTINEL.

VOL. XXV — GRAND JUNCTION, COLORADO, TUESDAY EVENING, NOVEMBER 12, 1918

THOSE WHO OVERTHREW THE KAISER FAVORABLE TO TERMS OF ARMISTICE

Their Acceptance of Terms as Outlined by Allies Removes Last Danger of a Complication Which Would Result in Further Warfare; Revolutionists' Peace Delegates Signed the Document at 5 O'clock Monday Morning.

REBELS ARE IN CONTROL OF THE NATION

General Hindenburg is Reported Adhering to Newly Formed Government; Revolutionists Now Hold Entire German Northern Fleet and Helgoland; German Troops in the Field Reported in Mutiny; Socialistic Parties Unite and Agree Upon a Joint Cabinet.

[By Associated Press.]

Paris, Nov. 12.—The new German government considered the armistice conditions at a sitting late Sunday at Berlin. Having decided to accept, it telephoned instructions to the German headquarters are located authorizing the delegates to sign the agreement. The courier left the Spa immediately, crossing the lines without incident. He reached Chateau de Franeort at about 2 o'clock in the morning.

After reading the instructions the German plenipotentiaries asked to see Marshal Foch, who, with Admiral Wemyss first lord of the British navy, received them. A discussion, which the Temps correspondent describes as being rather long, followed in regard to certain clauses, particularly concerning the maintenance of blockade. The German delegates signed the document at 5 o'clock.

Shortly afterward, on receiving the newspaper correspondents, Premier Clemenceau said:

The German plenipotentiaries insisted above all upon the food question. We will maintain the blockade during the armistice. Nevertheless as the situation in Germany and Europe is desperate, we will do everything possible to feed them that we can to fairness to ourselves. The question of transport dominates all these problems.

[By Associated Press.]

Amsterdam Nov 12.—The entire German northern fleet and the island of Helgoland are in the hands of the soldiers' council, according to a telegram from Bremen.

General Hindenburg is not in Holland, according to a telegram from the semi-official Wolff Bureau of Berlin, which says he remains at main headquarters and adheres to the new government. The telegram adds that Crown Prince Rupprecht of Bavaria, commander of the German northern army group, has not died as some reports declared.

[By Associated Press.]

Amsterdam Nov 11 (Monday)—The German socialists and independent socialists have agreed for a joint cabinet according to a Wolff Bureau announcement. The cabinet consists of Phillip Scheidemann, Herr Landsburg, Herr Gerbert, Hugo Haase, Richard Barth (editor of Vorwaerts) and Wilhelm Kattmann.

[By Associated Press.]

Amsterdam Nov 11 (Monday)—German troops at Beverloo camp, in Belgium, have mutinied and are marching with their guns toward Holland.

IMMEDIATE OPENING OF PEACE NEGOTIATIONS IS ASKED BY GERMANS

In a Plea to President Wilson, Foreign Secretary Solf Points to the Fact That His Country is in Pressing Danger of a Famine and Anxious That Final Terms Be Arranged That Permanent Peace May Be Declared.

[By Associated Press.]

London, Nov. 12, 4 p.m.—According to a German wireless message from Berlin, Germany has requested the president of the United States to arrange immediately for the opening of peace negotiations, there being pressing danger of famine. This message, which was sent by Foreign Secretary Solf to Secretary of State Lansing, adds:

An armistice being concluded, the German government requests the president of the United States to arrange for the opening of peace negotiations. For the purpose of their acceleration, the German government purposes, first, to take into view the conclusion of a preliminary peace, and asks for communication as to the place and time negotiations might begin. As there is pressing danger of famine the German government is particularly anxious for the negotiations to begin immediately.

STARVATION THREATENED IN GERMANY

Foreign Secretary Issues Appeal Against Stringency of Allied Armistice Demands.

STOP FOOD SHIPMENT

Official Washington Will Take Cognizance of Hun Plea. Terms Are Aimed to Prevent Treachery.

[By Associated Press.]

Washington Nov. 12.

FORMER KAISER NOW IN HOLLAND

[By Associated Press.]

Amsterdam Nov 12.—William Hohenzollern, former German emperor, arrived Sunday at Count Bentinck's chateau at Ledenlinke at noon near Arnhem, according to a Berlin Courant.

CHARLES OF AUSTRIA HAS ABDICATED

General Strike Will Be Declared at Vienna Tomorrow; Socialist Leader Dead.

[By Associated Press.]

London Nov 12, 9:10 a.m.—Emperor Charles of Austria has abdicated, according to an Exchange Telegraph company dispatch from Copenhagen quoting private advices from Vienna.

TO MANUFACTURE PASSENGER AUTOS AFTER JANUARY 1

That Date Had Been Fixed for Complete Curtailment of All Pleasure Cars; New List of Priorities.

CELEBRATION LASTED WELL INTO NIGHT

Merry Revelers Thronged Business District of the City; All Happy at Return of Peace.

COUNT OF VOTE CAST OVER MESA

No Changes Made in General Results as Announced on Day Following Election.

TAYLOR LED TICKET

Popular Congressman Polled 3,663 Votes Over County, a Majority of 1,718 Over Local Opponent. Vote on Amendments.

ACTIVITIES OF DRAFT BOARDS NOW WILL CEASE

Men Under 19 and Over 36 Not to Receive Questionnaires; Lessens the Work of Local Boards.

LISTING NO MORE APPLICANTS FOR OFFICERS SCHOOL

[By Associated Press.]

MYSTERY SURROUNDS PRESENT WHEREABOUTS OF DEPOSED EMPEROR

Kaiser is Thought to Have Sought Refuge at One of Three Country Seats in Holland; His Flight From the Land He Had Governed and Despoiled Was an Inglorious One; Travel-Stained Auto Carried Him From His Native Land.

BELGIAN REFUGEES ASK FOR VENGEANCE

[By Associated Press.]

Amsterdam, Nov. 11 (Monday).—A great mystery is still being made of William Hohenzollern's destination in Holland. Three different country seats of the Bentinck family have been mentioned as his temporary abode.

The kaiser and former German emperor made an inglorious entry into Holland, according to reports from Eysden. At 7:30 Sunday morning, ten travel-stained automobiles, driven by Prussian officers, were seen coming slowly through the fog along the Vise Maastricht highroad from the last Belgian village of Mouland, which is almost on the border line. The autos of the motors brought a crowd of curious villagers.

The former German ruler was dressed in a general's uniform with an officer's cap, and he carried a sword. The erstwhile martial figure was huddled and bent on a walking-stick while his eyes stared straight ahead.

Dutch frontier guards stopped the autos. After brief formalities the automobiles were conducted to the Eysden railway station and Dutch cavalry and military cyclists formed a cordon about the station. Crowds of Belgian refugees swarmed around the station crying "Assassin".

ONLY GLOW CAMP FIR MARK LIN

Peace Reigns Along the Front Where World's Battles Recently Rag

ONLY RUMBLE OF T

MANY TO SAV THE SENTIN

Yesterday's Big War Will Be Retained for toric Value in Many of the Valley.

MINNESOTA WA VOTED DRY MAJORITY

A picture of president Woodrow Wilson was featured on the front page of the Daily Sentinel with the caption: "The man whose name today is being cheered in every city and hamlet of every allied nation and who is referred to as a liberator by the great masses of people of Germany, Austria, Hungary, Bulgaria and Turkey." That same day President Wilson addressed a joint session of Congress, outlining the terms of surrender, which terms included: immediate evacuation of and full indemnity to occupied territories. The Germans were to cease operations on both land and sea within six hours; surrender all allied soldiers and civilians held as prisoners; surrender vast quantities of war materials and most of their high seas fleet, including one hundred sixty submarines. A just democracy was to be established throughout the world! (How about that?) The world was delirious with joy at the news of war's end!

There was cause for great celebration in all allied nations when the armistice was signed. Following is a story that appeared in the Mack news items, Tuesday, 19 November 1918:

Mack had a big parade last Monday, too, in the celebration of the ending of the war. Just two or three of us started out with cowbelles [sic] and inside of fifteen minutes everybody was in it. The housewives who were doing the regular Monday morning stint of washing, dried their hands on their aprons, seized a big spoon and a tin pan or whatever they could quickly lay their hands on ... The storekeepers closed up their stores and joined in with brand new tubs and hammers to beat them, what mattered it whether the tubs were made unsaleable [sic] or not, the war was over and we must voice our unbounded patriotism in some way. And the little boys and girls stopped their play and marched in true military style to the tune of their tin cans, etc. One little fellow was beating an old fruit jar with a silver spoon and thought he was making as much noise as anybody. We paraded about an hour, led by the stars and stripes in the hands of Mrs. Cooley and Mr. Falvey, followed by A. F. Lofquist carrying our fourth Liberty Loan flag which we earned by "going over the top."

We serenaded D & R G # 3 as it stood at the depot, after which we disbanded, before which though, we all stood at attention and saluted and gave three cheers for the flags of the Allies and of the United States. After dinner all who could, went to Grand Junction and participated in the big celebration there.

(The statement "going over the top" meant they had exceeded a goal in raising funds for the war effort by purchasing "Liberty Bonds.")

The Flu Epidemic

By this time also, the influenza epidemic was effecting the lives of thousands of citizens throughout the country. The following appeared in *The Daily Sentinel*, 10 October 1918:

"First Aid For Influenza ..."

- Take liberal doses of Epsom Salts.
- Go to bed immediately after first symptoms are felt.
- Keep warm in bed with blankets and hot-water bottles, but ...
- Keep plenty of fresh air in the room.
- Segregate yourself from other members of the family as much as possible.
- Attendants and nurses must wear gauze masks.
- If temperature is present and there is great pain, take Dovers Powders. This drug must be prescribed by either a pharmacist or a physician.
- Take no chances on home remedies aside from salts.
- Call a physician early. The plague is highly treacherous.
- A big dose of salts before the doctor arrives will do much to break up the disease ...

Records show that the lives of two whose names we'll recognize were lost to the dread disease. Lila M. (Fish) Saunders, first wife of Rowland F. "Roe" Saunders, died in Fruita of the "flu" on 13 November 1918. Some years later, Roe was to become a well-known farmer and civic leader in the lower valley. (More will be written about the Saunders' later.)

Then, taken from the Tuesday Evening, 14 January 1919 issue of *The Daily Sentinel* from the Mack items:

A Mr. Morrow, who lives about eight miles north of Mack, lost his young son, Thomas, aged 10 years , Sunday, 5 January, death being caused by influenza. His wife and two younger children were also stricken, but, through the timely aid of the doctor and good neighbors, they are now recovering nicely. The body of the boy was sent to the old home in Kansas for burial. We sympathize deeply with the bereaved family in the loss of their son.

(Records prove Thomas was actually 13, and the two younger children mentioned were Estellene and Elizabeth.)

Ironically, the "flu" epidemic had pretty well subsided by the end of January 1919.

To move ahead a few years ... several items in *The Daily Sentinel* of February and March 1924 noted that there was an outbreak of measles in the valley that became an epidemic. Several deaths occurred. We must remember that measles in those days could develop into a dangerous disease.

The Highline Canal

We have found a variation of the spelling of the name of the canal - Hi-Line; High Line, etc. We prefer the above, as it seems the most consistent.

In June 1902 Congress passed the Federal Reclamation Act with the aim to develop irrigation projects and "reclaim" desert land. No provision had been made by Congress for the new organization to operate the projects, so operation was temporarily provided by the Bureau of Geographic Surveys. Engineers of that bureau had previously made investigations of lands, soils, rivers, and water supplies in the western territories.

Soon after the Federal Reclamation Act was passed, the Bureau of Reclamation was organized and took over the planning and operations of new projects. Early in September

View of the Grand River looking along the axis of the proposed Diversion Dam for the Highline Canal, located in DeBeque Canyon, picture taken 21 August 1913. *(Grand Valley Water Users Association Collection)*

1902, J. H. Mathis, a government engineer, arrived in Grand Junction with a small party of engineers. Their purpose was to make a survey of the lands in the Grand Valley and determine the feasibility of an experimental irrigation project. He submitted a favorable report to the Bureau and soon a site was selected for a dam in DeBeque Canyon, several miles up river from the town of Palisade, Colorado.

By that time speculators and promoters had begun to try to muscle in on the plans and caused some delay in development through their schemes to try to convince the local citizens that the Bureau was not capable of developing irrigation of the lands, and that they, the developers, could do a better job for less money. Even *The Daily Sentinel* jumped on the band wagon and published negative editorials suggesting the futility of the project.

Consequently not much was accomplished until the Grand Valley Water Users' Association was organized in February 1905 to meet the requirements of the Bureau of Reclamation. The Bureau then opened an office in Grand Junction 20 February 1908, and field work began soon after. A construction camp was established near Cameo on 10 March 1908, and a field party was moved to Mack on 11 April 1908. Things had begun to happen!

At the suggestion of the Bureau, the Water Users then began a program of soliciting good, solid pledges from interested persons to establish a fund to provide a sound financial foundation for the project. The Water Users Association was successful in raising $134,000 in pledges. Then a proposal was presented to James A. Garfield, Secretary of the Interior, that the Bureau match funds of $125,000 from the Water Users, leaving $9,000 of their funds for "good measure." This would make it possible for construction to begin immediately.

After several more delays, created by various opposing factions, at 10 a.m., 4 May 1909, bids were let for $42,000.00 worth of construction. At 4 p.m. that same day a telegram was received from the Bureau in Washington stating that a "temporary suspension order" had been issued to stop construction.

Politics! More delays! There was a real danger for a time of the project being abandoned completely! However, owing to the persistence of a few dedicated individuals who straightened out all the political snags, work finally resumed late in the fall of 1912.

After a period of time required for reorganization, serious work began early in 1913. Construction proceeded then without further delays, and water was delivered to a limited acreage in 1916. The first public drawing for homestead units was held in April of 1917. (That did not include any units that came up in the drawing of March 1918)

The project was universally referred to as the "Highline Canal." Why was it so called? We have found no conclusive answer to that. Perhaps the fact that the location was the "highest" on the Grand River of any point of water diversion up to that time had some bearing on the name. Who knows?

The beginning of the Diversion Dam construction in DeBeque Canyon. This involved placing the forms for the cement structures, and hauling in the fill dirt for the coffer dam. *(Grand Valley Water Users' Association Collection)*

A general view of construction camp #1, south of the dam site, 20 August 1913. Houses were supplied for the men and barns for the horses. When you think of the food and supplies for the men and the hay and grain for the animals, it becomes a different picture. They couldn't go home every night as they do today, mainly because of the transportation and the time it would take to do that. Also, their hours wouldn't necessarily be from 9 a.m. to 4 p.m., but 5 a.m. to 10 p.m. or until dark. *(Grand Valley Water Users' Association Collection)*

Horse-drawn elevating graders and wagons working on Schedule 2, one mile above Cameo. This gives one an idea of how many horses it took to accomplish the job. There were no big dump trucks, dozers, scrapers, and other earth moving equipment to do the job with. Just horse and man power and lots of dust and sweat. *(Grand Valley Water Users' Association Collection)*

A steam shovel working on Schedule 4, below Cameo. Horse drawn wagons waiting, coming, and going with fill dirt for the coffer dam. They probably thought that shovel was a marvelous machine, as it could fill those wagons so quickly and get them on their way. Some of the men hired out their horses and themselves to the company. *(Grand Valley Water Users' Association Collection)*

65

(Above left) The Diversion Dam under construction in DeBeque Canyon facing north.

(Above) Looking at the dam from the east side abutment one can see the cement forms up close and the base for the dam. The Highline Canal gates on the far side are evident. Railroad freight cars are parked on the tracks across the river undoubtedly filled with supplies for the dam and canal outlet construction.

(Left) General view of the dam looking downstream from the east end.

(Below) Looking from the canal side on June 1917, the dam is complete and water is running in the canal. What an exciting day! It took four years to build the dam, with lots of sweat and hard work, and with primitive equipment. The dam was officially named the DeBeque Canyon Dam. *(All pictures are from the Grand Valley Water Users' Association Collection)*

(Above) Roller gates stretching across the river control the amount of water to be taken from the river into the canal. When the gates are closed the water level rises behind the dam and diverts the water to the canal gates. The roller gate in the picture above is closed to accomplish this purpose. (Upper right) This roller gate is wide open so the water flows freely under it. (Right) This gate is closed while the one next to it is open.

(Below) The canal gates are officially opened and the water is flowing into the canal for the first time in June 1917. The canal gates are raised and lowered by screw wheels on top of the deck. The water below the gates is measured in cubic feet per second (second feet) and a flow of 1.008 cubic feet per second will deliver one acre foot of water in twelve hours. The farmers are charged by the acre foot for the use of the water. *(All are from the Grand Valley Water Users' Association Collection)*

Main Canal Division #2: (Upper two) 1914, Excavating cut near Clifton by the 'trap tunnel' method. (Left) A view of concreting operations in Tunnel No. 2 showing forms in place. (Below) 11 April 1914, A steam shovel excavating the main canal. Material is loaded into wagons and dumped into railroad dump cars for use in track-raise. Looking north, loading trap and Camp No. 1 can be seen in background.
Opposite page: (Bottom) 11 April 1914, Looking south from lower portal of Tunnel No. 1, concrete canal lining, Jerry Creek siphon and Camp No.1, work-train on track handling the dirt cars. (Center right) A Maney wheel scraper. (Center left) Steam shovel and equipment used in making several cuts. (Top two: L-R) Two-yard dragline excavator driven by gasoline engine. Steam dragline excavator 2½ yard bucket, 85 foot boom working in a thorough cut. A preceding machine has made the right hand slope and bank and these machine are finishing the section. (*Grand Valley Water Users' Association Collection*)

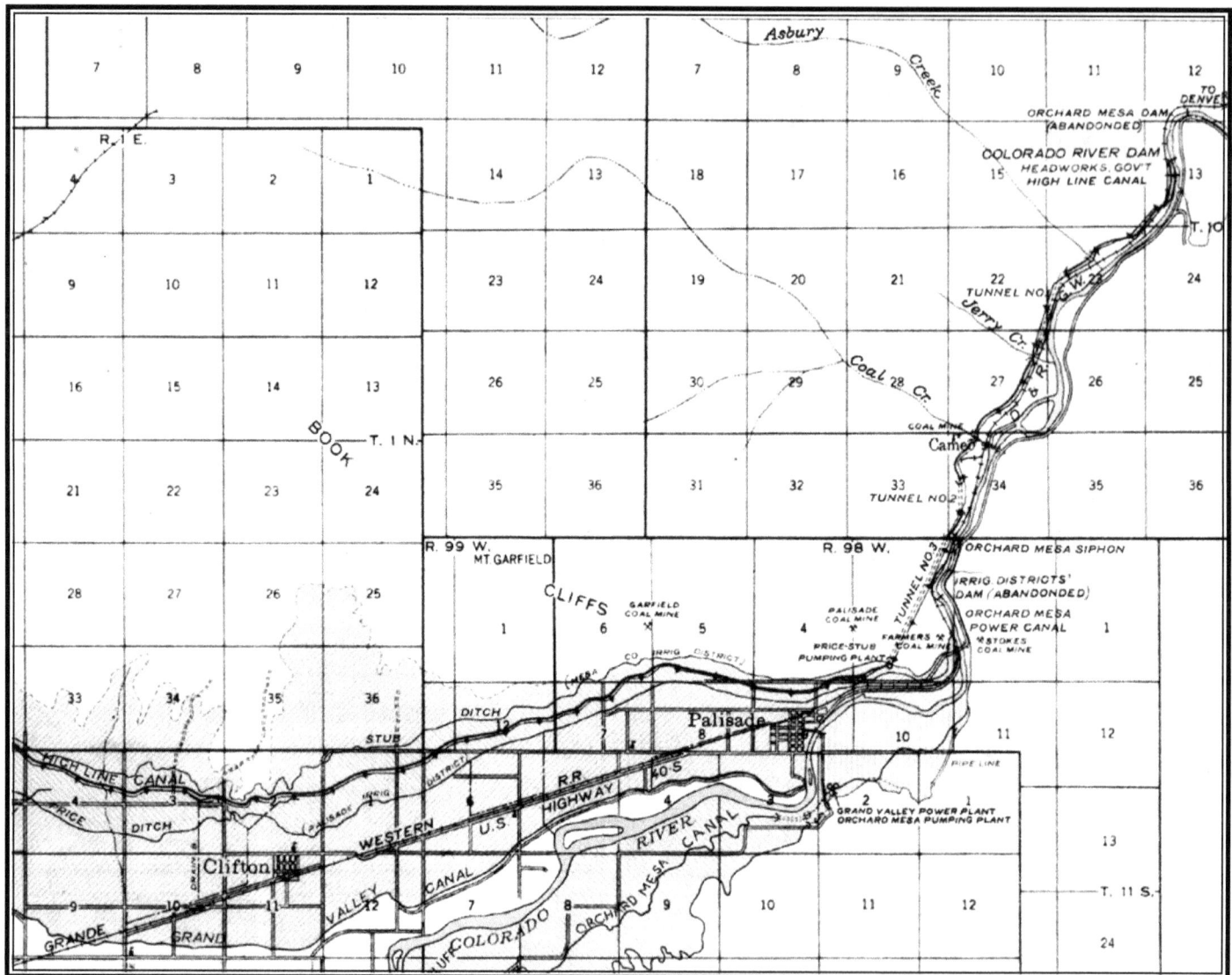

Opposite page: (Above left) A bridge carrying track of Rio Grande Railroad over the main canal just south of Diversion Dam, north of Cameo. (Above right) The Asbury Creek siphon above Tunnel #1, near the present Hayes farm. (Middle left) The concrete canal lining at Jerry Creek, siphon immediately south of Tunnel #1. All the above dated 16 October 1914. (Middle right) The Coal Creek siphon at Cameo March 1915. (Bottom) A crushing and screening plant at Orchard Mesa Power Canal near Cameo. This plant furnished gravel for practically all concrete work in the fall of 1923 and spring of 1924 for the Orchard Mesa siphon. *(All pictures from the Grand Valley Water Users' Association Collection)* **Above:** *(A section of the Grand Valley Irrigation Project Map of 1932, G.V.W.U.A.)* At the upper right corner of the map is the location of the Diversion Dam, now more commonly known as the Grand Valley Project Roller Dam, where the river water is diverted into the Highline Canal with a capacity of 1,600 cubic feet per second (cfs), more or less. From the dam, the canal flows under the railroad bridge, then through a siphon that runs under Asbury Creek, then through Tunnel #1, after which it is siphoned under Jerry Creek, then under Coal Creek at Cameo, and next through Tunnel #2, beyond which it comes to the inlets of Tunnel #3. At this location the water *may* be divided two ways: (1) When available, up to 860 cfs may be turned into the Orchard Mesa Power Canal through the Orchard

Mesa siphon that was built in 1923 (rehabilitated during the early 1980s) and runs under the railroad track, Colorado River, and Highway I-70. The Orchard Mesa Power Canal then transports the water some four miles to the Grand Power Plant (hydro-electric) and the adjacent Orchard Mesa Irrigation District's Pumping Plant where hydraulic pumps lift water up onto Orchard Mesa for irrigation. (2) The remaining water during the irrigation season flows through Tunnel #3 with a capacity *up to* 850 cfs and includes irrigation water for the Palisade Irrigation District (Price Canal, etc.) with a right for *up to* 80 cfs, and the Mesa County Irrigation District (Stub Ditch, etc.) with a right for *up to* 40 cfs, and the Highline Canal (G.V.W.U.A.) with a right for *up to* 730 cfs. The above said Roller Dam diverts water for five different entities according to priority of need with irrigation having the top priority. The previously mentioned hydro-electric power plant supplies electricity to Public Service of Colorado. During the irrigation season (approx April through October) the system is operated for both irrigation and generation of hydro-electric power. During the non-irrigation season, it is operated for hydro-electric power generation only with a decreed right of 800 cfs. The canal's length from the river diversion to its terminus, some five miles from the Colorado/Utah border, is approximately 55 miles, and as previously stated, serves a total of five different entities. —*Bill Klapwyk*

71

Silting Operation: 1916—When cuts were made through the shale formation, it was discovered that water would leak out through the cracks in the shale. So they conceived the idea of running silt into the canal so the silt would settle and seal the cracks. (Upper two) A giant stream using 3½ inch nozzle working on clay bank. (Left) The pumping plant used to provide water to make silt. (Below) 1917—A hydraulic giant at work at the silting plant. The canal is in the background so the silt pond is directly above the canal for the silt to flow into the canal. **Opposite page:** 1917 — (Upper left) A centrifugal pump with a 125 HP Weber gas engine at the silting plant. (Right and bottom) Cippoletti weir and distributing flume with notched semi-circular lipped openings with silting plant in the background on main canal. (Center) A view showing layer of silt deposited in shale cut about 3 miles below the silting plant. *(Grand Valley Water Users' Association Collection)*

Plans originally called for completion of the Highline Canal as far west as the Utah State line, but for one reason or another that never happened. The canal was completed to West Salt Wash, about five miles from Utah. Some water was allowed to waste into that wash for several years after the canal was in use. No land was developed that far west until years later. Eventually the canal proper fell into disuse beyond a lateral about a mile west of Badger Wash.

In September 1919 there was some excitement about a big irrigation project being planned for eastern Utah. A dam was to be built in the Colorado River near Westwater. It would provide enough water to irrigate 25,000 acres, and would generate enough power to electrify the Denver and Rio Grande Railroad from Grand Junction to Ogden! That was another dream that never reached fulfillment. There was certainly potential for many acres of good land that could be brought under irrigation in that part of Utah.

Sheep shearing sheds and pens were built at the end of the canal and were in use for quite a number of years. In the spring during shearing time the pens were a beehive of activity as herds were brought to the area and held on the desert nearby while the shearers and their helpers harvested the annual wool-clip.

We will include here a brief description of the shearing operation for the benefit of the younger generation who may have never seen such a thing.

The pens consisted of one or more large holding corrals from which at least one smaller pen branched off into an aisle. The sheep were directed single file into an area next to a shed where the shearers worked. One or two sheep would be kept waiting in little holding pens, separated from the shearers by burlap curtains. Since the sheep could not see through the curtains, they stood waiting in fear until a shearer could grab one and drag it into his enclosure and proceed to clip the wool off.

The shearing shed itself was a small temporary building made from materials that could be knocked down and moved easily. In each section where the shearers worked there was a small wooden floor about six to eight feet square, also temporary, arranged adjacent to the holding aisle where the sheep were kept waiting.

There were always a number of men —"helpers" — who kept the sheep moving for the shearers. There was also a man to gather up the loose fleece after the shearer finished with a sheep. He would gather the fleece into a bundle and tie it with special string. He in turn would move it down the line to the "stomper" who worked with a large bag tied to a special frame in such a way that the wool could be packed into the bag tightly until it was filled. After the bag was filled it would be taken down, sewn closed and marked with the brand of the sheep owner. The wool bags, each weighing several hundred pounds, would be kept together until such time as they could be loaded onto a wagon, rail car, or later, a truck, and hauled away. At the site we are telling about, it was loaded onto Uintah Railway flat cars.

The earlier method of clipping the wool was done with hand shears, much like you see gardeners use to clip grass around the edges of flower beds. These were kept very sharp, and if not used carefully could result in serious injury to the sheep, sometimes cutting off large patches of skin with the wool.

Later they perfected mechanical shears that were run by a series of belts and shafts. Still later these were replaced by electric -powered shears.

The Siphon

At East Salt Wash, near the Pollock farms a siphon was constructed to carry the canal water across the wash. That siphon was an interesting and unusual structure. It was a wooden tube about five or six feet in diameter, made up of tongued and grooved redwood boards approximately two inches thick by six inches wide and milled to match the specified circumference. The boards were doweled together at the ends to make the joints leak-proof. The tube was bound together and reinforced with adjustable iron bands. The siphon was supported on cribs or cement pilings with appropriate spacing, and a trestle to support it across the wash proper. It was nearly a mile in length from intake to outlet.

It became a yearly ritual to repair leaks in the siphon during the winter months. A crew of local farmers would assemble with necessary materials for needed repairs. The first item of business would be to drain the water trapped in the tube after the water in the canal was shut off. The siphon was lower in the middle than at either end, so it held a large amount of water. There was a large valve built into the bottom at the lowest point of the tube that could be opened for drainage. An anticipated bonus was the large number of fish, mostly carp, trapped inside. The crew would come prepared with tubs and sacks to carry the fish home for dinner. Once Clyde W. Likes, who was foreman of the crew several times, told of a large carp becoming wedged in the valve in such a way as to shut off most of the water flow.

The men would select a site in need of repair near the middle of the tube, and open a large window to give them access to the inside. This meant part of the crew could work inside and part outside.

The siphon was a death trap for livestock. If a cow or sheep got in the water too near the intake, the unfortunate animal didn't have a chance! Occasionally a cow or sheep carcass would come floating by at the swimming hole, but not necessarily because of the siphon. But that never delayed the swimming fun for very long!

The siphon crossing the East Salt Creek Wash on the main canal shown after a flood on 20 Aug 1925. There was no damage to the siphon or its pillars, thanks to the good construction, but the flood removed the highway bridge. See story by Viola Alstatt. The siphon was located on the SE ¼ of Section 3 Twp 9S Range 103W near the Pollock farm. *(Grand Valley Water Users Association Collection)*

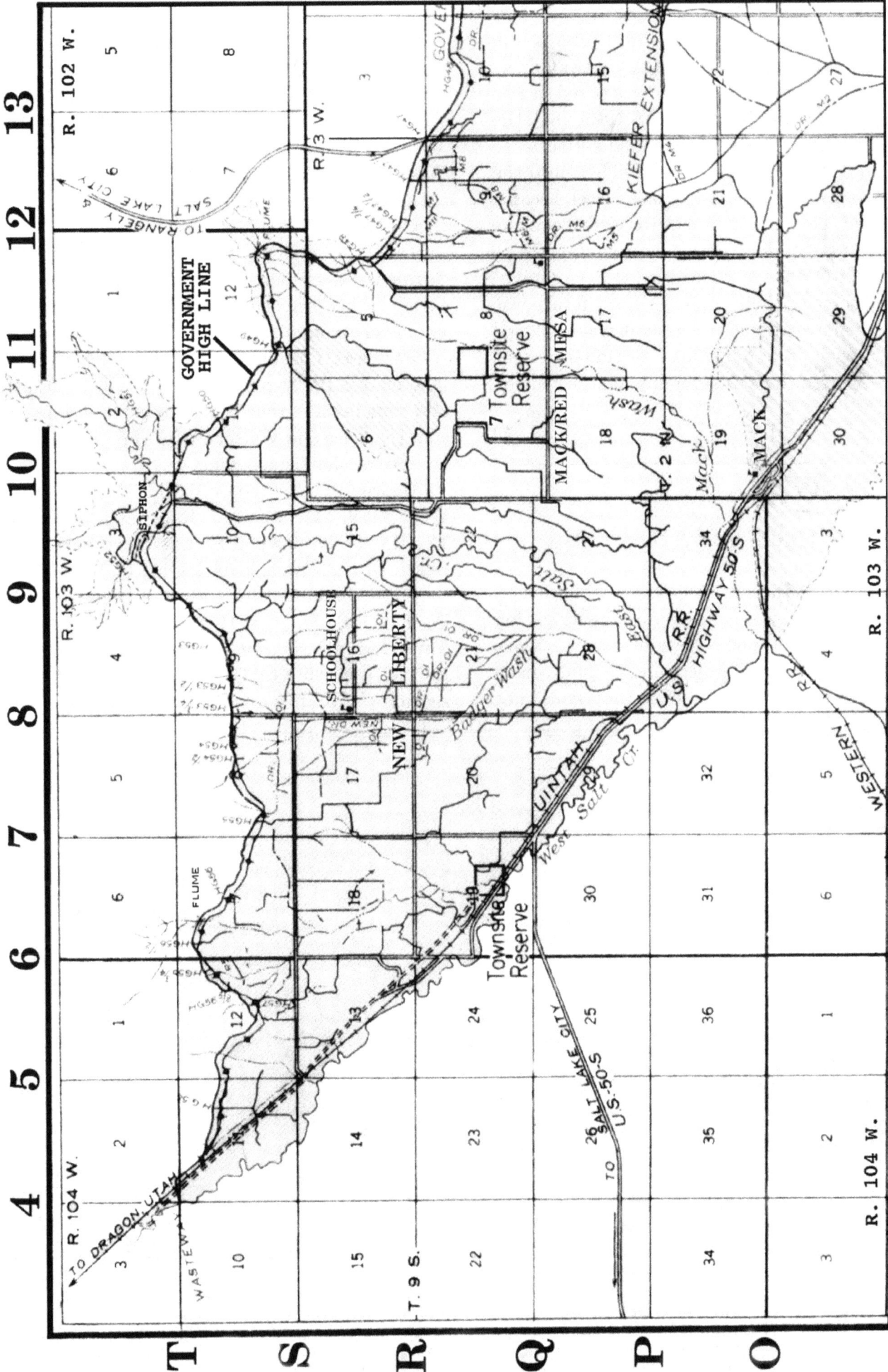

A section of a map of the GRAND VALLEY IRRIGATION PROJECT, MESA COUNTY, COLORADO. Drawn in 1932 by the Washington Office of the Department of the Interior, Bureau of Reclamation, J. H. Pellen, Chief Draftsman. W. J. Chiesman was Superintendent at the time. Thanks go to the Grand Valley Water User's Association, William Klapwyk, Manager when obtained.

To prevent livestock and trash from entering the tube, a trash screen was constructed near the intake. It was noted in *The Daily Sentinel* in the spring of 1929 that the intake to the siphon was washed out due to accumulation of excessive debris blown into the canal by a wind storm. The trash-screen became overloaded, causing the water to rise above the bank of the canal. The washout delayed the delivery of water, delaying the farmers' planting some of their crops. That structure was quite expensive to maintain, so it was replaced in 1952 with an underground sectional cement tube, which required little, if any, maintenance.

The First Settlers

We should mention a few settlers who filed on land in the lower valley before the irrigation project was developed. No doubt most were aware of the proposed project and possibly made their moves to "be there first" so they would not have to compete with other settlers when water was available. Many will recognize the names of a few of those early settlers: Joseph P. Kiefer, who was issued a tax deed 25 April 1901, on 160 acres in the Northwest Quarter of Section 16 Township 9 South Range 103 West; he was assigned water rights 30 January 1912 by the Grand Valley Water Users Association.

On 19 December 1918, Joe Kiefer filed a Quit Claim Deed for three acres in the southwest corner of his property on which to build a school for the new community.

Jervis B. Deacon filed 13 November 1905 on land on Sec 10 Twp 9 S R 103 W. J. B. Deacon and sons became well known as cattle ranchers; sons Clarence and Walter ran the operation many years after Jervis was gone.

George Bryan filed on part of Sec 16 R 103 W Twp 9 S, 11 June 1907; Robert M. Cox on Sec 17 R 103 W Twp 9 S, 26 December 1907; Charles Cavendish also on Sec 17, 17 June 1908.

Clyde Balkwill filed on land on Sec 15 R 103 W Twp 9 S, 11 June 1911 (owned by Milton & Lona Alstatt as recently as 1993). James Balkwill, father of Clyde, filed on the same section (adjoining on the south), 2 July 1911.

"Waiting for Water" Residence of H. B. Tyler on the NW ¼ of Section 21, Twp 9S Range 103 W; picture taken 21 August 1913. They didn't wait long enough. This may be the land that Luella McNaught won in the drawing in 1918 and abandoned later. If so, Clem Maluy was awarded the land as an amendment in 1931. He used the house for several years to house his hired help, the Romero family, who thinned beets for him. He provided them with a garden plot, irrigation water, and a cow. Mrs. Romero continued to come every summer with her children to work in the beets after her husband was killed in an auto accident on the way home from Mack. *(Grand Valley Water Users' Association)*

(Above) 1917 — Watermelon grown on the Robert M. Cox farm weighed in at 59½ pounds. The person holding the watermelon may be Ira Cox, brother of Robert. It looks like he is standing in a tomato field with a corn field in the background. (Top left) Lateral through new land. (Bottom left) Farmer on bridge over lateral with water irrigating new land. Last two taken June 1917. *(All pictures from Grand Valley Water Users' Association)*

Another was Fred M. Diehl, who filed on Sec 22 Twp 9 S R 103 W, 11 October 1905. There were others whose names are less familiar.

It should be noted that Robert M. Cox was employed in the canal construction, so there is little doubt he was much aware of the value of being there first. His homestead became one of the best in the lower valley, the soil was rich loam and well drained (presently owned by the Roberts' family).

It is worthy to note also that William H. Pollock contracted to build the laterals (ditches) to distribute the water from the main canal on the lower end of the project. The laterals were completed by the end of 1917.

Medical attention for employees on the project in the vicinity of Fruita and the west end was furnished by Dr. H. W. White of Fruita, under a contract of 25 May 1916. The contract provided for a payment of 95 cents per man month for all employees in that area, and for regular inspection trips to the construction camps.

In *The Daily Sentinel* of Monday evening, 3 September 1917, appeared this headline: "NEW LANDS OPEN FOR HOMESTEAD." The article describes land boundaries in Township 2 North in Ranges 2 & 3 West, and Township 9 South in Ranges 103 & 104 West. This land had been withdrawn from homesteading about two years earlier, until such time as it could be resurveyed because of obliteration of certain corners of the original survey. This area would soon be the location of the communities of New Liberty and Mack Mesa. Of course, by that time, construction of the canal and laterals was virtually complete, and water had already been delivered to at least one farm in the lower valley.

A map on file at the Grand Valley Water Users' Association office shows the land benefiting from the first irrigation in New Liberty in 1917 was in Sec 17 Twp 9 S R 103 W, belonging to Robert M. Cox. It is not known whether anyone other than Robert received water that first year. However, Charles Cavendish had land adjoining that of Robert, and since he too had filed before the completion of the Grand Valley project, perhaps he had developed enough land to have used some water.

In *The Daily Sentinel* of 4 September 1917 this bit of news appeared from Mack:

(Left) Exterior view of Loma Canning Factory 21 Aug 1913. (Above) Interior view of Loma Cannery 21 Aug 1913. They produced 1,600 cans per hour. (Lower) Ic refrigerated cars for packing and shipping fruit on t D&RGW RR Line, Grand Junction, Colorado 17 Aug 1913. (*All pictures are from the Grand Valley Water Use Association Collection*)

(Above) The sugar beet dump on a siding of the D&RGW RR in 1919 at Holland, Colorado, which later was named Appleton. Sugar beets were first grown in the Upper Valley as early as 1886, as W. E. Pabor exhibited a 26-pound beet at the Denver Exposition that year. In 1894 three carloads of beets were shipped to Lehi, Utah. In 1898 a sugar factory was built in Grand Junction and the first sugar was processed in 1899. In 1920 another sugar factory was built in Delta, Colorado. (*Grand Valley Water Users' Association Collection*)

(Right) The Mesa Flour Milling establishment 22 August 1913 in Grand Junction, Colorado. The output was 150 barrels per day producing the famous Mesa and Imperial flour, also, cornmeal, graham flour, etc. Farmer's grain could be utilized here and at the grain and feed supply stores. (*Grand Valley Water Users' Association Collection*)

Farmers who are farming land for the first time on the new lands under the Highline are well pleased with their crops, as everything is coming along fine. Cox brothers have delivered some fine potatoes to the stores here; also a load of fine watermelons. They report their grain and other products as being all that could be expected of brand new land ...

Facilities to handle the farmer's produce were already in place in the "Upper Valley" before 1918. There were grocery, grain, and feed stores in Mack, Loma, Fruita, and Grand Junction; canneries in Loma and Grand Junction; a flour mill and a sugar factory in Grand Junction; and the D&RGW RR was available to haul the produce where needed. All that was needed for the "Lower Valley" was *water*.

The Drawing

No doubt notice of "New Lands Open For Homestead" was published in many newspapers throughout the Midwest. As we can see from the response, it caught the attention of many people who lived a long way from Grand Valley.

On 28 February and 1 March 1918, formal notice of a drawing and further description of the land and instructions for the more than 200 applicants appeared in *The Daily Sentinel;* 102 farm units were to be offered.

On 18 March the paper noted that:

MANY WOMEN WANT LAND IN GRAND VALLEY, SAYS BLANCHARD

"No Place for 'Chickens,' However," Says Government Official; "Only Plucky Women Need Attempt the Farm Work; Talks of Opening."

"Women and men are very much alike when it comes to taking up government land and making a success of farming. It takes a particular type of person to make good. It is no place for 'chickens,' as we say when we mean young girls whose appearance cannot be reconciled to the life on a farm. It takes plucky women with grit and men who are willing to stick to the farm for a while until they have things going."

C. J. Blanchard, statistician for the United States Reclamation Service, who has arrived in Denver to meet the men and women of Colorado who are anxious to take up land in the Grand Valley and Uncompahgre projects, made the foregoing observation as he discussed the question in a *Denver Times* interview. Mr. Blanchard has spent several days in Chicago and Kansas City, meeting people who are interested in the two projects. In the first city he interviewed 1,100 people, each of whom was anxious to hear more of the projects. In Kansas City the daily average was over 200 persons.

"It is too bad that Uncle Sam has only 250 farms to give away in Colorado," he continued. "I know of no land in the United States that is equal to this. Anything but citrus fruit can be raised in the district, and a return of $44 an acre is the average. The section is irrigated by a complete system, the season is longer than it is in Denver, the sun is a little better for crops than it is in the section around Denver, and a man can get a crop the first year.

"The district is already settled. Some men have been farming it over there for 25 years. There are good schools which rank with any in the West and neighbors are not far away on any side.

"The reason that we are rushing this through is because we are anxious to get settlers located in sufficient time to allow them to raise a crop this year. It is in line with the government's plan to get the most from the farms this year. The principal crops are alfalfa, wheat, oats, sugar beets, corn, fruit and vegetables.

"We are not encouraging people to go over there unless they have sufficient capital. Without money to tide them over the first year or so, they are of no use in the plan. We are anxious to get permanent settlers — people who will make good and increase the food production of the United States. It is pioneering, and to a certain extent, roughing it; but it is so different from what this meant 25 years ago that it seems easy. It takes men and women with the pioneering spirit, however, to make such a venture. For such a capital of $1,500 may prove sufficient.

"Women are inquiring about the lands this year in greater numbers than ever before. Some are school teachers anxious to take on a plot. There are widows who think they would like to try this means of making a living. In Kansas City daughters of farmers who had left the farm to go to the city and were anxious to get back, came to inquire about the projects."

Though the number of women that filed is unavailable, seven women were successful in filing for land at New Liberty.

In *The Daily Sentinel* of 22 March 1918 was this article:

INITIAL RUN TO HIGH LINE WAS MADE TODAY

Thirty Home-Seekers Visit the Units in Great Drawing; Perfect Weather Greets Visitors to Valley; Eight Cars in Line Led by Project Engineer Harper.

There was a busy scene in front of the Chamber of Commerce rooms this morning and the noise of engines and the honk of the horns of a number of autos filled the air as the departure was made for the first sight-seeing contingent in the high-line drawing.

There were eight cars in the line which swung into First street led by the reclamation car with project engineer Harper at the steering wheel. Each car contained three and four strangers and those who had cars in the line besides the reclamation car were: J. A. Powell, C. N. Rhodes, W. P. Ela, Mark R. Bunting and the Western Slope Auto Company. A number of the wives of the home-seekers accompanied the party.

Owing to the number of late comers, the cars of Joseph Kiefer and Chas. F. Smith were added to the number of cars taking the trip today.

Family history reveals that three of the pioneers who went on that sight-seeing tour were Patrick and Clem Maluy and Clyde W. Likes. Too bad we can't name more of them!

The article continued by applauding the beautiful weather and the optimism of the people who had come to the valley with high hope of securing "free" land and a new home. The following day another article appeared labeling the initial trip a success. Try to imagine what an experience it must have been to ride out into the desert in those primitive automobiles where roads were almost non-existent — little more than wagon tracks!

The Daily Sentinel for 26 and 27 March 1918 suggested that local citizens should give the strangers sight-seeing tours of the nearby mountains and valleys so they could better appreciate Grand Valley as a place to live. Land seekers were labeled "High Character Of Men." A tentative list of registrants was published, giving their places of residence; some from as far

We believe this is possibly a scene taken on 22 March 1918 of the eight carloads of prospective homesteaders who were taken on a tour of the open land for the high-line drawing. They are parked in front of the Uintah Hotel in Mack, probably for a rest stop or lunch. *(Photo taken from a newspaper article and sent to us by Betty Booth Garber)*

away as Chicago and Indianapolis; quite a large number of them were from Kansas.

There were also headlines publicizing the Garmesa Farms:

If our transient guests who are interested in growing things and intensive agriculture and fine stock, they ought, by all means, to visit the beautiful Garmesa Farms. Located eight miles north of Fruita, in the midst of waterless waste, there is an oasis where the eye will never tire of the beauties that have resulted from the intelligent labor of man. Here one may see some of the very finest strains of Holstein cattle in the U.S., cows that are even now showing the very highest tests of butterfat production. This herd is headed by one of the best bulls in the country. One may also see fine specimens of the Duroc Jersey breed of hogs, and no one will take this trip without coming away fully repaid in many ways. It will show in a remarkable degree what a little water will do in desert country.

Scarcely two years were to pass before that show place had to be abandoned. An excellent water storage reservoir had been built to entrap drainage water from the canyons north of the farmland, but the designers had not reckoned with the amount of silt carried with that water as it comes racing down those canyons. It was soon discovered that the reservoir was filling up with silt, destroying the water storage capacity.

The Garmesa Farms had an auction in March 1920 and sold off all the buildings, machinery and livestock. The land was then abandoned to revert to desert. Today one would have to search carefully to find traces of the community that once existed on the desert near the Bookcliffs.

The Daily Sentinel of 28 March 1918 announced that a drawing would be held the following day at the Armory at 2 p.m., and that the Federal Courtroom would be closed to registrants at 9 a.m. Further details and instructions were given for the benefit of the registrants on 29 March:

Ad for the Garmesa Farms in *The Daily Sentinel,* Wednesday, 27 March 1918.

TWO HUNDRED FIFTEEN FILINGS ON THE HIGH LINE LANDS! INTENSE EXCITEMENT AT ARMORY DURING THE DRAWING; LIST OF THE LUCKY PEOPLE; MANY UNITS NOT SELECTED.

The article describes the interesting scene as the registrants completed their filings. Many had held off in hopes they would find a desirable unit that someone else had not already filed on, but such was not the case for many of them. The land seekers were willing to take their chances in the drawing! Still — many units were not filed on at all. On the other hand there were multiple filings in the more popular areas, particularly the red mesa units. It was told by one of the homesteaders that 40 applicants had filed on the forty acres won by Edward Hollinger on Mack Mesa.

The land-seekers organized a committee to publish a unanimous resolution praising the local citizenry and particularly the people employed by the Bureau of Reclamation for the excellent way the entire procedure had been handled and the way the visitors were hosted while in the valley.

A comparison was made between that method of settling the public domain with that of the Oklahoma Land Rush, which was characterized as "a survival of the fittest" - and - "every fellow for himself and the devil take the hindmost."

The following published list names the successful applicants, the first 22 having no contest:

William Baker, Kansas City, KS
Fillipi Palombo, Cold Creek, CO
Stephen Gould, Fruita, CO
John T. Stanoch, Chicago, IL
Frank M. Clark, Indianapolis, IN
Ira J. Hill, Grand Junction, CO
Charles E. Hollenbeck, Fruita, CO
William C. A. Hiatt, Grand Junction, CO
James. R. Ferrill, Dearborn, MO
Garfield Belden, Oakland, KS
Ray J. Ackerman, Washington, D. C.
Mrs. Jane Hayes, Grand Junction, CO

Mary A. Chamberlain, Los Angeles, CA
William H. Pollock, Fruita, CO
John B. Morrow, Conway Springs, KS
Burgeon D. Lofgren, Norton, KS
J. Paul Patten, Norton, KS
James. A. Strait, Kansas City, KS
Walter Sarles, Delta, CO
Edward L. Shires, Price, UT
May F. Boyden, Chicago, IL
Luella McNaught, Queen City, MO
William Evans, Clayton, MO
Lewis E. Musselman, Larned, KS
Elmer Harker, Frederick, KS
Early Clifton Waits, Aspen, CO
Edward C. Hollinger, Denver, CO
John R. Earp, Grand Junction, CO
Clyde W. Likes, Byers, KS
J. B. Perkins, Grand Junction, CO
Wm. A. Weick, Wilmont, MN
Clement Maluy, Marysville, KS
Lutman Harvey, Grand Junction, CO
A. Lucille Gnagey, Fruita, CO
Capt. J. Frank Smith, Chicago, IL
Alex. Schneider, O'Keene, OK
Jesse L. Keedy, Fruita, CO
Robert W. Partridge, Columbus, OH
Richard C. Horton, Pueblo, CO
John W. Blue, Ingersoll, OK
Frank O. Gustafson, Grand Junction, CO
John E. Graham, Chicago, IL
I. W. Charles, Palisade, CO
Robert M. Phillips, Colorado Springs, CO
Everett E. Freeman, Pierce City, MO
John Joseph Zeller, Grand Junction, CO
Oscar K. McLendon, Pueblo, CO

The next day, 30 March, the applicants who were unsuccessful in the drawing were allowed to file on the "free" units not registered for the drawing. Following is the published list of some of those persons:

James M. Morgan, Denver, CO
Oscar M. James, Grand Junction, CO
Orlando B. Garth, Pueblo, CO
W. J. Hoops, Okareal, OK
William E. Curtis, Dawson, NM
Harriet Terril, Dearborn, MO
Paul Ercrest, Aurora, CO
Mrs. Cornelia Moss, Emporia, KS
John M. Graham, Chicago, IL
J. R. Gladden, Fruita, CO
Franklin A. Coffman, Akron, OH
A. W. Alstatt, Marquette, KS
Arthur H. Cutler, Fruita, CO
Patrick H. Maluy, Marysville, KS
Hershell P. Evatt, Grand Junction, CO
George W. Fisher, Queen City, MO
Sam J. Barr, Fruita, CO
Bryan J. Hayman, Enid, OK

Few people today are aware that a drawing for lands in the Uncompagre Project was held at Montrose a week after the one in Grand Junction. Many who were unsuccessful in Mesa County quickly traveled to Montrose to register for that drawing, held 6 April 1918.

Land-seekers were permitted to file on the "free" units until about 1923; veterans being given preference. Several veterans we knew took advantage of the opportunity...some of whom were: Floyd Thomas, William Price, William E. Pollock, Athol L. Stotts, Benjamin A. Harrison and William A. Knapp. This list, of course, does not by any means name all of those who filed after the drawing.

Chapter Four

The Work Begins

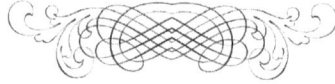

"Homesteading"

Homestead laws required that the applicant move onto the land within six months and begin improvements. This was accomplished in a variety of ways. Improvements included building of head ditches, fences, corrals, land leveling, and planting of crops. Some moved immediately and built homes, others lived in dugouts, some in tents. So, beginning in April of 1918, many new farm units in New Liberty and Mack Mesa communities began to show signs of life other than the prairie dogs, rabbits, coyotes, range stock, etc. Although much excitement and enthusiasm were shown at the time of the drawing, there were several farm units, some of them quite good ones, which were never developed.

It's interesting to contemplate how many of those named in the preceding lists *didn't* make their homes on the new land.

Of peculiar interest was this paragraph in *The Daily Sentinel* of 30 March 1918:

> One G. W. Fisher of Chicago, a conductor on the Chicago and Great Western Railway was successful in securing the lucky number in the drawing, but his sister lost out. However, the sister at once filed upon the unit adjoining that secured by the brother so that they have a nice big farm in a lump. The lady is the widow of a U. S. Soldier.

Evidently the reporter got the situation reversed. If you will read the preceding list again, you will discover that the widow, Luella McNaught, was the one who was lucky in the drawing and her brother, G. W. Fisher, made the later entry.

Also mentioned in the article above was this bit of news:

> Miss May Boyden of Chicago secured a fine piece of land near Mack without a contest, and will not go back east at all; she plans to go right to work erecting a house on her land and expects her brother from the farming section in Weld county to assist her in the improvements.

Another interesting bit of news was printed 9 April 1918:

The way the land looked when the homesteaders arrived; nothing but sagebrush, rabbits, prairie dogs, and coyotes. *(Grand Valley Water Users' Association.)*

(Upper) Plowing the new land. After plowing, they would disc and harrow in preparation for planting. (Middle) Making furrows in the prepared land. (Below) The trials of irrigating the new land; shows a lateral, head ditch, and furrows (creases). *(All photos courtesy of Grand Valley Water Users' Association)*

Miss Boyden of Chicago, an old time friend of Miss Lucille Gnagey, was one of the lucky ones in the land drawing in the High Line section. Miss Gnagey is also one of the fortunate ones, and these old friends may be near neighbors in the proving-up days to come.

There is little evidence that either of them did much "proving up" other than building homes on their new land.

No doubt many of the successful applicants were oozing with optimism as they made the move to their new destination — "Mack, Colorado." Many of the homesteading families came to Mack by train, as did some of their farm implements and household belongings.

The size of a homestead was limited to 40 acres on some "Red Mesa" units, and 60 acres on the "bottom" land units, with a few exceptions. So it was not possible for an individual or family to grab a disproportionate amount of land. However, no law prevented an individual or family from getting land in later years from someone who was willing to sell for a price. Thus Robert Cox, Bill and Clem Maluy, and the Deacons, were able to establish some large farm units in later years. Now there are even larger farm units owned by the Roberts and Arpke families that cover many hundreds of acres.

Irrigating the new land was a trying experience at best, since the soil would melt away like sugar when water ran over it. There was little vegetation growing naturally, so there was very little organic matter (humus) to tie the soil particles together. Many means were employed to control the water as it was directed down the furrows between the crop rows. Tumbleweeds, fox tail and other pests began to grow wherever the soil received moisture. Therefore, weeds, manure, hay and straw were used to try to control the washouts. Many a farmer would check his irrigation sets carefully in the evening before going to bed, only to get out the next morning and find most of his head of water

most of the farm land in the valley. In various areas the shale comes to the surface, in others it is as much as 20 feet under the surface. The loam soil lying over these areas leaches irrigation water down to the shale strata and then it follows the shale to the surface, bringing with it deposits of alkali salts too strong to grow crops.

A short time after irrigation began, the Bureau set about boring test wells both to learn where the water tables were and to follow the shale strata. They installed square wooden tubes in the wells so the rise and fall of the subsurface water could be monitored. Those square tubes were in place for many years, at least in the New Liberty community.

Drag lines were used to dig drainage ditches to drain off the subsurface water. Of course, there was always a certain amount of water from irrigating that was wasted into the drainage ditches as well.

Because of the width of the ditches, and the spoil banks where the dirt had to be piled, the

racing merrily down a huge gully. Several years later, grass and other vegetation became established along the head ditches, tying the soil together, thus making it much easier to control the water.

We've come a long way since! For a time in the 1940s some farmers experimented with siphons as an alternative method. That worked quite well, except for having to contend with the trash almost always present in the water. The trash would sometimes plug the small pipes used for siphons and cause the water flow to stop. If enough of them became plugged in a set, it would create an excess in the ditch that had to go somewhere and might cause problems.

At present the laterals are all underground pipe and gated pipe is used on the surface to direct the water down the furrows. This system has very nearly eliminated ditch maintenance. It has added acreage to the farms that used to be taken up by ditch banks, and unsightly growths of weeds and willows that were breeding places for insects. It also prevented loss of water through seepage and the resultant alkali patches.

It's interesting that there are undulating strata of shale under

(Upper) Excavating a drain ditch with a trenching machine in 1918. (Bottom) The old Monagon Dragline excavating Drain "G" ditch in 1918. *(Grand Valley Water Users' Association Collection)*

(Left) Dragline completing portion of Drain "G" ditch in 1918.

(Below left) Unloading prefabricated flume for Independent Ranchman's Canal, "J" Drain crossing.

(Below right) Placing flume on pile bents by use of dragline on Independent Ranchman's Canal, "J" Drain crossing.

(All three photos courtesy of Grand Valley Water Users' Association)

ditches caused the loss of much valuable land, especially when the ditches were engineered to follow the natural slope of the land. To further aggravate the problem many ditches were dug across a part of the farm land without regard to property lines, sometimes leaving small pieces that were not profitable to farm.

In recent years, many of those ditches have been filled in. In some instances, perforated pipe buried at appropriate depths has been used to collect the water and carry it out of the area.

Through the years excessive salt in the water in the lower reaches of the Colorado River has been caused by drainage off the farms in the Grand Valley. Because of that problem, plans are being made to route all of the drainage water to an area near the Utah state line, where it will be collected in a huge pond to evaporate. The salt will be collected and used for various purposes so it won't run down the river and continue to cause problems.

It was expected in the earlier days that a crew of men, sometimes with teams, would spend considerable time during the winter months cleaning the main laterals and sometimes sections of the main canal. Each farmer had to do this in the spring to his own distribution ditches in preparation for running water during the irrigating season. It was a lot of hard work!

Following is an interesting report from *The Daily Sentinel* of 10 June 1918:

As a result of the opening of a number of High Line tracts to settlement during the past spring, at least a thousand additional acres under the project have been planted to crops this spring, according to announcement made by Walt B. Smith, County Agriculturist†. Mr. Smith has been devoting a part of his time recently to instructing the new settlers in the art of irrigation, a majority of those who are new on their lands having come here from the rain belts. And he reports not only the planting of this thousand acres or more to crops, but also that crops are doing nicely to be on new land and tended in the most part by inexperienced irrigation farmers.

A considerable part of the acreage put in already this season is in the Mack district. Many of those successful in drawing claims have moved to their lands or have arranged for the planting of a small acreage this season, intending to break up the remainder of their land during the summer and fall months, that all of it may be put to crops next season.

The cultivated acreage under the High Line will be increased by several thousand acres next season as a result of the opening of the new units, as much of it will be planted by that time. The acreage of fall wheat planted on the project is expected to be large.

There appears to have been some misconceptions among a few of the people in Grand Junction about the success of the Highline settlers. After all, they may have reasoned, didn't those farmers receive free land from the government, so all they had to do was settle in and reap the benefits?

The following was published in *The Daily Sentinel* and dated Mack, Colorado, 6 January 1922:

Mr. Walter Walker
Grand Junction, Colo.

Dear Mr. Walker:
    The sentiments recently expressed in your paper regarding the prosperous condition of this section, and of the average citizen of Mesa County, certainly do not reflect the true facts when applied to the ranchers of the lower valley.
    If there is any section where conditions are

worse than they are down this way, we would be sorry to learn of it. And I can truly say if there is a single rancher living at this end of the Grand Valley who has prospered or has made a success of agriculture and a decent living at farming under the High Line project, for the past two years, I am not acquainted with him, and I know a lot of them.
    As a class, they are equal to any other section, just as intelligent, experienced, frugal and industrious men as can be found anywhere.
    Some of us have not actually sold enough produce off of our ranches to pay taxes, or for the water used in irrigation.
    The question of meeting our obligations and paying our water bills is a serious one with most of us.
    There are hundreds of tons of alfalfa hay, now on our ranches, for which we can find no market.
    We are all very much disappointed and dissatisfied with conditions that obtain here, and unless relieved in some way, a large number of High Line settlers will be forced to abandon their claims and seek a living elsewhere.
    Evidently the good people of Grand Junction are not acquainted with the true conditions, or the facts in regard to the High Line project, or the people striving to make a living under it.
    May we hope that some of your civic leaders will take the trouble to look us up, and lend a hand of friendship by using their influence to secure the cancellation of our water rentals for at least five years, until it is possible for the ranchers to recover from their losses, and get on their feet again.
    Respectfully, A RANCHER

There soon *was* a time when the settlers were given some relief on the payment of their water bills. According to need, a repayment schedule was worked out so they had a number of years to pay off their delinquent water charges — it eased the burden to some degree. Then a report of the Water Users' Annual Meeting, held 8 January 1924, as reported in *The Daily Sentinel*, reflected a change — the Highline farmers began to show a profit!

In the early days there was resentment on the part of some of the cattle and sheep men because the farmers had begun to move in and take up

†That title may have been changed later to "County Extension Agent."

89

some of their "free" range. This resentment created problems for several years. Even after fences were built to enclose the farm units, occasionally some of those fences were cut or gates thrown open. Livestock continued to run free in the area for some time, causing much anguish on the part of the homesteaders, who might arise some morning to find their precious hay stacks surrounded by stray cattle or horses, or to find some stray stock in a field destroying the crops or making a mess out of the irrigation system. In the spring and fall sheep herds were trailed through the farming areas. It didn't seem to be of concern to the herders when the sheep got into a field and damaged or destroyed a crop of hay or grain. To say ill feelings existed would be an understatement.

For many years the land above the canal was overgrazed, and because of that it was common to see, from miles away, huge clouds of dust billowing into the sky as large herds of sheep were being trailed to either summer or winter range. According to stories told by early stockmen, before the hordes of sheep arrived, grass grew in that area "high as a horse's belly." In 1934 the "Taylor Grazing Act" went into effect, eliminating most of the overgrazing. But some of the conditions told about by the old timers were already gone forever.

Crops and Machinery

The climate, soil, and length of growing season in the valley proved to be suitable for many different crops. Soon after settlement of the Grande Valley, fruit growing became a popular enterprise. Fruit crops were to become the principle means of income in the upper part of the valley. Presently there are still many orchards around the Palisade/Clifton/Orchard Mesa areas. Many orchards were established in the valley as far west as Fruita and Loma. No doubt the town of Fruita got its name from the fact there were so many orchards in the area. Some farms in the lower valley had a few fruit trees, but there was little fruit grown for commercial gain. Robert M. Cox had a peach orchard on his farm in New Liberty that produced commercial quantities for several years. On the red Mesa, north of Mack, the Davidson family established an orchard from which they sold fruit for many seasons.

Nearly every farmer had the usual variety of farm animals and poultry: horses, a few mules, cows, sheep, goats, pigs, chickens, turkeys, ducks and geese, with a few guinea hens and peacocks here and there. Much of the farm land was devoted to the raising of feed crops for the benefit of the animals. Those feed crops were mostly alfalfa hay, but there was some red clover, and also white and yellow sweet clover. The latter two were not very good for pasture or hay, but were excellent as green-manure crops to plow under to benefit the soil.

Haying was a major operation even though the acreage may have been small. Most farmers "traded work" and helped each other in "putting up" the hay. Seldom was there enough manpower within one family to manage the job.

Hay was cut and stacked in a variety of ways. In the early days, soon after settlement, some farmers resorted to old-fashioned scythes because there was simply not enough money to buy more expensive machinery. Within a few years, however, there began to appear a few horse-drawn mowers and sulky rakes. A few neighbors pooled their resources and purchased mowers and rakes and other machines in partnerships.

Mowers were interesting machines—the early ones usually had a five foot sickle bar. The sickle bars were an ingenious combination of moving and stationary parts. Every farmer had to have some means of keeping the sickles sharp. Most were equipped with more than one sharp sickle so that little time would be lost while changing a dull one. Sometimes the sharpening was done at a blacksmith's shop in town, but

(Above left) A three-horse, one-bottom, two-way plow in the 1920s. It was called two-way because the farmer would put the plow shear on one side down to plow when going up the field, and when he turned around and came back, he would put the other side down. The dirt had to be thrown to the same direction or side. (Courtesy of *Cross Orchards Living History Site, Museum of Western Colorado*) (Above right) John Morrow standing on a harrow pulled by four horses in 1920s. *(Morrow Collection)* (Right) Walter Weir plowing under sweet clover with a two-bottom, one-way plow pulled by three horses. With a one-way plow the farmer plowed around the field continuously, and a two-bottom would make two furrows instead of one. *(Weir Collection)* (Below) A field of red clover on the Patrick Maluy farm in the early 1920s. A herd of sheep are foraging in the clover. The Maluy residence is in the background. *(Grand Valley Water Users' Association Collection)*

(Above left) A manure spreader. In the spring the farmers would clean the manure from their corrals by forking it by hand into a manure spreader similar to this one, and then spread it on their fields for fertilizer. (Above right): A Fordson tractor. Sy Summers who had the first tractor in New Liberty, had a Fordson like this one. (Center left) A four-horse fresno. Most of the ground leveling in the Lower Valley was done in the early days by the use of this device . On the wall in the background are single-trees, double-trees, and a neck yoke in the middle. The neck yoke was hooked onto each of the two horses harness and the ring was placed over tongue of the implement. (Center right) A Planet Jr. Creaser used to make furrows (creases) for irrigation. *(All the above photos courtesy of Cross Orchard Living History Site, Museum of Western Colorado)* (Left) Ivan Likes discing the new land on the Likes farm in 1919. *(Homer Likes Collection)*

Clyde Likes Sr. and Clyde Jr., with horses, Prince and Nig, mowing the first hay crop on the Likes homestead during the summer of 1920. *(Homer Likes Collection)*

the shocks, it was loaded by hand onto "slips" (homemade sleds) or wagons, and hauled to the stack yard where a derrick was located.

Placed on the sled or wagon-bed was a "sling" of proper length and width upon which the hay was piled. This device was made with cables, ropes or chains with slats in the middle to maintain the width. It had rings on either end that could be hooked to special pulleys on the stacker cable. As the load was hoisted, the pulleys would draw the hay together, compacting it into a tight bundle about half the size it was on the wagon or slip. After the stacker man had located the load where he wanted to place it, he could pull a trip-rope, which made the sling separate in the middle and drop the load wherever he wished.

The derricks, also called stackers, were of several designs and built with poles hauled from the nearby mountains. Most were made with a "boom," or "arm" extending from a vertical pole at a forty-five-degree angle. All used a similar principle — the boom would swing with the weight of the load of hay to the far end of the stack if needed. Skids of various designs were built at the

some farmers equipped themselves with foot-powered wet grindstones with which they sharpened their own. Of course the grindstone was useful for other sharpening jobs as well.

Following the mowing, a sulky rake, pulled by a team of horses, first raked the hay into windrows (rows of hay). Then the same machine went the opposite direction and divided the windrows into piles, or "shocks," that could be handled by one man with a pitchfork. After allowing sufficient time for the hay to cure in

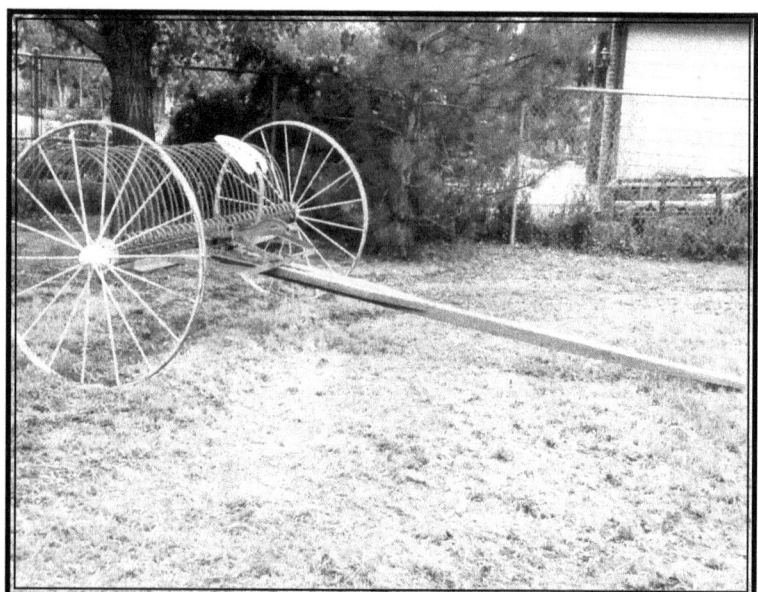

(Above left) A foot-powered wet grindstone used to sharpen sickle bars, shovels, hoes, etc. (Above right) A sulky rake used to windrow and shock the hay (see explanation above). *(Photos taken by Phyllis Likes at the Cross Orchards Living History Site, Museum of Western Colorado.)*

A field of third cutting hay that has been raked into shocks. *(Grand Valley Water Users' Association Collection)*

bottom end of the derrick to support the frame and to make it possible to move it wherever needed.

Building the stacks, sometimes holding fifty or more tons of hay, required much care and special technique. Indeed, some stacks were works of art. At times, though, if the man building the stack was a little careless, the stack would be built a little off center and would settle to one side —— a few even toppled over later, much to the embarrassment of the stacker man.

Another widely-used method of handling the loads was with a rope sling in the shape of a "V." The open part of the "V" was placed on the sled or wagon so it would face the stack where "hand ropes" were attached to it and held by the stacker man (or men). Another larger and longer rope, called a "pull rope," was placed over the top of the load and completely over and beyond the back end of the stack. One end of the rope was attached to the sling and a team was hitched to the other end and it was pulled over the stack, rolling the load until it reached the point where the stacker man wanted to place it.

"Jayhawk" overshot stackers and sweep rakes, while more popular in the higher country hay meadows, were used by a few of the farmers on the lower valley irrigated farms. A sweep rake consisted of a "fork" about six to eight feet wide,

made up of several wooden slats, two-by-two's about eight feet long, placed about one foot apart, carried on wheels and powered by two horses hitched some distance apart on either side of the machine. The rake would gather up a sizable pile of hay in the field and haul it to the stackyard where the load was placed on another fork, a part of the "overshot stacker." With the aid of a team hitched to a cable, this machine would pick up the load and hoist it overhead and dump it on the stack.

Despite the method used, there was always a sizable waste of leaves, the driest, lightest and most valuable part of the hay. Large mounds of leaves would be left lying near the stack and along the haulways — but no one seemed too concerned about the loss.

In later years after tractors had become popular, "Farm Hand" hydraulic loaders, attached to the tractors, were used by a few farmers. These machines could gather the hay from the field, then haul it to and place it on the stack. Thus two men could accomplish what formerly required five or more to do the same job.

Alfalfa hay was a natural cover for wild animals and birds such as skunks and rabbits, pheasants and quail etc., who chose to hide and/or nest in the standing hay crop. So there was always a danger of the sickle bar catching the birds or animals and either killing them outright or permanently maiming them. It was always a sad thing to see a pheasant, turkey, chicken, dog, rabbit, skunk, or other creature go hobbling away minus a foot or suffering other damage after being caught by the sickle bar.

Some farmers in later years cooperated with game officials and attached an apparatus called a "flushing bar" attached to the machine. Rods or wires dragged through the hay preceding the sickle to warn the birds or animals to move away before the sickle bar caught them. That was some help, but it was not an absolute cure for

(Above) A stacker in use. (Above right) A completed stack of hay with a "Mormon" stacker. *(Both photos courtesy of Grand Valley Water Users' Association)* (Center) Scene on the Morrow farm in the early 1930s. L-R: Al Daily, Al Alstatt, Floyd Thomas, Lawrence Morrow, John Morrow (on wagon), and Bud Larson. (Below) Mormon stacker minus boom on Morrow farm. *(Both from the Morrow Collection)* (Below right) Stacking hay on the Clem Maluy farm with a "Farm Hand" hydraulic loader in 1952. Darrell Maluy on the tractor and Clem on the stack. Leo Ertle, a friend from Kansas, on the ground. Hay was hauled in on a slip. *(Maluy Collection)*

the problem. That was still a dangerous part of the hay harvest that affected most farmers who had some feelings for the animals or birds.

Tractors did not become a common source of power on the farms until in the late 1930s. For years horses were among the farmers' most valuable assets. Some teams were prize possessions of their owners, but there were many very "ordinary nags" who could plod along and accomplish just as much work as the "classy" ones. Some farmers had more "horse savvy" than others — of course these men were looked up to and had many opportunities to offer advice; others offered advice whether it was asked for or not!

Nearly everyone had some experience with "runaways." They happened when the horses became excited or frightened by something or other. Some horses could not be trusted and would wait for just the right moment to take off on a run. If the driver was not watchful every moment, and left the team unattended only for a few seconds –– they were off!! Oftentimes there was much damage to whatever machinery the team happened to be hitched to. Sometimes there would be serious injury to the horses.

A variety of grain crops were grown: corn, oats, wheat, barley, and, in a few instances, maize and millet.

The ears of corn were harvested by hand for years. The farmers used a wagon box with a "bump board" attached on one side and above the box, which made it possible to toss the ears "at" the wagon without missing the wagon box target — the ears would hit the bump board and fall down into the wagon box. Husking the corn by hand was a long tedious process that required many long winter days — depending on the size of the field(s). The day's pick was hauled to the barn yard and shoveled into a crib or some other means of storage.

The corn was fed to the animals "on the ear," or if a grinder was available, it was sometimes ground into "corn and cob meal." Some corn was shelled either by simply rubbing the kernels off the cob by hand, or with a small mechanical device powered by a crank. In later years shellers powered by tractors or other types of gasoline engines were used to some extent. And still later came the modern "combine" machines that do the entire harvesting job in the field, with the shelled corn being the only thing hauled away.

After the harvest, the livestock were turned loose in the stalks to glean whatever feed may have been left. This was true of all the harvested fields. There would be enough feed left in this way to maintain several animals almost all winter. In many instances farmers leased this type of pasture to sheep-men who would keep their herds there for most of the winter. Much of the time hay was fed to the sheep on the same ground to augment the pasture. This practice proved to be beneficial for the soil because of the residue of feed and the manure left by the sheep where they were fed or

(Left) Patrick Maluy, Mary Maluy holding Darrell, and Clem Maluy in the fall of 1922, sitting on a corn wagon with a bump board. This is a typical corn wagon used when harvesting corn by hand, as described above. *(Mary Maluy Collection)*

(Upper left) John and Margaret Morrow with their prize stalks of corn in the early 1920s. (Morrow Collection) (Upper right) Corn in shocks to cure before shucking or running through the thresher. (Center) Cutting corn for silage on the Robert M. Cox farm in 1920. (Below right) The big silo on the Robert M. Cox farm in 1920 being filled with corn silage. *(Grand Valley Water Users' Association)* Below left: Mary Maluy standing in their first crop of corn in 1918. *(Mary Maluy Collection)*

Wheat in shocks on the Bill Knapp farm in 1928. The Knapp home is in the background. *(Grand Valley Water Users' Association Collection)*

"traction wheel" to transmit power to all of the components. It was equipped with a cutter-bar, much like a mower, above which a "reel" turned parallel to the cutter-bar and helped direct the cut grain onto a moving canvas platform where it was conveyed to another moving canvas, then into the tying part of the machine. Arms, called "gatherers" gathered the grain into bundles that were tied by an intricate device called a "knotter." The binding machine was a "mechanical marvel"— truly the work of a genius. Binders were more expensive than most farmers could afford, so

bedded.

Oats were grown either for a cash crop or to feed the livestock on the farm. They were a favorite horse feed. Oats were an easy crop to grow and were sometimes used for a nurse crop to start a stand of alfalfa. Sometimes the oats were mowed and harvested as a hay crop. But the usual method was to cut the crop with a "Self-Binder" which bound the cut oats into bundles that could be collected and stacked into "shocks," where they would complete the ripening process. Later the bundles would be loaded onto wagons and hauled to the thresher or stacked in the farmyard to be threshed at a more convenient time.

The stacks were unique. The bundles were placed with the heads of the grain facing the middle, with the cut ends facing out. The stacks would be built round and were brought to a round top as well. The rounded top would shed rain or snow to some extent and prevent the oats from being damaged from moisture. Other types of grains were handled in much the same way.

The binding machine was an engineering masterpiece. It was drawn by horses and had a

those who could afford them could get all the custom work they wanted.

Sugar beets were grown in Grand Valley at least as early as 1886. W. E. Pabor, Superintendent of the Fruita Town and Land Co., exhibited a 23-pound beet specimen at the Denver Exposition that year. However, that 23-pound beet became less significant after 41-pound specimens were found in both Montrose and Mesa counties in the fall of 1925.

Test plots of sugar beets were grown in the valley in 1894. Three carloads of beets were shipped that fall to Lehi, Utah, where the nearest processing plant was located. The Colorado Sugar Manufacturing Company was organized in 1898 and a sugar factory was built in Grand Junction where the first sugar was processed in 1899. But that year most of the crop was frozen in the ground and lost.

In 1920 another sugar factory was built in Delta, called the Holly Sugar Company, and that company began to contract with the farmers in the lower valley to grow beets for them.

As part of the contract the Holly Sugar Company provided the beet seed and the planter

(Above) Sebron "Si" Summers pulling his threshing machine used to thresh grain for the farmers in the community. The tractor is a gasoline powered Fordson. Before this he had a steam tractor. It was the only steam tractor ever used in New Liberty. *(Leroy Likes Collection)* (Upper right) Amos, Robert, and Milton Alstatt combining grain on the Alstatt farm in the mid 1940s. *(Alstatt Collection)* (Center) Edward L. Shires harvesting oats with a "Self Binder" in the early 1920s. *(Laura Berry Collection)* (Below) Threshing oats. The crop of oats has been cut, shocked, hauled in and piled into stacks. It is being forked by hand into the thresher and the grain goes into sacks and the straw from the grain is blown to form a straw stack. *(Grand Valley Water Users' Association Collection)*

machine. The planters would plant four rows at once. The seeds were planted in rows 24 inches apart and the irrigation furrows were spaced 48 inches apart, making two rows of beets between furrows.

Sugar beets required many hours of hand labor. Most of the natives did not like to do what they called "stoop labor," and as a consequence many Mexican laborers were imported to do the work.

When the beet plants came up they were too close together to develop properly and had to be thinned. So hand laborers were brought in to "thin" or hoe out the excess plants to a spacing of about four to six inches apart in the rows.

During the summer at least two "hoeings" were necessary to cut out the weeds that came up in the crop. The beets had to be cultivated at least once or twice to maintain good soil tilth and to help keep the weeds down. Some farmers at first used cultivators that would handle only one row, but later machines that would cover four rows became very popular.

Usually the harvest began in October, and again, much hand labor was required. A horse-drawn machine with two shares, or blades, was used to lift the beets loose from the soil one row at a time. Following that the laborers came along and pulled the beets the rest of the way out of the ground and tossed them into piles.

From these piles a specially built knife with a spike on the tip was used to pick up the beets one at a time and chop the tops off. Usually the tops were left in piles where they fell and the beets were tossed into other piles.

The beet dump siding on the Uintah Railway at Clarkton four miles west of Mack. The sign says Clarkton. Notice the beets were hauled in a wagon and how the wagon is dumped in the lower photo. *(Jim McCoy Collection)*

The tops were either left lying in the fields where livestock were allowed to feed on them, or they were hauled to the barnyard and fed to the stock. Almost invariably the tops would taint the milk from the cows with a taste that was unbearable to some people.

Later the beets were loaded into specially built wagon boxes with forks or by simply tossing them into the wagon one at a time. Then they were hauled to the "beet dump" where the operator would pull a sample from each load. These samples were kept separate and identified with the farmer who grew them, then sent in later to the sugar factory and used to determine the sugar content of the entire crop; the farmers were paid accordingly for their crop.

For the farmers in New Liberty the distance was too great to haul their beets to Mack to be loaded on the D&RG RR, so an unloading/loading facility was built in the southwest area of the community at Clarkton, between three and four miles west of Mack. There a siding was built beside the Uintah Railway track. The beets were then hauled into Mack by the Uintah Railway. According to Darrell Maluy, in order to transport the cars of beets from Mack to Grand Junction, the narrow gauge Uintah Railway tracks were laid between the wide gauge D&RG RR tracks. This service started in October 1920 and was operated the first fall by Hugh Gerry, brother of Guy Gerry. In later years it was operated by Bill Knapp, Clyde Likes Sr., and others.

In later years a by-product of the sugar making process: "beet molasses" became very popular as an additive to various livestock feeds. Some farmers would purchase large quantities from the sugar factory and pour it over the hay or grain as they fed it to their stock. However, much of it was used as a dried product that was mixed with grain.

In the late 1940s beet growing had evolved to the point that most of the work was done with machines. At first "pelleted seeds" were developed so that there could be more spacing in the row from the planter, eliminating much of the thinning by hand. But they also had "blocking machines" that eliminated almost all of the thinning. Harvesting machinery was also developed that eliminated most of the hand labor by lifting the beets out of the soil, cutting the tops off, and elevating them into a truck. Of course, by that time trucks were used to transport the beets to the loading facility.

But the demise of the sugar beet industry in western Colorado came when the sugar produced from sugar cane in the southern states, the Caribbean and Hawaiian Islands became so competitive it was no longer possible for the sugar beet growers and manufacturers to compete. Holly Sugar Company abandoned their plant in Delta and the farmers no longer had a market.

In the late 1920s pinto beans caught on and through the 1930s and 1940s became the major cash crop for most Grand Valley farmers.

Harvesting evolved through the years to a great extent. At first a horse-powered bean cutter, equipped with two wide blades set at opposing angles and running almost flat just under the surface of the soil, was used to cut two rows of beans at a time. Rods attached just above and parallel to the blades moved the cut bean plants toward the center into windrows. Men with pitch forks then came along and gathered the windrows into small shocks. The shocking process also eliminated much of the dirt that was mixed with the beans from the cutter. After the beans had cured sufficiently in the shocks, they were either hauled to the thresher or to the farmyard where they were stacked to be threshed later.

The threshing involved large crews of men with teams and wagons. Every farmer who wanted to have his beans threshed by the crew would become a part of the crew with his own team and wagon, or just himself and other family members with pitch-forks. This was motivated by a marvelous community spirit; it didn't matter if you had small or large acreage, you could be part of the operation. The ladies played a large part in this community exchange as well –– several women would work together to feed the men at noon with fabulous feasts. The women took a lot of pride in laying their tables with such delicious banquets! Certainly the men who benefited have fond memories of those times!

Planting beans with a two-row planter in 1918. The shaft at the side with the disc on the end was to mark the next row in order to keep the rows the same distance apart for cultivating. *(Grand Valley Water Users' Association Collection)*

As combines became available the harvesting process changed considerably. Tractors were at first equipped with cutters that cut two rows, similar to the horse-drawn cutters, but later four row cutters were used. The windrows were made larger and combines equipped with "pick-up attachments" would elevate the beans out of the windrow into the machine. Thus the large threshing crews with teams and wagons and the large stationary threshers were no longer needed.

Three or more bean-processing plants were built in Fruita, as well as one at Loma, and it was a thriving business for many years. During the peak of harvest the plants operated daily from early in the morning until far into the night. The beans were hauled to the facility from the threshing machines and unloaded and stored at the plants. Later the beans were run through cleaning and bagging

machinery and stored until they were shipped to market.

Then the government health agency got in on the act and brought about some changes in handling of the beans. After all, beans were raised mostly for human consumption. So processing and storage had to be cleaned up to avoid contamination from mice, insects, germs and dirt. This caused the processing plants in Fruita to close down, and for some time beans grown in the valley had to be hauled to Delta or Dove Creek, Colorado, or to Monticello, Utah, to be processed.

Tomatoes were raised by a few farmers on contract with

A later model planter with large fertilizer buckets added. Tubes ran down to the ground from the buckets and spread the fertilizer over the seeds in the ground. The seed buckets in front of the wheels had plates in the bottom of the buckets with holes in them that rotated and dropped the seeds into the ground at certain intervals. Corn, kaffir corn, sedan grass, etc. could also be used in the planters. (Photo courtesy of *Cross Orchards Living History Site, Museum of Western Colorado*)

102

(Upper left) A bean sprayer. Visible is the large wooden water tank, hoses for filling with water, the pump on top, and the hoses and nozzles for spraying. A bean sprayer was used for the infestation of the Mexican bean beetle. The beans would sometimes have to be sprayed twice if a second infestation from the eggs occurred. Arsenic was used for the insecticide in the 100-gallon tank of water on the sprayer. Also visible are pitch forks on the left, and single-trees, a treble-tree, and a double-tree on the wall in the background. A tree is bolted to the tongue of an implement and the horses harness is hooked to the tree. (Upper right) A well-used bean sprayer. (Center left) Beans being sprayed. *(All the above courtesy of Cross Orchards Living History Site, Museum of Western Colorado)* Center right: Bean field on the Wells' farm northwest of Mack. *(Grand Valley Water Users' Association)* (Right) Bean/beet cultivator in front and a peg-toothed harrow hanging on the wall. *(Photo taken at Cross Orchards Living History Site, Museum of Western Colorado)*

the Kuner Empson Company in Grand Junction. There was a cannery at Loma in the early days, but the name of the company is not known. The building was still standing on the south side of the D&RG RR track a few rods east of the county road as late as the early 1930s.

Much like the sugar-beet contracts, fertilizer, tomato plants, and a special machine for planting, were supplied by the canning company. The plants were placed in 48-inch rows with 48 inches of space between the plants in the row. Two people rode the planter and put the small plants onto a rotating wheel of sorts that placed the plants in the ground with a small shot of water.

Somewhat like sugar beets, the tomato crop was quite labor intensive. It was not easy to get help to harvest — in later years Mexican Nationals were imported to help with the picking. They made good money in the harvest if they were thrifty and ambitious enough to work hard. A few Mexicans were known to make enough during the harvest to support themselves and their families during the rest of the year. The exchange rate of 12 Mexican pesos to one American Dollar made it possible for the Mexicans to do well if they took their money home.

The tomatoes were placed along the rows in baskets in the 30s and boxes beginning in the 40s,

Tomatoes at the Kuner Empson Cannery in the 1930s. *(Grand Valley Water Users' Association Collection)*

then loaded on trucks and hauled to the cannery. That alone, was quite a job, since the cannery was in Grand Junction.

From very early potatoes were grown by many lower valley farmers, both as a cash crop and for family supply. The most common variety of potatoes grown was "Irish Cobblers." However, other varieties, such as Pontiac, were tried by some farmers.

Potatoes could be grown quite easily, but good soil was necessary to produce a good crop. They were planted when the soil was workable in the spring.

Orlin Corn always tried to plant his in February, but March was usually the best time. The potatoes were planted in 36-inch rows —that is, there was 36 inches of space between the rows.

The seed potatoes were prepared by the farmers and family members — occasionally hired help was needed. This was a process that always took place early in the spring, just before planting time. Usually it was done in the cellar where the potatoes had been stored through the winter. Good potatoes, sorted by hand for size and shape, were selected and cut up in small pieces, leaving an "eye" in each piece. A potato plant would grow from the "eye" after the seed potato was planted.

In the early days the seed potatoes were simply dropped into a furrow by hand, but later a

A tomato field on the Alstatt farm. *(Alstatt Collection)*

104

A one-row potato planter. *(Photo courtesy of Cross Orchards Living History Site, Museum of Western Colorado.)*

special machine was used for planting. A one-row planter was drawn by a team of horses; in later years tractor-drawn planters were developed to plant two or more rows. There was a bin on top to carry a supply of seed. It had a rotating device with hooks that would spear the potato seeds one at a time and deposit them in a furrow created by a "shoe" at the bottom. Following on the rear of the machine was a pair of discs arranged so they would plow up a "hill" of dirt around the row of seeds.

During the early summer months it would be necessary to cultivate the rows to control the weeds and to maintain a good "tilth," or soil condition. Sometimes it was also necessary to hoe the weeds by hand from between the plants in the row.

The harvest usually began in June, but would continue throughout the summer, depending on when the crop was planted or when all the conditions were favorable, such as maturity of the crop, machinery availability, hand labor, etc.

The digging was done in the early days by simply digging the potatoes out of the ground with a shovel. Some farmers used a walking plow to bring the potatoes to the surface. This was a tricky process that required skill. Later a walking digger came on the market. Pulled by a team, it had a share, or blade of sorts, that could be drawn through the soil to lift the plants and the potatoes to the surface. In the back of the blade was a system of rods with a roller underneath that would vibrate and shake the rods, separating dirt from the potatoes.

Later another type machine was developed, usually pulled by four horses. This was an upgrade of the machine just described. It had a single broad wheel in front that ran over the row of potatoes to firm the soil and mash down the vines and weeds. About midway down the length of the machine were two traction wheels equipped with spade lugs to provide power to run the shaker chain. There was a share designed to dig under and lift up the potatoes. The potatoes and dirt and vines were then propelled upward by the chain which was made up of crossbars and provided a lifting action. There were rollers under the chain on both sides to keep the chain constantly shaking. By the time the potatoes reached the rear of the machine, the dirt was mostly shaken out on the ground. As the potatoes dropped to the ground, they were easily seen and picked up.

Irish Cobbler seed potatoes in bloom on H. M. Long farm northeast of Mack. *(Grand Valley Waters Users' Association)*

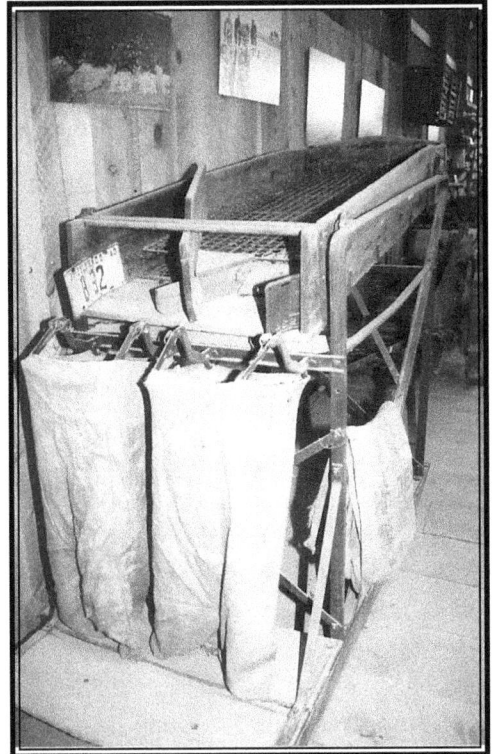

(Above left) A potato digger. (Above right) A potato sorter. License plates have been used to guide the potatoes into the sacks and keep them from falling on the ground. *(Both photos taken at Cross Orchards Living History Site)* (Left) A potato digger pulled by four horses. Visible are the potatoes rolling over the shaker chain and falling on the ground to be picked up. (Below) A potato harvest scene. Men sewing sacks closed in preparation to haul them in trucks to market. *(Both photos courtesy of Cross Orchards Living History Site, Museum of Western Colorado)*

The men, and sometimes women, who did the picking were equipped with specially made wire baskets with a bail. They would move down the rows picking up the potatoes and placing them in the baskets. When each basket was full it was carried over and dumped into the sorter. The sorter, a special machine on skids or runners, was pulled by a single horse and operated by one man. It had sloping screens over which the potatoes were moved by shaking. As they reached the rear of the screens, the operator would pick out the culls that were too large to fall through the screen and toss them over into the cull sack. Large clods and pieces of vines and other debris would be tossed out on the ground.

There were two sack holders on the back of the machine so the good potatoes would flow into one sack and the culls into the other. As the sacks became full the operator would unhook them and set them on the ground.

Then came the man who sewed the sacks. He had a special needle that could easily be threaded by simply snapping it over a loop of string. He kept a supply of string wrapped around his waste.

The full sacks were then picked up and loaded onto a truck and hauled to either home storage or to a railroad car on a siding at Mack. There would be a man there with the scales to weigh each sack of potatoes to be sure it contained 100 pounds. A sorter operator and sack sewer could estimate pretty closely the weight of the full sacks. So the "spuds," as we all called them, were then delivered to market. Farmers were often victims of the whims of the market. The author can recall one year when the price being paid was 20 cents per 100 pounds, delivered to the box car. Hardly enough to meet expenses!

During the 1930s the author was a member of a teenage potato-harvesting crew that took care of the "spud picking" for most of the growers in the New Liberty community. They were paid about 10 cents per sack of potatoes to be divided among the crew. Usually there were four pickers, a sorter man and a sack sewer. It was always a good project for earning money. The boys could each make around $2.25 per day when the going wage for other types of farm labor was $1 per day. Not

only that, we always had a good time working together, and it was hard work!

Head lettuce, melons and cucumbers were tried as cash crops by a few farmers on a small scale, but didn't catch on very well. At the present time a few farmers are growing onions as a commercial crop

Nearly all farms had a few dairy cows to provide milk, cream and butter for home use. Surplus cream was sold to creameries in Fruita and some was shipped further up the valley to Collbran, Colorado; some went to Eckert, Colorado. The skim milk from which the cream was separated was used to feed pigs and calves — much of it was used at the family dinner

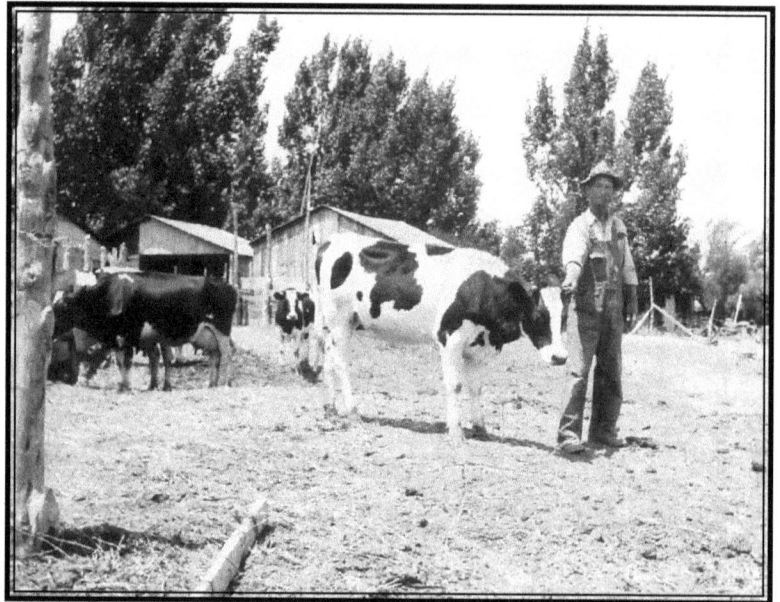

(Upper) Clyde Likes Sr.'s milk cows in 1920. *(Likes Collection)*
(Lower) Walter Weir with part of his dairy herd. *(Weir Collection)*

107

table. In the 1940s, near the end of World War II, a market was created for Grade-A milk, which was shipped daily to Delta to the Meadow Gold processing plant. There it was prepared for market as fresh milk and other products. Quite a large number of "Grade A" dairies were built up in the lower valley as a result.

Many farmers had chickens in varying numbers to provide meat and eggs for the family. Surplus was sold to local markets. A few farmers went into eggs and chickens on a much larger scale.

Pigs were raised in small to large numbers both for home consumption and for the market. There was a time when a marketing co-op was organized and occasionally members would collect enough pigs to make up a carload to be shipped to market in Los Angeles.

Turkeys were grown by many farmers — something that could be handled without too much cash outlay for buildings and equipment. Many turkeys were raised by simply letting the hens nest and feed wherever they pleased, and when the poults were large enough for market, they were caught and processed right in the barnyard.

A few farmers like M. W. Ray, and later Joel Brewster, made a big business of turkey-growing on the former Kiefer homestead. Henry Dalton also raised large flocks of turkeys on the adjoining farm near Mack. They raised their poults in a sheltered environment and cared for them much like sheep until they were ready for market. When time came for killing and de-feathering them it was a major undertaking, requiring lots of help from around the communities of Mack and New Liberty.

Mary Maluy raised turkeys for a few years as a cash-generating business. Maluys had a large flock in 1946 and hauled them to the Brewster farm at Mack for the killing and de-feathering. After that, the Maluys went into sheep.

An item of interest was found in *The Daily Sentinel* of 23 July 1939. As grasshoppers became a threat to the crops that summer, flocks of turkeys became a boon. For a fee, the turkeys were herded in the fields where they gleefully gathered the grasshoppers. The farmers were grateful to see an end to that threat to their crops and it was a cheap source of feed for the turkey growers.

(Upper) Turkeys on a local farm in the early 1920s. *(Grand Valley Water Users' Association)* (Lower) The Maluy turkeys in 1946 on the Brewster farm. *(Mary Maluy Collection)*

Turkey School

From *The Daily Sentinel* in January 1928 we learned that Mesa County Extension Agent Lauck and Professor Finch of the Fruita High School Agriculture Department conducted an evening "Turkey School" for the benefit of citizens of the New Liberty community at the schoolhouse. Over 100 were enrolled for the two-week school, and there was an average attendance of 45. A fund had been set aside to cover expenses for the school, but that was not sufficient, so there was a 5 cent charge made for each person enrolled for every night attended, to make up the deficit. The small fee charged not only paid the deficiency, but left a $7 surplus, which was turned over to the community club.

A grand program was planned for the final night, including a banquet and speakers invited from among prominent people such as, F. W. Bocking, Mayor of Fruita, and Edward T. Barber, agricultural editor of *The Daily Sentinel*. Included in the program was a reading given by Selma Snavely, a local resident. We feel it worthy to be included here. It was entitled:

"THE TURKEY"
(With apologies to James Whitcomb Riley)

The turkey biz is with us here to stay.

To eat the bugs and hoppers up
and drive hard times away.

And shoo the chickens off the farm
and bring the bossie cow and corn.

And when the evening work is done,
we gather at the schoolhouse
and have the mostest fun.

We listen to the turkey lore
Finch and Lauck tell about
to shoo off turkey troubles
if we just watch out.

Once there was a woman
so wondrous wise and nice
that she wouldn't go to turkey school
nor would she heed advice.

She knew raising turkey poults with
chicken hens was easy and so nice,

But the firstest thing she knew about
her poults were full of lice

and all the ills of turkey poults
and chicken pox and roup
limberneck and blackheads
and rickets too and croup

And when the market time arrived
she hadn't none to sell,
now who could this poor woman
blame, could any of you tell?

So we'd better pay attention
to the things here talked about
or the turkey ills will get us
if we don't watch out.

And Mr. Finch, he also says
that when the day is blue
and the lamp wick sputters
and the wind goes "w-o-o - w-o-o"
and you hear the coyote barkin'
and the moon goes gray, then out,
and our Colorado sunshine
is all squelched away,

You'd better heed your teachers
and your bulletins so true
and build sheds for your turkeys
and feed them careful too
and dust them well with powder
and vaccinate for roup
and watch for other enemies
that may cluster round your coop.

For success in raising turkeys
you must always be about
or these troubles will get you
if you don't watch out.

And when you've worked so hard
and true from spring to fall of year
it is fine to have the turkeys
to sell and bring good cheer
in the shape of well-filled larders,
debts and bank account.
Whatever else could you have done
to bring a like amount?

So, then just watch the coyote
the weasel and the cat
and all contagious troubles
and things like that,
and you'll have many turks to sell
and gobblers to eat
and even have some breeders
you would like to keep.

If only you'll
pay attention and always be about,
no turkey ills can get you
if you'll just watch out.

(Upper left) A couple of prize turkeys on the Shires farm in 1922. Laura is holding Leonard and Art is standing by. It looks like Art is about to sink into the adobe mud. (*Photo courtesy of Janie Starr*)

(Center left) Another view of the Maluy turkey herd of 2500 in 1946 on the Brewster farm waiting to be slaughtered.

(Bottom left) The Clem Maluy herd of sheep on the farm during the winter of 1954.

(Bottom right) The Maluy herd of sheep in the mountains during the summer of 1954. (*All three photos from the Mary Maluy Collection*)

Chapter Five

New Liberty

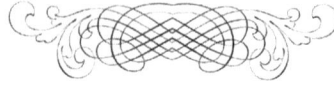

New Liberty School

As the New Liberty settlers were getting established on their farms they began to hope the proper officials would recognize their need of a school for their children. A few pupils from the new community attended school in Mack and Fruita during 1918-19.

Mack items in *The Daily Sentinel* Mon. 2 September 1918 :

Several farmers in the new farming section north of Mack have petitioned the school board for a school in their section. The school board is contemplating the erection of a school for them. There are about 20 children of school age in the section.

On 19 December 1918, Joseph P. Kiefer filed a Quit Claim Deed for three acres in the SW corner of the NW¼ of Section 16 to become School District #37 for a new school.

Mack items, Monday, 10 March 1919:

A special school election is called for next Wednesday to decide as to an appropriation to be used in building a new school house in the "High Line" District. There are about 20 scholars in that district and the parents are anxious to get the school started. A school house will have to be built in Mack also before fall, as the present quarters are entirely inadequate.

Mack items, Monday, 17 March 1919:

At a special school election held last Wednesday, it was decided to appropriate $800 for a school house and equipment in the 'High Line' District.

The school house was built during the summer of 1919; builders were still working that fall to finish before school began .

The following bit of history about the beginning of school at New Liberty, written by Clyde Likes Jr., 22 January 1982, seems consistent with other records:

We were called to school, I think, a little late in September by Miss Bonnie O'Bryan and we met out in the yard. The men were still building benches for us in the school room. She gave us all books and assignments for the first day of school. She had separated the kids into the proper classes and then in the school house on the first day she seated them accordingly.

Mack items, 17 Sept 1919:

School started in the northern part of the district this Monday; Miss O'Bryan from Fruita is the teacher.

The High Line District school house that was built in 1919. It was officially named New Liberty in 1922. *(Courtesy of Viola Alstatt)*

111

So we can calculate that the first day of school at New Liberty was Monday, 15 September 1919.

Educational Directories from School District #51 refer to the new school in 1919/20 as the "Highline School." The rest of the times it is referred to as "New Liberty School." It appears that the name New Liberty was being used sometime before the votes were cast as noted below.

The Board of Directors already serving for Mack took care of the new school as well for that year: President, Charles C. Kiefer; Secretary, Robert Cox; Treasurer, F. A. Kennedy.

In 1920/21 the School Board members were President, Donald MacTaggart; Secretary, Charles C. Kiefer; Treasurer, John E. Wesner. The 1921/22 School Board members were President, John E. Wesner; Secretary, Albert W. Alstatt; Treasurer, Donald MacTaggert.

Following is May Sanders' record for New Liberty, 27 June 1922:

The Board called a special meeting to choose new officers for New Liberty, also to name the district. The new School Board elected: President, W. E. Bowen; Treasurer, George W. Fisher; Secretary, Albert W. Alstatt.

Names were submitted, and votes cast to name the new district: New Liberty, 18; West Valley, 15; Valley Center, 1; Progressive, 1; Liberty, 1; Mt. View, 1; Paradise, 1.

Those who came to vote were: Lee [Roy] Wells, M. L. Wells, Mr. & Mrs. A. L. Stout [probably Stotts], Mr. & Mrs. John Morrow, George Bryan, W. A. Knapp, Mr. & Mrs. Vern Snavely, L. C. Snavely, Mr. & Mrs. Guy Gerry, Sara Clow, Andrew Saul, G. W. Fisher, B. A. Harrison, Mr. & Mrs. J. N. King, Mr. & Mrs. Robert Copper [probably Cooper], Mr. & Mrs. Clem Maluy, Mr. & Mrs. Ted Wassenburg, Mr. & Mrs. John Earp, Mr. & Mrs. E. L. Shires, Mrs. Raver, Mrs. Walter McCampbell, Mr. & Mrs. C. Winters, Charles Cavendish, Paul Arpke, Mrs. Schunter, Mr. & Mrs. Al Daily, Rudolph Johnson, Mr. & Mrs. A. H. Cutler, Mr. & Mrs. Walter Weir, Floyd Thomas, Mr. & Mrs. W. E. Bowen, Mr. Burket, Mr. & Mrs. C. W. Likes, R. M. Cox, A. W. Alstatt, Mr. & Mrs. Dean, Mr. & Mrs. B. D. Lofgren.

Apparently only one vote per household was allowed, as the votes cast totaled 38 and the number of voters present were 55.

We have learned that Arthur Cutler may have presented the name, "New Liberty."

The district was thus divided, and Mack became District #44; New Liberty remained #37.

Following are the names of teachers and pupils compiled by May Sanders. After listing all students for 1919-20, it appears she listed only new pupils each year thereafter:

1919/20—Teacher: Bonnie O'Bryan, 27 pupils:

1st grade: Milton Alstatt, William Bowen, Clyde Likes, Clifford Snow, Frank[lin] Manzanares, Elizabeth Morrow, Margaret McCampbell

2nd grade: none

3rd grade: Ruth Alstatt, Viola Alstatt, Hobart Cutler, Raymond Fisher, Fred Likes,

Wedding picture of Bonnie O'Bryan and Lee Roy Wells, Wednesday, 2 June 1921. *(Morrow/Thomas Collection)*

Peter Manzanares, Estellene Morrow, Elizabeth Stotts

4th grade: Charles Cutler, Laura Johnson

5th grade: Ivan Likes, Elmer Snow, John Pacheco

6th grade: Mabel Likes, Carmel Manzanares, Floyd Fleming, Frances Schunter, Maudie Raver

7th grade: Harold Carroll

8th grade: Nellie Schunter

1920/21 — Teacher: for 7 months, Gladys Hill; for remaining 2 months, Verda Weimer; 34 pupils;

1st grade: Manroe Snow, Edith Alstatt
2nd grade: Dorothy Dean
3rd grade: Lula Dean, Mildred Weir
5th grade: Frances Balkwell
7th grade: Dan Pacheco
8th grade: Frank Pacheco, Marie Blazon

1921/22 — Teacher: Selma Snavely; 29 pupils: Viola Alstatt, Ruth Alstatt, Edith Alstatt, Milton Alstatt, Frances Vivian Balkwell, Louise Clow, Lula Dean, Dorothy Dean, Laura Johnson, Mabel Likes, Ivan Likes, Fred Likes, Clyde Likes Jr., Estellene Morrow, Elizabeth Morrow, Maudie Raver, Francis Schunter, Mildred Weir, William Bowen, Harold Carroll, Charles Cutler, Hobart Cutler, Ralph Foss, Dan Pacheco, John Pacheco

May Sanders noted that Melba & Margaret McCampbell and Marie Blazon moved away that year. A picture published in the *Fruita Times* 2 May 1991 shows 29 pupils (see page 108). It includes Melba and Margaret McCampbell, but not Marie Blazon. Lephia Foss, Edna Weir and Vauna Clow are in that picture, but they must have been visiting. Lephia and Edna are listed below in the first grade 1923-24.

1922/23 — Teacher: Selma Snavely, no record of students.

New Liberty School students in 1919. Back row L-R: Mabel Likes, Frances Schunter, Laura Johnson, Teacher Bonnie O'Bryan. Middle row: Harold Carroll, Ivan Likes, William Bowen, Viola Alstatt. Front row: Elizabeth Morrow, Milton Alstatt, Clyde Likes, Jr., Ruth Alstatt, Estellene Morrow, Hobart Cutler, and Fred Likes (holding a rabbit). *(Mabel Likes Cox and Viola Alstatt Collections)*

New Liberty School students in 1921. (Back row) Mabel Likes, Nellie Schunter, Laura Johnson, Frances Schunter, Harold Carroll. Front rows: Milton Alstatt, Estellene Morrow, Ruth Alstatt, Bill Bowen (snowball), Elizabeth Morrow, Fred Likes, Clyde Likes Jr., Viola Alstatt, Hobart Cutler, Charles Cutler. *(Mabel Likes Cox Collection)*

(Left) New Liberty School students in 1922. Left to right—Front row: Vauna Clow, Louise Clow, Melba McCampbell, Edith Alstatt, Ralph Foss, Charles Cutler, Fred Likes, Bill Bowen, and Hobart Cutler. Second row: Dorothy Dean, Elizabeth Morrow, Milton Alstatt, Mildred Weir, Edna Weir, Margaret McCampbell, Harold Carroll, and Clyde Likes Jr. Third row: Viola Alstatt, Laura Johnson, Frances Vivian Balkwell, Ruth Alstatt, Estellene Morrow, and Lula Dean. Back row: Mabel Likes, Frances Schunter, Maudie Raver, Ivan Likes, John Pacheco, and Dan Pacheco. (*Mabel Likes Cox Collection*)

(Below Left) New Liberty graduating class of 1922 in front of the Snavely home. Maudie Raver, Mabel Likes, Ivan Likes, Frances Schunter, and teacher Selma Snavely. (*Mabel Likes Cox Collection*) (Below right) Mabel and Ivan Likes graduation picture taken 20 May 1922, apparently the same day as the one on the left. Mabel is 16 and Ivan is 14. (*Homer Likes Collection*)

114

The school building was remodeled in the summer of 1923 so it had two rooms. At that time two large coal/wood burning heaters were installed; one in a corner of each room. Surrounding each was a large galvanized sheet-metal reflector shield that prevented the students from getting too close to the hot stoves and also served well to radiate heat throughout the rooms. The areas close to those stoves were a favorite hangout for the students during the coldest winter days.

(It is not clear if the following lists are new students only.)

1923/24 — Teachers: Ralph and Gertrude Horn. The school board for that year: President, W. E. Bowen; Secretary, A. W. Alstatt; Treasurer, Lee L. Foss.

Lower grades: Ernest Frohn, Pedro Otero, Josie Otero, Mary Otero, Philip Marez, Fecundo Marez, Melba McCampbell, Lephia Foss, Edna Weir, Thelma Frohn, Cora Martinez, Mary Martinez, Frank Overbye, Helen Overbye

Upper Grades: Truman Sanders, Richard Weatherford, Charles MacIntosh, Netta Gadbury; Milton Alstatt, Edith Alstatt

1924/25 — The School Board remained the same. Lower grade teacher: La Cleta Shoemaker. Pupils:

1st grade: Merton Arpke, John Cavendish, Wallie Sanders, Clark Gerry, Charles Overbye, Arthur Shires, Eugene Waters, Jesus Cordova, Mary Cordova, Walter Cordova, Lena Cordova, Glen Lemon, Amos Alstatt

(No 2nd grade?)

3rd grade: Chester Haifley

Shirley Phillips taught the upper grades. Pupils:

5th grade: Victor Cordova

8th grade: Virginia Smith

1925/26—No record of School Board for this year. Lower grade teacher: Mable Henson.

1st grade: Victor Lofgren, Walter Cordova, Stella Trujillo, Arthur Nab, Erma Nab

2nd grade: Jesus Cordova, Merton Arpke, Amos Alstatt, John Cavendish, Clark Gerry, Arthur Shires, Clarence Porter, Joe Leach, Homer Likes

3rd grade: Marie Nab, Walter Nab, Edward Cordova, Lephia Foss, Edna Weir, Paul Cutler, Ernest Marez, Philip Marez

4th grade: Chester Haifley

Upper grades teacher: H. H. Henson

5th grade: Alene Leach, George Fisher, Edith Alstatt, Melba McCampbell, Ralph Foss, Lena Cordova, Frances Cordova, Thelma Frohn

6th grade: Franklin Manzanares

7th grade: Dorothy Dean, Clyde Likes, Margaret McCampbell

8th grade: Milton Alstatt, Lula Dean, Elizabeth Morrow, Mildred Weir

1926-27 — Teachers: Mr. & Mrs. James Sears for 2 months; Laurel Elbin, Mrs. Ida Smith and Margaret Lockard for the last seven months. The School Board elected for that year: President, B. A. Harrison; Secretary, A. W. Alstatt; Treasurer, W. E. Bowen.

[A teacherage was built in 1926]

1927/28 — Teachers: Grace Curtis and Laurel Elbin. School Board: President, B. A. Harrison; Secretary, A. W. Alstatt; Treasurer, Clement Maluy.

1928/29 — Teachers: Grace Curtis and Florence Chilson. [School Board was the same through school year 1937-38]

1929/30 — Teachers: Grace Curtis and Florence Chilson

1930/31 — Teachers: Reba and Wauneta Wing

1931/32 — Teachers: Faust M. and Claire Yates

1932/33 — Teachers: Dorothy Ellis and Claire Yates, 7 mos.; Pauline Geering, 2 mos.

[May Sanders seemed to have had an after thought here, as she added the names of some of the pupils for that year and the next, possibly because she wanted to show Floyd Carlson's class mates]

6th grade: Clyde Wright, Ruth Arpke, Edward Cutler, Bob Anderson, Gordon Lane, Barbara McKay, Lewis Likes, Helen Meglitsch, Leonard Shires

7th grade: Naomi Gerry, Darrell Maluy, Lawrence Morrow, Floyd Carlson, Eugene Goff

8th grade: Carl Alstatt, JoAnn Bowen, Wesley Lane, Art Shires, Harold Stotts

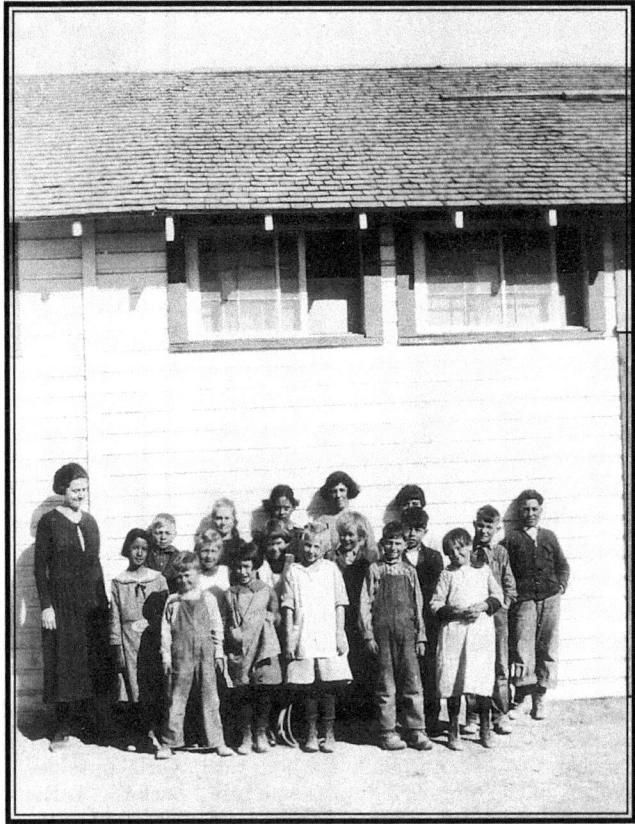

(Above left) Upper grades 1923/4. Not all are identified. Back row: Teacher Ralph Horn, ?, ?, Viola Alstatt, John Pacheco, and Lulu Dean. Middle row: Unidentified, Ruth Alstatt, Laura Johnson, Ellen Frohn, Estellene Morrow, and Charles Cutler. Front row: Margaret McCampbell, ?, Mildred Weir, Elizabeth Morrow, William Bowen, and Milton Alstatt. (Above Right) Lower grades 1923/4. Back row: Teacher Gertrude Horn, Frank Overbye, Helen Overbye, ?, ?, ?, could be Frank Manzanares. Middle row: Unidentified, Edith Alstatt, Melba McCampbell, ?, Hobart Cutler, and Ralph Foss. Front row: Unidentified, Edna Weir, ?, Paul Cutler, and Lephia Foss. *(Both photos from the Weir Collection)*

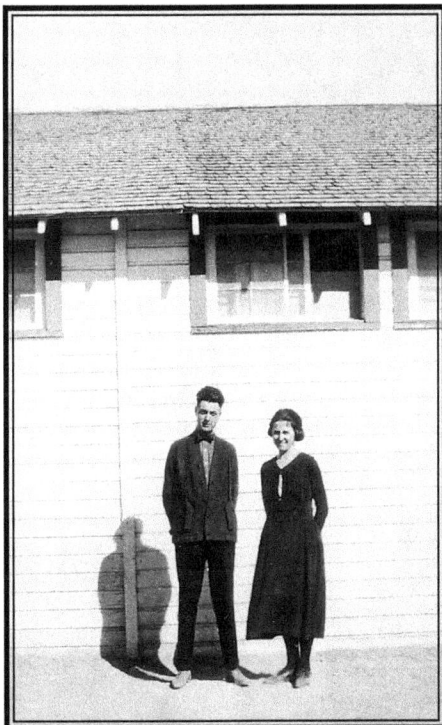

Teachers Ralph and Gertrude Horn for school year 1923/4. *(Weir Collection)*

The graduating class of 1924. L to R — Teacher Ralph Horn, Laura Johnson, Charles Cutler, Viola Alstatt, John Pacheco, and Ellen Frohn. *(Courtesy of Viola Alstatt)*

(Above) New Liberty School Teachers H. H. and Mabel Henson during the 1925/6 school year. *(Mabel Likes Collection)* (Upper right) New Liberty School pupils for the year 1929. Photo taken in school yard. Girls' outside toilet is in the center right of the picture. Back row L-R: Edward Cutler, Lewis Likes, Carl Alstatt, Darrell Maluy, ?, Don Clow, Lawrence Morrow, ? and Leonard Shires. Front row: Ruth Arpke, Barbara McKay, Helen Meglitsch, Virginia Likes, Mildred Raver, Eloise Foss, JoAnn Bowen, Sarah Leach and Agnes Alstatt. *(Shires Collection)* (Right) New Liberty 2nd grade, 1930. L-R: Virginia Likes, Allen Waters, Harry Cutler, Agnes Alstatt. The horse barn is visible in the distance. *(Likes Collection)* (Lower left) New Liberty 4th grade, 1930. Back row: Leonard Shires, Helen Meglitsch, Lewis Likes, Edward Cutler. Front: Barbara McKay, Naomi Gerry and Eloise Foss. *(Likes Collection)* (Lower right) New Liberty 5th grade, 1930. Boys: Lawrence Morrow and Carl Alstatt. Girls: Mildred Raver, Sarah Leach and JoAnn Bowen. They are sitting on the steps of the stile over the fence west of the school house. *(Photo courtesy of JoAnn Bowen Montague)*

New Liberty graduating class of 1930/31. Vauna Clow, Harold Sanders, Louise Clow, and Betty Curtis. (*Louise Clow Likes Collection*)

Part of the eighth grade, 1933. L-R: Harold Stotts, Art Shires and JoAnn Bowen. Missing are Carl Alstatt and Wesley Lane. (*Photo courtesy of JoAnn Bowen Montague*)

(Above) New Liberty school boys sitting on the running board of someone's 1928 Model A Ford in about 1932. L-R: Carl Alstatt, Lewis Likes, Lawrence Morrow, Bob Anderson, Ed Cutler and Clark Gerry. (Middle right) A party held in about 1930/31. In front: Barbara McKay. Second row: Naomi Gerry, Louise Waters, Edna ? and JoAnn Bowen. Third row: Lawrence Morrow, Allen Waters, Edward Cutler and Carl Alstatt. Back row: Clark Gerry, Joe Leach, Amos Alstatt, Darrell Maluy, Harold Stotts and Eugene Waters. (Right) New Liberty girls standing in front of the school house. Back row, L-R: Eloise Foss, Barbara McKay, Helen Meglitsch, JoAnn Bowen and Naomi Gerry. Front row: (2nd)Louise Alstatt, (4th) Marilyn Maluy. In the background is the horse barn. (*Photos courtesy of JoAnn Bowen Montague*)

In May of 1933 an item of interest was printed in *The Daily Sentinel*. The County Superintendent of Schools conducted a scholastic abilities test for all subjects being taught to children of the upper elementary grades in all schools in the county. The highest possible score for the test was 273 points. Three students of the New Liberty School were the highest in the county: Harold Stotts led with a test score of 196 points; JoAnn Bowen with 192 points; Carl Alstatt with 190 points and Douglas Booth of the Mack School scored 182 points. That says a lot for those little country schools and their students!

1933/34 — Teachers: Harold Carroll; and Esther Ziegler. Pupils:

5th grade; Agnes Alstatt, Harriett Cutler, Eloise Foss, Virginia Likes, Harry Cutler, Rex Maluy, Dale Maluy, James Pollock

6th grade: Charles Keith, Royal Elwess, Damon Eslinger [May noted that all three 6th graders left at midterm.]

7th grade: Lewis Likes, Glenn Forester, Clyde Wright, Leonard Shires, Edward Cutler, Bob Anderson, Gloria Higgins, Barbara McKay, Helen Meglitsch, Ruth Arpke, Margie McMillen, Lois Thomas

8th grade: Naomi Gerry, Darrell Maluy, Lawrence Morrow, Floyd Carlson, Edward Rouse

1934/35—Teachers: Harold Carroll and Inez Porter

[In 1935 B. A. Harrison resigned as president of the school board and Guy Gerry was appointed to fill the vacancy]

1935/36 — Teachers: Harold Carroll and Inez Porter

1936/37 — Teachers: Harold Carroll and Inez Porter, part; Josephine Price finished

1937/38 — Teachers: Harold Carroll and Josephine Price

1938-39 — Teachers: Russell Poley and Irene Gimple. School Board: President, Charles Brayton; Secretary, A. W. Alstatt; Treasurer, Clement Maluy.

(Board remained the same through 1942-43)

1939/40 — Teachers: Delbert and Fae Miller Jerome

1940/41 — Teachers: Delbert and Fae Miller Jerome

1941/42 — Teachers: Delbert and Fae Miller Jerome, LaRae Gosnell.

[Eugene Thomas says Fae had a baby within that school year, Gosnell finished for her]

1942/43 — Teachers: Thelma Brenton and Catherine Mowrer

1943/44 — Teachers: Zella Sanders and Dorothy M. Weaver. William E. Pollock was elected Secretary of the School Board

1944/45 — Teachers: Mary Katherine Bauman; Dorothy M. Weaver

[See following story about the third room]

1945/46 — Teachers: Hazel G. Ward, started; replaced by Nadine Mock; Dorothy M. Weaver; Beverly Maluy, 7 mos.; Lewis Likes, 2 mos.

A change occurred in the School Board — R. I. Wynkoop was elected Treasurer.

1946/47 — Teachers: Edna Cook, Fyrne M. Lyons, Ursula Thompson

School Board: President, William E. Pollock; Secretary, H. M. Sanders; Treasurer, Bernard Ebright

1947/48 — Teachers: Edna Cook, Clara Roach, Ursula Thompson

School Board: President, Merton Arpke; Secretary, H. M. Sanders; Treasurer, Floyd Thomas

1948/49 — Teachers: Mabel Cooper, Clara Roach, Ursula Thompson

1949/50 — Teachers: Mabel Cooper, Clara Roach, Ursula Thompson

Graduating class of 1934: Edward Rouse, Floyd Carlson, Teacher Harold Carroll, Darrell Maluy, Lawrence Morrow, and Naomi Gerry. *(Darrell Maluy Collection)*

(Above) Esther Ziegler, one of the teachers for the school year 1933/34. *(Laura Berry Collection)*

(Upper left) Upper classes 1933/34. Back row, left to right: Agnes Alstatt, Helen Higgins, Barbara McKay, Lois Thomas, Margie McMillen, teacher Harold Carroll, Helen Meglitsch, Eloise Foss, Naomi Gerry, Virginia Likes, and Harriett Cutler. Middle row: Leonard Shires, Lewis Likes, ?, Floyd Carlson, Darrell Maluy, Bob Anderson, and Lawrence Morrow. Front row: Dale Maluy, Frank Thomas, Ray Turner, Edward Cutler, Edward Rouse, Rex Maluy, James Pollock, and Harry Cutler. *(Darrell Maluy Collection)*

(Below) New Liberty School pupils for 1933/34. Teachers in the back: Esther Ziegler, Harold Carroll, and Helen Carroll. Helen taught music. Back row, left to right: Harriet Higgins, ?, Patty Maluy, Betty Pollock, Virginia Likes, Harriet Cutler, Naomi Gerry, Eloise Foss, Lois Thomas, Margie McMillen, Helen Meglitsch, Barbara McKay, Agnes Alstatt, Helen Higgins, Marilyn Maluy, P. Rouse, Blanche Meglitsch, Dorothy Cox, and Louise Alstatt. Middle row: ?, Ray Turner, Frank Thomas, Lewis Likes, ?, Bob Anderson, Darrell Maluy, Floyd Carlson, Edward Rouse, Lawrence Morrow, Leonard Shires, James Pollock. Front row: ?, Harold Blasdel, Robert Alstatt, ?, Burke Wright, Harry Cutler, Dale Maluy, Edward Cutler, Rex Maluy, Ben Rowe, Clifford McKay, Ray Likes, Billy Wright, Delores Calvert (kneeling). *(Darrell Maluy Collection)*

(Right) New Liberty Graduating class of 1935. L-R: Barbara McKay, Ruth Arpke, Helen Meglitsch, Gerald Colthorpe, Teacher Harold Carroll, Bob Anderson, Edward Cutler, Lewis Likes, Clyde Wright, Leonard Shires. *(Likes Collection)*

Opposite page: (Upper) New Liberty School boys. May 1936 is printed on back of picture. Left to right. Back row: Robert Brisbin, Robert Arpke, Harry Cutler, Rex Maluy, Edwin Berry, Teacher Harold Carroll, Francis Smiley, Richard Hastings, Dale Maluy, James Pollock, Burke Wright. Front row: Ray Likes, Robert Alstatt, Jack Grimsby, Fred Pacheco, Murray Phillips, Billy Wright, LeRoy Kinney, Kenneth Owings, Harold Blasdel, Sam Grimsby, and Glen Blasdel. *(Likes Collection and also courtesy Mildred Raver Means)*

(Below) New Liberty pupils for 1934/5 school year. Left to right: front row: Kenneth Owings, Sam Grimsby, Jack Grimsby, Harold Blasdel, Robert Alstatt, Ray Likes, Glen Blasdel. 2nd Row: Clifford McKay, Dorothy Cox, Betty Pollock, Delores Calvert, Marilyn Maluy, Blanche Meglitsch, Ruth Brisbin, Oliver Swyhart, Burke Wright. 3rd Row: Ben Henry Rowe, Robert Brisbin, Ray Turner, Robert Arpke, Harry Cutler, James Pollock, Virginia Likes. 4th Row: Leonard Shires, Clyde Wright, Joe Meyer, Lewis Likes, Edward Cutler, Agnes Alstatt, Harriett Cutler, Richard Swyhart. Back row: Mabel Brisbin, Ruth Arpke, Helen Meglitsch, Gerald Colthorpe, Bob Anderson, Eloise Foss, Barbara McKay, and Teacher Harold Carroll. *(Likes Collection)*

(Above) New liberty School boys. May 1936 is printed on back of picture. Back row, L-R, Robert Brisbin, Robert Arpke, Harry Cutler, Rex Maluy, Edwin Berry, Teacher Harold Carroll, Frances Smiley, Richard Hastings, Dale Maluy, James Pollock, Burke Wright. Front row: Ray Likes, Robert Alstatt, Jack Grimsby, Fred Pacheco, Murry Phillips, Billy Wright, LeRoy Kinney, Kenneth Owings, Harold Blasdel, Sam Grimsby, and Glen Blasdel. *(Likes Collection and courtesy of Mildred Rave Means)* (Below) New Liberty upper classes 1937. Back row: Louise Alstatt, Marilyn Maluy, Eloise Foss, Agnes Alstatt, Harriett Cutler, Virginia Likes, Helen Higgins, and Dorothy Cox. Front row: Harry Cutler, Dale Maluy, Rex Maluy, Robert Brisbin, Robert Arpke, Edwin Berry, and James Pollock. *(Likes Collection)*

(Above) Upper classes on an outing with chaperones in 1938. Upper group: Ray Banning, Harold Carroll, Louise Alstatt, Myrle Appier, Ruth Brisbin, Mary Maluy, Betty Pollock, Edith Currey, Helen Currey, Bobby Pacheco, Patty Maluy, and Naomi Banning. Lower group: Robert Arpke, Helen Carroll, Joe Appier, Marilyn Maluy, Dave Thomas, Robert Alstatt, Harry Cutler, Clifford McKay, Aaron Kenny, and Ray Likes. (Below) The chaperones. L-R: Harold Carroll, Helen Carroll, Ray Banning, Nellie Banning, Mary Maluy, Pansy Appier, and Viola Alstatt. *(Both photos courtesy of Viola Alstatt.)*

(Above) Class outing in September 1938. Not all are identified. Back Row: L-R — Harold Blasdel, ?,?,?, Lewis Sanders, Roy Homedew, Donald Wright, Wylie Sanders, Murray Phillips, ?. Next row: Georgia Wallace, Lee Ann Maluy, Barbara Wright, Thelma Burkett, ?, Robert Pollock. Next row: ?, Sandra Carroll, Dixie Wright, George Brayton, Phyllis Maluy. Next row: Norma Maluy, Anna Belle Alstatt, Wilma Maluy, Harriett Brisbin, Hazel Banning, ?, Helen Grace Carroll. Front row: Glen Blasdel, Junior Appier, ?, Eugene Thomas, ?. *(Phyllis Likes Collection)*

(Left) Teacher Delbert Jerome standing in front of the New Liberty Schoolhouse on the southwest corner. He taught from the fall of 1939 through the spring of 1942. (Above) Irene Gimple, teacher for the lower grades at New Liberty during the school year 1938-39. *(Phyllis Likes Collection)*

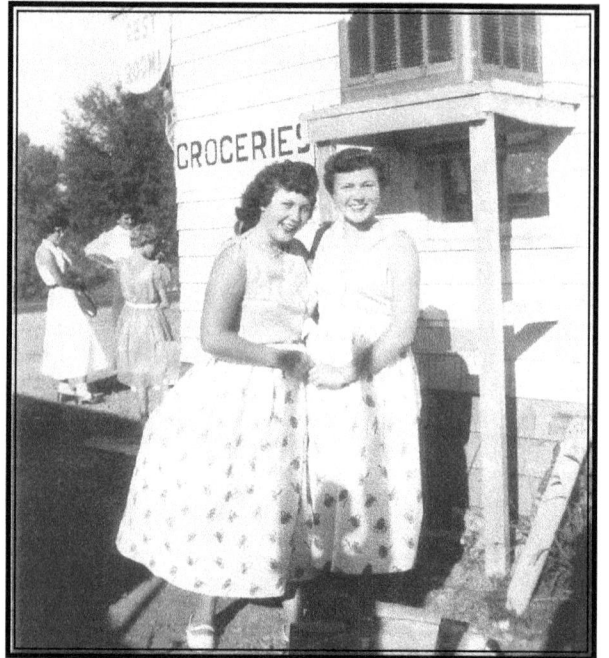

On the bus route to Fruita the high school students from New Liberty were let off at Mack while the bus made the run on Mack Mesa to pick up students, and then picked up the New Liberty students on the way to Fruita. These photos show some of those students. (Upper left) About 1942 in front of the Smith store. Standing L-R: Bobby Brisbin, Delores Smith, ? Downing, Jaye Rowe, Rose Ellen Adams, Myrle Appier, Richard Smith, Joe Meyers, Robert Pacheco, Naomi Banning, Robert Downing, Louise Alstatt. In front: Alta Smith, Agnes Alstatt, Charlie Smith. *(Delores Likes Collection)* (Upper right) About 1948 with Mack in the background. Left to right: Ralph Banning, Orlene Corn, Lee Ann (Bubbles) Maluy, Lewis Sanders, Ernest Paulson, Norma Maluy. *(Phyllis Likes Collection)* (Lower left) About 1944 beside the Smith store. Standing L-R: Anna Belle Alstatt, Wilma Maluy, Joan Marie Potzner, Phyllis Maluy, Linda Downing, Patty Maluy, Murray Phillips, Ray Sisler. Front: Billy Weihl and Robert Alstatt. *(Phyllis Likes Collection)* (Lower right) Taken in 1955 beside the Mack store is Maxine Cutler and Anna Jane Berry dressed alike in dresses that Modine Cutler, Maxine's mother, made them. Other New Liberty students in the background are unidentified. *(Photo courtesy of Maxine Cutler Stutler)*

(Above) Grades 5-8 in 1945: Standing, L-R: Leatha Wynkoop, Roy Homedew, Margie Sisler, A. J. Wynkoop, Thelma Burkett, Lester Wilkinson, Orlene Corn, Eugene Thomas, Dale Cutler, and Lee Ann (Bubbles) Maluy. In front: Bill Leach, Billy Appier, Alex Dale Wilkinson, Walter Pollock, and Dick Stutsman. *(Photo courtesy of Stanley Wynkoop)*
(Below) Grade 6 in 1946/7: Billy Likes, Jeanne Corn, Earle Denton, Darlene Lupton, Shirley Cotner, Abel Garcia, and Larry Paulson. *(Photo courtesy of Shirley Cotner Barsham)*

(Above) New Liberty lower grades of 1943\44. Back row: Teacher Dorothy M. Weaver, Shirley Ebright, Norma Burkett, Margie Sisler, Charlene Brayton, and Jeanne Corn. Middle row: Helen Sanders, Nettie Geeting, Anna Jane Berry, Maxine Cutler, Leona Belle Wynkoop, and Betty Tolle. Front row: Johnny Burkett, Paul Wells, Kay Geeting, Billy Appier, and Frank Berry. *(Photo courtesy of Anna Jane Berry Starr & Maxine Cutler Stutler)* (Below) Classes 1944\45. Back row L-R: Thelma Reed, Georgia Reed, Teacher Dorothy M. Weaver, and Norma Burkett. Middle row: Frank Berry, ? Pool, Darlene Lupton, Betty Tolle, Anna Jane Berry, Leona Belle Wynkoop, Maxine Cutler, Ernestine Lupton, Jeanne Corn, Shirley Ebright, Nettie Geeting, and Helen Sanders. Front rows: ? Leach, Basil Banning, ? Reader, Norma Pollock, Paul Wells, Curtis Thomas, Kay Geeting, Tommy Berry, Leon Ebright, and Johnny Burkett. *(Photo courtesy of Maxine Cutler Stutler)*

(Above) Lower grades 1945\46. Back row L-R: Curtis Thomas, Basil Banning, Kay Geeting, Bobby Cotner, Tom Berry, Paul Wells, ?Blank, Ernestine Lupton, Anna Jane Berry and Maxine Cutler. Front row: Dolores Cutler, Thelma Read, Peggy Arpke, Betty Leach and Norma Pollock. *(Photo courtesy of Maxine Cutler Stutler)*

(Below) Lower grades in 1946\47. Back rows: Jimmy Tomlinson, Norma Pollock, Basil Banning, Dolores Cutler, Curtis Thomas, Tom Berry, Tiburcio Garcia, Claude Denton, Bobby Cotner, and Teacher Fyrne Lyons. Front row: Carl Cotner, JoElla Brayton, Louie Denton, and Peggy Arpke. *(Photo courtesy of Dolores Cutler O'Connor)*

(Above) Upper grades in 1948/49. Standing L-R: Norma Pollock, Dolores Cutler, Peggy Arpke, Jimmy Tomlinson, Anthony Espinosa, Kenneth Gayman, Anna Jane Berry, Maxine Cutler, and Jeanne Corn. Front: Tom Berry, Curtis Thomas, Tiburcio Garcia, LaMoyne Jones, Ben Espinosa, and Edward Likes. *(Photo courtesy of Dolores Cutler O'Connor)*

(Right) The basketball team for 1948/49. Back row: Billy Likes, Able Garcia, Larry Paulson, Frank Berry. Front row: Bobby Likes, Coach Jim Cooper, and Johnny Burkett. Looks like Frank Berry has a broken finger. *(Photo courtesy of Anna Jane Berry Starr)*

(Right) The New Liberty Pep Club for the year 1948/49. Back row: Norma Pollock, Dolores Cutler, Anna Jane Berry, Leona Belle Wynkoop, Bernita Tufly, Dixie Cowden. Front row: ?. Kathleen Thomas, Darlene Tufly, Betty Jones. Cheerleaders; Peggy Arpke, Delena Dyer, Maxine Cutler, and Jeanne Corn. *(Photo courtesy of Maxine Cutler Stutler)*

(Left) The upper classes at New Liberty School in 1950\51. Back row: Tiburcio Garcia, Mrs. Mabel Cooper, LaMoyne (Rusty) Jones, Kenneth Gaymon, and Edward Likes. Kneeling: Tommy Berry, Anna Jane Berry, Maxine Cutler, and Pauline Ashburn. Sitting in the front is Curtis Thomas. *(Photo courtesy of Anna Jane Berry Starr and Maxine Cutler Stutler)*

(Below) Dressed up to attend the graduation for the class of 1951 at New Liberty School. The graduates are the four in the center: LeMoyne (Rusty) Jones, Maxine Cutler, Anna Jane Berry, and Edward Likes. Pauline Ashburn on the left and Dolores Cutler on the right are 7th graders. *(Photo courtesy of Dolores Cutler O'Connor)*

130

(Above left) The first grade at New Liberty School for the school year 1951/52. Back row: David Alstatt, Donna Jones, Trudy Maluy and Mableann Post. In front: Louise Wells and Johnny Komorrow. (Above right) Mrs. Mabel Cooper taught the upper grades at New Liberty School from 1948 to 1959, when the school closed down. She was involved with the children on the previous and following pages. Many special projects were accomplished under her tutelage. (Below:) New Liberty School students with their rock collection they accumulated for a school project. Photo published in *The Daily Sentinel* on 23 November 1952. Donnie Butt in front. Left to right: Jimmy Tomlinson, Darrel Barcus, Patricia White, Elizabeth Stahl, Betty Jones, Kathleen Thomas and Robert Drinnan. On the same page was a photo of a sculpture of the Colorado National Monument which the students made from sawdust and paste. The photo was not good enough to use. *(All three photos courtesy of Mableann Post Hawthorne)*

(Above left) New Liberty 7th & 8th grades 1951/52. Back row: Jimmy Tomlinson, Tiburcio Garcia, Curtis Thomas and Tom Berry. Front row: Max Barlow, Patricia White, Peggy Arpke, Bernita Tufly, Norma Pollock and Dolores Cutler. *(Photo courtesy of Jimmy Tomlinson and Dolores Cutler O'Connor)* (Above right) Upper classes 1952/53. Back row: Teacher Mrs. Cooper, Byron Scoggin, Hugh Scoggin, Jimmy Tomlinson, Daniel Valdez. Middle rows: Kathleen Thomas, Angelina Valdez, Betty Jones, James Scoggin, Luthera Barcus, Patricia White, Winnie Dean Butt, Darrel Barcus. Front: Allen Moss, Clarence

Barnes, Bill Hawthorne, Robert Drinnen, Jerry Hawthorne, Donnie Butt. (Left) Upper class girls 1952/53: Kathleen Thomas, Betty Jones, Winnie Dean Butt, Luthera Barcus, Patricia White, Angelina Valdez. (Right) Hugh Scoggin, Jimmy Tomlinson, Daniel Valdez and Darrel Barcus. (Below left) The 8th grade 1952/53: Hugh Scoggin, Mrs. Cooper, Darrel Barcus, Dolores Cutler, Jimmy Tomlinson, and Daniel Valdez. (Below right) The graduation of the 8th grade 1952/53: Hugh Scoggin, Darrel Barcus, Dolores Cutler, Jimmy Tomlinson, and Daniel Valdez. *(The above five photos courtesy of Dolores Cutler O'Connor)*

(Above) New Liberty upper grades of 1953/54. Back row: Teacher Mrs. Mabel Cooper, Kathleen Thomas, Patricia White, Max Barlow, and Bill Hawthorne. Middle row: Josie Brewster, Winnie Dean Butt, Betty Jones, Luthera Barcus and Rudy Wilkinson. Front row: Jerry Hawthorne, Donnie Butt, Clarence Barnes and Dennis (Rocky) Nichols. (Below left) 7th grade 1953/54: Bill Hawthorne, Winnie Dean Butt, Clarence Barnes, Patricia White, Max Barlow Jr., and Rudy Wilkinson. (Below right) One of the highlights of the year was a trip by train to Denver to visit the State Capitol and museum for some of the upper grades. The photo was taken on the steps of the State Capitol in the spring of 1954. Back row: Mrs. Mabel Cooper, Luthera Barcus, Betty Jones, and Petrea Barcus. Middle rows: Unidentified, Helen White, Donnie Butt, Reginald Berry, Janette Alstatt, and Chuck Roberts. Front row: Winnie Dean Butt and Kathleen Thomas. *(All three photos courtesy of Mableann Post Hawthorne)*

(Left) New Liberty 3rd grade in 1956. Back row: Geraldine Barnes, Donna Roberts, Virginia Anderson, Dennis Likes, Jim Shires, and Mrs. Shannon. Front row: Unidentified, Alla Komorrow, Sharon Koch and Jeri Jeffries. (Below) New Liberty classes of 1956: back row: Unidentified, Patricia White, Wesley Gribble, Cecil Gribble, Gene Wilkinson, Ronnie ?, and Jim Shires. Third and fourth rows: L-R; Ronnie Alstatt, Charlene Overbye, Vernon Barnes, Hallie Young, Molly Nelson, Geraldine Barnes, unidentified, Mableann Post, Alla Komorrow, Donna Roberts, Sharon Koch, Virginia Anderson, Linda Post, ?, and Annette Kelly. Second row: ?, Marjorie Smith, Kathy Wells, Mickey Puckett, Nila Puckett, Rita Berg, Gary Alstatt, Jimmy Barlow, and Jeri Jeffries. Front row: David Gunn, Larry Overbye, David Alstatt, Stephen Chaffin, Dennis Likes and ?. *(Dennis Likes Collection)*

134

(Above) Girls in the upper grades in 1957. Left to right: Alla Komorrow, Earlynn Barcus, Donna Roberts, Linda Post, Virginia Anderson, Louise Wells, Hallie Young (hiding) and Delene Barcus. *(Mableann Post Hawthorne Collection)* (Below) Lower grades 1955/56. Back row: Teacher Sue Thompson, Leslie Young, Annette Kelly, Mollie Nelson, Ronnie Alstatt, Reva Post, Retta Marie Likes, Allen Shires and Vernon Barnes. Middle row: Mickey Puckett, Marjorie Smith, Rita Berg, Kathy Wells, Ronnie White, Nila Puckett and Eddie Smith. Front row: Naida Young, Eddie Alstatt, Charlene Overbye, Louana Nelson and David Gunn. *(Retta-Marie Likes Brandow Collection)*

(Above left) Teachers for the school year 1956/57, Sue Thompson and Helen Andrews. (Courtesy of *Laurene Wells*) Above right: Teachers for the school year 1958/59, Sue Thompson, Helen Andrews and Mrs. Turman. *(Courtesy of Mableann Post Hawthorne)* (Below) Sue Thompson and some of the many students she taught at New Liberty School attending the Mack/New Liberty reunion in 1991. Sue taught at New Liberty School from the fall of 1946 to the spring of 1959, when the school closed down, which was the longest tenure of any teacher there. Some of the students have been identified. Front row, L-R: Mableann Post Hawthorne, ?, Sue Thompson, ?, Retta Marie Likes Brandow, Asha Wells (daughter of Louise Wells). Second row: Reggie Berry, 4th Tommy Berry, 7th Anna Jane Berry Starr, ?, Louise Wells, David Alstatt, and Reva Post Terrell?. Trudy Maluy Kareus is standing behind David and Reva. *(Photo taken by Phyllis Likes)*

(Right) The New Liberty School building during the late 1940's. (*Photo courtesy of Delores Cutler O'Connor*)

(Right) The New Liberty School building in the 1950s after the addition was built on the east side. (*Photo courtesy of Mableann Post Hawthorne*)

(Below) The New Liberty School building as it looked in 1994, changed very little from the time it was built in 1936. The flagpole, the goose neck lights over the west and south doors, and the railings over the foot scrapers at the south door are still there. Roger and Roberta Lowry now own the building. (*Photo used from the 28 January 1994 issue of the* Fruita Times*)*

The original one-room frame school at New Liberty was added to twice, according to various records. In the early 1930s the school began to experience growing pains again, and it became necessary to consider the possibility of a new school building. Accordingly, on 15 July 1935, New Liberty residents were given opportunity to vote on an $8,000 bond toward the construction of a new school building.

An article in *The Daily Sentinel* on 27 September 1935 announced that a building had been approved as a WPA project. (*Works Progress Administration* — a government program enacted during the depression years). The government was to furnish some $8,500 and the school district $2,300. Citizens must have been quite sure they were going to get the new building because by the time of the announcement of the approval, 20,000 adobe bricks had already been made, but another 20,000 would be required. The bricks were made in the schoolyard from what was called the "finest adobe material to be found."

The building was of Spanish design and was stuccoed on the outside while the inside walls were plastered; the floors in the hallway and classrooms were concrete, and the floor in the auditorium was hardwood. Construction began in 1935 and was completed in May 1936. A New Liberty news item in February 1936 said that work on the new building had progressed rapidly and was near enough to completion that students and teachers had already moved in. Of course, the old building had already been demolished, so they had no place to go but the new building. The building was not really complete until Rural Electrification Association electricity came in September 1937; gasoline lanterns were used for temporary lighting until that time.

The following article appeared in *The Daily Sentinel* on 30 March 1937 — it was a dual celebration, since it was also Easter Sunday.

NEW LIBERTY CELEBRATES ANNIVERSARY

Celebrating the nineteenth anniversary of the settlement of the valley, the New Liberty community Sunday (29th) gathered at the new community house for a basket dinner and to hear talks by old and recent residents of the valley.

C. W. Likes presided at the meeting, the outstanding feature of which was a talk by Bob Cox, one of the first four settlers at New Liberty. He told of the settling of the project early in 1908, and of the turning of water in the ditches in 1918. He outlined in detail the subsequent development of the community.

He emphasized that community progress is brought on by the sharing of individuals of their time, labor and wealth; that progress is not brought about by one person taking what is another's, nor by each person keeping his own to himself.

Musical numbers on the program, following the sumptuous basket dinner served to around 150, opened with the singing of "He Arose" by a mixed octet including Mesdames Maluy, Sanders, Arpke, Cox and Messieurs Likes, Brayton, Arpke and Cox. A violin solo "Melody by Dawes" was played by Mrs. Harold Carroll; W. J. Cox sang "The Holy City" the octet sang "The Awakening Chorus." Community singing, led by W. J. Cox, followed.

After the dinner and program in the community house, the afternoon was spent playing softball.

The above reflects such a wonderful community spirit!

Originally in the school there were two classrooms, a combined auditorium-gymnasium and a kitchen which was large enough to accommodate half the pupils at a time for school lunches. As nearly as we can determine from an article in *The Daily Sentinel* of 1 January 1942, school lunches began in January 1942. In 1945 the larger of the two rooms was divided and made into two classrooms, and beginning that fall there were three teachers.

In 1951 School District #51 was organized to include all elementary and high schools in Mesa County. Mack School was closed in 1953 and pupils were bused to New Liberty and Loma through 1958/59; then New Liberty was closed also.

The New Liberty building was modernized after it became part of School District #51 by adding a pressurized water system and restrooms.

The building is now (1994) being restored by

Roger and **Roberta Lowry.**

Here are some recollections of school by the author, Homer Likes:

The school played a very important part in the lives of the children who grew up at New Liberty. The school programs in the early days were vastly different from those of today — no videos, no computers. Students were taught basic "reading, writing and arithmetic," as well as geography and history. As I recall, a Latin class was offered for 7th and 8th grades, at least part of the time.

We were taught some music, depending on who the teachers were and their attitude toward music — I particularly remember Grace Curtis and her sister, Florence Chilson, who taught from 1928 to 1930. On the days scheduled for musical training the folding doors that separated the "lower" grades from the "upper" grades, were rolled back so the entire school could join together. As Miss Chilson played the piano, Mrs. Curtis led the chorus. I can hear ever so plainly today Mrs. Curtis' lusty soprano voice which overpowered the kids' voices. Her favorite song was "Spanish Cavalier."

Mrs. Curtis also organized a harmonica band — the students enjoyed that! She taught us to play parts and I was one of those selected to play "bass." If you are familiar with a basic "Marine Band" Hohner Harmonica, you will know there are serious limitations on the bass end of the instrument. But with music written just for those harmonicas, our music sounded quite good — to me, at least.

Occasionally certain individuals were asked to take part in a school play for special events such as Christmas or graduation. It was a great experience for those so chosen to try to overcome basic shyness and portray some character out of the past. Some students did pretty well—some were horrible!

I recall vividly being asked to sing a solo while holding hands with Cleo Dunston, who was the cute little daughter of a family then living on the Boyden farm at the west end of the community. Of course the teacher knew I was madly in love with Cleo (I was probably 11 years old), so that made it easier for me to accept the assignment. Cleo and I stood in the center of the stage, and while

swinging our joined hands; I sang in a quavering soprano voice ...

> School days, school days
> Dear old Golden Rule days
> Readin' and writin' and 'rithmetic
> Taught to the rule of a hickory stick
> You were my pal in calico
> I was your bashful barefoot beau
> And you wrote on my slate
> "I Love You Joe"
> When we were couple of kids

The school Christmas programs were always major events — always well attended by proud parents and other citizens of the community. With time to spare students were selected to play the parts of Joseph and Mary and the Shepards as well as the usual skit about Santa and his reindeer. Then came the daily rehearsals.

In plenty of time before the big night the children had a drawing to exchange names for inexpensive little trinkets for Christmas gifts — that way, no one was left out. There was always a pinon or cedar tree harvested from the nearby hills that would be decorated with strings of popcorn, paper chains, and real candles. How did we keep from burning the place down?

After the play was over, Santa, represented by one of the men of the community, would make an exciting entry. After a round of hearty "HO, HO, HOs," Santa would call out the names of each of the children in the school to come and receive a gift, as mentioned above, and a paper bag containing a popcorn ball, an orange (pure luxury!), and a few pieces of hard candy. For many of the children that was about the extent of their Christmas gifts.

The 8th grade graduations were always special events too. I remember the graduation of 1932, but some of the details I had forgotten. I'm grateful to have found the following written by Mrs. A. L. (Nellie) Stotts, dated 17 May and appearing in the New Liberty section in *The Daily Sentinel* of 20 May 1932:

Graduation exercises were held at the

schoolhouse Thursday evening. The program consisted of a prayer by C. W. Likes, followed by readings from John Cavendish, Homer Likes and Lephia Foss. Clark Gerry read the class will and Amos Alstatt read the class prophecy. T. A. Butcher [who was then Fruita High School Principal] gave a short talk to the class and the audience. Mr. Alstatt, a member of the school board, then presented the following graduates with their diplomas: John Cavendish, Homer Likes, Clark Gerry, Lephia Foss and Amos Alstatt.

I recall that John Cavendish always made a powerful delivery in a high-pitched voice which those seated in the back rows could hear very well. On graduation night, John was dressed in a brand new pair of bib overalls — he stole the show! I was dressed in my first suit with long pants — my mother had made it from a suit my brother Clyde had outgrown. By the way, John Cavendish never went to high school.

This seems the appropriate place to tell a story involving Russell Poley, one of the New Liberty teachers of 1938/39. Mr. Poley loved to associate with the older boys of the community, as he was interested in learning about their life-style. (Mr. Poley was quite naive in the ways of the country boys.) He was particularly interested in fishing and hunting.

In the fall of 1938 a deer-hunting outing to Dry Canyon, in the Bookcliffs north of New Liberty, was planned by Merton and Bob Arpke and Homer and Lewis Likes. When Russell learned of the plans he asked to be included.

The boys gathered up horses and camping equipment, and made elaborate (they thought) preparations for the big outing. Homer borrowed a mare from my Uncle Leonard Appier to use as a pack animal. The mare was nursing a colt and Uncle Leonard thought it best to leave the colt at home. Instructions were to milk the mare two or three times a day so her udder wouldn't become too congested.

Final preparations were completed by late afternoon on the day of departure, so we decided to leave then and travel across the desert as far as possible before dark, and make a dry camp for the night. All went well that far, until in the middle of the night we decided it was beginning to break day,

so we made breakfast and began to pack up to leave for our planned hunting area. (We found out later we had broken camp about 1:30 a.m.) Homer dutifully milked the mare, but decided, why throw that good milk away? All of us, except Mr. Poley, decided to use it as cream in our coffee. Mr. Poley didn't say anything more than just to refuse to use the milk.

We continued our trek until we were pretty well into the mouth of Dry Canyon, then we decided to take a short-cut up the side of a steep hill instead of following the established trail. We soon discovered we were in trouble when the horse Merton brought for a pack animal got about one-fourth of the way up the hill and refused to go any further — **up** or **down**. We all worked with that animal until almost dark, without any success. Then we realized we were faced with another dry camp. Merton stayed with that horse on the side of the hill throughout the night.

Mr. Poley was not used to that kind of rough life and it was beginning to tell on him. He had brought along equipment for bathing and shaving — complete with wash-cloth and towel. We made breakfast again as we had the morning before — complete with the mare's milk for coffee cream. We teased Poley about that a little bit too much! Shortly he threw all his gear together, took off and walked all the way home across the desert. We never heard any more about taking the school teacher along on any outings.

Mr. Poley was not the only one naive about "roughing it" in the wilds. The Likes and Arpke boys were also very naive in pretending they knew everything about camping, hunting, etc. We were in a strange area trying to do something we didn't know how to do and shouldn't have been trying to do. The balky horse? We just took off down the canyon without him — he soon caught up with us. He had been standing on that trail on the side of the mountain for about 18 hours.

New Liberty Sunday School

Probably within a few months after the school building was completed in 1919, a Sunday School was organized. Undoubtedly Rev. Clyde W. Likes was the kingpin in that organization. There were others in the community who also wished to maintain some kind of religious activity. It wasn't easy to travel the distance necessary to attend a church in Fruita or Grand Junction —almost the only options the settlers had.

The Sunday School was organized with the offices of President, Vice President and Secretary-Treasurer, and the necessary teachers for the various age groups. Officers and teachers were nominated and voted upon once each year by members of the congregation. There were also song-leaders and pianists selected to provide the music for the group. Many members served consecutive terms without being replaced, but always after the usual nominating and voting procedure. At least once a month there would be a short business meeting. Minutes of the previous meeting and a financial report from the treasurer were read. Also, a call would be put before the congregation for proposals of changes necessary or for an appointment of a new officer or teacher.

We can name several families who were active in the Sunday School: Alstatt, Cutler, Burket/Smiley, Weir, Gerry, Likes, Foss, Summers, Morrow, Brayton, Sanders, Sumnicht, Schunter, Bush, Wright, Shires/Johnson/Berry, Bowen, Wynkoop, McCampbell, Arpke, Banning, Wallace. There were probably others whom we haven't named. There were also some families who attended occasionally on days such as Christmas or Easter.

There was always someone who took care of the building preparations before Sunday School time — such as arranging chairs, building fires, etc.

We don't know if there were dues assessed each year from the membership, or if they had another means of funding. They may have used a practice such as the collection plate that is common in many church meetings. A small treasury was maintained — enough to buy the necessary study manuals, scriptures and other printed materials. We've noticed in different family stories that a prize of a New Testament was received for good attendance, etc.

The meetings were always conducted with opening and closing prayers, and the congregation sang songs from the hymn books. Sometimes responsive scripture readings were given

Occasionally the Sunday School would host a minister from up the valley who would preach a sermon, either in place of the Sunday School classes or after the class period was over. Clyde Likes Sr. was asked to speak on some of those special occasions.

Each year a sunrise service was held on Easter Sunday to commemorate the resurrection. Also, a picnic outing was held each year on the north side of Douglas Pass. (See Ada Bush's story.) On one of these outings Jim Wallace provided his farm truck for transportation. This turned out to be a near-disaster. On the switchback curves we used to have to negotiate on the south side of Douglas Pass, the truck would not turn close enough to get around a curve. Jim had to back up to make a shorter turn and very nearly backed off the mountainside. Later that day as the party was returning, Clyde Wright fell off the back of the truck and tumbled for many yards. We screamed at Jim to stop, expecting to go back and pick up a dead body. But Clyde was tough — he only had a broken arm.

As far as we know, the Sunday School was active until District #51 closed the school in 1959 — perhaps even longer.

(Above) A Sunday School group at the New Liberty Schoolhouse about 1923. Not very many have been identified. Adults: Margaret Morrow, 5th Viola Alstatt, Center back Mary Maluy, Mrs. McCampbell, Tom Gibbs, ?, Charles Brayton, Anna Belle Alstatt, Charles Cutler. Children, L-R: Paul Cutler, Edward Cutler, Homer Likes, Lewis Likes, Edith Alstatt, the last two in front are Carl and Amos Alstatt. *(Thomas/Morrow Collection)* (Below left) Sunday School class of 1932 in front of New Liberty Schoolhouse. Back row: Homer Likes, Lawrence Morrow, Amos Alstatt and Carl Alstatt. Front row: Harry Cutler, Ed Cutler, Bob Anderson and Lewis Likes. *(Darrell Maluy Collection)* (Below right) A Sunday School group in front of New Liberty Schoolhouse about 1946. Front row L-R: ?, ?, Reggie Berry, Carol Underwood, Kathleen Thomas, ?. Second row: ?, Jane Brayton, JoElla Brayton, Detra Reed, ?,?,?, Leon Ebright. Third row: Delores Cutler, Shirley Ebright, Tom Berry, Norma Pollock, Curtis Thomas, Kay Geeting, and Basil Banning. Back row: Jimmy Tomlinson, ?, Maxine Cutler, Dixie Cowden, Anna Jane Berry and Bobby Cotner. *(Photo courtesy of Lois Ebright Kimmel)*

Sunday School Classes: (Upper) L-R, Back row: Anna Belle Alstatt, Hazel Banning, and Sunday School teacher Mrs. Margaret Morrow. Front row: Leona Belle Wynkoop, Joyce Wynkoop, and unidentified. *(Morrow Collection)*

Middle: L-R, Back row: Joyce Wynkoop, Anna Belle Alstatt, Hazel Banning, Virgie Wynkoop, Mary Wynkoop, Ruth Banning. Front row: Lewis Sanders, Bobby Alstatt, Rev. Clyde Likes, Stanley Wynkoop, Billy Wiehl, Ralph Banning, and Wylie Sanders.
Lower: L-R, Back row: Joyce Wynkoop, Anna Bellle Alstatt, Virgie Wynkoop, Eloise Foss, Agnes Alstatt, Mary Wynkoop, Hazel Banning, and Naomi Banning. Front row: Ralph Banning, Stanley Wynkoop, Bobby Alstatt, Rev. Clyde Likes, Wylie Sanders, and Paul Wynkoop. Both photos were taken about 1945. *(Stanley Wynkoop Collection)*

Social Life

The people who came to settle in the New Liberty Community were an interesting mixture of society. Most of them had barely enough money to cover the expense of getting there, to buy only the very basic equipment and supplies, and to pay the necessary fees. Most of them had no previous experience with irrigation and some had never farmed before. Those who had a sincere desire to succeed and the will to "tough it out," were successful in establishing homes, but there were some who quit very soon after the beginning.

As the pioneers began to develop their farms, new and lasting friendships were established and occasional visits among neighboring families provided a means of getting better acquainted, as well as a break from the monotony of every-day farm drudgery. During those visits there were probably stories exchanged of earlier life in other areas, and perhaps much time was spent discussing current events. At that time television didn't exist and motion pictures were just beginning to be shown in some theaters. Automobiles were still a novelty, and a trip to the big city of Grand Junction by any means of transportation was a great adventure! Money was scarce — so it was a rare luxury to be able to see a circus, vaudeville, a wrestling or boxing match, a popular preacher, or whatever.

But those resourceful pioneers created their own entertainment! Many families owned "Victrolas" (windup record players), pianos, violins, guitars, harmonicas and other musical instruments. Many of them had good singing voices and loved to sing. Many had theatrical talent, and most of them loved to dance. Undoubtedly the New Liberty school building was used soon after its completion in 1919 for community gatherings for a variety of reasons.

From its very early days the community began celebrations of summer holidays such as Memorial Day, Independence Day, Labor Day. Nearly everyone attended! Except for the irrigating and milking, the farm work came to a standstill on

(Above) Neighborhood gathering at the John Morrow homestead in 1919. From left: Georgia "Jo" Bowen, Bonnie O'Bryan (first teacher at Highline School, which later became New Liberty School), Margaret Morrow, Estellene Morrow, Everett Bowen, Elizabeth Morrow, John Morrow, Billy Bowen, and Clem Maluy. Mary Maluy took the picture. (Below) The same day, in front of the Morrow house with prize pumpkins on display. L-R: Georgia "Jo" Bowen, Everett Bowen, Billy Bowen, Bonnie O'Bryan, Ada Williams and baby, Margaret Morrow, Clem Maluy, John Morrow, Howard Williams, Estellene Morrow and Elizabeth Morrow. (Both photos from the Thomas/Morrow Collection)

(Above) 1 January 1923. Not all are identified. L-R Men in back: Walter Weir, 4th Howard Williams, 6th Athol Stotts, 7th Guy Gerry. Women: L-R, Mrs. McCampbell, ? holding baby, Ena Sumnicht, Mrs. Williams holding baby, Bernice Gerry holding Naomi, & Mrs. Sumnicht. Children: L-R, Melba McCampbell, Merton Arpke, Edna Weir, Margaret McCampbell, Clark Gerry, & Mildred Weir. *(Photo Courtesy of Clark Gerry and Florence Chandler)* (Below) A watermelon party on the Walter Weir farm with Walter's famous watermelons. L-R: Walter Weir, Laura Weir, Edna Weir, ?, ?, ?, Mildred Weir. The rest of the people are not identified. On the back of the picture was written "Sanders and my folks" by Mildred Weir. It could also be Jesse Crane and family members, as he is Mrs. Weir's brother and lived in New Liberty. *(Weir Collection courtesy of Charlene Brayton Eldridge)*

(Above left) A Sunday dinner gathering at the John Morrow homestead in 1919. Adults L-R: Retta Likes, Clyde Likes holding Homer, John Morrow, Margaret Morrow, Bill Cox, Anna Alstatt, Albert Alstatt holding Amos, and Howard Williams. Children L-R: Clyde Likes Jr., Estellene Morrow, Viola Alstatt, Ruth Alstatt, Elizabeth Morrow, Edith and Milton Alstatt. (Above right) A closeup of the children in the above left picture. Standing: Estellene Morrow, Milton Alstatt, Viola Alstatt, Clyde Likes Jr., and Ruth Alstatt. Sitting: Edith Alstatt and Elizabeth Morrow.

(Left) The Alstatt and Morrow children in 1920. Standing: Milton Alstatt, Ruth Alstatt, Viola holding Carl, Estellene and Elizabeth Morrow. Sitting in wagon: Amos and Edith Alstatt with their dog.

(Right) Bill Cox being a clown with one of Margaret Morrow's famous pies at the Morrow residence. *(All four photos are from the Thomas/Morrow Collection)*

those occasions. Along with many of those gatherings were baseball games, horse races, horse-shoe pitching, etc. Also, much camaraderie! The children had their own entertainment in the form of games such as Pom-Pom Pull Away, Hide and Seek, Ante-Over, etc.

There were some "characters" among those early settlers whose peculiarities came to the surface from time to time. Some of them will be told about later, hopefully without offending family members. It would probably be better not to name one lady of the community who never failed to bring her assignment of food to the community gatherings, but would set it back so she and her family could enjoy it, and not have to take chances on the "unsanitary" foods offered by other ladies. How about the ice-cream furnished by another family that had a very distinct odor and taste of cow manure?

Homemade ice cream became an important part of those gatherings. Nearly every farm had milk cows, so it was no problem to have plenty of milk and cream. Some of the farmers had ice stored from the previous winter with which to supply the freezers. Frequently there were enough freezers to make it possible for everyone to eat as much ice cream as they wished. Much fun was created in the serious business of having one man or boy cranking a freezer while another sat on the top of it to keep it from tipping over when the cream began to freeze! Of course it was necessary to have something for insulation on top of the freezer to keep the posterior from freezing as well! The best part of all was for the people to mingle and have a good time together!

Celebrations of Independence Day were always great occasions. They were held many times at the Everett Bowen or Walter Weir farms, where there were good shade trees and some lawn. The children, as well as the grownups, always had much fun with fireworks. During the fireworks part of the celebration an occasional whimpering boy would be seen seeking the sympathy of his mother displaying a bruised and blackened hand — the result of a premature explosion, or because a giant firecracker was held a moment too long.

Occasionally there would be a farm auction — another exciting social event! The children would play together, and the adults would visit while the auctioneer's staccato chant could be heard offering the farmer's property to the highest bidder. Sometimes there would be vendors of refreshments or goods of some sort who would set up to sell their wares while the sale was going on. At one sale the author can recall, a man sold fresh-pressed cider — "all you can drink for 25 cents." A few boys unwisely went beyond the limit with that opportunity and

The Highline Canal in 1918 by the Morrow farm; this became the location for "Morrow's Hole." *(Thomas/Morrow Collection)*

147

Looking east at "Morrow's Hole" in the 1980s. *(Photo taken by Phyllis Likes.)*

drank more cider than they could hold. The upchucked cider was of no value to anyone, after all.

Then there were the excursions to the swimming hole in the canal near Morrow's farm. The swimming hole was known by almost everyone as "Morrow's Hole." At Morrow's head gate there was a check in the canal to raise the water level and the resulting gentle waterfall washed out a large cavity about seven or eight feet deep and perhaps twenty-five feet in diameter, adequate for many youngsters to

The canal looks very peaceful to swim in. Looking west from "Morrow's Hole" in the 1980s. *(Photo taken by Phyllis Likes.)*

play in. During the summer months it was a favorite place for young and old alike.

There was an interesting variety of "swimsuits" displayed at the swimming hole. Seldom did anyone dress in a genuine swimsuit — if so, it may have been one that reflected the styles of yesteryears. There were a few instances of "Mom" dressed in a pair of "Pop's" overalls over a blouse or shirt, or it could be simply a dress. For the men it could be overalls or underwear. If the boys were lucky enough to gather for a swim without females being present, they cast aside all inhibition and swam in the "buff." The girls, believe it or not, were known to do that also!

In retrospect, the author thinks it amazing that no one ever drowned in the canal in the lower valley even though youngsters were allowed to play in it for endless hours without the supervision of responsible adults. However, there were a few close calls!

It should also be mentioned that the canal was far from sanitary! It was a common sight while swimming to see cow and sheep droppings, even dead animals, floating down the stream. Yet Nellie Schunter Stotts, who for several years was *The Daily Sentinel* correspondent for New Liberty, complained in her items in July 1931 that "people should not be allowed to swim in the canal, as it is unsanitary and could lead to the spread of disease!"

The author is not aware of any disease that could be blamed on swimming in the unsanitary water except in August 1932 when Donald Knapp was afflicted with typhoid. Some thought it possible he caught that in the swimming hole — who knows?

(Above) Friends, 1925, Florence Wilson, George Darrow (Mary Maluy's brother) and Mabel Likes. *(Mabel Likes Collection)*

(Above right New Liberty school mates in about 1920. L-R: Frances Schunter, Viola Alstatt, Nellie Schunter and Harold Carroll. *(Thomas/Morrow Collection)*

(Right) New Liberty maidens, 1928. Standing L-R: Edna Weir, Vauna Clow, Elizabeth Morrow, Laura Johnson, Thelma Gunst and Estellene Morrow. Sitting: Mary Lou Gunst and Mildred Weir. *(Laura Johnson Berry Collection)*

(Below left) Ready for an outing. Ruth Alstatt, Ena Sumnicht and Viola Alstatt. *(Viola Alstatt Collection)*

(Below right) Best friends, 1920s. Viola Alstatt, Thelma Gunst, Laura Johnson, Vera Maynard? and Mary Lou Gunst. "Happy," the Clem Maluy family dog, in front. *(Mary Maluy Collection)*

(Upper left) A group picnic on DouglasPass in the late 1920s. Identification of some is questionable. L-R in back of table: Darrell, Mary and Clem Maluy, Blanche and (Densil?) Lofgren, Jo and Everett Bowen, (Victor?) Lofgren, ? and ?. In front of table: Olive Starbuck, Burgeon Lofgren, ?, ?, JoAnn Bowen and Clarence Porter. Sitting on blanket is Inez Porter and ? *(Photo courtesy of JoAnn Bowen Montague)*

(Middle left) Some of the Mothers and children in the community about 1923/4. Back row left to right: Margaret McCampbell, Estellene Morrow, ?, Viola Alstatt holding Agnes, Anna Shires holding Leonard, Frances Foss, and Margaret Morrow. Children standing: Amos Alstatt, Paul Cutler, ?, ?, Art Shires, Melba McCampbell, Darrell Maluy, Edith Alstatt, Edward Cutler, Naomi Gerry, and Carl Alstatt. In front: Billy Bowen. *(Thomas/Morrow Collection)*

(Lower left) 4-H group at the Morrow home, about 1926. Two back rows: Mrs. McCampbell, Selma Snavely, Edith Alstatt, ?, Lephia Foss, Sarah Clow Knapp, Louise Clow, Frances Foss, Melba McCampbell, Margaret Morrow, Edna Weir and Vauna Clow. In front: Lawrence Morrow (wheelborrow), Eloise Foss and Donald Clow. *(Thomas/Morrow Collection)*

(Above) New Liberty 4-H group about 1941. L-R standing: 4-H leader Lester Van Riper, Robert Pollock, Richard Van Riper, Murray Phillips, Lewis Sanders, Fred Pacheco, Phyllis Van Riper, Ray Sisler, Corky DeCrow, ?, Gale Cox, Donald Downing, Robert Alstatt, Eugene Thomas, Milton Cox, James Martinez and Wylie Sanders. Kneeling: Ralph Banning, Glen Martinez with dog, Walter Pollock, George Brayton and Ray Van Riper. (*Photo courtesy of Robert Alstatt*) (Below) New Libertyites in front of Mack Hotel in 1957, possibly a Sunday school group. L-R back row: Larry Overbye, Jim Shires, Allen Moss, Maymie Post, ?, Christine Shires, ?, Agnes Overbye, Helen Koch, Lona Alstatt, ?, Esther Daniels and June Alstatt. Middle row: Edna Shires, Sharon Koch, Terry Koch, Edward Alstatt, Ronald Alstatt and Roger Koch. Front row: Barnes twin ?, Virginia Anderson, next 4 ?, Janette Alstatt holding Karen Alstatt, Charlene Overbye, Lee Barnes, Barnes twin, Gerald Alstatt and next 3 ?. (*Photo courtesy of Mableann Post Hawthorne*)

(Above) 1928, Darrell Maluy's eighth birthday party at the Clem Maluy residence. Back row: Donald Clow Knapp, Homer Likes, ?, Clark Gerry, Amos Alstatt, Arthur Shires and Darrell Maluy. Middle row: Edward Cutler, Carl Alstatt, Lewis Likes, JoAnn Bowen, ?, Leonard Shires and Naomi Gerry. Front row: Rex Maluy, Patty Maluy, Dale Maluy, Virginia Likes, Agnes Alstatt. *(Mary Maluy Collection)*

(Left) Helen Grace Carroll's sixth birthday on 12 September 1936. Back row L-R: Norma Maluy, Anna Belle Alstatt, Dixie Wright, Louise Alstatt, Wilma Maluy and Phyllis Maluy. In front: Lee Ann (Bubbles) Maluy, Helen Grace Carroll and Sandra Carroll. *(Photo courtesy of Helen Grace Carroll Gingrich)*

(Left) Curtis Thomas' birthday in the 1940s at the Floyd Thomas residence. Left to right: Curtis Thomas with cake on head, Kathleen Thomas, Basil Banning, Kenneth Gaymon, Jim Tomlinson, Bob Cotner and Tom Berry. The dog is unidentified. *(Photo used from the 9 June 1991 issue of the* Fruita Times. *Original photo is from the Gene Thomas Collection)*

1946, Kathleen Thomas's fifth birthday with three cakes. Kathleen Thomas, Peggy Arpke, Jane Brayton, JoElla Brayton and Betty Leach. Front: Ruth Arpke, Elaine Arpke and Carol Underwood. *(Photo courtesy of Eugene Thomas)*

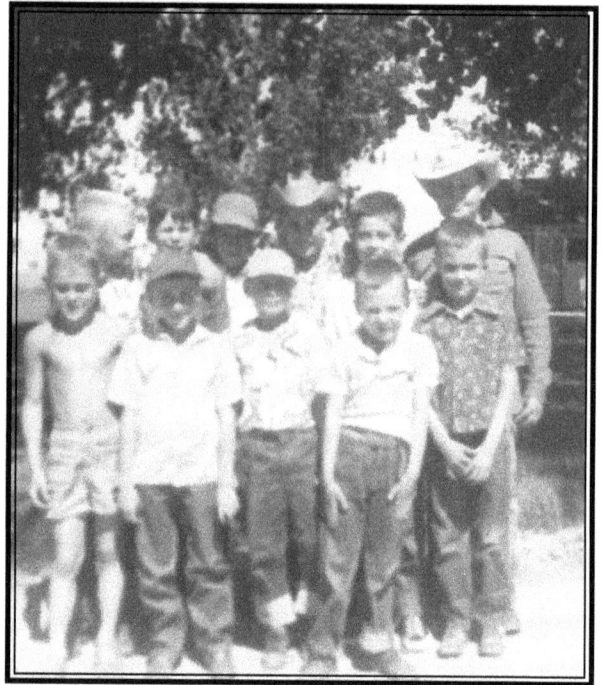

August 1956, Dennis Likes' ninth birthday. Back row: Dennis Likes, Stephen Chaffin, ?, Larry Overbye, Duane Arpke and James Shires. Front row: David Gunn, ?, David Alstatt, Edward Alstatt and Ronald Alstatt. *(Photo courtesy of Dennis Likes)*

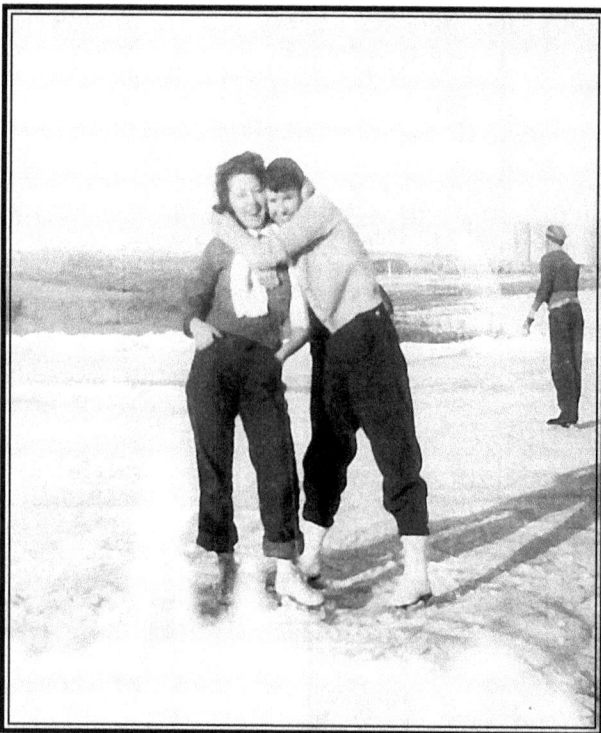

One of the favorite activities in the winter was ice skating on someone's pond. These two photos of ice skating were taken on Robert Cox's pond in the winter of 1942 or 1943. Jayne Snook and Helen Millie Keffalos. The person in the background is unidentified. *(Photo Courtesy of Helen Keffalos Dodson)*

Helen Millie Keffalos, Dorothy Cox, Marilyn May Maluy and Jayne Snook. On the back of the picture it states that they are trying to stand on their toes. But they weren't always on their toes; sometimes they were on their "ask me no questions." *(Photo courtesy of Helen Keffalos Dodson)*

Marriages and Births

As near as determined, the first marriage to occur among the settlers of New Liberty was that of Clyde L. Balkwill of Mack, and Ada D. Almond of Twin Lakes, Colorado. They owned adjoining properties in Sec 15 Twp 9S R103W in the New Liberty community. They were married in Grand Junction 30 August 1920.

However, a marriage of New Liberty people was recorded a year before that—Willard W. Stotts and Ella B. Stotts, 20 August 1919. That was likely a remarriage after divorce—one can only speculate. Land records show that Willard W. Stotts filed on a farm unit "A" of Sec 18 Twp 9S R103W in 1919, that land became property of Ella B. Stotts in 1921. It is not known when Willard left, but Ella lived in the community for many years. (See the Stotts story.) We should mention also, the marriage of Lee Roy Wells and Bonnie O'Bryan that occurred on 2 June 1921. Roy was one of the first settlers and Bonnie was the first New Liberty school teacher

The first baby in the New Liberty community was Arthur Shires, born 26 August 1918. There were several other boys (no girls) born elsewhere that same year who later lived in the community. Amos Alstatt and Homer Likes were born in Kansas, Merton Arpke in Nebraska and Clark Gerry in Fruita.

Anna Shires holding her son, Arthur, first baby born in New Liberty. Photo taken in front of Clem Maluy's pond by Mary Maluy. The Maluy barn is visible in the background. *(Mary Maluy Collection)*

New Liberty Community Club

Evidence has been found that New Liberty Community Club was organized about mid-April of 1926. A copy of the "Articles of Constitution of The New Liberty Progressive Farmer's Club," adopted 15 May 1926, were found in the personal effects of Bob and Bessie Phillips. Article II of that constitution reads ...

The purpose of this organization shall be to discuss current farm problems, to provide social and literary entertainment for the community, and to develop a spirit of fellowship and helpfulness among its membership.

The articles also included provisions for election of officers, the duties and powers of officers, etc. Membership was open to any resident of the community over age 18. Membership dues were to be 50 cents per year, and 15 cents per quarter thereafter, payable in advance. The following names were written on the back of the copy of the constitution: S. B. Snavely, C. W. and Retta Likes, B. A. Harrison, T. C. and Mrs. Wassenburg, showing they had paid their dues.

A presidency and treasurer were elected. Various committees were delegated by the president, to serve for a year, to take care of the food and entertainment, set up the chairs, build and maintain the fires in cold weather, and clean up after meetings. The club met on the third Saturday evening of each month at the New Liberty School house. The first order of business in a meeting was a brief time spent with some kind of literary program. Then roll call, minutes of the previous meeting, and a treasurer's report on finances was read, after which a discussion on any matters of business was held. The entertainment committee was then allowed time for their program, and fun was had by all!

Sometimes for entertainment a skit was performed by a group, or there could be readings by one or more people, or one or more people would provide a musical number, such as singing or playing the piano or other instruments.

Among the men, Bob Cox, Bill Cox, Clem Maluy and Al Daily were great singers, but the most popular male singer of all time was Ramsey Miller, a young farm hand who worked for various farmers and stockmen of the lower valley. He eventually married Alene Leach, a New Liberty resident. Ramsey was invited often to sing such ballads as "Strawberry Roan," "Big Rock Candy Mountain" and "Going to See My Mother When the Work's All Done Next Fall."

Among the women, the most popular singers were a trio consisting of Mary Maluy, May Sanders and Bernice Gerry. Mary and Bernice played the piano, and May played the mandolin. Their voices harmonized beautifully and they sang songs for all occasions — everyone loved to hear them! Among their favorites were such tunes as "Tiptoe Through the Tulips" and "When it's Springtime in The Rockies."

After Harold Carroll and his wife came to teach at New Liberty, Mrs. Carroll's music students would be featured occasionally as part of the entertainment. Leonard Shires and Barbara McKay were violin students who played very well — except they couldn't tell when they were off key. Their efforts were appreciated anyway!

There were others in the community who could play the piano or violin. A duo who may be remembered very well was a father-son team — Leonard and Floyd Thomas. Leonard played the violin (fiddle), and Floyd accompanied by chording on the piano. The duo played for entertainment on many occasions, and also provided music for dances.

After the business, entertainment and refreshments were over, people would begin to move the desks and chairs to the perimeter of the building in preparation for a dance. This was always the signal for the Likes' family and a few others who didn't dance to make their exit. Those dances lasted into the wee, small hours of the morning. Of course the little tykes could not stay awake that late, so they were bedded down among the desks and chairs, or if the weather was warm enough, out in the cars or wagons, while the parents had their fun dancing.

At some point in time the New Liberty Community Club purchased a seine to be used in the summer to catch fish from the Colorado River, usually at Horse Thief Canyon, south of Loma. A community fish fry would be scheduled for late July, when the water flow was very low and it was possible for the men to wade with the net and sweep the stream-bed, catching whatever unfortunate fish happened to be in the way. Many suckers and carp were netted; we didn't know they were "trash fish." The fish were prepared on the river bank and the women would be waiting with the corn meal and frying pans. Of course, there were always a variety of other delicious foods. Can you savor in your mind the fried fish, fried chicken, the salads, cakes, pies, ice cream and melons?

A community fish fry by the Colorado River at Horse Thief Canyon in the early 1920s. There is no identification of those present, but it looks like they are having a good time. (Mary Maluy Collection)

(Left) Schoolmates from the first school classes held in New Liberty in 1919 gather together at the Lewis Likes residence in 1987. L-R: Ivan Likes, Milton Alstatt, Louise Clow Likes, Maudie Raver Yates, Fred Likes and Viola Alstatt. (*Homer and Phyllis Likes Collection*)

(Left) Three more of the 1919 and 1920 New Liberty schoolmates as they looked in 1963. Left to right: Mildred Weir Brayton, Estellene Morrow Thomas, Laura Johnson Berry and their friend, Vera Lee. *(Photo courtesy of Charlene Brayton Eldredge)*

(Below) A gathering of some of New Liberty and Mack oldtimers in 1987 at Lewis Likes residence. Front row L-R: Homer Likes, Neta Rector, Robert W. Sanders, Mary Maluy, Fred Likes and Phyllis. Second row: Roy "Spark" Rector,. Gerald Colthorpe, Ivan Likes, Modine Cutler Deacon, Louise Clow Likes, Maudie Raver Yates, Viola Alstatt, Mildred Raver Means and Ray Barnes. Third row: Delores Smith Likes, Lona Alstatt, Milton Alstatt, Anna Belle Alstatt Thomas and June Spencer Alstatt Barnes. Back row: Darrell Maluy, Lewis Likes, Ruby Dodge Likes and ?. *(Homer and Phyllis Collection)*

Sew and So Club

In August 1926 the young women of the New Liberty community organized a sewing club that they named the "Sew and So Club." Ena Sumnicht was elected president; Maud Raver, vice president; Viola Alstatt, secretary-treasurer. Maud Raver was chairman of the bylaws committee, with Virginia Smith and Estellene Morrow as committee helpers. Estellene Morrow was chosen for the entertainment committee, with Ruth Alstatt and Mildred Weir as her helpers. Their next meeting, about two weeks later, was at the school grounds where a wiener-roast provided entertainment. Mrs. W. E. Bowen was named as their sponsor.

Sew and So Club members in 1928. Back row L-R: Laura Johnson, Ena Sumnicht, Vera Maynard, Estellene Morrow, Thelma Gunst and Grace Arbuckle. Front row: Mary Lou Gunst, Viola Alstatt, Allene Leach, Ruth Alstatt and Margaret McCampbell. *(Photo courtesy of Florence Brach Chandler)*

Sorosis Club

The following information was taken from the book of minutes kept by the Sorosis Club secretaries from 1929-1944, and an excerpt from the 17 June 1954 minutes.

If information we have is correct, the ladies of the New Liberty Community organized the Sorosis Club in September 1929. Records show that bylaws were written and adopted at that time. The first meeting of the Club was at the home of Fern Cox and the following officers were elected that day:

Margaret Morrow, president
Sara Knapp, vice president
May Sanders, secretary-treasurer

The first roster lists the following members:

Georgia Bowen,
Grace Carroll,
Fern Cox
Mary Cutler
Bernice Gerry
Elva Gunst
Sara Knapp
Retta Likes
Mary Maluy
Margaret Morrow
Dorothy Owings
May Sanders
Anna Shires
Selma Snavely
Olive Starbuck
Josie Summers
Anna Sumnicht
Ruth Wyant

Mrs. Watters, Estellene Morrow, Elizabeth Morrow and Laura Weir were added in 1930.

Constitution and By-Laws

Article I: Name — Sorosis Club.[†]

Article II: Object — The object of this club is to promote home interests.

Article III: Membership — All those in this community who are in sympathy with the aim of this club shall be eligible to membership.

Article IV: Officers — The officers of this club shall be a President, Vice President and Secretary-Treasurer, ... who shall be elected at the September meeting and serve for one year or until successors are elected and qualified.

Article V: Executive Committee — The officers of this club and the chairmen of standing committees shall constitute a board of directors for the transacting of business.

Article VI: Meetings — This club shall meet once each month, on the first Thursday.

Article VII: Dues — The dues of this club shall be 50¢ per year, payable in advance.

The dues proved to be flexible; in 1933 they cut the dues back to 15¢ per year and money would be raised as needed by contributions from the members. In 1935 it was raised to 25¢ and in 1944 raised back to 50¢.

The club was to meet on the first Thursday of each month, but this was also flexible and changed according to the needs. In 1938 they started having club meetings twice a month in the winter, and if it was not possible to have meetings during the summer, they canceled. They would have half or full-day meetings as needed.

In February 1931 a prayer was read by Mrs. Sumnicht and adopted as the club prayer. In January of 1939, they chose a creed, colors and club song. The creed which they were to memorize was:

†Reportedly suggested by Selma Snavely. The definition of the name is: "an organization of women or girls."

To promote the highest ideals of home and community life. To consider our children and their welfare the most important of our duties. To be willing to cooperate with others for any common good and to be ever ready to extend a helping hand to those in need.

The colors were blue and gold and the song was "Brighten the Corner." The meeting would begin with the song and prayer, then members would recite the creed

Year books were written and distributed among the members each year. They contained the creed and song, a schedule of the meetings, who was to be the hostess, where the meeting was to be held, the goals and projects to accomplish, etc.

In January of 1936 a motion was made to change the name of the club, but after the next three meetings with no success, it was given up.

Different activities were held during the meetings to make them fun and interesting. One year the club had a "market basket" in which those who wanted to could buy chances for 5¢ per chance (ticket). There was a drawing at the end of the meeting and the one with the lucky number got the basket. That person usually "took charge" of the basket for the next meeting. Another year members played games at every meeting with prizes for those being first or having the highest score of a game or games. The hostess was responsible for the prizes.

A roll call was taken at the beginning of each meeting. Each person would answer the roll with an answer relating to the topic that was assigned the previous meeting. Following are some of the roll call topics over the years:

- Current events
- Household hints, shortcuts, etc.
- Verse about babies and bring own baby picture
- Hints on chicken raising
- Flower bulbs, shrub and seed exchange
- Original four-line poem
- Place of birth and something interesting about it. (12 states and two countries were represented with 19 members present)
- Things to be thankful for (good health came first, then prosperity and happiness)

- Most embarrassing moment
- Table etiquette
- Pet Peeves
- A woman in history
- What would I do if I had a thousand dollars
- What can I do to help the Red Cross
- Advice to the new bride
- New Year resolutions or wishes
- Christmas customs

A study hour was held at some of the meetings. A member or volunteer would be chosen to present the subject and lead the discussion at the next meeting. At the March 1933 meeting Estellene Thomas led the study hour on the subject of Russia. It was reported, "A very interesting paper on Russia was read by Mrs. Thomas. Other members gave some unusual and interesting facts about the great country." Mrs. Anna Alstatt gave an interesting account of her childhood recollections of Sweden in the October 1933 meeting.

From the very beginning of the organization, the Sorosis Club members worked closely with the Mesa County Extension Office in Grand Junction. The extension office provided agents to come to the meetings and discuss different subjects. The first one to come on 21 October 1929 was Miss Callopy and the subject was, "Conveniences in the Kitchen." How interesting it would be to know what those conveniences were nearly 70 years ago. Miss Hall came during the years 1936-1939 and some of her subjects were salads and one dish meals, buying suitable colors and styles for our completion and build, making curtains, toy making, children's welfare and teenage problems, the child, helping children to grow-up emotionally and healthy.

The Sorosis Club ordered the Mesa County Extension Club's yearly programs (schedules) and would attend its monthly meetings held throughout the county. The Sorosis Club would take its turn hosting the meeting at its building, or be responsible for the program, entertainment or meal. For example, in May 1930 the Sorosis Club was responsible for the program at the monthly meeting held at the Brethren Church in Appleton. In February 1932, "the Sorosis Club paid 50¢ to Mrs. Ilk for their share of the rent for the hall in Fruita for the Extension Club's monthly meeting." March 1933, "The New Liberty ladies acted as hostesses at the March meeting held at Mack." During the summer vacation in 1933 the monthly meeting was held at New Liberty.

They would host the Highline Hustlers' Club from Mack Mesa and Highline communities, at least once a year. Then in turn the Highline Hustlers' Club would reciprocate, so they met together at least twice a year. Those were always such fun occasions, with entertainment and a special meal. Sometimes they would "let their hair down." On 20 February 1941 the ladies met with the Highline Hustlers Club at the Loma Community Hall and dressed up to represent the character they wished to be when they were grown-ups. First prize went to May Sanders, a hula dancer; second prize to Ruth Van Riper, a gypsy fortune teller; and third prize to Mary Maluy, a tight rope walker. The Sorosis Club members rode to and from Loma in a truck.

Taken from the 17 June 1954 minutes:

The Club entertained the Highline Hustlers' Club with a Slouch Day Party. There were 16 Sorosis Club members present and nine Highline Hustlers' Club members

.

The costumes were many and varied, ranging from the beautiful to the ragged and the ludicrous. A mock wedding in which everyone took part was the main entertainment. May Sanders attired as Charlie Chaplin, and Agnes Overbye, dressed as a Prima Donna, sang "I Love You Truly," accompanied by Laurene Wells, dressed as a grandmother in 19th century clothes. May Sanders was the preacher, reading an appropriate ceremony from the Montgomery Ward catalog. Mary Maluy, dressed in the scanty attire of a hula dancer with a lace curtain for a veil and train, was the bride.

Maurine Reed, dressed as a hobo in his leanest days, was the groom. Lois Saunders, dressed also as a hobo with a shot gun to see to it that her daughter was married, was the brides' father. Anna Shires was the groom's mother and Mabel Cooper was the bride's mother. Aileen Giles, attired in a beautiful 18th century gown, and Ward Ogle, also dressed as a hula dancer, were bridesmaids. Everyone took some part in the wedding party. Agnes Overbye sang, "I Wish I Were Single Again." Mabel Cooper, a reporter, read a comical write-up of the

(Above left) On 17 June 1954 the Sorosis Club and the Highline Hustlers' Club met together at the New Liberty school house and had a slouch day party. Back row: Anna Shires, Della Swyhart, Laura Berry, May Sanders, Laurene Wells,?, Christine Shires,?,?,?. Front row: ?, Agnes Overbye, Pearline Arpke, Willa Dean Butt, Betty Collins, Maurine Reed, Lois Saunders and Betty Rader. Children are unidentified. (Above Right) Mary Maluy, dressed up in a hula outfit for the Sorosis and Highline Hustlers' Club slouch day party, was the bride in the party's wedding ceremony. *(Both photos from Mary Maluy Collection)*

(Left) Just the Sorosis Club members at the combined party. Back row: Della Swyhart, Anna Shires, Mabel Cooper, Laura Berry, May Sanders, Mary Maluy, Laurene Wells and Christine Shires. Front row: ?. Agnes Overbye, Lona Alstatt, Pearline Arpke and Willa Dean Butt. The Children are not identified. Notice May Sanders being naughty with her cane; she used it to pull aside Mary Maluy's hula skirt, leaving her leg exposed What a character May was. *(Mary Maluy Collection)*

The Sorosis Club women entertaining the Highline Hustlers' Club with a costume party at the New Liberty school house in 1953. Standing: Maurine Reed, Estellene Thomas, Pearline Arpke, Mary White, ?, ?, Anna Alstatt, ?, ?, Lois Saunders, Phyllis Likes and Mary Maluy. Sitting: Neta Rector, (children; Janice Monger and Duane Arpke) Agnes Overbye, Laura Berry, (Dennis Likes), Lona Alstatt and May Sanders. This was a great opportunity for the women of the two clubs to socialize and let their hair down. *(Photo courtesy of Lona Alstatt)* *(Below)* Mary Maluy dressed up for the social above as "Mammy Yokum" of the Lil' Abner Cartoon strip. On the left with a scrub board and on the right with an ax chopping wood. Photos taken at Homer and Phyllis Likes' residence. *(Phyllis Likes Collection)*

wedding, describing in detail the groom's costume, but little mention of the bride's.

The refreshment committee served a beautiful wedding reception which would have done honor to a real wedding. A color scheme of pink and green was carried out, with green table linen and pink and green napkins. Angel food cakes decorated in pink and green frostings and beautiful strawberry jello salad was served. Also a delicious pink punch was served in glasses with frosted pink sugar-coated rims and a tiny pink rose bouquet on the outside of the glass. The center piece was two large wedding rings, 12 inches in diameter; one having a diamond setting.

Many pictures were taken, and each at the table, told of some extraordinary experience that occurred on her honeymoon.

—*Secretary, Mary C. Maluy*

One of the club's goals was to serve the community. It was responsible for getting the boys and girls 4-H club started. The club always raised money for it and assigned the leaders. They always bought the Christmas treats for the sacks given by Santa Claus to the children at the Christmas program held at the school house. It bought the material and made Santa Claus' suit for 1\underline{^{05}}$.

In the February 1930 meeting, the subject was brought up of earning money to buy a community house. A committee was appointed to see if they could buy the school house at Enterprise and what it would cost. There is no record that this ever happened, but in the October 1935 meeting the minutes report the club had obtained china for the club house. In February 1936, the Sorosis Club and the Community Club bought Mrs. Harrison's player piano for $50. Each club paid $25. In September 1936 club members decided to have the player piano repaired "that is in the Community Hall," and in April 1937 material was bought to make curtains for the "Club Hall."

In the summer of 1937 the new school house was completed and, from then on, that building was used for all community activities and some of the club's meetings.

The Sorosis Club immediately went to work

equipping the kitchen in the new building; lumber for tables, linoleum to put on the kitchen tables and curtains were bought.

In 1937 the club bought playground equipment for the school grounds (19\underline{^{60}}$ for equipment and 19\underline{^{19}}$ for freight) and a sander and sand-paper. The sander was undoubtedly to sand the new hardwood floors.

In 1938 it bought a Singer sewing machine for 12\underline{^{00}}$. A sewing class was held each Thursday, and was taught by Mrs. Smith Kilby from Fruita. Also in 1938 money was appropriated for a clock and first aid kit for the school, but the clock took all the money. In 1942 the club was finally able to get the first aid kit. In 1938, Lawrence Morrow was hired as janitor. Mrs. Morrow had been cleaning the "hall" the year prior.

In the 24 February 1938 meeting the club voted to try the WPA hot lunch program for a month. If the community hired a cook, members agreed that the following women were eligible for the job: Mary Cutler, Anna Shires (she rejected the offer), Mrs. Fry and Martha Wallace. The club bought two large kettles and six dozen two-quart jars (50¢ a dozen) with the WPA funds. The ladies were to furnish or can all their surplus vegetables for the next year's program. In June 1938 they went to a canning demonstration at Loma. In January 1939 they bought two bread pans, 35¢ each, for the school lunch.

The WPA program was tried at least the school year 1938-39. Mabel Brisbin Howes remembers the school lunches being served by the mothers before the Brisbins left in 1939. They served stew, beans, soups and homemade bread. New Liberty news items in *The Daily Sentinel* on 1 January 1942 states:

After much red tape, the school board thinks they will start the hot lunches. This school was one of the first to have hot lunches, but due to some misunderstanding, the lunches have not been started this year.

In the 13 November 1942 Sorosis Club meeting, the ladies voted to hire a head cook for school lunch with mothers to assist her. As far as we know, Retta May Likes was the first cook in New Liberty for the school lunch program. In the 24 October 1946 meeting she was given authority to order the pots and pans she needed to cook with. Margaret Morrow became the cook in the fall of 1948 and cooked until the spring of 1956. Jesse Hawthorne worked as a substitute for Mrs. Morrow from 1952 to 1956. Dora Tomlinson became the cook in the fall of 1956 and held that position until the school closed in 1959.

Before the school lunch program began and thereafter, the kitchen didn't sit idle. It was used by the students to eat their sack lunches, and community dinners for many occasions were cooked there. The Sorosis Club used it for its dinners and lunches. It was also the principal's office when a student was called in to be reprimanded or a parent wanted to meet with a teacher in private. The principal and teachers also held their meetings in the kitchen.

In 1940 the club bought basketball equipment and a basketball for the school for $33.82. Clem Maluy purchased it for them. A basketball team was begun with Jim Cooper as coach.

The Sorosis Club women took responsibility for a great deal of the entertainment and activities in the community. It entertained member's husbands at a dinner and party at least once a year; usually in January. For the first party held in January 1930, the members and their husbands went bob sledding, played cards and listened to the radio. Quite an active and interesting evening.

The ladies organized the annual fish fry at the Colorado River in conjunction with the Community Club. The women were responsible for the food and the men the seine and fishing. The activity was usually held in late July or early August, with plenty of fish and homemade ice cream. The ladies reported that at the August 1931 fish fry, 60 pounds of fish were caught and there were 76 people present. In several of their financial records, they mentioned having to buy ice for freezing the ice cream. So undoubtedly their private supplies in their "ice sheds" were depleted.

Some of the women attended the four-day recreation camp on Grand Mesa in July of 1936 and 1939. The Mesa County Extension Club's four-day recreation program, held in Grand Junction November 26-28, 1940, was well attended by the Sorosis Club women. The club paid for the transportation and lunches of those who attended. At the club's next meeting, a report was given by Estellene Thomas of how successful it was.

One of the club's best known contributions to the community was of compassionate service. The ladies gave showers and/or gifts for newlyweds and new babies; which proved to be quite numerous. The ill were remembered with gifts, flowers, plants, cards or letters. When Mary Maluy was ill with a long illness in 1934 and 1935, they gave her bedroom slippers and assigned members to send cards or write letters on different days to let her know of their concern, love and give her encouragement. She spent part of that time in California, convalescing at her sister's. At one meeting they reported giving flowers to five members that were ill that month. They also remembered family members of the club, when they were ill, with a gift. Some of those recipients were; Donald Knapp, Junior Appier, Anna Belle Alstatt, Eugene Thomas, Ray Likes and Rex Maluy (Rex was given a subscription to the *Fruita Times*).

They sent flowers for funerals and helped the families in their time of need. In the 27 March 1936 meeting members reported the passing of their president, Bernice Gerry. In the instance of illness and death, community members pulled together and helped each other with meals, caring for children, running errands, caring for livestock and assisting with crops. The Sorosis Club was always there to do its part.

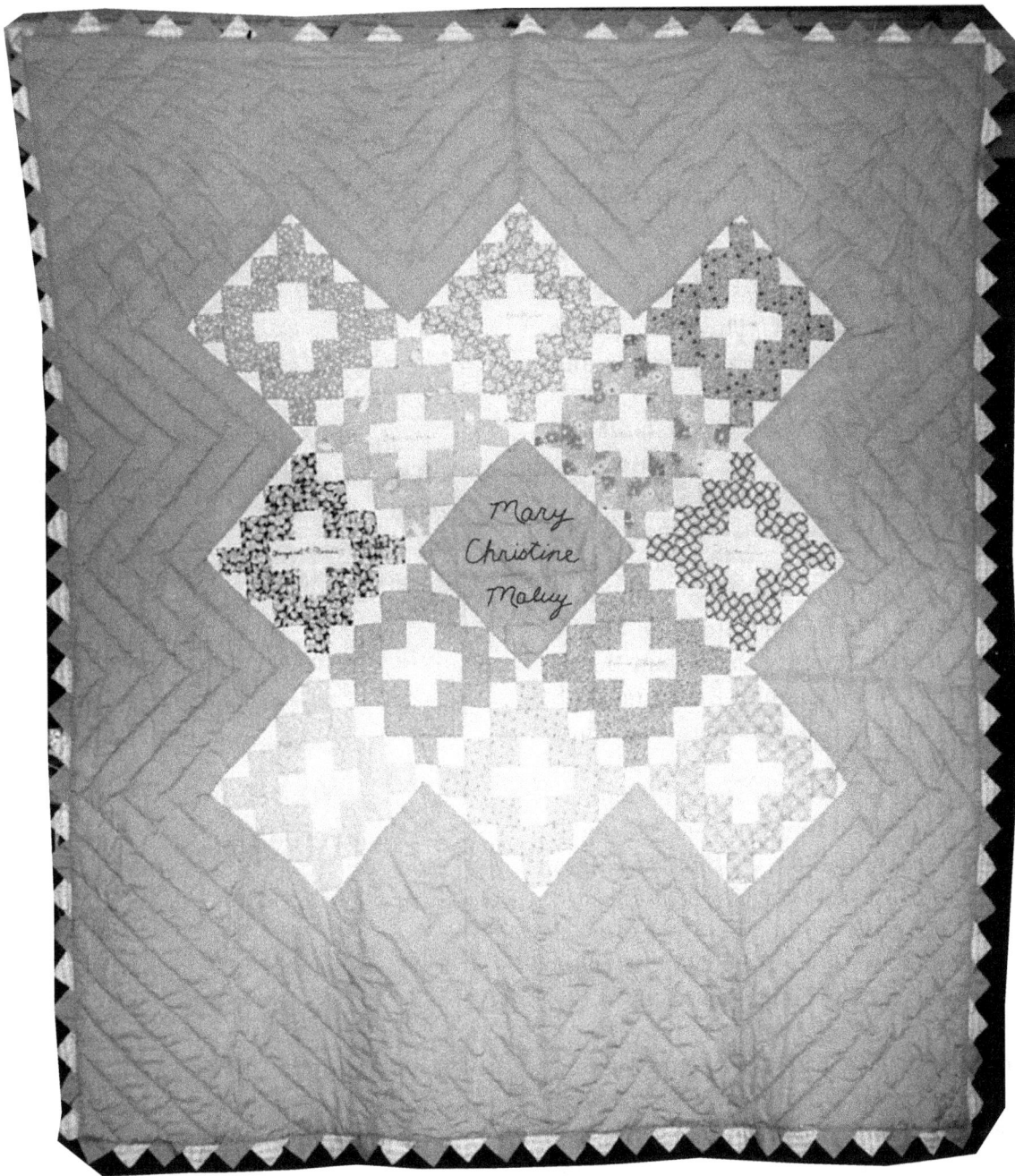

Quilt made by Retta Marie Likes Brandow for her grandmother, Mary Maluy, from twelve blocks
that were made by members in the Sorosis Club for Mary. Below: Closeups of three of the blocks
in the quilt above: Anna Alstatt, Retta M. Likes, and Margaret A. Morrow. Other blocks in the
quilt are from: Evelyn Likes, Ada Bush, Estellene Thomas, Helen Carroll, Grace Carroll, Laura
Weir, Bernice Gerry, Edith Harrison, and Letha Hardin. *(Photos taken by Phyllis Likes)*

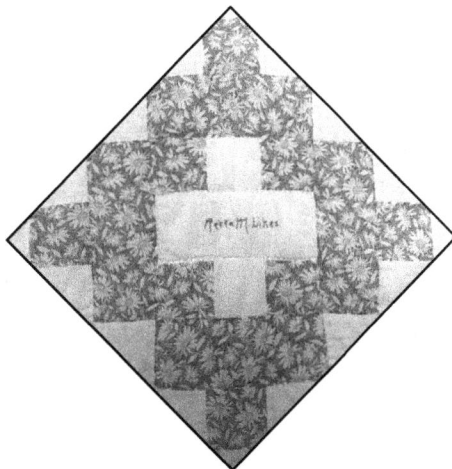

During World War II the club was involved with the Red Cross by sewing 12 dresses, diapers, quilts, splint pads and teaching first aid classes. It raised money to donate to the Red Cross, the "war fund," and the Infantile Paralysis Fund.

The ladies gave house-warming showers for those who built new homes. Three that were mentioned were the Van Ripers, Alstatts and Robert Sanders.

To be financially able to accomplish all the things they did, members were ingenious in creating fund-raising projects. Quilts were made and raffle tickets were sold to members, Community Club members, and at the county fair. They sold Mesa County Extension Club cook books, and served dinners or sold food at the Community Club, Mesa County Extension, Lower Valley Teacher's Association, Kiwanis Club meetings, and at farm sales and dances. They held bazaars with booths for hand-sewn articles, popcorn, candy, baked goods, a shooting gallery and a fish pond. In 1940 they received $20 and a ribbon as third prize for their booth at the Mesa County Fair, and Mesa Flour Mills donated a 25-pound sack of Mesa Flour and a package of Pikes Peak cake flour to their booth. At their next meeting, Mary Maluy bought the flour at the regular price.

Club members either brought in entertainers or they themselves entertained with plays and programs at the Community Club and charged an entrance fee. They also performed or served meals for a price at other clubs. They held parties and dances, then charged the people to participate. One way they had to raise money for the "war fund," was to fine the members when they were absent from their meetings.

As a keepsake, the women embroidered quilt blocks with their names on them and exchanged with each other. Enough were made so that all who wanted could make a quilt with the names of their friends — keepsake that many women were proud to display. Many of those quilts still exist today.

The Sorosis Club has been a choice experience for many ladies who have lived in the New Liberty Community. The club lives on — meetings are still held regularly, even though some of the members live in other communities.

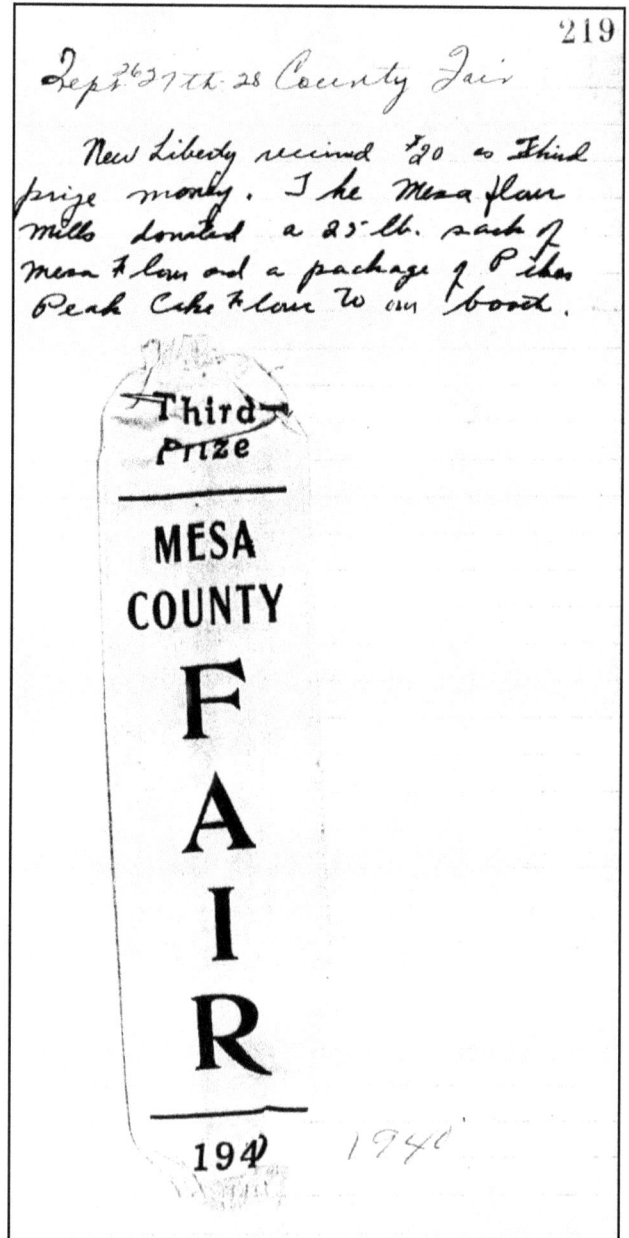

Page from the Sorosis Club book of minutes showing the third prize ribbon they won for their booth at the September 1940 county fair. *(Copied from the Sorosis Club Book of Minutes)*

FORD TOURING CAR

Delivered In Grand Junction Now

$481.00

Our Easy Payment Selling Plan Places the FORD CAR Within the Means Of Everyone.

For only $240.00 Cash you can start driving your new Ford Five-Passenger Touring Car. Pay the balance as you ride, in easy payments.

These prices are the lowest in the history of the Ford Motor Company and the car is the best car they ever made.

Millions have learned by experience that to own and operate a Ford is not an extravagance; they have learned that the many pleasures derived from a Ford takes the place of other pleasures, and the saving thus made often pays for the car and its maintenance.

The initial outlay and the after expense are so small that your Ford car will pay for itself many times over, whether used as a family car for pleasure, for business purposes, or both.

The sooner you place your order the sooner you will be enjoying your Ford car.

Call us by telephone, drop us a card, call at our salesroom, or let us call at your office or home and arrange a demonstration.

Cash $225
(Balance on easy payment)
$319.00 F. O. B. Detroit

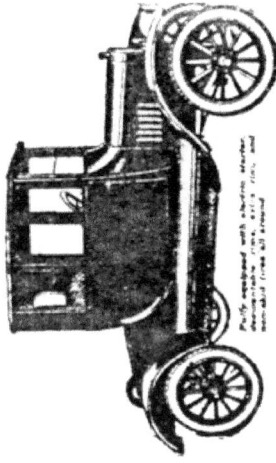

Cash $362
(Balance on easy payment)
$580.00 F. O. B. Detroit

Cash $280
(Balance on easy payments)
$430.00 F. O. B. Detroit

Cash $240
(Balance on easy payments)
$348.00 F. O. B. Detroit

Cash $395
(Balance on easy payments)
$645.00 F. O. B. Detroit

Cash $208
(Balance on easy payments)
$285.00 F. O. B. Detroit

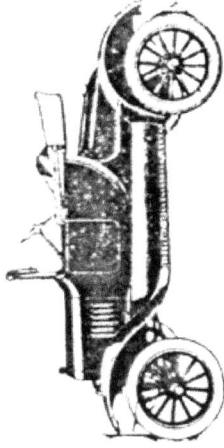

WESTERN SLOPE AUTO CO.

Second & Main St.

Phone Jct. 590

These are typical automobiles used by our homesteading parents in New Liberty and residents of Mack in the early days of the communities. How great it would be to pay these prices today. *(Ford Dealership's Advertisement in the Daily Sentinel, April 8, 1922)*

166

Chapter Six

Progress

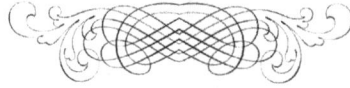

Automobiles & Roads

Back to the early days. Automobiles were beginning to be a popular mode of transportation at the time of the settlement of the lower valley. Some catchy little items about them appeared occasionally in *The Daily Sentinel* Friday, 17 August 1918, Grand Junction ...

"More tourist cars have passed through the city this summer than ever before... It is a rare day when at least half a dozen strange automobiles are not in the city."

Then on Monday, 2 September 1918, Mack item:

"Lots of auto tourists are passing through these days. Hardly an evening passes without finding one to six camps here for the night."

Those hardy travelers considered that dusty or muddy trail across the desert a highway !

In April 1919 it was noted that "the number of autos is far greater than last year — already this year licenses have been issued for 1,266 autos owned in Mesa county. The total for the last entire year was only 1,100." For comparison, the number of autos registered in Mesa County in 1993 was 112,586.

In those days one could buy gasoline at the pump for 15¢ or 16¢ per gallon. The pumps were much different than they are now. A long hand lever was attached to the side of an apparatus with which one could pump ten gallons into a "sight glass" container at the top and then dispense into the auto through a hose the amount needed.

About the first of July in 1931 some gasoline dealers endeavored to drive the price of gasoline up to 20¢ per gallon. A few of the less greedy kept their price at 16¢; but it was noted that by the end of the month of July the price was generally 20¢; a few places were even charging 21¢. Wouldn't it be nice to settle for that higher price now?

The Daily Sentinel for 6 April 1920, published some interesting statistics from the 1920 Federal census: the population in Grand Junction had grown to 8,665 citizens; Fruita had grown to 1,193, which was an increase of 35.4% over the 1910 count. The number of autos owned in the state of Colorado had risen to One for every nine persons.

By 1920 the farmers of New Liberty were beginning to feel a need for better roads. A few of them owned automobiles, but the roads already in use by horses and wagons or buggies were not suitable for auto travel. The road northwest from Mack that accessed the New Liberty community left the "highway" at about the vicinity of the present "10 Road." It then meandered

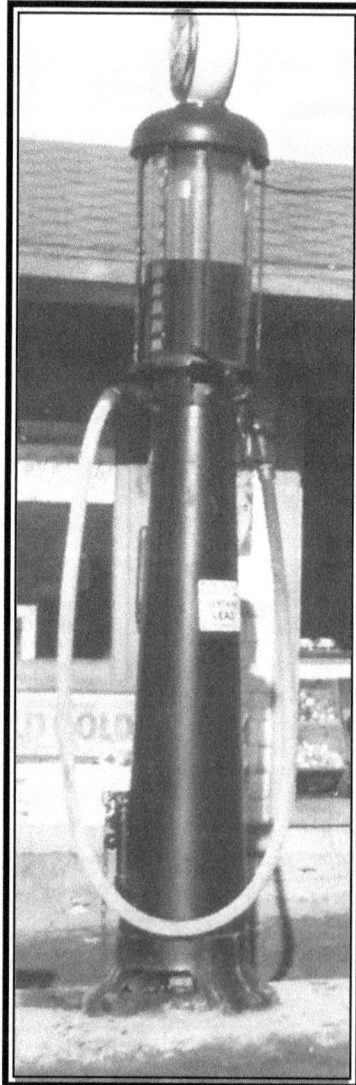

A gas pump in front of Mack Store like the one spoken of. One can see the "sight glass" container at the top of the pump. *(Taken from the photo of Mack Store, Evelyn Bush Welch)*

northwesterly toward the hills south of the George Fisher farm, which was situated west of the present "9" road, just south of "R" road. Other roads built on the section lines had been in use since the community was settled. The roads were not given the number and letter identification until many years later.

In April 1920 a delegation of farmers from the lower valley met with county commissioners to submit a request for aid to build about ten miles of roads in the New Liberty community. Delegates were: Robert Cox, Guy Gerry, Clem Maluy, A. W. Alstatt, J. B. Morrow, George Fisher and W. E. Bowen. They volunteered to provide labor if the county would supply machinery and materials to build bridges and culverts. The commissioners made an inspection tour of the area; soon there was an agreement and construction began. Roads were generally built on section or half-section lines (see map at end of this story).

For years the roads were maintained with a horse-drawn grader operated by various men of the community, including Max Sanders, Bob Sanders, Malcolm (Slim) Dean and Ernest Maynard.

In June of 1920 the State Highway Commission set the speed limit for autos on country roads at 35 miles per hour. The author recalls that 35 mph could have been "breakneck" speed!

In April 1925, citizens of Mack, with endorsement of the Fruita Chamber of Commerce, appealed to the Mesa County Commission to gravel the "Pikes Peak Coast to Coast Highway" between Mack and Fruita. The road was good during dry weather, but after a storm it was almost impassable.

The adobe soil created many problems during wet periods, making it virtually impossible to drive in some areas during or shortly after a rain. The slick mud, about the consistency of grease, sent many a "Model T" slithering into a fence or ditch. In some areas the roads would develop boggy spots where vehicles, including wagons, would become mired, sometimes having to be abandoned until sufficient power could be brought to pull them out.

Photo taken from the "Murphy's Law" poster in possession of Phyllis Likes. It is such a typical scene in New Liberty in the 1920s and 1930s. It seemed there was no bottom to the mud. East of the Clem Maluy gate was a dip in the road that would fill with water, becoming a small pond and turning into a pond of mud. Bubbles and Phyllis Maluy would run and swim in it in the summer and sled and slide on it in the winter.

During the fall of 1928 county commissioners awarded a contract for improvements on the road between Mack and Fruita. But after an unusual amount of rain, citizens of the lower valley complained bitterly to county commissioners about the condition of the road. The contractor had literally "bogged down," leaving the road in a terrible mess!

The school buses were easy victims to the road, as they were much heavier. Even though the roads had been much improved by then, as late as 1932 the school bus became mired in a soft spot in the *highway* about ¾ mile east of Mack. The worst part of that predicament was that the bus was on the way *home* from school!

Following is a story written by Viola Alstatt about another problem with a school bus:

I can recall some of the unusual events and difficulties endured by the high school students during the late 1920s to make the trip from New Liberty and Mack to attend Fruita Union High School. Ours was the longest route in the entire Union High School district.

Most of the roads were not even graveled, so when it stormed there was more than one time the bus slid off the shoulder of the road and all the students had to get out and push to get back on the road. Most of the students had good attendance records up to this time, but many times we would arrive in Fruita quite late and the classes that were missed had to be made up later.

I recall one day in the fall, about 1927, when the area had a heavy rain storm, maybe a cloud burst in the hills, which caused the water to come rushing down the wash and running the bank full. At this particular time the bridge that crossed the wash near the siphon was taken out by a flash flood. This was our road home, so we were stalled from completing our trip home that evening. Our bus driver, I believe, was Harold Carroll, who was also one of the students. Harold turned back and drove into the yard at the Deacon place. Charles and Hobart Cutler were near enough that they could walk on home, and I believe Harold walked home too. But there were several of us with no place to go. The Deacons made provision for the few boys to stay there for the night. There were at least five or six girls for whom they fixed beds on the bus by putting table leaves and boards across the seats and provided us with bedding, so we slept in the bus that night.

Since there were no telephones or other means of communication, Mr. Cutler rode a horse to the parents' houses to let them know

The Fruita Union High School bus that hauled the New Liberty students to Fruita, located at the Alstatt residence in 1932/3. Milton Alstatt is the driver with Carl and Amos Alstatt as passengers, petting the family dog. In the background is the family's Model T Ford car. *(Photo courtesy of Viola and Robert Alstatt)*

everyone was O.K. The Deacons fed us the evening meal, and fed us breakfast the next morning too. Of course, none of us had a change of clothes, and we remember putting on damp ones worn the day before. Even our shoes seemed damp when we dressed.

Soon we were on the bus schedule on the way to another day at school in Fruita. Before we left, Mr. Cutler came up and brought us all lunch money for the day.

Travel on lower valley roads while they were wet would create ruts that caused additional problems after they dried out. Many a driver cursed the maintenance crew for not being more prompt in grading. The steering in the autos of those days would cause unexpected and exciting things to happen if a driver got caught in a rut and then finally managed to climb out. The steering would be cramped to the extreme one way or the other — when the wheels would finally grab and cause the car to climb out there would be a frantic turning of the wheel in the opposite direction to try to keep from running into the ditch. Many times the ditch could not be avoided.

To move ahead a little in time, the roads in the New Liberty and Mack Mesa communities were graveled in the thirties under the direction of the Works Progress Administration, (WPA—a government program enacted during the depression) with men in the community providing teams and wagons. The wagons were equipped with specially built dump boxes that consisted of two-by-twelve side boards, with two-by-six boards laid loose in the bottom to form a floor. Handles were carved on the ends of the floor boards to make it easier for the teamster to lift and turn them, allowing the gravel to fall to the ground.

The gravel was hauled from a pit on the hill west of Floyd Thomas' on Road 8, and north of Joe Owings' farms on Sec 29.

The loading was another interesting process: A pit was constructed of timbers and posts with a trap door in a

floor above. The floor was high enough for a team and wagon to drive under and then other teams with slip scrapers would drag loads of gravel over the top of the pit, dumping the scraper so the gravel would fall through the trap into the wagon below.

When completed, the gravel on the roads resulted in much more reliable transportation and much more peace of mind when it was necessary to travel during inclement weather.

Above are examples of modes of transportation in 1913 for school students in the upper valley.

(Upper) A horse-drawn bus letting students out at the Consolidated School at Appleton. Also a girl riding by on her horse on the way home from school. You can also see a one-horse buggy in the background.

(Lower) Students getting off of a Consolidated School Suburban Railway which ran between Grand Junction and Rhone. *(Grand Valley Water Users' Association Collection)*

Siphon

East Salt Creek

To Douglas Pass

Government Highline Canal

Government Highline Canal

S 1/2 Road

To Baxter Pass

S Road

6 Road

7 Road

New Liberty School

9 Road

R 1/2 Road

8 Road

R Road

Badger Wash

West Salt Creek

Mack Mesa

10 Road

Pikes Peak Coast to Coast Highway

Gravel Pit

Q Road

First Road

Reservoir

Mack Mesa Reservoir

East Salt Creek

West Salt Creek

Salt Creek

Mack

Pikes Peak Coast to Coast Highway

To Fruita

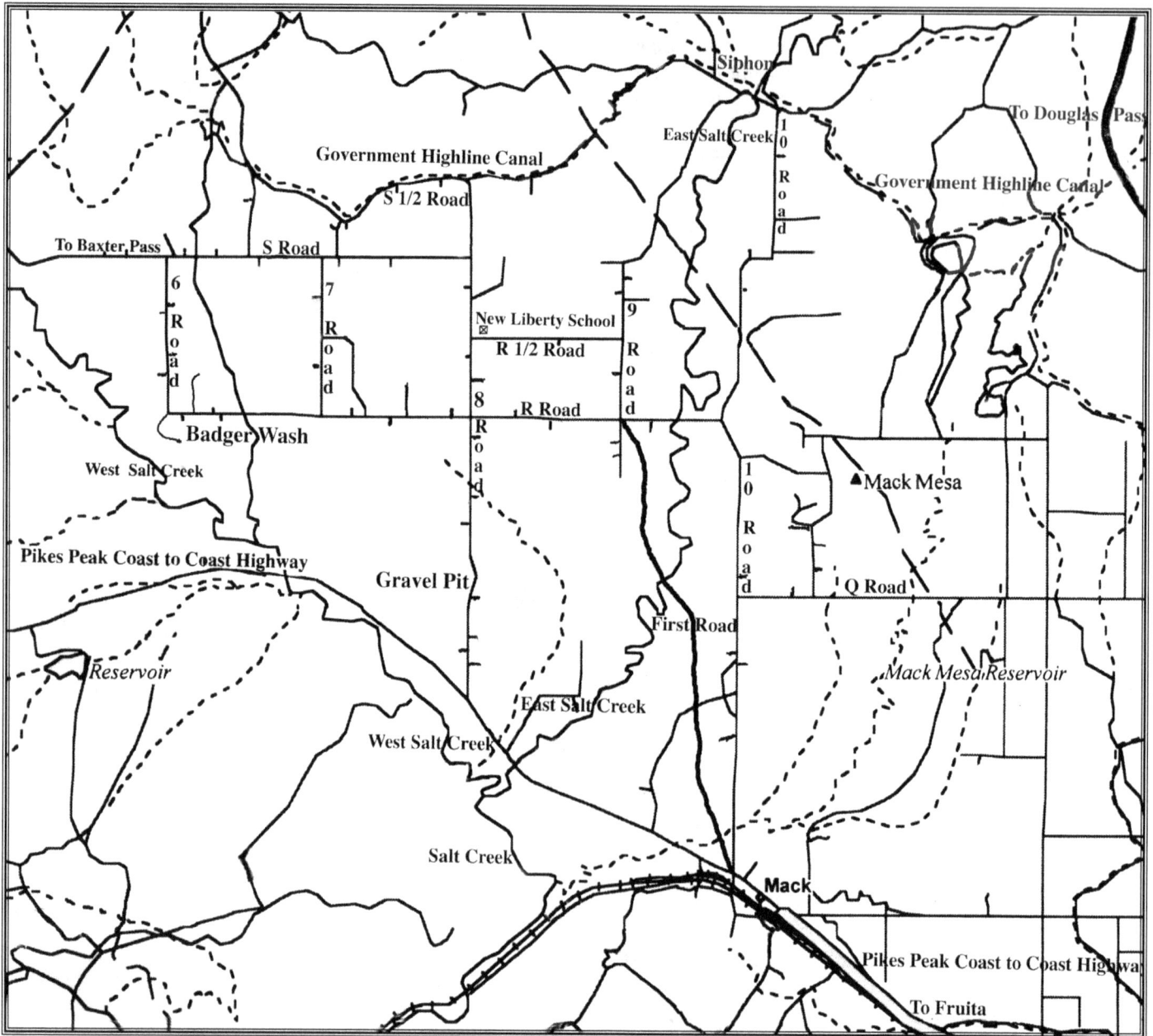

A road map of the Mack/New Liberty area in the 1920s. The map shows the first road (appropriately named "First Road") beginning at the highway and 10 Road and ending at the 9 and R Road junction; the crossing of First, 9, and R Road became the Don Weimer corner. The section and half-section lines became the main roads and also the mail route for Everett Bowen. A section equals a square mile and is divided into quarters. Those dividing lines are half-sections and are equal to a half mile between the main section lines, for example: roads R and S are a mile apart, just as roads 6 and 7 are also a mile apart. These roads are built on "section lines." Since R 1/2 Road is found on a "half-section line," it is only a half mile from R Road The roads are numbered from the Utah/Colorado State Line, for instance: 6 Road is six miles from the state line. The lettered roads begin at the south Mesa County line. The driveways to each residence in the communities have been drawn. The map shows the Pikes Peak Coast to Coast Highway which became Highway 6 & 50 and has been replaced by I-70. The section of improvement made in 1925 between Mack and Fruita, mentioned in the story, is visible. *(Map revised by Phyllis Likes)*

Fruita Union High School

Since nearly everyone in the Mack and New Liberty communities were involved in Fruita Union High School, we think it appropriate to touch briefly on the history of that school. Many of the older people will remember that the "old school," which was built in 1905, burned to the ground on 25 September 1934. The problem of continuing the school program was resolved by assigning the students to a variety of buildings throughout the town of Fruita—the Armory, Odd Fellows Hall, churches, warehouses, etc.

On 21 August 1935 *The Daily Sentinel* announced that citizens within the bounds of the Fruita Union High School District voted in favor of a bond for $80,000 to cover part of the cost of a new school building in Fruita. It was interesting to discover that Loma District voted against it; Mack, 11 for, 5 against; New Liberty, 15 for, 8 against. On 27 September 1935 another news article stated that a WPA project had been approved for construction of the new building. By 11 October a site had been selected and construction was to begin in the near future. Total cost of the project was to be about $156,000.

(Above left) The old Fruita Union High School when it was first built in 1905. Picture taken from the southeast, the front entrance. *(Photo courtesy of Frank Overbye)* (Above right) The day it burned down, 25 September 1934. (Below) The "old school" at it's prime, about 1915. The picture was taken from the northeast corner of the school grounds. *(The last two photos taken from the "Fruita High School 100 Years")*

When bids were let for construction only one contractor submitted a bid, W. O. Allison, for $127,384. An article in *The Daily Sentinel* of March 1936 noted that a corner-stone-laying ceremony was held with about 500 residents in attendance. Work was progressing very well. It must have been a happy day when the students and teachers moved into the new building in the fall of 1936, ending the inconvenience of the make-shift classrooms. The new building was dedicated 2 October 1936 with over 1,000 citizens in attendance for the ceremony.

In 1969 classes began at the new Fruita Monument High School located east of Fruita and near Highway 6 & 50. The former Fruita Union High School building became Fruita Junior High School.

(Upper) The "new" Fruita Union High School that was built in 1936 as it appeared in 1943. *(Phyllis Likes Collection)*
(Lower) In 1968-69, with the growth of the Redlands and Fruita, a new high school was needed. The Fruita Monument High School was built on 1815 J Road facing the highway. *(Photo taken from the "Fruita High School 100 Years")*

(Above) The interior of the gymnasium and auditorium of the Fruita Union High School where so many memories of games, dances, plays, assemblies and graduations, and the great Junior/Senior Proms that were so gaily decorated in various themes, were held. Laughter and cheering filled the walls of Fruita Union High for over 33 years . *(Photo taken from the "Fruita High School 100 Years")* (Below) In 1940 the Industrial Arts teacher, Harold Samuel Carroll, held a special display of the art work of his students for their parents and the public. Some magnificent wood work is displayed. *(Photo courtesy of Helen Grace Carroll Gingrich)*

Upper) The 1930 Fruita Union High School girls' basketball team. Back row: ? White, Wilma Rollins, Virginia Young, Lois Owens, Martina Klapwyk, Beulah Gourley and Bethel Jordan. Front row: Helen Overbye, Coach Ann White, and Jewel Pfaffenberger. They played Moab, Rifle, Glenwood Springs, Colbran, Grand Junction and Delta. They never beat Grand Junction, but beat the others teams easily. *(Photos courtesy of Helen Overbye Peterson)*

(Center) The 1931 Fruita Union High School boys' basketball team. Back row L-R: Harley Beeson, Wilson Weckel, Leo Markrud, Coach George Penner, Robert Murley, Blaine Standifird and Larimer Faris. Front row: Paul Watkins, John Rogers, Earl "Dick" Wagaman, Eldon Levi and Captain Robert Jordan. The Fruita Wildcats ended the 1931 conference season with Fruita in a tie with De Beque for runner up position. Fruita won the playoff 24-14 under the leadership of Captain Jordan, who scored 16 points.

(Lower) The 1931 Fruita Union High School Track team. Back row L-R: Billy Strawn, Bennie Pacheco, Robert Murley, Blaine Standifird, Coach George Penner, Leo Markrud, Eldon Levi, Clyde Nelson and Robert Jordon. Front row: John Rogers, Paul Watkins, Earl "Dick" Wagaman, Larimer Faris, Harley Beeson and Harold Moore. Boy in front is unidentified. The Wildcats entered a mile relay team in the Delta Relays. It was composed of Faris, Moore, Jordan and Wagaman with each man running 440 yards. Besides winning the race, they set a new record with a time of 3 minutes, 48.8 seconds. At the Western Slope track meet, someone on another team broke the discus record set by Leo Kiefer. *(Both photos above taken from the 1931 Fruita Union High School Annual courtesy of Leo Markrud)*

175

(Upper) Fruita Union High School 1931 football team. Back row L-R: 1-Glen Austin, 2-Eldon Levi, 3-John Rogers, 4-Captain Earl "Dick" Wagaman, 5-Leo Markrud, 6-Wilson Weckel, 7-Forrest March, 8-Ralph Arbuckle, 9-James Brenneman and 10-Porter Mogensen. Middle row: 11-Harley Beeson, 12-William Osborn, Coach George Penner, 13-Harold Moore, 14-Ted Lowenhagen and 15-Howard Mayne. Front row: 16-Robert Jordan, 17-Douglas Gorman, 18-Larimer Faris, 19-Paul Watkins and 20-Frank Peep. Football started under the leadership of Coach Penner, who was anxious to see the style of ball played on the Western Slope. After three weeks of work using the Warner style of play for the first time in Fruita, the Wildcats played a great game to tie Grand Junction 7-7 in a practice game. *(Photo courtesy of Leo Markrud)*

(Center) Fruita Union High School athletes that lettered in 1931. L-R: Leo Markrud, Wilson Weckel, John Rogers, Larimer Faris, Earl "Dick" Wagaman, Robert Murley, Harley Beeson, Paul Watkins, Robert Jordan, and Eldon Levi. *(Photo courtesy of Betty Booth Garber)*

(Below) Fruita Union High School 1932 football team. Front row L-R: Roland Hassell, Ted Lowenhagen, Kenneth Goff, James Brenneman, Rueben Maine, Fred Bessire and Sherman Kloster. Second row: Oscar Sweitzer, Jack Owens, Clyde Nelson, Benny Pacheco. Third row: Frank White, Ralph Arbuckle, Leo Sommerville and James Vanlandingham. Fourth row: Paul Watkins, ?, Ralph Wells, Willard Maine, Ralph McKinney, Lawrence Capps and Dwight Barcus. Top row: Coach George Penner, Delbert Jerome, Lloyd Sommerville, John Ingelhart, George Bessire, and ?. *(Photo courtesy of Oscar Sweitzer)*

Opposite page: (Upper) Fruita. Union High School Band, State Champions for 1935-36. Photo taken in Circle Park, downtown Fruita. Upper left corner: Band director, Charles "Chick" Nichols. Front row: Omar Brown, Douglas Booth, Raymond "Sammy" White, Marjorie Conrad, Joan Taylor, Miriam Sowers, Dixie Lew Young, Arlene Turner, May Nichols, Lucille Garrison and JoAnn Bowen. Second row: Aneth Quick, ?, Virginia Durkee, Alena Mogensen, Eleanor Reed, ?, Norma Pritchard, Marceline Capps, Leona Sommerville, Margaret Scoles, Frank Pritchard, Miriam Peep, Lee Smith and Clover Thirsk. Third row: Louise Thorpe, Margaret Capps, Velma Bass, Madge Watkins, Eleanor Vaughn, Blanche Crider, Theresa O'Connor, William Goss, Margaret Hassell, Evelyn Scoles, Chester Means, Percy Sheets, Jim McCoy, Guy Brown, Georgia Hemricy, Mary McCullough, ?, Betty Parish, Roberta Tucker, Weldon Vandenheuval and Leland Byers. Back row: Paul Crockett, Melvin Owens, Winifred Owens, Harold Mogensen, Bill Grant (Drum Major), ?, Walter Tufly, Willard Selke, Floyd Crider, Robert Scharf, Carol Standifird, Leon Daily, Clarence Porter and Wayne Nugent. *(Photo courtesy of Mildred Martin Van Dover)*

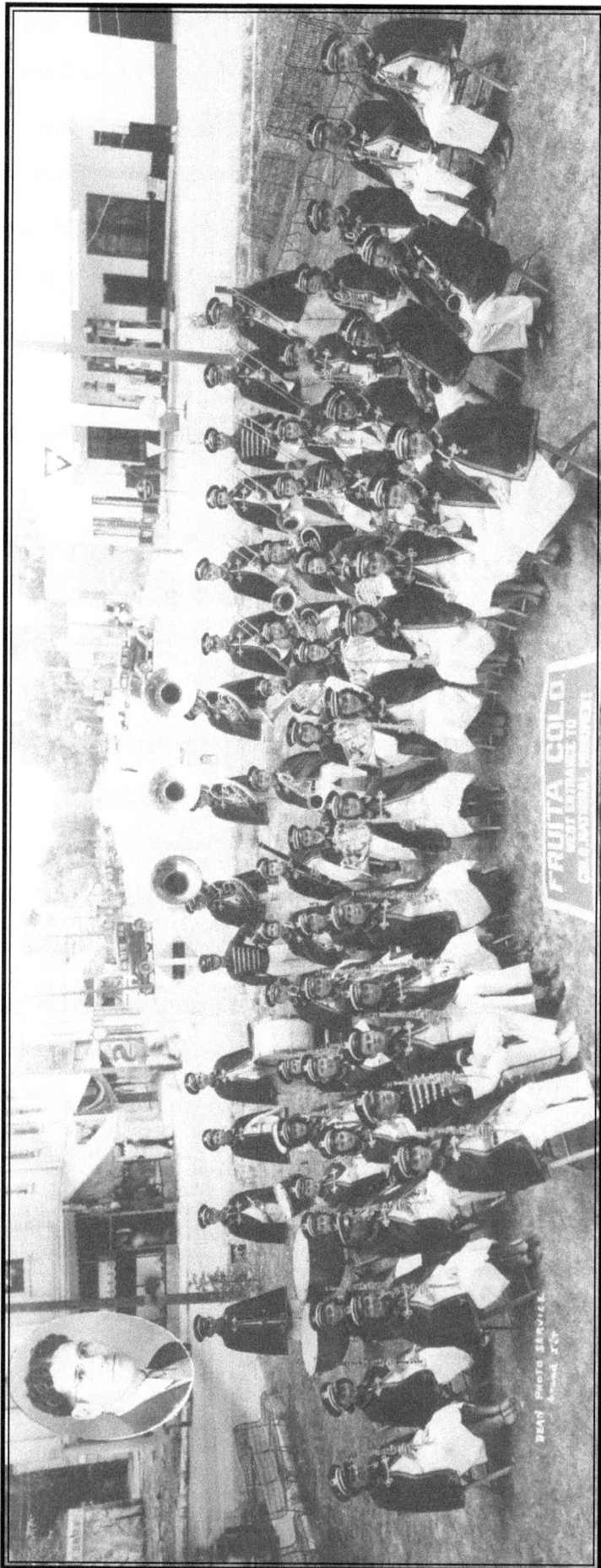

(Below) Fruita Union High School band, 1937-1938. National Champions at Provo, Utah. Front row L-R: Roy Eno, Virginia Durkee, Mildred Snodgrass, Raymond "Sammy" White, Joan Taylor, Patrice Pritchard, Dixie Lew Young, Miriam Sowers and Evelyn Scoles. Second row: Madge Watkins, Lois Gear, Theresa O'Connor, Eleanor Reed, Lucille Reed, Marie Havens, Eleanor Vaughn, Sarah Thirsk, LaVerne Somerville, Mary Crockett, Robert Burford, Betty Bird, William Goss, Rose Ellen Adams, Richard Goss, Clover Thirsk. Third row: Leola Cuddy, Delight Sheets, Sarah Ann Boughton, Mildred Roberts, Esther Bass, Sybil Mort, Jewel Crisman, Shirley Maile, Leland Hood, Lucille Glandon, Percy Sheets, Mervin Botkin, Lee Parish, Joyce Byers, Kenneth Rushing, Lawrence O'Connor, Howard Ilk, Floyd Crider, Raymond Botkin, Jim McCoy, Dean Glandon, Warren Nugent, Floyd Yourdon, Frank Pritchard and Lee Smith. Back row: Mildred Martin, Charles "Chick" Nichols-Band Director, Marvin Yourdon, Walter Tufly, Howard Ilk, Harold Mogensen, Lyle Barcus and Bill Beaslin. *(Photo courtesy of Mildred Martin Van Dover)*

177

Dick Wagaman who graduated in 1931 said the class of 1928 composed
the school fighting song "Wildcats" with Leland Lockett as spearhead.
Who ever or when ever they came into being – they still represent Fruita

wildcats

WILDCATS are we, Our team is backed with loyalty,

When the boys come on the field Let each one cheer,(Rah,
Rah,Rah.)

WILDCATS are we, The blue and white, Unfurled shall be

Ever o'er the conquest field, Fruita Union WILDCATS we.

**P
A
W**

POWER

Gay Johnson who graduated in 1927 said that the year he was a freshman
the coach had all the athletics teams choose the Wildcat for the mascot
and the colors of White and Blue for Fruita's High School.

(Page taken from "Fruita High School 100 Years)

178

The seniors dressed-up impersonating someone else on Senior Slouch Day. (Above) 1942, Johnny Rader, Tony Forilla and Earl Haller dressed as girls. Notice their figures. *(Photo courtesy of Helen Keffalos Dodson)*

(Center right) 1947, hobos in downtown Fruita: Genevieve Nichols, Wilma Maluy, Sally Chinn and Dorothy Bratton. *(Phyllis Likes Collection)*
(Lower right) 1947, seniors in downtown Fruita: Mary Ellen Cloyd, Uncle Sam; Albert Marinelli, cowboy singer; Deyon Davidson, you guess; Thelma Fry, Indian Princess; Betty Lynch and Dorothy Beaslin, cowgirls. Front: Dorothy Greer, Spanish Vaquero with Spanish maiden, Betty Gore. *(Phyllis Likes Collection)*

(Below) Freshman year, 1951. Maxine Cutler and Anna Jane Berry dressed in gunny sack dresses and carrying a sign around their neck that says "Olathe" when they were initiated into the Fruita Union High School Pep Club. The football team undoubtedly played Olathe that day. *(Phyllis Likes Collection)*

(Above left) Top Row: 1942, Mother goose, Helen Kovach; Bo-Peep, Jayne Snook; Miss Muffet, Anna High; Bottom Row: Jack & Jill, Helen Keffalos and Carmel Landini. (Above right) Hugh Wheeler, 1917 soldier; Helen Keffalos, Jack of Jack & Jill; Dale Parish, 1942 soldier. *(Photos courtesy of Helen Keffalos Dodson)*

Fruita Union High School Graduates

Fruita Times 12 Feb 1993, 5 Mar 1993

The class lists up through 1956 are taken from a booklet prepared by the Lower Valley Community Education Association. Later class lists are compiled from those published in the Fruita Times each spring.

Graduates from New Liberty:

1925 — Ruth Marie Alstatt
1926 — Milton Alstatt
1927 — Bessie Brayton
1928 — Viola Alstatt, Harold Carroll, Laura Johnson, Charles Mackintosh
1929 — Edith Alstatt, Billie Bowen, Thelma Gunst, Estellene Morrow
1930 — Dessie Black, Elizabeth Morrow, Inez Porter, Mildred Weir
1932 — Richard Kessinger, Vivian Porter
1933 — Ralph Foss, George Fisher, Arline Wassenberg
1934 — Rex Brisbin, Vauna Knapp, LaVerne Rowe
1935 — Merton Arpke, Paul Cutler, Edmund Daily, Edna Weir
1936 — Amos Alstatt, Lephia Foss, Clark Gerry
1937 — Carl Alstatt, JoAnn Bowen, Leon Daily, Mildred Raver, Arthur Shires, Harold Stotts
1937 — Darrel Maluy, Lawrence Morrow
1938 — Ruth Arpke, Ruth Banning, Edward Cutler, Lewis Likes
1940 — Mabel Brisbin, Mabel Currey
1941 — Rose Ellen Adams, Agnes Alstatt, Robert Brisbin, Thomas Currey, Harriet Cutler, Harry Cutler, Dale Maluy, Rex Maluy, Joe Meyer, Virginia Pacheco, Audie R. Potzner, James Pollock
1942 — Frank E. Currey, Louise Eileen Downing, Charles Pollock, Herman Jay Rowe
1943 — Elsie Louise Alstatt, Naomi Banning, Dorothy Cox, Marilyn May Maluy
1944 — Patty Maluy, Betty Pollock, Jack Pollock, Ben Rowe
1945 — Robert Alstatt, Edith Currey, Donald Downing, John Grimsby, Sam Grimsby, Frances Homedew, Clifford Kettle
1946 — Joan Marie Potzner, Claudia Taylor
1947 — Anna Belle Alstatt, Wilma Maluy, Murray Phillips
1948 — Ralph Banning, Earl Blasdel, Bruce Gerry, Norma Maluy, Ernest Paulson, Robert Pollock, Wylie Sanders
1949 — Glen Martinez, Becky Thompson, Lester Wilkinson
1950 — Orlene Corn, Dale Cutler, Lee Ann Maluy, Jimmie Martinez, Walter Pollock, Eugene Thomas
1951 — DeNelson Jones, Leatha Wynkoop, Fred Garcia
1952 — Leonard Gerry, Harold Martinez, Vernon Scoggin, Margaret Sisler
1953 — Ronnie Ashburn, Larry Paulson
1954 — Frank Alfred Berry, Nettie Ray Geeting, Reetus R. (Bud) Likes, Helen Sanders
1955 — Anna Jane Berry, Maxine Louise Cutler, Beverly Denton, Kenneth Gaymon, Cardon LeMoyne Jones
1956 — Charlene D. Ashburn, Tiburcio John Garcia
1957 — Darrel M. Barcus, Ruby Delores Cutler, Claude Harvey Denton, Ivan Leroy Likes, Jimmy Dick Tomlinson
1958 — Max V. Barlow, William W. Hawthorne, Patricia Ann White, Rudy R. Wilkinson
1959 — June Denton, Vic Thompson, Carol Underwood,
1960 — Luthera Barcus, Jerry Hawthorne, Kenneth Wynkoop
1961 — Madeline Jean Denton, Reginald Ernest Berry, Janette Kay Alstatt

1962 — Ronnie Ashburn, Glen Michael Denton, Eugene B. Wilkinson
1963 — Geraldine C. Barnes
1964 — David Kenneth Alstatt, Steven Faun Chaffin, Larry Eugene Overbye, Mabelann Post, Norma Louise Wells
1965 — Robert Duane Arpke, Delene Petrea Barcus, James E. Shires
1966 — Gary Lee Alstatt, Earlynn Elena Barcus, Linda Lou Post
1967 — Ronald G. Alstatt, Ernest Robert Denton, Leslie Ann Young, Edna Marie Shires
1968 — Edward Dean Alstatt, Reva Sue Post, Allen Lee Shires
1969 — Timothy Arpke, Patty Sue Maluy, Timmy Everett Tomlinson, Frances Young, Neta Young
1970 — Gerald Spencer Alstatt, Dale Russell Barnes, Warren Bruce Barnes, Donna Arlene Puckett
1971 — Nancy Gay Maluy, Vera Marie Post, Steven Lee Roberts, Rebecca Young
1972 — Gayle Marie Alstatt, Karen Joann Alstatt, Daniel Vincent Puckett
1973 — Ronald Eugene Puckett, Dale Allen Wells, Kathryn Young
1974 — Deborah (Debi) Kathleen Tomlinson
1975 — Betty Jo Young, Helen Young
1977 — John W. Young
1978 — Scott W. Young
1979 — Timothy Gale Puckett, Mikki Dora Tomlinson
1982 — Jimmy Dick Jr. Tomlinson

Graduates From Mack:

1924 — Roy Wagaman
1925 — John Kiefer, Margaret Trevarthan
1926 — Orval Wagaman
1927 — Eleanor Barr, Helen Trevarthan
1928 — William Eddings
1929 — Jerome Kiefer, Agnes Kiefer, Opal Wesner
1930 — Eula Rader, Henry Simpson, Madonna Weimer
1931 — Betty Booth, Earl Wagaman
1933 — Oscar Sweitzer
1934 — Naomi Cox, Josie MacTaggart, Bennie Pacheco, Mary Simpson
1935 — Barbara Barr
1937 — Douglas Booth, Manuel Pacheco
1938 — Tom Barr, Roy Eno
1939 — Jim McCoy
1940 — Vernon Brandon, Margaret Kiefer, Goldie L. Wesner
1941 — Delores Collins, Cecelia Anne Kiefer
1942 — Blayne Barr, Edward Collins, Helen Millie Keffalos
1943 — Floyd Edward Cook, George Keffalos, Charlie W. Pacheco, Ernest Robertson, Delores Imogene Smith.
1944 — Ralph Slaugh, Richard Smith, Wilbur Smith
1946 — Beatrice Cook, Gladys Davies, Shirley Smith
1947 — Milton Cox, Deyon Davidson, Erma Slaugh
1948 — Richard Keith
1949 — Emmett Collins
1950 — Gale Cox, Duane Wagaman
1951 — Josie Achuleta
1952 — Kathleen Komatos
1953 — Jacqueline Kelly
1954 — Robert Saunders, Thomas Saunders
1955 — Gracia Davies
1957 — Norma L. Eddings
1958 — Andrew J. Serve
1959 — Josie Brewster, Anne Serve, Tony Serve
1960 — Leah Kelly
1961 — Gerald Glen Slaugh
1963 — Nancy L. Eddings, Michael J. Serve
1967 — Annette Marie Kelly
1968 — Rita Colleen Kiefer
1969 — Danny Ross Monger
1970 — Byron Walter Kelly, Duane Michael Kiefer
1972 — Allen Leo Kiefer
1977 — Jennifer L. Kiefer

Fruita Union High School Graduates
Who Became Teachers or Land Owners

1902	Bessie Cox	Teacher	Mack
	Bessie Cox	Landowner	Mack Mesa
1909	Edna Penfield	Teacher	Mack
1910	Ethel Cox	Landowner	Mack Mesa
1911	Lucille Gnagey	Landowner	New Liberty
1913	William Pollock	Landowner	New Liberty
1914	Faye Wagner	Teacher	Mack
1915	Guy Gerry	Landowner	New Liberty
1917	Gladys Hill	Teacher	New Liberty
1918	Margaret Weimer	Teacher	Mack
1919	Lester Sumnicht	Landowner	New Liberty
1923	Ruth Smith	Teacher	Mack
1924	Ena Sumnicht	Teacher	Mack
1926	Enid Starr	Teacher	Mack
1927	Bessie Brayton	Landowner	New Liberty
1928	Harold Carroll	Teacher	New Liberty
	Mildred Hogsett	Teacher	Mack
1930	Inez Porter	Teacher	New Liberty
1932	Richard Kessinger	Landowner	New Liberty
	Mamie Hull (Post)	Landowner	New Liberty
1934	Dwight Barcus	Landowner	New Liberty
	Petrea Mogenson	Landowner	New Liberty
	Delbert Jerome	Teacher	New Liberty
	Josephine Price	Teacher	New Liberty
1943	Naomi Laurene Conrad	Landowner	New Liberty

Rural Electricity

A most wonderful thing happened in 1935 that greatly benefited the rural areas, not only in Grand Valley, but throughout the country. The Roosevelt administration established the **Rural Electrification Administration**—an agency authorized to finance low-interest government loans to Electric Cooperatives for the building of electrical power distribution systems in farming areas. The agency soon became known as **REA**; in 1936 Congress made it a permanent government program. Up to that time only one farm in ten in the United States enjoyed the luxury of electrical power. In the New Liberty community, electric lights were something that people hardly dared dream about. In the Grand Junction area a few farmers were fortunate enough to have Public Service power available to them. There were a few farms in the valley that had their own small power plants to provide electric lights, and perhaps radios, but that was all. To most farmers in the lower valley the luxury of refrigeration powered by electricity seemed beyond the wildest dream!

Then came **REA**! On 2 June 1936 a group of farmers met in Fruita to officially organize a cooperative named Grand Valley Rural Power Lines. Chosen as the first board of directors were Orval Herron, C. W. Likes, Rex Rankin, J. A. Edling, C. E. Blumenshine, G. B. Linton, C. S. Saxton, J. F. Shults and Stanley Cronk. Herron was named the first president of the association and immediately the services of Attorney W. R. Hinman were secured to prepare papers of incorporation signed 12 August 1936.

Committees were formed to tour various areas in the valley to sign up subscribers for the proposed power line.

Among those who served as committee-men in the lower valley were Orval Herron, Clyde W. Likes and Robert M. Cox. By late 1936 some 638 members in the valley west of Grand Junction were signed up for 139 miles of prospective line. Construction began on 1 February 1937, and power was turned on 27 September 1937.

Potential power for the new system was already in place since water from the dam built in Debeque Canyon to divert water into the High Line canal also sent water to a generating plant. Public Service Company of Grand Junction had leased the power from the plant at the time of construction. Its lease would expire near the time Grand Valley Rural Power Lines needed power.

Public Service soon began to realize that REA could possibly cut in on some of their territory, so the shenanigans began! Public Service first asked REA officials to bypass several thickly populated areas that were close to their lines, but the board, knowing that Public Service had their chance to serve these people for many years, stood firm and proceeded to plan to provide power in those areas. They did, however, make a gentleman's agreement not to parallel each other's lines. It was soon discovered that Public Service was trying to sign up some people north of Grand Junction and on east toward Fruitvale and Clifton—offering

Three of the original nine-member board of directors which first organized the oldest rural electric cooperative in the state of Colorado — Grand Valley Rural Power Lines of Grand Junction — are pictured above. They are L-R, C. W. Likes, G. B. Linton and Rex Rankin. Rankin, a prominent Grand Junction businessman, served from 1936 until he entered the military in 1942. Likes served from 1936 until 1949 and Linton completed a 19-year term in 1955 — without missing a single board meeting. *(Photo and data taken from the Colorado Rural Electric News)*

cheaper rates and quick completion of service.

By the time the initial phase of construction was complete many farm homes were wired and waiting for the big event. Almost without exception homes were wired for lights, refrigerators and radios, but nothing more. People could not imagine need for any more than that! Because that created a problem, many homes had to later upgrade their systems to fit the needs for additional electrical power.

Also, a government program to provide loans to bring telephone service to farm homes began about the same time as REA. Life on the farms began to change for the better from that time on!

In February 1996, in celebration of the 60th year since its organization, an interesting history of Grand Valley Rural Power Lines, written by G. B. Linton, was published in the *Colorado Country Life Magazine*. Mr. Linton was a member of the first board of directors from 1936 to 1955 and the written history covered that period of time. His history confirms our story.

Chapter Seven

More Challenges

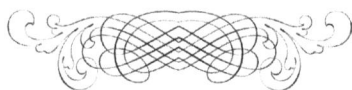

Prohibition & Moonshining

The hotly debated issue of prohibition made the headlines on 15 January 1919: "Nationwide Prohibition may be ratified by the states during the next 24 hours." On 1 July 1919 a new law, known as the 18th Amendment, (it was commonly called "Prohibition") went into effect, prohibiting the sale of' "alcoholic beverages" or "intoxicating liquors." Not everyone agreed with the new law; it led to "boot-legging," or illegal manufacture and sales of liquor. Government officials found the law hard to enforce. Anyone who desired to get some "white lightning" could do so if he knew where to go.

A headline on the front page of a January 1931 issue of *The Daily Sentinel* says: "A huge still was found near the state line." The article goes on to relate that W. F. Smiley was arrested in Fruita for drunkenness, and after being questioned by Sheriff Lumley and deputies, he admitted knowing about a still located on his property about five miles south of the State Line Store. Smiley had moved his family to Fruita and leased his property to a man by the name of Kelley. No evidence was found that Smiley was involved in the illegal enterprise.

Many were aware that Ola Lander of Mack had a still in the canyon down river near Cisco, Utah, which proved to be quite lucrative for him and convenient for the imbibers in the lower valley. His illegal business eventually led to the deaths of Ola's daughter, Ethel, age 14, and her cousin Tommy Keith, age 23, who went with Ola one Saturday night to retrieve some "white-lightning" for others who were having a high time at the Saturday night dance in Mack. To reach the still the youngsters attempted to cross the river in a small rowboat in the darkness. It

was during the spring high runoff and the boat was struck by a floating tree, causing the boat to overturn in midstream. The two young people drowned.

An article in *The Daily Sentinel* of 22 May 1933 telling of the accident, reported Lander and the youngsters were there on a "fishing outing." Their bodies were never recovered; however, months later a skeleton was found on the river bank several miles downstream that was believed to be the remains of Tommy Keith.

It was rumored that Vern Snavely operated a still in New Liberty. An article in *The Daily Sentinel* of 27 October 1934 removed any doubt we may have had about Vern's extra-curricular activities.

LOWER VALLEY RANCHER HELD AS MOONSHINER

Federal Agents returned late Friday afternoon from a raid on the Vernon Snavely ranch and reported the seizure of a 15 gallon still, 60 gallons of mash, three and one half gallons of moonshine liquor, together with other paraphernalia used in the manufacture of illicit booze.

A story about the Everetts brothers, written by Orlin Corn and included later in the Corn biography, tells of another illicit activity.

The situation with illegal drugs in the present day and age is similar to that time. In 1932 there was a political war being waged between the "Wets" and the "Drys." Wets claimed that prohibition was the cause of much crime. To a great extent their claim was right — illegal "Rum Runners," "Speakeasies" and "Bootleggers" were a force to contend with across the nation, but especially in the more populated areas.

Members of congress began drafting a bill to repeal prohibition (or the 18th Amendment), and in December of 1932 it passed the House, but the Senate rejected it. A couple of states, California and Arizona, took the bull by the horns and repealed the amendment on their own. The bill was passed by congress in March 1933. Individual State legislators were to pass on the bill for each state. By December 1933, 36 states had approved it. It was then legal to purchase 3.2% beer in any licensed cafe, pool hall, etc. As for Colorado, prohibition officially came to an end on 3 December 1933. It seems rather strange that there would still be need for bootleggers after prohibition had been repealed.

The Great Depression

Those who are old enough recall the "Great Depression" in the 1930s and remember the hardships brought on by the depressed economy throughout the nation. Herbert Hoover was elected president about the time of the stock market crash in 1928, which marked the beginning of the collapse of the economy. Banks went broke; businesses were bankrupted. Many farmers defaulted on their loans, so their farms, equipment and livestock were sold at a fraction of their former value. Soup and bread lines to feed the unemployed millions became commonplace across the country. People throughout the nation who were hard hit formed groups to march on Washington demanding something be done. An item in *The Daily Sentinel* in December 1932 claimed that farm income was only half what it had been in 1929. It is likely the income was very good, even in 1929.

Of course the blame was placed on Hoover's Republican Administration. At one point, late in the year of 1932, a bill of impeachment was introduced in Congress in an attempt to get rid of Hoover. That year proved to be a banner year for the Democrats — Franklin Delano Roosevelt was elected president in November in a landslide victory! To top that off, Democrats gained a majority in Congress!

Various "Reconstruction" bills were enacted by Congress, adding to our language several new acronyms such as "WPA" (Works Progress Administration), "CCC" (Civilian Conservation Corps, which began in April 1933), etc. The "Public Works" projects were very beneficial to both the nation and the individuals who provided the man-power for soil conservation, building of roads, and improving the park systems. It put a few dollars into the pockets of individuals who otherwise would have been unemployed. Slowly the nation's economy began to recover. The effects of the depression continued until the beginning of World War II.

Though times were tough for the farmers of New Liberty and Mack Mesa during the depression, they fared much better than many among the poorer classes throughout the nation. After all, farmers could raise much of their food supply — something that most city folks could not do.

Following is a poem that was printed in the *Fruit Times*. We don't have the date of the issue, but would like to use it for the same reason they did—in hopes it will strike a responsive chord in all our readers over the age of 55:

The Great Depression

Listen, let me tell you about a thing I know;
  About the great depression, when employment was low;
But we were sort of lucky, in a certain kind of way;
  For we lived on a farm and had no bills to pay;
We had no conveniences to lighten the load
  Sometimes a little hungry and sometimes a little cold;
We worked very hard, but it did us no harm;
  In the days of the depression down on the farm.
Our work began at 4 o'clock in the morn;
  We'd feed the cows and chickens, hoe the cotton and the corn;
We'd take a break at lunch time when the bell would sound;
  Then back to the hot field 'till the sun went down;
Didn't get in much trouble, for we had no time.
  And we didn't have no money, not even a dime:
But we were tired and happy when the day was through;

We felt we had accomplished what we set out to do.
When the vegetables all ripened, it was so grand;
  We were always so glad when we had them all canned;
We had milk and butter from our cows for sure;
  It tasted so delicious because it was so pure;
There weren't any Government sanitary laws;
  We'd strain the milk and drink as it was;
Or we'd put it in a bucket and drop in the well;
  It would come out so cold and tasted really swell.
We attended school at the old school hours;
  Where the teachers were so strict, we were quiet as a mouse;
From the old text books, our lessons we learned,
  By the light of the kerosene lamp we burned;
The teachers used paddles when we didn't behave;
  And the parents backed them every step of the way;
Dads and Moms were always seen and heard, and
  When we spoke to elders, "Ma'am" and "Sir" were the words.
We made up our own games, in our very own way;
  Using bottles for dolls, wrapped in rags, we'd play;
We played jump rope with an ole plow line;
  And we'd make a bed of straw from a tree of pine;
Used empty cans and bottles, in our house play;
  Which we'd sell at our grocery store that we made;
We'd play a game of Hopscotch or Hide and Go-Seek;
  And sometimes we'd go swimming in the water in the creek.
We used wood for fuel, that we cut off the land;
  And the family wash, it was done all by hand;
The iron was heated on an ole wood stove;
  Always a little too hot or a little too cold;
Life wasn't easy, but if you didn't mind the work;
  A whole lot of grit; a whole lot of dirt;
Then you'd be happy; it's a good place to rear,
  A family on the farm in the depression years.
So you see, we had a good time, as well as the bad;
  And we really feel better about the life we had;
To face such times of troubles, with little earthly goods;
  But the good Lord brought us thru it, as we prayed He
would;

And it wouldn't hurt the people of this day and time,
  To live thru a depression; maybe love they'd find;
If they had no conveniences, and they had to do without,
  Then they'd know what labor is and what it's all about.
Now, I could write a book about those old antiques;
  That you treasure so much and think are so neat;
But if we had to go back to those old-fashioned ways;
  It wouldn't be so easy; with those antiques, you'd slave;
You won't have time or money to run up and down the
streets;
  And you sure can't be too choosy about what you hope to eat;
I'm still very ignorant, but these lessons I've learned,
  by darn; About the great depression down on the farm.

Kate Godwin Mathews

World War II

Shortly after Hitler's coming into power in Germany in 1933 war clouds began to gather over Europe. It had been only a short time since the end of World War I in 1918, which was said to be "The War to End All Wars." After Hitler proclaimed that "Conquest is not only a right, it is a duty," several countries in Europe began to feel threatened. Shortly thereafter the "Third Reich" set about to take back all of the countries taken away from Germany at the end of World War I. France and Great Britain jumped in to help defend Poland, and after Hitler's attempt to invade Great Britain failed, he turned toward Russia, which resulted in a horrendous loss of life on both sides.

The United States went to great lengths to avoid being involved in the conflict, even though some U. S. ships were sunk by German submarines — Germany claiming the ships were illegally carrying munitions to Great Britain. Nevertheless, as the threat of war became greater, munitions factories in the United States began gearing up for production of weapons of war; aircraft factories began building various types of airplanes; shipyards began building ships, all in preparation for defense of our country. Restrictions were placed on production of civilian automobiles and auto factories began turning out military vehicles: tanks, trucks, artillery, and the new four-wheel drive Jeep.

This new activity soon phased out the unemployment problem — the great depression of the 1930s was over!

On 16 September 1940 a draft law was enacted by the U. S. Congress, requiring all men between the ages of 18 and 37 to register. Selective Service Administration was organized to oversee the registration and selection of men for military training. Selection was handled much like a lottery. Each registrant was assigned a number and each week in every draft board a large quantity of registration numbers written on slips of paper were placed in a tumbler and someone was selected to draw a specified number of slips. Notifications were sent out to those selected. Names of those selected by the Mesa County draft board were published in *The Daily Sentinel* each week.

After the beginning of draft registration and activity in defense industries, large numbers of young men and women across the nation began to enlist in various branches of the military. Then, on 7 December 1941, the Japanese Navy staged a sneak attack on Pearl Harbor on the Island of Oahu, destroying a large number of our ships and planes. Within hours the United States declared war and became fully involved in the conflict. For a time the United States suffered terrible defeats at the hands of the Japanese forces, both from sea and from land. The Japs had the advantage in the Pacific for some time — it seemed a very long time before the Allies began to show superiority.

In the Atlantic theatre, Germany mounted a very successful campaign with their submarine fleet, sinking almost as many ships as we could float in that direction, some in the Gulf of Mexico and others just off our eastern shore!

As the war effort took effect, the ship builders worked themselves into a frenzy, turning out cargo ships, aircraft carriers and warships of various sizes and shapes. Airplane factories began turning out B17s, B24s, P38s, P40s, etc. in unprecedented numbers, trying to gain an advantage and to offset the tremendous losses suffered in the early days of the conflict.

As the war effort increased, the shipyards and aircraft factories began working around the clock — in some instances seven days per week! Life in the cities near the factories adjusted accordingly. Cafes, theaters, dance-halls, bowling allies, etc., were open day and night, so that people who had to work the night shifts could be accommodated just as well as those working in the daylight hours.

Across the nation thousands of men were being trained to man the new ships and airplanes. During 1942, and particularly in 1943, the news media carried tragic stories daily of crashes of planes on all types on routine training flights, with the subsequent loss of crew members of up to 12 or more. At the same time, many men were lost at sea, in both the Atlantic and Pacific, as their ships and planes were destroyed by the enemy. It was a trying time! We owe much to the men who sacrificed their lives in the cause of freedom!

To offset our losses in the early days of the war, in August of 1944 the news media announced that in five years, 65,000 ships of all classes had been built by our ship-builders. It was also announced in September 1944 that in the *first eight months of that year* the nation's aircraft factories had produced 11,000 heavy bombers! Who would have thought such numbers were possible!

During that time women became a large part of the work force, becoming welders, riveters and assemblers, thus releasing men to serve in the military. There was even a song "Rosie The Riveter", which became popular during the war. Some of you youngsters might want to ask your grandmothers to tell about their experiences in building ships and airplanes! Women were also enlisted in branches of the military — WACS, WAVES, SPARS, etc. They did much of the clerical work in their respective organizations to free men for other duties.

Since so many of our boys and girls were involved in the military, both in training and in combat, United Service Organizations (USO) were set up to help keep them entertained and rewarded in some small way for their patriotism and the sacrifices they were making. Many thousands of volunteers operated recreation centers, both in the States and overseas. Military personnel could go to those centers to dance or to be entertained by well-known performers, or just to associate with the civilian population. USO provided libraries and free cigarettes and coffee, and in a few instances, free beer. Our soldiers and sailors appreciated having a place to relax and lay aside their cares!

Members of big name bands and popular comedians spent much time traveling overseas to entertain the troops at or near the battle fronts. Comedian Bob Hope probably spent more time doing shows around the world than any other entertainer. He always had a back-up group of well known singers, musicians, dancers and other comedians.

During that period of time many popular

bands, songs, singers and singing groups were born. Who among us in a certain age group would not remember a young singer who literally created riots when the teen-age girls would scramble over each other just to touch him, or even to see him, and would scream and yell "Frankie!" — some even fainted! Nowadays some of his fans fondly refer to him as "Ol' Blue Eyes."

Do any of you remember the "Zoot Suiters?" That fad began with an ethnic minority group, particularly in the Los Angeles area, who dressed in clothing that marked them differently than others. A song was written about the "Zoot Suiters," it became very popular! The song referred to the garb as the "Zoot Suit with the Reet Pleet." The pants of the Zoot Suit were made very full in the waist area, tapering down to extremely narrow cuffs. The coat was extra long, including, for an accessory, a long chain anchored at the belt and hanging in a loop almost to the pants cuffs.

As the war effort escalated and so many people left to join the military and to work in the war industries, a shortage of manpower to manage the farms across the nation became a real problem. Since many farmers did not have enough help to get their crops harvested, government officials began to bring in German prisoners of war as well as Japanese/American internees who had been uprooted from their homes on the west coast and placed in camps scattered throughout the western states. Mexican Nationals were also brought in from across the border.

At last the tide of war began to turn. The allies began to gain an advantage over both Germany and Japan! *The Daily Sentinel* published stories almost daily of heroic deeds by our men in battle.

It was reported on 25 May 1944 that 6,000 allied planes dropped 8,000 tons of bombs on various targets that day on areas occupied by the Germans. This was preliminary to the "D-Day" landing on the Normandy coast 6 June 1944. Thousands of Allied troops supported by some 11,000 planes and 4,000 ships stormed ashore. This was the beginning of a slow and costly march across German occupied territory.

General Dwight D. Eisenhower was appointed supreme commander of the Allied invading forces - he ordered the troops to accept nothing but complete victory!

Russian troops were marching with a vengeance toward Germany from the east! They had suffered some terrible defeats at the hands of the Germans, who, in the year before, had advanced far into Russia's home land. Russia's ally in that battle was the terrible winter weather; German troops were not as well equipped for extreme cold.

The steady march continued until the Germans surrendered to the Allies on 7 May 1945. That became known as "V-E Day."

As prisoners were freed the world began to learn of terrible atrocities committed by the Germans — many prisoners had been executed, or were starved, beaten, or overworked. This is not to mention the systematic execution of *millions* of Jews. After peace was established the Allied military leaders set about to identify, arrest and bring to trial the German leaders who had committed those crimes. It's interesting to read about the intense fear some of them exhibited with the prospects of being confronted in court with their terrible deeds. Hitler's brave officers proved to be cowards!

Some of the Germans assumed false identity and escaped before they could be captured. Some eventually worked their way out of the country, many of them ended up in North and South America. Even today, over 50 years later, some of those men are still being tracked down, arrested and brought to trial.

In the Pacific, Allied troops began to slowly and painfully regain various islands across the vast expanse of water until finally General Douglas McArthur was able to fulfill the promise he made as he left the Philippines in 1942: "I shall return!"

During the latter days of war in the Pacific Theatre a base for the B-29 "Superfortress" bombers was established on Tinian, one of the Marianas Islands. These huge bombers made nightly raids on the Japanese homeland destroying factories and military installations. Many of our planes were shot down and the crew members captured. A large number of those boys were executed and others were subjected to extreme cruelty and starvation.

Most of the islands of importance to U.S. military strategy were recaptured by the end of 1944, and on 9 January 1945 the Allies invaded Luzon, in the Philippines. In February, Iwo Jima was stormed by U. S. Troops, and on 1 April 1945 our troops landed on Okinawa. By this time Japan had begun to realize they were losing the war. The Philippines, Iwo Jima and Okinawa were extremely costly battles. The Japanese were dug in and defended those islands to the very death; our troops suffered severe losses.

On 6 August 1945 an American B-29 bomber named "Enola Gay" dropped an atomic bomb on Hiroshima, destroying more than half the city. Three days later another atomic bomb was dropped on Nagasaki. The next day, 10 August, Japan opened peace negotiations. On 14 August they accepted Allied surrender terms, and by 2 September signed the official surrender. This day became known as "V-J Day." At last the long war was over!

Then, as prisoners were released, the Allies began to hear tales of terrible abuse and starvation committed by the Japanese military upon prisoners of war — the same story as in Germany! Many of their generals and lesser officers were arrested and imprisoned as war criminals, soon to stand trial. Many of them committed suicide rather than face their accusers in the military courts.

Then began the process of discharging millions of men and women from the military. As they began to return to civilian life there were some unemployment problems. There was a period of labor unrest as well; many strikes occurred before we were able to settle into a life with some resemblance to prewar times.

We will not attempt to name here all the men and women from our communities who served in the military or were involved in some branch of the defense industry during World War II. However, as you read through the biographies you will learn of the involvement of different individuals in the war effort. At least three New Liberty and Mack boys were lost in battle, never to return: Lawrence Morrow, Delbert Slaugh and Vernon Brandon. Others made a career of the military or continued to live and work in areas where they worked during the war.

Several of our lower valley boys distinguished themselves in military service in World War II — look for stories of Bob Brisbin, Lawrence Morrow, Clark Gerry, Dale and Rex Maluy, Leon Daily, Vernon Brandon and others in their family biographies — they did more than their share! Some families had several children in the military: Felix Pacheco, five sons; Saul Pacheco, three sons; Leonard Slaugh, three sons; Alstatts, two sons and a daughter; Leonard B. Rich of Mack, six sons and a daughter — Marjorie in the WAC, Leonard, Steve, and Jerold in the Army; George, Frank and Bobby in the Navy. And there were others — talk about patriotism!!

Most of our men and women from Mack and New Liberty who were involved in the war effort returned home and became part of our communities again, but we can readily see that World War II changed Mack and New Liberty forever!

Let us not forget the price that was paid for the freedom so many of us take for granted. While the memories of horrors endured will always remain with the men and women who cam back, they at least came back. For that they are forever grateful. They will never forget their buddies who weren't so lucky. May the rest of the world also remember.

Freedom Is Not Free

I watched the flag pass by one day,
It fluttered in the breeze;
A young Marine saluted it,
And then he stood at ease.

I looked at him in uniform,
So young, so tall, so proud;
With hair cut square and eyes alert,
He'd stand out in any crowd.

I thought . . . how many men like him
Had fallen through the years?
How many died on foreign soil?
How many mothers' tears?

How many pilots' planes shot down
How many died at sea
How many foxholes were soldiers' graves
No, Freedom is not Free.

I heard the sound of Taps one night,
When everything was still;
I listened to the bugler play,
And felt a sudden chill;

I wondered just how many times
That Taps had meant "Amen"
When a flag had draped a coffin
Of a brother or a friend;

I thought of all the children,
Of the mothers and the wives,
Of fathers, sons and husbands.
With interrupted lives.

I thought about a graveyard
At the bottom of the sea,
Of unmarked graves in Arlington.
No. Freedom is not Free!

-Cadet Major Kelly Strong
Air Force Junior ROTC
Homestead Senior High School,
Homestead, Florida, 1988

A War Ration Book issued to Helen Keffalos in 1942 during World War II. Sugar, gas, and tires are three products rationed. The three stamps attached at the bottom are what is left of this book. Usually a ration book was issued every six months and that person could buy one of these products according to the amount of stamps/points one was issued. A person had to ration to be able to buy what was needed during that time period. (*Courtesy of Helen Keffalos Dodson*)

Chapter Eight

Nowadays

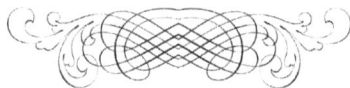

History in the Making

Gradually changes have come about in Mack and New Liberty. Most farms and businesses have changed owners, and new businesses have been developed. Some farms have been purchased as a place to live in the country while the owners work in town, or as a place to develop a business to serve the public.

Mack

Mack has lost some of its businesses and homes and has changed personality completely. The Mack School, the Last Chance Store, the old post office and Frank's Garage are gone and have been replaced by a pasture. The Mack Cafe is a private home, the liquor store next to it is gone and next to that a building was built for a business, but is presently empty. The Desert Gateway Store, Kelly's Rock Shop (now G G & M Rock Shop), the new post office, Doris Archuleta's Cafe (now Pork Barrel Cafe), two private homes, the Mack School teacherage owned and lived in by Billy and Charlene Ashburn Francisco, and Pappy's Country Store and Liquor Store are most of what now constitutes the town of Mack. West of Mack, the Harold's Desert Inn (now Colorado Club and Restaurant) is still in business. The D&RGW Railroad has a new name. It became part of the Southern Pacific Railroad in early 1997 which is now part of the Union Pacific Railroad.

But — history is in the making. Country Jam USA has come to Mack on the old Kiefer farm and Leonard Rich is in the process of subdividing the Rich farm, north and across the highway from Country Jam USA. There is a small airplane service airport north of Mack on Mack Mesa, a garden nursery north of Mack on 10 Road and a couple of out-of-the-home businesses.

Desert Gateway Store

Information is from courthouse records, thanks to Darrell Maluy's extensive research. Information is also used from Clyde Wright and Frank Overbye's histories.

Desert Gateway Store is the oldest business in Mack still in existence. The first information we have on the store is in Clyde Wright's history. He states that his folks, Chester "Chet" and Vera, bought a garage and store in Mack when he was four-and-a-half years old. That would make it the summer of 1925. We have no record who Chet bought it from. According to Clyde, there was a garage and store with a house in back.

On 1 October 1928 there was a warranty deed issued to Mattie B. Maltby for $500 for purchase of the property. Mattie was Chet's mother and undoubtedly helped him buy it. She doesn't appear on any other records.

Frank Overbye's history states that in 1928 he went to work for Ed Stout and Harley Wilkerson as a mechanic in a garage in Mack. We assume that it was Chet's garage, as there is no evidence of any other garage at that time.

In July, 1933, Chet Wright and W. C. Davis signed a lease for one year to White Eagle Oil Corporation, a Delaware company. The garage was to be known as Mack Garage and Service Station. White Eagle agreed to supply the following.

2 – 10-gallon clear-vision hand-operated gasoline pumps.
2 – 550-gallon underground gasoline storage tanks, pipe and fitting
3 – 30-gallon Bennett High Boy Lube tanks
2 – 60-gallon Milwaukee lubrication tanks

It was the first full-service gas station in Mack.

Chet must have sold his half interest in the garage in 1937. In January he took out a lien on his farm in New Liberty with Independent Lumber Company for material to improve the house on their farm. He paid the lien off 28 November 1937, apparently with the money from the garage and store.

On 13 December 1937, George A. Davis sold his one-half interest in the Mack Garage to Alice W. Davis. There is no evidence that W. C. Davis, partner with Chet in 1933, is related to or is the same person as George A. Davis. The authors remember that George and Alice Ward Davis were married.

On 7 September 1938 Alice W. Davis, also known as Mrs. Alice Hitner, took out a lien with contractors, Eric Hansen, J. A. Ambrose, H. H. Sypolt and R. T. Mayne. The lien states:

> The said lien is held for and account of a contract for labor and services, under which the claimants herein altered, added to, and repaired a building located in the Town of Mack, Mesa County, Colorado, owned by the said Alice W. Davis, also known as Mrs. Alice Hitner, said building being designated as "The Mack Garage," and also known as "The Desert Gateway Store."

This is the first record of the name "Desert Gateway Store."

Sometime during Alice's ownership, she undoubtedly added to the size of the property. When she sold the property to Ira Carpenter in November, 1946, it consisted of considerably more land. (See above drawing .) Interestingly, her name on the warranty deed to Ira was, Alice W. Ferrell, formerly Alice I. Ward. Ward is believed to be her maiden name. She evidently changed her name and husbands several times.

On 18 November 1957 Ira Carpenter sold to

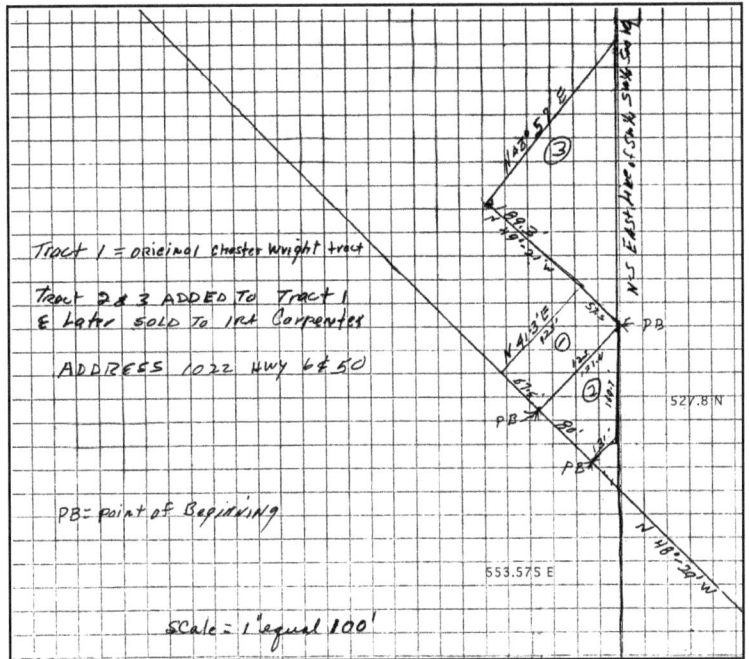

A drawing by Darrell Maluy from the property descriptions on the lien, lease and warranty deeds. *(Courtesy of Darrell Maluy)*

Ray and Fern Muths and they sold it to Delbert E. and Barbara K. Hahn, 27 March 1974. Raymond H. and Alice L. Wilson bought it in 3 October 1975 then sold it to Gary N. and Deanna L. Mead on 25 October 1977. Terrell L. and LaJetta Bowers bought it on 22 September 1981 and sold it to David W. and Patricia Lynch on 18 April 1986. David and Patricia sold it to the present owners, Tommy J. Smith and Barbara A. Stander on 20 November 1990. The business and building are still going strong after possibly 75 years.

G G & M Rock Shop

Information is from Walter and Ruth Gates.

G G & M Rock Shop is owned by Walter and Ruth Gates. They bought the shop and rock collection from Marie Kelly, in 1991. Walter does the cutting of the stones and makes the jewelry.

The building is part of the original Uintah Mack Hotel. After the hotel's closure in 1939, Frank "Red" Davies and family bought the hotel and made it their home. In 1953 Vern and Marie

Kelly bought it, and made a portion of it into Kelly's Rock Shop. Vern died in 1984, and Marie lived there until she sold it to the Gates in 1991..

Pork Barrel Cafe

Information from Sioux Robbins.

Pork Barrel Cafe was originally Doris Archuleta's Cafe. Doris built the cafe and started operating it in 1971. Sioux Robbins bought the building from Doris Archuleta in 1993 after it had been closed for two years. It is located in the center of Mack on the south side of U. S. Highway 6&50.

Sioux specializes in pork, which she raises on her farm in New Liberty. The pork is all USDA approved and very good quality. Besides regular meals, she has special diet dishes for senior citizens and also does catering. The cafe has a very "homey" atmosphere with good, homemade meals.

Pappy's Country Store and Liquor Store

Information from Ken Hansen.

The store is located on U. S. Highway 6&50 on the west end of Mack. The building was built in about 1956 by Robert Arpke as a sandwich and dairy freeze place. He had it quite a few years after which it changed hands a couple of times. It then became a liquor store and in November 1989 Ken and Jan Hansen bought it and changed it into a grocery and liquor store.

Colorado Club and Restaurant

Information from Virginia Nelson and Jake Smith.

The Colorado Club and Restaurant at 964 U.S. Highway 6&50, west of Mack, was originally Harold's Desert Inn. It was built by Charles Nelson and sons, Lloyd, Floyd "Tiny" and Elmer in the winter of 1949. The club was named in honor of Charles' son, Harold.

Harold had seen a cafe that he liked and started making plans to build one like it. That was interrupted when he joined the Air Corps during World War II. Harold was killed when his plane was shot down. Charles chose Mack near the desert to build the cafe in memory of Harold.

It was the first cafe to serve alcohol outside the city limits in Mesa County. Charles and Grace Nelson operated it as a family club. On Saturday nights there was live music and dancing. Families would bring their children with them and have a nice time.

When Charles' health started failing he sold it in 1963 or 1964 to Bennie Seavers. It has changed hands several times since then and most recently Jake and Mary Smith bought it from Edith Brow in January 1975.

Jake and Mary renamed the cafe "Colorado Club and Restaurant." They have a restaurant and dance hall, RV court with a dozen or more hookups and spaces. They serve Mexican/American food and have a country band Friday and Saturday nights, plus a jam session on Sundays. The club is open from 12-Noon to 2 a.m. Tuesdays through Sundays. They have hosted a few weddings held there during the last 20 years, and serve about six wedding receptions a year.

Patio Gardens

Information from Geri Robinson.

Patio Gardens is located on 1748 10 Road north of Mack. It is owned by Tim and Geri Robinson. They built the nursery themselves in 1994 with the idea of being primarily a wholesale contract business, but the retail business has done very well, also. They have retail customers from Cisco to Grand Junction. Tim and Geri feel there are very good people in the area and they appreciate how supportive the community has been.

Mack Mesa Airport

Information from Marjy Hartman and an article from the *Fruita Times*.

The Mack Mesa Airport is located on Section 6 Township 2N and Range 3W on the hilltop north of Davidson's former homestead which was later sold to Guy Leach. The address is 1048 R Rd., Mack, Colorado 81525. It had its beginning in 1964. Government land in Mesa County, that didn't qualify for homesteading, was put up for sale and the above parcel was included. The party that bought it had to qualify by already owning some land nearby. John Hartman owned what used to be the Hollinger homestead south of the airstrip property. He was involved with airplanes and so was very interested in the government land for its geographical possibility of supporting an airstrip. John bid on the government land and got it. He and his wife, Marjy, built their home and the airport strip on the new property and sold the Hollinger property.

Following is an article about the airport in the 11 July 1991 issue of the *Fruita Times:*

Mack Mesa Airport: A place out of time
by Stephanie Wenger

MACK — The hot dirt road that takes you to the Mack Mesa Airport is really an avenue back into time. Behind your car, plumes of pale dust drop a veil that shuts out forty years worth of transportation development.

The early evening sun gilds corrugated metal buildings and glows on the silver body and propeller of the Stearman biplane that just touched down in its own cloud of dust. Elongated shadows of the 1923 Model "T" truck rake the tire-edged runway as it heads out to meet the Stearman's pilots. To the north, the Bookcliffs turn rusty-orange.

The Stearman is in its own element here, joined by a 1946 Swift, a Stinson, a 1939 Fairchild 24-R, a variety of Cessnas, including a 1934 Airmaster, a rare N3N World War II trainer, and numerous vehicles without wings: three Model-T's, three Model-A's, an antique firetruck, a Packard.

Airport owner John Hartman has been into airplanes "all my life. I went into the Air Corps in 1943 as an aviation cadet," he said, and he just never got away from them. "In 1963 we bought a farm and I had to have a runway for my airplanes," he said.

The runway for his airplanes is now bordered by several metal buildings housing 32 locally owned airplanes. Jim Mullins' red crop-duster perches near the runway, looking like a lean crimson condor ready to launch. A walk into one of the hangars reveals a jigsaw of wings, tails and props carefully fitted together under a metal roof that whistles and ticks as the wind gusts through.

In the last few years, Hartman added a big hangar, housing 15 planes now, plus a maintenance hangar. Two other businesses share the grounds. Precision Aircraft Maintenance employs Russ Pearce, Rich Cottier, and Dave Wallace. Mack Air Service is run by Ernie Denton, who specializes in restoration work.

Also based at the airport is Chapter 19 of the EAA, the Experimental Aircraft Association which is a division of the Antique/Classic EAA. Chapter 19 is planning to restore a 1941 BC-65 Taylorcraft, and once the project is completed, all the members will have the chance to fly it.

The association defines antiques in airplanes as those built before 1956. Over half of Hartman's airplanes are antiques.

The Stearman was piloted by Carl Hays of San Diego and Victor Smolin, a champion acrobatic pilot from the USSR. The pause at Mack Mesa turned into an overnight stay, and the around-the-world flight entered its second day as dawn broke on Wednesday morning. It was also the final day.

The Stearman left Mack on the second day of its around the world flight on 26 June 1991. The flight ended on a downdraft in the Rocky Mountains. *(Used from the 11 July 1991 issue of the Fruita Times, photo by Ernie Denton.)*

196

Against local advice, the Stearman took off, heading across country to Maine where the pilots were scheduled to pick up survival gear for crossing the North Atlantic. In Europe the Stearman and its two chase planes were to be joined by a Junkers tri-motor and, eventually,

(Upper) The Mack Mesa Airport houses the old, new and not-so-new, and more than just airplanes. (Center) Nose to nose, wing to wing, planes are packed into a hangar. (Lower) John Hartman's 1923 Ford Open Wagon Express provides the airport's shuttle service. *(Used from the 11 July 1991 issue of The Fruita Times. Photos by Stephanie Wenger)*

the world's largest biplane for the Russia to Alaska leg. According to Ernie Denton, such a flight was last done by a biplane in the 1930s.

The three-to-four-month "Flight of the Northern Light," sponsored by a California contractor and accompanied by camera gear sponsored by the National Geographic society, came to an abrupt end in the Colorado Rockies on Wednesday. A sharp downdraft put the biplane upside down blocking two lanes of traffic on Vail Pass that afternoon.

"The Northern Light" went home in a U-Haul truck with a couple thousand dollars worth of damage. Hays and Smolin walked away with minor injuries.

At Mack Mesa, life has settled back to routine, the 1923 Open Wagon Express putting up and down between buildings with Hartman at the throttle and the wind singing in the wings of temporarily grounded old eagles.

At the present time (1997), the airport is still very active. It has two hangars for rental airplane storage and a plentiful supply of tie-downs for outside airplanes. There are two maintenance shops with qualified and certified mechanics. Ernie Denton, Hartman's son-in-law, still works part-time as a mechanic when needed. The crop duster is still headquartered there. Hartman also sells aviation fuel. Sometimes people land on the field if they can't get into the Walker Field at Grand Junction and then they drive into Grand Junction.

John had realized his dream before he passed away on 5 July 1994. Marjy still lives in their home at the airport.

Desert Sun Sensations

Information is from Connie Ferguson.

The Desert Sun Sensations is located at the Desert Sun Ranch which is owned by Scott and Connie Ferguson and lies north of Mack on 1010 Q 3/4 Road. The following was written by Connie:

My business name is "Desert Sun Sensations." I promote the shows called "Springtime in the Rockies" in Grand Junction; "The Pumpkin Patch" in Montrose,

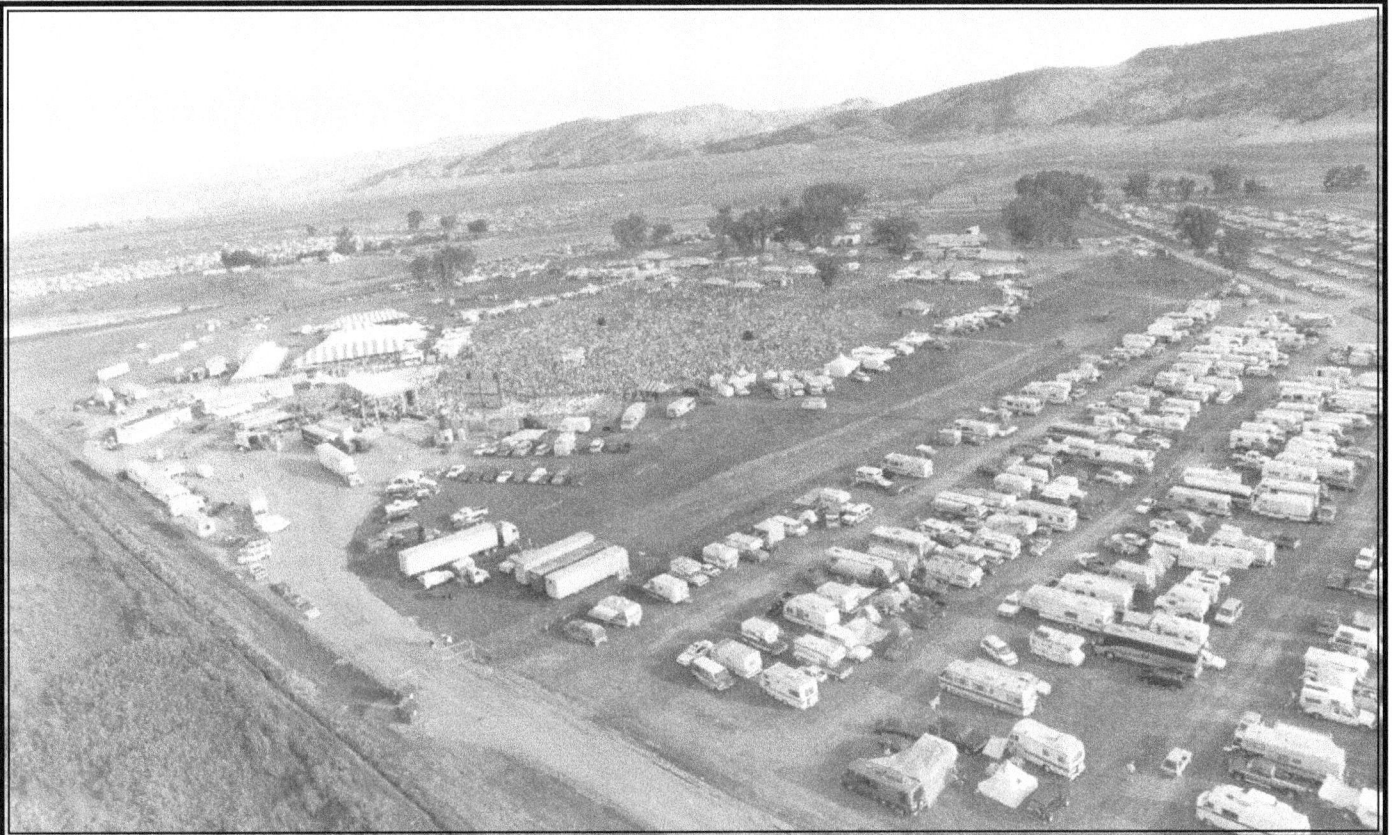

An aerial view of Country Jam USA in 1997. The main stage is center left with the striped dining tents and main food tents just left of it. Around the perimeter of the crowd of people are small stages and food tents. The original Kiefer house can be seen upper left (east) with a large vehicle parking lot behind it. The RV parking lot is immediately above with another vehicle parking lot in the upper right corner. (*Photo by Christopher Tomlinson, submitted by Lee Ann Maluy Blaney*)

Colorado and Farmington, New Mexico; and "Christmas in Colorado" in Glenwood and Grand Junction. This is my fourth year as a promoter. I bring artists and crafters from all over the Western United States to show and sell their handmade work. We are sponsored by KISS Country Radio and *The San Juan Silver Stage*, a newspaper celebrating creativity, editor Kathryn Retzler. My business also sponsors a newsletter called, *Colorado Creations*, that is produced by Barbra Boyce and promotes the arts in Colorado.

We just received notice that Connie Ferguson has moved to Collbran, Colorado. We are sorry to see her leave the area, but she can be contacted at P. O. Box 631, Collbran, CO 81624, or by phone 1-970-487-3544. Good luck Connie.

Bridal Carriage

Information is from Ronda Leischuck.

Bridal Carriage is located on 10 and Q Road. Ronda Leischuck purchased the business in 1995. She holds wedding planning workshops and coordinates between the bride and the merchant. She also is a distributor for Nutrition for Life.

Grand Valley Industrial Supply, Inc.

Information from Laddie D. "Rusty" Cupp.

The company is owned by Laddie D. "Rusty" Cupp who works out of his home located at 1535 101/2 Road, northeast of Mack. Laddie started the business in 1991. He is an engineer and does consulting for gold mines in Nevada, copper mines in Arizona, and power companies all over the western United States. He says he loves living in Mack.

Country Jam USA

Information from Melissa Jefferson in the office of Country Jam USA and John Tavoada.

Country Jam USA is a corporation owned by a group of investors. Two four-day jam sessions are held each year in the United States. The first session is held in Mack, Colorado, the last week of June, and the second one in Eau Claire, Wisconsin, three weeks later. Well-known country singers and performers are featured.

The first two Country Jam sessions held in Colorado were in 1991 and 1992, northwest of Grand Junction, and were very successful. In 1993, James and Pat Bischel of Chippewa Falls, Wisconsin, members of the corporation, bought the old Kiefer homestead southeast of Mack and hired John and Rose Tavoada to manage the property. Preparations were quickly made, and Country Jam USA was held in Mack that June in the open fields on the farm. The attendance was between 25 and 30 thousand people. This year (1997) the attendance was estimated at 100,000.

The following is taken from a Country Jam USA flyer:

What is Country Jam USA?

Country Jam USA is the nation's premier outdoor country music concert event which is host to the best entertainment Nashville has to offer. Entertainers that have graced the country Jam USA stage include: Reba McEntire, Willie Nelson, Vince Gill, Randy Travis, John Michael Montgomery, Brooks & Dunn, Alabama, Tanya Tucker, Clint Black, Kenny Rogers and Sawyer Brown, just to name a few.

What else does Country Jam have to Offer?

In addition to the entertainment on the main stage, the Country Jam USA grounds feature many other activities throughout the weekend. An assortment of merchants from around the nation offer a unique shopping experience guaranteed to offer a souvenir to match anyone's taste and price range. Between acts on the main stage, Country Jam USA showcases the best in regional country and variety entertainers and a thirst quenching selection of beverages at three different side stage entertainment areas. The Country Jam USA food court offers a wide variety of mouth-watering regional and ethnic cuisine that will satisfy even the most discriminating palette.

This year three more big-name performers were added to the list; Wynonna, Tim McGraw and Le Ann Rimes.

On the north end of the west field, is a permanent stage. It is a large cement slab with columns and cover. The main dining tents, food service tents and restrooms are located just east of the main stage. A new building built this year, 1997, houses the Campground Store, a full convenience store. Temporary stages and food service tents are located around the perimeter of the field south of the main stage. The center of the field is where the people cluster on their lawn chairs to listen to the music and entertainment. (See picture on previous page).

The equipment for the stages, sound systems, etc. is supplied by Stage Pro, a sub-contractor from Lawrence, Kansas. The kitchen equipment, grills, deep fat fryers, steam table, ovens, etc. are owned by Country Jam USA. They are shipped from Wisconsin a couple of weeks before the performance and then after the performance, quickly torn down and shipped back to Wisconsin for the performance three weeks later. John says it takes over two weeks to cleanup after the jam.

There are 3,000 camp sites for RV's and plenty of vehicle parking space on the property.

The property is still a working ranch, raising and selling hay. The original house built in 1910 by the Kiefers, and the Kiefer barn are still in use. The Kiefer Canal still meanders through the property.

In the summer, the Bureau of Land Management (BLM) uses the property as a base of operation for fire fighting, etc. Helicopters, trucks and tents are scattered throughout the property. The restrooms and showers are quite a convenience for them.

New Liberty

New Liberty farms are not only used for major incomes, some have also been purchased by entrepreneurs as a base for their businesses. It is very interesting how many businesses there are, but most interesting is the New Liberty Co-op that has been organized. The co-op was organized by Sioux Robbins who owns two businesses; one in Mack and the other in New Liberty. The purpose of the co-op is to gather community news and advertise the businesses that have been developed in the area and gain the support of the members and the community. The organization has a bulk mailing permit and sends out quarterly flyers.

Pig-A Sus Homestead Sanctuary

Information is from Sioux Robbins and a Pig-A-Sus flyer.

Pig-A-Sus is located on 506 S Road, on the northwest end of New Liberty, telephone 970-858-9628 It is owned by Sioux Robbins and Rocky Bartels. With the help of friends, volunteers and donations, Sioux and Rocky were able to open for business in June 1997. The following is taken from the Pig-A-Sus flyer.

The Pig-A-Sus Homestead Sanctuary is dedicated to a very special Potbelly Pig named *Thumper* whose tragic death ended her loving and caring friendship with many.

The Pig-A-Sus Homestead Sanctuary is nestled in a small acreage looking toward the desert and surrounded by the Bookcliff Mountains on the Baxter Pass Road. The sanctuary is open to the public, with focus mainly on preschools, kindergartens, nursing homes, handicapped persons or regular family outings. Tables and benches are available   for picnics on an expanse of grass.

The sanctuary offers "Adopt-A-Potbelly" for the families, school projects, individuals or businesses who do not have time for a full-time pet. Information is available for the Pig Owner, as we are here to serve the public, the first time Pig Owner and the Pig itself. The sanctuary is also a "Place of Protection" and is made up of numerous committees which have been formed to better serve the Pig.

The homestead is not only a potbelly pig sanctuary, as they also raise ordinary pigs to provide the pork cooked at Sioux's Pork Barrel Cafe in Mack and to sell the meat or pigs to the public.

Ed and Sons Lawn Care

Information is from Edson Miller.

Edson Miller lives on 561 S Road. He and his family moved to New Liberty in October of 1993 and started their business in 1994. He has four sons and at least three are working all the time. They do lawn maintenance on 125 lawns from 15 Road to Grand Junction and from Fruita to the Redlands. Ed and Sons use a special mower with three wheels, two in front and one in back, with the mower in front. It cuts a 42-inch swath and does an excellent job of manicuring with a high vacuum. These mowers cost $8,000 and are sold by Walkers of Fort Collins, Colorado. Ed and Sons do their own repair and maintenance on the mowers.

Ed's brother-in-law, Jason Gingrich, who lives on the corner of Q and 10 Road, started his own mowing business this year.

Lovell Sasser on Doc Talon with wither bag, front and rear bottle holders, cantle bag and special stirrup on the saddle, 26 April 1997. *(Photo courtesy of Lovell Sasser)*

Terrell Oil and Gas Service

Information is from David Terrell.

Terrell Oil and Gas Service is owned by David Terrell, 765 S 1/2 Road, the old Alstatt homestead. His office is on 20 Road and U.S. Highway 6&50. He has contracts to tend oil wells for independent oil well owners. David travels a large area, mostly western Colorado, Eastern Utah and the Bookcliffs.

Lower Valley Waste Service

Information is from Troy Latham.

Troy and Karen Latham created the Lower Valley Waste Service in 1993. They are located at 1847 7 Road on the old Van Riper place. They own two trucks and cover the area from Mack to Appleton.

Lovell of Mack

Information is from Lovell Sasser.

Lovell Sasser lives in New Liberty on the old Weir homestead at 647 R Road and runs her business out of her home. She has lived in New Liberty since 1973. In 1987 she began creating, sewing and making special accessories to place on her saddle when she went on trail rides. By 1989 this blossomed into a full-time business of making custom products for distance horseback riders.

Lovell draws-up prototypes, makes the patterns and sews or makes these custom creations herself. Her creations are almost too numerous to mention, but here are a few: cantle bags, withers or pommel bags, also made into a horn bag, water bottle holders, collapsible buckets and vet check bags. These all attach firmly to the saddle so nothing bounces. She says there is no saddle she can't or won't fit. She also makes special stirrups of leather covered aluminum, polar coolers and haunch heaters for the horse, and a hay feeder to place in the trailer or hang on a fence. The hay feeder also folds up. Aussie raincoats, slickers and riding tights are made to fit any size or shape.

Sasser Truck Repair

Information is from Loy Sasser.

Lovell's husband also has a business with the farm as headquarters. Loy Sasser has a portable diesel shop on his truck and covers all of Grand Valley repairing diesel engines, etc. He has been a diesel mechanic since 1983, and since so many repairs have to be done on the job, he decided to provide that facility.

PART TWO

FAMILY BIOGRAPHIES

The root of the kingdom is the state. The root of the state is in the family. The root of the family is in the person of its head.

—Mecius, 372-289 B.C.

All true work is sacred. In all true work, were it but true hand labor, there is something of divineness. Labor, wide as the Earth, has its summit in Heaven

—Anonymous

Family Biographies

A

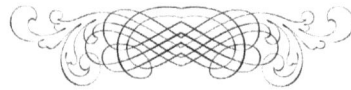

The following biographies will vary considerably in content. Some will be quite lengthy, owing to the kindly response of family members who contributed information. Others may be much shorter because they represent all the information we know or could find. Still others are simply not there because we had only names, nothing else. Since the stories we have included are largely from memories of the contributors you may detect some inaccuracies. In a few instances we have reinforced information with primary sources recorded at the time of the events. We have included birth and death dates when they were available.

Note that several of the early settlers were immigrants.

Alstatt

The Alstatt story came from a combination of obituaries and news items from *The Daily Sentinel,* stories contributed by Viola and Robert Alstatt, June Spencer Alstatt and Lona Groves Alstatt, and the author's personal knowledge.

Albert "Al" Wilford Alstatt was born 22 March 1882, at Marquette, McPherson, Kansas, to Swedish immigrant parents. He spent his childhood there and graduated from Marquette High School and later Salina Business College at Salina, Kansas.

Albert was married in Marquette, 21 May 1908, to **Anna Victoria Nelson,** who was born 30 November 1885 at Oscarham, Sweden. Anna had accompanied her parents from Sweden to Kansas in 1898 when she was 13 years of age. She became a citizen of the United States in 1908.

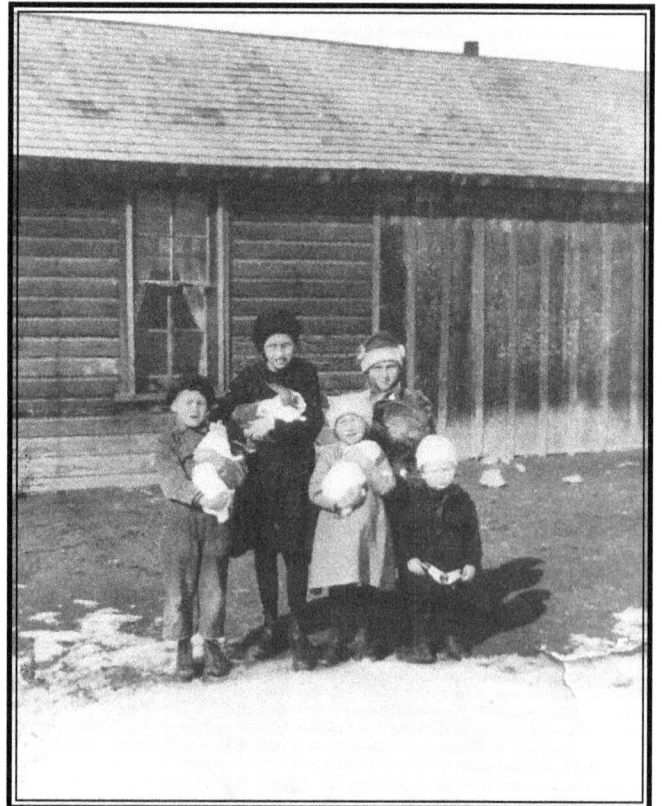

From the audio history tape of Anna on file in the Mesa County Library in Grand Junction, and in double-checking with Viola, we learned that Viola and her mother were still learning English when they came to New Liberty. Anna said Viola was her translator at the time. Viola can't remember that part, but she did say she spoke Swedish until she started to school.

Following are the names of the children of Albert and Anna with their birth-dates. The first five were born in Marquette, McPherson, Kansas, and the last five were born at Fruita and Mack, Colorado:

The Alstatt children standing in front of the homestead house in 1919 with their pet rabbits. Left to right: Milton, Viola, Edith, Ruth and Amos. *(From the late Margaret Morrow Collection)*

The Alstatt family in 1939 when Ruth came to visit from Wyoming. Back row L-R: Louise, Ruth, Viola, Carl, Amos and Agnes. Front row: Albert (father), Anna Belle, Anna (mother), Robert, Edith and Milton. (*Photo courtesy of Anna Belle Alstatt Thomas*)

Viola, 5 August 1909
Ruth Marie, 17 January 1911
Milton, 30 December 1912
Edith, 31 August 1914
Amos Edward, 16 March 1918
Carl Albert, 25 May 1920
Agnes Annette, 11 September 1922
Elsie Louise, 12 September 1925
Robert, 10 September 1927
Anna Belle, 23 January 1930

All 10 of the Alstatt children graduated from New Liberty School and later from Fruita Union High School. It was noted in school records that both Milton and Carl were outstanding students at New Liberty School.

Viola graduated from Fruita Union High school in 1928. She then enrolled at Ross Business College in Grand Junction and studied to become a secretary. She graduated from Ross in 1930

and worked wherever she could find a job, jobs being scarce because of the great Depression. In May of 1944 she enlisted in the Women's Army Corps (WAC) and served until May of 1946.

In October 1948 she secured a position with the Grand Junction Branch of the Rifle Production Credit Association. In April 1949, only a few months after she started work at that place, Viola had a harrowing experience. A teenage couple from Delta chose her place of employment for a holdup, after having recently burglarized several places in Delta. They had obtained guns in the course of their depredations and supposed Rifle Production Credit would be an easy place to get money. They demanded money of Viola, and as she told them there was no money there; the boy said, "Prove it" and then struck her on the head with the gun barrel and fired a bullet that struck her in the fleshy part of her upper right arm. The manager, Ward Torgerson, came to the rescue and the bandits fled, but were captured soon after. As Viola later described her experience she said, "I guess I'm just lucky." Viola retired after serving at that job for 28 years.

Following is a history written by Viola Alstatt and received by us in March 1988, and later updated and printed in the 2 May 1991 issue of the *Fruita Times*:

In the spring of 1918 Albert W. Alstatt left Kansas to attend a drawing for a farm in western Colorado, which had been scheduled by the government since an irrigation canal had been completed in 1917 to reclaim desert land. This Highline Canal brought water from the Colorado River diverted from a point in DeBeque Canyon and carried it about 50 miles as measured by the canal. This was desert land of sagebrush, weeds, prairie dogs, rabbits, coyotes and cacti. There was no sign of any trees or shade.

Albert Alstatt, in the drawing of 1918, got a homestead.[*] He returned to Kansas, sold his farm and most of his equipment and household goods, retaining just enough to start a farming venture in the new location. In April he left on a freight train, with a box car loaded with farm machinery, one team of horses, one cow, feed, and his new 1917 Model T Ford car.[†] On this new land Albert hurriedly built a one-room cabin, intended to later be the garage for the car when a home was completed. In late May of that year, after school was out in Kansas, Anna and five children arrived by train. Viola, eight years; Ruth, seven; Milton, five; Edith, almost four;

and Amos, the baby, two months.

There were several families who came about the same time, after water was available for irrigation, and soon the area was green as new crops and shade trees grew. Later cottonwood trees and willows could be seen sprouting along the ditches.

During that first growing season Al had to get up during the night, put on rubber boots and take the kerosene lantern to make sure the water was still running in all the furrows.

Some of the pioneer families living near the Alstatts were: W. E. Bowen, George Fisher, Clem Maluy, E. L. Shires, C. W. Likes, Bob Cox, John Morrow, Paul Arpke and George Bryan.

The first year was a pioneering life for the early families. There was no telephone, no electricity, no bathroom, no water in the house. In fact, water for house use was hauled from Mack in cream cans or barrels until a cistern was built. This had to be done before the water was turned out of the canal in the fall. To fill the cistern from the ditch, the water was run over gravel or charcoal and then through a screen to provide the house supply through the winter months. Ponds were filled with ditch water for the livestock.

During the first year, refrigeration was a screened box placed over an irrigation ditch. Later an ice box was used in the house, but ice had to be hauled from Mack or Fruita, and much of the time we were without refrigeration until a trip was made to town for supplies and ice, and in

The Alstatt homestead house in the winter of 1919. Standing in the yard is Ruth, Viola, Milton and Albert holding Amos. (*Maybelle Likes Cox Collection*)

The Alstatt house and barnyard in the winter of 1919. The entire family: Ruth, Albert, Milton, Anna, Amos, Edith and Viola. (*Maybelle Likes Cox Coll.*)

* Albert's name was not drawn in the original drawing. He was allowed to file on a homestead the next day after the drawing. See story about the drawing, pages 83 and 84. Al is listed on page 84.

† The author remembers the story that Al Alstatt and John Morrow leased a box car together to ship their belongings to Mack.

the busy growing season trips were not made very often. All other supplies, groceries and feed for the livestock had to be purchased in Mack or Fruita until a crop could be harvested.

There was no rural mail delivery; mail had to be picked up in Mack. There was no school or church the first year. All the children of the first settler families were behind a year in school when the one room school was built to accommodate all grades at the elementary level. About this time the Mack School District was divided, making a separate district for the new area, which became known as District #37; Mack became District #44. A meeting was called in the school building where all the residents were present to choose an official name for the community and school. New Liberty was the choice, and this then became New Liberty School. The first teacher was Bonnie O'Bryan. The school board for the new school was W. E. Bowen, President; G. W. Fisher, Treasurer; and Al Alstatt, Secretary. Al held this position from 1921 for 23 years after. He also was New Liberty representative on the High School Board for Fruita Union High School during all this time.

When the students from New Liberty were ready for high school they were taken to Fruita by bus. This bus route picked up students in Mack too, so they usually had a bus full by the time we got to Fruita.

In 1923 the school room at New Liberty was divided and there were about 43 pupils with two teachers. In 1924 another room was added to the school house, as there were now more than fifty students. New Liberty community was growing in all respects, and the desert was green and blooming wherever irrigation was available.

During the Government WPA program in 1935, a new school house was built with one large and one small classroom, a kitchen and large auditorium. During the early years the Community Club was organized with most families taking part in a variety of activities. The school building was the center of all meetings and activities. Al was the one on the board who had the key to open the building whenever anything was scheduled other than school. Many money-making projects were held there, such as pie and ice-cream socials, card parties, dances and bazaars. With money from these projects, the kitchen was completely furnished and a hot lunch program was then provided for the students. Books for the library were also furnished. Elections were held there, and each Sunday a non-denominational Sunday School met there.

In 1945 the large class room was divided,

making three classrooms; three teachers were then hired. In 1951 the school became part of School District #51. Students of the first six grades from Mack school were then bused to New Liberty. Students of the 7th and 8th grades from Mack school were sent to Loma and Fruita. In September 1960 the New Liberty School closed and the students were sent by bus to Loma.

Al Alstatt served as secretary for the Sunday School for several years and was also a member of the Farmers Union, both in Kansas and Colorado. He served on the Fruita Co-op board and the Grand Valley Water Users' Association for many years. In later years he worked with the Potato and Bean Grower's Association in Fruita

Through the years of growth in the community there was a variety of crops and livestock. The once barren desert land was producing alfalfa, sugar beets, pinto beans, corn and other grains and tomatoes for the canning factory.

The Alstatt homestead also had a small orchard near the home, with one or two trees each of several varieties of fruit. [Anna says in her taped history at the Mesa County Library that at the time, she was taking a Swedish Magazine from their former home in Kansas, and got her fruit trees for the homestead through that - author.] In addition, there was always a garden. For a number of years we had several dairy cows and sold cream to the Challenge Creamery at Eckert, Colorado. In addition to the dairy cows that many pioneers had, there were beef cattle, hogs, sheep, and all kinds of poultry. I've been told there were approximately 6,900 acres under irrigation in the lower valley farms and pasture lands when many families had settled in the area. In later years the farm locations and roads were numbered and the Alstatt homestead, located near the Highline Canal, 50 miles from where the water was diverted from the Colorado River in DeBeque Canyon, was numbered 765 S1/2 Road.

The farm acquired in 1918 was home for our family, where five more children were born, making 10 in all. Carl, Agnes, Louise, Robert and Anna Belle were all born in Colorado. Dad retired from the farm in 1946, selling the homestead to Amos after his return from serving in the Army during World War II. For a short time Dad and Mother lived near Clifton, but later moved to Grand Junction, and in 1954 moved to 2670 Patterson Road. Mother and Dad observed their 50th anniversary in 1958, with an open house at Carl's home in Grand Junction. All of the family were home for the event, plus some relatives of both Mother and Dad, who came from Kansas and Denver.

Now, in 1991, 73 years after Albert W. Alstatt filed on the homestead, the farm is no longer occupied by any of the Alstatts.

The family circle has been broken a number of times since the above mentioned anniversary. At this time there are only four of the ten children left.

(At present, February 1997, there are only three members of the Alstatt family left)

Ruth Marie Alstatt Wiant's family in 1958. Back row L-R: Paul, Ruth and Charles. Middle row: Shirley, Betty and Frances Ann. Front row: Jim, Peggy and Patty. *(Photo courtesy of Robert Alstatt)*

Paul
Betty (Dean)
Frances Ann (Kirby)
Shirley (Stillion)
James (Jim)
Peggy (Baluska)
Patty (Burns)

Charles M. died at Saratoga, Wyoming several years ago. Ruth died 15 June 1989, also at Saratoga.

The following information was obtained from Lona Alstatt in 1996:

ℛuth Marie graduated from Fruita Union High School in 1925. She married **Charles M. Wiant** 15 February 1930, at Mack. Charles had lived in the New Liberty community for a few years; he was a brother of Elva Gunst. After their marriage, Charles and Ruth moved to Saratoga, Wyoming, where they lived on a ranch.

Charles and Ruth had two sons and five daughters:

The Milton Alstatt family. L-R: Gary, Lona, Karen, Milton, Janette and Dave. Dale is not in this picture since he was born later. *(Photo courtesy of Robert Alstatt)*

ℳilton married **Lona Groves** 26 May 1939 at Fruita. They had two daughters and three sons:

Janette (Theuer), born 29 December 1943. Lives in Grand Junction and has worked for Northwest Transport Company since she was 17 years old. She is now Office Manager.

David, born 8 February 1946. Married Ellen Fouth. They live in Grand Junction and he works for the U. S. Soil Conservation Service.

Gary, born 16 March 1948. Married Dora Shmard. They live in Grand Junction and he works for Health Maintenance Organization (HMO).

Karen, born 1 June 1954. Lives in Grand Junction and works as the Director of Nursing at the Grand Junction Care Center for the elderly.

Dale, born 20 February 1960. Lives in Fruita in the former home of his grandmother, Orsa Groves. He is an electrician.

Milton and Lona lived many years on their New Liberty farm, which they purchased from Fred Likes. It was originally homesteaded by Clyde L. Balkwill. Milton worked part time at the Bean Growers Co-op Plant in Fruita. He served for 35 years as a substitute and a regular mail carrier on both the Mack and Loma rural routes.

Milton died at home in New Liberty on 26 November 1987. Lona sold the farm in 1993 and now lives in Fruita. She works as a volunteer for non-profit organizations.

Edith Alstatt Hamby's family in 1958. Back row L-R: Ida, Dewey, Edith and Dorothy. Front: Barbara and Donna. *(Photo courtesy of Robert Alstatt)*

*E*dith graduated from Fruita Union High School in 1934. She married **Dewey Tom Hamby** 17 November 1940, at Moab, Utah. Tom and Edith had four daughters:

> **Barbara (Blazer),** 12 June 1941
> **Donna Jean (Yeisley),** 3 January 1943
> **Dorothy (O'Brien),** 2 September 1944
> **Ida (Scott),** 6 April 1946
> They were all born in the old hospital in Grand Junction.

Dewey and Edith resided in Grand Junction since marriage. Dewey died in Grand Junction, 1 November 1987. Edith died in the Mesa Manor Nursing Home in Grand Junction, 21 December 1996. At the time of her passing there were eight grandchildren and seven great-grandchildren. Edith and Dewey are both buried in Orchard Mesa Cemetery, south of Grand Junction.

*A*mos **Edward** served in the U. S. Army in the Pacific theater during World War II. Seems he got more than his share of overseas duty. He entered the Army 13 October 1941, went overseas 20 May 1942 and did not get home until 16 November 1945. Even though he was still a young man when he came home, his hair had turned gray.

He married **June Spencer**, of Mack, 11 December 1945, at Rock Island, Illinois.

Amos and June had three sons and two daughters:

> **Joyce** (died at birth)
> **Ronald,** 19 December 1948
> **Edward,**
> **Gerald,** 21 August 1952
> **Gayle (Berry),** 9 August 1954
> They were all born in the old Fruita hospital.

Amos had a keen interest in sports, having participated in baseball and track during his school years at New Liberty and Fruita Union High School. He graduated from Fruita Union High School in 1936.

Amos and family lived on the Alstatt homestead from 1946 until Amos' death 26 September 1977. During that time he served on the Board of Directors of the Rifle Production Credit Association, and the Grand Valley Water Users' Association. After Amos' demise June and the children continued to live on the farm for several years, the boys doing the farm work.

June remarried to Raymond Barnes in August 1979 and they lived for some time on the former Likes farmstead. They are now living (1996) in Fruita.

The *Fruita Times* dated 23 February 1996 announced that **Gayle Alstatt Berry** was running for the office of Colorado State Representative for District 55. The article featured a picture of Gayle and told some interesting facts about her background. She graduated from Fruita Monument High School then from Mesa College in Grand Junction. She is self-employed, has operated a business support service, "Berry Inc.," in Grand Junction since 1982. She is married to A. C. Berry.

She is immediate past chair of the Board of Directors for the Grand Junction Area Chamber of Commerce. While serving a three-year term on the chamber board she chaired its Governmental Affairs Committee two years — plus many more services. We're proud of you, Gayle!

She won handily in the election in November 1996! *(Fruita Times, 8 November 1996)*

Carl Albert graduated from Fruita Union High School in 1937 and attended Mesa College for awhile before enlisting in the U. S. Air Corps in February 1942. He graduated from bombardier school 27 March 1943 and was commissioned 1st Lieutenant.

(Above) The Amos Alstatt family December 1967. Back row L-R: Edward, Ronald and Jerry. Front row: June, Gayle and Amos. *(Homer Likes Collection)* (Middle) An ad run in *The Daily Sentinel*, Saturday, October 12, 1996 by the Citizens for Gayle Berry. It is wonderful to see the support that Gayle received from the Lower Valley citizens. *(Ad sent to us by Mableann Post Hawthorne)* (Below) The Carl Alstatt family in 1958. L-R: Carl, Dee, Jessica and Alice. *(Photo courtesy of Robert Alstatt)*

Notice of his discharge was published in *The Daily Sentinel* column, "With the Boys and Girls in the Service," 20 January 1946. The article states he served as bombardier and navigator for 14 1/2 months with the 14th Air Force in China. He completed 24 missions in B-26 two-engine bombers with the 11th bombardment squadron of the 141st bombardment group. Mentioned in the article was an impressive list of medals

After his tour of duty, Carl married **Jessie McManaway** on 5 November 1949, at Colorado Springs, Colorado. Carl and Jessie raised two children, **Alice** and **Milton Dee**, Jessie's niece and son.

After marriage, Carl was employed as surveyor for the Colorado State Highway Department, as City Engineer for the City of Grand Junction, and as City Manager of Gunnison, Colorado. They moved to Arcadia, California in 1964 where he worked in the Engineering Department for the City of Arcadia. He retired in 1983, and died suddenly of a heart attack, 6 July 1992.

Agnes Alstatt Overbye family in 1958. L-R: Charlene, Agnes, Charlie and Larry. *(Photo courtesy of Robert Alstatt)*

Thereafter they lived in many different places in the Grand Valley, and were living in Fruita when Agnes died unexpectedly 6 August 1967. (See Charlie's biography with the Overbye's)

Son Larry lives in Fruita and has worked for National Park Service for 26 years and has been a member of the Fruita Volunteer Fire Department for 23 years. Charlene lives in Phoenix, Arizona.

Agnes graduated from Fruita Union High School in 1941 and married **Charles Overbye**, 7 March 1943. Charles and Agnes had one son and two daughters:

> **Helen Louise**, their first child, was born prematurely and died soon after birth.
> **Lawrence (Larry) Eugene** born 1 April 1946, Fruita
> **Charlene Marie**, 6 January 1949, Fruita

Charlie and Agnes bought the Ted Wassenberg (Uncle Ted, to Charlie) homestead in January 1947, and lived there for some time before selling out to Faun Chaffin.

Elsie Louise graduated from Fruita Union High School in 1943. She married **William H. Marshall**, 24 September 1948, in San Francisco, California. They had two sons: **Robert** and **Kenneth**. The family spent all their time in California. Louise died at San Carlos, California, 15 November 1962.

Robert graduated from Fruita Union High School in 1945 and then enrolled at Western State Teachers College at Gunnison, Colorado.

Louise Alstatt Marshall's family in 1958. L-R: Kenneth, Louise, Robert and William. *(Photo courtesy of Robert Alstatt)*

Following are some of Robert Alstatt's memories that he has written for the book:

"The Good Ol' Days at New Liberty"

I will attempt to write about things I remember after I arrived on the scene in 1927, but I don't remember much before I started to school at New Liberty. I really liked my first grade teacher, Esther Ziegler. She surely helped me get started on a good note. She was always so understanding; she didn't hesitate to help if needed. This was the school year of 1933-34. I was sorry to see her go after only one year. But she had better plans, as she soon married Lester Starr and lived in the Hunter area for many years. Janie (Berry) Starr has probably written a lot about her already, so I won't dwell on the subject.

I don't remember much about most of the other teachers I had. I didn't have Harold Carroll for a teacher, as he taught the upper grades. But I had plenty of contact with him and liked him a lot. Another teacher that I admired a lot was Delbert Jerome. He helped me finish out my eight years at New Liberty. My fifth grade teacher was one I didn't care much about. That was Mr. Poley. Since Dad was on the school board, I did not say much about it at home. Poley was definitely not one of my favorites.

The 8th grade graduation stands out as one of the highlights of my education. The ceremony and my salutatorian speech really meant a lot to me. Now that I look back on it, I will have to say that my eight years at New Liberty were memorable ones. Of course, I was not one to ever get in trouble with the teachers — if it did happen, I got another round of punishment when I got home. I think everyone understands about that.

My four years at Fruita Union High School were also good ones. I remember walking through our fields each morning to catch the bus for the long ride to Fruita. The mornings I spent at the Smith store at Mack were enjoyable ones. Those of us who rode the bus remember how we would get off at the corner west of Mack and walk up to the store and wait until the bus made it's rounds north of Mack picking up more students to go on to Fruita. The Smith's were always so good to us.

My senior year was different. I didn't walk to catch the bus, as I drove it to Fruita, making the long route through New Liberty and Mack and on to Fruita. Some days were pretty long driving the bus; especially during the winter when the weather was bad. Sometimes my day didn't end until after dark. But it gave me a little money that helped me get through my senior year at high school. I don't remember any real problems on the bus, except the usual things that probably happened to most drivers. But I felt closer to everyone, since I was a student.

Times were hard on the farm in those early years of my life. There never seemed to be any money to waste on frivolous things, but we always had plenty to eat and clothes to wear. I remember a few Christmases that we didn't get much, but we made do with what we had.

I have pleasant memories of the Sunday afternoon swims at the ol' swimming hole near Morrow's. Most evenings we would go for a dip in the canal right above our place; it helped cool you off after a long hot day in the fields.

Winters were cold and long, it seemed, but we survived. I really hated the early morning chores before going to school, but they were something that was expected of me, so I did them without too much complaint. The sledding parties on the weekends were fun. Many a Saturday or Sunday afternoon was spent on the hill near Walter Weir's place. Of course we dressed warm for the occasion, but we usually came home wet from playing in the snow.

The Alstatt family gathered for their parents 50th wedding anniversary in 1958. Back row, L-R: Carl, Amos, Anna Belle, Viola, Robert and Milton. Front and middle row: Louise, Edith, Anna and Albert (parents), Ruth and Agnes. *(Photo courtesy of Anna Belle Alstatt Thomas)*

My other memories of growing up in New Liberty are probably the same as many others have. The night melon parties in the fall, the usual Halloween pranks, and other things during the year, stand out in my memories, many times we were caught and paid our just punishments, but it was fun to try to get away with these things.

Family gatherings through the years were always enjoyable. With 10 children in the family there was never a dull moment. One such gathering stands out in my memory. My sister Ruth had married and left home in 1930 for a new life in the wilds of Wyoming. Nine years later she came home for a visit. She brought her two oldest children with her. I wasn't much older than they, so we had a lot of fun while they were there. We also had a family photo made at Dean Studio in Grand Junction while Ruth was there. To my knowledge there was only one other formal photo taken of the Alstatts; that was when my folks celebrated their 50th anniversary in 1958.

Dad never seemed to have much time for us kids, as he was busy with the crops. But I do remember on one occasion when he left Carl and Amos in charge and went with us on an outing on Grand Mesa. Some of the Kansas relatives were visiting, and he felt it was important enough to take some time off to spend with them and us.

I guess I always felt closer to my mother because Dad was always too busy to spend time with us. In later years, during the war, I spent more time with him since Amos and Carl were off serving overseas, and Milton was in defense work in California. We had to try and keep the farm going, just the two of us. It was also at that time that we went from horses to tractor. I enjoyed driving the tractor, and didn't mind it a bit if I had to be on it all day in the field. Soon after I left for college at Gunnison, Amos returned from the Army and took over the place, so Dad didn't have it all to do by himself.

Some other memories of community activities should not go without mention. The school house, of course, was the center of all community activities. I remember the many box socials that were held. Of course, I wasn't old enough to get in on the bidding. In later years, dances were held in the auditorium. I heard it said more than once that the hardwood floor was one of the best anywhere on which to dance.

I don't know if anyone has mentioned the Downings and the Curreys. They were families that were important in my life. They didn't stay in New Liberty very long, but Don Downing and Edith Currey were special to me since they were in the same grade I was. I had a lot of fun with them. The Maluys and Phillips were also special, as we spent a lot of time together. I can't forget the Braytons and the Bannings and all the good times we had together. The Coxs were close neighbors of ours and after they left we became well acquainted with the Wynkoops who moved in there. The Pachecos, Thomas' and Wrights lived further away and we didn't get to spend as much time with them. The Shires family along with the Berrys were always good friends as well as the Cutlers and Sanders families. I can never forget our close neighbors on the south, Charles and John Cavendish. I thought they lived a crude life. Likes' and Sislers were good neighbors also. The two Rays and I were quite close.

The 4-H Club would have never succeeded in New Liberty if it hadn't been for Les Van Riper. He gave a lot of time and effort to see that we had a good club each year that he was there. I have a picture taken in our front yard one summer, but I can't identify many of the kids in it.* I do remember that we came home from the fair each year with lots of ribbons.

I can't quit without telling about my memories of the Uintah Railway. It was a thrill to see the train slowly making its way toward Atchee on its daily run. We had a good view of it from our place, but it was brief. If you didn't look at the right time you would miss it. I don't remember what year it quit running, but I do remember seeing it make its last run, I was lucky to see history in the making.

I am now retired from a

career as a public school teacher[†]. I am sure that my beginning in the old school at New Liberty had a big influence on this career. I thought a lot about being a teacher like Mr. Carroll and Mr. Jerome. They were definitely role models for me. I guess that I was the only one in my family who went through at least four years of college. Some of the others went for awhile, but I stayed and got my degree. The first two years were difficult, even with a scholarship. It was then that I had a chance to teach on a temporary certificate. So I would teach during the school year and go back to college in the summers to work on my degree. There were several interruptions along the way, so it took nine years to finish. Along with four years of teaching, I spent two years in the Army (not my choice), and then back to Western State to finish my degree. So you might say that my education ran into many stumbling blocks after I left New Liberty.

Anna Belle graduated from Fruita Union High School in 1947 and soon went to work as a retail clerk for Montgomery Ward and later Woolworth Stores. She also worked as cashier/secretary for Meadow Gold and Stearns-Rogers. For the last 20 years she has worked for School District 51 as an Instructional Assistant.

Anna Belle Alstatt Thomas' family in 1972. L-R: Danny, Linda, Anna Belle, Duane, Charles and Diane. *(Photo courtesy of Anna Belle Alstatt Thomas)*

* See page 151.

[†] Bob taught at Clifton and Craig,, but most of the time in District 51 in the Grand Junction area.

213

Beginning when she was 18, Anna Belle developed a great love for bowling which has continued to the present time. Through the years she has been involved in competition all over the country. Her husband is also a bowler. She married **Charles Thomas** 20 August 1949, at Grand Junction. Charles worked for the Carpenter Union, and since retirement has been self-employed as a carpenter making cabinets, doing finish work, and repairing roofs.

Charles and Anna Belle have two boys and two girls:

> **Danny Allen,** born 17 September 1950. Married Carol Hunnziker.
> **Diane Louise,** born 20 Jan 1957. Married Royal Warinner.
> **Linda Marie,** born 1 January 1959. Married Kurt Johnson.
> **Duane Lee,** born 29 August 1966. Married Alice Casto.

The families all live and work in Grand Junction.

Anna Belle Alstatt Thomas' complete family in 1990. Back row L-R: Royal and Diane Warinner, Kurt Johnson, Carol and Danny Thomas, and Anna Belle Thomas. Front row: Joshua and Ryan Warinner, Veronica Thomas, Meadow and Forrest Johnson, Amanda Warinner, Linda Johnson holding Autumn Johnson, Duane and Charles Thomas. *(Photo courtesy of Anna Belle Alstatt Thomas)*

Anderson

The following is a compilation of obituaries and news items from *The Daily Sentinel*, a couple of letters from Alice Anderson Ahrens, some input from Agnes Kiefer and personal knowledge of the author.

John Frederick Anderson was born 7 December 1859 in Sweden. He came to the United States with other family members in 1882, becoming a citizen in 1890. About 1900, at St. Joseph, Missouri, he married **Lola Ellen King,** daughter of John Nelson King and Mary Alice Drury. (The Kings were New Liberty homesteaders.)

In later years John Anderson was employed by the Bureau of Reclamation and served as ditch rider at Camp #8 in the New Liberty District until his death 17 September 1930. Lola died years later, in 1958.

John and Lola had one daughter, **Alice Anderson,** born in St. Joseph, Missouri, 15 August 1901. The Andersons apparently moved to Grand Valley in about 1912.

Alice reports that she spent her "teen" years on the Tawney Ranch which, as she explained, was part of the original Charles C. Kiefer ranch. She attended both Mack and Loma schools, graduating from the 8th grade in 1917. The 1920 census lists the Andersons in the "Village of Mack." Alice's name appears as a student at Mack School in 1914-15. She reports that she attended Fruita Union High School for a time but had to give it up because of transportation problems.

Late in 1995 we heard a story from Agnes Keifer that shed some interesting light on the life of Alice Anderson. Apparently Alice and Agnes became friends when they were young and have corresponded and otherwise kept in touch through the years. Agnes shared with us a letter from Alice.

Alice learned when she was about twelve years old that she had been adopted by the Andersons when she was about eight months old. She had been the youngest of a family of eight children whose mother had died. An orphanage took in some of the older children, but thought Alice was too young for them to care for. Her name at that time was Elizabeth Wachter; the Andersons later named her Grace, but changed it still later to Alice. When she was about six they moved from a place near St. Joseph, Missouri to Omaha, Nebraska. After living there about two years they moved back to St. Joseph.

They moved to Colorado when Alice was about 11. One day when she was about 12, she and her Aunt Lietta King* were going through a dresser drawer looking for something when Alice picked up a letter marked — "adoption." Lietta grabbed the letter out of Alice's hand and said "you're not supposed to know." Lietta then decided she would tell Alice that she had been adopted, had a brother named Charles, who was a priest, and another sister, Mary Mildred, who was a nun. That, too, surprised Alice, since the Andersons had raised her as a Baptist.

In 1922 and again in 1924, Alice wrote to a Mr. Zimmerhoff of St. Joseph, a friend of the Andersons, who told her more about her family. She learned that her sister, Mary Mildred, was then living near St. Joseph, and brother Charles was living at Clyde, Missouri, and that she had another sister named Tillie living in Tulsa, Oklahoma. Tillie later came to see her and spent a day with her.

Alice vowed she would never tell the Andersons she knew, and so kept it a secret from them through all the years.

In 1920 Alice married **Bert K. Ahrens**, son of Henry Ahrens of Loma. Bert and Alice moved to Los Angeles in 1923, where he was employed by the Los Angeles Police Department. They had three children. After Bert's retirement they lived in Sun City, Arizona, for nearly 20 years. Bert died in September 1985, and since then Alice has been living in a retirement center in Corona, California. Her children are near enough to look in on her occasionally. We have had some communication

* See page 458, the J. N. King history.

from Alice, at age 92 in 1993.

Appier

The three Appier brothers from New Liberty taken about 1928 in California. Oren (Pete), John and Leonard. *(Homer Likes Collection)*

From Appier family history in possession of Homer Likes.

John Lewis Appier was born at Tecumseh, Pottawattomie, Oklahoma Territory, to David Marshall Appier and Susan Hester Solomon, 13 December 1898. Soon after his birth the family moved to Mardock, Cleveland, Oklahoma Territory, where he spent his childhood, attending Little River School. On 19 May 1918, he was married to **Vonnie G. Pittman** at

215

Wives of the three Appier boys taken about 1928 in California. Effie (Leonard), Vonnie (John) and Pansy (Oren). *(Homer Likes Collection)*

short distance the auto they were riding in hit a truck; both died instantly.

John died of cancer 3 January 1957, in Los Angeles. Vonnie died at Norco, California, 14 December 1994.

From Appier family history in possession of Homer Likes, obituaries and news items from *The Daily Sentinel* and *Fruita Times*.

Oren David "Pete" Appier was born 14 February 1894 at Nowata, Nowata, Indian Territory (later Oklahoma), to David Marshall Appier and Susan Hester Solomon. He moved with his family to central Oklahoma Territory about 1898 to a farm on the Cleveland-Pottowattomie County line where he attended Little River School.

Pete served in the Army in World War I, and was on the front lines during the push to defeat the German Armed Forces. He was exposed to great danger during that time, being wounded by shrapnel and exposed to poison gas. He said that he "went over the top nine times;" which meant that the soldiers left the shelter of their trenches at night to make raids into enemy territory.

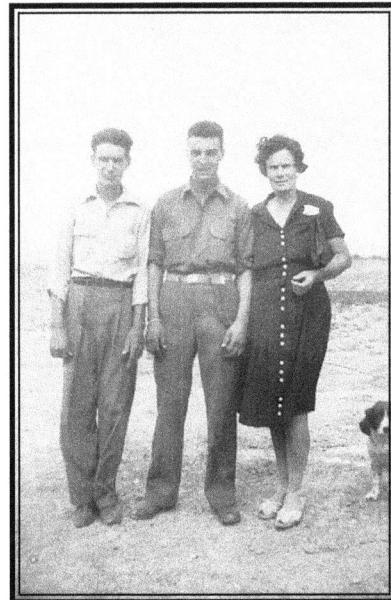

Mardock. They had one son: **Cleburn.** They later adopted a nephew of Vonnie's. In 1925 they moved to West Los Angeles, California, where John was engaged in a trucking business. In August of 1935 John and Vonnie purchased the 25 acres of land in New Liberty his parents had purchased from Charles Cavendish in 1931; the property joined the Likes' homestead on the west. In January 1936 John and Vonnie sold that land to Clyde W. Likes.

John, Vonnie and Cleburn came to New Liberty to live. They lived for a time on the Boyden farm at the west side of the community, and then returned to California.

Even though he had a wife and children, Cleburn enlisted in the Army during World War II. In late 1945 he and a companion were leaving the base on furlough and within a

(Left) Junior, Myrle and Joe Appier about 1944. (Right) Junior, Joe and Pansy Appier about 1944. Both photos taken on the Appier farm in New Liberty. *(Homer Likes Collection)*

216

(Above) Myrle and Joe Appier in Oklahoma about 1925.

(Right) Myrle Appier about 1940.

(Below left) Joe Appier about 1945. (Below right) Junior Appier about 1945. (*All photos from the Homer Likes Collection*)

In about 1926 the family moved to West Los Angeles, California, then about 1936 they came to Colorado and purchased a farm in the New Liberty community (originally the Walter McCampbell homestead). After the children were grown Pete and Pansy moved back to the Los Angeles area where they lived until 1970, when they again returned to Colorado and lived in Grand Junction.

During World War II both boys served in the military. Joe entered the service in February 1943 and was assigned as a Rifleman in the 187th Glider Infantry. He spent some time in Germany during and after the Normandy invasion. We do not have the date of his discharge.

Junior served in the Navy in the Pacific Theatre from 26 August 1944 to 9 June 1946. His letters home reflected a variety of experiences ranging from sea battles to typhoons.

Joe died at Grand Junction of cancer 2 June 1974, at age 49. Pansy died 14 April 1986 and Pete 27 August 1990, at Grand Junction. All three are buried in Memorial Gardens Cemetery at Grand Junction.

On 1 April 1922 he was married to **Pansy Mae Stewart** at Macomb, Oklahoma. They had one daughter and two sons:

> **Myrle Catherine Appier (McDaniel)** born 15 September 1922, Mardock, Cleveland, Oklahoma
> **Paul Austin "Joe" Appier**, 29 August 1924, Mardock, Cleveland, Oklahoma
> **David "Junior" Appier**, 17 August 1926, Oklahoma City, Oklahoma

From Appier family history in possession of Homer Likes.

William "Bill" Leonard Appier was born 7 November 1901, at Mardock, Cleveland, Oklahoma Territory, to David Marshall Appier and Susan Hester Solomon. He spent his boyhood years there, attending Little River School. He married **Effie J. Ellis**, 6 October, 1919, at Tecumseh, Pottawattomie, Oklahoma. Effie was born 16 October 1902 also at Mardock

Reford, Leonard and Effie Appier in about 1928.
(Homer Likes Collection)

They had two sons:

Reford Lee, born 4 July 1920 at Mardock, Oklahoma.
William Leonard Jr., born 25 October 1934, at Santa Monica, California

In 1925 Leonard and Effie moved to West Los Angeles to be near other members of their families. On 27 November 1934 they purchased a New Liberty farm from Dillbecks on the west side of Badger Wash, just south of the canal, the former Ira Cox/M. H. Dean homestead. They went back to Los Angeles for a short time, returning in February 1937. In December 1940 Leonard purchased a truck and moved the family back to West Los Angeles to begin a trucking business. They came back to the farm for a few years in the 1940s, but eventually sold out to David Thomas. The family lived in the West Los Angeles area for many years, but eventually moved further north. Leonard died at Lake Isabella, California, 21 June 1975. Effie, age 93 in October 1995, is living at Apple Valley near Victorville, California, close to Bill Jr.

Bill has had a trucking business for many years.

Reford worked at odd jobs in the Los Angeles area until the beginning of World War II. He realized that he was about to be drafted into the military,e so he joined the Merchant Marines. He sailed out of San Francisco with a large convoy, and went south through the Panama Canal. As the convoy crossed the Gulf of Mexico and proceeded up the Atlantic Coast toward New York, German submarines sunk over half the ships.

After that experience Reford had enough of the Merchant Marine — he jumped ship, went back to California and joined the Army. He spent considerable time in England and Germany serving as an MP (Military Police). After his stint in the service he went to work for the Los Angeles Police Department. He retired from that at an early age because of cancer and maintained residence at South Bend, Oregon for many years. He died in Los Angeles 20 January 1996.

Archuleta

Placido J. Archuleta was born 5 July 1907 at Abiquiu, Rio Arriba, New Mexico, to Amadeo Archuleta and Tonita Duran.

He was married 16 November 1926, in Grand Junction, to **Doris Ortega**. Doris was born 2 October 1911 at Monte Vista, Rio Grande, Colorado to Anthony Ortega and Emelia Albori.

Placido and Doris had three children:

Gilbert, born 10 August 1927
Mary Alice (Greenmun), 14 October 1928
Helen (Wellington), 5 June 1930
All were born in Grand Junction, Colorado.

Doris writes of her life in two different letters and we have combined them as follows:

I thought since we lived in Mack for 53 years I

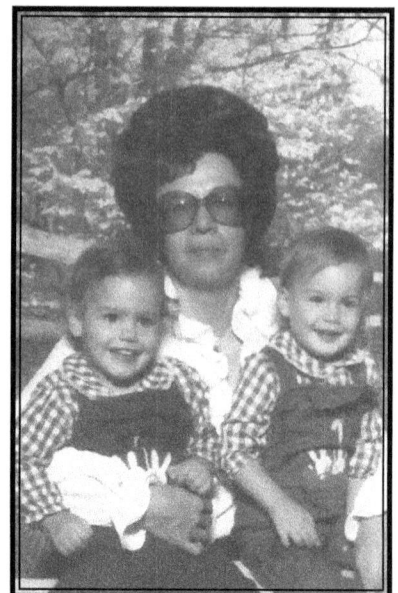

would add a few lines to your book.

I, Doris Ortega, was born in Monte Vista, Colorado on Oct. 2, 1911 to Anthony and Emilia Albori Ortega. My mother died in June of 1912 when I was eight months old. By then, our grandparents on both sides had passed away so my father was left to raise four children alone.

We left Monte Vista and came to Grand Junction by covered wagon in 1918. My sister, Eva, passed away in 1918 of the Spanish influenza. That left three of us and our father. In April of 1923 a car driven by a Mr. Hedgepath, who was learning to drive, ran over our father and he died of the injuries. My brother, Mace Ortega, 17 years old, had to quit high school to take care of my sister and I. Sarah, born June 6, 1908, was 14 years old and I was 11 years old. My brother became a boxer and became well known as "Kid Kare," the "Boxing Champion of the Western Slope." He picked that name because we thought that was our mother's maiden name, Karres. But it turned out to be her first husband's last name. We didn't know her maiden name, Albori, until I got my birth certificate. Mace was able to provide a good home for us. Sarah married at

(Above left) 1985, Placido Archuleta and great granddaughter, Erin Phillips. (Middle) 1985, Helen Archuleta Wellington and grandchildren, Erin and Kris Phillips. (Right) Mary Alice Archuleta and twin granddaughters, Mandy and Valerie Kenyon.

(Below left) Doris Archuleta and friend, Esther Trujillo, at the State Line Store. (Below bottom) November 1991, Doris "Dode"Archuleta in her cafe at Mack just before she closed it. *(All the photos above courtesy of Doris Archuleta)* (Below top) The State Line Store located on the Utah/Colorado state line about 1930 when the Baker Brothers owned the store and before the highway was paved. *(Photo courtesy of JoAnn Bowen Montague)*

18 just before I married. She married Mark Basta and had three children: Martha Joyce, Victor, and Mark Jr. Basta. I married at 15 to Placido J. Archuleta on 16 November 1926 in Grand Junction, Colorado.

We had three children by the time I was 18 years old, all born at home: Gilbert born August 10, 1927, Mary Alice born December 14, 1928, and Helen born June 5, 1930. I was very young, but our children never gave us any problems which made us very proud.

Placido started working for the D&RGW RR in 1934 and worked his way up from a section hand, to a relief foreman, to a track patrolman, and eventually retired as a truck driver after 38 years of service.

He transferred to Mack as a section hand in November of 1942. We moved to what was once the Uintah Hotel. That's when the railroad, "D&RGW," had a lot of men working. Red and Gladys Davies had purchased the hotel from the Uintah Railway when it went out of commission.

Our children remained in Grand Junction because we didn't know how long we would be in Mack. All three graduated from Grand Junction High School. Gilbert joined the Navy after graduation. He served for a year in the Navy then returned home and bought a truck and hauled for King Transportation to Denver. He met Charlene Marshall, who worked in the office

Gilbert Archuleta about 1945
(Photo courtesy of Doris Archuleta)

at King Transportation, and fell in love. She quit her job and came to Grand Junction and they were married. They have two children: a daughter, Vicki, married to John Folkestad, and they have one boy and two girls; and a son, Mark, married to Marsha Sage and they have three boys. Gilbert applied for a job in the Grand Junction Post Office around 1961 and retired four years ago after 32 years of service.

Our daughter, Mary Alice, married Francis Greenmun. They have two children: Mitzi, married to Dan Kenyon, and Gary Greenmun. Francis liked it in Mack, so by that time we had bought two lots from Glen and Susan Loveall. One lot had a house on it so we gave Mary and Francis the other lot. They built a cinder block house next to ours. She helped Alta Smith at the Post Office when needed. Their marriage ended in divorce and she got to keep the children. Mary Alice has worked in the office of Mountain Bell, now U. S. West Communications, for 34 years.

Our daughter, Helen, has two daughters, Donna Rodwell (Phillips) from her first marriage to Larry Rodwell, and Cheryl Lynn Wellington (Trumbo) from her second marriage to Jerry Wellington; they lived in Venezuela and Brazil. He was a supervisor for an oil company and passed away April 12, 1982 in Brazil of a heart attack. Helen came back to Grand Junction, Colorado, to live.

I went to work at the State Line Store for Lee and Lizzie Brogden. When they closed the store in 1970, I bought a lot next to our house and managed to have a small cafe built. I was there for 20 years. Helen Wellington, our daughter, helped me in the cafe until I closed.

It gave me great pleasure, 'cause I met the most wonderful people, like Lewis and Delores Likes, Alta Smith, Della Swyhart and George and Judy Harer who moved to Loma from California, all the nice guys who worked for Dowell Gas Company, Public Service, U. S. West, Nowsco, Great Western, Northwest Pipeline and many others too numerous to mention. I loved them all for the respect and help they gave me and my helpers.

I closed the cafe November 22, 1991. We sold out in Mack in April 1995 and moved to Grand Junction where all our family lives. Our daughter, Mary Greenmun, sold her place the year before.

Paul Gerhardt Arpke about 1917.
(*Photo courtesy of Robert C. Arpke*)

Elsie Emma Sandman Arpke at the time of
her graduation as a nurse about 1914.
(*Photo courtesy of Robert C. Arpke*)

Arpke

Obituaries and news items from *The Daily Sentinel,* land records, personal interviews with Robert, Pearline, Merton and Paul Arpke and personal knowledge of the author.

Paul Gerhardt Arpke was born 2 May 1879 at Sheboygan, Wisconsin to Adolph Arpke and Caroline Newman, German immigrants. Paul spent his childhood in Nebraska. He became a mortician and served in that capacity in Des Moines, Iowa, and Omaha, Nebraska He married **Elsie Emma Sandman,** 20 June 1917, at Fairbury, Nebraska. Elsie was born 4 September 1887 at Harbine, Nebraska to Paul Fred Sandman and Amanda Elizabeth Kratz.

Elsie spent her childhood at Harbine and attended Peru Normal School at Peru, Nebraska, and was a school teacher for a number of years. She received a degree in nursing in about 1914 and worked for a few years at the hospital in Beatrice, Nebraska. Her training as a nurse proved to be a valuable asset to the New Liberty Community. She was called many times to administer to sickness, injury or childbirth among her neighbors.

Paul and Elsie had three children:

Merton, born 24 June 1918, Fairbury, Nebraska
Ruth Elizabeth (Sampson) , 9 December 1921, Fairbury, Nebraska
Robert Calvin, born 20 August 1925, Fruita, Colorado

Paul, Elsie and son Merton moved to New Liberty in 1920 when they purchased a homestead that had originally been filed on by James M. Morgan.

A notice was found in the Mack items of *The Daily Sentinel* , 27 January 1926, that the Arpkes had a sale and rented their farm, as they were moving back to Nebraska.

They returned to the farm in New Liberty in the early 1930s and the children attended New Liberty and Fruita Union high schools. Paul died 7 August 1938 of Hodgkin's Disease.

(Above) About 1940, Ruth, Elsie and Robert standing in front of what appears to be a 1932 Chevrolet.

(Below) Elsie Arpke's posterity about 1971 in Fruita, Colorado. Back row: Robert Arpke, Merton Arpke, James Handley, Jim Anderson, Robert Duane Arpke, Paul Wesley Arpke, and Kevin Sampson. Middle row: Marlow Flitton, Denise Flitton, Susie Sights (Merton's step daughter), Velann Anderson, Elaine Arpke Flitton, Susan Anderson and Ruth Arpke Handley. Front row: Kristen Handley, James Ryan Handley, Sandy Arpke, Janis Dorene Moore Arpke, Pearline Arpke holding Tresa Arpke (granddaughter), Ruth Arpke Sampson, Carol Ann Wellington Arpke holding Cory Arpke (son), Elsie Arpke, Peggy Arpke Anderson and Natalie Kay Arpke. *(Photos courtesy of Robert C. Arpke)*

(Above) 1977—Photo taken on Elsie's 90th birthday. Robert, Ruth and Merton standing, and Elsie sitting in front. (Photo courtesy of Robert C. Arpke)

Elsie and the children continued on with the farm. Elsie will be remembered by all who knew her as a very frugal woman who was a firm believer in hard work. She is remembered as one who didn't mind donning men's clothing and working in the fields as hard as any man would.

One fall in the late 1930s, when bean harvest was under way, there came a terrible wind storm, as often happened in the fall, and it blew the shocked beans into huge piles wherever there was a wind break. The beans were picked out of the piles and hauled to the thresher, so it wasn't a total loss. But of course the beans were badly shattered out of the hulls and scattered on the ground. Normally the beans shelled out of the vines and the scattered loose pods would have been considered a total loss, but not to Elsie Arpke. She spent the fall and winter months picking up the wasted beans by hand and salvaging as much of the crop as possible. By today's standards she could not have been earning more than pennies per day — but to Elsie it was worthwhile.

1951—The Merton Arpke family on their farm in New Liberty. L-R: Lillian "Peggy," Mildred holding Paul, Merton, Elaine and Ruth. *(Homer Likes Collection)*

After the children had grown and married, Elsie moved to Fruita and built a four-plex dwelling. She also bought a car — she had to learn to drive since she had never driven before. It was quite amusing to see her driving down the road leaning over to the middle and peering past the steering wheel.

She had her children in mind as she acquired property — the New Liberty farm, the farm in Nebraska, and the four-plex in Fruita. When she died 7 March 1982, at age 94, each of her children inherited a portion of her property.

Merton married **Mildred Raver** of New Liberty on 11 August 1938, the day after his father's funeral. They had four children:

> **Lillian "Peggy" (Anderson),** 29 July 1939 in the same room her mother was born in on the Raver homestead.
> **Mildred Elaine "Clancy" (Mc Ginnis),** 15 October 1942, Los Angeles, California
> **Ruth Claudeen (Handley),** 24 June 1944, Fruita, Colorado
> **Paul Wesley,** 19 July 1949, Grand Junction

During World War II Merton was employed at Lockheed Aircraft in Burbank, California. He left Lockheed and worked for a time at Hill Air Force Base, in Clearfield, Utah. He later served in the Navy from 18 May 1944 until 4 November 1945, receiving training as Aviation Metalsmith. He was lucky enough to receive an early out through the point system because of his family.

After the war he and Mildred bought the S. S. Summers farm in New Liberty and lived there for several years. Then they moved again to Clearfield, Utah, where Merton again worked at Hill Air Force Base. While there Merton and Mildred were divorced. Merton remarried to **Elsie H. "Sandy" Hendrickson Sights,** 19 October 1954.

Merton retired from Hill Air Force Base in 1973 at 55 years of age, and became a devoted rock hound, hunting for stones in Utah and Colorado. He became a silver smith and has made beautiful jewelry with the stones he processed. Merton also took oil painting classes and became quite an accomplished artist. His paintings have been on display in different places and adorn the walls of many homes in his family.

1977—Merton and Elsie "Sandy" Arpke at Fruita, Colorado when they were attending his mother, Elsie's, 90th birthday celebration. *(Photo courtesy of Robert C. Arpke)*

For 15 years after retirement, Merton and Sandy spent their winters in Apache Junction, Arizona in Gerald Coltharp's trailer court. Then for several years they spent their winters at Beaver Dam near St. George, Utah. They presently live at Bountiful, Utah.

Merton and Sandy have traveled all over the world, mainly because they have visited his daughter, Elaine. She has worked many years contracting for the Air Force, and has lived throughout the world. Their last trip was to Greece and Turkey.

Merton has eight grandchildren and 12 great grandchildren.

Ruth Elizabeth married Merle Sampson about 1945. They lived in Grand Junction for a few years and Merle managed the Western Auto Supply store. Next he bought a Western Auto Supply store in Miles City, Montana, where their son, Kevin, was born. After several years they sold and moved to California. Ruth died in February 1986 in Simi Valley, Ventura, California.

Robert "Bob" Arpke married Pearline Monger of Mack on 8 September 1946. Pearline is a daughter of Nelson Dixon and Pearl Monger. Bob and Pearline had three children:

Robert Duane, born 24 June 1947
Timothy "Tim", 22 September 1951
(They lost their little girl at birth)

Bob became owner of the Arpke homestead. He enlarged his farm operation to include the Snavely and Morrow homesteads. Bob and sons, Duane and Tim, formed a partnership and the McKay and VanRiper farms were purchased in addition to the acreage already held making a total of 400 acres of farm land. Duane and Tim built their homes on those two farms.

Bob served as a board member with the Mesa County Tomato Growers Association in the 40s and 50s. He sat on the advisory board of the Fruita Future Farmers of America from 1961 to 1969 while his boys were involved during their high school years. He served on the Grand Valley Water Users' Association and the Rifle Production Credit Association boards for about six years.

Pearline has devoted her time to homemaking, growing gardens, cooking for farm help, and all the chores demanded of a farmer's wife. In her "spare time" she figures she has made over 100 crocheted bedspreads and afghans, tablecloths, and quilts over the years for friends, children, grandchildren and great grandchildren. She is still crocheting and has added liquid embroidery to her handicrafts.

Bob and Pearline became involved in square dancing about 1968. Bob became a professional caller for the square dances in 1970. They have taught square dancing in Fruita and Grand Junction. Between times they did a lot of fishing at Lake Powell

(Above left) Robert C. and Pearline Monger Arpke at the time of their marriage in 1946. (Above right) About 1963, Tim and Duane Arpke. *(Photos courtesy of Robert C. Arpke)*

About 1976, Duane and Carol Arpke and their three children, Natalie, Cory and Tresa. *(Photo courtesy of Robert C. Arpke)*

About 1979, Tim and Janis and their three children, Andrew, Brenda and Jennifer. *(Photo courtesy of Robert C. Arpke)*

and Lake Meramotte near Norwood, Colorado.

Bob and Pearline celebrated their Golden Anniversary in September 1996. They have six grandchildren and ten great grandchildren with one on the way (1997).

Duane and Carol have three children:

> **Natalie,** born 5 November 1967
> **Tresa,** 11 September 1969
> **Cory,** 24 February 1971

Robert Duane went to New Liberty and Fruita Union High School, graduating in 1965. He married **Carol Ann Wellington** 20 November 1965, in Grand Junction, Colorado. Carol was born 24 June 1946 to Bob and Lettie Wellington.

Duane then went to Salt Lake City, Utah, to attend Utah Trade Tech for two years. After graduating he worked as a machinist for a year, but didn't like the work or the area and came back to New Liberty. He then went into a farming partnership with his father and brother. For a few years Duane and Carol lived in a mobile home on the Bob Arpke farm, then they built a house on the Van Riper farm. About 1990 Duane gave up farming and became a truck driver. Two years ago he bought his own truck and has his own trucking business. He and Carol sold the farm and home in New Liberty and now live in Fruita.

Timothy went to New Liberty School and graduated from Fruita Union High School in 1969. He married **Janis Dorene Moore** on 13 June 1970. Janis was born 27 February 1953 to Fred and Helen Moore. After living a few years in a mobile home on the Bob Arpke farm, Tim and Janis built a house on the McKay farm. In 1994 Tim became the "Ditch Rider" at Camp #8, in the New Liberty area. They sold the farm and now live in the Camp #8 ditch rider's home near the highline canal.

Tim and Janis have three children:

> **Jennifer,** born 30 July 1971
> **Andrew Wade,** 10 July 1973
> **Brenda Gail,** 15 September 1974

Charles and Pauline Ashburn when they lived on the Sumnicht place in the early 1950s. *(Photo courtesy of Charlene Ashburn Francisco)*

Charles and Pauline had two children:

Charlene Donnis, born 15 March 1938, Grand Junction, Colorado
Ronnie Burlee, born 26 January 1944, Grand Junction, Colorado

Both children attended New Liberty School and Fruita Union High School. The family lived for many years in the Mack/New Liberty/Loma communities. They moved to New Liberty in 1950, living for a time on the Sumnicht place. They eventually purchased what was originally known as the McIntosh

Ashburn

From obituaries and news items from *The Daily Sentinel.* Some information from daughter, Charlene.

Charles "Charlie" Edgar Ashburn was born 7 December 1908, at Monterey, Putnam, Tennessee, to Robert Lee and Nina McDonald Ashburn. He came to the Mesa County area about 1924, apparently with his father and step-mother, and a brother and sister. They lived in the Loma district for several years.

Charlie married **Pauline Helen Long,** 7 August 1934, in Fruita, Colorado. Pauline was born 7 October 1910, at Elsmore, Allen, Kansas, to Albert "Bert" Edward Long and Pearle Baker. She spent her childhood at Elsmore, Chanute and Iola before moving with her parents to the Loma community in 1925. She attended Fruita Union High School.

(Upper) Charlene, Charles and Pauline in the 1950s on the McIntosh homestead after they bought it. (Below) July 1956 on their farm in New Liberty. L-R, Charles, Pauline, Ronnie and Charlene. *(Photos courtesy of Charlene Ashburn Francisco)*

226

homestead. After the children had grown and left home Charles and Pauline sold the farm and purchased the Mack School Teacherage, where they lived for many years.

Charles died at Cody, Wyoming, 26 July 1984, just two weeks before his and Pauline's Golden Anniversary. Pauline died in Fruita 6 September 1994 — both are buried in Elmwood Cemetery at Fruita.

Charlene married **Billy Dean Francisco** 29 November 1958 at Grand Junction, Colorado. They have three children: **William Scott, Diane Janell** and **Lee Ann.** Bill was in the Navy for 20 years — the Francisco's oldest daughter was born in Yokosuka, Japan. They spent nine years working in the oil fields in Wyoming, moving to Mack when Charlene's mother was in bad health. There are now seven grandchildren. Bill and Charlene currently live at Mack and deliver *The Daily Sentinel* throughout the area west of Fruita. Two of their children live in Grand Junction, one in Illinois.

Ronnie was married to **Judy Sack**, 14 August 1964, at Thornton, Adams, Colorado. They have two children: **Mathew Eugene** and **Christy Mae.** Ronnie and Judy were living in Littleton, Colorado, at the time of Pauline's death.

1991, Charlene's family. Back: Diane Janell, William Scott and Billy Dean. Front: Charlene and Lee Ann. *(Photo courtesy of Charlene Ashburn Francisco)*

B

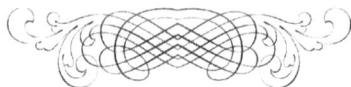

Baird

Elva Baird Beswick and Esther Baird Sproule sent the following story of the Baird family, who lived in Mack from 1911 until 1929. We have added some information from news items in *The Daily Sentinel* and the 1920 census.

Fred Buckham Baird was born 29 February 1880, at Langdon, Atchison, Missouri, to George Baird and Belle Hendrickson. Fred came to Mack from Missouri in 1907 and went to work for the Uintah Railway as clerk and telegraph operator. Later he was transferred to Dragon, Utah, where he was one day able to say

he "was sure he had seen his future wife" when she stepped off the train at Dragon.

Kate Blanche Innes was born 16 June 1886, at Doland, Spink, South Dakota, to Joseph Innes and Elva Burgess. Joseph and Elva moved their family from South Dakota to the Innes and Hoff Ranch east of Fruita in 1896. The family later moved into Fruita, where Joseph had a lumber yard, some mining property, and was very active in the development of the area. Blanche graduated from Fruita Union High School in 1905, worked at the drug store, was a telegraph operator for two years, then moved to Dragon, Utah, to teach school. In 1917, Joseph and Elva moved to Monticello, Utah.

Fred Baird and Blanche Innes were

The Baird family at Mack. Just a few minutes before leaving for California in May 1929. The car was all packed and ready to go. L-R: George Baird, Fred Baird Sr., Fred Baird Jr., May Daniels (cousin), Elva Baird, Lois Daniels (cousin), Esther Baird and Helen Baird. *(Photo courtesy of Esther Baird Sproule)*

married 23 May 1911 in Fruita. They took up residence in Mack, living for several years in what we have always called "the little house." Several years later, they moved to one of the railroad houses on the street facing the hotel lawn, the end one by the footbridge across the wash. Blanche was appointed town postmistress and Fred served as accountant for the Uintah. Later Fred was given the position of Assistant Secretary and Treasurer of the Uintah.

At some point in time, Fred, in addition to his duties in the Uintah office, became a correspondent for *The Daily Sentinel,* reporting the news of Mack and vicinity, including items of interest concerning the railroad. He continued with that until he moved his family to California in May 1929. Mrs. J. L. Booth took over as correspondent at that time.

Fred and Blanche had five children:

George Innes, 22 July 1912, Fruita
Fred Blanchard, 23 February 1914, Fruita
Elva Drusilla, 7 July 1916, Mack
Esther Belle, 14 March 1921, Fruita
Helen Marie, 18 November 1922, Grand Junction

We have always been glad we had our early life in Mack and remember it as a happy time. We often talk about the two-room school house, where we received a strong base for our education. We remember things like box suppers, pie socials and dances that were attended by the whole town. (Esther and Helen used to Charleston together.) At Halloween we remember holding jack-o-lanterns up to selected windows — then finding out the next morning that the footbridge over the wash had been turned over again, or that a ladies slip had been run up the flagpole. We remember silent movies in the school auditorium and sometimes church; and we remember the school plays that were presented there. Esther was not in school yet when a Mother Goose play was given. As there were more parts than students, and since Esther was the oldest child in town not in school, she was asked to fill in. There was also a musical about a gingerbread family, when Elva played the accompaniment on the piano and Esther and Helen were the gingerbread twins.

Elva had her 12th birthday party in July 1928. A few years before that she had a birthday party and forgot to tell Mama until the last minute. Needless to say, Mama rose to the occasion.

We also remember the 'golf course' where we took our sleds in the winter — and playing games in the schoolyard. Esther particularly remembers when the schoolyard had a merry-go-round — and riding a horse named 'Stockings', that belonged to MacTaggarts. There were baseball games with Loma — and skating on the sidewalks — and Chris (Pappas), who took care of the hotel lawn — and Uncle Henry (McCoy?). We remember May baskets and wild flowers,and we especially remember the trees of Mack.

George and Fred played in the Fruita High School Band and we can remember going by train to Denver to some kind of band competition — or maybe it was a parade (probably both). We saw our first 'talkie' movie while there. George sang a part in a musical presented at Fruita High in 1928 and Esther announced to all within earshot that it was her brother singing — it happened to be her 7th birthday.

In May 1929, shortly after school was out, the family moved to California. George had just finished high school, Fred was in the 10th grade, Elva the 7th grade, Esther the 2nd and Helen the 1st. We all drove out there in our Dodge car. It took us five days to reach our first destination at Lindsay, California, where we stayed a few days with relatives. It was quite a trip. George Jr. drove a good part of the way. We went through Salt Lake City, where we tried out the salty water in the lake and rode the roller coaster. Esther can remember seeing her first airplane there. We continued on through Nevada to Sacramento.

When we arrived at our destination at Pomona, the children there were still in school. We lived in Pomona the first summer, then moved to Pasadena, where we stayed for three years, and then to Los Angeles, where we all finished growing up.

George went to work in the trust department of the First Security Bank in Los Angeles shortly after we arrived there.

He married his first wife, Mildred Ball, in 1937, but they were divorced a few years later. In 1945 he married Jane Bessomette. They had three children and there are now eight grandchildren. George died in 1974 on Esther's birthday. He was deferred during World War II because he was working as an accountant in a defense industry.

Fred finished high school in Los Angeles and went into the CCC for two years. Then he went to work for S. E. Rykoff Foods, where he met his future wife, Mae. They were married in 1937 and had two children. Fred was in the Army during World War II and died in 1964, just before his first grandchild was born. There are now six grandchildren. Mae is still living.

Elva finished high school in Los Angeles and met her husband, Bob, in November of 1938 — they were married in March of 1939. Bob had been in the Navy and returned to that during World War II. During the last 10 years of his life he worked as a buyer for Disneyland.

Esther went to work after finishing high school and married Herb Sproule in August 1943. She met Herb when she was 11 years old and they sort of grew up together knowing they would be married someday — between arguments, that is. Herb was a pilot in the RCAF (Royal Canadian Air Force) during World War II. They had two children and now have three grandchildren.

Helen went to work for the telephone company after high school and married Bart Bartholomew in April 1950. Helen died 27 May 1955, leaving a boy just under two years and twin boys two and one-half months old. Elva and Bob had no children of their own, so they became legal guardians of the three boys three years later and raised them for Helen. Bob died in 1976 and now Elva has seven grandchildren.

Mother Blanche died in San Bernardino, California, 24 August 1938. Fred died in Los Angeles, 12 December 1943; both were buried in San Gabriel.

As mentioned before, we remember Mack as a very nice place to have started our lives, but we have also liked living in California. One of Helen's boys lives at Copper Mountain in Colorado. Esther and Herb like to travel by car, so have been to Colorado many times. They've stopped at Kelly's Rock Shop at Mack many times, and walked the old side walks, but there's very little left of the town as we knew it. Life in California

has been interesting and happy — and the changes we've seen in Colorado since 1929 have been truly amazing.

Bainter

Census records, obituaries and news items from *The Daily Sentinel* and personal knowledge of the author.

Max U. Bainter was born in 1905 in Illinois, the son of John R. and Orpha Bainter of the Redlands. Max married Ella Virginia Latham at De Beque in February 1932. Virginia was born 8 August 1910 at Clifton, Ashe, North Carolina, the daughter of Mr. & Mrs. John R. Latham. She moved with her family to DeBeque in 1918.

Max and Virginia moved from the vicinity of De Beque to the William A. Knapp farm in 1934.

Max and Virginia had two sons:

John Reigan Bainter, born 6 June 1934, Fruita
Bruce Latham Bainter, 1940, Fruita

The family made their home in New Liberty until about November of 1944, when they sold to J. M. Mogensen and moved to Naturita. Max was employed there as warehouseman for the Vanadium Corporation of America. In June of 1945 their son John, aged 10, drowned in the Delores River. The lad had attended schools at New Liberty, Mack and Naturita.

Max and Virginia moved to Denver about 1960, where Virginia died 25 November 1978. Both she and her son are buried in the Masonic Cemetery in Grand Junction.

Banning

Banning and Solomon family history in possession of Homer Likes.

Ray Banning, son of Walter E. Banning and Nettie Hawk, was born 22 September 1899, at Moore, Cleveland, Oklahoma Territory. He spent his childhood there and attended Little River School at Mardock, in Cleveland County.

(Upper left) Naomi Banning 1943. *(Delores Likes collection)* (Upper right) Ralph Banning 1948. (Lower left) Ruth Banning 1947. (Lower right) Basil Ray Banning 1954. *(Last three photos from Homer and Phyllis Likes Collection)*

He was married to **Nellie Francis Solomon,** daughter of John Thomas Solomon and Matilda Jane Barnett, 21 September 1919, at Mardock. Nellie was born 16 January 1901, at St. Joseph, Buchanan, Missouri.

Ray and Nellie lost their first two children at Mardock, a boy and girl who died at birth. There were five more:

Ruth Isabel (Schleicher), born 26 July 1921, Mardock, Oklahoma

Naomi Elizabeth (Underwood), 13 September 1925, West Los Angeles, California

Hazel Joyce (Porter), 21 October 1928, Mardock, Oklahoma

Ralph Nelson, 12 December 1930, West Los Angeles, California

Basil Ray, 10 October 1939, Fruita, Colorado

The Banning family moved from West Los Angeles to Colorado and purchased the Gerry homestead in March of 1938. The children attended schools at New Liberty and Fruita.

On 7 June 1946, the second daughter, Naomi, was married to **John "Jack" Underwood,** of New Liberty; we do not have marriage information on the other children. Ralph joined the Navy after graduating from Fruita Union High School in 1948 and continued with the Navy until retirement.

In 1948 Ray and Nellie, with children Hazel and Basil, moved to Missouri and settled on a farm at Phillipsburg, in Laclede county. Basil developed cancer in his upper right arm and shoulder not long after they moved to Missouri, which led to amputation of the arm. He passed away 29 January 1955, at age 16. Ray died about 1984 and Nellie in 1986 at Phillipsburg. Naomi Banning Underwood ended her own life a few years later.

Barcus

Dwight Earl Barcus was born 13 February 1917 at Yale, Guthrie, Iowa, to Harlan Earl Barcus and Della May Ulrich. Dwight and **Petrea Mary Mogensen**, were married 6 February 1938 at Fruita. Petrea was born at Fruita, Colorado, 5 January 1917, daughter of J. Marinus Mogensen and Gertrude Porter. Dwight and Petrea grew up in the same community, went to high school together; both graduated from Fruita Union High School in 1934.

They had five children, all born at Fruita:

Darrel Marinus, 27 October 1939
Luthera Ann (Hindman), 3 October 1942
Delene Petrea (Tufly), 26 February 1947
Earlynn Elena (Landini), 14 July 1948
Harlan Dwight, 11 August 1959

Petrea Barcus wrote the following about her family:

We moved to the New Liberty community in May 1951 into a new home we had built on the Pollock homestead, which we purchased from Clarence (Booze) and Walter Deacon. We combined that with the Joseph and William Dille homesteads which had been purchased in 1938 by my parents, J. M. and Gertrude Mogensen. That gave us about 300 acres of farm land which was connected to the desert permit that went with the ranch in Hay Canyon in the Douglas Pass area. My father bought it from Burns Fisher in 1936 or 1937 and we inherited it after my father's death in 1948. That made a good "set-up" for cow and calf operation.

We were welcomed into the community by our new neighbors, and the Sorosis Club had a housewarming shower for us. One of the nicest gifts brought was Canna Bulbs which we planted by the front door. The colorful blooms made a showing that were enjoyed by everyone.

The following year the nearby siphon was replaced with a new underground pipe. As they installed it we received a nice bonus in the form of a "riser" in front of our home to give us water under pressure for our yard.

The two oldest children had been going to

school at Fruita. We moved to New Liberty a couple weeks before school let out, but worked it out with the teachers that the children finished early at Fruita. Our children had to endure the trial of missing the students they had been used to and having to get acquainted all over again. One morning they looked out and saw a group of children and teachers in the bottom of the wash (East Salt Creek) having an outing, so Darrel and Luthera went down to meet them and were invited to join them. What a wonderful way to get acquainted!

We felt the children were fortunate to have had the experience of attending the New Liberty School during the time Ursula (Sue) Thompson and Mabel Cooper were the teachers. The students always had a good showing on the honor rolls as they went on to Fruita Union High School. One of the highlights of each school year for the older students was a trip to Denver on the train to visit the capitol and museum. The students also appreciated the school lunch program with Margaret Morrow at the helm. She handled it by herself and served the students good, nourishing home-cooked meals, bringing fruits and vegetables from her own garden as an extra treat.

The large auditorium gave the students a warm, dry place to play inside when the weather was cold and stormy. The community activities, graduations, and other school programs in the auditorium were especially appreciated.

There was an active PTA organization that served the Lower Valley Teachers Association a dinner about once a year as a money-making project. We had to bring dishes from home to serve that many — always a big undertaking. Remember the night the men dressed as women and put on a program? A fun time!

We became 4-H leaders for several years and again, our New Liberty members always made a

Dwight Barcus with some of his cattle on the farm in New Liberty. *(Photo courtesy of Petrea Barcus)*

233

(Above) The newly built home of Dwight and Petrea Barcus in May 1951. It was still in the middle of the hay field and they had just moved in. Notice the "B" on the chimney.

(Upper left) Another view of the home when they had the yard and trees planted. Delene is standing in the doorway. The home served them from 1951 to 1959, when they moved away.

(Center left) The Baracus family, Luthera, Earlynn, Dwight, Petrea, Delene, and Darrel in their home in the late 1950s shortly before they left New Liberty. Darrel died in 1961.

(Below left) Luthera and Darrel in back, and Earlynn and Delene in front, about 1953.

(Below right) The Barcus family in 1992 in their home in Portland, Oregon. Standing: Luthera, Delene, Harlan, Earlynn, and Dorothy Beaslin Russell, Dwight and Petrea's foster daughter. Sitting: Petrea and Dwight Barcus. *(All photos courtesy of Petrea Barcus)*

good showing at the annual fair in late summer. Some of the other leaders were Elizabeth Morrow and Julia Gosnell (Guy Gerry's sister) as sewing leaders. 4-H kept us active year around with meetings and contests. Our group participated in plays and talent contests and did very well. One time Tom Berry played a guitar and sang "Jambalaya." Excellent talent!

I enjoyed the fellowship and activities of the Sorosis Club with the ladies of the community. They always prepared a float for the parade during the festivities at the fair — always brought home some blue, red and white ribbons.

It was futile for us to try to raise chickens because of the skunks and bobcats that flourished in the creek bottom. One morning when feeding the chickens we discovered only three hens left and I decided to dress them out so *we* could have them instead of the bobcats. I bled them on two traps, one inside the chicken house, and one just outside the door. The children and I made a trip to the ranch that day and when we arrived home we could hear the trap chains clanking. Darrel and I went down to the chicken house with a flashlight and there was a full grown bobcat caught in not one, but both traps. Dwight was up at the ranch and had the guns. I saw that Spark and Neet's house was still lit up, so went over and got Spark to come shoot the bobcat. Neet came too!

The skunks made raising fryers impossible — they would go in the coop and kill the young chicks, even with the mother hen hovering over them. We took one injured baby that had been bit in the head up to the house. He was cockeyed, but thrived and did well. He became a nuisance as well as a pet at the back door.

We tried raising some guinea hens, as we thought their noisy cackle would let us know if there was a varmint around. Only saved one as the chicken hens pecked the little guinea chicks to death. No win! Again we had a pet and back-door nuisance. It roosted on the clothes line cross boards. One morning no sign of it was found. We think an owl just picked it off the roost at night.

We sold out in 1959 to a Mr. Brock from Utah. He soon sold to Ralph and Norma Eatinger from Nebraska, and a few years later they sold to Ivol Young.

We moved back to Fruita. At the time I was expecting another child and neighbors in the New Liberty and Mack community gave us a lovely white blanket for the expected little one. That little one was a *bonus baby boy*, Harlan Dwight, who is now 37 years old.

Dwight and Petrea's oldest son, Darrel, died 18 February 1961, at Colorado Springs, Colorado. He was buried in Elmwood Cemetery at Fruita. The others are all married — Luthera Ann to Robert Hindman; Delene Petrea to Roy Tufly; Earlynn Elena to Robert Landini; and Harlan Dwight to Joann Winteroth (They have since divorced).

Dorothy Marie Beaslin, born 13 March 1929 in Fruita, Colorado, has been a part of Dwight and Petrea's family since 2 October 1943. She married **LeRoy Earl Russell** 29 January 1949. LeRoy Russell died 23 March 1984.

Barnes

Obituaries and news items from *The Daily Sentinel.*

John Thomas Barnes was born at Center, Rio Grande, Colorado, 12 December 1912. He came with his parents to the Fruita/Mack area about 1929. He attended Fruita Union High School. On 2 August 1936 he was married to **Elva Carpenter** at Fruita. They had one daughter and eight sons:

Geraldine	**Clarence**
Floyd	**James**
Gene	**Vernon**
Dale	**Warren**
John	

John served in the Army during World War II. Sometime in the 1940s the family moved to New Liberty and lived many years on the Juan Pacheco homestead. John retired from the farm in the 1970s, leaving it in the care of one of his sons, and moved to Grand Junction. He died at the Veterans Hospital 25 March 1978, and is buried in the Rosebud Cemetery in Glenwood Springs, Colorado.

Barr

Obituaries, 1920 Colorado census and news items from *The Daily Sentinel.*

Sanford "Sam" J. Barr was born 15 September 1883 at Tate Springs, Tennessee. He spent the early part of his life in Tennessee and came to the Grand Valley in 1904. He worked as a telephone lineman for a number of years and later as an electrician. On 30 March 1918 Sam became a homesteader on Mack Mesa — one of the applicants who filed the day after the drawing. In later years he was involved in vanadium mining as well as farming.

Sam was married to **Minerva "Minnie" Louise Groves** in 1907 at Fruita. Minnie was a pioneer in the truest sense. She was born at Beatrice, Gage, Nebraska, 16 April 1881. She moved with her family by covered wagon to Kansas and later to Fruita. She attended schools in Fruita and then worked at Fruita Mercantile before she was married to Sam Barr. While she was clerking at the store she had the distinction of waiting on Chief Ouray and Chipeta, they returned several times because of her fairness in dealing with them.

Sam and Minnie had six daughters and three sons:[†]

Eleanor (Harris), 1911, Missouri
Ann (Leonard), 1914, Missouri
Sam Dalton, 1916, Colorado
Barbara (McFarland), 1918, Colorado
Blanche (Willey)
Blayne Elwood
James Thomas "Tom"
Betty Joan
Buelah Maxine

The latter two died young. The other children all grew up on the farm on Mack Mesa, attending Mack School and Fruita Union High School.

The 1920 census indicates that Sam and Minnie, then residing in Fruita, had lived in

[†] See page 151, MacTaggart story, for picture of the Barr children.

Missouri for awhile after their marriage. According to that record the two oldest children, Eleanor, age nine, and Anna, age six, were both born in Missouri. Dalton, age four years five months, and Barbara, age one year nine months, were born in Colorado.

Sam died at age 59 at the farm home 27 September 1942. Minnie spent the last four years of her life at Palisades Nursing Home. She died at age 89, 3 July 1970. Sam and Minnie are buried in Elmwood Cemetery at Fruita.

Blayne entered the Air Force in June 1944, after graduating from Fruita Union High School, and served as an "Airplane Armorer and Gunner" during World War II. He served overseas from January 1945 until February 1946. After the war he worked as a truck mechanic in Fruita. He died in an auto accident 7 November 1962 in Arapahoe County, south of Denver.

James Thomas "Tom" Barr served in the Army, as a Staff Sergeant, from 25 March 1942 to 6 December 1945 — overseas from 22 June 1944 to 29 November 1945. We have no other information.

Sam Dalton, the oldest son, died of cancer 5 September 1992 at Castro Valley, California. Both Sam and Blayne are buried in Elmwood Cemetery at Fruita.

Ann Barr; an interesting article concerning her was found in *The Daily Sentinel* of 19 February 1941. It states that Ann had graduated from Modesto Junior College in California and then took Beauty Training from Moss Beauty Shop in Grand Junction. She later worked in that and other shops in Grand Junction.

At the time the article was written she was on tour with Sonja Heinie, a popular (swimming) movie star, as her personal hair stylist. She had stopped to visit with her parents on the farm on Mack Mesa before returning to Hollywood. She had worked the previous eight years at Fox Studios in Hollywood as a hair stylist and had been a hairdresser for many actresses and actors, including Delores Del Rio, Shirley Temple and Tyrone Power.

Berry

Obituaries and news items from *The Daily Sentinel*, personal interviews with Laura Johnson Berry and Arthur Shires, a letter from Anna Jane Berry Starr (published in the *Fruita Times)* and personal knowledge of the author.

Oscar Edwin Berry was born 25 December 1894, at Cedar Vale, Chautauqua, Kansas, a son of Frank Merium and Nancy Jane Blanchard Berry. He spent the early part of his life in Kansas, coming to the Mack area in 1932. He brought with him a daughter and two sons from a previous marriage:

(Left) Oscar and pet bear in 1933. Oscar raised this bear from a baby, but it ate too many peach pits and died. (Above) Helen, Raymond and Edwin, about 1926. (Below) Emory and Helen Hestand in the 40s. *(All three photos courtesy of Anna Jane Berry Starr)*

Helen Viola (Hestand), 26 April 1920
Edwin Marion Berry, 28 Dec ember 1921
Raymond James Berry, 14 January 1924
Another son, **Francis Lloyd,** was born 8 July 1917 at Schoolton, Texas and died 16 November 1920 at Wheeler, Texas.

Helen Viola Berry was born 26 April 1920 in Bartlesville, Oklahoma. She married **Emory Hestand** and they lived in New Liberty for a couple of years after they were married on what became the Chaffin farm. They had two children; a son, David, and a daughter, Rosalie, and seven grandchildren. Helen died in December 1986 in Kansas.

Edwin Marion Berry was born 28 December 1921, at Cedar Vale, Chautauqua, Kansas. He came to New Liberty in 1932 with his father, Oscar Edwin Berry, and a brother, Raymond, and sister, Helen. He spent 12½ years in the

Navy during and after World War II and the Korean conflict. He was married to **Virginia Duncan** 28 December 1972, at Salida, Chaffee, Colorado. They had two children: **Cynthia Lee** and **James Edwin**. Edwin and Virginia were later divorced. Then he married **Gloria L. Ficco**. That marriage also ended in divorce.

Edwin died 16 April 1974, at age 52, at Veterans' Hospital in Grand Junction.

Raymond James Berry was born 14 January 1924 in Cedar Vale, Chautauqua, Kansas. He joined the Navy in 1942. In January 1945 he was reported missing in action; apparently he was taken prisoner after the ship he was on was sunk by a German submarine. No more was heard from him during World War II, but Anna Jane Berry Starr tells us he survived, later married **Lois** (unknown) and had five children. He passed away in December of 1974 in California.

On 1 August 1933, at Fruita, Oscar was remarried to **Laura Lucille Johnson**, of New Liberty. Oscar and Laura had three sons and two daughters:

Frank Alfred, 29 October 1934
Anna Jane (Starr), 19 April 1937
Thomas (Tom) Carl, 8 November 1938
Patricia (Patty) Lucille, 11 March 1941
Reginald "Reggie" Ernest, 27 May 1942

The family purchased a farm that had previously belonged to LeRoy (Roy) Wells, across 8 Road, east of the Edward L. Shires homestead.

In late summer of 1942, a committee of local citizens, led by Clyde Likes Sr. and Bob Cox, Bob being the spokesman, went to the Berry home and told Oscar that since they felt he was not taking proper care of his family, he would have to leave the community. Soon after that Oscar secured work as a coal miner at Horse Canyon Mine near Dragerton, Utah. He had high hopes of paying off his farm with the money he earned there.

(Above) Edwin Berry in the 70s. (Below) Laura and Oscar on their wedding day 1 August 1933. *(Photos courtesy of Anna Jane Berry Starr)*

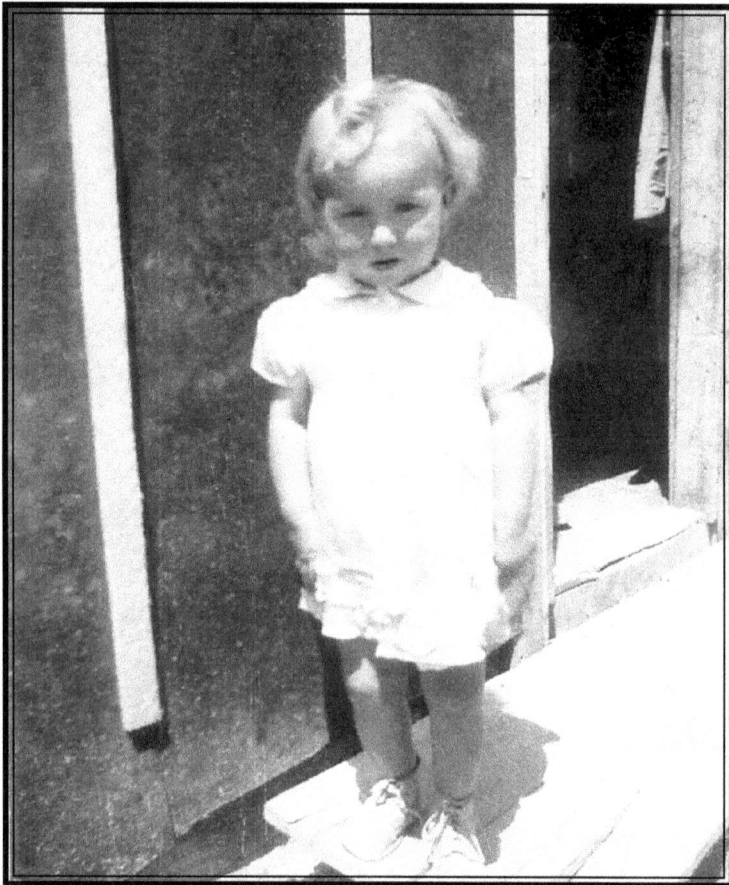

Patricia (Patty) Lucille Berry not very long before the accident that took her life. *(Photo courtesy of Anna Jane Berry Starr)*

On 7 September 1942, while Oscar was home briefly and helping at the school house making preparations for the beginning of school, tragedy struck the family. Anna Jane, Tommy, and Patty were playing with matches in a straw chicken house near the farm home. The straw caught fire and the children escaped safely, but little Patty, age 18 months, went back in the chicken house to rescue the bucket of eggs they had been gathering. Laura tried vainly to rescue the little girl, and was seriously burned. Laura was in the hospital in Fruita for a long time, then spent several months recuperating under her mother's care. She was badly scarred from her horrible experience.

In the spring of 1943 the family moved to Dragerton and Oscar went to work at Horse Canyon mine. They were living there when another tragedy struck — Oscar died of a sudden heart attack 30 October 1943. Laura then moved back to New Liberty with her family and continued striving to make the farm pay off.

Then later, still another tragedy; Frank lost his life in an auto accident south of Moab, Utah on 19 October 1955. Many people of the community rallied around the widow and her children.

The rest of the story can best be told by daughter Anna Jane Berry Starr. Anna Jane's appreciation is expressed in many ways in the following:

Mom moved her family back to New Liberty to the farm, being back among her family and friends and the neighbors she needed, and this is where we spent the remainder of our growing-up years. And they were good years, the best place in the world for Mom to raise her little family. Mother worked hard to keep her little farm and to make those payments; she was determined to keep her farm on which to raise her children. And she did, with lots of hard work and many tears on her part. But she also had the help of her brothers, Rudolph, Arthur and Leonard.

My brother, Frank, as soon as he was old enough, worked hard not only in helping Mom, but helping our uncles also. Mom only asked for help when it was impossible for her to do it herself. And then she hated to ask.

Mother had many heartaches and hard times, but she was a fighter, a hard worker, and determined to take care of her family. She was very kind and loving, and the dearest mother. She needed lots of encouragement, love and support, which she got from all the wonderful people, friends and neighbors who lived in New Liberty, Mack and other areas.

Going to Sunday School was very important to Mom, her only goal now was to love, provide for, and raise "good kids" and she did a good job! I know that we didn't miss going to church and Sunday School very many times, as we earned lots of perfect-attendance New Testaments and Bibles.

I remember many Sundays when we went to someone's home for dinner. If the weather was too bad to walk, Zella and Bob Sanders always came for us. I'm sure there were others, but my memory is of the Sanders'. We ate many Sunday dinners in their home. Zella Sanders was such a dear lady whom my mother loved very much. Bob always came to get our family so we could enjoy the fireworks he would get for his family for the 4th of July, and of course, we were always fed. We always looked forward to that. Bob always thought of

239

(Above) Laura, Oscar and new born, Reggie, May 1942. This was the last picture taken of Oscar before his death.

(Above) 1944—Anna Jane, Laura, Reggie, Tom, and Frank in front of their house right after Oscar died. (Below) 1944—Tom, Frank, Anna Jane and Reggie at "Aunt Mary" & "Uncle Clem" Maluy's house 1944. When Laura was burned, the Maluys took care of Reggie for almost a year while Laura was in the hospital and recuperating. The Maluy home was a second home for them.

(Below left) 1946—The Berry boys on "Old Smokey." Reggie in the saddle, Tom standing on the horse, and Frank standing next to the horse. *(All photos courtesy of Anna Jane Berry Starr)*

"Laura and her little ones" when he went to get fruit and vegetables for his own family, and would bring us some too, never costing Mom a dime. Wylie, Lewis and Helen — I'll always love you. And Bob, thank you for your kindness and love shown to our family!

Aunt Mary, what would we have done without you and Uncle Clem? [Maluy] You were Reginald's second parents for almost a year. I can still hear Uncle Clem who, whenever he saw Reg, would say, "How's my little fiddler?" Because of you two wonderful people, Santa would always come to our house. I still remember some of the gifts you gave us, especially I remember the year Reg got his little red wagon. You seemed to know when Mom could only get the oranges, nuts and candy to put in our stockings. I always loved to come to your house, and I did a lot, as did the other kids. Mom used to tell us, "Don't you go pester Aunt Mary today; if I catch you down there, you will get a spanking-now, I mean that!" But we would watch for Uncle Clem, and away we would go.

Lee Ann, you were always so patient with me. I loved to play in your play-room; I think I just liked being with you. Marilyn and Charlie, Darrell and Beverly, Phyllis and Homer, thanks for all the hugs and for being so good to Mom and us kids.

Aunt Mary, thank you for your love and kindness in helping to make our childhood a happy one. We love you!

Then there was another Maluy family, the Bill Maluy family — Uncle Bill, Aunt Martha, Dale, Rex, Patty, Wilma, Norma, Jody and Audie. We needed you! All of you showered us with love and attention. Uncle Bill and Tom became real buddies; Tom spent every minute possible at his side or at his heels. They became quite the story-tellers, and Tom still is a good story-teller. His nephews and niece think he is the greatest!

Uncle Bill took us to our first movie; he took us to the Fruita theater to see Uncle Remus in "Song of the South." I'll never forget! He got us each a treat, then took us inside the theater, sat us down and said, "I'll be right out here when the movie is over." And he was. No one loved Uncle Bill more than the little Berry kids! I also remember the day when we called Bill "Uncle Bill" and Aunt Martha said, "Now this 'Uncle Bill' has to stop. If I can't be 'Aunt Martha' then Bill can't be 'Uncle Bill'." From that day on it was Uncle Bill and Aunt Martha. Aunt Martha made sure the Easter Bunny always came to our house.

What wonderful, dear people!

As I sit here writing this and remembering, I think of another dear friend of Mom's; they were friends all during their school years. Viola Alstatt, do you remember the day you brought the little black and white T.V. to us? Our first T.V. I can't remember the year, but I do remember our excitement and the many hours of entertainment we enjoyed for several years! Thank you, Viola!

Modine, you and Hobart put up with me a lot. You were so good to me; you took me when you took Maxine and Dolores, especially during the high school days. Had it not been for you, I would not have gotten to do many things that I did get to take part in. Maxine and I ended up marrying cousins, so became family. Dolores and her husband Jim, and their family are very close and dear friends. Thank you, Modine, for many, many things. I know Mom didn't have money for me to go with you many times, yet I was always treated as if I was one of your girls. I love you!

I used to baby-sit for Jim and Mildred Cooper. And I remember Don and Jessie Weimer. We all knew Don, and he loved all kids. (His real name was Dominic. Most everyone knew him as "Don")

I worked for Jessie during the summers for a few years. I helped her clean and wash windows for which she paid me 50 cents a day. I thought I was getting rich! I remember when I was in the 8th grade I started fixing Aunt Martha's hair; and did that all through my high school days. She paid me $2 each time; that was my favorite job.

Mr. Bowen, our mail carrier, was always very patient with us kids. If he saw us running to the mailbox he would wait for us and hand us our mail. He would always say "Hi" and always told us, "Tell your mother Hello."

Then I must not forget Della Swyhart. She was the one who always came to stay with us when Mom needed to go someplace. We all liked Della. We also knew that we had to mind her. When she said, "Get to bed," we did, with the covers over our heads. She laughed about that, as we did, years later.

Clyde and Ruby Likes, Billy, Bob and Ed, we had lots of fun at their home, and many good meals. When they lost Billy, our hearts were broken.

Bill and Lois Pollock, Betty, Robert, Walter and Norma. Cardon and Hattie Jones, Nelson, Rusty, Betty and Donna. Merton and Mildred Arpke and their girls Peggy, Elaine and Ruth. Lois and Howard Tufly and their

1952—Anna Jane, Laura, Reggie, Tom, and Frank standing in front of the newly remodeled home. They had a right to be proud of their accomplishments. *(Photo courtesy of Anna Jane Berry Starr)*

family. George and Ann Underwood. I remember visiting in each of their homes many times as a young child, also the help many of them gave to our family.

When I was in the 8th grade, Mom was able to get our first refrigerator. Boy! Were we kids happy! That meant we no longer had to carry our milk home from Grandma Shires' in those big coffee jars. Many times we dropped our jar of milk and then there was no more until the next day, or sometimes for a couple of days.

I think my mother's happiest day was the day the little farm was truly hers. She had done it! Now she was able to fix up a few things about the house. With the help of neighbors, family and friends doing the labor, getting the materials needed, our house became a mansion.

She built a big, long room across the front of the old part, giving us a nice living room and kitchen, not to say how much warmer the new part was. My brother, Frank, built the sink and cupboards in shop at school. We also got an electric kitchen range. We were so proud of the new addition!

We never had indoor plumbing, but we never missed having it either. For many years we used big wooden barrels to keep our water supply in. In the winter we melted snow for

our water supply, then when the water came into the ditches, we used ditch water. Then one year after Uncle Bill no longer used his stock cistern, he told Mom she could use it. We cleaned it and filled it, but the only bad part of it was, Mom had to carry water in buckets for probably a block and a half from our house. I guess you know we were conservative with water.

Saturday nights were bath nights. Mom would get the little round tub down and start bathing us; the cleanest one first (that was usually me). Then when we were all clean we read our Sunday School lesson. Mom then tucked us all in bed and we were clean for Sunday School the next morning.

Mom used to worry that she didn't keep us clean enough. But one day Sue Thompson said, "Laura, you keep your little kids so nice and clean; I can't say that for the rest of my students." Mom quit worrying after that. We always had to change our clothes as soon as we got home from school. We almost always wore the same clothes for all five days of the school week.

Mom always bought each of us a new pair of shoes at the beginning of the school year. We wore hand-me-down clothes, but Mom always said it would ruin our feet if we wore someone else's shoes. The boys each got two new pairs of overalls and those two pair had to last the whole nine months of the school year. If I remember correctly, most of our shoes came from a Sears or Montgomery Ward catalog. Mom would trace our feet on a piece of paper, send that with the order, and the shoes were always the right size.

We were a very happy family; we never wanted for more. The only thing I ever really wanted and couldn't have, was a bicycle. And that was something Mom said we could get along without. She always reminded us "how rich we were," and we were, in so many, many ways. I'm glad I grew up in New Liberty; that was one of our riches.

I lived there for 18 years, going to school there left me with many good friends and memories, and a good start on my education. We were lucky we had so many good teachers. Mrs. Weaver started me out (see New Liberty School history). I loved her, she was so good to me, always taking me home for the weekend with her. I loved that so very much! Mrs. Clara Roach was another of the teachers who took me to her home many, many times. She had a daughter, Jean, who, the last I knew, was living in Grand Junction. And Jean Mock, whom I think married Johnny White. I remember when Lewis Likes taught, and I especially remember Sue Thompson and Mabel Cooper. They were not only good teachers but good friends as well. They remained our friends and kept in touch for all these many years. We had lots of fun wiener roasts over at Mrs. Cooper's. I remember when our school used to go to Mack for Play Day or a Track Meet quite often, so we knew most of the kids at Mack School.

Our school Christmas plays were a big thing, and so were our big music program at the end of the year. Our Young Citizens' League group, that Mrs. Cooper worked very hard for, was a wonderful program. At the end of the school year all the schools would go to Fruita for May Day. We would take our sack lunches for a really big day! As I remember, the New Liberty kids excelled in almost everything.

We had hot lunches at school. Through the years 1943 to 1950, Mrs. Margaret Morrow and Dora Tomlinson were the cooks.

Frank graduated from high school and had decided that if he could get a good job he could earn enough money to buy a tractor and some equipment, then he could farm our little farm himself. He got a job with Moab Drilling Company of Moab, Utah, but lost his life 19 Oct 1955, in a tragic traffic accident. I graduated that year and moved to Grand Junction to work for Mountain Bell. Tom had joined the Navy and was gone from home, so this left Mom and Reg on the farm until Reg graduated and joined the Army. Mom stayed on the farm for awhile, but we didn't like for her to be out there alone. We felt she shouldn't have the worry of finding someone to run the farm, so we talked her into selling the place.

My brother Edwin came back from the Navy, bought a house in Grand Junction and Mom lived there with him for a few years. Then Edwin got a job in Leadville, Colorado, so Mom moved to Leadville with him. Tom and his wife, Marilyn, were living there also by that time.

They were there for several years, then Mom got a trailer and moved into a park in Grand Junction for awhile. But she was never happy there, so we moved her to Fruita to the K Road Mobile Home Park, where she lived until she sold her trailer and moved into Independence Village in Fruita. She lived there almost five years before she passed away 8 May 1985, at age 77 years.

Mother, you are always in our hearts. For as long as we remember, you always provided stability within our family, full of laughter, full of tears, full of love. Whatever we became was because of you. And we thank you forever for that relationship.

I think we all got a good honest start from being born and raised in New Liberty. After all, how could we go wrong? We were one big family out there.

Where are the Berry kids today? (1991)

Tom and his wife **Marilyn Musser** live in Hawthorne, Nevada. Tom retired for medical reasons and has many health problems. He has his own welding shop and works when he can. They have two sons, **Tom Jr.**, who lives in California, and **Ronald (Ron)** and his wife, **Susie**, live in Hawthorne, Nevada.

Reg and his wife, **Freida Nolan**, live at Ridgway, Colorado. They have one son, **Reg Jr.**, who also lives at Ridgway.

My husband, **Fred Starr** and I farmed near Fruita for 32 years at 21 and M roads. Then a big change happened in our lives and we were no longer farmers.

We had to start over again. Fred is now with the United States Department of Agriculture. Our home is now in Meeker, Colorado, where Fred has been the County Executive Director (CED) for the past three and one half years. (1991) Fruita will always be home, but we do like Meeker very much, it is beautiful in the summer.

We have three children. **Richard** and his wife, **Sharon Buller**, and their children, **Trenton** and **Marissa**, live at Fruita. Richard works for Western Slope Auto.

Darren and his wife, **Cindy Coulson**, and

The grandchildren of Anna Jane and Fred Starr. Back row L-R: Megan and Trenton Starr, and Derek Dodson. Front row: Ashley Dodson, Shay and Marissa Starr. (*Photo courtesy of Anna Jane Berry Starr*)

their two children, **Megan** and **Shay**, live also at Grand Junction. Darren works for the City of Grand Junction.

Our daughter, **Tamara**, and her husband, **Richard Dodson**, and their two children, **Ashley** and **Derek**, live at Fruita. Derek and Tamara both work for City Market.

We are especially happy to include the foregoing heartfelt tribute to the people of New Liberty Community, the story points out the wonderful caring attributes of the people who lived there. And a special tribute to that GIANT mother — Laura Lucille Johnson Berry, who was truly a saintly woman. Here is a verse of scripture that fits Laura: "*Many daughters have done virtuously, but thou excellest them all.*" (Proverbs. 31:29) More will be told about Laura with the Shires/Johnson story.

Oscar, Laura, Patricia, Frank and Edwin Berry are all buried in the Elmwood Cemetery at Fruita.

1970 - Anna Jane Starr, Tom, Reginald and Laura Berry in Fruita, Colorado. (*Photo courtesy of Anna Jane Berry Starr*)

Noah Earle and Allie Mae Reece Raver
Blasdel, 1924. *(Photo from Maybelle Likes
Cox Collection)*

Blasdel

Information from family group sheets, stories
from James Blasdel and Mildred Raver Means,
obituaries and news items from *The Daily
Sentinel.*

Noah Earle Blasdel was born 15 July 1889, at
Coffeyville, Montgomery, Kansas, to Ira John
Blasdel and Lettie Bell Proctor. He spent his
childhood and attended schools in Kansas and
Colorado. Noah came to Colorado in a covered
wagon with his parents, two brothers and one
sister and settled at Del Norte. He married **Allie
Mae Reece Raver** at Del Norte, Rio Grande,
Colorado, 13 August 1924 (see Raver).

Noah was previously married to Goldie Staples.
They had a girl named Gloria Mae. She is now
deceased.

The Fruita news items of *The Daily Sentinel,*
18 September 1924, reported an interesting bit of
news that was extracted from the *Del Norte
Prospector:*

With Rev. White officiating, Mrs. Mae Raver
and Mr. Noah Blasdel were married at the H. J.
Kreps home last Thursday evening. The bride and
groom are both well known and liked. They will
make their home in Del Norte, at least for some
time. The bride at one time resided in the Fruita
area and has a number of friends there who

extend congratulations and best wishes. Mrs.
[Allie Mae] Blasdel's daughter, Miss Maudie
Raver, is attending school at Del Norte, and after
she finishes her high school course the family
expects to return to Mesa County to make their
home.

Noah and Allie continued to live at Del Norte
until 3 March 1926, when they moved to the Raver
homestead in New Liberty.

Noah and Allie had five sons:

John Harold, born 14 August 1926
Glen Harvey, 30 May 1928
Noah Earl, 7 July 1930
Donald Eugene, 24 December 1932,
James Marlin, 29 June 1934
Harold, Glen, Earl, and James were born on
the Raver homestead at New Liberty. Donald
was born in Del Norte, Colorado.

About 1930, Noah purchased a homestead
formerly owned by Martin Wells, father of Lee Roy
Wells, which was located just west of the New Liberty
School. About 1936 he sold that farm to Clem Maluy

In April 1940 they sold the farm to Walter E.
Weir and Jesse Crane and moved to a place on 18 and
M Road, near Fruita. After farming for over 40
years, Noah and Allie retired. In 1981 they moved to
Grandview, Washington.

Their son, Harold, died 31 May 1973 from
injuries received in a tractor accident. Noah died 16
October 1982; Allie, 7 April 1985; both had lived past
90 years. They were both buried at Grandview,
Washington. At that time there were 17
grandchildren.

Following is an excerpt from Mildred Raver
Mean's, daughter of Allie Mae, story of the Ravers
and the Blasdels:

When I was six years of age we were blessed at
our house with a sweet baby boy, John Harold,
named after his paternal grandfather, John Blasdel.

We grew up on pinto beans, potatoes and
wonderful garden vegetables my mother grew, and I
well remember one of the first two words Harold put
together. It was at the table. He sat in a high chair
by one of the parents and suddenly said, "Daddy —
beans." We all got excited over that.

The combined Raver and Blasdel family in 1974 at Allie and Noah's 50th Wedding Anniversary. Standing, L-R: John Harold, Donald Eugene, Noah Earl, James Marlin and Glen Harvey. Sitting: Mildred Raver (Arpke Shultz Means), Allie Mae and Noah Earle Blasdel and Maudie Raver (Yates). *(Photo courtesy of Mildred Raver Means)*

When Glen Harvey (named after one of dad's brothers, Harvey Blasdel) came to the home two years later, our family was beginning to grow. Mother desperately needed help, so I was conscripted. I rocked, changed, fed and did various other jobs when asked. One evening we had company and the women were all working in the kitchen. Not wishing to be left out of the circle, I was holding Glen on the cupboard in front of me. He suddenly jerked from my arms with a little push of his legs and struck his head on a crock. My horrified mother cried out, "Oh, Mildred, you've killed him." She grabbed the limp body of my brother and began trying to revive him, while I stood in struck terror. Thank God he had been knocked out momentarily and seemed none the worse for the wear.

He got even with me. When I was a teenager, we were wrestling one day and my head hit the wooden arm of the couch resulting in my momentary "knockout."

Glen had Bright's disease and was bed ridden for three months. He said three, but it seemed more like six months to me. His bed had been placed in the living room. One day when I was sweeping the linoleum around the room, I saw one of those little farm creatures, which occasioned the sanctity of our home, run across the floor and hide behind Glen's bed. With good aim and accuracy, I swished at that mouse with the broom and killed it on the spot. I felt so heroic.

Speaking of brooms — one day Harold and Glen came in from playing outside just as I had gathered a dust pile of sweepings and I asked them not to step in it. Glen playfully drug his feet through the mess and I retaliated. Getting a good hold on the end of that broomstick, I whacked him across the seat of his pants. It must have been one of my best wallops because that broom handle broke off right in my hands while I stood in utter disbelief at what I had done. Not that I was sorry for the deed I had done, but that was the only broom my mom had.

Next was a move to Del Norte again for awhile, but not before another little brother, Noah Earl, came to live with us. This one had blonde hair and blue eyes like me. His hair curled playfully around my finger while with his winning blue eyes he absolutely stole my heart away. Sometime before he was school age he shook his head at me and seriously said, "Leave my hair alone." How could I? It would curl into a small scroll around my finger and stay that way for hours.

About this same time, Earl was afflicted with

246

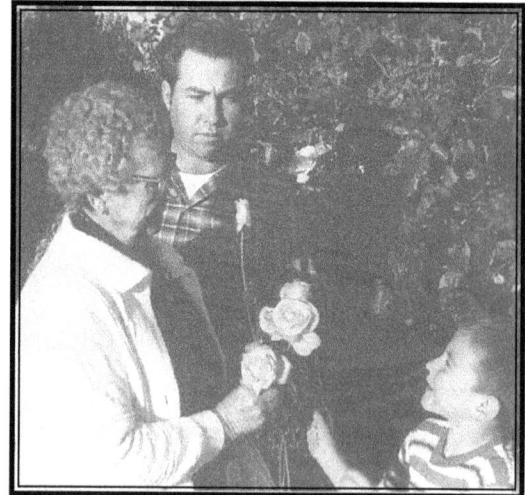

Harold and wife, Peggy, had two children: Minnie (Jerry Spaeth) and Dan (Karen) Blasdel. **Glen** and Roberta Schaffer Blasdel had three children: Terry (Becky), Glenda (Douglas Watts) and Lonnie (Kathy) Blasdel. **Earl** and Mae Schultz Blasdel had two children: Mike (Jeannie) and Michelle (Daniel Richard Babcock) Blasdel. **Donald** and Ivel Lee Ehart Blasdel had two children: David Eugene and Dennis Earl Blasdel. **Jim** and Marcella Blasdel had four children: Marsha (Mel Barbee), Jimmy G. (Michelle), John (Vanessa) and Joe (Sharon) Blasdel.

(Upper left) About 1929 on the New Liberty homestead. L-R: Maudie Raver, Harold Blasdel, Glen Blasdel, Allie Mae Blasdel and Mildred Raver sitting on a hay mower in the hay field. *(Photo courtesy of Mildred Raver Means)* (Upper right) A neighborly gathering at Merton and Mildred Arpke's residence in New Liberty, 1948. Front to back on left side: Noah, Earl and Allie Mae Blasdel, Mildred Raver Arpke, Glen Blasdel in front of tree and Harold Blasdel sitting on chair. Center: Donald and James Blasdel. Front to back on the right side: Ruth, Elaine and Peggy Arpke, Robert Arpke holding son, Duane, Merton Arpke, Phyllis Likes holding son, Dennis, and Homer Likes sitting on chair. *(Homer and Phyllis Likes Collection)* (Center left) Ada Bush and Allie Mae Blasdel at Ada's home in Santa Cruz, California, 1965. (Center) Harold Blasdel in 1972 in Prosser, Washington with his roses he loved to grow. (Center right) Allie Mae, Glen and Harold's son, Danny Ray, with Harold's roses. (Below) Marsha Blasdel Barbee of Mack, Colorado, with her dad, Jim Blasdel, in 1996. *(The last four photos courtesy of Mildred Raver Means)*

extremely large, diseased tonsils, and it was imperative he have a tonsillectomy as soon as possible. They were chronically obstructing his breathing. The doctor's orders were to get him to Denver immediately to be operated on. We had no durable auto. Uncle Harvey and Aunt Pearly had a nice sedan, but did not, for some reason, see fit to let it be used for this purpose. A friend, Earl Wates, who had a truck, offered to drive Mom and Earl to Denver if they were willing to ride in the back. There was no choice and the offer was gratefully accepted. The trip was successfully made and both survived the ordeal.

Later, in New Liberty, he had pneumonia. Dr. White did not put him in the hospital but left instructions as to his care and some medication with mother. A bed was set up in the living room again for close care. She worked day and night with hot fomentations off and on and liquids and some food offered frequently to keep up his strength. I recall she became extremely weary. One time as she placed a pack on Earl's chest I heard him say in a small, tired little voice, "Oh, Dod, not again."

A neighbor, Mrs. Mackintosh, came to see Earl and to give mother a short rest. She gently picked him up in her arms and carried him to a rocking chair. She slowly rocked and sang to him. Before she left, she had prayer with the family and asked God for His blessings. When Dr. White came the next morning, he fully expected to find Earl dead. He complimented mother for her tireless and successful care, and advised her to place the hot packs only to his back for the weight was just too much for that little body and heart. Breathing itself was all he could manage. I listened and looked on, watching carefully and was learning to pray. I know now God is not to be bargained with, but I promised if He would save my brother's life, I would acknowledge Him all my life. God heard and answered a young girl's prayer.

Donald Eugene, a healthy boy, was born in Del Norte on one of our trips there. It was Christmas Eve and mom was trying to nail a Christmas tree onto cross boards for us kids to decorate. It was a futile job for her and she began to cry. It was not long before I was told she was going into labor and dad was not home. I ran to Uncle Harvey's, perhaps a quarter of a mile away, to have him telephone the doctor. Don was born before midnight and we had a new, real baby doll for Christmas.

James Marlin was born last, but not least. A little, dark-skinned, brown-eyed boy was totally different in the home. He took the looks of the Cherokee Indian blood from dad. His black eyes were like dad's and Grandma Lettie Bell Blasdel Carver's, who lived with us off and on.

What a darling Grandma Carver was, the only grandparent I ever had. Her snow white hair was fun to shampoo, set and dress up with pretty pins. We used a touch of laundry bluing to keep the yellow out, and wave set to keep a good curl. Her white hair and black eyes were beautiful to me.

Here are some personal memories from James Blasdel:

My father, Noah, came to Colorado from Kansas in a covered wagon with his parents, two brothers and a sister. It was quite a hard trip; they settled in Del Norte. My mom and dad met in Del Norte, thanks to family and friends. They were married there, then moved back to the homestead where four out of us five boys were born. After our oldest sister, Maudie, was married, her husband put a kitchen over the pitcher pump and mom had water in the house. What a thrill that was in those days. Wash days were very full with having to haul water and then bring it all into the house with a bucket and heat it for mom to do the laundry.

Mom always had a big garden and did lots of canning to feed all of us boys. I know now it had to have been very hard.

I remember Charlie Cavendish and his son, Johnny. They got a Model A Ford. They would go by the school and old Charlie would be riding in the car with the door open so he could jump if need be. I guess he was afraid of Johnny's driving.

I am the youngest of the family, born in June 1934. We lived on the old homestead until I was about five years old, then we traded the homestead for the place in Fruita on 18 and M roads, where I actually grew up.

When the roof was redone at the school, all of us would get into the tar and chew it. I can't imagine now how terrible it must have tasted. The school also had the floors done and the school ordered tennis shoes for all of the kids, but the parents ended up paying for them.

My brother, Earl, was able to take our old Studebaker truck to Moab for the senior sneak day. Some of the kids had to ride in the back, but they didn't care as long as they were all able to go. What fun!

Blasier

Obituaries and news items from *The Daily Sentinel*.

Percy D. Blasier was born 16 February 1902 at Orlando, Logan, Oklahoma, to Fred and Jennie Blasier. He grew to manhood there, moving to Castle, Okfuskee, Oklahoma, when he was 21 years old.

He married **Ola Langwell** 2 December 1923 at Castle. Ola was born 24 February 1904 in Oklahoma. Her father was Washington Langwell.

Percy and Ola moved to the Lower Valley in 1934, and purchased the P. A. Daily farm in the New Liberty community. Percy owned a thresher and spent a large part of the summer and fall months threshing grains and beans for his neighbors in New Liberty. He also did some trucking of farm produce.

Percy grew excellent watermelons, so his patch was the target of many night-time depredations by the youth of the area.

Percy died 3 September 1947. After that Ola moved to Compton, California to live with her father. She died at Norwalk, California, 7 April 1975; both she and Percy are buried in Elmwood Cemetery at Fruita.

Booth

Obituaries and news items from *The Daily Sentinel* and letters from Betty Booth Garber and Charlotte Booth Cass.

James Leonard Booth was born 24 August 1883, at Tallula, Menard, Illinois. His parents were James Alan Booth and Sarah Arnett. He spent his childhood in Nebraska, attending high school at Pawnee City, Pawnee County, Nebraska. He married **Charlotte "Lottie" M. Shoults** 25 April 1909, at Cheyenne, Laramie, Wyoming.

Charlotte M. Shoults was born 16 January

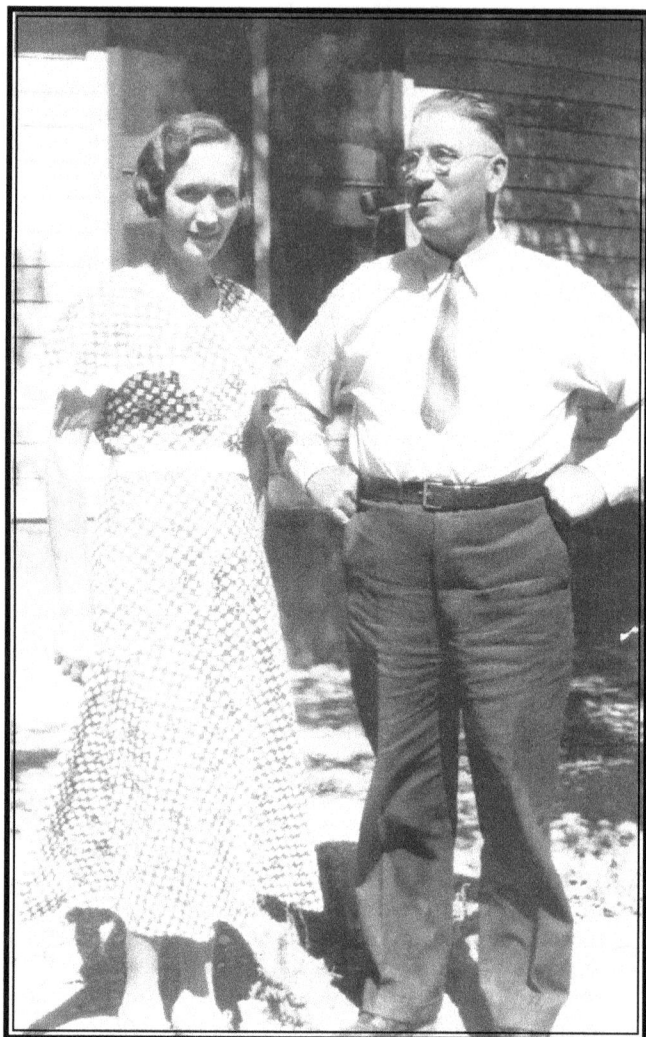

James and Charlotte Booth at Mack, Colorado, in front of the Uintah Railway Office in the early 20s *(Photo courtesy of Betty Booth Garber)*.

1889 at Chadron, Dawes, Nebraska. Her parents were James Madison Shoults and Cora Diets. She spent most of her early life in Wyoming.

James and Charlotte had four sons and two daughters:

James Harold, 11 Oct 1910, died in 1912
Gordon Everett, 21 Feb 1913, Denver, Colorado
Betty Louise (Garber), 6 July 1914, Grand Valley, Colorado
Woodrow Edward, 17 March 1917, Minatare, Scotts Bluff, Nebraska
Douglas Alan, 26 October 1920, at Fruita, Colorado

Charlotte Jeanne (Cass), 1 February 1925, Mack, Colorado

James L. Booth was employed by the Burlington Railroad for 10 years as agent and telegraph operator. Then he transferred to the Rio Grande, and continued working in that same capacity for another 10 years. They moved from Minatare, Nebraska, to Salt Lake City, Utah, and then to Grand Valley, Colorado. While there they homesteaded 160 acres of land and lived there long enough to prove up on it. (That property is still in the family).

They moved to Mack in 1918 where James continued to work for awhile for the Rio Grande. About 1924 he went to work for the Uintah Railway at Mack as train dispatcher and general freight agent, and worked in that capacity until 1939, when the Uintah went out of business.

After Fred Baird moved to California in May 1929, Lottie assumed the duties of correspondent for *The Daily Sentinel*, providing news items from Mack and vicinity, she continued with that until after the demise of the Uintah Railway. James retired at that time and they moved to a farm east of Mack, which they had purchased some time previously. Some time later the family moved to the Redlands, near Grand Junction. Charlotte (Lottie) died 29 March 1963 in Grand Junction, Colorado. James died at Rifle, Colorado, 21 April 1966, from a heart attack.

Following are some of Betty L. Booth Garber's recollections:

When we moved to Mack, Gordon, Betty and Woodrow were the only children. Later, Douglas was born in Fruita and Charlotte at home in Mack.

The Uintah Railway furnished homes for their employees. The homes were well cared for, painted and kept in good repair. Each house had electricity, steam heat and water. Ice was also delivered every other day.

Chris Pappas was caretaker of the Hotel and office grounds. Aunt Agnes Lee (sister of Lottie Booth) was manager of the hotel after Maud Levi left. Mr. Walter Rader, Superintendent of the Uintah, and his wife and their two daughters, lived in an apartment in the hotel.

Sometimes the young people of the town would gather at the hotel and listen to Deone Standifird Wagaman play the piano; she was very talented.

Other times we listened to the player piano. Occasionally in the summer, we would gather on the hotel lawn and listen to music played by Marshall Eddings on his guitar.

The town had two grocery stores, one owned by Luke Crews and the other by W. H. Cox. Clem Miller ran the lumber yard and hardware store. Mr. and Mrs. Boyden ran the Post Office. Chester Wright had a garage and small store. Mr. and Mrs. Coles ran a cafe and pool-hall.

Most of the Mack children graduated from the 8th grade at Mack School. Then they went on to Fruita Union High School and graduated from there. They had to ride the bus; there were several good bus-drivers. I remember Harold Carroll and George Fisher, to mention two of them.

Gordon, Douglas and Betty graduated from Fruita Union High School. Charlotte graduated from Grand Junction High School, as the family had moved to the Redlands by that time.

The Mack Community had most of their entertainment at the school house auditorium. I remember the moving pictures shown there by Judge Kennedy at the cost of ten cents for children and twenty five cents for adults. All the school plays, graduations and Christmas programs were held there. On Saturday nights there were dances there.

The town also had a baseball team and played teams from other places such as Atchee, Fruita and New Liberty.

The most excitement I can remember in Mack was when Mr. Crews' grocery store burned in the middle of the night. [17 February 1928] Of course, everyone in town came to watch after the fire-whistle blew — I can remember hearing the cans of food exploding all night.

And then the time when the wooden water tank broke apart and the planks and water came crashing down. Mr. Eagan saved his life by standing in the doorway, which somehow shielded him. I happened to be at Eagan's house with Hazel, daughter of the Eagans, and we saw the tank fall apart.

My brothers and sister all had special friends — Gordon and Henry Simpson; Betty and Lola Rector (Dunlap); Woodrow and Keith Wright; Douglas and Leon Daily; Charlotte and June Spencer. The Booth parents were good friends with the W. E. Bowen family, visiting them often when they lived at New Liberty, and then after they moved to Mack.

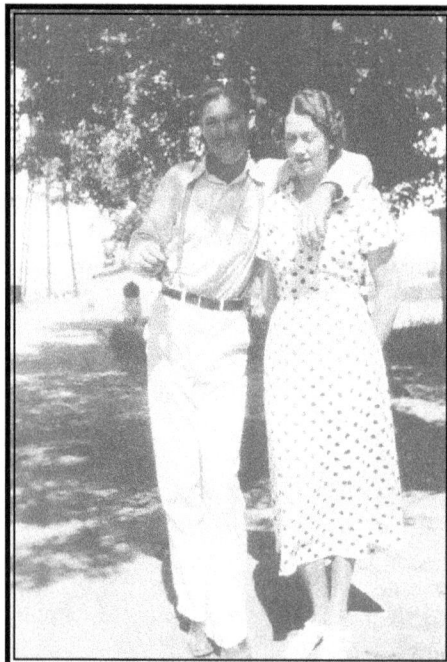

(Upper left) 1925, James and Lottie with Charlotte in yard at Mack. (Upper right) James Booth with Doug and Charlotte and dog in front of their house in Mack. (Center left) Lottie Booth in the 30s in front of their house in Mack. (Center right) Betty Booth standing in the gate at the entrance of the Uintah Golf Course in Mack about 1932. (Lower left) Woodrow (Woody) and Betty in their front yard. Visible in the background is the base of the water tower for the water tank that supplied water for the town. (Lower right) Lottie and parents, James and Cora Shoults, standing in front of the Booth home in Mack. It was located where the post office is now. (*Photos courtesy of Betty Booth Garber*)

Betty Louise Booth and Paul Marion Garber were married at Fruita, 14 November 1934. [They celebrated their 60th Anniversary in November 1994] Paul was born 9 April 1910 at Marquette, McPherson, Kansas, to John L. Garber and Hannah M. Saylor, who had come to Kansas from Tennessee. Paul started school at Little River, Kansas. The family moved to eastern Colorado when Paul was about six years of age — when there were no roads, just wagon trails. Then they moved west and homesteaded a parcel of land near Cisco, Utah, near several other families. They lived there for several years, most of that time in tents, before they gave up and moved to a farm in the Loma area. Paul and his brothers, Jack (Cecil), Lee, Chester and Elmer, attended Loma school. They returned to Kansas occasionally to work in the wheat harvest. Paul came back to Mack about 1932 and soon met Betty Booth.

After Paul and Betty were married, they lived at Lake McAndrews [on the north side of Baxter Pass] for about a year, and then lived in Atchee until the Uintah folded. They then moved to Loma and later to Grand Junction. During World War II they lived at Portland, Oregon, where Paul worked in the shipyards.

They had two children:

Gary James
Paula Susan (Peach)

There are now four grandchildren.

Paul died in Grand Junction 6 June 1996 at age 86. He was buried in Memorial Gardens Cemetery.

Paul and Betty's home in one of the cabins at Lake McAndrews in the winter of 1934. *(Photo courtesy of Betty Booth Garber)*

Gordon married **Grace E. Miller** at Delta, Colorado, 21 January 1939. They had two children:

Robert Douglas
Patricia Louise

Grace died 21 July 1966. Later Gordon married **June McCoy**, and they had a daughter, **Theresa**. Gordon worked for the Rio Grande RR and was a conductor before retirement.

Woodrow "Woody" married **Mildred Gronning** 18 January 1937, at Meeker, Colorado. They had two children:

James Edward
Sondra Jean

Woody also worked as a conductor for the Rio Grande until retirement. He died 14 June 1992.

Douglas married **Mildred Verna Reed Owens** 10 February 1948, at Ely, Nevada. They raised three children.

Chalma Owens, stepdaughter
Norma Owens. stepdaughter
Alan Reed, son

Douglas served in the Air Force for 22 years as an instructor in electronics, and retired as a senior master sergeant. Mildred died 14 June 1974 and Douglas, 2 September 1984.

Charlotte Jeanne married **Erwin Douglas Cass** 20 September 1944, at the home of her parents on the Redlands. They had three children:

Charlotte Candace (Phipps) born 2 August 1946
Daniel Clyde, born 8 Feb 1952
Kimberly Joanne (Brophy), born 12 May 1956

Charlotte Jeanne worked for Mountain Bell Telephone Company (now U. S. West) for 32 years and retired in 1982. She belongs to the Telephone Company Pioneers who do community service. She has been helping with the Adult

Reading Program at Mesa County Library since she retired.

Erwin served in the Navy from November 1942 to November 1945. He was a carpenter and sheet-metal worker for 30 years. He worked for Lane & Co., Mt. Garfield, and Becham Heating until retirement in 1982. He died 21 January 1989. Charlotte still lives in their home on the Redlands.

Charlotte Jeanne wrote the following in 1996 for this book. While some of her information is repetitious, her story adds a lot to our history of the family. We have done some editing.

The Booth Family

James Leonard Booth and Charlotte M. Shoults Booth came to the Grand Valley in 1918. Jim and Lottie, as they were commonly known, felt as though they had reached a wonderful place to live. They especially appreciated the delicious fruit and the beautiful scenery. Jim was a Station Agent - Telegrapher for the D&RGW Railroad. He had been stationed in various places in Nebraska, Colorado and Utah.

While stationed at Grand Valley, Colorado, Jim and Lottie took up a homestead on Wallace Creek. In 1910 their first child, James Harold, was born, but later died in 1912 at age $1\frac{1}{2}$ years.

After awhile Jim went to work for the Uintah Railway and served as General Freight Agent for most of the years until the railway was abandoned and his subsequent retirement. He had an office in the office building next to the hotel, and a freight office located perhaps a quarter mile west along the tracks. Walking between the two offices made him a very healthy person!

Lottie was busy caring for her home and several children: Gordon Everett, born 1913 in Denver, Colorado; Betty, born 1914 in Grand Valley, Colorado; Woodrow Edward, born 1917 in Minatare, Nebraska; Douglas Alan, born 1920 in Fruita, Colorado; and Charlotte Jeanne, born at Mack in 1925. While Lottie was very dedicated to her home and family, she always found time to help in community affairs — especially the Mack Sunday School held in the auditorium of the Mack School. She also contributed a column of Mack news items for *The Daily Sentinel* of Grand Junction. She enjoyed the Annual Correspondent's Party the *Sentinel* gave each year. There was always fine and unusual entertainment provided, along with lovely gifts.

Some of the entertainment of that time in Mack were the Saturday night dances with local talent playing good music. There were "Silent Movies" played by "Judge" Kennedy from a projection room built into the school auditorium. Judge Kennedy also took many photographs of places in Mack which later helped to preserve the history of Mack. For those who enjoyed sports, Mr. Byron Boyden supervised the building of a golf course on the hills north of town as well as a lovely tennis court right in town. There was also a baseball field west of the school with a backstop and benches.

The Uintah Railway maintained an excellent hotel and office building with a great expanse of lawn and good sidewalks (wonderful for roller-skating). Company houses where the Uintah employees lived were routinely painted and repaired. Electricity was generated at the pump house beneath the water tower where the train engines were left between runs. Throughout town the generator engine could be heard running while in use. Electricity was made available in the evenings, and on predetermined mornings for washing and ironing needs. The large water tank suspended on iron legs was the source of the town's water supply. In the winter time the steam heating system in the pump-house supplied steam for radiators in the company houses. The radiators clanged and banged but kept the houses pretty warm.

After abandonment of the railroad in 1939, Jim and Lottie moved to Fruita briefly, tried a winter in Washington State, moved back to Grand Junction, and finally settled on the Redlands where they had a small peach orchard. They enjoyed their life in this location until Lottie's death in 1963 and Jim's in 1966.

After his graduation from Fruita Union High School in 1930, son Gordon followed his father Jim into railroading, starting on the section crew at Mack, traveled with the bridge construction crew, then to train service as brakeman and ending up as conductor before his retirement. All of this was with the Denver and Rio Grand Railroad.

Gordon married Grace Miller of Glade Park in Delta in 1939. They established a home on Orchard Mesa, near Grand Junction, where two children were added to their family: Robert Douglas and Patricia Louise. Grace had worked at Mountain States Telephone and Telegraph before her marriage and through the years was called back to help in busy times.

Grace died suddenly in July 1966, leaving a great void in the whole family. Gordon then married June McCoy in 1967, and they had a daughter, Teresa. Gordon and family lived for several years at Mesa, Colorado, and enjoyed raising animals. That marriage ended in divorce.

Gordon, after suffering some health problems, now lives in an assisted-care home. He still likes to visit and can tell you much about the early days in the Grand Valley and the people he has known for years.

Betty Louise graduated from Fruita Union High School in 1931. She married Paul Garber 14 November 1934. They started married life living at Lake McAndrews on the north side of Baxter Pass, where Paul worked for the section crew of the Uintah Railway. They had a great garden and plenty of fish to eat. McAndrews was where ice was cut to supply the large ice-house in Mack, where it was packed in saw-dust until it was used in the following summer to maintain the employees' ice-boxes. The ice was delivered regularly in a "Model A" Ford truck and children would run after it for "ice chips."

After several moves, Paul and Betty bought property on the Redlands near Grand Junction. They had two children: Gary James, born while they lived at McAndrews, and Paula Susan, who was born after they moved to the Redlands. Both babies were born in St. Mary's Hospital. There are now four grandchildren.

Paul was a fine fisherman; he loved to hunt too. Betty was very good at cooking whatever was brought home. Paul also had a "Green Thumb" and had a great vegetable garden as well as beautiful roses.

In 1975 Betty retired from Goodwill Industries, where she assisted in training handicapped people. Paul retired the same year from School District #51.

As has been reported previously, Paul died 6 June 1996.

Woodrow also followed his father's choice of a railroad career. He, like Gordon, also started on the section crew at Mack, then the bridge construction crew until he was able to join train service. He also worked as brakeman and later conductor before his retirement.

Woodrow married Mildred Gronning of Meeker on 18 January 1937. They lived for a short time in Mack, then moved to the Grand Junction area, starting out on Orchard Mesa, then later settling on South Redlands. They had two children: James Edward and Sondra Jean. There are now several grandchildren and great-grandchildren.

Woody enjoyed hunting and fishing and also knew a lot about the area and people who lived in the Valley in the early days. Mildred enjoyed being a home-maker, liked to bowl, and was active in the Railroad Ladies Association. Her sister-in-law, Grace, joined her in the bowling and Railroad Ladies activities.

After Woody's retirement they moved to the family property homesteaded by Jim and Lottie, at Grand Valley (now called Parachute). Woody's health began to be a concern, so they decided to move back to the Grand Valley and settled at Clifton. As has been previously reported, Woody died in 1992. Mildred still lives in the family home at Clifton.

Douglas enjoyed his childhood days in Mack and began his lifelong interest in music in those days by learning to play the violin. He later played clarinet in the Fruita High School Band and served as Drum Major in the Marching Band. He graduated from high school in 1937.

He played in several dance bands in the area and was a member of a band while he was serving in the Air Force in India. Doug enlisted in the Air Force when news of the impending problems started in Europe and were becoming more serious in the United States. After receiving his training as a bombsight technician, he spent three years in India near Karachi. After serving his first tour of duty, he came home and attended Mesa College.

In February 1948, during the time he was in college, Doug married Mildred Verna Reed Owens. Mildred, also known as Mickey, had two daughters, Norma and Chalma, by her former marriage to Melvin Owens. Melvin, who had grown up in Fruita, died at a young age. Doug was happy to take over being a father to the little girls and a strong bond developed between them.

Doug reenlisted in the Air Force, and while he was stationed at Lowry Field near Denver, a son, Alan Reed, joined the family in 1950. As military families do, they traveled to several different bases in the United States. Then Doug spent a year in Korea while the family stayed in California.

After Doug's retirement, he and Mickey lived in several places, trying to decide where they would like to live permanently. They settled in Reno, Nevada, but a short time later, in 1974, Mickey died suddenly. Doug returned to live in Fruita, and later established a home in Clifton. He died in 1984.

Charlotte spent many happy years in Mack, attending Mack grade school and the freshman and sophomore years at Fruita Union High

School. In 1940 she moved with her parents to the Redlands and graduated from Grand Junction High School in 1942. Then she went to Ross Business College and later went to work for Mountain States Telephone and Telegraph. She started out as a telephone operator, and through the years witnessed many changes in the way telephone calls are handled.

In 1944 she married Erwin (Erv) Douglas Cass while he was on leave from the Navy's Aerial Patrol in the North Atlantic.[†] After he left the Navy, Erv worked with his father for many years as a Sheet Metal Mechanic.

Erv and Charlotte had three children: Charlotte Candace (Candy), Daniel Clyde and Kimberly Joanne. The family enjoyed outdoor activities such as hiking, picnicking, fishing and watching Erv play in football games. Charlotte kept up an active interest in Sunday School and working with Cub Scouts through all those years.

Charlotte worked with the telephone company until retirement in 1982; Erv retired in 1982 also, then they spent some enjoyable times traveling and going boating on Lake Powell and Flaming Gorge.

Erv died in 1989 and Charlotte continues to live in the family home on the Redlands.

William Everett Bowen   Georgia "Jo" Starbuck Bowen
Both photos taken in 1943. *(Photos courtesy of JoAnn Bowen Montague)*

Bowen

Most of the following was contributed by JoAnn Bowen Montague. There are some additions from *The Daily Sentinel* news items, obituaries, and author's personal knowledge.

William Everett Bowen was born 2 July 1892, at Osborne, Osborne, Kansas. His parents were **W. B. Bowen** and **Ruth Nullender**. Everett attended schools in Osborne and played football on the Osborne High school team. He was later employed by Standard Oil Company as a tank truck driver, which was originally a horse-drawn vehicle. Everett was visiting with a cousin in Smith Center, Kansas when he met **Georgia "Jo" Starbuck**, a sister of his cousin's wife. They promptly fell in love and were married 3 May 1912, at Kansas City.

Georgia was born at Smith Center, Kansas, 30 December 1892, to **Lee Starbuck** and **Olive Morris**. She graduated from high school in Lansing, Kansas, where she had been active in the drama society and in "Elocution Lessons." After marriage Everett and Jo lived at Norton, Kansas, where they became acquainted with

† AM3c Erwin Douglas Cass served from 22 November 1942 to 9 November 1945.

255

Burgeon (Burge) and Blanche Lofgren.

Everett and Jo's son, William "Bill" L. Bowen, was born 19 November 1913, at Logan, Phillips, Kansas, a short distance from Norton.

In 1918 Everett, in company with Burge Lofgren, journeyed to Grand Junction, Colorado to participate in a drawing for homestead rights on the new land opening up for homesteading in the Lower Grand Valley. Everett and Burge were successful in acquiring homesteads near each other. However, there is some confusion as to the date Everett filed — his name does not appear with the early applicants. One source says he filed in 1918, another says he filed in 1919. According to daughter JoAnn, he left Jo, and son, Bill, behind with her parents in Smith Center while he went to Colorado to establish their new home.

Son, Bill, tells about the transition this way:

Jo and son, Bill, about 1917. *(Photo courtesy of JoAnn Bowen Montague)*

Burge Lofgren came out and looked the place over and came back and talked Everett into coming out. And further — Jo had the flu and nearly died the winter before (likely the flu epidemic), and the doctor told them to get her to a higher and drier climate. Everett and his younger brother (age 16) came out and built the house, then sent for Jo and Bill to come out on the train. The younger brother then went home.

The Mack items of *The Daily Sentinel* dated Tuesday., 15 April 1919:

"W. E. Bowen and family arrived here last week to move on one of the homesteads near here."

Another *The Daily Sentinel* item from Mack dated Saturday, 6 December 1919:

"W. E. Bowen, one of the ranchers near

Mack, has gone to Atchee to work for the winter."

The 1920 census lists William E. Bowen, 27, Machinist, in Atchee.

Bill recalled his first experience at the homestead:

The day I arrived in New Liberty I made a terrible mistake. There wasn't a tree or bush in sight. I went to the toilet and instead of the toilet I opened the door to the chicken house and let all the chickens out.

The Bowen house and large yard that everyone in the community enjoyed in the summertime. *(Photo courtesy of JoAnn Bowen Montague)*

Everett, Jo and Bill established a home in a typical homestead shanty and became a part of the community. Everett and Jo were both active in community affairs; Bill was one of the first grade students at the "new" New Liberty School in September of 1919. Everett was a member of the school board for several years, and Jo was involved in the Sunday School many years as a teacher. Soon after they set up house-keeping on the farm, they planted a large yard of blue grass and shade trees. This later was one of the favorite spots for the community's summer activities.

Some of JoAnn's memories:

Anywhere there was a picnic, the Bowens were a part. Good food and good horseshoe games. Often on the Fourth of July picnics were held at the Gerry's, Morrow's, Alstatt's, Maluy's, or on Douglas Pass. The homemade ice cream, fried chicken, fresh peach pies, and a myriad of other delicacies were in evidence. In the early days, however, our family didn't socialize outside of the New Liberty

(Left) The Bowen family at the Clem Maluy residence in 1923. L-R: Everett, Bill, Jo holding JoAnn. Patrick Maluy in the background. (Above) L-R: Lee and Olive Starbuck, JoAnn, Georgia (Jo), Everett and Bill Bowen about 1929 or 1930 in front of the Bowen yard and house in New Liberty. (Below) Everett and JoAnn with the family washing machine on the Bowen farm in New Liberty about 1925. *(Photos courtesy of JoAnn Bowen Montague)*

(Middle above) "The long and the short of it." Everett and JoAnn standing in the field on the Bowen farm in New Liberty about 1923. (Above) Grandpa Starbuck with the Bowen turkey herd standing in front of the turkey roost and shed, 1920s. (Right) Everett and friend, Odis Simpson, admiring Everett's pigs, on the Bowen farm in the 30s. *(Photos courtesy of JoAnn Bowen Montague)*

community. We did, of course, sled down Hollinger's Hill as well as Gerry's hill in the wintertime. A memoir would not be complete without the Sunday School experience. The congregation was faithful — no minister (although the senior Clyde Likes would occasionally preach). Once in awhile, I recall all the *old* hymns we sang. Some of the congregations of the church I now attend have never heard of the revival hymns. My mother taught Sunday School; I played the piano, as I recall. It was a weekly experience to look forward to — all classes held in the White schoolhouse!

Bill and I attended the New Liberty school when it was a two-room edifice, by the virtue of folding doors in the middle. Activities were riding a horse to school, playing marbles in the spring, and later attending Fruita Union High School — getting there by riding a bus driven by an assortment of "local" bus drivers. Participating in extracurricular activities was very difficult due to transportation problems! Still, we had a great experience.

Bowens always had dogs on the farm, and sometimes as many as 27 cats (to control the sparrow population?). Here it must be mentioned that cows and horses were pets back in the "olden days." Dee was Bill's horse as he and Clyde Likes explored the territory around the Bookcliff Mountains. Shorty was a workhorse, and occasionally, against his will, a saddlehorse. When neighbors came to borrow him, my father would agree to the barter because he *knew* that when Shorty reached the end of the quarter-mile section, he would *stop*, and never budge, no matter the words of encouragement. Shorty was also the horse I would occasionally ride to school and tie up in the barn provided for the ponies (Shorty was

The Bowen horses about 1929 or 1930. JoAnn Bowen, Palmer "Dinty" Simpson, and Bill Bowen with the horses. *(Photo courtesy of JoAnn Bowen Montague)*

not a pony). The bell would ring and Grace Curtis or Mr. Yates would be in the middle of the first activities, story, drill, or whatever, when a racket would be heard from the barn. Some young person (be it Darrell Maluy, Don Knapp, or Carl Alstatt) would say, "There goes Shorty!" Sure enough, Shorty would have reared back, broken his bridle straps, and trotted through the schoolyard back to the Bowen farm.

Our very small house was the center of our family life. My favorite memory was coming home in the winter (farm work was at a low ebb during that season) and mother and dad would have made doughnuts as well as *snow ice cream.* With all of today's pollution problems, snow ice cream would probably be considered "hazardous to one's health." My granddad and I played cribbage, checkers and pitch a lot.

My grandparents, Lee and Ollie Starbuck, often came to stay with my parents. My father built a "cabin" out back, in which my mother's parents could stay. As I recall, my mother's sister and my mother decided that my grandparents (at age 50) were too old to stay alone, so they had them "break-up housekeeping" and the Starbucks would live six months with the Bowen family in Kansas and six months with the Bowen family in Colorado. Granddad Starbuck was very gregarious and knew everyone in the entire New Liberty community. His goal was to sell everyone in New Liberty the *Kansas City Star* (a weekly publication). He came close! He would contact them in the field, in the byways, and at their homes. In between he hunted pheasants, helped with the chores at home, and generally took on any task he was assigned. I recall our family would drive to Denver and pick up Grandpa and Grandma Starbuck once a year

Jo feeding one of the many cats that they had on the farm. *(Photo courtesy of JoAnn Bowen Montague)*

Olive and Lee Starbuck. *(Photo courtesy of JoAnn Bowen Montague)*

and then drive back to Denver, meet Aunt Chloe and Uncle Walt Bowen, and they would take my grandparents home with them for six months.[†]

Grandma Starbuck quilted from morning until night, but never on Sunday. I used to thread a spoolful of needles when I left in the morning for school, since her eyesight was failing. The stitches on the quilts never indicated that. She had the tiniest stitches ever. When I look at quilts today, I compare the stitches to hers, and none ever measure up!

My mother, called Jo by her friends, was an expert at needlework, especially crocheting, with those infinitely fine needles and thread. She did beautiful embroidery and "cutwork" as well. She had a great market for her embroidered articles through a shop in Grand Junction on Main Street, and through the mail from people who admired her work. She was also an antique collector of some renown. My father refinished furniture that she brought home. They were both interested in antiques and collected beautiful pieces throughout the years.

A story about Jo and her collecting would be appropriate here: She loved to attend auctions in search of rare items and it became well known by others that she would bid pretty high for some valuable pieces. She would frequently ask someone else to bid for her so that no one would know she was interested in a certain item. On one occasion she had forgotten that she had asked a friend to bid for her, so asked another. The bidding became pretty lively between the two with neither of them knowing the other was bidding for Jo. She went home with the antique, but it cost her quite a bit extra.

Here's a story about Bill that should be told at this point: He and Clyde Likes were pals from the time they entered school together at New Liberty. Seems like there was always some sort of mischief on the make when those two were together! On one of their escapades when they were about 15 years of age, they were in the desert somewhere north of the canal on a Sunday afternoon and stumbled on to a cache of dynamite and caps that someone had left to blast some rock. Of course it was impossible for Bill and Clyde to just ride away and forget what they had found. They built a fire and threw the caps into the fire just to see what would happen. But it didn't go as they had planned. The caps exploded with a BANG as expected, but the boys were much too close to the fire. The explosions peppered them thoroughly with bits of copper that penetrated their clothing and their skins. They had to ride home and confess what they had been doing, then spend that Sunday evening enduring the humility and embarrassment (and pain) of having a doctor dig the bits of copper out of their skins. They were hurting!

The Mack Rural Route was established in December 1924, with Byron Boyden, husband of the postmaster, serving as temporary carrier. Everett Bowen became the first official mail carrier for Rural Route #1, on 2 March 1925. He used a model T Ford when the weather was favorable and horse and buggy when the weather made the roads muddy and slippery. On most days with an automobile he would make the run

The Bowen home in Mack in the 40s. Jo sitting on the front step. *(Photo courtesy of JoAnn Bowen Montague)*

[†] Jo and sister, Chloe Starbuck, married cousins, Everett and Walter Bowen.

259

in three to four hours, but when he had to resort to the buggy it would take most of the day. In 1930 he purchased his first Chevrolet and, as far as we can tell, stayed with Chevrolets for the rest of his career, trading for a new one every other year.

In November 1935 the Bowens moved to Mack into the former Dick Stewart home. JoAnn says the main difference was running water and an inside bathroom!

For some time, after completing his day of mail-carrying, Everett would drive out and work his farm at New Liberty, but eventually rented it and later sold it.

Everett was well known and well liked by everyone on the mail route — he was always ready to take a few minutes to visit with someone at a mail box. He must have had special joy in his work when it entailed the delivery of some of the parcel post shipments such as small farm implements, fruit trees from nurseries, incubators, brooders, and live baby chicks.

He retired from the Postal Service 31 July 1962; then he and Jo moved to Grand Junction in 1968. Everett died 27 June 1968 and Jo, 31 May 1980. Both are buried in the Orchard Mesa Cemetery.

Bill was a dedicated student who excelled in all his studies. He graduated from New Liberty about two years ahead of the other students in his age group, then graduated from Fruita Union High School in 1929, before he had reached his 16th birthday. He enrolled at Ross Business College in Grand Junction in the fall of 1929 and completed the two year course there by the spring of 1931. Later he graduated from Colorado State University with a degree in Forestry. He married **Gertrude Casto** of Unaweep, Colorado 16 August 1934 at Mack, and they both taught school in Gateway for awhile. He was employed by the Civilian Conservation Corps on Grand Mesa for a short time and then

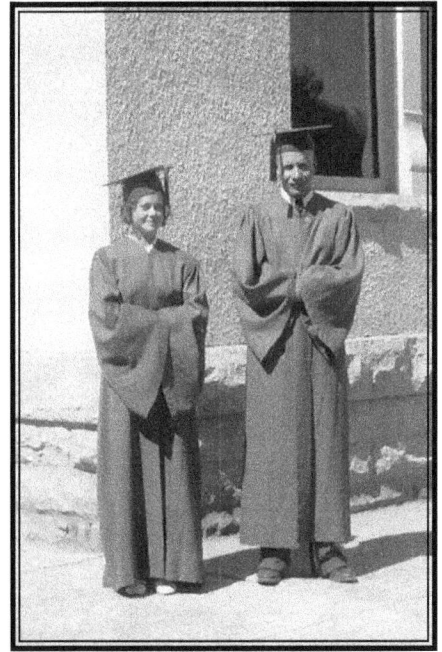

(Above) Left: William "Bill" Bowen about 1929. (Right) Gertrude Casto and William "Bill" Bowen 1933-34 when they graduated from Colorado State University. *(Photos courtesy of JoAnn Bowen Montague)*

worked for the National Park Service until retirement except for time in the military during World War II) They raised a son named **Steve**. After Bill retired (about 1980?) they lived on Orchard Mesa for a few years, then moved to Elizabethtown, Kentucky, to be near their son, who works at Fort Knox. They are not far from JoAnn.

JoAnn Bowen about 1937

Jo Ann was born 13 October 1921 in the Fruita hospital. On that occasion Everett had to ride a horse over to enlist the aid of Al Alstatt and his Model "T" Ford to take Jo to the hospital.

Within a few years JoAnn began studying piano and soon became an accomplished concert pianist and teacher. Several youngsters in the community benefited from her expertise as a tutor, learning to play piano well.

JoAnn was also an outstanding student. She excelled in all her studies and finished her grade school two years before the other students in her age group. She did the same in high school and probably entered and graduated from Mesa College as one of the youngest graduates that school ever had. Even after she was married and raising a family she continued her studies, ultimately graduating from Florida State University, Southern Illinois University, and Saint Louis University. JoAnn and Hal have lived in Louisville, Kentucky since 1979. Both have served as part-time teachers at the University of Louisville.

JoAnn and **Hal Montague** were married 4 September 1942 in Denver. Hal made a career of the Air Force, so they were required to move often. He retired in 1973. They raised two daughters: **Judee** and **Susan**. They have four grandchildren.

JoAnn, Judee and Hal Montague in 1944. *(Photos courtesy of JoAnn Bowen Montague)*

Boyden

The information we have on the Boyden family is quite sketchy, but feel we should include what little we have. We don't know when they came to Mack. Some census and land records, news items from *The Daily Sentinel.*

Byron Boyden was born in Wisconsin about 1866. His wife, **Sarah (Sara),** was born in Illinois about the same year. In 1920, according to the census, Boydens were living on the New Liberty homestead. Byron and Sarah had purchased a relinquishment from Jesse L. Keedy on Unit H Sec 18 R103W. It adjoined the homestead belonging to their daughter, **May F. Boyden,** who won hers in the drawing 29 March 1918. Daughter May was also living on her homestead in 1920. (See story on Annie Gnagey).

We have discovered the Boydens had a son named **Donald,** living in Chicago, who visited them in Mack occasionally.

261

As has been noted previously, Sarah was appointed postmaster at the Mack Post Office in 1924. She held that job until 31 January 1940.

In December of 1924, a rural route was established and Byron served as temporary carrier.

Byron was very active in civic affairs in Mack; serving as committee member in the Uintah Country Club. He was largely responsible for development of the golf course at Mack.

(Author's memory) Byron had a vintage Model "T" Ford touring car which he kept in mint condition, and which he probably drove for the rest of his life. One time as the Likes family drove into Mack, they were just in time to see that Model T take a dive into the "sewer ditch" on the south side of the highway, across from the pool hall. The car was damaged only a little; Byron and his daughter, May, were not hurt badly, but were quite visibly shaken. Byron had no explanation for the sudden and unexpected detour.

Brandon

Information sent by Emmett Russell Brandon of 240 28 1/2 Rd, Grand Junction, Colorado We also used census records, obituaries and news items from *The Daily Sentinel*.

James Henry Brandon was born 22 February 1884 in Kansas to James A. and Sophronia Brandon. He spent his youth in Kansas; and was married to **Emma Johannah Lander** in November 1906 at Lyndon, Lyon, Kansas.

Emma Johannah Lander was born 27 December 1881 at Urbana, Champaign, Illinois, fifth of 14 children born to John P. and Jane N. Lander. (See Ola Lander). She spent much of her youth in Lyon County, Kansas.

They had two sons:

Henry Vernon, born 1922, Topeka, Kansas
Emmett Russell, 13 August 1925, Topeka, Kansas
(A daughter died in infancy)

The family moved from Miller, Lyon, Kansas, to Mesa County, Colorado in 1934, and lived variously at Mack, Loma, Fruita and Grand Junction. They lived for several years in the house formerly occupied by Clarence (Red) and Garnet Davidson on Mack Mesa. The boys attended Mack School and Fruita Union High School. Vernon graduated in 1940.

Henry and Emma were involved in community affairs. Quoting from Deyon Davidson's story in the *Fruita Times,* "Route 1, Box 10":

> Mrs. Brandon loved to put on skits, give recitations and monologues, and she was quite good at it. One time she got the Red Mesa kids together and put on a skit at Mack Community Club. We played the part of her unruly children and the setting was a Thanksgiving dinner. As we sat at the table she put a pie (carrot, as I remember) before us and began to say grace. We fidgeted and squirmed and giggled and finally passed the pie which was fully consumed before the "amen," at which time we bolted to protection behind the curtain. It was hilarious!

Both Brandon boys served in the Army in World War II and were involved in crucial battles in German-held territory. Russell tells us that he and Vernon crossed paths in the war zone — they were in a field hospital compound at the same time, but didn't know it until later. Vernon was assigned to Normandy and died in a battle on 5 March 1945.

Russell was a paratrooper with the 82nd Airborne in the Battle of the Bulge, and during that time his feet were frozen — hence the stay in the hospital. He was just released from the hospital at the time his brother, Vernon, was killed.

At some point in time Russell reenlisted — probably after the war was over. While home on leave he met his future wife, **Geneva Moore,** who was working in the telephone office in Grand Junction. They were married in 1946 in South Carolina. Russell was stationed at Fort Bragg, North Carolina, at the time.

Emma died 26 December 1943, while the boys were away serving in the Army. After Vernon's death, Henry began to have some problems. The deaths of both his wife and his son were more than he could handle emotionally. He went to live with Russell and family for some time. When Russell was discharged from the Army, Henry went with his family to Las Vegas (where Geneva was from).

Russell and Geneva had two sons:

Russell Jr. born 1947, Fayetteville, North Carolina
Roy V. "Bud," 1948, Las Vegas, Clark, Nevada

When their second son, Roy, was three months old, they decided to move back to Grand Junction, where they have lived since.

James Henry Brandon died at Lincoln Park Hospital in Grand Junction, 17 November 1958, and was buried beside his wife in Elmwood Cemetery at Fruita.

Russell and Geneva had the misfortune of losing their oldest son, Russell, Jr., at age 24. His little daughter turned two years old the same day.

Russell Sr. worked as a tire recapper at Standard Tire Company for 35 years before retiring. His son, Roy, is general manager and part owner of Standard Tire. Roy's son, Nathan, worked for some time at the same place. (Keeping it in the family!) Roy's wife, Judy, has a shop in the new Cottonwood Mall called "Perfect Nails."

Russell and Geneva have lived at 240 28 1/2 Road, Grand Junction, for 35 years.

Brayton

The Brayton story was written mostly by Charlene Brayton Eldridge, daughter of Charles and Mildred Weir Brayton. There are some news items and obituaries added from *The Daily Sentinel* and a little input from author's personal knowledge.

Martha Josephine "Josie" Hess was born 14 March 1873 near Hume, Bates, Missouri, to Joseph Dudley Hess and Martha Jane Mitchell. She spent her childhood years in that area. On 10 September 1893 she married **George Louke Brayton** at Worland, Bates, Missouri. Their children were:

George, born 13 October 1894 (died shortly after)
Lawson Wonnel, 15 March 1896
Stanley Louke, 11 March 1898
Josie Edna, 14 July 1900
Charles Arnold, 13 October 1902
Phillip Walter, 22 February 1905
Bessie Mable, 17 June 1907
Ethel Ellen, 20 May 1911

In May 1915, as George was taking a load of calves across a river, the wagon tipped over, injuring him. He died about two weeks later, at age 54. That left Josie, age 42, with seven children, ages 19, 17, 15, 13, 10, eight and four. They stayed on the farm, with the boys working anywhere they could. The oldest daughter, Edna, worked as a telephone operator until she married Ollie Hawk. She gave birth to a son, Raymond Hawk, on 3 January 1921, and died from complications of childbirth on 12 January 1921.

In the summer of 1923, S. S. Summers came to Missouri for a visit. His wife, Ida, had died in Colorado in 1921. He had been a friend of the Brayton family previously, and he and Josie got married on 1 August 1923. Bessie, then age 16, and Ethel, age 12, went back with Mr. Summers

(Left) The Brayton brothers in the early 20s L-R: Charles, Phillip, Lawson and Stanley. (Above) 1923— Ethel Brayton, Seabran Silas and Josie Brayton Summers, and Bessie Brayton. *(Photo courtesy of Charlene Brayton Eldredge)*

and Josie to his homestead in Colorado.

Josie Brayton, the mother of the Brayton clan, lived in the valley for many more years. she was well known for her tendency to say what she thought, regardless of the circumstances or the end result. She also had a way of getting a point across that sometimes caused hurt and distress. On one occasion her husband, Si Summers, had left the house to go about his farm work and had forgotten to bring in fuel for the kitchen stove before he left. When he returned for lunch at noon she was resting and seemed unconcerned that Si was expecting to be fed. When he mentioned that he would like something to eat, she, not very politely, told him that whenever he brought her some wood and coal, she would fix him something to eat.

On another occasion Josie was hosting the ladies' Sorosis Club. It was customary and expected that the hostess would provide the refreshments after the meeting. Josie was ready — she served them pinto beans! It may have been embarrassing for the ladies at the time, but they joked about that for years after! Josie apparently never changed her name from Summers after she divorced Si. She died 19 September 1956, and

was buried in the Elmwood Cemetery at Fruita.

Of Josie's eight children, Charles, Phillip, Stanley, Bessie and Ethel, each lived at some time or other in the New Liberty community.

Charles made his first trip to New Liberty in 1924. He had been taking a correspondence course in auto mechanics, and was accepted by a school in Lincoln, Nebraska, where he finished his training. In March 1925, Charles received a letter from his mother asking him to rent a farm, as she and the girls were coming back to Missouri. Lawson, Stanley and Phillip had been working in Iowa — Charles had gone there too, as there seemed to be plenty of work. He did rent a farm for two years, and his mother and the girls joined him, but in the spring of 1927 mother and the girls moved back to Colorado.

Charlene submitted the following story:

Charles came to Colorado to stay in 1928 and soon started dating **Mildred Weir**. They were married 7 October 1930. They first lived on the Summers' place, then moved to the Boyden place. **George Kenneth** was born at St. Mary's Hospital, 23 October 1931, while they lived on the Boyden place. They then (July 1931) moved to the Watters place, where they lived when **Charlene Louise**, was born (at St. Mary's) 3

1952—Back row L-R: Charlotte, George and Charlene. Front row: Charles and Mildred Brayton. *(Photo courtesy of Charlene Brayton Eldredge)*

February 1934. Dad said they did not have a car at that time, so he had to ride a horse over to Weirs and borrow a car to take mother to the hospital in Grand Junction. Mother was not well after I was born, so they hired a girl to come and help with the work. Mother said she was a girl from Collbran who "sure knew how to work."

They moved back to the Summers' place just before **Charlotte Lois** was born 15 March 1935 (also at St. Mary's).

In February 1936, Josie and S. S. Summers were divorced, but Dad and Mr. Summers always remained friends.

We moved to Fruita for a year, rented the first house, then Dad bought one for $500 (it was the same house Grandmother Weir bought years later). George started in first grade while we were in Fruita and Dad worked in a garage with Mr. Summers.

We then moved back to the Summers' farm in New Liberty and stayed there for seven years. We kids had many happy times there. Our mother cut our hair, Dad pulled our teeth (after dipping the pliers in boiling water). If we got

sick, it was a dose of castor oil. Saturday night was cornbread and beans for supper. We listened to the "Grand Old Opry" on the radio while awaiting our turn for the bathtub behind the kitchen stove. The shoes were polished for Sunday School the next morning. Mother sewed Charlotte's and my dresses, but she bought George Kenneth's clothes. We changed our school clothes and put on everyday clothes as soon as we got home from school. All clothes were washed once a week on Monday in a gas-powered washer (this was before electricity came). On Tuesday she ironed the clothes. For winter there were two pairs of long underwear, two pairs of long stockings for the girls, and one pair of new shoes for each child for the year. In the summer we went bare-footed.

Homemade bread was baked and the butter churned as used. Dad butchered a calf each year and mother canned the meat. A pig was butchered, cured, and hung in the cellar. We raised chickens to eat and to provide eggs. Dad always milked several cows.

Just as soon as we were big enough we were given jobs to do. Charlotte and I brought in the coal and wood for the stoves. When I was nine, Dad had us hoe 15 acres of potatoes, he paid us each $1. I asked Dad years later why he had us

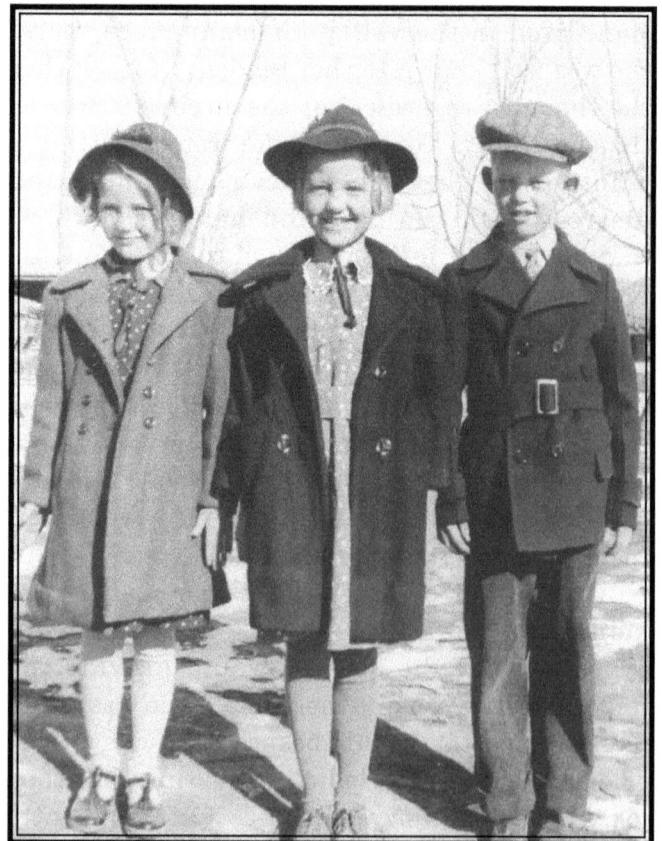

1944—L-R: Charlotte, Charlene and George Brayton. *(Photo courtesy of Charlene Brayton Eldredge)*

265

hoeing at such a young age. I said "I was only nine, and I know you had to go out and do the job over." He said; "I thought I was doing you a favor waiting so long — I was only five when I started working in the fields." We put our money together and bought a Monopoly game. Many hours were spent with that game and with checkers, marbles, paper dolls, mud pies, and our little farms on the hill close to the house.

We had a big black dog named Giggs and a little dog named Bob. Dad told of a time when they loaded us kids in the car and left a forgotten lunch sitting there. When they got back at the end of the day dad could see a path around the basket where the big dog had kept the little dog from the food. Giggs always walked us to the school bus — one day he was hit by the bus and was in such pain Dad had to shoot him. Dad thought he had buried him way off from the house where we could never find him, but for several years we would go down to the wash bank and look at the remains.

Dad had two work horses, but Charlotte and I loved to ride them. Hers was named Barney, mine was Nig. We spent a lot of time on those horses. Then George got a new man-sized bike. We girls soon learned to ride that, even double. We took lots of spills on the graveled roads. In the winter we skated on the pond that was close to the house.

We enjoyed the New Liberty School — two rooms, four grades in each room. I still remember Mrs. Jerome teaching: "Dick, see Dick; Jane, see Jane, etc, etc." George completed seven and one-half years there, five and one-half for me, and four and one-half for Charlotte. I remember a Christmas play that was put on there, Jackie Bray was an elf. The older girls had really pretty dresses made out of crepe paper. I remember how hard the teachers and parents worked to get ready for that.

Then there were the community dinners and all the faithful saints who kept the Sunday School going. I received my first New Testament and Bible there.

Sometimes the roads were so muddy we could hardly get to the school house and back, but Dad would put the '35 Ford in the deep ruts and just keep going; we always made it.

Our house had three small bedrooms, a living room and a kitchen. It had a big screened-in porch across the east end and half-way around the south end. There was a hand pump for water on the cistern right outside the door. We cleaned the cistern each year and filled it with water from the irrigation ditch. Dad would choose a day to fill it when the water was running clear.

Over the kitchen door, up high, hung a long-barreled shotgun. It was used many times to shoot predators that were after the farm animals. By the back door near the water bucket and the wash pan hung the razor strop. Dad never used the strop on us kids, but he did shake it a few times.

In the spring of 1946 we moved to the Pear Park area, east of Grand Junction, where we all three completed our schooling, married, raised families and are now grandparents. As my 13 year old grandson tells me: "Welcome to the '90s, Grandma."

Charles and Mildred were divorced, and Charles later married Marion Hintz Smith on 14 January 1959. (There will be more information about Mildred with the Weir family) In addition to his experience as a farmer and auto mechanic, Charles also served as Mesa County Court Bailiff for twelve years. He then worked as financial clerk for Denver and Rio Grande RR, and retired in 1970. Charles died 17 February 1988, and is buried in the Orchard Mesa Cemetery.

George Kenneth married Erma Isley and they have lived for several years in Senagal, West Africa, serving as missionaries. (George Kenneth and family came home from Africa in 1994 and are now living in Grand Junction)

Charlene married James F. Eldredge and lives in the Pear Park district near Grand Junction.

Charlotte married Monty Carlisle and lived at Lakeland, Florida, until her death 18 December 1995 from liver cancer.

Stanley married quite late in life to a girl named Etta. She died giving birth to their first child — the baby boy died also. On 13 June 1939 he married **Ruby Mae Kennett**, a native of Grand Junction. They had five girls and one boy: Donna, Norma, Martha, Velma, Lillian and Paul. In 1943 the family moved to Utah, and lived in Orem in a home on State Street on the property now occupied by K-Mart. Stanley and Ruby are credited with being the founders of the Rock Canyon Assembly of God Church of North Provo.

Stanley died at Provo, Utah, 18 December 1966. Ruby died 26 August 1979, also in Provo. Both are buried in the Timpanogos Memorial Gardens Cemetery in Orem.

Phillip lived around New Liberty for many years also. He too married late in life, but his is a little different story. His was a mail-order bride whose name was **Ella May Horr**. They were married in the Baptist Church at Palisade, 21 May 1939. Phillip bought a farm from Fred Likes (where the Frank Wells' family now live) and built a nice home for his bride. They had two daughters, **Jo Ella** and **Jane**. As far as we know at this time (1995), Phillip and Ella are living in the area of Stockton, California.

Bessie married **Robert Marion Phillips**, 15 October 1928, at Fruita, Colorado. More will be written about her with the Phillips' family story.

Ethel attended school at New Liberty for some time after moving to Colorado. She was married at one time to **James Stotts**, son of Ella Stotts, but the marriage didn't last very long. Ethel had a baby boy from that marriage, but he died soon after birth. She married **Stanley Stacy** 18 September 1937, and they had three sons and a daughter. Husband Stanley, a farmer and miner, died in **1966**, and Ethel continued on in the Fruita area until her death, 9 July 1989, and was buried in the Elmwood Cemetery.

1940s — Ella and Phillip Brayton with daughters, JoElla and Jane. *(Photo courtesy of Charlene Brayton Eldredge)*

Brewster

Family group sheet and outline provided by Josie Brewster Johnson of P. O. Box 454, Fruita, Colorado, with additional information from obituaries in *The Daily Sentinel.*

Joel Eugene Brewster was born 22 July 1894 at Ophir, San Juan, Colorado. He spent most of his childhood and attended schools there and later attended schools at Fruita, Colorado.

He served in the Navy during World War I, and then moved to California. He married **Edna Mathson** 26 December 1919 in California — she died 15 July 1920.

He met **Jennie Ellen Menter** while working as bridge foreman for the railroad at Needles, California. They were married 11 June 1927 at Needles. Jennie was born 19 January 1903 in Nebraska, where she spent her childhood and attended schools.

About 1961. Jennie, Joel and Josie Brewster. *(Photo courtesy of Josie Brewster Johnson)*

Joel and Jennie had an unnamed stillborn son before they left California. They moved to Colorado some time in the early 1930s, settling for a time at Atchee, where they lived on a ranch. They moved later to a farm north of Mack, on Red Mesa on 10 road, near Herron's. While living there Joel worked for a time on the D&RG Railroad at Grand Junction. Their daughter, **Josie Ellen (Johnson)**, was born at Fruita, 16 December 1941.

In 1946/47 they moved to Mack and took over the M. W. Ray turkey operation on the original C. C. Keifer ranch one mile east of Mack. They were well known in the Mack community and became friends with everyone.

Jennie served as a nurse, delivering babies and nursing several sick people back to health. She also worked at both grocery stores at Mack, and later went to work for the Quality Meat Market in Fruita, and became the head of the Poultry Department.

While living on the turkey ranch, Jennie would order a large supply of fireworks to put on a big display on the hill to celebrate Independence Day for the enjoyment of the neighbors, young and old. On Thanksgiving and Christmas there was always a big turkey in the oven and the house was full of neighbors and friends.

Josie remembers going to the Harold's Club (west of Mack) when it was a family place. She would baby-sit for the Mongers and Nelsons. One of her fondest memories was when she was in school, Kay Rich's

pigeon danced on the piano while they sang the morning school songs. She remembers the bingo games and the parties and the merry go-round, and many other happy times.

In the meantime Joel went to work for the Mesa County Highway Department and soon became a bridge foreman — seems natural, as he had done the same for the railroad in California about the time he and Jennie were married. Josie mentions that Joel had only a fifth grade education.

An item in *The Daily Sentinel* of 24 December 1944 says that Lester Whetten had purchased the turkey ranch. According to daughter Josie's memory, the family moved to the turkey ranch in 1946 or 1947. We are not sure if both the Whetten and Brewster families lived there at the same time.

In 1955 Joel and Jennie purchased the Fruita Washeteria and moved to Fruita, leaving Josie broken-hearted and crying for two weeks even though she had been going to school at Fruita for two years because they had closed the Mack School and sent the students to other schools. She and Vic Thompson were the only seventh graders to make the move. She has many happy memories of life at Mack.

Joel died at the Lower Valley Nursing Home in Fruita, 18 March 1984 at age 89. Jennie died at Family Health West, 25 November 1985 at age 82.

Josie graduated from Fruita Union High School in 1959, then went to Parks School of Business in Denver through 1959 and 1960. On 31 December 1961 she married **Larry Dean Johnson** at Fruita. Larry lived at Loma most of his life.

Larry and Josie have three daughters:

Virginia Ann, born 9 August 1962
Victoria Renee, 3 November 1965
Veronica, 29 October 1969

Larry worked at logging and cutting fire wood for several years, then drove a truck for awhile. Josie helped with the logging and fire-wood and has been driving a school bus and doing other part-time jobs through the years. Larry died at the Veterans Hospital in Grand Junction, 4 December 1982, of leukemia. There are now (1992) four grandchildren and two great grandchildren.

The Brisbin family on 4 July 1941. The family was gathered for the parent's 25th Anniversary. Back, L-R: Robert "Bob" Lee, Mabel Virginia, Rex Milton and William "Bill" Long Brisbin. Front row: Harriett Louise, Milton "Milt" Smith (father), Ruth (mother), Mary Pearl and Ruth Marie Brisbin. *(Photo courtesy of Bill Brisbin and Mabel Brisbin Howes)*

Brisbin

Written from information provided by Bill and Jean Brisbin, histories by Mabel Brisbin Howes; a marriage record from Montrose County, Colorado; obituaries; 1900 census record for Mesa County, Colorado; 1920 census record for Kern County, California; and news items in *The Daily Sentinel*.

Milton "Milt" Smith Brisbin was born in 1890 near Spooner, Wisconsin to **Daniel Lee Brisbin** and **Marian Wonch**. He moved into the Plateau Valley in the early 1900s and, on 31 August 1911, was married to **Ruth Long**, daughter of **Joel J. Long** and **Hattie Shattrich**, pioneer ranchers of Plateau Valley. Ruth was

born 21 April 1893 in Plateau Valley and spent her childhood there, attending school in Collbran. Ruth is listed as a 7-year-old in the 1900 census of Mesa County for the Collbran area, 8th Precinct

The story is told by their children that when Milt and Ruth wanted to get married, her parents objected, so the young couple eloped. In company with some of Milt's family, they drove a covered wagon to Montrose, Colorado, and were married there. Ruth's obituary says they were married in Placerville, which is in San Miguel County, but the marriage record does not support that.

They had four daughters and three sons:

Mary Pearl (Garlitz), born 20 May 1914
Rex Milton, 29 September 1915
William "Bill" Long, 22 September 1917
Mabel Virginia (Howes), 20 September 1921

Robert "Bob" Lee, 8 December 1923
Ruth Marie (Becher), 5 October 1926
Harriett Louise (New), 9 May 1929
All the children were born in Collbran except Mabel, who was born in Bakersfield, California.

After their marriage Milt and Ruth met with Milt's cousin, Charlie Mason, at Mancos, Colorado, then they traveled to Arizona where Milt worked for a cattle company.

Ruth's obituary says they spent some time in Arizona before returning to Plateau Valley. We know they were in Kern County, California, for at least some time in 1920 since the 1920 census, taken in February, shows Milt and Ruth with the first three children, Mary, Rex and Bill.

According to Ruth's obituary, in 1932 the family moved to the Hunter area where they operated a farm for a couple of years. Bill and Jean say they moved to Hunter in 1930. According to land records, they purchased the Snavely farm in New Liberty in February 1935; they stayed there until about 1939. They rented their farm and went to California to work in defense. They sold out in New Liberty in 1941 (this information from land records) and moved away. Milt became interested in the Cortez area, but they lived a few years in Los Angeles, California, before coming back to Cortez to live again on a farm.

Mary, Rex and Bill attended schools at Hunter and Fruita. All of the younger ones, including Mabel, Bob, Ruth and Harriet, attended New Liberty School. Rex graduated from Fruita Union High School in 1934, Mabel in 1940 and Robert in 1941. As far as we know, they were the only ones to graduate in Fruita.

Following are histories of Milt and Ruth Long Brisbin and each of their children, written by Mabel Brisbin Howes of Chugiak, Alaska. We have done some editing.

Ruth Long was Joe and Hattie Long's third child. She was born 21 April 1893 in the Long family log house located near what is now Collbran, Colorado.

She was a pretty child with black hair and brown eyes. She was not an aggressive child, her two older sisters were the aggressive ones in the family. This made Ruth the sweet one. At a young age she had rheumatic fever. She had recurring attacks during her life which left her with a weak heart. This sickly child was spoiled, causing resentment by her sister Susan, who was just two years older. Ruth was not required to carry her share of the work load, like picking up potatoes in the fall. These heavier tasks fell to the rest of the family of six girls and only one boy.

Ruth was the little daredevil. She once told me the following story; Ruth and the other children were playing follow-the-leader when she looked out the upstairs window and saw a featherbed sunning on the ground — common practice after a long winter. The big bag of feathers looked soft to her so she jumped onto it. Feathers have a way of moving when one lands on them. Needless to say, she was a bit bruised.

The other kids did not follow her but told their mother, who promptly "jawed" her saying, "You will get a licking when your father gets home!" That evening Ruth met her father at the gate and said, "Papa, I'll put your horse up." That was no easy task for a child, it required taking off the saddle and bridle and feeding and watering the horse. She later did get the spanking but, she said, "I wasn't killed."

When Ruth was about 15, she went with her parents to Kansas to visit some of her mother's relatives. They hoped Ruth's health would improve in the process.

In 1992, her younger sister, Harriet, then 92 years old, told me this joke Ruth had told her when she returned from Kansas: "A priest and a girl were on a ship. The priest said to the girl, 'For me to sin would be a rarity, for you to sin would be for charity.' The girl said, 'For me to sin would be no rarity, for I sin for cash, not for charity.'" My Aunt had remembered that story after 78 years!

Ruth was pretty, and, I do believe, somewhat of a flirt; after all, she had been to Kansas.

Her father had been grooming a cow-hand for a son-in-law. Jess Hittle had worked for him faithfully for six years. What grandfather did for men who stayed with him for a long while was to give them 10 heifers to start their own herd. By always saving the heifers, in a few years a man could have quite a start. I'm sure Joe felt Jess would take good care of his weaker daughter.

Ruth had accepted an engagement ring from Freeman Wilson Howes, but gave it back. Norman Hill, a quite short guy, was also in love with her. Next she took a ring from Jess Hittle, I think to take the pressure off from home. How happy Joe and Hattie were! — until a drifter named Milt Brisbin came along. Joe needed some help, so he hired him. Milt's mother was a divorced woman; in those days that was a sign of a "marked lady." Joe and Hattie considered Milt less of a man than Jess Hittle, and certainly not worthy of their daughter. However, Ruth had met her "tall dark and handsome!" He had dark hair and hazel eyes and stood about six feet tall. Ruth fell in love, "hook, line and sinker!" She once told me that when Milt danced his coat tails swung back and forth.

Milton Smith Brisbin was born near Spooner, Wisconsin, to Daniel Lee Brisbin and Marian Wonch. He was the youngest of five children. His father was a civil war veteran and not well. They lived in a cabin in the backwoods and they lived mostly off the land, hunting and trapping. Milt once told me a story about a scar on his wrist When he was a small boy they were fishing on a lake in a boat. Milt caught a big carp and when he brought it in, it bit him. Another time he told of visiting a man at a distant cabin. The man showed him how to aim the rifle higher so as to carry the bullet farther.

Marian Brisbin left Daniel Brisbin and went back to Iowa, where Milt's Aunt Marion (Tompkins) Wethrill's mother lived. Milt and his cousin, Charlie Mason, rode with Aunt Marion to Mancos, Colorado. Benjamin Kite Wethrill had come west with his older boys to establish a cattle ranch. Milt and Charlie were to work on the ranch for safely bringing their aunt to Colorado.

One morning after they had been there awhile, Milt got up and found Charlie with his horse already saddled. He said, "Milt you do whatever you want, but I'm leaving for Oregon. Those boys (Wethrills) are rustling cattle, holding them up in the box canyons."

(Those canyons are now in Mesa Verde National Park. Much has been written about the Wethrills in Colorado history). In those days when a cattle rustler was caught, he was hung to the nearest tree.

Milt decided to go on over to Craig, Colorado, where he worked at a mine for awhile, then stayed on during the winter while the mine was closed. The next spring he rode his horse over the hog back[†] into Plateau Valley. His sister, Pearl, and his mother, Marian, and grandmother, Anna Towers, were there.

Joe Long needed a hand, so he hired Milt. Later that spring the dirt-fill dam of Atkinson Reservoir went out and down the creek came rocks and trees and everything else in its way. One man said the bridges looked like ferry boats floating by! That evening Milt was on one side of the creek and his girl, Ruth, with whom he had a date, was on the other side. Some fellow said to Milt, "No one will be crossing that creek tonight." Milt's response, "You want to bet?" Milt backed his horse up a good distance, then, with the horse on the run, he spurred him so he would jump out into the middle of the turbulent water. Luckily, both man and horse came out on the other side. Joe Long was watching and said, "Damn fool could have killed the horse!" Needless to say, Milt didn't make any points with Ruth's father!

In August Milt was preparing to go with his mother, who had married Walt Hawkins, and his sister, Pearl, who had married Mel Palmer, to Arizona to take up land. What an opportunity! Ruth sneaked out and went with Milt in his covered wagon. They were married at Montrose, Colorado, on 31 August 1911, and were headed out for their honeymoon!

On the way Ruth had a change of heart and got out of the wagon and sat on a rock. Milt went on without her, but at dark he did come back after her and she decided to go on with him. One time they camped near a ranch owned by some Mormons. During the night someone stole their team. The Mormons loaned Milt a horse to try to track the horses. A ranch-hand said, "It was another Mormon, but they will never tell on each other, even if they do wrong." The Mormons were good folks and hired both Ruth and Milt until they could earn enough money to buy another team. (This could have been on their way back).

[†]A hog back is a mountain ridge with a sharp crest and abruptly sloping sides, often formed by the out-cropping edge of steeply dipping rock strata.

There were no roads, they just followed old wagon trails. One time on that trip they saw a Stanley Steamer automobile. It scared the horses; if Milt hadn't been such a good driver they would have ran away. Milt could really handle horses. He told me he could handle teams of four or six horses. Perhaps he learned that at Craig as he hauled ore in wagons.

Things did not go well in Arizona. It was hot, dry land with rattle snakes and scorpions. But they did file on land. They had to haul water in barrels and managed to raise some squash and pumpkins and took them to sell at Jerome, a mining town. They got two or three dollars for a wagon load.

Although in love, Ruth got Oh! so homesick! Milts brother, Ed, died there at Cottonwood, Arizona, of tuberculosis. His sister, Pearl, had been taking care of him.

Milt and Ruth wanted to go back to Colorado, but didn't know how they would be accepted. After two years they did go back. As Ruth's sister once said, "If Ruth cries, all is forgiven." Ruth cried, but all was not forgiven!

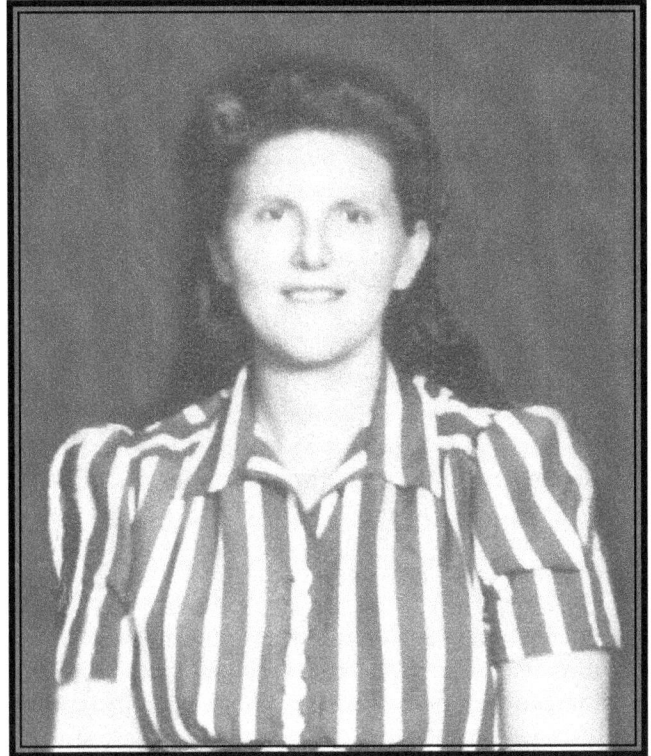

Milt and Ruth Brisbin, on their honeymoon in 1911, ferrying across the San Juan River with their wagon and horses on their way to Arizona. *(Photo courtesy of Mabel Brisbin Howes)*

Mary Pearl Brisbin in 1941
(Photo courtesy of Mabel Brisbin Howes)

Mary Pearl Brisbin was the oldest of our family, she was born 20 May 1914, at Collbran, Colorado. She was a beautiful child with bright red hair. Mary was a self-willed child and could really get her way! She and Rex went to school together and if anyone picked on Rex, she would light into them with both fists.

Since Mary was the oldest of seven children she had to work hard, especially because her mother was not well. Mary was not only well organized but worked quickly and independently. She once decided the folks had a lot of old junk papers in a big trunk. She burned up the papers, including my folks marriage certificate! She could clean a big house in just a few hours. She told me once she had the kitchen linoleum just shining and the oil cloth as clean as could be. Rex and Bill came into the kitchen and dumped their pockets out. They had a lot of wheat in their pockets. She screamed at them until they had cleaned up every kernel!

She rode a horse named Cleo to school. The horse would try to turn in at Joe Long's place, which was about a mile from our house. Mary had trouble controlling her. Aunt Dorothy, Ruth's youngest sister, would strap Cleo on the butt and then she would buck Mary off and Dorothy would laugh. Mary said Dorothy was mean to her. I believe it was Dorothy who broke the horse. Any teenage girl that could break a horse to ride had to be tough. Aunt Dorothy was only seven years older than Mary.

Once, when I (Mabel) was just a baby, a huge tarantula jumped about four feet toward me. Mary was an "in charge" person, she grabbed me and put me on the porch and screamed for help, thus saving my life. She would have been only about eight or nine years old.

She and Rex got a job picking strawberries; remember, I told you how quick she was. She got paid $35 and she bought herself a dress for $1.98 and spent the rest buying presents for everyone else. She was so generous!

Mary took piano lessons when she was quite young. She loved to practice and would play everything she could get her hands on. She played the tuba in the high school band and could substitute on most instruments. She also had a beautiful voice, our doctor's wife taught voice lessons and Mary worked for her on some Saturdays in exchange for lessons.

One Saturday Margaret, the doctor's wife, put Mary to washing out some things in dry cleaning fluid of some kind in an unventilated room. Mary was found passed out, she was gassed. She suffered from the effects of that for many years.

In her teenage years Mary was a very popular young lady. She was so full of fun as long as she got her own way. Once she got in a peck of trouble because she went with one boy, then ditched him and came home with one she liked better. There was another guy named Homer Cory who was what you would now call a "dork," but he liked Mary. The other girls would tell Mary. "You go with Homer so we'll all have a way to go. Homer's dad had a two seated car that would hold four couples seated on each others laps. Mary also had a boy friend named Harlan who was quiet and reserved. For some reason he had stayed for supper one day. Our little brother, Bob, who was about four years old, stood up on his stool and said, "Mary are you going to marry Homer or are you going to marry Harlan?" Needless to say, we all enjoyed that except the poor embarrassed guy. Even our straight-laced father, Milt, choked on his food. Mary vowed to kill her little brother Bob! He would run to the front window and in

a loud voice announce, "Mary, your boy friend is here!"

She organized lots of home parties at our house. She would bring home other girls to help with the cleaning and cake-baking. Mother would make a big pot of cocoa. With Mary at the piano, what else could kids need? They would sing and play parlor games: Post Office, Fine or Super Fine, or Spin the Bottle.

After high school Mary decided she was going to college. By hook or crook she would go. She borrowed $10 from everyone she could. She went to McFarland, California, where Aunt Mary Newby and family lived. She enrolled in Junior College at Bakersfield, California. She had a cousin also going to school there. Mary got a job there working for her board and room. She won a contest as best in the state for singing "A Capella." We were so proud of her, everything seemed to be going well for her until Aunt Mary got real sick.

Mary and her cousin, Jim, went to McFarland to see if they could be of any help. Aunt Mary died of diphtheria and most of the family contacted it, including Mary. They were all put in an isolation ward and, as you may know, this was an awful experience for her. She later came home with what was diagnosed as tuberculosis. The doctor later said she had valley fever. I remember she ate from separate dishes and everything she ate or drank from had to be boiled.

After we moved to Hunter she fell in love with a young man in the neighborhood named **Earl Price Garlitz.** His family called him "Dude," because he was so clean and wanted to dress nice. Earl loved Mary and put up with her temper all these 61 years. From this marriage came two lovely daughters: **Norma** and **Mildred,** and a fine son, **Lee.**

Rex Milton Brisbin was born 29 September 1915 at Collbran. Rex seemed to always see the sunny side of any situation. I remember one time when my mother was "jawing" him. He said, "We are mad, aren't we, Mommy? We are all mad; when we get over it we will be glad." She tried to catch him as he ran around our big kitchen table. But about the time she would reach out to grab him he would dive under the table and come up on the other side. By then both were laughing.

Rex always took a lot of the responsibility of Bill, his brother who was two years younger. I think he even took a few whippings for Bill, as

Rex Milton Brisbin in 1941.
(Photo courtesy of Mabel Brisbin Howes)

the older kids never told on each other, no matter what the cost. They always worked hard. On the ranch we all got up at five o'clock to milk 10 or 12 cows and feed all the stock before going to school. That was routine for most ranch kids. They would also raise 4-H calves which needed special care.

At about 12 to 14 the boys began to help with the hay stacking right along with the men. These were depression times and parents were trying to feed their families and little else. One summer Milt couldn't afford to hire any help and the family was trading work with the neighbors. Often everyone's hay or grain needed to be put up at the same time; rain could ruin a crop fast, once it was ready to harvest.

That summer Milt told the boys, "When we get the hay in the stacks you boys can take horses and, with the neighbor boys, go to the mountains for a vacation." They really started making plans. They were to take with them Bobby and Junior Stoddard, who were about their age. The Stoddards were a kind of

dysfunctional family who lived about a mile from us down under the hill. The boys spent a lot of time at our house.

The Stoddards made their own brew. On the south of our ranch was a place called the Dowden place. No one lived there and the old log house was in a bad state of disrepair, but there was a pretty good cellar there hidden by an over-growth of Tanzy. Well, guess what! With my brothers, having such a good hide-away, and with the Stoddard boys' expertise, they decided to make their own batch of home-brew. Milt knew what they were doing and would go by there when he was irrigating up there; he used that land for pasture. One day he told Ruth,"We are going to have some sick boys one of these days. That stuff is getting pretty ripe." I remember hearing him say that but I never told the boys — law of the family, you know.

The boys had a team and two saddle horses. They loaded their supplies in a light spring wagon for a week in the hills. They took a sack of spuds, eggs, a side of bacon, canned milk, some canned goods, flour, sugar, baking powder and lard. They also took fish hooks and lines plus other essentials to eat for a week. They also bought a bag of "Bull Durham" tobacco and a package of "Golden Grain" cigarette papers, so as to have makings for home-rolled cigarettes. They stopped off and picked up their home-brew. They didn't have to carry water, as that was plentiful; there was lots of pure water everywhere. They were all set to spend a week in the mountains.

They were going to Grand Mesa, the highest flat-top mountain in the world. There are over 200 lakes up there. Also several reservoirs and old and new cabins used by the cattle men and forest service people. They were headed for the old "Englehart Ranger Station," no longer in use by the rangers. The area where they were going was called "Mesa Lakes." It is now known as "Purgatory Ski Resort."

The road ended a few miles short of where they were going, so they unhitched from the wagon and loaded everything on the four horses. Of course the younger boys were riding the work horses. They got to camp about dark and still had to unload all their gear, unsaddle the horses and "picket" them out on ropes.

They got a fire going, peeled some spuds, cut off several slices of bacon. Since mother had tucked in a couple of loaves of bread, they didn't have to make biscuits the first night. Oh! How hungry those boys were, with such

274

good food to go with home-made cigarettes and home-made beer! To say the least, they got drunk and sick, everyone of them! Needless to say they slept late the next morning. They managed to catch a string of fish for supper that night, being too sick to eat breakfast or lunch. They were really having fun!!

Rex, being the oldest, took responsibility for all the boys. He also cooked and made the biscuits. They were called "cowboy biscuits." They were made by mixing baking-powder and salt into the top of the flour in the flour sack. Then that was stirred into some thinned canned milk. Then the soft dough was dropped by spoonfuls into a hot greased pan to bake. If there was no oven they were spooned into a cast iron skillet with a heavy iron lid, called a "Dutch Oven," then pushed it into the hot coals of the fire.

They rode the horses all over the mountain, fishing in the lakes and exploring old cabins. In the mountains one often has to contend with afternoon thunder storms. The sky gets black and thunder roars and lightning flashes. Then the rain will come down in torrents. Shortly the storm will leave about as fast as it came. The boys tried to always be back at the cabin by late afternoon. But one day it got dark before they made it back, but they did manage to make it to the Leon Creek cabin.

There was bedding hung by wire from the rafters. So they built a fire and looked for something to eat. They found a big can of dried beans that had been left for a hungry traveler. So, what did they have to worry about? They had food and heat! So they put the beans on to cook, and after about four hours they were still hard as rocks! At 10,000 feet elevation one has to soak beans overnight, or twelve hours. So Rex devised a plan to cook the beans all night, he and Bobby would stay up three hours and keep the fire going and the beans from boiling dry. Then they would wake up Bill and Junior for their three hour shift. But really what they did was stay up for two hours, then turned the clock ahead and woke the other boys up, thus they were able to sleep for four hours. So like boys!

For breakfast they caught some fish and ate them with the half-cooked beans. Then they put everything back as they found it and got on their horses and rode back to the Englehart Cabin.

One of the things they did for fun was find a stand of small quaking aspen trees and they would shinny up to the top of a tree until it bent over with their weight, then grab onto another tree and go around the other trees like a bunch of monkeys. They did this until they were exhausted. Then they would lie on the ground and watch the clouds float by in the bright blue sky. I do believe the sky is bluer in Colorado than any other place in the world.

As their food supply began to dwindle Rex was trying to get everyone to eat more fish. But they were getting tired of fish. Since they had sold their 4-H calves, they did have a little money, so they decided to ride over to Land's End where they knew there was a little store. Since they knew it was an all-day's ride, they got up early — they had learned their lesson about being caught out in the mountains in the dark! It was about six miles to the store, with no roads, just trying to follow the trails over hills and around the lakes. They made it and bought more spuds, some canned goods, more flour, a can of milk, syrup for the biscuits, and a candy bar for each.

Milt and Ruth thought the boys would run out of grub after about five days, but with their "survival smarts" they lasted for 10 days. On the 10th day they packed up and left the cabin as they had found it, even splitting wood for the next guy to come by — "The Law of the Mountains." While this was an unwritten law, it was seldom, if ever, broken.

They were a tired, weary bunch of boys when they got home! I can still remember how much fresh milk they drank when they got home! Think of the wisdom of Milt, who taught them how to survive in the mountains. They probably never forgot what they had learned, and, moreover, it made them more determined not to be bachelors!

When Rex got out of Fruita Union High School in 1934, he went to Massachusetts to work for the Dewight family. Ruth's oldest sister, Frances, had married into a proud New England family at Hatfield, Massachusetts. Myron Dewight had a portable circular saw driven by a kerosene-burning engine. They sawed 10,000 board-feet of lumber per day. Rex worked for him for perhaps two years during which time he got tangled up with a log and broke a leg.

About 1936 Ruth sent for Rex to come home because Milt had to go to a hospital in Kansas City for a hemorrhoid operation. He was losing so much blood he was weak, it was a pretty serious thing in those days. We were all so worried about him, praying that he would live. So Rex came home for the rest of the summer. In that same summer he got a big, old, motorcycle and once drove it clear through the barn. With Rex's luck he was not killed or even seriously hurt.

I think it was the winter of that year that Rex and Bill went to a Diesel Mechanics School in San Francisco. This turned out to be a waste of time and money for Rex, as he was not mechanically inclined. After that he got a job on a 1,000-acre wheat farm in the San Joaquin Valley, near Shafter. After harvest was over he went up along the northern coast, and tried sluicing gold with a fellow who cheated him. Rex never learned much from that experience as he always trusted folks. Next he went down to Los Angeles with a guy whom he had worked with at Shafter. They got a room together and the next morning the guy was gone and also Rex's money. Rex had to send home for some money to pay for the hotel room — he thinks it was only $2. He learned later he could sleep in an all-night movie theatre for only ten cents. He spent a lot of time hitch-hiking and riding freight cars and hunting work along with hundreds of other younger and older men. Those depression years were tough!

On 3 October 1940, when Rex was 25 years old, he went to Durango, Colorado, with two friends and joined the Army, as they were trying to get ahead of the draft. They were sent to Fort Bliss, Texas, for basic training. Rex wrote home that at Fort Bliss you could stand in mud and have dirt blow in your face.

After basic training he was sent to Fort Sill, Oklahoma. As a Cadre†, he was assigned to the 6th Regiment and was given first class stripes. The Army decided to eliminate the 6th Regiment. That left Rex unassigned, so he didn't get any stripes. Next he was attached to central headquarters and was used as a utility man (an all-around flunky); he did everything from paper work to chauffeuring the General. A supply officer noticed that he could straighten out paper work, so he took him to the section that issued beds and furniture etc. He told Rex to get it straightened out — half the items had been unaccounted for. He did the job and during that time he trained two supply sergeants. But he was still unassigned and did not get any rating.

A Personnel Lieutenant needed him, so he was sent to work in Personnel. The lieutenant seemed to be a good guy, so Rex asked him to sign him up for an overseas assignment, which he did. A week later he ran into a Captain who said, "I took your name off the list, as I need you to run a public address system." It was a bull-horn type thing mounted on a truck, he was to meet incoming troop trains and tell the men where to go. He also went to the rifle range to blast information. The job was never authorized — after awhile the Captain he worked for was transferred. So here was Rex with no job or assignment. He made up new issue receipts, and changed to quarter master. It took months to straighten out, he was lost in the paper work at Fort Sill.

He finally went to a new outfit to service Piper Cub Aircraft, which were used for artillery observation. He thought he finally had a home, but he had a bleeding ulcer and was put in a hospital. The doctor did not X-ray him for ten days, but was keeping him under observation. Ratings for the servicemen came out and there was a regulation that said a man in the hospital could not be promoted. So he lost out again! Then a week later the doctor told him to go back to work, as he didn't have an ulcer. They just needed his bed.

So Rex was sent back to his crew chief job on the Cub Aircraft. They transferred into his crew two men who had washed out in pilot school — a Tech Sergeant and a Staff Sergeant. Since Rex was a private, this caused some problems. He went to the Captain, who backed him up. He told him they will follow your orders, or else! Boy! Did he ever feel important without any stripes!

A few weeks later he was on a week end pass. He was standing on a street corner across from the bus depot waiting for a girl he had met at the USO the week-end before. She didn't show, so he was wondering what to do when a guy drove up and said, "Soldier, do you want a date with a pretty girl? She rooms at our house and we want her to go to a Norwegian dance with us." This is how he met **Zella Manning**, a young country girl who had come from Tulsa, Oklahoma, to work for an oil company. This turned out to be a whirlwind love affair. They were married 19 August 1942 by a Baptist minister in Oklahoma City. Rex was made Corporal three weeks later.

Rex lived off base with Zella and ate her cooking, during that time he had very little trouble with his stomach. A year later they were expecting a baby and Zella went home so her brother-in law, who was a doctor, could do the delivery. Rex went back to eating Army chow and his ulcer began to act up again. He was bleeding and had to be admitted into emergency. This time the doctor said, "We will discharge you because you had an ulcer before you came in." Rex said, "Wait a minute. It is in my records that I did not have an ulcer two years ago." Thus, by this fluke, Rex has drawn

† He was a member of a cadre which is a unified group organized to instruct or lead a larger group.

276

20% disability for the past 52 years.

This marriage has lasted 52 years and at this writing Rex is 80 years old and still works part time for the Santa Rosa Fire Equipment Co. He gardens with a passion! Zella is still a very pretty woman. She waits on Rex and spoils him rotten. She has always enjoyed the art of home-making and has been faithful all her life to church work and to prayer. They have two beautiful red-headed boys: **Warren Rex**, born 3 November 1943 and **Joe Milton**, born 28 September 1945.

The following was written by Bill and Jean Turner Brisbin, with a little input from the author.

William "Bill" Long Brisbin married Jean Turner, daughter of **Bert** and **Rhoda Turner**[†], on 27 June 1938, in Salt Lake City, Utah, Jean had moved to New Liberty with her parents in 1936; they lived on the Claude Taylor farm, the former Howard Williams/Athol Stotts place. Bill and Jean met at an end-of-school activity; both had been attending Fruita Union High School.

They had four girls:

Billy Jean, born 22 May 1939, Collbran, Colorado

Judith Arlene, 24 November 1940, Cortez, Montezuma, Colorado

Linda Kay, 28 November 1944, Dolores, Montezuma, Colorado

Christine Ruth, 29 October 1951, Roosevelt, Uintah, Utah.

In the summer of 1938, right after their marriage, Bill worked for his grandmother Long at Collbran. During World War II, he worked in a shipyard in California, probably at Long Beach. In the spring of 1943 the family moved back to Colorado and rented a farm and orchard at Dolores, living there for three years; they continued to live in the Cortez area for four more years. Then, in 1948, they

[†] See Turner story, page 733

William "Bill" Long Brisbin
(Photo courtesy of Mabel Brisbin Howes)

purchased an 80 acre farm near Roosevelt, Utah, where they raised hay and cattle. The farm was located about three miles east of Roosevelt, on Whiterocks Road.

The four girls all continued their education and married. Billy Jean taught Business Ed and Computer at Vocational School at Roosevelt, Utah. After marriage Judith moved to Logan, Utah, and operated a flower shop for several years before retirement. Linda Kay still works as a Librarian in Roosevelt. Christine earned a Law Degree and is now working as a lawyer in Salt Lake City.

During 27 of the years Bill and Jean lived at Roosevelt, Bill worked as Service Manager at Labrum Ford. He began to have health problems that led to open heart surgery. That curtailed his activities considerably and they rented the farm to others for a few years. In the meantime, Jean kept busy with her daughters and grandkids and community

Bill Brisbin family in 1980. Back row, L-R: Billy Jean, Judith Arlene, Linda Kay and Christine Ruth. *(Photo courtesy of Bill and Jean Brisbin)*

pretty well ended the fight — who wants to have a fight without an audience? Why they each felt they needed the cap, I don't know, 'cause they were going to the pond to skinny dip. (A boy's privilege). This was the ice pond located at the Kinney place — folks sawed chunks of ice out of it in the winter time. The ice was put in bins of sawdust and used for special occasions in the summer, like making ice-cream on the 4th of July.

Bill and Rex were real pals. They were more like twins; they even weighed the same for many years.

Bill was a marble-player — most boys kept a few marbles in their pockets. Boys always had a can full of them stashed somewhere. There were the shooters, the glassies and the agates. I can remember them playing mumbley peg. In this game they dug little holes in the corners of a square and a hole in the middle. The object was to shoot around missing the holes and back to the center. If one shooter had his thumb outside the hole another would holler, "He fudged." Then an argument would ensue. Some times they would put all the best marbles in the center of a big ring with a pre-established line to try to shoot the other guy's best marble out. Sometimes it was for keeps. I do believe all boys played marbles to some extent. It was some years later when girls were allowed to play.

Once when spring had sprung they took their horses and skipped school. As usual they got caught and the teacher made a big deal out of it. It was decided they were to apologize to the teacher. Rex said, "I am sorry." Bill said, "I'm sorry, but not really, after the way you acted."

The boys took a lariat and climbed high up in a shade tree and tied one end to a high limb. A gunny-sack filled with straw on the other end. With this long swing they could swing up to the roof of the two-story house. They would jump off on the swing and really go! For kids that was quite a span — so many things kids could do for fun before radio and television.

Once the boys built a crystal radio set, Bill was the mechanic. He took a coil of copper wire with a phonograph needle attached to it. The needle was positioned on a spot on a piece of "fools gold" (iron pyrite). They also had a set of

activities. She worked for some years in Roosevelt as a Title 1 aid in reading and mathematics. They finally sold the farm in 1993 and moved to St. George, Utah.

More about Bill, written by Mabel Brisbin Howes

Bill was born 22 September 1917 at Collbran. He was the third child born to Milt and Ruth — a "tow-head." What a contrast to Mary's red hair and Rex's black hair! Bill was a very mild-mannered child.

The stories I remember being told about Bill when he was very young are cute. Bill said, "I'll be glad when I can get home so I can have a pitto† with a sheet on it." At times when Milt had to make a trip somewhere he often took just one child at a time, thus we all remember a trip with our father. One time Milt had taken Bill with him when he went to haul a load of wood from the Sunny Side. It was getting late and Milt said, "Bill are you getting hungry?" His answer was: "I is if you is, Daddy."

I never knew Bill to fight except one time with Rex over a cap. Milt told the boys, "If you want to fight, go out in the back yard." This

---

†A "pillow."

ear phones. Some way they were able to pick up radio stations, perhaps only one. Thus my brothers had a primitive type of radio.

About this time of growing up there was a traveling show that would come to our little cow-town (Collbran). It was after the medicine show and before the carnival. In our part of the country it was called a Chautauqua. It was an event that brought out about everyone. They stayed several nights, putting on a different show every night — drama one night, comedy another night, and black comedy another night. (Nowadays that would be socially unacceptable). They had music with a pretty girl singing and some one-man acts. They sold stuff; I remember they sold little boxes of taffy with crackerjacks. One box was guaranteed to have a diamond ring in it. Before movies that was considered good entertainment.

As far as I know Bill had only one real girl friend. Her name was Jean Turner. She was a pretty girl. They loved to go to dances. Jean was at our house with other girls most Sunday afternoons. Once Milt said, "Bill were you thinking about Jean when you missed a couple of rows?" Bill's reply was, "I speck so, I think of her most all the time."

As I recall, while Bill was at Diesel Mechanic School in San Francisco, Jean and her parents moved to Salt Lake City. Bill went there after he got out of school. He and Jean were married in Salt Lake City 27 June 1938. After they were married they came back to Colorado and their friends and neighbors had a big chivaree for them. It was the custom in those days for friends and neighbors to come to the newly-weds' place and make a lot of noise to give them a send-off on their married life together. Actually it was a well-wishing demonstration, but it would get to be rather raucous sometimes. It usually started late at night when the couple would begin to think they had missed the celebration. Sometimes the groom would be required to push the bride down the road in a wheelbarrow. At Bill and Jean's chivaree they took Jean one way and Bill another, telling each they would bring them home in the morning. While they were gone some of the neighbors did naughty things like "short-sheet" the bed or put rice in the bed.

To finish off the party the bride would serve cake and cookies and the groom would offer cigars to the men. Sometimes the bride and groom would fool their neighbors by hiding out so they couldn't be found for several nights. Lots of fun! That old custom of chivarees faded out after World War II.

Bill and Jean farmed several years at Cortez, Colorado, and Bill raised fine crops. One time when Billy Jean, their oldest girl, was about four years old, she said, "See that grain out there? It's my Dad's, the best in the country." She was so cute and so right!

Bill wanted a boy in the worst way. When their third girl arrived, Milt and Ruth received a telegram that said, "Linda Kay arrived today. No Robert Ray." I understand Jean cried, she wanted so bad to give Bill a boy. I don't believe I ever knew a woman, except my mother, who loved her man so much as Jean. Bill loved cake and she baked him one every day.

Bill and Jean ranched in the area of Roosevelt, Utah, and Bill worked at the Ford Garage in Roosevelt, as well as his ranch. They have been sweethearts for 57 years at this writing. They've been blessed with four lovely girls: **Billie Jean**, **Judy**, **Linda Kay** and **Christine**.

Mabel Virginia Brisbin — I have not wanted to write about myself, but I do have some feeling that I have shunned my responsibility. I find it difficult to be objective about myself. However, my life is interwoven with other stories.

I was the only child of Milt and Ruth Brisbin not born at Collbran. My father was a restless man who did not like farming. He would leave the ranch and try to make a living at something else, but with a big family to provide for, he always had to go back to the farm.

In about 1920 Milt and Ruth left Collbran for California, as mother had a sister, Mary, and a brother, Al Long, who lived at McFarland, in the area of Bakersfield, California.

My Dad was working at the Doul pumping station between Bakersfield and McFarland. They had a nice, comfortable company house to live in. While they were there Dan Brisbin, Milt's father, lived with them for awhile.

On 20 September 1921, mother went into labor about noon and told my father to go to town to get the doctor. That was before there were phones in the homes. Dad cranked up the old Model T Ford, (cars did not have self starters in those days) and went for the doctor. He told the doctor to, "Come out after awhile, as Ruth is in labor and it always takes her awhile." When

Mabel Virginia Brisbin
(Photo courtesy of Mabel Brisbin Howes)

butterflies, and bugs of all kinds. I had three brothers and several big cousins who teased me about being a "carrot top." So I grew up believing red hair was bad. My grandfather Long lived down the road about a mile; I loved that old man, but I can remember him holding me up in front of the mirror in the side board and saying, "Ginger, you will never be a beauty, you better learn to be useful." I felt to him I was special. Grandpa Joel Jackson Long died in 1933.

I did grieve for my grandpa, but I had a cousin I really loved — Jerry Jackson Long. He was just one year younger than me. We played together and were going to get married when we grew up and live over by Sunnyside. We all went to school over at Eaglelite, a one-room school. I was put back to take 1st grade over , so Jerry and I were in the same grade. Jerry died the next year from Rheumatic Fever. I thought my world had caved in — I told no one how I felt.

Around this time Dad had a ranch sale and sold every thing at auction, maybe to pay our debts, I don't know. He hired George Brown, (my husband Fred's uncle) to haul our stuff down to Hunter, Colorado, about four miles east of Fruita. I know Rex graduated from Fruita Union High School that year, so that would have been 1934. The Hunter grade school was a nice building with two rooms — grades one through four in one room and grades five through eight in the other. A really nice building.

Our close neighbors were the Garlitz family. This is where Mary got her husband, Earl Price Garlitz. These were the hard years; depression was in full bloom. I remember Dad got a job with his horses helping build a road; it may have been a WPA job. Dad was proud and would not accept charity. Many folks went to Fruita to get food stuff. I remember we did not wear shoes in the summer months, so as to save them. Maybe I didn't even have any shoes!

It was here Dad put a big wooden barrel at the side of the stove with pipes running into the barrel from the stove, to heat water. It took a lot of filling-up, but one could have enough hot water for a bath in the galvanized tub without having to heat it on the stove.

Dad built a little store at Hunter, perhaps 10 x 10 feet in size. We sold canned goods, sugar, flour, and big pieces of candy for a

my Dad arrived back home I was just making my entrance into the world. Dad tied my cord and had me and my mother pretty well cleaned up when the doctor arrived. The doctor retied my cord as Dad had left it about five inches long.

I believe Dad always wished he had gone to Oregon with his cousin, Charlie Mason. From McFarland he moved us to Oregon, as the grass was so tall and green he just knew he could make money on cows. Seems the grass had too much rain; when the cows ate it they did not produce much milk.

I do not know the year when we moved back to Collbran, but it must have been before 1923, when Bob was born.

This red-headed freckle-faced kid (me) loved the outdoors. I collected birds, penny. And I remember a "Nehi" (a brand name of soft drinks) square ice chest with pop in it like Orange Crush and Grape and Cream Soda. This stuff was to sell and we did pretty good with it. I remember Dad telling someone it paid for our groceries.

We also had a hand-operated gas pump. I remember folks would drive in and buy one or two gallons of gas, enough to get to town and back. I remember Bob and I sitting all day by the road to sell maybe two or three big watermelons at ten cents each. Some truckers, as they went by, would stop and buy. Local folks had watermelons in their own gardens.

We lived at Hunter for about two years, as I recall. One day a man by the name of Vern Snavely came by and made Dad an offer he couldn't turn down. The place at Hunter was 40 acres with a dump of a house and the little store. Mr. Snavely wanted to trade the place in New Liberty with twice the land and a very good farm house (yes, it did have an out-house for several years before we finally got rid of that inconvenience) and nice out-buildings. We traded straight across.

Seems that Vern had been arrested for boot-legging and had spent 20 years fighting with a neighbor. This, I think, was the women's war between Mrs. Snavely and Mrs. Morrow, more than anything else.

The Snavely's were real characters — I remember Mrs. Snavely coming to try to teach Mother about her faith. When Mother found out Mrs. Snavely wouldn't salute the flag she became irate and ordered her off the place. I remember she also said the world would come to an end, I think, in 1938. Guess what? — it didn't.

One of the things I remember about New Liberty was the teacher giving us that awful cod liver oil at school. I think we all took it from the same spoon. Also the mothers came to school and started the school lunch program; they served stew and beans. I remember Mother was one of the first PTA presidents. I was so proud of her!

Mr. Likes taught bible classes at the school. The Likes' had a retarded child, a sweet little boy that liked me and he would come to our house to sit on my lap.

There were lots of neighborhood parties. There would be popcorn and cookies, cake, and homemade ice cream when we had ice.

One year Dad got a herd of cattle and ran them on Glade Park. Next year he couldn't get the permit, so the cattle had to be sold. I remember one night someone stole and butchered a calf; they came from the direction of the Morrows. Whoever it was wanted it to look like Morrows did it. My folks always got along good with the neighbors, so we never accused anyone.

After the cattle I think we raised mostly beans. Restless Dad then rented the place out for a year or two and went to California to work in defense work. [When that happened, Milt built a small travel-trailer on an automobile running gear and axle in which to live and travel.] He got a job in a ship-yard at Long Beach. At that time Price Garlitz, Mary's husband, was working at Douglas Aircraft, and Bill was also working in the ship-yards. I also ended up out there working for Lockheed at the Burbank plant, building bombers.

Then the folks came back to New Liberty, sold the Snavely place and moved to Cortez, Colorado. By that time Rex and Bob were both in the Army.

My boyfriend, **Frederick V. Howes**, who grew up in Collbran, came back from Alaska. We didn't want to wait until the war was over, so we went to Reno, Nevada, and were married by the Justice of Peace on 16 March 1943. Fred, who was in the Army, had to report at San Antonio, Texas, so I went back to work at Lockheed in Burbank, California as a production Engineer. I worked there until Fred got a place for us to live in San Antonio.

Our first son, **Frederick**, was born in San Antonio; he lived only ten days. Our second son, **Freeman Milton**, was born in Del Rio, Texas. After the war Fred re-enlisted and was sent to Korea. Our son, Freeman and I, went back to Cortez to live with my folks. When Fred came back from Korea, he was stationed at Denver for a few months before being sent to Tucson, Arizona.

Freeman and I rejoined Fred in Tucson and our third son, **Monty Douglas**, was born there. Two weeks later Freeman died of Polio.

Two years later we had **Ronald DeWayne**, a big, bouncing healthy boy. We stayed in Tucson for 12 or 13 years. Then we were stationed in Okinawa for two years. Fred retired then and we went back to Arizona, sold out there and went to Alaska in the spring of 1962. Fred died there 28 February 1988, at age 74, after a gallant fight with coronary artery disease.

I still live in Chugiak, Alaska, which has been my home for 35 years. My oldest son, Monty, lives about seven miles away at Eagle River, Alaska. My son, Ronald, is in the Army and stationed in Korea. I have six grandchildren and three great grandsons. I have been blessed with a good life.

Robert Brisbin on his horse, Maude, at New Liberty. *(Photo courtesy of Mabel Brisbin Howes)*

(Mabel is telling this portion of the story)

Robert "Bob" Lee Brisbin was born 8 December 1923, at Collbran. I consider him my "little" brother as he is two years and three months younger than I am. Mary recalls that he had a little "kiddie car" and he rode it so fast the family was afraid of losing him. He started to school at Eaglite, a one room school. His teacher's name was Miss Wompler. Bob was always smarter in school than I was; he learned quickly and had to do very little home work. But he did love to tease the younger girls.

I don't remember any special events about Bob in school except when he got mad at me one time for not giving him a sandwich I had promised him. It was my fault because I hadn't done what I said I would. One time Bob had a bad fall on the cistern. He had a bad sunburn and really got skinned up when he fell. The abrasions got infected with fungus, or it could have been ringworm, as we always had cats and dogs. I remember feeling so sorry for him 'cause it took Mother a long time to get it healed up.

Most of my memories of him were after we were living at New Liberty. He wanted to do everything his big brothers did, even though they were six and eight years older than him. They would take off and leave him, but he would try to keep up with them; he was a pretty tough little kid. Dad had a horse named Prince that was hard for others to ride, but Bob rode him bareback. Prince would back up to the fence so Bob could get on him easily. Bob also had a little toy terrier he loved. The dog slept at the foot of his bed and kept Bob's feet warm.

Mary told me that when Bob was little he once stole a knife from Uncle Jack and our parents made him take it back. Mary asked him why he stole it and he said, "To get in the jail house." he loved the song "I'm In The Jail House Now."

After we moved to New Liberty he would ride the tractor and yodel, in many ways a happy young man. I remember when he wore an old cowboy hat that was about four sizes too large for him. We girls thought it looked awful and would try to get it away from him. But Mother would stick up for him about that hat.

I found among his records a certificate showing he was a member of the Colorado State Rural School Choir. He also belonged to a 4-H club and learned to make excellent oatmeal cookies.

William "Bill" with family dog, Robert and Rex in a corn field at New Liberty. *(Both photos courtesy of Mabel Brisbin Howes)*

Bob thought Dad was rough on him. Dad was a stern disciplinarian who did not spare the belt when the boys would disobey him. The older boys, Rex and Bill, thought Bob had it a lot easier than they did and got away with more. But, of course, as men get older they usually mellow somewhat.

Bob graduated from Fruita Union High School in 1941. By that time the United States was becoming involved in World War II and many of us went to California to work in defense jobs. It was in Long Beach, California, where Bob received his "Greetings from the President of the United States." He was instructed to go back to Colorado and report to his draft board. From there he was sent to Fort Logan, Colorado, and was inducted into the Air Force in June 1943. He finished technical school at Amarillo, Texas, and then was sent to gunnery school at Las Vegas, Nevada. While there he got the mumps and began to fear he wouldn't be able to graduate with his class.

After graduation he had hoped he would get to come home on leave, but instead he and his crew went to Nebraska and picked up their B17 Flying Fortress and flew it to England. Bob was trained as a tail gunner — the most dangerous position on the aircraft. He was 19 years old.

They had flown 15 separate missions, taking flack (bits of metal from the exploding anti-aircraft shells) on every mission. It was on the fifteenth mission when they were shot down — on 25 June 1944. They were about 20 miles off the coast in the vicinity of Caen, France. Their plane took a direct hit, believed to have been in an oxygen tank behind the pilot's and co-pilot's seats. Bob was wounded from a piece of flack in his leg.

At about 7:05 AM the pilot ordered all crew members to bail out. The pilot, co-pilot and another gunner named Wyett, refused to leave. Wyett said, "I'll ride it down." They saw the plane explode a little later; seven men got out of the plane alive.

The Daily Sentinel of 2 July 1944 reported that Bob had recently been awarded an Air Medal for participation in five separate combat missions over Europe. Then, following is the account of his being reported missing in action in *The Daily Sentinel* of 12 July 1944:

Sgt. Robert Lee Brisbin, son of Mr. and Mrs. M. S. Brisbin, former Fruita residents, was reported missing in action from a flight over France, 25 June, according to a War Department message to his parents.

Sergeant Brisbin, tail gunner on a Flying Fortress of the eighth air force base in England, was recently awarded the Air Medal. A graduate of Fruita Union High School, the young man entered the Army in January 1943, and received his training at Las Vegas, Nevada, and Amarillo, Texas.

The young man was well known in the lower valley community.

His name appears in several articles in *The Daily Sentinel* during the months following his capture by the Germans.

Mabel's story continues:

Robert (Bob) Lee Brisbin in 1943
(Photo courtesy of Mabel Brisbin Howes)

Where Bob landed there was a valley with trees on one side. As he knew the Germans would try to kill him, he hit the ground running in spite of his wounded leg. A Frenchman helped by hiding him in a pig pen. The pig pens were holes dug into the side of a hill. Since it was dark, one German soldier came into the pen but didn't find him. But they had seen him come down, so they knew he was around somewhere. Soon another German came in and lit a match and was then able to see him. They put Bob in a motorcycle side-car and

Prisoner

Black barbs of war that fetter me, and scowling towers
Only the least of me is hostage — mere limbs and voice
Which were imprisoned in one pattern or another anyway.
I was a veteran prisoner before you; these feet know well
The slavery of patter-roads close followed;
The voice is trained answer low in meekness
The overseeing tones of tyrant custom.
I am used to the black bread of dogma
And the tasteless water of convention, so you see
Black barbs and scowling towers, you do not chain me
No more than I am used to being chained.
I have learned well the articles of servitude
To which a man must submit his flesh,
Learned them so well indeed that they are role
And no longer interfere with that of me which is beyond the chain,
Forever reaching — forever free.

Anonymous

Both of these drawings and the one on page 286 were drawn by fellow prisoners of Bob Brisbin when they were in prison in Germany. After they returned home from prison, a book was put together with all the drawings and poems that were written, and made available to all of the prisoners that wanted one. The drawing above was done by prisoner Hittel in 1944. It represents the building Bob was in at Stalag Luft IV. These drawings and poem were copied from Bob's book by his sister, Mabel Brisbin Howes, and made available to us.

took him to a ranch house and put him in a hen-house type enclosure. When they had about forty prisoners they started them marching. The guards were mounted on horses.

They marched across France and ultimately reached Berlin where they slept one night in an underground train station. By this time many had died from dysentery, pneumonia and starvation. For those who became too weak to keep up, the cruel guards would stick them with a bayonet, hit them over the head with a rifle butt, or just shoot them. Bob said whenever he fell, or was otherwise able to, he would get a mouth full of grass or a stalk of grain. Being a farm boy helped him to survive. He remembered that his Dad had once told him, "A man can live on food a cow would eat."

They would pick up more prisoners as they marched along the way. Once in Germany the guards also had to protect them from the civilians who were angry at the "fly boys" who had been bombing their home land.

Somewhere along the way they were herded into box cars about half the size of box cars in the United States. These were cattle cars that were so old they had been used in World War I, back in 1918. They were called "40 Hommes 8 Chevaux."

After the boys were packed in, there was no longer any room to lie down or sit. The doors were locked on the outside. Without food or water the men soon became as swine. The smell grew steadily worse as the men became sicker. With vomiting and with the need to relieve themselves because of dysentery they couldn't move and so had to remain in their filth. The stench was enough to make a strong man sick. The greatest suffering was from thirst; tongues began to swell and throats felt as if they were closing, too dry to swallow. Their lips became parched and their eyes were burned red. By now most were without any equipment as the cumbersome flying boots had worn out or had been lost in the bail-outs. They were a ragged, filthy bunch, to say the least.

Bob was finally placed in Stalag Luft IV, as Prisoner of War #80758. For awhile life was not so miserable; not good, but without physical pain. The camp was located near the Baltic about two miles from the small village of Kiefeide, between Danzig and Stettin; about 75 miles north of Stettin.

(From this point on we will attempt to quote from Bob's story as closely as possible in his own words.)

Prisoners arrived at Stalag Luft IV from hospitals in Vienna and Frankfurt and from German transit and interrogation centers at Wextlar and Budapest; also from camps at St. Wendell, near the French border, and from Heydekrung in East Prussia. Many were evacuated from paths of the advancing Allied Armies; also from numerous points where enemy fighters and flak had spilled them (or caused them to crash).

The camp had been activated early in May and prisoner arrivals trickled in throughout the next two months. On 18 July more than 2,000 men were admitted from the recently-evacuated Heydekrung camp. Other groups ranging from 20 to 200 men, joined us each few days. By the end of the year there were 10,000 men in the camp. With the exception of about 800 British and Canadian Airmen, most were American non-commissioned officers. (Bob was a Staff Sergeant).

The camp was divided into four compounds, or lagers, each containing a separate unit. These were arranged in a square and bisected by a road from which a single gate led into each unit. Twin barbed-wire fences about nine feet high, running parallel and about the same distance apart, surrounded each of the four compounds as well as the entire camp. And along the perimeter were carefully spaced log towers, serving as vantage points for the guards. Search lights and machine guns were mounted on the towers between which flood lights had also been erected. Guards on foot, with police dogs, patrolled around and beyond all this. A cozy place, to say the least!

The barracks were of standard German type construction — 40 by 130 feet, each containing 10 rooms, with a central hallway running the full length of the building. Two washrooms and a pit latrine for night use were located in the rear of the barracks, although it was soon necessary to use that space for additional sleeping quarters. Each room, approximately 15 by 23 feet, was designed to provide facilities for sixteen men in double bunks.

It later became necessary to change to triple bunks, thus making 24 men to a room. In addition, eight or nine men were required to sleep on the floors. The men on the floor fared just about as well as the men on the bunks, as the bunks were so crude. They contained only six slats, no more, no less, and the only buoyancy for one's bones was an elongated paper sack filled with wood-shavings. That would soon compress to form a mattress not unlike a sheet of wallboard. A small stove, a table and a few stools constituted the furniture.

The International Convention Relating to Treatment of Prisoners of War had been signed at the Geneva Convention in July 1929, and was ratified by most nations, including Germany and the United States. These regulations had the most immediate effect on the routine activities governing the little incidents in the everyday lives of the prisoners.

All rules were promulgated by Der Kommandant, whose assistant was

coldest of nights and necessitated long periods of shivering in the hallway while a check was made of each prisoner's rank and P. O. W. number.

The barracks were locked up at prescribed hours every night. The outer doors were closed and barred, and shutters were placed over all windows. Somewhat similar regulations prevailed in case of air raids. The men were given three minutes to clear the lager grounds and return to barracks. After that the guards would shoot anyone not inside.

Food was not only inadequate in quantity, but lacked quality as well. No breakfast was served. Dinner consisted of barley soup; supper

Gruppenleiter. A Lageroffizier was directly in charge of each compound and his orders were carried out by a Lagerfeldwebel, a Sergeant. The language of the camp was proclaimed to be German. All Prisoners of War were required to salute all German Officers, regardless of rank. They were superior to those detained.

Most important to Der Kommandant, of course, was the accounting of the continued presence of his wards and to this end roll calls were held in each compound twice daily. It was not unusual to be awakened in the middle of the night for an "identity check." It was a hell of a nuisance which seemed to occur on the

was plain boiled potatoes. Occasional substitutions for dinner might include cabbage soup or stewed greens. On rare occasions they would serve a cup of barley cereal, that being a deluxe meal by comparison, and the camp favorite. Needless to say, this diet contributed greatly to weight loss.

The kitchen staff cooked the available rations in two or three huge vats for each 2,000 or more men. These were the only utensils with which to cook the food. Nor did the facilities for serving the food add to its attractiveness. It reached the 25 men in each room in ten-quart galvanized pails of the mop-bucket type so familiar in the American household. It was no wonder that the few personal packages from home and the food packages brought by the Red Cross played an important part during this period of existence. It was supposed that the Red Cross intended for their parcels to be issued once a week to each man. But the Germans did not prescribe to this idea. Instead, all parcels were opened and searched, the cans punched and the contents distributed at the rate of two or three items through a week. All the cans had to be returned and accounted for.

What to do with spare time was not an especially important problem; with a newly arrived P.O.W., rest was foremost in his mind. Those who reached Luft IV during the summer months found an ideal climate and sky under which to stretch out and just relax. But after a week they would be beating a path around the edge of the compound, and by the third week life had become very monotonous.

Games or athletic equipment did not arrive in any quantity until late in the fall. A couple of soft balls and improvised bats plus a few decks of cards, some homemade, served to entertain the P. O. W.'s for several months. A few hobbies sprang up, such as writing poetry, even an epidemic of knitting took over the camp. Men unraveled old sweaters and tried to work the yarn into scarfs or caps. (Even I did this).

Later in the fall other equipment arrived; some musical instruments from the Y. M. C. A. came through Geneva. Meanwhile, the more serious-minded P. O. W.'s had not been idle. A committee on education canvassed the camp and rounded up a respectable faculty and instituted daily classes on dozens of subjects. Later a shipment of books came — Armed Forces Editions of current best sellers, published by the Council on Books in Wartime, which, we believe, did a splendid job.

Few events in camp proved more popular than the various religious services. Bible study classes, masses, choir rehearsals and prayer meetings were well attended each week. Participation in regular Sunday services far surpassed attendance goals set by optimistic chaplains elsewhere in the world. But it was also due in no small measure to the popularity and tireless efforts of a few men whom the fortunes of war had thrown in their midst: P. O. W., Reverend G. Rex Morgan of the Church of England; and another P.O.W., Reverend Father T. J. E. Lynch, a Captain in the British Army. There was also Reverend Anthony Jackson, whose parish was on the Isle of Guernsey, taken by the Germans during the early stages of the war. Credit is due also to the assistants of these churchmen, particularly T/ Sgt. Major V. Mears of Copperas Cave, Texas, an ordained Baptist minister; he had been a first engineer on a bomber that failed to return. There were also Hamlin R. Cathy of Charlotte, North Carolina, Charles M. Doss of Morris, Illinois, and a Peter Smith, all who performed their tasks well and were largely responsible for the success of the religious programs. Achievements in these programs are all the more creditable when one fully realizes the handicaps under which the program was carried forward.

As the bombs grew closer and battles could be heard being fought on each side, the P.O.W.'s became alarmed and began to wonder what would happen to them. Three rumors ran through the compounds: 1. The German guards will surrender this camp to the Russians. 2. The high command will be ordered to Berlin and put us all to death. 3. They will evacuate us on a long march across Germany. All knew that in the latter event there would be many casualties. It would be a march of death, as the Russians were close and the Germans were afraid of them.

On 6 February 1945 we were ordered to roll up packs as quickly and orderly as possible. (Remember there were 8,000 men). The guards were heavily armed and ordered to shoot anyone who broke ranks. We were divided up in groups of about 100 men to each unit and were marched in columns of five. The guards warned us, "We will shoot any prisoner who falls out from exhaustion. Remember, we will shoot without hesitation." The S. S. never argued, a rifle shot saved time. The guards were all frightened, so the prisoners believed what they were told. It was a march of great hardship. For 45 days we were marched long distances in bitter weather and on starvation rations; we lived in filth and slept in open fields or in barns. Clothing, medical facilities and sanitary facilities were utterly inadequate. Hundreds of the men suffered from malnutrition, exposure, tuberculosis and other diseases. No doubt many men still suffer, even today, as a result of that ordeal.

There were depressing scenes of civilians along the roads — old men being helped by boys, mothers carrying babies, young children carrying bundles of belongings and food. Most were poorly clothed and half frozen from the bitter cold. The highways were almost paralyzed by the thousands of people all moving in one direction. These civilians were bitter and demoralized and would rather have surrendered to the Russians than continue. They were, in fact, prisoners of the S. S. troops who moved them by force with rifles and bayonets. An occasional rifle shot would allow a civilian to sit at the side of the road forever. Occasionally even a guard would fall down from exhaustion. German morale was near the breaking point, as they knew the end was near for Hitler's Germany.

Prisoners or "Kriegies" suffered from frostbite and pneumonia; hundreds had severe cases of dysentery. Our numbers were steadily growing smaller. If possible the prisoners were put up at nights in barns or church buildings, or wherever shelter could be found. Enough heat was generated from the hundreds of men's bodies to warm the barn or whatever building. Snow was melted for water, if any wood was available for fire, and tea was made from the boiling water. Because of their already weakened condition, many men became desperately sick to their stomachs. They were often not able to reach a door in time and would step on or vomit on others as they tried to get outside. Sometimes the stench would get so bad they would try to sit outside, but then their hands and feet would freeze. Sometimes in barns they were able to cover their bodies with hay.

I managed, on a few occasions, to steal potatoes, or grain from the shocks, even eggs or a chicken — anything for food. If Kriegies had cigarettes they could trade with the Germans for bread or potatoes or onions, which they ate raw. Many died from eating snow; their thirst would get so bad they could not resist.

Miles and hours passed into weeks. We were marched back and forth across Germany; crossing the Elbe River several times. We knew the war was about over, but it seemed to drag on and on. We could often see bombers flying toward us and we tried always to stay in sight on the road, always hoping we would be identified. The march lasted a total of 45 days — General Patton and General Patch were on one side and the Russians closing in on the other. We knew we were in a tight squeeze. By this time some of the guards would mysteriously disappear at night, no one knew where they went.

The prisoners got weaker and thinner; not only dirty but lousy. They had no way to comb their hair, let alone shave or bathe. Some times we were housed in abandoned factory buildings and this alarmed some because there was a chance we could be bombed. However, some of those factory buildings had toilets and water. The numbers of prisoners became fewer each day, as we became too weak to go on. There were occasional beatings by the guards — yet we knew we were so near the end of this "HELL."

The first of April we were again forced to march. This time we went in an easterly direction, running from the American and British forces. We doubled back and covered again a good bit of the same territory we had just marched over from the other direction the month before. We doubled back and forth across the country for over 200 kilometers and 30 days, getting weaker and sicker by the day. We crossed the Elbe River three times.

On May 2nd, 1945, near Bonn, a British tank brigade suddenly came upon us. The German guards immediately threw down their weapons and a British squad marched them off to an Allied prisoner of war compound where they soon found out what kind of treatment prisoners of war got from their captors.

Many of us could not stand alone. There were about 200 of us left out of 1,500 that had started on February 15 — 76 days of HELL and misery. I weighed 75 pounds, down from a normal weight of 165 pounds when I was shot down.

The British tank outfit told us to get across the river before dark. Somehow we made the 2 kilometer walk to a British command area where everyone got emergency medical care and we were immediately fed, bathed, deloused and refitted from the skin out in complete uniform (but not necessarily in that order). The very sick were put into field hospitals, others were transported by British lorries[†] to British units where they went into hospitals. (I did not go into a hospital).

"Chattanooga" (a Tennessee boy who was the turret gunner on the same plane with Bob) was with me at this time. A British officer came by in a jeep and picked us up.

The Germans surrendered on 7 May 1945. All kinds of confusion followed, as everyone alive seemed to scatter in every direction.

Later we got a new Hupmobile from off the street and stayed overnight in the Mayor's house, where we ate and drank until we got sick. We stayed there a week and by then we could manage a little better and had gained some strength. We went to a bank and got some invasion money from Brussels, Belgium. Next we went to Lahr, France, a sea port,

[†]A British lorry is a motor truck.

where we waited two weeks for a boat. We left the car there on the street, I always wondered what happened to that little Hupmobile.

A tank carrier took us back to New York harbor; then we were sent to Camp Shanks. There were thousands of soldiers arriving there. As soon as we were processed, I was given a 90-day furlough. (No debriefing or attention to adjustment problems). Transportation wasn't all that great to get home. I had to ride a narrow-gauge railroad to Dolores through Alamosa and Durango.

(The end of quoting from Bob, now back to Mabel)

Our brother was home! We thanked God and cried for joy! Little did we know or understand how much he had been through. The Army did not have a debriefing time or any psychoanalysis program, so they really didn't know how well he was — be it physically or emotionally — or if he could stand the stress of returning to civilian life.

Fred (Mabel's husband) and I got a leave and went home to see Bob. He was still thin and haggard. I can remember him sitting off alone and just staring off into space. At night he had terrible nightmares. One night Dad jumped up, as Bob was yelling and was about to throw a rocking chair out the window.

I have never been able to get Bob to talk about the war. To write this story I have done a lot of probing. His friends tell me when Bob is drunk he will talk about it. Perhaps that is why he drinks; to forget about it if only for a short time. There are still a lot of scars in him, maybe too deep to heal.

Bob was given an Honorable Discharge from the Army Air Corps, 8 October 1945. He also received a Purple Heart, Air Medal with two Oak Leaf Clusters and a Prisoner of War Medal.

On 8 December 1945, the same year he came home, and on his 22nd birthday, he married **Dorothy Jean McConnell**. We all loved Dorothy and felt it was such a good thing for him to marry her. Their first daughter, **Donna Jean**, was born 20 December 1949; she was a beautiful child with blue eyes. They had two other little girls: **Susan**, born 4 May 1953, and **Nancy**, born 5 May 1958.

Bob worked as a carpenter for building contractors in the Cortez area. Later he built a beautiful home for he and Donna and girls; one of the most beautiful homes in Cortez. But

Donna and Bob drew apart and eventually she filed for divorce and they separated.

We know now that Bob had been suffering from Post Traumatic Stress Disorder (PTSD) caused by the terrible ordeal he went through during the war. That disorder causes men to be nervous, withdrawn, hostile, restless and paranoid. They have nightmares, flashbacks, and are unable to concentrate. They have difficulty establishing strong emotional ties with others, they sleep poorly, they are irritable, and they have trouble controlling their tempers. They suffer from depression and have a tendency to cry at inappropriate times. They are often estranged from their families

Bob was sent to the mental hospital at Pueblo, Colorado, where he was finally able to get the psychiatric help he should have had before he was discharged from the Army Air Corps.

After he was released he went to Alaska and was married again; that marriage also ended in divorce. He worked in building construction in Alaska, was foreman on many big jobs. He also worked on the Alaskan pipeline.

He decided to go to Arizona for the past winter (1996/97), but expects to go back to Alaska in the spring. He has been having some health problems.

Isn't it ironic that the real heroes of war seldom, if ever, get the credit they deserve? We are grateful to have been able to retell Bob's story. We sincerely hope Bob's reluctance to talk about it will not cause him to be offended by our sharing his story by this means. We are proud of you, Bob, for having guts enough to survive in spite of all the hardships!

Ruth Marie Brisbin was born 5 October 1926, at Collbran, Colorado. She was named Ruth after her mother, and correctly named, as she is so like her mother. She had lots of dark brown hair and her mother's dark brown eyes. I was five years old when she was born, and as soon as she could leave her crib she slept with me. (Wet on me now and then). Later, because she had broken off her front teeth, she was unable to talk plain. We thought it was cute and we and our cousins would tease her until her fiery little temper would appear. "I tan too tot tain!"

Ruth Marie Brisbin
(Photo courtesy of Mabel Brisbin Howes)

The hard part of Ruthie's early life was caused by the birth of her little sister, Harriet. A "blue baby" who had to have much care. Needless to say, the weak child got all the attention. Perhaps Ruth was not a well child, or just needed more attention. I can remember waking up at night several times and she would be crosswise in the bed with her feet across my stomach. When I complained she said, "Duh hutt."

I believe Ruth started to school at New Liberty. By this time Harriet had out grown much of her frailty, and she and Ruth became great pals, always playing jacks or building playhouses. By the time she was in high school our restless Dad had moved to Dolores, Colorado, near Cortez. She grew into a pretty young woman and she was bright and ambitious. She went to college at Fort Collins long enough to be able to teach, since there was then a shortage of teachers. Later she taught for some time at a one-room school at Mesa Verde. She should have gone further in college.

It was during this time, 22 December 1947, that she married **Thomas Arthur Becher**. They lived at Dolores, where the Becher family had lived for 50 years. Ruth taught as a substitute and as a teachers' aid for many years. She also took correspondence classes and later was able to get a real estate license and a broker's license.

They had not been married long — Dee and Tommy were still babies — when Tom was working up at Rico as a mechanic. Before he went to bed at night he would wind the clock, set the alarm and set the clock on Ruth's side of the bed. In the morning she would get up, fix breakfast and then try to get him up. This aggravated her no end, until one day she said, "Keep the clock on your own side of the bed!" But some time during the night, Tom moved the clock to her side of the bed. When it went off, Ruth threw the clock right through the window. That was the last time Tom did that.

If Ruth wanted a new washer and dryer, or other appliances, she would go out and get a job. When she had enough money for the appliance she would just quit her job. We all loved her independence.

When her children needed a kindergarten and the town didn't have one, she started one and taught other kids in town as well. After her children no longer needed kindergarten, she quit, and it upset many of the town folks who were depending on her.

A plywood factory came into the little town of Dolores and brought many new people with it. Ruth started a welcome wagon to call on and welcome many new folks into the community. She belonged to the Methodist Church and many members of that church went fishing and camping on Sunday, so she organized a kid's bible class that met on Friday or Saturday evening.

Ruth and Tom were a fun family and they did lots of crazy things that we all enjoyed. We visited them one time when the home-brew bottle caps were popping off. Another time they decided to raise frying chickens in their garage. The trouble began when they discovered they had twice as many chickens as they had space for. We arrived and began dressing out the biggest fryers each day so the smaller ones had more room to grow. We ate lots of good fried chicken on that visit.

Another time they had read about raising mushrooms, so began hauling river-bottom dirt and manure and mixing it in the no-longer used coal bin. When everything was ready they ordered $100 worth of seed. Then began the long vigil of waiting and watching for the mushrooms to begin to grow. Nothing happened, so next year they hauled all that wonderful soil out to the garden. Guess what, they had mushrooms in the garden! They didn't know it takes two years for the spores to grow.

They bought a one hundred year-old, three-story, four-bedroom house near where the Bear Creek dumps into the Dolores River. It was a marvelous old house and Ruth and Tom made us all feel welcome. The Bechers swam in the river, floated on inner-tubes and fished for trout, in the winter they skated on the ice. As if that wasn't enough, they bought a double-wide trailer and made a summer camp by the river-side. Every one of us six families have so many wonderful memories of Ruth's family and their hospitality.

When our parents, Ruth and Milt, retired and moved into the town of Cortez, Ruth's family were the only ones who lived nearby. It was eight miles from Dolores to Cortez. So Ruth took on the responsibility of seeing to their needs. As the years went by she was not only the care-giver for Ruth and Milt but for Milt and his second wife, Jessie, after Ruth was gone.

In 1992, because of ill health, Ruth and Tom sold the big house and moved to a single-level country house halfway between Dolores and Cortez. They had several acres and a fish pond where birds visited. It was also a delightful place for us to visit with Ruth and her wonderful family. They have now been married 47 years (1994) — we hope they'll make it to 50 and beyond. They have three great children: **Dee Elda**, 9 June 1959; **Thomas Arthur Jr.**, 28 November 1968; and **Leslie Ann**, 13 May 1969. (Tom died of cancer in July 1995.)

arriet Louise Brisbin was born 9 May 1929, at Collbran, Colorado. She was called a "blue baby", very frail, due to a congenital heart problem. Our oldest sister, Mary, who was then 15 years old, told us she was not allowed to pick Harriet up because she was so frail. As the years passed Harriet did grow out of it, but she remained small and always somewhat pale. When she was a teenager she had to work at it to weigh 100 pounds when she was soaking wet. But she had a sweet disposition, we all loved her.

I remember one time when one of us said to our mother, "We have too many children." Mother said, "Which one should we have left out — Harriet?" That settled it. Harriet is the only one of us who remembers sitting on her Daddy's lap. He called her his "snooken tater."

Harriett Louise Brisbin
(Photo courtesy of Mabel Brisbin Howes)

Harriet was light on her feet and at about age five she would do a little jig and kind of tap dance for us and for company. We would all laugh and applaud.

We lived at Collbran until she was about four. She loved to gather the eggs. She would reach up into the manger where the hens liked to lay their eggs and once she touched a bull snake. She was as white as a ghost, we were afraid she was going to die. Dad went out and killed the bull snake, even though ranchers did not object to having them around, as they were good at killing the mice around the barns and grain bins. They were considered harmless by most people.

Harriet became great pals with her older sister, Ruth. I remember them sitting on the floor a lot, playing jacks. This is a game that's played with little metal jacks that have eight spokes about one-half inch across and a little rubber ball about an inch in diameter. The idea is to bounce the ball, pick up one jack before the ball hits the floor, then on the next bounce, pick up two jacks; "onesy, twosy, threesy" etc., until you were able to pick up all the jacks in that order, or until you missed. Then you would have to let your partner have a turn.

We all jumped rope, but we did not have individual ropes then. We would use a piece of rope about eight or ten feet long and tie one end to a post, then someone would swing the rope in a big loop. Then Harriet, Ruth, Bob, or myself, would take turns jumping until one made a mistake. Then, we would have to let someone else take a turn. We would sing out, "One, two, buckle my shoe; three, four, shut the door; five, six, pick up sticks; seven, eight lay them straight; nine, ten, big fat hen, etc." Harriet loved this game and we had to be careful that she wouldn't get too tired. Because of her we would do "Rock-a-bye-baby," swinging the rope slower, or back and forth instead of over the loop.

Other variations included two kids swinging the rope going very fast, which was called, "Red Hot Pepper," and swinging the rope about six to 10 inches above the ground, which was called, "High Water." Then there was the "Double Dutch" — two people swinging two ropes in different directions. That one was usually played by older kids at school.

After Harriet started going to school, probably when she was in first grade; she had a part in a Christmas school play. She was the littlest angel and sang the song: "I don't believe in Santa Claus." The principal carried her out on the stage; she was so little, she made a big hit!

By the time Harriet was about 10, the family lived in Dolores, Colorado. She remembers riding a horse to town with eggs to sell, so she could have money to go to a show. This reminds me of another story to tell about our older brothers, Rex and Bill, who would sneak out two or three eggs per day until they had saved up a dozen. Then would take them to town and sell them for perhaps 10 cents per dozen so they'd have money to buy a sack of "Bull Durham." They would sneak out behind the barn and they started smoking at an early age.

Another memory of Ruth and Harriet... As they washed dishes together Ruth would say, "I have them all washed and she has just finished polishing one cup." Harriet was very slow and thorough and neat in every thing she did.

In high school Harriet met **Bob Wood** and fell in love and wanted to quit school and get married. My folks said, "Finish school and then you'll have our blessing." They were married 15 May 1947. Bobbie got a job with Safeway Stores and they were doing good. **Robert**, their first son, was born 22 March 1948. He was a cute little red head, but he cried night and day. He had eczema and they tried everything and finally took him to a doctor in California who told them Robert would have lost his legs because he had so

much infection from the eczema. The Colorado doctor had not been treating him properly. The California doctor discovered he was allergic to almost everything, including the soy-bean milk they had been feeding him. They started giving him goat's milk at first, then started him on one kind of food at a time until he developed tolerance.

Her next child **Michael Dean**, another red-head, was born 11 April 1951 without fingers on his left hand. It was determined to be a genetic thing, somewhat like Harriet's congenital heart problem. Mike adapted well, as he had Harriet for a mother. He was truly a human monkey who climbed everything and swung with one hand from anything higher than his head.

I remember visiting her once when I found her sitting on the floor playing blocks with her kids. She loved her kids and devoted her life to their well-being. **Mitchell Dean**, another red-head, was born 20 February 1954.

Bob was made store manager and was transferred to Albuquerque. When Mitch was about three years old, Bob decided he wanted a lady who worked in the store as a meat wrapper. Harriet received notice in the mail that Bob had divorced her. She moved back to Colorado and really did a wonderful job raising those little boys, though with many difficulties.

Once Harriet had to go to Grand Junction for some training. It was while I was in Colorado waiting to take my boys to join Fred in Okinawa, so we stayed at her house with her boys. What a fun time that was with five little boys, all between the ages of four and 10! Once they came home with big sacks of plums. I found out they had climbed over the fence to steal a few and the owner came out with sacks and told them to take the sacks home full.

Another time, the boys brought home a skunk that had been shot. Perhaps he had been someone's pet, as he had been descented. He did not stink — (much). He was cute and he did get well; he would stamp his feet when he wanted to be fed.

Robert had a chemistry set and one time he filled the house with pink smoke. Another time the boys went hunting and shot a white pigeon. They had it on the stove, boiling; they had plucked it's feathers but had not taken out it's entrails. One time Harriet even let her kids keep a monkey — what fun memories at Harriett's house!

Harriet married **Kenneth Graham** on 3 February 1962. We all liked Ken, as he was so good to Harriet and her boys. But Ken had a bad heart and died 29 December 1977. Harriet grieved so and perhaps still grieves for Ken. He was buried at Lancaster, California, where they lived most of their married life.

On 3 February 1983, Harriet married another good man by the name of **Joe New**. As of 20 March 1995 they are living at Lancaster, California. It has been a good marriage.

In recent years Milt's and Ruth's children and grandchildren have developed a tradition of gathering at Quartzsite and/or Yuma, Arizona, during the winter months, to spend time together. However, they did not do that in the winter of 1996/97.

Ruth, the mother, died 9 February 1963 in Cortez. Milt married Jessie B. Cody Johnson, 31 October 1966, in Cortez, and they continued to live there until Milt's death on 9 October 1971. Jessie Brisbin died in Fruita at age 97.

George Bryan
(Photo courtesy of niece, Reta Massey Foy)

Bryan

We have combined information we had on George Bryan with a history written by Weston Thomas Massey, oldest son of Mary Bryan Massey (George's sister), sent to us by Reta Massey Foy, Weston's daughter. Also census and land records, an obituary and news items from *The Daily Sentinel.*

George Bryan was born in County Cork, Ireland, 1 January 1880. His sister, Mary, had come to the United States in 1892, and eventually married Eben T. Massey. They lived on a ranch in Unaweep Canyon. Eben Massey was shot to death in 1903 in a dispute with a neighbor, leaving Mary a widow with four young sons: Weston Thomas, Eben B., Phillip W. and James.

George came to the United States in 1904, spending a couple of years in North Dakota with another sister, Bessie. In 1907, Mary wrote George and asked him to come to Unaweep to help her with the ranch; George did so. While working on the ranch, he filed on a homestead, 11 June 1907, in what was to become the New Liberty community. In 1909 Mary and George received word that their parents had passed away in Ireland. George was the only surviving male heir, so he decided to go back to Ireland, as he would then be eligible to inherit the property. He told his sister goodbye — not expecting to return. But Mary said: "You'll be back. I've been away from that place longer than you have; I haven't forgotten what it's like." In 1911 Mary received a letter from George asking her to send money for his passage back saying, "I want to return to the States; I don't want this damn place." She sent the money, but the delay because of slow passage of mail at that time caused him to miss being booked on the ship he had expected to sail on — the Titanic. On its maiden voyage, 15 April 1912, the Titanic struck an ice-berg and sank, drowning 1,250 passengers. The ship he *did* sail on was the Lusitania, which, in 1915, was sunk by a German submarine.

By the time George returned, Mary had moved to Gateway. In 1912, George bought Judd Hatch's place in Unaweep and Mary moved back to the Massey ranch in Unaweep. Before long George sold his place to William Graham and took a preemption on another

PUBLIC SALE

Having sold my ranch, I will sell at my residence 2 miles west and 2 miles north of Mack, and ¼ mile south of the New Liberty school

WEDNESDAY, MARCH 24

Sale Starts Promptly at 11 A. M. Lunch Served on the Grounds
Following Described Articles

LIVESTOCK

Bay gelding, 8 yrs., 1,600 lbs., extra good one; bay mare, smooth mouth, in foal 1,550 lbs.; brown mare, smooth mouth, in foal, 1,400 lbs.; black horse, smooth mouth, 1,500 lbs.; filly, coming 2 yrs., good one; sorrel horse, smooth mouth, 1,100 lbs.; Jersey cow, 3 yrs., fresh; Jersey cow, 2 yrs., fresh; Holstein cow 3 yrs, fresh; Durham cow, 8 yrs., giving 6 gallons; Holstein heifer, 2 yrs.; registered Durham Bull, 2 yrs., no better bull in county; 3 yearling Durham heifers, fat; yearling Durham steer, fat; 3 good Durham vealers; Holstein cow, 4 yrs., fresh soon; 2 brood sows.

IMPLEMENTS

McCormick-Deering mower, new; 2 hay slings; McCormick-Deering hay rake, new; 3-horse fresno; Bailer bean harvester; John Deere riding cultivator; hay stacker, complete; 8-foot disc; 2-way plow; Mormon alfalfa creaser; spring tooth harrow; 2-section harrow; McCormick-Deering corn and bean planter; 2 hay slips; McCormick mower; wagon and hay rack; Bean power spraying machine 150-gallon tank, a good one; 14-inch walking plow; blacksmith forge, new; Royal Blue cream separator; 2½ sets work harness, good as new; lots of extra collars; iron wheelbarrow; sickle grinder, new vise, good 2-row Bailer cultivator.

HOUSEHOLD GOODS

Range stove with reservoir; dining table, dresser, 2 beds, springs and mattresses; 2 rocking chairs; Heatrola, new; library table; refrigerator, 2 Linoleum rugs; 5 kitchen chairs; dishes and cooking utensils, million articles not mentioned.

MISCELLANEOUS

Lot chicken and turkey roosts, 6 full spools new barbed wire, 200 bushels good yellow corn, shelled; 100 bushels wheat, 500 pounds seed beans; 10 dozen Rhode Island pullets, extra fine birds; 75 chicks, 6 weeks old; 25 chicks, two weeks old; 5 turkey hens, gobbler; chick brooder, 1,000 capacity; 200 cedar posts, 7 tons hay, some new woven wire; lots of poles and corral lumber; 500 lbs. alfalfa seed.

The Above Articles Are in First Class Condition, So Be Sure to Attend This Sale

Hale & Jordan, Auctioneers   TERMS: CASH   Lee Warner, Clerk

GEORGE BRYAN, Owner

place in Unaweep — then later sold that to Mary.

George became a citizen in 1913 during the time he was proving up on his homestead in New Liberty. It was several years before water would be available for his farming. He made final proof on the homestead 7 February 1919, with Robert Cox and Charles Cavendish as his witnesses.

Some time after he was established in his new home on the farm, his sister, Mary, visited him and advised him to hire a housekeeper. Apparently that is when **Lucie McCoy** came on the scene. George and Lucie were married 21 August 1925, and before long George built a new house for her. They couldn't get along and were separated and divorced after a couple of years. There were other housekeepers after that, but no more marriages.

George had a good relationship with neighbors Charles and John Cavendish. They worked together and helped each other quite often. He had lots of other friends in the community, but he seldom joined in social gatherings.

George had two brothers and a sister who never came to the United States. Jim, the oldest of the family, came over, but didn't stay. There were three other sisters, Bessie, Eva and Frances, who came to this country and stayed the rest of their lives. Eventually Esther's children, the sister who stayed in Ireland, inherited the parent's property.

George sold his New Liberty farm to Bill Maluy in March 1937 and moved to Fruita, then a few years later moved to Grand Junction.

Gene Thomas tells the story that when George sold his farm several neighbors went to his house to have a farewell party. George thought they were celebrating because they wanted him to leave. He hid in one of the outbuildings and wouldn't come out. The neighbors finally gave up and went elsewhere to have their party.

After leaving the farm George didn't seem to have much to occupy his time. He would be seen often at the livestock auctions near Grand Junction, and at farm auctions in various places throughout the valley. Those auctions apparently provided social activity for him. It appears likely from a newspaper account that George died in his sleep on 14 April 1961, at age 81. He was the last of his family; all his brothers and sisters had died before him. George was buried in Elmwood Cemetery at Fruita.

Burkett

Information was gleaned from land and census records and news items from the *Fruita Times* and *The Daily Sentinel*.

Wesley Burkett — little is known of this pioneer. Land records show that he bought a relinquishment from Annie Lucille Gnagey in 1918, on Unit J, Section 18, R 103 W (just west of Gerry's). The 1920 census lists him as a widower, age 57. He was living on the farm alone. Wesley died 22 January 1926. We learned from the Fruita items of *The Daily Sentinel* of 26 January 1926 that his funeral had been held at the Love and Truehart Funeral home in Fruita and he was buried in Elmwood Cemetery at Fruita.

Leland Burkett, his nephew, may have been living with Wesley not long after 1920 — we can only speculate. He continued to live on that farm for several years after his uncle Wesley died.

Leland became well known for his expertise with a team of horses he had trained to pull. With that team he won the pulling contest at the Mesa County Agricultural Fair at Fruita in October 1933. A story in *The Daily Sentinel* explained that Leland's team pulled 5,500 pounds of cement loaded on a 1,700 pound wagon (with wheels locked) farther than six other contenders. (The author recalls that Leland later won the pulling contest a second time.)

Leland owned some land to the southwest of where he lived, but he sold that to Chet Wright in 1931. In the early 1940s Leland began operating a dairy, selling milk from a herd of Jersey cows. But in the mid to late 1940s he found that he could not gain title to his uncle's land because of some legal twist, so he and some of the Smiley's abandoned the farm and moved to Idaho. There must have been family there to influence that move.

Blanche Loraine Burkett, Leland's sister, was born 25 July 1901 at Ottawa, Franklin County, Kansas. We do not have the names of their parents. She spent her childhood in Kansas, Colorado and Idaho.

In September 1921, at Ottawa, Blanche married **William "Bill" F. Smiley.** They came to western Colorado about 1926 and spent at least some of the time at New Liberty with Leland. Leland and Blanche's mother lived with them for a time also.

William and Blanche had three sons and five daughters:

Francis Eugene
Ruhannah Elizabeth (Dial)
Vernon Leroy
Emma
Thelma Loraine
Norma Lee
Marceline Mildred
John Edward

We know Francis, Thelma, Vernon and John attended school at New Liberty.

At some point in time Bill Smiley acquired some land in Rabbit Valley, south of The State Line Store and moved the family there for awhile. It appears they moved to Fruita in late 1930 and leased the farm to a man by the name of Kelley.

In January 1931 Bill Smiley made the news when it was found he owned the land south of The State Line Store where Sheriff Lumley and deputies found a "huge still." (See "Bootlegging")

In 1932 the Smileys moved to Grand Junction. It is believed some of the Smiley children continued to live with Uncle Leland after the parents moved.

Blanche Loraine Smiley died in Grand Junction 12 January 1943 and was buried in the Orchard Mesa Cemetery.

Francis Smiley made the news 1 January 1946:
PFC Francis E. Smiley, 1121 S. 5th St.; Cannoneer in Field Artillery, Veteran of Normandy, Northern France, Rhineland and Central Europe Campaigns. Holder of American Service, European-African-Middle Eastern Victory and Good Conduct Medals. Overseas 26 April 1944 to 3 December 1945; in service 24 March 1943 to 22 December 1945.

Looks like Francis had his share of the war, doesn't it?

Bush

Information from letters and family group sheets from Evelyn Bush (Likes) Welch, her daughter, Betty Likes Smit, and her son, Leroy Likes.

Reetis "Reet" Otheral Bush born 20 September 1889 at Hindsboro, Douglas, Illinois, was one of five children born to **James Ford Bush** and **Lavina Chilcote.** When Reet was 15 years old, the family moved to a farm near Worland, Missouri. He worked on the farm and went to school called "Red Top," a little school with one teacher for all eight grades.

While attending "Red Top" school he met a young lady named **Henrietta Ada Summers.** Ada was the youngest of five children born to **Matthew Reason Summers** and **Minnie Marie Helwig.** Matthew Summers was a miner and prospector. Ada was born 23 May 1893 in a mining camp at Copper Rock, Colorado, not far from Boulder, but she spent most of her growing-up years in the Worland, Missouri area. Her father disappeared mysteriously when Ada was quite young. He had gone on a prospecting trip to Idaho and, while they did get a letter from him after he left, that was the last they heard from him.

In 1911, with the aid of a new buggy, Reet began courting, Ada. On 25 May 1913, they were married at Worland, Bates, Missouri. They had one daughter, **Evelyn Leona,** who was born 3

Reetis Bush and Ada Summers in Reetis' new buggy on an Easter Sunday, 7 April 1912, during their courting years. *(Photo courtesy of Evelyn Bush Welch)*

Reetis Bush in the Peabody Oilfields at Orlando, Kansas, in 1921. *(Photo courtesy of Evelyn Bush Welch)*

Ada and Evelyn Bush at Craig, Colorado, in 1918, when the family was living in a tent. *(Photo courtesy of Evelyn Bush Welch)*

January 1914, at Worland.

At that time Reet was working in a coal mine for 25 cents per day. In 1918, they decided to leave there and moved to Craig, Colorado, where they lived in a tent while Reet searched for a job. While there Reet received notice from his draft board to report at Worland for induction into the Army. But the day they arrived back in Worland the war ended, so he didn't have to serve. From there they moved to Florence, Kansas, where Reet secured a job in the oil fields. Later he was transferred to Orlando, Kansas, where he continued to work in the oil fields. While they were living at Orlando, Reet became involved in baseball and became a very good pitcher. His accuracy was so good he amazed people by

knocking birds out of trees by throwing rocks!

In 1931 they moved to Colorado and farmed for a time with "Uncle Seab" Summers in the New Liberty community. Probably in 1933 Reet and Ada leased a store in Mack. The store was not agreeable with Ada's health, so they moved to a farm in the New Liberty community — the Ted Wassenberg farm. Some confusion exists about the time Reet and Ada had the "Last Chance" Service Station and store. We don't know if Evelyn believed that the store mentioned above was the "Last Chance" or some other store. A Mack news item in *The Daily Sentinel* of 21 January 1939 says: "Charley Smith sold the store to Reet Bush." That may have been the store in question.

Ada, Reetis and Evelyn at home in Worland, Missouri. Evelyn was 5 years old. *(Photo courtesy of Evelyn Bush Welch)*

Ada, Evelyn and Reet with their new 1926 or 1927 Chevrolet. *(Photo courtesy of Evelyn Bush Welch)*

(Above) 1939, L-R: Ada holding granddaughter, Loretta Likes, Lee Ann "Bubbles" Maluy, Betty Likes, Thelma Likes and Reetis "Bud" Likes. The Last Chance Service Station is in the background, also see page 30 for a picture of the Last Chance Service Station. (Right) L-R: Ada Bush, holding granddaughter Betty Likes, and Reetis Bush about 1935. *(Both photos courtesy of Evelyn Bush Welch)*

The Bush's were involved in community affairs, always taking part in gatherings for all occasions. Ada was a member of the New Liberty Sunday School and was a regular attendee. Each year the Sunday School would plan a picnic outing to the north slope of the Douglas Pass area. Even though Ada knew she would run into problems with the altitude at Douglas Pass, she never hesitated to go along on those outings. Perhaps she had hopes she would get away with it "just this once." But each year at some point during the day she would begin to feel faint and create anxiety and excitement which caused her daughter, Evelyn, to become hysterical and usually cutting short the time planned for the picnic. The other participants in the outing could plan on this annual bit of excitement, or entertainment, if you will. Despite her apparent heart problem, Ada lived a long life.

Eventually Reet's sister persuaded them to move out to Salinas, California, where Reet went to work for a trucking company. They left New Liberty in November 1941.

After retirement Reet and Ada lived for many years at Santa Cruz. Reet died of a heart attack 27 March 1958. Ada, in spite of many years of poor health, lived to the ripe old age of 88. She died at Santa Cruz, 11 July 1981. Both she and Reet are buried at Santa Cruz.

Ada and Reetis Bush in 1949 at Salinas, California. *(Photo courtesy of Evelyn Bush Welch)*

298

Evelyn Leona Bush
in 1932, at 18 years of age.
(Photo courtesy of Evelyn Bush Welch)

Ivan and Evelyn with children, Loretta, Bud, Leroy (in front) and Betty, soon after they arrived in Santa Cruz, California, in 1942. *(Photo courtesy of Evelyn Bush Welch)*

Evelyn and Elmer Welch in 1992. Evelyn is 78 and Elmer is 86. *(Photo courtesy of Leroy Likes)*

Evelyn Leona began her schooling while the family lived at Florence, Kansas. But her schooling was interrupted after her dad was transferred to Orlando, and she experienced some ill health. At Orlando she did complete the eighth grade.

After they came to Colorado, Evelyn attended Fruita Union High School for a time. Later she worked for awhile as housekeeper for Bob and Fern Cox, then went to work for Clem and Mary Maluy. While she was at Maluy's she helped care for the Maluy's new baby girl, Lee Ann. It was Evelyn who gave baby Lee Ann the name, "Bubbles."

On 17 August 1933 Evelyn was married to **Ivan Likes**. (See biography of Ivan Likes)

Ivan, Evelyn and children moved to California, in 1942, where her parents lived. Ivan and Evelyn's father, went to work for a trucking company owned by Elmer Welch. Ivan and Evelyn were later divorced, and Evelyn was married to **Elmer Welch** in 1946. In 1960 Evelyn and Elmer began to manage motels, which they did for 26 years before they retired. They moved to Sparks, Nevada, in 1986, to be near Evelyn's children: Bud, Betty and Loretta. Elmer passed away 2 January 1996. Evelyn still lives in Sparks.

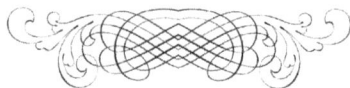

Carroll

The following was written mostly by Helen Grace Carroll Gingrich, daughter of Harold and Helen Carroll. Some information from obituaries in *The Daily Sentinel.*

Bernard Daniel Carroll was born 26 January 1861, at Fairbault, Rice, Minnesota. His parents had immigrated there from Ireland. Bernard spent much of his early life in Nebraska. There he met **Grace Mary Smith** who was born 11 May 1872, at New Lexington, Perry, Ohio. She spent her childhood in Ohio and Nebraska. She may have been living at Sutton, Nebraska, when she and Bernard met at a community dance. Bernard lived several towns away, but each week he would travel across the country to see Grace. She was a lovely young lady who won a beauty contest when she was 16 years old.

On 10 October 1891, Bernard and Grace were married at Grafton, Fillmore, Nebraska. They had six children:

Maida (Rouviere)
Homer
Thomas
Cecil J.
Raymond
Harold Samuel

As the family was growing, they moved to Brush, Colorado. Their youngest son,

Harold, was born at Hillrose, Morgan, Colorado, 18 April 1909. They moved to Montrose in 1910, where Maida graduated from high school, and then to Fruita in 1914. In 1918 Bernard filed on a homestead in the New Liberty community — Unit A Sec 3 R103W. That farm was located due west of Pollocks and just north of the west end of the siphon which lay across East Salt Creek. The three youngest boys, Cecil J., Raymond and Harold, were included in the 1921 school census, which indicated Cecil and Raymond had both attended the 9th grade within the census year. Harold was one of the first students at New Liberty school in 1919-20. He is the only one of the three whom we know attended New Liberty school.

The following was written by Helen Grace Carroll Gingrich:

Bernard and Grace were musical. While Grace played the piano, Bernard would do an Irish Jig. He played the violin. Among their

1891—Bernard Daniel and Grace Mary Carroll. *(Photo courtesy of Helen Grace Carroll Gingrich)*

musical instruments were rattlesnake rattles.

Grace was an adept seamstress. She also loved to do fancy work. She made a friendship quilt that has the names of most of the families in the New Liberty area embroidered on it. Some of the linens were unbleached linen, the stitches are fine. If there was illness and a doctor had to come to the house, she had special pillow cases she used for the occasion. Her guest towels were made from linen and the old type cotton. Most of this work was done in the winter by kerosene lamplight. Much of her time in summer was spent in her garden. This was also a time for canning tomatoes, pickles, peaches, pears and plums. The apricot-pineapple preserves were everyone's favorite. Mornings and evenings, she milked her little brown Jersey cow.

Bernard tilled the fields with the help of his sons and a team named Buster and Rex. It was in a field on 21 September 1934, that Bernard had a stroke that led to his death. Grace had prepared the noonday meal. After ringing the bell several times, she put sunbonnets on her two little granddaughters who were spending the day with her, and went to look for him. She found him lying on his back in a furrow in the field. Taking the sunbonnets off the girls (Sandra was 2 and Gracie was almost 4), she asked them to hold the bonnets to shade his face from the midday sun while she ran for help. She crossed the wash and got Mr. Cutler and his son to help her get Bernard to the house. He asked for Mentholatum to soothe the pain in his head. A few days later he died. He is buried in Calvary Cemetery at Grand Junction.

Several years later, 1937, Grace went to live with her son, Harold, and his family in Fruita. She spent the summers with the Rouvieres (Louis, Maida, and Louena) in Gunnison. In January 1945, Grace died from colon cancer in a hospital at Denver. She was buried next to her husband in Calvary Cemetery at Grand Junction.

Of the six children, **Maida** got her teaching certificate in Greeley and taught school. She married Louis Rouviere in 1914 and settled on Rainbow Ranch on the outskirts of Gunnison. They had one daughter, Louena. They were original settlers in that area and are mentioned in Colorado history books.

Homer was a friend of Jack Dempsey and boxed with him when he was young. Homer joined the Army in World War I and was sent overseas where he was exposed to mustard gas. He spent the rest of his life in veterans'

hospitals. He is buried in Ft. Logan Cemetery at Denver, Colorado.

Tom suffered from infantile paralysis (polio) as a boy. After leaving the farm at New Liberty, he went to California where he worked as a longshoreman. He never married. In his later years he was in a wheelchair, but was very self-sufficient until his death in May 1990.

Cecil, who was born 19 May 1901, at Fairmont, Nebraska, graduated from Stanford University in California. He married Tress ? and they had two boys — Jay and Terry. He was a chemistry teacher in high schools in San Francisco until he retired. He and Tress are buried in San Francisco.

Raymond, was born 24 May 1903, at York, Nebraska. He and his wife, Helen, moved to Oakland, California. He worked as a house-painter and managed apartment buildings. They had an adopted son, Fred. Raymond and Helen are buried at Longmont, Colorado.

Harold Carroll History

Harold Samuel Carroll in 1928.
(Photo courtesy of Helen Carroll Gingrich)

Harold **Samuel Carroll** was born in Hillrose, Colorado, on 18 April 1909. His family moved to New Liberty when he was a boy. He graduated from Fruita Union High School in 1928. That fall he enrolled at Western State College in Gunnison, Colorado. He became a member of Sigma Delta Phi and played on the football team. When he was a sophomore, **Helen Cook,** a southern belle from Mississippi, came to Western State as the new music teacher. Harold quickly signed up for a music class.

Helen Elizabeth Cook about 1929. *(Photo courtesy of Helen Carroll Gingrich)*

Helen Elizabeth Cook was born at Hattiesburg, Forrest, Mississippi, 15 August 1905, to Alexander Cook and Eunice Vick. Helen's mother, Eunice, died when Helen was three. When Helen was nine, her father, a jeweler, died instantly from injuries he sustained in a fall while repairing a clock high on a bank in Hattiesburg. Helen was raised by her aunt, Inez Pritchett, and attended private girls' schools throughout high school. Later, she graduated from the Louisville Conservatory of Music in Louisville, Kentucky. She became a talented violinist, and this led to her job as the teacher of violin at Western State College in Gunnison in the fall of 1929.

Harold and Helen were married 9 November 1929 at Colorado Springs, Colorado. In 1933 they moved to New Liberty where Harold taught school. They lived in the "teacherage," which was next to the school. Miss Josephine Price also had a room at the teacherage, as she taught the pupils in the early grades. During those years Harold and Helen acquired a family:

Helen Grace, born 12 September 1930, at Gunnison
Sandra Alice, 23 April 1932, Fruita
Harold Samuel Jr., 9 February 1937, Fruita
Jerry Lee, 15 July 1948, Denver

Helen and Harold were deeply involved in the social life of the New Liberty community; most of those events took place at the school. The pupils put on skits, sang songs, played musical instruments and recited poems for holiday entertainment. Dances were also held in the school auditorium.

Helen gave private music lessons, often in exchange for fruit or vegetables or whatever the family could provide. An important part of her life was teaching her own children. She started Helen Grace on violin lessons at age three on a very small violin. Sandra was given piano lessons. For the girls, half-hour practice sessions and recitals became a way of life throughout high school.

The family left the New Liberty area in 1938, as Harold had taken a job teaching English and Industrial Arts at Fruita Union High School. Being a practical joker, he once served rattlesnake meat at a teachers' banquet, only telling them what it was after it had been eaten. Another time, he put moth balls in Principal Phillip Griebel's overcoat pockets. He would laugh for days over the reactions these pranks brought. He joined the Navy in 1943 (World War II), as an Ensign. During the war he taught at the Naval Academy in Annapolis, Maryland, Cornell University in New York, and served as a gunnery officer on a cruiser, the U.S.S. Houston. From there, he and the family went to San Pedro, California, where he was the base commander. He retired as a Lieutenant Commander in 1946 and fulfilled his dream of getting back to Colorado. Resuming teaching, he taught at Westminster High School in Denver. Before retiring in 1973, he was nominated as Colorado Teacher of the Year. Helen died in 1988 and Harold in 1990. They were buried in Boulder, Colorado.

All four of their children graduated from the University of Colorado.

Helen Grace earned a B. A. Degree and was an elementary school teacher. She married **Roy Gingrich**, a civil engineer with the Federal Highway Department. They live in Ellicott City, Maryland. Roy and Grace have four children — Carolyn, Gary, Daniel and David.

(Left) Harold Samuel Carroll in 1937 when he was teaching at New Liberty.

(Right) Helen Cook Carroll in 1937 when she was teaching music at New Liberty.

(Middle left) Helen Grace and Sandra Carroll. Gracie (as she was called in New Liberty) was already taking violin lessons from her mother.

(Middle right) Harold Jr. (Robyn) in 1936 with beautiful curls.

(Lower left) The Harold Carroll family in 1979. Back row, L-R: Helen Grace, Sandra, Robyn and Jerry. Harold and Helen in front.

(Lower right) Harold and Helen Carroll in 1978 picking out a pumpkin for Halloween in their dear Colorado. *(All photos courtesy of Helen Grace Carroll Gingrich)*

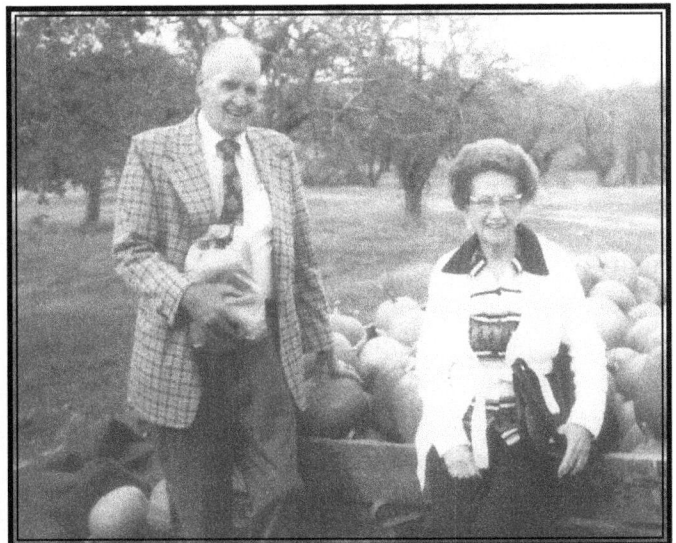

Sandra earned a B. A. Degree and also taught school. She married **Robert Royce**, an aeronautical engineer. They had one daughter, Linda. Bob died of a heart attack in 1975. In 1985, Sandra married Jack Streeter. Sandra died 8 October 1993 in Denver. In her later years, she often returned to the Fruita, Mack, New Liberty area and retraced her happy childhood memories.

Harold Jr. (Robyn) graduated with a B. A. Degree and became Vice President of First Interstate Bank in Fort Collins, Colorado. He and his wife **Jan (Hobson)** have two daughters —**Debra** and **Tamara**. Later he owned and operated two Champion Automotive stores in Colorado Springs, where they now live.

Jerry went to Mesa College in Grand Junction. He met his wife, **Linda Beezer**, while going to school there. After getting his B. A. Degree from the University of Colorado, he became a stock broker. Jerry and Linda have two daughters — **Christine** and **Amy**. They live in Boulder.

Caruthers

Frances Caruthers and family contributed most of the following. Some of the information is from author's personal knowledge.

Herbert Lester "Les" Caruthers was born 11 March 1914 at Salem, Arkansas. (There are three places called Salem in Arkansas). His parents were Warner Monroe Caruthers and Josephine Thomas. Les attended schools in Arkansas and Kansas.

When he was still a young lad his mother died and his father remarried. Les couldn't cope with his stepmother, so in 1927, as a young teenager, he went to Colorado. He spent some time in Eagle County, Colorado, working at Copper Spur. In the spring of 1928 he came to Mack and began working wherever he could find work as a ranch hand. Bob Cox took him under his wing and Les spent quite a bit of time in

Herbert Lester Caruthers
1938, New Liberty
(From Frances Caruthers)

Frances Morrow Caruthers
1940, Grand Junction
(Homer Likes Collection)

Bob's employ. Les made acquaintance of several of the teen-age boys in the Mack/New Liberty area — Clyde Likes, Billy Bowen, Milton Alstatt, and Gordon Booth — so he didn't lack for friends. (Seems like Les had an uncle, or some other relative, in the Grand Junction area).

In 1934 Les went back to Arkansas for a visit. In September he caught a ride on a school bus from Union to Salem, Arkansas, where his uncle lived. On that bus he met **Frances Morrow**. Frances said, "It was love at first sight." They were married the following 28 April 1934 at Salem. Frances was born at Milo, Carter, Oklahoma, 30 November 1914, to Homer and Ethel Morrow.

Les and Frances soon came to Mack to make their home. In 1936 Les went to work as a section hand for the D&RGW Railroad at Mack.

For some time they lived in a rented house in Mack with a wood/coal stove for heating and cooking, with an outdoor toilet and no indoor plumbing. During those years they established a close relationship with the Likes family — the Likes were "family" to the Caruthers.

Les and Frances had seven children:

William Herbert "Bill", born 29 March 1935, Mack
Carolyn Annette(Clark),29 January 1937, Mack

305

Westwater, Utah, 1949. Back row, L-R: Bruce, Carolyn and William "Bill" Caruthers. Front row: Thomas "Tom," Eleanor, Terry Caruthers, and Dennis Likes. *(Homer Likes Collection)*

Bruce Alton, born 3 June 1939, Fruita
Eleanor "Elly" Frances (Baumbauer), 26 July 1941, Mack
Larry Russell, 11 October 1943, Mack
Terry Lee, 24 May 1945, Mack
Thomas Keen "Tommy", 31 August 1947, Fruita

In 1941 Les became a telegrapher and moved to Green River, Utah. He continued in that position until the end of World War II (1945) when he became section foreman at Price, Utah. He later transferred to Westwater, Utah. The first school the children attended was in Loma, since the Mack school was closed during World War II.

The family moved back to Colorado in 1949 when Les became foreman of the section at Red Cliff, Colorado. They lived in Red Cliff until Les retired in 1974. The children all attended Red Cliff schools.

At the time Les retired the children were all grown and doing their own things. Two or more of them were then living in Tuscon, Arizona, which was why Les and Frances decided to take up residence there.

In the 1980s Les began to have health problems which gradually lead to his death at age 75, 7 November 1989, at Tucson. Frances continues to live in Tucson, where her daughter, Carolyn, and sons Bruce, Larry and Tom also live. Terry lives in Arvada, Colorado, and Elly in Denver. Frances now has 13 grandchildren, 17 great grandchildren and 2 great great grandchildren.

ℬill was stricken with polio when he was a baby, so he had a pretty tough life. As a young child, he spent lots of time in the hospitals at Denver and Colorado Springs, Colorado, enduring operations and a few experimental treatments.

Bill was 14 when the family moved to Red Cliff. He graduated from Red Cliff High School when he was 20. He was older than his classmates because he had spent so much time in hospitals for surgeries related to his crippling sickness. As a young adult, in spite of being hampered with a severe limp, he enjoyed hunting,

Lester and his section gang at Westwater, Utah. Winters were always very snowy and cold so it was quite a task to keep the railroad tracks clear. *(Photo courtesy of Frances Caruthers)*

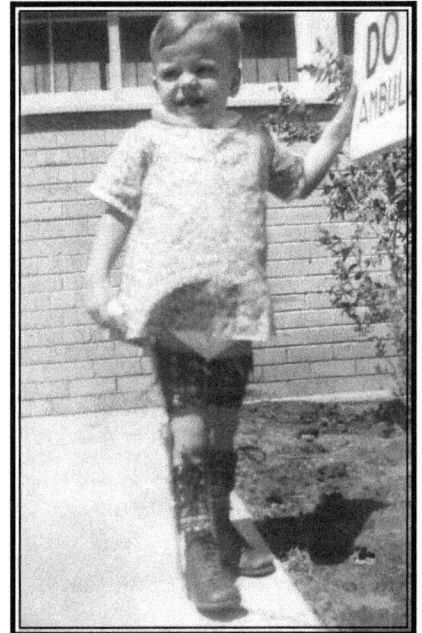

Bill at the Bethel Hospital, Denver Colorado, in 1938. He adjusted to his braces remarkably well. *(Homer Likes Collection)*

306

The Caruthers family at the Likes residence in the early spring of 1946. L-R: Larry, Eleanor, Frances (holding Terry) Caruthers; Retta, Richard and Clyde W. Likes; Carolyn, Bruce and Billy Caruthers. *(All pictures on this page courtesy of Frances Caruthers, and the Likes Collection)*

(Above) Bill Caruthers—1955

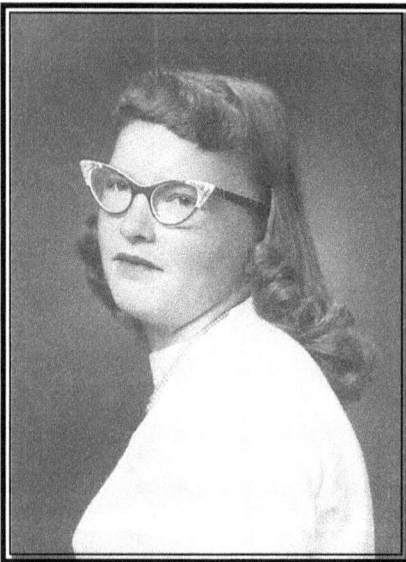

(Above) Carolyn Caruthers—1957
(Below) Larry Caruthers—1961

(Above) Bruce Caruthers—1958
(Below) Terry Caruthers—1963

(Above) Eleanor Caruthers—1960
(Below) Thomas Caruthers—1966

hiking to high mountain lakes for fishing and other outdoor activities.

The author can vouch for Bill's zeal for outdoor activities. Once in the 1950s the Likes brothers were planning their annual deer hunting camp-out in the Baxter Pass area. Les and Billy wanted to come along. We had some real concern for Bill's going with us since we had to hike several miles up West Canyon. We tried to discourage Bill's going because we felt sure he would become a liability. He insisted he could handle it, so we consented. He did just fine — our fears were soon proven to be unfounded.

Bill led a very active life even though he was quite severely handicapped. He attended business college and in 1962 was appointed Acting Postmaster at Red Cliff. He married Genny Jo "Jody" Chambers in Eagle in 1963, and they had two daughters: Suzette and Celeste. During this period he served as a member of the Red Cliff Volunteer Fire Department.

Bill and his wife and daughters made several moves during the next 10 years: First to Eagle, then to Aurora, and back to Eagle, where they lived for the next 22 years.

During those years he was a member of the Independent Order of Odd Fellows and Rebekahs, the Encampment and the Patriarchs Militant/ Canton. He served in several offices with the Odd Fellows and Rebekahs in Gypsum, including Noble Grand of Odd Fellows and Vice Grand of Rebekahs. He also became a charter member of the Rifle Encampment, serving as scribe and chief Patriarch.

During his years in the Eagle Valley he was appointed to the Royal Gorge Manor Board, a senior citizens' complex owned and operated by the IOOF, on which he also served as president.

He joined the Eagle Lions Club, where he achieved 15 years of perfect attendance, received the 100 percent President's Award, served as zone chairman, worked with the Eye Bank and received a variety of other honors for serving on many community service projects. He also served for more than 15 years as secretary for the Greater Eagle Fire Protection District Board.

Bill's employer, PTI Communications, transferred him to La Junta in 1994. Despite suffering the loss of mobility because of his bout with polio, he still continued to give his time to the community and IOOF.

Bill died 23 August 1996, at age 61, in Pueblo, Colorado. Surviving, in addition to his wife, Jody, are daughters, Suzette Schlund of Littleton, Colorado and Celeste Hauser of Avon, Colorado, and five grandchildren.

Cavendish

From land records, Charles' obituary in *The Daily Sentinel* and from author's personal knowledge. Also from birth, marriage, and death records from Nicholas County, West Virginia.

Charles "Charlie" Cavendish was born 6 November 1877 in Nicholas County, West Virginia. A search of the 1880 census revealed Charles W. Cavendish, age 2, with his parents, **Benjamin** and **Martha A. Legg Cavendish** and sister, **Ermina**, in Nicholas County. There were also three other Cavendish families living nearby. One family was his grandparents, Alexander and Sarah A. Dorsey Cavendish. In 1881, both his mother and his 18 month old sister died. His father remarried and had seven more children.

Also stated in his obituary, Charles graduated from Huntington High School and then completed a law course at Elliott Commercial College, but he did not practice that profession. He was a veteran of the Spanish-American War, probably serving in 1897-98. Soon after that he was involved in the Alaska gold rush, probably in 1899-1903. He occasionally shared some of his experiences of that time; but other than that, he revealed very little of his personal life. Much of his history will remain a mystery, but it's probably safe to assume that something happened in his life that caused him to withdraw somewhat from society. We can't really call him a recluse, but he remained single and wasn't integrated into community life like other people.

He loved to visit with his neighbors and seemed

to get special pleasure out of having anyone come to see him for any reason. He had a particular zeal for trying to extract gossip from his visitors about various neighbors. There seemed to be a special interest in Ella Stotts, for whatever reason. Perhaps he had some romantic interest in her — maybe he had been spurned. The author often heard him refer to Ella as "the old skirt." He and John both had peculiar expressions that we all heard quite often—"Old biggety Bob, though!" or —"Old D. C. M., though!"

It is not known exactly when Charlie came to the Mack area, but we do know he filed on land in the New Liberty area on 17 June 1908, years before irrigation water was available. It was rumored that he had taught school at Mack at one time, but the author has found no evidence to support that rumor. He did live in Mack for a time and worked on the Uintah Railway Gilsonite transfer gang, in addition to "proving up" on his homestead.

While living in Mack he fathered an illegitimate son, **John "Johnnie" William**, born at Mack, 17 May 1915. John came to live on the homestead with Charlie when he was about ten years old. Apparently no secrets were kept from him — he knew all about his family background. For some reason or other John had not progressed normally in school, so he was a couple of years older than his classmates when he enrolled at New Liberty School. His name first appears on the school rolls in 1925. He was probably not the dummy that most people assumed he was — he seemed to do very well in his studies. We could probably accurately say he was a victim of his peculiar environment. When he was a young teenager, he had an astonishing ability to name all the Presidents of the United States in proper order, and with great gusto!

Charlie and John lived a crude life; they weren't very clean, seldom bathed, and seldom swept the floor in their cabin. In the early days they lived in a typical tar-paper-covered shack, much the same as the other homesteaders of the day. That shack was located near the south end of their property. In 1930 they built a house with home-made adobe brick at the north end of the farm, much closer to the road. Neighbor George Bryan assisted them in building that home. For years neighbors speculated that the house would fall down, because the walls were neither square nor vertical. None of the farm homes in the community had indoor plumbing until in the late 1930s, but Charlie and John didn't even have an outhouse.

John, being somewhat different, was victim of lots of teasing and cruel jokes. While he was a member of the New Liberty teenage potato harvesting team, his team mates made sure he never had a dull moment. There was one instance when they were harvesting potatoes at Arpke's farm and decided to send John to the house to borrow a "sky-hook." John, in total innocence, dutifully went to bring the sky-hook. He even asked Mrs. Arpke to help him find it — she didn't catch on either! She and John spent some time looking for the sky-hook!

John was hanging around a dance at New Liberty School one Saturday night and was victimized by a group of boys from Mack, who ran up behind him with a rope between them and tripped him; he fell and struck the back of his head on the cement sidewalk and was unconscious for some time. That really put the fear into that bunch of rowdy boys!

In the 1930s, shortly after they built their new house, Charlie and John sold some horses and used the money to buy a 1926 Chevrolet touring car. Neither of them knew anything about driving. Charlie had no desire to learn, so he left that responsibility to John. Things were quite hectic before John began to get the hang of it. On one occasion, they approached a corner a little too fast and Charlie bailed out. He always rode with both hands firmly gripping the door — just in case! Later that Chevy was traded for a 1931 Model A Ford Roadster. We now call them convertibles.

John served some time in the Army during World War II and was assigned to an armored tank training base in Arkansas. No one knows the truth for sure, but he told some pretty convincing stories about his expertise as a tank driver. He was discharged early for medical reasons.

Charlie died 10 December 1955 at Fruita, and was buried in Elmwood Cemetery. John continued to live for some time on the homestead, but the loneliness apparently overcame his better judgment. He began to frequent the beer parlor at Mack and was known to stay away from home for extended periods of time. He was eventually committed to

Homelake Colorado State Soldiers and Sailors Home at Monte Vista, Colorado, where he died in October 1983. He was buried in the Fort Logan Cemetery in Denver.

Chaffin

From a letter and recordings from Stephen and Maureen Chaffin, an obituary in *The Daily Sentinel* and some personal knowledge of author.

Faun "L" Chaffin was born 19 August 1899 at Torrey, Wayne, Utah, the oldest of 12 children of Louis Moses Chaffin and Martha Elizabeth Alice Brian. Wayne County is known by southern Utahns as "Wayne Wonderland" — it has a range of spectacular mountains on the south and drains to the east via the Fremont River, which runs through the Capitol Reef National Monument before it joins the "Dirty Devil River" at Hanksville, Utah.

Among Faun's fondest memories of childhood was spending Christmas with his grandmother, Ellen Barnes Brian, a Utah pioneer who, when she was six years old, walked across the plains with a handcart company after her people were driven out of Nauvoo, Illinois, by mobs. Faun told of being fed by an Indian family in their wickiup — he didn't know what was being served "but it was good." He was often fed at sheep-camps also.

Faun led a full

Faun "L" Chaffin, 1960s *(Photo courtesy of Wiladeane Chaffin Hills)*

Faun Chaffin on the Chaffin ranch on the San Rafael River in Utah. He is standing by the first new car the Chaffins owned. A 1927 or 1928 Azax built by Nash. *(Photo courtesy of Wiladeane Chaffin Hills)*

and varied life — as a teenager he served as a cowpuncher and teamster. He later worked as a rodman for Negovia Association Drilling Company as they surveyed large areas of Utah as well as the Douglas Pass area in Colorado. He then worked for a short time for the Texas Well Co. He helped build a section of Highway 6 & 50 at Woodside, Utah, using his own team of horses.

For 25 years he was partners with his father and brothers, running cattle on the Chaffin Ranch, "Under the Ledge" on the Green River south of the town of Green River, Utah. During those days they had many trying experiences, such as losing cattle and horses off 1,000 foot cliffs and driving herds of cattle across the rivers. The Chaffin Ranch covered a lot of territory — from Flint on the San Rafael River to the Colorado River and to the Dirty Devil River near Hite, Utah, where Faun's uncle ran the Chaffin Ferry that crossed the Colorado. That place is no longer visible, as it is now covered by the waters of Lake Powell. Today much of the Chaffin Ranch grazing land is within the boundaries of Canyonlands National Park. The ranch is now owned by Utah Power and Light Co.

On 25 July 1927, at Green River, Emery, Utah, Faun married **Mary Violet Hunt.**

They had three children:

Wiladeane (Wubben, Hills), born 29 April 1928, Green River, Utah
Ina Claire (Morrow), 14 November 1933, Green River
Stephen "Steve" Faun, 11 April 1946, Fruita, Colorado
They also raised **Merridy Irene Chaffin,** a down syndrome child who was born to **Wiladeane Wubben** on 1 September 1949, but raised and eventually adopted as Faun's and Violet's daughter. They had her until Violet's death. Then, after Faun had kept her awhile, she was taken back by Wiladeane and sent to a special school where she learned some skills and is presently employed at Red Lobster Cafe.

ary Violet Hunt was born 23 December 1907, at Aldrich, Wayne, Utah, to Charles Alford Hunt and Alta Curtis. She spent her childhood at Caineville, (situated on the Fremont River west of Hanksville) and attended schools at Caineville and Salt Lake City.

In 1944 Faun and Violet moved from Green River to Grand Junction, Colorado, to live on a ranch on North 7th St. They moved to the New Liberty community in 1948 after purchasing the Ted Wassenberg homestead, in November 1947, and then the Burge Lofgren homestead, in April 1949. After the Highline Canal tunnel collapsed in March 1949, the family moved to Starr Valley, Nevada, where Faun worked as cattle foreman for the C/C Ranch.

After the New Liberty School was closed, the Chaffins purchased the school building from a man who had bought it and decided he didn't want it because of difficulty in settling the title. Son Stephen and family lived on the farm, while Faun and Violet established residence in the school building. The old school building was sold to the Lowry's in the fall of 1994.

During the 1960s Faun worked at the Chaffin Lime Quarry owned by his Uncle George Chaffin at Leamington, Utah. Geneva Steel now owns that quarry.

Violet Hunt Chaffin, 1960s
(Photo courtesy of Wiladeane Chaffin Hills)

Violet died on 12 June 1987 and was buried in the Elmwood Cemetery at Fruita. Faun continued to live in the school building until a few months before his death on 30 March 1994 at age 94. He had moved to "The Oaks" in Fruita for a short stay. He was buried in the Elmwood Cemetery near Violet.

Wiladeane and Merridy live in Grand Junction, Ina Claire, Nevada. Faun's and Violet's posterity has grown to 16 grandchildren, 22 great grandchildren and three great-great-grandchildren

(Upper left) Bill Racy and Faun Chaffin, 94 years old, in front of old coal cook stove used in New Liberty to cook on and heat the house with. Maureen uses it as a heater in her den at their home in Fruita. (Upper right) New Liberty farm in 1970. L-R: Ralph Hills on Rajo, Wiladean Hills on YoYo, Merridy Chaffin, Cathy Wubben on Princess, Faun Chaffin with shovel and Steve Chaffin standing on right. (Center left) Steve breaking Rajo, a racehorse, to ride in 1970. (Center right) On the Chaffin farm in the 60s, Faun Chaffin on Playboy Jones, father of Rajo. (Lower) 1970, horseback riding in the field on the Chaffin farm in New Liberty on 9 Rd. L-R: Cathy Wubben, daughter of Wiladeane, on Princess; Wiladeane Hills on Rajo; and Steve Chaffin on YoYo. *(Photos courtesy of Wiladeane Hills)*

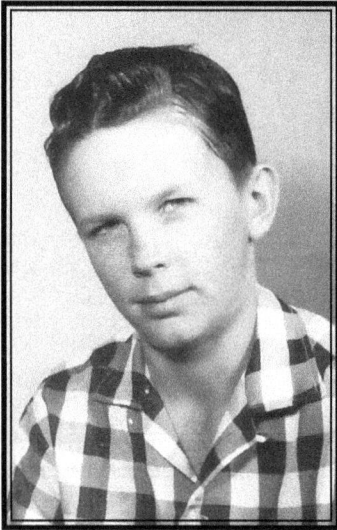

Steve was about 14 years old when the photo at left was taken.

Steve and Maureen sent us a collection of Steve's boyhood memories tape recorded as they were driving from Vail to Fruita, Colorado. Sounds like a lot of mischief! We have done some editing but tried to retain the integrity of Steve's stories:

My dad, Faun Chaffin, was 21 and was helping run cattle down on the Henry Mountains. My Grandpa Hunt, mother's dad, ran sheep on the Henry Mountains in the summer and wintered them on the Muddy and Dirty Devil Rivers, between Green River and Salina. They didn't have penicillin then and, as a matter of fact, Wayne County didn't even have a doctor until the 1930s. My dad kept getting boils. People would sometimes die from boils. He had one that covered his entire back, and was terribly painful. He was out on the range and got so bad he couldn't eat anything. Charlie Hunt put some pine tar on to boil, and dad knows that he saved his life. Charlie took dad down to his place and put him in the back room where it was dark and he stayed there nearly a month; he was delirious part of the time. He remembers the Hunt girls would come in and feed him soup. Charlie had nine girls and three boys. My mother, Mary Violet Hunt, was 13 years old when this happened. Faun got up one day feeling good, thanked everyone, got on his horse and rode away.

In those days if anyone wanted to get more schooling they had to go away to get it. At 13, Mary Violet (called Violet) went to Salt Lake City to go to school. She "nannied" for the Wirthlin family and took care of Joseph Wirthlin, called little Joey, and also worked in the millinery factory making hats. When she was 19 (1927), she decided to go back home to see her parents. On the 24th of July, the train laid over at Green River, a wild, gentile town. She was walking down the wooden sidewalk on Main street, which then ran north and south. There was a dance at the big armory. All the cowboys came in twice a year; once for the 24th of July and the other for the Christmas program. Violet had on a big pink hat that she had made. She had beautiful coal black hair and looked like a pretty porcelain doll. The cowboys came runnin' in. Faun took the tip of his boot and flipped the brim of her hat and said, "How about a date tonight redhead?" She recognized him and turned on her heel, stuck her nose in the air and walked off. He just laughed and started shooting up the town with the rest of the cowboys.

Her girlfriend said, "Let's go to the dance tonight." Of course nobody missed the big dance of the year, so they went. They were sitting out a dance when Faun walked in. Faun said he looked into those lovely eyes and knew that she was the girl for him. His heart skipped about three beats and jumped up into his throat and stayed. I can remember him saying, "Look out, this is the girl that will hurt you." They danced and danced. Knowing my dad, I would say he was soon doing all the sweet talking he could to convince her to marry him.

The band took a break at about 2 a.m. They walked down the street to the Justice of the Peace for a license, then walked up the street and got the bishop out of bed, and were married on the spot. The only other ones present at the wedding was her girlfriend and her boyfriend. They then went back and danced till dawn, keeping it a secret from everyone.

The next day a Texas gas company boss came into town looking for a cook. It appears they were drilling oil wells on the flats and had fired their cook. He asked dad, who was a tool pusher for them at the time, if he knew of anyone that could cook for them. He said, "May I recommend my wife." Everybody laughed and said, "Sure, you're married." But they found out sure enough he was married.

We lived in New Liberty for a time before we moved to Nevada. While in New Liberty I ran away from home at three years of age, going in the direction of Arpkes. I saw Dad on his horse galloping along looking for me. He was following my tracks in the soft dirt as I ran toward Arpkes. I hid in the grass by the canal; he didn't see me and went on down to Arpkes. I took off for home. I thought, if I could get to Mom she would protect me. I saw him come galloping, so I ran fast and got in the house to Mom just as he came in the yard. When he came in I was drinking hot chocolate. He wanted to whip me, but he knew if he did he'd have to whip Mom first. So he calmed down and I didn't get a whipping that time.

The Highline Tunnel broke about 1949 and it looked like there would be no water and it would be a long time before they could get it fixed. So Dad took a job out in Elko, Nevada, running cattle for someone out there. We were there for four years. Mr. Jordan rented our place in New Liberty. He was an old gentleman.

I went to a small school called Star School, in Nevada. There were only nine students in the whole school, grades one through eight. A friend and I were the only ones in the first/second grade. Actually we skipped the 1st grade and went to the 2nd grade. When I came back to New Liberty I had already had the third grade in Nevada, but the New Liberty school board said I had to stay with my age group, so I had to take the third grade over. There is a real bond in those little country schools with the teachers and students.

I remember when Mrs. Thompson was the school principal and she rattled Larry Overbye's teeth. Larry Overbye and I were sitting in the southeast classroom, side by side, at a table near the teacher's desk on the north side of the room. Larry and I were supposed to be studying, but we started to talk. Mrs. Thompson was quite a disciplinarian. Our backs were to her, and all of a sudden we heard this clunk, clunk, clunk, sound of her high-heeled shoes on the hardwood floor. Both of us hunkered down, as we just knew we were going to get it. She grabbed Larry and shook the "daylights out of him." His front teeth protruded a little and she shook him until they rattled. We were good boys for quite awhile after that. We were in the fourth grade.

At one time we had three teachers at New Liberty: Mrs. Cooper, Mrs. Thompson and Mrs. Reeves. In the northeast corner of the school lot was a large, open area near the boys' toilet. We got the idea of building a prairie dog town. We brought shovels and things to dig with to school. We dug a hole in the ground, three or four feet, and deeper sometimes, and put a big piece of plywood on top. Then dug another hole a ways from that one and connected that with a tunnel. We had quite a prairie dog town there after awhile. Had the master club house which wasn't even open at the top. It was covered with plywood and covered with dirt and connected by two or three tunnels. In order to get into it you had to crawl into one hole and through an under-ground tunnel, through another hole and into the club house.

The teachers tolerated it for awhile, but it got to be quite extensive. We would have trouble hearing the school bell ring when it was time for the recess to be over. Mrs. Cooper, and Mrs. Thompson too, would ring the school bell vigorously to make a lot of noise in order for us to hear. Then we would come running. We were disappointed when we were informed that the tunnels were unsafe and would have to be dug up and filled in. They were filled with a lot less enthusiasm than when they were dug.

Shires' field was next to the northeast corner of the school lot and we just loved it when they grew corn there because we could sneak through the fence during recess and build little hideouts out in the corn field. Little men always like to build hideouts; it is kind of a bonding. There was always a teacher on the play ground during recess, so we would post guards. We would always work it so two or three of us could sneak out in the corn field.

There was a district music teacher, Mrs. Hines, that would go to the different schools and teach music appreciation classes. She came to our school once a week and would take about an hour to teach us some songs to sing. It mainly was a lot of fun. Some of the songs we learned were: "She'll be Coming Around the Mountain When She Comes," "Red River Valley," "Who's in the Kitchen with Dinah," and "Shenandoah."

Then there was the Tonette experience. She brought some flutes — pipes that you blew in to make a tune, called Tonettes. We learned different songs on them. We had a Tonette band for a short while. It didn't last too long, as we didn't develop enough interest in it — especially the young men. Mrs. Hines had a pitch pipe, a circular thing. When we got ready to sing she would say: "OK, here is your pitch." She would start pulling on that little circle thing and go hum, hum. So that was our music appreciation classes.

We would put on Christmas programs for the parents. One time, it wasn't a Christmas program. Tim Arpke played the part of a rain drop. He was to come on the stage at the right cue, disguised as a little rain drop and do this little dance and sing, "I'm a little rain drop." He made his grand entrance on the stage, made his hop like a little rain drop, sang his part, and his hat just flip flopped on the floor. He was so embarrassed and everybody laughed.

Everybody liked the teacher, Mrs. Cooper. She lived on the old Cooper (Diehl) place on the hill, on R road between 9 & 10 roads. She was real pleasant, entertaining and interesting. She was probably past retirement age. She had a way of piquing your interest and getting your curiosity aroused on a subject or topic. We discussed a lot of things. We would read a lot in class as our school day was "up" for reading period — a novel or good classic that was entertaining, or an action-packed and interesting western.

One time Mrs. Cooper got an idea for a project for the class. She had seen an advertisement on some strange variety of grass that would grow anywhere — it would turn a hillside green on any old piece of alkali or drought-resistant soil. So she sent off for some seed. I don't know what it was, Siberian or something. I don't think the people who developed this grass had any idea of the degree of desolation on some of these hills. She decided that we would seed the dry hillside north of Coopers where Peter Daniels built his house. She had us all pumped up and we thought we would change the world, revolutionize the valley to a beautiful hillside, help the cattlemen, and make a pretty place instead of a bare hillside. Of course we were ready to do anything she wanted. We got up there with our hoes and seed. Someone would make a trench with the hoe, someone else would drop some seed in the trench and then someone else would cover it with dirt. We spent a whole spring morning on this project. Later we would drive by there to see if there was any sign of grass, but we never did see any change, grass or green.

There was basketball, high jumping contests and track meets between schools. Mr. McGraw was the district physical education teacher, came once a week. He was our childhood hero. He was a man's man — tall, straight, distinguished looking, and athletic. He taught us all the sports — high jump, relay walk races, basketball, baseball, and tag football. I played the quarterback. In tag football you would put a strip of cloth in your back belt; no one could tackle anyone. You would have to run up and pull the tail out. That was our pre-football.

There was the "fabulous three," Dave Alstatt, Larry Overbye and myself, and some of the younger boys: Jim Barlow, Gary Alstatt and Ron Alstatt who formed the basketball team. We were so excited!

We had a game with the Hunter school, and it was the first time we had ever competed with another school in a sport activity. Mr. McGraw

had us all pumped up. He said, "Those guys in Hunter are really good. You will have to work hard to beat them." He then taught us all sorts of tricks and strategies. Of course, Mr. McGraw coached those guys, too. They beat us bad! We were so chagrined because we thought we were big and tough country boys; we were tougher than those city guys. They cleaned our plow!

I had one moment of glory in the game, though. They were about eight points ahead of us and one of their guys made a basket and they threw up their hands and shouted "Hoorah." As soon as that ball went through the hoop I grabbed it, stepped out of bounds and threw it up to Larry Overbye on the other end of the court. He threw it in the basket and made two points. We all yelled, "Hoorah!" Mr. McGraw never missed a chance to teach a lesson. He said, "See there boys, while you were hoorahing they were hooping." We had our moment of glory.

Once in a while the community would have entertainers come to the school house. I remember when Jim Barnes was hypnotized. They had this hypnotist come. Nobody believed that he could hypnotize anybody; it was just an act. Jim Barnes, who was in high school, was one of the non-believers. So this guy got him to come up front. He dangled his watch in front of Jim's eyes and did this lyrical talking to him. It seemed so simple. "OK," he said, "he is hypnotized and in my control now." Nobody believed him until he asked Jim to do these strange things. Jim would do it, and everybody thought, "How can he do that?" He pretended that he was roller skating and skated all around the floor. What really convinced us that he really was hypnotized was that he (the hypnotist) set two chairs there about four feet apart, facing each other. He told Jim that he was a board and he laid him on the floor and told him that he couldn't bend or anything, that he was a straight board. He raised Jim's head up and put his head on one chair and his feet on the other chair. There was this space between the two chairs and there was Jim suspended just as peaceful as could be, as straight as a board. Jim said he didn't remember anything about that afterward.

They had dances at the school. Bob Arpke would get a caller and they would have a square dance. He and Pearline were real good square dancers. Bob later became an expert caller himself. I was interested in dancing as a young lad, but I had two right feet and one left. I had a hard time remembering the square dance calls.

Murray Phillips was our faithful school bus driver. We called him Sunshine. He was a neat guy, a confirmed bachelor, a striking looking fellow with dark hair, and tall. He was so easy going it was easy to take advantage of him. He drove the bus for years. I remember when three of us got kicked off the bus for flying kites out the window or something. The Muth boy used to raise a lot of heck, but he was not vicious. One time the Muth boy and some others beat Murray up. I wasn't there that time.

I remember one time when Reg Berry and Jim Barnes got into a fight. They were pretty good buddies, but they use to get into fights once in awhile. This one time they got to fighting on the school bus and Murray says, "Oh, blankety blank, all right you guys get outside." We all piled off to see the fight. They pounded on each other until they were both bloody, then got back on the bus and we went on. Do anything like that today and you would be sued for everything.

Discipline was more lax then than now. One time there was a new kid and we were kind of mean to him. He was pretty heavy set and he was always spouting off his mouth. On one occasion we squished him down in between the seats of the bus so that he was sitting on the floor and his feet were sticking out forward of the seats. We took the laces out of his boots and tied his feet to the seat in front of him so he couldn't get out. He was crying and when it came time for him to get off the bus; Murray got mad because he had to cut his shoe laces to get him out. He was screaming and hollering what his dad was going to do. We were disappointed when Murray lost his job as bus driver.

Mrs. Leonard Rich replaced Murray and she ripped us up in no time. No one talked back to her. Her husband, Leonard, used to drive once in a while too. He wore real fancy cowboy boots and a felt hat. As a prank one day, I brought a little package of ripe cattails onto the bus. On the way home from school that evening we opened the windows and released those cattails into the air. Man! The effects were much better than I expected. The bus was like it was full of snow. All the girls hair and blouses were covered with cattail fuzz. But the funniest thing was Leonard's black felt hat covered with cattail seeds and such. He was a mighty unhappy camper.

There was a back door in the bus that could be opened in an emergency, but we used it quite often to sneak things into the bus. When they got the new buses, they had an alarm system on the rear door. If you opened the door the alarm would go off. Leonard Rich was driving and was showing us all the neat things on the dash board. We sat in the back, as someone was going to sneak some water balloons or something through the back door. They opened the back door and the buzzer went off. Leonard couldn't figure out what was happening. Because he was watching us through the rear view mirror, we couldn't shut the door so it would turn off. He was trying frantically to turn it off. I can still see his hand moving up and down flipping switches. He couldn't get it to stop so he got out and raised the hood of the bus to see what was wrong. When he had the hood up so he couldn't see us, we slammed the door shut. The buzzing stopped so he slammed the hood down and thought he had solved the problem. The next day he watched us closely, as he had figured out what had caused the problem.

Some of the "old timers" in the community were kind of intimidating. As a kid I gave them a wide berth. Mother would get real mad at Booze Deacon because when he would bring his cattle down from the summer mountain range, he would turn his cattle loose in the area and let them graze the roadsides. If the fence was down or the gate open, they just entered the fields.

Another one of those intimidating old timers was Dean Thomas who bought the Barcus place north of the siphon. There was a bridge that covered the salt wash west of his house and pigeons would roost under the bridge at night. I had a black 1952 Commander Studebaker, one with the suicide doors; it was pretty old then in about 1960. I was about 13 or 14 and didn't have a driver's license yet, but I drove on the back roads. Me and my two partners in crime, Jimmy Barlow and Dave Alstatt, decided to drive over to the bridge after dark one night to get some of the pigeons. We took flash lights along and would blind the pigeons, then grab them and put them in boxes. Later we would turn them loose so we could catch them again another time. We drove up to the bridge from the west with our lights out. East of the bridge and on the north side of the road were Mr. Thomas' range cows and it was calving time. We got out of the car under the bridge and we heard a vehicle coming. We said, "Oh, no! someone is coming. Hurry! we'd better get out of here." We just got in the car and got it started to go east when this pickup pulled up going west. He stopped about two feet from my open window with a double barreled shotgun pointed at me. Old man Thomas, as we called him, asked us what we were up to. He had been missing some calves and he would like to talk about it. Before I had a chance to say anything about it, I think there was an "act of God, or something." A meteorite came down out of the night sky about the size of the full moon going from east to west. It was a bright fluorescent blue and lit up the country side. He couldn't see it very well because of the pickup and he had his back to it, but he could see the light from it. I said, "Look at that!" and my mouth was left open. He pulled the shot gun in and hung his head out the window and craned his neck to see it. Just as he did that I goosed that old Commander's all eight cylinders, gravel flying, and tore out of there before he could get his gun out again. We drove 60 miles an hour down by Booze Deacons, terrified as usual.

Another time we went to the bridge and retrieved several boxes of pigeons. We couldn't decide what to do with them, as some of them were beautiful, but we didn't want to feed and take care of them. We decided to mail them to people. So we went around New Liberty and stuffed them in peoples mail boxes. The next day we got the idea that things weren't going too well when Esther Barlow was up there with soap and water cleaning out her mailbox. My Dad was curious what she was doing and she said, "Didn't your mailbox get it, too?" He said, "No, I don't think so." She said, "Oh, I'm so mad at who ever did this dirty trick — I'd like to get them." I was beginning to quake in my boots. My Dad kind of looked at me. About an hour later a deputy sheriff came to the house and asked my Dad if he knew anything about this. Then he asked me if I knew anything about it and, of course, I lied through my teeth. I had a big laugh. I think this guy kind of guessed what was going on because he started telling me, "Do you know that this is a federal offense? Mailboxes are federal property." He went on how it was punishable by 40 years in jail, etc. He left, but that was the end of our pigeon projects.

The siphon was quite a curious attraction for us. In the 60s, the siphon was no longer a wooden siphon above ground, but was replaced in 1952 by a cement tube about 4 feet in diameter and went under ground beneath East Salt Wash and was about a mile long. It went from the canal on the high bank above the wash, down under the wash, and back up the

bank on the other side to the canal. In the winter they turned the water off in the canal and drained the siphon. Twice they would turn the water back in the canal during the winter; sometime before Christmas, and possibly in February, so the farmers could fill their ponds. When it was drained you could walk through it. Jim Barlow, Dave Alstatt, and I decided to go in it. I had my B B gun and flash light.

At first we were really brave, but after a while it was really dark and spooky. We had to stoop to walk along, and it smelled like musty fish and stale water. Sound would ricochet off of those walls. We got a ways down and spent quite a bit of time experimenting with the sound effects, yelling, etc. We decided to shoot the B B gun. The pellet would ricochet off the wall and echo until it sounded like a full war going on. We got to the bottom where the wash was and couldn't go any farther as it was full of water. Our minds got to playing tricks on us, and the flash light started to weaken. We got to thinking about what if they turned the water back in. Thoughts of large torrents of water and we would be trapped and buried there. We started hurrying back, in a panic, stumbling over each other trying to hurry to get out, but we made it. But we went back three or four times after that. It was pretty neat.

One time Jim Barnes, Jerry Hawthorne, and Joe Sloggenhoff found an old abandoned row boat near Mack Mesa Lake. They floated it down the canal and when they came around a bend in the canal, right in front of them was the siphon opening. Jim and Joe jumped out and swam to shore, but Jerry Hawthorne, I guess, thought there wasn't enough time and stayed with the boat. There was a bar that went across the entrance to the siphon and Jerry grabbed for that and pulled himself up as the boat went in the siphon. He managed to get out. They wondered if the boat would come out the other end of the siphon. They decided to see. They waited for an hour or two and it never came, so they left. The ditch rider found it a couple of days later, but don't know what condition it was in.

Dave Alstatt, Dick Bale, Gene McElhaney and I thought it would be fun to dynamite an outhouse. We got in the black Studebaker and went up on the hill where Guy Leach lived. There was an abandoned place with an old outhouse. We dynamited it, but it didn't do much damage. We decided to push the thing down the lane and onto the county road. We pushed it over onto its roof so we would have a smooth surface. It was a big out house and we couldn't push it. So I got the black Studebaker and with no lights on pushed the out house down the lane with the three other boys holding it upright and guiding it. The county road in front of the lane is in an L shape (corner), west to north. I was pushing the outhouse from east to west to get it out on the road good.

Just as we got it on the county road, all of a sudden, instant headlights right into my eyes! I almost pushed the outhouse into the vehicle. It was Guy Leach in his 2-ton farm truck. He had heard all the commotion and came to see what was going on. He had sneaked over with his lights off and waited in the road. The only thing that saved us was that he was so close to the outhouse that he couldn't get around to catch us. That put everyone in action. Dick Bale ran into the corn field; I could hear the corn stocks going snap, crack, snap. I slammed the car in reverse and backed up and headed north away from him. He had to back his truck up and go around the outhouse to go after me. I could see his headlights bouncing in the rear-view mirror as I tore along without my lights. My heart was in my throat!

I went over a little hump and turned left where T. J. Baer used to live, where Charlie Roush lives now. He thought I had gone on straight on down the road east toward the creek. It was quite a relief to see him go on. I turned around and went back to the scene of crime. The outhouse was still sitting in the road. I whispered and the boys came out and we went home worrying if he recognized the car — saw the license plates or what. The next day we went on the school bus and came around the corner and there sat the outhouse on its roof in the middle of the road. We all looked at each other sideways and didn't know whether to congratulate ourselves of not.

Bob Sanders was one of my favorite people I liked to visit. When we first moved out from Nevada, we didn't have any farm equipment. My Dad would trade work with him. He would go over and help Bob and then he would bale our hay, chop our silage, etc. He had hands the size of a toilet seat — the biggest hands I'd ever seen. He was always such a big, pleasant fellow.

His wife worked beside him all the time; milked cows and really worked hard. I used to love to go over and work with him because at 11 o'clock she would quit to go in and get dinner. Dinner was a huge meal. They had a big circular table, and they would always keep jams and everything on the table. They cooked herds of chicken and I think he ate the whole herd. He used to say that if a man couldn't eat five chickens at one sitting, he didn't like chicken. There were mashed potatoes and gravy and all good kinds of things to eat. I loved to go there and eat homemade bread and jam.

Bob had quite a style of farming and I liked his style. When we cut ensilage in the fall, he had what he called a "gravy train." He hooked two or three wagons behind a tractor and he'd bring them all in from the field at the same time and dump the silage. He was neat! Mother used to get kind of mad at him though, because he would show up to work about noon — just in time to eat. Dad would say, "We can't start now; it's almost lunch time." So they would have to eat before going to work. Mother felt she'd prepare a big meal and get a half days work. If you feed men, you want a whole days work. He would eat about a dozen eggs for breakfast.

Bob was a big man, and did a lot of work with a gift of gab. My dad and he would work together shucking corn by hand. Bob would bring his team of horses over and that team was trained so that when he wanted them to move up a ways, he would just yell at them and they would go a little ways and stop. Bob used to work with me. I had my own shucking peg and helped as much as I could. I wasn't very old. He would say to me, "See if you can keep an ear of corn in the air all the time." He could do it. He could even shuck an ear of corn with one hand sometimes, if everything was just right.

Bill Young was one of the finest people I ever met. Everyone had a lot of respect for him as he was real honest, a hard worker, and helpful. I loved to go to his home. He and his wife were the ranchers extraordinaire — they had all of Baxter Pass and everything that was real cattle country. Bill and my Dad got along real well because they came from the same kind of background. My dad rode with him a lot to help get the cattle off the mountain. Great friends! Dad had owned the old Standifird homestead in South Canyon, and sold it to the Youngs when we went to Nevada.

Bill Young was no farmer; he was a cattleman and did a real good job with the cattle. He left the farming up to his son, Dick, who did the best he could, but it seemed like nothing ever worked out too well. I was always impressed because they always had new tractors, but they never seemed to last very long for them. They had a Case tractor that Lloyd Nelson raked with, and I was helping them mow with our old John Deere Model A, the one you turned the fly wheel to start. Their Case tractor was rather new, but it was using a lot of water and oil. I guess it had a broken block or something, as they were constantly putting water or oil in it. Bill Young came and someone said "This tractor needs oil." We were already working on other things, so he gets a half gallon container of oil and starts pouring it in. Someone looked over and said, "Bill, you're putting the oil in the radiator." He said, "That's OK, it will probably end up in the gas tank anyway." So he poured the rest of it in.

Much time each year was spent planning and looking forward to deer hunting season. We worked feverishly so we could get the crops in or whatever needed to be done so we could go hunting.

Youngs had all that country up there with cabins and they never kept anyone from going hunting up there. They had a cabin at Atchee and one at "21." (21-mile post on the Uintah) Deer were so plentiful then, if you didn't see 100 deer in a day it was a bad day.

My Dad, Schulties from near Fruita, Harold and Bill Young and myself, were hunting up at 21 and I had gotten my deer. It started raining. The tradition was that the liver of the first deer killed was eaten in camp. We would cut the liver from the new kill into slices and fry it with lots of onions. It wasn't that good, but we thought it was. Hovering down in those warm blankets in the cabin at 21 and the rain coming down on the roof made everything right with the world — there wasn't anything wrong! Every year the Youngs had a 4th of July cow puncher picnic at Atchee. Everyone in the community was invited.

Max Barlow was one of the nicest guys. He had what you would call a liquid laugh. It was like water pouring over a brook or something as it was so melodic. It was so pleasant to listen to it, and he laughed a lot.

I was always a little afraid of Lona Alstatt. Milton was a real mild-mannered person, but if I didn't get chewed out by her every day or two, I wasn't living right. Mercy! I got some good chewing outs! But I probably deserved them. She was one of those neat ladies, too. She was one of those people that you knew where you stood if she didn't like something. If she didn't like something, she let you know in a hurry.

I was about three years old when we lived in New Liberty just before we moved to Nevada. We had a big cistern made of cement with an iron lid that covered it. We didn't have Ute water then, but had water hauled from town by truck and put into the cistern. Sometimes we would run the ditch water in and let it settle, then use it. My Dad had told me to never, ever, to fool around that cistern. I was not to look down in it or anything, because I might fall in and drown. One day Dave Alstatt, the same age as me, was visiting us and I felt I had to show him the sights. That cistern was quite an attraction. I got a stick and pried the lid loose and Dave and I were peering into the cistern, singing and talking. It sounded like we were in a big chamber or something. About that time I felt a hand grab the back of my pants and my Dad put me over his knee, and I got a good whipping. I don't know whether Dave got one or not.

I was always getting a whipping and I hated it. My dad let me choose the instrument of torture. He'd say, "Go get me a willow." I'd have to cut a stick from the willow. I hated tamarisks as they were so tough on the skin!

Maxwell Sanders and his wife lived north of Bob Sanders. Maxwell and Bob didn't get along too well. Max was a real sweet man; he didn't have the line of bull that Bob did. Very sensitive; he really liked kids. When Max and May lost their son at seven they said they didn't have the heart to start over again. He was always really nice to me, treated me like a king. One time my dad said he was going to have to whip me. Max stood up and said, "You are not going to whip that kid. If you whip that kid you'll have to whip me first. I don't have a kid, by golly, and you aren't going to whip that kid!"

I was so impressed how Clem Maluy, Phyllis's dad, could mow hay. I thought I was pretty good at mowing hay, but I didn't hold a candle to Clem Maluy mowing hay. He had a size bigger tractor than us; a John Deere Model G, which was a pretty good-sized tractor then; we had a Model A John Deere. He would put that thing in fifth gear and would just sail down the field. It looked like he was going about 15 miles and hour. Hay was really falling down.

Don Weimer didn't have any kids. He was another guy that was real good with kids. He watched out for them, taught them, worked and played with them, and loved them. He would call on me when he needed help with castrating lambs because of my sharp teeth.

Steve after a slight mishap on the John Deere "G". It rolled off the hill while excavating for the old farrowing house. Steve in background on old John Deere "A." *(Photo courtesy of Steve Chaffin)*

couldn't control it. The wagon skidded off the road and almost turned the tractor over. The tractor got stuck and the tongue on the wagon broke. Don came down and kind of chided me. He said, "Don't you know how to drive this thing? Use your brakes a little bit on each side to steer it down the hill." The next time I tried it I didn't use the brakes or anything; I just took it out of gear and flew down the hill as I just wanted to stay ahead of the wagon.

It wasn't very long after that when Don came down the hill with his tractor pulling the chopper and a load of silage on the wagon behind it. I got up so I could see, as I knew what was going to happen. I was feeling a little sore because he had chastised me for wrecking that wagon. Sure enough, here he came down the hill sliding and loosing control because he had too much weight. Finally he kicked it out of gear and let her sail. By the time he hit the bottom he must have been going 40 miles an hour. The dust was flying and he bounced about five feet in the air and then went up the other side of the hill and gradually came to a halt. He just stood there, took his hat off and said, "Whew! That was quite a ride!"

Maymie Post sold Avon. Mom always bought something from her. It couldn't have been too productive for Maymie though, as they would visit so long. Maymie was known as the

The others would take a drink of beer afterwards, and I would get a drink of lemonade. Don chewed his tobacco. I will always remember his dark blue 1955 Chevy pickup. You could always tell it was his, because it always had a big streak of tobacco juice all the way from the front window to the back of the pickup on the driver's side. When my dad was gone to the mine, Don always checked on us to make sure we were doing fine. He was putting up ensilage at our place one time and he had a Massey Ferguson tractor, a pretty powerful tractor to pull a chopper with and pull a wagon behind the chopper. We had a little Farmall tractor, a Cub, to pull the silage wagon with. There was a hill to go down by the pond that was quite steep. I was going down the hill the first time and the wagon was too heavy for the tractor. The tractor started skidding and I

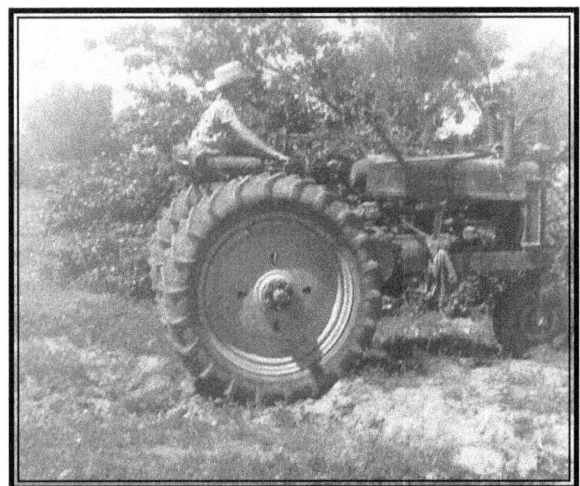

About 1960, Steve Chaffin on John Deere "A" pushing trees over in preparation to level the field on the Chaffin farm in New Liberty. *(Photo courtesy of Steve Chaffin)*

The Faun Chaffin family, June 1971, on New Liberty farm on 9 Rd. L-R: Faun Chaffin holding Brooks Morrow, Rob Morrow, Russell Hills, Violet Chaffin, Wiladeane Chaffin Hills (in back and in front of her), Merridee Chaffin and Vivian and Brian Morrow, Maureen and Steve Chaffin, (in front of them) Elizabeth "Lis" Morrow, Claire Chaffin Morrow and Bob Morrow leading Sand Baby. *(Photo courtesy of Wiladeane Chaffin Hills)*

Grand Madam of New Liberty. If you wanted to know anything about politics, ask Maymie.

We always had John Deere or Farmall tractors. Whoever had them said they were the best. They called a John Deere "Popping Johnnie," as it had only 2 cylinders. The one we had, we started by turning the fly wheel, and setting petcocks and choke just right. Sometimes it would start real good and other times not at all. We still have it, as a matter of fact.

Then the new generation John Deere came out and it was said that there would be no more "Popping Johnnies." They were replaced with a six cylinder turbo-charged diesel engine with a fuel tank in the front and the radiator in the middle. Taylor Roberts bought one to pull a three-bottom plow. Can you imagine? A three bottom-plow! Early one morning Taylor was out plowing and saw me down at the end of the field watching him. He waved to me and said, "Come go a round with me." He took me on that new generation tractor with a three-bottom plow, and that was great. Taylor was so proud of that new tractor! He sat there straight as a string and told all about the horse power, what this did and what that did, and how much more land he could handle. He was so proud!

When did my folks buy the schoolhouse? We didn't get it first. There was a sealed bid and someone else got it. The guy that bought it didn't want it because there was a problem with the title. Kiefers had donated that land and there was a clause in the deed that said that if it ever sold that the property was to go back to the Kiefers. The second time it was up for bid they were to provide a good title. The folks were the only bidders and got it. But they had to go to court to get the title cleared, about 1964.

Stephen and Maureen and family now live in Fruita where their children have been outstanding students and have made notable achievements in school. They are a family of achievers! Following is some additional information about each member of their family:

Maureen and Stephen Chaffin, 1980
(Photo courtesy of Maureen Chaffin)

Then he went back to Colorado State University, where he met **Maureen Ann Mangan.** They were married in the Salt Lake Temple 14 December 1970. Steve graduated from CSU in May 1971 with a bachelor's degree in agricultural business. He did some work on a master's degree in agricultural economics.

While in college he became involved in the ROTC program and was commissioned a Second Lieutenant in May 1971. He served in the Army Reserves for about eleven years at Fort Benning, Fort Riley, and Fort Knox. He eventually achieved the rank of captain.

The Chaffins returned to New Liberty in October 1971. In 1976 Steve started the "Bar-U-Bar Supply," an agricultural fertilizer and chemical business. He raised corn, grass seed, cattle and hogs for 20 years, but they lost the New Liberty farm in 1983.

In 1995, when Faun died, Steve inherited 90 acres, along with his sisters.

Stephen was born in the old Fruita hospital, which later belonged to the Slaugh family. He passed the first and second grades in New Liberty School in one year. He enjoyed music and breaking horses. While growing up he was active in 4-H, showing livestock, and was a two-time winner in the State Tractor-Driving Contest. Once he won in the National competition. He belonged to the National 4-H Club Congress.

After graduating from New Liberty he went to Fruita Junior High School and Fruita Union High School, graduating with the class of 1964. Then he went on to Colorado State University for two years. While at CSU he won a campaign for student Legislator — Representative at Large for the College — and was on the Dean's list for outstanding performance.

He served a Spanish-Speaking LDS Mission from October 1966 to January 1969 (he was asked to extend for 3 extra months) in the West American Mission in California, Arizona and South Nevada.

Maureen was born 6 June 1951 at Delta, Colorado, to James Mangan and Velda McCabe. She is a fourth generation Coloradoan on the McCabe side. Maureen takes pride in being a granddaughter of Bus McCabe, who, during the 1940s, used to spend time on the desert west of Mack checking on Dan McIntyre's sheepherders. He spent lots of time with the Kelly's at the rock shop in Mack. An old man named Stoner from Mack, who worked for Bus on the Muddy River, claimed that Bus was the best cowboy in the world.

Her great-great uncle, Henry Gillespie, founded the town of Aspen, Colorado. He had a ranch nearby called "El Jebel."

When Maureen's mother, Velda, was a little girl she used to write letters to her father, Bus McCabe, when he was at Mack, never dreaming that one day she would be writing to her grandchildren at that address.

James Mangan worked for the Forest Service and consequently had to move around a lot. When Maureen was 18 years old her father was transferred to Fort Collins and she enrolled in CSU. In college Maureen majored in art and music, with a minor in drama and dance. She said she put herself through college by doing "gigs and contracting art work." She did a lot of acting and produced an album in Denver at age 19. She had already developed her talents so she was able to help do one-half hour T V specials at age 16 and 17. She taught art at Elizabethtown College when Steve was stationed at Fort Knox. She became a published illustrator — note the drawing of our historic mail carrier, Everett Bowen, in the front of this book.

She started teaching music when she was 14 years old; she taught for 30 years before she retired. She has had an interesting musical career — learned to play seven instruments and has also led choirs. She led the Fruita Centennial Choir when Fruita celebrated its 100th birthday.

After their marriage Steve drove Maureen over the mountain from Fort Collins to the ranch in New Liberty and the next morning she found herself driving the mower, cutting hay. She had been one of those city girls who refused to believe milk came from a cow! That is how she made the transition!

She and Steve bought the Curt Young place at 6 and S Roads in 1974. (That must have been the Williams/Stotts/Taylor homestead). They also farmed the Cheeney place, about half way to Delta, and they farmed at Cisco for many years. They also farmed in Washington and Nevada. She said in some of their experiences they had to pack in water and sleep on the ground. She thinks they have cooked more over a camp fire than a stove. They have never owned a TV, nor have they ever subscribed to newspapers. With all of that, Maureen says her greatest joy and sense of accomplishment has been as a mother.

Steve and Maureen had three boys and one girl:

Shannon "L", born 12 April 1972, Fruita
Dustin Brian, 8 December 1973, Grand Junction
Travis John, 30 December 1976, Grand Junction
Anna Sophia, 30 November 1978, Grand Junction

Shannon graduated from Fruita Monument High School in 1990, and was president of Future Farmers of America. He enjoys music and made All-State Choir as a tenor. He was an Eagle Scout, earned a black belt in Karate, and is a Certified Scuba Diver. He served an LDS Mission to Thailand from 1991 to 1993.

Shannon graduated from Hillsdale College in Hillsboro, Michigan, in 1997, with degrees in history and political science; he was on the Dean's List all four years. He has chosen the J. Reuben Clark Law College at Brigham Young University in Provo, Utah, to get a Doctorate in International Law or Constitutional Law.

Dustin graduated from Fruita Monument High School in 1992. He was president of Future Farmers of America and became an Eagle Scout. He served as an LDS missionary in the Oregon, Portland, Mission. He graduated from Ricks College in Rexburg, Idaho, in 1997, with honors and a degree in soil sciences. He is going on to Utah State University in Logan, Utah, and expects to eventually take over the family Agricultural business.

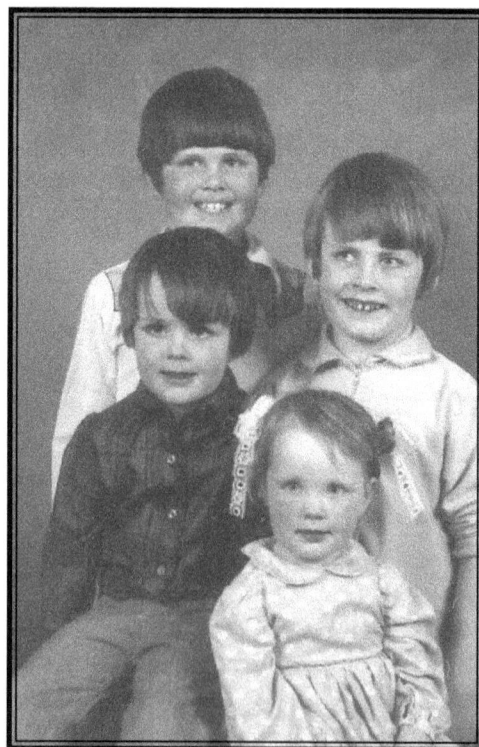

1980, Stephen and Maureen Chaffin's children. Standing L-R: Shannon and Dustin. Sitting: Travis and Anna. *(Photo courtesy of Maureen Chaffin)*

ravis graduated from Fruita Monument High School in 1995. He is a musician, and he became an Eagle Scout and a heavy-equipment operator. He is serving in the LDS Ecuador, Quito, Mission and will complete that in 1998. He learned to speak the Quechua (K-Chew-Wah) language.

Travis wants to go to college and major in physics or chemistry. He enjoys physical labor and being a cowboy.

nna graduated from Fruita Monument High School in 1996, a year early for her age, and made the National Honor Society. She was selected as 1987 Fruita Fall Festival Princess and in 1995 was Fruita Fall Festival Queen. She has earned her Young Women's Medallion (comparable to Eagle Scout for the boys), was first Soprano in the All-State Choir. She enjoys art (She restored the Dinosaur in Fruita Circle Park), drama, dance, and music. He has been involved in equestrian and marshall arts activities.

She started teaching music lessons in percussion and beginning piano at age 14. She works right alongside the Chaffin men on the farm. She is currently attending Hillsdale College and is working three jobs to earn money to put herself through school. One of those jobs is with a construction crew building straw houses.

Maureen says none of the children are married because they don't take time to date.

The Steve Chaffin family, about 1990. Back row L-R: Dustin, Steve, Maureen and Shannon. Front row: Anna and Travis. *(Photo courtesy of Maureen Chaffin)*

Chilson

Stories of Florence Chilson and Grace Eleanor Chilson Curtis and her husband, Leslie Curtis, are from obituaries in *The Daily Sentinel.* Some personal knowledge of author.

lorence Hazel Chilson was born 26 August 1893, at Bridgewater, Hanson, South Dakota, to Sanford A. Chilson and Lavantia A. Parker. She spent her childhood in Missouri, and attended Plainsfield School of Music in South Dakota and Western State College at Gunnison. She married **Jackson R. Dennis**, 6 January 1938, at Grand Junction, Colorado. They had a son, **Carl R. Dennis.**

During the school years 1928/29 and 1929/30, she was known as "Miss Chilson" to the students of New Liberty School, where she taught with her sister, Grace E. Curtis. Teaching was her life's work. She died 9 July 1977 in Grand Junction.

race Eleanor Chilson was born 27 February 1887 at Bridgewater, Hanson, South Dakota, a daughter of Sanford A. Chilson and Lavantia A. Parker. She spent her childhood at Mount Hope, Wisconsin, where she graduated from high school. She later graduated from Western State College at Gunnison, Colorado, and then began a career of teaching. She married **Leslie P. Curtis** at Crawford, Nebraska, 30 June 1911. They had a daughter, **Betty.** Betty attended school at New Liberty, graduating from the eighth grade in 1931, while living with the Snavelys.

Grace was known as "Mrs. Curtis" to the students of New Liberty School. She taught there in the year 1927/28 with Laurel Elbin, then 1928/29 through 1929/30, with her sister, Florence Chilson.

Mrs. Curtis had a peculiar method of punishing students — she would make them hold a hand in front of them with the palm up and then she would spat the hand with a ruler.

It was effective!

She and her sister, Miss Chilson, gave the students a good foundation in music as well as the usual "reading, writing and 'rithmetic." The author well remembers the music sessions when the folding doors dividing the two classrooms were rolled back so all classes could be together. Miss Chilson would accompany on the piano while Mrs. Curtis conducted and sang along with the students. Her powerful soprano voice could always be heard above the voices of the students.

Another novelty was the harmonica band told about previously (page 139) — the students were quite excited with that!

Leslie Curtis went to California in 1944 and found work as a time-keeper at Kaiser Shipyard at El Cerrito. Grace Curtis had just joined him after teaching at Glade Park the previous year. Leslie died suddenly on 9 June 1944. Grace Curtis went back to Colorado to continue her career as a school teacher.

Mrs. Curtis's teaching career ended when she died in the school room at Riverside School, 26 March 1958. She was buried in Elmwood Cemetery at Fruita near her parents and husband.

Christofferson

From census, obituaries and news items in *The Daily Sentinel.*

Christian "Chris" Peter Christofferson will be remembered by many people who lived in the Mack area. He was born in Denmark in 1874, immigrated to the United States in 1892, and became a citizen in 1918. He may have lived in Iowa for a time, as he had a son named **Florian D.**, whom the 1920 census says was born in Iowa about 1900. Nothing is known about the mother of Florian. The census enumerator had a little trouble with the name Florian, listing him as wife of Chris. You will see that they are both named in the previously noted draft list of October 1918.

Chris was married on 2 February 1934, in Grand Junction, to **Mary May Green (Ingleright)**. She died 29 May 1947. Apparently the Christoffersons moved to a farm west of Fruita, where they lived for a number of years. Then Florian moved to Salina, Kansas, and in 1958 Chris joined him there. Chris died at Salina 28 August 1961, but he is buried in Elmwood cemetery at Fruita.

Cole

From obituaries and news items in *The Daily Sentinel.*

Fred A Cole was born 29 September 1876 in Illinois to Orvie and Martha Cole. When he was a small boy the family moved to Atchison, and later to Muscotaw, Kansas. He married **Mary V. Vining**, 1 January 1899, at Muscotaw.

Mary was born 17 June 1880 at Ottawa, Kansas. She spent her childhood at Muscotaw, Kansas, where she met and married Fred Cole.

Fred and Mary had two daughters: **Wilma L.** and **Thelma L.**

The couple came to Colorado in 1901 and lived at various times at Salida, Hotchkiss, Olathe, Delta, and Paonia. They moved to Mack in 1931, where they operated a cafe and grocery store until 1943. After Fred's death 25 March 1945, Mary made her home with her daughter, Thelma Beluchie at Glenwood Springs, Colorado. She died there 1 May 1959. Both Fred and Mary are buried in Elmwood Cemetery at Fruita.

Collins

From obituaries in *The Daily Sentinel* and personal knowledge of author.

Lois and Emmett Collins on Red Mesa farm.
(Photo courtesy of Maurine Collins Reed)

E mmett David Collins was born 27 June 1899 at Lincoln, Lancaster, Nebraska. His parents were Kenneth F. and Laura B. Collins. He lived in the Grand Valley all his adult life, coming to the Mack area about 1920. On 28 October 1922, at Mack, he married **Lois Maurine Hollinger**. (See Hollinger & Saunders stories)

Emmett and Lois had four children:

Delores Belle (Slaugh) (Hutchison), born 17 April, 1923
Kenneth Edward, 19 June 1924
Maurine Maxine (Reed), 15 October 1929
Emmett David Jr., 5 April 1931
All born in Fruita, Colorado.

Emmett and family were living on the Hollinger farm on Mack Mesa at the time of his death, 9 November 1933. (He reportedly died of injuries sustained in a fight at a dance at Mack School). He was buried in Elmwood Cemetery at Fruita.

D elores Belle Collins was born 17 April 1923 at Fruita. She spent her childhood in the Mack area, attending Mack School. She graduated from Fruita Union High School and from Ross Business College of Grand Junction. She later taught school in Fruita.

On 1 November 1942, she was married to **Delbert Slaugh** of Mack. They had one son: **Gerald "Jerry" Glenn Slaugh**. Delbert died in battle in the Philippines during World War II. (See the Slaugh story).

On 2 November 1945, in Salt Lake City, Utah, Delores married **Lenn Hutchison**. They had one daughter: **Kathleen "Katy" Lois Hutchison**.

Delores died at age 31, 3 October 1954, at St. Mary's Hospital in Grand Junction.

K enneth Edward Collins was born 19 June 1924 at Fruita. He spent his childhood in the Mack/Loma area and attended Mack School. He graduated from Fruita Union High School in 1942. On 14 May 1947, at Fruita, he was married to **Betty Pearl Hiatt**, daughter of **Edwin A. "Red" Hiatt**.

They had five children:

James Albert, born 13 February 1949
Diane Lynn (Bailey), 27 July 1950
Barbara Gail (Botkin), 3 October 1952
Kenneth Clayton, 12 April 1961
Bruce Rowland, 29 January 1964

M aurine Maxine Collins was born 15 October 1929, at Fruita. She attended Mack School and Fruita Union High School. On 2 December 1946, in Salt Lake City, Utah, she married **Robert A. Reed**.

They had six children:

Linda Lucille (Heiny), born 16 April 1947
Richard Alden, 30 June 1950
Lawrence Dean, 21 Apr 1952
Thomas Edward, 10 November 1957
Cindy Rae (Keresey), 25 September 1959
Ronald Lee, 19 March 1961
All were born in Fruita.

Emmett David Collins Jr. was born at Fruita, 5 April 1931. He attended the Mack School and Fruita Union High School. He married twice: **Joan Hule** and **La Rue Nixon**. He has four children:

Cheryl Dean, born 28 January 1955
David Gene, 17 May 1956
Nancy Eileen, 2 February 1958
Todd Douglas, 26 March 1962
All were born in Fruita.

Cook

The following was sent to us by Billie Beatrice Cook Hutton of Dixon, Wyoming.

Frank and Icy Cook about 1922
(Photo courtesy of Bea Cook Hutton)

Frank Cook was born 27 October 1893 at Olpe, Lyon, Kansas. On 27 January 1922 he married **Icy Leona Cowan** at Newkirk, Kay, Oklahoma. Icy was born at Cestos, Dewey, Oklahoma, 27 March 1901.

Frank and Icy had 10 children:

Floyd E., born 27 August 1923 at Springfield, Missouri

Dorothy L. (Harper), 31 March 1925, Swink, Colorado

Frank C., 27 November 1926, LaJunta, Colorado.

Billie Beatrice "Bea" (Hutton), 20 July 1928, Rocky Ford, Colorado

Joseph P., 25 August 1929, La Junta, Colorado

Betty L. (Varney), 24 February 1931, La Junta, Colorado

Alice B. (Alberts), 8 April 1933, La Junta, Colorado

Charles W., 3 August 1936, La Junta, Colorado

Nancy Joan (Wilkins), 27 February 1939, Mack, Colorado

James R., 9 August 1943, Fruita, Colorado
Verna J. (Enz), December 1920, (A half-sister on the mother's side who grew up with the Cook children).

Taken in 1929 at La Junta, Colorado. L-R: Bea, Dorothy, Frank and Floyd Cook. *(Photo courtesy of Bea Cook Hutton)*

All the children are still living except Frank, who died in 1989 at Rawlins, Wyoming.

Here's Bea's story in her own words:

The Cook family moved to Mack in the fall of 1937 from La Junta, Colorado — fleeing the "dust bowl." We traveled in a large truck with living quarters in the back. Frank worked variously as a mechanic, blacksmith, horse shoe-er and machinist; a "jack of all trades."

Taken in July 1988, at the Cook family reunion at Winchester Bay, Oregon, of all the Cook brothers. L-R: Floyd, Charles, James, Frank and Joe. *(Photo courtesy of Bea Cook Hutton)*

Before coming to Mack, the family stopped first on the Redlands and picked fruit. What a joy after the dust bowl days in La Junta!

Dad leased the Conoco Station at Mack. (This must have been the station Chet Wright had.) My brother Floyd and sister Dorothy worked there too. (They're still complaining about how hard they worked) Sometimes Dad would accept cases of eggs in payment for his work.

I was in the fourth grade when we moved there. We lived in the old "Forrey" house about a mile west of Mack on Highway 6 & 50. Joan, my youngest sister, was born in that house. I recall that our mother used to take us along the railroad track to help pick up chunks of coal to burn in our stove. My Dad would farm out my brother Joe, and I, to hoe beans. We hated that!

My mother always had at least two goats to provide milk for the family. Of course she thought goat's milk was best for her children. We always had fun riding the kid goats.

My childhood memories of Mack are very special. I remember when I was so glad when I could get on the merry-go-round and take my shoes off 'cause I had no holes in my orange anklets! When the new cement steps were built at the school, we all willed parts of our bodies, eyes, etc. and those notes were put in a shoe box and buried in the cement steps. I don't know why I have remembered that so well. (Wonder if that's still there?)

We just about froze walking to school, so my brother, Floyd, would build small fires on the way to warm us. We didn't live far enough out of town to be allowed to ride the school bus. They said even the New Liberty bus would turn out on the highway in front of us. Our teachers, Mr. and Mrs. Claycomb, excused us when we were late.

Bums were really prevalent during those years and used to stop by the house for food. My mother always had chickens, so she never refused to feed them canned peaches and egg sandwiches. Even families, parents with children, would stop for food. They would leave the empty jars outside behind the house.

I remember one time when my brother, Frank, had new shoes that pinched his feet, so on the way to Mack he hid them under the bridge. When he returned to get them, his shoes were replaced by a bum's worn out shoes. We never let Frank forget that!

We used to go with Dad to pick turkeys for Thanksgiving. What a job that was! My parents taught all of us how to work. Those years were tough, but I believe it made better people of us.

Some of the names I remember from Mack were Slaugh — I believe Mr. Slaugh was a trapper at that time. The children's names were Delbert, Ralph, Calvin, Irma, Vesta. I remember also Russell Brandon, Mary Catherine Daily and Shirley Smith. My brother Floyd and sister Dorothy graduated the same year from the eighth grade at Mack. Dorothy was Valedictorian and Floyd was salutatorian.

I went to school at Mack in the fourth, fifth, and part of the sixth grades, then my Dad moved us to Fruita in the fall of 1939. I graduated from Fruita Union High School in 1946.

My dad had a blacksmith shop in Fruita and I used to stop by on my way home from school and turn the forge for him. We lived in Fruita until 1947, when my parents and younger siblings moved to Lebanon, Oregon, where dad became a millwright at a saw mill. He worked there until retirement.

Taken in July 1988, Winchester Bay, Oregon, of the Frank and Icy Cook children. L-R: James, Joan Wilkins, Charles, Alice Alberts, Joseph, Bea Hutton, Frank, Dorothy Harper, Floyd and Verna Enz Cook. Deceased and not in picture, Betty Cook Varney. *(Photo courtesy of Bea Cook Hutton)*

Cooper

Information from obituaries in *The Daily Sentinel*

William Orlen Cooper was born 6 October 1883, at Weatherby, DeKalb, Missouri. He spent his childhood in Missouri and moved to San Louis Valley in Colorado as a young man. He was a farmer and stone mason. On 2 November 1919, at Monte Vista, Colorado, he married **Mabel Angela Lovejoy**. They had a son, **James "Jim" Lewis**, and a daughter, **Jessie (Hawthorne)**. Jim was married to **Mildred——?** and they had two children: **James D.** and **Anna**. Jim and family moved to California in 1953. Mildred died at San Jose, 2 August 1985.

Jessie married **Victor Hawthorne**. (See Victor Hawthorne story).

The Coopers, with son James and family, and a young man named **Howard Milema**, moved to New Liberty in 1947 and established a home on the Fred Diehl homestead. Beginning in 1948 Mabel taught at New Liberty School, and continued until the school was closed at the end of school year 1958-59. We are assuming she continued to teach for some time at Loma School. William died at the New Liberty farm of a heart attack 17 September 1950 and is buried in Elmwood Cemetery at Fruita. Mabel died 17 January 1989 at Sacramento, California, at age 96.

The beautiful house that William and Mabel built on the Diehl place. Jim and Mildred lived in the mobile home to the right. *(Photo courtesy of Ann Post Hawthorne)*

Corn

From land records, news items and obituaries in *The Daily Sentinel* and author's personal knowledge.

Graves Franklin Corn was born 4 March 1879, at Florence, Colorado. As a young man, he traveled by covered wagon to Montrose. He spent most of his life working with livestock in the Ridgway, Uravan and Rifle areas, as well as in Mesa County. On 1 October 1905, he married **Edna Mae Joyce** at Appleton, Colorado. Edna was born 17 May 1885, at Syracuse, Nebraska, but she spent her childhood in Mesa County.

Graves and Edna had a son: **Orlin H. Corn**, born 17 March 1908 in Grand Junction, Colorado. There was a daughter, **Ila C. (Bennett)**, whom we know nothing about, only that she was living in Thousand Oaks, California at the time of Orlin's death.

Orlin married **Thelma Mock** on 26 November 1927. She was born at Springfield, Missouri, 12 October 1908. Thelma attended Colorado Women's College and Barnes Business College at Denver. At some point in time she was employed by the Colorado Department of Revenue. While living in New Liberty she was a 4-H leader and was president of the Home Economics Club.

Orlin and Thelma had two daughters:

Orlene (Murphy)
Jeanne (Haley)
A son died at birth.

There are three grandchildren and at least two great-grandchildren.

Orlin and Thelma eventually divorced. Orlin remarried, 30 October 1962, in Boulder, to **Mary Lou Nohr**.

The Corns moved to New Liberty in the 1930s after purchasing land from John and Frank Everetts, in Section 12 Range 104 W, in the northwest corner of the community. Later Graves developed 53 acres of land adjoining on the west, which had also been filed on by the Everetts

Brothers.

In 1948 Graves Corn sold his 60 acres to Red Geeting, then he and Edna built a new home in Fruita. Land records show that in 1947 Orlin sold out to Young and Jones and moved to Loveland, Colorado, where he was employed as a brand inspector.

In 1968 Graves and Edna moved to Loveland to be near Orlin. Graves died there at age 90, 10 September 1969. Edna died at Loveland, 21 December 1972. Both she and Graves are buried at Crown Point Cemetery near Grand Junction.

Orlin was notably short in stature and fell heir to the nicknames "Shorty" and "Nubbin." He had a little cattle spread in the Bookcliffs, which he had also purchased from the Everetts brothers. It was located in West Canyon, the place he tells about in the story which follows.

Shorty was also well known for his early potato crop. He would plant in late February or early March, weather permitting, so he was always first in the community to harvest potatoes.

Orlin became a writer — had several of his stories published. A couple of his efforts appeared in "Echoes of A Dream" by Earlynne

Orlin H. Corn
(Photo courtesy of Ann Post Hawthorne)

Barcus and Irma Harrison (published 1983). We have copied one of his stories that appeared in a June 1984, "Rodeo Edition" in *The Daily Sentinel.* It adds dimension to the character of Orlin Corn, as well as John and Frank Everetts.

An Era Gone Forever
by Orlin Corn

The Bookcliff Mountains. A last frontier looking northwest from Fruita, Colorado. The Bookcliffs look like a book standing on end with the pages half open.

Each canyon inviting those who choose to challenge this rough and rugged land, giant bluffs of gray and rusty brown rim rock with sheer face hundreds of feet high. The cedar and pinon trees that cling to the steep hills seem to beckon to the passerby when the wind blows.

At the heads of these canyons lie big basins with spring water laughing as it pours over a rocky course. Pine trees stand among oak brush, grass and sage fills in between.

This is cow country.

Ute Indians were in this country when the west end of Colorado was occupied by the first white settlers.

The events to follow are true...

I grew up with a rope in my hand. Had to lead my horse to a prairie dog mound in order to climb on.

My father and uncles were cattle men when this country was young.

I never grew big and tall; some said it was because my stirrups held my feet, which were fastened to my legs, so they didn't have a chance to get long.

I was named after Orlin Gavin, who was one of the top cowboys in this untamed land around the first part of this century. My name is Orlin Corn, born March 17 1908. I went to work for Tom Kelley in 1930. Tom owned cattle and sheep and lots of horses and mules.

Tom told me about two old men by the name of Everetts who showed up in this country in 1918. No one knew anything about their past. Tom said John Everetts took up a homestead in the head of West Canyon.

His cabin nestled among the aspen with cold spring water near the door.

Tom sent me over to the Everetts' range to look for any W-over-X branded cattle.

This was Tom's brand. This was the first time John and I met. It was a sudden surprise to both of us.

Out of nowhere we came together on this narrow trail. His dark eyes seemed to drill a hole in me. With heavy black eyebrows edged under a big, gray felt hat, his ragged blue jumper told of hard times. Depression — the Thirties. His right hand rested close to his six-shooter handle. The overflow of a few meals dotted the front of his blue shirt. On his bronzed, sun-scorched face, grooves of fine lines registered his 70 years. He sat straight in his saddle, though.

John asked with a growl, "Who are you? State your business for being here."

"I work for Tom Kelley. He has cattle around here."

All this time his squinty eyes darted over my horse for a brand. This would tell him something he wanted to know now, this very moment.

His face muscles twitched while he read me with suspicion. He wished I was somewhere else.

"Look, young fellow, we'uns don't like strangers ridin' around in these parts."

"Because you never met me before doesn't make me a stranger to this country." I turned my horse to leave.

John gave me a frantic yell. "Hold it, wait a minute!" His eyes had dead aim on the brand my horse was wearing.

"I guess you do work for Tom Kelley. That's his horse you're glued to."

"What makes you say I'm glued to my horse?" I asked.

"Well now, young fellow, don't think for one minute this old man can't see good. You ride like you are part of the horse. Tom Kelley told me about you. It just now caught up with me what he said. Tom told me that one should never underestimate you. Said you could rope a critter by the horns or both hind feet. Very seldom waste a loop. Tom said he didn't know of a horse that ever put you on the ground and made you walk home."

John shoved his raspy hand toward me. We shook hands as my horse shied away from him.

"Come to my cabin anytime you're near." John let a slight smile creep over his face. Said he was supposed to meet a man at the mouth of West Canyon. (This is where the road ends and the trail begins).

My curiosity about a man I had just met made unanswered questions claw at my brain while I rode toward the Kelly ranch.

That evening Tom asked, "Did you find any cattle of mine in West Canyon?"

"Sure did, Tom, and met old John Everetts. Tell me, Tom, what makes John so suspicious?" "I don't know," he answered, "but after he knows you, he'll calm down. One thing I do know is he sleeps with 'Old Betsy' under his pillow. Also takes it with him to the outhouse. Fact is, he never goes anywhere without Betsy. Sure a funny name for a six-shooter."

Tom's round face held a sober expression as he said, "Don't try to change it's name in front of John. Don't rub salt on a wound that never did heal. In other words, don't say or do anything to ruffle John."

"Okay Tom, thanks for the advice."

The first ray of sun was creeping over the backbone of the Bookcliffs. We had just caught fresh mounts for the day.

Tom motioned with his hand, "Go back to West Canyon and make sure all my cattle are out of there. The Everetts brothers would like to save all that grass for their own cattle."

Oak brush scratched and clawed at me while the heart of West Canyon came closer. My thoughts were: "These old men aren't able to chop out the trails." My horse splashed water with his feet while I looked for fresh cow tracks along the little creek.

A month went by real fast. A particular day was used for packing salt to the cattle. With four blocks of salt on a horse that had spilled another fellow the day before, I thought maybe he would keep all four feet on the ground with this load. Wagon Canyon was the place for the salt. This was only two miles from John and Frank's. Why not eat dinner with them? My thoughts started to magnify as West Canyon spread out bold and wide under the eaves of the divide above.

The last remnant of snow in a big ravine displayed like white clothes on the line. Blue smoke curled up from the rusty stove pipe. This told me someone was fixing a meal at John's cabin.

The bark of a dog gave warning sound of my appearance. John stood in the doorway for a moment, then came out to meet me.

"Howdy," he said. "Get down, tie your horse to that oak, you're just in time for dinner. How would you like to have a drink of high-life?"

"No thanks," I answered. "Coffee or good mountain water would suit me."

"Aw, come on now," John insisted. "The world will look brighter to you."

"No, John, are you out to prime me into something?"

"Yes and no. We will talk about it later."

Frank and Tobe came through the cabin door as John spoke. "Howdy," they said. Both gave a suspicious glance at each other.

John set the table with four tin plates with cups to match. Knives and forks, which had been used for something other than table use, were bent out of shape.

We ate venison steak, sour-dough biscuits, gravy, cranberry jam, all topped out with coffee that would float a horse-shoe.

I thought of all the honey they had packed in, but none was used for what it was meant for. They used honey to replace the sugar to make 'high-life' as John called it.

Everyone was sort of silent as the meal was devoured.

John put his hat on, squinted at the sunlight, and felt the handle of Betsy, which he wore as he fixed dinner. With a motion of his hand he said, "Come with me, I'll show you our operation."

We walked up a brushy trail. About 200 yards from the cabin was a big still. A tiny stream of whiskey poured out into a five-gallon keg. It went through a strainer first, then into the keg.

"Liquid gold," John said with a sneaky grin. "You know we'uns make the best. Tobe knows how and showed Frank and me. Tobe has a market in Price, Utah, for all we'uns can make. Right now we'uns are really making big money. We hope the revenue agents never get wind of what we'uns are doin'."

"We'uns have made an agreement between the three of us to never let the government agents or sheriff take us alive."

John gave a quick glance in all directions as he told of the many places where a dead man could disappear and never be found.

Orlin died at Loveland 9 May 1984, and was buried in the Mountain View Cemetery at Longmont

Thelma died at Wheat Ridge, Colorado, 3 December 1985. A private burial service was held at Chapel Hills Cemetery. Her remains were cremated.

Cotner

Submitted by Shirley Cotner Barshaw in November, 1992.

Ora Preston Cotner was born 25 March 1913, at Benedict, York, Nebraska, to Ira E. Cotner and Adena Sands. He spent his childhood in that area. On 4 September 1935, he married **Frances Osman**, daughter of Frank Powie Osman and Lillian Nichol, at Clifton, Colorado. Frances was born 13 September 1915 at Hermosa, La Plata, Colorado.

They had 5 children:

Shirley (Barshaw), born 1 March 1936, Fruita
Robert "Bob" Eugene, 24 April 1938, Mack
Carl Wayne, 11 November 1940, Grand Junction
Ida Elaine (Cooper), 22 October 1942, San Diego, California
Richard Curtis, 6 February 1944, San Diego, California

In 1936 Ora and Frances moved to New Liberty, where Ora went to work as a farm hand for Don Weimer. While in Don's employ, Ora was allowed homestead rights to a plot of land south of Don's and began to prove up on it. Later, in 1941, the family moved to San Diego, where Ora was employed in an aircraft factory during World War II. They returned again to the homestead in 1945, built a house, and began to cultivate some of the land. During that time Ora also operated the Mack Garage.

The Cotners stayed only five years before heading off to "greener pastures" at Salem,

Oregon. Ora worked for the Southern Pacific railroad and operated a small berry farm in his spare time. Frances was employed by the State of Oregon doing clerical work. There the children finished their schooling and married. Ora and Frances are both retired and enjoying eleven grandchildren and nine great-grandchildren.

Shirley spent some time in the Army. She is a divorced mother of four children and has seven grandchildren. She now lives in Portland and is employed by the State of Oregon as a management- level supervisor.

Bob has one child and owns a State Farm Insurance Agency in Seattle, Washington.

Carl works for the State of Oregon as a supervisor of governmental painters. He has two children and lives in Salem, Oregon.

Ida has two children, two grandchildren and lives in Salem, Oregon. She is also employed by the State of Oregon in the Motor Vehicle Division — on the front line.

Richard has two children and works in private industry as the manager of crews of installers/repairers of heating and air-conditioning equipment. He also lives in Salem, Oregon.

The Cotner family in Salem, Oregon, May 1992. Back, L-R: Shirley Barshaw, Ora (father), Carl, Ida Cooper and Robert. Front: Richard and Frances (mother). *(Photo courtesy of Shirley Cotner Barshaw)*

Cox

The following was gathered from numerous sources, including census and land records, obituaries and news items from *The Daily Sentinel*. Milton Cox contributed some information and some came from the author's personal knowledge.

Samuel **Milton Cox** was born 3 February 1857, in Bartholomew County, Indiana, probably in Sand Creek Township, several miles south of Columbus, to Samuel and Catherine Ann Cox. In the 1860 Federal Census, Samuel (Jr.), at age 3, is listed with his family in Sand Creek Township, Bartholomew, Indiana. The family's post office was at Elizabeth Town. There was also an older sister named Jurah C., age 4, and a younger brother named Ira B., age 2. Ten years previous, Samuel's parents are listed in the same area in the 1850 census with two children

Taken about 1915-16, Mary Cox and children. Standing L-R: Margaret, Bessie and Robert Cox. Sitting: Edward, William, Mary Ethel, Mary (Mother Cox) and Ira Cox. *(Photo courtesy of Milton Cox)*

named William Hardin, age 6, and John T., age 3. Apparently those two children had died or left home for other reasons before 1860.

In 1881, probably in Bartholomew County, Samuel M. married **Mary Agnes "Mamie" Herron,** who was born 27 June 1859, in Indiana, to William and Mary Herron.

Samuel and Mamie had seven children:

Bessie C. (Brown), born 9 January 1883, Columbus, Bartholomew, Indiana
Edward E., February 1884, Indiana
Robert Milton, 22 March 1886, Columbus, Indiana
Margaret "Maggie" A. (Hobson), October 1887, Nebraska
Mary Ethel, October 1890, Nebraska
William J., January 1893, Indiana
Ira W., 18 October 1894, Columbus, Indiana

We believe it's likely that Samuel and Mary Agnes' children were born in the area of Elizabeth Town— not actually in Columbus.

The family lived many years in Indiana, then moved to some place in Nebraska to live for several years, where Margaret and Mary Ethel were born. They went back to Columbus, and a short time later, in January 1895, came to Fruita, Colorado, settling the following spring on a ranch four miles east of Fruita. The children went to school at Hunter, then Fruita, and later at Mack. The family is listed in the 1900 census in the Rhone Precinct, the oldest child, Bessie, was then 17.

Samuel died of Typhoid Fever 28 September 1904, at age 47, and was buried in the Elmwood Cemetery. *The Daily Sentinel* of 28 September 1904 published this notice of his death:

S. M. COX DEAD

Mr. S. M. Cox, a prominent ranchman of the lower valley and a gentleman widely known in the county, died this afternoon about two o'clock at his home near Fruita. He suffered from typhoid fever and was ill for several weeks.

Mr. Cox leaves a large family to mourn his loss. His wife and several children were at his bedside when death came. He was a brother-in-law of John Herron of Herron and Cassell of this city. He was a good citizen and a successful farmer.

The following story was told by Milton Cox, S. M.'s grandson:

"Dad (W. J., or Bill Cox) was sick with the fever at the same time as Grandpa. When Grandpa died his body was slipped out the window so Dad didn't know his father had passed on until after he (dad) had recovered.

About 1908 Mary Agnes and children moved to a homestead north of Mack, in Sec 7 T 2N R 103W. Mary Agnes and daughter Bessie each filed on land (adjoining plots) at that time. That was the same farm on which son William J. lived years later. It appears likely the family just lived there for a time, not farming, as they probably had no irrigation water, unless they got water from the Kiefer Extension. The 1910 census lists the widow Mary Agnes living in the Loma Precinct (on Mack Mesa) with the three youngest children—Ethel, William and Ira, as well as Mary Agnes' 79-year-old mother, Mary Herron, who was born in Ireland.

After proving up on the homestead, Mary Agnes moved to Grand Junction to live with her daughter Ethel. Later, on 12 October 1926, she moved to Portland, Oregon, to make her home with another daughter, Margaret (Mrs. C. C.) Hobson. She had been there only a short time when she suffered a stroke and died 20 October 1926. Her body was transported by train to Fruita, where she was buried beside her husband in the Elmwood Cemetery.

Bessie, Robert, Mary Ethel, William and Ira were all very involved in the Mack and New Liberty history, as they either homesteaded or taught in the area. Not much has been found on Edward or Maggie.

$\mathcal{B}$essie Catherine Cox was born at Columbus, Bartholomew, Indiana, 9 January 1883 and came with her parents to Fruita in 1895, graduating from Fruita Union High School in 1902. The following school term she began teaching at Rhone School; later she taught at Mesa, Colorado. She was the first teacher at Mack School beginning in 1906.

Cox family, 1929. Standing L-R: Mary Ethel Cox; Freddie Cox (Edward's wife); Helen Cox (Bill's wife); Edward Cox holding son, Glenn; Bessie Cox Brown; Haywood Brown; Zarna (Edwards' daughter); Persis Brown (Bessie's daughter); Careen Cox (Edward's daughter, died at age 21); Fern, Robert and Dorothy Cox. Front: William Cox holding Milton, and Clayton (Edward's son). *(Photo courtesy of Milton Cox)*

On 18 June 1906, she was married to **Haywood Brown** at Fruita. Haywood was then an employee of the Uintah Railway in Mack. They had two children: a son, **Cantwell**, whose name appears in the Mack school student list of 1914-15, and a daughter, **Persis**, who later became Mrs. Wilford Carson.

Cantwell's name appears in the Mack news items of 5 February 1942 as "Cap't" Cantwell Brown, who had been serving in an Artillery unit in the Army; he had been transferred to the Intelligence Division of the War Department and was to be stationed in Washington, D. C. The article also stated that Cantwell had been the first baby born in Mack.

Bessie and Haywood moved to Norfolk, Virginia in 1916, later living in Richmond and Arlington. After Haywood died in 1950, Bessie returned to Grand Junction, where she died 3 December 1963. She was buried in the Cox family plot in Elmwood Cemetery at Fruita.

$\mathcal{R}$obert (Bob) Milton Cox was born 22 March 1886 at Columbus, Bartholomew, Indiana. After spending 11 years of his childhood in Indiana and Nebraska, he came to Fruita with his parents and brothers and sisters in 1895. He attended school at Rhone and Hunter, later graduating from Fruita Union High School. He then attended Denver University.

Fern, Robert and Dorothy Cox, 1929

Dorothy Margaret Cox, 1943

(Photos courtesy of Milton Cox)

As was reported earlier, in December 1907, Robert filed on land in an area that was to become part of the New Liberty Community. He was employed for a time in the construction of the Highline Canal and, in the summer of 1917, was the first in the community to run irrigation water and the first to market produce from the new land. Robert's brothers, William and Ira, worked with him in the early days of homesteading and acquired parcels of land adjacent to his, the end result being that all of that land eventually became one large farm belonging to Robert.

One night in the late 1920s Bob and his brother, Ira, became involved in a melee at the pool hall in Fruita that turned out to be almost fatal for Bob. Seems there had been a long-standing feud going on between the Cox brothers and some cowboys whose names are not known. The fight ended when Bob was struck on the head with a billiard cue, fracturing his skull. He was taken to St. Mary's Hospital where he remained unconscious for several hours. Surgeons implanted a silver plate in his head, which remained for the rest of his life.

Robert married **Fern Margaret Walker** 22 March 1923. Fern was born 10 September 1898 at Pitkin, Gunnison, Colorado, second of two

children born to David Walker and May Elizabeth Hager. Fern spent her childhood in Pitkin and Gunnison, coming to Grand Junction with her parents in 1917. She graduated from Gunnison High School and then from Hoel-Ross Business College at Grand Junction. She was a stenographer at C. D. Smith Drug Co. for five years before her marriage to Robert Cox.

Fern's mother and father spent some time in San Diego, California, where her father died in June 1930. Fern's mother (it appears she and husband were separated) spent considerable time with Bob and Fern, and after the father's death, lived with them at New Liberty until her own death in November 1930. She was buried in Elmwood Cemetery at Fruita.

After suffering from poor health for several years, Fern died at the New Liberty farm home on 6 April 1942. Robert lived on the farm for a few more years, then rented it out and moved to Grand Junction. He died there 12 December 1957, and is buried in the Cox family plot in Elmwood Cemetery at Fruita.

Bob and Fern had one daughter — **Dorothy Margaret,** born 18 December 1925 in Grand Junction. She spent her childhood in New Liberty, attended New Liberty School and graduated from Fruita Union High School in 1943.

Dorothy was employed for several years at U. S. Vanadium Company in Grand Junction, then moved to Portland, Oregon, in 1955, where she worked in a bank. She married 2 June 1956 to Ben Dietz in Portland.

Dorothy died from heart failure at age 32 in Portland on 16 October 1958. She was buried in the Cox family plot in Elmwood Cemetery in Fruita.

Mary Ethel Cox was born in October 1890 in Nebraska. (Milton reports that Ethel weighed a little over 3 pounds at birth). She came to Fruita with her family in 1895, attending schools at Hunter and Fruita. She graduated from Fruita Union High School in 1910.

Ethel became well known in Grand Junction for her business interests and became a charter member of the Business and Professional Women's Club of Grand Junction. In the late 1930s she secured employment in Washington D. C. and worked there until 1944 when she moved to Portland, Oregon, to live near her sister, Margaret (Mrs. C. C.) Hobson. Ethel continued her business interests and her membership in the Club at Grand Junction.

Ethel never married, but raised a girl named Laurette Wills, whose father had deserted her mother and three children. Laurette lived with Ethel from the age of three until Ethel's death. Laurette Wills McComber is now a widow living in Grand Junction.

Ethel died 25 May 1946 at Portland, Oregon and was buried in the Cox family plot in the Elmwood Cemetery at Fruita.

The William J. Cox story was contributed by Milton Scott Cox — there are other sources: census, obituaries and news items from *The Daily Sentinel.*

William "Bill" John Cox was born January 1893 at Columbus, Bartholomew, Indiana. He moved with his family to Fruita in 1895 and attended schools at Hunter, Fruita and Mack. For some years he lived with his widowed mother, Mary, on a homestead on Mack Mesa.

Bill was drafted into the Army late in 1918 (note that he was among those registered for the draft in September 1918). He was trained in the Coast Artillery at Presidio, California, and then sent to France. He spent about six weeks in France. Then, just as his unit had been notified they were going to the Argonne, the Armistice was signed. Bill soon was sent home; he saw no action.

Land records show his brother, Ira, relinquished his rights to Bill to farm unit A in R 103 W Sec 7 in 1919. In 1920 Bill relinquished his rights to Malcolm H. Dean. This was the farm just west of Badger Wash and just below the canal. Apparently he was associated with his brother Robert in farming in the New Liberty district in about 1919 and 1920.

Bill had a desire to go into the ministry, so he enrolled in the Kansas Wesleyan University at Salina. But he soon dropped out because of financial and health problems.

While working in Grand Junction he met **Helen Constance Scott** of Delta. He and Helen were married on 8 September 1926 at Portland, Oregon, (just before his mother died). Apparently Bill and Helen continued to live in Portland for a time while Bill managed a grocery store there. They returned to Colorado and Bill got a job managing another grocery store at Montrose. He lost that job and they moved to Grand Junction where they started a candy store. The depression soon wiped them out, so they went back to farming. They farmed two farms on Ash Mesa, southeast of Delta, until 1934, when they moved to Mack and began

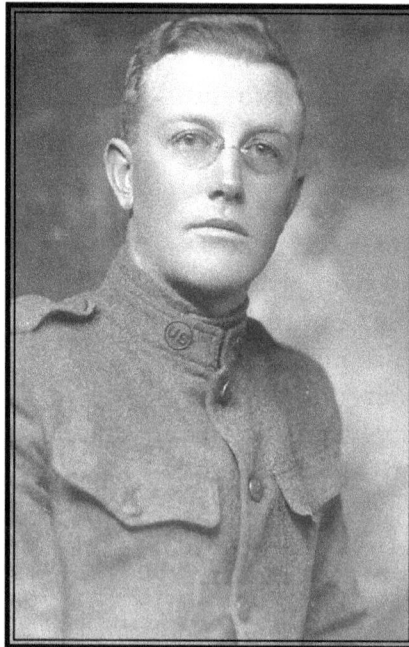

William John Cox, 1918   William and Helen Cox, 1926

(Photos courtesy of Milton Cox)

337

Bill Cox irrigating his corn field on the Red Mesa farm, north of Mack. *(Photo courtesy of Milton Cox)*

June 1947 on the Bill Cox Red Mesa farm. L-R: Gale, Helen, Bill and Milton Cox. *(Photo courtesy of Milton Cox)*

farming the land on Mack Mesa belonging to Bill's sister Bessie as well as the land owned by his mother's estate.

Bill and Helen had two sons:

Milton Scott, 23 March 1929, Maize, Kansas
William Gale, 23 January 1932, Delta, Colorado

Taken 1936. William Gale Cox, 4 years old and Milton Scott Cox, 7 years old. *(Photo courtesy of Milton Cox)*

They operated a dairy for several years, and then Bill and Helen moved to Fruita in 1957. Bill died 29 May 1961 at the Veterans Hospital in Grand Junction and was buried in the Cox family plot in Elmwood Cemetery at Fruita. Helen (age 94 in 1996) still lives in her home in Fruita at 252 North Maple.

Milton Scott Cox was born 23 March 1929 in the old St. Mary's Hospital in Grand Junction. He attended grade school at Mack and graduated from Fruita Union High School in 1947.

Here are some of Milton's reminisces, with a little editing:

Favorite Swimming Places: The lateral on the west side of the farm (was a place to get wet, anyway); Headgate 49; Camp 7; the flume across Mack Wash; and the canal at Arpke's. One time after 4-H we all went swimming by Arpke's. The water was so muddy that when we would come up out of it, the mud ran down our faces. We had to bathe after we got home.

Flat Rock Hill south of Mack was a great place to hike, roll boulders, hug and smoke cedar bark. There is a big rock there shaped like a teepee — it even has a hole at the top, almost like a smoke hole and one can crawl inside. (See Norma Eddings Levitt story).

We liked to ride our bikes to school at Mack in good weather and in the winter sled down Hollinger's Hill.

Miss Hogsett was my first teacher — what a wonderful young woman! Her mother was Sadie Hogsett, who was Mesa County Superintendent of Schools for years. The children loved Miss

(Left) Milton Cox at Glenwood Springs swimming pool on Sneak Day, April 1947. *(Photo courtesy of Milton Cox)*

Hogsett! One Christmas at Community Club, Bill Cox was playing Santa and handing out gifts. When Miss Hogsett walked in the east door of the room all the little kids left Santa for Miss Hogsett. Miss Hogsett married and had one little girl, but passed away before she was 35. (See J. V. Kelly story).

Mack School had three classrooms: little room, big room and middle room. The middle room was the auditorium. One winter afternoon we all smelled smoke and later one of the students walked out into the hallway and discovered the wainscoting by the south door was smoldering. The problem proved to be a faulty flue. Had this happened during the weekend the school would have burned down. During one weekend most of the ceiling in the middle room came down. If school had been in session some students could have been seriously injured or killed.

Remember when Bob Alstatt drove the school bus? It was an underpowered Diamond T. One spring when the road below the south side of the Red Mesa thawed, the mud got so thick the bus wouldn't go any farther and we had to walk home. On a field trip to Fruita Monument the bus just powered out. Bob sure had a tough time getting to the top.

Franklin D. Roosevelt was Phyllis Maluy's hero. One evening on the bus during Roosevelt's last election, as we were about to go up on Mack Mesa, politics got to be a hot subject — mostly teasing. Phyllis was about ready to whip all us Republicans!

Silo Romero, a very good friend, and some other boys hiked down into Box Canyon. They crossed the river in a boat that was there. Silo had a .22 rifle and picked it up by the barrel. He was accidentally shot and died.

Two Uintah cattle cars somehow lost their brakes and coasted away from Mack toward the stockyards to the west and wrecked on the siding. Jim Herron and I took off at noon to see the wreck— one of the cars had ended up with it's leading trucks back under the middle of the car. While we were on that hike a lone D&RGRR engine and tender came up out of Crow Bottom. When the engine went past us the engineer opened a valve and squirted water on us. I about outran the engine back to Mack as I thought it was steam. The engineer was leaning out of the cab until out of sight laughing at us!

One way we could earn money was to pick turkeys for the Maluys, Don Weimer, or the Rays east of Mack. Today the Health Department would shut that operation down.

I remember the World War II years and some of those who never came back. Delbert Slaugh died in the Philippines and Vernon Brandon on "D-Day" in France. The Morrow and Mitchell boys went down in their planes in the Pacific.

Milton served in the Army from 13 May 1954 until March 1956. After receiving his basic training at Fort Ord, California, he was assigned to the 5th Reconnaissance Company of the 5th Infantry Division at Munich, Germany.

After the military Milton attended three semesters at Mesa College in Grand Junction, then transferred to Colorado State University at Fort Collins. He graduated in 1962 with a degree in Agriculture, majoring in Agronomy. After graduation, he worked for a time in the soils laboratory at Colorado State University, and later went to work for the Adolph Coors Company of Golden, Colorado, as a field man in the Commodities Department.

On 17 June 1962, at Billings, Montana, Milton was married to **Dixie Elaine Manor**, daughter of Harold Manor and Blanche Matlock.

They had two sons:

Gregory Scott, born 23 July 1964, Longmont, Colorado
Brian David, born 28 May 1967, Delta, Colorado

Both sons now **(1995)** live at Longmont, Colorado. There is one grandchild.

Through the 31 years Milton worked as an Agronomist for Coors, he received numerous assignments in Colorado, Wyoming and Montana. In July 1992, in his 30th year with Coors, he was given special recognition and was the subject of a write-up in the *Denver Post*. He retired 30 November 1993, after completing 31 years. He had a cancer scare a few years ago, and after chemotherapy he has been in remission since September 1993.

Milton and Dixie currently (1995) live at 814 Sherman, Longmont, Colorado.

William Gale Cox was born 12 January 1932. He also attended Mack School, graduating from Fruita Union High School in 1950.

After graduation he left Mack and went to

Taken in 1953. Gale and Helen Cox and their dog in front of their 1953 car. *(Photo courtesy of Milton Cox)*

Ephraita, Washington, to work on a reclamation project.

He was married to **Helen McKenzie** of Fruita. She is a daughter of Bud McKenzie, who once owned Fruita Super Service. Gale and Helen have four children:

Micky Allen
Gail Marie
Sharie Lee
Michael David

July 1953. Gale and son, Micky, 2 years old, mowing the lawn on the Cox Red Mesa farm. *(Photo courtesy of Milton Cox)*

There are now three grandchildren.

After a time in Washington, Gale and Helen returned to Fruita and he worked for Denver and Rio Grande on the signal gang for a number of years. When American Gilsonite opened their new refinery at Fruita, Gale was among the original crew.

Later he resigned from American Gilsonite and went into partnership with Ray Thompkins in a grocery distributorship. Gale and Helen later bought the business, which supplied groceries to schools and restaurants. They sold that business and are now at Price, Utah, operating a gift shop.

Ira W. Cox was born 18 October 1894 at Columbus, Bartholomew, Indiana. He came with his family to Fruita in 1895 and attended schools at Hunter, Fruita and Mack. Note that Ira's name appears in 1908-09 at Mack School. In 1918 he filed on a homestead on the West bank of Badger Wash, but later relinquished to his brother William. Ira was also associated with his brother Robert in farming interests in New Liberty. He spent many years in the Mack and Fruita areas, then moved to Oregon in 1943.

Ira died at Rockaway, Oregon, 8 March 1967, leaving his wife Leala, two sons and one daughter and six grandchildren.

Cox

Information from obituaries and news items in *The Daily Sentinel*, "The History of Ottawa County" *and* personal knowledge of the author.

(No relation to the Samuel Cox family)

Benjamin and Hazel Cox on their 50th Wedding Anniversary, December 1964. *(Photo courtesy of Joan Cox Evans)*

Benjamin "Ben" Harrison Cox was born 2 February 1889, at Fairland, Indian Territory, youngest of nine children born to John Wesley Cox and Unice (Unica) Jane Braden. Later that area became known as Ottawa County, Oklahoma.

We quote from a paragraph in the "History of Ottawa County" at Miami Public Library, Miami, Oklahoma, part of the story of the John Wesley Cox family :

> On 7 September 1887, the family started to "the territory." They crossed the Mississippi River 11 September 1887, daughter Nettie's 20th birthday. They arrived in the Indian Territory 15 October 1887, and shortly thereafter moved to Seneca, Missouri, where they lived until 27 January 1888, when they moved to the Frank Lamar place located south of the present town of Fairland, Oklahoma. In the spring of 1900 they moved to Afton, Indian Territory.

Ben spent his childhood in the Fairland/Afton area, and came to Mack, Colorado in 1908 where he joined his brother, William Henry, in the merchandising business.

On 24 December 1914 he married **Hazel I. McCoy**, who was born at Brooklyn, Powashiek, Iowa, 22 February 1895. She was a sister of V. L. "Roy" McCoy who worked for the Uintah in Atchee and Mack for many years. The McCoy family came to Fruita in 1911.

Ben went to work for the Uintah Railway and spent one year in Atchee. After about two years he transferred to the Denver and Rio Grande Railroad, becoming a conductor in 1917. In 1918 he entered the Army and served about 10 months overseas with the 348th Field Artillery.

When Ben returned from the military he resumed his job with the Rio Grande. He and Hazel lived at Helper, Utah, until 1930, when Ben was transferred to Grand Junction. He retired in 1949. Ben was a 55-year member of the Brotherhood of Railroad Trainmen.

Ben died in Grand Junction in June 1967. Hazel died, also in Grand Junction, in February 1979. There were no children.

William Henry Cox was born near McLeansboro, Hamilton, Illinois, 14 January 1876, to John Wesley Cox and Unice (Unica) Jane Braden, fourth in a family of six boys and three girls. In 1887, when William was about 11 years of age, the family moved to the vicinity of Afton, Ottawa County, in Indian Territory (which later became part of Oklahoma).

W. H. Cox began working as a store clerk quite early in life. One day he showed a pair of shoes to an attractive young lady, and from that meeting began a romance that led to marriage. On 28 August 1898, at Afton, Ottowa, Indian Territory, W. H. married **Jennie Maude Jackson**, who was born 18 April 1881, at Pierson, Woodbury, Iowa, to Francis Marion Jackson and Jerusha Loomis.

(Left) William Henry and Maude Cox, 1926. (Above) Taken 29 May 1950. L-R: Judy, Greg and Naomi Cox Smith, Lynette and Lucille Cox Schultz, and Maude and William Henry Cox. (Center left) L-R: Leonard, Maybelle, Maude, William Henry, Minnie and Earl Cox, and Naomi Cox Smith; in front Judy Smith. (Center right) Orval and Josie Cox Wagaman, 1968. (Lower left) L-R: Chuck Frank, Maybelle, Maude, Leonard, Eugene and Earl Cox. (Lower right) Naomi Cox Smith. (*Photos courtesy of Joan Cox Evans*)

Willie Paul, Jennie Maude holding Leonard Melvin, William Henry and Earl Otis Cox, 1905
(Photo courtesy of Eugene Cox)

They had six children:

Earl Otis, born 16 August 1899, in Afton, Oklahoma
Willie Paul, 8 April 1902, Lamar, Colorado
Leonard Melvin, 19 September 1904, Grand Junction
Josephine "Josie" Maude (Wagaman), 15 March 1907, Grand Junction
Lucille Bessie (Schultz), 21 April 1910, Grand Junction
Naomi Maxine (Smith), 28 November 1916, Fruita

William and Jennie Maude Cox lived in the Afton, Oklahoma, area for a time before moving for a short stay at Lamar, Colorado. In about 1904 they moved to Grand Junction, and then to Fruita, where William was a partner with F. A. Brewer in the mercantile business (Cox and Brewer Mercantile). During that time William served as mayor of Fruita. We are not able to determine clearly all of the times and places the Cox family lived after they came to Colorado, but it appears likely they lived in Grand Junction for some time before coming to Fruita and Mack. The third, fourth and fifth children were born at Grand Junction.

However, the 1910 census shows they were living in the Loma Precinct. William's occupation is stated as "Proprietor of Department Store." That record also shows a baby daughter just two months old (that would have been Lucille). They lived at Mack for awhile after William became manager of the Mack Mercantile. The Mack School records of 1909-10 show the names of Earl and Leonard Cox. We have in our files a snapshot showing Leonard with a group of students in front of the Fruita Central School in 1912, but in 1913-14, Earl, Leonard and Josie are listed as students at Mack School. The family went back to Fruita again for a time, where the sixth child, Naomi, was born in 1916. At that time William went into the cattle business with another man— that turned out to be a bad experience.

In the Fruita items of *The Daily Sentinel* dated 23 January 1922: "W. H. Cox has secured the Horse Thief Canyon Ranch, south of Loma." During the time they lived there the children attended school at Loma.

During the years 1924 and 1925 the names of members of the Cox family appeared often in the news items of the Highline Community. They lived on the Lynch or Finch farm. Daughter Lucille was named in 1925 as one of the graduates from the eighth grade at Loma School; Josie may have graduated at Loma also.

Mack Items of 24 September 1925 gives us the news that "W. H. Cox has purchased the Mack Mercantile from W E. Roberson and E. L. Smith." Cox's took over operation of the store on 2 October 1925. We found in the Mack items of 10 August 1928 that W. H. Cox made a deal with Biggs and Kurtz Co. to trade the store for some orchard land on the Redlands. In 1930 W. H. ran for Mesa County Assessor on the Republican ticket, but was defeated.

After living in the Grand Junction and Redlands area for some time, William Henry and Jennie Maud apparently came back to Mack for a time beginning in February 1932. We found in the Mack news items of 11 October 1936 that "owing to ill health, W. H. Cox is disposing of all his stock in the Mack

Mercantile." They had a big sale, offering prizes to attract more customers. Finally, they moved the remaining stock of the store to another store in Palisade and closed the Mack Mercantile for good on 24 July 1937. We don't really know if anyone else operated the store after that. We found in the Mack items of 23 November 1941 that the Cox's were living in Cedaredge and had been to Mack for a visit. It may have been soon afterward they moved to Riverside, California. We believe Earl was living there then. William Henry died at Riverside 28 December 1951; Jennie Maude 3 April 1969. Both are buried in the Olivewood Cemetery at Riverside, California.

Earl Otis Cox was born at Afton, Ottawa, Indian Territory, 16 August 1899. He attended schools at Fruita, Loma and Mack. On 23 September 1918, Earl registered for the draft in Mesa County; nothing is known of his service in the war. On 14 August 1920 he was married at Fruita to **Oleta Gardner**. They had a son, **Eugene Cox**, who presently lives at Delta, Colorado. The marriage ended in divorce, and for years Earl would not claim Eugene as his son. Years later, after he was a married man, Eugene contacted his uncle Leonard and because of Leonard's friendly welcome, began again to be a part of the Cox family.

In 1930 Earl married **Minnie Dorman**, and in 1942 they adopted a daughter whom they named **Darlene**. Earl died 4 September 1968 at Riverside, California.

Willie Paul Cox was born 8 April 1902 at Lamar, Prowers, Colorado. He passed away when not quite five years old on 16 January 1907 at Grand Junction, and is buried in the Orchard Mesa Cemetery.

Leonard Melvin Cox
(Photo courtesy of Joan Cox Evans)

Leonard Melvin Cox was born 19 September 1904 at Grand Junction. He attended schools at Fruita, Loma and Mack and spent most of his boyhood years helping his father with the farming and mercantile business. He worked for a short time on the Uintah Railway when the big slide occurred in 1929.

He was married to **Mabel Dean Likes**, daughter of Clyde W. Likes and Retta May Appier on 13 July 1926, at Delta, Colorado. The following account of the event appeared in the Mack News Items in *The Daily Sentinel* Friday, 23 July 1926, F. B. Baird, Correspondent:

Mr. Leonard Cox and Miss Mabel Likes stole a march on their friends and were quietly married in Delta July 13. The young people kept it a secret until it came out in the paper Sunday. Mr. Cox assists his father in the Mack Mercantile, and Mrs. Cox, daughter of Mr. and Mrs. Clyde Likes of the High Line [sic], has been working at the hotel for the past year and a half. They have the best wishes of their many friends in the vicinity. The young people of Mack gave them their good wishes with a shivaree Monday evening.

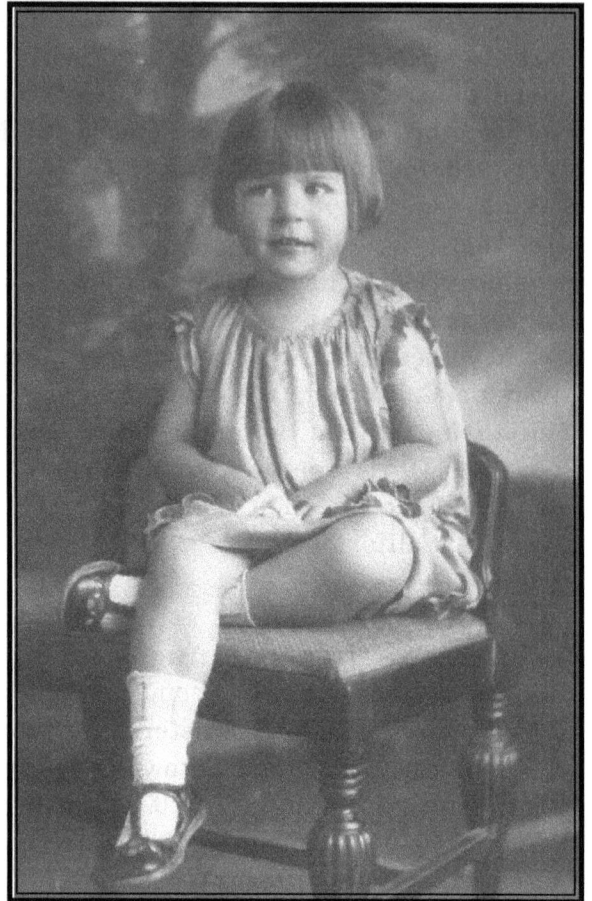

(Upper left) Leonard and Joan Cox, 1928. (Upper center) Mabel and Joan Cox, 1928. (Above) Joan Lucille Cox, 1931. (Center left) Leonard Cox in 1926 with his 1924 Model "T" Ford. (Center right) Leonard, Mabel and Joan, about 1936. (Lower left) Joan and Mabel, about 1932 in California. (Lower right) Leonard, Mabel and Joan in Grand Junction, Lincoln Park, 1958. *(Photos courtesy of Joan Cox Evans)*

Leonard and Mabel Likes Cox on their wedding day, 13 July 1926, on Grand Mesa in Colorado. *(Photo courtesy of Joan Cox Evans)*

Leonard and Mabel resided in Mack for a short time, then went to California where they spent some time in the Imperial Valley and in Los Angeles. On 2 January 1928, at Grand Junction, they were blessed with a daughter, **Joan Lucille Cox**. (See Mabel Likes biography.)

Leonard stayed with the mercantile business for most of his life. As an employee of Safeway Stores for many years, he was required to move several times. After he left Safeway, they lived in California for awhile and then, during World War II, went to Hawaii for a year and worked as a storekeeper in a shipyard, leaving Mabel and Joan in Los Angeles. After his return, he and his brother-in-law, Ed Schultz, went into the grocery business together in Los Angeles. They jokingly referred to their business as their "Carrot Shop."

Later, Leonard and Mabel moved back to Colorado, and after a two-year stay at Paonia, moved to Denver. Still later, they moved back again to the Los Angeles area, spending several years managing apartments. Leonard's working years ended in 1969 when he was diagnosed with cancer. He died at Fruita, 25 September 1971, and is buried in the Memorial Gardens Cemetery at Grand Junction.

Joan Lucille Cox had her first school experience at Mack. She recalls the school as having only one room. She went to elementary school at Paonia, and then graduated from high school in Riverside, California. She attended a Dorothy Prebble Modeling School in Hollywood, California at 16 years old. She modeled from 1943 to 1946 as a runway model. Once she even hosted the Jack Benny radio program. Her first marriage occurred in Los Angeles to **Fred Henry** 5 March 1945, and her first child, **Charles (Chuck) Leroy**, was born there 2 September 1946. She and Fred were divorced. Then Joan, Chuck, Mabel and Leonard moved back to Paonia. Joan was married for the second time in Paonia to **William "Bill" Palmer** in 1947 and her second son, **Donald William**, was born 29 March 1948 while living there. In 1949, she was ready to restart her modeling career when she and Bill were in a car accident. Joan was thrown through the windshield, incurring serious facial injuries which abruptly ended her career. Her marriage to Bill ended shortly after the accident. She was married the third time to **Oren Ivan Frank** at Denver, 1 November 1951. The third son, **Douglas**, was born 31 March 1954 in Denver and his father adopted the other two sons, making a family of three **Frank** sons. Oren and Joan divorced and Joan married **Harold "Hal" Evans** 26 May 1973 in California. They currently reside in Concord, California.

Oren Frank died 24 July 1977, and while in Denver to attend the funeral, the oldest son, Chuck, drowned 27 July 1977 in a swimming pool.

Joan attended a business college in Denver and worked as an executive secretary for Gates Rubber Company. When she went to California in 1972, she worked as a secretary for Liberty House in Concord. She then worked for Blendow, Crowley and Oliver. For several years she traveled Europe with her husband, Hal, with his business. In 1984 she purchased her own business, Danville Secretarial Services. She retired in 1995 and currently works part time out of her home.

Joan has nine grandchildren.

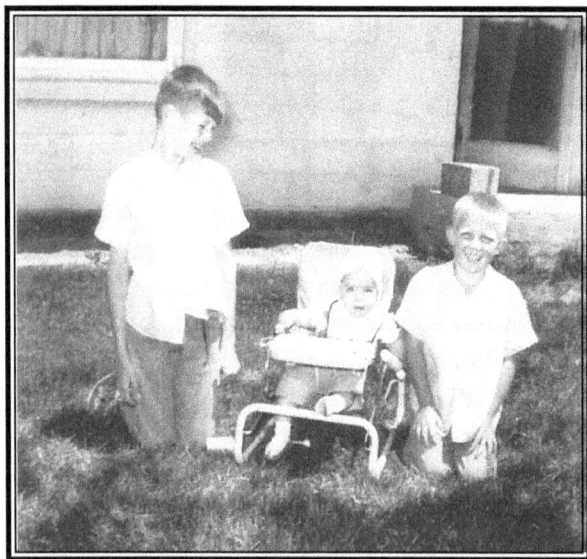

(Upper left) Joan and first husband, Fred Henry in 1945 in California. (Upper Center) Joan and second husband, William Palmer, 1947 in Paonia, Colorado. (Upper right) Joan and third husband, Oren Frank, and son, Douglas, 1955 in Denver, Colorado. (Center left) Joan and fourth husband, Hal Evans, taken recently in Concord, California. (Lower left) The three Frank boys, Chuck, Douglas and Donald Frank, 1956, in Denver, Colorado. (Right) Joan Cox, 16 years old, at the beginning of her modeling career in Los Angeles, California. *(Photos courtesy of Joan Cox Evans)*

347

Josephine "Josie" Maude Cox was born 15 March 1907, at Grand Junction, she attended schools at Fruita, Loma and Mack. On 9 June 1928, at Grand Junction, she married **Orval Hugh Wagaman,** of Mack. (The following account by Mabel C. Kiefer appeared in the Fruita items in *The Daily Sentinel* of 11 June 1928). "Fruita friends are interested in a wedding which took place Saturday evening in Grand Junction. The contracting parties are Miss Josie Cox and Orval Wagaman of Mack. The young people have been attending the Fruita High School and are well known to many here. They belong to old and respected families of the valley, the bride being the daughter of Mr. and Mrs. W. H. Cox of Mack and the groom is the son of Mr. and Mrs. Frank Wagaman of Mack. The ceremony was performed at the Baptist church with Rev. Franklin Fenner officiating, using the impressive ring service. Mr. and Mrs. Leonard Cox were witnesses. The bride and groom have made their homes in the valley during their entire childhood, and Fruita friends join with others in extending congratulations and best wishes. They will continue to live in Mack."

Orval and Josie had two sons:

James L. (died as an infant)
Charles Richard "Dick"
(see biography of Orval Wagaman)

The family spent many years in Minnesota. Orval and Josie died and were buried there.

Lucille Bessie Cox was born 21 April 1910, at Fruita. The 1910 census shows the family living in the Loma Precinct when Lucille was two months old.

On 12 March 1933 Lucille was married to **Edward Schultz** at Grand Junction. Ed also followed the store-keeping trade and probably worked for his in-laws in the Mack Store at some time or other. After World War II he and his brother-in-law, Leonard Cox, operated a vegetable stand in downtown Los Angeles.

Ed and Lucille had two children: **Ronald Gene,** born 8 October 1934 at Grand Junction, and **Lynette,** born 31 July 1939 at Cedaredge, Colorado. Ronald now lives at Hemet, California, and Lynette at Bellflower, California.

Lucille died 19 February 1977 at San Jacinto, California; Ed remarried and lived several more years in the Grand Junction area.

Naomi Maxine Cox was born at Fruita 28 November 1916. She attended schools at Loma, Mack and Fruita, graduating from Fruita Union High School in 1934. On 8 September 1940 she married **Clarence "Smitty" Smith** at Littleton, Colorado. They had a daughter, **Judith,** born 31 August 1941 at Paonia, Colorado, and a son, **Gregory,** born 17 February 1947 at Riverside, California. Naomi and Smitty lived in Denver, Los Angeles and Riverside for many years, and then moved to Las Vegas where Smitty died several years ago. Naomi continued to live in Las Vegas until some time in 1992 when she moved to Littleton, Colorado, so she could be near her children. Naomi died in Littleton in January 1995.

Crews

From obituaries and news items in *The Daily Sentinel.*

Luke J. Crews was born in Illinois in 1873, according to the 1920 census. He was married 11 September 1899 in Montrose, Colorado, to **Lena Reynolds,** who was born 12 September 1867 in Decatur County, Indiana. The Reynolds family lived for a time in Kentucky and then moved to Colorado in 1874. After marriage, the Crews lived in Illinois and Arizona before coming back to Grand Junction, Colorado, and then to Mack. They had one son, **Matt** (likely Matthew), who was born in Colorado in 1900. Matt started school in Mack in 1915-16 with Ida Davis as teacher.

The Crews family was owner-operator of a grocery store in Mack for about 11 years. On the night of 17 February 1928 Luke and Lena had gone to a party in Grand Junction, leaving the store and home in the care of son Matt. Late in the evening Matt stoked up the fire in the stove in the store before going to bed and in the early morning hours he was awakened by smoke and heat and had to run for his life. The entire building was engulfed in flames, which consumed the building, the stock in the store, and all personal belongings.

The Crews had a farm north of Loma, where they lived after their loss; the store was never rebuilt.

Matt was married in August of 1936.

Lena died at Mack in July 1943. At the time of his mother's death, Matt was living at Henefer, Utah.

This is all the information we have on this family.

Currey

The following was compiled from letters from Helen Currey Sumner and Tom Currey, with some editing. It was also compiled with information from obituaries for James and Nova Currey.

James Ervin Currey was born 7 August 1883 at Lamar, Barton, Missouri. He was married to **Nova Emma Slawson**, 4 March 1908 at Girard, Crawford, Kansas.

Their children were:

Christia Anne (Barton), born 17 April 1909
Paul Emmett, 13 November 1910
Hillary "Hux" Slawson, 14 April 1913
Dorothy Maxine (Brenneman) (Heller), 10 January 1916
Jennie Beatrice (McKeel), 18 March 1918
Mable Margaret (Moore), 4 November 1920
Thomas "Tom" Woodrow, 16 February 1922
Frank Erwin, 17 August 1923
Helen Martha (Sumner), 16 May 1925
Edith Marie (Hansen), 1 February 1927
Donald Edmond, 18 November 1929
Betty Jean (Anderegg), 23 September 1931

This information comes from Tom and his wife:

After marriage the Curreys lived at Lamar, Missouri area, where three of their children were born. Then they moved to Belltower, Montana, where eight more were born. They lived there until about 1931, when they moved to Collbran, Colorado, where the last child, Betty, was born. In 1934 they moved to the New Liberty community where they lived on the Tom Adams' farm on the north side of the siphon, between Pollocks and Carrolls, where they raised turkeys in partnership with Tom Lemmon of Collbran.

Mable, Tom, Frank, Helen and Edith all attended school at New Liberty, and later, all of them graduated from Fruita Union High School.

The family moved to Orchard Mesa about 1940, and then to the Rhone area. James and Nova later moved to Fruitvale on Florence Road.

James Ervin passed away on 8 February 1965 at home in Fruitvale, and Nova Emma passed away in the La Villa Grande Care Center in Fruitvale, 30 September 1981 at the age of 89. She had been resident of Mesa county for 50 years.

Following are some of Helen's memories. Her dates conflict with her brother Tom's:

Our dad moved his family from Collbran to Mack in 1937 to raise a large number of turkeys for Tom Lemmon of Collbran. Those turkeys were dressed out for the Thanksgiving market. I remember the Currey kids got to pick turkeys and more turkeys!

School was a fun time with our friends at the small New Liberty school house. I remember one time a bunch of my friends, including me, thought it was neat to tear the rubber caps off our shoe heels. Some of the kids found themselves flying through the air when the protruding tacks hit wet spots on the cement floor around the water cooler. It was a good laugh for the rest of us, of course.

Another thing I recall was how pretty our teacher's wife was. Mrs. Carroll had beautiful snow-white hair, although she was quite young. The story was it turned silver overnight. I cannot remember why.

I got to see "Snow White and the Seven Dwarfs" for the first time when I lived at New Liberty. One of my friends' parents took Dorothy, their daughter, and me to the special

(Above) The Currey family, 8 March 1958 at the parents' 50th Wedding anniversary. Standing, L-R: Betty, Donald, Edith, Helen, Frank, Tom and Jennie. Sitting: Hillary "Hux," Christia, James and Nova (parents), Paul and Dorothy. Mabel was missing as she was expecting a baby. *(Photo courtesy of Lois and Tom Currey)* (Below) The Currey family in 1961. Standing, L-R: Edith, Frank, Donald, Hillary "Hux," Paul and Tom. Sitting: Jennie, Mabel, Christia, James and Nova (parents), Betty, Dorothy and Helen. *(Photo courtesy of Mabel Currey Moore)*

movie. Movies weren't in the Currey budget.

There was a big siphon connecting two parts of the canal near our home. When they drained it we would walk inside as far as we dared. It was slick and scary. Fish drained out with all the water. We also walked the top of the siphon. One time we saw a dead cow spinning around in front of the intake gate — sad sight!

We had many good friends to spend happy hours with at New Liberty! To this day I remember those times with the Maluy girls, Pollock kids, Dorothy Cox and our other classmates.

Before we left New Liberty, for some reason I can't remember, we lived for a short time in an old one-room school house. We had beds all around the outside walls with curtains hung in front of them. Oh! The things you must do with a house full of kids! We had a good, good time doing them!

We soon moved to the Orchard Mesa area, only to return and attend high school at Fruita. There we renewed our New Liberty friendships.

Cutler

Edward Cutler and Harriett Cutler Blau provided most of the following family information. Also compiled with information from obituaries and news items from *The Daily Sentinel* and personal knowledge of the author.

Arthur and Mary Alice Russell Cutler, in 1907
(Courtesy of Dolores Cutler O'Connor)

Arthur Howard Cutler, was born 9 January 1878 at Heath, Hampshire, Massachusetts and spent his childhood there. His mother died when Arthur was about 13 years of age. His father remarried and Arthur did not get along well with his stepmother. He left home for a time at about age 19, but went back to try it again. Then, at age 24, he left again, following the admonition of Horace Greeley to "Go west young man, go west!"

Arthur did go west as far as York, Nebraska, where he found a job as a farm hand on the Russell family wheat farm. David M. Russell and Ida Smith had a large family of nine daughters and two sons. In the early 1900s the mother and the first and third daughters died of tuberculosis, leaving **Mary Alice**, the second daughter, to take over the responsibilities of mothering the family. After this terrible ordeal David Russell said, "I'm taking my family to a healthy country." So they moved in 1906 to Fruita, Colorado, settling on a farm in the Starr community. They shipped the livestock on the railroad and Arthur Cutler traveled with them.

Arthur and Mary Alice were married in the Russell family home at Starr, 31 January 1907. Mary was born 28 October 1882 at York, Nebraska. When she and Arthur were married she was past her 25th birthday, Arthur was 29. The morning after their marriage, Mary helped her five younger sisters get off to school; she was still in charge of the family.

Arthur and Mary had seven children:

Charles David, born 6 March 1908 (in the Russell home at Starr)
Hobart Arthur, born 6 January 1910, supposedly at Collbran
Vera Esther, born 1913 (died at about 6 months)
Paul Russell, 4 February 1916
Edward Harding, 6 March 1921
Harry and **Harriett** (twins), 22 October 1923

A couple of years after their marriage Arthur and Mary moved to a dairy farm in the Collbran area where Hobart is said to have been born. After a short period there they moved back to Starr, where they lived until 1918, when Arthur acquired a homestead in the New Liberty community. The homestead was located on Unit J Sec 10 R 103 W on the east bank of East Salt Creek.

They lived for awhile in a typical tar-paper shanty built on land formerly owned by Tom Carroll before building an interesting home against the hill about a quarter mile away. To the south of the new home they planted a row of poplar trees; one for each member of the family.

The house had two levels. The north wall of the lower story was a cut bank in the hill. The lower floor contained a bedroom for parents, a kitchen and dining area; the upper floor was a large open attic which also served as bedroom for the boys. The north end of the upper room had a door opening onto the hillside. The interior of the house was whitewashed.

The Cutler's had access to their farm from two directions. There was a drive that connected to what is now called "10 Road" on the east; but they had a wagon trail out to the west, which crossed East Salt Wash and joined the road on the hill near Burge Lofgrens' place on what now would be about "9 1/4 Road." That road was used more than the other because school and Sunday School were to the west of them, and that's where most of their social activities took place. However, when they would go to Mack or further up the valley, they always went to the east.

After Mary gave birth to Edward she volunteered to provide sustenance for a neighbor's baby in addition to her own. The **Padilla (Padia?)** family lived on the hill to the east of them and that mother had a baby born about the same time as Edward. Mrs. Padilla could not nurse her baby for some reason. Mary Cutler would nurse Edward then get on a horse and ride over to the Padilla's and nurse that baby too.

The Cutler family was always active in New Liberty Sunday School and Community Club; they rode in a wagon for many years to those functions. The children remember being given 25 cents to come early and light the fires for Sunday School; this may have done the same for Community Club. Thus the school house would be warm enough to be tolerable when the rest of the people arrived.

The Likes and Cutler families were very close and had lots of association. They visited together often and helped each other with haying and other harvesting.

Here's a story Edward recalls: on a Sunday afternoon the Likes family came to dinner at the Cutlers' house and after dinner the boys, Paul, Edward, Homer and Lewis, went to explore some caves the Cutler boys knew about in the cut bank of the wash near their house. They crawled into a cave some distance and as Edward looked back he thought, as he told the story, "what if there had been a cave-in?" The boys may never have been found!

There was often a small-fry Cutler/Likes rodeo involving the younger boys roping and/or riding the calves in the corral. The calves would have liked very much to be left alone.

Some time during 22 October 1923, Mary began to experience labor pains and it soon became apparent she was about to give birth. Arthur hurried over to neighbor Joe Fessler's who came to

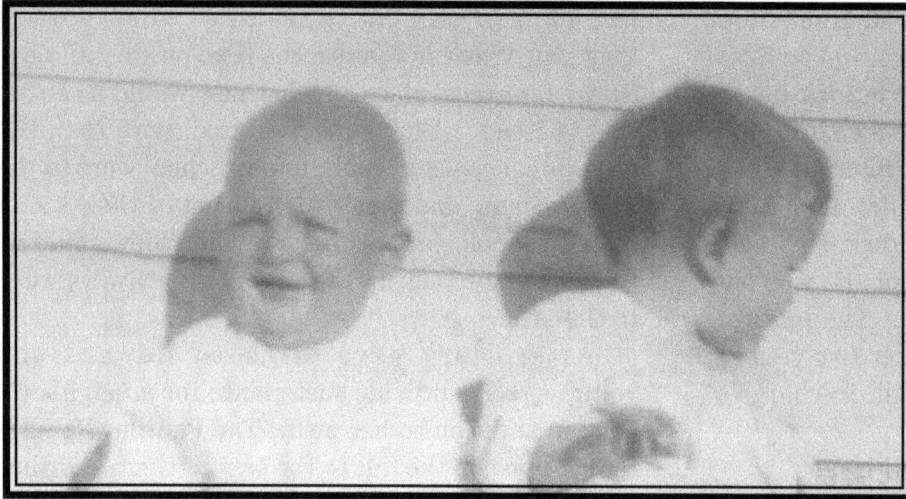

Twins Harry and Harriett Cutler, nine months old. *(Photo courtesy of Harriett Cutler Blau)*

the rescue with his truck and they sped toward the hospital in Fruita. For many years the author believed the story that they didn't make it in time, but Harriet wouldn't confirm that story. She says it *may* be true that she was born in the truck. Whatever the truth, she was born first. Mary was not aware up to that time that she was pregnant with twins, so she was quite surprised when the doctor informed her there was a second baby about to be delivered. Harry was born about 15 minutes later. The doctor overseeing the birth was Dr. Harry White and the attending nurse's name was Harriett (Hattie) Hunter, so the twins were given their names: Harry and Harriett.

Arthur was partial to Ayrshire dairy cows and had a pretty good looking herd — the only Ayrshires in the lower valley. He also had his own ideas about feed for those cows; in addition to the usual alfalfa hay and grain, he once grew artichokes to feed them.

In the summer of 1927, Arthur and his friend, Clyde Likes Sr., who was partial to Jersey dairy cows, conceived the idea to rent pasture for their combined dairy herds from Josh Meniece at his ranch on the north side of Douglas Pass. Hobart Cutler, age 17, and Fred Likes, 16, were elected to

spend the summer with the cows and tend to the milking and separating of the cream, to be picked up weekly and taken to the creamery at Fruita.

So, on 16 July 1927, they began trailing the combined herds toward the mountain ranch — a major undertaking. They went as far as R.O. Brown's ranch the first day and penned the stock up there for the night, then continued on up the mountain the next morning. The cows and bulls were trailed together, and of course, had some contact with range cattle in the Douglas Pass area of the Bookcliff range as they traveled through that area. The Hereford bulls gave the Ayrshire and Jersey bulls a sound thrashing, and the local cowboys warned the Cutlers and Likes' that their bulls were in real danger of becoming steers.

However, they arrived safely at the Maniece ranch with the dairy outfit and Hobart and Fred spent a pleasant summer producing cream. A weekly trip was made by the Likes' or Cutlers' to check on the boys and bring the cream to market. The younger Likes and Cutler boys had high hopes of spending some time with the older brothers, but, owing to the salty language of Josh Maniece, their fathers, Arthur and Clyde, decided it was no place for young boys. The boys had to be satisfied with going along on

Arthur Cutler and one of his prize Ayrshire bulls, in 1929-30. *(Photo courtesy of Harriett Cutler Blau)*

the weekly trips — still a major adventure.

Josh was a cowboy of the old school who wore a six-shooter on his hip at all times. That six-shooter was later used by Josh in the killing of one of his neighbors, Russell A. Darr, a son-in-law of A. W. Rector. Seems there was an on-going feud over rights of way over the Rector property. The feud ended in a store in Rangely when Josh began an argument with Darr, then pulled his six-shooter and shot him. Josh was subsequently charged with murder, found guilty and sentenced for the rest of his life in the Colorado State Penitentiary.

One summer of that Cutler/Likes dairy venture was enough.

In October of 1931, Arthur became despondent over his many cares and ended his life by suicide. He left notes for his family explaining that he had too many worries to continue on.

After Arthur's death, mother Mary moved with her family to another location on some land they had purchased from Rex Rankin, east of where they had been living. Hobart had been married the previous May, so two new homes were built adjacent to each other by the same contractor. Harriett and Edward report they moved into the new homes at Thanksgiving time.

As Mary became older and her health failed, she went to live in the Mesa Convalescent Home in Fruita. She died there at age 82, 8 March 1946, and was buried in Elmwood Cemetery at Fruita.

All of the Cutler children graduated from the eighth grade at New Liberty School. Hobart, Paul, Edward, Harry and Harriett graduated from Fruita Union High School as well. During World War II Charles, Paul, Edward and Harry all served in the military.

Charles spent most of his early life in New Liberty doing farm work. At some point in time he began working during the summer months for a survey crew.

The Daily Sentinel of Monday, 1 September 1929 gives the following account of an incident in Charles' driving experience:

Charles Cutler, resident of the Mack district, was released this morning from the Fruita Hospital, having started on recovery from injuries sustained in an automobile collision on Hollinger Hill a short distance

from Mack on Saturday night.

Cutler received a broken rib and numerous cuts in the collision. His brother, Hobart, who was with him, escaped uninjured. Mrs. Jake Saunders, who, with her husband, occupied the other automobile, received several cuts, none of which were serious, while Mr. Saunders was also cut and bruised.

Cutler and Saunders were each driving Ford cars and met head-on on the steep grade of the hill, which is a side road in the vicinity of Mack. It was reported Saturday night that both cars were driving without headlights burning, thus making the collision almost unavoidable. The Cutler automobile was almost completely wrecked, while that owned by Saunders received but little damage and was able to continue on under its own power.

Charles went into the Army Engineers in May 1942 and served 27 months in the Aleutian Islands. He was on a troop ship headed for the South Pacific when the war ended in 1945. The ship, which had been underway for nine days, turned around and headed back to the states.

Charles spent about seven years working the Morrow farm after John Morrow died. Then he went back to the survey crew from which he finally retired. Charles wooed several young ladies in the

Charles David Cutler, four years old
Hobart Arthur Cutler, one-and-a-half years old
(Photo courtesy of Dolores Cutler O'Connor)

354

New Liberty community, including Elizabeth Morrow, but never married.

He lived in Montrose for about 30years near his brother Harry, but recently (1994) moved to Canon City, Colorado. He died in Canon City, 6 September 1994, a funeral service was held in Montrose and he was buried in the Elmwood Cemetery at Fruita. It might interest you to know that Charles and Elizabeth Morrow reserved burial plots side by side many years ago.

(Above left) Mary Cutler and grandchildren, Dale, Maxine and Dolores Cutler. (Above right) About 1943, Hobart Cutler and children Maxine, Dolores and Dale. (*Photos courtesy of Dolores Cutler O'Connor*) (Below) Hobart Cutler, as a teenager, on his pinto horse at the Likes'. (*Homer Likes Collection*)

Hobart spent most of his early years as a farmer in New Liberty. On 5 May 1931, at Green River, he was married to **Modine Jaynes**, daughter of Ed Jaynes and Zenie Taylor. Modine was born 12 June 1916 at Speer, Choctaw, Oklahoma. Evidently the family moved to Colorado when she was still quite young. Her obituary says she spent her childhood (on the Uintah) at McAndrews and Dragon, Colorado.

Hobart and Modine had three children:

Hobart Dale, born 2 December 1932
Maxine Louise (Stutler), 22 February 1937
Ruby Dolores (O'Connor), 19 June 1939

The children all attended New Liberty and Fruita Union High Schools. Hobart continued farming on the home place after the other brothers had gone elsewhere.

After Hobart and Modine's children were grown Modine sued for divorce. Hobart later left the farm, selling to a family by the name of Noetzlemann. He drifted around for a time, becoming involved in construction work at various locations from Rangely to Cortez. He later married Leona Hilton in Cortez; but they too divorced. His last business venture was a tire shop in Cortez.

Hobart died 20 June 1976 in the Eventide Nursing Home in Montrose, and is buried in Elmwood Cemetery at Fruita.

Paul graduated from the eighth grade at New Liberty in 1931 and from Fruita Union High School in 1935, after which he farmed for a year. He worked at a dairy in Grand Junction for a time, then went to Uravan where he worked in a vanadium mine.

In May of 1937 he married **Margaret Scoles**, in Green River, Utah. Paul and Margaret had met while attending high school in Fruita. They had three sons:

Robert Russell
Melvin Leroy
George Paul

Paul and family moved to Santa Maria, California, in 1940, and Paul went to work for Union Sugar Company. Later he found employment with Union Oil Company as a service station operator. Still later he became a book keeper for the company.

Some time during World War II Paul was called up by the draft board. Even though he had three children he was drafted and was kept

The Cutler boys on the homestead in New Liberty about 1919. L-R: Charles, Paul and Hobart. *(Photo courtesy of Harriet Cutler Blau)*

in the Army for about a year.

After his sons were old enough to become involved in the business, Paul went to Reno to set up the same business operation there. About that time his health began to fail, so he came back to Salinas, California, and there he died, 13 May 1972. Currently there are eight grandchildren.

Edward graduated from New Liberty in 1935 and from Fruita Union High School in 1939. During the following summer he worked at Fruita Co-op. The next summer he too, worked for the survey crew that Charles had been working for. During that summer he accidentally cut his toe with an ax and was laid up for awhile. In the next year he went to California where Paul and family were and went to work for the same company.

Edward went into the Army on 30 April 1942 and was assigned to the Signal Corps. He received basic training at Camp Crowder in Missouri, then went to Kansas City for radio school. While there he was billeted in the Pickwick Hotel (pretty classy!). He was then shipped to Camp Murphy for radar training. Next he was sent to Brisbane, Australia, spending 31 days on a troop

Photo taken about 1943 when Edward was home on leave before shipping overseas. L-R: Hobart, Mary (mother) and Edward Cutler. *(Photo courtesy of Edward Cutler)*

ship with 4,500 other servicemen. After arriving in Australia he volunteered for duty at Port Moresby, New Guinea; at that time he was as far away from home as one can get. He once volunteered for a night patrol, but luckily wasn't called. The entire group was killed in a fire-fight with the Japs that night.

Next he spent time at Leyte, Luzon and Mindanao in the Philippines. He was overseas from 30 April 1943 until 20 November 1945. He received his separation 29 November 1945.

Let's go back to Kansas City now, where Ed met **Rosalee Cheatham** while in training there. Their meeting was set up by a friend of hers. They had several dates and then were separated for three and one half years while he was overseas. The chemistry must have been right, because when he came back again she was waiting for him!

Ed arrived home at New Liberty on the day after Thanksgiving in 1945. After communicating with Rosalee, he went to Kansas City to see her on 12 December. Because of a mix-up in schedules he did not arrive at the station as expected and she had waited all day before giving up and going home. Ed arrived shortly after and called her at home, a little perturbed because she hadn't waited.

They were married 31 December 1945 at Olathe, Kansas — Rosalee says that gave her a tax deduction worth $113 for that year! They went immediately to Santa Maria, California,

Cutler Family Reunion June 1994. Lee and Janet Cutler, Tony, Rosemary, and Kyle Williams, Rosalee and Ed Cutler, Nancy, Lynn, and Kevin Cutler. *(Photo courtesy of Edward Cutler)*

where brother Paul had a job for Ed.

Edward and Rosalee had three children:

Lee Edward
Lynn Sherman
Rosemary Lois (Williams)

There are currently three grandchildren. The family has resided in Santa Maria continually through all the years.

In January an article in the Fruita Times, along with a portrait, told of Edward and Rosalee celebrating their Golden anniversary 7 January 1996 with a steak dinner in the Cabana Room in Santa Maria, California. The celebration was hosted by the Cutler's two sons and daughters-in-law, with fifty family and friends in attendance.

Harriett graduated from Fruita Union High School in 1941 and then enrolled at Ross Business College in Grand Junction, about the time Ross Business College became part of Mesa

Twins Harry and Harriett at seven years old sitting on the family car's bumper. *(Photo courtesy of Harriett Cutler Blau)*

College. While attending school there she roomed with Ruth Banning. One day, after reading an item in the news paper telling about a Civil Service Examination coming up, Ruth challenged Harriett to go with her to take the exam. Harriet passed but Ruth didn't.

On 26 March 1942, when she received a letter from Dr. Briggs, Director of the National Bureau of Standards, Harriett moved to Washington, D. C. and went to work there as purchasing agent for the Heaton Power Division.

On 2 June 1946 she was married to **Robert Blau** in Washington, D. C.

In 1949 Harriett changed jobs and went to work for the Arlington Virginia County Library, continuing there until 1954 when she took time out for family. She had two boys:

Robert
Edward

In December 1975 Harriett went to work at Smithsonian Institute and is still employed there.

Harry also graduated from Fruita Union High School in 1941 and before long went to work as a Railroad Telegrapher for the Southern Pacific Railroad at Hazen, Nevada. He served in the Navy during World War II and got as far away from home as Shanghai.

After Harry got out of the Navy in 1946, he went to work for Monarch Airlines (later Frontier Airlines) as station manager at the Montrose Airport. In 1947 he obtained a private pilot's license. He retired from Frontier after 25 years, then, for a short time, took over operation of the Montrose Airport for Montrose County. Then he started working for the flight department of Colorado Ute Electric and retired from that after 15 years.

Harry was married 26 August 1948, at Montrose, to **Faye Moore.**

They had seven children:

Maurice
Renice
Nannette
Marshall
Jeanine (died at age one year)
Lynnae
Rogene

There are currently ten grandchildren.

Harry and Faye were divorced and then Harry remarried to **Marion King** in June 1977.

Harry suffered some serious health problems brought on by complications developing from open-heart surgery in 1992. He passed away in the Valley Manor Care Center in Montrose on 24 July 1994 and was buried at Montrose.

The Cutler family had a reunion at the Redlands Community Hall on 18 June 1994. There was a large crowd in attendance, representing many descendants of Arthur and Mary Cutler. However, Harriett and Edward were the only ones present representing the second generation; Harry and Charles were still living then but unable to attend.

(Upper) The Cutler siblings on the farm in 1965. L-R: Harry, Harriett, Edward, Paul, Hobart and Charles. (Center right) The Cutler boys home on leave in 1943. L-R: Charles, Harriett, Edward, Hobart, Harry and Paul. (Lower left) Hobart, Harry, Mary (mother) and Charles in November 1944. (Lower right) Cutler sisters-in-law: L-R: Harriett, Rosalee (Ed's wife), Margaret (Paul's wife) and Modine (Hobart's wife). (*Photos courtesy of Dolores Cutler O'Connor and Harriett Cutler Blau*)

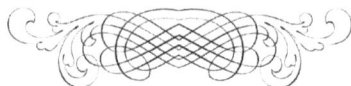

Daily

The following history was written by James Leon Daily. A few changes have been made to include obituaries and news items from *The Daily Sentinel* and personal knowledge of the author.

Patrick Allen and Hazel Daily in the '50s. *(Photo courtesy of Mary Catherine Daily Beede)*

Patrick "Pat" Allen "Al" Daily was born 11 August 1892 at Jamestown, Jewell, Kansas, to **John Uriah Daily** & **Mary Ellen Duffey**. He spent his childhood at Jamestown and graduated from high school at nearby Randall. Al received

a college education at Western State College at Gunnison, Colorado. He married **Hazel Arminda Crane** 23 August 1916 at Esbon, Jewell, Kansas. Hazel was born 5 December 1890 at Pueblo, Pueblo, Colorado, and spent her childhood and attended school at Randall, Kansas.

Allen taught school for a few years in Kansas and was manager of a mercantile and creamery for a time. While still living in Kansas, their two sons were born:

Joseph Edmund, 20 October 1917
James Leon, 15 July 1919

At that time, Kansans became aware of a new irrigation project being constructed near Grand Junction, Colorado. A lot of land had been opened up for settlement and a farmer could be assured of a crop every year due to the new canal that had been constructed to lead the water from the Colorado River to the farms. Hazel's sister and brother-in-law, Walter and Laura (Crane) Weir, had made the move and reported on the great opportunities.

Allen & Hazel made the trip to the Mack/ New Liberty area for the first "look-see" during the year 1920. The next year, 1921, they collected all the money they could and packed all the essential equipment, such as kitchen and household effects, that would be needed. Most of the early settlers brought their own cook-stoves and sewing machines. The one thing the Dailys brought to Colorado that was not a necessity was a Victrola record player and many records, because they loved music. Everything was loaded into an immigrant box car and shipped to Mack, Colorado.

As it turned out, they had waited too long in getting to Colorado; the good flat lands, including all the lands near the canal, had already been homesteaded. What they did find was a place at the end of the laterals, a flat piece of land between two salt washes next to where Lee Foss had recently located, and just to the east of Floyd Thomas's farm. Lee Foss had built on the west bank of the West Salt Wash and Allen & Hazel built their one room house on the east bank, the wash ran between the two. They knew the Fosses from Kansas, as Hazel had gone to grade school with Lee.

Allen bought a team of horses and enough equipment to clear a ten-acre plot of land which was covered with greasewood and some sagebrush. He brought water to the land and planted a crop of alfalfa. A good crop came up, but the alkali burned it up. This was a new and disappointing experience to the Dailys; they had never seen alkali before. After this happened, they started scouting for a place where they could buy the homestead rights. The first person contacted was Floyd Thomas, but he declined to sell. It happened that the homesteader to the west did not want to stay, so they were able to buy him out. [It appears from land records that they bought the homestead that had originally belonged to William Evans, of Clayton, Missouri, a winner in the drawing of 29 March 1918.]

Allen then took two teams and wagons and moved the house to the new location on the hill about a half mile south of Floyd Thomas. The house was placed over a previously excavated cellar.

The closest neighbor was Bill Knapp, just across the fence to the north. Floyd Thomas was the next neighbor to the north, and Lee Foss lived about a half mile to the northeast; the east side of the Daily place bordered on the Foss property. Later, across the road to the west, was Joe Owings. Being neighbors was very important to these settlers; they would get together to help each other harvest their crops — this was a necessity. If it happened to be a crop of alfalfa hay, it had to be taken off as soon as possible so the next crop could start growing. The whole community worked well together to harvest beans and any other crop needing a threshing machine, as the thresher went from farm to farm. These were big days for Hazel, who prepared large dinners for the harvest crew. The Daily boys grew up helping; when old enough they drove the hay stacker teams, and they also learned at an early age to hoe weeds from the crops.

It was a struggle to make a living on the mediocre farm land, and, like other farmers in the community, they searched each year for a crop that would pay enough to get them through the winter. No money came in through the summer months; groceries and supplies were bought on credit and not paid for until crops were sold in the fall.

The land was fenced with posts cut from the cedars that grew on the hills about five miles south of the farm. The cedars that were too crooked for posts were used for fuel for the cook stove and the pot-bellied heating stove. Each fall the family made a trip by wagon to the coal mine in the Bookcliffs to the north to bring back enough coal to last through the winter. Once a year, in the fall, Allen and Hazel and two or three neighbors went to Palisade, Colorado, where they picked peaches for canning. Nearly all farmers in the community raised hogs, cattle, chickens and turkeys, both for cash and to supply their needs.

The second year (1923) of farming didn't look good for the Dailys, so when they learned the school district needed a teacher for the upper four grades at the new Mack school, Allen applied for the job. Teaching was a great love of his anyway, and from all reports, he was an excellent teacher. His son, Edmund, rode with him to attend school at Mack. Allen couldn't do all the farm work and the teaching too, so occasionally he hired a young man, a neighbor to the north, to work for him. That young man was John Pacheco, a well-liked and good worker who didn't mind showing the Daily boys how to work.

There were no other farms on the south side of the Daily farm. Their acreage was divided by the right of way of the Uintah Railway and Highway 6 & 50, a major route from east to west. On the south side of the highway lay several acres of good land; on the west side of this was a natural place to build a large pond of about ten acres for a winter water supply for the farm animals. This turned out to be a wonderful skating pond; during the colder winter months it attracted people from throughout the Mack/New Liberty communities. Everett Bowen, the rural mail carrier, was a frequent visitor whom all watched and learned from; he was an outstanding figure skater. Many of the local children learned to skate from watching Mr. Bowen. The pond was also used for cutting ice in the winter to be stored in cellars for making ice cream in the summer.

Allen quit teaching in 1925 so he could spend more time on the farm. This meant that Edmund and Leon had to walk two and one-half miles to attend school in Mack. Later, about 1927-28, the high school bus started picking them up.

In the fall of the year 1927, Allen Daily, Joe Owings and Bill Knapp all decided it would be profitable to raise chickens for cash income. Each built a large chicken house. They all took a trip to the big chicken-producing area at Heber, Utah. They learned what to feed the chickens to get the best egg production. They also came back with an idea that if they could put lights on the chickens in the evenings to keep them from going to roost they would eat more and thus increase egg production. Gasoline lamps were then used each evening. They also came back singing the theme song of Al Smith of New York, who was running for President of the United States. The song was "East Side, West Side, All Around the Town." For the next few years the Daily farm had about 1,000 chickens and sold fryers to the Mack Hotel for its famous "Fried Chicken Sunday Dinners." They shipped eggs on the train to Grand Junction and Leadville.

Allen & Hazel were still trying to find extra things to do to bring in a little more money. They had plenty of hay, so they fed some of it and sold some for extra cash. They decided that raising sheep would be profitable and so bought about 500 head.

Ed Daily (see biography following), Allen's younger brother, with his wife, **Louise** and daughter **Corrine**, decided to move to Colorado from Kansas City to become farmers. **John Uriah Daily**, father of Ed and Al, also decided to move to Colorado from Kansas.

To find a place to pasture the sheep in the summer, the three of them plus Edgar Rollins, a friend in Fruita, who also had sheep, all found open land to homestead in the Douglas Pass area. This gave them a place to run the sheep in the summer.

In 1928, a baby girl was born to Allen and Hazel; she was named **Mary Catherine**. Mrs. Anna Shires, a neighbor who lived about a mile north, attended Hazel and the new baby for about ten days after the birth. Mrs. Shires was quite good at this type of work and was called on by many of her neighbors.

The big entertainment each month was the meeting of the New Liberty Community Club. Allen & Hazel took an active part, acting in the plays and singing in quartets. Both Allen and Hazel loved to dance, and they also took turns chording on the piano during the evening. The wives brought food that was served after the entertainment and before the dancing started.

As the Depression set in, it became more and more difficult to make money at any endeavor. After President Roosevelt was elected, he started many "New Deals" to help people make enough to eat. One was the "WPA" in which Allen was involved in building a new teacherage at Mack School. He sold the sheep

herd for enough to pay off the bank loan, and they were again back to farming. Allen and Hazel always made enough to pay the grocery store's yearly debt, and never got behind. They also made enough to buy a new car and a new tractor now and then, and to enlarge the house and install electricity and a phone when they came to the district in 1937. Allen was always active in community affairs and was a school board member for many years.

Joseph Edmund, Allen & Hazel's oldest son, died on 7 October 1935, as the result of an accident a week earlier. He was hit by a car as he was riding his bicycle in Grand Junction. Edmund, 18, was attending Mesa College.

Joseph Edmund Daily in the spring of 1935, high school graduate. *(Photo courtesy of Mary Catherine Daily Beede)*

James Leon attended New Liberty School during his seventh grade year, but graduated from Mack School the following year. In 1937 he graduated from Fruita Union High School, then stayed on the farm for awhile to help. In 1938, after Leon left for college,

1937 — James Leon Daily, high school graduate. *(Photo courtesy of Mary Catherine Daily Beede)*

Allen & Hazel looked at their situation and decided they were tired of farming and wanted to change their occupation. They sold the farm to Percy Blasier, and bought a rooming house in Grand Junction. Allen sold real estate, built a few houses in Grand Junction, then finally built a house on some property they had bought on the Redlands. The place had a 20-acre peach orchard. Allen ran for State Representative on the Democratic ticket, but was defeated. He was called to teach one year at the Loma Elementary School during World War II. He and Hazel lived on the peach ranch until Allen's death, 26 July 1963. Hazel then moved to an apartment in Grand Junction and enjoyed Golden Age dancing until her death, 1 January 1977.

Leon graduated from Mesa Junior College after two years, then attended Western State College at Gunnison, Colorado, for one year. While at Western State he enrolled in one of President Roosevelt's "New Deals" that allowed the college to teach pilot training under a Civilian Pilot Training Program (CPT), at no cost to the student. He enlisted 17 March 1941 in the U. S. Navy and, in December 1941, after completing pilot training in carrier based fighter planes, he received a commission as Ensign. He retired after 21 years in the Navy. By then he had attained the rank of Commander.

Early in his Navy career, he married **Anita Mae Wilson** of Grand Junction, 21 June 1942. They raised a family of six children. Before leaving the Navy he graduated from the University of Maryland and did graduate work at George Washington University at Washington, D. C. Upon retirement, he and Anita moved to the Daily farm on the Redlands where they built a new home. He taught for two years at the Orchard Mesa Junior High School, then 11 years at Mesa Junior College in Grand Junction.

Leon and Anita observed their Golden Anniversary, Saturday, 25 July 1992, at the Elks Lodge in Grand Junction. The celebration was attended by 85 relatives from both the Daily and Wilson families. Leon and Anita's six children coordinated the many family reunion activities prior to the celebration and were in complete charge of all the activities during the gathering. In addition to the six children and their spouses, 15 grandchildren and two great-grandchildren were present.

Leon died at Veterans Hospital in Denver, Colorado, 21 September 1994 at age 75.

Leon and Anita Daily, with family, at their Golden Anniversary celebration, 25 July 1992. Back row L-R: Janice, Michael, Sharon, Patrick, Kathleen and Jim. Anita and Leon sitting in front. *(Photo courtesy of Anita Daily)*

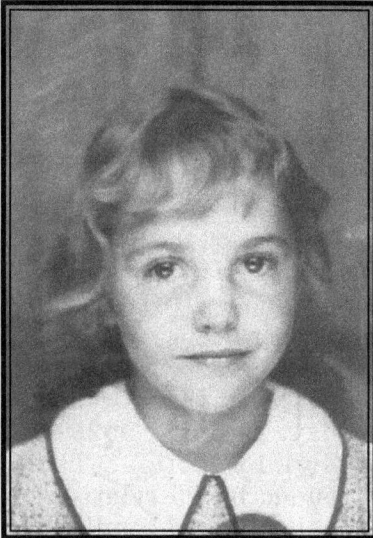

(Above) Mary Catherine Daily about 1935. (Right) 1967 — Mary Catherine's family. L-R: Mary Catherine, Dale, Joan, Carol, Ross and Wayne Beede. *(Photos courtesy of Mary Catherine Daily Beede)*

Mary Catherine married **Wayne Beede** from Loma, Colorado, after graduating from high school.

From *The Daily Sentinel* of Sunday 17 August 1947:

DAILY-BEEDE WEDDING EVENT OF SATURDAY

At 11:30 o'clock Saturday morning, Miss **Mary Catherine Daily**, daughter of Mr. and Mrs. P. A. Daily of Grand Junction, became the bride of **Wayne Edward Beede**, son of Mr. and Mrs. T. W. Beede of Loma. Msgr. F. P. Cawley read the double-ring ceremony, which took place at St. Joseph's Catholic Church.

Given in marriage by her father, the bride was attired in white net and taffeta with sequins, and her fingertip veil had a tiara of sequins. She carried an orchid and stephanotis with a white prayer book. Her maid of honor, Miss Jean Balliger, chose turquoise, and the two bridesmaids, Miss Doris Clark and Mrs. Ray Cheedle were in pastel shades. The three young women wore matching hats and mitts and carried nosegays. Joyce Beede, sister of the groom, was flower girl, and Bruce Kapaun was the ring bearer. The groom's attendant was Grant Huntley of Fruita, and ushers were William Guccini and Robert Arpke.

The wedding processional and recessional were played by Miss Mary Louise Giblin on the organ. Bouquets of gladiola decorated the church.

A dinner at La Court Hotel was held for the wedding party after the ceremony, and a reception was held from 2 to 4 o'clock at the C. E. Daily home, 545 Hill Avenue. Around 125 guests attended the reception.

After a two-week wedding trip to Yellowstone Park, the couple will make their home in Boulder, where Mr. Beede will attend Colorado University.

Mrs. Beede is a graduate of Grand Junction High School and attended Mesa College for one year. Mr. Beede served with the Army in Japan for 18 months. He is a graduate of Fruita Union High School.

Mary Catherine and Wayne raised a family of four children on a farm north of Loma. They now reside at 2630 G Rd near Grand Junction. Mary Catherine is the lone survivor of the P. A. Daily family.

Cousins. Back row, L-R: J. Leon Daily and Mary Catherine Beede, children of P. A. Daily. The other three L-R: Corrine Dawson, Margaret Cheedle and Chris Daily, children of Ed Daily, who ran the filling station in Mack. *(Photo courtesy of Mary Catherine Daily Beede)*

Christopher Edmund "Ed" Daily was born 2 June 1896 at Randall, Jewell, Kansas, to **John Uriah Daily** and **Mary Ellen Duffey**. Born and reared on a farm, Ed spent his childhood in that area, graduating from Randall High School in 1916. After one year at Kansas University, he entered the Army Aviation Corps and served two years during World War I. After discharge he finished his college training at Kansas University. On 10 Feb 1921, at Kansas City, Kansas, he married **Louise Rebecca Shotts**, who was born at Decatur, Decatur, Iowa, 14 September 1902, but spent her childhood at Chanute, Neosho, Kansas.

Ed and Louise had five children:

Christopher "Chris"
Paul Richard
Ellen
Margaret Ann
Mary Corinne

Ed and Louise lost two of their children at an early age; Paul Richard apparently died young, and daughter Ellen died in Children's Hospital in Denver, 7 February 1943, at age nine.

After a visit to the Allen Daily home in 1925, Ed and family decided to move to Colorado to live. He began work as a partner in a sheep-ranching operation with his brother, Allen, and Edgar Rollins. In December 1931, Ed and Louise bought a service station/store at Mack called "Last Chance" from C. P. Simpson. The place had four or five motel rooms (cabins) in back, and was located on the west side of Mack near the east gate of the Mack School yard. In addition to managing the store, Ed did janitorial work at the school. The business was sold in 1936 to Charlie and Alta Smith; this was where Alta Smith later located the Mack Post Office.

After a short period as a car salesman, Ed worked from 1939 to 1944 with the Mesa County Welfare Department. After a short time in Ogden, Utah, he returned to Grand Junction and opened the railroad retirement office, but resigned in 1946 to return to the Welfare Department. Also in 1946 he was Democratic candidate for Mesa County Assessor. In addition to his work with the Welfare Department, he was a volunteer Veterans' Service Officer for Mesa County, helping veterans with pensions and other problems.

Ed died at St. Mary's Hospital, 16 July 1953, after suffering a heart attack while on an outing on Grand Mesa. Louise died 28 June 1965 at the home of her daughter, Corrine, after enduring ill health for three years.

Chris married **Rachel Boyer** of Grand Junction; they have two children. **Corinne** married **Leo Dawson** of Grand Junction and raised three children. Leo and one son are deceased. **Margaret Ann** married **Ray Cheedle** of Grand Junction and raised four children.

John Uriah Daily was born 9 December 1867 in Appanoose County, Iowa. He moved with his family to Kansas when he was nine years old.

He was married **Mary Ellen Duffey**, and they were parents of four sons and three daughters, all born and raised in the area of Randall and Jamestown, Kansas. Two of the sons, Patrick Allen and Christopher Edmund, have been featured in the foregoing stories.

After the two sons moved to Colorado, mother Mary Ellen died, and John came to live with the sons and spent the remainder of his life in Colorado. As John became older he moved to an apartment in Grand Junction. It has been said that he and Leonard Thomas, another New Liberty old-timer, roomed together for a time. John died in St. Mary's Hospital in Grand Junction on Christmas Eve 1951 at age 84, and was buried at Jamestown, Kansas.

Davidson

The following was provided by Deyon Davidson Boughton. Much of this information was published in the *Fruita Times,* 14 February 1991 under the title "Route 1, Box 10, Mack." We have included some quotes from that writing.

James F. Davidson was born in 1858 in Owenton, Kentucky, to Samuel F. Davidson and Alvira T. Southworth. His father died when James was young, and he was taken under wing by P. T. Barnum. He performed at least one circus show as a high-wire aerialist under the name "Flying Frenchman."

"COLONEL" (An honorarium bestowed on prominent Kentucky gentlemen) James F. Davidson moved to the Grand Valley in 1917, living temporarily in a stone house which still stands north of Park Square in Fruita. He later settled on 60 acres on the mesa north of Mack, where he farmed and tended a substantial orchard. The mesa was known as Hildreth, later as Garnet Mesa, and more currently as Red Mesa.

James Davidson had been a promoter in St. Louis, Missouri, during the St. Louis World's fair and later in the newly opened Indian Territory oil lands near Duncan, Oklahoma. When he moved to the Mack area, one of his concerns was water, and he immediately sought and obtained a position on the Grand Valley Water Users' Association Board of Directors. He would walk from his home to Mack, where he caught a train and rode to Grand Junction to attend meetings. After the meetings were over, he would catch a train back to Mack and walk from there, home.

He had previously served as a geological survey photographer and carried his equipment with him, developing the pictures along the way. (His camera is still operable and in good condition.) Before the turn of the century, he became superintendent of St. Louis Transit Lines. The Transit Lines went out of business due to the advent of automobiles. Photography

James F. Davidson,

1880s; he is in his 20s

Emma Duff Fisher,

1894; she is 23 years, 4 months

(Both photos courtesy of Deyon Davidson Boughton)

continued to be a hobby, as did watchmaking, jewelry designing and engraving.

James F. Davidson died 2 November 1929 at Mack, and is buried in the Elmwood Cemetery at Fruita, Colorado.

$\mathcal{E}$mma Duff Fisher was born 10 June 1871 at Stillmanville, New Jersey, to Captain Richard Fisher and Emma McDuff. Richard Fisher was captain of the S.S. Emily S. Snailer that went down in the Bermuda Triangle with a cargo of Cuban sugar on Christmas Eve, 1884. Emma was provided nurses' training at the Philadelphia Hospital through auspices of the "Seamen's Dead Man Fund." Her older brother was also lost in the tragedy, and another brother paid off the loss of the uninsured sugar.

She first met James Davidson when he was a patient of Dr. Brokman. Later she moved to St. Louis, Missouri, with Dr. Brokman to help establish his medical practice. She again met James, and they were married 11 October 1893.

The couple lived in St. Louis until 1906,

Clarence Davidson,
1918 World War I Soldier

Garnet Hatcher,
about 1923

(Both photos courtesy of Deyon Davidson Boughton)

when they moved to Oklahoma, and then to Colorado in 1917.

While living north of Mack, Emma was a member of the Highline Hustlers' Club. Emma died in Grand Junction, 3 September 1955, and is buried in the Elmwood Cemetery at Fruita.

$\mathcal{C}$larence "Red" Fisher Davidson, the only child of James and Emma, was born 30 September 1895, in St. Louis, Missouri. When the family moved to Oklahoma he became best friends with the son of an Indian chief.

He acquired advanced education at Stillwater, Oklahoma. He served in the Army from March 1918 to May 1919 as Wagoner in the Toulouse area of France, carrying munitions to the front lines. He was at the front at the time of the Armistice, and received a World War I Bronze Victory Button. The family received a plaque signed by President Reagan in recognition of his military service. After the war he rejoined his family at Mack and bought 60 acres of land adjoining that of his parents.

Clarence married **Garnet Hannah Rachel Hatcher**, 30 December 1925, at Loma. Garnet was born at home 16 November 1906, in Osborne County, Kansas, to Charles David Hatcher and Lyda Mae Patterson. She weighed less than 4 pounds at birth.

The Hatchers moved to Mesa County in 1913. They homesteaded in the Loma area in 1920 and lived there until they moved to Grand

About 1925. Two lovebirds, Garnet Hatcher and Clarence Davidson, on a ladder. *(Photo courtesy of Deyon Davidson Boughton)*

Clarence "Red" Davidson — 1975   Garnet Davidson — 1980s
(Both photos courtesy of Deyon Davidson Boughton)

Charles and Lyda Hatcher — 1940s
Garnet Davidson's parents.
(Photo courtesy of Deyon Davidson Boughton)

Junction in 1947.

After marriage, Clarence and Garnet built a house on their 60 acres on the Red Mesa, north of Mack. In 1935 they built a larger home on the original James Davidson property, where they resided until 1948, when they moved to Grand Junction. They had two children:

Mary Deyon (Boughton), 24 October 1929, at Grand Junction
James Charles, 28 March 1940, at Grand Junction

Clarence was interested in civic affairs and was a member of Veterans of Foreign Wars and the Methodist Church. Garnet was active in the Highline Hustlers Club. More than just a social club, the Hustlers owned a building that was used to house indigent farm laborers.

The Hustlers also served meals to neighborhood men as they went around to the various farms in the area harvesting crops. Dances were well attended at the Highline Hustlers Club House with music provided by local musicians. The income from tickets sold at those dances was used to support local activities. (A history of Highline Hustlers Club appears earlier in this history)

Garnet was also active in Mack Community Club, and, with several other parents, worked hard to keep the Mack School open when the School District threatened to close it in 1947.

After Clarence and Garnet moved to Grand Junction in 1948, they built a home on the Redlands . Clarence became produce manager for City Market for several years. Later he went to work for the U.S. Postal Service and retired in 1960. While on the Redlands, Garnet became involved in the School Hot Lunch program and worked at that for fifteen years.

Clarence died 30 October 1983 at Florence, Colorado, and is buried in the Elmwood Cemetery at Fruita. Garnet now lives with James and family part of the time.

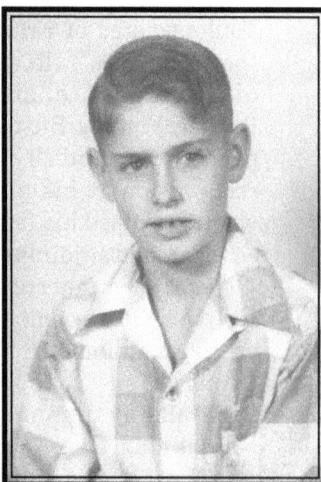

Mary Deyon Davidson, 1938   James Charles Davidson, 1950

(Both photos courtesy of Deyon Davidson Boughton)

Mary Deyon Davidson was born 24 October 1929 at Grand Junction.

We include here some excerpts from Deyon's article, "Route 1, Box 10, Mack," published in the *Fruita Times*, 14 February 1991:

The Depression hung heavily over the continent during 1929. Black Thursday and I arrived on the same date: October 24 1929. I think my father always felt I was somehow responsible for the Great Depression.

My grandfather Davidson died a few days later and I have always regretted that I didn't have a chance to know him. My Grandfather Hatcher told me that I would have liked him.

My folks built a little house across a field and road from my grandmother's home. There was a small dugout west of the house, where we raised baby chicks. Domestic water was stored in a cistern and I remember the day when a kitten fell in. Mother held me by the heels and I caught the kitten as it swam by. We warmed the little fellow in the coal stove oven.

There was a big willow tree and I could swing from it's limbs and drop into the irrigation ditch, which was great fun.

In 1934 my folks attended the Chicago World's Fair. I recall being with my grandparents Hatcher when they arrived home with a box turtle. Have you any idea how interesting a box turtle can be? I had lots of animals as companions. One in particular was a lamb who chased me through the house, hunted me in closets and jumped over boxes I put in its way. The lamb was my friend until shearing time. Somehow the shearing ruined my friendship, and I never liked the little fellow after that. Then there was "Red," the one-horned cow who tried to remove my appendix.

Outbuildings and corrals for both farms had been moved from Quaker Oats recently-defunct venture known as the Garmesa Ranch.

I was a first grader in 1935 with Mildred Hogsett teaching first, second, third and fourth grades. We moved to a new house next to my grandmother's home that year, and I came down with scarlet fever on Christmas Eve. Dr. Herman Graves came from Grand Junction to treat me and I woke up several days later. The first thing I saw was a porcelain bride and groom set given me by Jimmie Herron. I liked the groom best because he had a black top hat and black tux. The bride was all white and colorless. I played with them for many days while I recovered.

My grandmother Davidson read to me, listened to me read, and talked with me. She was a strong influence in my life, but she also abused me with stories of kidnapping, white slavery and other dangers. She pitted me against my little brother rather badly, but I remember many hours of bicycling with him in the basket on the handlebars.

Donna MacTaggart was my best friend. Donna was a year younger, but during her fourth grade year she was allowed to skip a grade and caught up. It was a practical move because with one teacher, 20 or more kids, and four classes, condensing was necessary. Besides, Helen MacTaggart was on the school board, which probably made the move easier. With four age groups together and with big kids helping little ones, everyone moved along pretty smoothly. I believe we received a much better education than many youngsters are receiving today. But then the demands of society have surely changed.

Across the road from MacTaggarts at Route 1, Box 8, were the Coxes, Bill and Helen. Milton was a few months older than I, and we were in the same grade. We were friends and enemies for the next 12 years of school. Gale was his little brother, and I always liked him best, but I liked both boys and have fond memories of our times together.

The Cox house was within walking distance from my bus stop and I often walked to Coxes to wait. Helen made bread and there was absolutely nothing better than going into her kitchen and receiving a hot slice of it. I'd walk half a mile for that bread any day, especially if the day was frigid and the bus was late.

Bill Cox was the community patriot. He had enlisted, or was drafted, into the war effort and was on his way to France when the World War I Armistice was signed. He never made it into battle, but his good intention was upper-most in his mind and he never failed to remind people of his contribution. It always irked my father, who had been in battle and under fire for months, to hear Bill talk of his conquests.

One day after World War II was declared, Bill hitched his team of horses to the wagon and Milton and I and other neighborhood kids headed out toward school picking up scrap metal. We picked up a wagon load of empty cans, old license plates, bed springs and even the remains of an old car. Bill got his picture in the paper for our efforts, which peeved us kids. After all, we were the ones who had done the work. But, after all, it was a great way to get out of going to school.

Route 1, Box 5. That brings back lots of memories. That was the Collins, Emmett and Lois. Emmett died at an early age and Lois married Roe Saunders. I remember much about the whole family. Something was always doing at the Saunders' — Monopoly, Old Maid, tag, hide-and -seek, baseball — many games could be found going on, there was always room for another player.

Delores (Dody) was the oldest. She married Delbert Slaugh, from Mack, and had a baby named Gerry. Like Vernon Brandon, Delbert was killed in World War II. Dody taught commercial classes in Fruita Union High School and later married Dave Hutchison, but died very young. Next was Edward (Eddie) who teased me, but was always nice. I probably would have had a crush on him, but he was so much older than I (maybe five years). He married Betty Hiatt of Fruita, and they still live in the area.

Then there was Maurine (Meme), and Emmett (Mutt or Boy, depending on how people felt about it), and Bobby. Bobby was the only Saunders; the others were Collins.

There were only nine days between Maurine's birthday and mine. Mother let me have Maurine stay all night quite often and I think would have kept her if she could. We fought and made up and told secrets and shared dreams and did all the things little girls have to do to grow up. I loved Maurine dearly. (Mrs. Bob Reed of Fruita).

Deyon graduated from Fruita Union High School in 1947, then acquired college credits through night classes. She worked for Rio Grande Motorways, was advertising manager for City Market stores for several years, and did freelance secretarial and advertising work in Grand Junction.

On 30 August 1949, Deyon married **Lynn E. Boughton,** son of Reuben Byron Boughton and Irene Frazer of Fruita. Lynn attended Fruita Elementary School, Fruita Union High School, Mesa College, then Colorado State College at Greeley.

He taught at schools in the valley for a time. Then, in 1954, he became a Research Chemist at the Atomic Commission Compound at Grand Junction. In 1958 he moved his family to Canon City, where he became Chief Chemist for Cotter Uranium (Commonwealth Edison). He retired in 1979.

In 1969, Deyon started Lynde Garden Center, Inc. Currently Boughtons both work at the retail/contracting business and are active in community activities.

Deyon and Lynn have three children, who are also achievers:

Keith Lynn was born at Grand Junction, 6 August 1953. He attended Denver University and later obtained a law degree from Columbus School of Law in Washington, D. C.

Keith married Janet Porton 21 March 1987.

Jeri Leah, born 2 August 1955, at Grand Junction. She graduated from Mesa College. On 4 September 1976 she married William

Lynn and Deyon Boughton family — about 1962
L-R: Jeri, Lynn, Deyon, Keith and David Boughton.
(Photo courtesy of Deyon Davidson Boughton)

Michael Fry. They have two boys: Christopher Byron and Devin James. The family resides in Canon City, Colorado.

David B., born 13 November 1957 in Grand Junction. He attended New Mexico Institute of Mining and Technology at Socorro, New Mexico. He married **Eileen O'Neill**. They have three children: **Orion Gareth, Emily Corinne** and **Erika Kathryn**. They live near Florence, Colorado.

Lynn and Deyon now have five grandchildren.

James Charles Davidson was born 28 March 1940 in Grand Junction and was named after both grandfathers. He attended schools at Mack, Fruita and Grand Junction. He served in the Navy on the Aircraft Carrier Kitty Hawk during the Vietnam conflict and was Honors Man in the Naval Radar School. He graduated from Mesa College and Colorado State University.

On 11 May 1983 Jim married **Gertrude "Tula" Barajas** of Colima, Mexico. Jim is

Gertrude "Tula", James and Ansan Davidson, Christmas day in 1987.
(Photo courtesy of Deyon Davidson Boughton)

employed with the Colorado State Division of Employment and Training at Glenwood Springs, Colorado. Tula works with the school lunch program in New Castle and the family currently resides near New Castle, Colorado. They have one son named **Ansan Immanuel**. Ansan is a direct descendant of Hernando Cortez.

Davies

The following was contributed by Gladys Davies Howser, and we are thankful for her very informative letter! We did some editing. Additional information came from obituaries and news items from *The Daily Sentinel*.

Frank "Red" Merritt Davies was born 18 August 1898 at Braceville, Illinois, and spent his childhood and school years there. He moved to Topeka, Kansas, in 1920, and was married to **Gladys O. Callighan** on 7 June 1922 in Topeka. Gladys was born 3 March 1900 at Kansas City, Kansas, to Charles V. and Sarah J. Crawford Callighan. She spent her childhood and graduated from high school in Topeka, Kansas. She received a B.A. degree in music from the American Conservatory of Music in Chicago.

Frank and Gladys met when she went back to Topeka for her mother's funeral. At the time, she was studying music in Chicago. After a few weeks of corresponding, Frank proposed by mail and Gladys accepted. Gladys' musical career was suspended at that time as Frank was working for the Santa Fe Railraod in Illinois.

They had six children:

Rosemary (Casto), born 12 February 1921
Frank Merritt Jr., 8 April 1925
Gladys Larraine (Howser), 11 September 1927
Charles "Chuck" LeRoy, 8 December 1931
Gracia Elizabeth (Bare), 26 February 1936
Marcia Electa (Albert), 26 February 1936
The first three children were born in Topeka, Kansas; Charles LeRoy in Holly,

Colorado; the twins, Gracia and Marcia, were born in Garden City, Kansas.

Red worked for the Santa Fe Railroad at La Junta, Colorado, from 1922 to 1936. At the time the twins were born, the family was living in Holly, Colorado. During that time Frank was out of work and riding the rails in all directions trying to find work so he could support his growing family. Gladys Larraine remembers when her mother was carrying the twins; she became so huge she could barely sit on her piano bench. The birth of twins was quite an occasion for that part of the country. The townspeople turned out to welcome them home from the hospital. At the time the twins were born the family was still living in Holly, Colorado.

Frank had been out of work for some time when he got a job with the Denver & Rio Grande Western Railroad and was sent to Silt, Colorado, where he worked as telegrapher. During this time he was on the "extra board" and had to work at Rifle and Glenwood Springs, or wherever he was needed. He had to move often and ultimately worked in almost every small town in western Kansas and eastern Colorado

On 24 September 1939 he was sent to Mack,

still on the "extra board." This meant that he had to work at the various "whistle stops," such as Thistle, Helper, Price, Ogden and Cisco, in Utah. He was also sent to places in Colorado, such as Leadville, Tennessee Pass, etc.

Eventually he became permanent Station agent at Mack. When he sent for his family at Silt to come live in Mack, it was an answer to prayer.

He served at Mack until 1953, when he moved to Palisade and continued as station agent there. Not long after that he retired and he and Gladys moved to Grand Junction.

Gladys Larraine recalls:

Life in our household was a series of experiences. We were never very well off. We had a kinship within the family structure, though, that comes, I think, from the hardships and controversies.

There was lots of sadness, sometimes anger, but lots of love and loyalty within our family. We had some religious strengths. My mother was determined to give us as much as she could. My dad was a religious man in his own right but he was not much for "church going." You lived by his rule with some of God's rules thrown in.

When it was possible, we went to church, as my mother usually played for the choir, or sang in the choir. She had a beautiful singing voice; she had studied voice under J. Courtland Cooper in Chicago. She had been accepted by the Hayden Choral Society, but when her mother died she was unable to go on tour with the choir, thus losing her place.

Mother had studied piano all her life. The most pleasant times in our home came when we all gathered around the piano to sing and have fun together.

Most of the homes we lived in were depot family housing, usually in

1964 — The "Red" Davies family at Red and Gladys' home in Grand Junction. L-R: Marcia, Chuck, Gladys (mother), Frank "Red" (father), Gracia, Gladys and Rosemary. *(Photo courtesy of Gladys Davies Howser)*

1947 — at Mack. Frank "Red"; Gladys, 20; and Chuck, 15. Taken when Chuck was home on leave. *(Photo courtesy of Gladys Davies Howser)*

the back of the depot. Our first real home was in Mack; it was the old Uintah Hotel that my parents purchased when the Uintah Railway shut down.

All of us went to elementary school in Mack; all attended Fruita Union High School. Rosemary never finished high school, she went to Arizona for a while to live with an aunt. During the war years she enlisted in the Army. I, Gladys, went to Fruita Union, and quit when I was a sophomore, due to family strife. I moved away, but with the persuasion of parents, moved back home and went back to high school to finish. I lost my sophomore year, so I finished a year later than I should have.

Chuck (Charles LeRoy) went as far as the ninth grade, then quit and ran away from home and joined the Army at age 15. After getting all the way through basic training and being sent to Hawaii, the Army found out he was under age and sent him back home.

Gracia was the next; she graduated from Fruita Union High School. Then she attended Mesa College for some time. Marcia, her twin, quit school after the ninth grade and, even though very young, her parents allowed her to

marry Vestal Rich, whose family lived in the Loma area.

My brother and best friend in the whole world, did not get to go on with his life. He and I were both in the eighth grade at Mack when he lost his life. He was such a wonderful person! He gave my life purpose and was my best friend in all things. He was my hero and my protector; we were only 17 months apart. I really believe that from that time on, Mack was a nightmare for me and my family. Things were never the same after that!

Losing Frank Jr., my dear brother, was the worst thing to happen in my life. It was the most devastating thing to happen to our whole family. I was visiting my friend in Silt at the time. At 3 o'clock on the day he died, I knew — I didn't know what happened, but I knew. Even though I had a few days left to spend with them, I insisted my friend's mother take me to catch the train so I could go home that night

Frank M. Davies Jr., age 14, died of an accidental gun-shot wound at Crow Bottom, southwest of Mack, on 21 November 1940. Not only was it a tragedy for his family, but for his companions as well. Frank, in company with Ralph Slaugh, Delbert Slaugh, Richard Simpson, Phillip Goodwin, and Richard Smith, had gone on a hunting outing on the Colorado River. They had secured a boat to cross the river, and after they were through hunting, were loading the boat to return. Frank was placing a couple of guns in the boat when one of them discharged; the bullet struck him near the heart.

I remember most of all the community meetings and dances at the community hall in the Mack School building. The Slaughs, who

Place where Frank Jr. was killed in November 1940. *(Photo courtesy of Gladys Davies Howser)*

lived in the old Uintah Office building next door to the hotel, all played instruments. I played the violin, and Rosemary played the accordion. Sometimes we would all get together and play for dances.

I remember Halloweens and some of the pranks we played. Mostly, though, we were severely punished if we were caught doing things that were not acceptable to our father. We did tease each other and did some ornery things, as most kids do, but I can't remember any bad things.

I remember so many friends in and around Mack — too many to mention them all. At one time I considered Irma and Ralph Slaugh as extra good friends. When I occasionally sang in public, Irma was always there to accompany me on the piano. Ralph and I were close to the same age. He was also a friend of my brother. I guess one could say I had a crush on Ralph! After my brother died many of those friendships ended.

I also have many memories of horse-back rides with you (Phyllis) and other friends. I remember the Pachecos as being good friends; some of those friendships carried into my adult life. Alice Hitner, who owned the store in Mack, gave me my first job and taught me the workings in the store, is also dear to my heart. I talked to her when my mother died; she now owns a motel in Grand Junction.

My Dad's death was hard for all of us. He had been so ill for ten years! He was so cancer-ridden and it took a long time for him to give up; he was a survivor! My Dad and I had become so close over the years — I forgave him for many things. I learned that he had so much love and wisdom, it was almost uncanny! He was really a very good person.

My mother — what a person! How strong she was all her life! She raised six children under some very hard conditions — gave up luxury to marry my Dad and had to learn to live as she did. Only the last ten years of her life did she have peace. She died with much dignity. I loved her very much and she is sorely missed!

Rosemary was in the Army near the end of World War II. Chuck was in the Army until they found out he was too young and was sent home. He went back into the Army in the '50s and served in Germany. I (Gladys) joined the Navy in 1949 and served until 1954. I was an Aviation Metalsmith (worked on airplanes) until they took the mechanical ratings away from the WAVES. I was already rated, so they sent me to Aviation Storekeeper School in Florida. From there I was sent to Hawaii, where one of my jobs was training supply officers from all branches of service.

Rosemary was married twice. She had four children from the first marriage — two boys and two girls; the boys are deceased. Rosemary lives in El Cajon, California, one daughter, Roxiena, lives near her, the other one, Corrine, lives in Minnesota.

Chuck is married and lives at Loma. For many years he has had a very successful guide business. His business was based in Clifton for many years but is now based at Loma. Chuck and his wife, Marilyn, had two sons. One died of cancer in 1988. The other son, Mark, and his wife, Shauna, live nearby in the Loma area. They are now taking over the business, as Chuck and Marilyn are preparing to retire.

Gracia married Norman Bare from Appleton. They have two children: Scott and Shauna. Scott has one son and another on the way. Shauna is a single mom with one daughter, Marie. Norman was a soil scientist working for the Federal Government, now retired. Gracia worked in various fields, but retired from the State of Idaho, where she worked as a Job Placement Counselor with the State Employment Agency.

Marcia was married first to Vestal Rich. They had five children. Marcia is now married to Don Albert, they have one daughter. Don and Marcia live in El Cajon, California, where Don works for a local paper. Marcia worked for the school lunch program until she was injured and had to retire. All her children are married and there are grandchildren.

Gladys Larraine — I married Lewis Howser 44 years ago. We met while we both were serving in the Navy. We have three sons, all are married and all live nearby. We have one granddaughter and a step granddaughter from our oldest son, Michael, who is Agricultural Inspector for the State of Idaho.

Stephen, our middle son, has no children, but they have a wonderful dog, named Lucky, whom we call 'our granddoggie.' Stephen is finishing his Ph.D. in Ecology. He has been in school all his life!

We have two grandsons from our youngest son, Patrick. Patrick is Safety Engineer and #3 man with a division of Raytheon, out of

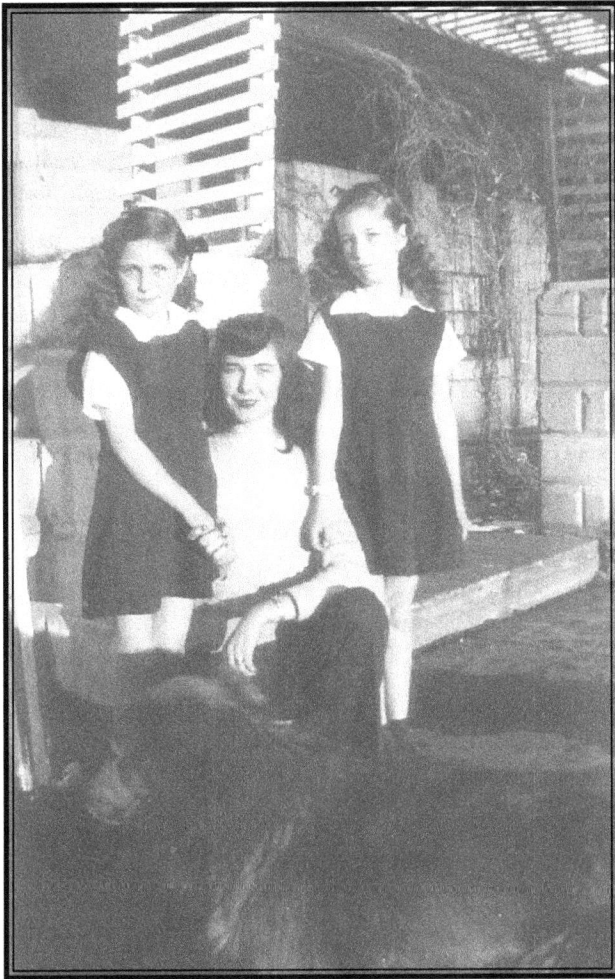

1945 — in front of the Mack Hotel, their home. Gracia and Marcia, twins, 8½ years old, and Gladys, 18, with their dog, Trerri. *(Photo courtesy of Gladys Davies Howser)*

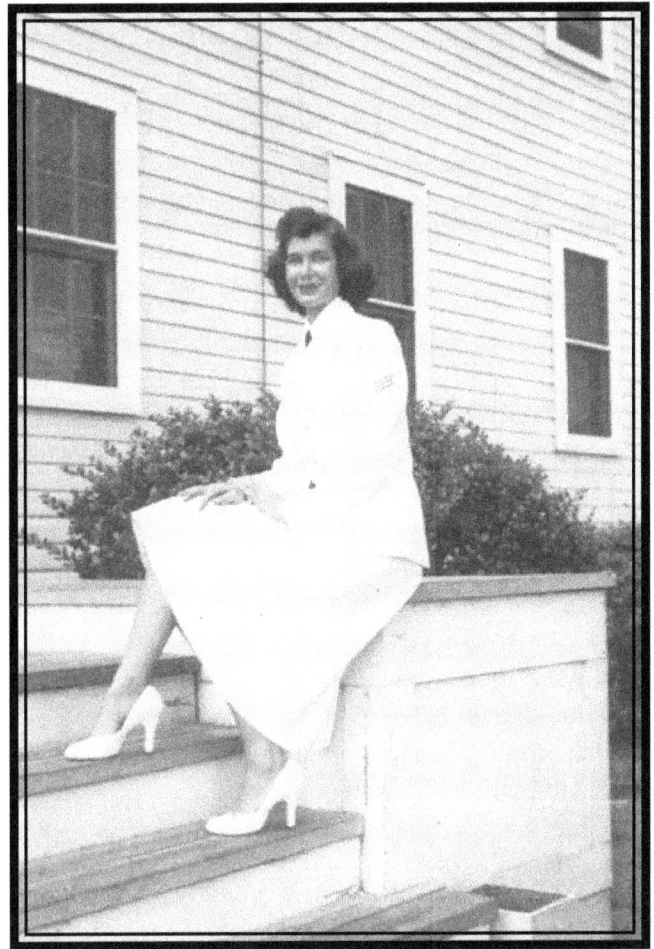

1952 — Gladys Davies at Jacksonville, Florida in her Navy uniform. *(Photo courtesy of Gladys Davies Howser)*

Massachusetts.

My husband, Lewis, works for the State of Idaho as an Investigator for the Industrial Commission. He has been in police work almost all of his life — in the Grand Junction and El Cajon police departments. He has previously earned retirement from Frito-Lay as a District Sales Manager.

After the Navy we lived in Ohio, where Lewis had a business with his parents. I worked as a legal secretary in Ohio, and also did appraisals and was a Public Notary for the State of Ohio. I worked in the credit department at Montgomery Wards in Grand Junction,and also worked at J. C. Penneys in California until illness brought me down. From then on I became a "stay at-home-mom" and didn't work until my children were raised and we moved to Pocatello in 1978. I went back to work at 50 years of age. I managed the store for the Boy Scout Council in Pocatello, and was also the Registrar and Assistant to the Activities Director until I retired in 1992.

My husband hopes to retire next year; he has lost many months of work due to illness.

We love being together as a family. My passion is sewing, and writing journals. Our grandchildren are also a big priority in our lives. We are building a cabin in the mountains and love working on that together. We work and stay there many weekends in the spring and summer. We can only get in on snowmobiles in the winter months. Our dream is to get it finished and have an old-fashioned Christmas there with all the extended families. We all love being in the outdoors with camping, snowmobiling, four-wheeling and rebuilding classic cars.

Frank (Red) M. Davies died at St. Mary's Hospital, 9 January 1969.

Gladys (Sr.) died at Bannock Geriatrics Center in Pocatello, Idaho, on 19 October 1989, at age 89.

Frank (Red), Gladys and Frank Jr. are all three buried in the Masonic Cemetery on Orchard Mesa, south of Grand Junction .

Deacon

From land records, obituaries and news items in *The Daily Sentinel.*

Jervis Butterworth Deacon was born 29 January 1863, at Princeton, New Jersey, where he spent his childhood. He came to the Grand Valley as a young man in 1884, and worked as a ranch hand for many of the old-time cattle outfits at Unaweep Canyon, Piceance Creek, and other parts of Mesa, Garfield, and Rio Blanco Counties.

He was married to **Margaret "Maggie" Elizabeth Smith (Quinlan)**, about 1893, probably in Grand Junction. She was born at Pioche, Nevada in 1877, a daughter of N. N. Smith. Maggie moved with her family to Grand Junction when she was quite young.

There were four Deacon sons:

> **Samuel Leroy**
> **Clarence**
> **George W.**
> **Walter Lee**

Samuel Leroy died in Grand Junction, May 1898, at age four, and is buried in Orchard Mesa Cemetery.

Maggie's obituary, found in *The Daily Sentinel*, 16 October 1905, says that she was the oldest daughter of N. N. Smith of Grand Junction. Margaret died of blood poisoning, at age 28, 15 October 1905, in Grand Junction, and is buried in Orchard Mesa Cemetery. The obituary also said that she was survived by two young sons, who were probably Clarence and George W.

Jervis was married twice more after he lost Maggie. First to **Minnie Voorhees** and then to **Josephine Ford**. Walter Lee was probably a son of Minnie.

Jervis filed on land north of Mack on Sec. 10 & 11 Twp 9S R103W, 13 Nov 1905, making him one of the earliest pioneers in the New Liberty area. In 1909 he moved to Glenwood Springs, where he operated a livery stable for a time. Later he lived in the Grand Junction area, until about 1925, when he returned to New Liberty and, with his sons, Clarence and Walter, began to build up a large cattle operation They owned grazing land in the Douglas Pass area where they kept cattle through the summer months. The farm land in the New Liberty area was used for raising feed crops and as a place to feed their cattle through the winter months.

Jervis died at his home at New Liberty 7 September 1949 and was buried in the Orchard Mesa Cemetery.

Clarence "Booze" Deacon was born at Grand Junction, 15 May 1902, to Jervis and Margaret Smith Deacon. He spent most of his life involved in cattle raising with his father, Jervis, and brother, Walter, in Rio Blanco, Garfield and Mesa counties in Colorado. Most of his life centered around the home place in New Liberty. However, he worked for a time on the Gilsonite Transfer Gang at Mack. He was an active member of the Colorado Cattleman's Association, the Rifle Production Credit Association, and the Colorado Farm Bureau. He was also a lifetime member of the Fraternal Order of the Eagles.

After the death of his brother, Walter, Clarence sold the ranching operation and purchased the farm formerly owned by Max Bainter (the former Knapp farm), and lived there for a number of years before his death, 10 November 1989. He was buried in Orchard Mesa Cemetery.

George W. Deacon in 1968, at the time of Walter's death, was living in La Verne, California. We have no other information on him.

Walter Lee Deacon was born 9 September 1909, at Denver. He spent most of his life farming and cattle ranching with his father Jervis and brother, Clarence. He was a member of the Elks Lodge in Rangely and the Eagles in Grand Junction. In 1956 he moved to a ranch in the Rangely area. On 24 January 1958, at Vernal, Utah, he married Modine Cutler of

Mack. Walter died 5 March 1968 at Rangely of a heart attack.

Walter Lee Deacon on the ranch in the 40s.
(Lewis Likes Collection)

He was buried in Orchard mesa Cemetery. Modine died of cancer at Grand Junction 8 December 1995 and was buried in Elmwood Cemetery at Fruita.

Dean

From land and census records, obituaries and news items in *The Daily Sentinel.*

Malcolm "Slim" H. Dean was born in South Carolina in 1887. He was married to **Laura** ? They had two daughters:

Lula Mae (Sanders), born 18 August 1912
Dorothy Lou (Love), born 28 April 1914
Both were born at Trinidad, Las Animas, Colorado.

The family moved to Mack in 1919. The girls were listed in both the Mack and New Liberty School rolls in 1920-21, so there must have been a move during that school year from Mack to New Liberty, as they were in New Liberty School during the year 1921-22.

Slim purchased a relinquishment on farm unit "A" on Section 7 R 103 W from William J. Cox in 1920. This farm was located west of Badger Wash, just south of the canal. At some point in time they lived on the east side of the wash on the William Price farm. The family may have lived for a time on the Balkwill farm, where Fred Likes and then Milton Alstatt lived in later years. We know they lived in Mack more than once.

Lula was married to **Robert Wylie Sanders Sr.** 2 July 1927. (More about Lula in the Sanders biography).

Daughter **Dorothy Lou** married **Lyle Love**, but that's all we know.

Slim spent a considerable time as maintainer and supervisor of the roads in the lower valley. On 5 October 1929, he was driving across the railroad track between the Mack depot and Mack Mercantile when he was struck by a west-bound freight train. He was thrown about 60 feet from his car and suffered serious injuries. He was in the Fruita Hospital for some time and spent many months gaining enough strength to be up and around — actually he never fully recovered.

We have learned that Slim and Laura lived on the Redlands for a time, as he was manager of the county farm at the time of daughter Lula's death in 1931.

DeCrow

Most of the following information was provided by Hester Davidson (formerly De Crow), who lives at 535 West Aspen, Space 9, in Fruita.

Grand Junction
Donald Lee, 28 November 1949 at Grand Junction
Allen Eugene, 6 August 1953 at Delta

Carl, Hester and son Duke, Carl's parents, Lewis and Elsie DeCrow and brother, Clyde "Corky" DeCrow moved to the Don Weimer farm in New Liberty in 1941, where they farmed for one year.

Carl and Hester were later divorced and he was remarried to **Elvena Fugate**. Carl died of a heart attack on 2 June 1966 and was buried in Elmwood Cemetery at Fruita.

(Above) in back, L-R: 1946 — Joe Koffer, (Carl's brother-in-law), Carl DeCrow, Florence DeCrow Koffer, Hester DeCrow holding daughter, Laura, Elsie and Lewis De Crow. Front: Duke DeCrow and Barbara Harper (Hester's sister). *(Photo courtesy of Hester Davidson)* (Right) 1937 — Carl DeCrow at the CCC camp at Glenwood Springs. (Far right) Corky DeCrow about 1943. *(Both photos from Homer and Phyllis Likes Collection)*

Carl William DeCrow was born at Beatrice, Nebraska, 26 October 1916, a son of **Louis** and **Elsie DeCrow**. He spent his early life in Topeka, Kansas, moving with his family to Fruita about 1935.

Carl spent part of 1937-38 in the Civilian Conservation Corps, assigned to Camp SP 10C at Glenwood Springs, Colorado. He was married to **Hester Wright**, daughter of Joe Wright and Leona Hindman, 16 January 1940 at Moab, Utah.

They had four sons and a daughter:

Lewis Edward "Duke", born 22 July 1940 at Fruita
Laura, 9 December 1944 at Grand Junction
Carl William Jr. "Abie", 12 February 1947 at

Demaree

From census records, obituaries and news items in *The Daily Sentinel, and* personal knowledge of the author.

Robert "Bob" P. Demaree was born 5 November 1874 in Indiana. Many of the residents of Mack/New Liberty may remember Bob Demaree, a bachelor who lived in Dry Canyon in the Bookcliff Mountains north of New Liberty. He and his brother, **Jesse Taylor Demaree**, had come to the region about 1910; the census for that year shows them in Garfield County in the Roan Creek area. Bob was listed as a rancher and his brother as a "camp cook." Jesse Taylor Demaree was buried in the Elmwood Cemetery at Fruita, 6 August 1915. One can only speculate as to the cause of Jesse's death at age 27.

Bob, perhaps with his brother's help, had built a cabin on a ledge high up on a cliff near the mouth of Dry Canyon, where he spent the winter months. Another cabin, which served for the summer months, was situated at about the 7,500 foot elevation, near the northern boundary of his property. He had built both residences so that he had water and food/feed storage and comfort for both himself and his livestock. He was seldom seen in town, but when visited at his ranch he was very friendly and loved to hear about things going on in the lower valley.

Eventually, because of advanced age, he could no longer care for his ranch and livestock, so he sold his property and moved to Fruita about 1948 and lived there for three or four years before moving to Palisade.

He had made arrangements for his funeral and cemetery plot, grave marker etc. several days before he was found dead on a park bench in Palisade Town Park. He had ended his own life. His faithful dog was standing watch and attempted to climb into the ambulance when the body was taken away. It was reported that Bob had a substantial savings account, and this seems a reasonable assumption since he probably sold his ranch for a sizable sum. There were no known heirs. Bob was buried beside his brother, 27 May 1952, in the Elmwood Cemetery at Fruita.

Denton

From obituaries and news items in *The Daily Sentinel* and personal knowledge of the author.

Thomas "Tom" Martin Denton was born 15 October 1908, to James Edward Denton and Ida May LeGrand, at Doniphan, Ripley, Missouri.

Tom moved to Fruita at age 8 with his family and attended school at Fruita.

He was married 10 November 1929 to Marguerite Wesner in Fruita. Marguerite was born 20 March 1911, at Glade Park, Colorado, to Arthur John Wesner and Augustus Bailey. She spent her early childhood in Oklahoma, New Mexico and Colorado.

Tom and Marguerite had ten children:

Edward A.
Earle D.
Louie L.
Claude H.
Glen M.
Ernest R.
Eugene
Harry Jerry
Beverly (Means)
June (DeVries)

Tom became a well-known farmer in the Fruita, Loma, New Liberty and Mack communities. He rented the Bob Cox farm in New Liberty for several years, and later purchased a farm northeast of Mack.

Tom and Marguerite lost two of their children: Harry Jerry died when just 11 days old; Eugene died in a truck accident in Glenwood Canyon 21 May 1968, at age 36. He left a wife and two daughters.

Tom and Marguerite were involved in an auto accident in December 1977, and Marguerite died of injuries incurred at that time. She was buried in Elmwood Cemetery at Fruita.

Tom remarried to **Lora Gallatin Layton**, 1 April 1988, in Grand Junction.

Tom spent some time at LaVilla Grande Care Center in Grand Junction before his death, 1 September 1990. He was buried in Elmwood Cemetery

Diehl

Information is from an interview with Leona Watson, obituaries, and news items in *The Daily Sentinel.*

Fred M. Diehl was born at Woodsfield, Monroe, Ohio, 22 May 1867. He moved to Rico, Dolores, Colorado, in 1892, then to Grand Junction in 1896. He was married 20 December 1901, in Grand Junction to **Edith Grace McCabe** who was born 7 January 1880, at Selbyville, Sussex, Delaware. Her parents, J. Q. and Kate McCabe, brought Edith and three brothers to Grand Junction in 1883. At that time Grand Junction was only a few log cabins and tents.

Fred and Edith had two daughters:

Leona C. (Watson), born 3 March 1904
Frieda A. (Anderson), 13 December 1909
Both were born in Grand Junction.

Fred was a carpenter and later a building contractor who had much to do with the building of Grand Junction. In October 1905, for a little change in scenery, he homesteaded 40 acres (later it was amended to 69 acres) in the New Liberty district. Edith refused to live out there with him, so Fred would go out at odd times to do his development work. His daughter, Leona, accompanied him and stayed with him on the homestead in the summer months during school vacation. During these times Leona became friends with Mary Maluy and other nearby neighbors. Leona vividly remembers riding horseback down to the Maluy's to get milk for her and her father to drink. It appears that Fred didn't live there very much after the proving-up work was done.

The "Diehl Place," as we knew it, had many renters through the years, but was finally sold in 1947 to James Cooper and Howard Milema.

Fred was a joiner; he was a member of the First Methodist Church, a charter member of Local 244 of the Carpenters Union, the Mesa Lodge of IOOF. He retired in 1946.

Soon after celebrating their 52nd anniversary, Edith died 16 June 1954. Fred died 1 June 1959 at age 92.

Leona became an accomplished pianist and organist. She taught piano and organ until late in life. She joined the Rebekah Lodge at 22 years of age and has been very active since. She became the Noble Grand in 1937 and has been the official musician until recently. Leona married **Frank Watson** 20 June 1937, in Grand Junction. Frank was a teacher and a car salesman during his lifetime. When Frank and Leona married they moved into a new home that her father built for them in 1936 on Chipeta Avenue in Grand Junction.

Frank and Leona adopted their daughter, **Gayleen (Eubanks)** shortly after her birth, 13 December 1944. She lives in Denver and has two sons and one daughter.

Leona is now 93 years old (1997). She moved into the Mesa View Retirement Residence in Grand Junction in March of 1997. Leona left her home of 60 years and her organ, but says she has taken her piano with her. She is very happy in the retirement center with all the new neighbors, and also gets the opportunity to go downtown via the driver and van supplied. This way she gets to see what is going on and feels a part of things.

Frieda married Harry Anderson and they had two boys and one girl. The boys live in Cedaredge and the girl lives in Maryland. Frieda died in California in 1996.

Dillbeck

Information from obituaries and news items in *The Daily Sentinel*. Some information provided by Virginia Selke Eddings and the author.

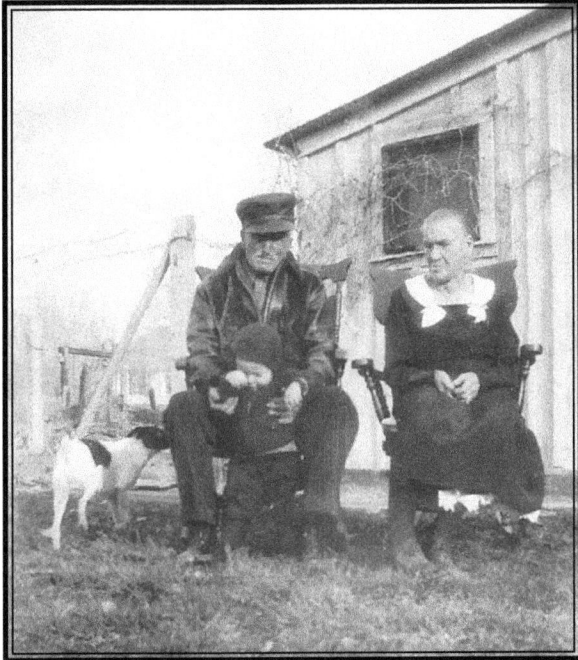

(Above) William Dillbeck with great-grandson, Ronald E. Eddings, and Sarah Dillbeck, 1935, in Mack. (Below) L-R: Ronald E., William "Buss," and George Eddings, William and Sarah Dillbeck, 1935. *(Photos courtesy of Virginia Eddings)*

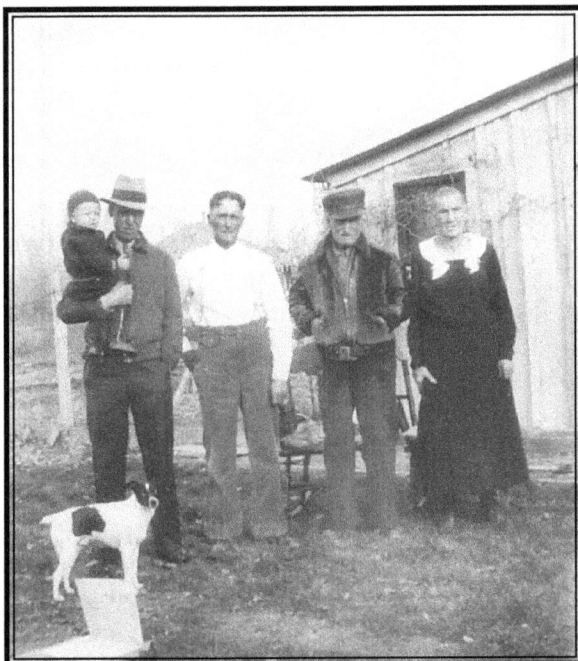

William "Bill" A. Dillbeck was born 18 December 1860, at Mount Vernon, Lawrence, Missouri. He married **Sarah Elizabeth Stewart**, 29 July 1879, at Marionville, Lawrence, Missouri. Sarah was born 7 May 1861, in Pulaski County, Missouri. The couple had three daughters:

Mary Lee (Eddings)
Berta (Sparks)
Cordie (Dennis)
(A son died as an infant)

While living near Strafford, Missouri, Bill and Sarah Dillbeck had given a home to a young man by the name William Matlock. Matlock had come to Colorado and worked for the Oscar Turner family. He returned to Missouri and told the Dillbecks and the Eddings about all the beauties and advantages of Colorado. Because of that influence the Dillbecks and the Eddings all came to Fruita, Colorado in 1912 on the same train. Isn't it strange that young Matlock later returned to Missouri and lived the rest of his life there!

Sometime in the early 1930s, before Eddings moved to Mack, Bill and Sarah Dillbeck moved to the Malcolm Dean homestead west of Badger Wash in New Liberty, south of the Highline Canal. When they retired in the mid-1930s they purchased the Wagaman home just north of the Mack Mercantile. They wanted to be near their daughters, Mary Eddings and Berta Sparks.

It was noted in the Mack items of 31 July 1941 that William and Sarah celebrated their 63rd wedding anniversary. Both were said to be past 80 years old. They lived in Mack until 13 August 1943, then moved to Denver to live with their daughter, Cordie Dennis.

William died in Denver 18 May 1944, buried in the Riverside Cemetery in Denver. Then Sarah lived with daughter Mary Eddings until she died 20 December 1947. She was buried next to her father, Francis Stewart, in the Elmwood Cemetery at Fruita.

Dille

Information from obituaries and news items in *The Daily Sentinel* and personal knowledge of the author.

William "Bill" Clarkson Dille was born 13 October 1887, and Joseph "Joe" L. Dille was born 19 April 1895, at Casey, Iowa, to I. S. and Emma Eva Dille. The family moved to Tonganoxi, Kansas, for a time and then to Palisade, Colorado, in 1902.

In 1918 Joe filed on farm unit "A" on Sec. 2 R 103 W and Bill on unit "B" which was partly in Sec. 2 and partly in Sec. 3. Their farms bordered each other and also joined the Carroll and Pollock farms on the south. The records show that Joe sold out to Ernest E. Ball in 1920 and apparently moved to Oakland, California, in the 1930s, where he died 1 September 1965. He was buried in the Palisade Cemetery. Joe had married, but we do not have the name of his wife.

Bill continued to live on the farm until about 1933. He never married. He died in Grand Junction 24 May 1959, and was buried in the Palisade Cemetery.

(Above) Ed, Ida and grandchildren. L-R: Robert Gene Likes, Ida Bailey Dodge, William Ray and Edward Lee Likes; Edward Waite Dodge in back. (Below) Ida Mary Bailey and Edward Waite Dodge, 1944. *(Photos courtesy of Robert Likes)*

Dodge

Information from family records and personal knowledge of the author

Edward Waite Dodge was born in Missouri and spent his childhood there. In about 1914 he married **Ida Mary Bailey** in Barton County, Missouri. They had two children:

Ruby Pearl, born 22 April 1915, at Golden Barton, Missouri
Cecil Russell, 4 June 1919, at Bradleyville, Barton, Missouri

Ruby and Cecil attended schools in that area.

Ruby graduated from high school in Jerico Springs, Missouri.

In April 1933 the Dodge family moved to western Colorado and purchased the George W. Fisher farm in New Liberty. Cecil attended Fruita Union High School, and Ruby was employed for a time in the Clem Maluy household.

Edward was quite a trader, so he didn't stay in one place very long. Within two years he and Ida moved to a farm east of Whitewater, near Purdy Mesa, on Kannah Creek. Not much later they moved to Grand Junction, where, for several years, they ran a second-hand store on Colorado Avenue. In 1937 Ed became interested in another second-hand store in Twin Falls, Idaho, and did some more trading. The Dodges lived in Idaho from then on. Ed and Ida died about 20 years ago.

Ruby married **Clyde William Likes Jr.**, 25 November 1933. (See Clyde Likes story). Some time after Clyde's death Ruby married Ivan Thelander; they made their home in Ozark, Missouri. She died there in 1990. Clyde, Ruby

Clyde Likes Family, October 1981. Back Row, L-R: Edward, Clyde, Ruby Likes, Sherry holding Annabeth and Frederick holding Michelle Frahm. In front: Kathleen holding Leigh Ann Likes, Rose and Bobby Likes, Susy holding her two kids, Venessa and Chad, and Kelly Bess *(Homer Likes Photo Collection)*

and their son Billy are all buried in the Elmwood Cemetery at Fruita.

Cecil married **Vera Lohr** at Twin Falls, Idaho, and they have two daughters. Cecil and Vera currently live at Pocatello, Idaho.

Ruby Dodge and Clyde Likes
(Likes Photo Collection)

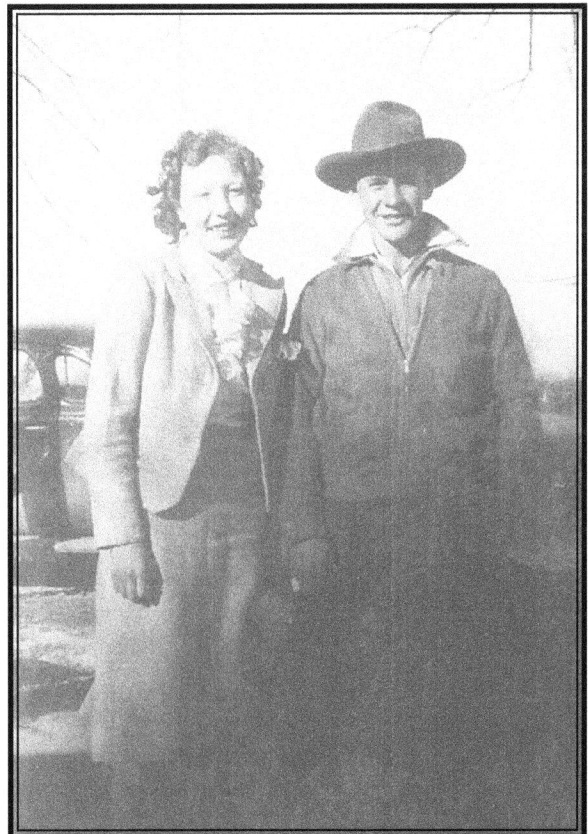

Cecil and Vera Lohr Dodge
(Photo courtesy of Robert Likes)

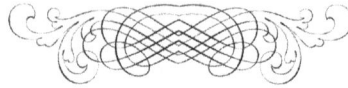

Earp

The Earp/Clow/Snavely story was compiled from census records, obituaries and New Liberty news items from *The Daily Sentinel.* Plus information from Louise Clow Likes, and personal knowledge of the author.

John Randolph Earp was born 27 October 1854 at Indianola, Warren, Iowa, to Lorenzo Dow and Cerena Iler Earp.

We don't know if John had any particular pride in being a first cousin of the infamous Earp brothers of Tombstone, Arizona. However, his granddaughter, Louise Clow Likes, said her grandfather, when asked, *did* admit that he knew he was a first cousin of Wyatt Earp, but never talked about it otherwise. Wyatt's father and John's father were brothers.

Research has revealed that Cerena was Lorenzo Earp's second wife. He had nine children by the first marriage while living in Kentucky and Illinois. The first child of the nine children born to Cerena was born in Warren County, Illinois. Lorenzo and family lived in Warren County, Illinois, until about 1853, then moved to Warren County, Iowa. In about 1860 they moved to Jasper County, Iowa, and lived near the town of Galesburg, 30 miles east of Des Moines, at least until John was about 25 years old. It appears that Lorenzo may have believed that it was his personal responsibility to "multiply and replenish the earth." Eighteen children — wow!

Many years later, at age 85, John recalled for *The Daily Sentinel* reporter, his experiences as a boy growing up on the Iowa farm where the family raised hogs. At market time the hogs were trailed (not hauled) some 80 miles to the nearest rail-point at Eddyville, Iowa, from whence they were shipped to Chicago where they were sold at two to four cents per pound. He also recalled memories of the Civil War and the assassination of President Abraham Lincoln.

John left Iowa in 1883 and moved to Wheeler County, Nebraska, where he filed on a homestead. He married **Mary Elizabeth Apple** at Spalding, Greeley, Nebraska, 3 March 1886. Mary Apple was born at Fairfield, Indiana, 27 November 1857. In 1870 she moved with her family to Jasper County, Iowa, where they lived near the Earp family.

Picture taken at Florence, Colorado, in 1919. L-R: John and Mary Earp, Sara and George Clow with Louise and Vauna Clow in front. *(Photo courtesy of Louise Clow Likes)*

While John and Mary lived on the homestead near Bartlett, Nebraska, they had four children. Their third child probably died young, as the information in the 1900 census is that she had four children and three were living. Those three were:

Selma Bertha, born 21 September 1888
Elmer Victor (Vic), 20 August 1890
Sara Belle, 3 June 1894

Between 1899 and 1900 they moved to Guthrie Center, Iowa, and lived there until coming to Green River, Utah, in 1907. At Green River John hoped to get land under a proposed irrigation project on the river, but that failed to materialize.

Selma Snavely with nieces, Vauna and Louise Clow, 11 May 1919 at Florence, Colorado. *(Photo courtesy Louise Clow Likes)*

Early in 1918, John and Mary moved to Grand Junction, and on 29 March his name was drawn for a homestead on Mack Mesa. It is not understood why he was allowed to homestead in Colorado after having homesteaded in Nebraska, since according to law, a person was allowed to homestead only one time.

For some reason the names of Mr. and Mrs. John Earp appear in the list of those who voted for the name of the New Liberty school district in June 1922. One would suppose they would have been part of the Mack district.

They lived on the farm until 1925, when they sold out to Blair MacTaggart and moved to Grand Junction. Mary died of cancer 26 June 1927, at age 69, and was buried in the Earp family plot in the Elmwood Cemetery at Fruita. John continued living in Grand Junction for nearly 17 more years, the last four of which were spent with his daughter Selma. He died 16 February 1943, at age 89, and is also buried in Elmwood Cemetery.

Selma Bertha Earp, was born at Bartlett, Wheeler, Nebraska, 21 September 1888. She attained her elementary and high school education at Green River, Utah, and then studied for her teacher's certificate at Salt Lake City. She taught at some point in time at the school in the little community of La Sal, Utah, south of Moab. She also taught for a time at a little known school at Dewey Bridge, south of Cisco, Utah. While there she boarded with the Cato family. It may have been while teaching there that she met her future husband. On 7 June 1911, she was married to **Lewis Vernon "Vern" Snavely** at Green River. They had no children.

After marriage Vern and Selma continued to live in Utah for about seven more years, spending some of the time in Castle Valley, upriver from Moab.

Selma taught at New Liberty School for two years, from 1921 to 1923. During the 1924-25 school year she taught at Atchee. (See the Snavely story for more; see also "The Turkey")

(Upper) Elmer Victor Earp, retired railroader who saw the old Uintah Railway through its heyday, checks the battery-run clock which once occupied the station at Atchee. (Center) Engineer Earp (in cab) fired up No. 51 for the first time after it was unloaded at Mack, in 1928. He was the first man to take the "Old 51" on its run from Atchee to the gilsonite works in Utah when the new super engine was added to the Uintah line. (Lower) As superintendent of the line, Earp had at his disposal this luxurious converted Model "T" Ford which served as scout car, delivery room and ambulance when occasion warranted. It could haul two motor cars loaded with section men and their tools up the 5 per cent grade from Wendella to Baxter Pass — in low gear, no faster than a walk. *(The Daily Sentinel, 17 September 1962, Section "Western Slope Living," article "When Enough's Enough," courtesy of Betty Booth Garber)*

&lmer Victor "Vic" Earp was born 20 August 1890, at Bartlett, Wheeler , Nebraska. In 1899/1900 he moved with his family to Guthrie Center, Iowa; then in 1907 to Green River, Utah. While in Green River he began his career in railroading as call boy for the Denver & Rio Grande Railroad.

Vic was married twice; his first wife was **Sarah Elizabeth Davis**, who was born 27 Sept 1894, at Naples, Uintah County, Utah. Her parents were William George Davis and Margaret Lucina Bird. Victor and Elizabeth had two daughters: **Barta Helen**, who died shortly after birth, and **Margaret Elizabeth**. We know very little about Sarah Elizabeth and Margaret Elizabeth except that their names appeared occasionally in Atchee and Mack news items. The 1920 census shows the family in Atchee with daughter Margaret age 2½ (born in Colorado). Victor and Elizabeth were later divorced.

In 1912 Vic went to work as a fireman for the Uintah Railway. A few years later, around 1916, he became an engineer. In 1928, he was the engineer who piloted the new No. 51, an articulated[†] locomotive built by Baldwin, over Baxter Pass after it arrived in Mack.

During the years Vic served as engineer he lived at Atchee, but after he became superintendent he moved to Mack. As superintendent he saw the Uintah come to the end of its operation in 1939.

After the demise of the railroad he moved to Morenci, Arizona, and worked for Phelps-Dodge Mining Company. On 3 March 1941, he married **Ila F. Switzer** at Safford, Arizona. In 1955, at age 65, Vic retired with pensions from both Phelps-Dodge and Barber Asphalt Co. A more complete account of Victor Earp's life and career may be found in *The Daily Sentinel* of 17 Sept. 1962. After retirement Vic lived several years in Grand Junction, where he died 11 Aug 1967. He is buried in the Orchard Mesa Cemetery.

[†] No. 51 was an articulated locomotive, but was called a Mallet (Mal'-lee). A Mallet is a compound locomotive — one which uses steam twice, first in the rear or high-pressure cylinders and then in the large low-pressure cylinders, before exhausting it to the atmosphere. The articulateds were simple locomotives, utilizing high pressure steam in all four cylinders.

Sara Belle Earp was born at Bartlett, Wheeler County, Nebraska, 3 June 1894. She moved with her family to Guthrie Center, Iowa, when she was five years old; she moved to Green River, Utah, seven years later. She attended schools in Green River and then sought employment in Salt Lake City. She was working at a candy factory in Salt Lake City when she met **George Francis Clow**, a resident of Garfield, a town no longer on the map, located near the present site of Magna, in Salt Lake County.

With the help of some information provided by Sara Belle's daughter, Louise Clow Likes, and with a little research, we have compiled some interesting information on George Francis Clow.

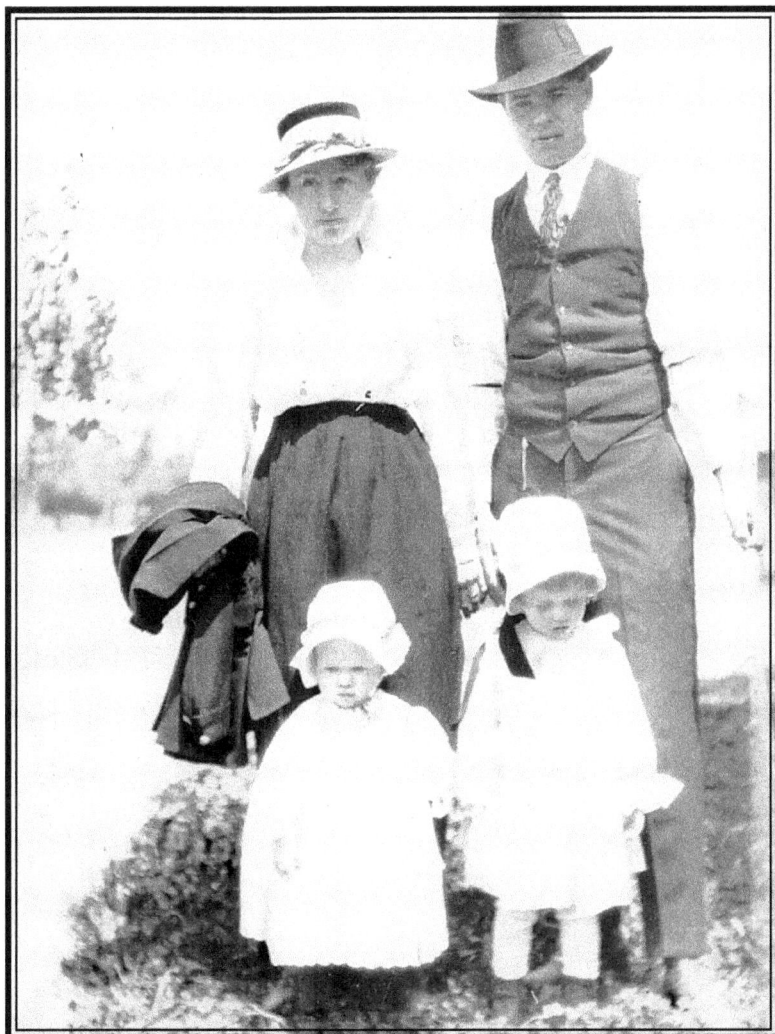

1919, Sara and George Clow with their daughters, Vauna Marie and Louise Berthel. (*Courtesy of Louise Clow Likes*)

George Francis Clow was born to George Clow and Lillian Frances Bloom 19 March 1889, at Leadville, Lake, Colorado. While he was a very young child George's father died in a mine accident and within a short period of time his mother remarried and left. The family never heard from her again. George was raised by his grandmother, Marion (Mary) Bloom; George went by the name Bloom until he was grown.

George moved to Salt Lake City, Utah, at least as early as 1911. At that time he is identified in a Salt Lake City Directory, as George F. Clow, "Laundry Worker." In the 1915 through 1918 directories he is identified as a barber. Of course, through those later years he had a young family. We learned of other Clow families in the Salt Lake area, but we don't know how they were related.

George and Sara Belle Earp were married at Farmington, Davis, Utah, 19 October 1914. Soon after marriage they set up housekeeping in Salt Lake County, at a place called Pleasant Green, in the vicinity of Magna. They moved around a lot, as you can see from the birthplaces of the children.

The children were:

Louise Berthel, born at Green River, Emery, Utah, 24 July 1915 (Remember, Sara's parents were living there at that time)
Vauna Marie, 31 January 1917, at Magna, Salt Lake, Utah
Donald Vernon, 3 May 1919, at Florence, Fremont, Colorado.

We found the family listed in the 1920 census at Florence, the children were then very young. George's occupation at that time was given as foreman in a smelter.

The family was living in the Grand Junction area when George and Sara separated; she was awarded a divorce in Grand Junction in 1923.

George had no automobile and on one occasion after the divorce, got off the train at Mack and walked out to New Liberty to see his children, who were staying with Vern

388

and Selma Snavely. Vern and Selma saw him coming and Vern met George at the gate and told him he wouldn't be allowed to see the children. George was devastated, but went away peacefully and was not heard from for a long time. He ultimately remarried, settled in Portland, Oregon, and died there 6 September 1957. It appears George had more than his share of hard knocks.

Contrary to the opinion of most who knew of him, George was never a homesteader in New Liberty.

Sara continued to live in the Mack/Grand Junction area with her children while she worked at various jobs. On 17 April 1926, she was married to **William "Bill" A. Knapp**, in Grand Junction, at the home of her parents.

Bill, a New Liberty homesteader, was born 17 October 1892, at Red Bud, Randolph, Illinois. He attended Valparaiso University, at Valparaiso, Indiana, and later, in 1918, enlisted in the Army and served in the Philippines. In 1920 he filed on 60 acres of land — Unit F Sec. 21 of R 103 W. The homestead was located south of Clem Maluy's, and east of Ben Harrison's.

Soon after marriage Bill and Sara and Sara's children moved to a farm in Sec. 28 Twp 9 S, just north of P. A. Daily and south of Floyd Thomas. Records show the farm was purchased 20 October 1927, in Sara's name, from Ralph M. Todd, one of the early homesteaders who filed on land years before the irrigation project was started. Bill and Sara built a new home on that property soon after acquiring it.

In 1933 Bill and Sara Knapp traded their New Liberty farm to Max and Virginia Latham Bainter for property in the Roan Creek area, near DeBeque, Colorado. Bill and Sara, Vauna and Donald, soon became dissatisfied with living there and subsequently moved to a farm north of Grand Junction on North 7th St.

Sara's life came to an untimely end; she had some sort of ailment for which she was receiving treatment from a doctor in Moab. On 27 May 1937, as she was in Moab for treatment, she died at age 42. She is buried in the Earp family plot in Elmwood Cemetery at Fruita.

After losing Sara, Bill remarried to **Farrie**

Veatch Croley on 8 May 1938. Bill died 10 August 1973, and was buried in Grand Junction Municipal Cemetery.

Louise Berthel Clow spent most of her childhood in the Mack/New Liberty area. However, she began her schooling at Hawthorne School in Grand Junction, she attended Mack School, then later New Liberty and Fruita Union High Schools. Louise said that when she was very young she was so shy she had a tough time with school and as a consequence failed a grade and spent the rest of her school years in the same grade as sister Vauna.

Louise, Vauna and Donald had to walk from the Knapp home (they went by the name Knapp at that time, though they were never legally adopted by Bill) for over two miles to get to New Liberty School. Many times during the winter they would come into the school building with their hair, eyebrows and clothing covered with frost created from their breathing as they walked. They would immediately get close to the stove standing in the corner and would have to stay there for a considerable time to thaw out. Hardship most of us will never know!!

During their early years, Louise and Vauna often spent time with Grandpa and Grandma Earp at their home on Mack Mesa and later in Grand Junction. Donald was a favorite of Aunt Selma Snavely and spent a lot of time at her home. Aunt Selma had no children of her own, so she lavished a lot of affection on her sister's children, especially little Donald.

If you will look in the lower left hand corner of the picture of the New Liberty School student body taken in spring of 1922 (page 114), you will see Louise and Vauna seated together. They graduated from the eighth grade at New Liberty in the spring of 1930, along with Betty Curtis and Harold Sanders.

Louise Clow Likes and sister, Vauna Clow, on Fred and Louise' residence at New Liberty in 1940. *(Homer Likes Collection)*

Louise married **Elmer Fred Likes** on 3 March 1933. (See biography of Fred Likes). She was a student at Fruita Union High School and not quite 18 when she and Fred decided to get married without her parent's approval. Then she had to endure the indignity of her parents not accepting her marriage and disowning her. Eventually amends were made, but the experience left scars that never healed. In spite of that experience she had a happy marriage with Fred that lasted nearly 60 years. (They were married during the worst of the depression — Fred had to borrow $5 to pay for the marriage license).

Vauna Marie Clow spent most of her childhood in the Mack/New Liberty area. She started her schooling in the original Mack School building that stood north of the Mack Mercantile. (Her name doesn't show in the Mack student lists).

She graduated from the eighth grade at New

Liberty School in 1930 and from Fruita Union High School in 1934. She married **Roy Humphries** at Moab, Utah, 9 March 1941. They had one child: **Sharon**. Vauna and Roy were later divorced. Vauna remarried **William Carrington** and now lives in Las Vegas, Nevada.

Donald Vernon Clow spent most of his childhood in the Mack/New Liberty area, attending school at New Liberty and Fruita Union High School.

In August 1932 he became very ill with typhoid fever. It was feared, for awhile, that he would lose his life. He lost all his hair and was in bed for a long time.

He moved with his mother and step-father to the De Beque area and later to the Grand Junction area. On 10 March 1940, he married **Mary Smith** at Moab, Utah. They had one son, **Gary**. Donald and Mary were later divorced.

The Daily Sentinel of 1 August 1946 gave notice of discharge of Donald Vernon Clow, MP, stating that he had served from 29 August 1944 until 27 June 1946. Don died at Portland, Oregon, in June 1975.

Ebright

The following is from a history written by Lois Wilson Ebright, obituaries and news items from *The Daily Sentinel, and s*ome input by the author.

Bernard "Fat" Earle Ebright was born 23 May 1913, at Concordia, Cloud, Kansas, to Scott C. Ebright and Mae Carter. On 22 April 1935, at Pomona, Los Angeles, California, he was married to **Lois Maurine Wilson**, who was born 25 November 1916 at Walsh, Baca, Colorado, daughter of Henry Edward Wilson and Bertha May Noble. We have no other information about their childhood.

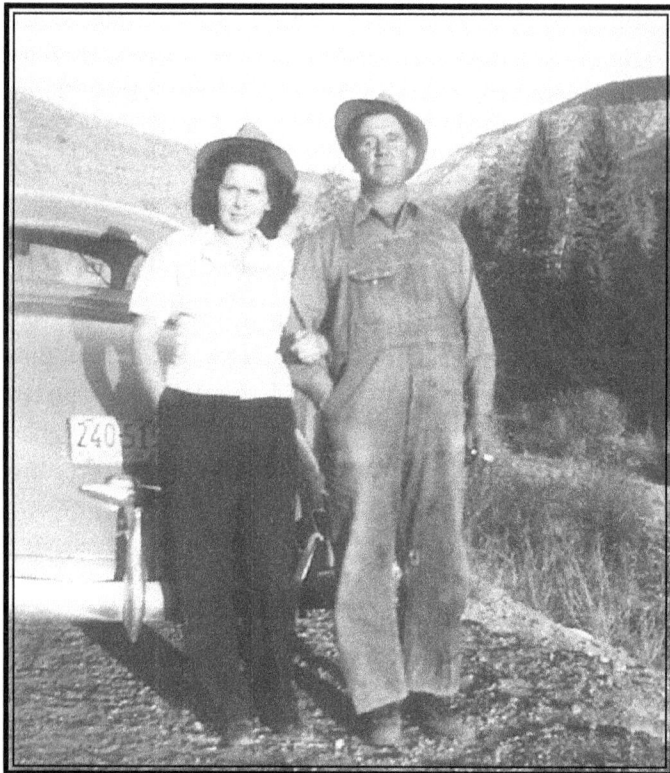

(Above) Lois Maurine and Bernard "Fat" Ebright, 1945. (Below) Shirley Ebright, Grandmother Bertha Wilson and Leon Ebright in front of the Ebright house in New Liberty, 1943. *(Photos courtesy of Lois Ebright Kimmel)*

They had two children:

Shirley Mae (Johnson), born 7 February 1936
Leon Earl, 16 May 1940
Both were born at Burbank, California.

Lois' related story:

We were among the later settlers in the New Liberty area. In 1938 we bought desert land at the east edge of the community adjoining Hobart and Modine Cutler on the south. While the family was still living in Grand Junction, my father, Ed Wilson and Carroll Wing helped Fat haul ties from the recently abandoned Uintah Railway tracks with which they built a small house and a barn. While living in a tent the men built a small barn on a hill, then later built a two-room house. The family finally got moved about 1942. The house was about three-fourths of a mile from the main road, so it was hard to get in and out during stormy weather.

Using some of the railroad ties we had left we later added another room and a small porch, which we used for a bedroom,

Fat's grandfather, Smiley M. Carter, had quit ranching up in the Smith Fork Canyon near Crawford, Colorado, and gave us a nice team of Belgian mares (Lady and Liz), some pieces of farm equipment, five head of Guernsey cows and a thousand dollars, which was a lot of money in those days. He also gave us his old brand he used for his ranch which was an upside down Y and a lazy U. We used this brand for our cattle for several years. After leaving the ranch, we let the brand lapse. Later I contacted Jay Rowe, when he was Colorado State Brand Inspector, in Denver; he found that no one had picked it up, so I have paid the assessment on it since.

Grandpa Carter liked to come down to the ranch quite often to help, but he was around 75 years old and couldn't do very much. One time, when harrowing, his foot slipped off the harrow and he injured his foot, then the horse stepped on his foot, also. When he was a boy and lived near Pueblo, Colorado, he would go on those cattle drives out of Texas. A cowboy taught him how to read, but he never learned to write. He let grandmother Carter do that for him after he married her. Later he mined at Crested Butte, Colorado, broke horses for ranchers at Maher, Colorado, and then owned

(Above left) About 1945. L-R: Leon, Lois and Shirley Ebright.

(Above center) Shirley Ebright showing her 4-H guernsey calf at the fair in Fruita, about 1948.

(Above right) Leon and Shirley with their favorite toys, about 1943, in front of their home in New Liberty.

(Left) The Ebrights and the Cutlers about 1944. Children L-R: Leon and Shirley Ebright and Maxine and Dolores Cutler. In back: Lois Ebright and Grandma Mary Cutler.

(Below) The cow and horse corral on the Ebright farm in New Liberty. *(Photos courtesy of Lois Ebright Kimmel)*

392

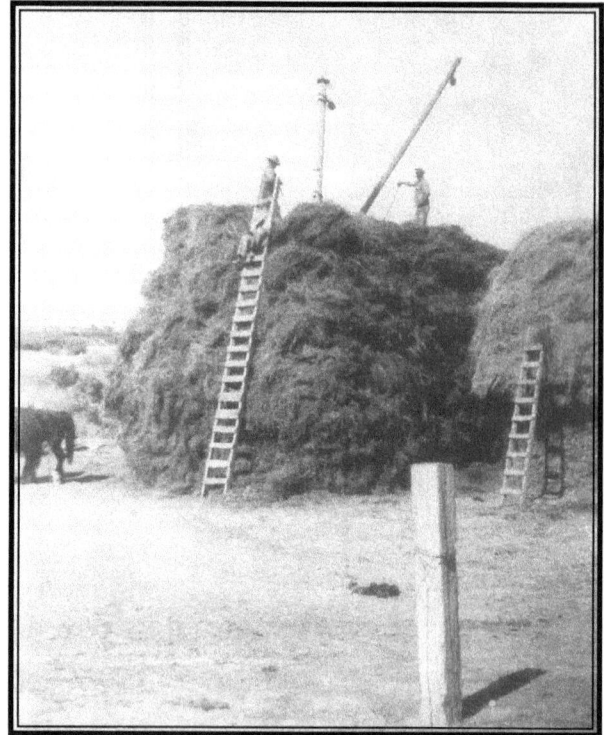

(Above) Bertha and Ed Wilson with grandchildren Shirley and Leon Ebright, along with horse, Dutch, and her colt, about 1942-3. The Wilsons, Lois' parents, were proving up on a homestead farm located west of the Mack Mesa reservoir and joining the Ebright farm on the south. It had an airstrip on it that was used by Betty Clark, who dusted the crops in New Liberty during the 40s. The Wilsons built a house, fences, plowed the fields and placed a pump in the canal to irrigate with, but because of government red-tape, lost the farm. The house and fences later disappeared. Undoubtedly they melted into another person's farm. (Above right) The guernsey dairy herd owned by Fat and Lois from 1942 to 1947 in New Liberty. The Ebright house is in the background. (Center) Stacking hay on the Ebright farm in the 1940s. Fat and his brother, Merle, on the stack. Quoting Lois: "Sometimes we had to stack after sundown, as the wind would go down some at that time. One year there was a bad infestation of grasshoppers. We used rolled barley, molasses and Paris Green at the edge of the field to poison them, but there were still a lot in the stacked hay. The cows didn't seem to mind eating them." (Below left) Pinto bean threshing on the Ebright farm in the 1940s. The crew is unidentified. (Lower right) Shirley attempting to milk a cow with Leon looking on, 1942. *(Photos courtesy of Lois Ebright Kimmel)*

Grandpa Smiley Carter with Leon and Shirley Ebright on the New Liberty farm, about 1942. *(Photo courtesy of Lois Ebright Kimmel)*

his own ranch in Smith Fork Canyon, near Crawford.

As soon as we were set up we began to sell cream from the cows at Fruita or Salt Lake City, or wherever we could get the best price.

There were no fences on the place yet so we set up some electric fences to try to control the cows, but the range cattle had no respect for the electric fences and kept breaking in and eating up the crops, making a good fence a necessity.

We finally had enough acreage and cows so we had enough units to qualify for the Rural Electrification Association to put in electric power to our place. It sure was nice to have a washing machine, refrigerator and milking machine. We had been using a cooler that grandpa Wilson made to keep our milk cool at the house. It was a screened-in cupboard with a pan of water on top from which a piece of flannel soaked and dripped down the sides so the evaporation would make it cool inside.

In those days farmers didn't have much

money — their worth was calculated by what they were able to accumulate. Lots of the time it was necessary to operate on borrowed money, paying it back in the fall when the crops were sold. At least it could be said there was more freedom in a farmer's life than in working for someone else. I'm grateful for the experience but still wish I could have had a pressure cooker to help in feeding the harvest crews.

Shirley started in the first grade at New Liberty School. We enjoyed all the Christmas plays and graduation exercises. Bob and Agnes Alstatt and some of the Maluy girls graduated while we were there. One of the Maluy girls (Phyllis) sang a song I thought was nice. Leon was little then, almost six.

The school house was our community center for all sorts of activities. Bernard even had a wrestling match with Earl Lacey there one night. We thought all of the people were really nice. The women were superb to have survived all the hard work involved in raising families, gardening, and canning, and yet finding time to meet with the other ladies of the Sorosis Club. It was always a pleasant get-together — Mrs. Kiefer always gave such nice readings.

Lots of Sundays we would take picnic lunches and go along with Cutlers, Pollocks and Edna Rowe up to Booze and Walt Deacon's mountain cabin on Douglas Pass. It was always so beautiful and cool up there and we all enjoyed being together. We spent many evenings playing cards with the Rectors, Cutlers and Pollocks.

Mrs. Schunter and Bill lived over in that area and I visited with her many times. Everyone seemed to work together to help each other and we enjoyed the friendship very much. We could see that this friendship is still alive, judging from the enjoyment we felt at the Mack/New Liberty reunion held at the High Line Lake (1991). We missed some of the older folks who are gone. We were some of the younger couples with children and now we are the older group. We miss that life now, but remember that it was hard getting started. I often think of Mrs. Alstatt, Mrs. Morrow, Mrs. Likes, Mrs. Weir, May and Zella Sanders, the two Mrs. Maluys and so many others. I remember Mrs. Swyhart telling about how when their house caught fire she was able to drag out a big trunk, but after the excitement was over she couldn't budge it.

The rural mail carrier was important to us as we looked forward to mail from the family. We sure didn't have many bills in those days.

World War II was going on during part of

the time we lived out there. We were all on ration stamps for sugar, shoes, gasoline and tires. Grandpa Carter gave us his sugar and shoe stamps sometimes. We were asked to save all the excess fats so the government could use them in making explosives.

In the mid 1940s, Fat went to work for Meadow Gold as a field man, so we moved back to Grand Junction, leaving the farm with Fat's brother, **Merle** and his wife **Pearl** and their two children. They stayed several years before deciding to move back to Oregon. Merle and his wife are the last ones left of the older Ebrights.

We moved our dairy up to Grand Junction, then sold the Mack farm. We built a new milking parlor which made milking much easier. Of course, with 90 acres of farm land to care for as well, it was a full-time job. From 6 a.m. to 10 p.m. made long days, but we look back on it with some fondness.

At some point in time Bernard and Lois separated and divorced. Lois remarried to **Leonard Lowes Kimmel** 15 June 1971 in Denver. Lois and Leonard lived for many years on Orchard Mesa in the Wilson family home Lois had inherited from her father. She now lives there alone, since Leonard passed away a few years ago.

As far as we know, Bernard did not remarry. He died in Grand Junction 1987 of Hodgkin's disease.

Shirley, their daughter, has five children. She currently works for "The Industrial Company" in Idaho Falls, Idaho. They are building a hydro-electric dam. She plans to come back to live in the Grand Junction area after that job runs out.

Leon, their son, has two children. He has spent many years in the building trade, 17 of those years in Canada.

Eddings

George Marshall and Mary Lee Eddings
(Photo courtsy of Nancy Eddings Wiswell)

Most of the following was contributed by Dana, Norma, Nancy, and Virginia Eddings. Also included are some news items and obituaries from *The Daily Sentinel*.

George Marshall Eddings Sr. was born 23 September 1881, at Strafford, Greene, Missouri. He spent the early part of his life in Missouri and married **Mary Lee Dillbeck**, 26 June 1908, at Springfield, Greene, Missouri. She was born 25 February 1891, in Douglas County, Missouri, to **William A. Dillbeck** and **Sarah Elizabeth Stewart**. (See Dillbeck biography) She spent her childhood at Strafford, Missouri, where she met George Eddings.

They had two sons:

William Madison "Buss," born 25 August 1909 in Strafford, Greene, Missouri
George Marshall Jr., 9 April 1915, Fruita
(A daughter died at birth)

George, Mary and William (two years old), moved to Fruita in 1912. We are told by Virginia Eddings (Buss's wife) that the Eddings family came to Fruita on the same train as Mary's

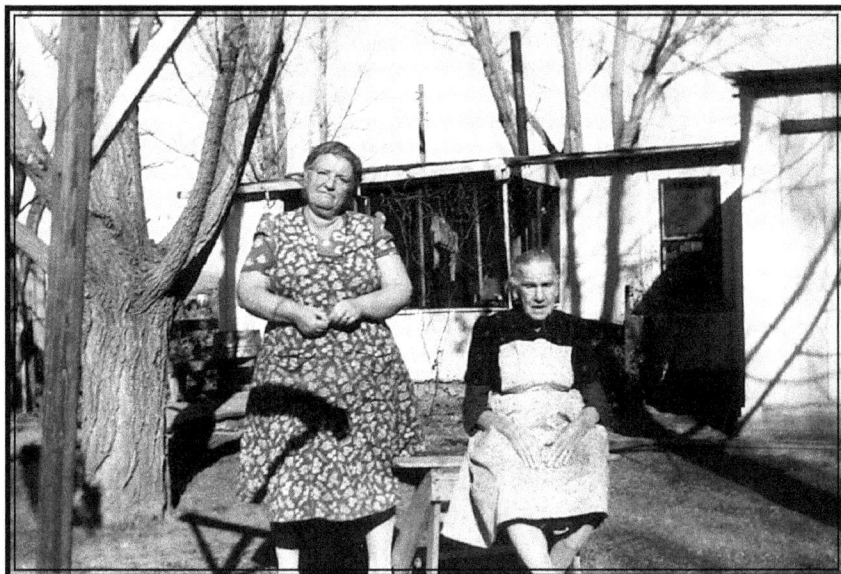

Mary Lee Eddings and mother, Sarah Dillbeck, in front of Mary's home. (Photo courtesy of Nancy Eddings Wiswell)

parents, William and Sarah Dillbeck (see Dillbeck biography). George went to work for the D&RGW Railroad in 1915, where he continued to work until he retired at age 65.

George, Mary, Marshall, Buss and his new bride, moved to Mack in the fall of 1932. George and Mary lived for awhile in a home they purchased from a sister of Ephraim Winkle; later they purchased another home from Odis Simpson, where they lived the rest of their lives.

Mary Lee died 22 October 1955. George Sr. died 10 July 1956. Both are buried in Elmwood Cemetery at Fruita.

William "Buss" Madison Eddings was born 25 August 1909 at Strafford, Greene, Missouri, and moved to Fruita, Colorado with his parents in 1915. He graduated from Fruita Union High School with the class of 1928. He was married 8 September 1932, in Grand Junction, to **Virginia Selke**, who was born 7 July 1913, at Salida, Chaffee, Colorado, a daughter of William F. Selke and Alice Myers.

Shortly after Buss and Virginia were married, the family moved to Mack, living for a time in a house owned by Tony Overbye, across the road south of the Keifer's. They divided the home into two apartments, the newly-weds occupying the front two rooms while George, Mary and Marshall lived in the back four rooms. They paid

$10 per month rent; $4 were paid by Buss and Virginia and the remaining $6 by the rest of the family. Buss worked for the Uintah Railway and George for the D&RG Railroad.

Buss and Virginia raised three children:

Ronald Eugene, born 27 October 1934, at Fruita
Alice Lee (Mair), 31 July 1937, Fruita
Kathryn Berniece (Whaley), 5 June 1940, Fruita

Virginia wrote that they spent a memorable winter in the Overbye home in Mack. They would get together in the evenings for pop-corn, apples and fudge. Often-times grandma Mary would make her delicious hot biscuits for all at breakfast. Virginia and Mary made several comforters during that winter.

In the spring of 1933 Buss and Virginia bought a little house in Mack from Bill Wells, a Uintah employee who worked with Buss. Not long after that Buss was promoted to Track Foreman at Dragon and had to move his family there. The Buss Eddings family lived in Dragon until the Uintah closed down in 1939.

After the Uintah closed down, Buss and Virginia lived on a small farm near Fruita for two years. Then, in 1942, they moved to San Diego where Buss went to work for Consolidated Aircraft Co., which later became General Dynamics.

Buss died at their home in San Diego 15 August 1996 at age 86. He was buried in Holy Cross Cemetery at San Diego. His obituary revealed that their son, Ronald, died at Hayden Lake, Kootenai, Idaho, 1 January 1994.

Surviving are his wife, Virginia, two daughters, six grandsons, two granddaughters and eight great-grandchildren.

Dana Foster and Marshall Eddings, 16
February 1937
(Photo courtesy of Nancy Eddings Wiswell)

George **Marshall Eddings, Jr.** was born 9 April 1915, at Fruita, and spent his childhood and attended schools there. Everyone who knew Marshall (he went by his second name) admired his guitar playing; he played in several bands throughout the Grand Valley. On 16 February 1937, he was married to **Dana I. Foster** of Appleton. She was born at Grand Junction, a daughter of Allison H. Foster and Hariett Robinson. The Foster family had moved to the Appleton community when Dana was about three years old.

Dana recalls that when she was 16, Marshall Eddings would bring his guitar to the home of Dow Jones, whose wife was Dana's cousin. Dow was a banjo player. She says, "I loved music and kept asking the red-headed fellow (Marshall) to play all the songs I liked. I was a shy little girl, kept giggling, because Dow kept teasing me." About a year later she met Marshall at the Copeco dance hall and let him take her home. They began dating and a romance developed that eventually led to marriage.

Mrs J. L. Booth of Mack, correspondent for *The Daily Sentinel*, wrote this account of the wedding in the Mack items of 26 February 1937:

A wedding of interest to many occurred 16 February in Fruita when Miss Dana Foster of Appleton and Marshall Eddings of Mack were united in marriage. Reverend Methvin performed the ceremony. Both of the young people are well and favorably known in the lower valley and have a host of friends who wish them worlds of happiness in their future. Mrs. Eddings has been employed in Grand Junction. The groom is night patrolman for the D&RGW Railroad here at Mack. They will make their home in Mack in the near future.

The couple had two daughters:

Norma Lou (Levitt), born 13 October 1939, at Grand Junction.
Nancy Lee(Wiswell), 12 November 1945, Vancouver, Washington

Nancy Lee and Norma Lou Eddings
(Photo courtesy of Nancy Eddings Wiswell)

Marshall and Dana purchased the house that had belonged to Buss and Virginia Eddings; they paid $75 for it. Evidently someone else had lived in it for some years and had left it in a mess. Here is Dana's impression of it when she moved in:

When we moved to Mack in 1937 we moved into an old beat up Uintah railroad house with tar paper on the outside and cardboard on the inside. It had a cold water pressure pump and an old rusty sink. The water was hauled to Mack from Dragon, Utah. The place was really a fire trap; cold in the winter and hot in the summer. There were some shade trees and a

(Upper left) Dana Foster before she became Dana Eddings. (Upper right) Marshall with Hap Harris' Band at Harold's Desert Inn, Mack, Colorado, about 1950. Marshall is the guitarist and Hap Harris the drummer. All others are unidentified.

(Center) Marshall with his 1928 or 29 Chevrolet when he and Dana were dating. Taken in front of his parents home in Mack. (Lower left) Nancy Eddings, about four years old, with her dog, Nikki, in 1949. The two Eddings' homes are in the background.

(Lower center) January 1940, Dana and baby Norma, 3½ months old, in front of their home in Mack. (Lower right) About 1952, Nancy Eddings in the Eddings back yard with the town of Mack in the background. L-R: The school teacherage, Last Chance Grocery Store, school house, post office and Alta Smith's house. *(All photos courtesy of Nancy Eddings Wiswell)*

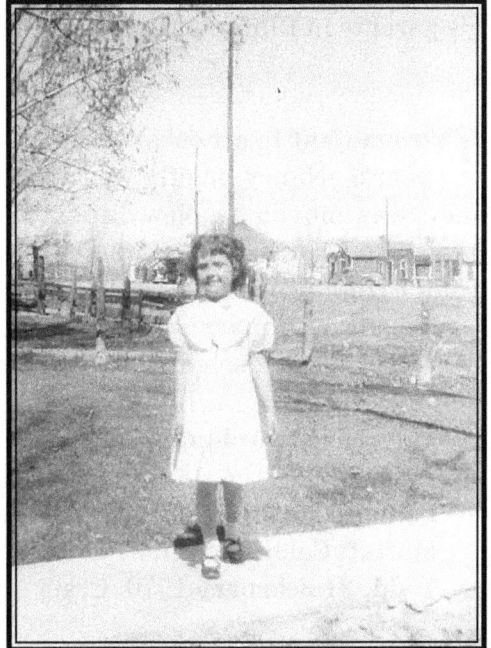

dried-up lawn. We did have irrigation water to flood the lawns, which was all free.

We fixed the place up inside and had some nice furniture later. Marshall and his dad built on a bed-room and porch. During World War II we were gone for three years to work in the war industry. We kept the place for 16 years, then sold it and built a home in Fruita.

Dana tells of a "real thrill" in riding the Uintah train over Baxter Pass to visit with Buss and Virginia at Dragon. Said the ride was "long and tiresome and scary." The round trip took all day, but they had fun playing rummy with Buss and Virginia and playing with three year old Ronnie.

One night as Marshall was patrolling the track west of Mack on his motorcar, a wheel broke, throwing the car off the track, seriously injuring him. He was laid up for a long time; finally losing a section of bone from his injured arm. He eventually accepted a cash settlement from the Rio Grande Railroad, and for some time operated a truck in the Mack/New Liberty area. Later he went to work for the Mesa County Highway Department.

During World War II Marshall and Dana lived three years at Vancouver, Washington; Marshall worked in the ship yards at Portland, Oregon. Their daughter Nancy was born while they were living there.

George Marshall Jr. died on 12 May 1976 following a four-month illness. He is buried near his parents in Elmwood Cemetery at Fruita.

Norma went to school at Mack for a total of six years. Nancy briefly went to Loma School, then was moved to New Liberty. After they moved to Fruita, Nancy was enrolled at Fruita Junior High School.

Norma was married in September 1958 to **Carroll M. Levitt**, son of John and Carrie Levitt.

They have two children:

Pamela, born 10 November 1963, Craig, Moffat, Colorado
Todd, 21 February 1970, Craig

Nancy married **Allen Lee Wiswell** at Fruita on 28 September 1967. Allen was born 24 February 1940 at Greeley, Colorado, a son of Lea A. Wiswell and Leola McGarvey. He grew up in Colorado and Utah, graduating from Fruita Union High School in the class of 1958.

After graduating from high school Allen enlisted in the U. S. Navy and served for 20 years. After he got out of the Navy he moved his family to Emery County, Utah, where he worked at the Huntington Canyon Coal Mine. They lived there for ten years before moving to Price in 1988.

Allen and Nancy had three children:

Jennifer (Leichman)
Nicole (Atwood)
Shane Alan

Allen passed away from heart failure 21 March 1996.

Following is a story written by Norma Lou Eddings Levitt:

When I was a baby my parents lived at Mack, Colorado. My father, George Marshall Eddings, had been employed by the D&RGW Railroad, until he was hurt in an accident with a motor car in Ruby Canyon (southwest of Mack). This was while my mother was expecting me, as she has told me about going to the Railroad Medical facility at Canon City, Colorado with my dad for treatment on his arm.

When I was a toddler, my parents moved to Portland, Oregon where my dad was employed as a welder in a ship yards where they built aircraft carriers for the war.

We lived there approximately three years. I started first grade school there, and my sister, Nancy, was born in Vancouver, Washington.

The war ended, the ship yards closed down, and the family moved back to Colorado in January 1946, and settled in the little house in Mack. I was six years old, and my sister a small baby.

We lived in Mack all of my childhood. My parents did not move to Fruita until I was a young woman, married and living in Craig, Colorado.

My first real recollections of childhood was moving back to Mack from Oregon/Washington area. I finished my first grade at the Loma school (apparently Mack School was not open that year). I rode the bus to Loma, a Mrs. Baker was my teacher. I remember there were a lot of little kids riding that bus, so perhaps that is why, the following school year, the little school at Mack was opened.

I went to the three room Mack School from second grade through the eighth grade. As in all small communities, the school was the hub of not only school activities, but also community gatherings.

Our little house in Mack, was next door to my grandparents, George and Mary Eddings. As a child I played as much in their yard as my own. Growing up in Mack holds a lot of special memories. It was a rather busy little community, especially in my early childhood years.

The railroad seemed to be the main center of activity for quite a few years. I can remember the railroad depot, where the trains would stop. Gilsonite was trucked in, along with the big, long bags of wool. I believe these were loaded on the train. There was also a stockyards, where cattle and sheep were shipped out.

The houses that the Davies and Slaugh families lived in had been railroad houses. I don't think they were there when I was at Mack, although I am not certain about this. There was also a house that the section foreman lived in; in later years it was the Montoya family. I went to high school with their daughters, Mary Jane and Charlotte.

The first few years going to Mack School, it seems there were quite a few children of all ages, as there were three rooms and three teachers teaching the eight grades.

As I recall the first teachers were a Mr. & Mrs. Stites. They lived in the teacherage which was provided for the teachers. The school had running water in it, as there were drinking fountains and a little room that was actually called the kitchen, with a sink and a little stove (don't know about a refrigerator).

There were no indoor bathrooms, as we would all make trips to the outhouses. I don't know about the teacherage.

At one time, a Miss Kiefer was my teacher (a favorite). She was from a family that lived in the area (perhaps between Mack & Loma). I remember she only taught one or two years and then got married and moved away. This is quite clear to me as my grandmother, Mary Eddings, and other family members, went to her wedding and reception. This was probably the first wedding I attended and I was quite impressed.

Some of the kids that attended Mack School when I was going there were Kay and Maxine Rich, lots of older kids, Betty Weber, Rachel Slaugh (she was the youngest), Marcia and Gracia Davies, Elmer Ortego (there were other siblings), Bobby Saunders, the Thompson kids, Rudy and Jughead Wilkinson (don't know what Jughead's real given name was), and Josie Brewster.

One of the main activities while I was in school was the CYCL (Colorado Young Citizen's League). This was at a state wide level, for seventh and eighth graders. Each school would have their students write an essay on Citizenship and there would be district competitions, as I remember going up to what was then the old Central School at Fruita and having to read my essay on stage in front of all the kids and the teachers from the area.

Winners of the essay contest would then get to go to the State Convention in Denver. I went on this trip two times, once as an essay winner and once as an eighth grader.

The Mack school and community would pay the eighth graders expenses on this trip. There were always money making projects by the community for this purpose. I can remember one of the money-making projects during my eighth grade year was a raffle for a quilt (or afghan) my grandmother, Mary Eddings, had made and donated for that purpose.

Kay Rich and I would talk the teacher into letting us have several afternoons off, and we would ride our horses out to the outlying farm areas toward New Liberty to sell raffle tickets on the quilt. We had a lot of fun and actually sold quite a few tickets.

We would take the train to Denver, along with our teacher, to spend three days. A lot of the western slope kids were on this train, as I remember, including Dolores Cutler, (she later became a very good friend in high school)

Curtis Thomas, the Berry kids from New Liberty, a lot of kids from the Appleton, Fruita, Loma area, who would all eventually become high school classmates.

The delegates would stay at one of the downtown Denver Hotels, the Kenwood, I believe. (I am sure it is long gone). We would go to the state capitol for meetings and to see and tour the capitol building, visit the museums, go to the top of the Daniel & Fishers Tower and do some downtown shopping. At that time the big Woolworth store was awesome to us young Mack-ites.

My dad, Marshall Eddings, was a trucker at that time, so I had the chance to go to Denver with him several times, but I know that this was the first trip that some of these kids had made to the big city.

I think going to school in a little country type school was a very good experience. I have often told my children about some of the experiences and how good they were. I also think the quality of education for that time period was OK, as I didn't seem to have much trouble when I went on to high school at Fruita.

I can remember another money-making project the community would have to raise money for other special purposes was box socials. The ladies and young girls would make up box lunches (usually a shoe box), decorate the box real, special, and put in a lunch (fried chicken, potato salad and pie were popular). The boxes would be auctioned off, and the gent or boy that bought the box had supper with the lady or girl that brought the lunch. It was always a big secret whose box belonged to what lady, or grandmother.

Another community affair that I can remember, were the Halloween parties. It was always a costume affair, for both the kids and adults. I can remember one year when I was about ten, my mother fixed me a beautiful, long dress made out of a net material which was quite full (I have no idea where she found this material), and piled curls on my head, and I went to the party as Cinderella. I was quite sure I would win the best costume prize, as she had put a lot of effort into this costume.

During the course of the evening, my mother sent word with my dad, sister and grandparents that she would not be coming, as she did not feel well. I remember thinking she wouldn't get to see me win the prize for best costume. To make a long story short, the headless horseman and his horse showed up, and won the prize. I was so disappointed,

until the headless horseman revealed himself. It was my mother, Dana Eddings! Doris Archuleta and another lady (it may have been Eva Rich, I am not sure) were the horse. There were always games to play, along with apple dunking, pin the tail on the donkey and such.

As the children got older, I don't recall any more of these gatherings at the school. The outhouse of Mrs. Smith, the postmistress, was always a prime target for the older "tricksters," along with Mrs. Brewster's (who had a turkey farm) outhouse.

Mrs. Slaugh gave piano lessons to quite a few of the kids in Mack. Her little music recitals were another event that everyone seemed to like to attend.

As I mentioned before, the railroad was kind of a hub at that time. My grandmother, Mary Eddings, had a close lady friend (I don't remember her name) that I think had lived in Mack at one time, and now lived in Glenwood Springs. Grandma would visit her at least once a year, and usually would take me with her. We would catch the train at the little depot in Mack and ride to Glenwood Springs. I did this several times with her. It seemed to take quite a while to get to Glenwood Springs, as the train stopped at what we called "all the milk crossings." I do not know if they actually picked up milk, but the train did stop a lot. Sometime later, during my years in Mack, they shut the depot down, and the train did not stop any more in Mack, and we would have to go to the Grand Junction depot to catch the new California Zephyr.

My eighth grade graduation class had three kids in it: myself, Kay Rich and Elmer Ortego. We started catching the bus the following year to go to high school in Fruita, which I did for four years, until high school graduation. I don't think either Kay or Elmer finished high school at Fruita. Sometime during my high school years, the little Mack school closed down, as my sister, Nancy, went to New Liberty school, until she and my parents moved to Fruita.

My dad, Marshall Eddings, was an accomplished musician. He was well-known in the area for his guitar playing and played with several local bands. His band played for a number of years at Harold's Desert Inn, west of Mack, and at the Loma community dances.

Summers were the most fun. Some time during my younger years, I learned to ride horses. I would ride with Marcia Davies and Maxine & Kay Rich. Mr. Rich had a lot of horses, and we girls spent a lot of time riding in the summers. I had a great love for horses and became quite determined to have my own horse.

Eventually my dad bought me my own horse and some of my best times growing up was riding my horse (Star) with my girl friends. This love of horses has never diminished, as my husband and I have always had horses from when we were first married, and now have registered paint and quarter horses that we breed, show and sell.

Mr. Rich had a little herd of cows, and the Rich girls, Marcia Davies and myself would spend the summers herding the cows. We would take them from the Rich farm to the Mack wash. We would get the cows settled and then have all day to ride the wash, lay in the tall grass watching the clouds, eat our sack lunches, talk about girl things, and dream about living on a huge cattle ranch in Texas. This was a fun time. Toward late afternoon we would gather the cows up and take them home. I didn't get to do this every day, but a couple of times a week during the summer.

As I started going to high school, I found new friends from Fruita and Loma who rode horses, and lots of times we would ride to Loma and meet each other.

Another fun thing we did was lots of hiking. The hills south of Mack had a lot of neat things for kids to see, in fact the interstate now goes close by. There was a big flat rock that we all called "Flat Rock." We would hike to Flat Rock and near by was also a big tall rock called "Hollow Rock" that was a favorite place for all of us. It was big enough that several people could crawl into it and sit comfortably.

There were also some ponds where we would swim in in the summer and ice skate in the winter time. I don't remember any one having very much money (if any), but we didn't really need any.

While growing up, a lot of Saturday's were spent going to "town" — being Grand Junction. My mother, Dana, did not drive at that time, like a lot of women in Mack. There was a bus that we would catch early Saturday morning, which would go through the Fruita, Appleton and Hunter areas (known as the old highway) and eventually get us to Grand Junction. We would spend the day, do whatever needed to done, catch the bus late afternoon and be home in time for my mother to make supper. Sometimes if my mother had lots of errands or shopping to do I would take my sister Nancy to the matinee movie, usually cartoons, and be out in plenty of time for us to catch the bus.

After I started high school in Fruita I didn't spend as much time riding the horse or the hiking. I would go with my dad a lot in the truck in the summer time. He had a trucking business and hauled livestock and hay. Later he hauled mainly produce for Tompkins of Fruita.

Some of us would work in the fields, picking tomatoes, cucumbers and other crops. There was a farmer (it may have been a Likes but I am not sure) who, with his wife, lived northeast of Mack, but not as far as Loma, who would have us pick crops for him. I don't remember what we made, but I am thinking I would work from early morning to early afternoons in the fields and maybe make $2.

As I became high school age I would sometimes help Mrs. Carpenter at the grocery store during busy times, stocking shelves, dusting cans and helping with customers.

After graduating from high school I worked in an office in Grand Junction for about 1½ years before getting married. I married Carroll Levitt of Fruita, (son of John & Carrie Levitt, both deceased) and we moved to Craig, Colorado, where we still reside.

We have two children, Pamela, of Craig, Colorado, and Todd, an Army Officer at Clarksville, Tennessee.

Following is a story by Nancy Lee Eddings Wiswell.

One of my first recollections of being in Mack, Colorado, as a child begins with Mama and me walking home from Cole's store one day. We had crossed the highway and our little dog, Nicky, was with us but he hadn't crossed the highway with us. From my yard I called, "Here Nicky, here Nicky." As he started across the highway a vehicle came speeding along, hitting and killing him. My big sister, Norma and I cried a lot. I was not yet five years old.

I can remember Saturday nights when Daddy would go out to play his guitar for dances. He'd be dressed up in nice dress slacks, white shirt and tie, and smelling of Old Spice Cologne. I thought he was very handsome and smelled better than anybody in the whole world! Lots of times he would play with the Hap Harris Band at the old Desert Inn Club west of Mack. Sometimes he would play at the Loma Community Dance Hall or the Copeco Dance Hall. Generally a lot of local people came to those places to dance.

Daddy was a self-taught musician. He started playing at the Avalon Theatre in Grand Junction and at the Rialto Theatre at Fruita, winning talent competitions by the time he was 14 years old. He became very well-known for his music by all the local folks. He never had lessons, nor learned to read music. He played by ear and could really belt out some old rag-time tunes on the piano as well!

Sometimes my mother would dress up and go with him. She loved black dresses and high heels. She had dark brown hair that was almost black. She and my father were an attractive couple when they were all dressed up to go out for the evening.

My sister and I would be sent next door to Grandma's house to spend the night. We would be put to bed in a large bed that was high off the floor. I can remember having to stand on a foot-stool to climb in. We were tucked in under many homemade quilts and comforters.

In the morning Grandma Eddings would fix pancakes, and always her Pekingese dogs, Nina and Boots, would get pancakes also. They liked to bury themselves under pillows on the couch, or wherever else they wanted to. They had the run of the house!

Daddy was a truck driver — seems he always had a truck when we lived in Mack. He hauled livestock for many of the years we lived there. After we moved to Fruita, though, he drove a truck for awhile for Ray Tompkins, hauling groceries and goods for the store. He and I always had names for the trucks. One of his livestock trucks was named "Bessie" — the grocery van was called "Louie." Eventually, he quit driving trucks and went to work for the Mesa County Highway Department.

It seems Mom worked hard in Mack to keep our home going. She did lots of laundry on a wringer washer — had lots of clothes to hang out to dry and lots of ironing! Seems like we had fried chicken every Sunday — lots of homemade cookies, pies, and bread. She sewed lots of pretty dresses for Norma and I when we were little girls. I learned how to sew on her treadle sewing machine. She also taught me how to do embroidery. She was a very good homemaker and a good mom!

Sometimes on Saturdays we would ride the bus to Grand Junction and stay all day. Grandma Eddings would go too. We'd return late in the day. I remember also Daddy,

Marshall playing his guitar at about age 18.
(Photo courtesy of Nancy Eddings Wiswell)

Marshall and his truck "Bessie" in 1951.
(Photo Courtesy of Nancy Eddings Wiswell)

Mama, Norma and I would sometimes go to Fruita on Saturday. Norma and I would go to Walker's theatre and stay in there all afternoon watching the old-time movies that were popular then — most of which I have long ago forgot the names of.

We always had dogs and cats at our house to play with. When Daddy drove the grocery van he occasionally made trips to Kansas. On these occasions he would bring me back big desert turtles. I had three or four of them over a course of several years. They all eventually ran away.

I loved to make play houses. Wherever I could find an empty shed I would set me up a little house. Once when I was about ten years old I was in my playhouse smoking driftwood. Daddy caught me and just the look on his face made me very ashamed! I wouldn't doubt that Norma got in trouble for that one — for she is the one who showed me how!

One of my more memorable experiences was taking piano lessons from Mrs. Jennie Slaugh. I started at the age of five. Once a week I would have my lesson at the big house where the Slaugh's lived; 50 cents per hour for the lessons.

I also belonged to the 4-H Club. Mrs. Barcus taught the cooking class and later on I took a sewing class.

In 1951 I started first grade at Mack School. Mrs. Stites was my first teacher. She and her husband, who also taught there, lived in the house on the school grounds. After I completed the second grade the Mack School was closed permanently. We children of the Mack School had a choice of either going to Loma or to New Liberty. I started out at Loma, but was so lonesome for the familiar faces of the other Mack kids (seems they all went to New Liberty) that my folks transferred me after only two weeks. Mrs. Sue Thompson was my third grade teacher and Mrs. Marylou Reeves my fourth grade teacher. Mrs. Cooper taught the upper grades.

I had a lot of respect for those ladies! They taught us well! They were very strict — didn't put up with a lot of nonsense, but they were also good to the kids. I remember some outings we all went on. The teachers organized games for us to play at recess and stayed right with us to supervise. It was a fun little school!

We played basketball inside in the winter months and baseball outside in the spring. We had Christmas programs, plays and programs with music too. Mom and Dad were always there in the audience to cheer me on!

When I was a fifth grader there was a program in effect called "CYCL" — Colorado Young Citizens League. It was for the fifth and sixth graders throughout the state of Colorado. I only got to go one year, as it was discontinued. What a good time we had! As part of the program we boarded the train at Grand Junction (the "Prospector?"), Ronnie Ashburn, Gene Wilkerson, Helen White, Geraldine Barnes, Janice Monger, Luthera Barcus, Nancy Eddings and Mrs. Cooper, our chaperone and teacher. (If I left anyone out, please understand, it was awhile back). It was the highlight of of our school days of long — ago getting to go to Denver!

We visited the State Capitol Building, museums, the top of Daniel and Fisher Tower, shopped for souvenirs and attended a banquet and conference for CYCL.

I have fond memories of Community Club at the Mack School building: the ladies and unmarried girls would make box lunches to be raffled off, the gentleman who bought a box lunch would then share it with the lady who made it. I wonder if any romances ever started that way? Those times are fun to recall. Seems like that little auditorium was full of folks from the community — laughing, talking, dancing, music, kids playing. It was a good time when folks got together!

My best friend when I was growing up in Mack was Janice Monger. It seems we were really inseparable through those years. We were the same age — both our families spent time in Oregon/Washington during the war years. We didn't know each other then, though. Janice was born in Portland, Oregon, 15 September 1945 and I in Vancouver, Washington, 12 November 1945. The two cities are separated by the Columbia River.

We were not yet five years old when we first discovered each other. We were separated by the highway, she on the north side and I on the south. We would wave to each other. As soon as we were able to cross that highway, we formed a friendship and played together often. We played at her house, my house or my grandma's house. We loved to play with paper dolls. We played on the hills and in the fields. We rode bikes together and when we were older we would ride our bikes out to New Liberty to visit Geraldine Barnes.

Janice and I remain friends even today — that childhood bond has never been broken!

My childhood at Mack was fun and memorable. Life seemed much simpler then. A little community tucked away in a little space in the world. All too soon it came to an end. I finished growing up as a teenager in Fruita, got married, went away and had a family. Life has changed! The memories I have of those days will never be forgotten!

Everetts

The Everetts story came from obituaries in *The Daily Sentinel* found through the obituary index at the Mesa County Public Library in Grand Junction.

Frank Everetts was born 2 February 1861 in Dallas, Texas, to William Harrington and Amanda Everetts. He and his brother **John Everetts,** filed on 120 acres in the west end of the New Liberty community on Sec. 12 of R 104W some time prior to 1918.

We know very little about these two pioneers, but herein is a bit of their history gleaned from obituaries: Frank spent his childhood in Texas and came to Colorado as a young man. He had been engaged in freighting ore for many years — somewhere.

The brothers ran cattle in West Canyon in the Bookcliffs area. In December 1931 they sold the New Liberty farm, and, we suppose, the land in the Bookcliffs to Graves and Orlin Corn and moved into the Ray Stewart home in Mack. They hired Bertie Dillbeck Sparks to keep house for them.

John died in January 1936 and Frank, 23 April 1948. Both were buried in Elmwood Cemetery at Fruita.

(A story about the Everetts brothers, written by Orlin Corn, is included with the Corn story. More about John Everetts is in Clem Maluy's history).

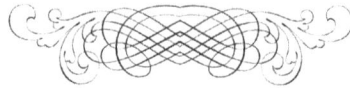

Fisher

The Fisher story is compiled from news items from the *Daily Sentinel.*

George W. Fisher: We have very little family history on George and sons, but we'll include such information as we have. George came to Colorado to participate in the homestead drawing of 29 March 1918. It was noted erroneously in *The Daily Sentinel* news item of 30 March 1918, that:

> One G. W. Fisher of Chicago, a conductor on the Chicago and Great Western railway, had been successful in the drawing the previous day, but his sister had lost out.

His sister was the one who was successful in the drawing. George's name appears further on in the same article among the list of those who filed on land after the drawing. In that instance his residence was listed as Queen City, Missouri.

George's farm was Unit A Sec 21 R 103W. His sister, Luella McNaught, filed on Unit D of the same section. Unit A was east and Unit D south of Clem Maluy. Unit D was later abandoned because of alkali and eventually became part of the Clem Maluy homestead.

George settled on the homestead with two young sons: **Raymond** and **George Jr.** Nothing is known of the mother of those sons. However, she was mentioned in two or three articles in the *Daily Sentinel* in the early days, but only as "Mrs. Fisher."

We have discovered in newspaper accounts that George had an older son, **Lloyd,** who was a stunt aviator for a circus. He crashed his airplane in May of 1922 at Macon, Georgia, and was seriously injured. George and family were

notified 1 September 1922, that Lloyd died of his injuries. It appears that George Sr. and sons, Raymond and George Jr., were living in Mack at that time.

George Sr.'s name appears as a voter on 22 June 1922, when the New Liberty School district was organized, so the Fishers may have been dividing their time between Mack and New Liberty. We wonder if George had something to do with the Uintah Railway, since in the foregoing article his connection with Great Western Railway was mentioned. And, why else would he be living in Mack?

According to May Sanders' records, Raymond Fisher was enrolled in the third grade at New Liberty in 1919-20; and in the "upper grades" at Mack in school year 1920-21.

George Jr. was enrolled in the fifth grade at New Liberty in 1925. Later, in the 1930s, George Jr. was driver of the New Liberty/Mack school bus for two or more years. George graduated from Fruita Union High School with the class of 1933. Ten years later, in April 1943, we found notice that he had graduated from Army Air Corps pilot's training school. His home address was then Rural Route 1, Fruita, Colorado. On 21 January 1946 notice was posted in the *Daily Sentinel* column, "With the Boys and Girls in the Service" that "1st Lieutenant George W. Fisher, U. S. Air Corps Pilot, of Route 1, Fruita, has been discharged." He had served from 22 April 1943 to 3 January 1946.

The Fishers sold their New Liberty farm to Edward W. Dodge about 1932. Later Don Weimer lived on that place.

Foss

The Foss history is compiled from census records, and a family group sheet and history outline from Lephia Foss Garlitz. Information was also gleaned from obituaries and news items from *The Daily Sentinel*, land records and author's personal knowledge.

Levi L. "Lee" Foss, was born 3 March 1886, at Randall, Jewell, Kansas, one of six children born to Alvin B. and Martha E. Foss. He spent his childhood in that area, and became a telephone lineman. On 7 September 1910 Lee married **Frances Alberta Harford,** at Randall. Frances was born 16 June 1890 at Randall.

They had three children:

Charley and Lee Foss, with Eloise in the basket, on a trip from Kansas to Colorado. *(Photo courtesy of Lephia Foss Garlitz)*

> **Ralph Leroy,** born 17 May 1914, at Randall, Jewell, Kansas
> **Lephia Marie (Garlitz),** 21 June 1916, Jamestown, Cloud, Kansas
> **Eloise Martha,** 17 February 1921, Esbon, Jewell, Kansas

In 1921 the family moved to Colorado from Esbon, Kansas in two Model "T" Fords. Lee's brother, Charley, came with them and stayed until the house was built. They settled on a homestead on Unit B Sec. 28 R 103W. It was located on East Salt Creek a short distance north of Highway 6 & 50, and northeast of the Daily farm.

That homestead proved to be unsatisfactory because of alkali. Lee made a deal with the Bureau of Reclamation and Grand Valley Water Users' Association to abandon that farm and

Ralph, Lee, Frances and Eloise Foss, 1 January 1953. *(Photo courtesy of Lephia Foss Garlitz)*

move to 60 acres on Sec. 7 R 103W, north of Ella Stotts, and immediately west of Camp #8 on the Highline Canal.

On 11 February 1927, with the help of neighbors, the Foss house was loaded on timbers and wagon running gear and hauled to the new place. It created quite a sensation in the community to see that house being moved up the road behind several teams of horses. Fortunately, there were no telephone or power lines to contend with in those days. Several years later the Fosses were able to add 40 acres more of desert land to that property, making a total of 100 acres.

The Foss children all attended New Liberty and Fruita Union high schools. In 1938 Lephia married **Marshall F. Garlitz** of the Hunter community. They have one daughter, **Sharon**.

Ralph farmed with his father until he enlisted in the U. S. Army for two years from January 1941 to December 1942. He worked for a time in the Oil Shale operation at Grand Valley (Parachute), Colorado.

The Fosses sold their New Liberty farm in 1952 to Victor Hawthorne, and moved to a home on 29 Road, near Grand Junction. Lee died 15 August 1959, at Pueblo, Colorado. Frances died 8 July 1960, at Grand Junction. Both were buried in Memorial Gardens Cemetery at Grand Junction.

Ralph and Eloise never married; they continued to share living quarters for several years until Ralph entered the Colorado State Veterans Center at Homelake, Colorado (in the San Luis Valley). He died there 5 February 1991. Eloise currently resides at the Grand Junction Care Center on Teller Avenue in Grand Junction.

Marshall, Lephia and daughter, Sharon Garlitz.
(Photo courtesy of Lephia Foss Garlitz)

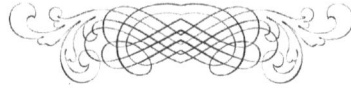

Gadbury

It seems that everyone who lived in New Liberty in the early days knew of a family who lost two children in a house fire, but no one was able place the date of the tragedy, the name of the family, nor the actual place. We found the story in *The Daily Sentinel*.

B.A. and **Katherine Gadbury:**

On 7 February 1924, a terrible tragedy struck the Gadbury family who were living near the east end of the New Liberty community in a house owned by Clyde Balkwill, on what is now "10 Road," about four miles north of Mack.

Mr. Gadbury had left that morning for Bingham, Utah, to seek employment, leaving the mother and children at home. The story, as told by neighbors and *The Daily Sentinel*, was that shortly after noon the mother, **Katherine**, stoked up the fire in the stove and left the two young children, **Richard**, age four, and **Virginia**, age two, asleep in their beds while she went for a brief visit to the home of her brother, **Paul Padilla**, who lived nearby. A short time later the Gadbury home was discovered to be completely engulfed in flames. Frantic efforts by neighbors and family to rescue the children were unsuccessful.

The father was located in Utah and he returned on the first train available. The little children were buried in a single casket in the Orchard Mesa Cemetery.

Mrs. Gadbury's father came from Missouri to be with his daughter in her grief and to take her back home with him until her husband found permanent employment.

A little girl named **Netta Gadbury** was listed as a student in New Liberty School in 1923-24;

we think it safe to assume she was a member of that family.

Garber

The following was taken from an obituary in *The Daily Sentinel*.

Cecil (Jack) L. Garber was born 1 September 1903, to John L. Garber and Hannah M. Saylor, at Marquette, McPherson County, Kansas. He spent his youth and attended schools there. (See history of Paul Garber with the Booth story)

Jack worked for many years as a welder for the Denver & Rio Grande RR and retired in the 1960s.

He was married in the 1920s to **Effie Richardson**. She died some years later and he was remarried to **Billie Rice** in 1969.

Jack died in the St. Mary's Hospital 28 November 1991 at age 88, and was buried in the Orchard Mesa Cemetery.

Garcia

The following was contributed by **Joe Lino Garcia** of 713 Santa Clara, Grand Junction, Colorado.

Jose Garcia was born at Durango, Mexico, in 1888 to Andres Garcia and Josefita Rivas. Jose was married in 1916 to **Josephita Cordova** at Tucumcari, Quay, New Mexico. Josephita was born in 1892 at Logan, Quay, New Mexico, to **Jose** and **Valeria Cordova**.

Jose and Josephita had eight children:

Tony, born 1918 at Logan, New
Mexico
Phyllis (Mason), Pueblo, Colorado
John, 1924, Pueblo
Consuelo "Connie" (Rivas), 1926,
Pueblo
Louis, 1927, Pueblo
Joe Lino, 1930, Pueblo
Two other children were born at
Logan, but died young.

Following is the story as told by Joe Lino
Garcia.

Jose Garcia was born at Durango, Mexico,
in 1888. At the age of 7, he and his parents
moved to New Mexico where he spent his
boyhood. He met and married Josephita
Cordova in 1916 at Tucumcari, New Mexico.
Josephita was born in 1892 at Logan, Quay,
New Mexico.

Mr. and Mrs. Jose Garcia made their home
in Logan, New Mexico, where Mrs. Garcia's

Josephita and Jose Cordova Garcia, 1968.
(Photo courtesy of Joe Lino Garcia)

parents owned a ranch. The family moved to
Pueblo, Colorado, where Jose worked at the
steel mill. Mr. And Mrs. Garcia had four sons,
Tony, John, Louis and Joe Lino, and two
daughters, Phyllis and Connie.

As the depression began in the early 1930s,
Jose was one of many men who was laid off. He
and his familiy moved to Cisco, Utah, where he
was offered employment with the D&RGW
Railroad, along with his two eldest sons, Tony
and John. While living in Cisco, Mr. Garcia,
along with a nephew, purchased a farm south
of the train depot in Mack, Colorado. He was
later transferred from the Cisco Section to the
Mack Section.

The Garcia's had several friendly neighbors
living nearby who shared in their daily living.
To mention a few of many, across the road lived
Mr. and Mrs. Bowen, Mr. Bowen being a rural
mail carrier. Also across the road lived Mr.
and Mrs. Garber who had a very nice Model "T"
pickup. Mr. and Mrs. Slaugh lived in the old
Uintah Railroad office. Mr. Slaugh was a
government wildlife employee. Mr. and Mrs.
Davies lived in the house which is now a Rock
Shop. The Brewsters, on top of the hill, had a
turkey farm where the locals had many a good
time "picking turkeys." The Vigils from Cisco,
Utah, lived briefly in Mack and two of the girls
eventually married two Garcia boys. Mr.
McCoy, had his little Model "B" pickup, which
everyone liked. The Rich family lived on a
nearby farm and shared the same ditch rights
and cleaning as the Garcias, as did Mr. Wilcox,
who was also a next door neighbor. And along
the path to the store owned by Mr. And Mrs.
Carpenter was Mrs. Swyhart and the Snook
family. The Archuleta family, another
railroader, were close neighbors, as were the
Komatas family. There was also Mrs. Smith,
the postal clerk, the N. D. Monger family and
the elementary teacher, Mrs. DeQuasie. The
school house quarters still stand but the school
building is "history." The Wilkinson brothers
lived up the highway. These and many others
were all friendly people.

Mr. Garcia and the family farmed while
Jose continued working on the railroad until
retirement. As the children grew, the boys
eventually served in the military and two of
the boys, John and Tony, purchased homes in
Mack, where they raised their families. Both
daughters, Phyllis and Connie, worked in
Grand Junction. Phyllis married and moved to
Fruita, Colorado, where she raised her family.
She now resides in Salt Lake City, Utah.
Connie also married and moved to Pueblo,

Colorado, where her brother, Louis Garcia, and his wife and family currently live. Louis worked for and retired from the Pueblo Army Depot. Lino worked for and retired from the Veteran's Administration Hospital in Grand Junction, Colorado. He and his family currently reside in Grand Junction, Colorado.

The Mack farm was sold in the late 1970s. Mr. and Mrs. Garcia worked hard on the farm. Sons, daughters and their families, friends and relatives have many special memories of the Mack farm.

Jose passed away at the age of 92 in 1981, while his wife, Josephita, passed away in 1983, at age 90. A son, John, passed away in 1989 at age 64. At the time of Josephita's passing there were 22 grandchildren and four great grandchildren. Annual reunions are held to reminisce and keep up the Garcia tradition.

Lorenzo T. and Juanita Marez Garcia, 1965.
(Photo courtesy of Cecelia Garcia Chavez)

The Lorenzo T. Garcia family history outline was provided by Joe R. Garcia of Grand Junction, Colorado, received November 1992. We include his history outline, with some editing. It is quite an interesting story! We also included information from obituaries of daughter, Christina, from *The Daily Sentinel*, and of wife/mother, Juanita Marez, published in the *Fruita Times*, 21 March 1997.

Lorenzo T. Garcia who was born 19 April 1899, in Belen, Valencia, New Mexico, to Tiburcio and Lucia Garcia. On 14 August 1924, Lorenzo was married to **Juanita M. Marez**, at Gallup, McKinley, New Mexico. Juanita was born 24 June 1907, at San Rafael, Cibola, New Mexico, to Christino and Piedad Marez. She grew up in San Rafael.

Their ten children were:

Anthony T., born 11 July 1925 at Atarque, New Mexico
Cecelia (Chavez), 2 February 1927, San Rafael, New Mexico
Elsie (Torres), 8 July 1929, Mancos, Colorado
Emilio "Joe" Ramon, 25 October 1930, Mancos
Frederico "Fred," 23 May 1933, Mancos
Abel P., 3 February 1935, Mancos
Tiburcio "Tim" John, 25 April 1937, Mancos
Christina, 21 March 1942, Mancos
Eugene E., 3 June 1946, Grand Junction
Ernest, 14 October 1951, Grand Junction

We quote from the history outline contributed by **Joe R. Garcia:**

This family is very large and its circumstances are quite complex. The family came to the Grand Valley not by itself, but with an extended family, several brothers and sisters and their children, to work in the fields of the Western Slope. The family roots were in the amalgam of the indigenous and Spanish families of northern New Mexico, even before the annexation of that area by the United States at the time of the treaty of Guadalupe Hidalgo. That treaty promised sovereignty to all individuals residing on the land annexed by the United States — they became citizens of the United States. In short, the United States *came* to this family, they did not come to the United States.

In short order after this annexation, the Garcia family lost all their land to foreign carpetbaggers, individuals who used new property tax laws foreign

413

(Above left) The Garcia family, about 1952, in New Liberty. In Back, L-R: Juanita, holding granddaughter Cathy, and Lorenzo Garcia. In front: Ernest and Eugene Garcia. (Above center) Frederico "Fred" Garcia in his Airborne Patrol uniform. (Above right) Lorenzo, Eugene and Juanita at Eugene's graduation from University of Utah when he received his B.A. Degree. Eugene graduated from Lawrence University in Topeka, Kansas with a Masters and a Doctorate Degree in 1970. (Below) The Lorenzo Garcia family, 3 September 1994. L-R: Tiburcio "Tim" Garcia, Emilio "Joe" Ramon Garcia, Cecelia Garcia Chavez, Abel P. Garcia (in back), Ernest Garcia (in front of Abel), Elsie Garcia Torres, Frederico "Fred" Garcia and Dr. Eugene E. Garcia. Mother, Juanita Marez Garcia, in front. *(Photos courtesy of Cecelia Garcia Chavez)*

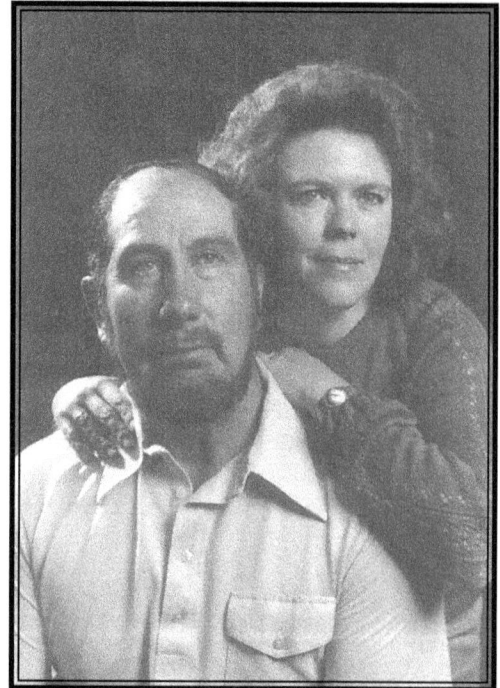

(Above) Joe and Cora Sandaval Garcia's wedding day, 16 October 1945 in Grand Junction, Colorado. L-R: Joseph Chavez, Joe Garcia, Cora Sandaval Garcia and Cecelia Garcia Chavez. Cecelia and Joseph Chavez were married 21 July 1945 in Grand Junction. (Upper right) Couple in front is Abel and Irene Moldonado Garcia on wedding day, 6 June 1959, Fruita, Colorado. They were divorced summer of 1974. The couple in back is unidentified. *(Photos courtesy of Cecelia Garcia Chavez)* (Center right) Abel and second wife, Opal Barnes (Bond), married 24 December 1974. *(Photo courtesy of Opal Garcia)* (Below left) Dr. Eugene and Erminda Holguin Garcia's wedding day, 3 July 1969, Grand Junction, Colorado. (Below right) Anthony and Angelina Garcia's wedding day, 10 January 1949, Grand Junction, Colorado. *(Photos courtesy of Cecelia Garcia Chavez)*

415

to local residents, to "legally" procure land to which they had no actual rights. The Garcia family, once prosperous ranchers, found themselves employees of the new landowners, without a claim to their own land, vagrants in what was once their own ranchos.

Over several generations members of the family sought a working livelihood. One brother, Lorenzo, and his wife came to work in the Colorado agricultural fields as migrant farm workers in the beets, peaches and apples, and settled in the Mack/New Liberty area as share croppers. Their large family, six boys and two girls, with a willingness to work hard, made such a relationship a good one for all concerned.

The family's stay in the Mack/New Libery area was short; some five years. During this period a seventh son was born. The work on the farm was hard and required long hours, but no one complained and the family prospered. The harvests were good during those years; the family felt particularly blessed by the availability of work on the neighboring farms.

One of the sons (Joe R.) married and brought his new bride to live with the family on the farm. Grandma Piedad Marez (we called her "Nana") also joined the family, extending the physical members of the family, while at the same time making the environment a full and warm place for the younger children.

The highlight of those years was the purchase of the family's first pick-up truck. That was no easy feat! Father had no formal education and spoke mostly in Spanish and conducted negotiations with the salesman through his eldest son, Anthony. Borrowing money to purchase anything, including this much-needed shiny new vehicle, was an absolute "no no." Therefore the negotiations required the right price — from the cash which the family had scraped together over several years.

After a long afternoon of confusing negotiations in Fruita, father and son arrived at the farm in that shiny vehicle, a 1950 blue "Chevy" pick-up truck, to the applause of the usually sedate family.

It took only two days to organize a trip to Salt Lake City with father, mother and "Nana" up front with Anthony driving (father and mother both refused to learn how to drive), with all the remaining family members happily packed in the back of the truck. You might say this was the first family trip taken for pleasure.

Two sons joined the U. S. Army, one serving in the Korean War. The two daughters married and moved to Salt Lake City, Utah.

On a cold winter day the owner of the farm advised the family that his oldest son was now ready to occupy the farm residence and return to farming. The Garcia family was asked to find new quarters by

spring. What might have been a lethal blow to the family became an opportunity to occupy another farm in a share-cropping relationship just up the road from Appleton.

Two remaining sons followed the lead of the older brothers and served in the U.S. Army, both serving extended assignments in Europe. The family survived on that farm and yet another as long as there were enough of them to work the fields.

But as the members of the family grew older and began to form their own families, working a farm became impossible. Mother and father and the two youngest boys, Eugene and Ernest, moved to the "big city" of Grand Junction to share the residence of the oldest son, Anthony, and his family. Eugene went to college, the only family member to have that opportunity.

Three brothers and one sister continue to reside on the western slope; two are retired (1992) and one continues to farm. One brother works in Denver, one sister continued to live in Salt Lake City after retirement. One brother is a doctor, Eugene, and is working in California. The oldest son, Tony, and daughter, Christina, have passed away and are buried near their father. Mother lives in her own house in Grand Junction, sharing with her daughter, Elsie, who tries to care for her 85-year-old mother; a difficult task to accomplish, just ask any son or daughter of a hard-working farm veteran.

The Garcia family holds biannual reunions at which time mother, the remaining eight children, 29 grandchildren, 21 great-grandchildren and one great-great-grandchild celebrate the Garcia tradition and enrich the expansive roots which have blessed this family.

Wife and mother, Juanita, died in the Grand Junction Care Center, 15 March 1997, at age 89. She was buried in the Calvary Cemetery, near her husband and two children. At the time of her passing there were 31 grandchildren, 52 great-grandchildren and four great-great-grandchildren.

Geeting

The Geeting story was written from an obituary in *The Daily Sentinel.*

Kenneth "Red" Geeting was born 29 May 1908, at Running Water, South Dakota, and spent his boyhood there. He lived in White Bird, Idaho, for a time before moving to Dragon, Utah, in 1929. He moved to the Fruita area in the early 1930s, where he was married to **Opal Mae Gunther** on 20 September 1934. They had a daughter, **Nettie Rae** (wife of Gene Barnes of New Liberty and Fruita), and a son, **Kenneth Jr.** The family farmed in the New Liberty community for a time on land they had purchased from Graves Corn. That land had been part of the Everetts Brothers' homestead; Red in turn sold it to Clyde Likes, Jr.

For many years Red owned and operated a saw mill, working mostly in the Baxter and Douglas pass areas.

He and Opal had lived on 17 Road, in the Fruita area, for several years before his death on 2 March 1981. He was buried in Elmwood Cemetery at Fruita.

Gerry

The Gerry history was gleaned from obituaries, census records, land records, items from *The Daily Sentinel*, a letter from Clark Gerry, and personal knowledge of the author.

Guy Gilbert Gerry was born 17 June 1896, at Glenrock, Converse, Wyoming, to Henry A. Gerry and Mary Beeman, the oldest of seven children. Guy's father was a well-known farmer who had settled in the Grand Valley about 1902; the family lived in the Loma community many years. Henry Gerry accompanied a load of hogs to Los Angeles, California, in November 1928 and while there he became ill with influenza.

He tried to make it home, but died in Las Vegas, Nevada.

On 26 February 1917, Guy married **Bernice Clark.** Bernice was born 9 June 1892, at Geneva, Fillmore, Nebraska, to Horace M. Clark and (unknown) Larson. Guy and Bernice had three children:

> **Clark Henry,** born 2 June 1918, Fruita
> **Naomi,** 16 March 1921, Fruita
> **Donald Bruce,** 20 November 1929, Fruita
> **Leonard Gerry,** a son of Guy's deceased brother, Albert, joined the family in 1935; Leonard was then three years old.

In 1919, the Gerry family settled on a New Liberty homestead originally filed on by Harvey Lutman. The children attended New Liberty and Fruita Union high schools.

The Gerry farmstead was situated on a hill near the west end of the New Liberty community, across

The Gerry house located on Weir's hill. This home and yard were enjoyed by the Banning family and now the Posts. *(Photo courtesy of Ann Post Hawthorne)*

the road north of Walter Weir's farm, which is presently known as "R Road." The hill became known as "Weir's Hill" (why wasn't it called "Gerry's Hill"?) and was one of the favorite places for the community, young and old alike, to gather for sledding in the winter. With good sledding conditions one could start a ride at the top of the hill a few rods west of Gerry's gate, and ride at least a half mile to the east. What fun!

That hill also presented a challenge to the early "Model Ts" and other autos. Many a driver was heard to boast that he was able to get up enough speed to make it up that hill "in high gear."

Guy Gerry farmed some land on the hill and several acres of bottom land on both sides of Badger Wash, which runs through the property. Guy also occasionally rented land, including the Boyden farm to the north and west.

Gerrys also had a large yard with a well-shaded lawn, a favorite spot for people of the community to gather for picnics on special days.

On 27 March 1936, Bernice died of pneumonia; she was buried in Elmwood Cemetery at Fruita. Two years later, Guy sold the farm to Ray Banning and moved to Loma, and later to Rangely. On 31 December 1948, at Meeker, Colorado, Guy was joined in marriage to **Minta Byers,** formerly of Fruita.

Guy died 16 April 1982 at Rangely, Colorado, and was buried in the Elmwood Cemetery at Fruita.

Clark Henry Gerry made the news in the Fruita items of *The Daily Sentinel* of 6 June 1918, when he came into the world:

> Mr. and Mrs Guy Gerry welcomed the arrival of an eight-pound baby boy into their family last week — the mother and babe are doing nicely at the Fruita Hospital.

Clark graduated from New Liberty School in May 1932 and from Fruita Union High School in 1936. He attended University of Arizona at Tuscon in 1940-41, and then enlisted in the Army Air Corps and was assigned to Pilot Class of 1942. In July of 1942, he was sent overseas to the Middle East Theater as a B24 Pilot.

In June 1944 an article about Clark, including a picture, appeared in "With the Boys and Girls in Service" column of *The Daily Sentinel*:

> The name of Captain Clark Gerry, 25, son of Guy Gerry of Loma, and former Mesa College student, is one of those listed on a scroll on the tail of the famous Liberator bomber, "Wash's Tub," which is making a bond-selling tour of the nation at the present time. Vivid memories of air battles over hostile territory in the Mediterranean and the Middle East were brought back to the officer when the battle-scarred but proud old ship rolled down the landing strip of his present station, Gowan Field, Boise, Idaho, to pay a short visit. Captain Gerry was one of the pilots who guided this historic ship, now being given a well-earned rest from combat, on some of her many missions, during which she chalked up

> 551.35 combat hours, downed 22 enemy planes, sank three Italian and five German warships, and dropped 219 tons of bombs on Axis targets. The officer, who entered the Army Air Force as an aviation cadet in November 1941, was a civil engineering student at the University of Arizona at the time of his enlistment. He is now engaged in training other heavy bombardment crew pilots at the Idaho flying school for overseas duty.

After the end of the war Clark indulged in a playful low-level "buzzing" of the New Liberty community in a B24. Perhaps bending the rules a little — but Fun!

Clark returned to the University of Arizona in 1946 and graduated in 1949 with a degree in civil engineering. After that he worked for the Geological Survey and the U. S. Air Force until retirement in 1982. He has since lived at Peoria, in the vicinity of Phoenix, Arizona.

Naomi Gerry was married 15 July 1938, in Denver, to **Raymond F. White** of Fruita, after attending Fruita Union High School.

They had four children:

H. Gerry
Kim O.
Jon R.
Karen

The family lived in Ogden, Utah, for many years. During World War II Naomi worked at the Ogden Arsenal. She served also as a nurse's aid and was a member of the Ogden Family Counseling Board. She was also a member of the Order of the Eastern Star and Daughters of the Nile. At age 71 and after nearly 54 years of marriage, Naomi died 5 July 1992, in Ogden. She was buried in Washington Heights Memorial Park, Ogden, Utah.

We have very limited information on the other children in the Gerry family. Bruce is reported to have died in Amarillo, Texas, some years ago. Leonard is said to be living near Hotchkiss, Colorado.

Glass

All of the following came from news items in *The Daily Sentinel*.

Charlie Glass never actually lived in Mack or New Liberty, but he was probably in the vicinity many times. As the author I think it fitting to include a few words about Charlie, a black man, who in the early 1900s, came to the Grand Valley from Oklahoma and New Mexico. He worked on Pinon Mesa as a cowboy for the Seiber Cattle Company and later went to eastern Utah, where he worked for the Turner Brothers. The color of his skin made him quite a novelty among the cattle and sheep men of the area. I can remember people who, with a certain amount of awe, told many "tall tales" about the legendary cowboy.

His many friends reported that Charlie was a kindly and courteous man. But misfortune caught up with him on the desert north of Cisco, Utah, when he had a confrontation with a Basque sheepherder. Charlie caught the herder grazing his sheep on the Turner property, though he had promised previously to stay off. It was reported that the sheepherder attempted to kill him, but Charlie shot him in self-defense. There were no witnesses, and Charlie was charged with murder. *The Daily Sentinel* of 30 November 1921 told quite a story about the court proceedings, and the Fruita items in *The Daily Sentinel* of 2 December reported he had been acquitted. The story is told (but not confirmed) that friends of the Basque sheepherder set about to get revenge.

Early one Monday morning in February 1937 Charlie died in an auto accident on highway 6 & 50, about one and one half miles west of Cisco, as he and two sheepherders were returning to that town from Thompson. An account of the accident was found in *The Daily Sentinel* of 24 February 1937. The investigating officers reported that the pickup in which Charlie and the two sheepmen were riding was traveling too fast for road conditions. There was also evidence the men had been drinking. Charlie was thrown out of the pickup and died immediately of a broken neck. The other men were badly bruised but survived.

Some believed the auto accident that claimed Charlie's life was a conspiracy.

The newspaper account of his death made this observation:

> Cattlemen, former employers and acquaintances of Glass all agree that fiction could produce no more colorful nor picturesque a character than Glass. He arrived in the Grand Valley about 39 years ago and from that time on his name has been closely linked with range-riding exploits. As a cowpuncher, those who worked with him declare he was as expert as anyone in the game — a good rider and a top-notch man with a lariat. The fact that he was one of the few negro cowboys in the west added to his notoriety. He was a familiar figure at Western Colorado rodeos.

A funeral was held at Stark's Funeral Home in Fruita; burial was in Elmwood Cemetery. Pall bearers were Ute Osborn, Lester Tomlinson, Lou Young, Claude Taylor, Bert Mahaney and Don Weimer, which seems to say there was a lot of respect for Charlie among his fellow cowboys.

Gnagey

The following is from census and land records, obituaries and news items in *The Daily Sentinel*.

Annie Lucille Gnagey was born 25 December 1889, at Grantsville, Garrett, Maryland, to Abraham Lincoln and Effie Lillian Gnagey.

Annie moved with her parents to Colorado and lived for a time on the eastern slope before moving to Fruita. She graduated from Fruita Union High School in 1911, and later graduated from McPherson College in Kansas.

She achieved some notoriety when she and her friend, May Boyden, were noted in *The Daily Sentinel* as two of the few women who were successful in drawing for homesteads on 29 March 1918. (We wonder if Gnagey and Boyden attended McPherson College together?) Their

40-acre tracts on Sec. 18 R 103W were near each other. Annie was registered as "A. Lucille Gnagey." She probably built the house on her homestead — a better than average house which was probably the same one Burketts lived in later. Annie relinquished to Wesley Burkett in 1919.

Annie must have traveled around some because she married **Ross Gourley** in Waco, Texas, 24 June 1926. They moved to Wenatchee, Washington, in 1929, and then to Seattle in 1945. She died in Seattle in April of 1972 and is buried near her parents in Elmwood Cemetery at Fruita.

Griebel

The following is from news items and obituary in *The Daily Sentinel.*

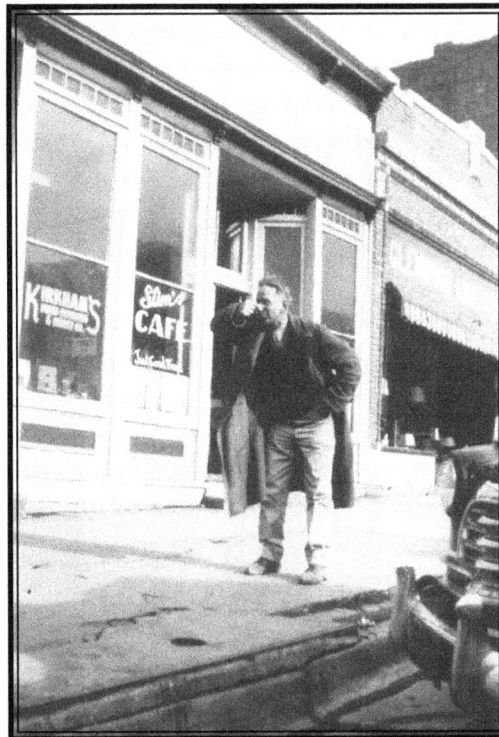

Phillip Griebel shows a sense of humor as he pretends to blow his nose on the sidewalk in downtown Fruita. *(Courtesy of Deyon Davidson Boughton)*

Phillip Griebel, was another legendary character whom students of Fruita Union High School knew as "Mr. Griebel," and whom we chose to include in our history, even though Phillip never lived in Mack or New Liberty. Many students from the two communities were taught mathematics, science, or coached at Fruita Union High School by him.

He was born 28 November 1889, at Warrensburg, Missouri. He attended schools

Teachers, Merton Bergner and Phillip Griebel, standing in front of old Fruita Union High School building that burned in 1934. *(Taken from the "Fruita High School 100 Years, 1893-1993")*

there and later earned a teaching degree in mathematics and science at Missouri State University. He served in the Army in World War I and never married.

According to his obituary in *The Daily Sentinel*, he moved to Fruita in 1927 from Houston, Texas, where he had been both a coach and teacher. At Fruita Union High School he taught mathematics and science and coached; he later served as principal. The athletic field at Fruita Jr. High School (formerly Fruita High) was named in his honor.

He was an avid golfer, photographer, stamp and coin collector, and rockhound. He had an uncanny ability to remember students long after they had left his classroom. He died 28 February 1985, at the age of 96 and was buried in the Elmwood Cemetery at Fruita.

Grimsby

The following information was sent to us by John "Jack" Grimsby. His parents' marriage took some strange turns. We found Sam's obituary in the *Ogden Standard Examiner*.

(Upper) The Grimsby family, 1930. L-R: Ella, Glen and his mother, Minnie Grimsby. In front: John, Sam and Lennis. (Lower) L-R: John "Jack" Avery Grimsby, Ella Foster (Grimsby) O'Brien, Glen Samuel Grimsby and Samuel Orie Grimsby, 1945. *(Photos courtesy of John A. Grimsby)*

Glen Samuel Grimsby, 1919, standing in front of army barracks in Texas. *(Photo courtesy of John A. Grimsby)*

Glen Samuel Grimsby was born 26 November 1898 at New Hampton, Chickasaw, Iowa, to Avery Samuel Grimsby and Minnie Mack. He became a machinist, miner and farmer. In 1925, at Gateway, Mesa, Colorado, he married **Ella Sarah Etta Foster**, who was born at Norwood, San Miguel, Colorado, 25 November 1905.

They had two sons:

John "Jack" Avery Grimsby, born 11 August 1926
Samuel Orie Grimsby, 17 November 1927

The mother, Ella, had a daughter, **Lennis Forman (Clement)**, by a previous marriage, born March 1925.

Ella left Glen and the children, including Lennis, when Sam was a small child; about 1931. Ella's mother and her mother's husband, **Orie and Laura Craig**, took Lennis to raise, and Glen kept the boys.

Glen and the two boys moved from Gateway to New Liberty in the fall of 1931 and lived on the Fred Diehl farm, near East Salt Creek. They lived there until about 1938, then moved to the Fruita area.

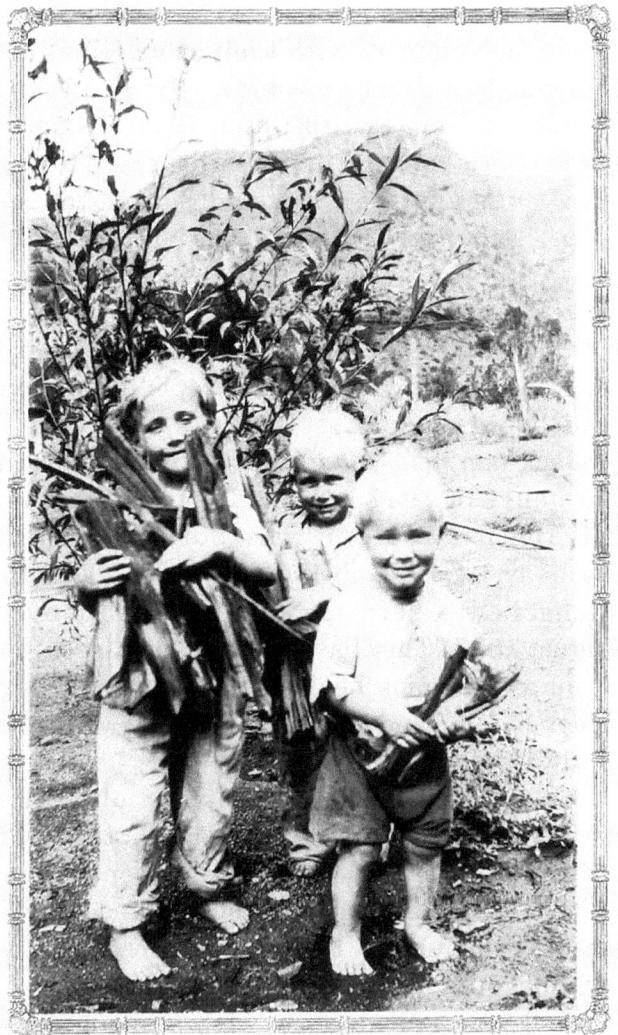

(Upper left) Anna, Tim, John and Monika Grimsby, 1963 in Ogden, Utah. (Center left) I Corps Pistol Champs, 1966 Olympics in Korea. John wrote, "I spent 15 years shooting and training pistol teams, and we generally won." John is the third from the left. (Lower left) Clement family. L-R: Gene, Lennis and Glen. In front: Lenola and dog, Seraffy. (Above) 1930, mother's helpers. L-R: Lennis Edna, John Avery and Samuel Orie. (Below) Michael and Connie Grimsby, 1986. Michael is the son of Samuel Orie Grimsby. *(Photos courtesy of John A. Grimsby)*

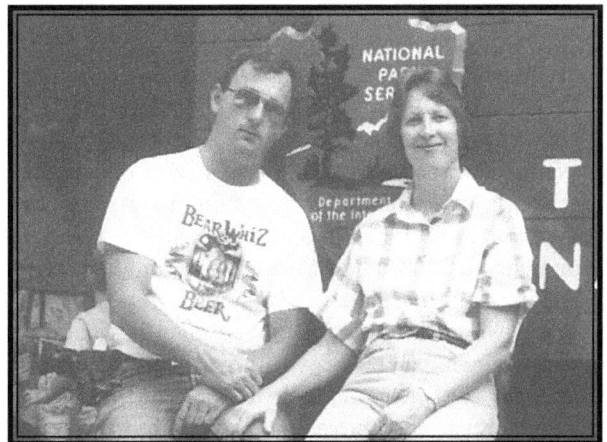

When the boys were about 12 they began to spend the summers with their mom (Ella) and Clinton (her third husband). Sam and Jack graduated from Fruita Union High School in 1945. Both enlisted in the military that same year — Jack in the Army and Sam in the Air Corps. Both made a career of the military.

Jack served in Germany with the Artillery, and was active with the rifle and pistol shooting teams. He built match pistols and one year shot in the Far East Olympics.

Jack married **Anna Louise Sagel** in Berlin, Germany, in 1947. Their daughter, **Monika Elizabeth (Wooley)**, was born in Berlin, Germany, 12 December 1947. A son, **Timothy Michael**, was born in Neu Ulm, Germany, 9 August 1957. They have four grandchildren.

Jack had some health problems — a heart attack in 1968 and another in 1974 — which led to a by-pass operation in 1988.

He retired in 1969 after 25 years of service. After retirement he worked in the photographic industry in Grand Junction. After that he worked for the Oldsmobile, Cadillac and General Motors dealerships. He and Anna presently live in Grand Junction.

Jack now spends time with his computer, talking to politicians, reloading and shooting his rifles and pistols, and working with photography as a hobby. He also enjoys going fishing with his grandchildren. His wife, Anna, is involved with her children and grandchildren and in church and women's organizations.

Following are some memories of New Liberty written by Jack:

New Liberty School is a few miles north of Mack, which is west of Fruita. We lived nearly two miles from school and walked every day. When I started to school we had a one-room schoolhouse with a folding door to divide the lower grades from the upper grades. Grades one through four had the east end and the fifth through eighth had the west end. Each room had a wood-burning heater to keep it warm in the winter. Each stove had a high, tin wall around it to keep the children from burning themselves. The boys used to climb on the tin walls during recess when the stoves were not being used. During winter we all liked the stoves because we could bring potatoes to put in the hot ashes to cook. By noon they were nicely baked so we could have something hot to eat, otherwise we just ate sandwiches and fruit. We drank water from a cistern that was filled just before school started in the fall.

During recess we played marbles, tops, softball, and on the swings, teeter-totter and merry-go-round. Our tops had two kinds of points: one was ball-shaped (called a walker, because it traveled as it spun) the other had a point so it stood still as it spun. It was thought that it would knock the other tops over quicker.

Since we had to walk to school, we started early enough so that we could take our time. We didn't have to be there until 9 o'clock, so we enjoyed the walk. When the roads were muddy, the cars left deep ruts. The driver would put the car's wheels in the ruts and then didn't have to steer the car till it got to the corner, or needed to turn off.

Of course, all the land along the roads was farmed. Most farmers had watermelon or cantaloupe fields. After the first frost we were allowed to eat as much as we wanted to, as long as we put the seeds in a large can that was in the field. The farmers washed the seeds and dried them for sale to the seed companies.

We had quite a few springs on our farm on the west side of the creek, but the springs were so salty that crystals grew in the water. On the other side of the creek the springs were pure, sweet water. The good water was only about 50 feet from the bad.

We had community gatherings called "sings" about once a month. Everyone brought food to share. The kids sang and put on skits. There were also songs for everyone. These took place in the evenings and went into the night. One night some young men put someone's "Model A" car up on the school's roof. My brother and I worried about that all the way home.[†]

I seem to remember you (Phyllis), Sam and I helping some chicks out of the shells, for which we got a scolding. I also remember bringing a box of .22 shells to school. One of the boys found a piece of metal, kind of like a golf-club, with which we took turns hitting the shells so they would go "bang." The teacher took them away from us.

As Sam and I were quite shy, it was hard for us to make friends, so we usually played at home.

The first years we went to school, it was a

one-room school. Then the old school was torn down and a new school was built. We enjoyed that, as there were lots of shingles around from the old building with which to make whip arrows. The competition was to see how high they would go.

During my third year at school we found that our sister, Lennis, was going to school at New Liberty with us. One afternoon, Lennis and her two cousins came over to our farm and took Sam and I to our grandmother's farm a couple of miles north of our place. We hadn't seen our mother for several years, so she seemed a stranger to us.

During our third year we sold our farm and went to Fruita, where we lived in a tent just outside of town. My brother and I went to Fruita Elementary School till the end of the school year, then we moved to Bonanza, Colorado, in Sagauche County. As Bonanza was a bit over 9,000 feet, it was a big change from New Liberty (which is 5,600 feet).

Sam entered the Air Corps in 1945 and made it a career. He retired as master sergeant in communications in 1971.

He married **Margaret Bingham**, 2 February 1950, in Ogden, Utah. They had a son, **Michael**, born in 1958 in Ogden.

Sam died 2 July 1975 at Trout Lake in Montrose County, Colorado, of an apparent heart attack. He was 47 years of age.

We assume he was buried in Ogden. His wife and son continue to live in Ogden. Son, Michael, works in social services with troubled teens. Michael's wife, **Connie**, works for Internal Revenue Service in Ogden. They have two children: **Amanda and Aaron.**

†The story above is not remembered by the author, but I do remember when a number of local teenage pranksters removed the boy's outhouse and parked Glen's Model "T" over the hole.

H

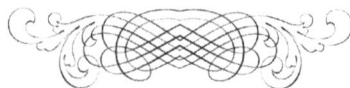

Harris

The following is from a letter written by **Lois Harris Currey**, wife of Tom Currey:

My family lived at Mack for awhile, so I'll include a bit of my own history for you:

John E. "Jack" Harris and **Emme B. Edwards** traded their ranch at Collbran, Colorado, to Dean Waters, and we moved to Mack on 18 August 1933.

My parents, along with my oldest sister, **Cora Belle Harris Parsons** and her husband, **Jake**, ran a dairy and shipped milk on the Uintah Railway as well as running a local route throughout the town of Mack. The milk shipped on the Uintah went to Atchee, Watson, and other small towns on the route. I was only eight years old at the time, and didn't pay too much attention to individual addresses!

My mother made butter and molded it into one-pound cubes with a wooden mold. She also made cream cheese, which was sold on the route and at Mr. Cox's Mack Mercantile.

Mack, at that time, was a really personable little town with two grocery stores, a pool hall and a twenty-room hotel with dining room. There were also two service stations and three streets full of houses.

How it has changed! The house we lived in was between Mack and Loma and sits on a hillside south of the old highway, but can be seen from I-70, looking toward the north. It was built by Charles Kiefer (Cecelia Ann's father) and the Hirons family was involved in its history somewhere. It is currently headquarters for "Country Jam USA," its fields a glorified parking lot.

The school house at the west end of Mack was a pretty building with the "Big Room" grades five through eight and the "Little Room" grades one through four. There was a nice wide hallway with a drinking fountain and a sink for washing hands.

There was also a scaled-down gymnasium that served the students well in bad weather. We had more plays than most schools; I really did like that part of school.

This is a wild guess, but there must have been between 40 and 50 students attending school at the time I did. I finished third grade there and most of the fourth. My teacher was Mildred Hogsett, and what a lovely lady she was! My sister, **Eloise Harris Jones**, also attended school at Mack. There is a lot to be credited to small schools; we had all the advantages we needed, and certainly no disadvantages

We moved from Mack on 15 March 1935 and I enrolled in Appleton Consolidated School. You might be interested to know that part of the Mack School building was moved to Appleton on 24 Road, just south of H Road. It was remodeled and became part of a larger dwelling.

Harrison

From an obituary in *The Daily Sentinel* and land records.

Benjamin "Ben" Arthur "Art" Harrison was born 15 July 1873, at Wakefield, Clay, Kansas. He spent much of his childhood at Clay Center, Kansas. He enlisted in the Army and served in the Spanish-American War. After the war he spent some time in Alaska, after which (1919) he settled on a homestead in the New Liberty community. His farm was Unit G, Section 21, R 103 W, between Robert M. Phillips and Floyd Thomas.

He was always active in community affairs and served for some time on the New Liberty School Board. Virtually nothing is known of his family life. He was still a resident of the Mack area at the time of his death, 6 September 1944, at St. Mary's Hospital in Grand Junction. He was buried in Elmwood Cemetery at Fruita.

Hawthorne

The following information is from a letter by Victor L. Hawthorne and interview with Vic and Jesse.

Victor Lemoyne Hawthorne was born 23 April 1917 at Trumbull, Clay, Nebraska, to Wayne Hawthorne and Ruby Etta Smith. When Victor was one year old the family moved to a homestead near Holyoke, Phillips, Colorado. After a year

Victor, Jesse and William Howard Hawthorne in front of home at Fruita in 1994. *(Photo courtesy of Vic and Jesse Hawthorne)*

there they went back to Trumbull and farmed a year, later selling the homestead at Holyoke, and buying a farm near Burlington, Kit Carson, Colorado, where Victor attended school during his growing-up years. He went back to Trumbull to attend high school.

In **1936**, during the dust-bowl years, Victor left Kit Carson and went to work on a large cattle ranch in the San Luis Valley where he met his future wife, **Jesse Ellen Cooper**. Jesse and another girl were cooking for the crew of upwards of **60 to 70** single men who ate at the cook-house. Jesse was born 25 November 1919 at Hotchkiss, Delta County, Colorado. She was raised by **William Orlen** and **Mabel Angela Lovejoy Cooper**.

Victor and Jessie were married 5 March 1938 at Alamosa, Alamosa, Colorado.

They raised three sons:

William Wayne, born 5 July 1940 at Alamosa, Colorado. He married **Sue Davis**, 12 August 1966, in Sacramento, California. She had two children from a previous marriage: **Wayne Darwin** and **Nannette Fisher**. **Jerry James** and **Mark Hawthorne** were born to them later.

Jerry James, born 20 November 1942 at Gunnison, Colorado. He married **Mableann Post**, daughter of Charlie and Mamie Post of New Liberty, 15 November 1974, in Grand Junction. They had one daughter, **Kathryn**. Jerry and Mabel were divorced. Jerry works at Colorado State Prison at Canon City, Colorado; Mableann and Kathryn live on the old Raver homestead, presently owned by Victor Hawthorne.

William Howard (adopted), born 21 April 1962 at Sacramento, California, married **Karen Serve**, 21 March 1986 in Grand Junction. They had no children as of 1994.

Victor worked for a large cattle ranch at Gunnison for several years, then they moved to Clifton, Colorado, for one summer (1943). That summer Victor and Jim Cooper planted 15 acres of tomatoes about one mile west of Clifton, "making a profit of $25" for their summer's work. Then they went back to Kit Carson County where Victor worked for the Coke Cattle Co. until 1952, when Vic and Jim came to New Liberty and purchased the Lee Foss farm. However, they lived on the Diehl farm (where the Coopers lived) the first year, and didn't occupy the Foss farm until the next year. During the time they lived on the Foss farm, Victor worked part time for the Young Cattle Co. (Bill Young & Sons) helping with the cattle feeding and farm work. During that time also Jessie served as custodian at New Liberty School, substituting occasionally for Mrs. Morrow as cook in the school lunch program.

In October 1956 Victor went to work at the State Home and Training School at Grand Junction. They sold the Foss farm about 1962 and moved to a place on "D" road, near Grand Junction, where they raised sheep, selling lambs and wool, with Jessie serving as sheep herder. They bought the Anderson farm in New Liberty in 1977 (the Raver homestead). Vic retired from the State Home and Training School in February 1978 and in 1980 bought a home in Fruita where they currently live.

Vic still keeps some cattle on the Anderson place (Raver homestead); we visited there in 1995 and saw a peculiar addition to the Hawthorne cattle herd — a yearling bull elk that had been orphaned by poachers in the area. He took up with Vic's cattle and had come to believe he was a bovine instead of a wapiti and also the boss of the herd. At that time Vic was negotiating with the fish and game officials to take him away, as he had become quite a nuisance. (He should have put him in the freezer).

A bull elk raised with Vic Hawthorne's cattle on his farm in New Liberty. *(Photo courtesy of Ann Post Hawthorne)*

Henderson

The Henderson story is from census records, obituaries and other news items in *The Daily Sentinel.*

Darie L. Henderson was born 5 April 1879, at Franklin, Johnson, Indiana, spending his childhood there and in Nebraska. He came to the Grand Valley with his parents in 1895, traveling by covered wagon. He married **Jessie Alameda Norine** at East Lawn, near Grand Junction, 30 September 1904.

Jessie was born at Prairie City, Jasper, Iowa, 14 March 1877, to Swedish parents Andrew and Carrie Norine, and spent her childhood at Oakland, Nebraska. She came with her parents to the Grand Valley in 1894. Her father operated a fruit farm east of Grand Junction known as East Lawn. Jessie became a school teacher and taught for several years before her marriage to Darie Henderson.

Darie and Jessie had four children:

Josephine (Reseigh)
Richard C.
Roger L.
Ben A.

According to the 1920 census, the family was then living in the Mack area, probably at Camp #8.

Darie joined the Bureau of Reclamation, 24 October 1902, six months after it was organized, beginning as a rodman on the Grand Valley (Highline) Project. He worked on preliminary surveys on the Uncompahgre Project (Delta County) in 1903, was assigned briefly to survey work on the Pecos River Project near Roswell, New Mexico, returning to the Uncompahgre until 1909, then heading back to the Grand Valley project.

Except for brief assignments in Boise, Idaho, and Utah, he worked for the

Grand Valley Project until retirement; at that time he was serving as watermaster. He held the national record for longevity with the bureau when he retired in January 1947.

Jessie died 22 September 1944. Darie died 20 October 1960, at age 81, of injuries received in an auto accident. Both are buried in the Grand Junction Municipal Cemetery.

Herron

The Herron story was compiled from obituaries in *The Daily Sentinel*, land records, census records and author's personal knowledge.

Orval R. Herron was born 19 October 1885 at Hartsville, Bartholomew, Indiana, to John H. and Jessie W. Herron. Orval was a first cousin of Robert and William Cox — his father and the Cox brothers' mother, were brother and sister.

The family moved to Mesa County when Orval was 11 years old. He spent the remainder of his life in the Grand Valley, attending schools in Grand Junction and Fruita. On 14 December 1918 he married **Lillian Anderson** in Grand Junction. Lillian was born 30 April 1900, in Grand Junction.

Their children were:

William Frederick "Fred," born 22 January 1922, Grand Junction
Margaret Gaye (Coyle), 29 February 1924, Grand Junction
James "Jim" Anderson, 16 September 1930, Grand Junction

We have found evidence that in 1925 Orval and his family assumed management of the Loma Hotel (see the Sweitzer story). The Herron family lived for many years on a farm on Red Mesa, north of Mack, just across the road south of the Hollinger homestead. While the children were attending schools at Mack and Fruita they were able to catch the school bus almost at their front door.

The Herron's farm always appeared to produce well and the home and outbuildings were well-kept. The farm produced diversified crops and livestock,

leaning somewhat toward the production of milk and cream. One of the farm's added attractions was a spring of water that surfaced a short distance south of the house, enhancing the livestock operation. Water from that spring was also used for irrigation a mile or so farther south. But the spring is now dry since the Highline canal was sealed and the laterals replaced by underground pipes.

In addition to his farm interests, Orval was involved in the real estate business as a member of the Rankin and Herron firm. In the mid-1930s Orval played an active part in the organization and development of the Grand Valley Rural Power Lines

Orval died in an auto accident on the "new" highway east of Fruita on 3 May 1947. He was buried in the Grand Junction Municipal Cemetery.

Son James "Jim" continued on the farm for a number of years with a new milk barn and a Grade -A dairy business.

Lillian worked for several years in the Mesa County Budget Office. She died 21 April 1970 and was also buried in Grand Junction Municipal Cemetery.

Hiatt

The Hiatt story was compiled from obituaries and other news items in *The Daily Sentinel* as well as information obtained from Goldie Hiatt Arbuckle.

Edwin "Ed" Dalbert Hiatt was born 5 February 1879, in Wayne County, Indiana, to Lyndon C. and Samantha Hiatt. He spent his childhood in Indiana, moving with his parents to western Kansas as a young man. They moved to Fruita, Colorado, in 1900. He had three brothers and three sisters. Two of the brothers lived close to Ed in Fruita. Ed's parents lived in a home close to the river south of Fruita.

On 25 December 1902, at Fruita, Ed married **Ida Maude Young**, a daughter of George Young. Ida had auburn hair, brown eyes and was beautiful and trim. She was a good cook, sewed beautiful things, and grew wonderful gardens. Ed and Ida did everything together and for each other. They had six children:

Ed Hiatt's children in 1953, when they were reunited as a family. Left to right: Goldie, George, LaDean, Edwin "Red," Myrle and Vernon. *(Photo courtesy of Donna Hiatt Guccini)*

Myrle (Brumfield), born 23 August 1904
Edwin "Red" Albert, 17 May 1907
Goldie (Arbuckle), 21 January 1910
George, 22 May 1912
Vernon, 8 April 1914
LaDean (Stobaugh), 9 April 1920
All the children were born in Fruita.

Ed built a lovely home for his family on his farm between Fruita and Grand Junction by the railroad tracks. They were the first ones in the area to get modern things, such as a car and phonograph.

On his farm Ed raised a few cattle, turkeys, pigs, chickens and beautiful horses. He was very proud of his horses and took special care of them. He used them not only to do his own farming, but to dig potatoes and bind grain for other farmers with his binder.

Ida died from Bright's disease in Fruita, 17 February 1922 at age 39, leaving Ed alone to care for six children ranging in age from 2 to 17 years. Perhaps he thought to make the situation easier by marrying **Allie Mae Raver,** of New Liberty, widow of John Raver, 27 October 1922, at Fruita, but that marriage was short-lived.

Ed tried to hold his family together, but was unable to. When LaDean was about four years old, she was adopted out to a nice couple in Grand Junction, Joseph and Sylvia Newlan. Goldie knew where she was and visited her a few times, but that became too difficult for both of them. LaDean came back into the family when her adoptive parents passed away. Goldie went to live with her married sister, Myrle, and then later with her grandmother. She eventually rented a room until she finished school and got married. The boys stayed at home and helped on the farm until Ed lost the farm.

Ed became very bitter and did things during this time that he normally would not have done. George was living on a farm in New Liberty and in about 1935 Ed rented the Everett Bowen farm in New Liberty. Vernon and George both lived there with him for a time.

Ed was well known for his fiery temper, and, on more than one occasion, got into trouble because of it. One time, as a threshing crew was waiting to start the day's work, a neighbor, **Joe Owings,** confronted Ed, accusing him of stealing a pitchfork. Ed drew his pocket knife and roared: "I'll cut a ring around your G__ D___ neck!" Joe let the accusation drop as members of the crew subdued Ed. [Homer Likes was a personal witness of this episode.] Ed was very outspoken; it could never be said that he didn't speak up when he felt he had something to say.

On 17 October 1937 Ed married **Agnes Evelyn Shoults Lee,** a widow who had lived in the Mack/New Liberty communities for many years. Agnes was born 17 July 1877 in Iowa. A pioneer in the truest sense, she left Iowa with her parents when she was 12 years old and they traveled in a covered wagon to Chadron, Nebraska, where her younger sister, Charlotte (Mrs. J. L. Booth), was born. Agnes was married previously and had a daughter, Helen, by that marriage.

Agnes was associated with the Uintah Hotel at Mack for several years as cook and manager. She leased the hotel in June of 1930 and had sole control of it for some time. She was keeping house and caring for Bill Maluy's children at the time she married Ed Hiatt.

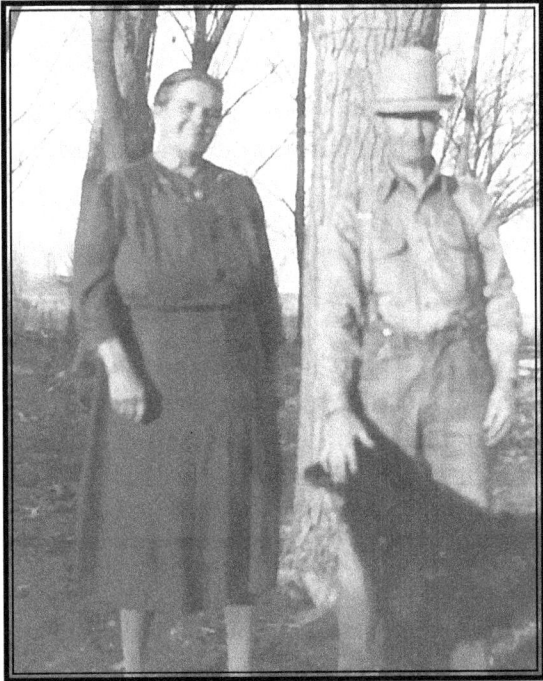

Agnes and Ed Hiatt on Ed's 64th birthday, 5 February 1943, at their farm in New Liberty. *(Photo courtesy of Donna Hiatt Guccini)*

The Red Hiatt family, about 1946. L-R: Edwin "Red," Betty, Pearl and Donna Hiatt. *(Photo courtesy of Donna Hiatt Guccini)*

The family says that Agnes was the best thing that ever happened to Ed. He mellowed and became more like himself. Phyllis Likes remembers how particular and meticulous he was with everything he had, and was a good farmer. She remembers being at the Hiatt's home on the Bowen place one time when he proudly showed Phyllis and her sister, Bubbles, his chickens and garden. Another time Phyllis, and other Maluy family members, was visiting with Ed and Agnes when they lived on the Diehl place. Ed was proudly showing off his garden and his beautiful strawberries. As they talked, Ed would periodically say to Agnes, "Agnes, please don't step on the strawberries." Pretty soon Agnes said, "Oh, the hell with your damn strawberries," and proceeded to stomp right up through the middle of them. The Maluy family has laughed about that for all these years.

Agnes died at Pueblo, Colorado, 22 July 1945. Ed died 2 August 1949 in Grand Junction. Both are buried in the Elmwood Cemetery at Fruita.

$\mathcal{E}$dwin "Red" Albert Hiatt, oldest son of Ed Hiatt, was born 17 May 1907, at Fruita, where he spent his childhood and attended schools.

On 8 September 1925, Red married **Pearl Bickel** in Grand Junction.

Red and Pearl had two daughters:

Betty (Collins), born 14 May 1927, Fruita
Donna (Guccini), 21 September 1931, Fruita

Red worked at various jobs throughout his life, most of them related to farming. In August 1948 he was operating a Caterpillar tractor (bulldozer) on a construction job in Unaweep Canyon, when the Cat overturned, pinning Red under it. The resulting injuries caused him to lose an arm, and then a leg years later. After that, he carried mail under contract from Grand Junction to the Loma and Mack post offices.

Red died 15 January 1984, at age 76, in the Lower Valley Nursing Home. He was buried in Elmwood Cemetery at Fruita. Pearl lives in Grand Junction with her daughter, Donna.

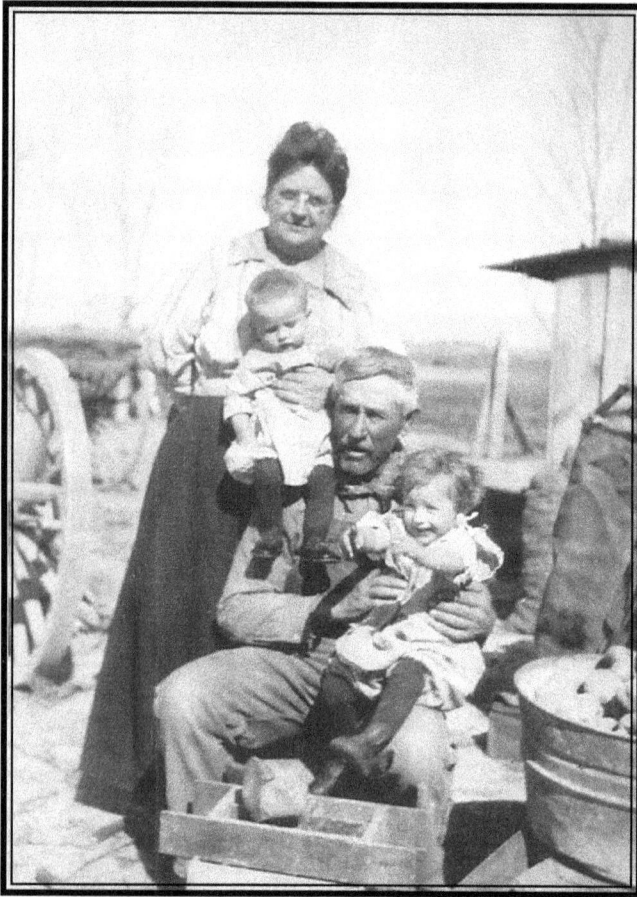

Edward and Blanche Hollinger with grandchildren, Edward and Delores Collins, on March 1925 at the Hollinger farm. *(Photo courtesy of Maurine Collins Reed)*

Hollinger

The Hollinger story comes from obituaries and other news items in *The Daily Sentinel*.

$\mathscr{E}$dward Clayton Hollinger was born 25 May 1867, at Chambersburg, Franklin, Pennsylvania. He spent his childhood there, then moved to Missouri where he met and married **Blanche Eveline Friz** at Kansas City, 7 October 1896. Blanche was born 1 December 1873, at Chester, Michigan. She lived there until she was six, when the family moved to a farm near Abeline, Kansas.

After marriage, Edward and Blanche established a home at Salina, Kansas, then, in 1900, moved to Abilene, where Ed was a banker. They had two daughters:

Edna Blanche, born 10 November 1897,

Salina, Saline, Kansas
Lois Maurine, 5 August 1899,
Abilene, Dickinson, Kansas
(See Smith, Collins and Saunders stories for more on Edna and Lois).

In 1909 the family moved to Bailey, Colorado, where Ed raised purebred cattle for a few years.

They came to the western slope in 1918, and settled on a homestead on the Red Mesa north of Mack. That homestead had the distinction of being one of the most sought-after units in the Bureau of Reclamation drawing of 29 March

(Upper) Identified on back of picture as first home of Ed and Blanche Hollinger when they homesteaded the ranch at Mack (Red Mesa), taken 20 September 1919. (Lower) Identified as homestead of Ed and Blanche Hollinger in Mack, Colorado, 1 June 1918. The lower photo is the home the Hollingers lived in located at the top of what was known as "Hollinger's Hill." This property became the property of Edna B. Smith and the Smiths enlarged the home. The upper photo is possibly on the land that was deeded to Blanche Hollinger and became the property of Lois M. Saunders. *(Photos courtesy of Maurine Collins Reed)*

1918; 40 applicants had signed up for it. They owned two parcels of land. The one by the hillside, consisting of 70.7 acres, was deeded to Edward C. Hollinger. The other parcel just east of it was deeded to Blanche E. Hollinger and consisted of 40.0 acres. The daughters fell heir to the farm some years later. Edna inherited the hillside property of Edward, and Lois the property of Blanche.

The Hollinger farm seemed to be a focal point for the area. Not only was there an excellent hill for sledding on the road which ran north and south on the west side of it, but for people who were unfamiliar with the neighborhood, the Hollinger farm was used for a reference point in giving directions.

Edward Hollinger died at his farm home 27 July 1938; Blanche died 6 February 1944. Both are buried in Elmwood Cemetery at Fruita.

Homedew

Samuel Abyron Homedew
(Photo courtesy of Barbara Peterson Homedew)

Information from obituaries in *The Daily Sentinel*; telephone conversations with Charles Homedew, Frances Homedew Mercer and Colleen Homedew; an interview with Barbara Homedew and the use of family records in her possession.

Samuel "Sam" Abyron Homedew was born 12 May 1886 in Oxford, Sumner, Kansas, a son of Charles Henry Homedew and Emma Frances Randall. He spent his childhood there before moving to eastern Colorado.

The Homedews have an interesting ancestry that has been traced back to 1417 in France. The name was originally L' HommeDieu; they were Huguenots. Following are extractions from the books, "Universal Book of Peerages of France, " Volume XX, by St. Allairs Lords of Tranchant and Lignerolles, and "Southold and Its People in the Revolutionary Days," by Wayland Jefferson.

In LaRochelle, France, lived the family of Pierre L' HommeDieu. They were Huguenots or French Protestants. At the time, the prevailing religion was Catholic. King Louis XIV at first allowed this religion to be practiced, later he revoked his approval and those who followed the Protestant Religion were persecuted. Their names were placed on lists which were posted in public places and their goods were confiscated. On one of these lists was the name of Martha L' HommeDieu and family; this was on 29 September 1685.

Pierre L' HommeDieu had died previous to this date. The family consisted of Martha L' HommeDieu whose maiden name was Peyron. She married a man named Bourchard and had a son, Jean. She married a second to Pierre and had three sons: Benjamin, Hosea (Osee) and Pierre. The father Pierre lived in LaRochelle 1629–1685.

At the time of the persecution in 1685, Jean and Benjamin were in the French Navy. They jumped ship and became stowaways on an American ship and came to America.

At the time of the flight, Martha went to England with Pierre and Osee. Pierre's name appears on a ship passenger list to America on the ship William and Mary on 31 January 1690. Martha came to America and lived with Pierre in Kingston, New York (then called Old Hurley). Later she returned to England, and as Pierre's will stated, he left all to his mother, Martha, living in England. The will was signed 10 February 1691. Pierre was on a visit to New York City (then New Amsterdam) when he died.

Benjamin L' HommeDieu and Jean Bourchard (L' HommeDieu) applied for citizenship in New York City on 19 August 1687; they were granted citizenship. Jean was granted citizenship under the name of John L' HommeDieu.

The book about Southold mentions a "visit of General George Washington to Honorable Ezra L' HommeDieu." Ezra would be from one of the later generations in the 1700s.

Rosa Effie Hall
(Photo courtesy of Barbara Peterson Homedew)

Sam married **Rosa Effie Hall**, on 27 November 1912, in Springfield, Baca, Colorado. Rosa was born 21 March 1895 in Yates Center, Woodson, Kansas, the youngest of six children born to Daniel Sylvester Hall and Mary Rachel Morrow.

Samuel and Rosa had five sons and one daughter:

John Valentine, born 14 February 1914 in Hugoton, Stevens, Kansas
Charles Daniel, 28 March 1916, Hugoton
Henry Harold, 11 September 1918, Hugoton
George, 25 May 1922, Springfield, Baca, Colorado
Mary Frances (Mercer), 30 December 1927, Holly, Prowers, Colorado
Roy Leslie, 15 November 1930, Noti, Lane, Oregon

Sam and Rosa homesteaded in Hugoton, Kansas, after their marriage. The first three children were born there. The family moved to eastern Colorado in the early 1920s where the next two children were born, and then they moved to Oregon in the late 1920s where the last child, Roy, was born. They returned to Holly on the eastern slope of Colorado for a short time before coming to western Colorado.

Rosa and Sam Homedew
(Photo courtesy of Barbara Peterson Homedew)

In 1938 they purchased 22.4 acres of land in the New Liberty community formerly owned by Thomas Carroll, just south of the siphon. Frances says the boys bought it in John's name.

Since there wasn't enough land to make a

living, Sam and the boys worked for farmers in the Lower Valley. When working Sam always wore a red kerchief around his neck, a long sleeved shirt and overalls. His philosophy was that the kerchief around his neck helped keep him cool. It would cause him to sweat and then the breeze blowing on his wet neck would work like an air conditioner. He believed that if a person kept his neck cool, the rest of the body would stay cool.

The Homedews owned burros and one would see Sam and Roy riding around the neighborhood in a special homemade cart pulled by the burros.

The Homedew's home was like lots of the homes in New Liberty: small with rough wooden floors. It was only one big room when they moved there. It didn't have any modern conveniences like running water in the house, refrigeration or a bathroom, just a "two-holer" outside and a coal oil lamp for lights. Water had to be hauled in by the bucket for culinary use, baths and laundry. It was heated on the coal stove. In 1942 they moved to Appleton for two years; when they returned in 1944 they added two rooms on the back of the house. They also put false brick siding on it and wired it for electricity. In the late 1940s they got a telephone. Rosa said that this was the best house she had had since she was married.

Frances and Roy attended school at New Liberty and Frances graduated from Fruita Union High School.

Rosa and Sam separated in 1950 and Rosa moved to Grand Junction. She worked as a professional seamstress for a dry cleaning business doing alterations and repairs, then she worked for a men's clothing store until she qualified for Social Security. Rosa died 26 June 1961 in Grand Junction.

Sam continued to live on the farm in New Liberty until 1959 when he moved to Fruita. John moved in with him when he retired from the Army in 1965. Sam died at the Lower Valley Hospital in Fruita on 20 September 1966 at the age of 80.

John Valentine Homedew
(Photo courtesy of Barbara Peterson Homedew)

John Valentine never married, but made a career of the military. He retired after serving 22 years in the Army (1943 to 1965) as a Mess Sergeant. He was in Europe during World War II, served two terms in the Korean War, and spent 10 years on duty in Germany. He

John Valentine Homedew sitting at his desk during the time he was in the Army. *(Photo courtesy of Barbara Peterson Homedew)*

434

(Upper left) Sam plowing with his mules on the Homedew farm in New Liberty..

(Upper right) Mary Frances and the burros, about 1944. Charles titled this picture, "Two Jacks and a Queen.".

(Center left) Roy and Sam Homedew in their grain field, about 1946 Looks like they have a reason to feel proud.

(Center right) Roy with a new calf on the New Liberty farm. This calf may have become his 4-H calf.

(Below right) Rosa Homedew, Ina Mae Beesley, and Mary Frances Homedew, about 1946 on the Homedew farm in New Liberty. The Homedew house is in the background. *(All photos courtesy of Barbara Peterson Homedew)*

loved Germany; he said it was beautiful there and he did extensive touring. When he retired in 1965, he moved in with his father in a mobile home in Fruita. On the morning of 20 October 1976 John was found dead under his trailer, evidently a victim of choking to death on his morning bacon. He had been living alone since his father's death in 1966.

Charles Daniel Homedew, 1941.
(Photo courtesy of Barbara Peterson Homedew)

Charles Daniel was in the Civilian Conservation Corps stationed on Grand Mesa during 1935–36. He also helped build the road on the Colorado National Monument. He went to New Liberty in 1936 to work for his Uncle John Hall who had rented a farm from Don Weimer. He worked for Rudolph Johnson in 1937 and 1938. His parents and family followed him to New Liberty in 1938. In 1939 he rented and farmed the Bill Dille farm. He joined the Army in December 1941. He said he was stationed at boot camp when he heard the news over the loud speaker that the United States had declared war on Japan. He served in England, France, Belgium and Germany before being discharged in October 1945. After he got out of the military, he worked for farmers, road

construction companies, and oil rigs. He was working for an oil rig company when he left New Liberty and went to Blanding, Utah.

Charles married **Barbara Lucille Peterson** in the Salt Lake Temple on 9 May 1960 after five years of courtship in Blanding. Barbara was born 10 August 1928 in Salt Lake City, Salt Lake, Utah, the seventh of 12 children of Lorenzo Stowell Peterson and Ida Mae Turley. Barbara had been married previously to Lester Neil and had three children:

> **Nancy Lucille,** born 14 July 1953, Salt Lake City, Salt Lake, Utah
> **Rebecca,** 6 July 1954, Monticello, San Juan, Utah
> **David Lester,** 6 September 1955, Monticello

Charles and Barbara lived in Blanding and had five children:

> **Ruth,** born 24 January 1962, Monticello
> **Samuel Lorenzo,** 24 June 1963, Monticello
> **Beth,** 31 August 1964, Monticello
> **Rosamae,** 22 August 1966, Cortez, Montezuma, Colorado
> **Heidi,** 23 August 1969, Monticello

Charles and Barbara were divorced in 1985 after 25 years of marriage. Charles went to work on road construction in Green River, Montezuma Creek and then Olathe, Colorado where he retired in 1987 and presently lives. He is very talented with wood and leather. He makes wooden tops and lamps to sell to enhance his income from Social Security.

Barbara went to work for the school district in Blanding and the district paid for her education at Brigham Young University in elementary education. She got her teaching degree at age 49 and taught school in Blanding for 20 years. She presently lives in Provo, Utah.

(Above) Harold and Edith Homedew's family. L-R: Marie, Kaye, Harold, Paul and Edith Homedew. *(Photo courtesy of Barbara Peterson Homedew)*

George Homedew, 1943.
(Photo courtesy of Barbara Peterson Homedew)

Henry **Harold** served in the Army during World War II from August 1941 to late 1945. He was wounded in Germany in 1944 when a piece of shrapnel hit him in the right elbow. He suffered from a frozen elbow for the rest of his life. Harold married **Edith Meyhew** on 17 May 1947 in Lamar, Prowers, Colorado. They had three children:

> **Kaye**, born 13 January 1948, Lamar, Powers, Colorado
> **Paul**, 21 May 1952, Clayton, Union, New Mexico
> **Marie**, 9 December 1954, Lamar

Harold owned a wheat farm for several years in Lamar and then owned and ran a feed store there until retirement. He lived in Lamar until his death in Denver on 26 December 1977. He was buried in Lamar.

George also served in the Army during World War II from October 1942 until late in 1945. His service was a tour of duty in Japan driving a Jeep for the Red Cross. When he came home he went to work for oil rigs as a driller. Over the years he worked in Texas, Wyoming, Colorado and Utah. He married **Esther Littleton** 2 November 1952. George and Esther had three children:

> **Galen**, born 26 October 1953, Grand Junction
> **Barbara**, 10 January 1955, Grand Junction
> **Judy**, 19 July 1958,

George and Esther's marriage ended in divorce. He had two other marriages; **Josphine Skiels** (before Esther) and **Velma Peterson** (after Esther).

When he quit the oil work, George and family moved to Meeker, Rio Blanco, Colorado and he worked for several years at a Conoco gas/service station. He became restless and decided to go back to work on an oil rig. As he was preparing to go to work on the morning of 3 November 1976, he had a heart attack. He died at the Pioneer Hospital in Meeker at age 54. He was buried in Meeker.

(Above) The family of Charles & Barbara Peterson Homedew, 1992. Standing L-R: Samuel and Deanna Homedew, Rosamae Homedew and Thomas Daleboul, David and Pat Homedew, Ruth Homedew and Craig Heninger, Beth Homedew and Casey Nielson, Nancy Homedew and William Player, Rebecca Homedew and Kevin Rocque, and Heidi Homedew and Dale Brown. Sitting in front is Barbara Peterson and Charles Homedew. (Center left) George and Esther Homedew's family. L-R: Galen, Esther, Judy, George and Barbara Homedew. *(Photos courtesy of Barbara Peterson Homedew)*

(Left) Mary Frances and Robert Mercer with four of their five children, about 1955. L-R: Mildred Ann, Mary Frances, Donald Wayne, Melvin Lester, Robert A. and Larry Gene Mercer. *(Photo courtesy of Barbara Peterson Homedew)*

438

Mary Frances Homedew, 1945.
(Photo courtesy of Barbara Peterson Homedew)

Mary Frances and Roy Leslie Homedew before coming to New Liberty in 1938. *(Photo courtesy of Barbara Peterson Homedew)*

Mary Frances married **Robert A. Mercer** 18 August 1946 in Fruita. They had five children:

Larry Gene, born 1 March 1948, Grand Junction
Mildred Ann (Sturgeon), 28 December 1949, Montrose, Montrose, Colorado
Melvin Lester, 18 March 1951, Montrose
Donald Wayne, 10 December 1954, Denver, Denver, Colorado
Beverly Joyce (Rosenow), 9 February 1956, Denver

Frances had been called Frances until 1981 when she decided to be called by her first name, Mary. It was quite a challenge for friends and family, but she is now known as Mary.

Mary and Robert lived in Grand Junction and Montrose for several years as Robert was involved in farming. Then Robert went to work for Gates Rubber Company and they lived in Denver for 28 years, then Olathe for 12 years, and have now lived in Colorado City, near Pueblo, for the last four years.

Roy Leslie was born with a hairlip and had surgery at the Denver General Hospital to correct the disability when he was three years old.

Roy worked as a cowboy for the S. S. Cattle Company in Blanding, Utah, for many years. He was also a cowboy for the Redd Cattle Company in LaSal, Utah and Paradox, Colorado.

He married **Mary Franklin** on 9 September 1957 and they were later divorced.

Roy was afflicted with diabetes and went blind by the time he was 32 years old. He went to an Auto Mechanics Training School for the Blind in Denver. Before he could use that training, he died from complications of his diabetes at St. Mary's Hospital in Grand Junction on 30 May 1964, only 33 years old.

Mary Franklin and Roy Leslie Homedew, 1957. *(Photo courtesy of Barbara Peterson Homedew)*

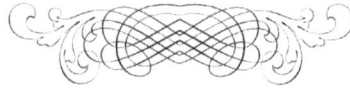

Jones

The Jones story comes from a letter and family group sheet from Hattie Guyman Jones, an obituary from the *San Juan Record* and author's personal knowledge,

Cardon De Jones, the oldest of five children, was born at Bluff, San Juan County, Utah, 27 September 1912, to Thomas DeAlton Jones and Anna McElprang. When Cardon was about five years old the family moved a few miles north to Blanding, where he attended schools.

On 24 February 1933 he was married at Blanding to his high school sweetheart, **Hattie Louise Guyman.** Hattie was born at Grayson (later Blanding), Utah, 20 December 1912 to Willard Richard Guyman and Hattie Black. Except for the time she spent in Colorado, she has spent the remainder of her time at Blanding.

Cardon and Hattie had five children:

De Nelson, born 24 April 1934, at Murray, Utah
Cardon LaMoyne, 25 January 1937, Blanding
Betty Ann (Stevens), 11 March 1942, Blanding
Donna Louise (Slade), 16 April 1946, Blanding
Hattie Marie, 20 November 1947, Monticello.
(Hattie Marie died shortly after birth)

The Cardon Jones family in 1951. Back L-R: Betty, Nelson and LaMoyne "Rusty." Front: Cardon, Hattie and Donna.
(Photo courtesy of Hattie Jones)

Cardon spent his entire life working with livestock and raising feed crops. In 1947 the Jones family entered into a partnership with Bill Young and Sons and purchased the Tom Kelley ranch in Colorado, in the Atchee area, along with farm land in the New Liberty community; namely the former Bill Price and M. H. Dean farms. Cardon and Hattie and children stayed through the summer of 1947 at New Liberty and Atchee, but moved back to Blanding when school started that fall. The following year they came back to establish residence on the Price farm.

Hattie said that when they moved into the house on the Price farm, there were no modern conveniences, so Cardon and Clyde Likes went right to work building a cistern and wiring the house for electricity.

Cardon and Hattie and children spent most of the summer months on the ranch at Atchee, taking care of the cattle, but spent the winter months on the farm so the children could go to New Liberty School. In the winter they kept the cattle on the farms and the surrounding desert and did some feeding through the coldest months, especially if there was snow on the ground.

In 1952 they moved into the lovely home on the Corn place that the company had just purchased. In 1954 the Jones' sold out their share to the Youngs and purchased a ranch in the Nucla, Colorado area, where they lived until 1966, when they moved back to Blanding.

Nelson graduated from Fruita Union High School in 1951. About a year later he enlisted in the military, where he spent the next four years. While in the military, he married **Clayre Elgin Banks** at Fort Worth, Texas, 3 April 1954. After his release from the military he attended Colorado State University at Fort Collins, Colorado, and earned a degree in Veterinary Medicine.

Nelson worked as a veterinarian for a large dairy in the vicinity of Phoenix, Arizona, for many years. Through those years he and Clayre had six children and raised five of them. Nelson and Clayre still live in the Phoenix area.

LaMoyne (Rusty) graduated from the eighth grade at New Liberty School then later graduated from Fruita Union High School in the class of 1955. He married **Nellene Parry**, 22 September 1961, at St. George, Utah. They had five children.

LaMoyne was diabetic, so his life was relatively short; he died at Monticello, Utah 3 November 1976 and was buried at Blanding.

Betty attended Fruita High School but moved away before graduating. She married **William Reed Stevens**, 25 October 1963 at Manti, Utah. They have seven children.

Donna attended New Liberty School until the fourth grade before the family moved away. On 2 September 1983, at Provo, Utah, she married **M. Dale Slade**, a widower with nine children. They have two children.

Cardon died, 27 February 1979, at age 67, in Blanding. Hattie continues to live in their home in Blanding. Their daughter, Donna, and family live in Blanding also.

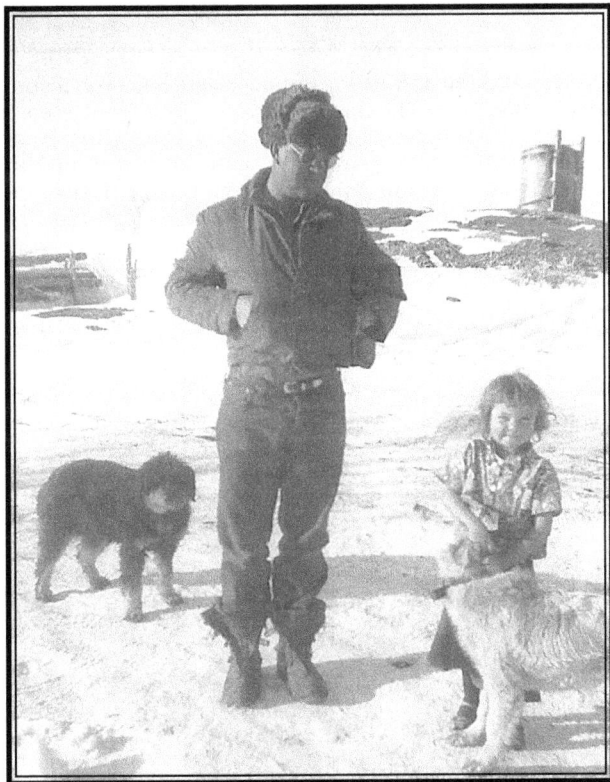

Winter of 1949 at the old Kelley house on the Price homestead in New Liberty. Cardon and Donna Jones with dogs, Sminky and Ronnie.. *(Photo courtesy of Hattie Jones)*

(Above) Cardon and Donna in the corn patch at the Kelley place on the High Line canal in 1949 *(Photo courtesy of Hattie Jones)* (Below) Donna and Betty Jones in front of the New Liberty School house in 1953. *(Photo courtesy of Delores Cutler O'Connor)*

(Upper) Betty, Nelson, Donna and Rusty outside their house on a sunny wintry day in 1949. (Center) The Jones family on the front steps of their house on the Corn place in New Liberty, October 1952. L-R: Rusty, Donna, Cardon, Betty and Hattie. (Lower) The Jones family in 1951. Back row, L-R: Hattie and Cardon Jones, Maxine Cutler, Nelson and Rusty Jones. Front: Betty and Donna Jones. *(All three photos courtesy of Hattie Jones)*

Family Biographies

K

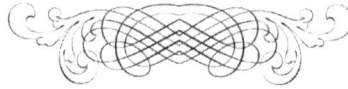

Keffalos

Information is from a letter and family group sheet by Helen Keffalos Dodson. It is also from the 1920 census, obituaries and news items from *The Daily Sentinel*.

Scop Keffalos was born at Zacinthos, Greece, 18 January 1886. He came to the United States in 1902 and was processed through the Ellis Island immigration station in New York Harbor. He worked for a time in New York for a cousin and also served in the court in that area as an interpreter to help other Greek immigrants. He was befriended by a Railroad official and brought to the Grand Valley where he began his career with the Denver and Rio Grande Railroad about 1906. He became a section foreman on the railroad in 1916 shortly before he entered the military service. He served in France and Germany during World War I. He became a citizen of the United States in 1918, apparently after his military service. The 1920 census shows him living in Mack and lists his occupation as a section foreman. In that capacity he served also at Mack and Fruita.

In 1922 he was married in Salt Lake City, Utah, to **Millie Lehr**, a native of Fruita.

They had three children; all were born at Fruita:

George Scop, 11 January 1923
Helen Millie (Dodson), 17 December 1924
Dorothy Victoria (Lucas), 23 July 1927

The children all attended Mack School and Fruita Union High School.

George Jr. married **Dorothy Hulse** in October 1943 at Grand Junction. They had five children; 3 boys and 2 girls. George Jr. served in the Navy during World War II. After the war George and Dorothy moved to Farmington, New Mexico, where he was employed as engineer for the El Paso Natural Gas Company. They lost one son in the Vietnam War, and George passed away in October 1985 of cancer.

(Upper) George Scop Keffalos, Jr. in his navy uniform, about 1943. (Lower) The Scop Keffalos family, about 1940. L-R: Millie, Helen, George, Dorothy and Scop Keffalos. *(Photos courtesy of Helen Keffalos Dodson)*

Helen was married first to **Guy Krohn** in July 1945 at Fruita. Guy was employed by Western Neon Sign Company of Grand Junction. He served in the Army during World War II in Africa and Italy. Guy and Helen had a boy and a girl, and there are now three grandchildren and one great grandchild. Helen later married **Don Dodson.**

Dorothy was married in October 1948 at Fruita to **Dan Lucas,** who served in the Navy during World War II in the South Pacific Theatre. After the war Dan worked for El Paso Natural Gas in El Paso, Texas. They had three children: two girls and a boy. Both Dorothy and Dan died of cancer in 1971 at El Paso; both are buried there.

In 1948, after having served with the railroad for 42 years, Scop died in a motor car accident in Ruby Canyon, west of Mack. Millie passed away at age 82 in Grand Junction.

Helen is the only survivor of the Keffalos family. She says she speaks for all in saying they were fortunate to live in the Mack community.

Kelley

Information from the 1910 census, obituaries and news items in *The Daily Sentinel.*

Thomas "Tom" W. Kelley was born 22 March 1877 in Barber County, Kansas, and at the age of five moved with his parents to Paradox Valley (Montrose County, Colorado) by covered wagon. He moved to Fruita in 1899.

He became involved in the sheep business while he was a young man and worked at sheep ranching in eastern Utah and western Colorado. He is listed at age 32 in the 1910 census of Grand County, Utah, as a "sheep foreman." For years he owned and operated a ranch in the Atchee area, until selling to Young and Jones from Blanding, Utah, in 1947.

Tom first married **Myrtle Page,** but she died in 1917. It is assumed his son, **James Thomas** "Jim Tom," was born to his first wife. On 6 January 1920, Tom was married to **Mrs. Hawley (Holley) Fitzpatrick** at Glenwood Springs, Colorado. Holley had a daughter, **Cleone Elizabeth Fitzpatrick,** who married **Ellery Burford.**

At one time Tom and wife had a nice home in Mack, which was headquarters for the family. The son, **Jim Tom,** went to Mack School and Fruita Union High School.

We have no other information on any of the family except that Tom died in the Lower Valley Hospital at Fruita, 16 July 1959, and was buried in Elmwood Cemetery at Fruita.

Kelly

Information from obituaries and news items in *The Daily Sentinel* and personal knowledge of author.

Julius Vernon "Vern" Kelly was born 20 May 1914 at Oronoque County, Kansas, coming to Colorado with his family when six years of age. He spent the remainder of his childhood and attended schools at Hotchkiss and Fruita, Colorado. He later attended Ross Business College.

Vern was married first to **Mildred Hogsett** in June 1941. They had a daughter named **Leah Elizabeth (Walz).**

Mildred was born 24 June 1911 at Olean, Miller, Missouri, to Sydney and Sadie Hogsett. The family resided on a farm near Olean until 1916, when they moved to Fruita, Colorado. Mildred attended schools in Fruita, graduating from Fruita Union High School in 1928. She later graduated from Western State College and then taught school at Salida for one year, after which she taught nine years at Mack. Mildred died unexpectedly from an embolism, 1 November 1944.

On 18 October 1947 Vernon married **Frances Marie Hamilton,** who had a daughter, **Jacqueline (Barkley),** by a former marriage. They had two children: **Annette Marie (Loucks)** and **Byron Walter.**

Vern was employed for many years as a signal maintainer for D&RGW Railroad.

The Kelly family lived for a long time in the old Uintah Hotel at Mack. In later years Vern and Marie became intensely interested in rock hunting ("Rock Hounds") and eventually converted part of the old hotel into "Kelly's Rock Shop." They made a prosperous business of dealing in gem-quality rocks and fossils. Before retirement Vern kept up with this as well as his signal maintaining.

About the time of his retirement Vern was diagnosed with cancer. He died at Hilltop Rehabilitation Hospital at Grand Junction, 27 December 1984.

Kennedy

Information from the 1920 census, obituaries and news items in *The Daily Sentinel.*

Frank A. "Judge" Kennedy was born about 14 September 1865 at Galena, Daviess, Illinois, and came from Texas to Colorado about the time the Uintah Railroad was being built. He worked first for the Uintah as a superintendent, but the 1920 census lists him as claims agent for the railroad. Later he served as auditor.

Judge (must have been an honorary title) Kennedy was well known by nearly everyone in and around Mack. Many recall having seen the first motion pictures in the Mack School through the efforts of Judge Kennedy. He was well known for his photographic hobby — many of us are familiar with his photos of the Uintah Railway and the people and towns associated with the railway. He also had one of the first automobiles in Mack.

Prior to his death, 13 January 1944, he had been living in an upstairs apartment in the former Uintah Office building, which was then the home of the Leonard Slaugh family. Judge Kennedy

Frank A. "Judge" Kennedy
(Photo courtesy of Agnes Kiefer)

somehow started a fire in his bedding and became asphyxiated. The tragedy was not discovered until the next morning. He was buried in Elmwood Cemetery at Fruita.

Kessinger

From a letter and phone calls to Dick and Evelyn Kessinger

Richard "Dick" Kessinger was born 25 December 1913, at Delta, Colorado, to Charles Arthur Kessinger and Mary Prowers. The Kessingers came to Delta from near Phillipsburg, Kansas, shortly before Dick was born. There were three sons and one daughter in the family: **Esther, Fred, Richard,** and **Stanley.**

When Dick was still quite young the Kessingers

447

They had three children:

Richard Arden, born 24 January 1939, in Grand Junction.
Lanny Ray, 11 May 1941, northwest of Loma
James Gary, 8 December 1942, Oregon City, Clackamas, Oregon

After marriage Dick and Evelyn farmed in the Loma community for awhile before moving to New Liberty. For two years they rented the Phillip Brayton place, which was the former Dean Waters farm, east of Lofgrens and Wassenburgs. (It is presently occupied by Max Barlow). Then they lived on the Brisbin place (the former Snavely place). They may have rented from the Garners, who bought from Brisbins.

Dick tells us he had "an English Bulldog named 'Jiggs' that could whip anything in the area, including Deacon's cows, when they were in our haystacks." He also reveals that his favorite mischief was hunting deer out of season and sharing the meat with his friends.

In 1941 they went to Oregon City, Oregon, and Dick went to work as a section hand on a logging railroad. The Kessingers were soon joined by Fred and Louise Likes; Fred went to work for the same company as fireman on the "donkey." Then they went to the Oregon coast and worked in a shipyard for some time.

In 1944 they went to Bickleton, Washington, where Dick and Fred Likes formed a partnership in an auto and machinery repair shop. Evelyn secured the position of postmaster in Bickleton and ran the office for 22 years, retiring in 1972.

Fred Likes eventually sold Dick his share of the business and moved away. Dick continued with it and developed a heavy equipment repair and metal fabricating business. He retired in 1974. Dick and Evelyn spent the winters in Quartzsite, Arizona, and eventually sold everything in Washington, and in 1985 moved to Arizona for good, "or bad."

Since living in Quartzsite Dick has pursued a hobby of silver-smithing and making jewelry. They told us they stayed in Quartzsite through the summer of 1996, it was like living in an oven!

(Above) Dick, Evelyn, and their two sons, James and Arden, in 1973.

(Left) Dick and Evelyn sitting in Arden's apartment in 1977.

(Photos courtesy of Dick and Evelyn Kessinger)

moved to the Loma area. Dick and his siblings attended Loma Elementary and later Fruita Union High School. Dick graduated in 1932. His two brothers served in the Navy during World War II. Both are deceased. One of the Dick's sons served in the Army.

In the Loma community he met **Evelyn Long**, daughter of Albert "Bert" Edward Long and Clara Pearl Baker. Evelyn was born 25 January 1916, at Elsmore, Woodson, Kansas.

Bert and Clara had four children: **Albert Edward Jr.**, **Norma Jean (Rogers)**, **Pauline (Ashburn)**, and **Evelyn (Kessinger)**.

The Longs came to the Loma area in 1926 from eastern Kansas and settled on a farm northwest of Loma. Evelyn and her siblings attended Loma Elementary School, and later, Fruita Union High School. Evelyn graduated in 1934.

Dick and Evelyn were married 30 March 1935 in Grand Junction.

Kiefer

Information from a history written by members of the Charles Kiefer family. This also includes information from the 1920 census, obituaries and news items in *The Daily Sentinel*.

Charles "Charlie" Casper Kiefer was born 14 December 1870, at Brookville, Franklin, Indiana, to **John Kiefer** from Indiana and **Anna Marie Schmitt** from Germany. He attended school at Tipton, Indiana. On 30 January 1906, at Toledo, Lucas, Ohio, he married **Mary "May" Francis Kopf**, who was born 25 November 1878, at Chicago, Cook, Illinois. May was a daughter of **Simon Kopf**, from Germany, and **Margaret Ryan**, from Ireland.

Charles and May had six children:

John Simon, born 14 December 1906, at New Castle, Henry, Indiana,
Charles Leo, 21 October 1908
Agnes Ruth, 24 December 1910
Jerome Aloysius, 20 January 1913
Margaret Mary (Scheetz), 13 December 1921

Following is a story contributed by Agnes, Jerome, Margaret, Cecilia and Leo Kiefer, with some editing.

Charles Kiefer came to the western slope of Colorado in 1890, at age 19, following his uncles, Joe, Frank and Ben, and widowed grandmother, Caroline Kiefer, who came from Indiana in 1882–83. In 1892 Charlie filed preemption on 160 acres of desert land one-and-a-half miles east of Crevasse (Crevease), a siding[†] on the D&RGW Railroad where a house and water tank stood. He signed the final papers in 1895. Charlie stayed part of the time with his uncles in Fruita and would hop on a D&RGW Railroad train there and hop off again at Crevasse to visit his farm.

The gilsonite mines to the north brought in the Barber Asphalt Company to plan and build the Uintah Railway, with headquarters at the town of Mack. Crevasse was abandoned after Mack was established, but for several years there was still a siding at that location, about a mile west of Mack. Charlie saw the building of the Uintah, the town of Mack, and was still there to see the demise of the Uintah in 1939.

In 1902, Carl Osborn, a Fruita grocer, opened a branch store at Mack, named it the Mack Mercantile, and hired Charlie Kiefer to manage it. Charlie was then living in a small cabin on his farm. His obituary tells us that he ran a traveling commissary during the construction of the Uintah Railroad.

On a trip back to Indiana Charlie was engaged to his sweetheart, Mary Kopf. Then in 1905 he went to Indiana to marry her, and stayed there until 1908, when Carl Osborn contacted him and asked him to again take over the management of the Mack Mercantile. This was the incentive Charlie needed to return to

Charlie and May Kiefer's family, 1925. L-R: Charles Casper, Cecilia Anne, Agnes Ruth, Margaret Mary, Mary Francis, (in back) John Simon, Jerome Aloysius and Charles Leo. *(Photo courtesy of Agnes R. Kiefer)*

† A siding is a short railway for unloading, bypassing, etc.; sidetrack.

(Above left) Benedict "Ben" Kiefer. (Center left) Joseph "Joe" Kiefer. (Below left) Frank and Mabel Steele Kiefer. Ben, Joe and Frank Kiefer are the three Kiefer brothers that built the Kiefer Extension to the Grand Valley Ditch Canal in 1894–1898, which brought water to Loma, Mack and the Redlands. They are uncles of Charles Kiefer, and all came from Indiana in 1882–83. (Above center) Leopold "Labe" Kiefer. (Above right) Valentine "Val" Kiefer. Labe and Val were brothers of Ben, Joe and Frank. They homesteaded and had nice farms between Loma and Mack. Ben and Frank settled in Fruita, and Ben owned a jewelry store there. Frank was completely involved in the Kiefer Extension project and died about 1909. His widow, Mabel, was *The Daily Sentinel* correspondent for Fruita for a long time and her daughter Ila took over after her. Joe, Labe and Val were all three bachelors. Joe never had a permanent home. The family says that "Joe's home was where he hung his hat." He went to the Alaskan Klondike gold rush and brought back about $65,000. He bought land in Loma, Fruita and the Redlands, but died a pauper in California. *(Photos courtesy of Agnes R. Kiefer)*

(Above) The Kiefer and Brown kids, about 1916, on the Kiefer farm in Mack. Standing, L-R: Agnes, John and Leo Kiefer, and Cantwell Brown. Sitting: Jerome Kiefer and Persis Brown. *(Photo courtesy of Agnes R. Kiefer)*

(Above) The Charles Kiefer corral, east of Mack, in 1930. This picture was taken from the Kiefer pond looking a little southwest across the corrals toward the town of Mack, which is in the background. The Kiefer children are sitting on the fence.

(Below left) Charles Kiefer corral and stable east of Mack, 1924. Standing on the right is Simon Kopf, father of May (Mrs. Charles) Kiefer. Agnes Kiefer says, "This is part of the Jersey herd of milking cows whose milk raised two generations of children in Mack and 'up the Line' on the Uintah Railway."

(Below right) Butchering a sow that weighed 800 pounds dressed out on the Kiefer farm. L-R: Jerome, Charles and Leo Kiefer.

(Photos courtesy of Agnes R. Kiefer)

his beloved Colorado, and with his wife, May, and his small son, John, they made a permanent move. They lived in the "Hughes" house south of the tracks in Mack, and it was there that their second son, Leo, was born.

But Charlie's interest was in farming, so as soon as irrigation water came to the lower valley he left the store and became a full- time farmer. May was a city girl who learned to love Colorado. In 1910 they built a house on the hill on their acreage — the house still stands on what was his original preemption one-half mile east and a bit south of Mack. Here Agnes and Jerome were born. A recent article in *The Daily Sentinel* told of the eagles who winter in the "Eagle Tree" near Mack. We believe the tree is on Papa's original place and that, in all probability, he planted that tree — he planted many shade trees in the valley.

A few years later Charlie and May lost part of their place — that part where the new house stood. They moved onto the part they were able to save, north, across the D&RGW RR tracks and the highway. The little log cabin they moved into was built by Caroline Kiefer of aspen logs hauled on the Uintah Railway from the Bookcliffs. In this little house Margaret and Cecilia were born and, with additions, was our home for many years. The house was a quarter mile east of Mack on Highway 50. Our mail came to the post office, Box 47, and until recently that box has been used by a Kiefer. Allen Kiefer, Leo's son, lives where Leo and Genevieve lived and raised their family. The foundation of that place was bought by Charlie and May during the early years.

Charlie was friends with many of the Ute Indians who had been moved to a reservation in northeastern Utah; some lived in the Bitter Creek area in Utah. Those friends were Chipeta, McCook and Sam Atchee. Atchee and some of his tribe sometimes camped in the Kiefer yard. Some of the older children remember that.

In about 1920 Charlie noticed someone painting his fence posts and, accompanied by Leo, went to investigate. They learned the "painters" were marking the route of the "Pike's Peak Ocean to Ocean Highway," which later became Highway 50, going through Mack by the Kiefer's front door.

Along with the farming, the family operated a dairy and delivered milk to Mack families and shipped milk on the Uintah to Atchee, Dragon and Watson. It was Jerome's job, while he was still quite young, to herd the cows out on the desert and ditch banks. He spent many hours reading in the shade of his horse while herding the cows. Jerome began delivering milk the year before he started going to school so the older boys who helped with the milking could sleep a little later in the mornings. Jerome, at first, made those deliveries with a cart, but later, when he was about 15 years old, he was able to buy a 1915 Model T Ford for $20, and sold it a few years later for $20. But of course, all of the family helped with the dairy chores. Even the girls remember delivering the milk with a car.

All six Kiefer kids went through the Mack School, beginning in 1913. All graduated from Fruita Union High School, the last one finishing in 1941. So, for 28 years the family had students in one or both of the schools. The four older children started school when the Mack School was located north of the Mack Mercantile. The building had been only one room, but a lean-to had been added to make two rooms with four grades each.

[The Mack items in *The Daily Sentinel* of 29 August 1941 noted that for the first time in 25 years there was not a Kiefer child in the local schools. All six had graduated from Mack School, then Fruita Union High School; John in 1925, Leo 1928, Jerome 1929, Agnes 1929, Margaret 1940 and Cecelia 1941 — author]

A new school building was built in Mack in 1922 at the west end of town on the north side of the highway. It too had two rooms with four grades each, but there was also a nice auditorium that was used for many school activities, including Christmas programs, with visits by Santa. Roller skating was allowed in

Charles Kiefer and Chief Atchee in the 1890s. *(Photo courtesy of Agnes R. Kiefer)*

the auditorium for a time, but that proved to be too hard on the floor. Community meetings for various purposes were held there, including silent movies shown by "Judge" Kennedy (for 25 cents), with Maude Levi providing background music on the piano. Many good times were enjoyed when Community Club was held there.

"Judge" Kennedy had the first car in Mack, and was very kind to accommodate anyone for trips to Fruita or Grand Junction.

During World War I the students learned to knit and a certain time of each day was set aside for knitting squares to be put together for blankets for the soldiers. Students made candles by cutting the newspapers by the columns, starting with a string and rolling the paper very tightly to about ¾ inch in diameter with a part of the string exposed at one end for the wick. The rolls were then dipped in wax and sent to the soldiers.

One of our recreational activities was hiking around the hills south of Mack, and we now wonder how much of the new Kokopelli Trail we may have hiked in the old days. We also remember school picnics on Flat Rock south of town. In later years we made trips to Lincoln Park in Grand Junction for the end-of-school picnic. But during the depression years we sometimes held the school picnic on the Kiefer lawn.

Mack teachers we remember include Bessie Cox, (who was the first teacher at Mack), Lillian Robinson, Faye Wagner, Ruth Smith,

(Above) Threshing grain on the Kiefer farm at Mack, in the fall of 1910. Sitting on the sacks of grain, R-L: Mary Kopf Kiefer, John Simon, Charles Leo (standing) and Charlie Casper Kiefer (with hand supporting Leo). Man standing left of two women in the center with hand on hip, Leopold "Labe" Kiefer. The two men forking grain into threshing machine behind the two women, L-R: Valentine "Val" Kiefer and Bernard Hughes. Others are not identified. The house was finished in time to move in for Agnes' birth 24 December 1910. This property is now the location for the Country Jam USA held every summer. *(Photo courtesy of Agnes R. Kiefer)*

Miss Jex, and Miss Davis. In the new school the teachers were Margaret Weimer and Al "Pat" Daily (a favorite of Agnes and Jerome), Miss Jerome, Miss Francis, Miss Palmer, Miss Lockett (who became Mrs. Patterson during the term), Mildred Hogsett, Enid Starr, Pauline Geering, Mr. Yates, Dugger Saunders, Walter Poirier and Mrs. Chapman, who sometimes substituted. Margaret Kiefer taught in Mack School in 1948–49 with Mr. and Mrs. Clarence Stites. At least for that year there were three classrooms; ordinarily the first four grades made up the "little" room and the next four grades the "big" room. Agnes Kiefer and Opal Wesner attended 12 years of school together, as did Cecilia Kiefer and Dolores Collins.

The school bus brought the students in from Red Mesa, north of Mack, as well as taking high school students from New Liberty and Mack on to Fruita. Can you imagine those ungraveled, unpaved early roads?

It was from the high-schoolers returning home on the bus that we, at grade school, learned that the Fruita Union High School had burned down in 1934.

Mack, as we knew it, was an oasis in the desert. We all have pleasant memories of the cool park-like atmosphere around the hotel and office building, with the beautiful poplar trees surrounding the lovely lawn. Chris Pappas was caretaker of the Uintah grounds and none ever had better care; the lawn was like a velvet carpet with never a dandelion. Mr. Pappas mowed the immense lawn with an old-fashioned push-type reel mower and kept it watered just right. His duties probably included janitorial work in the hotel and the office building. The sidewalk ran in front of these two buildings and then at the east end turned 90 degrees to go north in front of the "row" of five houses which housed some of the Uintah employees. This sidewalk was the only concrete walk in town and we kids used to roller-skate there by the hour. On July 4th there was always a big celebration on the hotel lawn, along with foot races, horse races, and fireworks. Many dinner parties and dances took place in the hotel which had a lovely dining room. The Women's Guild may have

454

been responsible for these dances, and they sewed regularly for the poor.

The domestic water supply originated at the water tower where a steam engine pumped water up into the tower from railroad tank cars that hauled the water from on the north side of Baxter Pass. The steam engine also powered a generator to supply electricity for the town. Mr. Skogle tended the boiler on the night shift and sometimes on cold winter evenings our boys, while delivering milk, would stop there to warm up and visit with Mr. Skogle. He had a barrel of water with a steam pipe bubbling through it, and usually had a pair of his overalls in it getting washed. His wife was a fastidious person who probably didn't want those dirty overalls brought home. She covered her floor with newspapers and wrapped ice in her ice box in newspapers to keep it from melting. Some time in the 1920s the steel hoops around the large wooden tank gave way and the tank burst. The town was without power until a new steel tank was erected on the north side of town, and a new pump house built. We outside of town had no such power until the REA came into the valley in about 1937.

The fire alarm was the school bell and when it rang at the wrong time of day for a school summons all knew it meant FIRE! Everyone came running to do what they could with whatever was available to extinguish it. Mack had a forest fire in 1942, which started in Crow Canyon and swept up the hill south of town. It was thought to have been caused by a carelessly thrown cigarette from someone walking in the canyon. Pickups full of men finally put the fire out, fighting it with shovels.

There were several tragedies on the Uintah Railway due to runaways, and damage to the roadbed caused by mud and snow slides and flash floods. The death of young Roy Wagaman when, in 1924, a steam shovel tipped over on him, was the greatest shock to the citizens of Mack. (See the Wagaman story). Not all accidents were on the railroad; Ethel Landers and Tommy Keith were drowned as she and Tommy attempted to row across the river west of Mack in a small boat at night. Their bodies were never found. Malcom Dean suffered serious injuries when he attempted to beat a train to the Mack D&RGW Railroad crossing. Edmond Daily died after being hit by a car as he rode his bike in Grand Junction. Don Robertson was badly hurt when he fell off the roof of a building he was dismantling. It was always a risk to work with horses and they caused their share of accidents, including the time Charlie Kiefer was kicked in the chest by one. There was a train wreck in Ruby Canyon with one or two of the crew killed and fruit scattered all over. Many of the Mack citizens gathered up fruit from the wreckage.

West of Mack, on the desert beside the Uintah tracks, were some permanent sheds and corrals used for the yearly shearing of thousands of sheep that ranged the Colorado/Utah desert. The sheep were sheared by hand and then they were driven through vats containing an antiseptic solution to kill the ticks. This scene was a diversion from daily work and many people went to watch the interesting operation. Then in the fall came the shipping out by railroad of the hundreds of cattle and sheep from the Mack stockyards. The fences would be lined with kids from five to 75 years of age fascinated by the animals, the sweat soaked cowboys, the clouds of dust, and the long line of stock cars backed up on the siding. This illustrates that though Mack was a Uintah town, there was surrounding it a wide farming and stock-raising area. With the shipments on both the Uintah Railway and D&RGW Railroad, Mack was a busy place.

A different form of "stock" raising on a commercial scale came to the neighborhood in the 1930s in the form of poultry. The Mennal Ray family moved their turkey-raising equipment from Moab after purchasing the former Charlie Kiefer place on the hill. They brought in timbers for brooder houses, windows, stoves — everything by truck. The brooders for the poults (baby turkeys) were made with boards into which rolls of turkey feathers were inserted into holes to imitate the "mother hen." These were heated from underground pipes fed from fires in oil barrel furnaces. It was quite an operation! The poults were shipped in by train early in the spring and upon arrival each poult had to be fed with an eye-dropper. We neighbors and other people from Mack would go over to help with the process. This was for 5,000 turkeys! Sometimes the neighbors would stay with them at night to see that everything was working right for the poults' survival. This was volunteer work by the neighbors, but the Rays always distributed nice big turkeys in the fall to all who had helped.

During the growing months the turkeys were herded there on the ranch, much like herding sheep. For several years Margaret did this herding with her dog and a .22 caliber rifle to ward off coyotes. In November slaughter time came and again the neighbors provided the work force, being paid by 'the head,' or by the number of birds plucked.

We were always close friends of whomever moved into that house Papa had built in 1910. It was such a blow to the family to lose that part of the farm! Perhaps it helped to know the succeeding owners well, and to visit them in that house. We started to list all the families who lived there, then realized it was not only those families but many others whom we knew as friends through the years. These included those who lived in the three houses directly across the road from us, many in the town and to the west and north on the Red Mesa, and many in New Liberty. Though Mack was but a little village, railroad people moved in and out a lot, so over the years we knew many residents there.

We always had a post office, one or two stores, a cafe, lumber yard, pool hall, garage, one or two service stations, motel, etc. We believe the original post office was in the Uintah Office building, then there were three other locations, from south of the tracks, to the north and west end of town and to it's present location, a very attractive building.

After Charles Kiefer had the Mack Mercantilc it went to W. H. Cox. He was there for a time, then left, but returned later. There was a Mr. Hepson, Mr. Robinson and a Walter Kurtz. We think the latter was operating the store when the Uintah was abandoned in 1939. At one time Luke Crews operated a store over by the post office, south of the tracks. Chet Wright had a store, service station and garage some time in the 1920s on the north side of the highway. That may have been the same building that later became the Desert Gateway Store and station, which was operated by Alice Ward Davis Hitner.

With the dismantling of the Uintah, the office building, part of the hotel and all the company houses were moved out. Our pretty little oasis is not the same anymore. It was a nice place to grow up and a nice place to call home. Charles and May Kiefer retired and sold the place to Joe and Lupe Tafoya in 1945, 50 years after Charles had homesteaded. Allen Kiefer, a grandson, still calls Mack home. The people of Mack gave the elder Kiefers a picture of the Last Supper as a going-away gift. It is now on Cecilia Anne's dining room wall. We also have two water colors of the Baxter Pass area painted by Edith Maguire, showing the little train. We hope that someone might identify her.

Charlie and May moved to Jerome and Florence's place near Grand Junction, where Charlie and Jerome built a new home for the parents. That house in recent years has been moved to north of Mack. Now two houses built by Charlie are standing in the Mack area. The area will always have a place in our hearts. We like to go there to hike the old trails, Box Canyon, the Indian Camp, and have lunch on the Flat Rock! The "Old Grey Mare" still stands as a sentinel over the lower valley from her place on the Bookcliffs to the east, and we salute her. Some say nostalgia is a sign of old age. We prefer to think of it as love and caring for the friends and places of days gone by.

A final note: there are two streets in Fruita named for the Kiefer family: Carolina Ave., which should be "Caroline," for our great-grandmother; and Kiefer Ave., named for our great-uncles.

Four of the six children of Charles and May are still living: Agnes, Jerome, Margaret and Anne. Charles died 28 April 1953, May on 16 February 1946 and Charles Leo on 17 January 1977, in Grand Junction. John Simon died 14 August 1935 in Elwood, Indiana.

Leo Kiefer family in 1988. (Insert of Leo was taken in 1972) L-R: Charles Leo, Rita Colleen (Cowen), Genevieve, Barbara Anne, Duane Michael, Allen Leo and Carl Steven Kiefer. *(Photo courtesy of Genevieve Kiefer)*

Leo's wife, Genevieve, sent us a history of herself, Leo and their family. Information was also used from Leo's obituary and news items from *The Daily Sentinel.*

Charles Leo Kiefer was born in the "Hughes" house in Mack on 21 October 1908. He was the second child born to Charles C. and Mary Frances Kiefer. He spent his entire life in Mack, except about two years in 1934/35 when he went to Illinois and Indiana and spent some time with his brother, John S. Kiefer. He was also away from Mack while he was in the Army from 1942-45.

According to Mack School records, Leo was a new student at Mack School in 1915, with Ida Davis as his teacher. He is named in the school census taken 16 March 1921 by his father, Charles C. Kiefer. The record states Leo had last attended the fifth grade. He graduated from Fruita Union High School in 1928. While attending high school he was active in football and discus throwing.

Leo Kiefer served in an anti-aircraft unit of the Army during World War II, with a T-5 rank, from 3 April 1942 until 9 November 1945. Eleven months of that time was spent overseas in Germany. He was, at some point in time, near Hitler's hide-out. It's worthy of note also that Leo crossed the ocean, probably on his home-coming voyage, on the "Queen Elizabeth."

In 1946, following his return from the war, he started farming on the hill about a mile northeast of Mack; very much like in the homestead days. He dug a cistern entirely by hand, built fences, etc. He moved a house on the property with two rooms, each 10-by-14 feet. In the spring of 1949, just before he was married, he added another room which was 14 by 14 feet. For indoor plumbing, there was a hand pump in the kitchen.

After their youngest child, Barbara, was born, Leo hired three carpenters to remodel the house, adding a bathroom, new kitchen and living room.

While they were doing the remodeling the Mack School building was being torn down. Leo acquired the book-case from the school, and installed it in the living room. Genevieve says to get it out now would require cutting some of the wall out of the house.

On 30 April 1949, Leo married Genevieve Willers, at Grand Junction. Genevieve was born 14 August 1921, at Roy, Harding, New Mexico, a daughter of Christopher R. Willers and Elizabeth Alice Vessels.

They had six children:

Rita Colleen (Cowen), born 6 May 1950
Duane Michael, 12 February 1952
Alice Marie, 9 June 1953, died 18 June 1953
Allen Leo, 28 September 1954
Carl Steven, 20 November 1956
Barbara Anne, 13 October 1961
All were born at St. Mary's Hospital in Grand Junction.

In 1957 when the Kiefer's oldest, Rita, was ready to start to school, the Mack School had been closed for about five years, so they had to choose between sending Rita to Loma or New Liberty. They chose Loma. Subsequently all their children went there. When they started there were eight grades, but by the time Duane reached the seventh grade there was a junior high in Fruita which included seventh through ninth grades. Among the first graduates from the new Fruita Monument High School was their son, Duane. Since then there have been other changes. Now the Loma School has grades first through fifth; middle school has sixth through eighth; and high school is again ninth through twelfth.

In March 1965, through the urging of Jean Rich, Genevieve started driving the school bus; she continued that for 23 years. She also drove for the "Summer Migrant School" for several years. That was during the time sugar beets were grown in the valley and Navajo Indians were brought in to work in the fields.

Genevieve tells of some curious incidents happening during those years. One morning, as she made a stop to pick up the Navajo children, a youngster about four or five years old came up to her and pointed at his mouth. He had a ring stuck between his two upper front teeth. She finally got it out, after much effort.

During the years while their children were growing up, the Kiefers had two swans who took up residence on their pond. Another time when they were checking the cows near the pond there was an elk with them. For a time they had large frogs [likely southern bull frogs] living on or near the pond; they were quite noisy.

Rita was in the Army from 1974 to 1976 and

was assigned to the same area where her father was during World War II. Rita and her husband, John (Jack), have two children and live in Pueblo.

Duane and his wife, Sandy, and their two boys, live near Fruita. Allen and his wife, Kathy, and their three children, live on the homestead at Mack. Carl served four years in the Marines, from 1979 to 1983. He now lives in San Diego. Barbara lives near Grand Junction. Neither of the latter two are married.

King

Information from a letter by Alice Anderson Ahrens, the 1920 census, obituaries and news items from *The Daily Sentinel,* personal knowledge of the author.

John Nelson King was born 27 December 1851, in Andrew County, Missouri, to Wingate A. King and Sarah Miller. On 23 April 1884, he married **Mary Alice Drury,** who was born at St. Petersburg, Minnesota. (Mary Alice is said to have been 1/4 Cherokee.)

They had six children:

Lola Ellen, who married **John Anderson** (the ditch rider at Camp 8 in New Liberty)
Loren E.
Clara
Lietta Dell (Boling)
Virtie Ruby
Vardie "Vern" J.
(There was also a son named **Fred,** whose birth order is not known.)

The Kings came to Colorado from St. Joseph, Missouri, in 1912. John filed on a homestead in the New Liberty area in May 1918. He was one of the oldest, if not the oldest, of the New Liberty homesteaders The Kings lived there for several years and then moved away, renting the homestead; eventually it was sold to W. B. Maluy. Land entries show that for a short time son Loren owned an adjoining homestead in the same section, acquired from William Hargraves. It was later relinquished to Thomas Gibbs.

John N. King died 4 March 1925 in Grand Junction. He was buried in the Grand Junction Municipal Cemetery. His wife, Mary Alice, continued to live in the Grand Junction area. We have no further information on her.

Koch

Information from a history and family group sheet provided by Helen Johnson Koch.

Alvin Theodore Koch was born 19 July 1922, at Galatea, Kiowa County, Colorado, one of six children born to Andrew William Koch and Clara Jane Dale. He attended elementary school at Chivington, Colorado, and graduated from high school at Eads, Colorado. Alvin was a member of that school's football squad, and they became good enough, in his senior year, to win every game except the last one, which they lost by a very narrow margin. Alvin served in the Navy during World War II.

In May 1948 he met a young lady named Helen Mercedes Johnson at a skating rink in Lamar, Colorado. They were married at Eads, Colorado, 18 September 1949. Helen was born at Kit Carson, Colorado, 3 December 1922, a daughter of Arthur William Johnson and Cecilia Maria McQuillin, one of six children. Helen tells of herself and brothers and sisters having to ride 2 1/2 miles on horses to a little school called Pleasant Valley, until it was closed in 1935. In the fall of that year they began riding a bus that transported the grade-school students to Arena and the high school students to Kit Carson High School.

Alvin and Helen had four children:

Sheryn Lorraine (Overholt)
Terrel Elayne (Felkins)
Roger Allen
Cynthia "Cindy" Marie (Kribari)
The first three were born in the Eads area, the fourth in Grand Junction.

The Koch family, in September 1973. Back row, L-R: Helen Mercedes, Sharyn Lorraine and Terrel Elayne Koch. Front row: Alvin Theodore, Cynthia "Cindy' Marie and Roger Allen Koch. *(Photo courtesy of Helen Koch)*

Alvin and Helen lived in eastern Colorado and Missouri until May 1954, when they moved to Mack, Colorado, and operated the Last Chance Store and service station for eight years. In May of 1962 they moved the grocery stock from the Mack Store to a store at Whitewater, Colorado, (southeast of Grand Junction). (Gene Thomas says a family named Clements had the Last Chance store after the Kochs.) While operating the store at Whitewater, they lived on a 20-acre farm on B 1/2 road , near Grand Junction and commuted to Whitewater for four years. After they closed that store Alvin worked for School District 51 as a warehouseman.

Alvin loved hunting and fishing. While on a hunting trip near Kremmling, Colorado, on 10 October 1981, he died suddenly at age 59.

Helene Behrendt and George Spiros Komatas, Sr.
(Photo courtesy of Kathryn Komatas Prince)

Komatas

The following information was sent by George Komatas, Jr. and Kathryn G. Prince, son and daughter of George Komatas, Sr. Their information differs in some respects, so we decided to include both. The first part is taken from Kathryn's answers to our questionnaire. Following is George Jr.'s history. We have done some editing. We also include information from the 1920 census and from marriage records of Salt Lake County, Utah.

George Spiros Komatas, Sr. was born at Steno, Greece, 5 January 1881. His parents were Sam and Christine Komatas.

(Marriage record says George was born 23 April 1882; his parents were *Spiro* (Spiros) Komatas and Christine Stanropoulous. George's occupation was section foreman.)

George grew to manhood in Greece, spending his boyhood on the family farm helping with the farm work and sheep herding.

In 1901 George and his brother, Tony, came to Chicago to go to work for the railroad. They also went to Little Rock, Arkansas and St. Louis, Missouri. While in Missouri Tony died of tuberculosis.

George eventually found his way to Carbonera, Colorado, and went to work for the Uintah Railway.

(The 1920 census shows George as an alien, age 44, a laborer for a steam railroad, immigrated in 1901. Listed with him is a brother, Sam, age 46, an alien, also a laborer for the same railroad, immigrated in 1911. They were then living at Carbonera, Garfield, Colorado)

At Carbonera George met **Helene Behrendt**, who was born on 4 July 1910, in Memel, Germany, to Godlip and Anna Behrendt.

Helene's mother died when she was a young girl. She came to the United States to live with her Aunt Anna and Uncle Rudy Neff. They adopted her. Uncle Rudy was employed at the coal mine at Carbonera. Aunt Anna was a cook at the boarding house.

The marriage record says she was born 4 July 1911. Her parents were *Gutley* (Godlip) Behrendt and Anna Burkschat. Helene was just a few days short of her 16th birthday when Mrs. Rudolph *Naef* (Neff) signed consent as her guardian. Helene was a resident of Mt. Pleasant, San Pete, Utah. The marriage was performed in Salt Lake City by George Graham, an elder of The Church of Jesus Christ of Latter-day Saints. George and Helene were married in Salt Lake City, Utah, 29 June 1927. After their marriage Helene went to Grand Junction to stay with a friend for about six months while George and some of his fellow-workers built a house for them in Carbonera.

They had three children:

Crystal Ann, born 25 January 1932
George, Jr., 27 April 1933
Kathryn G. (Prince), 24 June 1934

All were born in Grand Junction.

The Komatas' lived in Carbonera until the Uintah Railway went out of business in 1939. Then they moved to Mack and George got a job for the D&RGW Railroad.

The children were enrolled in Mack School.

Kathryn recalls the time during World War II when the Mack School was closed for a time and the students bused to Loma. After a couple years they returned to Mack School. Kathryn graduated from Fruita Union High School in 1952.

Kathryn said that she, Crystal, and George, Jr. were raised in a two-bedroom home in Mack. In the summer they worked in the fields picking potatoes and cucumbers, and in the fall picked peaches at Palisade.

The family enjoyed the community activities at Mack; the dances, plays, and Christmas programs. Always at Christmas time the people in the community collected donations, using the proceeds to buy fruits, nuts and candies for the children.

George, Jr. served in the Army during World War II . After the war he worked for the D&RGW Railroad for a time. He then worked for *The Daily Sentinel.* He retired in December 1995. He and his wife, **Wilda,** had three daughters: **Cindy, Pam** and **Patricia.** Cindy lives in Palisade with her husband, Jeff, and daughter, Jasmine. Pam and her husband, Scott, live in Mesa, Arizona, with their boys Derek and Brandon. Patricia, "Trish," lives in Grand Junction with her twin girls, Kaylene and Katrina.

George Jr.'s history:

In 1898 Dad (George S. Komatas) started from Greece with three brothers. They were unable to get visas or passports from Greece to America, so they got visas and passports to France. They had to stay in France for at least one year to obtain a French citizenship paper. This would allow them to get passports to America. After staying in France for one and a half years, they got visas and passports to America.

Starting from France on a ship, they worked part time to pay for the trip. One of the brothers died about half way. The trip took about six months. They arrived in America in 1901, at Ellis Island. They stayed there about six to ten weeks while they were being processed. Upon leaving Ellis Island they made their way to Chicago, where another brother

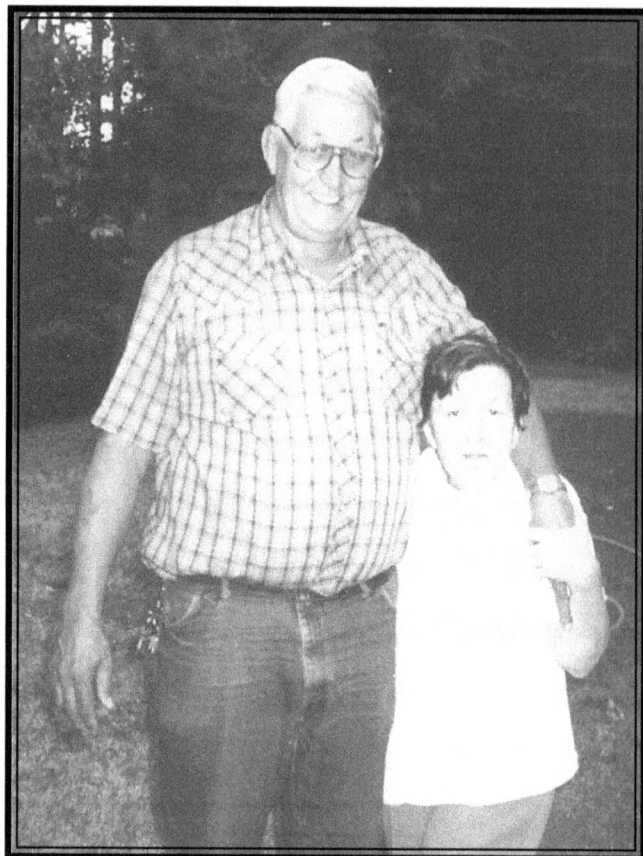

George Jr. and Crystal Ann Komatas.
(Photo courtesy of Kathryn Komatas Prince)

died. The third brother said that he'd had enough of America and went back to Greece.

Dad continued to travel to Little Rock, Arkansas where he worked for the Santa Fe Railroad. After some time, he went to Galveston, Texas, then to Salida, Colorado in 1905 to work for another railroad. In 1908 he heard about the Uintah Railway, and moved to Carbonera in 1909. He worked for the Uintah as a section foreman.

He married Helene Behrendt in June 1927, in Mt. Pleasant, Utah. They had three children: Crystal Ann, George and Kathryn.

Dad worked for the Uintah until 1939, when the railway folded. Then he went to work for the Rio Grande Railroad as a night watchman in Ruby Canyon, just below Mack. He retired in 1948.

Crystal Ann and Kathryn now live in Seattle, Washington. I live in Grand Junction.

After graduating from high school in 1950, I went to Utah and worked for a while driving trucks. Then I went to work on the signal gang for the Rio Grande. While working there, Dad got sick and was taken to the hospital. At that time, I met Wilda. Jim Thayer's wife set us up. After that we started to dating steadily.

This page includes Kathryn's sons and families. (Above) Tina, Shawn and Nathan Prince (Above right) L-R: Wayne, wife Suzi, children, Joel and Lana, with their dogs. (Below left) Mark and his daughter, Sara. (Lower right) Billy and his new bride, Brandi, on their wedding day, 10 July 1994, at Stanwood, Washington. *(Photos and information courtesy of Kathryn Komatas Prince)*

About a year later, my brother-in-law, Don Prince, called me and told me to come to work for *The Daily Sentinel*. I took a leave of absence from the railroad to work for *The Daily Sentinel* in 1957.

George and **Wilda Barlow** were married in May 1959. They had three daughters:

Cynthia "Cindy"
Pamela
Patricia

They have three granddaughters: Jasmine Janell, Kaylene Rae and Katrina Rose, and two grandsons: Brandon James and Derrick Scott.

Wilda died in March 1989. George, Sr. died in Grand Junction, 17 February 1972. Helene died in Grand Junction, 13 September 1985. Both Helene and George are buried in Memorial Gardens in Grand Junction.

Kathryn met **Don Prince** through a friend in high school. Don saw her picture in a high school year book and asked the friend to introduce them. One Saturday, while she was in the midst of housecleaning, Don came to meet her. They made a date for the following Saturday and they were married 12 May 1956 at Grand Junction, 20 days later.

Don and Kathryn had four sons:

Mark, born 9 April 1957
Bill, 2 June 1959
Wayne, 20 January 1961
Nathan, 12 July 1962
All were born in Grand Junction

Don and Kathryn lived in a trailer until their second son was born. During that time Don was working in the uranium mines. He later worked as a machinist for *The Daily Sentinel*. They then bought a house in Grand Junction and lived there until 1962, when they moved to Washington State.

Kathryn was a grocery store clerk for 24 years in the Seattle area. She retired on 19 October 1996 after her company was sold. She didn't mention what kind of work Don did.

Mark has been in management at Boeing

Kathryn G. Komatas Prince
(Photo courtesy of Kathryn)

Aircraft for the past 18 years. He is divorced and has a thirteen year old daughter, Sara, who lives in Burlington, Washington, with her mom.

Bill is a special education teacher with the Monroe School District and lives in Sylvana, Washington with his wife, Brandi.

Wayne is a machinist at Boeing Aircraft. He lives in Mountlake Terrace, Washington with his wife, Suzi, their seven-year-old son, Joel, and four- year- old daughter, Lana.

Nathan is a cable technician with North West Utilities. He lives in Seattle with his wife, Tina, and their five-year-old son, Shawn.

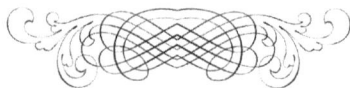

Lander

Information is from Emmett Russell Brandon, Richard Keith, John Edward Arbuckle, 1900 federal census and obituaries and news items from *The Daily Sentinel.*

Ola E. Lander was born 23 May 1898, at Admire, Lyon, Kansas to John P. and Jane M. Lander. John P. Lander came to America in 1865 from Sweden. Ola was 11th in a family of 14 children. He spent his childhood in Kansas, becoming a farmer as an adult.

He married **Ruby Hiatt**, on 23 June 1918, at Horton, Kansas, where she spent her childhood. The couple moved to Mack in 1921. They returned to Kansas for a short time years later, returning in 1956.

Ola spent 40 years as a farmer in the Lower Valley. He lived for a time in Mack. He and Ruby had two children: **Ethel**, who died from drowning in the Colorado River in May 1933,† and a son named **Arthur**. Arthur was allowed to smoke cigarettes and drink beer and whiskey when he was very small. His parents thought it was funny, as did most everyone else. Needless to say, he didn't live to a ripe old age.

Ruby died in Fruita, 2 June 1961 and was buried in the Elmwood Cemetery in Fruita.

Ola had three sisters who also lived in the Mack and Loma areas: Emma Joan, wife of James Henry Brandon; Minnie M., wife of Olin Reese Arbuckle; and Josie, wife of Richard Keith.

Ola married **Ruth Blum** in Delta, 23 August 1963. He died 30 September 1967, at St. Mary's Hospital in Grand Junction, and was buried in the Elmwood Cemetery at Fruita.

† See story "Prohibition and Moonshining" in the section "More Challenges," page 185.

Leach

The following was contributed by Eula Mae Leach.

Guy and Eula Leach, 23 February 1966
on their 39th wedding anniversary.
(Photo courtesy of Eula Leach)

Harold Guy Leach was born 18 June 1902 in Grand Junction, Colorado, to Fred and Amy Leach, second of seven children. His parents met and married in Kansas. Guy met and married **Eula Mae Mulford** in the Appleton, Colorado, area. They had no children.

Eula Mae Mulford was born at Stuart, Holt, Nebraska, 18 August 1906, to Linden and Edith Mulford .

Here's the story in Eula Mae's words in 1992.

My parents met in Grand Junction. Dad came to Grand Junction to meet my mother; they had been writing to each other. He married her in Grand Junction and took her with him to Stuart, Nebraska. I was three years old when they decided to return to Colorado. Dad rented a car on the railroad and brought his farming equipment, household goods, horses, cow and dog. He put Mama and me on the train, and we all came to Grand Junction. My Dad was a school teacher and farmer, but ended up being a carpenter. He worked on the building of the Highline Canal.

Guy drove a sprinkler wagon on the highway.

One day when my folks and I were going to town Guy waved and I waved back. I'm sure I fell in love before I even knew his name. He was my ideal.

Later he met me at the Appleton store and asked if he could take me out. I said, "Come meet my folks." They liked him and after that we went together and one night he asked me to marry him, but I said, "We are too young." My mother agreed.

My folks went to California and, of course, I had to go, too. So, we didn't see each other for four years and two months.

Guy had started to go to California to get a job, but instead went to work for Rust Engineering Co. in Utah building concrete smoke stacks and was sent all over the United States, Canada, Mexico and South America. We met again when he returned on February 21 — too late in the day to do anything. The next day was Washington's birthday so we couldn't get a license, but we got a ring and made all the necessary arrangements and were married on 23 February 1927.

After the depression began we farmed at Appleton and Fruita, then eventually bought a home north of Mack. It was a neat home and we were proud of it. We made a lot of wonderful friends in Loma, Mack and New Liberty. I have wonderful memories of all our years there. Guy was the ditch-rider for Mack and New Liberty for 22 years. We had been married 62 years and eight months when Guy died 2 November 1989. He was buried in Masonic Cemetery at Grand Junction.

Likes

The following was written by Homer Likes. He has told this story as though he remembered all the events, though he was just a babe during the time of the early part of it. However, he's heard the stories many, many times. Some information is from the 1900, 1910, and 1920 census, obituaries and news items in *The Daily Sentinel.*

Clyde William Likes was born 27 March 1882, at Lincoln, Lancaster , Nebraska, to Nimrod Likes and Elizabeth Driskell. Lincoln, in 1882, was still a comparatively small frontier town. The family lived there until Clyde was about 10 years of age. He told of herding cows on the prairie surrounding Lincoln where they found evidences of the great buffalo massacre that occurred not many years earlier.

In about 1892 Nimrod filed on a prairie homestead near Binkleman, Nebraska, but this venture "dusted out" after a couple of years. Then the family traveled by covered wagon to Oklahoma Territory and settled for a time near Durant, just

(Above) Nimrod Likes (Below) Retta and Clyde Likes *(Likes Photo Collection)*

across the state line from the town of Denison, Texas. They didn't stay there very long before going back north to Cleveland County, Oklahoma Territory, and settling near Mardock, about 17 miles east of Norman.

About this time his parents separated, leaving young Clyde to shift for himself. His mother, Elizabeth, continued to live in the Norman area; Nimrod went back to Nebraska. Clyde attended Little River School at Mardock, living for a time with the Coffman family. Later, in 1902, he attended "normal" school, at Norman, Oklahoma. (Normal school is the equivalent of high school today).

While living in the area near Mardock, Clyde became acquainted with **Retta May Appier,** a daughter of David Marshall Appier and Susan Hester Solomon. Retta was born 15 October 1888, at Chelsea, Rogers, Indian Territory. The Appier family lived in several locations in Missouri, Kansas, Indian Territory, and Oklahoma Territory, all frontier environments, so Retta and her siblings had little chance for schooling. But Retta did have the distinction of going to school with Will Rogers before he became the famous country humorist. The Appier family moved to Cleveland County, Oklahoma Territory, about 1899, and about two years later David filed on a homestead in the vicinity of Mardock. The Appier children attended Little River School near Mardock.

466

The Big Jim Mission in Mardock, Oklahoma where Clyde and Retta were married. *(Likes Photo Collection)*

Clyde William Likes and Retta May Appier married 10 April 1904. *(Likes Photo Collection)*

Clyde was not readily accepted by Retta's father. However, Grandpa Appier did travel to Norman with him to sign consent for Retta to be married; she was not yet 16.

Clyde and Retta were married 10 April 1904, at a little church called Big Jim Mission. A Friends minister, who was affectionately known as "Uncle John Mardock," performed the ceremony. In 1901 John Mardock had built the little church and established a post office and store which were subsequently named after him. The post office and store are long gone but the little church is still standing (1993), however it hasn't been used for church for many years.

Clyde and Retta had nine children:

Mabel "Maybelle" Dean, born 14 August 1905, Mardock, Cleveland, Oklahoma
Ivan Randle, 20 July 1907, Mardock
Elmer Fred, 30 August 1910, Shawnee, Pottawatomie, Oklahoma
Clyde Williams, Jr., 29 July 1912, Ottawa, Ottawa, Oklahoma
Homer Chilson, 5 June 1918, Byers, Pratt, Kansas
Lewis David, 21 March 1921, Fruita
Virginia Ellen, 14 June 1923, Colorado Springs, El Paso, Colorado
Ray Marenus, 22 August 1927, Grand Junction
Richard Allen, 17 September 1931, Fruita

Clyde and Retta set up housekeeping on a farm near the Mardock post office, and their first two children were born there: **Mabel Dean,** 14 August 1905, and **Ivan Randle,** 20 July 1907. In November 1907, Oklahoma Territory became a state. Also in 1907 Clyde and Retta (with some financial assistance from Clyde's mother) bought a homestead from Retta's uncle, Bill Solomon. This may have been the same farm they were living on.

Ivan Randle, Elmer Fred, and Maybelle Dean Likes
(Likes Photo Collection)

467

(Above left) Pupils at Prairie Center, Oklahoma, 1917. Third row: Ivan is third and Mabel is eighth from the left. Second row: Fred is fifth from the left. Front row: Clyde Jr. is third from the left. (Above) Reverend Clyde Likes Sr. standing at the pulpit at the Mount Ayers Friends Church, Alton, Kansas, December 1916. (Left) Pleasant Plains Friends Church and congregation, Byers, Kansas, 1917. (Below center) L-R: Clyde William Jr., Mabel Dean, Elmer Fred, and Ivan Randle Likes, 1914. *(Likes Photo Collection)*

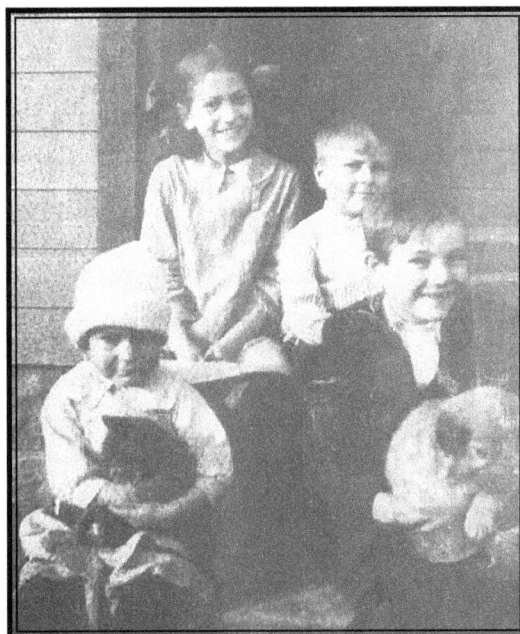

Around this time Clyde began to have a feeling he wanted to become a minister. We don't have the full story, but Clyde told of his first experience with preaching under the watchful eye of "Uncle John Mardock." It probably occurred in the little church called the Big Jim Mission. Big Jim was the chief of one of the area Indian tribes.

Clyde and Retta gave up farming in about 1910 and moved to Skiatook Mission in the northeast part of Oklahoma. That is where they were living when the census was taken in 1910. Clyde's occupation was listed as "minister" in that census. The family must have moved soon after that, as the next child, **Elmer Fred**, was born at Shawnee, 30 August 1910. On Fred's birth certificate his father's occupation is given as "Hostler on the Rock Island Railroad." Clyde often mentioned his experience working for the Rock Island. He was required to work 12 hours per day, seven days per week, for 15¢ per hour. They rented a house in Shawnee for $7 per month.

Clyde then became a full-time minister and gave up his job as hostler. He soon became pastor of a church at Wyandotte, in Ottawa County, in the northeast corner of Oklahoma, where the fourth child, **Clyde William Jr.**, was born on 29 July 1912.

The family later moved to a place called Prairie Center, still later to Pond Creek, and we must not forget Muskogee, where Clyde Sr. was employed as a street car conductor. It seems likely that it was necessary for him to have a job in addition to his ministry as he probably did not receive sufficient income as a minister to support his family.

Some time in 1917 Clyde became pastor of a little country church called Pleasant Plains Friends Church, a couple of miles southwest of Byers, Pratt, Kansas. About this time Clyde had also learned of an irrigation project under construction in the Grand Valley in western Colorado. In March of 1918 he journeyed to Grand Junction to have a look. Many years later he told of having taken the auto tour to see first-hand the land to be settled. He was one of the "lucky" winners in the drawing held in Grand Junction 29 March 1918.

On 5 June 1918, the fifth child, **Homer Chilson**, was born at Byers; it had been nearly six years since the birth of Clyde Jr.

Not long after Clyde Sr.'s return from Colorado, the family began preparations for the move to the homestead. One of the first things was to sell "Old Nelly" and the buggy and purchase a nearly new (1917) Model "T" Ford touring car. Probably some time in July the five children and parents, plus all of their personal belongings, were loaded on or in the Ford. Away they went to Oklahoma to visit relatives before venturing on into the "wild west."

After arriving in Oklahoma, Retta had opportunity to show off her new little boy while becoming acquainted with a new niece and nephew, children of her younger and older sisters. Retta was very close to her family and truly enjoyed getting together with them.

Clyde Sr.'s mother and half-sister also lived in the same area of Oklahoma. I'm sure he had a good visit with Aunt Mabel, but this may have been the last visit he had with his mother. She was not happy with his choice to become a poorly-paid minister in the Friends Church, when he could have been a well-paid reader in the Christian Science Church. It was probably then that she showed him the door and told him she never wanted to see him again!

After the visit to Oklahoma, the family set out on the long trip over the Rocky Mountains to their new adventure on the homestead. Think for a moment what an undertaking that must have been! Five children and two adults loaded in an open car with all their personal belongings, traveling into an unknown area on roads that were little more than wagon trails!

The route they chose through the mountains was over Monarch Pass, which, according to present-day maps, reaches an altitude of 11,312 feet. The Ford lacked power to climb the steep grades near the top of the divide, making it necessary for Mom and the older children to

The "new" Model "T" Ford owned by the Likes family from 1918 to 1925. *(Likes Photo Collection)*

469

walk along behind the car and push whenever necessary. Clyde Jr. was assigned to sit in the front seat holding Homer while Clyde Sr. drove. When they reached the top of the pass, a man with a much more powerful car observed the Model "T" and its burden and exclaimed in amazement: "You drove *that* up *here*?!"

A new problem developed as they began to descend the other side of the pass; Model "T" Fords were not equipped with very good brakes, so the brakes soon wore out. Clyde Sr. followed standard procedure for Fords of that day and used the reverse pedal for a brake. That got them into Gunnison where he had the brake repaired.

The family arrived in the Grand Valley too late to plant any crops, but Clyde Sr. soon found opportunity to take over a lease from a man who was farming Dr. Harry White's farm in the Appleton District. The older children, Mabel, Ivan, Fred and Clyde, were enrolled in the Appleton School that fall. The man from whom Clyde Sr. took over the lease neglected to mention that he had the crops mortgaged to the limit. So Clyde Sr. didn't get much out of his venture that year except a team of horses, some farm implements, cows, chickens and pigs. But he did get some experience in whom to place his trust!

The flu epidemic was taking it's toll that winter, and the Likes' had their share of anxiety. Dad and Ivan both came down with the sickness and Ivan became seriously ill. The school was closed at Appleton for a while that winter because of the flu.

Retta sent Fred and Clyde Jr. to the neighbors' house nearby to ask for some advice in caring for Ivan. That family had a daughter who was down with the flu. The advice was to soak Ivan in hot mustard water, "as hot as he could stand." Clyde Jr. reported years later that the water must have been about as hot as Ivan could stand, as "he yelled pretty loud." Clyde also told of the neighbor stopping by the next morning to report that his daughter had died during the night. The neighbor announced, "Sis croaked last night." How crude! In recent years a news article was found that gave a more civilized account of the girl's death.

During that winter Clyde Sr. and his two oldest sons, Ivan and Fred, went out to the homestead to make some preparations for the family to move out in the spring. They built a two-room cabin out of two-by-fours and one-by-twelves with no foundation, no insulation, no decorations, no indoor plumbing — typical of the homestead shacks of the day. It would afford shelter from the wind and rain. Perhaps we could say it *was* better than a tent!

At that time Ivan turned over the first soil on the homestead with a disc drawn by a team of horses. It was a beginning!

Sometime in May 1919, after school was out in Appleton, the Likes family loaded all their belongings on the hay wagon and, trailing the cows behind, began the move to the homestead. They journeyed to Loma the first day and corralled the cows and horses in the lumber yard for the night while the kids and Dad and Mom slept in the Loma Hotel. What an adventure that must have been! Pure luxury!

It seems that Retta had never seen the homestead until she arrived there to live. Upon seeing nothing but shadscale and rabbit brush, she turned to Clyde and asked: "What do you think you're gonna do with that?" But she hid her surprise and disappointment and set about to make a home for her family. Hardship was not new to either Clyde or Retta. Both had been raised in a pioneer environment; we have already had a glimpse of Clyde's and Retta's backgrounds.

The family settled into their new life with great expectations. No doubt much of the first year (1919) was spent building ditches and fences; at least some land leveling was done also. Within that first year Clyde planted a few acres of alfalfa; probably with a nurse crop of oats or wheat. Surely there were other crops.

Retta was strong for gardening, so there must have been peas, potatoes, carrots, beets, beans, etc. As she had learned as a child, Retta harvested plants that grew wild and served them to her family as "greens" to supplement their diet. Many of the things fed to the family then would be looked upon with suspicion today. Perhaps they were then!

No doubt the building of the New Liberty

School in 1919 caused excitement among the Likes' children and others in the community. Clyde Jr. and Fred contributed their bit by carrying boards for the carpenters. (They may have been more of a nuisance than help.) The new school was less than one-half mile from the Likes' home.

In March 1920, Clyde Sr. attended an auction at Garmesa Farms, as did several of his neighbors. It's not known what else he bought, but he did bring home a registered Duroc Jersey gilt (female pig) with a plan to start his own swine herd. A snapshot sent soon after that to Mom's sister, Zella Banning, shows the pig with the full pedigree name written on the back of the picture. Also, in the spring of 1920, the Likes' acquired some "bum" (orphan) lambs.

During the summer of 1920, they harvested the first crop of alfalfa hay and built the first haystack on the homestead! That must have created a lot of excitement in the Likes family!

About that time also it became customary for the Likes boys to herd the milk cows along the roadside, ditch-banks, and vacant land in the area; thus eliminating the necessity of using precious farm land for pasture and cutting down considerably on the amount of hay and grain that otherwise had to be fed to the cows. Fred and Clyde fell heir to that job first; but years later it was turned over to Homer and Lewis.

Clyde Likes Sr. was

instrumental in organizing a Sunday School in the community as soon as the new school building was completed. The Sunday School afforded Clyde opportunity to further his ministerial work. (It's amusing that several people who have written to us referred to Rev. Clyde Likes as their "pastor." More is written about the Sunday School elsewhere).

Clyde also commuted to various places up the valley to preach whenever opportunities arose. He would drive the Model "T" or ride a horse to Fruita and catch the Interurban (Electric Train)

(Upper) Retta with sons, Homer, Fred and Clyde with the cows on the Likes' farm, 1920. (Below) The Duroc pigs that were bought from the Garmesa farm, 1920. On back of picture it reads: "The one on the left is Betsy Brookwater Garmesa, Registered Duroc." *(Likes Photo Collection)*

(Upper left) The Likes' homestead, about 1928. (Upper right) Clyde Likes Sr. in Kansas when he worked for Elijah Williams, 1900, 18 years old. (Left) Two-year-old Homer feeding the bum lambs acquired in the spring of 1920. (Lower left) The first hay crop, 1920. L-R: Ivan holding a lamb, Mabel, Homer, Retta and Fred. On the back of the pictures it says, "Clyde Jr. was not there, as he was hunting his hat." (Lower right) The first haystack, 1920. L-R in back: Mabel, Retta and Clyde Sr. Front: Ivan, Fred, Clyde Jr. and Homer. *(Likes Photo Collection)*

from there to Grand Junction or points in between. Other times he would catch a Denver & Rio Grande passenger train at Mack.

No doubt Clyde and Retta had hopes that their children would follow their religious training. But, sad to say, not one of the nine followed their teachings.

On 21 March 1921 the sixth child was born. He was given the name **Lewis David** and was the first in the family to be born in a hospital, the Fruita Hospital, and the first of the children to be born in Colorado.

Mabel and Ivan were among the graduates from the eighth grade at New Liberty in the spring of 1922. Mabel lost a year at some point in time and Ivan was advanced beyond his age group while in the seventh grade, thus they graduated together.

Some time during the 1921-22 school year there arose a problem between the Likes family and teacher Selma Snavely. Selma had a fiery temper, and the students were made to feel that temper occasionally. One day Clyde Jr., being a mischievous nine-year-old, pushed his luck too far and provoked Selma to the point she felt he should be disciplined. She grabbed a lock of Clyde's hair, probably intending to haul him up to the front of the class room, but she pulled so violently the lock of hair came out by the roots, leaving a bald spot of noticeable size. Clyde, of course, was hurting, and ran home to tell his parents about the "cruel and unusual" punishment. Dad and Mom were furious and went to the school board to complain. Dad demanded that Selma be dismissed at once, but the school board took the stand that replacing her was nearly impossible, because it was mid-term and school teachers were not easily found.

A community meeting was called for the purpose of allowing the principle complainers to blow off some steam. A lot of bitter feelings were expressed, but nothing was accomplished. Dad was determined that Selma should go, but conceded that he would abide by the decision of the school board for the rest of the school year. If she was still there the following year, though, his children would not return!

It appears the school board did not take Clyde's threat seriously, as Selma was still at the school in the fall. So it became necessary for him to make good on his promise. He accepted an offer to become pastor of the Friends Church at Colorado Springs. In the fall of 1922 the homestead was leased to neighbor Howard Williams and the Likes family moved to Colorado Springs.

I do not remember any of the details of that trip to Colorado Springs, but I'm sure it must have been somewhat like the one I do remember a few years later when we traveled over there to a Yearly Meeting. It was late enough in the fall that it had begun to be pretty cold on the mountain passes. We camped out one night along the side of the road and the warmth of the campfire was most welcome. In the car, Mom had us bundled up in a nest of warm quilts and blankets. We carried along heated flatirons from the stove and heated rocks from the camp fire to help keep us warm. Remember, Model "T"s were not equipped with heaters!

The family set up housekeeping in a "temporary parsonage" in Colorado Springs while another house was being readied. Later they moved into the permanent parsonage; a home purchased by the church and remodeled to accommodate the growing family of the new preacher.

Mabel and Ivan had enrolled at Fruita Union High School that fall, but the move to Colorado Springs disrupted school at New Liberty and Fruita for all four of the older Likes children. All were enrolled at the schools in Colorado Springs.

On 14 June 1923, while in Colorado Springs, the seventh child was born — the second girl in the family. She was named **Virginia Ellen**. Virginia was a special joy to her parents, brothers and sister. Consequently she was spoiled to the extreme! She was quite an attraction to the teenage girls in the church group as well. They were always contesting for the privilege of holding her or changing her diapers. Once, when one of the girls changed her, Virginia began crying and didn't stop until Mom investigated and found that one of the safety pins was pinned through the skin on her thigh. She had good reason to cry!

Homer survived his first school experience

(Above) Retta holding baby Virginia on porch of the parsonage in Colorado Springs, 1923. (Upper right) The Likes family standing in front of the new parsonage being remodeled in the spring of 1923. L-R: Clyde Jr., Clyde Sr., Ivan, Homer, Retta, Lewis (in front) and Fred. (Lower right) The church where Clyde preached in Colorado Springs. The people are unidentified. *(Photos courtesy of Mabel and Homer Likes Collection)*

in Colorado Springs, and Mabel, Ivan, and Fred all became teenagers with part-time jobs. Fred had a paper route, and Mabel worked as a telephone operator. Typically, they endured the feelings of frustration most teenagers experience when not allowed to make all their own decisions. Ivan had a row with his Dad and ran away from home. He headed to Oklahoma where he felt sure relatives would give him shelter — maybe some sympathy.

Mabel enrolled at the Friends Academy (similar to a high school) at Haviland, Kansas, probably in the fall of 1923. In the late summer of 1924, shortly after she had returned to school, the family went to see her as they traveled to Oklahoma to visit relatives. Clyde Jr. told years later that Mabel was clever at deceiving her parents. As the family journeyed

on toward Oklahoma they stopped at the home of some friends to spend the night. During that night, while all were sleeping soundly, a telephone call came from Haviland informing Clyde and Retta that "Maybelle" had been in an auto accident, was hurt and calling for her "Momma." So, the kids were all hauled out of bed to make the trip back to Haviland, arriving in the wee, small hours of the morning. Before long Mabel began to beg to go to Oklahoma with them. Whether or not she was seriously hurt is questionable, but she *did* go to Oklahoma with the family and never went back to school.

It must have been about that time that Mabel decided her name should be spelled **Maybelle**; perhaps the original spelling was not sophisticated enough. From then on her name was "Maybelle." We have learned since that her

474

name had come from her Aunt Mabel (her father's half sister), her great grandmother, Mabel Timartha Lewin Driskell and her great, great, great, grandmother, Mabel Timartha Hunt Lewin.

Apparently during the winter of 1924-25, Clyde Sr. had a major misunderstanding with the elders of the church. He resigned his pastorate, severed connections with the church, and proceeded to move his family back to the homestead in the spring of 1925. They started out in the Model "T," but it broke down at Salida. Dad sold it (more than likely gave it away) and we all continued the trip by train.

After they returned to the farm, Maybelle went to work as a waitress/maid at the Mack Hotel where she soon met Leonard Cox, son of W. H. Cox, proprietor of Mack Mercantile. In the summer of 1926, Maybelle and Leonard, and Leonard's sisters, Josie and Lucille, were on an outing on Grand Mesa with other young people. Josie and Lucille began to tease Maybelle and Leonard into getting married. They had been making plans to be married in January 1927, but at the insistence of the sisters, they were married that day at Delta, Colorado, 13 July 1926. Maybelle then had to work out a plan to inform her parents in a way that would lessen the shock, and before they found out from someone else. They had big plans for her to marry a "preacher-type," which Leonard, by any stretch of imagination, did not measure up to! But they accepted her choice and made the best of it. What else could they do? (See Leonard Cox story).

Soon after the family returned to the homestead, Ivan came home to live and vowed never to live in a city again. He would soon be 18 years old and felt that he had the world by the tail on a down-hill pull! He had some interesting experiences while away from the family; one of which should be told here.

While in Oklahoma he was hired by a family acquaintance to drive a team and wagon to somewhere in Texas — quite an undertaking for a 17-year-old. He arrived in Texas safely, but even though a wage for the trip had been previously agreed upon, he was never paid.

After Ivan returned to Colorado in 1925 he went to work wherever he could find a job. During the summer of 1925 he found work in Unaweep Canyon helping the Massey's and Casto's harvest their hay crop. The following summer (1926) Fred, age 15, went there too. They were there during the summers of 1927 and 1928 also. It was fascinating to hear the stories they told of working there. Oh, how the younger brothers wished they were big enough to share in those experiences!

For the school year 1925-26 the teachers were H. H. and Mable Henson. Mr. Henson had a very effective method of punishing errant boys. Soon after school began, Homer and his new-found friend, Arthur Shires, were playing during recess in the drainage ditch across the road west of the school. They heard the bell ring but one challenged the other to ignore the bell. What fun! Such daring! But they soon had the sobering thought that they would have to face the music some time, so they surrendered. But they didn't get any credit for repentance. The deed was done! They must be punished!

About this same time Clyde Likes Jr. and Franklin Manzanares had been caught, or at least "squealed" on, for smoking. They too must be punished! So the Hensons called a general assembly of all the school so all could witness the punishment of those errant boys. One by one, Clyde, Franklin, Arthur and Homer, were marched up in front of the students and flogged with a length of rubber hose. Mr. Henson knew how to lay it on so it counted! Homer has never had to suffer such humiliation since, but he learned a lesson — crime doesn't pay! The punishment probably provided excellent entertainment for the other students.

In the spring of 1926, with the assistance of neighbor John Morrow, Clyde Sr. built an addition on the west side of the Likes' home. It was a lean-to that would provide another bedroom, something the family never had enough of — a new kitchen was also included. After the addition was completed the cook stove was moved into the new part and the large dining table was set nearby. A heater was set up in the old part of the house, so they had two sources of heat now, instead of just the cook stove; one could toast shins and posteriors wherever room was available.

This is an appropriate place to tell a story about the stoves. Clyde Sr. developed a ritual that continued for many years, much to the chagrin of the growing-up children. He would be the first to arise in the morning and would loudly shake the grates in the stoves in preparation for stoking up the fires. Then, as if that were not enough to get everyone awake, he would get the violin and proceed to play a few tunes. By that time, the teenagers were only pretending to be asleep. Then he would start yelling to finish the waking-up process.

During the summer months bedrooms were no problem, for there was the whole outdoors to sleep in. There were boys sleeping in the barn, in the cellar, on the haystack, etc. That was just fine except when there were thunderstorms! But in the winter it was wall-to-wall boys. There were never less than two boys to a bed; by necessity most of the beds were on the floor. The boys had a little trick to keep warm: they would undress (usually we slept in our underwear) and back up to the heater and soak up all the heat they could stand, then run and jump under the covers before that heat dissipated. Retta always kept plenty of home-made quilts on the beds for warmth.

Some time in 1925 or 1926, the family acquired a puppy named Jerry. He was probably half Airdale, but the other half could have been Heinz-57. Jerry became as much a part of the family as any of the kids. An excellent stock dog, he just loved to work with the cows and horses. Many times he would be seen to nip the heel of a horse and then drop back and down just enough so the expected kick would graze over the top of his head. It's a good thing he never misjudged!

Later, Jerry would go with Homer and Lewis to herd the cows and was a valuable help with that chore. The boys also spent lots of time, while the cows were grazing, hunting rabbits, prairie-dogs, snakes, skunks, etc. Jerry was always right in the midst of those ventures!

One night at the farmstead all were awakened by Jerry raising a terrible ruckus! Clyde Sr. could not really see by lantern light what it was that had made Jerry so excited, but he said to Jerry: "Get him!" Jerry dutifully "got him." We heard Jerry

The new addition to the Clyde Likes home in New Liberty, 1926.
(Maybelle Likes Cox Collection)

yelp and soon discovered he had a nose full of porcupine quills! Jerry endured somewhat less than patiently as the quills were extracted. But one was missed. Months later a quill was discovered protruding from his chest.

Jerry liked to roam at night, as most robust male dogs do. Early one morning he was discovered burying a large object in the field west of the house. Upon investigating, it was found he had raided someone's home storage and stole a large smoked ham. Jerry must have traveled far that night, for it was never learned who had lost the ham, even though all neighbors were quizzed about possible missing items.

In spite of being ran over by a car, gun shot,

476

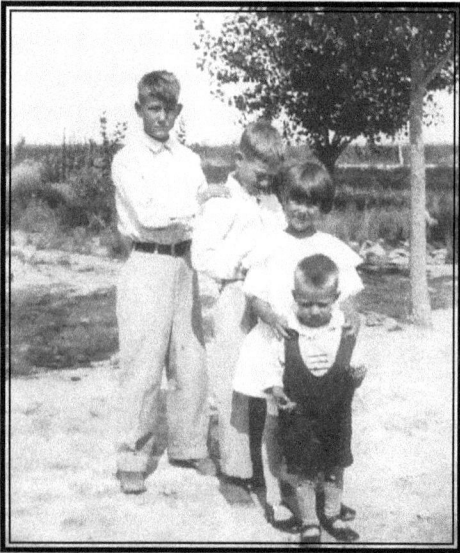

Back to front: Homer, Lewis, Virginia and Ray Marenus Likes, about 1930. *(Likes Photo Collection)*

poisoned, distemper, etc., Jerry lived to a very old age.

Number eight in the family, another baby boy whom they named **Ray Marenus**, joined the family on 22 August 1927. He was born in St. Mary's Hospital in Grand Junction. Ray seemed destined to live a life of hard knocks; quite early he was victim of numerous childhood diseases. At age four he was hit by a car on a street in West Los Angeles, suffering a fractured skull and a broken leg and arm. When he was about eight or nine he was kicked by a mule. While he seemed to recover from all of these rough knocks, all of them probably contributed to later health problems.

He later had St. Vitus Dance, an ailment that caused him to shake and vibrate. When he was 12 he had rheumatic fever, which left him with an enlarged heart. He was told by doctors that he could live a long time if he would be careful and not tax his heart unnecessarily. But he did not heed that advice and tried to do everything that all young boys want to do. Consequently he died at a young age. He was swimming with friends in Kansas City when his heart gave out; he had to be rescued from the pool. He died a few days later, on 2 August 1949, in a hospital in Lebanon, Missouri, just prior to his 22nd birthday. He was buried at Climax Springs, Missouri.

About 1928, Ivan and Fred bought a Model "T" Ford truck with which they began to haul hay, grain and salt to outlying ranches and to road-building crews. That proved to be quite a job; it entailed long hours, plus having to contend with horrendous road conditions caused by mud and snow. They soon realized that they must get a bigger truck, so they bought one of the earliest Model "A" Ford trucks (with dual wheels, even). Much of the

Ray Marenus Likes, 1928

Ray Marenus Likes, 1931

Ray Marenus Likes, 1946

(All three photos from the Likes Photo Collection)

Clyde Likes Sr. family, spring of 1940. Standing L-R: Ray Marenus, Clyde William Jr., Ivan Randle, Maybelle (Cox), Virginia Ellen, Clyde William Sr., Richard Allen, Retta May and Elmer Fred Likes. Front: Homer Chilson and Lewis David Likes. *(Likes Photo Collection)*

hay they hauled had to be baled out of the stacks, so they were involved in the baling much of the time. The trucking venture continued well into the depression years; then money became so scarce they could no longer meet the payments on the new truck. It was soon repossessed, thus ending the "Likes Brothers" trucking business.

By that time the three oldest boys, Ivan, Fred, Clyde, and their Dad began to enlarge the farming operation to include some rented land so there could be more income for the family. This led to the purchase of a John Deere model "G P" tractor in the spring of 1930. Then they rented the King farm, the Bill Price farm, some of Deacon's farm, etc. That turned out to be a good experience for all involved; there was still not much income, but a sense of satisfaction for all the hard work.

Early in 1931 after Retta learned she was pregnant with her ninth child; she began to

have complications with uremic poisoning and had to be under a doctor's care. She was nearing her 43rd birthday when she gave birth on 17 September 1931, to a Down's Syndrome child; he was given the name **Richard Allen.**

Only families who have had that experience can really understand what a great burden it is! Mothers and other family members can love a mentally retarded child as much as any other, but there comes a long period of testing to raise to maturity one with such a handicap. Not much was known at that time about training children with Down's Syndrome; but Richard was closely nurtured as a *family member.* Many children like that have been placed in institutions at an early age and more or less forgotten; others were just kept out of sight.

478

Richard Allen Likes
(Likes Photo Collection)

Retta Likes chose to raise her handicapped child as near like her other children as possible — and it was not easy.

At one time Richard was placed in the State Home and Training School at Grand Junction, but it was a short stay. He didn't adapt well and Mom couldn't stand to see him suffer from homesickness, so she soon brought him home. He learned to talk to the degree that most family members could communicate with him quite well, but his learning capacity was very limited. Mom worried that he would not be properly cared for after she could no longer handle the responsibility. She kept him until her death in 1958; then he was placed in the State Home and after several years there he was farmed out to other homes.

He lived for some time in a home in downtown Grand Junction, but there was a fire that caused them to close the place. He was sent to Plateau Valley Nursing Home near Collbran on 17 February 1981. There he adapted very well and had excellent care. He used to be overjoyed to have family members come to visit him but near the end he showed no sign of recognition and did not seem to care if anyone came to see him. Richard lived past 63 years of age. He died at the Plateau Valley Nursing Home on 19 January 1995, and was buried in the Elmwood Cemetery at Fruita. It was noted during the funeral service that he was likely the oldest survivor of Down's Syndrome. Usually they do not survive the teen years.

Here is a poem written by Marilyn Eidson, one of Richard's nurses, and read by her at his funeral service:

Richard was an angel
Although we didn't know it.
He was sent from God to dwell
With us mortals here below.
His job on earth wasn't easy;
In fact it was quite hard.
He tried to teach us lessons
That came straight from his heart.
He couldn't speak like you and me;
Yet we could understand
By a twinkle of his eye
Or a shake of his hand.
He loved to do his book work
With paper and pen;
And he wrote many a letter
Sitting at Mary Lou's right hand.
If we could have read his writing,
It might have taught us lots
Why he was on earth at all —
And why he was in this spot.
I'd like to think he taught us
How to love and care and trust
For those who might be different
Than most of us.
Richard had a family who
Held him very dear;
And they loved and cared for him
While he was here.
Now he's gone back to heaven
Where he's met family and friends.
His earthly duties are over;
But his love he will to us still send.
Now when we get to heaven
And the angel choir we see,
There will be a cute rotund angel
Close to God he will be
And when he sees us coming
I would like to think
To each he'll give a smile
And a shy little wink.

Clyde Sr. served many years on the Board of Directors of the Grand Valley Water User's Association. In the mid 1930s he played a major part in organizing the Grand Valley Rural Power Lines and then served on that Board of Directors for many years.

Clyde and Retta left the New Liberty homestead two or three times. During World War II Clyde went away and worked as a carpenter in various areas such as Pasco, Washington, where he helped build a facility

Clyde William and Retta May Appier Likes, 1954, married 50 years. *(Likes Photo Collection)*

which was involved in the development of the atomic bomb. At Orem, Utah, he helped build the Geneva Steel Plant. He became a member of the carpenters' union.

Clyde and Retta bought a home on Orchard Mesa and lived there for a couple of years. That home was sold, and they went back to the farm about the end of the war. After Homer came home from the war he and Clyde Sr. farmed together for awhile. Then in about 1947, some time after Homer and Phyllis were married, Clyde and Retta left and went to California for a time, then came back and lived in the teacherage at New Liberty School. In 1948 Clyde and Retta sold the homestead to Homer and Phyllis and moved to Climax Springs, Missouri. They bought another farm there but soon sold that to Fred and Ray. They then came back to Colorado and bought another house on Orchard Mesa, where they stayed until Retta died.

Retta never enjoyed good health after

Richard's birth. She eventually became overweight and then began to suffer from hypertension. She had several strokes before she died in the Community Hospital in Grand Junction on 16 August 1958, at age 69. She was buried in Memorial Gardens at Grand Junction.

Clyde Sr. survived for 12 more years in reasonably good health — physically. He lived for short periods of time with each of his children; but as he became older he became severely senile and ever harder to care for. He lived in a nursing home for some time, but again became too difficult to care for and finally had to be placed in the State Hospital at Pueblo. He died there on 23 March 1970, just four days short of his 88th birthday. He too is buried at Memorial Gardens. After he was gone the doctors decided he was a victim of Alzheimer's disease — the disease was just then beginning to be recognized.

Clyde and Retta left a large posterity; they had reared a family of nine children, but none of their offspring had more than four children. Nevertheless, when Clyde died there were 25 grandchildren, 23 great-grandchildren and four great-great-grandchildren. That count has expanded considerably since then.

Mabel "Maybelle" and **Leonard Cox** were married 13 July 1926, at Delta, Colorado. They lived in Mack for awhile after their marriage and then moved to California where he worked in the mercantile business for Safeway Stores Inc.. While working for Safeway, they were required to move quite often, even to other states. On one of those moves they lived in Paonia, Colorado. While there Virginia lived with them and went to high school.

Mabel and Leonard had a daughter, **Joan Lucille**, born 2 January 1928 at Grand Junction. (See Leonard Cox history).

During World War II, Leonard went to Hawaii for a year and worked as a storekeeper in a shipyard. Maybelle and Joan lived with Maybelle's sister-in-law, Lucille Schultz and family, for quite awhile and then moved in with Clyde and Ruby and family until Leonard came

(Above left) Mabel Dean "Maybelle" Likes, 1923. (Above right) The Friends Academy, Haviland Kansas, 1923–24. (Above right) The girl's dormitory at the Friends' Academy, Haviland, Kansas, 1923–24. (Below left) Leonard and Maybelle Cox with their new daughter, Joan, 1928. (Below center) Joan, Maybelle and Leonard Cox in California, 1944. (Below right) Leonard and Maybelle Cox and their poodles in Denver, early 1960s. *(Likes Photo Collection)*

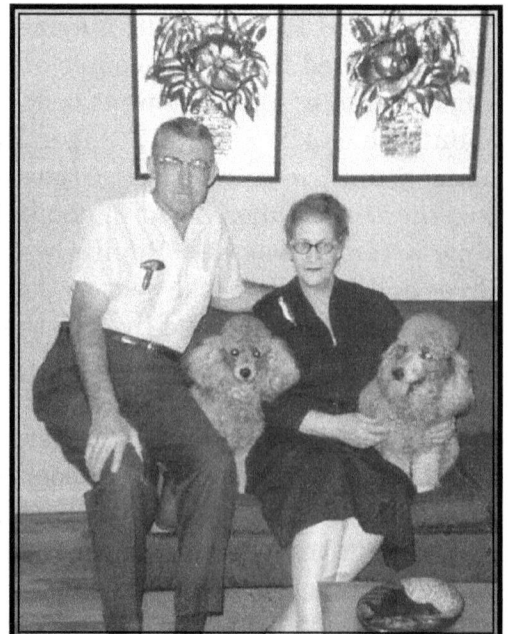

home. Maybelle worked at March Field during that time. The winter of 1946–47, Maybelle, Leonard, Joan and her son, Chuck, moved to Paonia, Colorado. Leonard went into partnership with brothers-in-law, Fred and Lewis Likes in a grocery store for two years. Maybelle and Leonard then moved to Denver where Maybelle worked for J.C. Penny's for five years as manager of the yardage department. She would sew sample dresses and etc. for the floor and when the store was through showing them, Maybelle gave them to Joan. She had made them Joan's size just for this very purpose. She also made drapes for the store and eventually turned this to her advantage. She quit Penney's and opened a drapery business in her home. She sewed draperies under contract for companies who built new homes for home shows in Denver. She had this business for about 10 years, when she and Leonard moved back to Watts and then Alhambra, California. Maybelle managed apartments while Leonard managed a fruit stand and then he worked for a liquor store.

Leonard was diagnosed with prostate cancer in 1969, then they moved to Fruita. Leonard died there 25 September 1971.

After Leonard's death, Maybelle lived near her daughter Joan in the Sacramento, California area. She also enjoyed a close relationship with Joan's son, Chuck, and his children, who lived there also. Eventually she came back to Colorado to live and spent some time with Lewis and Delores near Mack. Then she moved into the "Village" in Fruita and was there for several years. In the spring of 1986 she was stricken with pneumonia. She entered St. Mary's Hospital and hovered near death for several weeks. She finally recovered enough to return to the Village but continued to decline in health, both physically and mentally. Eventually she was moved to Family Health West in Fruita and diagnosed with Alzheimer's disease, where she lived out her remaining days. She died there at age 87 on 9 December 1992. She was buried beside her husband, Leonard, at Memorial Gardens.

We might mention at this point that all three of the older boys; Ivan, Fred and Clyde Jr., were married in 1933. It was almost as if

some disease affected them!

Ivan married **Evelyn Bush** (see Bush story) 17 August 1933.

They had four children:

Betty Alene (Smit), born 4 May 1934, New Liberty (Betty has two sons and four grandchildren)
Reetis Randal "Bud", 12 June 1936, Fruita (Bud has three daughters).
Loretta Jean, 2 May 1938, Fruita
Ivan Leroy, 18 February 1940, New Liberty (Leroy has five children and seven grandchildren)

After their marriage Ivan and Evelyn rented the Ted Wassenberg farm, where Evelyn's parents, Reet and Ada Bush, had been living. They lived there until 1941, then moved to the Leonard Appier farm west of Badger Wash.

Ivan was a good farmer and a good man with livestock. His pride and joy was a team of horses he had raised from colts. They were quite large, probably weighed over 1,800 pounds each. Those horses did most of his farm work for several years.

Ivan was an avid hunter and outdoorsman, so he spent as much time as possible in the Bookcliff Mountains north of New Liberty. He loved to go to the hills to get cedar wood or fence posts for use at home.

(Left) Ivan and his horse, Two Steps. (Right) Ivan, with a broken leg, and Ramsey Miller in front of the Likes house in New Liberty, about 1935. (*Likes Photo Collection*)

(The following is told in first person, since I was there — author) On one of those outings Ivan came home with a leg broken from being run over by the wagon. Previously the end of the wagon tongue had been broken off and Ivan repaired it by forging a wagon tire into a loop to replace the broken end.

After we had loaded the wagon with wood in the hills northwest of New Liberty, we "rough-locked" the wagon to hold it back as we proceeded down a steep hill. But the grade was so steep it put too much strain on the repaired tongue and it broke, allowing the wagon to run up on the team. Rather than ride the load of wood to the bottom of the hill, Ivan jumped off and as he hit the ground he fell under the wheels. The horses were badly frightened, of course, but they stopped running as soon as the wagon stopped pushing them. Ivan was lying on the ground, helpless. I remember very well riding one of the horses about 10 miles to get help. It was late in the evening before we got him to Dr. White in Fruita to get his leg set in a plaster cast.

On another occasion Ivan and his son, Bud, were victims of the outdoors becoming seriously ill with "Rocky Mountain Fever" from tick bites.

After Ivan quit farming in 1942 he went to California and got a job driving a truck. He and his family were living at Santa Cruz, California when he and Evelyn separated and divorced.

Ivan was a born mechanic, so he worked at that trade many years after he left the farm. He worked as a mechanic for a considerable time in California until he began to have serious back problems, which eventually led to surgery.

Ivan married **Leota Redfern** 27 October 1947, in California, but that marriage was short-lived. He came back to Colorado to make his home again among family and friends. He worked for a season for the Morrow family, and it looked for a time as though he and Elizabeth Morrow would marry. — But it never happened. He later had a garage in Mack which kept him occupied for some time.

On 17 July 1952, Ivan married **Leda Helen Cato Smith**, a divorced mother who lived in Fruita. She had three children

living at home: Madalyn, Maxine and Patsy Smith. With Ivan's two boys, Bud and Leroy, they made a pretty lively family; all graduated from Fruita Union High School.

In 1957 Ivan went to work as shop foreman for Moab Drilling Co., in Moab, Utah, and early in 1958 Leda moved there. In 1962, he was offered a good job at Silverton, Colorado, as a mechanic for Westwood Trucking Company Ivan and Leda bought a home in Silverton and lived there for several years. Leda became county assessor and Ivan was sheriff while they were living there.

In late 1972 Leda was diagnosed with cancer and died at Durango Community Hospital 25 January 1973. She was buried in Elmwood Cemetery at Fruita.

On 14 September 1981 Ivan married **Dorothy Dove Palmer**, a widow from Fruita. They lived at 1310A Highway 50 West, Delta, Colorado, for several years, but in 1994 bought a home in Fruita at 224 South Sycamore.

Before they moved to Fruita, Ivan began to have some serious health problems from diabetes. Then, not long after the move to Fruita, it was discovered he had Alzheimer's and it soon became impossible for Dorothy to provide the care he needed. He was placed in Family Health West where he would have the benefit of around-the-clock care. On 20 July 1996, he had his 89th birthday. He became unable to recognize family members before he passed away 21 May 1997. He was buried beside Leda in

Ivan Likes the mechanic at a garage in Santa Cruz, California, about 1945. *(Likes Photo Collection)*

483

(Above left) Evelyn Bush and Ivan Randle Likes, 1935. (Above right) Ivan and family in front of the house they rented on the Ted Wassenberg farm fall 1939. L-R: Bud, Ivan with Loretta, Evelyn with Betty in front,. (Center left) Ivan and family in front of Clyde Likes Sr.'s house, 1940. L-R: Richard Likes in background, Ivan and Bud in back, and Loretta, Betty and Evelyn holding Leroy in front. (Center right) L-R: Bud, Betty, Loretta, Ivan and Leroy, 1950, California. (Below left) Loretta and Bud Likes, about 1950. (Below center) Ivan and Leda Cato Smith Likes, 1952. (Below right) Dorothy Dove Palmer and Ivan Likes, 1983. *(Likes Photo Collection)*

Elmwood Cemetery.

Ivan's two daughters, Betty and Loretta, live in Sparks, Nevada, as does their mother, Evelyn. Bud lived in Mississippi for awhile, but is back in Nevada. Leroy lives in Aurora, Colorado, near Denver. There are 10 grandchildren and at least 10 great grandchildren.

Fred married **Louise Clow** (see Earp story) on 3 March 1933, at Grand Junction. They lived for a short time with Fred's parents until they could find something more suitable. They bought the Andrew Lane homestead through a tax sale and moved a tiny shack there in which to live. In October 1937 they sold that farm to Phillip Brayton and bought the farm on the hill formerly owned by Clyde Balkwill.

Fred and Ivan Likes on the Likes farm in New Liberty, 1927. *(Likes Photo Collection)*

Thelma, Fred and Louise Likes, 1935
(Likes Photo Collection)

Fred and Louise had three children:

Thelma Louise (Faulkner), born 30 December 1934, Mack (Thelma has five children and four grandchildren)
Donald Fred, 23 March 1937, Fruita (Don has one child)
Marvin George, 6 August 1940, Grand Junction (Marvin has three children and 1 grandchild)
All three of Fred and Louise's children were born while they lived at New Liberty.

Fred and Louise sold the farm around 1941 to

Louise, Fred and children, 1943. Children L-R: Thelma Louise, Donald Fred and Marvin George Likes. *(Likes Photo Collection)*

Milton Alstatt and moved to the northwest. Upon recommendation of New Liberty friends, Dick and Evelyn Kessinger, they went first to Cottage Grove, Oregon, with a homemade travel trailer they had bought from Frank Overbye. Louise said that living in that trailer was not the most comfortable home she has lived in! Fred found work in a logging camp as fireman on a "donkey," a steam-powered machine built for dragging logs.

After a time, the family went to Albany, Oregon and Fred got a job helping dynamite stumps from an area being cleared for an Army base. He then learned about a welding school that would qualify him to go to work in a shipyard at Portland. So they moved to the Portland area. Louise soon learned she could go to welding school, also, and after 10 days of training she was hired at the same shipyard; both were working for Oregon Ship Builders.

After a time Fred learned of an opportunity to train as a diesel mechanic; shortly after he completed that he was called by a man who needed a

mechanic at Bickleton, Washington. Dick Kessinger, formerly of the New Liberty/Mack area, joined the family and he and Fred formed a partnership to operate the garage. Fred and Louise's two oldest children, Thelma and Donald, went to school in Bickleton.

Sometime in 1946 Fred and Louise decided they had had enough of the partnership and Fred sold out to Dick and they moved back to Colorado. They invested in another partnership with Leonard Cox and Lewis Likes in a grocery store at Paonia, Colorado. Fred also had a truck that was utilized by his brothers, Clyde, Homer and Ray, to haul logs from an area on the north fork of the Gunnison River, east of Paonia.

In about 1949 they moved to Climax Springs, Missouri, where they lived for a time on the Likes farm near the Lake of the Ozarks. During that time, their daughter, Thelma, married a boy from Arkansas. She has continued to live in the south, and has lived for many years at Ardmore, Alabama.

Fred and Louise moved from Climax Springs farther north to Marysville, Missouri, where Fred was employed as a mechanic for a branch of the International Harvestor Company. With Fred still working as a heavy equipment mechanic for International Harvestor, they lived for a time at Hollister, California. Then, after a couple of short stays at Moab, Utah, and Silverton, Colorado, they moved to Shelton, Washington, where their sons, Donald and Marvin, were living.

Some years earlier, as Don was doing a stint in the Navy, one of his buddies, who was from Shelton, introduced him to his cute sister. Don and she were married within a year, and after living in Moab for awhile, migrated back to Shelton to be near her family. The rest of the Fred Likes family, except Thelma, decided they wanted to live there also.

On 18 May 1980 Fred and Louise had a harrowing experience. They had taken a job watching some mining equipment on the weekends at a location approximately four miles north of Mount St. Helens. They were out for a walk on the morning the volcano exploded, and shortly after the explosion they were threatened by mud-balls falling from the sky, then dust and darkness. They took refuge under a safety canopy on a tractor sitting nearby. They sat there for some time before venturing on to their trailer. They endured many hours of fear and anxiety before they were able to get out of there. It was a month before they could get their trailer out because of the six-inch layer of volcanic dust covering everything. They were thankful to live to tell about it.

Fred began to have heart problems which culminated in open-heart surgery in October 1983. After surgery, as he was in recovery, he managed to get a hand free and ripped away the life-support equipment attached to him. Of course, he immediately went into cardiac and respiratory arrest. It was some time before the doctors and nurses revived him. He suffered some brain damage from that episode. Fred's quality of life went downhill from that time on. His health gradually worsened and eventually he began to exhibit Alzheimer's symptoms. He died in the hospital at Olympia, Washington, 13 February 1993, at age 82, and was buried in the Municipal Cemetery at Shelton, Washington. Louise continues to live in their home close to their son, Marvin. On 24 July 1997 she celebrated her 82nd birthday There are seven grandchildren and five great-grandchildren

Clyde William, Jr., William Ray, and Ruby Dodge Likes,1935. (*Likes Photo Collection*)

Clyde Jr. married **Ruby Pearl Dodge** 25 November 1933, at Grand Junction. They lived in the Mack/New Liberty area for several years.

They had three sons:

William "Billy" Ray, born 7 February 1935, Mack

Robert "Bob" Gene, 18 May 1936, Fruita (Bob has two children, one stepchild, and four grandchildren)

Edward "Eddie" Lee, 21 November 1937, Fruita (Ed has four children and three grandchildren)

The boys all attended New Liberty School, each graduating from the eighth grade there.

The family moved to the Horse Thief Canyon Ranch south of Loma, Colorado, in August 1936, then, in November 1938, moved to the Ella Stotts farm in New Liberty, where they were to live for several years. During the time they were at Horse Thief Canyon they had signed a sales contract to purchase some livestock and farm

Louise Clow and Elmer Fred Likes, 1972. (*Likes Photo Collection*)

equipment from Alice Davis, who owned the Desert Gateway Store in Mack. During that year Alice married a man by the name of Hitner, who proceeded to take over all of Alice's business interests.

The next fall, after they had moved to the Stotts place, Clyde and Ruby did not have enough money to make the payment on their indebtedness, so the vindictive Hitner promptly foreclosed on them, taking virtually everything they had. It was quite a blow, but they slowly recovered from the experience.

In 1940 and 1941 they were living on a farm in the Loma area when Clyde decided to move to California in hopes he could make enough money to get started on a farm of his own. He was sure that if he could accumulate $500 to buy equipment and livestock; he would soon be able to buy some land. They never realized that dream. By the time they had the $500, it was not sufficient to do what they wanted.

L-R: Edward Lee, Robert Gene, Clyde William Jr, William Ray, and Ruby Dodge Likes summer of 1949 taken on Baxter Pass *(Likes Photo Collection)*

Clyde secured employment at the Lockheed Aircraft Factory in Burbank, California, in 1941. Later he took advantage of the company's program offering employees opportunities to train for better jobs. He trained to be an electrician and continued to work at that trade at Lockheed for several years.

They lived temporarily in Idaho and Oregon, but returned to the Los Angeles area. Clyde never lost the desire to live on a farm, so in the late 1940s they came back to New Liberty and bought the Kenneth "Red" Geeting farm at the west end of the New Liberty Community (the former Everetts/Corn property). This was not very good land and they had a tough time making a living on it. They lived for a year on the McIntosh homestead and the next year bought the McCampbell homestead across the road at the corner of S and 6 Roads. Since Grade-A milk production was quite popular at that time, they built a dairy barn and acquired some milk cows.

On 13 September 1949, shortly after beginning high school, Billy, their oldest son, died of polio. Ed, the youngest of the other two boys, was afflicted with polio also, but in time recovered without any lasting effects. The loss of Billy was a major trial — they never fully recovered from that.

The family then moved back to California. Clyde worked as an electrician in construction for a few years, then went to Idaho and found work there while doing a little farming on the side. (Ruby's parents and brother lived there). Eventually Clyde had the opportunity to work with the Idaho Department of Law Enforcement as an electrical inspector. That worked into a pretty good job, and soon he was spending some time writing electrical code for the building trades. Ultimately he played a major role in writing the National Electrical Code, which regulates electrical installation in buildings for the entire nation.

Susie Colleen Lee and Sherry Ann Likes
(Likes Photo Collection)

In December 1960, while in Idaho, Clyde and Ruby adopted two little girls who were sisters:

Susie Colleen Lee, born 20 March 1958, Ontario, Oregon, (Susie has two children)
Sherry Ann, born 22 May 1960, Burley, Idaho (Sherry had three children, but lost the first one)

The girls became a welcome part of the Likes family.

Then came at a time that was hard for all to cope with — Clyde developed cancer! He endured eleven years of chemotherapy with alternate periods of terrible sickness. In late 1981 he discontinued treatments because he simply did not want to endure anymore. In March 1982 he entered the hospital in Boise for exploratory surgery and they discovered that cancer had invaded his stomach. They removed his stomach, and while he was in recovery he went into cardiac arrest; it was some time before he was revived. After spending 19 days in intensive care, he died 27 March 1982.

Clyde, Ruby and Billy are all buried in the Elmwood Cemetery in Fruita, Colorado.

The extended family at present consists of 11 grandchildren and seven great-grandchildren.

At the present time, 1997, Bob lives near Paso Robles, California; Ed lives in Nampa, Idaho. ;Sherry in Boise, Idaho; and Susie in Sparks, Nevada.

Homer: Perhaps it would be appropriate at this point to bring you up to date on my (Homer's) adult years. In 1936 I was employed for about a year in the construction of the Grand Valley Rural Power Lines in the Mack and Loma areas, then went with that same contractor up to Mesa, Colorado, during the following summer.

After working as a farm laborer during the summer of 1937 Cecil Dodge and I made a trip to Idaho to work as farm laborers there. I became homesick and returned. After that I decided to try the Civilian Conservation Corps (CCC) and was assigned to Camp SP 10 C at Glenwood Springs, Colorado. While there I worked in the mess hall, and as a truck driver and cat operator. I learned to run a bull-dozer — that came in handy later.

The following year, 1938, my Dad asked me

(Top) Camp SP10C at Glenwood Springs, Colorado, 1937-38. (Bottom) Homer Likes and Relman McCroskie, CCC Camp SP 10 C, summer of 1937. *(Likes Photo Collection)*

489

to farm with him. He bought a new John Deere tractor for added enticement. This arrangement continued until December 1940. My brother Lewis enlisted in the Navy at that time; I tried that too, but I couldn't meet physical requirements because of poor vision. On the day after Christmas 1940, Darrell Maluy and I hitched a ride in the back of my Uncle Leonard Appier's new dump truck and went to West Los Angeles to make our fortune. At the time work was pretty scarce in the Los Angeles area, except for a few Works Progress Administration (*WPA*) jobs. The depression was lingering on, but it was soon to end.

At that time World War II was already going on in Europe and the United States was gearing up for the defense effort. In the spring of 1941 riveters were in demand at the Lockheed Aircraft Factory in Burbank, California. After taking an aptitude test and agreeing to start wearing glasses, I was accepted to become a riveter in the P-38 center section assembly line and went to work there in April 1941.

I had a good job there, even though I had to work a straight swing shift. It was not too difficult to become accustomed to working nights because by that time everything was geared to the war effort. All entertainment, cafes, etc., were open around the clock.

On 7 December 1941, the Japanese bombed Pearl Harbor. Very soon after that the United States became fully involved in World War II. I had registered for the draft in 1939 in Colorado, but because I was working in a defense industry I was given a deferment, supposedly for 18 months. In 1942 I was called up and traveled all the way to Grand Junction expecting to be inducted, but, while standing around waiting for orders, I was called into the office and told that I was excused and could go back to work.

I discovered early in 1943 that I was locked into my job after I tried at one point to enlist in the CB's (*Naval Construction Battalions*), but was refused on the basis of my defense job. I continued working at

Lockheed until the following October when I received another letter of "greetings" from my draft board. I notified my superior on the job; he advised me to forget it, as they would get me another deferment, but I chose to go see what would happen. It had been jokingly said that if you were able to breath and could stand, you would be inducted! After reporting to my draft board in Grand Junction I was sent to the induction center in Denver where I was surprised to learn I had a choice between the Army and CB's. Since I had already tried to get into the Navy branch of the military, I did not hesitate to opt for the CB's.

I was sent to Camp Peary, Virginia, for my "boot" training, so I had a train ride from coast to coast within a seven-day period. I received additional training at Davisville, Rhode Island,

Homer Chilson Likes, 1943.
(Likes Photo Collection)

Homer at the airfield construction on Okinawa, 1945. Front left is Homer Likes and next one to the right is Commander Cook. *(Likes Photo Collection)*

and later at Gulfport, Mississippi. In February 1944, at Biloxi, Mississippi, I boarded a combination troop/cargo ship with 1,000 black Marines and my own CB battalion and shipped out to the South Pacific Theatre. After the ship left Biloxi we went to New Orleans and loaded 20,000 cases of beer. Needless to say, this created a lot of mischief. We traveled across the Gulf, through the Panama Canal, and then spent endless days crossing the Pacific. I was aboard that ship for 90 days! I was then assigned to the 20th CB Battalion, stationed on Banika in the New Hebrides Islands. But that didn't last very long, as that unit was scheduled to return to the States within a short time.

Soon I was sent to another unit, the 87th Battalion, which was building an airfield on Stirling Island in the Northern Solomon Islands group. That place was just two degrees south of the equator, so you can well imagine that we had little difficulty keeping warm. That can be further illustrated by the fact that the men in our camp could be seen outside their tents during the daily rainstorms soaping down as if in the indoor showers. That rainwater was blessedly cool!

After that job was completed we were sent to New Caledonia for a sort of "R & R" (Rest and Recreation), though the military was not using that terminology at that time. We were issued

new equipment there (bulldozers, trucks, etc.) in preparation for a new assignment. The men and equipment were loaded aboard LSTs (*Landing Ship Tank*) and we sailed north to the Marianas Islands and set up camp at Saipan, which was to serve as a staging area. While there we began to experience battle conditions. Saipan had not yet been secured; there were still Japanese soldiers and civilians hiding in caves throughout the north half of the island. Almost daily we would see U. S. Military patrols marching Japanese military and civilian prisoners through our camp after ferreting them out of their hiding places.

Just a few miles from our camp there was a B-29 bomber base on Tinian, a neighboring island so we were able to hear those planes warming up every afternoon. Then we would see them take off and fly over our camp on the way to Tokyo; that was when much of that huge city was destroyed. The bombers would fly all night to deliver their bomb loads, returning early the next morning.

On 27 April 1945, we arrived at Okinawa on an LST, 27 days after the initial assault on the island. I remember quite clearly our ship being anchored in Naha Harbor the first night and watching with awe the battleship New York and a British battleship, HMS King George, lobbing shells into Naha, a city of 200,000. (Later, I had an opportunity to visit Naha. Except for two damaged buildings still standing, nothing was left but huge piles of rubble).

That same night there was a Kamikaze attack; the Japanese had learned there was a ship in the harbor loaded with munitions. We could see quite clearly an airplane dive into that ship and the explosion and fire that followed. The ship was soon scuttled. During that melee, I was standing on the deck watching the show, as were most of the men on the ship, when a piece of shrapnel ricocheted off the deck about three feet from where I was standing. I quickly sought cover, realizing almost too late how dumb it was to be exposed to the danger of flying bits of metal!

Our unit set about repairing Japanese airfields so they could be used by our own planes. We had little sleep in those first weeks, as we were bombed almost nightly by the Japanese airplanes and, of course, our anti-aircraft guns made a terrible racket blasting away at them. During that time we saw many more Kamikaze attacks. Early one morning a single plane flew over our camp less than a hundred feet off the ground and dove into an LST anchored a couple of hundred yards away. We could see the facial features of the pilot very plainly as he flew over.

On several occasions as we were working nights on Yontan airfield the lights would be doused while night patrols would go looking for snipers. The snipers would hide out during the daylight hours, then would try to pick us off as we worked in the lights.

One night during a blackout we watched as several Kamikaze planes were shot down near us. Many of us were standing around some shelters watching the show when we saw a ball of fire rolling down the landing strip a short distance in front of us. Soon we heard small-arms fire and very shortly a man ran up and told us to get out of sight; we were silhouetted by flashes of light from the anti-aircraft shells exploding above us. The man who came to warn us didn't use very kindly language, perhaps that's what we needed to wake us up to the real danger we were in!

We learned the next morning that a plane had landed on the airstrip after it had been damaged by an anti-aircraft shell on the way in to land, so one engine fell off as the plane touched the ground. The ball of fire we had seen was an engine from a "Sally Bomber" which was loaded with soldiers on a suicide mission! The Japanese soldiers aboard were armed with phosphorous grenades and managed to destroy all our aircraft sitting around the perimeter of the field before they were dispatched by our soldiers. The Japanese bomber was cut to shreds the next morning by "souvenir-happy" U.S. military men!

Within a month we were building a giant B-29 airfield at Bolo Point near the north end of the island, which was nearing completion when the war ended. Many times during those final months of the war, as the Japanese were trying

desperately to hold on, we spend most of our nights in "fox holes." We became so used to seeking protection in the night it seemed we could fall into the shelters in our sleep.

In August we learned that atomic bombs had been dropped on Hiroshima and Nagasaki. Then came the night that the end of the war was announced over the air waves — what a wild celebration!! It sounded as though every firearm, large or small, expended all available ammunition that night. The formal surrender took place a day or two later on Ie Shima, an island just a few miles from our camp. But there was another historic signing some time later in Tokyo Harbor for the benefit of General Douglas McArthur

In September we experienced the first of two typhoons that struck the island. While the first was bad enough, we learned that it was actually pretty mild compared to the next one! Soon after that our camp was moved some distance to a hill overlooking Buckner Bay, where many ships were unloaded and reloaded.

We had adequate warning before the next typhoon hit in October. We were issued rope to tie our tents down and were advised to stow all our gear so it wouldn't blow away. When the big blow hit we found we were not very well prepared! Wind gusts up to 178 miles per hour were clocked on the beach below our camp. We lost all our camp, including the quonset huts which were pretty sturdy metal buildings. At the height of the storm we had real reason to believe we may not survive! One cannot adequately describe the experience of a typhoon — it is impossible to help anyone to understand what it is like to cope with wind blowing in excess of 150 miles per hour. One must have a personal experience!

As the storm picked up in its fury my tent-mates and I left our tent. Just as we stepped out and our tent was relieved of our weight, it literally took off! My buddy and I sought refuge in the quonset hut housing the Galley and Mess Hall. It was a metal building forty feet wide and about eighty feet long. Within a short time the walls of that building began to buckle, so we left there and went to the camp laundry hut. That was also a quonset hut, twenty feet wide and forty feet long with all sorts of laundry equipment in it. Within an hour or so the intensity of the wind increased so much it was beginning to move that building off it's foundation. We decided to leave that place and, just as we stepped out of the door, my buddy disappeared into the torrent of wind and water roaring down the company street. I never saw him again until the next day after the storm had abated — I supposed he was dead! I worked my way about a hundred yards to a truck that was parked beside a stone wall and stayed in that truck until the storm was over about sixteen hours later. It was a great feeling of relief to find my buddy alive and well the next morning! The experience of that storm was far more frightening than being bombed and shot at by the Japanese military!

After the storm was over, we picked over the debris where our camp had been. I lost everything but the clothes I had on — all my clothing and personal belongings. I did find some of my photo collection which I had stored in a Japanese military cigarette container — but that was all. I still have those photos.

We then began to realize why the Japanese built their villages in low places surrounded by rock walls and trees.

Recently a report telling of the severity of that storm was found in Grand Junction's *The Daily Sentinel* of 14 October 1945. The report said 28 Navy men died, 70 were missing and 428 injured. One hundred and thirty Naval craft were beached or damaged — 80 percent of the Navy's shore installations were damaged or destroyed. Food shortages resulting from damaged supplies and levelled warehouses were relieved by superforts flying in supplies from Guam and other bases.

Soon the process of bringing all the troops home began. The older men were sent home first. I remember the impression I had at the time — how ancient those 40-year-olds seemed! Forty seems quite young to me now!

I recently discovered, in *The Daily Sentinel* of 20 November 1945, a New Liberty item that noted a letter had been received by Mrs. C. W. Likes informing her that Homer would be leaving Okinawa 17 November. Then on 7 December another item saying the Likes family had received a telegram stating that Homer was in San Francisco — soon to be home on furlough.

I came back to the States with the remainder of my battalion on a hospital ship. No, we weren't wounded — the ship had been pressed into service to help out with the huge task of transporting the troops home. *Home* for Christmas! Needless to say, I was *happy* to get *home*!

Then, during the week of Christmas, the following appeared in the New Liberty items (it has been edited):

Mr. and Mrs. C. W. Likes were happily surprised on last Wednesday evening after being in Grand Junction in the afternoon and as they were nearing home they saw the house lighted up. On arriving they found their son, Fred and wife with two boys from Bickleton, Washington, their son Clyde Jr., wife and three boys from Los Angeles, California, their son Ray, who had gone to California about a month ago, their son Ivan from California, and also their son, Homer, of the Seabees, home from overseas. Fred and family left Saturday and took Ivan back to California. Clyde and family will remain here for a short visit. Homer will report to Denver on 7 January, as yet he doesn't know if he is to be discharged or not. Quite a homecoming!

After spending some time at CB bases at Port Hueneme and Camp Pendleton in California, I received my separation papers in February 1946, then began to get back into civilian life. I had no desire to be anyplace but back on the farm in New Liberty. I had thought of that a lot in the five years I had been away!

Homer and Phyllis Maluy Likes
(Likes Photo Collection)

and acquired some more milk cows so we could sell Grade-A milk. That continued for 14 years — it became such drudgery!

In the summer of 1948 Phyllis and I bought the homestead, milk cows and farm equipment from Clyde and Retta and they moved to Climax Springs, Missouri.

We traded dollars for many years. The cash out-flow always seemed to be a little greater than the in-flow. We struggled along until one day in 1955, probably as I was having some particularly trying problems, I went to the house and called an auctioneer and began to make preparations to auction off all our cows and dairy equipment. The end of an era!

But I want to take a moment to tell about something that has crossed my mind several times through the years since then.

We often refer to farm animals as "dumb" animals — but they are not "dumb" animals; they are much more intelligent than we want to give them credit for. Recently I had a dream that made me think about that. For some reason, in my dream, I was reliving the days

Then, at a dance at Loma one Saturday night I danced with a girl I'd hardly noticed until then. She had been just a freckled-faced little imp, the younger sister of one of my best friends. But there she was, still freckled, but I do love freckles! She was now a young woman! **Phyllis Clemene Maluy** and I began dating and were married 2 December 1946 in her parents home. My father performed the ceremony. We made the same mistake that Fred and Louise had made when they were married; we lived with my parents for a while.

We had two children, both were born at St. Mary's Hospital in Grand Junction:

Dennis Wayne, born 9 August 1947 (Dennis had seven children; they lost the last one. There are three grandchildren)
Retta-Marie (Clayburn, Brandow), 9 February 1950 (Retta Marie had five children, and raised three stepchildren. There are 11 grandchildren).

In January 1947, Dad and I built a milk barn

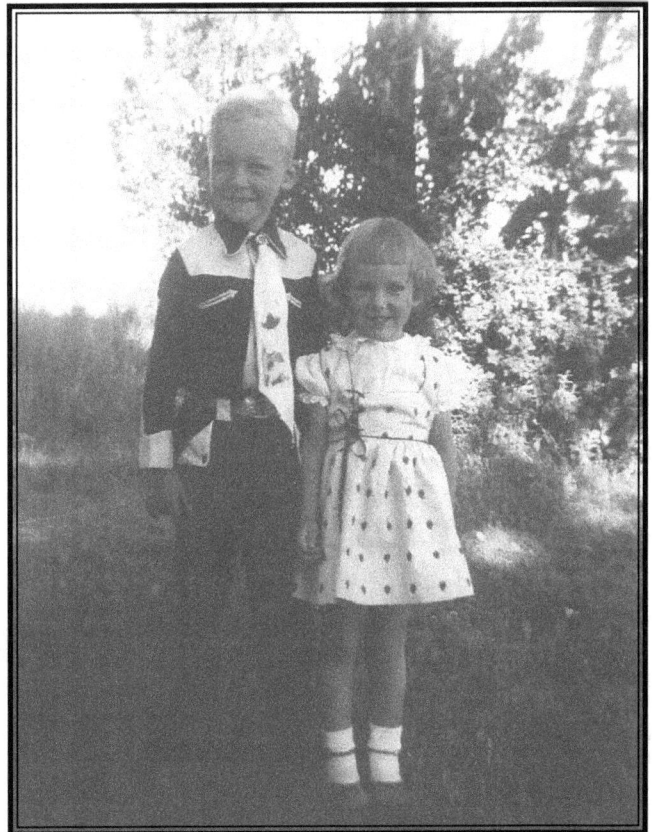

Dennis Wayne and Retta-Marie Likes
(Likes Photo Collection)

494

(Above left) Clyde and Retta packed and ready to leave for Missouri, July 1948. L-R: Clyde, Retta, Homer and Dennis Likes. (Above right) Phyllis holding the chain that secured their bull, Herkimer, in front of the pond and milk barn, 1952. (Center) The Likes house after Homer and Phyllis had new siding put on it, 1955. (Below left) The milk cows coming in from the pasture at 5:30 p.m. to be milked at 6 p.m. (Lower right) Cows waiting at the milk barn for their turn to be milked. *(Likes Photo Collection)*

when we built the "Grade-A" dairy barn on the Likes farm. (And I often do that; "reliving" must go with the territory as we grow older). I was reminded of how we trained those cows to come into that new barn — to accept the new-fangled milking machine; all the sights, sounds and smells of new surroundings. The amazing thing was that within a relatively short amount of time those cows would come to the little holding pen just outside the barn door as soon as they heard us making preparations for milking. They would wait patiently until their turns came to enter the barn. After attaching the milker to two of the first group to come into the barn, we would release the first cow after she had been milked, put the grain ration in the trough for the next, open the door and the next cow would enter. It would always be the one who was supposed to come in a proper order and go to that particular stanchion. At the time we gave it very little thought, but now, as I think back, it was uncanny!

In 1956 I decided to try tomatoes as a cash crop; a couple of my neighbors seemed to do quite well with them. But I had lessons to learn! Since I was new at the game, hadn't learned all the tricks, and was dependent on the cannery company for the plants and planter, I was not able to get my first crop planted until quite late. Things went well, however — until harvest time. I had bought a truck with which to haul tomatoes to the cannery and it turned over on its side as we were pulling out of the field with the first load. (John Cavendish was in the cab with me when that happened. The way he reacted was just hilarious!) Then, just as we were getting into the picking full force, we had an early frost which wound up the harvest in a hurry! We had only hauled about three truck loads to the cannery when the freeze came.

In 1957, I had the tomatoes planted in good time and the plants were healthy and growing well. I was farming on four different farms at that time and had tomatoes on two of those farms, with a variety of crops elsewhere. On June 14, as I was irrigating on the "Graves Corn" farm at the west end of the community, I noticed a dark cloud approaching from the northwest. That was not unusual, so I thought little of it and went over to Youngs (on the Summers place) for some reason I can't recall. About the time I drove in the yard golf-ball-sized hailstones had begun to fall out of the sky. I took shelter in a shed and soon began to wonder if the roof was going to cave in. That storm only lasted about 15 minutes, but as I was soon to discover, it destroyed all my crops! The storm had traveled across the community at such an angle that it covered all the fields I was farming. The tomatoes, alfalfa and grain were completely devastated! Nothing like that had ever happened in the New Liberty community before. We had hail storms but never severe enough to do that kind of damage.

I had about 20 acres of ground ready to plant into pinto beans — that crop was excellent! As for the tomato ground, since it was mid-June, I decided to disk up that ground and replant that to beans also. These did well until harvest time. After I had the beans in windrows waiting for them to dry enough to thresh with a combine, it began to rain. It rained off and on for about six weeks. Every time we'd get a little sunshine I'd turn the windrows so the beans would dry; then it would rain again. During that time, since it was usually too wet to do anything else, my father-in-law, Clem Maluy, and I did lots of deer hunting. This went on for about six weeks.

By the time I was able to combine those beans they were so discolored they were not marketable. In addition to that, I had threshed out about half of them from turning them so many times. Was someone trying to tell me something?

That fall my brother Ivan went to work as shop foreman for Moab Drilling Company at Moab, Utah (owned by Charley Steen, the Uranium Millionaire). I told Ivan if he could get me a job with him there, to give me a call. He called about two weeks later. I went to work at Moab Drilling on 17 December 1957. The following spring I had another auction and got rid of all my farm equipment and burned all my bridges behind me!

We bought a home in Moab and lived there until the end of 1964. During that time I also worked at a couple of the uranium mines and then went to work on the construction of the potash mine downriver from Moab, which involved sinking an open shaft 1,100 feet down to the potash deposit. While I was working there a peculiar thing happened: I came down with the flu and stayed home for about three days, sending word to my boss via members of my crew.

When I went back to work I found that my boss had not received my message and had terminated me. But wait — I'm thankful for that! Within a couple of days the fellow who had taken my place went down the shaft to begin work on the swing shift, and as he lit his acetylene torch, he touched off a huge explosion that killed him and several other men. The explosion wrecked the hoisting equipment so no rescue work could be done. It was several days before they were able to get a rescue operation underway and in the meantime several more men died from lack of oxygen. In all 13 men died in that accident. If I had not lost my job it would probably have been me who caused the explosion. Was someone watching over me?

On the last day of 1964 we moved into a rental home in Price. By then I was working for H.& E. Lowdermilk at Helper, Utah, a construction company that was based at Englewood, in the Denver area. After my experience with heavy equipment in the CCC, the Navy, Moab Drilling, and the work at the potash shaft, I came to realize I was well adapted and enjoyed that kind of work. In all I had gained a lot of valuable experience with trucks, tractors and drilling/mining equipment. I joined the Union of Operating Engineers and continued for 19 more years working as a repairman on heavy earth-moving equipment. The pay was good and I earned a good retirement.

Homer and family when they were living in Price, Utah, 1965. L-R: Homer Chilson, Phyllis Maluy, Retta-Marie and Dennis Wayne Likes. *(Homer Likes Collection)*

In June of 1966 we moved into another rental home in Provo, Utah, and began looking for a home to buy in Orem, where we had previously decided we wanted to live. Five weeks later we bought a nearly new home and moved into it on 13 July 1966. We have been here over 31 years. We feel that this is home; we have no desire to live in any other area. We can truthfully say we live in a neighborhood where "neighbors love their neighbors."

After working in Utah 23 years, I retired on the last day of 1980 and began a home business repairing small engines: lawn mowers, chain saws, tillers, etc. That has given me something to do, a little added income, and has been a much-appreciated service for my neighbors and other clientele in Utah Valley. Recently I've slowed down with the small -engine repair business and hope to spend more time writing this and other histories. Maybe I should admit the calendar has something to do with it — I'm now 79 years old!

Phyllis acquired more education since coming to Utah. She worked for several years as a bookkeeper and did some time as a police-dispatcher in Moab. She attended Brigham

Young University after we moved to Orem and worked for a travel agency for four years and then for the county assessor's office for four more years. She did a lot of traveling while doing that work. In recent years she has developed considerable skill as a genealogical researcher and has built up quite a clientele. She has also become interested and quite adept at using the computer and publishing applications. For some time she and I have both devoted a lot of time to writing this book.

Our family has now grown to include 14 grandchildren; seven of whom are married. Both our son and daughter and families live near us in Utah Valley, for which we are grateful. We often have family gatherings (so many birthdays, etc.) and have a good time together. Of course, the married grandchildren are beginning to be scattered all over the country! We may never get all the family in one place again! If our kids learned nothing else, they did learn to multiply! It's really neat to

have a large posterity! We now (1997) have eight great-granddaughters and six great-grandsons. We really love and appreciate our extended family!

At the end of July, 1995, we had the first official "Homer and Phyllis Likes Family Reunion." We had a grand time! All of the family came home except one of our grand-sons-in-law who is in the air force and stationed at Spokane, Washington. Dennis' oldest son, Jared, and his wife, Kelley, and their little daughter, Taysha, didn't attend either. They spent the summer in Atlanta, Georgia, making it too much for them to attend and return for school at BYU a little later.

In late April and early May of 1996 we were invited to spend 10 days with Dennis and family on Maui. Dennis' mother-in-law was along on that vacation also. We had a grand time! As we flew along in excess of 500 miles per hour, far above the Pacific ocean, I couldn't help but remember having traveled across that same

Homer and Phyllis and family in 1990, consisting of their children, daughter-in-law, son-in--law and grandchildren. Back row, L-R: Susan Munzell Likes, Dennis and Jared Likes, Retta-Marie Likes Brandow, Warren III, Brian and Warren IV "Butch" Brandow. Middle row: Denise, Christina and Jennifer Likes, Kenneth Brandow, Carl Clayburn, Lance Brandow and Kimberli Clayburn. Front row: Joshua, Justin, Homer and Phyllis Maluy Likes, Benteen and Shauntai Brandow. *(Homer Likes Collection)*

expanse of water over 50 years previous. What a contrast! In the airplane we crossed the water to Hawaii in four and a half hours, while it had taken over a week to return from Okinawa on a ship!

On 28 December 1996, our kids and grandkids hosted a celebration of our 50 years of married life. A large crowd attended and we all had a grand time! All of our grandkids were home except Butch and his family, and Lance, who is serving an LDS mission in Japan. Butch is in the Air Force, stationed at Abilene, Texas.

Dennis, after doing a four year hitch in the Navy, married **Susan Mary Munzell** on 4 September 1971. He then attended Brigham Young University for four years and graduated in April 1975 with a degree in electrical engineering. He is employed by a large company that specializes in computer software design. He has had little opportunity to exercise his engineering skills since he has been called to do supervisory and managerial work and be part of the corporation almost from the beginning. He has to do lots of traveling and has begun to dislike that part of it. They have six living children. Two of their children are married and there are three grandchildren.

Retta-Marie has spent most of her time since graduating from high school being a mother and homemaker. She married **Alan David Clayburn** on 10 August 1968, and they had two children. The marriage ended in divorce. On 16 May 1975 she married **Warren Francis Brandow III** and they combined families: her two and his three. They then had three children between them. Warren has flown airplanes for United Airlines for over thirty years. He is currently assigned as Captain on 747-400s flying from Los Angeles to Sidney, Australia, Tokyo, Japan and Seoul, Korea. They have five married children and eleven grandchildren. Retta and Warren are now (1997) divorced.

In 1993, Retta-Marie decided to go back to school to study to become a registered nurse — she plans to eventually become a midwife.

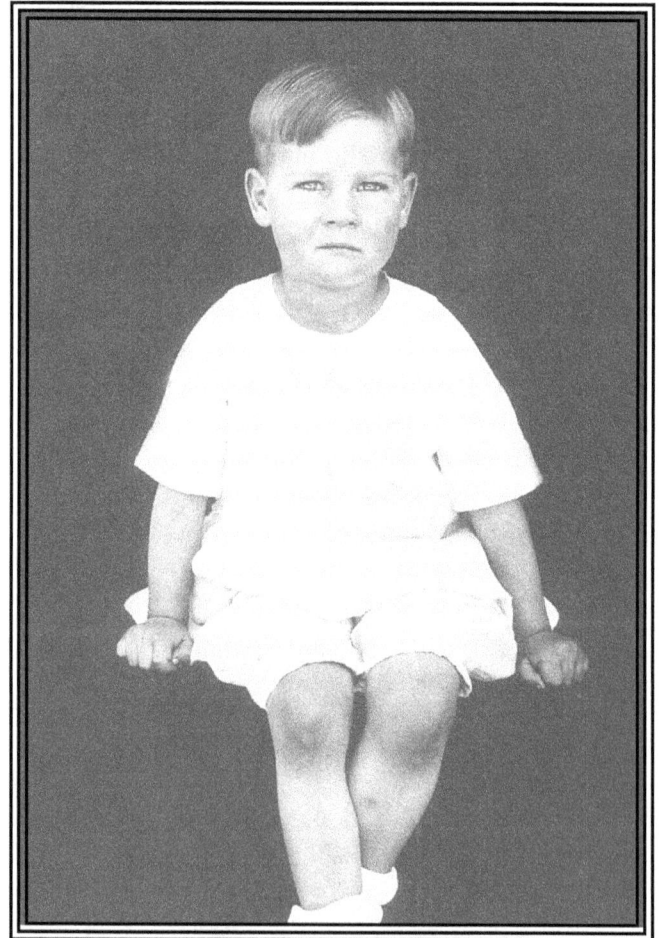

Lewis David Likes, 1924.
(Likes Photo Collection)

Lewis David has several firsts in the family that should be mentioned. He was the first of Clyde and Retta's children to be born in Colorado and the first to be born in a hospital. He was also the first to graduate from high school and the first to enter the military.

When we lived in Colorado Springs, Lewis

was just learning to talk and had a cute saying that has long been remembered. Some prisoners had escaped from the Colorado State Prison at Canon City and had made their way to near where we were living. Several members of the family saw the escapees in the alley in back of our house, and a little later members of a posse running up the alley in pursuit of them. Of course that was cause for much excitement among family members and Lewis was heard exclaiming: "I saw them 'stinking' up the alley!"

At some point in time Lewis took piano lessons. But, like the other Likes children, didn't like the restrictions imposed by the need to practice, so he became a dropout. However, as time passed he continued to retain interest in the piano and began to put together chords to various tunes and before long developed his own style of playing so it sounded pretty good.

Lewis David Likes, 1941.
(Likes Photo Collection)

He continued that for many years and became a notable musician much in demand. He gained a lot of satisfaction from his playing and other people loved to hear him play. Through the years he played often at community dances and other social activities. Eventually, after removed to the Serve farm, he added an electronic organ next to his piano and gained a lot of satisfaction out of that. He played the two together in some arrangements to the delight of his audiences.

Lewis graduated from Fruita Union High School in the spring of 1939, then worked around the community that summer helping various farmers with the harvest. With $50 help from his Dad he started school at Blair Business College in Colorado Springs, but he couldn't make ends meet, working for his room and board as well as study, so he came home. In the summer of 1940 he got a job with the Bureau of Land Management as part of a crew doing geological surveys. After that came to an end in September he went to work for the contractor building the Grand Valley Rural Power lines in the Mesa and Collbran area.

As has been mentioned before, Lewis enlisted in the Navy near the end of 1940; he left home the day after Christmas of that year for San Diego for his "boot" training. It was a difficult parting for him, as he realized he was committed to leave home and be gone for a long time.

Near the end of his basic training it was determined he was qualified to go to Aviation Machinist Mate School and learn to repair airplanes. He believes that was the second school of that type the Navy had ever been held at North Island.

In July 1941, not long after his training was completed at San Diego, he was assigned to the Naval Air Station at Kaneohe Bay, across the Island of Oahu from Pearl Harbor. On 7 December 1941, when the Japanese made their sneak attack on Pearl Harbor, Kaneohe Bay Naval Air Station came under attack also. Lewis' unit were as unprepared as the Navy people across the island, even though they had been warned to be on the look-out for any suspicious activity. Lewis awoke on the morning of the infamous day to the sound of machine-gun fire. In all the haste and confusion, he and one of his buddies set up a machine gun for some sort of defense, but the Japs soon discovered their position and promptly bombed and strafed them. There was considerable damage to the hangar and all of their planes were destroyed on the ground, but there was no loss of life. Of course, there was much cause for concern among Lewis' family members before it was learned he was safe.

During his assignment at Kaneohe he was working on a plane one day and noticed someone on the mat beside him and asked him to hand him a wrench. He then looked down and discovered it was Lawrence Morrow. Lawrence was later assigned to the same unit. This led to a singular experience that you may read about in the Morrow biography.

Lewis left there in June of 1943 and returned stateside to go to Flight School, but dropped out after a year and was restored to his former rank as Machinist Mate.

On 17 June 1944 Lewis married **Delores Imogene Smith** of Mack (see Smith biography). The marriage was performed by Rev. Clyde W. Likes at the Likes farm home. The newly-weds went to Pensacola, Florida, and spent the remainder of World War II there.

They had three children:

Deana Lou, born 27 February 1945, Pensacola, Escambia, Florida
James "Jim" Dean, 10 September 1946, Fruita (Jim has five children)
Janice Sue (Bentley), 9 June 1950, Lincoln, Lancaster, Nebraska (Janice has five children, stepchildren, and grandchildren)

Their first child was born prematurely on 27 February 1945. Delores was home alone when she unexpectedly began to experience labor pains. Soon a little girl was born and there was no one there to help. She finally got the attention of a neighbor who promptly called an ambulance. Lewis had gone to work only a little while before this happened. As soon as he was notified he

Lewis David and Delores Imogene Smith Likes, 1944.
(Likes Photo Collection)

Lewis and Delores' wedding. L-R: Reverend Likes, Naomi Banning, Delores Smith, Virginia Likes Sandifer, Richard Smith, Lewis Likes, Robert Arpke. In the background: Margaret Morrow and Retta Likes holding Sharon Sandifer. *(Likes Photo Collection)*

hustled to the hospital, arriving shortly after Delores and the baby did. The baby lived only six days; they gave her the name **Deana Lou**.

James Dean, Delores Imogene, Janice Sue and Lewis David Likes, 1962.
(Likes Photo Collection)

Lewis left the Navy for about three years after the war. He and Delores went to Washington and worked for awhile. Then he tried a venture with his brother, Fred, and brother-in-law, Leonard Cox, in a grocery store in Paonia, but that was not very successful. In the meantime their second child, **James "Jim" Dean**, was born 10 September 1946.

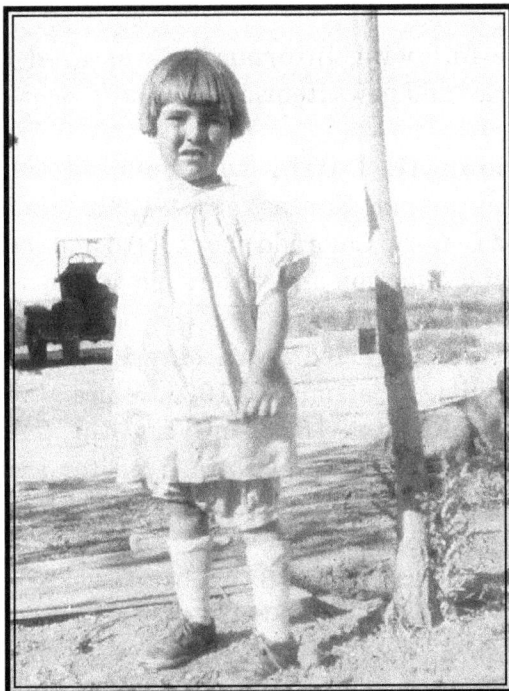

Virginia Ellen Likes on the farm,
(Likes Photo Collection)

Then they moved to the area of Shelton and Tacoma, Washington, where Lewis worked for the Army Air Corps for awhile. After a period of time he found that the idea of being back in the Navy appealed to him, so he reenlisted and was able to return to his former rank. He was first assigned to a Naval Air Base at Lincoln, Nebraska, then later the family lived in Philadelphia, Pennsylvania; Cherry Point, North Carolina; and San Diego, California. While they were at Lincoln their third child, **Janice Sue**, was born on 9 June 1950.

Lewis retired 1 November 1966, after serving a total of 26 years. After living in Grand Junction and Mack for a time, they purchased the Serve farm, a short distance to the northeast of Mack, and lived there for 22 years. Some time previous to their leaving the farm they purchased a home in Fruita. That is where they live at the present time (1997).

On 19 June 1994 they celebrated their Golden Anniversary with an open house held in the dining room of "The Village." A large number of friends and relatives were present on that occasion.

They have 10 grandchildren and one great-grandchild.

Virginia Ellen was born in Colorado Springs. After the family moved back to New Liberty, she attended New Liberty and Fruita Union High schools. For her senior year, she went to live with her sister, Maybelle, at Paonia, Colorado and graduated from high school there. During her senior year, she became acquainted with a boy named **Edwin Sandifer**. They were married in Los Angeles, California, 7 March 1942. They had a little girl, **Sharon**, born in 5 February 1943, at Redwood City, San Mateo, California. Edwin served in the military during World War II and just before he returned from overseas, Virginia filed for divorce.

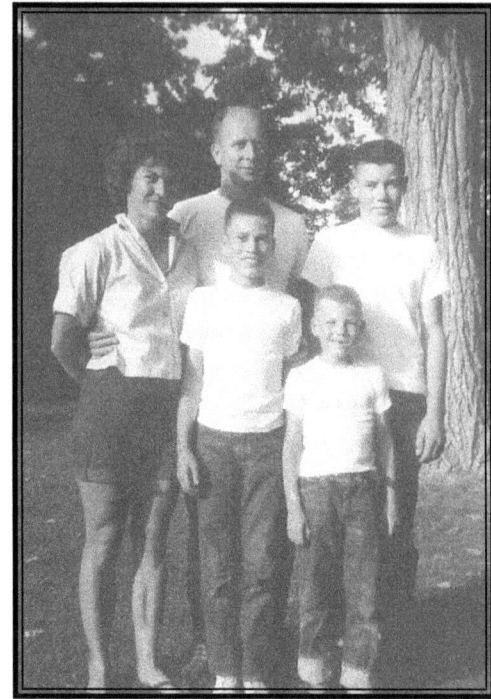

(Above) Virginia Ellen Likes, 1937. (Center) Virginia and daughter, Sharon Sandifer, 1945. (Right) In back, L-R: Virginia, Bill and Jack Birka. In front: Gary and Randy Birka, 1962. *(Likes Photo Collection)*

She married **Bill Birka**, 29 December 1945, and they moved to Tacoma, Washington to live.

Bill and Virginia had three boys:

William Jack., born 1 December 1946, Tacoma, Pierce, Washington (Jack has a daughter).
Gary Lee, 21 March 1949, Tacoma (Gary has a daughter).
Randy Lynn, 6 August 1954, Tacoma (Randy has a daughter).

Virginia and Bill lived near Tacoma and raised their boys. They had a nice home and yard, with a large pond, in a beautiful location. They did a lot of boating and fishing as a family. Eventually Bill and Virginia had problems and were divorce.

Virginia later married **John Haggerty** in Tacoma. They were separated and divorced for awhile, but were remarried 7 October 1977.

Virginia and John purchased property and built a home near the town of Rainier, Washington. In 1983, Virginia began to have health problems and it was soon discovered she had cancer. To further complicate her problems, her youngest son, Randy, drowned in a fish pond at his father's home in the same year.

She later had extensive surgery with the hopes that the cancer could be arrested, but it soon recurred. She died 13 July 1984, in a hospital in Olympia, Washington. She was buried at Spanaway, Washington.

Loftin

The following information was used from obituaries and news items in *The Daily Sentinel.*

Norman H. Loftin was born at Elgin, Chautauqua, Kansas, about 1890. He came to Mesa County, Colorado about 1910 and lived in the Grand Junction area before moving to a farm in New Liberty in 1932.

Norman married **Nora May Lockhart**, at Fayetteville, Oklahoma, in 1925. Nora May was born 17 August 1883 in Virginia. After marriage, Norman and Nora lived for a short time near Oakwood, Oklahoma. They had one daughter, **Thelma**.

Nora died at Fruita 8 October 1948. Norman died at Fruita 10 July 1962. Both were buried in the Elmwood Cemetery at Fruita.

503

Lyman

The following is compiled from a combination of census records, newspaper stories, marriage records from Mesa County, Colorado, and the Ancestral File at the Utah Valley Regional Family History Center at Brigham Young University.

George Alonzo Lyman was born 6 July 1884, at Fillmore, Millard, Utah, second of six children born to Ira Depo Lyman and Elizabeth Ann Rowley. The 1900 census lists the family in Carbon County, Utah, when George was 15 years old. According to the 1910 census they had moved to Uintah County, Utah, and were living in a community called Randlett, southeast of Roosevelt. George and his father were both listed as "Homestead Farmers."

George was married 13 July 1910, at Grand Junction, to Dora Maggie Dennis, daughter of Joseph Rogers Dennis and Senith Arvilla Davis. According to the marriage record, George and Dora were both living at Dragon, Utah, at the time of their marriage.

Dora was born 1 January 1891 at Gilson, Knox, Illinois. She moved with her family to the Vernal, Utah area when she was a teenager.

George and Dora had two sons:

Ira "Jack," born 1912
George Jr., born 1913

The 1920 census lists the family in Mack and gives the birthplace of both sons as Colorado. They could have been born at Mack, Fruita or Grand Junction. The school records list son Jack in the Mack School in 1918-19, it is possible George Jr. went to school the next year, but we have no record of it. They are not listed in the 1921 school census, so it may be safe to assume they moved back up the line somewhere for a short time.

We can only speculate on how George worked his way up so quickly to become Locomotive Engineer for the Uintah Railway. He was living on a homestead near Randlett, Utah, at the time the census was taken in 1910, though he may have been working for the Uintah at that time. But as you will see, he was running a locomotive in September 1911. George's career was plagued with accidents, almost as if a dark cloud of trouble was following him around for several years.

The first accident occurred during a run from the north on 30 September 1911, when he was piloting the passenger train back to Mack and running late due to several washouts caused by heavy rains. At about 1 a.m. on 1 October, he eased the engine onto the trestle spanning Salt Wash, two miles west of Mack, but the flood-weakened bridge gave way and sent the locomotive tumbling into the raging flood waters below. After being rescued George was immediately rushed to St. Mary's Hospital in Grand Junction where he was given medical attention.

The fireman, Charles Pasano, and a

Engine No. 10 located on the "wye" at Mack with Engineer George Lyman in front with oil can and Fireman Vic Earp in the cab; the conductor is unidentified. *(McCoy Collection)*

section hand, **C. M. Kipros**, who was riding illegally in the cab, were trapped in the engine and drowned. According to *The Daily Sentinel* story, it was not known until some time after the accident that the section hand was in the cab. It was two days before their bodies were recovered.

Here is an eyewitness account as told by Miss Katherine Tawney, a passenger who was traveling on the train from McAndrews to Mack. The story was published by *The Daily Sentinel* on 1 October 1911:

The track was very bad in many places and the going had been slow all the way from Dragon. We were due in Mack at 5 p.m. and the accident occurred at 1 a.m. A section gang had crossed the bridge about an hour before we reached it and reported it safe. The engineer approached the bridge carefully, the train barely moving as we crawled over the span. Suddenly we felt a slight jar, the noise of the crashing bridge and the scream of the engineer. Instantly the conductor called that the engine had gone down. The passenger coach and an ice car which preceded it, were on the bridge, but the north approach was safe and steady. It was very dark and the conductor looked out and saw merely a blacker mass in the water than the surrounding dark.

Engineer Lyman was brave and plucky, despite his injuries and the strength of the powerful current which threatened to tear him loose from his engine and sweep him down the wash. He coolly directed the Greeks toward his rescue and although every effort seemed to be put forth it was nearly an hour before he was taken from the water.

I am not a good judge of distances, but I remember that it took a bell cord and four ropes from trunks in the baggage car to reach him on the engine.

Men who were on the train

Scenes of the flash-flood train accident that claimed the lives of two men, 1 October 1911. In the bottom photo is Engine No. 10. *(Photos from the McCoy Collection)*

declared that if the train had been moving a little faster or had not been loaded so heavily, the passenger car would have been pulled into the abyss with the engine. As it was, the engine broke off cleanly from the rest of the train and the front end of the ice car projected several feet over the broken span.

The rescuers worked heroically and, handicapped by the darkness and the current, they could make but slow progress. When the engine broke down the fireman's side of the cab fell undermost, pinning him under the wreckage, and if he had not been crushed to death he most certainly would have drowned in a few moments. The engineer could not have lived at all had he lost his hold. The next morning we had a clearer view of the bridge and the engine, but by that time the current had subsided some what and at that I could hardly have told that the engine lay beneath the turgid waters where the fireman met his death.

When taken out of the water, Mr. Lyman was suffering intensely from the cold and the bruises but was bravely repressing any expression of pain and talked coherently of his injuries without a sign of fear.

Another accident involving George and a passenger train occurred during the afternoon of 8 September 1918. George was bringing the train down the Grade-Above Atchee when he lost control because of wet rails and failure of the sanding equipment on the engine. George sensed a problem and immediately signaled for the conductor, **Patrick J. "Patsy" Fitzpatrick**, to apply hand brakes, but the engine was already moving too fast. When they came into a curve near milepost 31 above Atchee, the engine and coach left the track and rolled down the mountain side crushing conductor Fitzpatrick to death. The fireman, **Roy Eno**, jumped to safety just as the engine left the tracks. Engineer Lyman remained in the cab trying to slow the runaway but jumped just as the engine overturned. The wreckage caught him and dislocated both shoulders and fractured one elbow. The accident left him crippled for the rest of his life.

A third accident occurred in approximately the same area on the afternoon of Thursday, 4

Company houses at Atchee, about 1910. Patrick J. "Patsy" Fitzpatrick standing on the far right.
(McCoy Collection)

506

January 1923. In that instance, according to *The Daily Sentinel*, George was riding as "Traveling Engineer" (*The Vernal Express* says "Road Inspector") on a train of gilsonite with **Richard Griffith** as engineer, **Roy Eno** as fireman and **Lee Allison** as conductor.

As the train was approaching "Shale Hill," about four miles above Atchee, when the engineer lost control and the train began to run away. The engine left the track at a sharp curve, turning over on its side with the cars of gilsonite piling up behind it. George Lyman was caught in the wreckage and died instantly. It was late in the evening before his body could be extricated from the wrecked flat cars and bags of gilsonite. The engineer was badly scalded in the wreck, but the fireman and conductor were able to jump off safely and were not injured.

Thus George Lyman's life and career as an engineer came to an untimely end. He would have been 39 on his next birthday. A special train brought George's body and the injured engineer to Mack, then they continued on to Grand Junction on D&RGW #4. Engineer Griffith was taken to St. Mary's Hospital for treatment; he never completely recovered from his burns. On the following Sunday afternoon a funeral was held in the Elks' Club in Grand Junction for George Lyman, with the LDS elders officiating. A special train was dispatched to accommodate about 75 family members and friends from the Vernal area and on down the Uintah line. The D&RGW Railroad again ran a special train from Mack to bring the funeral party to Grand Junction. George was buried in the Orchard Mesa Cemetery at Grand Junction.

The following appeared in the Mack Items of *The Daily Sentinel* of 19 December 1926.

Friends on the Uintah will be interested in hearing that Mrs. George Lyman, formerly of Mack and Atchee, recently married J. E. Lawler of Los Angeles. Jack and Junior Lyman, who have been attending school in Pueblo, will join their mother in her new home soon.

The wreckage that claimed George Lyman's life, 4 January 1923.
(McCoy Collection)

M

MacTaggart

Information is from obituaries and news items in *The Daily Sentinel*. Some history from Josie MacTaggart Simmons. Also 1900, 1910, and 1920 census and land records.

Donald MacTaggart was born at Sonya, Ontario, Canada, 1 June 1858, to Scottish immigrant parents, Duncan MacTaggart and Mary Melony. According to the 1920 census, Donald came to the United States about 1868, becoming a U. S. citizen in 1875. He was married to **Margaret Marshall** 15 November 1882 in Iowa. Margaret was born 15 September 1865, at Eagle Grove, Wright County, Iowa, her father was George Marshall.

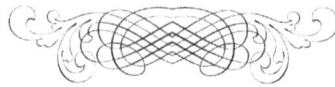

The 1900 census of Iowa shows that Margaret, had given birth to five children of whom four were then living. The third child died at birth on 30 November 1893. The other four were:

Mary Ethel (Burkitt), born 23 February 1884, Washburn, Blackhawk, Iowa
Blair Kenneth, 12 July 1888, Washburn, Blackhawk, Iowa
Hazel Verne (Blackstone), 22 October 1894, Vinton, Benton, Iowa
Virgil Prescott, 7 April 1897, Vinton, Benton, Iowa

Donald and his family left Iowa and moved to Colorado about 1901. From daughter Hazel's obituary we learned that the family lived in Fruita for a time before moving to Mack. However, the 1910 census shows the family living in Grand Junction. Apparently they lived in the Mack area for some time before the settling of Red Mesa and New Liberty. (See land records below and Ethel's school records)

Donald was active in community affairs, serving as president of District #37 School Board in 1920-21 before the district was divided. He filled other positions on the school board later.

Donald, Blair, Ethel, and Alvin W. Blackstone, all filed on land in Sec. 27 of Twp. 9 S R 103 W, according to records in the Patent Book in Mesa County Court House. Ethel filed 21 December 1907, but we don't have the dates of the others. To help your perspective, section 27 is located immediately west of 10 road about two miles north of Mack.

The MacTaggart family, about 1922, in front of the MacTaggart House north of Mack. In back, L-R: Virgil, Hazel (Blackstone), Donald, Margaret, and Blair MacTaggart. In front: Bob, Jessie, Josie MacTaggart, Shirley Blackstone, and Helen MacTaggart. *(Photo courtesy of Josie MacTaggart Simmons)*

Donald's obituary tells that he worked for the Denver and Rio Grande Railroad "for years."

On 11 June 1932, when he was 74 years old and living in Fruita with his son, Virgil, Donald was reported missing. Searchers traced him to Palisade. Someone had given him a ride to that place and it was found he had stopped at a restaurant in Palisade, asking for a drink of water. Later it was learned that two small boys had seen a man who fit the description north of the canal in the Clifton area. The search party assumed it likely he had fallen into the canal, so they drug the canal with grappling hooks. Later, they drained the canal to search - but did not find him.

Not until 25 October 1932 did they find the body near the Bookcliffs north of Fruitvale, where he had apparently become exhausted and laid down to rest. He had apparently become confused and wandered off in the wrong direction. In June the search party had been within a short distance of where the body was found.

Funeral services were held in Fruita, 26 October 1932, and he was buried in Grand Junction Municipal Cemetery.

Margaret died at Crawford, Colorado, 8 July 1948, at the home of her son, Blair. She too, was buried in Grand Junction Municipal Cemetery.

Mary Ethel MacTaggart was born 21 February 1884, in Iowa. (Possibly Vinton) She graduated from high school at Vinton, Iowa and came to Colorado with her parents in 1901. According to school records, Ethel was the third teacher at Mack School. She taught for three years from 1908 through the end of the school year in 1911.

She married **William R. Burkitt** at Glenwood Springs, Colorado, 20 June 1912. (An interesting biography of W. R. "Mose" Burkitt appears on pp 167-170 of "Echoes of A Dream" by Earlynne Barcus and Irma Harrison)

The Burkitts had two children:

Dorothy, born 1914 (died at age 12)

William Hollis, 1916

Dorothy was born in 1914 and died at the age of twelve from a ruptured appendix. William Hollis was born in 1916. He lives in Billings, Montana.

William R. "Mose" and Ethel lived in Ridgway, Olathe and Montrose in western Colorado before retiring. Ethel died in Montrose, Colorado, 3 March 1957, and was buried in the Dallas Park Cemetery at Ridgway. William R. died at Billings, Montana, 12 December 1978. Funeral services were held in Fruita and he also was buried in Dallas Park Cemetery at Ridgway.

Blair Kenneth MacTaggert was born at Washburn, Blackhawk, Iowa, 12 July 1888. He came with his parents to Mesa County in December 1901. He attended schools in Vinton, Iowa and Fruita, Colorado. He was listed in the census record of 1910, at age 21, working as a sheep-herder in the Cisco, Utah area. He also worked for the Young brothers on Glade park before going into business for himself.

On 16 March 1916, at Fruita, he was married to **Helen M. McKnight,** who was born 27 January 1895, at Minturn, Colorado, to Edward J. McKnight and Josephine Landis.

Blair and Helen had five children:

Josie Helen (Barnes, Simmons), born 13 February 1917, twin
Jessie Blair (Graham), 13 February 1917, twin
Robert "Bob" Edward, 25 February 1918
Donna LaVon (Deutsch, Fuller, Rondell), 9 May 1930
Donald Bruce, 23 March 1932
The twin girls, Josie and Jessie, were born 13 February 1917 at home in Fruita.

Josie was married to **William (Bill) A. Barnes** 12 September 1943 in Moab, Utah. They had two children: Lynda Joanne and William A. III. Bill II died 24 February 1984. Josie married Ray Simmons 8 June 1991 in Grand Junction.

The MacTaggart and Barr children, in about 1921. Front row, L-R: Bob and Josie MacTaggart, and Blanche Barr. Back: Jessie MacTaggart, Joan (baby), Blaine, Eleanor (holding baby), Anna, Barbara, and Dalton Barr. *(Photo courtesy of Josie MacTaggart Simmons)*

Jessie was married 3 May 1941 in Grand Junction to **Rubin R. Graham.** They had three children: Roger, Cheryl and Cindy. Rubin died 14 March 1958. Jessie died 31 August 1981 at Grand Junction, Colorado. She is buried in Elmwood Cemetery at Fruita.

Robert "Bob" was born 25 February 1918 in Fruita, Colorado. In July 1938, he was married to **Alice Wanetta Kruse** in Grand Junction. They had four children: Janet Alice, Robert Blair, James LeRoy and Jerry Richard.

Bob died 25 May 1979 at Moab, Utah.

Donna, born 9 May 1930, in Fruita, lives in Waubay, South Dakota. (Mrs. Calvin Rondell) She was married to **Kale Deutsch** 19 May 1947 in Crawford, Colorado. They had a son named Val Adair. Donna and Kale were divorced. She married and divorced Ronald Fuller, then married Calvin Rondell 25 May, 1995 in Sisseton, South Dakota.

Donald Bruce was born 23 March 1932, at Fruita. He was married 13 September 1951, at Midwest City, Oklahoma, to **Early Dawn Everett.** Bruce died 23 August 1984 at Salida, Colorado. He was buried in Fairview Cemetery at Salida.

Blair, Helen and three older children,

Josie, Jessie and Bob, moved to the farm on Red Mesa north of Mack in 1920. This was the farm just north of the Donald MacTaggart property. The children attended Mack school and Fruita Union High School. Helen was a charter member of the Highline Hustlers Women's Club. She also served on the District #44 (Mack) School Board.

In 1925 they purchased the John R. Earp homestead east of where they had been living and were there until sometime after 6 December 1940. The Mack news items of 6 December 1940, written by Mrs. W. J. Cox, told of the school having a party for Donald and Donna, just before the family moved to Crawford, Colorado.

According to obituaries, Blair and Helen lived at Crawford for ten years. In 1951, they bought the South Side Laundry in Grand Junction and operated it until 1954. After that they returned to Crawford for three years. They sold their home there and went back to Mesa County, finally residing at Clifton, Colorado.

Blair died in the Lower Valley Hospital at Fruita, 11 December 1959. Helen died 9 May 1971 at St. Mary's Hospital in Grand Junction. Both are buried in Elmwood Cemetery at Fruita.

Here are some of Josie's memories of growing up in the Mack area:

The only other kids we had to play with were the Sam Barr kids: Eleanor, Anna, Dalron, Blanche, Barbara and Blaine. Barrs lost Joan, a beautiful little girl, at age four. Later, there were the Orval Herron children: Fred, Jim and Margaret Gay, who lived across the road from us. We all walked to school together - the only kids going from Red Mesa at the time.

The school was in a new building erected in 1922. It included eight grades in two rooms with two teachers, sometimes three. Mr. P. A. Daily was principal and the teachers were Misses

Elizabeth Smith and Minnie Francis, as I remember.

There were two cloak rooms, one for the girls, one for the boys, a nice library in the wide hallway with a set of World Book encyclopedias. There was also a nice auditorium across the north end of the building where programs, plays etc., were held. Now it is all gone!

We three older kids started to school at the same time in 1930, walking one and a half miles to get there. When it rained hard our dad would take us via a team of horses and a lumber wagon because of the dirt roads. On bad snow days we just trekked on through!

Jessie and I nearly froze our legs one winter because we cut the legs off our long underwear above the knees before winter was really over.

Sometimes, if our work horses were not working, we could ride them to school. They had to be tied to the school fence all day. Then they would be ready to hurry home in the later afternoon.

The MacTaggart kids never had cash to spend. Some of the Mack kids whose dad's worked for the Uintah Railway fared better. They would often bring candy to school and share it. We knew our folks sometimes charged groceries at the Mack mercantile. So we tried that *once!* 'Til our parents got their next bill! That was the end of our generosity.

When we went to high school in Fruita, we were transported by a bus that picked up kids from New Liberty, Mack and Loma. That's how we got acquainted with the New Liberty kids. That's also when some teenage romances started, some lasting only a day or two, others ending up some years later in marriages. Great memories!

As kids, we made up our own entertainment: Hide and seek, kick the can, run sheep run, etc. *No TV!!*

We always had to help with the work around the farm, for which I have always been thankful. We herded cattle when they had to be put out on the hillside for feed. We weeded the bean and potato fields; picked up potatoes during the harvest.

Our mother was the one who milked the cows and helped with the irrigating. We girls did a lot of the housework and

Sam Hill's threshing machine and crew. Far right: Helen and Blair MacTaggart. Others are unidentified. *(Photo courtesy of Josie MacTaggart Simmons)*

herded the two little kids.

Threshing season was an all-neighbor event. Sam Hill would come out with his threshing equipment and go from one farm to the next. All of the men worked together on each farm. The host farmer would provide the dinner, and it was always the best! Besides helping at home when it was out turn, I remember working for Mrs. Hollinger when she fed the crew.

As a small child about five years old, I remember the wedding of Roy Smith and Edna Hollinger, who lived about one-fourth mile north of our place at Hollinger Hill. Jessie and I were the little flower girls. I was so thrilled with the little glass baskets we carried. That was the social event of Red Mesa on Easter Sunday, 16 April 1922. Donna and Bruce were so much younger than we three, about all I remember about them was, they were my young siblings. I left home in 1934 when they were four and two respectively.

I attended Ross Business College in Grand Junction and later married Bill Barnes in 1937. I never felt as though I really knew them until they, too, were adults. Now, Donna is truly my best friend!

One more thing I remember that affected our lives, and something none of us were very proud of, but what every man (and probably his wife) in the Mack community knew, was that our Dad, Blair, and Sam Barr played poker every Saturday night. I suppose there were others, too, who participated. We and the Barr kids would argue about whose dad came home the latest. My dad always dressed up and left the house wearing a long black overcoat and black hat. I thought he looked so handsome! We had no idea what poker was, but we knew our mother was not real happy when he would leave. The only poker we knew about was the coal stove poker.

Hazel Verne MacTaggart was born 22 October 1894 at Vinton, Benton County, Iowa. She was married to **Frank L. Blackstone** about 1917, probably in Grand Junction.

They had a daughter, **Shirley Anita (Anderson)**, who was born 16 June 1918, in Grand Junction. She now lives in Napa, California.

Frank Blackstone filed on land in the Loma District, but sold that and moved to Grand Junction. He then invested in the Blackstone Jewelry store with his brother (who was probably Alvin. See land records with Donald MacTaggart) at 441 main Street in Grand Junction. Frank and Hazel lived in Grand Junction until 1921, then moved to San Bernardino, California.

Hazel died at San Bernardino 11 October 1925 and her body was shipped back to Colorado. She was buried in Grand Junction Municipal Cemetery. Frank Blackstone remarried and they had a son, Donald, who lives in Riverside, California

Virgil Prescott MacTaggart was born 7 April 1897, at Vinton, Benton County, Iowa. He came to Colorado with his parents in 1901. He served two years in the military during World War I. Apparently he returned to Mack as he is listed with his parents in Mack in the 1920 census.

He was living in Fruita in 1932 at the time of his father's death. (see Donald MacTaggart) He married **Elsie Hill** of Fruita 19 October 1932. They had no children.

While living in Fruita Virgil had a garage and repair shop. He serviced the buses for the School District and also served as a bus driver for some time. In 1939 they moved to Vallejo, California, then in 1940 to Palm Springs, California, then back to Vallejo in 1941, where he was employed in a shipyard as a machinist.

While visiting family in Fruita in 1956, Virgil was stricken with a massive stroke. He died in the Fruita hospital, 20 May 1956. He was buried in Grand Junction Municipal Cemetery.

Maluy

Information is from family records, tapes, of interviews, Mary Maluy's histories, articles from *The Daily Sentinel,* along with information from Darrell Maluy, Marilyn Maluy Pacheco, Lee Ann Maluy Blaney, Dale and Rex Maluy, Patty Maluy Huntley, Wilma Maluy Walker, Norma Maluy Klapwyk, and personal knowledge of Homer and Phyllis Maluy Likes. The history is written by Phyllis.

Clement, William Benedict and Patrick Henry Maluy
(Maluy Photo Collection)

The Three Maluys of New Liberty

Patrick Henry Maluy was born 20 October 1861, at Sycamore, DeKalb, Illinois, the third child and the third son of William James

Maluy and Catherine Bennett, who were Irish/English immigrants. Patrick was christened Patrick Peter, but later in life he chose to use Patrick Henry. In 1869 the William Maluy family moved from Illinois to Hanover, Washington County, Kansas, settling on a homestead near Hanover.

The name Maluy is apparently not the original family surname. The family opinion is that the original name was O'Malley. William James Maluy came to America from Galway, Ireland in 1855. The family story is that when he exited the ship in New York, he was asked to spell his name. Since he could neither read nor write, the immigration person wrote Maluy. On all business and church records since then it is written Maluy. On the tombstones in Kansas it is O'Maluy. Patrick's older brother, William, attended the Kansas State Agricultural College in Manhattan, Kansas under the surname, O'Malley.

In 1887 the family came down with diphtheria which took the life of Patrick's

Patrick Peter Maluy about 1880

Mary Agnes Chloetilda Reel, about 1886

(Maluy Photo Collection)

brother William. In 1890, his oldest brother, Thomas, died of a massive heart attack. Neither William nor Thomas left any descendants to carry on the Maluy name. Patrick has only one descendant, grandson Rex, who has a child to carry on the name. The name Maluy is unique to our family in the United States.

On 24 April 1888 Patrick married his childhood sweetheart, **Mary Agnes Chloetilda Reel.** She was a lovely lass born 24April 1868 in Galena, Jo Daviess, Illinois, to Irish immigrant parents, Patrick James Reel and Margaret Gertrude Burke. The Reels had also homesteaded near Hanover, Kansas a mile from the Maluys.

Patrick built a house for his bride on the family farm, and he and his father farmed together. He later purchased the farm from his father.

Patrick and Mary had six children:

Mary Loretta "Mae" (Williams), born 8 February 1889
William Benedict "Bill," 20 May 1890
Gertrude Kathryn "Gertie" (James), 14 February 1892
Adalyne Margaret "Addie" (Warner), 12 July 1893
Clement "Clem," 3 October 1895
Thomas Patrick "Tom," 22 July 1897

All the children were born on the farm near Hanover.

Patrick Peter and Mary Agnes Chloetilda Reel Maluy, wedding picture, 24 April 1888 *(Maluy Photo Collection)*

Patrick was a dignified, honest, and charitable man who had to endure the loss of his wife Mary, who died soon after the birth of their sixth child; leaving him alone to raise children ranging in age from newborn to eight years. But with the help of Patrick's mother and sister, and later his daughters, he raised a happy and close-knit family.

In February 1917, Patrick sold his farm and auctioned off his equipment and livestock. By that time daughter Mae was married to Evan Charles Williams and living in California; Bill was single and living on the farm; Gertie was married to Oliver "Ollie" James and living on a homestead near Flagler, Colorado. Addie was single, living and working in Marysville, Kansas; Clem had married Mary Christine Darrow and was living on the farm. Tom was married to Cecil Worley and living at Rawlins, Wyoming.

Patrick, Bill, Clem and Mary all moved to Marysville after the auction. Patrick moved in with Addie, while Bill, Clem and Mary lived in a hotel in town. During the summer of 1917 Bill joined the Army and was soon sent to France. Clem and Mary moved to Rawlins, Wyoming, where Clem went to work for the Union Pacific Railroad.

(Upper right) 1916, Maluy Homestead at Hanover, Kansas. L-R: Patrick, Adalyne, Thomas Maluy, William Maluy holding Lola James, Mary and Clem Maluy. (Above left) 1962, Salt Lake City. L-R: William Benedict Maluy, Mary Loretta "Mae" Maluy Williams, Adalyne Margaret "Addie" Maluy Warner, Gertude Kathryn "Gertie" James, and Clement Maluy. (Above right) Thomas Patrick Maluy. *(Maluy Photo Collection)*

It was Patrick's desire to set up each of his three sons on a farm, and he had been looking for irrigated homestead possibilities. He had read about the Bureau of Reclamation Project about to be opened up in the Grand Valley in Colorado, and was quite interested in it. Bill was serving in the Army in France and couldn't come home; Tom was working for the railroad in Wyoming and wasn't interested in farming. So Patrick and Clem went to Colorado to investigate.

They arrived in Grand Junction in time to join the auto tour that was being hosted 22 March 1918, by the Chamber of Commerce and the Bureau of Reclamation to give applicants an opportunity to see the new land being offered. They liked what they saw and each filed on a farm unit.

On the day of the drawing, March 29th, Clem was successful in the drawing, but Patrick wasn't. However, the next day unsuccessful applicants were allowed to file on the remaining "free" units. Patrick filed on 60 acres of land located less than a mile from Clem. They were both pleased with their homesteads of good, level land.

Patrick and Clem didn't go back home to Kansas after the drawing. Instead, they purchased horses, farm equipment, and the necessary materials to build a house. They built a 12-by-24 foot tar paper covered shack, a good sized barn and a chicken house. They also prepared about 20 acres of ground on Clem's farm for planting. Clem then sent for Mary.

The next year Patrick planted crops on his own homestead. After living with Clem and Mary for two or three years, Patrick built a house on his farm and settled there. He loved his farm and felt it a blessing to raise beautiful crops with irrigation. Patrick became well known and respected by his friends and neighbors, who knew him as "Pat."

During the winter of 1925, Patrick went to San Francisco, California to visit his daughter Mae. Her widowed mother-in-law, **Emily Josephine "Mully" Williams**, lived with

Emily "Mully" Williams and Patrick Henry Maluy
(Maluy Photo Collection)

Mae and family. Patrick and Mully had been exchanging letters and pictures for some time. So his visit had two purposes and he fulfilled them both. He visited his daughter and family, and he and Mully were married that winter. In the spring of 1926, he brought Mully back to Colorado to live.

Mary Maluy had this to say about Mully:

She was a lady, very sweet, and had a good sense of humor. Before she came to Colorado she was used to a home with the conveniences of that time period in San Francisco. She was out of her element here as there weren't many conveniences. All she had to wear for shoes when she came were her dress shoes. There were no sidewalks on the farm and it was very dusty, so Patrick went to town and bought her a pair of high topped button shoes. She said, "Just look at my feet, that doesn't look like my feet," and laughed. She probably didn't like them either, but she wouldn't complain.

She became very lonesome for her family in San Francisco. My daughter, Marilyn, was nearly the same age as Leroy (Mae's son) and she became very attached to her. She was quite a seamstress and made a beautiful coat for Marilyn.

Patrick sold his farm to his son Bill in 1927, and Bill and his family moved in with Patrick and Mully. Patrick's dream was nearly fulfilled with his sons settled on irrigated farms.

Patrick loved chickens and he decided in 1928 that he and Mully would go to San Francisco, near Mae, and have a chicken farm. It was more expensive than they planned and they were unsuccessful. They returned to Colorado in 1930 by train. Mary tells about their return.

> Clem met them at the train in a wagon and drove them out to our farm. When Mully got down out of the wagon, she put her arms around my neck and said. "I'm just a broken old stick, Mary." I felt so bad as she looked so old and worn out. They moved into the White House Hotel in Fruita and she only lived three weeks. One day, before she died, I went to see her and she was washing the wood work. What a waste of energy, but she was so meticulous. She died of some kind of cancer.

Mully died 31 October 1930 and was buried in the Elmwood Cemetery in Fruita.

Patrick then purchased the Piggly Wiggly store in Grand Junction, across from Lincoln Park. He married Mrs. Stella Chappell, the Maluy's called her "Granny," 1 June 1934. They lived in Grand Junction with Stella's children, Bill and Tommie Chappell, on 5th and Colorado. Patrick died there in his sleep 29 July 1936 and was buried in the Elmwood

Patrick Henry Maluy   Stella Chappell Maluy

(Maluy Photo Collection)

Cemetery next to Mully.

Clement Maluy was born 3 October 1895, at Hanover, Washington, Kansas, and attended school there through the eighth grade. As there was no high school near, he didn't have the opportunity for more schooling. He worked with his dad on the farm and also hired out on other farms. In 1914, when he was 18, he traveled around the country with a cousin, Jim Farrell, and hired out as a farm laborer. On the train returning to Kansas at the close of harvesting, Jim told Clem he wanted to marry his sweetheart when he got home, but didn't have enough money. Clem said, "I've got $20, I'll keep $1.00 and you take the $19, then you go home and marry that girl. I'll get off at Beloit and see if I can find a job."

Clem got off the train at Beloit and approached the Pennsylvania Hotel to see if he could get board and room. Clem informed Anna Darrow, the proprietress, that all he had was a dollar, but he would get work and pay her. She said that he looked like an honest person, and if her son was in the same situation, she would hope someone would be kind enough to help him out, so she rented him a room.

Clem found a job working for the Girl's Industrial School firing the furnace and he paid his rent consistently. He also took notice of Anna's 18 year old daughter, Mary, and started courting her.

Mary Christine Darrow was born 3 April 1896 at Asherville, Mitchell, Kansas, the fourth of six children born to George Allen Darrow and Anna Lautrup. Mary spent her childhood years in Asherville. When Mary was a teenager, the family moved to Beloit where her parents bought the Pennsylvania Hotel. Shortly after moving to Beloit, Mary's parents were divorced and her mother continued to manage the hotel. Mary went to Beloit High School and helped her mother in the hotel by cleaning the rooms and serving the meals three times a day. She also took care of the finances and business, as her mother's English and writing weren't very good.

Mary Christine Darrow and Clement Maluy on their wedding day,
1 May 1916 *(Maluy Photo Collection)*

When her mother came to America from Denmark at 17 years old, she couldn't speak or write a word of English. She first learned English by reading cookbooks when she worked as a cook.

After two years Clem and Mary were married on 1 May 1916 at Salina, Saline County, Kansas. Clem and Mary moved out to the Maluy farm in Hanover that summer to help his dad and brother, Patrick and Bill, with the farming and harvesting.

The next spring Patrick sold his farm and they all moved to Marysville, Kansas. Clem and Mary lived in the only hotel in town. Mary went to work at the hotel, and Bill and Clem went into business selling "Puncture Proof," a sure cure for punctured tires. After they had a call-back because all four of the man's tires went flat, they decided it wasn't so puncture proof after all!

Clem then went to work for the Union Pacific Railroad and he and Mary moved to Rawlins, Wyoming. Clem studied to be a fireman and brakeman, but they soon realized that this job would keep them separated for lengthy periods of time. Clem said: "We got married so we could be together," so he quit. They went to Twin Falls, Idaho, and found a job picking apples. A week later there came a freeze that ruined the remainder of the apple crop. They then moved to Fowler, Idaho, and Clem got a job with a threshing crew and Mary did the cooking for the crew. After two months of this they went to Salt Lake City where both of them went to work for the railroad; Clem worked in the yard doing maintenance work and Mary cleaned passenger cars. They enjoyed their work and were making good money.

Early in the spring of 1918, Clem received a phone call from his sister, Addie, asking him to come home, as their father was quite despondent. Patrick was concerned because his money was dwindling away and nothing was coming in. So Clem and Mary went back to Marysville. Patrick told him about the homesteading prospects in Colorado, so the two went to Colorado to investigate. They each acquired a parcel to homestead.

Mary was sent for after Clem and Patrick built the house. She arrived in Mack by train on 7 June 1918, and Clem met her with a team and wagon. She was very excited to see their new home; but upon arrival at the homestead, she could see it was no Garden of Eden! It was a hot desert with no houses or trees in sight and "dust six inches deep." Her first thought was, "There is no place to hang my hammock."

The first summer was very hard with the three of them living in that tiny house with no shade, and a wood/coal burning cook stove that added to the heat. Mary says there were days that the thermometer in the kitchen would register clear to the top of the thermometer which measured 130 degrees. The ceiling was

(Above left) Clem and Patrick standing in their first grain crop in 1918. (Above right) Mary and Patrick Maluy with the bum lambs Mary raised the summer of 1918. (Center) 1918, the first horses they bought in Colorado. Clem with Bill and Barney, Patrick with Babe and Maude, Mary with the colt, Betty, and the dog, Wee Wee on Betty's back. That is barbed-wire fence in front. (Below) Clem Maluy homestead in 1918. In front is the horse barn, with the hay wagon and haystack behind it. The building in the distance is their little house with Clem and Patrick standing in front of the chicken house and pig pen. (*Maluy Photo Collection*)

so low, and their heads were near where all the heat was, so Mary would get very ill. There was no relief, as there were no shade trees, so they built a lean-to on the side of the house where she could go when it was intolerable.

The family hauled wood and coal from the Bookcliffs about 15 miles away to use in the cookstove. To start the fire, they soaked corn cobs in coal oil (kerosene), lit them, added small kindling, then wood, and then the coal. They would open the windows to let air circulate, but they didn't have screens, so the flies were a big problem. The water supply was deplorable. All they had was ditch water that had sheep manure and many other kinds of debris in it. They would fill barrels with the water to let the mud settle to the bottom and the debris rise to the top. They would skim the stuff off the top and then put the water in canvas bags in hopes it would cool and be somewhat drinkable.

Because of World War I, sugar was rationed and flour and butter were very scarce. The family used what was called "war flour" made from barley and rye. It didn't make very good bread. They could get a little cornmeal so they had corn bread once in awhile. They had to buy all their staples.

There was no refrigeration, so the only meat available was bacon and ham that had been cured and highly salted. They had to boil the meat for a long time to get enough salt out to make it edible. Pinto beans were available, so the combination of ham and beans became a regular staple. They had their own chickens and milk cows to supply eggs and milk. They bought a couple of pigs to raise for meat.

They had to buy hay to feed their five horses, two cows, and the pigs. The hay cost $30 to $35 per ton and had to be hauled by wagon from 10 miles distant. It required almost a full day to get a wagon load of hay and return with it. On one occasion they were on the way home with a load of hay and it tipped over as they crossed the Uintah Railway tracks. They were late in the night getting home after having to reload the wagon.

The greatest challenge for Patrick and Clem was to learn to irrigate. The soil was silt loam and it washed away like sugar as the water ran through it. Yet, it would become hard as brick after it dried out.

The Maluys raised a beautiful garden the first year and since it was pristine soil, they didn't have many weeds. The cabbage grew so large, 20 pounds each, they could only get two heads in a bushel basket. Mary put up 28 gallons of sauerkraut that first fall. She also canned some fruit, but because of the distance they had to travel to get it and the expense of the jars, etc., they were limited on the amount they could bottle.

Winter presented a new challenge — the cook stove that added to the heat misery in the summer was not quite adequate to keep them warm in the winter. It wouldn't hold a fire overnight, so when they got out of bed in the morning, their blankets were frosted from their breath and frozen around their chins. The water would be frozen in the bucket on the cupboard. They had built a cistern in the fall, so they had a good water supply. Clem and Mary met their challenges though, and as Mary said, "They were young and madly in love, so didn't resent it too much, and were happy."

Clem and Mary had four children:

Darrell Claire, born 15 December 1920 in New Liberty
Marilyn May, 5 October 1925, New Liberty
Phyllis Clemene, 29 January 1930, Fruita
Lee Ann "Bubbles", 20 February 1933, New Liberty

Their first child, **Darrell Claire**, was born at home. He was such a joy! Clem and Mary were so proud of him. This added extra laundry to Mary's already heavy burden. After hauling the water by bucket from the cistern or ditch, she had to heat it on the cook stove in pots and pans. She washed all the clothes, diapers, and bedding on a scrub board in a #3 tub, then hung everything out on the line to dry in the sun and wind.

(Above left) 1936, Phyllis, Darrell, Bubbles in front, and, Marilyn Maluy. (Above right) 1939, Back row, L-R: Mary, Clem and Darrell Maluy. Front: Bubbles, Phyllis holding Brownie, and Marilyn with Happy. (Center)1944, Darrell, Phyllis, Clem, Marilyn, Mary, and Bubbles Maluy. (Below) 1953, Back row, L-R: Marilyn Maluy Pacheco, Lee Ann "Bubbles" Maluy, and Phyllis Maluy Likes. Front: Darrell, Mary, and Clem Maluy. *(Maluy Photo Collection)*

Clem and baby Darrell standing in front of the homestead house, spring of 1921. *(Maluy Photo Collection)*

Eight year old Billy Bowen made this remark one day, "Rain or shine, Darrell's pants are on the line."

Mary later acquired a hand powered washing machine. A metal tub with a long wooden handle on it that one would rock back and forth to wash the clothes. Mary would rock it 200 times to wash the clothes, and Darrell, as a small child, would rock it 50 times to rinse. Mary bought a washer powered by a gasoline engine in the winter of 1929 — a real luxury. She had raised turkeys to earn the money to buy it.

In 1925 they knew they were going to have an addition to their family, so they built a 10-by-24 porch on the north side of the house for a bedroom. It was built with boards half way up and screens and canvas the other half making it half-screened. They also built a half-screened in porch, without canvas, on the south side of the house to place the ice box and cream separator in. A dirt cellar was dug underneath the house with a stairway from the porch, and shelves to store fruit on. So Mary wouldn't have to haul

water by the pail anymore, a hand water pump was installed near the sink connected by a pipe to the cistern. They were very pleased with the improvements.

Their first daughter, **Marilyn May**, was also born at home. A red-head! Mary said when Marilyn was little and standing in the sun, it looked like her head was on fire. Marilyn was a very cheerful, freckled beauty. Mary always called her "my rock of Gibraltar."

Another red-headed daughter, **Phyllis Clemene**, was the only child not born at home. She was born at Maude George's Maternity Home in Fruita. Phyllis became Clem's "right-hand man" during World War II. She was the next boy he needed.

And then **Lee Ann "Bubbles"**, a blonde, joined the family. Bubbles came down with the whooping cough when she was only 6 weeks old and Mary spent days and nights for six weeks keeping the phlegm out of Bubbles' throat to save her. Actually, all the children and hired man contracted it. What a spring! Bill and Clara Maluy lost their little son that spring from the whooping cough; he was only five weeks old.

Mary's health was broken after that and it took her two years to recuperate. The fall and winter of 1933–34 Mary stayed with the Gerry's and Bernice took care of her and Bubbles. Bubbles was around nine months old and stayed in her crib by Mary's bed all the time. She would rock her crib and blow bubbles with her saliva to entertain herself. Consequently the name Bubbles replaced Lee Ann, and she still goes by that name.

In the winter of 1934–35 Mary, Phyllis and Bubbles spent the winter in Los Angeles with Mary's sister, Claire, while Mary recuperated. Phyllis went to kindergarten while they were in California, the only child in the family to go to kindergarten.

Mary was able to return the love, devotion and care to Bernice Gerry when Bernice came down with pneumonia in March of 1936. Mary cared for her in the Gerry home, but she died 27 March 1936 in Mary's arms.

Clem acquired more land and became one of the prominent farmers in the community. For many years he farmed over 200 acres of good silt loam. In April 1929, he bought a John Deere Model "D" with a two-bottom two-way plow and 10-foot tandem disc; while this was not the first tractor in the community, it was the first tractor purchased new. Clem's neighbor, Bob Cox, advised him that within a few years that tractor would be sitting against the fence with weeds growing up around it. Clem was undaunted. When there was plowing or discing to be done, neighbors would hear that tractor going from before sunrise until there was no longer enough light to see in the evening.

Clem raised a variety of crops. Along with hay, grain, and corn he raised sugar beets, pinto beans, and potatoes; also sudan grass, alfalfa and red clover for seed. The family always had a large garden.

In later years Clem and Mary also invested heavily into livestock. From 1944 to 1949 they raised turkeys, some years as many as 3,000 head. Gertrude Rader wrote in her Loma/Mack news items in the *Fruita Times*, dated 13 December 1946:

(Upper) Clem's 1929 John Deere Model "D" tractor restored by Darrell Maluy. (Below) Bubbles and Clem sitting on the new 1939 John Deere Model "B" tractor. *(Maluy Photo Collection)*

Turkey picking is keeping a good many people occupied this week. Don Weimer and Clem Maluy have several thousand and many farmers have smaller flocks.

In 1947, Clem and Mary bought some sheep and kept an average of 500 to 600 head for the remainder of their years on the farm. Clem acquired some wintering ground on the desert southeast of Mack and there he would spend his winters herding the sheep and "baching"† in the camp wagon. It was like a vacation for him!

Clem was a friendly fellow — he had no enemies. However, something happened to him one day because of his friendliness that deserves to be told. He always waved to people as he drove by. In this particular instance he waved to Bertie Dillbeck as he was driving through Mack. It so happened that Bertie was then keeping house for John and Frank Everetts. John saw that friendly wave and assumed Clem had a romantic interest in Bertie. As Clem parked in front of Desert Gateway Store at Mack, John followed very shortly and, with a .45 pistol shoved against Clem's belly for emphasis, told him not to flirt with Bertie anymore. Clem tried to apologize and convince John that he had no more than just a friendly interest in Bertie. It took a little while for John to cool off and put his pistol away!

† Baching is a term used when a man lives alone and cooks for himself, playing the bachelor role.

523

(Above left) The Clem Maluy house in 1943 with Mary, Stella "Granny," and Marilyn Maluy sitting on the patio.

(Above right) The Maluy house in about 1967 when Darrell owned it. He had added a roof over the patio and brick flower beds across the front of the patio.

(Below) An aerial view of the Clem Maluy farm yard in 1957. From the bottom: 1-The orchard; 2-the house with the circular driveway to the left , 3-the chicken brooder houses and lambing pens to the right; 4-the big trees around the original yard with the extra little house on the left; 5-beyond the trees is the original barn with the pond in front, 6-the chicken house and granary to its left; 7-the cow corral and haystacks are beyond the pond.
(Maluy Photo Collection)

Clement Maluy, about 1950
(Maluy Photo Collection)

Mary Christine Darrow Maluy, about 1950
(Maluy Photo Collection)

Clem and Mary designed and built a lovely home on the farm, their "dream home." The New Liberty items of *The Daily Sentinel* dated October, 1936, noted that construction was underway on the new home. It was completed in the summer of 1937. The family anxiously awaited the arrival of electricity before moving into the new home. Electricity and telephones came to New Liberty in the fall of 1937. The new house had running water, electricity and beautiful, shining hardwood floors. It seemed like a glittering castle. There were three bedrooms on the main floor for Clem, Mary and the girls. Darrell's bedroom was downstairs along with a playroom for the girls, a big fruit room, a furnace room and big area in the center. The family was in all new surroundings — what a change! They brought nothing but their clothing from the original homestead shack in which they had lived for years, and the clothing was washed thoroughly so the bedbugs wouldn't come with them.

The old house was torn down except the porch, which contained the cream separator and the old ice box. These were moved to another location near the barn. The cellar was filled in with dirt, and there was always a big dip in the lawn that was planted where the cellar had been.

Clem served 18 years as a member of the New Liberty School Board, nine years as a member of the Grand Valley Water Users' Association Board of Directors and the board for the Lower Grand Valley Soil Conservation District, seven years on the state board of the Farmers' Grain and Bean Co-op Association, and six years as a committee member for the AAA Farm Program. He was also an active member of the Wool Growers' Association and the Farmers' Union.

Clem and Mary sold the farm in 1964, expecting to spend their "golden" years in retirement. But Clem received severe burns from an explosion as he was pouring gasoline into the baler gas tank near its engine. He died 21 days later, on 10 November 1964, at the

Fruita Hospital. The irony of it was that he had just half of a row to go to finish baling hay, and he was through farming for good. He was buried in Memorial Gardens Cemetery.

Mary moved to Grand Junction and lived for some years in an apartment, eventually buying a home. She learned to play golf and also became an avid bowler. She spent much time with her friends at the bowling alleys. Her teams went to state championship tournaments in 1967, 1972, 1974 and 1976 in Denver. In 1976, they also played in the WIBC Bicentennial Championship tournament. Mary didn't get to play the year they won state and went to Nationals in Las Vegas, as she had a broken wrist. She went anyway because she had helped them win state. She also belonged to a bridge club and won the majority of the time. She played bridge until a few months before her death.

Mary loved to travel and toured most of the States, including three trips to Hawaii. She also toured some of Canada, traveled to Europe on two occasions and went on three Caribbean Cruises. Her last cruise, when she was 94, was with her two daughters and their spouses.

All of these interests, however, were second to her devotion to her children and grandchildren. Mary always had time for her family, as she was very proud of everyone of them.

Mary joined The Church of Jesus Christ of Latter-day Saints on her 80th birthday and was active in its programs. She attended the temple in Provo, Utah, when she visited her daughter, Phyllis.

When Mary became older, she determined she was not going to spend her last years in a rest home. She made her children promise that they would not allow that to happen. Mary lived in her own home, with the help of a housekeeper, until the very end. When she died 17 January 1992 nearing her 96th birthday, she was the last original homesteader. She had 11 grandchildren, 30 great-grandchildren and two great-great-grandchildren. She was buried in Memorial Gardens Cemetery near her beloved husband.

Back,L-R: Mary and her bowling partners at the 1974 Colorado State Championship Tournament. Back row, L-R: Irene Knoche, Edith Eckert, Jane Tucker. Front: Mary Maluy and Vivian Foster.
(Maluy Photo Collection)

Mary after her baptism on her 80th birthday 4 April 1976. L-R: Homer Likes, who baptized her, Mary Maluy, and Dennis Likes, who confirmed her. *(Maluy Photo Collection)*

Darrell Claire Maluy, 1921. *(Maluy Photo Collection)*

Darrell was the first child born and the only boy born to Clem and Mary. This honor comes with a lot of attention, responsibility, and leadership, which Darrell handled very well. He was the apple of his parent's and grandfather's eyes, and as he grew he was expected to carry his part of the load. As a farm boy that meant early hours and heavy work at a very young age. He arose with his father before sunup to milk the cows, and worked beside him in the field till sundown. He was expected to be a protector, leader, and example for his sisters, and they responded with adoration. Mary tells of what a help he was to her:

Darrell was always good to help me when he was small. He helped me with the old washing machine that we had to turn by hand. He would help me churn the butter and peel the peaches when I canned. One time I was sick for three weeks. Darrell was about nine or 10 years old, and we had a hired man, too. Darrell would do the cooking, scrub the floor and do everything needed. One day I told him, "I'm so sorry that you have to do all this." And he said, "Oh, you just don't know how happy it makes me to be able to help you." I thought

what a wonderful boy he is.

While growing up, Darrell was prone to accidents with broken bones and unusual catastrophes. His first broken bone was when he was only five years old. It got to be kind of a family joke, with everyone wondering, "What's next?" There was never a dull moment, but, as his mother said, "his guardian angel always seemed to be on his shoulder." One such incident happened when he was about eight years old. He was visiting the Shires boys and they were on top of an old shed. He either fell or jumped off and landed on a railroad tie with his head landing between two spikes sticking straight up in the tie. He ended up with only a broken nose.

Another accident happened in the fall of 1934. Darrell and several of the community boys formed a potato-picking crew. Darrell was the person who made the deals with the farmers and collected the money for the labor. The crew had just finished picking Leland Burkett's potatoes, and Darrell was collecting the money from Leland. Out of nowhere, Leland's dog came up and bit Darrell on the leg and ran off. Two days later Leland contacted Clem and told him he thought the dog might be rabid. He had killed the dog, cut his head off and sent it in to have it tested. Sure enough, the test came back positive, the dog was rabid. Darrell had to have a series of 14 shots, one every day, in the abdomen. At the time, he was attending high school and since the school had burned down, they were holding classes in different buildings throughout town. One of his classes was held in the Odd Fellows Hall directly over the doctor's office. Darrell would go to class and then go down and get his shot. The shots were very painful and he said it was a terrible experience.

Even after Darrell was a grown man he was still prone to accidents and miraculous outcomes. In the late spring of 1960, about midnight, he was driving his pickup on Highway 6&50, near Loma, when he hit a large pothole. He lost control of the pickup and it rolled into the burrow pit. When it stopped it was laying on its left side across Darrell's legs, but was barely touching him as it was crosswise the ditch banks at the bottom of the burrow pit. Darrell had been thrown out of the pickup and landed prone on his back in the ditch. He was nearly scalped, as his head hit the door frame when he was thrown out. He had a big hole in his forehead above his left eye, a large cut down his nose, and his right cheek was cut open from the corner of his mouth to his ear. He was lucky again, as he wasn't seriously hurt.

Darrell loved to hunt and fish. He would go duck hunting in the fall with his 12 gauge pump shotgun and bring home sacks full of ducks. His record was 30 at one time. Mary's policy was that whatever anyone got when hunting or fishing, they had to clean it for eating. Marilyn, and later Phyllis, would act as his "bird dog" at different times. Marilyn remembers one time when he shot 12 ducks with one shot with his 12 gauge shot gun.

It was quite a process to clean the ducks. First he ruffled the feathers and dunked them in boiling water, wrapped them in newspaper and then rolled them up in gunny sacks to steam and loosen the feathers and down. This invention worked slicker than slick, as he could rub all the down off. Before this, paraffin was melted and the ducks dunked in the paraffin after the feathers were removed, and when the paraffin cooled it would peel off and the down would come with it. After the feathers and down were removed, the entrails had to be removed. Well, Darrell had some little sisters that he managed to bribe into doing most of that for him. He

also hunted pheasants, rabbits, and deer, and never came home empty handed.

Darrell fished on the Colorado River for catfish and the Grand Mesa for trout. Phyllis remembers once when he brought home enough catfish to fill two #3 tubs. The count was 100 catfish. He bribed her into cleaning the last tubful of them for him and she spent hours hitting the catfish on the head with a hammer to kill them or just cutting their heads off. She then cut them open and took the entrails out, and she had to be careful they didn't stick her with their spines on their jaws and back. What a job! She also picked and cleaned many ducks and pheasants for him. The family enjoyed the meat and were proud of his accomplishments.

Darrell was also an accomplished athlete. In high school he played football and basketball and was on the track team. He held the record in discus for a long time. He and Roger Swan were the only athletes from Fruita to attend the BYU Invitational Track Meet in the spring of 1938. Roger was in the pole vault competition and Darrell in the discus. Darrell got first place.

In 1936, while running at one of the track meets, Darrell fell and scratched his right knee. He didn't think much about it until sometime later when it became red and feverish. Mary took him to see Doctor Orr who discovered he had blood poisoning. This was before penicillin or any other antibiotic. Doctor Orr would lance it, drain it, use an ultra-violet ray machine on it (it would just smoke), and then pack it with gauze. This had to be done every two or three days for several weeks. Darrell wasn't given anything for pain. He would sit there and hum and hum through it all. Mary usually took him and she said, "It just made me sick to see what that boy had to go through." One day she asked Clem to go with her and she would wait outside while he went in with Darrell. Clem hadn't been in the office with him very long when he came outside "as white as a sheet and sick."

Darrell and Orval Mayne after a successful rabbit hunt in 1938/9. *(Maluy Photo Collection)*

528

Darrell Maluy at the track meet held at University of Utah in 1940. The scars from blood poisoning are evident on his right knee. *(Maluy Photo Collection)*

Mary tells of another incident involving Marilyn:

One day Marilyn said, "Well, I want to go with him this time." So she went with me. When she saw the doctor working on him like that, she said, "Mama, I'm sick," and fainted on the floor. There was an electric fan on the floor and the Doctor said, "Put her there in front of that fan, she's just fainted." I put her there and he just went on working on Darrell and didn't pay any attention to her. I said, "Well, aren't you going to do anything for her?" He said, "Oh, just leave her there, she'll be alright." She was so white, but she finally started to come around. I thought she was never going to.

At one point the Doctor was afraid he would have to amputate Darrell's leg or he wouldn't live, but Darrell declined. Miraculously it finally healed. This happened in March, and in August Dr. Orr said, "Well, all you have to worry about now is that he doesn't get married too young." This was his way of saying he was now out of danger.

Darrell graduated from Fruita Union High School in 1938 and attended Mesa Junior College in Grand Junction the next two years. He was on the football, wrestling and track teams at Mesa. He was also in the BYU Invitational Track Meet the two years he attended Mesa and the intramurals with other junior colleges in western Colorado, eastern Utah and Idaho. These were held at the University of Utah and he threw the shot put, javelin and discus, and was high point man at the track meet in the fall of 1940. He was also on the football team.

He only attended the one semester at the School of Mines, as on 26 December 1940 he and Homer Likes snuggled into the back of Leonard Appier's new Ford truck and rode to West Los Angeles, California, to earn their "first million." He worked at various jobs until he went north and secured a job in the ship yards at San Francisco. The shipyards were building ships for World War II. In 1942 he transferred to the shipyards at Wilmington and it was there he met **Beverly Bayne Busgen**, a welder.

Beverly was born 19 October 1923, in Oglesby, LaSalle, Illinois to John Antone Busgen and Gladys Olmsted. She graduated from high school in LaSalle, then worked two years as a telephone switchboard operator while attending LaSalle Junior College at Peru, Illinois. In 1943 she moved to California and lived with her Uncle Bob and Aunt Gertrude Leonard in Hollywood while she worked at the Consolidated Shipyards in Wilmington. Bob Leonard was a movie director.

Darrell and Beverly were married 28 August 1943, during their lunch hour, on the ship they were building; a minister who was part of their crew performed the ceremony.

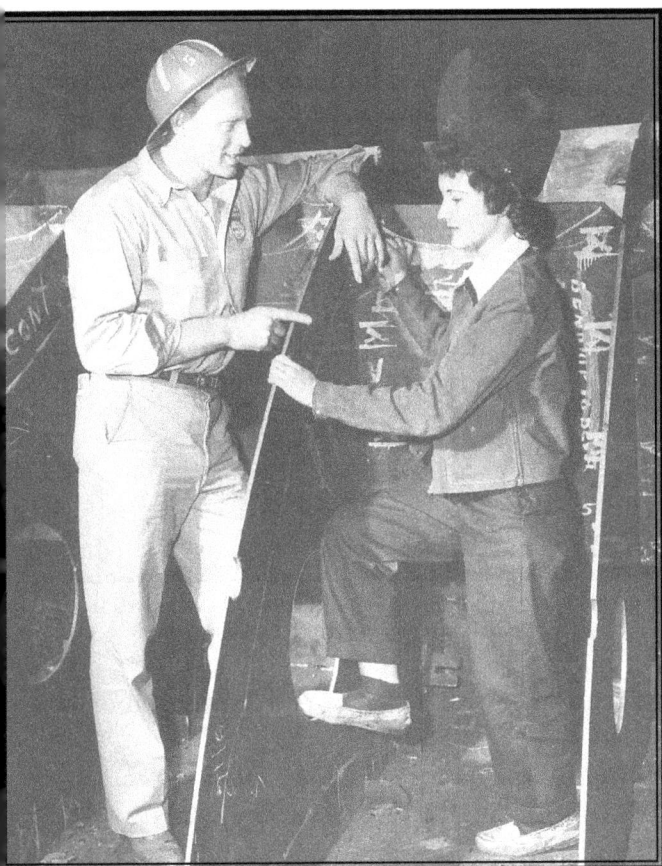

Darrell and Beverly Busgen Maluy the night of their wedding
at the shipyards, 28 August 1943.
(Photo courtesy of Darrell Maluy)

Darrell Claire and Beverly Busgen Maluy, August 1943
(Maluy Photo Collection)

Their wedding ceremony captured nation-wide media attention for their patriotism in not taking any time off from work to get married. Later they did go on a brief honeymoon.

Darrell had told his mother that when he got married it would be very private and that he wasn't going to have any children. It was quite a surprise to the family when they heard the news that he had gotten married before the movie cameras and news media. In The Los Angeles Times the headlines read:

Leadman Married Welder at Shipyard Night Lunchtime

It was lunchtime under the lights at Consolidated shipyard. The clamor died away. Only a giant derrick stirred through the night and that was to plump a piano out of the sky alongside an assembly skid. Then a tin-hatted quartet sang "Sweet Adeline."

And so they were married — and went back to work.

Brunette Beverly Busgen, 19, in her welder's hood and orchid-decorated leather jacket and blue overalls, and Darrell Maluy, 22, a blond giant in a steel helmet and the khaki overalls of a shipfitter leadman.

A shipfitter married them — Rev. Ray Pool of the Church of Nazareth when he's preaching, but he's working on the same assembly skid for the duration.

There wasn't any TV then and Phyllis remembers the family going to the theater in Fruita to see Darrell and Beverly's wedding on the news reel that was always shown between the movies with the cartoons.

Darrell enlisted in the Army Air Corps (now the Air Force) in November 1943. He began training to be a navigator in San Antonio, Texas, and Beverly continued to work and attend school at UCLA in California. Darrell graduated from the schools of navigation, bombardier, and radar. He earned all four wings possible and the rank of Second Lieutenant.

Second Lieutenant Darrell Claire Maluy, 1945.
(Maluy Photo Collection)

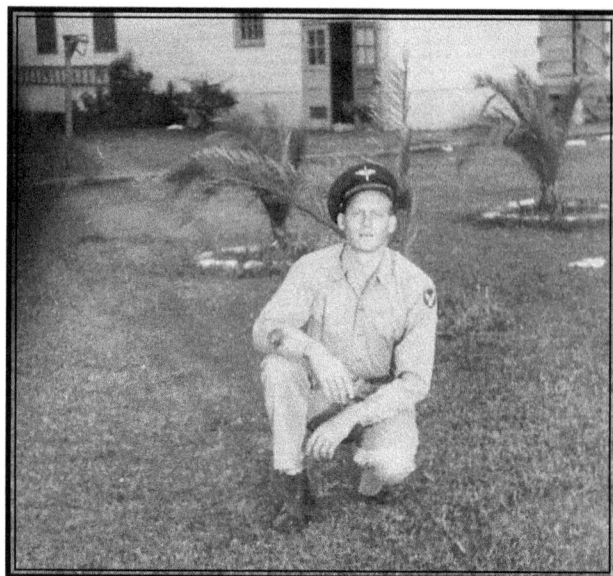

Darrell at SAAC Camp in San Antonio, Texas in 1944
(Photo courtesy of Darrell Maluy)

The United States was bombing Japan at the time of his training. He was being trained to fly bombing missions over Japan at night in a flight simulator when the atomic bomb was dropped and ended the war. Consequently Darrell didn't serve active duty overseas.

When the war ended in the fall of 1945, he was sent to Bakersfield, California. There he played defensive tackle on the Air Corps football team, which consisted of 50 players, who were officers from all over the country. The Air Corps team competed with the Navy, Marines, and Army teams throughout the United States, and also the University of Los Angeles. The football team flew to the games in an Air Corps C-47.

Darrell was discharged in 1946 and he and Beverly moved home to Colorado to start family life.

Darrell and Beverly had five children:

Trudy Lee (Kareus), born 13 September 1946
Cindy Lou (Baker), 18 May 1948
Patty Sue (Miller, Christopher), 22 June 1951
Nancy Gay (Prosence), 25 February 1953
Dwight Darrell "DD," 25 February 1956

All the children were born in the Fruita Hospital.

Darrell farmed with his dad from 1946 to 1954. Darrell and Beverly lived in a small house in Clem and Mary's yard for three years and then rented the house now owned by Jimmy Dick Tomlinson on 8 Road.

In the winters of 1953 and 1954 Darrell did some prospecting for Tri-State Uranium Company in the Henry Mountains in Utah, and mined there from 1954–1956. This was the beginning of many years of mining experiences in Utah, Wyoming and northern Colorado.

Darrell and family moved to Grand Junction on 29 Road and Partee Drive in 1955. Their only son, Dwight Darrell "DD" was born in February, 1956. After having four girls, Darrell and Beverly finally got their boy, and he had curly, red hair. He was Clem and Mary's only red-headed grandchild.

Trudy Lee Maluy, 1960

Cindy Lou Maluy, 1962

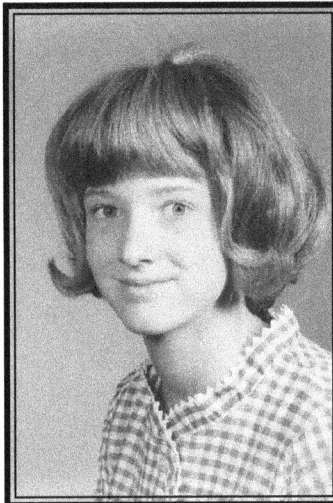
Patty Sue Maluy, 1965

Nancy Gay Maluy, 1967

(All four photos above from the Maluy Photo Collection)

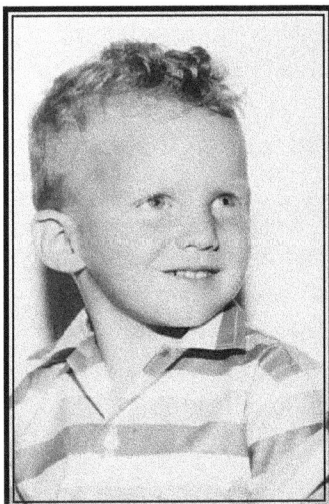
Dwight Darrell "DD" Maluy
November 1958
(Maluy Photo Collection)

DD was a very outstanding and brilliant child. Beverly taught home kindergarten with several students, and when DD was only two, he was able to do many of the things that the five-year-olds were doing. But the family's great joy and happiness was suddenly darkened when a terrible tragedy occurred. DD lost his life 22 April 1959 at age three, the result of an auto-pedestrian accident.

Darrell and David Sigismund formed the Sigma Mining Company in March 1959 and did open-pit mining of uranium in the Gas Hills in south central Wyoming near Baggs.

Another tragedy struck the family when Clem died from burn injuries in November 1964. He had just previously sold the farm to a Mr. Richardson who was a colonel in the military, and he wouldn't be retiring and taking over the farm until June 1965. Clem had agreed to do the harvesting in 1964 and plant the crops in the spring of 1965. Darrell took care of Clem's obligations on the home farm until Richardson took over the farm in June 1965.

In the fall of 1965, Darrell bought 1,100 head of Navajo sheep and kept them on Don Weimer's farm. He bought the hay from Richardson, and Don fed them for him. Darrell bought the Maluy farm from Richardson in June 1966 and moved the family there.

In the fall of 1969, he sold the farm and bought a home on the Redlands by Grand Junction. He went back full-time in the mining business in the Arizona Copper Mines and the Gas Hills in Wyoming doing research and developing underground mines.

In 1973 Darrell bought land in Fruita and on the Redlands for subdivision developments. He also bought 1,200 head of cattle to feed in the feed lots in Garden City, Kansas. All of the 22,000 head of cattle in the feedlot got scabies† and had to be run through dip vats in order to clear up the disease. Darrell invented a procedure with three 3,000-gallon heated dip vats that would handle 200 head of cattle at one session. The cattle had to be dipped twice at 10-day intervals. Through this process they were able to cure the problem and fatten the cattle for sale.

† Scabies is a contagious skin disease caused by a parasitic mite that burrows under the skin to deposit eggs, causing intense itching. The animals will lose all their hair and rub against anything until they even rub off their skin. They lose weight quickly and the disease may become life threatening.

In 1974, Darrell started the Robison Manor Subdivision in Fruita. The utility lines went underground and by 1975 he had it finished with a sewer system and sidewalks. Also, in 1975 he signed a lease with the Consolidated Coal Company on property near Walden, Colorado, for an open-pit coal mine. He later bought the coal company out and operated the open-pit coal mine until he sold it in 1979.

From 1978 through 1985 he developed the three phases of the subdivision on the Redlands. In 1981 he bought 640 acres in Devil's Canyon for subdivision development. He installed a pump in the Colorado River and pumped water up a 300-foot lift through 8,000 feet of 12-inch lines to four reservoirs and 3,000 feet of pipe lines with sprinklers on them with the intent of people building homes and utilizing them. He also built four-and-a-half miles of roads. His dream of having beautiful homes in Devil's Canyon didn't come true, and the Bureau of Land Management now has the property.

Darrell then retired to be with Beverly, as she had been ill. Since that time he has fulfilled one of his dreams. He has completely restored his father's 1929 John Deere "D" tractor, making it look like new. He also found a two-bottom, two-way plow like his father had and restored it.

After the family left the farm in 1969, Beverly attended Mesa College for two years and got an Associate's Degree in Business. She then worked for eight-and-a-half years as a postal clerk at the Fruita and Grand Junction post offices. She became too ill with asthma and other complications to continue, and has been mostly homebound since.

Darrell and Beverly have 13 grandchildren.

The following are some of Darrell's memories of homestead life in New Liberty recorded on video.

When Dad and Grandpa settled on the homestead, they built a shack for a chicken house, and we lived in it for 19 years. It was a two-room shack with a flat roof, coal/wood cook stove, no running water, no shade trees and an outdoor toilet. When mom used the cook stove in the summer, it would get to be around 115–120 degrees in the house. There was an irrigation ditch with running water by the house. I sure enjoyed paddling in that ditch to keep cool.

The homesteaders had lots of trials and tribulations trying to reclaim the desert land with irrigation. The land had a lot of ditches and rills from natural erosion throughout the centuries, so it had to be leveled. Each farmer had a fresno pulled by three head of horses. The farmers were out there continually, when they weren't farming some small patch, trying to level more land to put into production. They would move dirt from the high spots to the low spots, fill up a little rill and so forth to try to get it level enough to irrigate.

Dad and Grandpa had never irrigated before, so they didn't know how to work with the soil. It had very little humus in it, so when the water ran through it, it would melt like sugar. They didn't have any humus or sod to use, so they used straw to try to hold their dams, checks, etc.

Most of the land sloped to the south and the head ditches were on the north end of the fields. The creases were thirty inches apart and little streams of water ran down them. If the ground wasn't level enough, the water would cut over to

Darrell trying out the 1929 John Deere "D" tractor and two-bottom, two-way plow he restored in memory of his dad. *(Photo by Phyllis Likes)*

the down-hill side of the furrow, pick up a little more water in the next furrow, and then that one would do the same thing and pretty soon all the water would be going down a gully diagonally across the field. Prairie dog holes were a big problem also, as the water would run in them and wash out underneath the topsoil until a large pond and then a gully would form. The field would then have to dry up enough to be able to re-level and re-crease it. They had a heck of a time getting started! Eventually the grass and weeds grew along the head ditches and dad and grandfather were able to stabilize them. Over a period of time they were able to handle the water quite efficiently.

Another problem homesteaders had was marketing their produce. There wasn't a ready market for cereal grains at that time. There wasn't any organization buying those particular products. Most of the crops they raised were alfalfa they fed to the livestock and grain to feed to the chickens, hogs and cattle. So the cash crop was mostly eggs from the chickens and cream from the milk. They separated the milk and put the cream in cream cans, gathered the eggs and took them to town to sell. If any money was left over, that would buy their groceries and clothing.

There weren't any slaughter houses to buy the farmers' animals for meat until Mr. Mogensen built a slaughter house outside of Fruita and started marketing meat throughout the western slope area — Grand Junction, Palisade, Delta, Montrose, Gunnison, etc.

Mr. Mogensen was an immigrant from Denmark. He was a very brilliant young man and quite an entrepreneur. When he got here he learned the language quickly. He married a girl by the name of Porter whose brother was a doctor (by the way, Dr. Porter is the one who delivered me).

Mr. Mogensen had a refrigerator truck and hired butchers who butchered every day all year long. He also fed livestock all year. He went around the valley in another truck and bought cattle, hogs and sheep from the farmers. If the animals needed to be fattened, he would feed them until they were ready to

butcher. That was the first market for meat that was raised by the farmers. Dad always raised hogs and after he separated the cream from the milk, the skim milk was fed to the hogs.

Dad built a chicken house with nests and roosts for the chickens. The hens were kept in the chicken house so we could gather their eggs. They had a self-feeder and wheat and barley was ground into mash for them. He then built a granary to store the grain in. He generally raised wheat, barley, or oats. One side of the granary was for the oats or barley and the other side for the wheat. The oats were used to feed the horses and milk cows and the wheat was for the chickens. Dad built a corn crib, and in the fall corn was shucked by hand and the ears of corn were stored in the crib. Later the corn was fed to the hogs to fatten them.

The second cash crop that dad and grandfather raised was beets. The Holly Sugar Company had built a sugar factory in Grand Junction. At that time the Uintah Railway was hauling gilsonite from Baxter Pass. Holly Sugar Company built a beet-dump adjacent to a railroad sidetrack located at what would now be about 7 Road. The beets were hauled there by team and wagon. The wagons were called beet racks.

Dad had two beet racks. Beets were pitched onto the beet racks with beet forks; there was about two tons per rack. The dump was approximately three-and-a half miles from our place. When the beet racks first arrived at the dump, they were driven on a scale and weighed. There was a lift at the dump that would hook onto rings on the rack and tip the rack bed over and dump it into a hopper. The beets were then elevated into the narrow-gauge railway cars (see page 100). The elevator vibrated so all the dirt and stuff was shaken off the beets into a hopper. Then the dirt or tare, as it was called, was elevated back into the rack and the rack was reweighed. The difference between the two weights was the tonnage of beets that was brought in.

The D&RGW Railroad had standard-gauge railroad tracks in Mack, so instead of transferring the beets from the narrowgauge Uintah Railway cars to the D&RGW cars, the Uintah Railway placed narrowgauge rails between the standard-gauge rails from Mack to the sugar factory in Grand Junction. This way they were able to haul the beets via the D&RGW Railroad engines to Grand Junction and unload the beets there.

Farmers needed to raise more than beets and eggs and cream to get by. Farms got larger and also increased in production. Pinto beans and potatoes grew well there. The farmers in the Lower Valley organized and became District No. 10 of the Colorado Bean Growers' Association. Potato growers was not included in the name, but it was called the Bean and Potato Grower's Association by the farmers, as potatoes were also included in the program.

We don't have an exact date when District No. 10 was organized, but we do know it was active in 1927. A letter, notice of an annual meeting, copy of By-Laws, and a list of members dated 4 June 1927 were found in Robert Phillips' collection. A copy of the letter is copied on the next page and the list of members for Mack and New Liberty is as follows:

A. W. Alstatt	Clement Maluy
Noah E. Blasdel	P. A. Maluy
W. E. Bowen	William B. Maluy
Leland Burkett	G. E. Maynard
Charles W. Cavendish	John B. Morrow
C. Christofferson	Conrad Nab
Joe A. Cordova	Juan Pacheco
M. A. Cordova	R. M. Phillips
Robert M. Cox	W. R. Price
P. A. Daily	H. M. Sanders Jr.
C. F. Davidson	Robert Sanders
G. W. Fisher	W. E. Schunter
Guy G. Gerry	Vernon Snavely
B. A. Harrison	S. S. Summers
William A. Knapp	David N. Thomas
Clyde W. Likes	Floyd R. Thomas
Blair MacTaggart	E. D. Winkle

Darrell: The Association members built a warehouse in Fruita near the railroad tracks so they could load the produce into railroad cars. The beans were hauled to the warehouse in Fruita by truck and sometimes the driver had to wait in line until 1 a.m. to be weighed and unloaded. The warehouse had a huge cleaning machine that cleaned all the dirt, chaff, etc. out of the beans and sacked them in the labeled sacks. The potatoes were loaded on railroad cars at Mack, Loma or Fruita and shipped to market. They were evenly weighed at 102 pounds per sack. The two extra pounds allowed for shrinkage.

The farmers in the Lower Valley incorporated and set up a Board of Directors and a program with the bank where they could borrow money. The corporation was named Colorado Bean Growers' Warehouse Corporation, Fruita, Colorado. They had warehousing where a person could store their beans if they didn't want to sell them. There was always a market for beans where they could ship them to market in car-load lots throughout the country. Wherever the market was, Omaha or Chicago, that would be the price, less haulage or freight.

A list of the stockholders of the Colorado Bean Growers' Warehouse Corporation for 1934 was also found in Robert Phillips' Collection. The following is the list of stockholders from Mack and New Liberty:

A. W. Alstatt	Blair MacTaggart
Paul G. Arpke	Clement Maluy
O. W. Berry	William B. Maluy
W. E. Bowen Brayton	G. E. Maynard
Bros. George Bryan	C. C. McKay
Leland Burkett	John B. Morrow
B. D. Carroll	Joseph A. Owings
Charles W. Cavendish	Frank Pacheco
C. Christofferson	Juan Pacheco
Robert M. Cox	R. M. Phillips
P. A. Daily	W. E. Pollock
C. F. Davidson	H. M. Sanders Jr.
Lee L. Foss	Robert W. Sanders
Guy G. Gerry	W. E. Schunter
B. A. Harrison	Vernon Snavely
E. C. Hollinger	A. L. Stotts
J. F. Holt	S. S. Summers
Mary E. & F. R.	David N. Thomas
James Rudolph	Floyd R. Thomas
Johnson	T. C. Wassenberg
G. H. Kilby	E. D. Winkle
Clyde W. Likes	

COLORADO BEAN GROWERS

ASSOCIATION

INCORPORATED
TELEPHONE MAIN 7644
301-306 COOPER BLDG.
DENVER, COLORADO

NOTICE OF DISTRICT MEETING

MEMBERS OF COLORADO BEAN GROWERS ASSOCIATION
IN DISTRICT NO. TEN

You are hereby notified that a meeting of members in your district will be held on Saturday, June 4, 1927, at Loma, Colorado at Potato Warehouse from two to four o'clock p. m.

This meeting is being held for the purpose of electing eleven delegates who shall represent the membership in your district in selecting a member to serve on the board of Directors of the Colorado Bean Growers Association for one year from June 22, 1927 or until his successor is duly elected and qualified.

Take the inclosed ballot with you to the meeting, or if you cannot attend write in the names of the men you wish to vote for, sign the ballot and mail to A. W. ALSTATT, Mack, Colorado.

M. H. HASSTEDT, Secretary.

May 20, 1927

The notice of the Colorado Bean Growers Association's Annual Meeting that was found in the Robert Phillips Collection.
(Courtesy of Charlene Brayton Eldridge)

Darrell:

If a farmer wanted to keep his beans for speculating on them, they called it warehousing. The association would borrow money from the bank, a person could borrow 30 or 40 percent of what the price was at that particular time. Say the beans were $3 per hundred pounds, you could borrow a dollar a hundred on them. You could operate on that for awhile if you wished. The farmer would keep the beans there and pay storage on them. That would pay for the insurance and labor of the people managing the warehouse.

Dad ordinarily warehoused his beans and waited to sell until the next spring or summer when the beans were a better price. He usually did a little better then than if he had sold at the time of harvest.

Potatoes were perishable and whatever the market price was at the time of harvest, that was what the farmers received for them. That would be from 25 cents to $2 per hundred pound sack. In the early days beans were from $2 a hundred to $5.50 a hundred.

Dad had warehoused beans starting about 1932 and kept them until 1936; four years of beans. They had been bouncing around between $2 to $3 a hundred. Something happened making the price go up to $5.50. So he sold them and did quite well. That year, 1936, he also had a good year of potatoes, and that's when they built our new home.

Between 1928 and 1930 the Osborn Mercantile Company set up a warehouse adjacent to the Bean and Potato Growers' Association warehouse, and went into competition with them. Osborn's bought directly from the farmers, and the competition for produce was good for the farmer. They also bought wool from the sheep men. There was a Wool Growers' Association, and the company competed with them which kept the price right up there where it should be. Their coming into existence was a very fine thing for the farmer.

When I was born the folks didn't have a car, so they went everywhere in a wagon or buggy. When Mother started to have labor pains, Grandpa took off in the buggy and went to Fruita for Dr. Porter and brought him back with him. He spent the night and delivered me.

When I was a little boy Dad and Grandfather worked together a lot. I just adored Grandfather and used to follow him around. I remember one experience at grandfather's place. Dad had a team of horses hitched to a wagon with a walking plow and some other tools loaded on it. I was on the wagon when the horses took off and ran at a full gallop all the way to our home about a mile away. Dad and Grandpa were really concerned about what would happen to me and the equipment as they couldn't catch up with us. When they got home everything was still intact. I was still on the rack and nothing had been thrown off. That was quite a relief to them.

When I was four to six years old, Mother would hitch the horse to the buggy and we would go to Fruita. The road was a dirt road, and not even the highway to Fruita was graveled. There was a livery stable in Fruita where we would leave the horse and buggy. From Fruita to Grand Junction there was a trolley called the Interurban which ran on DC current. It picked up people, chickens and produce or whatever else, and made stops at Appleton or wherever it was flagged down. We would go to Fruita early in the morning, about a three hour buggy ride, catch the Interurban out of the Fruita station (where the fire station is now). We would get a hotel room and shop that afternoon and the next morning until about noon, then we would get on the Inter-urban and ride back to Fruita, get the horse out of the livery barn, hook up to the buggy, and get home about dark. I can remember the trip so well because in the home we had nothing but kerosene lamps while in town the brightness of the electric lights just dazzled me. How bright they were!

I started school in 1926 at age five and I rode a horse to school. There was a horse barn at the school house to keep our horses in during the day, as most of the kids rode horses to school.

One evening when I was coming home from school I was involved in an accident. North of our place near the mailbox the road wasn't quite straight as it made a curve around a patch of willows there. On this occasion I was riding at a full gallop. Bowens had bought a new Model "T" Ford and Jo was driving it on the curve, but I wasn't visible until she came around the curve. The sunlight hit the windshield and the glare scared the horse. He came to an abrupt stop and I flew over his head and broke my arm. That was the first broken arm I had. They took me to Dr. White in Fruita and he X-rayed it. He said I had what they called a "green-stick" break. It didn't break clear through, just half way. I recovered from that quite nicely.

(Upper left) 1929, cousins: Bobby Warner, Marilyn, Dale, Darrell, Rex and Patty Maluy. (Upper right) 1929, Bill Maluy with Patty on his shoulders, Dale, Clara, Darrell, Rex, Mary holding Bobby Warner, and Clem with Marilyn on his shoulders. The turkeys and turkey roost are in the background. (Center left) 1939, Rex, Darrell and Dale Maluy. (Center right) 1929, Bill Maluy holding Patty, Clem, Mary, Clara Maluy, and Addie Warner holding Bobby. Dale, Rex, Marilyn and Darrell Maluy are in front. Clem Maluy's homestead house is in the background. (Lower left) 1922, Darrell and Dale Maluy. (Below) Rex, Marilyn, Darrell, Dale and Patty Maluy. Bobby Warner is in front. Bill's new 1928/9 Chevrolet car. *(Maluy Photo Collection)*

Grandpa sold his place to Uncle Bill Maluy in 1927. Dad and Uncle Bill worked together trading work back and forth. Aunt Clara, Uncle Bill's wife, was a very fine, lovely person, who passed away in 1934 of pneumonia. That was a terrible tragedy for the family, as she left five children for Uncle Bill to raise alone.

We had our Thanksgiving, Christmas and New Year's at each other's house, and we had a wonderful time getting together like one great big family. We cousins were awfully close, and still are. Dale, Rex, and I had an awful lot of fun together as kids. Dad and Uncle Bill were hard workers, and we had to work hard, too. By the time we were nine or ten years old we were expected to work in the fields driving teams of horses when we started out. Dad and Bill never took a weekend or Sunday off; it was always seven days a week during the summer time and that's the way we worked — long hours. We got by OK and enjoyed each other's company a great deal.

When I was growing up I liked to climb trees. One summer, when I was seven years old, my folks had company and I was climbing a tree. When I got in the top of the tree, a limb broke and I fell down head-first on the road below. I broke my left arm in many different places. Dad took me to Dr. Orr in Fruita. The elbow was broken quite badly and the wrist and bone between the elbow and shoulder were also broken. He got the wrist and bone between the elbow and shoulder set, but the elbow wouldn't stay in place.

During the next year, Dr. Orr re-broke and reset the elbow three different times. He never did get it back into the original position. The last time he said, "That's the best I can do, this boy will probably never have more than 50 percent use of this arm. There's nothing more that I can do." Back in those times they didn't have pins, etc. to hold things in place.

When he took the cast off of the arm I couldn't get it to straighten out more than 90 degrees. In other words, it had a 90degree bend in it. Dr. Orr said, "Have this boy carry a five pound pail of water or rocks around and start pulling those tendons out to straighten that arm out." Well, I did that and I was determined I would get the use of that arm. When I got a little more mobility out of it I started throwing rocks with it. I got it completely straightened out and I had just as good use of it as my right arm, except it was crooked. It didn't come out straight. I threw with it and could do anything with it

that anyone else could do with their left arm. In fact, when I went into the Air Force they were very particular about having complete coordination and passed me right through. I got through that and have never had any problem with it since, except the deformity and look of it. I was quite conscious of that in high school playing basketball and track, but I think all young people care if they aren't 100 percent.

When I was about seven or eight, Dad bought a Model "T" truck with a bed on the back of it. There weren't very many pickup trucks in the valley at that time. The folks would then go to town in style. It didn't have a heater so we would take a lot of blankets and so forth. Marilyn and I would be in the back, and we would be all bundled up in those blankets trying to keep warm.

One time I remember going to Grand Junction in the summer. Coming back there had evidently been a big rain in the Bookcliffs, and the wash west of Mack was at flood stage. There was probably four or five feet of water going down the wash and roaring like a freight train. We sat there a long time and finally Dad said, "I guess the only way we're going to get across here is to cross on the railroad bridge." (That's when the Uintah Railway had a bridge there). He backed up and drove onto the railroad bridge. We bounced across on the ties and on home. When we got home we could still hear the flood in the wash about a mile east of us. It was a terrific flood!

I remember we still had the Model "T" in 1931 when they dedicated a monument at the Utah/Colorado State Line† and both governors were there. It was Governor Johnson from our state, if I remember correctly. Mother took me with her to the celebration and dedication. There were a lot of people there and that was quite a sight for me. At that time I believe the road was still dirt, though it might have been gravel.

That old Model "T" served us until about 1931 or 1932 when Dad bought a used 1929 Nash car. That thing was like a freight train — a great big old car. From then on we started getting better automobiles.

Luella McNaught's 60 acre homestead south adjoining the folks' homestead went to seep and was abandoned.

Dad was able to acquire it from the Bureau of Reclamation. There was a one-room, 20by-24 house on the place, and Dad used it for the Mexican Nationals. They would come up each spring and work in the beets — thin, hoe and

† See page 32 for photo of monument celebration on 25 September 1931.

top the beets. They also picked potatoes, put up hay, or whatever manual labor had to be done.

As long as I can remember from when I was five years old, the Romero family came up from Mexico each summer and occupied that house until World War II. The children didn't go to school here, as they went back to Mexico in the fall. I got well acquainted with the kids and spent many hours playing with them. I learned to speak a little Spanish, but not good. Mrs. Romero was a fine lady. She made tortillas and cooked them on top of the coal cook stove. She made fine chili, too. Dad provided a cow for them to milk, and always saved one pig for them to butcher. We had an acre of garden, and they had access to anything they wanted out of the it. They lived quite well and ate good. They had about as much as anyone since no one had much money in those days They were fine people.

Mother set some setting hens to hatch out little chickens. She also had an incubator with a kerosene heater that would handle 200 eggs. She would put eggs in there and place them where it was dark. Later she would candle them to see if the little embryos were starting to grow. When they hatched out we had a little brooder house with a kerosene heater for them, and they would get under that to keep warm. There were also little feeders and drinking fountains. Mother raised several hundred chickens and some turkeys that way.

Some of the roosters were caponized. When the chicks were about two months old, she opened them up in the back and took out the little testicles. They were then called capons and grew considerably larger than the other roosters. These were usually Rhode Island Reds or Plymouth Rocks. They would get up to about eight to 10 pounds. In the fall when we had threshing or haying crews to cook for, she would send me down to kill three or four of those capons. She would fry them and have enough for the whole crew. We kept the Leghorn hens for laying hens, so we had three different kinds of chickens.

One year the Schunters had several turkeys being developed called Broad Breasted Bronze. They brought us over a big tom, as mother wanted to breed the hen turkeys she had. She paid quite a price for it. I was probably five or six years old and we had a dog named "Billy" that was a doggoned good cattle dog, and he was always with me. This tom turkey would attack me, knock me over, and tromp on me. It scared the heck out of me!

Dad said, "Take the dog and a stick and see if you can't chase him off." Well, I got the best of that turkey, and when I was all through the turkey was dead. Dad was so upset he gave me a spanking — he felt bad about it later. Money was so hard to come by and they had bought that turkey thinking it would be good for the flock. Then I, a little kid, turned around and killed the darn turkey.

Each fall Dad would butcher the turkeys we raised to be eaten for the holidays. He'd share them with Uncle Bill and the neighbors.

There was no refrigeration, but we did have an ice cellar that dad built. In the winter time, when the ice would get thick on the pond, we'd take a timber saw and saw the ice into about 50-to-60 pound chunks and store them in the cellar and cover them with straw. The ice would keep all summer long. Each day we took out a chunk of ice and put it in our ice box to keep our milk, butter, and things like that cool. However they didn't keep very long.

The only fresh meat we had in the summer was chicken or turkey. In the winter time we butchered a beef and we would have fresh beef as long as the weather was cold. What we couldn't keep mother would can, so we ate canned beef in the summer time. Also Dad would butcher a couple of hogs in the fall. We had a smoke-house, and he'd smoke the hams and make sausage out of part of it. The bacon was cured and Mother would boil the real fat part with lye to make soap. The chunks of hide left over from that process became "cracklings," and we would go around chewing on those. The cooked sausage and its grease was placed in 10-gallon crocks. The grease would come to the top and seal and preserve it all year. I remember coming home from school, getting one of those sausages, heating it up, and eating it for a snack. It tasted pretty good, as I would be hungry as heck.

The schoolhouse was also used for church and social functions. In those days very few people had cars, so we were quite isolated. The families in New Liberty became a very close-knit group. They entertained themselves and each other. In the wintertime dances were held in the schoolhouse nearly every Saturday night. I don't remember who furnished the music, but I do remember Mr. Thomas (David and Floyd's dad, Eugene's grandfather) played a violin. There was generally a violin and a piano. At midnight they had an intermission and the women served coffee and sandwiches.

Mother and Dad loved to dance. They took Marilyn and me along with them, plus plenty of blankets for us to sleep with on the chairs. Sometimes they danced till three in the morning. This was one of my good memories of the early days. The people were really jovial and had lots of fun. I remember mother telling me how in the spring a person could tell the men had been hauling manure out of their corrals. The men would work up quite a sweat dancing and even though they had taken a bath, the smell would get pretty strong in the building. The stench was ingrained in them.

In the summertime the community held pot-luck dinners and the women would bring their favorite culinary dish. The men played baseball and the kids would play different games. I always looked forward to those meals because of the good food. In those days people had ice cellars and we had lots of homemade freezer ice cream. Later in the year there was watermelon and cantaloupe. It was very festive and enjoyable.

One time when I was about 10 years old a little white mare came to our place and stayed. I started riding her, and we called her "Queenie." We found out that she belonged to a fellow by the name of Jake Saunders. He herded sheep for Fitzpatrick and other people and also leased the old Diehl place for a year or two. He took Queenie with him up to the Uintah Basin near Vernal, Utah. The government supplied them with good stallions to upgrade their horses, and Queenie got bred by one of them. She wouldn't stay with Jake and she kept coming back to our place, and I would ride her. Jake said, "Aw the heck with it, you just keep her, she won't stay with me." So I inherited Queenie. She had a little mare colt and we called her "Coshee." I broke the colt when she was about two years or so old. She

was-good sized, well-built, and turned out to be a real fine animal.

When I was in the seventh or eighth grade I rode Coshee to school and she loved to run. Nellie Stotts used to go around in a horse-drawn buggy to pick up the local news. She'd talk to different people and find out what they had been doing during the week, who had a birthday, and any local gossip that was available. After school one evening, there were five of us on horses and we were racing down the road, five abreast, from the schoolhouse to Shires' corner, about half a mile away. Leonard Shires was on behind me, and we were on the left-hand side of the road going south. Nellie, with her horse and buggy, was going north on the same side of the road as Leonard and I were. I could see we were going to have a collision, so I tried to stop that pony of mine. By golly, I couldn't stop her! My horse's chest hit the front wheel of the buggy and Nellie, the buggy and her horse went flying over into the fence. My horse fell down and Leonard fell off and broke his arm. We gathered everything up and I got Leonard back on the horse. I took him home to his mother with his broken arm. She was boiling mad! She thought I was delinquent anyway.

On one 4th of July the residents of New Liberty went to the top of Douglas Pass to have a picnic. There were some people from East Douglas by the name of Coltharp who came to join us. They had a boy about my age named Gerald. We became friends, and they invited me to come up there to spend some time with them.

Darrell, 12 years old, on Queenie with the colt, Coshee, packed and ready for one of his excursions to the mountains. *(Photo courtesy of Darrell Maluy)*

541

In August I got some supplies and took off for East Douglas on Coshee, not knowing exactly where it was. The first day I got as far as the bottom of Douglas Pass and there was an old cabin there, so I stayed in that all night. The next day I rode as far as Josh Manice's, a fellow who kept dairy cattle up there for us in the summer. I stayed with him for a day or two and he pointed me in the right direction to East Douglas. I had to go up the mountain and on up East Douglas Creek. Well, I found it okay and then Gerald and I had a heck of a time the next couple of weeks. I shot the first deer I ever shot. We did some great fishing at some beaver ponds at the head of East Douglas Creek. We roped some calves and rode them, and wild horses were up there. It was a heck of an experience!

The Coltharps made their living trapping coyotes, bobcats, bears and different other animals that preyed on the sheep and other animals on the mountain. They had a trap line, horses and pack animals. Gerald went to school sporadically in Rangely where the Coltharps had a home. When I got back dad said, "You know, that boy ought to go to school." So arrangements were made for Gerald to come and stay with us and attend school at New Liberty. He stayed the next two years with us and got his diploma from grade school. That was a great thing dad did to give Gerald that opportunity. Gerald has done real well. He owns a big trailer court in Apache Junction, Arizona and is a millionaire.

On the homestead there weren't any trees or anything to use for fuel in our stoves, so we had to find fuel outside the area. In the fall Dad and I took a couple of teams and wagons with hay-racks on them and headed toward the Utah state line to a mesa where there were lots of cedar trees about seven or eight miles from home. He then unhitched one of the teams and a double-tree from one of the wagons. Pulled the old dead cedars down and tore them apart. We then loaded them on the wagons and took off for home. We piled the cedar across the back yard and made a pile about 15 or 20 feet across by about 10 feet high. We used that old dry cedar for kindling, as it burned real hot. We would put a bunch of kindling in the cook stove or heater, start a fire and then add coal. The fire would ignite the coal and burn for a long time.

We had to haul the coal, also. We used the two wagons that were used to haul beets to the beet dump. We started out early in the morning with two teams and wagons and drove to the Stove Canyon Coal Mine. It was about 15 or 20 miles from home. We got there in the evening and loaded the wagons with about five tons of coal altogether. We would then grain and hay the horses, and water them in the wash. After we cared for the horses, we ate the lunch mother fixed for us. We then took our bedrolls into the coal mine where it was warm and slept there all night. The next morning at daylight we'd get up and head for home. This had to be done when the roads were dry — it couldn't be done when they were muddy or frozen. The horses would do fine going up the hills and I could drive the wagon; but going down the hills I couldn't hold the wagon back with the heavy load on it. So Dad drove his wagon to the bottom of the hill, then walked back up and drove my wagon down. Usually the brake would be on so hard it would make the wheels slide and the horses even had to pull a little to go down the hill. If it wasn't for the brake, the wagon would have run over the top of the horses. We would get home about dark. Some times that coal wouldn't last all winter and we would have to go back in January or February to make another trip for more.

In the summertime Dad would light the cook stove when he got

Darrell Maluy and Gerald Coltharp after a successful deer hunt in October 1943. *(Maluy Photo Collection)*

up, then go do the chores. By the time he got back an hour and half later Mother would have breakfast cooked. In the winter time when I was a little boy we only had the cook stove and the house would get real cold and freeze at night. Later Dad built a half screened-in porch on the back of the house. The lower half was made of boards and the upper half was screen. He installed canvas on rollers that could be rolled down to keep the cold air out or rolled up in the summer to let the air in. He put a big pot-bellied stove in there. In the winter we would fire that stove up and try to keep it going all the time. It would die down at night but it would still have chunks of live coals in it to keep it warm. It still got mighty cold by morning! Dad would roust me out to help with the morning chores, and it sure felt good to get back into the nice warm house. By the time we got back the stoves had warmed things up.

We planted about an acre of garden. My parents would share some with the Nationals from Mexico, and we canned string beans, corn, and tomatoes. In the fall the carrots, parsnips, turnips and potatoes were placed in a root-cellar for winter storage. We made sauerkraut out of the cabbage and put it in a 20-gallon crock. We also had crocks of pickles we made out of the cucumbers. In the fall when the peaches and other fruits came on we would get 10 or 12 bushels of peaches, four or five bushels of pears and can about 250 quarts of peaches and 100 quarts of pears. We had cherry, plum, apricot and apple trees at home. Mother would can pie cherries and plums and apricots to eat. She raised strawberries for strawberry jam. All in all we canned about a thousand quarts of fruit every year.

Dad dug out a cellar under the old shack. It was dark and cool and the canned fruits and vegetables, sauerkraut, pickles and crocks of sausage would store there very well. We also put our eggs down there as we gathered them, and once a week we candled them and put them in an egg crate. There would be three dozen to a layer, as I recall, and it was about twelve layers deep, so we would take about 70 dozens of eggs to Fruita at a crack. We kept our cream in the cellar and in the ice box and took the cream and eggs into town at the same time to sell them.

Since Gerald was so much a part of the Maluy family we decided to include him here.

Gerald Coltharp was born 25 July 1918 in Olney Springs, Crowley, Colorado, east of Pueblo, to Ed Coltharp and Cora Williams. Ed and Cora homesteaded on Douglas Pass before Gerald was born, then Cora went to her parents at Olney Springs to give birth to Gerald. Ed and Cora also owned a small home in Rangely, Colorado. In the summer they farmed, raised cattle and had a trap line on Douglas Pass, then spent the winters in Rangely. They also worked the trap line during the winter.

Gerald attended his first seven years of school at Rangely, then attended the eighth grade at New Liberty School and graduated from there. He lived with the Clem Maluys while going to New Liberty School. Gerald says he milked cows for Clem. He always called Clem "Mr. Malleysoup." After graduating he worked for Clem on the farm then went to work for the D&RGW Railroad for a while in the shop repairing engines. He then went back to Rangely and worked in the oil fields for the next 35 years. He also had a junk business in Rangely called Beacon Heights and Salvage.

Gerald married **Venis Smuin** 24 July 1939, in Vernal, Uintah, Utah. Venis was born in Vernal, the daughter of Hyrum and Idell Smuin. Gerald and Venis had three children:

Vernon, born 1 August 1940, Vernal, Uintah, Utah
Raema, 9 June 1942, Vernal
Roger, 1 July 1944, Grand Junction

In 1944 and 1945 Gerald took a break from the oil fields and worked for Clem Maluy on the farm. Clem built a little two-room house just southeast of his house for Gerald's family to live in. The water was piped into the house from the cistern and a hand pump installed at the sink to make it possible to have water in the house. Other than that there weren't any modern conveniences.

One time Gerald visited an aunt in California who lived in a mobile home park. He liked the looks of the park and decided he would like to have one, so he went to the library and read books on how to develop one. He visited some friends who lived in Apache Junction, Arizona, and looked at property there. Gerald found a piece of property he liked, returned home, sold his business and building to the oil company, and bought the Arizona property. He drove a gravel truck for several years to raise money to build the cement pads in the park. In 1970 he opened the park and people started moving into the completed spaces. He continued to expand and add spaces, and in a few years had a 150-space park making him financially secure. Gerald and Venis bought a home in Vernal so they could spend the summers in Vernal and the winters in Arizona.

A tragedy struck in September 1979 ; Venis was killed in an auto accident. Gerald sold the mobile home park soon after. The next year, 1980, he built another mobile home park with 140 spaces in Queens Creek, Arizona, about seven miles from Apache Junction .

Gerald married a school teacher, **Valry Webster**, 6 March 1991, in Las Vegas, Nevada. This year, 1997, they sold the home in Vernal and bought a home in Pinedale, Arizona.

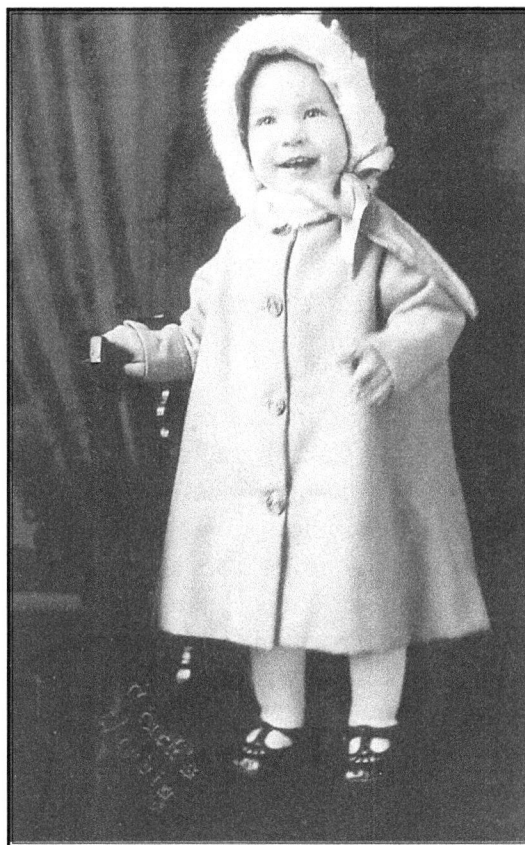

Marilyn May Maluy, 1926.
(Maluy Photo Collection)

Gerald and Valry Coltharp.
(Photo by Phyllis Likes)

Marilyn was the second child born to Clem and Mary Maluy. She had bright red hair. Mother always called her "a Rock of Gibraltar," as she could always withstand adversities. She also said Marilyn was a happy, cheerful child — she could always see the funny side of things and was a good sport.

Being the first daughter, she and mother were very close and Mother depended on her a great deal. She took over helping in the house and being a big sister, especially during the first two years of World War II when mother had to work in the field so much. She and Mother were the best of friends and had a lot of good times together.

Marilyn was always involved in activities going on in the community, school or with her friends. In high school she was head girl in her class, a member of the Pep Club and a cheerleader. She also took part in sports and other activities in school. I remember one of the performances the Pep Club put on at half time for a basketball game. It was choreographed to the tune of Skater's Waltz. We went to see the performance, and I thought it was the most beautiful thing I had ever seen — she was the star.

Marilyn loved to dance and never missed a dance at the Loma Community Hall if she could help it. She received shoe ice skates for Christmas one year and would skate every chance she could during the winter. She got pretty good on them — spinning, stopping fast, doing figure eights, etc.

Marilyn took piano and tap dancing lessons from Mrs. Helen Carroll. She advanced to the 6th level in the piano books and was playing quite advanced music. However, she decided that things were going too slow; she didn't want to learn about theory, composers, etc. she just wanted to play music. She discovered she could play by ear with chords and didn't have to read the music. From then on she played anything and everything she wanted to. She also took some tap dancing in high school under Mrs. Stivers.

Marilyn's main boy friend in high school was a football player, Charlie Pacheco. Marilyn graduated from Fruita Union High School the spring of 1943. That fall she worked at the peach sheds in Grand Junction, packing peaches for shipping. She saved her money and bought a fur coat, some nice clothes and, unknown to her parents, a train ticket to Sacramento, California.

She married **Charlie William "Chuck" Pacheco**, 11 October 1943, in Sacramento, Sacramento, California. Charlie was born 6 April 1924 at Hotchkiss, Colorado, a son of Saul and Cassandra Cisneros Pacheco (see Pacheco biography). Charlie was serving in the U.S. Navy at the time, and was in port on leave. The family was in quite a state

(Left) Marilyn and her new fur coat just before she left for California. The cat is the family pet, Cutta. (Right) Charlie and Marilyn Pacheco after Charlie returned from the war. Clem Maluy farm, 1945. *(Maluy Photo Collection)*

of shock when she called and said she was in Sacramento and married!

Marilyn and Charlie have three children:

Beau Allen, born 11 March 1947 in Fruita
Kathi Mae (Beard, Wisdom), 23 November 1953, Burbank, Los Angeles, California
Darrell Alvin, 1 February 1955, Van Nuys, Los Angeles, California

Beau Allen Pacheco

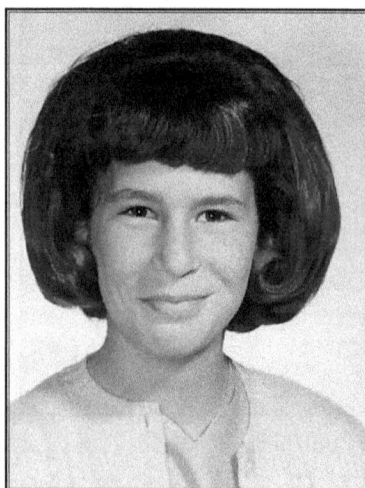

Kathi Mae Pacheco

Darrell Alvin Pacheco

(Maluy Photo Collection)

(Left) Marilyn in her Skater's Waltz Costume for the Pep Club performance.

(Above) 1938, Marilyn and friends on a horseback ride. L-R: Laurette Wills (raised by Ethel Cox), Dorothy Cox and Marilyn Maluy.

(Right) Marilyn May Maluy, high school graduation picture, 1943. Sweet eighteen. *(All photos on this page courtesy of Marilyn Maluy Pacheco)*

(Lower left) The Charlie Pacheco family in 1958. Back, L-R: Beau, Charlie, Marilyn Pacheco. Front: Darrell and Kathi Pacheco. (Lower right) Marilyn and her ice cream vendor bike in Sparks, Nevada.

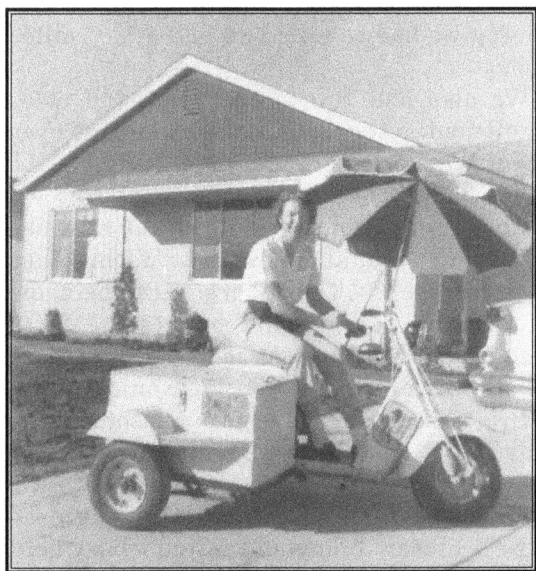

Since Marilyn and Charlie's marriage they have lived nearly all over the United States, but returned to Fruita in 1990 to retire.

Marilyn tells the rest of the story.

I was born 5 October 1925, to Clem and Mary Maluy. Dr. James Orr said I was the first bright red haired baby he had delivered. I was born in a little two-room house half-a-mile from "Shires Corner," which is the only descriptive address we had in those days. But that was good enough! I was the second child of four, and we all think we grew up in the best of times, and that New Liberty was the perfect place to be.

We were very close to our cousins, Dale, Rex, Patty, Wilma and Norma, "Uncle Bill's kids." Aunt Clara, their mother, died when Norma was almost three years old. Patty and I were good pals, and we have lots of memories of the good and the bad times. Dad and Uncle Bill helped each other with the farming. That meant the kids got together to help with the threshing, stacking hay, picking seed spuds, or whatever else there was to do. Nonetheless, we always found time to go to the canal and swim. That's where we met all our friends during the summer.

The winters were more severe with temperatures in the 20s and 30s. I remember Mom and Dad dressing me in long underwear, long cotton stocking's and a warm snow suit over my clothes to go to school a mile away. Darrell and I would ride Queenie to school then put her in a stall until time to go home. Sometimes she would take off her bridle and beat us home. She was good at that! Once in awhile Patty and I would ride her to visit Betty Pollock and she would pull her "trick" meaning we had to walk two and-a-half miles home.

We also had fun in the snow and cold. Darrell made a toboggan and we would go over to Don Weimer's hill and slide down it. At the bottom of the hill was a big wash (ditch). We would get going so fast down the hill that the toboggan would fly over the wash. That was great sport! Then there were the snow sledding and tobogganing parties at Weirs or Hollinger's hill, or the ice skating parties on the Daily or Cox ponds. We would build a bonfire to keep warm and provide some light at night. There was always a big gathering of kids.

Everyone in the community belonged to the New Liberty Community Club. They held summer ice cream socials and picnics away from New Liberty, sometimes as far away as Douglas Pass or Horse Thief Canyon, and once I remember going to the Big Salt Wash west of Mack. The Community Club held their meetings at the schoolhouse. With the regular meetings there were different social activities; dances, three-act plays, and local entertainment with good desserts served afterward. They had an auction at Christmas time, and all the women would bring their special projects of sewing, baked goods, and candy. All the money from this would go to buy school supplies and equipment for the playground. I remember after the new schoolhouse was built, we got all new playground equipment. There were swings, a teeter-totter and a slide. That first day was a fun day! There were lots of skins, bruises and arguments to see who was next in line.

Harold Carroll was my favorite teacher, and Dorothy Cox was my special friend. One of my sweet memories of her is at one of the Christmas auctions. Mrs. Della Swyhart had made and donated a doll bed and dresser set. It was made from apple crates and painted green. It was so cute. Dorothy and I both wanted it. After the bidding started it looked like someone else was going to get it. So Dorothy bid three dollars, then I bid four dollars, and so on until we had the bid up to 50 dollars. Everyone was getting a laugh out of this, but finally, Bob Cox stopped us bidding and it started all over again. This time Dorothy and I weren't allowed to bid! Bob Cox won the bid, and I felt so bad that I cried. When Christmas morning came — surprise! Under the table with a sheet to hide the gifts was the little green doll furniture for me. I was so happy I had to cry again. Dorothy and Santa had given it to me.

Through the efforts of the Community Club and the Women's Sorosis Club, our school had everything we needed. It was great!

Louise Alstatt, Dorothy Cox, and I went all 12 years of school together. Needless to say, we were very close friends. We graduated in 1943, Dorothy died in 1958, and Louise died in 1962. I miss them very much.

While I was in high school I was a cheerleader two years and head girl in my junior year.

Charlie Pacheco was my high school sweetheart. He joined the Navy in his senior year. A lot of our classmates joined some branch of the service during World War II. We were married in October 1943 and 10 days later he went overseas for two years. What a way to start a marriage, but it has lasted 54 years.

During the time Charlie was overseas, I worked in the shipyard in Vallejo, California, as a welder and managed a Tool Crib. In 1945 I came home, and Mom and I raised 600 turkeys. Some of the toms dressed out at 32 pounds. We took them to Mack, packed them in crates with dry ice, and shipped them to market by train. Every time we took a load to the depot the agent would say, "Here comes another load of mules." We **were very proud of our "crop."**

Charlie was discharged October 1945. He came home safe, healthy and ready to go on with life. We lived with my folks that fall while Charlie helped Dad with the harvesting. He then went to work for the D&RGW Railroad as a telegrapher and was stationed at Eagle, Colorado. This was the beginning of many different occupations and homes throughout the United States [see Charlie Pacheco's history].

While we lived in Sparks, Nevada, I had an ice cream vendor route, and then I worked for Harrahs Club in Reno from 1962–1965 managing the snack bars. We then moved to Grand Junction, and I worked at the Mesa National Bank in Grand Junction from 1966 to 1970. From 1971–1988, I worked with Charlie on all his projects selling real estate and campgrounds. In 1988–1990 we sold kitchen appliances at army bases in Texas and California.

In 1990 we came to Fruita because of health problems. We are glad to be home and healthy again. I work for my sister, Lee Ann, at Impact Promotional Products. I do all her embroidery work for promotional garments, hats, etc. on a special embroidery machine run with a computer.

Charlie and I raised three children: Beau, Kathi and Darrell. We now have five grandchildren and three great-grandchildren.

Beau married Jeanne Larson 4 February 1967, in Grand Junction, and they had two children, Tamara Kay and Travis Larson. Jeanne died 24 May 1992. Beau was an entertainer and emcee for 23 years. He then worked for the Rider magazine, and is now an editor for the Big Twin Magazine.

Kathi married Lynn Beard March 1969, at the Lake of the Ozarks, Missouri.

They had two children, Casey Don and Shauna Lynn Beard. That marriage ended in divorce, and Kathi married Ford Wisdom 29 February 1987, in Texas. That marriage also ended in divorce. Kathi managed Pizza Huts in Texas for several years and then worked for seven years as a building contractor in Las Vegas. Kathi still lives in Las Vegas and is raising and showing dogs.

Darrell had a daughter, Amy Monica, by his first marriage. She was born 8 June 1973, at the Lake of the Ozarks, Missouri. He married Kathryn Page 2 November 1982, in Grand Junction. Darrell works for the prison system in North Carolina, and does surveying as well. He also is in the National Guard Reserves and served in the Gulf War.

Mother and Dad are both gone now, but my heart is still at New Liberty. Every time I go past the homestead, I shed a few tears. Things are never the same when you go back.

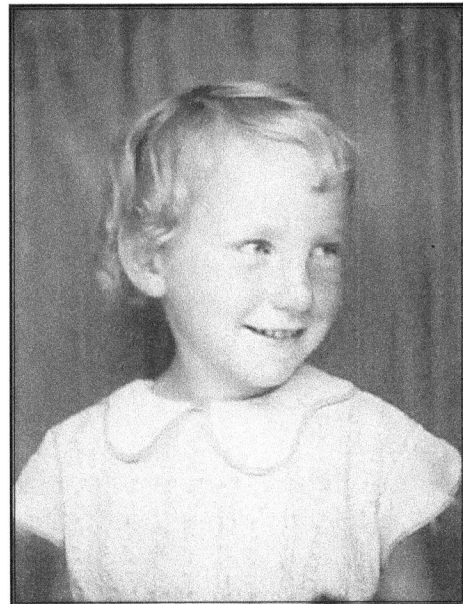

Phyllis Clemene Maluy
(Maluy Photo Collection)

Phyllis Clemene was the third child born in the Clem Maluy family, another redhead, and aptly named after her father. I became my father's next boy. I worked beside him in the field with all the different equipment, digging ditches and irrigating, milking cows, attending rodeos and auctions. I also herded the cows in the lower desert property and sheep on the barren hills. Being with my father and around other men I learned a man's language, which wasn't always very "lady-like." My mother kept me well corrected at home though.

Phyllis Clemene Maluy, sweet sixteen.
(Maluy Photo Collection)

I wasn't very enthusiastic about going to school. Mother said she had to coax me into going to school nearly every morning. There were too many things to do besides going to school. However I did have a talent for singing and sang the lead in the grade school operetta Mrs. Brenton directed. I also sang two solo numbers in my eighth grade graduation: "The Bubble," by Rudolph Friml and "Alice Blue Gown."

Teachers in grade school and high school approached Mother at different times telling her that I should have an opportunity to develop my singing, but there wasn't enough money for that. I loved classical music; also Nelson Eddie and Jeanette McDonald were my idols. I always dreamed of being a singer just like Jeanette. I practiced while driving the tractor or horse drawn equipment in the field. At least I got to sing for the horses! I sang in the high school chorus and with a range of three octaves, I always got the obligatory parts. I loved musicals, so when it was my turn to go to town with Mother to spend the day shopping and going to a movie, Mother made sure there was a musical showing. I remember seeing, Oklahoma, Phantom of the Opera, and many

others. Mother knew better than take me to a mystery or scary movie as I would spend my time hiding under the seat. I can still hear her saying, "Phyllis get up and sit in your seat, it's not going to hurt you, it's just a movie."

I took piano lessons from my mother, but after a couple of years I felt I should have the opportunity to have lessons from someone else (like Marilyn did), and refused to take anymore lessons from Mother. I continued to play and teach myself. My favorite piano music was by Chopin. I bought a book of Chopin's music and memorized the "Minute Waltz," then learned to play them all.

After I married and moved to Moab I took lessons from Aloyes Ivie. When both the Ivie and Likes families moved to Orem, Aloyes and I played duets together for several years and took lessons from a professor at BYU. Later I took lessons from Margaret Brown, a well known teacher in Orem, then from another teacher who taught composing. After I composed one number and played it at a recital, the teacher moved and I got too involved with family and other things to continue.

I attended Fruita Union High School. I sang in the chorus, played basketball, belonged to the Pep Club, Spanish Club, and was a cheerleader during my junior and senior year.

I quit school in the middle of my senior year and married **Homer Chilson Likes**, 2 December 1946 in my parents' home. Homer was also a son of homesteaders, Clyde William Likes Sr. and Retta May Appier (see more on Homer in the Likes history). We moved in with his parents after our marriage.

Homer and I have two children:

Dennis Wayne, born 9 August 1947, Grand Junction
Retta-Marie (Clayburn, Brandow), 9 February 1950, Grand Junction

Homer and I bought his parents' farm and ran a Grade-A dairy for 12 years. We had Jersey cows and two registered Jersey bulls. The bulls were kept tethered to a pole by a chain hooked to a ring in their noses. I tamed them and was

Homer and Phyllis Maluy Likes *(Maluy Photo Collection)*

Dennis Wayne Likes
(Maluy Photo Collection)

Retta Marie Likes
(Maluy Photo Collection)

able to ride one of them (Herkimer), I slid down his neck and bounced on his head onto the head of the other bull and back to the first. It soon became evident that only I was able to handle

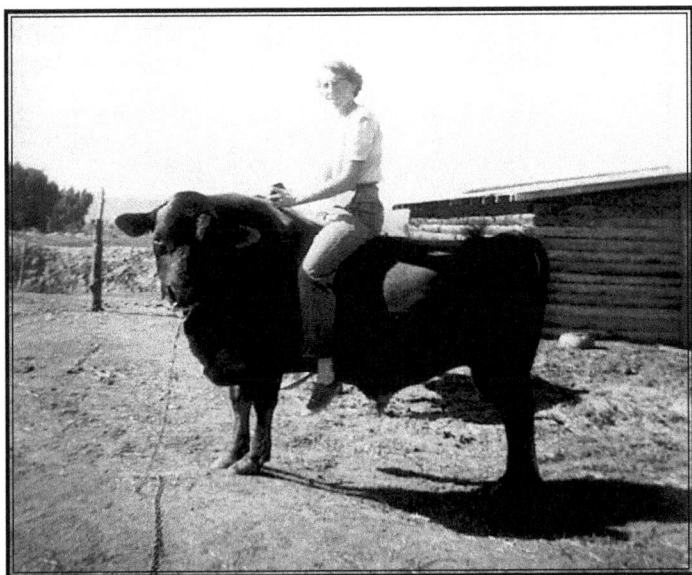
Phyllis and Herkimer the Bull, 1954.
(Maluy Photo Collection)

the bulls when they were to be used with a cow or needed to be led for any reason.

The only modern facilities the house had was a hand pump at the sink piped from the cistern. In the milk barn there was an electric water heater that we filled by carrying two buckets of water from the house. Hot water was needed to wash the milking machines and milk cans. Cold water was poured in the top of the water heater and when the spout was pulled down hot water would come out. I decided that this hot water would be nice to use in the #3 tub on Sunday mornings for the children's and my weekly baths before going to church. This caused one of my most embarrassing moments.

Homer and I put our farm up for sale. This certain Sunday morning I was sitting naked on a milk stool, bathing my two children in the tub. Suddenly the door flew open and there stood the realtor with two possible buyers. They stood there with their mouths open and looked. Finally I said, "Well!" The realtor asked where he could find Homer and after I told him where, he slowly backed up and closed the door. They then peered in each window as they went around the barn — as if to make sure they had really seen what they thought they had seen.

Homer, the children, and I moved to Moab in January 1958 without having sold the farm. We rented it out for a year or two and then took out a second mortgage on it and let that person sell it.

In Moab, I worked two years in Nordfelt's Dairy Freeze and then two years as a dispatcher for the Sheriff and Utah Highway Department. I decided to go back to school and finish getting my diploma. I took a stenographer course on a government MDTA grant held at Moab High School. Since my son, Dennis, attended high school there, we had the opportunity to attend school together.

On New Years, 1965, the family moved to Price and I attended the College of Eastern Utah (CEU) for a year-and-a-half. Dennis and my nephew, Beau Pacheco, attended a year at CEU with me. We moved to Orem, Utah June 1966 and I attended Brigham Young University (BYU) for two semesters. I worked for Halstrom Motors in American Fork, Utah, as a secretary and parts person for a year, then worked four years for Deseret Travel and four years for the Utah County Assessor as an accountant.

I did extensive traveling while working for Deseret Travel. The trip that was the highlight of that career was the six-week tour I organized for my mother and Auntie Claire through Spain, Italy, France, Switzerland, Holland, Germany, Denmark, England and Ireland. I joined them in Holland and we toured all the countries that my ancestors came from.

In 1976 I quit working after discovering I had breast cancer. During the next six months I had two surgeries for a double mastectomy and implants. Everything went well and I received a clean bill of health.

I was interested in genealogy research before I quit working. I had attended many classes on genealogy research and had been doing research on my family since 1954. I became a volunteer consultant at the Regional Family History Center in the BYU Library in 1968. By 1980 I was seriously involved in family research, teaching classes, and helping others in their research. Also in 1980, Homer and I decided we wanted to write a book on New Liberty and began doing research and interviews.

Homer and I served a mission in West Virginia for the LDS church from November 1984 to May 1986. On our return, I started doing genealogy research professionally and established quite a clientele. Computers became an important way to store, organize and have a quick access to genealogy information, so I learned how to use the computer.

I knew that the computer would not only help with the genealogy research data, but also with our goal of writing the community history for New Liberty. I attended classes on how to write and publish histories. The

Phyllis working at Deseret Travel, 1971.
(Maluy Photo Collection)

Phyllis and Homer at the BYU Library, about 1980.
(Maluy Photo Collection)

process seemed so tedious and expensive. While the text was being typed, spaces had to be measured and saved for the pictures. The pictures had to be half-toned, before they could be glued to the text layout. A publisher then made a negative of the complete layout before it could be printed. I felt there must be a way that pictures and text could be combined in the computer. I looked into those possibilities and discovered with the right kind of computer, scanner, photo and computer publishing programs, it could be done. In 1992 I bought the first set of equipment and programs to accomplish this goal. With the help of Dennis and his son, Jared, I have learned how to use the computer and programs. I have started my own publishing company, Likes Publishing, and have published three books for clients in addition to this book. I have more waiting for this book to be completed. This book has been a great learning experience and one of much joy. Homer and I have communicated with so many people and received such wonderful response with stories and pictures. The trust everyone has had in sending their pictures has been overwhelming. The experience of publishing the book has been very stressful, but also very gratifying.

Homer and I are very proud of our children and grandchildren. See Homer Likes' history for a family picture and more information on Dennis and Retta-Marie.

Dennis married **Susan Mary Munzell,** 4 September 1971, a daughter of Peter James and Frances Marjorie Althoff Munzell. Dennis and Susan had seven children: **Jared Christopher, Jennifer Lynn, Denise Marie, Christina Louise, Joshua Clement, Justin Peter and John David.** John David died shortly after birth. They have three grandchildren.

Retta-Marie married **Alan David Clayburn** on 10 August 1968, a son of Theron and Cora Clayburn. Retta-Marie and Alan had two children: **Kimberli** and **Carl David.** That marriage ended in divorce and she married **Warren Francis Brandow III** on 16 May 1975, a son of Warren Francis II and Beverly Rose Brandow. Warren III already had three children: **Warren Francis IV "Butch," Kenneth William** and **Brian Patrick.** Retta-Marie and Warren had three children: **Lance Edward, Shauntai Marie** and **Benteen Darrell.** They have 11 grandchildren. Retta-Marie and Warren divorced in 1997.

Some of my memories of home and growing up in New Liberty:

I feel like I grew up in the perfect home and place. Our home was full of love, happiness, patience, positiveness, respect, trust, work, play, and harmony. When I think of New Liberty I think of serenity, security, brotherhood, fun, togetherness, cooperation, compassion, and love. We were one big family!

Our family worked hard together as a team. I can't remember any grumbling or complaining. We looked positively on work and knew our part was important. We also played hard together. Each one was an integral part of the family and took part. We sang, danced, played games, pulled pranks, told stories, joked, laughed and cried together. Mealtime was always a fun time — one of our favorite things was to get Daddy to tell the story about "Old Man Koothie's Pears." The story wasn't the important thing, it was how Daddy always got so tickled when he told it; he laughed till tears ran down his face. We also laughed with tears running down our faces and holding our stomachs. A laugh fest!

Another fun time at the table was when the Clem and Bill Maluy families had holiday dinners together. The adults and boys ate in the dining room and we girls ate in the kitchen — unsupervised. There was plenty of mischief and laughing going on. We looked forward to those times. Whenever we get together now, we still laugh and talk about those special times.

I idolized my brother Darrell, and would do anything to meet his approval. I was his bird dog while hunting, and cleaned the ducks he shot and the fish he caught. I was his ball catcher when he practiced pitching the hard baseball. No matter how hard he pitched I would clench my teeth and smile, even when he pitched faster and harder to see what I could take. I would even let him and his friends sleep in my bed when they came home on weekend visits from college. But he wasn't allowed to tease or mistreat my animals. This was one way he knew he could get my goat, but most of the time he treated me with love and respect — a typical brother!

The housekeeping responsibilities were divided up between we three girls. Even when I worked in the field I did my share in the house. I took sewing and cooking in 4-H and one of the assignments was to bake bread in the home for the family. I was working on the tractor in the fields west and east of the house at the time and would mix the dough before going to the field, and then return several times to punch the dough down two times, another time mold the dough into loaves in the pans, another put the bread in the oven, and then another to take the six loaves out and butter their tops. This was done with three different batches of bread over a week's time.

Being the middle girl I had a close and special relationship with both my sisters. I looked up to my older sister, and felt very flattered when included in many of her activities. I especially enjoyed tagging along on Marilyn's dates going to movies, ice skating on the neighbor's pond, or just going for a ride with a group in a car. Of course, some of these dates or activities Marilyn wouldn't have been able to go on if her little sister wasn't along to "chaperone." This worked also for me also when I took Bubbles, my little sister, with me. Marilyn was a good example for Bubbles and I in so many ways. She was obedient and respectful to her parents, was very loving, and lots of fun.

Bubbles and I did more things together, as we were closer in age. Since Bubbles was younger, I was always getting her into some adventure, such as using her to get permission from our mother to do things that I felt I couldn't get permission to do. But I also knew that I had to be careful because if anything happened to Bubbles, I was in big trouble. One time Bubbles was riding on back of a horse with me. We were going full speed across the yard when we came to the clothesline. I drove the horse under it and ducked under the wire. However Bubbles didn't see the wire and was pulled off the horse by her throat. Yes, I was in big trouble. Bubbles lived through this and many more adventures like it.

I loved animals and had a lot of different pets. One was a male bum lamb that Bubbles and I raised named "Lumma." He and I became the closest pals, and he followed me everywhere. Clem decided to keep him a buck so he grew to be very large and ornery. I was the only one who could handle him. I was continually being asked to save someone from him. One time I was in my bedroom and heard mother yelling from the back porch, "Phyllis, hurry! Come get your lamb." As I got closer I could hear a big thud. When I got to the porch I could see Frankie Berry plastered against the door outside. Frankie had come up the stairs and knocked on the door. Lumma saw him, ran up the stairs behind him, and butted him against the door. Then Lumma backed down the stairs, braced himself, charged back up the stairs, and butted him against the door again. Poor Frankie, he just stood there and screamed. Phyllis to the rescue!

One time Lumma followed me to school, but stopped off at Shires' corner. Mrs. Shires came out of the house with a dishpan full of water to dump in the irrigation ditch. The next thing she knew she and the dishpan had landed in the ditch of running water. Lumma had come up behind her and given her a big boost and then he stood there, daring her to

Bubbles, Phyllis and Marilyn with the family dogs and Lumma, the lamb.
(Maluy Photo Collection)

get out. I certainly heard about that one when I got home that evening.

My first experience I can remember on a horse was when I was two-and-a-half years old. Marilyn rode Queenie to visit the Bill Maluy cousins a mile away and took me along. I was sitting in the saddle and Marilyn was riding in back. When we got to their gate at the entrance of the driveway, it was closed. Marilyn got off the horse to open it and handed me the reins. I remember taking the reins and taking hold of the saddle horn as per instructions from Marilyn. She was busy opening the gate when Queenie decided to go home. Queenie turned and started galloping down the road and Marilyn couldn't catch her. As we galloped down the road with me hanging on for dear life and crying, I could see Uncle Bill running across the field to try to catch her. But he didn't make it. Then when we ran by the north end of our field, I could see Daddy running along the fence trying to catch her. The gate was closed at the entrance of our driveway and she stopped. Daddy was right there to comfort and rescue me. That was the beginning of my horse riding experiences.

I rode horses a lot, but Wilma, Norma and Bubbles didn't ride as much. One time I had Norma on the back of the horse with me. It had rained a few days before and the road had dried with big ruts in it from the cars and trucks. Norma had made the remark one time that she wished she had dimples. I started galloping the horse. Norma pulled her feet back into the horses flanks. The horse started bucking and Norma and I literally flew through the air. I landed on my bum a straddle one of the truck ruts and Norma landed on her face on the flat surface. She got her wish. She ended up with a dimple on her cheek from the injury. I ended up in surgery a year later to have my broken tail bone removed. At least her dimple can be seen — mine can't!

One of Daddy's closest friends was Don Weimer who had a farm just east of us. They were like brothers, and shared work and ideas with each other. Don and Jesse didn't have any children and they practically adopted me. Don always had a herd of riding horses that he used on Grand Mesa during the summer at a lodge for people to rent and ride. One summer he decided to keep a beautiful thoroughbred named Jimmy at home, and asked me to work with him and prepare him to enter the race in the fall festival at Fruita. I was so thrilled to have that beautiful horse for the summer! I rode him everyday as I herded the cows in the lower desert property just south of the corrals and fields.

I always rode bareback like an Indian as a saddle was too restrictive. I rode Jimmy in a big circle that had a ditch running through the center so that he jumped it twice when he went around the circle. At the end of the run, while going full speed, I turned him into the field entrance with a closed gate so he had to make a sudden stop on all fours. What a thrill! We did this over and over all afternoon.

When the time came for the big race, Daddy and Don decided that I wouldn't ride him, as it was too dangerous. They got one of the Haller boys to ride him. The Hallers had some of their horses in the race, also. I was very hurt and angry, after all, I had trained and prepared him for this big event! But the thing that really made me angry was that the person riding Jimmy held him back. He wasn't used to riding such a big, fast horse and appeared afraid or, as I felt, didn't want him to win. I stood on the sidelines "faunching at the bit" because I knew that if I had been riding him, he would have won. Of course! Don took Jimmy home after that and it wasn't two weeks before Jimmy foundered and died. My hopes of owning him were dashed!

Next year Dad bought me a horse I called Smokey. Right away it became obvious that he had ring bone on his right front ankle. Daddy and Don tried to treat him with something that would eat the damaged part away. But after horrible suffering for several weeks, Daddy had him put down. A year or so later he bought me a Morgan mare named Jenny from Ray Likes. She was a wonderful horse, very gentle and easy to train. I rode her herding the cows and began doing acrobatics on her. I stood on Jenny, frontwards, sideways and backwards and galloped across the desert. Jenny followed me like a puppy. I could get on her anywhere and ride her without a bridle.

I learned to drive the tractor and vehicles while quite young. By the time I was 12 years old I had experience driving the tractor and truck in the fields. When I was 14 I drove the truck on the road from one field to another. Once when I was about 15 I drove the truck on the back roads to Fruita to get something for Dad. I was trusted to drive the family car quite often by the time I was 15. We didn't worry about driver's licenses as long as we drove in the country on the dirt roads.

There were times when I proved I wasn't quite that trustworthy. One time I had been creasing the beans in the field across from the schoolhouse with the John Deere tractor. When I finished, I picked up Norma, Wilma and Bubbles at Uncle Bill's house to take them home with me. They were standing on the creaser bars on the back of the tractor. We were nearly to Laura Berry's driveway when we decided to go back to Uncle Bill's house for something. I attempted to turn the tractor at too high a speed and we ended up in the ditch on the side of the road. The ditch was full of water and mud so the back wheel sunk down and the tractor ended up laying on its side. Of course everyone was thrown off. It was a miracle someone wasn't hurt, but we were fine — I was scared and they were angry. We had to get Daddy to pull it out. Needless to say, he wasn't very happy.

Another time I was driving the Model "T" Ford that Daddy had bought for my use. A bunch of us had been swimming in the canal and decided to go for a ride. I had kids all over that car — inside, sitting on the front fenders and standing on the running boards. I couldn't see anything but the middle of the road. We came around a curve and right in front of us was a narrow bridge over a wash that I couldn't see. The kids in front started yelling to stop. When I finally did, the right front wheel was hanging over the edge of the beginning of the bridge and we were teetering. Miraculously, again, no one was hurt. Everyone gathered together and lifted the car while I put it in reverse. We got it back on the road and went on our merry way.

In the summertime we would have some large thunderstorms and lightning. There were several incidents with lightning. One time I was roller skating on the sidewalk in front of the steps to the back porch. All of a sudden I saw this big red ball of fire coming toward me, then going past me. Mother happened to be standing on the back porch and looking out the window. I ran up the stairs without any trouble on my skates, and yelled at Mother that someone had shot at me. She said, "No, that was lightning." She had seen it and a big puff of smoke on the sidewalk behind me. We looked at the sidewalk and there was a big black burned spot where it had struck. It had gone between me on my roller skates and the steel hand rods at the top of the stairs and struck cement. Miracles do happen!

Another time lightning struck Uncle Bill's house. He and Aunt Martha were sleeping on the screened in back porch. All of a sudden they heard this big bang and found themselves on the floor. Lightning had struck

the corner of the porch and pulled all the nails half way out of the wall from the roof to the ground, and moved their steel framed bed from the wall. They were stunned but OK.

Growing up in New Liberty one had such a sense of freedom. There was no fear of anything day or night. During the summer, we slept on the cistern top or the lawn under the beautiful sky of moon and stars. We listened to the crickets, the dogs barking at the coyotes' howling, and the train going through Mack. We mimicked the coyotes and they would howl back at us. We went for long walks at night, swam in the canal at night, and went watermelon swiping at night. No one in the community locked their doors. I doubt if anyone had a key.

Our parents never worried about us. Bubbles and I many times packed a lunch and left for a day tramping in the hills looking for rocks or some type of adventure. Then we would return sometime in the afternoon or evening. A bunch of us would go horseback riding all day, go swimming at Morrow's Hole day or night, or go into Mack (five miles) on foot, bicycle, or horse to get some candy and pop. When we weren't working in the field or house, we were as free as birds.

That doesn't mean there wasn't some kind of mischief, though! One time I drove Dad's flat bed truck to the swimming hole at night, and a group of us, including Norma and Wilma Maluy, Lewis and Wylie Sanders, Robert and Anna Belle Alstatt, Ralph Banning, Bubbles and I, went for a ride after the swim. We drove by Lupton's (the old Weir place) and noticed a large limb from one of his apple trees had broken off. So we loaded that limb full of apples on the truck bed and took off. We all had fun eating apples and laughing at what we had done. Then I delivered each person to their homes before going home. Maxwell Sanders was the country deputy sheriff. Mr. Lupton called him the next morning and reported that someone had stolen some of his apples. Maxwell and Mr. Lupton simply had to follow the trail of apples down the road to each person's home. Bubbles and I thought we had gotten off free, but they ended up on our doorstep, as they had been told we were the transportation providers. Yes, every parent backed Maxwell and Mr. Lupton up with some kind of punishment. Ours was a little more hard work.

We were very proud when Darrell, Dale and Rex entered the military during World War II. In those days people were very patriotic and it meant a great deal to have one of your family in the service of our country. They all three entered the Army Air Corps, and we all did our share to support them. We bought war bonds and did double duty at home to supply food and anything that the government needed to win the war. Sugar, tires and gas were the main things rationed. We had the advantage on gas, though. As a farmer, my dad had a large allotment, and we had free access to the 50-gallon barrels.

The community was deeply saddened when Lawrence Morrow, Delbert Slaugh, and Vernon Brandon lost their lives during the war. It made us all more determined to win the war.

Another tragedy in the community was when little Patricia Berry burned to death in the Berry family's chicken house. Laura was severely burned trying to rescue her. My parents took three month-old Reggie home and cared for him during the months that Laura was in the hospital. We had him until he was nearly a year old. We became very attached to him. My Dad always called him his "little fat fiddler." We took him to see Laura at the hospital regularly. I remember my turns. It was so difficult to see how badly she was burned and how sad it was that she couldn't hold Reggie, only look at him. Other families in the community helped with Frank, Anna Jane and Tom. They also had help from the farmers with their livestock and crops.

Yes, we felt and shared each others sorrows, joys, and accomplishments. We were one big family!

Lee Ann "Bubbles" Maluy, three years old.
(Maluy Photo Collection)

Lee Ann "Bubbles" was the last of the Clem Maluy children, the baby of the family. She was also born at home. Dr. White came out from Fruita and made the delivery. She was born with dark hair, very pretty, with a little pug nose and small mouth. Darrell said, "When I came in and saw her in the crib, I thought she was the prettiest little thing I'd ever seen," She became a platinum blonde when her new hair came in. Bubbles was very sweet and shy, not adventurous like her siblings. She was called Bubbles because, as a baby, she blew bubbles with her saliva as a pastime. Evelyn Bush, who was working for Mary, gave her the name, and it stuck. She is still known mainly by Bubbles.

Bubbles entered New Liberty School in 1939. She skipped the second grade. As she became older she overcame most of her shyness. She was talented in singing, dancing and comedy. She sang leads in the operetta put on in grade school by her teacher, Mrs. Brenton. She also sang and yodeled at the New Liberty Community Club. Phyllis just knew Bubbles was going to be a movie star someday — then Phyllis could be her agent and promoter. Phyllis made that remark to her cousins one day, and Wilma's retort was, "She can't be a movie star

Lee Ann "Bubbles" Maluy, sweet sixteen.
(Maluy Photo Collection)

because she has a crooked finger." Phyllis said it could be fixed and she'd be a movie star. When Bubbles was a baby, she stuck her index finger in the car door and when it was closed, her finger was crushed. It healed crooked and she can only bend it halfway.

By 1943, Darrell and Marilyn had left home, leaving Phyllis and Mary to work in the fields quite often and Bubbles responsible for the house cleaning and cooking. Being the baby of the family backfired. She was only 10 years old, but did remarkably

well. After the war was over in 1945, Marilyn and Charlie and Darrell and Beverly came home, and Bubbles was relieved of those duties. Then Phyllis married and left home. Bubbles then got the attention and opportunities afforded the baby of the family and the only child at home.

Bubbles graduated from eighth grade in May 1946 as salutatorian and entered Fruita Union High School that fall. During high school she had lead roles in plays and played GAA (Girl's Athletic Association) sports. Also during that time, she and cousin Norma were charter members of the Rainbow Girls when it was first organized in Fruita. Rainbow Girls is a young girls' organization sponsored by the Masons and Eastern Star. Norma was the first Worthy Advisor; later Bubbles became Worthy Advisor, then Grand Nature, an officer in the state chapter. In this calling she gave speeches at all the chapters in Colorado.

Bubbles graduated from high school in 1950. She was the only one of the three girls to go to college after high school. She attended Mesa Junior College and finished a one year business course. During the first two quarters she lived with Phyllis Muhr at her Aunt Reba DaLee's. The last quarter she stayed at home and drove back and forth with Dale Cutler.

In the summer of 1951 she began employment as a teller with Mesa Federal Savings and Loan Association, when it was on Main Street.

Buddy Raymond and Lee Ann Maluy Blaney
(Maluy Photo Collection)

Brett Michael Blaney

Brook Sean Blaney

(Maluy Photo Collection)

557

She was later promoted to loan officer.

Lee Ann married **Buddy Raymond "Bud" Blaney** 7 November 1954, in Grand Junction. Bud was born 19 June 1929, a son of Raymond John and Jennie D. Hatch Blaney. He grew up in Grand Junction and attended Emerson Elementary School. He graduated from Grand Junction High School in 1947 and attended Mesa Junior College for two years. He played baseball and football for the college.

Bud and Lee Ann had two children:

Brett Michael, born 24 October 1961, in Grand Junction
Brook Sean, 13 February 1969, Grand Junction

Lee Ann's career ended at Mesa Federal in 1961 when Brett was born. The next year she did bookkeeping at home for Sigma Mining Company, which was owned by her brother, Darrell, and David Sigismund.

Bud started Bud's Custom Shop, a custom auto body business, in 1952. Bud and Lee Ann purchased a large piece of land on 28 Road, where K-Mart is now. Bud built a large facility for the body business and moved the Smoke Shack building from North Avenue over next to it. The Smoke Shack was a landmark which was owned by Lloyd Files. Bud and Lee Ann remodeled the building and re-opened the Smoke Shack business. Two years later all of the properties were sold to Dave Perry.

In 1960 Bud studied insurance law and became an insurance claims adjuster for McMillan Claim Service and Lee Ann began investing in rental income real estate. Bud worked until 1971 as an adjuster, he then began working for Western Slope Auto Company as a sales representative.

Bud retired from Western Slope Auto Company in 1978 and he and Lee Ann started Busy B's Balloon & Novelty Company out of their home. They were the first people on the Western Slope to do balloon bouquets. Brett joined the business in 1982, at which time the advertising specialties part of the business was added under the name of Impact Promotional Products. The business was then moved into Solarus Square on North Avenue.

Black Sunday came in 1984 when Exxon pulled out and deserted the Oil Shale Project, at Parachute, which put the entire Western Slope into a black depression. The business no longer could support two families and Brett was forced to start another profession. The business was moved to 904 North Avenue for cheaper rent. As the economy began to change, the business began to grow and in-house apparel screen printing and computer embroidery were added. Marilyn Pacheco, Lee Ann's sister, was employed to take charge of the embroidery. Brook, the second son, came on board when he was in high school and is with the business at this time.

In 1984 Bud and Lee Ann bought the building on 904 North Avenue. In 1994 they sold it and bought a larger building at 407 Glenwood Avenue where the business is now located. The

Buddy Raymond and Lee Ann Maluy Blaney
(Maluy Photo Collection)

558

business has grown to nine employees. Their rental income properties have accumulated to 10 properties including duplexes, apartment buildings and single family dwellings.

Lee Ann has done many things besides these businesses. She designed and manufactured costumes for "Grease Monkey" franchises all over the United States. She opened a studio for Mark Wahlberg who is now a renowned sculptor in Hollywood. She and Mark designed a Denver Bronco mask in 1982, which was licensed by the NFL to manufacture and sell.

She and Bud were active in the Jaycees and Jayceettes in the first years of their marriage. Bud became acting Jaycee president and Lee Ann became Jayceette president. Bud was well known as a catcher in softball in Grand Junction. He played in two World Tournaments in Salt Lake and Phoenix. They were very active in Little League when their sons were playing. Bud and Lee Ann have lived in the same home since their marriage, but due to numerous remodeling projects, the home looks very little like it did when they bought it.

Bubbles deserves great credit for the love,

devotion and care she gave her Mom and Auntie Claire, Bud's dad, Uncle Sam and Aunt Bertha in their later years. She devoted 20 years in caring for them along with raising two sons that were very active in sports, caring for a husband that was ill part of the time, running a business and managing rental property. Since Marilyn and Phyllis lived out-of-state, they were only able to help periodically.

Brett played Little League baseball while growing up and continued to play baseball in high school. He was chosen All State first baseman. He continues to play ball and manages a traveling tournament softball team sponsored by Impact Promotional. He was also an excellent boxer and boxed Golden Gloves. He later trained a team, which included his brother, Brook, and took them to a Golden Gloves Tournament in Salt Lake City.

Brett married **Jennifer Chandler** 28 November 1980 in Grand Junction. They have two children, **Sean Michael** and **Meghan Lee Ann**.

Brett worked as a district manager for Campbell's Food Company and earned a national award. He is now in retail delivery for Meadow Gold Dairy.

Brook followed his big brother in sports. He also played Little League baseball and boxed in Golden Gloves. Brook is a people person. He joined the Grand Junction Jaycees and became the youngest Jaycee president in the nation at 20 years old. He also received the highest possible national award from the United States Jaycee president. Brook then became the youngest Exalted Ruler in the nation for the Elks Club at age 25. He is also a member of the Kiwanis Club.

Brook and Shonna's wedding.. L-R: Sean , Jennifer, Brett Blaney, Shonna Martin and Brook Blaney, Lee Ann and Bud Blaney. Meghan Blaney is in front. *(Photo courtesy of Lee Ann Blaney)*

Brook married **Shonna Martin** 7 November 1994, in Redstone, Colorado, on Bud and Lee Ann's 40th Anniversary and Shonna's parent's 25th Anniversary. Brook works with Lee Ann at Impact Promotional Products.

Following are some of Bubbles' memories of life in New Liberty.

I made my first appearance in this community on 20 February 1933. Old Doc White made the long trip out from Fruita for the big delivery. I was born to Clem and Mary Maluy and became part of a brood of four children. Darrell, the oldest, was tall, blonde, and good looking; he won my admiration immediately. I always thought of him as a big strong Danish Viking (our grandmother came from Denmark) who was out to conquer the world. He was serious and intense, yet had a wee bit of Irish orneriness and humor that made him really interesting. The second sibling, my oldest sister, Marilyn, had "fiery' red hair and a happy, happy, happy disposition. She and Mom were always smooching and loving me. She made me feel like the world was made just for me and I gained a lot of confidence from that. The third sibling, my sister with the golden hair, Phyllis, the head strong, adventurous one, became my buddy and playmate. She was responsible for any courage I might have gained as I went through life. My experiences in life were certainly broadened through my relationship. Nothing was impossible!

I'll never forget the old homestead shack. One bedroom with three regular beds and a crib for me. There was a big trunk and a rod, which held our measly wardrobe.

The dining/living room barely had room enough to hold the big round table and eight chairs, with the kerosene lamp in the middle, and Mom's piano, which she had shipped from Kansas. Mom played the piano in the evenings and we all sang. Grandpa Maluy used to say, "Mary, you just make that piano dance." Mom and Dad harmonized, "When you wore a tulip, a sweet yellow tulip, and I wore a big red rose." They could really sing nice together. They were a real pair. They had so much love for each other and that love was given in abundance

to us children.

Our small kitchen contained an old wood/coal cook stove, cupboards and a sink with a pump to draw water from the old cistern, which we filled with ditch water. Our baths were taken in the old tin tub in the middle of the floor of that tiny kitchen. Off the kitchen was the porch that held the cream separator and ice box. From the porch we entered an old dirt cellar under the house that was used for food storage and our winter play room. We used to build roads along the sides of the dirt walls, using empty thread spools and film spools for cars. Sometimes they were small blocks of wood.

Dad and Mom were hard workers and good business people. Some good bean crops and some wise decisions regarding the marketing of beans, afforded them the opportunity to build a new house in 1936/7. I'll never forget when we moved to the new house, — wow! — inside amenities, lots of space and electricity!

Uncle Bill, Dad's brother, and his family lived just a quarter of a mile away. We spent much of our time with his children, Dale, Rex, Patty, Wilma, and Norma. Oscar and Laura Berry between our Maluy farms, and the Berry kids were most always involved in whatever the Maluy kids had going. I remember the time we were all dying to go skating on Uncle Bill's pond and it was questionable whether or not it was solid enough to get on.

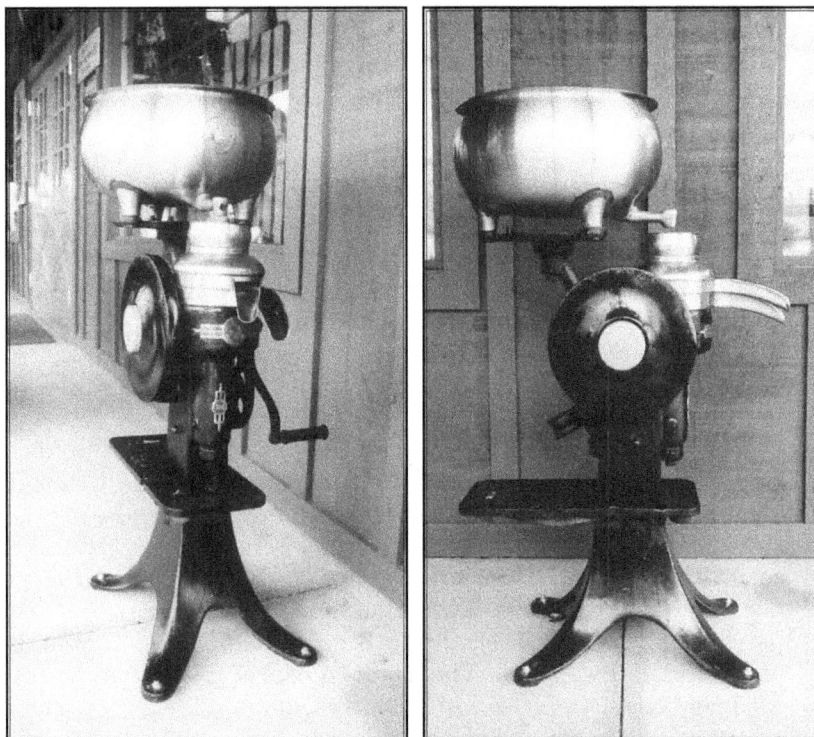

A cream separator somewhat like the one used on the farm.
(Photo by Phyllis Likes)

So, since I was the smallest, the big kids sent me out on it to test it. I got out in the middle and the ice gave way, and away I went into the ice cold water. Fortunately the pond was low and they were able to get me out before I froze or drowned. But I lost my shoes in the thick, black mud at the bottom of the pond. Believe me, shoes were a luxury in those days. The big kids had a lot of explaining to do as to why my shoes and I were out in the middle of the pond, especially since I was only four years old.

The two Maluy families always worked together to get their crops harvested. One year Uncle Bill raised a crop of red clover. The rains came after he cut it and it was covered with black mildew. At the time, Phyllis was diving the team of horses on the stacker, and Willma, Norma, and I were driving the horse-drawn wagon loads of clover. By the end of the day our faces were black as coal — all you could see was our white eyeballs and teeth. We were bringing in our last loads when Wilma hollered, "Race you!" The race was on. Dude and Dime were pulling Wilma's wagon and Jerry, our mule, and Bolo were pulling mine. We were nip and tuck all the way until we reached Shires' bridge. The bridge was a little too narrow for two wagons and Wilma's wheel slipped off the edge of the bridge. The wagon and the whole load were dumped into the deep drainage ditch below. Thank goodness Wilma wasn't hurt. When Uncle Bill arrived on the scene, all you could see was great big eyes peering out of black faces — no smiles — no white teeth. We knew we were in trouble.

Don Weimer, our neighbor, whom we kids loved dearly, called me his little "swamp chicken." He brought me a little runt pig. It had scabies on its skin and was nearly starved to death. Don said that if I could save the pig's life, I could have him. I bathed him in boric acid water, fed him with a little doll bottle, getting up two or three times a night and all day long. I doctored him, fed him and gave him lots of love. He grew up to be a great big fat red hog. I named him Henry. He and I were great buddies. He would allow me to ride on his back all over the corral. One sad, black day I came home from school, and as I turned into the gate of the driveway, I saw something hanging from the scaffolding Dad used to hang the carcasses of animals on when he was butchering. There hung Henry, dead and skinned. I was broken hearted! Of course, we knew when we raised pigs, calves, lambs or any kind of fowl, what the end result was going to be. Either they would be sold or used

for food on the table. We couldn't afford to feed these critters until they died of old age. However, I mourned the loss of Henry. I had a real hard time forgiving Dad, and believe me, I did not eat any of that pork.

The year we had the large herd of turkeys, we were having a lot of losses to coyotes. The turkeys roosted at night just west of a tall shelter Dad built out of tall timbers that were erected in a big square, and covered with wire stuffed with straw. It made a great shelter and a neat place for a sleepover. Dad had planned to keep a vigil for a few nights to see if he could possibly get that coyote. He allowed me to go with him. We waited quietly on top of the shed, Dad with his loaded gun and me with the big spotlight. Two nights had passed and on the third night the turkeys started rustling and making noises. Dad pulled the gun at an aim and I quickly turned the spotlight down on the herd. Just as luck would have it, the spotlight happened to shine right on the coyote. Dad pulled the trigger and got him! What excitement! Dad grabbed me and gave me a big hug, "Great job Partner." Sometime in my younger years Dad nicknamed me "Partner." Maybe that's when it started. Dad had a nickname for all of us, Darrell, "Dairdo," Marilyn, "Marnie," Phyllis, "Phiddy" or "Phlits" and mine was "Partner."

During World War II, all of the young men had been called to service. That left the girls and women to help in the fields, as there were no men to hire. Darrell was in the Air Corps and Marilyn was working in the shipyards in California. Mon and Phyllis helped Dad in the fields, and I took over the housekeeping and cooking duties. Phyllis was 13 and I was 10. My poor family! Everyday I cooked the same for noon meal. I hooked a chicken, cut its head off, dipped it in hot water, plucked and cleaned it and cut it up and fried it. I peeled, boiled, and whipped potatoes, made gravy from the chicken drippings, gathered and cooked vegetables from the garden, made homemade ice cream from the wonderful fresh cream and milk and froze the ice cream in the trays in the refrigerator — same thing everyday, everyday. They never complained!

One day Norma, Wilma, Phyllis and I were walking back to Uncle Bill's house from our house. We always crossed through Laura Berry's yard to get there. Laura had been flooding her grape vines and in the process had flooded our normal path. Unfortunately,

1939, Marilyn, Patty, Wilma, Phyllis and Norma Maluy, Georgia Wallace, Mary Warner and Lee Ann Maluy. *(Maluy Photo Collection)*

1941, the new Schwinn. Marilyn, Phyllis and Lee Ann with the family dogs. *(Maluy Photo Collection)*

Laura's strawberry plants happened to be there. Now understand, we girls loved Laura, and she was always so good natured. However, upon seeing her strawberries being trampled, she felt it only right to give us a little scolding. Well, we had never been scolded by Laura. After the scolding and we were on our way, we overheard her say, "Sure hope it doesn't rain." You know kids — that was all we needed. We decided to do an Indian rain dance. The sky definitely had dark clouds, but didn't look all that threatening. We proceeded with our dance. We danced around in a circle, making all the noises and gyrations we had seen on the Tom Mix shows. Round and round we danced, the Apaches couldn't have done it better. Suddenly the wind started blowing, the thunder and lightning began to crack and flash. Then the rain began to come down in torrents. The sky just opened up!

We all shed our muddy shoes on the 18 inch high cistern top in front of Uncle Bill's house. At the same time, Marilyn and Mom were at our house trying to keep the windows intact in the dining room. The wind was literally blowing the frames right out of the walls. Dad was zapped by lightning while on his tractor up on the north forty. He didn't get hurt badly. He commented how, "It felt like someone had hit him over the head with a sledge hammer." We stood on the porch watching all this in amazement, when all of a sudden we noticed our shoes floating off the cistern top and into the swirling flood of water. Later, we finally found my shoes about three quarters of a mile away on Art Harrison's place. Now, I'm quite

sure the storm would have occurred without our rain dance, but you couldn't have convinced us at that time. We all made a pact to never do rain dances again.

In 1941, Marilyn, Phyllis and I raised bum lambs to sell, cleaned the separator room for 5 cents each time, and any other job we could do to raise money so we could buy a bicycle. Phyllis kept track of her hours in the field and received 5 cents an hour. That fall the great day finally came when we had enough money saved up. We bought a beautiful blue and white, big balloon-tired Schwinn. We were so proud of it and ourselves. The bicycle took us on many adventures.

Uncle Bill brought Martha Potzner from Kansas, with her children, Audie and Joan Marie "Jody," to keep house and care for his children. We decided to show Jody the swimming hole at the canal, a mile from Uncle Bill's house. Jody had a beautiful, big racing bike with the large narrow tires. Jody took Wilma on her bike and Phyllis took me on our balloon tired Schwinn. I'll never forget the ride home! We took off at the same time. Every time Jody pumped, those big tires would cover twice as much territory as our Schwinn balloons. Phyllis was a fierce competitor. She just pumped twice as hard. We were flying down the road neck and neck. We came to a place where the two roads came together, hit some loose gravel and our bike flew out from under us. We slid down the road, me on my knee. Phyllis got up and demanded I get back on the bike as we were going to catch them and win. My retort, "We can never catch up with them!" Phyllis, not willing to give up the race to the new girl on the block said, "Just stop bawling and get on the bike. You never know, they might have a wreck and we can still beat 'em!" The next thing I knew we were sailing down the road in pursuit, me with my injured knee, blood running down my leg and my mouth wide open bawling, and Phyllis with jaw set in determination, pumping frantically, the sweat running down her red, determined face. They didn't wreck and needless to say we didn't win. I can't remember, but I'll bet Phyllis challenged them to a rematch.

I guess I feel like I am probably the luckiest person in the world to have been born to two of the greatest parents anyone could ever have and to have been raised in a loving, happy family. The frosting on the cake was to have been raised in the little community of New Liberty. I can still smell the fresh new mown hay, hear the crickets and frogs, see the bright stars and moon in the sky when Phyllis and I slept out on the old cistern in the summertime. We had no fears of anything or anyone; we didn't even own a key to lock our doors. The people in the community, ah, the salt of the earth — the friendship, the comradery, the caring and support in times of need or sorrow. It was just a special place in time that I hold in my heart and wish I could pass on to my children and grandchildren.

I took my grandchildren, Sean and Meghan, out to see the old school building awhile back. The new owners generously took their time to show us around and let us just take our time remembering and being nostalgic. The old cinder filled playground was still the same — I could just see us kids playing pump pump pullaway, softball and football. I recalled that during the war, zippers weren't available because of the shortness of metal. Jeans had little spindly snaps to hold them together. Norma Maluy and I were playing football with the big boys, Wylie and Lewis Sanders were among them. We were in the heat of the competition when Wylie tackled Norma. The snaps gave way and so did the britches. Poor Norma tried to limp off the field with her jeans around her ankles. However, we discovered, she not only had lost

her drawers, but had broken her leg.

The merry-go-round is gone, along with the two old outhouses that we all trudged to through the snow, sleet, and hail. The old swing set with the slippery slide, rings, bars, teeter totter (see-saw, margery daw) and three swings are still there. I will never forget when Charlotte Brayton was hit by one of the swings and received a large hole in her forehead. We all stood in horror as the blood literally poured from the wound. The old cistern is still there. That's where Roy Homedew and I had the fight of the century. I still bear the scar on my knee to prove it. He was chasing me and trying to kiss me when I suddenly turned on him and gave him a big punch in the stomach. I knocked the wind out of him which scared us all to death. When he came around, he kept his temper enough to give me a big shove, and I landed on the cistern top and handily cut my knee. Roy and I were grounded to the classroom (together) for a week.

As my grandchildren and I entered the building, I couldn't help but think how many times I had stood in line, in front of the big double doors, while the teacher rang the bell. This brought to mind the time that Phyllis and I had walked to school as usual, without the knowledge that our lamb, Lumma, had followed us. It was time for the bell to ring. Mrs. Mowrer appeared at the door and began ringing the old hand-held brass bell. We all began lining up, when suddenly old Lumma came from out of nowhere behind Mrs. Mowrer and sent her, bell and all, sprawling and rolling. Bless her heart, she got up, dusted herself off and informed the open-mouthed crowd that "whoever owned that blankety-blank sheep had better have it off of that school ground — and now!!!!" All you could see on Phyllis and my faces was white skin and eyeballs. Well, we could see that Lumma had worn out his welcome, so Phyllis made sure he found his way home.

I remember how Norma, my cousin, and I got bored one day because our teacher had fallen asleep during poem recitals. We jumped out the open window, with the help and encouragement of our classmates, took a spin around the two-mile block on our Schwinn, made our re-entry through the window, woke up the teacher and class resumed. She never knew! Zella Sanders was our teacher at the time, one of the finest, hardest working women in the community. At this particular time, she was trying to get the yearly canning done at night. Her hubby's back was on the bum so she had to help the boys with the milking and feeding the stock, get breakfast, then get cleaned up and ready to face the day trying to teach four different grades of hearty farm kids. Of course, we hated to miss poem recital, but we figured she really did deserve a nap!

There were hundreds of memories as we walked through the building. We entered the old kitchen. I could still see Mrs. Morrow and Mrs. Swyhart serving up those wonderful hot lunches, and the wrath of Mrs. Morrow because I wouldn't eat the sauerkraut — missed a couple of noon recesses because of that.

The big kids, my sisters, cousins and whoever else they could get to join us, were always playing school in the summertime and I got to be one of the students. That is probably the reason when I started to school I knew about all that was usually learned in the first grade. In the first grade I got my work done and then did the second graders' work. Mrs. Jerome, my first and second grade teacher, who I thought was the most beautiful lady in the world, pushed me past the third grade into the fourth grade. Of course, this didn't hurt my feelings. I joined up with Orlenc Corn (my best friend through the elementary years), Walter Pollock, Dale Cutler, Roy Homedew, Thelma Burkett, Ray and Phyllis Van Riper. Dickie Stutsman joined our class during the winter. He came to live with Orlene Corn's family. Marilyn used to love to hear me say Walter's name when my two front teeth were missing. I had a real eye for Walter. However, when Mr. Stutsman came on the scene, I thought he was just about the "cat's pajamas."

Eugene Thomas joined our class later. He had lost a year because of a bone infection in his hip, and spent a great deal of time in the Denver Children's Hospital. We loved having Eugene in our class, except he was smarter than the rest of us. He was always acing me out in the spelling contests. He and I made it up through the ranks to get to the Mesa County contest — he beat me out by one word. He came in first, and I came in second.

Since I skipped the third grade, I had Irene Gosnell for the fourth; Catherine Mowrer the fifth; Zella Sanders the sixth; Mary Katherine Bauman the seventh; and Hazel Ward, Beverly Maluy and Lewis Likes for the eighth. Miss Bauman was a young lady from Palisade, She was a good teacher, but I sometimes think we took advantage of her youthfulness. One time Betty Likes, from California, was visiting her grandparents, Clyde and Retta Likes. She went to school with me one day and our whole class was showing off for our visitor — getting completely out of hand. In desperation Miss Bauman made one of the boys go out to the drainage ditch across the road and cut her a big willow switch. She proceeded to whack each one of us with the switch, including Betty. Betty's eyes got big and she said, "I can't believe this, I never have been spanked or whipped once in the California schools. I visit one day in Colorado and I get whipped with a switch." In my eighth grade, Mrs. Ward started the school year, but became ill and had to quit. Beverly Maluy, my brother's wife, who I was very close to, taught for the next seven months. Beverly was very intelligent and we learned a lot from her. Lewis Likes taught the last two months of that school year. He was an excellent teacher.

When it came time for the eighth grade graduation, Eugene aced me out again. He got to be valedictorian and I was salutatorian. Seems like I was always coming in second.

Our graduation ceremony was as follows:

America . . . . Congregation

Processional . . . . Mrs. C. Maluy

Invocation . . . . The Rev. C. W. Likes

Salutatorian . . . . Lee Ann Maluy

Class History . . . . Orlene Mae Corn

Reading — " Johnny's History Lesson"
                Thelma Loraine Burkett

Class Prophesy . . . . Walter Pollock

Class Wishing Well . . . .
                Roy Leslie Homedew

Class Will . . . . Hobart Dale Cutler

Valedictory Address . . . .
                Hubert Eugene Thomas

Speaker . . . . Mr. Roland Powell

Presentation of Class to School Board
                Lewis D. Likes

Presentation of Diplomas . . . .
                Mr. A. W. Alstatt

Benediction . . . . The Rev. C. W. Likes

(Above and below) Bubbles Maluy during her performance of "Rag Mop." (Upper right) 1946, the New Liberty eighth grade Sneak Day. L-R: Roy Homedew, Walter Pollock, Orlene Corn, Bubbles Maluy, and Eugene Thomas. (Right) Miss Mary Katherine Bauman, New Liberty School teacher for the school year 1944/45, standing in front of the New Liberty Teacherage. (Below right) The queens chosen to represent the local communities in the Highway 6&50 celebration in about 1950. Standing L-R: Charlene Jones, Mack; Patricia Anderson, Star; and Billy Jean Evans, Loma. Seated: Betty Borland, Appleton; Jean Ann Naeve, Enterprise; and Lee Ann Maluy, New Liberty. Seated on the ground: Connie Morgan Hunter. *(Photos courtesy of Lee Ann "Bubbles" Maluy Blaney)*

All kinds of memories came to mind when we entered the gym. The wonderful hardwood floor that now lay in pieces readying for the new cement floor. I took a piece of the floor home with me. The gym was the heart of our community. It held all of the wonderful monthly Community Club's night activities when different people were responsible for entertainment: reciting, singing, dancing, and playing their favorite instruments. It didn't matter if they were good or not, they received a hearty applause. Mae Sanders could sing really well and so could our mom, Mary Maluy. Mom could also play the piano quite well and Mae the mandolin. Mom and Mae entertained quite often and they sang at almost every funeral.

Some great Christmas programs were performed on that stage through the years. However, the greatest production that ever had to be was the operetta Mrs. Brenton, the teacher at the time, produced and directed. She was such a knowledgeable and talented musician. She later became the music director for Grand Junction High School. What we may have lacked in talent, she made up for in knowledge.

I got to have a solo part in the operetta, as did Walter Pollock and my sister, Phyllis. Just before the performance Mrs. Brenton told us, "During the operetta, no one is to touch or put their hands near their faces." Probably so there wouldn't be any nose picking. Well, while I am chortling away, "Too witt, too wee, too witt, too wee, the little bird sang from the top of the tree," I could hear my dear sister, Marilyn, laughing so hard she was doubling over. I couldn't imagine what could be so funny about my song. She was almost rolling in the aisles. I looked around and there was Dow Pittman with a great big fly on his face. He took the teacher at her word. Believe me, he was not putting his hands anywhere near his face! The fly crawled around his nostril, down his cheek to his chin, back over his lips, over his nose and back up to his forehead. Dow skewed his nose around and around, crossed and rolled his eyes every direction following the journey of that fly. But the hands never came near his face! The fly was relentless and kept on exploring. By this time Dow's eyes were watering and his whole face had become a mass of wriggling and twitching and the fly kept on exploring! But the hands never came near his face. Such discipline! I so often think that Dow should have received some kind of a special award for following the teacher's

directions — or for the "Best Performance" anyway. He certainly was the star of the show at that moment. Dow was a great guy and one of the smarter kids in school. He definitely knew how to follow instructions.

When the new Highway 6&50 was built between Fruita and Grand Junction in about 1950, a big celebration was held in Fruita. Each of the surrounding communities, New Liberty, Mack, Loma, Star, Enterprise, Rhone, Hunter, etc., were to supply a candidate for queen. I was chosen by the Sorosis Club to represent New Liberty as their queen candidate. I was lucky and made it to the final four. Then I'll be darned if Jean Naeve didn't ace me out with that beautiful smile of hers and again I came in second. That's me — always the bridesmaid and never the bride. Oh, yes, I did get to be lead singer with the New Liberty Hot Pots Band.

Now there was a famous group! Band members included Mae Sanders on the vacuum hose; Nita Rector on the comb; Bessie Phillips on the gas funnel; Mary Maluy, my mom, on the bass viol (made of a broom stick connected to a # 3 tub with a wire running from the top of the broomstick to the tub); Agnes Overbye on the eggbeater; and I got to play the bucket, pots and lids (drums). Laurene Wells was our piano player. I have a feeling that without her talent we might not have succeeded. I did my "Rag Mop" rendition and my Elvis Presley impersonation while Mae Sanders and Mother harmonized in the background. Mae Sanders would recite some of her homespun poetry; and the band played on. A real professional production! Believe it or not, we won first place in the big Fruita Talent Show. We were asked to entertain at a number of functions after that. Phyllis, my sister, was added with the washboard and a hot pan, and she and I did our "I Love You Truly" song and dance. We had a great time! The band went on for two or three years and different people participated.

Reverend Clyde Likes, Al Alstatt and Charlie Brayton were responsible for the opportunity everyone had to go to church and Sunday School every Sunday in the gym. When crops were harvested and winter came, it was time to start having the Saturday night dances. Most of the families in the community would be there, kids and all, along with many people from miles around. Great Adults and kids alike danced to some of the hottest fiddlin' and guitar pickin' around. Most of it was local talent. The room reeled with the fox trot, two step, waltz, polka,

Virginia Reel, and a lot of square dancing. The Sorosis Club served a scrumptious meal at midnight. The kids would then start curling up in their respective quilts and coats on the stage and the adults would continue to dance, sometimes until time to start morning chores.

Joe and Sue Thompson joined our community in 1946, along with their daughters, Becky and Virginia. Sue had taken a teaching position at New Liberty School and they lived in the teacherage just north of the school. The girls and I became acquainted and we had a great time. Becky and I had both just received our drivers licenses. We kept the Fruita highway hot driving her folks old green Lincoln (Becky always said it was held together with bubble gum and baling wire) or my folks' old 1939 Dodge. Becky and Peggy Hayes were my very best friends my last two years of high school.

After we left the schoolhouse, I took my grandchildren to see the old swimming hole in the canal by John Morrow's old place. In the spring before the water came down we sometimes gathered together with shovels and dug out a big hole in the canal so there was a

In front: Bubbles Maluy and Becky Thompson in the hallway of Fruita Union High School, about 1950.
(Photo courtesy of Lee Ann "Bubbles" Maluy Blaney)

place deep enough to dive. This was much to the chagrin of Ed Sisler, the ditch rider. None of us had a chance to take swimming lessons, for a matter of fact, we never heard of such a thing. The way I learned to swim was Marilyn threw me in the canal to sink or swim. I paddled for dear life until I reached the shore.

There are so many great memories they are too numerous to tell. The 4th of July celebrations at the school when everyone ate more homemade ice cream than they should. The winters when we went sledding and tubing on Banning's or Hollinger's hill. Seems like we had a lot more snow then than now. Phyllis and I would walk to school in the snow and it seems like it was an everyday occurrence for the teacher to have to get buckets of tepid water for us to put our frozen fee in. Even though Mom and Dad bundled us like we were going to the arctic. We wore good old long underwear with those horrible ugly, long brown socks over them that were held up by a very attractive garter harness and of course, our black boots. Can't tell you how many times we shed the harness, rolled the socks down and rolled the underwear up after we left the house.

Though there was lots of happiness and fun, there were the trying and sad times also. Times when the farmers lost their whole years' work when the weather either destroyed the crop or it stormed so they couldn't harvest it. There were illnesses and losses of loved ones and friends. Uncle Bill lost his wife Clara to an illness, and his little boy, Jackie, to whooping cough. Uncle Bill was left to raise his five children without their mother. During the war the young men had to leave the community to go to the service; Morrow's lost their son, Lawrence. Clyde and Ruby Likes lost their son, Billy, in the polio epidemic. Laura Berry lost her little girl, Patty, and was severely burned herself. Then her husband, Oscar, died of a heart attack and Frankie, her oldest son, was killed in a truck accident. She was always so thankful to still have Tom, Anna Jane and Reggie. Laura's courage, strength and sweetness has been a tremendous inspiration to me in living my life.

We were so devastated when our Dad lost his life due to a hay baler explosion and he was burned over 65% of his body. He lived only six weeks. The excruciating pain he endured with so little complaint. My Dad, a man with courage, integrity and tenacity and so much love and kindness for his family and friends. I shall cherish him always and regret that my children and grandchildren never got to know him.

Our Mom, Mary, was with us until she reached the age of 95. Our Rock of Gibraltar, a great gal and a great parent. I was lucky enough to get to spend lots of time with her in her retired years. Mom was very competitive. She and I played lots of golf and bridge together. She was an excellent bowler and won lots of tournaments. Her sister, our Auntie Claire, lived to be nearly 100. She lived close to Mom and I in Grand Junction, so we spent a lot of time together. We had some real hot three handed bridge games. We miss all of them so very much.

One of the most important things I feel I accomplished in my life was the care of my Mom, Auntie Claire and Bud's Dad, "Speck" Blaney, in their later years. They had all expressed the wish that they not be put in a nursing home. I was able to see that they had care and were able to remain in their homes.

Our most rewarding experience has been raising our two sons and watching them grow into wonderful, responsible men. They both married lovely young ladies. And of course, the greatest experience and blessing is loving our two grand children, Sean and Meghan.

This book is such a tribute to all of the people who had the courage, ambition and tenacity to withstand all the hardships that came with homesteading in this little community. I would personally like to pay a special tribute to Phyllis and Homer Likes for their courage in writing this wonderful history book. The time they have devoted, the traveling, phone calls and money spent can never be repaid monetarily. I salute them and thank them. I just wish all of the old pioneers (especially their parents) could be here to enjoy it.

William Benedict Maluy, 1919.
(Maluy Photo Collection)

William "Bill" Benedict Maluy was born 20 May 1890 near Hanover, Washington, Kansas. He lived with his father on the Maluy farm near Hanover until he was about age 20 and then he went away from home to find work. He was in California in 1910, shortly after his sister Mae married and moved out there. Bill played professional baseball in Sacramento for awhile. He had played in Hanover before leaving home. He played the position of catcher and his hands got so badly battered he had to quit.

For the next few years he traveled all over the western United States riding the freight trains to various destinations. He worked in the grain harvest, following that into Montana and Canada. He came home in 1916 and helped his father farm that summer and fall. Clem, his brother, and Clem's new wife, Mary, and Bill's youngest brother, Tom, came home. Addie, his sister would visit often from Marysville.

568

Mary told Phyllis about some of the fun times the family had together on the farm. They were always pulling pranks on one another, having water fights, evenings of singing, etc. Bill had a nice horse and buggy that he was very proud of. He was dating a young girl five miles south of the farm, and was to pick her up at 5 p.m. to bring her to a dance . He was a person that was very punctual. He had groomed his horse and shined his buggy and came in to bath and get ready by about three o'clock. Mary and Addie decided they would pull a prank on him to get even with one he had pulled on them. They replaced the shampoo in the bottle with syrup. They heard him yelling all kinds of words from the wash room, but he couldn't do anything to them, as he wasn't dressed. When he did come out they laughed at him, but he was very upset to say the least. But he couldn't respond, as he had to hurry so he wouldn't be late.

Another time Clem and Mary were in their buggy and Bill in his buggy and they entered the long driveway at the same time. Bill challenged them to a race to the house. They were running neck and neck when all of a sudden the wheels on their buggies got too close and Clem's hub on his wheel stripped the spokes out of Bill's wheel. That quickly ended the race.

Bill's father sold the farm in February 1917, and Bill went to Marysville with Clem, Mary and his dad to live. Bill and Clem sold a puncture proof product for tires for awhile, but that didn't last long.

In the summer of 1917 Bill enlisted in the 35th Regiment of the National Guard. World War I began soon after and that unit was activated as the Army Infantry. He was sent to Fort Sill, Oklahoma, for basic training. After basic training he was assigned to serve with the 35th Division of the 128th Field Artillery, Battery E, as a gunner on field artillery, and was shipped to France. The gunner is the one that pulled the lander (chord) that shot the artillery gun. He took part in four campaigns: The Vosges Mountains, entrance to the Alps; St. Mihiel; Muese-Argonne; and he was in Verdun when the war ended. He did not return home until some time in 1919.

He went to Oriziba, Mexico soon after returning home, looking into an investment scheme in which his father and brothers, Clem and Tom, and sister, Addie, became involved. It didn't prove to be successful for any of them and Bill returned to Kansas.

Clara Rosella Griffis
(Maluy Photo Collection)

On 28 February 1921, Bill married **Clara Rosella Griffis**, at Atchison, Atchison Co., Kansas. Clara was born 6 October 1893 to Henry A . and Anna E. Griffis, at Washington, Washington Co., Kansas. Bill and Clara lived in that general area in Kansas for a number of years and Bill worked as a telephone lineman.

Bill and Clara had six children:

Dale Clair, born 12 January 1923, Marysville,
Marshall Co., Kansas
Rex Loren, 3 January 1924, Linn, Washington Co., Kansas.
Patty Jean (Huntley), 17 September

1926, Grand Junction
Wilma Colleen (Walker), 23 February
1929, Fruita
Norma Mae (Klapwyk) 10 October 1930,
Fruita.
Jackie Lee, 30 April 1933, Fruita,

Their first two children, Dale and Rex, were born while living in Kansas. In 1925 Bill, Clara and the two boys went to California. Bill worked in the fruit harvest and they lived for awhile in Oakdale, California. He worked as a telephone lineman for a company in San Juaquin Valley. Dale remembers riding the ferry from Sacramento to San Francisco. They also lived in Klamath Falls, Oregon where Bill worked as a telephone lineman. They planned to homestead there, until Patrick, his dad, asked them to come to Colorado. The family moved to Colorado late in 1925 and lived for a time in Grand Junction, where the third child, Patty Jean, was born in 1926. During that time Bill was employed as a lineman for the Bell Telephone Company.

The following year (1927) Bill and Patrick struck a deal for Bill to buy his Patrick's homestead. Bill and his family moved in with Patrick and Mully, who returned to California in 1928.

The rest of Bill's children were born in Fruita. During this period Bill was involved in the Mack Baseball Team and the IOOF at Fruita. Clara was involved in the Rebeckahs. Bill was

Bill Maluy and his new 1935/6 Chevrolet with the old Patrick Maluy house in the background.
(Maluy Photo Collection)

also very active in the VFW in Grand Junction and Clara in the auxiliary.

Within a short time after he started farming, Bill began to have a desire to expand his farm operation. He wanted more land to farm than was available on his dad's homestead. At various times he rented land from Bob Cox, Bob Phillips, Joe Owings, etc., using a McCormick Deering tractor he bought from Si Summers to do the heavy plowing and discing. In 1933 he bought the J. N. King farm on a tax sale.

Then a tragedy happened in the family. Their youngest son, Jackie Lee, came down with the whooping cough. He died at six weeks old on 5 June 1933. Then Clara was stricken with uremic poisoning and pneumonia and died on 17 May 1934, leaving Bill alone with a family of five young children.

Mrs. Higgins, who lived on Art Harrison's place, cared for the children that summer. Bill moved with his children to Grand Junction in September and Mrs. Higgins went with them. During the 1934/35 school year Dale, Rex and Patty attended Hawthorne School. Dale and Rex were in the sixth grade and Patty in the third with Mrs. Pinger as their teacher. The family then moved back to the farm in New Liberty in the spring and finished the school year there.

Through the next few years Bill hired several different women to keep house and help care for the children. Some were Virginia James, his niece from the Eastern Slope of Colorado; Mrs. Burkett, the mother of Leland Burkett; Mrs. Blasdel; and Agnes Lee. Agnes married Ed Hiatt in October, 1937, and Bill rehired his niece Virginia, and then Mrs. Blasdel.

In 1937, Bill purchased the George Bryan farm and a new Model A John Deere tractor. By this time Dale and Rex were big enough to help with the farm work. Dale developed quite a reputation for making straight rows with that John Deere tractor. His half-mile long rows were straight as an arrow.

Bill remodeled the Bryan house with Mary Maluy's assistance. She helped Bill with the remodeling plans and picking out all the furnishings. Quite a step up from the old Patrick Maluy homestead house.

(Above) The remodeled Bryan house from the south side. *(Courtesy of the Shires/Johnson Collection)*

(Left) Martha and Bill Maluy in June 1942. *(Maluy Photo Collection)*

A woman whom Bill had known in Kansas years earlier, **Martha Potzner**, came to take over the housekeeping chores in about 1939. Martha brought with her two children by a former marriage to Adam Potzner, **Audie** and **Joan Marie Potzner**, and they were integrated into Bill's family. Bill and Martha were married in Fruita, 21 June 1941.

Bill was a successful farmer, but was known to gamble on unusual crops. It was he who began to grow red clover in lieu of alfalfa for hay; he raised seed from that crop as well. He did well with hay, potatoes and pinto beans, growing a large acreage of those crops. At one time he planted about 100 acres of radishes for seed. After harvesting the seed he bought 200 head of pigs, hauled in by the truck loads, to root up and eat the radishes. It worked, believe it or not! It was said by one of his neighbors that "Bill could fall in a toilet and come out smelling like a rose!" The pigs were quite intelligent and became pets to the Maluy children. When they heard the school bus coming around the hill at Thomas' about a mile away they would start running toward the gate so they could meet the children as they got off the bus. It was a sad day when the pigs had to be taken to market! Phyllis has quite a memory of assisting several family members in herding the pigs to the stockyards in Mack — it created quite a sensation! The pigs made a good conversation piece in the community.

In 1953 Bill retired and rented the farm to Taylor Roberts. He and Martha lived in Fruita for about three years. Then they sold the farm to Taylor Roberts and moved to Grand Junction where they bought a home and lived comfortably the rest of their lives.

Bill was one who had a good understanding of the dangers of older people driving. When he realized that the time had come when he might be a danger to others, he simply quit driving.

Bill always stood very straight and erect and walked very briskly. Phyllis can remember seeing her Uncle Bill walking down the sidewalk toward the hospital to visit Clem when Clem was in the hospital suffering from his burns. He looked so stately and proud. She realized how much she loved him. It was pretty hard for him to see his brother in that condition.

Bill died in Grand Junction 28 March 1970, eight days after his 80th birthday. Beautiful tributes were paid to him by friends and family. A grandson, Rex Huntley, wrote the following, which was read at the funeral by Rex's brother Mark.

For Daddy Bill

And now the days will be shorter by one,
One whom we all loved and held dear.
A someone so close, warmer than any sun
One gentle, one fun, whose face is clear
And the earth he leaves, the wind takes his place
But in our hearts, he will forever live
And in our thoughts he'll walk without a trace
But in you, in me, he will still live
For of him we are all a part;
And even death cannot change it.

(Upper left) Bill Maluy family,1941. Audie Potzner is missing. Back row, L-R: Patty, Dale, Rex, Martha, and Bill Maluy. Front row: Norma and Wilma Maluy, and Joan Marie Potzner. (Upper right) Bill and Martha Maluy, 1960s. (Above) Rex and Vernette Maluy, Christmas, 1954. (Left) Back row, L--R: Patty Maluy Huntley, Wilma Maluy Walker, and Norma Maluy Klapwyk. Rex and Bill Maluy in front, 1953. (Lower left) 1970, Grand Junction. L-R: Joan Marie Potzner Tuttle, Dale Maluy, Patty Maluy Huntley, Rex Maluy, Martha Maluy, Audie Potzner, Wilma Maluy Walker, and Norma Maluy Klapwyk. (Lower right) Patty Maluy, graduation from nursing school, 1948. *(Photos upper right and lower left, courtesy of Marilyn Maluy Pacheco. The rest are from the Maluy Photo Collection)*

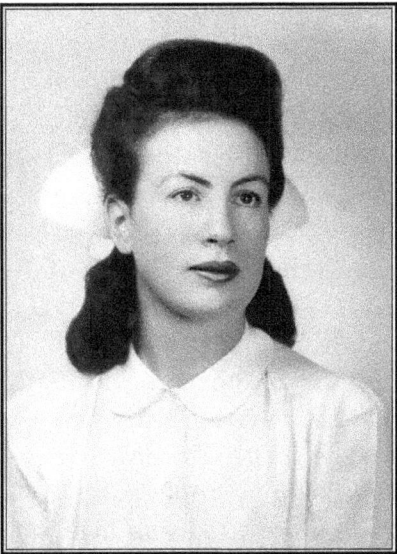

Dale Clair Maluy, 1944.
(Maluy Photo Collection)

Dale and flight squad that flew bombing missions over England in 19443/44. Dale is second from the left in the front row. *(Photo courtesy of Darrell Maluy)*

Dale graduated from Fruita Union High School in 1941 and enlisted in the Army Air Corps 6 January 1942. He was promoted to staff sergeant after he had completed training in the technical branch of the Air Corps. He became an air cadet in November 1942 and was trained to become a bomber pilot.

Dale went on to achieve fame in the Air Force as he flew B 17 Bombers from England to Germany. An item in *The Daily Sentinel* of 3 September 1944 says that Lieutenant Dale Maluy was awarded the "Air Medal for 17 bombing missions over Germany." - Then another article on 19 December 1944 tells that "Captain Dale Maluy, 21, veteran of 30 daylight bombing raids over Germany, was recently awarded the Distinguished Flying Cross."

He married **Mae Croitz** of Roswell, New Mexico, 10 November 1945. Dale was soon stationed at Salina, Kansas They had one daughter: **Linda,** born at Salina, 20 July 1946. Dale and Mae were later divorced

Later, in the Korean War, he flew 59 bombing missions from Japan to Korea in B 29 bombers. After that was over he was able to realize a secret ambition . . . he flew a B 29 over the New Liberty community at very low altitude. In his words he flew low enough to "flush the toilets." That got the attention of the citizens in New Liberty! The following article found in *The Daily Sentinel* of 1 September 1947 refers to that incident:

> The Mack area was buzzed by a large unidentified aircraft which flew around the Mack/New Liberty area for over 1/2 hour. It was rumored to have crashed; but the story was later determined to be unfounded.

Dale retired from the Air Force with the rank of Lieutenant Colonel and has since lived in New Mexico. His interest in education continued and he has earned a Bachelor's Degree from New Mexico Highlands University and an Master's from University of New Mexico. He does volunteer work helping people with their income tax reports and any problems they may have with the IRS.

Rex and Dale graduated from Fruita Union High School together in 1941. Rex also enlisted in the Air Corps on 25 November 1942, and trained to be a navigator at Hondo, Texas. He was commissioned 2nd Lieutenant. He then went to gunnery school at Harlingen Air Base at Harlingen, Texas. After he went overseas, *The Daily Sentinel* article of 7

Rex Loren Maluy, 1944.
(Maluy Photo Collection)

November 1944 said, "Lieutenant Rex Maluy was recently awarded the 3rd Oak Leaf Cluster." Another article on 11 December 1944:

First Lieutenant Rex Maluy received the Distinguished Flying Cross for extraordinary achievement in navigating Flying Fortresses for more than 35,000 miles during 8th Air Force Bombing attacks on German military and industrial targets. He also has the Air Medal with Four Oak Leaf Clusters.

He flew 35 missions in B-17s over Germany and other parts of the European theater of operations with the 96th Bomb Group, 8th Air Force.

He was discharged 11 October 1945 and became a coach and physical education teacher at Fruita Union High School. An article in the *Fruita Times*, issue 19 October 1945 states:

Rex Maluy (physical education and coaching) added to Fruita Union High School faculty. Maluy, recently discharged as a Flying Fortress pilot with 35 missions in Europe, will relieve Philip Griebel, veteran Fruita Union High School principal, teacher,

and athletic director, who has served in many capacities during the wartime shortage of teachers.

Rex married **Vernette Mathews Harker**, from California, 16 June 1946, in Fruita, Colorado. He had met Vernette in California during the war.

In September 1946 it was discovered Rex had tuberculosis. He was sent to Fort Bayard Veterans' Hospital in Silver City, New Mexico on 18 October 1946. Rex and Vernette moved to Silver City, New Mexico, in December. He recuperated enough to do part-time work in 1948. During recovery he worked in a sporting goods store and in 1950 went to work for Don Johnson Photography. Vernette worked in Silver City for Mountain States Telephone Company from 1948 to 1957.

Good things happened for the family in 1957. In May they moved to Lordsburg, New Mexico and Rex went to work full time for the New Mexico Highway Department as a project supervisor over highway construction projects. Their son **Mike "M"** was born 17 October 1957.

While working for the highway department the family lived in a trailer house in the following places: Lordsburg, Alamagorda, Clovis, Albuquerque, Taos and Espanola, New Mexico. In 1965 Rex went to work for O. D. Cowart Construction Company as a superintendent over highway construction in the area north and south of Truth or Consequences, New Mexico, living in Truth or Consequences until 1971. In May 1971 they bought their present home in Santa Fe, New Mexico, and Rex went to work for KNC Construction Company working as a superintendent on various highway construction jobs in New Mexico; Arizona; Cheyenne, Wyoming; and Meeker and Rangely, Colorado.

Rex retired in July 1986 and has enjoyed fishing, hunting and taking it easy.

Mike married **Nellie Olivas** in 1976 and they had a daughter, **Laura Michelle**, born 11 June 1977, in Santa Fe, New Mexico. Mike and Nellie divorced in 1977. In 1984, seven year-old Laura, went to live with Rex and Vernette and they have enjoyed raising her.

Patty Jean Maluy, 1944.
(Maluy Photo Collection)

Laura is now 20, has her own car, is working for Cedarwood Veterinary Clinic and goes to Santa Fe Community College part time.

Mike then married **Laura Garner** in 1978 in Oklahoma. Laura had two boys by a previous marriage, **James** and **Randy**. Mike and Laura have two children: **Melissa Ann**, born 12 January 1983, and **Rex Loren II**, born 5 January 1986, who was named after his grandpa. Both children were born in Oklahoma City, Oklahoma. The family now live in Enid, Oklahoma, and Mike works for Penske Trucking and Truck Rental.

Patty was the oldest girl in the family and had to take on quite a bit of the responsibility without a mother in the home. In high school she was head girl of her class during her senior year. She was a member of the Spanish Club and Pep Club. She graduated from Fruita Union High School in 1944 and then entered the U. S. Air Force as a nurse cadet at Trinidad, Colorado. She took her nurses training at the Seton School of Nursing at Colorado Springs, living in the dorms. She graduated in 1948 receiving her Registered nurse degree. She worked at St.

Mary's Hospital in Grand Junction and then in Reno, Nevada. She married **Grant Hugh Huntley** 8 February 1948, at Raton, Colfax, New Mexico. They had six children.

Wilma graduated from Fruita Union High School in 1947 and went to work as a telephone operator for Mountain Bell Telephone Company (now U. S. West) in Grand Junction. She worked there from 1947 to 1952. She married **Louis Mac Walker** 27 December 1951 at Grand Junction. Louis was born 4 August 1927, in Farmington, San Juan, New Mexico, a son of Andrew Mac and Ione Marie Page Walker. Louis worked for the First National Bank in Albuquerque, New Mexico, then served in the U. S. Army before coming to Grand Junction and working for the First National Bank there. Wilma and Louis have two children:

Norma Lou (McKittrick), born 18 November 1953, Eugene, Lane, Oregon
Garrett Lynn, 11 December 1955, Grand Junction

Louis transferred to Eugene, Oregon, with the First National Bank in 1952, and Wilma went to work for the Medaland Creamery as a bookkeeper. She quit to have her first child, Norma Lou in 1953. Louis then transferred back to Grand Junction in 1955 and worked as

Wilma Colleen Maluy, 1947.
(Maluy Photo Collection)

575

assistant cashier, then became vice president of the Grand Junction branch. Wilma went back to work for the telephone office in 1955 and retired in 1965.

In 1964 Louis helped form the Mesa National Bank in Grand Junction and became its president. He then became president of the Bank of Orchard Mesa, serving in that position from 1976 until 1981 when he retired. Louis was president of the Grand Junction Chamber of Commerce in 1967, treasurer for the Boy Scouts for eight years, and has done a lot of community service with different organizations. His hobbies are trout fishing, gardening and golf.

Wilma's hobbies are trout fishing, gardening, flower arrangements, sewing and reading. She and Louis moved in with their son, Garrett, in 1986 to help him out. At present Louis' mother is living with them so Wilma can care for her. Wilma and Louis have two grandchildren.

Garrett never married. He got his contractor's license in 1987 and is very successful at building and remodeling houses and business buildings

Norma Lou married **Michael Arn McKittrick** 7 June 1974, in Carbondale,

Garfield, Colorado. They had two children: **Jacabe William** and **Sarah Colene**. Norma Lou and Micheal divorced in 1976 and he lost his life 12 November 1985 in Anchorage, Alaska. Norma Lou has become a successful business woman. She is a self-employed real estate broker and salesperson, dealing mostly in commercial businesses, land and timber buying and leasing.

*N*orma, like Patty, was head girl of her class in her junior year at Fruita Union High School. She belonged to the Pep Club and was a very good forward on the girl's basketball team. She graduated from high school in 1948, then also went to work for Mountain Bell Telephone Company in Grand Junction as an operator. She married **George William "Bill" Klapwyk** 14 February 1953, at Salt Lake City, Utah. Bill was born 2 August 1927, in Fruita, a son of John and Viola Pauline Goddard Klapwyk.

Norma and Bill have three children, all born in Grand Junction:

Kurt, born 1 August 1957
Lisa Ann (Crouser), 9 May 1960
Tana Kay, 8 December 1965

Norma worked for the telephone company from 1948 until she retired in 1983. For something to do, she began to work two hours a day for the Grand Junction School District helping serve hot lunches. She enjoyed this so much, she did it for eight years. She says she is fully retired now and only does things around the home.

Bill graduated from Fruita Union High School in 1945 and joined the Army in 1946. He served in the Army Corp of Engineers until the middle of 1947. When he returned he attended Mesa College for two years, graduating in 1949 with an associate degree in science. Right out of school he was asked by the Grand Valley Water Users' Association if he would work temporarily for the ditch rider in the Fruita district near his home. He said as long as he didn't have to stay when the ditch rider came back. Well, the ditch rider couldn't come back, and Bill hired on permanently. In 1953 Bill was called to work in the office as assistant to the manager, a position called water

Norma Mae Maluy, 1948.
(Maluy Photo Collection)

master. A ditch rider is the lifeline to the farmers for their irrigating water, and the water master is over them. Later Bill became assistant manager and in 1966 he became manager of the Grand Valley projects, covering the Highline Canal and the Orchard Mesa Canal. He retired 1 October 1994, but has continued to be on call and assist when needed. He owns 110 acres of farmland in the valley and farms about 40 acres. He calls this his recreational farming.

Bill and Norma have two grandchildren whom they enjoy very much.

Kurt is not married. He lives in Reno, Nevada and works as a courier for businesses in Reno. He is also involved with a gold mine.

Lisa Ann married **Mitchell Steven Crouser** 9 September 1960 in Portland Multnomah, Oregon. They have two children, **Ryan** and **Matt**.

Tana Kay is not married and works as a bookkeeper in Gresha, Oregon.

Audie F. Potzner was born 31 January 1923 to Adam and Martha Gertrude Rechtien Potzner in Milwaukee, Waukesha Wisconsin. Audie attended school four years at St. Boniface Catholic School in Milwaukee and then four years at St. Johns Catholic School in Hanover, Kansas. He attended two years high school at Marysville High School in Marysville, Kansas. He moved with his mother and sister to New Liberty in 1939 when his mother came to take care of Bill Maluy's home and children. He then attended Fruita Union High School, graduating in 1941 with Dale and Rex.

After graduation Audie moved back to Milwaukee. He married **Ruth** (last name unknown) at West Allis, Wisconsin. They had two daughters, **Rita Lee** and **Mary Lynn**. Their marriage ended in divorce.

Audie worked for Drott Tractor Company, then Allis Chalmers, and then at Maynard Steel, all located in Milwaukee. After retirement he moved back to the home town of Hanover, Kansas, took it easy and traveled between Grand Junction and Milwaukee. He died in Hanover of lung cancer on 22 July 1995.

Joan Marie Potzner, 1945.
(Maluy Photo Collection)

He had three grandchildren at the time of his death.

Joan Marie "Jody" Potzner was born 25 November 1928, in Milwaukee, Waukesha, Wisconsin a daughter of Adam and Martha Gertrude Rechtien Potzner. She attended two years St. Johns Catholic School in Hanover and two years at Marysville Grade School in Marysville, Kansas before moving with her mother and brother to New Liberty in 1939. She attended four years at New Liberty School, then graduated from Fruita Union High School in 1945. She attended three years at St. Mary's nursing school in Denver, then one year at Ohio State to become a nurse anesthetist. She worked one year at Columbia Hospital in Milwaukee. She then moved to Eugene, Oregon, and worked in the Eugene Hospital.

Jody married **Edwin Tuttle** in 1957 in Grand Junction. They had three children, **Jan, Mark,** and **Paul.** Jody worked at the Eugene Hospital until her death, 21 May 1986, in Milwaukee, Wisconsin, while visiting Audie.

(Upper left) Audie and Ruth Potzner's wedding in West Allis, Wisconsin. (Above) Audie's granddaughter and great-grandson, Sarah, Brian, and Audie. (Center) Audie and daughters, Mary Lynn and Rita Lee Potzner. (Below) Joan Marie's wedding to Edwin Tuttle, 1957, Grand Junction. L-R: Norma Maluy Klapwyk, Grand Huntley, Wilma Maluy Walker, Patty Maluy Huntley, Mary and Clem Maluy, Joan Marie Potzner Tuttle, Edwin Tuttle, Martha, Rex, and Bill Maluy. *(All photos courtesy of Audie Potzner)*

Martinez

Lloyd Martinez was born in Gardner, Huerfano, Colorado, 20 November 1901, to Lucas Martinez and Dora Aragon. He married **Carmel Manzanares** on 12 April 1926 at Fort Collins, Larimer, Colorado. Lloyd and Carmel had five children:

Priscilla (Poulin), born 13 March 1928
Glen, 2 January 1930
James, 1 January 1932
Harold, 7 January 1934
Donald, 11 January 1937

All were born at Greeley, Weld, Colorado except Donald, who was born at Pierce, Weld, Colorado.

The Martinez family moved to the Diehl farm in the New Liberty community in February, 1942, and the children attended New Liberty School. In 1943 the family moved to the Starr area, then to Fruita in 1946. They moved to Los Angeles, California, in 1953. Lloyd worked for an auto parts store and Carmel worked in a school cafeteria in the Los Angeles School System. She retired in 1972 after nearly 20 years of service.

Lloyd died in California in January, 1981. Carmel lives in Virginia Beach near Priscilla.

Priscilla graduated from the eighth grade at New Liberty in 1942. Priscilla married **Robert Poulin** 14 August 1953, in Honolulu, Hawaii. They have two children, **Steven Robert** and **Michael Thomas**.

Robert was in the Navy so they traveled around extensively: Hawaii (twice); Portland, Oregon; Washington, D.C.; Athens, Georgia;

The Lloyd Martinez family in 1948. Back row, L-R: Donald, Priscilla, and Harold Martinez. Front row: Glen, Carmel, Lloyd, and James Martinez. *(Photo courtesy of Carmel Martinez)*

579

and the last tour was in Norfolk, Virginia. They bought a home in Virginia Beach, Virginia and that's where they presently live. Priscilla worked as a secretary for the government and retired as computer analyst for the Navy.

Glen went to New Liberty School and graduated from Fruita Union High School in 1949. He worked for the Operating Engineers Union on heavy duty equipment on road construction jobs in Colorado, Utah and California. He married **Patricia Martin** 1 May 1955 in Las Vegas. They moved to California where Glen continued to work in construction. He then became a licensed state of California sewer contractor in Wrightwood and Palmdale, California. Patricia worked as a managing officer for a corporation of internal medicine practice in Lancaster, California until she was unable to work anymore due to a back problem that has required extensive surgeries. Glen and Patricia had seven children: **Glen C., Susan C. (George), Bruce, Gary, Laurie (Ross), Gail**, and **Ellen (Britt).**

In 1993 Glen and Patricia moved to Paonia, Colorado. Glen continues to work in road construction, only now with the Steelworkers Union, as the Operating Engineers isn't active in the Paonia area.

James also went to New Liberty School, graduating from Fruita Union High School in 1950. He married **Alda** (last name unknown) and adopted her two sons. James became afflicted with multiple sclerosis, his marriage failed, and he went to live with his parents as he became quite ill. He was in a nursing home seven years before he died 24 November 1985 in Sun Valley, California.

Harold also attended New Liberty School and graduated from Fruita Union High School in 1952. He married **Renee Lindstrom** in 1960 at Sylmar, California. She had two children from another marriage, and she and Harold have five children. Harold belongs to the electrician's union and worked as an electrician for Los Angeles County. He lives in Sylmar and retired a year ago. Their son Harold lost his life

trying to save two of his children. The children were in the car on a fishing trip when one of the boys accidentally put the car out of gear and it rolled into the lake. Harold and children drowned.

Donald married **Darlene Stephan** in 1958 at Glendale, California. They had four children. Donald sells insurance and is also a financial advisor. Donald and Darlene have five grandchildren and live in Grass Valley, California.

McCoy

The following history is compiled mostly from information sent to us by James L "Jim" McCoy. Jim has sent us a large portion of the V. L. McCoy photo collection. Among them are some photos by "Judge" Kennedy, prominent figure of Mack.

Vernon Leroy "Roy" McCoy was born at Fulton, Poweshiek, Iowa, 9 August 1893, to Tom and Harriett McCoy. He moved with his family to Colorado in 1912. On 12 December 1917 he was married to **Julia Helen Brassell** at Fruita. Julia was born on 24 June 1893 at Mattoon, Coles, Illinois to James and Elizabeth Brassell. Before the Brassell family moved to the Fruita area, they lived for a time at Salida, Colorado, where Julia graduated from high school.

Roy and Julia had three children:

Thomas "Tom" V., born 6 May 1918, at Grand Junction
James L., 1 December 1921, Fruita
Helen (Ross), 30 January 1923, Fruita

Roy began his career on the Uintah Railroad about 1917. He took time out during World War I to serve in France in the Army Engineers, where he acquired additional railroad experience. He served in various capacities for the Uintah . . . Fireman; Brakeman; Hostler; Engineer; Water Serviceman; Machinist. For most of that career he worked out of Atchee and Dragon, Colorado. He moved his family to Mack in September 1935. At that time Roy began operating the power plant and water system.. During all the time they lived in Mack Roy managed a baseball team made up of men from Atchee and other points on the Uintah with son Jim serving as bat boy. The men from Atchee and other points up the line would occasionally ride a special train to Mack for games.

After the family moved to Mack the children were enrolled in schools at Mack and Fruita. Roy then managed the Mack School baseball team.

Perhaps Roy was able to see the handwriting on the wall because, in April 1936, before the Uintah folded, he moved his family to Grand Junction and began working in the shops for the Denver and Rio Grande. Later he became an engineer. Julia died 21 December 1968 and Roy 29 September 1982. Both are buried in Calvary Cemetery on Orchard Mesa.

We have a little information on Tom and Helen:

Tom went to work at age 16 for the Denver and Rio Grande Railroad as a call boy and worked there for 36 years until retirement. He was married to **Leona J. Ogden** 10 June 1938 at Grand Junction. They had a boy and a girl. Tom died in Grand Junction 5 August 1988.

Helen married **Dr. C. L. Ross** of Grand Junction. Dr. Ross went to Mesa College. He worked as a doctor in Burlington, Colorado for 32 years before his death in 1991. Helen worked most of her life at different occupations. She also boarded young people and helped them get their education. She now lives in Colorado Springs.

Jim writes that he was . . . "One year old" (December 1922) when he moved with his family to Atchee . . . went through all eight elementary grades in school there. He was the only boy in the school from the fifth through the eighth grades, graduating from that school with a class of two. Being the only boy automatically placed him in position to captain the football and baseball teams.

Jim says that one of the requirements in hiring a teacher at Atchee was that "she" be able to play the piano. I suppose that expertise came in handy in community functions as well as school.

He tells of having broken a leg in a bob-sledding accident at Atchee. The Uintah ran a special train to take him to Mack. Then they hauled him by automobile to Grand Junction for medical attention.

During the years the McCoys lived in Atchee "Judge" Kennedy would bring films from Mack, so they could have a movie once a month at Atchee.

After the family moved to Mack in 1935, Jim attended Fruita Union High School, graduating in the class of 1939. He has fond memories of catching the school bus each morning at Mack, and of the friends he acquired during that time, especially the ones who played in the Fruita High School Band.

He had an interest in band, so, since Chick Nichols needed someone to play baritone, Jim and his mother went to Grand Junction to find a horn and contracted to pay for it at $4 per month. He was also active in the drama group in high school. He was in every play.

During and after his high school days Jim worked for various farmers around Mack, harvesting hay and beans. He worked on a turkey farm. He also delivered milk for the local dairy - driving a Model "T".

After graduation from Fruita Union High School Jim attended one year at Mesa College. Then he taught for one year in a log cabin school on Divide Creek near Silt, Colorado. Additional duties included cooking the noon meal for the students. The school year started with eleven students but ended with seven.

(Above left) Senator Barry Goldwater of Arizona and Jim McCoy, when Senator Goldwater visited the Madison Rose Lane School in Phoenix, Arizona. (Above right) Jim on one of his many trips. (Below) The Jim McCoy family. L-R: Anna and Jim McCoy, Jeff McCoy, Jean McCoy Colosanti, Mary McCoy Kelley, Joe, John, and Jim McCoy, and Analee McCoy Emery. (*Photos courtesy of Jim McCoy*)

He enlisted in the Army Medical Corps in June 1943 and served in England as a Surgical Technician. He specialized in burn cases and has the distinction of administering the first penicillin that was received in the general hospital in England. That made history!

Not long after he enlisted in the Army he stopped to visit his sister Helen who was going to school near Kansas City. She was rooming with a girl named **Anna Wright**. It was love at first sight! Jim altered his plans and spent a whole week there with Helen and with Anna's parents. Jim and Anna were married at New Orleans 6 November 1943.

They had seven children:

Annalee (Emery), born 6 November 1944, Kansas City, Johnson, Kansas
James L. Jr., born 14 July 1946, Kansas City
John, 3 August 1947, Kansas City
Joe, 24 July, 1948, Kansas City
Mary (Kelley), 30 January 1950, Kansas City
Jean (Colosanti), 18 April 1956, Delta, Delta, Colorado
Jeff, 23 September 1959, Grand Junction

After military Jim came back to Grand Junction and, through the G I bill, attended Mesa College for two more years. Later he taught at Mesa College and was involved in adult educational programs. Eventually Jim attained a master's degree in education with an additional 56 hours toward a doctorate. All he lacks is the dissertation.

In 1985 the family moved to Arizona where Jim taught at Northland Pioneer College at Eager, Arizona. Anna spent her career years as an elementary teacher.

All seven children attended college and all but two received degrees. Anna, Jim 's wife, received a master's degree in education from Arizona State University, the same year daughter Annalee received hers.

Since retirement the Jim McCoys have become involved in raising and showing dogs and horses. They have received much enjoyment from that.

In January, 1996 we received a communication from Jim that included a tribute and news article about their intended move to a new home at 2613 N. 122 Ave., Avondale, Arizona 85323. Since they moved to Eager they have both been involved in community and civic activities.

Anna was involved in an auto accident on St. Patrick's Day last year. (1995) She has had respiratory problems since that seem to require a lower elevation.

Jim has sent us some verse he composed:

A Teacher

They bend and sway and sing.
No, I'm not talking about willows.
I'm talking about students.
They see themselves, they set goals.
Why? How do they evaluate self?
I'm talking about a teacher.
Who demands more from them than
They can give. Yet-
They give that more,
That last drop of sweat,
That last burst of energy,
That last sweet note,
growing, learning, smiling, liking self.
The gift that will follow,
as one mother said.
All through their lives
I'm talking a teacher!
I'm talking Mr. Bill!
I'm talking Mr. Bill!
Students bending, swaying, and singing,
not as willows, but,
As gifted, mature, talented kids,
who will never forget, never forget!
I'm talking Mr. Bill!
I'm talking Mr. Bill!

We want to thank Jim for the generous number of pictures he submitted for use in the book. He owns his father's collection of Judge Kennedy's pictures, which includes 2,000 pictures and slides.

Morrow

The following is a history of the Morrow families, written by Eugene Thomas, editor and publisher of the *Fruita Times*. The history appeared in the *Fruita Times* 15 August 1991. There are some additions from personal knowledge of the author.

John Burrell Morrow was born 31 October 1884 at Grainfield, Gove, Kansas, to John Burrell and Mary Elzina Morrow. He spent part of his childhood at Grainfield and part in Colorado. I recall his telling of time spent with relatives in the Denver area and attending Columbian School there (which is still in use the last I knew). **Margaret Adelphia Gibbs** was born 30 November 1884 on the farm which her father homesteaded near Russell, Russell, Kansas (that farm is still in the family — the land is now rented out and there have been no residents on the place, 1991). Grandma Morrow always liked to talk about her childhood in Kansas and I know a great deal about that. On the other hand I'm very fuzzy on John Morrow's childhood. His father had a homestead near Russell also and my grandparents met at community events and were subsequently married on the Gibbs farm in 25 December 1904. Their two older sons, Thomas and Edward, and my mother, Estellene, were born on the elder Morrow's homestead

John and Margaret had five children:

Thomas Burrell, born 28 October 1905, Russell, Russell, Kansas
Gordon Edward, October 1909, Russell
Marjorie Estellene, 18 June 1911, Russell
Elizabeth, 19 August 1913, Castile, Wyoming, New York
John Lawrence, 30 October 1920, Fruita (Gordon Edward's birthday was calculated from the 1910 census)

I remember Grandma telling how John Morrow's father became ill and went to stay with other family members in Castile, Wyoming, New York. John and Margaret Morrow and the three children went back there to be with the elder Mr. Morrow. John got a job doing orchard work and also learned carpentry during that time. It turned out to be a difficult time for them. Their youngest son, Gordon Edward, became ill and died. He was buried at Perry, New York. Their home was at Castile, New York, and their second daughter, Elizabeth, their fourth child, was born 19 August 1913, there. There was a fire in the house and Margaret had a nervous breakdown.

The family returned to Kansas where they had a farm near Conway Springs in Sumner County (quite a distance from Russell) for a while, and their fortunes weren't the best there, either. Among other things, their horses died and money was short, so Granddad got a job in the mines at Cripple Creek, Colorado,. The family lived at Victor, Colorado, for two winters, I think. My mother had memories of that time.

They heard of the land in Colorado under the Highline Canal in the Grand Valley opening up for homesteading, and John Morrow got one of the first places at New Liberty. Grandma used to tell how John (J.B.) Morrow and Albert Alstatt got acquainted on the immigrant train from Kansas to Colorado and ended up with farms next to each other at New Liberty. John brought the farm equipment and I suppose the household stuff, too, sometime in early 1918.† By fall he had a small house built and the livestock set up near the canal. Margaret Morrow and the three children — Thomas, Estellene and Elizabeth — came on out in the fall. Thomas died a few months later, 6 January 1919, during the flu

The Morrow's barnyard in 1919.
(Estellene Thomas Collection)

† The author remembers John telling him that at the time of the drawing, John and Al Alstatt became acquainted and, upon learning they had adjoining homesteads, leased a railroad box car together to transport their belongings from Kansas to Colorado.

(Above) The John Morrow family about 1940. L-R: John Lawrence, John Burrell, Margaret Adelphia, Elizabeth, and Marjorie Estellene Morrow. (Below) About 1944. Back row, L-R: Robert and Sarah Galbraith, John and Margaret Morrow, Floyd and David Thomas. Front row: Kathleen, Eugene, and Curtis Thomas. *(Photos courtesy of Eugene Thomas)*

Margaret Morrow standing by the coal/wood cook stove in her home. An almost exact setting could be seen at the New Liberty Schoolhouse during the 40s when she was a cook at the school. *(Photo courtesy of Eugene Thomas)*

epidemic. His body was returned to Kansas and is buried in the Gibb's family plot in the Russell Cemetery.

There was no school at New Liberty in 1918, so my mother (Estellene) went back to Salina, Kansas, to stay with relatives, and went to school that year. Apparently Thomas did not go to school that year — I don't recall any mention of that question in our family.

John and Margaret Morrows youngest son, John Lawrence, was born 30 October 1920, in the hospital at Fruita.

Grandpa moved the house several hundred feet south of its original location because of Grandma's fear that the baby would fall into the canal. I think they added to the house at that time, also, but it was still small and I recall there was always a bed set up in one end of the kitchen, or in the living room, and sometimes both. More additions were made later.

Margaret was a fastidious housekeeper; her house was always

spotless. The floors were very nearly worn out from her efforts to keep them swept and mopped. She had a peculiar habit of sweeping the yard as well; there was never any loose dirt around to be tracked or blown into the house. As was typical of homestead families, there were never enough bedrooms; beds set up in the kitchen or living room were an accepted part of pioneer life.

*E*stellene finished grade school at New Liberty and graduated from Fruita Union High School in 1929. She attended Ross Business College in Grand Junction. She and **Floyd Thomas** were married 20 December 1930, at Fruita. My brother, Curt, says Dad said he met Mom when she was 11 years old and decided he wanted to marry her, but had to wait for her to grow up. Grandma Morrow always had a special likening for Dad, and I feel sure that eventually helped them along.

*E*lizabeth graduated from Fruita Union High School in 1930, and as the family story goes, ran off to Texas with a traveling man and the family didn't hear from her for awhile. I recall going along to meet her when she came home, which must have been in 1935 or 1936. I don't remember how long she stayed, but she went back to Texas. The next time we saw her she had a new car, and I think the next time after that, a new husband — **Louis Davis.**

Estellene Morrow   Elizabeth Morrow
(Photos courtesy of Eugene Thomas)

586

Elizabeth and Louis moved to the farm for a time and Lewis helped John get started on the new house he always planned. Granddad planned to build the house out of railroad ties and had bought enough to do this after the Uintah Railway closed down. But things went awry with Elizabeth and Louis's marriage and they were later divorced. Louis returned to Texas and work on the house stopped and was never resumed. Elizabeth also went back to Texas and married another Texan, J.C. Dyer, but this marriage also ended in divorce. She fought cancer for several years and succumbed to it in 1960.

The author remembers John telling a story about the foundation poured for the house. John said, "We were coming along very well with building a new house when Maggie started talking about having her sister come to live with us. So I just quit building."

In May 1932 John Morrow was stricken with "Rocky Mountain Tick Fever." The following report, written by Nellie Stotts, correspondent for *The Daily Sentinel*, was included in the New Liberty items dated 17 May 1932:

Mr. J. B. Morrow was taken to Grand Junction Saturday in the ambulance where he will receive treatments for tick fever. Mr. Morrow isn't improving as much as his friends and relatives would like him to. He was quite sick Saturday night and unconscious all night. We are hoping Mr. Morrow will recover. Several of his neighbors called on him Friday afternoon.

In the same items it was noted that Paul Arpke and family, who had recently returned from Nebraska, were taking over the Morrow farm for the season.

Later we discovered in *The Daily Sentinel* that John's "Tick Fever" had been re-diagnosed as "Tularemia," a very dangerous viral infection. Some investigations were made because of John's infection and it was discovered that both the rabbits and ticks in the area were carriers of the disease. There were other incidents of the disease in the valley after that, but by that time new methods of treatment had been discovered. John recovered after a long battle.

John had been chewing tobacco since he was a young man but because of the fever during his sickness, he lost his taste for tobacco. This lasted for some time, but in John's own words. "I was feeling around above the kitchen door one day looking for something and discovered a forgotten plug of tobacco. The temptation was too strong; I bit off a chew and went back to where I was before I quit."

Lawrence graduated from Fruita Union High School in 1938. He and John did considerable improvement work on the Morrow farm, leveling until most of the place was in large fields and easy to irrigate. The south end of the farm was very productive in the beginning, then was lost to alkali that came up due to seepage from the canal.

At one time there was a field with rows nearly a half mile long. Later that was found to be impractical and a ditch was added to cut the length of the rows in half. A drainage ditch was dug across that part to alleviate the problem. The land below the drainage ditch was not farmed, but John worked for some time leveling it in preparation for bringing it into production. He never completed the project. Arpke's now farm to the south boundary.

Lawrence joined the Navy before the United States entry into World War II, and became a pilot. His plane was shot down in April, 1943, by a surfaced Japanese submarine in Kaneohe Bay, on the opposite side of the island from Pearl Harbor. He was declared officially dead, but the family held some slight hope that he might have survived — so the gradual acceptance of his death was a rough time for all, including me as I had no older siblings, and Lawrence was a hero, in

Lawrence Morrow, 24 August 1941.
(Photo courtesy of Eugene Thomas)

fact taking me places and teaching me things (probably often at the insistence of Grandma Morrow).

As noted in *The Daily Sentinel* of 24 December 1940, Lawrence came home on furlough for the first Christmas after he enlisted. It was also noted that he was enrolled in a mechanics school and was doing outstanding work.

Notice of his "missing in action" appeared in *The Daily Sentinel* 22 April 1943. Announcement of his being "officially declared dead" was made on 24 June 1943. The article states that after he completed machinist training he was transferred to the naval air base at Corpus Christi, Texas, and was promoted to AMM3c. He was accepted for flight training in February, 1942, and sent to Pensacola for that training, which began in March; he graduated in August, and then was sent to active duty in the Pacific. At the time of his death he held the rank of AP2c.

Margaret Morrow had, on several occasions, mentioned something in her New Liberty news items about Lawrence's activities in the Navy. Just days before his being reported missing she reported that he and Lewis Likes were at the same base and that they had told how much they enjoyed receiving *The Daily Sentinel*, even though it was weeks old before they received it. Then, after Lawrence was reported missing, she didn't mention his name again.

April 8, 1993 marked the 50th anniversary of the loss of Lawrence Morrow. Following is a tribute written by Gene Thomas and Lewis Likes and published in the Fruita Times, 2 April 1993.

Lewis Likes has been a friend as long as I can remember, and was a friend of my mother, Estellene Thomas, and her family, before I was born. He was a particular friend and schoolmate of my mother's brother, John Lawrence Morrow, who graduated from Fruita Union High School in 1938.

Not too long ago, Lewis mentioned that it might be a good idea to commemorate the 50th anniversary of Lawrence's death, and I agreed, hence this writing, which I find easier to do in first person than the news-style third person.

Lawrence was the third son in the Morrow family, but the other two had already died before he was born, so the family pinned a great many hopes for a future on him.

He was quite a hero to me — about ten years older than I, taught me about a lot of things and how to do a lot of things, and in the earliest period that I remember was in high school and was the person I always talked to about school in the time before I was old enough to go to school. I particularly remember talking about the new high school (opened in 1936) and how impressed I was when we got to go see him in a play in the school.

After the United States' entry into World War II and Lawrence's entry into the Navy, there was a lot of worry in the family that something would happen to him, and when the word came — first that he was missing and then that he had been declared dead — the effect was devastating.

The situation with Lawrence and Lewis must not be that common — two good buddies who were not only stationed together, but would have been together on the plane that went down had it not been for the fact that Lewis got orders at the last minute to prepare another plane for flight, and Donald Eppard was sent to fly with Lawrence instead.

In preparing for this commemoration, Lewis and I got together and went through a number of Lawrence's things that have remained in the family for the past 50 years, including his log book, which shows the last flight, and the letter Lewis wrote to Lawrence's parents shortly after his death. This brought back lots of memories for both of us. We agreed that printing the letter might serve to get a lot of feelings as well as some history into print.

There are probably several people among our readers who were school-mates or friends of Lawrence and who have memories of him.

Lewis says he has carried many thoughts and feelings with him over the years, such as the thought that some slight change at the time Lawrence took off in the plane could have resulted in a different outcome. Lewis has summed up some of his feelings in a tribute which is printed here also, along with the letter he had written to Lawrence's parents 50 years ago. (By way of explanation, the Lura Mae mentioned in the letter is Lura Mae Russell, Lawrence's fiancee who lived at Corpus Christi, Texas, whom he had met while he was stationed there).

U. S. Naval Air Station
Kanehoe Bay, T. H.
April 12 1943

My Dear Friends:

Knowing that you have already been notified of your son's and my very best friend's death, makes it very difficult to write to you about him for fear of increasing your great grief. I can in no way have the grief in my heart that you must have, but if yours is more than mine, your heart will surely break.

God alone knows for sure what happened that awful night to Lawrence and his radioman second class Donald C. Eppar. I saw it myself and can't imagine what it was.

Lawrence died in the line of his military profession and in the act of destroying our enemy and protecting our country. I am not allowed to tell his mission, but after the war is over I can.

At the time, our last evening seemed no more unusual than any other. (I mean by "unusual" that our friendship and being together was unusual because we never tired of each other's company, talking and planning for our future). But now I remember that Lawrence and Donald were both exceedingly quiet all evening and spent most of it writing letters. I was the last person to talk to him before he left and those words were: "Take it easy kid, it's pretty dark out there." And he replied, "Don't worry, I'll be back in a few minutes."

Everything in our power was done to save them, and we worked all night and through most of the next day trying to find some trace of them, but it was to no good. I went in a plane the next morning and satisfied myself for you that they were not to be found. Please believe me that our search was extensive and complete and our plane did not return until I gave up and I was the last one to do that.

Both boys were true "captains;" both went down with their ship with Lawrence trying to save the other's life and our country's much needed equipment. They now rest in a watery grave not far from the last place that I talked my last to him. Lawrence was an excellent man for his profession, an always concerned "Buddy" and an example that if all men would follow, this would be a grand, cheerful and easier world to live in. God will surely take care of his soul. He loved all of his shipmates

and they all loved him.

I am truly lost with myself because we were together so much. He never missed a day coming to see me during my need for him in my long illness. I could have never repaid him for that. We planned a lot together for our future and now those plans are left alone with me and they are no good without him. He was very much in love with Lura and had planned a great future happiness with her.

He probably wrote you about his pictures. He had only one pose developed, but three different ones taken. I have already ordered eight prints of each pose to send to you. I thought you might like them as they were his last. All other pictures of him that I may find I will save and send to you.

I have taken care of his belongings as far as I was allowed and they will soon be on their way.

I plan to see you in the near future and I will be certain to come and tell you about him.

This entire unit and myself send you our deepest sympathy.

Please see my father and mother and let them share your grief. It may help console you.

I have bothered you long enough, but if there is anything that I can do, feel free to ask me to do it.

God bless you and I pray that He will be near to comfort you and yours at this time of grievance.

I remain your friend and your friend forever.

Lewis David Likes AMM1C USN

IN MEMORY OF
LAWRENCE MORROW
Born 31 October 1920
Died 8 April 1943

He died while piloting a Navy J2F-2 aircraft in a night attack against a surfaced Japanese submarine. The submarine was lurking near the shipping channel entrance to the U. S. Naval Air Station, Kaneohe Bay, Territory of Hawaii, and was attempting to sink a vessel in the channel to close it to shipping to this major patrol plane base.

His radioman, Donald Eppard, was also killed.

A place (in my mind) is all that's
 there
  where he died
  in the service of his country.
No Cross is there to mark   the spot where
his body fell,
  it is water —- his body was
  never recovered.

He can never say:
"I love you wife."
"I'll fish with you son."
"My dreams have been
  realized"
  I will not forget.
                    His friend, Lewis D. Likes

John Morrow ran the farm until 1951 and also bought the neighboring Snavely or Brisbin place, removed all the buildings from it and leveled it out. He suffered two heart attacks in early summer, 1951, and died that fall, 7 September 1951.

Some years earlier, John and Margaret had engaged in a melee with Vern and Selma Snavely at the mail box — yes, both the men and the women — and the two couples were never on speaking terms again. Snavelys had established a much better-than-average farmstead, a good house and out buildings, fruit orchard and lots of good shade trees. Brisbins purchased the Snavely's farm in 1935 and lived there a few years. Eventually John Morrow bought the farm from Brisbins and proceeded to destroy every trace of the Snavelys as he had vowed he would do.

Margaret and Elizabeth stayed on the farm until 1960, with long-time family friend Charles Cutler doing a lot of the heavy work. They moved to Fruita in 1960 after Elizabeth had become almost totally disabled by the cancer that took her life that fall, 29 November, 1960, in the Fruita Hospital.

Margaret and Elizabeth made the move after the farm was sold to Bob and Pearline Arpke. The Arpkes added it to the original Arpke farm just to the east, and Bob and Pearline still live there in the house they built not too far from the site that John Morrow had picked out for a new house many years earlier.

After Elizabeth's death, Margaret continued to live in the house on Maple Street in Fruita until 1969 when she and my parents went together and bought a duplex at 306 and 308 Pine Street, Orchard Mesa, Grand Junction. Margaret lived there until shortly before her death in 1976, at age 91, on 1 August 1976.

John and Margaret Morrow and Elizabeth Dyer are all buried in New Elmwood Cemetery at Fruita.

There is also a marker on the family plot in memory of John Lawrence Morrow.

Margaret Morrow became *The Daily Sentinel* Correspondent for the New Liberty community in July 1937, succeeding Nellie Stotts. We do not know how many years she continued in that position.

Margaret was always active in community affairs and the Sunday School at New Liberty, she was a 4H leader, and cooked at the school for several years. John Morrow had a keen interest in national and world affairs and would spend much time discussing them with anyone who would take the time.

While on the Morrow and Gibbs families, I will mention two of Margaret Morrow's siblings who also lived at New Liberty. Her brother Thomas Gibbs (always Uncle Tom to us) farmed for a while there. (Helen Sanders Quain mentioned in her account of the Sanders' family that Bob Sanders bought the Tom Gibbs place.) I think Uncle Tom might have been there at the time his first wife died in childbirth. The baby, their first, also died. I remember Uncle Tom mentioning that he had also sold subscriptions for *The Daily Sentinel* at one time while he lived at New Liberty. He moved back to the Gibbs farm in Russell,

Kansas, where he and another brother, Theodore (Uncle Pete), farmed it as long as they were able. Uncle Tom married again in the 1940s, as I recall, but that marriage only lasted a short time. He visited New Liberty many times through the years, the last time being late fall of 1966. He died in Kansas the summer of 1967.

Margaret's sister, Sarah "Sadie," also lived at New Liberty at different times beginning in 1929. She and her daughter, Madge Howie, moved here after Sarah separated from her first husband, Jack Howie. Things did not work out for Madge at the New Liberty School, so the family moved to Grand Junction where Madge went first to Hawthorne and then to Lowell School. Sarah's son, Howard Howie, did not come with them at that time, but I believe may have spent some time here later. Howard is now deceased; Madge lived at Lee's Summit, Missouri, for many years. She died in the spring of 1994.

Aunt Sarah married Bob Galbraith and they lived in Grand Junction for some time during the 1940s. Ben and Jay Rowe probably remember him, as he was a friend of the Deacons. Sarah and Bob were divorced.

In 1951, Sarah was married to my Dad's brother, Dave Thomas. They lived for a time on the place at the end of 6 Road where the Charles Brayton's and then Merton Arpke's had lived. Dave later worked for Charles Wilsea and he and Sarah lived on the

Wilsea farm just west of Grand Junction. Dave and Sarah went back to Fairport, Kansas, (near the Gibbs' farm) for awhile, then returned to Colorado and Dave was caretaker of the old Mesa College farm on the Redlands, which was 4-H headquarters at the time, and Dave worked for John Frezieres. In the late 1960s Dave and Sarah went back to Kansas and Aunt Sarah bought a house in Russell. They lived there until her death in 1977.

Muths

The following information is from Fern Muths and an obituary for Ray Muths from the 11 June 1993 issue of the *Fruita Times*.

Ray Muths was born 4 September 1912, at Tipton, Mitchell, Kansas, a son of Joseph M. and Katharine Yunk Muths. Ray spent his childhood and attended schools at Tipton, Kansas. He married **Fern E. Pavola** on 26 December 1938, at Sterling, Logan, Colorado. Fern was born 2 March 1918 in Reliance, Sweetwater, Wyoming, the daughter of John and Jennie Pavola. They had two sons:

John Pavola, born 28 June 1942, Sterling, Logan, Colorado
Joe Michael, 4 November 1951, Sterling

Ray farmed at Sterling and Proctor, Colorado, before he and the family moved to Denver. They lived there until 1957, when they moved to Mack. In Mack Ray and Fern purchased the Desert Gateway Store from **Ira** and **Thelma Carpenter** in November 1957. Fern's parents, John and Jennie Pavola, made their home with the Muths at the store. In 1974 they sold the store and moved to an acreage near Fruita. Ray farmed and Fern commuted to Grand Junction, working at Conrad's, a women's clothing store, and then at Price Tag, until 1986.

Ray was a member of the Moose Lodge. He passed away at home 7 June 1993. Fern stayed on the farm until moving to Grand Junction this year (1997). She lives at Monterey Park with other senior citizens and is enjoying herself. She has two granddaughters.

John married **Lotus Bottom** in June 1961 at Grand Junction. They have two daughters: **Tohn Fayette** and **Heather Su.** They live in LaHabra, California, where John is in management work in the cement industry.

Joseph lives on the Muths' farm, near Fruita. He has worked at Lake Powell for many years, and is presently employed at the Fruita City Maintenance Department.

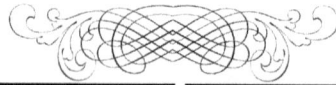

Charles Logan and Grace Sanborn Nelson, 1912   Charles Logan and Grace Sanborn Nelson, 1962

(Photos courtesy of Virginia Labrum Nelson)

Nelson

Information is compiled from family group sheets, a letter, and a history outline written by Virginia Nelson.

Charles "Charlie" Logan Nelson was born 27 March 1886, at Colby, Thomas, Kansas a son of Isaac Newton Nelson and Lydia Ann "Eliza" Tittus. He married **Grace Sanborn** on 21 April 1905, at Pueblo, Pueblo, Colorado. She was born 2 March 1887, at Pueblo, Pueblo, Colorado, a daughter of Triston Sanborn and Mary Ella Bayles.

Charlie and Grace had nine children:

Charles Jr., born 21 March 1907, Pueblo, Pueblo, Colorado
Grace, 18 August 1909, Pueblo
Arnold, 10 January 1912, Pueblo
Vincent "Shorty," 20 May 1914, Pueblo
Elmer, 30 March 1916, Fruita
Lloyd, 24 September 1918, Fruita

Floyd "Tiny," 24 September 1918, Fruita
Harold, 8 April 1922, Fruita
Larry, 4 May 1928, Rifle, Garfield, Colorado

Charlie, Grace and their four oldest children moved from Pueblo to Fruita, Colorado, in about 1914, in a covered wagon. Grace's brother, Frank, and his wife, Cora, and their small daughter, Dorothy, accompanied them. Charlie's mother, Eliza, and her husband, Will Cunduff, had moved to Fruita previously and told them how nice it was there.

When the twins, Lloyd and Floyd, were born, Dr. White was in attendance. He said to Grace, "Come on Grace, have another one, I've never delivered triplets."

Grace was a tiny lady about four feet, ten inches tall and weighed about 75 to 80 pounds. She told him, "Two is enough and if you don't get out of here I'm going to get out of bed and get after you with the broom!"

Charlie and Grace couldn't decide what to name the twins until she was reading the names of soldiers who had died in World War I and discovered the names of two who were Lloyd and Floyd and decided those were the names she wanted for her new twins.

The family lived in Fruita several years while Charlie worked as a farmer and chef; he loved to cook and was head chef at the Mack and Loma hotels for a number of years. A few of the older folks around Fruita remember Charlie — he made the best hamburgers around and always had a stand at the Hunters' Roundup. And he always loved to bet with someone on the horse races.

The Nelsons left Fruita and moved to Rifle around 1928 or 1929, then moved back to Grand Junction around 1938. At that time Lloyd went to work for "Rock" Labrum at the Western Slope Foundry. Soon Lloyd discovered that Rock had a teenage daughter named **Virginia**.

Virginia was born 22 October 1922, at Grand Junction, to **Rocco "Rock" Jeffords Labrum** and **Catherine Rose Hicks**. At the time of her birth, Virginia's parents were living at Castle Gate, Utah. Since Virginia was Catherine's first child, Catherine wanted to be with her mother when Virginia was born, and she also wanted to can some fruit. So Virginia was born in the home of her grandmother, Mary Hicks, in Grand Junction. Afterwards, Virginia's dad came to get them and moved them back to Castle Gate. Then Virginia got asthma so bad the doctor advise them to take her back to Grand Junction. They moved back and forth for awhile; Virginia would get better and they would move back to Castle Gate; then she would get bad again and they would go back to Grand Junction. When she was four years old the family moved back to Grand Junction to stay.

In 1938, when Lloyd came to Grand Junction, 16year-old Virginia wasn't interested in boys. Lloyd went back to Rifle where he worked as a ranch-hand until 1940. When he came back to Grand Junction he and Virginia started dating and were married 11 January 1941, at Moab, Utah.

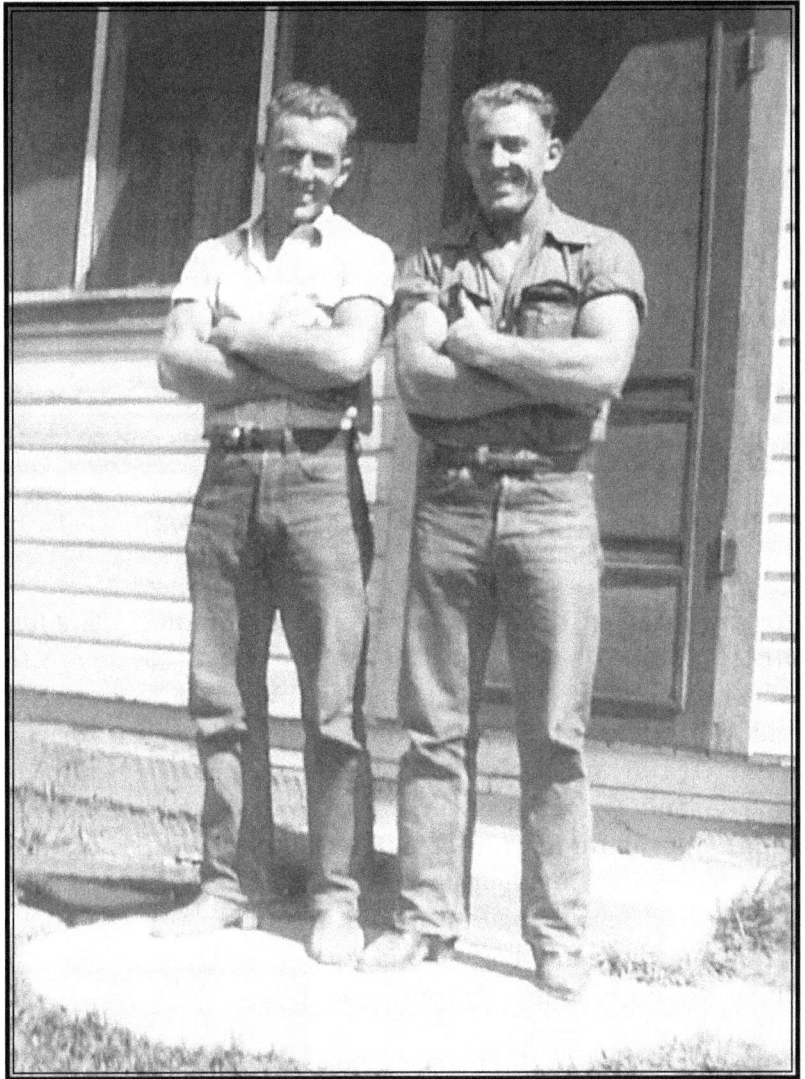

Lloyd and Floyd "Tiny" Nelson
(Photo courtesy of Virginia Labrum Nelson)

After Lloyd and Virginia were married, her folks, Rock and Catherine Labrum, moved back to Castle Gate and her father worked there in the coal mine until it closed down. In the 1950s Rock went to work in the Lone Park Uranium mine at Uravan, Colorado. He was killed in a mine cave-in on 25 September 1957, at age 57, leaving Catherine alone with four boys still at home. There were 11 children total in that family — five boys and six girls. One of the boys was lost in an accident at some point in time.

In June 1942 Lloyd was drafted into the Army. Virginia stayed with him as long as he was stationed in the States. He went overseas and served in the 89th Division. He came home from the Army in January 1946. On 10 September 1948, Lloyd and Virginia had a little

Harold's Desert Inn at Mack, in the spring of 1950, when the club was first opened.
(Photo courtesy of Virginia Labrum Nelson)

girl they named **Louanna Rose**, born at Canon City, Colorado.

At the end of March 1950, Lloyd, Virginia, and daughter, Louanna, moved to Mack from Grand Junction. About a month later Charlie and Grace also moved to Mack and began operation of Harold's Desert Inn, which they had built during the winter of 1949/50. Their son, Harold, had seen a club similar to that somewhere and began to make plans to build one. Harold was killed in a plane crash near Florence, Italy, while serving as a Navigator Bombardier with the 15th Airborne Division during World War II, so did not get to realize his dream. Charlie and his sons, Lloyd, Floyd and Elmer built the club and named it "Harold's Desert Inn" in honor of Harold. (There is more about Harold's Desert Inn under "Colorado Club and Restaurant" in the "Nowadays" section on page 195.)

Charlie was the chef at the inn, but he also loved gardening. He had planted a lawn and shrubs all around the club. He loved Zinnias, so he always had a small plot of them. Whenever he was needed to cook something, someone always had to go find him somewhere out in the yard planting or tending

his flowers and shrubs.

Lloyd, Virginia and Louanna moved to New Liberty about 1961. They lived in the former Summers house where Merton and Mildred Arpke, and later, Dick and Edith Young, lived. Louanna attended school at New Liberty and was among the last students to attend school there.

Charlie and Grace moved to the Pete Appier

Behind Harold's Desert Inn. Back row, L-R: Ricky (kneeling), Louanna, Judy and Jerrie Nelson. In front: Mollie, Sandy, and Carlin Jo Nelson. Charlie Nelson, baby crawling in front. Ricky, Judy and Charlie are Larry's children. Judy, Jerrie and Mollie are Tiny's, and Louanna is Lloyd's daughter. *(Photo courtesy of Virginia Labrum Nelson)*

place in 1967 and lived there until 1969, when Charlie died at age 80. Tiny moved in with Grace, but soon after, Grace moved into Fruita and Tiny bought a trailer. He died there on 13 February 1975. The Appier house burned down in the 70s after Grace had moved into Fruita.

In 1977 Lloyd and Virginia bought 10 acres between the Appier place and Badger Wash. They moved a mobile home onto the property and Grace moved in with them. She remained with them until her death 7 September 1978, at age 92. Lloyd and Virginia sold the Appier place to Vern and Jean McNeal in 1980 or 81.

Grace Nelson's 90th birthday, 2 March 1977. In back, L-R: Lloyd, Louanna (Mackey), and Virginia Nelson. *(Photo courtesy of Virginia Labrum Nelson)*

Lloyd worked for Bill Young and Sons for several years. When Bill needed help with the cattle or farming he would come and get Lloyd. Bill finally talked Lloyd into working for them full time. In the fall roundup and during the winter and spring Lloyd would help Harold Young with the cattle. Then during the farming season he would help with the farming. He worked for the Youngs until 1970, when he started having health problems, but he still occasionally would help Harold. Louanna was Lloyd's little helper — she would drive the tractor and help in doing the creasing, hay baling, or whatever else needed to be done. The highlight of her summer days would be when she and the Post girls, Mableann, Reva and Vera,

would ride their horses to the Young's summer camp at Atchee and spend a few days together. Harold would then load up the horses and girls, and bring them home. Happy years! Louanna married Mitchell Dean Mackey, 2 July 1969.

Lloyd died 22 March 1997, at his home in New Liberty at age 78. Elmer lives in Fruita; he's past age 80. Virginia still lives on the home place in New Liberty.

Family Biographies

O

1884, when Tony was three months old, the family immigrated to Twin Lakes, Minnesota. A little later they moved to Rushville, Nebraska, and lived there for a time and then moved to Fort Dodge, Iowa. Tony went back to Nebraska alone in 1908 where he had previously met **Cornelia "Cora" Victoria Wassenburg.** Cornelia was born at Hay Springs, Sheridan, Nebraska, 10 August 1889, to Laurence Frank Wassenburg and Mary Jane Heesacker. Tony and Cora were married at Fort Dodge, Iowa, 10 Aug 1910, where they resided for a short time before moving back to Rushville. They lived on a homestead near Cora's parents for several years. Their children were:

Helen Marie, born 5 June 1911
Franklin Leroy, 20 March 1913
Charles Webster, 5 February 1919
All were born on a farm in a community known as "Sand Flats" near Rushville, Sheridan, Nebraska.

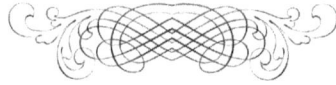

Anthony and Cornelia Victoria Overbye, 1910
(Photo courtesy of Helen Overbye Peterson)

Overbye

The following stories came from Helen Overbye Peterson and Frank Overbye. There are some additions from obituaries and news items in *The Daily Sentinel* and from the author

Anthony "Tony" Overbye was born 28 December 1883, at Christiana, near Oslo, Norway, to Andrew Overbye and Bertha Anderson. In the summer of

The Tony Overbye family, Grand Junction, Colorado, 1923. Back row: L-R: Franklin Leroy and Helen Marie. Front row: Anthony "Tony", Charles Webster and Cornelia "Cora" Overbye. *(Photo courtesy of Helen Overbye Peterson)*

(Above) Cora Overbye standing in front of the new 1923 Model "T" Ford that cost $700. In the background is the new corn crib that was built on the Wassenberg farm in New Liberty by Tony Overbye and Ted Wassenberg. (Left) Matt Heesacker, grandfather of Cora Overbye, with wife and children. The girl in center front is Mary Jane Heesacker (Wassenberg), mother of Cora Wassenberg Overbye. (Below left) Frank and Mary Jane Wassenberg with grandchildren, Helen and Frank Overbye, 1913. (Below right) Bertha Overbye, grandmother of Helen and Frank Overbye, of Fort Dodge, Iowa, 1928. *(Photos courtesy of Helen Overbye Peterson)*

After Helen was born the family lived a short time at Spokane, Washington, where Tony was employed by the Diamond Match Co. Back in Nebraska Helen and Frank started school at "Sand Flats" in 1918 in a sod school house. About this time also, Tony became a citizen of the United States.

In May 1919 they sold the place at Sand Hills and moved to a farm on the Niobrara River in a community known as "Mirage Flats." There they farmed and milked cows. Helen did not start to school until her brother Frank was old enough to go, because their mother was afraid for Helen to walk the three miles to school alone.

After World War I, Cora's brother, Ted Wassenburg, went to Colorado and bought a homestead in the New Liberty community. He was successful in convincing Tony and Cora that they should move out there too. So, the Overbye family arrived at Mack, 20 March 1923. Ted met them at the Mack depot with a team and wagon. They stopped at Allen Daily's the first night and then drove on to Ted's farm the next day. They farmed with Ted that first year, then the family moved to Grand Junction where Tony was employed for a short time icing railroad cars — filling the ice compartments to keep the fruit cool.

They rented a farm in the Appleton district northwest of Grand Junction and Helen and Frank went to school there for part of a year. They moved back to New Liberty in the spring of 1924 and rented the Clyde Balkwill farm across the road east of Ted's farm. (Where Milton and Lona Alstatt recently lived) Helen and Frank enrolled again in school at New Liberty. Charles started school there in the fall of 1924.

In the winter of 1924 Tony bought four building lots about a quarter mile east of Mack on the south side of the highway, and built a new home on one of them. He moved the family there in March of 1925. The children were then enrolled in school at Mack. Tony went to work for the Uintah Railway on the gilsonite transfer gang.

Helen and Frank both graduated from the eighth grade at Mack school in May 1927. Both were enrolled at Fruita Union High School that fall.

In 1936 Tony and Cora bought a farm 10 miles south west of Grand Valley, Colorado. In the fall of 1940 Tony and Cora moved to Weir's farm, in the New Liberty area. Then, in 1942, Frank and Velma bought 40 acres from Charlie Smith on the west edge of Mack, adjoining the school grounds. They built a house and out buildings on that property, and later a garage. Five years later they gave Tony and Cora two acres on the south end of this property where they built a small house and retired from farming. In the summer of 1962 they moved to Grand Junction where Cora died 27 October 1962. On 28 February 1963 Tony died; both are buried in Elmwood Cemetery at Fruita.

Helen developed a great interest in basketball while in high school and after making the first string she traveled with the team all over the western slope under the coaching of Philip Griebel. She met **Harley Wilkerson**, a resident of Mack, who was employed at the Mack Garage,

Helen Overbye and Harley Wilkerson
(Photo courtesy of Helen Overbye Peterson)

Lloyd and Helen Kendall and family, December 1958, Springville, Utah. Back row, L-R: Daryl and Kaye Dauwalder, and John David and Joan Wilkerson. Front: Tracy Lloyd Dauwalder, Lloyd Kendall, Tina Dauwalder and Helen Kendall. *(Photo courtesy of Helen Overbye Peterson)*

Virgial and Helen Overbye Peterson, 1995, Springville, Utah.
(Photo courtesy of Helen Overbye Peterson)

and after a relatively short courtship, they were married 21 October 1930, at Marietta, Love County, Oklahoma. After living about a year in Texas, they moved back to Fruita, Colorado, and lived on a farm for a few years. While living there Helen gave birth to two sons, the first of whom did not survive, the second, named **John David**, was born 18 August 1933. Then they bought a large home in Grand Junction and remodeled it into apartments.

On 18 March 1937, while visiting Helen's parents on the farm near Grand Valley, Colorado, Harley, who was doing some farm work, came to the house complaining of pain in his chest. A short time later he died. He was only 34.

Helen and her small son continued to live in the big house in Grand Junction and her brother, Frank, came to board with her for awhile. She later sold that place and, on 24 March 1939, at Price, Utah, was married to **Lloyd Kendall**, a widower with a small daughter named Kaye. Lloyd at one time lived on a ranch near Atchee, Colorado.

Lloyd and Helen moved into a new home in Springville, Utah, 3 July 1941, where they raised their two children. After the children were grown and married, each made their homes in the Provo area. Lloyd had a heart attack in July 1954 and spent nineteen days in the hospital, finally gaining enough strength to return home. He was never very well after that, and died in 1962. (Lloyd's daughter, Kaye, died in Provo in 1993 from cancer.)

On 4 April 1974, Helen married **Virgial Peterson**, a next door neighbor. They are living in the home in Springville she and Lloyd built in 1941. They have done a lot of traveling since their marriage.

$\mathcal{F}$rank went to live with his parents on their farm near Grand Valley for a while and it was while living there he met **Velma Power**; they were married 2 July 1940 at Provo, Utah. They have two children:

> **Carolyn Louise,** born 21 February 1945
> **Leon Franklin,** 29 June 1950
> There are two grandchildren.

Following are excerpts from an unpublished autobiography by Frank Overbye, some of which was printed in the *Fruita Times* of 8 August 1991. We have included several pages of it because of its humor and because it gives us

L-R: Leon Franklin, Franklin Leroy, Velma Power and Carolyn Louise Overbye, December 1953, Springfield, Oregon. *(Photo courtesy of Frank and Velma Overbye)*

years, or until the fall of 1919. During that six years my sister and I, along with our dog, Budger, roamed the sand hills, playing in the "blowouts" for entertainment, sometimes stepping on sand-burrs or cactus with our bare feet. If Mom lost sight of us for too long she would call the dog and he would go to her, then she would follow him back to where we were. Budger was our best friend, I remember well the day when he was kicked by a horse and died soon after. I was about four years old. Dad got another dog, a red and white one, we named him Rover. Rover saved us from some serious problems. Several times when we kids were playing in the yard, a big goose or turkey gobbler would attack us. Rover would always come to the rescue.

My sister Helen and I started school at the same time; age didn't make much difference in those days, I was five and she was six and a half. Our first school

good insight into the lifestyle of a young man growing up in a "sometimes harsh" farm environment during the depression. We have done some editing.

The Sandhill Kid

by Franklin Leroy Overbye

My life started during one of the worst blizzards that ever hit Western Nebraska on Thursday, 20 March 1913. I was born at 5 A.M. in a little sod house about 19 miles south of Hay Springs, and Rushville, Sheridan, Nebraska, in the heart of the Sandhill country.

My parents were Anthony (Tony) Overbye, born in Oslo, Norway 28 Dec 1883, and Cornelia Victoria Wassenberg, born at Mirage Flats south of Hay Springs, Nebraska, 10 August 1889. They were married 10 August 1910 at Fort Dodge, Iowa, where they lived a few months, then moved back to Nebraska, where they homesteaded a section of land near my maternal grandparents, Lawrence Frank Wassenberg and Mary Jane Heesacker, who also had a large cattle ranch.

It was there that our family started, I was the second of three children. First was my sister Helen Marie, born 5 June 1911. Six years after my arrival our brother Charles Webster was born, 5 February 1919. We lived in the sod house on the homestead for about six

The Sandhill kids, Helen Marie and Frank Leroy Overbye, 1913. *(Photo courtesy of Helen Overbye Peterson)*

601

house there was also made of sod. A wood frame horse shed stood in the corner of the school yard. One night a storm came up, tornado-like, and lifted the horse shed and dropped it over the fence in a pile of rubble.

Our next school was a little homestead shack about a half mile from our home, but in the opposite direction, a change to accommodate more families in the area. When walking to this school in the late winter, we could never see the fences, they were covered over with drifted snow. School terms were three to four months of the year, depending on the winters.

One winter morning during a hard snow storm, Dad could not get out the door, the snow had drifted as high as the house. The wind had blown snow in the keyhole and formed a snow pyramid three feet high inside the house. Dad had to crawl out the top of a window to get outside and shovel his way back to the kitchen door. Our house was barely visible under the snowdrift. Dad had stretched a wire from the door of the house to the barn so that, in case of a blizzard, he could find his way between the house and barn

I can't remember the water ever freezing in the water tank, even at below zero temperatures, the windmill was always left running and the underground water was warm enough, with the continuous flow, to keep it from freezing.

In the summer of 1918 my mother's brother, Ted Wassenberg, left to join the Army in World War I. Before he left he sold my Dad his violin for $25, which I inherited and still have. The violin was to play a good part in our lives. Later my dad played it for dances while my mother played the organ. Dad said he would give it to the first kid to learn to play it. I won the violin and had the privilege of playing it in later years for dances too. Our son, Leon, also played it in later years during his fifth grade in school.

Our brother Charles was born, 5 February 1919, while Helen and I were in school. A short time later Uncle Ted came home. Uncle Ted was lucky to not get even a scratch in the war. He spent 21 months overseas and said he always followed a hunch.

About that time my parents sold the homestead for $5000 and bought a ranch 11 May 1919, for which they paid $3200. It was a section of land about ten miles east on the Niobrara River. Dad built a big barn on the ranch the first year in which to keep his milk cows and horses. During our stay there we milked up to 25 cows. My sister and I always helped; we broke in on the strippers. Dad harvested wild hay, alfalfa, wheat, barley, maize and potatoes. Mother picked all the wild berries she could find along the river and made jams and jellies.

On this ranch I had the most enjoyable time of my growing-up years. There was always work to do, but after the work was done we had our time to play. In addition to the cows, we always had about 25 hogs to feed, as well as chickens, geese and turkeys. In the summer when our chores were done we kids would wander up and down the river eating wild currants, choke cherries, wild grapes and ground cherries. We also fished along the river and lakes for sunfish, bull heads, catfish, suckers and carp.

At least once a day we would go swimming, and it was here that our dog, Rover, played the life saver. Helen got into some swift water and could not swim out. Rover saw the trouble, jumped in and helped her to the bank. He always sat on the bank watching us, if he wasn't swimming with us. About this same time our younger brother, Charlie, was with us one day when Helen and I decided to see who could stay under water the longest. Before doing this we noticed Charlie sitting safely on a sand bar, but when we surfaced all we could see of him was first a hand come up, then a leg, as he rolled with the river current. We ran and pulled him to a sand bar and pumped all the water out of him. There were no ill effects. We never told our parents until years later!

In the summer time pocket gophers would dig holes and make mounds of dirt in the alfalfa fields. Dad bought some traps and wanted me to trap them. I would put traps in some holes with apples for bait, in others I'd use nuts for bait. We never caught gophers by the apples, we always caught them by the nuts!!!

The school we went to from this ranch was three miles away. It was located on Peter's Flats. Our teacher was Cecelia Heesacker. Helen was one grade ahead of me when we started to school there, but I made 2nd and 3rd grades in one year.

We rode a horse named "Old Jim" to school and left him standing tied all day in a barn. In cold weather we would get on him and start home. Being cold and wanting to warm up, he would buck us off and run to the next gate, there we would catch him and ride on home. Our school had outdoor privy's, one for the boys and one for the girls. The boys' favorite pastime was peeking through the knotholes of the girls privy!!

One fall day Helen and I walked to school and on the way home we spotted a pack of wolves coming over a hill heading in our direction. We started running and were still about a mile from home and plenty scared! Dad had spotted the wolves also and grabbed a shotgun and came to meet us. We were sure tickled to see him!

In those days there were no pesticides to spray for bugs, so we had to pick the bugs off the potatoes and other garden plants one at a time and drop them into a bucket of coal oil. (sure death!) It was a slow and tedious process.

It was when we lived on this ranch that Mom talked Pop into joining the Sacred Heart Catholic Church, which was about a mile and a half from home on Mirage Flats, just north of Peter's Flats. To the best of my knowledge, we kids were all christened in this church, although Helen has record that she was christened, 29 Sep. 1911, at St. Mary's Catholic Church in Rushville, Sheridan, Nebraska. My Wassenberg grandparents and one aunt are buried in the church yard there. My grandfather Wassenberg drowned in the stock water tank, 30 July 1919, on their homestead in the sand-hills. They said he always got up early and sat on the edge of the tank to soak his feet in the water. The cause of his death is unknown, but he was found floating in the water.

Several relatives lived near us there, such as Pete and Frank Weyers, second or third cousins of Mom's. Also several of the Heesacker families who were cousins and aunts and uncles of Mom's. Our nearest neighbors were the Sweiners, who lived one half mile up the river. John Peters and Frank Weyers lived west of us. To the east lived Charles Grossenbeck, Charley Peters, Nick Kozal and the Skudlocks. Down river were VanDorens and a bachelor named Andy Brown, who lived in a dugout, and who usually made it to one of his neighbors regularly for a meal. When he came to our place for a meal in cold weather he would park a chair in front of the kitchen stove, sit down and put his feet into the oven. Much to Mom's disgust, she had to walk around him to get the meal.

It was at Nick Kozal's barn where Mom and Dad played for dances. Dad had the fiddle and Mom the old pumper organ. This barn was about a mile from home. We would milk the cows and do the other chores, then Dad would put the fiddle under his arm and we would walk up the fence line to the barn. We always had a midnight supper, then everybody would dance until daylight, walk home, milk the cows and go to bed. Helen and I learned to dance there.

Another early settler in this area was "Old Jules Sandos", who had the Post Office and trading post a couple of miles east of us. He also had the first and only orchard in the area. It was next to Sweiners, a half mile up river. Old Jules died in 1927, his daughter became an author and wrote a book about her dad and his trials and tribulations in trying to settle this sometimes harsh country.

We had five horses on this ranch, three of which were work horses. They were named Jim, Fan and Nell. The other two were fast horses and were used only to pull our two seated surrey. I remember one day in about 1920 when we drove those horses to Hay Springs, 19 miles north, and while there we saw our first automobile. It scared the horses and we almost had a runaway,

Shortly thereafter Dad bought a used 1919 Ford Touring car. I'll never forget when he drove it home, all went fine until he came to the wire gate to turn into our place. He intended to stop at the gate and open it before going through, but as he approached the gate he hollered "Whoa", but the durn (sic) car just kept right on going through the gate. Needless to say, he had to build a new gate, those new-fangled motors just wouldn't listen!!

When we wanted to go west from our place we had to ford the river because there was no bridge. We tried to get across by driving like lightning through the water and sand bars, but sometimes Dad's foot would slip off the low-pedal and there we would sit in the middle of the river, stuck! It was always my duty to take off my shoes and pants, wade out, go back and harness old Jim and go to the rescue; pulling the old Ford on across. If we were headed away from home, we would just take the harness off the horse and send him back to the barn.

When we left home going to the east, we had to climb a sand hill to get up from the river bottom. It was on this hill we sometimes had a problem getting stuck in the sand. Sometimes we had to get a horse to pull us up the hill.

A graded road was not to be found in that country in the early days. The road consisted of two ruts, one for each wheel to run in and if you happened to meet another car, which was very seldom, you would have trouble getting out of the ruts as they were so deep sometimes the car would high-center and we'd have to jack up a wheel and put chunks of sod or cow-chips under it to get traction. When the gas was low in the tank, which was under the front seat, Pop would have to turn around and back up the hills. Mom learned to drive the Model T by driving around and around on the prairie flats.

One winter when the snow was deep, we started to Hay Springs, which was 19 miles. We came to a small canyon where the snow was drifted to several feet deep in the bottom. Dad decided he would have to make a fast run through a narrow cut in the snow bank. At the bottom the Model T jumped to one side and dove into the snow bank which almost covered the car. We were stuck good and nobody came along to pull us out, so Mom and Pop shoveled snow till almost dark before finally getting out. So we went to a hotel to stay the night, then went on home the next day.

In the late fall a trip to town by team and wagon was always planned to take a load of hogs to market and bring back a wagon load of groceries and coal for the winter. Also in the fall we always had to go out on the prairie to pick up dried cow chips. Helen and I would take a basket between us and pick until the basket was full, then dump it in the wagon. These chips were used for fuel in the winter, we always had a shed full of them. (Cow chips were piles of cow manure that had dried during the summer - author)

After she sold out in the sand hills, my grandmother Wassenberg came to stay with us one summer. She was not feeling too well at the time, but she left to go visit the Maston family near where she had lived. A few days later we got word that she had passed away. She had just come back from a trip to Mack, Colorado, to visit her son Ted.

My grandmother on my Dad's side came to visit us one time during World War I, when we lived in the sand hills. This was the only time we ever saw her; she lived at Fort Dodge, Iowa. She died in 1930. We never did see grand dad Overbye, he died in 1920.

When we first moved to the river ranch Mom sent to Montgomery Ward for a nice mantel clock which would chime on the hours; a hanging kerosene Rayo lamp with a pretty Tiffany shade, a rug, a nice table and some easy chairs for the living room. The clock is now in my possession and it's running good to this day.

Our irrigation system for the garden was unique, being an old wooden-tub washing machine and two buckets. The washing machine stood on the bank of the river with a pipe running from it to the garden rows. It took three of us to make it work. I would stand next to the water, dip a bucket full, hand it to Mom, who would pour it into the machine. When the tub was full we would pull the plug and let the water go down the rows.

In the spring and fall the ducks migrating north or south would sometimes land on the river and Dad would quite often shoot some. They made good eating.

One winter when Charlie was about four years old we were sleigh-riding down the hill behind the barn. Helen and I put him on the sled and started it down the hill. We were going to run along side and stop him if it got to going too fast. But the sled got away from us and we were unable to catch up. There was a barbed wire fence near the bottom which we knew he was going to hit. We yelled at him to roll off , but he didn't hear us and when he went under the fence a barb on the wire caught him under the chin and tore a three-inch gash through his mouth. He was bleeding bad and when we got him to the house Mom bandaged him up, but he always had a scar.

Every spring when the snow would melt the river would flood. It would always tear out all the fence that crossed the river, and it also took a little more of the garden patch every year.

Uncle Ted Wassenberg went to Colorado in 1920 and bought a homestead in the New Liberty community near Mack. He thought it much better than Nebraska, so he talked to Dad and Mom about it and they too decided to move to Colorado. About the first of March 1923, my parents had a public auction, sold the farm and all their possessions.

We had to leave behind our dog Rover, our best pal! He would never ride in a car before, but as we got in the car on the train to leave he crawled in too and hid under our feet. He knew we were leaving! We left him with Frank Weyers but he only lived a few months and died apparently of a broken heart.

It took us three days and nights on the train. We arrived in Mack on my birthday, 20 March 1923. Uncle Ted met us at the train with a team and wagon and drove us six miles out in the country to his farm in the New Liberty district. Everything looked so dry and barren, we were all pretty depressed. On the way to the ranch Helen and I kept asking Uncle Ted; "How much further is it?" Finally he got tired of saying "a mile or two" and then said: "See that big mountain over there? Well, it isn't on top of that".

My Dad and Uncle Ted farmed his place together that first year. The first thing Dad did was buy a new 1923 Model T Ford car. As I remember, it cost about $700.

That year Dad built a 14 by 14 homestead shack on Ted's place. We lived in it until late August 1923. We had to walk close to a mile to New Liberty School. There was no road, just a trail across the alkali flats and deep seep ditches. In wet weather the mud would stick to our shoes so we could hardly walk. We learned why they called it "Gum-boot Flats". . .

In August 1923 we took a tent and went to Grand Junction and camped in a tent park on 5th and North Avenue. For about a week Dad worked at the ice house icing railroad cars for shipping peaches. After about a week we rented a house and Helen and I started at Washington school. Peach harvest was over in about a month, Dad was laid off, so we rented a farm at Appleton, west of Grand Junction.

It was there Dad bought three horses and four cows and began farming. The school there was tough, I had to fight everywhere I went. But Helen always helped me.

In the spring of 1924 we moved back to New Liberty and rented the Clyde Balkwill place, across the road east of Uncle Ted's place. Helen and I went back to New Liberty School again.

The Balkwill place was all in alfalfa, so Dad worked on the Highline ditch part of the summer while Mom and we kids irrigated the hay. We had several tons of hay stacked that summer and that fall our landlord came to the place while we were gone and sold all our hay to a sheep man and took off with the money. Dad hunted him down, found him running an auto paint shop in Grand Junction. All Dad ever got out of his hay money was a paint job for his Ford. He told Dad he needed the money worse than Dad did and refused to pay up.

That fall Dad got a job on the transfer gang on the Uintah Railway at Mack. That winter Dad bought two lots just east of Mack for $100 per lot and later bought two more lots adjoining them. They built a new house on that property, between the highway and the railroad track.

We moved into the new house 1 March 1925 and Helen, Charlie and I all started to Mack School. This was another tough school, we had a few "smart alecks" who were always

The new Tony Overbye house east of Mack

Left is the front and right is the back of the house. (Photos courtesy of Frank Overbye)

promoting fights among the smaller kids. I was one of those smaller kids and had to fight all the way home every evening. Helen was always there to help me out.

Helen and I both graduated from Mack School in 1927. We both started to Fruita Union High School that fall.

During the time I was going to High School I delivered milk for Kiefer's Dairy, which was across the road from our house. I pulled a little two-wheeled cart loaded with about forty gallons of milk to and around the town of Mack, which was about a quarter mile from home. Part of the milk went to local customers and the rest of it to the Uintah Depot to be shipped to Watson and Dragon, Utah. For this job I received the enormous sum of $5 per month.

School was never one of my best projects. I did enjoy the Agriculture class, where we learned blacksmithing, carpenter and mechanic work. We also learned how to caponize chickens, repair harness and saddles, build hog and dog houses and other farm-related structures. I was selected to drive the Model T truck to haul those latter items to country schools around the valley to demonstrate to the farmers in the various communities, etc. The first few months weren't bad, but as the weeks drug on and the grass started to get green, my feet just wouldn't stay under the desk anymore.

So I quit school to do more important things . . . I thought!

I went to work in the Mack Cafe for George Rittenhouse washing dishes (pearl diving) for a dollar a day and board. The cook was Harry Warfle. I thought I had it made . . . easy work, lots of money and good food. That lasted a few weeks until they hired a new cook.

I quit there and went to work for Ed Stout in a garage at the same big wages. But I worked sometimes for nothing just to learn the trade and to be with Harley Wilkerson, who later was to become my brother-in-law.

I remember Mom sending me to town for fifty cents worth of steak, which was enough to feed about six people at that time. If I lucked out I got to drive the car on those kinds of errands.

The first car I remember driving was a 1920 Dodge Commercial belonging to Ed Stout. He would let me drive it to the Post Office to pick up packages and mail for him. I was about 13 then, at that time driver's licenses weren't required. All the mail and freight in those days came in on #3 D&RG

passenger train every morning at 10 o'clock. That train was almost our only means of transportation in those days as roads were almost non-existent, especially in winter.

I had another job in 1928 driving a Graham 1½ ton truck for Mack Mercantile, hauling groceries and supplies from Grand Junction to Mack and an occasional delivery of hay and grain to local stockmen. Every morning about 10 o'clock I hauled grocery orders over to Uintah Depot to be shipped to Atchee, Dragon and Watson. My wages were $1.50 per day.

Helen moved to Fruita to work in a restaurant for Dow Jones and stayed with them while going to High School. About this time she started dating Harley Wilkerson. We could always tell who it was when he brought her home because he always said, "if you put the brakes on hard it makes a smoother stop as the wheels slide on the gravel."

One Sunday Harley and Helen went for a ride on Douglas Pass with Russell Rector and Etta Simpson. They were driving Russell's 1926 Chrysler Roadster. They were almost to the top of the pass when they stopped to take some pictures. They had left the car and walked up the road some distance when one of them looked back and saw the car rolling down off the road into the brush. A small tree lodged under the front axle and over the bumper and stopped the car about 100 feet over the bank.

They caught a ride home and the next day several of us went up and winched the car back up on the road then pulled it home. It was sort of bent out of shape, but Russell had it repaired in Grand Junction so it looked good as new.

Harley helped me buy my first car — a 1917 Model T bug that cost $17. The former owner had burned out a rod. I worked on it for about a year and never did get it to run very good, every time I left home with it I had to be towed home. I finally bought the running gear of a 1921 Model T for $3 and built an airplane style body on it out of tin highway signs. This was a good running Ford with a good motor. One day a young man saw it and wanted to trade me a 1924 Ford Touring. I jumped at the chance, took it and dressed it up with windshield wings, several horns, a new paint job, exhaust whistle, radiator ornaments, etc.

One thing that stood out on this car was a small box that came from the Uintah RR office with a slot in the top. Painted on the side were the words: "Suggestion Box". The suggestions I found in it ranged from matches to horse turds.

While living at Mack I also helped Judge Kennedy run the movie projector for silent movies in the school auditorium. One night during the show the film caught fire and everything else caught on fire. We had to go down a ladder to get away, but we got out alright. The volunteer fire department soon put the fire out with a bucket brigade.

Dad worked for the Uintah until about 1929. After that he rented a farm at the edge of Mack from Chris Pappas and farmed it for about two years.

Harley and Helen were married 21 October 1930 at Marietta, Love, Oklahoma. They lived in Cleburne, Texas for awhile, then bought a farm about 20 miles out of town with a truck and hay baler. The following spring Harley and Helen came back to Colorado on vacation. When they went back they asked me to go with them.

That summer we hauled grain from threshing machines to storage in various places. We had been hauling from one big machine for several days when we woke up one morning and it was raining hard. 3 o'clock AM was the time we normally started, but that morning we didn't go out until 6 AM. It hadn't rained at the thresher, so we were docked a half day's pay for being late. We were only being paid $1.50 per day plus a little extra for the truck and our day was from 3 AM until 10 PM.

I "plowed" or cultivated a lot of cotton that summer and had my first experience picking cotton as well. Harley could pick close to 200

Frank's first car he bought at 14 years of age, 1927. It was a 1917 Model "T" Bug. *(Photo courtesy of Frank Overbye)*

pounds per day but my top was 108 pounds.

Harley got several jobs with his hay baler and worked the rest of the summer at that - baling Johnson grass and prairie hay. When Harley and I were hauling hay from the baler to Glen Rose one time we had it stacked pretty high on the truck. As we rounded a curve in the road we met a car, a new roadster, when several of the top bales rolled off, caving in the top of the nice car. The man driving the car was very nice. He said when he saw the bales coming he said to himself, "This is going to hurt". But he didn't get a scratch. After he talked to us for a few minutes, he just put the top down and drove on down the road. Harley was afraid he would have to pay for the damage. But I guess the old boy driving the car decided he got off pretty lucky at that!

That fall Harley decided he wanted to go to Colorado to hunt deer. To help pay expenses he bought several barrels of cheap oil, about 500 pounds of pecans, loaded them on the truck along with his sister, Bea, her husband, Virgil, Floyd C. (Virgil and Bea's boy, about 6 or 7), Helen and myself. About 100 miles north of Amarillo, Texas, with the wind blowing hard and cold, a valve spring broke in the truck engine. We "just happened" to have one, so, with the aid of a flashlight, we got it installed. It took two days and two nights to travel the 1,000 miles to Colorado.

Harley sold the oil and the pecans; he and Virgil were successful in their hunt. During the time we were in Colorado, Harley and Helen decided they wanted to move back to Colorado. So, Harley, Virgil, Bea, Floyd C., Harley's mother, Jenny, and Dad, Wiley, boarded the truck, covered up with a tarp, and went back to Texas to haul their belongings back to Colorado. (Helen stayed with mother and Dad Overbye at Mack)

Coming back from Texas I drove the truck and Harley drove his car. Harley's Dad and Floyd C. rode with me while Harley and his mother rode in the car. We left first as Harley said he would catch up with us. After a couple of hours driving Floyd C. began saying, "I'm thirsty by now." While we were stopped at a stand to get him a drink, we thought we saw Harley go flying by in his car. We drove till midnight but never did catch up with Harley, so we pulled off the road so we would see him if he did happen to be behind us. Then we crawled in the back of the truck under the tarp and slept until daylight.

Dad, Wilkerson, and I only had about $3 between us, we bought a tank of gas. That broke us and we were beginning to feel a little desperate. We had about 200 pounds of pecans in the truck, so when we got to Texline we sold the pecans. We drove all day and then all night until about 5 A. M. the next morning when we found Harley in a motel in Trinidad, Colorado. We slept a couple of hours then took off again for home. Harley went on ahead again, saying we had made it so good so far we just as well drive it on home. By the time we made it home I was so tired I couldn't sleep. I had driven every mile of the way.

After their return, Harley and Helen bought an old school building at Atchee, tore it down and used the lumber to build a house on 10 acres 4 miles east of Fruita. Harley and Helen's son, John David, was born while they lived on that place.

Every fall Harley and I would go toward Atchee to get a load of wood. But wood wasn't all we got, we usually brought home a deer also. We would cover it carefully with the wood. One time when we were going home we stopped at a station to get gas and the operator told us that was the first load of wood he ever saw bleeding!

About 1932, when the depression was beginning to get bad, my parents decided to sell their house at Mack and rent a 20 acre farm one mile west of Pomona School. They stayed there a year, then bought a 20 acre farm 2 miles west of Appleton for $800.

In 1933 this area was a very poor place to find work. I tried for a year but only found two weeks work driving a Uintah Railway passenger and freight bus between Grand Junction and Mack, for Johnnie Hayden while he was sick. I was paid $1.00 per day and board. I went back to work at the Mack Garage in 1934 on commission. But it hardly paid enough to pay for batching expenses.

In the spring of 1935 my folks sold their 20-acre farm west of Appleton and rented a summer pasture in the hills above Collbran. In the meantime, Uncle Ted bought a starter motel in Gillette, Wyoming. I helped the folks move to Collbran. Then I went back to Mack and helped Uncle Ted get ready to move to Gillette. He built a semi-trailer on the 1927 Buick to haul all his belongings to Gillette. I helped drive and move his family up there.

I stayed all summer and hauled gravel on the Buick trailer from the Bell Fouche River, 38 miles east of Gillette. I loaded gravel on

and off by hand, and mixed all the cement with a mixer for the foundations. These included three basements for the ten units we built onto the motel that summer. I got $1.25 a day, with board and room, for 10 hours work.

I stayed till the last of October, then helped my folks move to about 10 miles northeast of Fruita for the winter.

In 1936 Harley and Helen traded their Fruita place for one on Wallace Creek, 10 miles southwest of Grand Valley. My folks bought a place there, also, and farmed both places, as Harley was called to work on the railroad.

Harley bought a big, old house at 540 Hill Avenue, in Grand Junction, and I helped him make it into four apartments.

Harley and I became interested in flying, so we joined a flying club and bought shares in a plane. I got 33 hours of flying time in a Piper Club plane and received my solo license. I lacked two hours of being eligible for a private license.

In the spring, 18 March 1938, Helen and Harley went up to their farm at Grand Valley, to visit our parents. Harley was out burning weeds when he had a pain in his chest, went to the house, laid down on the bed and passed away. It was hard to believe, as he never had a problem that any of us were aware of.

Later that spring, I sold my interest in the plane and went back to Grand Valley and did custom plowing for farmers with my Fordson tractor for awhile. I opened a garage in Grand Valley for a short term, then went back to work for Otto Letson, running his station in DeBeque.

Fall and winter of 1938 and 1939 I went to work for the Mt. Streeter Coal mine, loading coal in the mine for 50 cents a ton. Walt Kramer and I batched together in my trailer house.

It was about this time that I met and started dating Velma Power. We were married on 2 July 1940 by the Justice of the Peace in the Utah County Courthouse in Provo, Utah, My sister Helen and Margaret Wilkerson stood with us.

We went back to Grand Valley. In August I went to work for U.S. Geological Survey at Salida. Velma stayed with her mother until I returned in October, when it got too cold to work. I hauled coal for Bud Main from the Mt. Streeter mine, north of Meeker to Glenwood Springs, Aspen, Carbondale, Rifle, Grand Valley, and DeBeque.

In the fall of 1940, my folks moved to the Weir place in New Liberty. In the spring of 1941 I plowed their fields for them with my

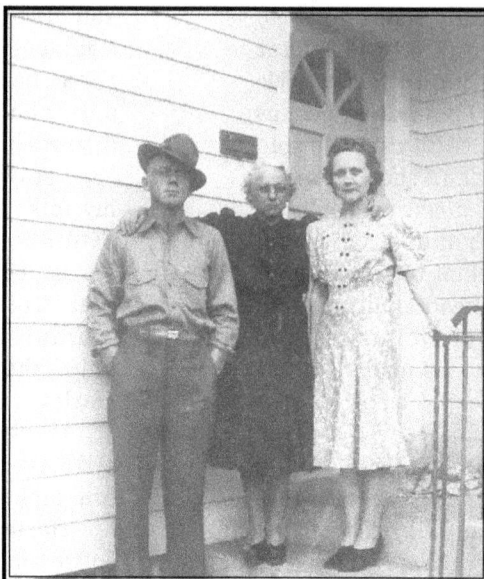

(Left) Frank and Velma Overbye the winter of 1942–43 in Springville, Utah at his sister, Helen's, place. (Above) Frank and Cora Overbye, and Helen Overbye Kendall, the same time and place as above. *(Photos courtesy of Frank Overbye)*

tractor. Then I went to work on the survey crew at Creede, Colorado. We finished there in October and went to Mack to work in a garage for Mike Stroud. We parked our trailer in back of the garage on 7 December 1941, the day Pearl Harbor was bombed by Japan.

In early 1942 we bought our 40-acre farm next to the town of Mack. This was all virgin land. We bought it from Charley Smith.

We traded our trailer house for several hundred railroad ties, a chicken house and some chickens, a sewing machine, a radio and a heating stove. We built a railroad-tie cow barn. We also bought a two-room house and moved it onto our farm. Then we borrowed $100 from the Government (F.F.A.) and bought a cow and some more chickens. About a month later the chicken house burned down one night, killing all of the chickens but one old setting hen.

The first year or two our drinking water was hauled from Fruita — eight miles in a steel tank. Needless to say, it got a bit warm in summer. Then we built a cistern on top of the hill and piped it to the house, but the water still had to be hauled and put in the cistern. We used the Fordson tractor and a scraper to dig out space for the house, brooder house, and pond. I then traded the Fordson for parts to build a tractor.

In October, we went on to Springville, Utah. I got a job driving trucks for Midwest Pipe, hauling pipes to the steel plant addition in Ironton, and to the new steel plant being built west of Provo called Geneva Steel. We lived with my sister, Helen Kendall, that winter, for no rentals were available because of the war.

In March of 1943 we bought three more cows, more chickens and rented two more farms for that summer. In June we bought an old John Deere combine, spent a month fixing it up, then went out and combined for hire. With our 1933 Chevrolet truck we hauled the grain from the combine. With these we paid off the farm the first year. Velma was kept busy chasing parts for the combine.

In 1944 we added two rooms to our house to make room for our expected increase in the family. We also put asphalt shakes on the outside of the house to make it more attractive and warmer in the winter. We dug a cellar into the hill, with a milk room in the front.

About this time, Stove Canyon Coal mine quit working and auctioned off all the buildings at the mine. We bought the engine house, which was made of galvanized tin, for $20, tore it down in sections and hauled it home. We made a hip roof on our railroad tie barn, including a hay loft.

At 4:50 a.m., 21 February 1945, our daughter, Carolyn Louise, was born at the Fruita Community Hospital.

I wired our house for electricity, had it inspected and had the electricity turned on 1 April 1946, a greatly appreciated convenience. Soon after, we bought a used refrigerator. We felt lucky to find one, as they were scarce because of the war. Our only cooling system before this was a screened-in box with a tub of water on top and a sheet of burlap. One end was in the tub and the rest hung down over the screen. The breeze caused it to cool everything inside.

In early 1947 we gave my parents two acres of land on the south edge of our place, and they built a small house on it. Dad had retired from farming then, at age 65.

In late 1947, Don Severson, of Mobil Oil Company, requested we build a garage and station on the front of our property adjoining the highway, so the company would have an outlet for their products in the Lower Valley. Our

(Upper left) Frank and the Fordson tractor that he used for many years and traded for parts to build a tractor. (Upper right) Frank and his John Deere combine he bought in 1943 and tractor that he built. (Center left) The tractor that Frank built to fit his needs. (Center right) A view taken from the hill on Frank and Velma's farm, showing the 1933 Chevrolet truck and house, after they had added the asphalt shakes, about 1945. (Lower left) Frank's railroad tie barn with the galvanized tin roof that he built. All pictures were taken on Frank and Velma's 40 acre farm in Mack. They show Frank's creativity, ingenuity and thrifty talents. *(Photos courtesy of Frank Overbye)*

business was good for about a year. At times we had three mechanics. Velma was bookkeeper and parts chaser, and she and Dad helped some with the gas pumps. I did all the welding, towing and field work. We operated the garage for about two years. The second year, credit got to be a problem. After the war was over, my health forced us to lease the garage, in late 1948, to Jim Rousch from Telluride, Colorado.

I went to work for W & M Supply, an auto parts house in Grand Junction. In the fall of 1949 I decided to do custom farm work again, so we bought a large International tractor, large plow, and another combine. During the spring of 1950, the tunnel for the Irrigation Project for the entire lower valley, which went through a mountain, slid away and left the valley without irrigation water. Therefore, all the farm work was stopped, and we didn't get any custom work of any kind. The tunnel was rebuilt by the middle of June, but was too late for many crops.

With nothing else to do, we went to Grand Valley and I went to work on a water well drill rig, drilling water wells all around the valley from Aspen to Mack.

In my spare time, I started to build us an 8-foot-by-24foot trailer house in Velma's mother's yard. We had it livable by the middle of June. On 29 June 1950, our son, Leon Franklin, was born in St. Mary's hospital in Grand Junction. When he was two weeks old, we moved into our new trailer house and moved to Carbondale, Colorado and spent several weeks drilling wells. That fall we moved to Mack to drill several wells for Deacons, Ebrights, Swansons, Merton Arpke and the Bureau of Land Management at Appleton.

When it became too cold to drill, we decided to make a big move. We sold our 40-acre farm to my brother, Charlie, and had a public auction the last of November. We sold most everything we owned, and leased our garage and station to Ora Cotner. He was our only former mechanic that was honest.

We were packed and ready to leave Mack in about the middle December 1950. We did not have the slightest idea where we were going or what we were going to do. It was very hard to leave there after spending 10 years and a lot of hard work building up our first home and place. We were just like the proverbial "boll weavel just looking for a home."

Frank,Velma and family arrived in Tooele, Utah, west of Salt Lake City, on 15 December 1950, and stayed there until they moved to Springfield, Oregon in 1952. In 1953, they built two houses on the property they bought in Springfield. They sold one of the houses and still live in the other.

Frank and Velma's home they built in Springfield, Oregon in 1953; They still live there. (Right) Velma, Frank, Leon and Carolyn when they arrived in Springfield, Oregon in 1952. *(Photos courtesy of Frank Overbye)*

L-R: Charles Webster, Laurence "Larry" Eugene, Agnes and Charlene Marie Overbye, 1960s. *(Photo courtesy of Helen Overbye Peterson)*

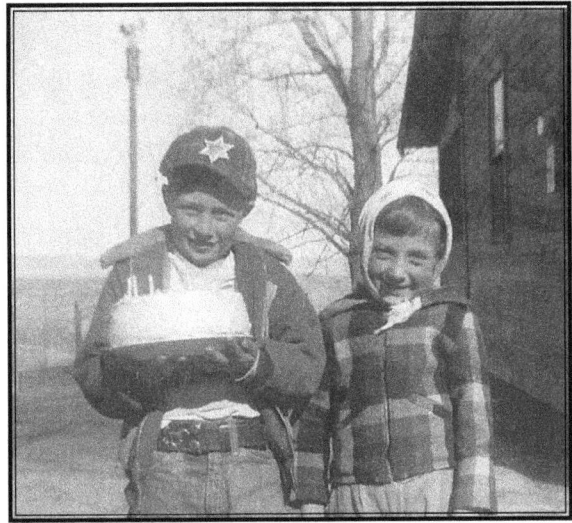

Larry Eugene and Charlene Marie Overbye, 1957. *(Photo courtesy of Larry Overbye)*

Information from an article in the *Fruita Times*, obituaries, and interviews with Larry and Charlene.

Charles married **Agnes Alstatt** 7 March 1943, at New Liberty. Their first child, a little girl, was born prematurely, weighing only 24 ounces. She lived only two days.

> **Helen Louise (Peterson),** born August 1943 at Fruita
> **Laurence "Larry" Eugene,** 4 January 1946, at Fruita
> **Charlene Marie (Marciano, Dedmon, Grounds),** 1 June 1949, at Fruita

Charlie and Agnes lived at a number of different places in the Grand Valley. Charlie farmed part of the time and worked at various trades for other people.

Agnes died in Grand Junction, 6 Aug 1967, and Charlie died there also, 8 June 1971.

Larry attended all eight grades at New Liberty School and graduated from Fruita Union High School in 1964. Larry remembers one incident in New Liberty School where Patsy Butt and Earlynn Barcus gave him his first kiss and he cried. He also remembers when he was about 10 years old, he and a friend, George Mussleman, decided to get into his dad's

Bull Durham and roll themselves some cigarettes to smoke. They hid over a ditch bank on the north side of the house, thinking they were out of sight. They tried and tried to roll the cigarettes, but they couldn't get the tobacco to stay in the paper and they were smoking mostly paper. Unbeknownst to them their dads, Charlie and Bud, had been watching them. Finally Charlie decided to come help them.

He said, "Boys, if you are going to smoke, you need some tobacco in that paper so let me roll you one." He rolled each a cigarette and then made them smoke the whole thing. Larry says he got so sick and has never smoked one since.

He met his future wife, **Connie Bartman**, of Fruita while going to Fruita Union High School. They were married at Fruita, 22 April 1966. Larry was drafted into the military in May 1966 a month after he was married. He took his basic training in Fort Bliss, Texas and did a tour in Munich, Germany. Connie accompanied him to Germany. When his mother died in August 1967, he came home for her funeral and the military transferred him to Fort Carson in Colorado Springs, Colorado. They lived there until he was discharged in 1968.

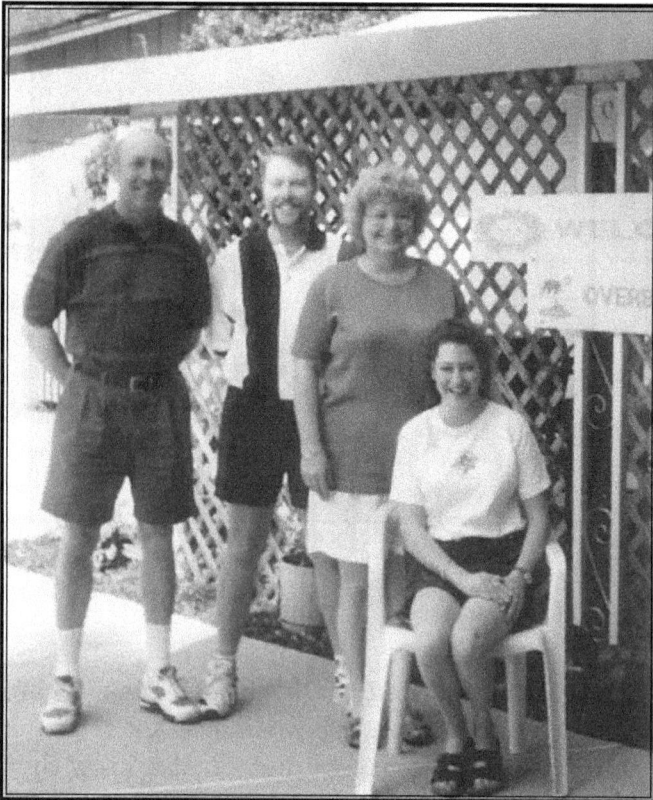

Larry, Todd, Connie and Lori Overbye, 1995, at Overbye Reunion at Charlene's in Arizona. *(Photo courtesy of Larry Overbye)*

Larry and Connie have two children:

Todd Eugene, born 5 December 1967, at Fort Carson, Colorado Springs, Colorado
Lori Ann, 30 April 1972, Grand Junction

Larry has worked for the National Park Service at Colorado National Monument Park for 30 years (1997) and has also been a member of the Fruita Volunteer Fire Department (FVFD) since May 1970.

In 1973 the FVFD became the Lower Valley Rural Fire Protection District (LVRFPD) taking care of fires and rescue calls outside the city limits of Fruita and a part of the LVFPD (Lower Valley Fire Protection District).

An excellent article written by Gayle Meyer was published in the *Fruita Times* of 29 March 1996 announcing Larry's retirement after 26 years in the above organization. She shares in that article many of the experiences Larry told as he remembered his years of service, some humorous, some tragic.

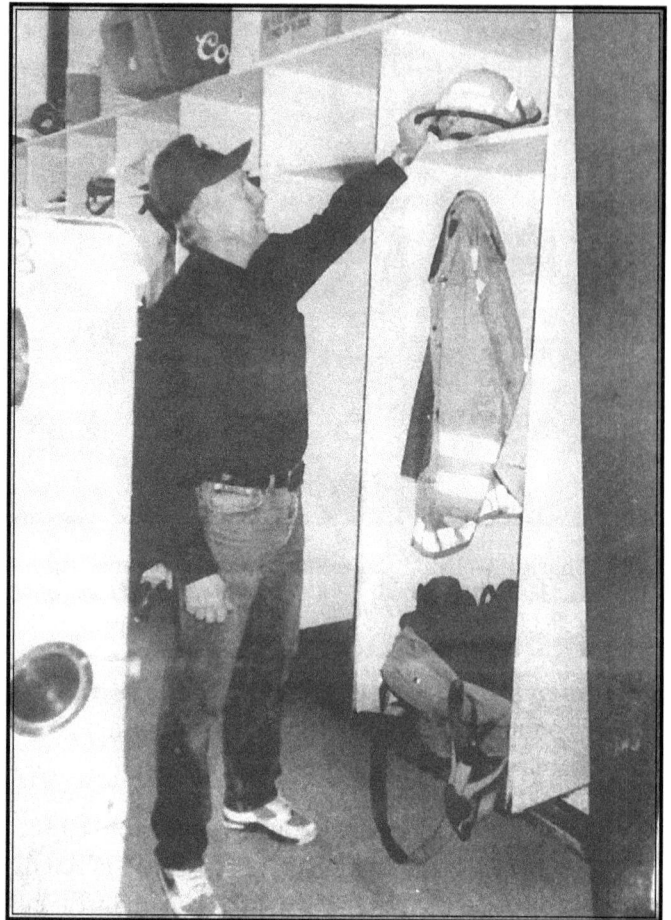

Larry Overbye checks some of the gear that has seen him safely through 26 years of fire and rescue squad calls for the Lower Valley Fire Protection District. *(Fruita Times, 29 March 1996)*

Fighting fires is only half the job of the volunteers of the LVFPD. Rescue squad work and life support is the other. Both disciplines — fire fighting and life support — require many hours of training. "Today, there is so much mandatory training, for fighting fires, for patient care," he said, "and every call brings something different. Just when you think you've seen it all, something comes up and you realize, once again, that you haven't seen it all. I'm still learning every day." On the medical side, Overbye is an EMT-I (Emergency Medical Technician-Intermediate) capable of administering advanced life support care.

For over a quarter-century, Overbye has answered emergency calls. ... The calls range from odd predicaments to unspeakable tragedy: An elderly woman must be extricated from her own bath tub; a young man's twisted body must be removed from a corn grinder on a long ago Thanksgiving Day; ... a baby delivered in the squad; rescued

Charlene Overbye Dedmon-Grounds and husband, Bruce Grounds, 1997, on a cruise. *(Photo courtesy of Charlene Overbye Dedmon-Grounds)*

a treed cat; tried to resuscitate the baby of a young couple he knew personally, a victim of Sudden Infant Death Syndrome and was unsuccessful.

He recalled a time when the squad was paged to a heart attack victim. "I didn't drive the squad and didn't realize until we got to the address that the victim was my uncle. I had to forget he was a relative and do what I had been trained to do." Overbye has also participated in some memorable rescues on the Colorado National Monument. He recalled one that started with a young fellow hiding from his girlfriend, so that he could leap out from behind a rock and scare her. It was dark. The young man jumped over a rock near the edge of the road and plummeted some 30 feet down a storm drain, breaking both legs, both ankles and his pelvis. It took hours to get him out, Overbye recalled, but he was rescued and survived. "And he managed to scare his girl friend, that's for sure," Overbye said.

"This has always been a highly respected fire department," Overbye said. "I've always been proud to be a part of it."

Larry and his son, Todd, are avid sports fans. They play softball and basketball. His hobby is collecting sports cards. His wife, Connie, has worked at City Market for 18 years as a checker and produce clerk. They live in Fruita.

𝕿odd Eugene graduated from Mesa State College in Grand Junction with a degree in recreation management. He works for the Colorado National Monument as an interpretive ranger and the City of Grand Junction with the recreation program department.

𝕷ori Ann was born with a heart defect and had four major open-heart surgeries. She is a graduate of Technical Trade Institute with a medical secretarial degree. She works at St. Mary's Hospital as a medical secretary.

𝕮harlene attended New Liberty School through the third grade. She went to Clifton Elementary for the fourth grade, Fruita Central Elementary for the fifth and sixth grades, and attended junior high and high school at Fruita through the 10th grade. She graduated from Grand Junction High School in 1967.

She married Chuck Marciano in 1968, and as he was a military man they traveled all over the southeast United States. That marriage ended in divorce. She moved to Flagstaff, Arizona, in 1970 and lived there for three years, moving and then moved to Phoenix in 1973. She married Harvey Dedmon in 1973 and gained five stepchildren. That marriage also ended in divorce and she married Bruce Grounds in 1981. Over these years she has helped with 11 stepchildren, but has had no children of her own. She goes by the name of Dedmon-Grounds.

Charlene worked for Cory Food Services in Phoenix for 13 years as an operations manager. She then worked three years as an office manager and bookkeeper for M. H. Hintz Construction. Since 1993 she has worked for Orco Construction Supply in the accounting department and just recently was made office manager for the Phoenix Branch.

In 1981, she and Bruce started their own tour service, XTC Excursions, as something on the side. They specialize in group travel to destinations such as Mexico and Hawaii, also coordinate cruises to different places, and plan sporting activities to include skiing and football games. Charlene and Bruce also do a lot of boating.

considerable information in church, school and census records.

Juan Pacheco was born 18 June 1858, in New Mexico. (We have conflicting information on the year) His parents were Ramon Pacheco and Ascencion Marques. Some of Juan's grand children have raised a question about his parentage. Felix's sons say that Juan may have been adopted. This story has some merit, since some who remember Juan say that he was light complexioned; one story says he had blue eyes.

Juan was born during the latter part of the revolution in New Mexico. His parents lived in Taos, New Mexico, where the revolt between the Taos government and Father Antonio Jose Martinez erupted in 1837, followed by the Mexican-American War in 1847. The Pacheco and Marques families were members of Father Martinez' church, as he signed the marriage and baptismal records found in the Taos Church Records. The following are abstracts from the book, New Mexico: *A History of Four Centuries*, by Warren A. Beck.

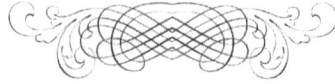

Mary Porfiria and Juan Pacheco
(Photo courtesy of Delia Pacheco)

Pacheco

The following was gathered from several of Juan and Porfiria Pacheco's grandchildren . . . Margaret and Hazel, daughters of Abedon (Abe), who live in the Delta/Hotchkiss area. Raymie, Virginia, Bob and Fred, children of Felix. Bennie and Charlie, sons of Saul. Carmel and Franklin Manzanares, children of Priscilla. We found

The new governor of Taos was levying heavy taxes on the people and Martinez, "a champion of the people," disapproved of this. Martinez and Manuel Armijo, a displeased custom-house official who had been removed from office, organized a revolt. Armijo carried out the plans; plus making it beneficial for himself.

Soon large groups of Pueblo Indians formed and began marching on Santa Fe. Governor Perez gathered a force of about 150 militia, including some Pueblo Indians, and marched to meet the insurgents. The Governor's forces were defeated in the ensuing battle and were forced to flee. The rebels captured Perez and a number of his associates and murdered them...

They elected a Taos Indian, Jose Gonzalez, as governor, reappointed Indians to most governmental posts, and seized the property of the former political figures. On the eighth of September Armijo raised a force and marched on the capital against the rebels.

His position was vastly strengthened by the arrival of approximately 300 troops from Chihuahua. Ultimately, the government forces met the rebels in January, 1838, defeating them and executing Gonzalez and his leaders.

Then came the Americans in 1847. The book, The Leading Facts of New Mexican History, by Ralph Emerson, Esq., enlarges on Father Antonio Jose Martinez' position with the Americans.

Rev. Antonio Jose Martinez was regarded by many as one of the principals in the revolution of 1847. He realized that the coming of the American was a death blow to his power and prestige in the country and he is said to have done everything he possibly could to create a sentiment of suspicion and distrust against the American people.

Rev. W. J. Howlett, in his Life of Bishop Machebeuf, says of him: "It was said that he had much to do with the uprising of the Indians and Mexicans at Taos, when Governor Bent and about 15 Americans and their Mexican sympathizers were massacred on 19 January 1847."

Juan's parents, Ramon and Ascension, lived in Taos and were married there in 1848. They had three children, Juana, Rafaela, Cleofas in Taos County between 1850 and 1855. Their marriage record and the baptismal records of the two oldest children were signed by Father Martinez. They were in Arroyo Hondo, Taos, New Mexico when Cleofas was baptized and his record was signed by Mariano de Jesus Lucero. Martinez and Lucero were both suspended from the church for their activities in the revolution and other activities.

This must have been a very difficult time for the Pacheco family. They started migrating north. In the New Mexico 1860 census, Ramon and Ascension still live in Arroyo Hondo. The only child enumerated was Cleofas, so Juan was still not a member of the family. The girls were not present so we don't know if they died or were somewhere else at the time. The family moved to Rio Arriba, New Mexico, then later we find them in Walsenburg, Colorado.

The first record of Juan is in Walsenburg. On 9 February 1880, Juan married Mary Porfiria Archuleta, in Walsenburg, Huerfano, Colorado. Porfiria was also born in New Mexico, 12 April 1864 (there is some conflict on this year also). Her parents were Pablo "Paul" Archuleta and Encarnacion Vellarde. According to the Colorado state marriage record, at the time of their marriage, Juan's residence was Crestone, Saguache, Colorado, and Porfiria's residence, Gardner, Huerfano, Colorado, but the church record gives residences of both as Huerfano County.

Records show that they had 14 children:

Jose Felix, born 4 April 1881
Agapito "Pete," 14 August 1882
Maria Lucia (Blazon), 9 December 1883
Placida "Priscilla" (Manzanares), 8 December 1885
Saul, 5 September 1887
Abedon "Abe," 18 June 1889
Juana Teresa, 22 April 1892
Abel (Dutton), 4 January 1894 (Abel changed his last name to Dutton)
Anastocia "Oscar," 22 January 1896
Telesforo "Ted," 5 January 1898
Maria Rosita "Rose" (Autabee), 16 June 1900

All born in Huerfano County, Colorado.

Francisco "Frank," 2 April 1902
Daniel Boldasar "Dan," 13 January 1905
Juan Custobul "John," 2 June 1906
The last three were born in Pueblo. Juana Teresa died before June 1900. All of the names on the christening records are written in Spanish and Latin.

Juan and Porfiria are listed in the 1885 Colorado State Census, in Gardner, Huerfano County, Colorado, with three children: Felix, Agapito and Lucia. Juan's occupation was "merchant." Listed with them is a man named "M.P. Belside," who was identified as Juan's father-in-law, also a merchant.

We found the family living in Pueblo County, near the town of Boone, as per the 1900 census. Juan is listed as a "railroad laborer." The record states that Porfiria had given birth to 10 children, of whom eight were living.

There were eight children listed in the family, but Teresa and Oscar were not listed. Teresa is said to have died about 1900, but Oscar, we've since learned, lived until 7 January 1951. So Oscar must have been visiting another family at the time. The enumerator counted eight and Porfiria said she had 10.

Abel, Oscar and Ted served in World War I. In the 1920 census we found Agapito, age 37, listed as a "mail contractor" at Powderhorn, Gunnison, Colorado.

Juan and Porfiria could have lived in Pueblo County until just before they came to New Liberty in 1919, the year Juan filed on the homestead. However, it is most likely they spent some time in the Hotchkiss or Delta area. Their daughter, Priscilla Manzanares, died 21 November 1919, in the Hotchkiss area and was buried in Delta. Priscilla left a husband and five children, ages six to 13. Porfiria and sons Frank, Dan and John stayed with Priscilla's family, Peter Manzanares and five children in Delta County while Juan went onto New Liberty and prepared the homestead for the family to live there.

The family, including the five Manzanares grandchildren, moved to New Liberty in 1920 by team and wagon from Delta. They lived in three tents for several years until the house was built. The house was built with adobe bricks sometime during the 20s by John and Abedon with the help of a Spaniard from Mack.

The Manzanares grandchildren lived with them for three years and went to New Liberty school with Frank, Dan and John, and another granddaughter, Marie Blazon. The Manzanares children then moved to Fort Lupton, Colorado to be with their father and his parents. Franklin Manzanares returned to New Liberty two years later and stayed with Juan and Porfiria for several years.

Frank Pacheco and Marie Blazon graduated from the eighth grade in New Liberty about 1921.

Frank Pacheco was a poet. He wrote the following, dated 21 June 1921. It was written for Mabel Likes, who was in the seventh grade:

Fred King, as I guess all know
Is Mabel Likes' dearest beau
She received a note from him last night
I saw her reading it by candle light
As I looked on from where I stood
Her eyes with tears of joy and gratitude
For one from her heart she could not exclude
Then I lingered there a little more
She finished reading and closed the door
I heard her mutter as she went to bed,
If only I could be with Fred
I'd be content until I were dead.

Dan Pacheco probably graduated from the New Liberty School in 1922, however he is not included in the picture of that class. John Pacheco graduated in 1923 and Franklin Manzanares in 1927.

After Dan graduated from the eighth grade he wanted to go on to high school, so an arrangement was made for him to live with Felix and family and attend Appleton High School. Felix's son, Raymie, came to stay with the grandparents and attended New Liberty School during that time. That was probably during the school year of 1922-23, when Selma Snavely was the teacher.

Another tragedy struck Juan's and Porfiria's family on 24 May 1934, when Frank was spraying potatoes on the farm. According to the story in *The Daily Sentinel*, a large bolt connecting the tongue to the body of the spray machine broke. The machine tipped forward and threw Frank onto the ground, against one of the horses. He was entangled in the double-tree and couldn't get loose before the horse he had fallen against started kicking him in the head. The horses then started running and dragging him. Frank's brother Dan and a neighbor saw the runaway and ran to Frank's assistance. When they reached him, even though he was seriously injured, he was still alive. They immediately placed him in a car and went to Fruita for a doctor's assistance, but Frank died before they could reach Fruita. Funeral services were held in St. Michael's Catholic Church in Delta, where he was buried.

Juan and Porfiria may have moved to Denver within a short time after Frank's death. Juan died in Denver 12 December 1936. Porfiria lived for another nine-and-a half more years until 12 April 1946. Both are buried in Mt. Olivet Cemetery in Denver.

The following article is from a Denver paper sent to us by several of the children:

A pioneer mother of Colorado who passed away recently had a record family of children, grandchildren, and great-grandchildren to mourn her passing. She is Mrs. John Pacheco, a resident of Denver, formerly of Grand Junction, who was the mother of 16 children, grandmother of 69, and great-grandmother of 52. She lived all of her 84 years in Colorado, and most of her large family live in Colorado and Utah.

The article gives her credit for 16 children instead of the 14 we have record of. The article may have been submitted by her daughter Lucia, who lived to be 103.

Felix Pacheco was married at Pueblo in June of 1902, to **Theodora "Dora" Farley**, the daughter of Peter and Anna Farley. We have learned that Theodora was raised by a Gonzales family. Her surname appears as Gonzales on her children's' christening records. Theodora was light complexioned, with red hair; she showed distinct Irish heritage.

Felix and Theodora had 12 children according to christening records:

Carolina Beatrice (Peterson), born 9 February 1904
Alberto "Albert," 28 February 1906
Domesio Epinso Jose "Pete," 15 November 1909
Filiberto, 8 June 1910
Ramigio "Raymond" and **"Raymie,"** 8 July 1911
Antonio Noperto "Tony," 7 December 1914
William "Bill," 28 February 1917
Priscilla, 27 September 1920
Virginia (Bennedetti, Rockvam), 1 April 1923
Robert Felix "Bob," '4 September 1925
Fred, 27 August 1929

The first six children were born at Pueblo, the remainder were born after the move to the Grand Junction area. We are not sure if Bill was born in Mesa County, but we are quite sure the younger children were.

Filiberto died while he was young and they may have lost another child in infancy. Priscilla, who had Down's syndrome, died 16 April 1946, at Grand Junction, and is buried in the Calvary Cemetery. We have only minimal marriage information on Tony and Bill. They are both deceased; Tony died in West Los Angeles 25 December 1969, and Bill at Johnstown, Pennsylvania, 28 January 1970.

The family was listed in the 1910 census living in Pueblo. At that time Felix was employed at the Bethlehem Steel Mill.

It appears the family moved to the Grand Junction area some time between 1914 and 1917. The 1920 census shows them in the Pomona District; perhaps we can assume they lived in that area until in the late 1920s. The New Liberty items in *The Daily Sentinel* tell us that Virginia started school at New Liberty in April 1929, but we don't know where the family lived until March of 1930, when they moved to the J. N. King homestead, about one-half mile west of the New Liberty School.

Around 1937, Felix and family moved to the Pacheco homestead and lived there until about 1944, when they moved to Dragerton, Utah, where Felix and other members of his family were employed in the coal mines. By that time several of the sons and daughters had moved to California. This led Felix and Theodora to move out there, too. Felix and Theodora had five sons in the military simultaneously during World War II: Raymie, Tony, Bill, Bob and Fred. We have learned that Tony was shot in the neck during a battle and suffered from serious headaches from then on.

Felix died 14 January 1970, in Ventura, California; Theodora died 28 October 1974, also in Ventura. Both are buried there.

We have a little family information on some of the other members of the family.

(Above) The Felix Pacheco family, 1946. Back row, L-R: William, Pete, Fred, Raymond, Albert and Robert. Front row: Virginia, Felix, Dora and Beatrice. (Below) Taken at Felix and Dora's 50th wedding anniversary, June 1952. Back row, L-R: Robert and Alberto Pacheco, John Bennedetti, Raymond and William Pacheco, Roland Peterson, Pete and Tony Pacheco. Middle row: Lorraine and Vesta Pacheco, Virginia Pacheco Bennedetti, Dora and Felix Pacheco, Beatrice Pacheco Peterson, Bertha and Piper Pacheco. Front row: Kay Pacheco, John Bennedetti, Linda, Carol, Bill, Janet and John Pacheco. *(Photos courtesy of Raymond Pacheco and Virginia Pacheco Rockvam)*

(Upper) Raymond Pacheco family. L-R: Evelyn Rohl, Karen Ruth, Raymond and Ronald Richard Pacheco. (Lower) Raymond's family, 1991: Karen, Raymond, Evelyn and Ronald. *(Photos courtesy of Raymond Pacheco)*

Raymond, or **Raymie**, as he was known, worked on the farm until he was inducted into the army in 1942. He served in the Aleutian Islands for two-and-a-half years. His unit came back stateside and was ready to go out again when the atomic bombs were dropped and the war ended. He was discharged in July 1945 and went to Reno, Nevada, and worked for a lumber molding company. He married **Evelyn Rohl** on 21 February 1954, at Northridge, California. Evelyn was born 17 March 1917, in Lancaster, Niagara, New York. They have two children.

Ronald Richard, born 26 October 1955, Reno
Karen Ruth (Hatch), 7 June 1957, Reno

In 1959 Raymie leased and eventually bought a gas service station on Virginia Street in Reno where they sold and delivered fuel oil. During the time he owned it, he was in a auto-pedestrian accident. He was crossing the intersection at the station and someone hit him and threw him quite a distance. He was severely injured and didn't work for six months. Raymie sold the station after 13 years and leased a gas station on the corner of 4th Street. It was open 24 hours a day and sold the largest volume of gas of any station in Reno. He retired after running the station for three years and has been retired for 24 years. Evelyn was the bookkeeper and did the taxes for the stations all those years.

Raymie and Evelyn now live in Oroville, California.

Virginia graduated from Fruita Union High School in 1941. She then went to Cheyenne, Wyoming, and lived with her brother, Pete, and graduated from beauty school. She worked as a beautician for two years. Then she worked as a clerk and bookkeeper at Western Union Telegraph for three years, and then for the Veteran's Administration as a transfer clerk for three years. Virginia was living in Trinidad, Colorado, when she met and married **John Bennedetti**, 20 November 1948, in Raton, New Mexico. They had two sons:

John Lee, born 1 September 1949, Trinidad, Las Animas, Colorado
Dale Paul, 26 August 1953, Trinidad

That marriage ended in divorce in 1958 and Virginia and the boys moved to Ventura, California. She went to work at the Pacific Missile Test Center at Point Mugu, California as a visual information officer and retired in 1983, after 25 years. She married **Albert Rockvam** on 18 March 1986 and they live in Ventura, California. Virginia has three grandchildren.

ob graduated from Fruita Union High School in 1943. He then went to Dragerton, Utah, and worked in the coal mines until he joined the Navy in December 1943. He served in the South Pacific as a signalman on a demolition ship for 29 months. He was discharged in May 1946. He went to Beverly Hills, California, and worked for Standard Oil Company. He married **Lorraine Marie Hamilton** on 31 August 1947, at Las Vegas, Nevada. Lorraine was born 26 November 1925 at Colome, Tripp, South Dakota They have three girls and one boy.

> **Linda Rae (Flora),** born 28 November 1948
> **Carole Ann (Matheson),** 28 June 1950
> **James Allen,** 3 March 1956
> **Jan Susan (Olivero),** 2 March 1959
> All the children were born in Van Nuys, Los Angeles, California.

(Above) Robert Pacheco family, 1975. L-R: Robert, Jan, Lorraine, Carole, Linda and James. (Below) Robert Pacheco family, 1991. Children, L-R: Jan, James, Carole and Linda. Robert and Lorraine in front. *(Photos courtesy of Robert Pacheco)*

(Upper) Albert and Virginia Rockvam, 1986. (Lower) Virginia and sons, left to right: Dale Paul and John Lee Bennedetti. *(Photos courtesy of Virginia Rockvam)*

In 1952 Bob went to work for an independent service station in Van Nuys. In 1959 they moved to Sparks, Nevada, and Bob went in with Raymie in a fuel oil service station in Reno. Then, in 1961, he leased a service station and the owner sold it to a Savings and Loan Company in 1969. Bob then went to work for the Western Mountain Oil Company and worked his way up to Terminal Manager. He retired in 1991. Bob enjoys golfing and plays with the senior softball team in Sparks.

Lorraine worked for the Federal Government in the General Service Administration Office for 20 years, and is now retired.

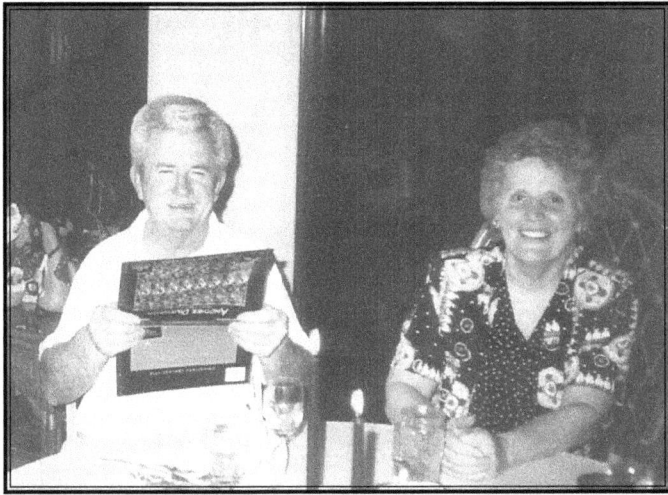

Fred and Cecelia "Sue" Pacheco, 1996.
(Photo courtesy of Fred Pacheco)

Dennis (standing), Roger, Kathleen and Diane Pacheco, about 1969. *(Photo courtesy of Fred Pacheco)*

Fred graduated from Price High School in Price, Utah, in 1947. The next two years he worked for a butcher market, gas station and in the coal mines. He joined the Navy in 1950 and served in the Korean War as a radioman on a mine sweeper. He was discharged in 1954 in California. He stayed in Van Nuys, California, and went to work in house construction installing cabinets in houses, apartments and condos.

Fred married **Cecelia Mary "Sue" Sessler** on 12 January 1957, at Canoga Park, California. Cecelia was born 10 October 1945, in Red Bank, Monmouth, New Jersey. They have two boys and two girls.

Diane Claudette, born 28 February 1958
Dennis William, 20 February 1959
Kathleen Mary, 20 October 1963
Roger Frederick, 15 March 1965
All the children were born in Van Nuys, Los Angeles, California.

Fred retired after 30 years in the house construction work, but has been working two days a week cleaning beer lines for restaurants and beer joints. Cecelia has worked the last year-and-a-half as a secretary for the Episcopal Church.

Fred and Cecelia live in Canoga Park, California.

The following is a letter Fred wrote to Eugene Thomas, and it was published in the *Fruita Times*, 8 August 1991.

Gene Thomas: I don't know if you will remember me, but I remember you very well. When I knew you it was Eugene, not Gene.

We used to walk to New Liberty School together on the days when your Dad didn't drive us, and on the way we would pick up Murray Phillips. When I tell my children (four of them, all grown now) about that long walk, they won't believe me, but we know it's true. We usually got a pretty early start 'cause I don't remember us getting into too big a hurry to get there.

Delbert and Faye Jerome were the teachers then; I remember them well.

After New Liberty I went only a half year at Fruita Union High School, as my parents had moved to Utah, and I stayed with Bob Arpke and his mother to be able to go to Fruita. When I went home to Utah for Christmas, I was talked into staying there, so I finished my high school at Price, Utah. They are having their

(Upper left) Virginia Pacheco, 1941. (Upper center) Robert Pacheco, 1943. (Photos courtesy of Delores Likes) (Upper right) Fred Pacheco, 1943. (Photo courtesy of Phyllis Likes) (Center left) Fred with his 4-H calf, about 1939. (Center right) Fred and his convertible in Price, 17 years old. (Lower left) L-R: Fred with his two brothers, Tony and Bill, in Dragerton, Utah, 1946. (Lower right) Dora and Felix on their 60th wedding anniversary, 1962. The priest is unidentified. *(Photos courtesy of Fred Pacheco)*

high school reunion the same weekend as the New Liberty reunion. Theirs will be on Friday night and Saturday night, so I plan on being there Friday night and part of Saturday, then going on to New Liberty and being there for Sunday.

Looking at the papers you sent me I see a lot of names I recognize, and some I don't. There's a lot of people I remember; hope they will remember me.

I don't know who to thank for all the *Fruita Times*, but whoever it was, thanks a million. I have thoroughly enjoyed them.

Hopefully I will see you August 18, Fred Pacheco.

Placida "Priscilla" Pacheco married **Pedro "Peter" Manzanares**, 27 August 1905, in Avondale, Pueblo, Colorado. Peter was born at Gardner, Huerfano, Colorado, in 1886. They had six children:

Stella, born 1906
Carmela "Carmel" (Martinez), 23 December 1907
Agapito Eugenio "Peter," 1909
Adolpho, 8 March 1911 (died in infancy)
Raphael Franklin, 29 February 1912
Charles, 28 December 1913
Stella, Carmel and Peter were born at Avondale, Franklin and Charles at Crawford, Colorado.

On 21 November 1919, at age 34, Priscilla died and was buried at Delta. Grandparents Juan and Porfiria then took over the motherless children and moved with them to the homestead in New Liberty. The 1920 census of Delta County, recorded in January of that year, shows Peter Manzanares and children with their grandmother, Porfiria, and her three youngest sons, Frank, Dan and John, all living together. Juan was not found in the census for that year; he must have been somewhere in transit.

Granddaughter Carmel Manzanares told the story of Juan and Porfiria and their children and grandchildren, traveling from Delta by team and wagon to the New Liberty homestead. She said their ages when they arrived were Stella, 13; Carmel, 12; Pete, 10; Franklin, 8; and Charles, 6. They lived in three tents for some time. Then, several years later, perhaps in the mid 1920s, some members of the family built a house with adobe bricks.

School records show there were three Manzanares children enrolled at the new New Liberty School in 1919-20: Carmel, sixth grade; Peter, third grade and Franklin, first grade. John Pacheco was also a student in the fifth grade that year. Likely the Manzanares' and John did not start to school in New Liberty until some time after 15 January 1920, since the census record shows they were still in Delta County as of that date. The following year, 1920-21, all three Pacheco boys: Frank, Dan and John, were enrolled at New Liberty, along with a granddaughter of Juan and Porfiria, **Marie Blazon**, daughter of Lucia. For some reason the Manzanares' children were not listed in the 1921 school census, even though Marie Blazon and the three Pacheco boys were.

Carmel has informed us that the Manzanares children lived with the grandparents three years, then moved to Fort Lupton to live with their father and paternal grand parents. Franklin returned to live with grandparents Juan and Porfiria a couple of years later, and was with them for several years.

After losing his wife in 1919, Pedro Manzanares lived, at various times, at Delta, Hotchkiss, Paonia, and Fort Lupton, Colorado. Several years later, in 1941, he moved to Los Angeles, California, to live with his son, Charles. He died there 14 July 1947, but was buried in the Delta Colorado Cemetery.

Saul Pacheco   Cassandra Cisneros Pacheco
(Photos courtesy of Marilyn Maluy Pacheco)

Saul and Cassandra's children, 1931. L-R: Charlie William, Arela "Della," John Manuel, Benigno Venantis "Bennie" and Beatrice. *(Photo courtesy of Bennie Pacheco)*

Saul Pacheco was born 1 September 1887, at Los Chavez, Huerfano, Colorado. He spent his childhood in Huerfano County and moved to Pueblo around 1908. He married **Cassandra Cisneros** in 1909 in Pueblo. Cassandra was born 16 September 1887, at Turkey Creek, Huerfano, Colorado, to Manuel Cisneros and Mary Natividad Vallejos. She was previously married to **Felix Sierra**, and they had one child, **Consolacion "Connie,"** born 1905 at Avondale, Pueblo, Colorado.

Saul and Cassandra soon moved to Delta County, Colorado, where their six children were born:

> **Beatrice (Rivera),** born 7 August 1910, probably at Lazear, Delta, Colorado
> **Mary Emma,** 31 December 1912, Lazear
> **Benigno Venantis "Bennie,"** 5 October 1914, Lazear
> **John Manuel,** 7 January 1917, Delta
> **Arela "Della" (Law, Dickson),** 30 September, 1919, Delta
> **Charlie William "Chuck,"** 6 April 1924, Hotchkiss

On 9 July 1930, their daughter Mary Emma died at Austin, Colorado, at age 17. She was buried in Delta.

The family left Hotchkiss soon after and moved to Fruita for a time. While living in Fruita they had another death in the family. Their daughter, Beatrice, died suddenly on 30 July 1937. She had married **Ralph Rivera** on 3 August 1935.

The family then moved to a farm in the Appleton area until 1938, when they moved to the Golden Hills ranch near Loma. They lived there until 1941, and then moved to Mack, where Saul managed the Mack Pool Hall and the Mack Cafe until April 1945.

Saul and Cassandra moved to Sacramento in 1945, where they lived until 1946. Saul then went to Rifle, Colorado, and operated a pool hall there until 1954,

Cassandra on Charlie's horse. *(Photo courtesy of Marilyn Maluy Pacheco)*

when he returned to Sacramento. He died in August 1975 and Cassandra died in July 1977. Both are buried at Sacramento, California.

The children all attended schools in the various areas. Bennie, Manuel and Charlie all graduated from Fruita Union High School; all three excelled in the athletic programs of the school and all three served in the Navy during World War II.

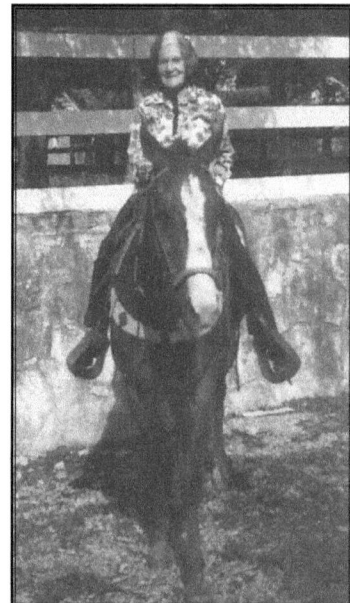

Lela Davison and Bennie Pacheco, 1945.
(Photo courtesy of Bennie Pacheco)

Bennie graduated from Fruita Union High School in 1934. He had been very active in the athletic program in track and football. He joined the Navy in 1942. On 18 October 1943 he married **Lela M. Davison** at Syracuse, Hamilton, Kansas. Lela was born 25 August 1913, at Alva, Woods, Oklahoma to Phillip Davison and Delia Smith. She spent her childhood at Springfield, Colorado, attending schools at Vilas, Colorado.

Bennie and Lela adopted and raised a boy and a girl:

Charles Kent, born 24 September 1946
Delia Ann (Garcia), 2 February 1949
Both are married and have children.

After World War II Bennie and Lela settled in Fruita and Bennie opened the Owl Cigar Store. This article was found in the "Fifty Years Ago" section of the *Fruita Times*, 14 June 1996 issue. It had been written in a June 1946 issue:

The Owl Cigar Store, owned by Bennie Pacheco, will open today in the new building just constructed between Lee Warner's office and Hutchison Brothers Appliance Shop. All games will be on the house on opening day, Pacheco announced.

Sometime later he became involved in construction work and became a proficient heavy equipment operator, always in demand. He worked in construction until he retired. Since retirement Bennie has developed a hobby into a business. He does beautiful woodwork making clocks, salt and pepper shakers, mirrors with etchings, etc.

Bennie and Lela raised wonderful gardens and kept a beautiful yard. Their yard has been chosen more than once as "Yard of the Month." Lela's specialty was her rose garden. She and Bennie arrowhead hunting and made beautiful displays of their arrowhead collections. They have been involved in several organizations: The Sacred Heart Catholic Church, Veterans of Foreign Wars and pinochle clubs. They have also spent many happy times camping and attending recreational activities.

Lela worked for years as a waitress in Fruita. She also built a business out of her talent of oil painting. Besides wall paintings, she painted on saws, wood, mirrors and made many handy craft articles. She died of cancer 21 November 1995, at Fruita and was buried in the Elmwood Cemetery. At the time of her death she and Bennie had five grandchildren and two great-grandchildren.

Bennie still lives in their home in Fruita and just received another "Yard of the Month" award.

Bennie Pacheco family: L-R: Bennie, Charles Kent, Lela Davison, Delia Ann Pacheco. *(Photo courtesy of Bennie Pacheco)*

*J*ohn **Manuel**, besides being a scholar, was an outstanding athlete in high school. The following article was found in the *Fruita Times* of 23 May 1935, under the headline: "Coach Penner Announces Next Year's Captains."

Manuel Pacheco, by virtue of scoring the largest number of points in the Western Slope Track meet, will hold the captaincy of the track team in 1936. Pacheco will be a junior next year. He has earned letters in three sports in his two years in high school. He will be, according to Coach Penner, probably the only three-star captain Fruita ever had.

He graduated from Fruita Union High School in 1937 with a football scholarship to Brigham Young University in Provo, Utah. During the summer he and several of the football players worked for Rohl and Connley Contractors building the Deer Creek Dam up Provo Canyon. Manuel also played softball for a local team. He attended BYU for two years and then transferred his scholarship to Clemson Agricultural Military School in Clemson, South Carolina. He attained a bachelors degree in engineering.

A headline was found in *The Daily Sentinel* in the fall of 1939: "Manuel Pacheco, Ex-Fruita, Thumbs Way to South Carolina to Try at Clemson's Team."

Clemson Gets a Star

Manuel Pacheco thumbed his way from Utah to South Carolina "because Clemson was the school of his choice."

"And the fact that he picked out Clemson _ though Clemson knew nothing of him while a dozen other big universities of the west and middle west were dangling all sorts of offers in his face — the fact that this boy hitchhiked his way across the continent to Clemson proves conclusively that Clemson has acquired not only a fine physical specimen but a boy of intelligence and sound judgment," said Mr. Brennecke.

Clemson's college paper, The Tiger, says of Pacheco: What looks like one of the best football discoveries of the year came floating in "by air" from far away Utah last week. Eleven days it took Manuel Pacheco, fast but husky youth from Utah, to "bum" his way

across the country to his adopted Clemson. Eleven days, with food only occasionally, with sleep an unknown luxury and then one long Thursday night of studying signals, his first night in Clemson. That was the long hard road of preparation.

But it didn't take Pacheco long in the Presbyterian freshman game to show his wares. In that short game he filled three backfield positions and contributed a 22-yard run toward his team's victory.

The hitchhiker's thumb brought more than a football player to Clemson. Pacheco plays basketball, has quite a reputation in baseball, and his record shows a consistent 9.9 for the 100-yard dash.

Pacheco was a star in high school and attracted much attention. But he liked something about Clemson and wrote Coach Nelley asking if transportation could be sent him — that he had picked Clemson as his school. There is no fund at Clemson for the transportation of a boy under such conditions and Pacheco received word that it would be impossible to send the money. So the young man took the matter in his own hands, starting for Clemson on the pneumatic tires of motorists.

(The foregoing article found it's way to *The Daily Sentinel* from *The New Orleans Times-Picayune*, one of the south's leading newspapers).

After graduation from Clemson Manuel worked for the construction company that built the John Martin Dam in Lamar, Colorado. He joined the Navy in 1942 and served in the Pacific until 1946. He was out of the Navy for one year and then returned for four more years.

When he got out of the Navy he coached football for three years at St. Francis High School in Pasadena, California. He then owned a salvage business in California for seven years. He sold that business and went to Alaska and started another salvage business. His company had the first telephone answering service in Alaska. While in Alaska he started a boys club. After three years he returned to California and drove truck for Associated Transportation for 12 years. He then moved to Las Vegas, Nevada, and worked in casinos until he retired a year ago.

Marcia Bankston, Manuel, and Bennie John "BJ" Pacheco, 1986.
(Photo courtesy of Marilyn Maluy Pacheco)

Manuel was married to **Cleo Halloway**, a movie actress, for eight years. He was then married to **Frances Archer** for 28 years. On 26 August 1978 he married **Marcia** (pronounced Mar-see-a) **Lynn Bankston** in Las Vegas. Marcia was born 3 November 1947 in Rockford, Winnebago, Illinois. They have one son, **Bennie John "BJ,"** born 27 January 1980 in Las Vegas. BJ works in a bicycle shop and is an accomplished BMX rider. He is a senior in high school.

Marcia and Manuel met in one of the casinos in Las Vegas where they were both employed. After they married, she had to quit as two of one family cannot work in the same casino. She went to work at the Imperial Palace 16 years ago and has worked her way up to kino manager.

Manuel has also turned a hobby into a business. He does beautiful woodwork with natural forms of wood. He never uses a saw.

He makes desk sets, jewelry boxes, mirrors, etc. He sells a large amount of his woodwork in Hawaii. He has also done some nice carvings, but Marcia says those are hers.

Della didn't live in Mack, as she was already married, so we don't have much information on her. She married **George Law** and they had three children, **Claudia**, **Dennis** and **Connie**. That marriage ended in divorce and she married **William Dickson** 4 September 1976. They live in Sacramento, California.

Charlie "Chuck" also excelled in athletics in high school. He lettered all four years in football, track and basketball. In his junior year he broke the state record in discus and high hurdles. That record stood for many years. He also took first place in shot put. The interesting thing is that he accomplished these feats with quite a handicap. He had one kind of track shoe on one foot and another kind on the other foot, and they were both too big for him. His mother had managed to scrounge up these shoes for him. Track shoes in those days weren't available like they are today, and it was also financially quite a burden. But besides his mother, Charlie also had another reason for his motivation. Dale Weldon was the big track star at that time, especially in the high hurdles. The media were interviewing Dale about his feelings of winning that day. And, of course, he felt very confident. Charlie overheard the interview and told himself, "No, you won't win today Dale. I'll do all in my power to see to it that you won't." Well, he did all in his power, and broke the state record in the hurdles by quite an amount. Everyone was awed by the outcome. Then he went on and broke the state record in throwing the discus, and got first in shot put — quite a day! Charlie also wrestled on the wrestling team. At that time wrestling was not an interscholastic competition, just competition within the school. He took first in his division.

Charlie William and Marilyn May Maluy Pacheco,
11 October 1943 *(Photo courtesy of Marilyn Maluy Pacheco)*

Kathi Mae, Darrell Alvin and Beau Allen Pacheco, about
1960. *(Photo courtesy of Marilyn Maluy Pacheco)*

Charlie joined the Navy in October 1942, during his senior year in high school, as so many of his classmates did. When he came in on leave into Vallejo Port in California, he married **Marilyn May Maluy** on 11 October 1943, in Sacramento, Sacramento, California. Marilyn was born 5 October 1925, in New Liberty, a daughter of Clement Maluy and Mary Christine Darrow. Ten days after their marriage he was shipped overseas and served two years in the Pacific. What a way to start a marriage! But that was very common during the war.

We found the following account of his service in *The Daily Sentinel* of 5 August 1945:

Charles [sic] W. Pacheco, Signalman 3rd Class, from Mack, fought aboard the light cruiser U.S.S. Oakland when it helped sink a Jap destroyer and a 7,500 ton transport, and shot down 12 Jap planes as highlights of its combat career of 40 Naval actions. The ship has traveled more than 170,000 miles, crossing the equator 24 times and seeing action in nearly every major invasion.

Chuck was discharged from the Navy in October 1945. He and Marilyn lived with the Clem Maluy family while Chuck helped with the fall harvest. Chuck then went to work as a telegrapher on the D&RGW Railroad for awhile, and they lived in Eagle, Colorado. That kept him away from home too much, so he quit and worked in the Rifle Pool Hall with his Dad for a year. He and Marilyn rented an apartment in Rifle from Max and Virginia Bainter, ex-New Libertyites.

Charlie and Marilyn have three children:

Beau Allen, born 11 March 1947, Fruita
Kathi Mae, 23 November 1953, Burbank, Los Angeles, California
Darrell Alvin, 1 February 1955, Van Nuys, Los Angeles, California.

In 1948 Chuck went to work as a lumber grader in Lake Tahoe, California. Then in 1951 he went to work as a milkman in Los Angeles, California.

Chuck played semiprofessional fast-pitch softball from 1947 through 1958. He played in Grand Junction, Lake Tahoe and Los Angeles. His fast pitch was clocked at 90 miles per hour.

From 1955 to 1958 Chuck worked for Model Dairy Distributors in Reno and owned his own milk route. In 1958 he bought and operated the Tahoe Creamery in Lake Tahoe, California. Then in 1963 he sold the creamery and worked

Chuck Pacheco standing beside a Tahoe Creamery truck.
(Photo courtesy of Marilyn Maluy Pacheco)

Chuck Pacheco family, 8 May 1966: Beau standing behind
Darrell, Kathi Mae, Chuck, and Marilyn Maluy Pacheco.
(Photo courtesy of Marilyn Maluy Pacheco)

for Meadow Gold in Sparks, Nevada. Meadow Gold transferred him to Grand Junction, Colorado in 1965. In 1967 he quit Meadow Gold and went to work for Clymer's Dairy. He worked there until 1970, when the family left Grand Junction to start their adventure in selling real estate. From 1970 to 1988 Chuck and Marilyn sold real estate and campgrounds in Missouri (near the Lake of the Ozarks), Texas, New Mexico, Oklahoma, North Carolina, South Carolina, Virginia, New York, California, Arizona, Tennessee, Georgia and Arkansas. From 1988 to 1990 they sold kitchen appliances at Army Bases in Texas and California. Chuck and Marilyn had many good and bad experiences throughout the United States, but enjoyed themselves.

In 1990 Chuck and Marilyn moved to Fruita (home) because of health problems and bought a mobile home in the Red Cliff Mobile Court south of Fruita. Chuck is now employed in the Mesa Mall in Grand Junction working for Cutlery USA selling knives. He is also selling roofing for mobile homes, and is cutting firewood to sell this winter.

(There is more information on Marilyn in the Maluy history). There are five grandchildren and three great-grandchildren.

an moved to Denver in the late 1930s and worked for a time in a cement plant and then for a short time at a railroad. While there he met **Delia Lopez**, daughter of Jose Lopez and Louisa Sandoval. Delia was born at Pagosa Junction, Archuleta, Colorado, 1 May 1910. Delia and Dan were married 9 October 1939, at St. George Catholic Church, Denver, Colorado

They moved to Dragerton, Utah, in 1943, where Dan went to work at the Horse Canyon Coal Mine. They bought a home in Dragerton (now East Carbon City) and lived there until Dan retired.

Dan and Delia had four daughters:

Juanita Louise (Foley), born 25 June 1940, Denver
Terry Jean (Salazar), 7 April 1944, Dragerton, Carbon, Utah
Danniel Marie (Harter), 13 December 1946, Dragerton
Carol Ann (Rose), 11 June 1949, Dragerton

After retirement Dan and Delia moved to Lakewood, California, where Dan died 19 July 1989. Delia continues to live there with her daughter, Danniel.

(Above right) John Pacheco family, 1951. Back row, L-R: Joyce, 13; John, 45; Phyllis, 32; Loretta, 18; and Mrs. Ulibarri, grandma. Middle row: LeRoy, 11; Richard, 7; Norma, 9; and Linda, 4 in front. (Above left) John Pacheco with burro, "Rosita," at his son LeRoy's place in Castle Valley, Utah, 3 April 1994. (Photos courtesy of LeRoy Pacheco) (Center) Dan and Delia Pacheco's daughters L-R: Louise, Terry, Daniel and Carol Pacheco. (Below right) John, Delia and Dan Pacheco with Terry Pacheco in front. (Below left) Brothers, John and Dan Pacheco, in Price, Utah. *(Photos courtesy of Delia Lopez Pacheco).*

Juan "John" Pacheco lived on the New Liberty homestead until some time in the 1930s, probably when Felix and family took over the farm. He found employment in Grand Junction and rented a room from a woman by the name of Mrs. Ulibarri. Mrs. Ulibarri had a daughter named **Phyllis**, who was born 20 August 1920 at Canjilon, Rio Arriba, New Mexico. Phyllis and John were attracted to each other and were married in Grand Junction, 11 March 1936. The New Liberty items in *The Daily Sentinel* dated 22 March 1936 noted the marriage:

A large crowd gathered at the Pacheco home Friday evening, 20 March, to celebrate the marriage of John Pacheco and his new bride.

Juan and Phyllis had six children:

Loretta (Carter), 4 February 1937
Joyce (Crain), 7 February 1939
LeRoy, 3 August 1941
Norma (D'Ambrosia, Lohmeyer), 2 July 1943
Richard, 1946
Linda (Belville), 13 December 1948

The first three were born in Grand Junction; Norma was born at Dragerton, and the other two were born at Price, Utah.

John and his family moved to Dragerton, Utah, shortly before his daughter, Norma, was born. John's brothers Felix and Dan, and their families, moved there at about the same time. John went to work at the Horse Canyon Mine where he remained until retirement. After living in Dragerton for a few years they moved to a home in Price.

In the early 1950s John and Phyllis were divorced. Phyllis remarried and John has since spent a lot of time with their daughter, Norma. After their son LeRoy retired he built a small home for John beside his new home in Castle Valley, up-river from Moab. John broke an arm while living there, and since it was slow to heal, he went back to live with Norma in Salt Lake. To add to his problems, not long after he went to live with Norma he fell and broke a hip. John healed very well under Norma's watchful care. In the late summer of 1994 we, the authors, had a delightful visit with John and his daughter Norma and husband and found John in good spirits. While his memory of recent events was not very good, it was a delight to hear him recite readings that have stayed with him since his younger days. He recited "Charge of the Light Brigade," "Hiawatha" and "The Village Blacksmith" with little or no hesitation.

But at present, 1996, he is not in good health. He celebrated his 90th birthday in June and has, for several years, shown the effects of osteoporosis. Since his birthday in 1995, he fell and cracked a vertebrae and has been confined to a rest home in Salt Lake City. John is the youngest and sole survivor of the 14 children of Juan and Porfiria Pacheco.

We've been told by various family members that there have been several Pacheco family reunions, some attended by as many as 150 descendants of Juan and Porfiria Pacheco. What a family!

Paulson

The following is from an interview with Larry Paulson plus obituaries and news items from *The Daily Sentinel.*

James "Jim" Lawrence Paulson was born at Grand Valley, Garfield, Colorado, 26 May 1906, to Martin Paulson and Martha Wolfe. The family lived on a homestead. When Jim was still quite young his father sold out and moved the family to Victor, Teller, Colorado, where he operated a livery stable. Jim started to school there, then the family moved to Collbran, Colorado where he had more schooling.

James "Jim" Lawrence and Eunice Sager Paulson
(Photo courtesy of Larry Paulson)

Larry Wayne, Martha Marie, Ernest Edward Paulson
(Photo courtesy of Larry Paulson)

Larry, Bethine and Marie Paulson, 1947, in New Liberty. *(Photo courtesy of Larry Paulson)*

He was married to **Eunice Sager** at Collbran in January, 1928. She was born 12 February 1906, at Laveta, Colorado, the daughter of Mr. and Mrs. A. E. Sager. She moved with her family to Plateau Valley when she was a small girl. She attended schools and grew to womanhood in that area.

After marriage Jim and Eunice lived on a ranch in Plateau Valley until Eunice's health began to fail. Then they moved to Grand Junction, where Jim went to work for the D&RGW as a boiler-maker.

They had three children:

Martha Marie (Brown), born 9 December 1929, at Collbran
Ernest Edward, 18 November 1930, at Collbran
Larry Wayne, 31 January 1935, at Collbran.

Eunice died of pneumonia 24 March 1936, at St. Mary's Hospital and was buried in Grand Junction Municipal Cemetery. She was only 25.

Jim married **Bethine Mulnix** about 1937/38. In 1942 they bought a chicken ranch and motel at Fruitvale corner. The children attended school at Fruitvale and their daughter, Marie, graduated from Fruitvale High School.

They sold out in Fruitvale in 1945 and moved to the New Liberty community, buying the former Boyden homestead from **George Blank** in 1946. During the time they lived there they wintered 35 to 40 head of steers. The boys attended New Liberty school and graduated from Fruita Union High School.

(Above left) Jim Paulson on his horse in front of a haystack on his farm in New Liberty. (Above right) Larry, Marie and Jim Paulson, 1947. (Center left) The Paulson's pigs, 23 September 1948. They sold for $29.75 per 100 pound weight. *(Photos courtesy of Larry Paulson)*

(Above) The Paulson's horses, Goldie and Silver, mowing the third cutting of hay, 1947. Others are not identified. (Right) Ralph Banning, and Ernest and Larry Paulson, about 1945. *(Photos courtesy of Larry Paulson)*

In 1952 Jim and Bethine sold the New Liberty farm and moved to Fruita. Jim served as Town Marshall for the town of Fruita for five or six years. Then he and Larry started building houses together until Jim retired in 1970. He didn't stay retired, but built a couple more houses and retired again in 1975. Jim died 29 November 1996 in Fruita.

Martha Marie graduated from Fruitvale High School and then went on to college and became a registered nurse. She married **Warren Brown** in Montrose, Colorado. They have three children; **Debbie**, **Jeff** and **Randy** and live in Palm Springs, California.

Ernest was active in student affairs while in high school; he served on the student council, was vice president of the sophomore class, played basketball in his junior and senior years, was secretary of the Chess Club in his junior year, was on the track team in his senior year, on the school newspaper staff in his senior year and in the school letterman's club in his junior and senior years. He graduated in 1948.

After high school, Ernest spent some time in the Marines during the Korean War and achieved the rank of Staff Sergeant. He was married three times, the last to **Doris Myrel Morris**, 16 November 1969 at Las Vegas, Nevada. Doris had a son **Billy**, by a former marriage, and then she and Ernest had a daughter, **Shawna Marie**.

Ernest ran a garage in Seattle, Washington, then lived for a time in Albuquerque, New Mexico, and Montrose, Colorado, then came back to Fruita and worked as an electrician for several years. Then he started building houses and began the Ernest Paulson Construction Company. Ernest died 15 November 1992, at St. Mary's Hospital in Grand Junction.

Larry graduated from Fruita Union High School in 1953. He went to Mesa College in Grand Junction for two years, then he went to work for his Uncle Leonard Paulson in Grand Junction for four years building houses. He

married **Lucille Mackey** 19 August 1956, in Grand Junction. Lucille was born 16 July 1937 at Greeley, Weld, Colorado, a daughter of Chester Mackey and Kathryn Opal Doctor. They have four children: two boys and two girls.

Linda Lucille (Kovach), born 12 June 1958
LuAnn Kay (Gauna), 28 April 1960
Lanny Duane, 6 June 1961
Loren Wayne, 17 July 1965
All were born in Fruita.

In 1957 Larry and Lucille moved to Fruita and Larry and his father started building houses together. Larry has continued the building business on his own since his father retired.

Larry was on the Fruita City Council for seven years, between 1973–1980, and was a member of the volunteer fire department for 10 years, between 1970–1980. He played on softball teams in Grand Junction as a pitcher for 20 years. Larry, his sons and two sons-in-law decided to help form a Class A softball team after his sons were out of college. He coached that for three years and two out of the three years the team qualified for the Nationals; they took 5th one year and 4th another.

Lucille has worked for School District 51 as a nurse's aid for 27 years. She also served as a food leader in the 4-H club from 1966 to 1973. She and Larry have seven grandchildren.

Penfield

Here is a little information from an obituary in *The Daily Sentinel,* about one of the early teachers in Mack School,

Edna Penfield, was born 5 April 1889, at Burwell, Nevada, to Edward Penfield and Mary Ellen Fulton. She spent her childhood in Boone,

Iowa, and Fruita, Colorado. She graduated from Fruita Union High School in 1909, then graduated from Colorado Teacher's College at Greeley, Colorado, and attended University of California at Berkeley.

She taught at Mack School in 1912-13. She is listed in the 1920 census at age 30, living with her parents in Fruita. She was then teaching in Fruita. She also taught at Utah Mine, Clear Creek, Rollap and other mining camps in Carbon County, Utah, before she moved to Moab. She then continued to teach in Grand and San Juan Counties until retirement.

She was married to **George Owthit Patterson**, 25 November 1922, at Moab. They raised a boy and two girls. The children attended school in Moab. George died 19 November 1962; Edna died 28 August 1992, at age 103. Both died at Allen Memorial Hospital in Moab and both were buried in Moab.

Phillips

Information is from obituaries and news items in *The Daily Sentinel*; 1860, 1870 and 1880 Kentucky Federal Census records; and contributions from Charlene Brayton Eldridge, who inherited the personal effects of the Phillips, Braytons and Weirs.

Clifton Jackson Phillips was born 28 May 1858, near Elizabethtown, Hardin, Kentucky, the oldest of seven children and the only son of Francis Marion and Sarah Jane Phillips. He spent most of his childhood on a farm near Elizabethtown. The 1880 census enumerates him at home at age 22, and going to school. He must have attended one of the colleges in Elizabethtown. In 1899 he went to Florida and later to North Carolina, where he resided for one year before returning to Kentucky in 1900. Clifton married **Mamie Augusta Beasley** at Osceola, Volusia, Florida, 8 November 1892. Mamie was born 18 May 1886, at Oxford, Granville, North Carolina, where she spent the early part of her life. Their son, **Robert "Bob" Marion**, was born at Osceola, Florida, 22 July 1893. There was also a daughter who apparently died young. In 1910 the family moved west and settled in Colorado Springs, Colorado, where they lived until 1918, when they moved to the New Liberty community. Clifton was a carpenter by trade, but always combined that occupation with farming.

Clifton Jackson, Robert Marion, and Francis Marion Phillips, three generations.
(Photo courtesy of Charlene Brayton Eldridge)

The following was contributed by Charlene Brayton Eldridge, a niece of Bob and Bessie. It was published in the *Fruita Times*, 4 December 1992.

Probably within two years of the time Clifton and family arrived in New Liberty, he recorded the following: "My life's desire has been to earn a little home on a small farm, well influenced by my own work and near a small town. Just such a place we now have on this Grand Valley irrigation [project], except in process of improvements that in some ways the conditions here are far better than anything I ever knew or dreamed of. I came here with a whole lifetime of home hunger. That made light of the hardships to pioneering and gave me a hearty appreciation for the really great advantages of the valley. In less than two years we made greater progress toward developing a farm than I had in thirteen years of hard work at our timber tract in Kentucky, or before that, eleven years at the hundred [acre] tract in Florida. Though perfect strangers, we were quickly established at the lumber yard, bank and grocery, for anything we needed. I never spent money for liquor nor money for tobacco nor any other nonsense, but devoted my energy to the one great purpose - a little farm and home. It has been done."

Robert M. won rights to the homestead in the drawing of 29 March 1918. He and his parents began proving up on it that same year.

Robert was married 15 October 1928, at Fruita, to **Bessie Mabel Brayton**. They had a son, **Murray Hess**, who was born at Grand Junction, 2 September 1929.

Robert and Bessie were active in community affairs; we find evidence of that in records of community organizations: Sunday School, Community Club and New Liberty School, etc. Robert had also learned the carpenter trade from his father.

Bob and Bessie were meticulous records keepers, as evidenced by the following excerpts from information submitted by Charlene Brayton Eldridge, as mentioned below:

"19 April 1921 . . . Land broken, 55 acres; land leveled (perfect), 25 acres; land leveled (partly), 25 acres; land in alfalfa, 5 acres; in fall wheat, 3 acres.

Buildings, 1 house, $100; fencing, $60; cistern, $25.

"Miscellaneous assets, 139 grain sacks, $13.50; 1 float, $5; 1 hayrack, $10; barbed wire, $5.50; cedar posts, $15; canvas, $5 — total of $53.90.

"Feed, 4 tons hay, $40; 80 bushel. oats, $55.10; 10 bushel. corn, $5; 3 bushel. wheat, $3.60.

Negotiable assets, 14 April 1921: 1 plow, $20; 1 plow, $4; 1 Wagon, $40; 1 disk, $41.70; 1 harrow, $20; 1 fresno, $15; beet implements, $82.50; 1 set harness, $40; 1 set harness, $30; — Total $293.20.

"Livestock: 1 team horses, $200; 1 brood sow, $25; poultry, $15; — total $240"

Bessie Mabel Brayton and Robert Marion Phillips.
(Photo courtesy of Charlene Brayton Eldridge)

Murray Phillips, 1947.
(Photo courtesy of Fred Pacheco)

637

(Above) Bob Phillip's house in New Liberty, taken 1983. *(Photo courtesy of Phyllis Maluy Likes)* (Right) Bob, Bessie and Murray Phillips, about 1932. (Lower left) Bob, Bessie and Murray Phillips, about 1933. (Lower right) Murray and friend, Fred Pacheco, with their best friends, their dogs. Photo was taken at the Felix Pacheco residence looking northeast; the New Liberty community is in the background. *(Photos courtesy of Charlene Brayton Eldridge)*

Included in Bob's personal effects was a lease written by Bill Knapp and dated Mack, Colorado, 9 April 1921. Bill may have then been staying, or soon would be, at the Roselyn Hotel in Los Angeles. The paper authorized Bob to be in charge of Bill's homestead for a period of three years; water and taxes were paid.

Bob had a mind of his own, he did not adhere to his father's philosophy of avoiding such 'nonsense' as tobacco. He rolled his own 'Bull Durham' cigarettes. But his frugal nature caused him to recycle the butts to cut down on the waste. He was afflicted with asthma, so the Bull Durham couldn't have helped that very much.

Bob was a member of the Colorado Bean Growers Association and had preserved a notice dated 20 May 1927, of a meeting to be held 22 June 1927, at the Potato Growers Warehouse at Loma, for the purpose of choosing delegates from whom one would be selected to serve on the board of directors. This letter also includes a list of all members of the association at that time; a rather interesting document.

In the newspaper article submitted by Charlene were included also a foreman's report of men who worked on the ditches in the winter of 1934, including the names of Oscar Berry, George Bryan, John Pacheco, Rudolph Johnson, Arthur Shires, R. M. Phillips, Allen Daily, J. A. Owings and J. M. Appleby.

Bessie came to New Liberty from Missouri in August 1923, with S.S. Summers, who had recently married Bessie's mother, Josephine Brayton.

Bessie was active in the New Liberty Sunday School and helped organize a young people's study group on 8 January 1928.

Many were present at the organizational meeting: Phillip Brayton, Milton Alstatt, Clyde Likes, Charles Cutler, Viola Alstatt, Ruth Alstatt, Elizabeth Morrow, Hobart Cutler, Mrs. McCampbell, Melba McCampbell, Ethel Brayton Bessie Brayton, Bob Phillips, Mrs. Summers, Mrs Morrow and Estellene Morrow.

Phillip Brayton was elected president of the new organization; Estellene Morrow was elected Vice President, Bob Phillips, Secretary and Treasurer. Phillip Brayton was also elected to lead the singing at the meetings, Hobart Cutler to take up a collection every third Sunday, Charles Cutler and Viola Alstatt as membership committee. Bessie was elected to the devotional committee with the privilege of choosing two members to assist her. Clyde Likes and Milton Alstatt were elected to take care of the song books.

Bessie was also instrumental in organizing the New Liberty Community Club and assisted in writing the Articles of Constitution, which were adopted 15 May 1926. (Turn back to the article about New Liberty Community Club for further information.)

Bessie graduated from Fruita Union High School in 1927. After her marriage to Bob she devoted her life to making a home for her husband and son and Bob's parents.

Time began to take it's toll; Mamie became ill and was taken to the hospital in Grand Junction where she died 10 March 1938. Clifton was already well up in years (60) when they came to New Liberty, in fact, he was one of the oldest settlers in the community. After his wife died he became senile and was confused much of the time. There was one instance when he was discovered by someone who recognized him, walking along the highway almost to Cisco. He passed away at home Sunday morning 19 November 1939. He and Mamie are both buried in Elmwood Cemetery at Fruita.

After suffering for years from asthma, Bob died 22 June 1950. Bessie wrote the following after Bob passed on.

> We had our cup of joy
> We'll live in memories' garden,
> For memories are a gift of God
> That death cannot destroy.

Bessie and Murray continued with the homestead. Murray had grown up on the farm. He attended New Liberty School and graduated from Fruita Union High School in 1947. He drove the school bus in 1952 and 1953. On 25 August 1953 he entered St. Mary's Hospital with a perforated appendix. He developed an abscess after the operation and had a lengthy stay in the hospital until 3 October 1953. He was left with a bad lung from that episode.

In the meantime Bessie went to work for an elderly couple in Grand Junction and was with them for 15 years. In 1970 she completed an "in service course" at the Palisade Nursing Home. She worked there for a couple more years, then she and Murray moved to a farm in the area of Silt, Colorado, in 1972.

Bessie entered a retirement home in June 1981, in Rifle, and died at Clagett Memorial Hospital in Rifle, 27 June 1988, at age 81.

Murray caught a bad cold before the Christmas holiday of 1991 and died 26 December 1991, in the Clagett Memorial Hospital at Rifle. He was 62. Among his personal notes was found this observation: "I grew up in a caring community."

Robert, Bessie and Murray are all buried in Elmwood Cemetery at Fruita.

Information from obituaries and news items in *The Daily Sentinel*.

Ħomer Marshall Phillips was born 22 May 1867, at Fort Scott, Bourbon, Kansas, the son of John Phillips.

He graduated from Fort Scott High School and later graduated from Missouri State College in Warrensburg, Missouri, where he prepared to enter the newspaper business. In 1889 he moved to Chicago where he was employed as a printer.

He was married in Chicago 17 March 1895, to **Agnes Marie Kane**. Agnes was born 15 August 1876, in Troy, Rensselaer County, New York. (We don't know the names of her parents)

They had six children, including a daughter who died in infancy:

Helen Margaret (Gore)
Homer Marshall Jr.
Harold K.
William
Clyde "Chirp"

In 1917 the family moved from Chicago to Fruita, where Mr. Phillips took over the Fruita Mail (Newspaper), which he edited until 1920, when he resigned to accept employment with the Uintah Railway as assistant dispatcher at Mack. He resigned from that position in 1936 because of failing eyesight.

The family all lived around Grand Valley for many years. Helen Margaret married Wade Gore of Fruita and raised two children. Clyde lived in Mack for many years and was, at one time, appointed temporary post master at the Mack post office.

Homer II worked for the Barber Asphalt Co. at Dragon, Utah, and then later for the American Gilsonite Co., where he served at Bonanza for many years as chief clerk.

Pollock

From obituaries and news items in *The Daily Sentinel*, plus a history written by Betty Pollock Benson, daughter of William E. Pollock. A few items from land and marriage records are included.

Ŵilliam "Bill" Hill Pollock Jr. Was born 24 October 1866 at Oil City, Venango County, Pennsylvania, to **William Hill Pollock Sr.** and **Mary Anne Pollock**. Bill was one of six children and was a genuine pioneer. He came with his parents to Colorado in 1878 and to Grand Junction in 1882 via Black Mesa, traveling by wagon. William H. Sr. established the first bakery in Grand Junction. In 1883 they moved to a homestead in "Pollock Canyon" on the south side of the Colorado (Grand) River between Fruita and Loma. Around 1900 William and Mary Anne built the Park Hotel at Fruita. (There is some controversy about the date it was built.)

The family then moved back to the Rico-

William "Bill" Hill Pollock Jr. family. L-R: Bill Jr., Elmer Harley "Duke", William Ernest "Bill", and May Agnes Hay Pollock. *(Photo courtesy of Betty Pollock Benson)*

William H. Jr. was a teamster; he did hauling over a wide area of the western slope with horses and wagons. During the construction of the Highline Canal, William contracted to build the laterals in the New Liberty section of the canal system. That job was finished in time for the first water run in 1917.

Son William E. was about eight years old when he came to Fruita with his parents. He graduated from Fruita Union High School in 1913, and later from Colorado State University at Fort Collins. He served in the Navy Medical Corps during World War I. After the war he became a partner in the Pollock - Brennan garage business in Fruita.

On 29 March 1918, William H. won rights to a homestead in the drawing held that day. It was

Leadville-Silverton areas of Colorado, where William H. Jr. met **May Agnes Hay.** They were married at Rico, 22 September 1894.

May Agnes Hay was also a genuine Colorado pioneer. She was born 10 December 1877 at Utica, LaSalle County, Illinois. In 1881 she moved with her family by covered wagon to Colorado and settled in the area of Rico. The family later moved to the Cripple Creek and Victor mining areas where her father worked as a master mechanic in the mines.

William H. Jr. and May moved to Fruita in 1903. In 1916, after the death of William's mother, Mary Anne, they took over operation of the Park Hotel.

They had two sons:

William "Bill" or **"Willie" Ernest,** born 10 September 1895, at Rico, Delores, Colorado

Elmer "Duke" Harley, 26 December 1898 at Almont, Gunnison, Colorado.

The Park Hotel in Fruita, Colorado, built by William H Sr. and Mary Anne Pollock in the 1890s. In 1993 it was still functioning as a hotel under the same name. *(Photo used from the Fruita Times 15 October 1993 issue)*

farm unit "C", located in Sec. 2 & 3. Later that year, son William E. filed on unit "D", Sec 2 and 11, joining his Dad's on the south.

Following is an account of a wedding as written in the Fruita news items by Mabel C. Kiefer, correspondent for *The Daily Sentinel:*

"Miss Lois Righdenour and William E. Pollock were quietly married Tuesday evening, 12 September 1922, at the Congregational Parsonage by Reverend I. J. Tripp, in the presence of the bride's mother, Mrs. D. V. Righdenour, and the groom's mother, Mrs. William Pollock, and brother, Elmer Pollock.

The bride was tastefully attired in a traveling costume and the groom in a black business suit. The young couple are distinctly Fruita people, having grown to manhood and womanhood here, where they attended our schools and engaged in business. The bride was for some time one of the efficient operators at the local telephone office. She is the daughter of Mr. and Mrs. D. V. Righdenour, and her attractive personality has won her many friends. The groom is a young business man, one of the partners of the Pollock - Brennan Garage, and is a young man of sterling qualities. He is the son of Mr. and Mrs. William Pollock.

Mr. and Mrs. Pollock left immediately after the ceremony for Grand Junction and later motored to Mesa, Glenwood Springs and Norrie. They expect to be away about a week and on their return will be at home at the William Pollock residence on So. Coulson St., to which they will take with them the hearty congratulations and best wishes for a happy future, of many friends."

Bill and Lois had three sons and two daughters:

James William, born 3 April 1924
Elizabeth (Betty) May, 17 November 1925
Robert Price, 16 January 1931
Walter Henry, 23 April 1932
Norma Lois, 10 June 1938
All were born at Fruita.

Here is a history written by Betty Pollock Benson, which was published in the *Fruita Times,* 1 August 1991.

(Upper) Bill E. Pollock family, 1971. Standing: Betty Benson, Jim, Walt, Bob and Norma Gobbo. Lois and Bill are sitting in front. (Lower) The Bill E. Pollock children, late 1980s. Back row, L-R: Bob, Walt and Jim Pollock. In front: Betty Benson and Norma Gobbo. *(Photos courtesy of Betty Pollock Benson)*

Wake-up call came early on the farm, if you dared to catch an extra wink you might get cold water on your face.

My Grandpa and Dad each homesteaded 60 acres 5 1/2 miles north of Mack. It took a lot of work clearing the land but the ground was very fertile. Our land was on a hill above Grandpa's.

My grandparents owned and operated the Park Hotel in Fruita. Grandpa much preferred farming to making beds, so he spent Monday through Friday at the farm. My Dad owned and operated a garage at Fruita, but he had to prove up on the land or lose it, so we moved to New Liberty.

He bought a "mining shack" to live in . . . three rooms and an added porch with the promise of a new house, but a tractor or farm implement took it's place. I think the old house is still standing (Ed Young's place).

We had a lot of milk cows and fed the separated (skim) milk to lots of pigs. My job was washing the greasy separator. We sold the cream to the creamery in Fruita. That was our grocery money.

The Highline canal was above our place (south) and there was a siphon that carried the water about a mile into the canal by Carroll's farm. The intake to the siphon was dangerous and we were not allowed to go near it or suffer the consequences. We suffered a few times.

The canal carried the water to the west end of New Liberty. I spent a lot of time on that siphon . . . it was easy to get up on, but hard to get off, so I usually jumped. No wonder I have flat feet!

Hay and potatoes and corn were the main crops, but later Dad raised a lot of beans.

My three brothers . . . Jim, Bob and Walt - and myself, spent a lot of our summers hoeing crops. Mom and Dad helped too. If we dared miss a weed, my Dad spied it. But we were a family working together, laughing and teasing.

My Dad didn't believe pastures were necessary, so we took turns (grudgingly) herding cows. We had certain places to herd them and boy was it a job trying to keep them out of the hay, etc.

It was a good thing my Dad studied to be a vet, as we had a few cows bloat. One cow in particular was the instigator, "Dot." She choked on a potato one day and after my Dad lectured me about how easy it was to choke, I said, "Well, I was hoping she would." She was always hiding in the cornfield.

Grandpa took pride in his team of horses. We had several teams, and until my dad bought a tractor, we used them all. Once in awhile one of those teams would "run" and it would cause a lot of excitement.

We had lots of fun on the farm. We did a lot of exploring and I could climb a tree as well as any of my brothers.

Now, I'm not forgetting my sister, Norma, she joined us later in life. She got out of a lot of work.

We lived by a creek (East Salt Creek) that was usually a small stream but when it rained, especially in the mountains to the north, we didn't go near it. It was like a river then.

There were lots of coyotes in the creek and I didn't know what I would have done if I had seen one. I was deathly afraid of them. Daddy couldn't raise lambs because the coyotes always ate them and they were well fenced. They had a lot of good meals off Mom's chickens, too.

We had several stock ponds on the farm and we swam a lot, I tried to, but my brothers kept trying to drown me. It wasn't fun being the only girl.

There were two roads leading to New Liberty, one was 8 Rd. and one was 10 Rd. We lived on 10 Rd. We had our own little community. We were the flatlanders. Lots of good times were had.

During the haying season the men would go from farm to farm stacking hay, and the women cooked such good food. My Mom was an excellent cook, but she outdid herself during haying. Mary Cutler was such good help. She was a widow with several children to raise, and my good friend. Sometimes when I really got mad at Mom I would go down to Mary's place and tell her my troubles and she'd always listen. And I can't leave Modine out, either.

After haying was over, several families, Cutlers, Schunters, Ebrights, Rectors, Rowes, all went to Deacon's summer camp to picnic for a day.

My Dad hated picnics and tried every way he could to get out of going, but Booze and Walt ganged up on him. One day we started to the cabin and our car kept acting up, and we all thought it was my Dad trying to get out of going. All of a sudden the radiator cap blew off and lots and lots of peach seeds blew out. The field mice must have had a "heyday." I never heard anyone laugh so hard as Booze and Walt did. It was hilarious, a real "old faithful."

School was 3 1/2 miles from where we lived, and the first year of school we had to either walk or ride a horse. We had a little Indian pony and our Dad wouldn't let Jim and me use the saddle and the horse was always shying, so we fell off almost every day. He finally bought us another horse. We still fell off. Finally the bus went our direction and we could ride. What a relief.

Our school building was only two rooms with a teacher for four grades in each. I doubt if we ever had over forty students at a time. I'm sure they were relieved, as some of the students were characters.

They built a new schoolhouse when I was in the third grade and we even had hot lunches. No more soggy sandwiches. It was fun trading lunches, though.

The whole community shared in activities and "special days". We always put on a play at Christmas time and had a "real" Santa Claus and lots of goodies in our sacks, especially candy and oranges. Some of the kids only got oranges at our Christmas parties.

Some of the teachers stick out more in my mind . . . . Esther Zeigler (Mrs. Starr), Delbert Jerome, and dear Mrs. Harold Carroll. They really influenced my life. Mrs. Carroll was our music teacher and she also taught a lot of us piano and violin and tap dancing. Gene Thomas' grandmother, Mrs. Morrow, was our 4-H leader, and boy, could she cook. His mom, Estellene, was our sewing leader. She was an excellent cook also. Harriett Cutler and I rode horseback to the different farms because it was too far to walk.

When Adamses moved to New Liberty we went in Rose Ellen's "puddle jumper." What fun we had at the Adamses . . . pulling taffy.

We didn't have electricity for a long time, so most of us had to bake on coal stoves. Patty Maluy and Marilyn Maluy were probably the only ones who had electric stoves . . . but I prided myself in my cakes. Coal stove or not, we all did real well at the 4-H Fair. Most of us got to go to camp on Grand Mesa. That was the highlight of my summers.

We all went to college. Jimmy and Bob both went to the University of Colorado and Walt went to Colorado State University, Norma and I both went to Mesa College.

Jim is retired and lives at Cedaredge. He is a bachelor and my husband said he was the only smart one of us.

Betty married **James A. "Jim" Benson** of DeBeque on 19 January 1949. Jim worked at American Gilsonite for several years and then went into his own building construction business, J. B. Construction. We had cattle and leased a summer pasture on Bitter Creek. Chipeta's cabin was on the property. We had four children: **Sharon Dent, Ed, Rick**, and **Linda Hudson** and twelve grandchildren. We lost Jim in 1982, but I keep very active. I love to fish.

Bob **and Veva** own Laser Print West. They have five children and six grandchildren. Bob is very active in Lions, church, and anything that comes along.

Walt **and Pat** live in Boulder. He works for the National Center for Atmospheric Research. They have three children. He loves to fish.

Norma **Gobbo** lives on 23 and L roads. Her husband, **Don**, is with Gobbo Land and Livestock. They have three girls and seven grandchildren. So the Bill Pollocks are well represented.

So the Bill Pollacks are well represented. The older generations of Pollocks are all gone. May Agnes Pollock died at the Park Hotel 31 October 1942. William H. Pollock moved to the Carlson Rest Home in Clifton, where he died 2 July 1952. William E. Pollock retired from the farm in 1947 and he and Lois moved back to Fruita. Bill died in the Lower Valley hospital at Fruita, on 23 October 1977. Lois was in the Lower Valley Nursing Home when she died 4 April 1982. All four are buried in Elmwood Cemetery at Fruita.

Descendants of William H. Pollock Sr., the man who established the homestead in Pollock Canyon, and for whom the canyon is named, met in Fruita, 2nd and 3rd of October 1993, for a reunion. They were joined by some members of Clan Pollock, who trace their ancestry to Scotland. The group toured the old Pollock homestead (south of Fruita) and the Park Hotel, had a barbecue at Reed Park and breakfast at Odd Fellows Hall.

Gene Thomas, editor and publisher of the *Fruita Times*, featured a number of pictures and a story of the gathering in the *Fruita Times* of 8 October 1993.

The Charlie Post family, Easter 1962. In back, L-R: Charlie, Maymie and Mableann. In front: Vera, Reva and Linda. *(Photo courtesy of Ann Post Hawthorne)*

Post

We express gratitude to Maymie Post and Mableann Post Hawthorne for most of the following. We also included an obituary and news items from *The Daily Sentinel*.

Charles "Charlie" Clifford Post was born 6 June 1906 at Grand Junction, to William Henry Post and Sarah Annette Coulter. He spent most of his childhood in the home of his grandparents, Samuel and Elizabeth Coulter, who lived east of Fruita in the Star District. Charlie attended the Star School and Fruita Union High School. As a young man he farmed in the Star community for several years.

In 1893 Charlie's father, William Henry Post, was awarded the original patent to the land comprising the Horse Thief Canyon Ranch. It was he who built the road down over the cliff to the river bottom.

On 6 October 1944, Charlie married **Maymie Grace Hull**. Maymie, an identical twin, was born 11 May 1913, at Colona, Montrose County, Colorado, to Charles Henry Hull and Mable Maude Smith. The family moved to Fruita when Maymie was five years old. She graduated from Fruita Union High School in 1932.

Maymie had an unusual experience before she married; she was a chauffeur and assistant of "Doc" Hapes of Fruita. Doc Hapes was a controversial figure who was not a licensed veterinarian but became in much demand by many farmers and stockmen of Grand Valley because he was able to cure a "sleeping sickness" that at one time reached epidemic proportions among horses in the valley. Hapes claimed to have obtained his "secret potion" from England while serving in the Army. To the end of his life he never revealed his secret to anyone.

There were two licensed veterinarians in the valley who were unable to attain the same results with their treatment of the sickness. But with some success they were able to legally block Doc Hapes' activities. After their efforts to put him out of business, Doc was not allowed to charge for his services, but he could and did accept donations.

Maymie and her sister traveled with Doc all over western Colorado and eastern Utah. She said that during one run they vaccinated 89 head of horses.

Charlie and Maymie had four daughters:

Mableann, born 18 March 1946
Linda Louise, 22 November 1947
Reva Sue, 15 March 1950
Vera Marie, 27 July 1952
All were born in Grand Junction.

After they purchased the former Clifford McKay farm, Charlie and Maymie and their little daughters, Mableann and Linda, moved to New Liberty in 1948. After rearranging the outbuildings and reorganizing the corrals and pastures, they remodeled the home, building an addition to serve as a kitchen and living room.

Maymie had an accident while they lived on the McKay place. She was loading coal into the heating stove one time when a dynamite cap or .22 caliber cartridge, exploded as it hit the

(Above) Charlie Post and a sample of his corn he raised on the New Liberty farm in 1951. (Upper left) Charlie Post cultivating beans on his New Liberty farm on 7 Road, 1954. (Middle) The Post's first house in New Liberty, 1949. (Left) The Post house in New Liberty, 1957. (Below left) Vera, Mableann, Reva and Linda on the horse, Tag. (Below center) LR: Unknown, Linda and Reva Post, 1959. (Below right) Mableann standing on her trained horse. *(Photos courtesy of Ann Post Hawthorne)*

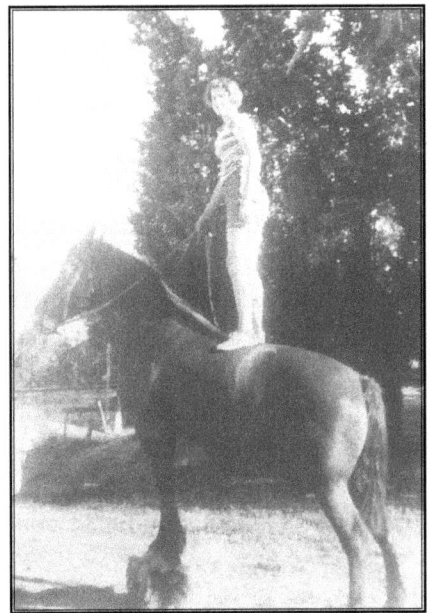

burning embers. A particle of metal hit her in the eye, destroying the sight in that eye permanently.

They lived on the McKay place until June 1957, when they sold out to Delbert and Ruth Oliver, when they moved to the former Guy Gerry farm. They later bought the former Burkett homestead, making a total of 160 acres in cultivation. Charlie was ambitious enough to farm additional acres, so he rented the Claude Taylor farm for several years. It was originally the Howard Williams' homestead. As if that weren't enough, he also bought a threshing machine and did custom threshing. The old thresher still sits at the bottom of the hill next to Badger Wash.

The girls grew up in New Liberty and attended New Liberty School and Fruita Union High School.

Mableann married **Jerry Hawthorne** 15 November 1974. They later divorced. Mableann and her daughter, **Katherine**, or **"Katie" Hawthorne,** presently (1997) live at the Blasdel (formerly Raver) farm in New Liberty.

Linda married **John Richard Dalton** 21 November 1978. John and Linda live at Durango, Colorado.

Reva Sue married **Lawrence Richard Terrell,** 4 November 1969. They have two children and live at Loma, Colorado.

Vera Marie married **David Keith Terrell,** 23 September 1972. They have two children and live in New Liberty.

Maymie and Charlie retired from farming in 1973, turning the operation over to daughters and sons-in-law. Somewhere along the way Maymie started selling Avon products, she continued with that until **1991.**

Charlie died at the farm home 19 April 1993, at the age of 86. Maymie still lives there — a "plucky old gal" who still has a lot of "get-up-and-go," she will soon be 84 years old. (1997)

Puckett

The following information was provided by Miles Puckett.

Miles Raymond Puckett was born in Fruita, Colorado, 14 July 1923, a son of John Arthur Puckett and Laura Myrtle Meadows. He attended schools at Fruita, Redlands and Crawford.

Miles was inducted into the Navy 7 January 1944 and eventually served aboard an LST - # 838 (Landing Ship Tanks). He was involved in the Philippines Liberation Campaign and was discharged 30 March 1946.

On 24 September 1948, he was married at Glenwood Springs, Garfield County, Colorado, to **Willie Sophronia Vincent.** She was born 12 August 1921 at Colony, Washita County, Oklahoma, to George Washington Vincent and Stella Ruth Garretson.

Miles and Willie had nine children:

Edwin Leo, born 4 February 1940
Robert Hoyt, 22 September 1941
Miles Raymond Jr., 1 July 1949
Nila Ann (Wise), 22 July 1950
Donna Arlene (Willden), 23 January 1952
Daniel Vincent, 22 December 1953
Ronald Eugene, 22 June 1955
Randall George, 11 November 1956
Timothy Gale, 2 August 1961
All were born at Grand Junction except Miles Raymond Jr., who was born at Kansas City, Missouri.

In 1949 Miles attended a mechanic school in Kansas City, Missouri, funded by the "G I Bill," a special fund made available for Veterans of World War II to help them with education, home or farm loans, etc. Most veterans took advantage of it in some way. Willie and the two oldest boys accompanied him while he was in Kansas City, and while they were there the third boy, Miles Jr., was born.

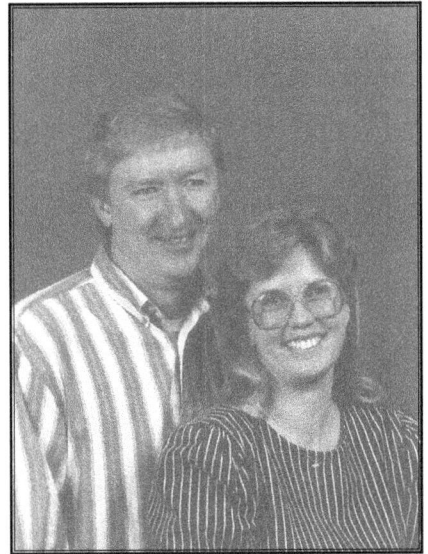

(Left) The Miles Puckett Sr. family. Back row, L-R: Donna, Daniel, Miles Jr., Tim, Leo and Robert. In front: Nila, Miles Sr., Willie and Ronald. (Above) Randy and his wife. *(Photos courtesy of Miles Puckett Sr.)*

After returning from Kansas City Miles was employed for a time as a truck driver, but lost his job for some reason and his family was about to be evicted from their rental home. They were then living in the vicinity of Whitewater, nine miles east of Grand Junction.

The family moved to the west end of New Liberty in 1954. There they "squatted" on some vacant desert land adjacent to the west end of the High Line canal, just to the west of the Clyde Likes Jr. farm. Miles related a story of his sons, Leo and Robert, constructing a make-shift cabin from lumber salvaged from an old flume taken from the Highline canal in the vicinity of 19 Road. That was home to the family for several years.

Miles tells of the hardships when they first settled out there:

Firewood was gathered by the two oldest boys in whatever quantities they could find large enough to make heat in a small pot-bellied stove. Our water was hauled in a barrel and was frozen most of the time. Most of the water for drinking, cooking, laundry, etc. came from melting snow on the stove. We were truly pioneering — the winter was cold and it was hard to keep warm in the make-shift cabin.

The older children began attending New Liberty School, walking 1½ miles to catch the school bus. (At the corner of S and 6 roads)

The land they had settled on was poor, being laced with alkali and bentonite, so they had little success with crops. They had to depend on waste water for irrigation since they had no water rights from the High Line canal.

In January 1956, while continuing to live in New Liberty, Miles went to work for the Mountain States Telephone and Telegraph Company. He held various positions through the years, such as janitorial work and building maintenance; for the last 13½ years before retirement he worked in the supply department, occasionally making deliveries to Aspen and Gunnison. He retired in August 1982.

In 1965 the family was able to make improvements on their home, but by that time many of the older children had finished school and had gone out on their own.

At present the girls, **Nila** and **Donna**, are homemakers, busy raising their families.

Leo has been self employed as a cement contractor for nearly 30 years. He has a hobby of raising different breeds of chickens, doves and pigeons and spends lots of time building special pens, nests and brooders.

Robert worked for the state highway department for more than 30 years. He now has a small farm near Palisade.

Miles **Jr.** joined the Navy in December 1967 during the Vietnam War. He served on several Aircraft Carriers for a total of 13 years. At present he drives an eighteen-wheeler for C. R. England from Los Angeles, California to Atlanta, Georgia.

Daniel spent 17 years working at the refinery west of Fruita. He is now in Thailand.

Ronald works as a mechanic for Jim Fuoco Motor Company in Grand Junction.

Randy is also a mechanic for Jim Fuoco Motors. He is one of their specially trained mechanics who has worked there for 18 years.

Tim is also a mechanic. He and his brothers Ronald and Randy rebuild and maintain auto engines and carburetors.

In 1978 the Puckets had a disastrous fire that destroyed their home and most of their belongings. They were fortunate to be able to collect enough insurance to rebuild, but they opted to move instead. They now live on 20 acres at 1264 12½ Road in the Loma District.

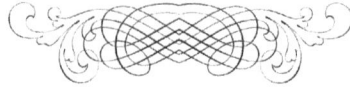

Raver

From stories written by Maudie Raver Yates, Mildred Raver Arpke Shultz Means, obituaries and news items from *The Daily Sentinel,* and personal knowledge of the author.

John Wesley Raver was born 23 February 1885 in Illinois. He married **Allie Mae Reese** at Arbor, Missouri, 8 August 1905. Allie Mae was born at Advance, Stoddard, Missouri, 28 April 1891, to John Franklin Reese and Allie Victoria Anderson. Both Allie Mae's parents died when she was a young child, so she was raised by foster parents.

The newlyweds lived in the area of Allenville, Stoddard, Missouri, for a time, where their daughter, **Georgia Maud "Maudie" Agnes Mary**, was born, 3 March 1907.

The family moved to Louisiana for several years, and then came to Grand Junction, Colorado, in about 1916. John had been advised by a doctor to move to Colorado in hopes the dryer climate would be helpful for his tuberculosis. He worked in the Denver and Rio Grande Shops at Grand Junction as a Railroad Pipe Fitter. His tuberculosis became worse, so his doctor advised him to get away from the shops. In 1918 he filed on a homestead in the New Liberty community in hopes this change of life style would give him some relief from his illness; but that was not to be.

The following was quoted to daughter, Mildred, by her mother:

I beheld a rosebud
Kissed by the morning dew
My heart thought of a fairer one
So, I'll send this one to you.

That was sent to Allie Mae when she was 17-18 years old by Ernie Hepner, brother of Zelma Reese, who was Allie Mae's sister-in-law.

Mildred informed us that her mother, Allie Mae Raver, kept diaries throughout much of her life, which she said would make a fine book. Included with some of her mother's writings was a letter to Howard Williams, a homesteader who in the early days lived just north of Ravers. Williams apparently had written Allie Mae asking her to write a story of their homestead experiences. What she wrote is pretty well covered in Maudie's and Mildred's writings.

Following are some quotes from Allie Mae's diaries:

John W. Raver and Allie Mae Reese married 8th of August 1905 at the residence of W. L. Hitt, in presence of Annie Christian and Lula Raver. Minister, J. B. Bright.

On the 19th day of December 1910, a water tank at Aquilla, Missouri, on the St. Louis and Santa Fe Railroad, burst, throwing J. W. Raver 30 feet, breaking his left arm just above the wrist and cutting his head and face in three places. He was sent to the St. Louis Frisco Hospital on the 20th day of December 1910. He left the hospital in January 1911, and he left Broomfield, Missouri for DeQuincy Louisiana., in March 1911. Mrs. J. W. Raver left Bloomfield, Missouri for DeQuincy, Louisiana., in April 1911.

On the back page of a diary were the words, "Presented to me by my dear husband, January 1st 1913, Mrs. J. W. Raver."

Georgia Maude Agnes Mary and Mildred Lucinda Raver
(Photo courtesy of Mabel Likes Cox)

Found in the fly-leaf of that diary, started at DeQuincy, Louisiana, 2 January 1913, were the words:

J. W. Raver, age 28 years ,23rd February.
Mae A. Raver, age 22 years, 28th April.
Maudie Agnes Raver, age 6 years, 3rd March.

August 2nd 1921, Sunday — Today is sad and lonely. John is so bad, none of us feel well. Our hearts are sad, our bodies wearied. No one has time to come to say one cheery word of comfort. Surely God will not forsake us in our hour of deep sorrow.

Little sweet Mildred, the joy of our hearts; what pleasure we have at all is from watching her cunning baby ways.

Sweet Mildred does not know Daddy is so bad. Maudie knows but does not realize to the fullest extent. Young hearts don't grieve until face to face with death. Hard and bitter the cup we must drink to the very dregs. Parting is a terrible thought.

Even though it may be only for a little while. Jesus is coming soon. Then the gathering of the worthy ones and the resurrection and the righteous dead. O God, comfort us now. Our hearts are grieved. Give us strength, courage and faith in thee. Mae Raver.

Their second daughter, **Mildred Lucinda,** was born at New Liberty, 5 August 1920. She was 14 months old when her father passed on. He died 20 October 1921, at age 36, and was buried in the Elmwood Cemetery at Fruita.

January 7, 1922 — John Wesley Raver was borned (sic) at Mt. Vernon, Illinois, February 23, 1885.

Died at his home, 5 miles northwest of Mack, Thursday, Oct. 20, 1921.

Was buried in Elmwood Cemetery at Fruita, Colorado., Sunday October 23, 1921.

Dressed in dark blue serge/white casket.

Services conducted by Elder Sutton, Seventh-Day Adventist Minister at Methodist Church at Fruita.

At the cemetery the Masons of Fruita took charge — also with all the funeral arrangements. All were kind. Our hearts were sad. Mrs. John W. Raver.

My life is all I have to spend
My flowers are but few
The happiest hours I ever spent
Were those I spent with you.

On 27 October 1922 she was married to **Edwin "Ed" Dalbert Hiatt,** but that marriage didn't last very long , and proved to be heart breaking for Allie, as you will see reflected in an entry in her diary which follows.

July 10, 1923 — Sick, broken-hearted, love, but not loved. Ed hates me; wants me to leave him. Says if I don't he'll make life so miserable for me that I will be sorry I did not. If I stay he'll have a bit of heaven on the side and all hell at home. Heaven to him is the association with fast women. In the front pages of this book is written many pleasant items of my sweetheart that was my true husband and is gone. This is written of my

Allie Mae and Ed Hiatt
(Courtesy of Mildred Raver Means)

were the McKays. On the hill to the south were the Gerrys and across the road from them, the Weirs. The Sumnichts lived on the hill to the west. The Shires' lived about two miles to the east, and I well remember Rudolph and Laura walking over to get acquainted when they learned there was a new little girl in the community. I think Rudolph was about 17, I was about 11 and Laura was a little younger than I.

Because of my father's health, he had been told to get out of the shops in Grand Junction, so we moved to the homestead. It was a mistake. They should have gotten a small place already proved up on; my Daddy wasn't a farmer and he wasn't about to learn. Of course, he couldn't take any dust, so I did the harrowing. We had a team named Topsy and Eva, and they were smart enough to know a kid was driving them and worked accordingly. I would get so angry! But of course they knew I couldn't hurt them. This was all a new experience to me, as up to this time I had lived in town.

There wasn't any schoolhouse, so I went to school in Fruita and stayed with the Arbuckles. Mrs. (Mollie) Arbuckle was Ena Sumnicht's sister. Ena was staying there also and going to school. My Daddy went back to Grand Junction and worked at the Latimer Chemical Co. and I stayed with him and went to school. My darling mother stayed at the ranch, for as you know, so much time had to be spent on a homestead to prove up on it.

Daddy had hired Guy Gerry to irrigate and mother watched him and felt she could do that. When Daddy came home she told him she had fired his irrigator and he wanted to know why. "Well," she told him, "I can do it myself."

second husband; both I have loved. The first loved me, the second does not. Little Mildred will know nothing of Mother's broken heart. Neither does little LaDean. Goldie and Maudie are sorry. Goldie wants me to stay. I want to be with my sweetheart, but he is tired of me. Fairer ones are calling, he hears the voices in the distance. Voices that destroy all manhood and all that is pure in a man or woman. The wages of sin is death. The gift of God is Eternal Life through Jesus Christ Our Lord. Mrs. Raver Hiatt.

Allie Mae and her daughters, Maudie and Mildred, continued to live in the New Liberty and Fruita areas until some time in 1924, when they moved to Del Norte, Colorado. Allie married Noah Earle Blasdel at Del Norte 13 August 1924. (See Blasdel).

Here are some of Maudie's memories published in the *Fruita Times*, 21 March 1991:

I remember we lived in a dug-out at Camp 8 while our house was being built on the homestead. It was no surprise to get up in the morning to see new houses or cabins going up in different directions from where we lived: The Williams and McCampbells to the north, Summers beyond that, and directly east of us

Georgia Maude Agnes Mary Raver
(Photo courtesy of Mabel Likes Cox)

653

A school house was built in 1919 and I went to the eighth grade there, with five students graduating in the spring of 1922: Ivan and Mabel Likes, Frances Schunter, Dan Pacheco and myself.

By this time there were lots of families and children in the community — friends still very dear to me. My sister, Mildred, was born at New Liberty, as were Art and Leonard Shires, Clark and Naomi Gerry, some of the Likes children and some of the Alstatts and many others.

We lost Daddy in the fall before I graduated from the eighth grade.

People can be so cruel and thoughtless! Mother had a fence around the hay-stack to protect the hay to feed the cows, and at night someone who had range cattle would open the gate and let them in. So when I would get up in the morning, I would have to drive the cattle to the highway before I went to school. Mrs. Snavely, bless her, knew why I was late and never marked me tardy.

Neighbors and men in the community were very kind and helped us in many ways. They dug our cistern and finished it for use, which was very helpful.

In the early years I remember many good times. Someone would learn that someone else had a birthday and they would go around with a hay wagon and gather up everyone and have a party. They'd make ice cream and we'd have such a good time.

After Maudie graduated from the eighth grade at New Liberty she attended Fruita Union High School for two years. Then, in 1924, she and her mother and sister, Mildred, moved to Del Norte where she later graduated from Del Norte High School. She then went to Grand Junction and graduated from Ross Business College, working part time to help pay for her room and board and tuition.

She met **Edgar Lawrence Yates** in Del Norte. Lawrence was born 24 November 1906 at Amy, Lane, Kansas. Lawrence and Maudie were married 16 June 1928, at Grand Junction and lived in the New Liberty area for a time. They had five sons:

Richard Wesley, born April 1929 in Fruita
Eldon Lloyd, June 1930, New Liberty
Wayne Ellsworth, 12 October 1932, New Liberty

Kenneth Raverne, 31 March 1935, New Liberty
Billy Ray, 9 September 1940, Fruita

Richard Wesley lived only a few hours. He is buried in Elmwood Cemetery at Fruita.

Laurence died 26 January 1978, at Grandview, Washington, where the family had lived for many years.

On 7 February 1982 Eldon Lloyd, at age 51, was seriously injured in an airplane crash and spent the rest of his life in hospitals and special care facilities. He died 29 October 1990, at age 60. Maudie and her three remaining sons still live at Grandview or nearby.

Sometime after Maudie and Lawrence moved to Washington, Maudie studied to be a Licensed Practical Nurse (LPN). She worked for 30 years as Medical and Treatment Nurse at the Grandview Hillcrest Nursing Home.

She suffered a stroke in 1992 and also became diabetic. She celebrated her 90th birthday 3 March 1997.

The following is a story told to Mildred by Maudie on 14 August 1994:

Mom, Daddy and I lived in Grand Junction during the terrible year of the influenza, when many died. The three of us were on a tonic plus some medicine in the form of tablets that the doctor gave us. If Daddy had contracted the flu along with his tuberculosis he surely would have died sooner. We were living in an apartment on Pitkin Avenue across from Whitman Park. Later we moved again to the ranch (homestead). Apparently Mother was pregnant with you (Mildred), so this was late 1919 or early 1920.

After you were born the family moved to Fruita one/half mile west of the Fruita Cemetery across the road from Mrs. Dittlinger. Her large house still stands there today.

Daddy lived in a tent by now, away from the family, but died at New Liberty on the "ranch." He died on the front porch there, which was screened in. This is the same porch where you slept for many years, weather permitting.

Mr. C. B. Ellis and son Harold lived in Mack. Mr. Ellis had worked with Daddy. They were present when Daddy died, 20 October

(Above) Maudie and Lawrence Yates on their 40th Anniversary, June 1968. (Upper right) The whole Yates gang, June 1968. Front, L-R: Tamara, Denise, Debbie, Darla, Brian and Diana Yates. Middle: Theresa, Lawrence, Maudie and Sheila Yates. Back: Steven, Bill, Judy, Shawn, Kenneth, Bernadine, Joyce, Duayne, Wayne, Dolores, Eldon, Dennis and Connie Yates. (Below right) Lawrence, Maudie and children, Thanksgiving, 1964. Back, L-R: Wayne Ellsworth and Eldon Lloyd Yates. Front: Billy Ray, Maudie, Lawrence and Kenneth Raverne Yates. *(Photos courtesy of Lorry Yates)* (Bottom left) Lawrence Yates and his miniature pioneer wagons on display. Miniature prairie schooners, ranch wagons, buckrakes, Wells Fargo stagecoaches and lots more are among the creations of Lawrence Yates. His roomful of treasures had been lovingly constructed over a 20-year period. The vehicles are mostly of cedar, with glove leather harnesses for the miniature horses. *(Photo and information used from The Grandview Herald, Grandview, Washington)*

1921.

Dickersons of Grand Junction were friends of the family and mother Allie Mae, Mildred and I spent some time with them after Daddy's burial in the Fruita Elmwood Cemetery.

When we went back to the ranch everything was just as we left it at the time of his death: The boards on which he was "laid out" for the undertaker, the bed in which he died, the sheets, the pillow, the cup made of steel with the release bottom. The cup held a paper in which Daddy expectorated and folded over. The bottom of the cup could be tripped to release the paper of sputum into the fire. (This cup is in Mildred's possession today)

Here are some memories by Mildred dated May 1997:

Daddy contracted consumption while he was still in Missouri, the dreaded disease for which there was no cure. He had previously lost a brother to this disease who was also sent to Colorado "for his health;" he went to Del Norte. Their father and mother also succumbed to tuberculosis.

New Liberty was a challenge for anyone who was healthy, let alone someone who was ill. My mother, Allie, and sister, Maudie, tried to help and mother stayed alone on this lonely piece of hard-pan desert to "prove up" on it, as was required in those days. Daddy and Maudie moved to Grand Junction so Daddy could work for the Denver and Rio Grande Railway and Latimer Chemical Company while Maudie attended school.

A medical doctor removed Daddy's tonsils and the throat never healed. He died 20 October 1921 at the young age of 36 on the front porch of the nice home they had built with the help of kind neighbors.

I, Mildred, came on the scene just 14 months before my father passed away. I was born there in the farm house. What a chore I must have been! Dr. James L. Keen, physician, had been summoned first by my sister running to Mr. Gerry's or Mr. Weir's, and they in turn going to Mack to place a phone call to the doctor's office.

Then the doctor lost his way by going north from Loma toward Douglas Pass. He arrived very late to take over a very prolonged and distressful labor, but saved both mother and baby. Horse and buggy were Dr. Keen's means of transportation.

Roads in those days were of clay composition, having, of course, no paving of any sort. They would get deep ruts when traveled on after rains. A grader was used on occasion to shore up and somewhat level the road beds. They remained that way until in the late 20s before they were graveled. (Actually they were graveled in the 30s — author)

I was told that when Daddy was bathed and had clean linen, he would hold a clean cloth over his face and cuddle me.

Years later, when I was 35 years old and taking a nursing course at Weber College in Ogden where I lived, the class affiliated with the Tuberculosis Sanitarium in Ogden. Each student had a complete check-up there and I was told that scar tissue in my lungs was an indication of my having had tuberculosis as an infant. The story is told that I cried for long hours and it was also discovered that while mother was trying to breast feed me she apparently did not have enough milk.

A large cement cistern was built and filled from the High Line Canal. The hole was dug prior to Daddy's death and the cement work was done by the Masons after his burial. It was well built, for it never leaked through all the years it was used. It eventually became my chore to clean it before each new filling.

Tubs of clean water were saved and sent down by rope to me to wash down the walls and then the floor with a new broom until all the residue of mud and water had been hoisted up and dumped out. Once in awhile I think a frog or two was in there.

Then the cistern was filled with a trickle of water that ran only at night and came in a small ditch about a quarter of a mile up the hill from us. The last few feet of the ditch was lined with small rock and gravel to purify and clarify the water. It was always tasty, cool and good the year around and served us well for culinary, house and laundry purposes.

A large salt wash (Badger Wash) ran through our farm, which carried the run-off from the distant Bookcliffs during and after rain storms, as well as the overflow from the High Line. One could hear the roar of the water coming, and if Dad, my stepfather Noah Blasdel, happened to be using the horses across the wash, he had best make haste to unhitch, jump astride one of the horses and run for the house, for that wash filled from side to side with rushing muddy water carrying debris of trees, broken banks of sod, etc. Sleeping on that porch as I grew up, I would lie awake at night and listen to that roar and hear huge banks crash loose and carry a part of the farm

The Raver home as it stands today. Ann Hawthorne occupies it at this time, and she is the person standing in the shade. Photo taken by Mildred Means, 1991. *(Photo courtesy of Mildred Raver Means)*

health was concerned. She was an avid reader and had many medical books which she poured over through the years.

In later years I realized she would have liked to have been a nurse, and yet she did a lot of nursing in raising her large family. She was a very capable and ingenious woman, and had life provided her with money and schooling, I am sure she would have been a very knowledgeable and caring doctor.

Her mother, Allie Victoria Reese, died when mother was four and her father died when she was seven. Her maternal grandfather was Dr. C. M. Anderson and one of his brothers was a lawyer.

A family history compiled by a cousin in Hollywood established that one Mary Anderson, M.D., was the first woman surgeon in the United States. I have one grandson, Ryan Handly, and a granddaughter, Susan Anderson Arnett, who are registered nurses. Also, my sister, Maudie, was a nurse. She worked over 25 years at Hillcrest Nursing Home in Grandview, Washington, as a medical and treatment nurse.

My brother-in-law, Lawrence Yates, taught me to ride horseback. Dolly, a "cow pony" was given to me by Dad's nephew, Jack Blasdel, to ride the two-and-one-half miles to school. Naturally I had to learn to ride this rather small critter, probably 14 hands. Her smallness was a godsend, for I was a wisp of a child with short legs. While Dolly was small in height, she was wide in girth, so my legs stuck out at an angle whenever I was astride her. Though she always seemed fat enough, she had a backbone that I recall felt as if I were riding a rail.

Dad had an old Army McClellan (saddle), you know, which was a split wooden tree with most of the leather worn off. The difference

away.

I enjoyed our house; it was large for the time and era. It had two bedrooms, a kitchen and living room, a back porch and the front porch, which ran across the width of the house. Later, after Maudie married Lawrence Yates, he built another kitchen that extended over a portion of the cistern so mother could have water in the house with a sink! Not running water, but a pitcher pump which had to be primed each morning, It seems the sink was a used one, but it was large enough to place a dishpan or two in and drained through a pipe to the outside of the house. The pipe extended ten or twelve feet beyond and I am sure caused some drainage problems in the winter time.

There was also a small porch attached to this kitchen and it remains the same size today, except the present owner, Mrs. Anderson, had enough room to use the back portion of the kitchen for a small bathroom.

Our bathroom was a good old outdoor privy. A hole several feet deep was dug and the shanty placed over it until a move was necessitated. When that time came, the shanty was moved to a newly-dug hole and the old hole was carefully covered.

As I look back and after having had nurses training myself, I can see where my Mother, who had only a fifth-grade education, was meticulous and cautious where the family's between the hardness of the saddle or bareback was just about the same. I became an avid bareback rider, and as I try to ride bareback now I wonder how I ever stayed on. Many times I fell off Dolly during those years. Once, when giving a ride to a girl on the way to school, she put her legs along Dolly's flanks and we both went flying off because of one little buck. By that time the roads had been graveled and we had some little rock burns.

I now ride a registered Tennessee Walker with an Australian saddle. What joy! My mare, Shadow, did a 180 degree turn with me not long ago, and I remained "up."

Winters were cold, with wind, snow and freezing. One morning the weather was especially cold and I was not dressed for it. (No snow suits or moon boots then). About two miles into the ride I remember feeling like I was not going to make it to school. I felt so cold and sleepy, but reasoned it would be farther back home than to continue on to school. I do not remember arriving at school. Someone must have removed me from my horse and put her in the shed built on the school grounds to provide shelter for the horses kids rode to school. After that I was told to stop at a neighbors on my way on cold mornings to warm up and I think I did that on more than one occasion.

Dolly was smart. In the summertime the pastures looked good to her and she wouldn't let me catch her on my own. One afternoon Dad had caught her for me to ride to 4-H or somewhere. I mounted and started up the lane when she began to limp. That limp became so bad that I turned her around for home and she limped all the way back, right up to the pasture gate. After I turned her loose her tail sailed high over her back, and with her head swinging low she was off with a husky gallop. Being a cow pony, if I should get on one-sided, like happened on several occasions, I would have fallen off, except for the fine growth of mane she had. She would stop suddenly and if I was not prepared I would land on the ground.

Anyway, I loved Dolly and shed many tears when she died when I was 18. She was perhaps about 36. Dad buried her on the far side of the farm in a hole he dug because she was too important in our lives to go to the glue factory. I say "our lives" because the boys rode her too as they were growing up.

When I was in the sixth grade the family rented the farm and moved to Del Norte, Colorado. There the distance to school was approximately the same, but I got to ride a school bus. In my freshman year in high school we moved back to New Liberty and I graduated from Fruita Union High School when I was 16 years of age. Edna Weir and I walked a mile to catch the school bus for the 25 mile ride to Fruita on the back roads. Those roads were not always well maintained and on rainy days we slowly rutted our way home. Boys were boys even in those days, and those long rides were sometimes torture for us girls as well as the driver, Milton Alstatt. Those long hours on rough roads were hard on me physically and I was most happy to finally graduate.

Mother borrowed money for me to attend Mesa College, which I did for one year. The latter part of that year was very pleasant, for by the grace of God I was privileged to live in the home of Lawrence and Ilene Sardoni. He was the music teacher for orchestra and voice. It was in their home I learned to enjoy classical music, for they would ask me to sit down and listen to the Philharmonic Symphonies with them while Mr. Sardoni explained and enlightened my knowledge of music.

One quarter he asked me to try out for the choir. By no means was there a singing voice within me, but he had abilities of which I was unaware. How happy I was at the end of our concert that quarter when he said to me, "You did very well, Mildred." I asked how he knew I did well with the large orchestra and nearly one hundred voices all going at the same time. He said he could hear each voice and instrument, at which I marveled. I will always be grateful for the appreciation he taught me and my enjoyment through those years of wonderful music.

On August 11, 1938, I was married to a neighbor boy named Merton Claude Arpke. We were married in my home by "Pastor" Clyde W. Likes, who held the only Sunday School and was the only preacher I knew up to that time. Merton and I spent our honeymoon in an underground cellar on the Arpke farm. We helped on the farm for a little while. The land in that community was demanding of hard labor yet yielded little in return. The valley has had hard times since I can remember and still affords little. Women helped in the fields, shocking beans, growing gardens and helping to raise cattle, chickens, turkeys and anything to help out in raising the children and eking out an existence. Everyone around us were poor in worldly goods.

On July 29, 1939, came our darling dainty **Lillian**, named for a paternal aunt. She was soon dubbed **Peggy** by grandpa Arpke and is still called Peggy to this day. (Grandpa Arpke died 8 August 1938 — author) I wanted a girl— I got one. I wanted a brown-eyed girl — I got one. I also wanted a baby with all its fingers and toes and that was the first thing I looked for. She had the most beautiful tiny hands and feet I had ever seen! Another answered prayer!

At the time I was very ill with the flu and spent several days in bed and Grandma Arpke came to help with her nursing abilities, caring for me and the baby while I regained my strength. I tipped the scales at 90 pounds when I got up from the bed.

Dr. White delivered our Lillian in the same room on the Raver homestead in which I was born.

While we lived in Glendale, California, (Mert was working for Lockheed Aircraft) our next little girl, **Mildred Elaine**, was born at P & S Hospital in Los Angeles. I was given too much anesthesia and did not know anything for three days. When bedpans and food were passed, I was asleep and awakened only briefly at other times. Elaine had long arms and legs and looked mighty shriveled to me. I called her my little mouse, but she blossomed into a lovely butterfly.

Then the war beckoned and Merton enlisted in the Navy. We lived at that time in Ogden, Utah, in a rented unit in Washington Terrace. My folks lived in Washington state at the time and I wanted to go live near them. But Peggy, Elaine and I, with one more on the way, were moved to Fruita into a little house rented from John and Elizabeth Snook. It was a bewildered and sad wife Mert left as he answered the unrequired call.

Ruth Claudeen was born in the old Fruita hospital with Dr. James Orr in attendance, only he did not arrive until the delivery was over. Ruth was a beautiful baby — plump and pink, and very active. The date was June 14, 1944. She was born on Merton's birthday.

In July 1949 **Paul Wesley Arpke** was born in the old St. Mary's hospital in Grand Junction with Dr. Merkley, a specialist, in attendance. Thanks to Dr. Merkley we had a viable birth. Paul was born breach — upside down and backward with the cord wrapped around his neck. My mother-in-law, Elsie Arpke, was an R.N. just getting off duty, and she was allowed in the birthing room. I heard the doctor say, "Give her more anesthesia" as he was pushing the baby back into the canal. I was alert enough to later hear him say — "Damn little shit, he looks just like his dad!" The rest of the story, as I recall, was Mom Arpke in the mother's room telling me it was a boy. I argued the point with her to the extent that she went to the nursery and brought the boy to me to show me the facts!

He was a beautiful baby and won a baby picture contest when 11 months old. We were living again in New Liberty at the time of his birth, having purchased the Summer's homestead.

A short time after his birth, at home, I discovered Paul's heart was not rhythmical and a trip to the doctor's office was in order. He

Home on leave, 1940s. L-R: Merton Claude, Mildred Elaine, Lillian "Peggy," Mildred Lucinda and Ruth Claudeen Arpke. *(Photo courtesy of Mildred Raver Means)*

(Above) Mildred and children, 1997. Standing, L-R: Lillian "Peggy" (Anderson), Mildred Elaine (Flitton, McGinnis), Ruth Maudeen (Handley) and Paul Wesley Arpke. Mother, Mildred Raver Arpke Schultz Means. *(Photo courtesy of Mildred Raver Means)* (Below right) Mildred Arpke R.N. and son, Paul, at the Sacred Heart hospital in Spokane, Washington, recuperating from heart surgery, 1959. (Below center) Maudie Yates retiring after 25 years service at the Hillcrest Nursing Home as an L.P.N. She was 80 years old and continued to work "on call." She also took care of her son, Eldon, after his tragic accident that debilitated him for several years before his death. *(Last two photos courtesy of Lorry Yates)* (Bottom right) Mildred Raver Arpke graduated with an R.N. certificate from the Weber College of Nursing at Ogden, Utah, in June 1959, motivated by her sons illness. *(Photo courtesy of Mildred Raver Means)*

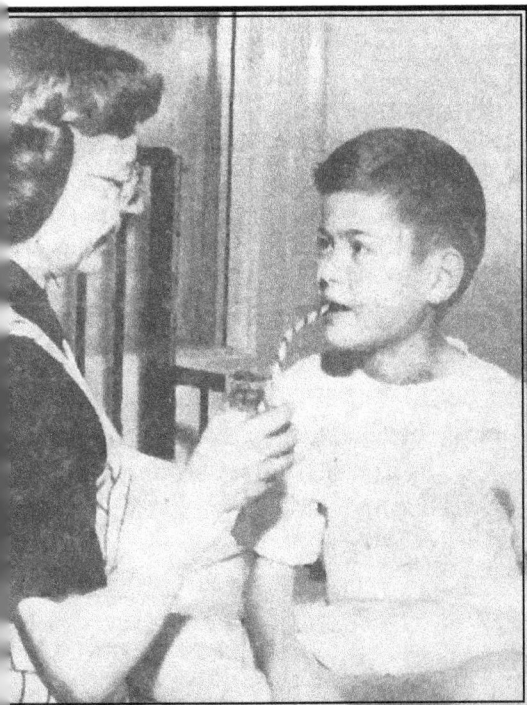

explained that a valve had not closed as usual at the time of birth and that Paul was probably what we would call a "blue baby."

That was the beginning of a whole new story. To make it short — he had open-heart surgery at the age of ten in Spokane, Washington, and nearly lost his life more than once.

It was at that time also our neighbors, Clyde and Ruby Likes lost one of their boys to polio. My husband would not let me go visit for fear of contagion. I felt badly, being restricted.

On the Summer's place we lived in an old house with four small rooms and a large kitchen. I painted the kitchen linoleum with bright green paint to liven up the place. The house sat beside a hill where the girls used to pick pink butter cups to bring in to me. One day I asked Peggy to run get an egg for me from an old shed . In just a few moments after she returned to the house we heard a loud crashing noise. As we looked out we could see that the old lean-too from which she had just retrieved the egg had crashed, caving in completely. God takes charge again.

As to our marriage, may I use a quote from Karen Scalf Linamen from the April 1997 Reader's Digest: "Courtship is exciting and romantic because it thrives on the edge of disaster. It co-exists with the threat that, at any given moment, it could all fall apart and be lost forever. To expect the lifelong commitment of marriage to evoke excitement and adventure created by the fragility of courtship — Well, as they say in Texas — "That dog just don't hunt."

To sum it all up:

I treasure the memories of a valley called New Liberty, five miles as the crow flies to the Utah State border. The Bookcliff hills to the north of us, Grand Mesa to the east and the desert we learned to love. If everyone in this world could have wonderful home-raised fruits and vegetables and home-grown meats, there would be no hungry and starving people. If all could have the fresh air and horses, cats and dogs to love and watch them bring babies to life, there would be less crime. If all could enjoy God, our loving Savior and know how He loves us . . . What a joyous world this would be! My roots are in New Liberty.

By Mildred Lucinda Raver Arpke Schultz Means. Age 77, at Weston, Oregon.

Rector

Information from a letter and family group sheet from Nita Baughman Rector.

Roy Lester "Spark" Rector was born 13 February 1904, at Lamar, Barton, Missouri, to **Benjamin F. Rector** and **Jennie Lee**. When Spark was 11 years old the family, including his parents, sister **Minnie**, and brother **Russell**, traveled by covered wagon to the vicinity of Rangely, Colorado, where his father had homesteaded with his brother, Jim Rector. Ben later moved the family to Ordway, Colorado, where Spark spent his teen years. He worked for a time on the railroad there.

In March, 1924, they moved to Atchee, Colorado, where Spark worked as hostler for the Uintah Railway until 1929, when they moved to Mack.

On 7 October 1933, he married **Juanita "Nita" Baughman** in Grand Junction. They had no children. Nita was born 9 September 1916, to J. C. and Jessie Baughman at Grand Valley (now Parachute), Garfield, Colorado. The newlyweds worked for several sheep and cattle outfits in the Grand Valley area before moving to Mack. Then they worked for Tom Kelley, Ross Brown, A. A. Kirby, Dale Mitchell, Sam Kinsey, and in 1946 started to work for C. A. "Chick" Hitchborn. They were all in the Douglas Pass area.

Spark and Nita lived for many years on the old Carroll homestead, near the west end of the Highline Siphon at East Salt Creek.

Nita tells us they were with Hitchborn about 37 years, finally retiring 2 February 1981. Then they moved to a trailer court in Mack and lived there until 15 August 1983, when they moved to Fruita.

Nita tells us also that Ben and Jennie Rector ran a small cafe at Mack that became popular with the cattle and sheep men because they could not eat at the Uintah Hotel unless they had on a coat and tie.

Looks like Spark is still going strong — he celebrated his 93rd birthday in February, 1997. He and Nita currently live at Fruita.

Robert Jean, 24 April 1944, Mack, Mesa, Colorado

Rich

Information from obituaries in *The Daily Sentinel* and *The Fruita Times*, history outlines by Mae Belle Rich Sasser and Maxine Rich Bethea.

Leonard Bush Rich was born at Winthrop, Buchanan, Iowa, 11 January 1880, to Frank Arthur Rich and Hilah Adelaide DeLaMater. He spent his childhood years in Iowa and came to Colorado with his family in 1910. He was married 4 December 1915, at Burlington, Kit Carson, Colorado, to **Frances Adele Sly**. Frances was born 17 July 1898, at Maryville, Nodaway, Missouri, to Samuel Guilford Sly and Mary Margaret Boyer.

Frances was a pioneer who, at age two, rode in a covered wagon with her parents to Deadwood, South Dakota. They later traveled through Nebraska and Kansas to a homestead south of Burlington, Colorado, on the banks of the Smoky Hill River.

Leonard and Frances had five daughters and six sons:

Beatrice "Becie" Lucille (Owens), born 11 November 1916, Arapahoe, Cheyenne, Colorado
Leonard C., 7 March 1919, Arapahoe
Marjorie Lois (Chappell), 14 January 1921, Burlington, Kit Carson, Colorado
George Arthur, 10 November 1923, Arapahoe
Stephen "Steve" Gerold, 29 December 1925, Burlington
Mae Belle (Sasser), 13 January 1928, Mountain Grove, Texas, Missouri
Frank A., 21 April 1930, Chouteau, Mayes, Oklahoma
Jerold "Jerry" Louis, 21 August 1932, Chouteau
Kay Frances (Beagley, Kern), 5 August 1938, Encenata, New Mexico
Maxine Lovern (Watts, Bethea), 12 April 1936, Tierra Amarilla, Rio Arriba, New Mexico

After marriage, Leonard and Frances and their older children lived in Arapahoe County for many years before moving away when they became victims of the "dust bowl" days. They had to leave their ranch because Leonard had "dust pneumonia," which affected his breathing.

Leonard and Frances sold everything they could and outfitted three covered wagons and a buggy with a forge mounted on it. They and five children drove the wagons and buggy, trailing 100 head of wild horses and 32 head of mules from Arapahoe County, Colorado, through Kansas and down to Mountain Grove, Missouri, where Frances' parents lived. Frances drove the lead wagon all the way. They were on the road three months. Every other night they shod the horses and mules, which were to be auctioned off at a big sale.

From there the family went through Oklahoma to Texas. In the fall of 1934 they moved to a ranch near Tierra Amarilla, New Mexico, where they lived for 10 years. For two or three years before they had school buses, the children had to walk three miles to school, which was a Catholic school taught by Nuns. Mae Belle says they were the best teachers she ever had.

In November 1942, the family moved to Mack, Colorado, and bought a smaller place.

The Rich boys, 1953, Mack, Colorado. L-R: Frank, George, Jerry, Steve and Leonard "Pop" Rich. *(Photo courtesy of Mae Belle Rich Sasser)*

Leonard Bush Rich with his granddaughters, 20 July 1956. Leonard died 1 September 1956. *(Photo courtesy of Maxine Rich Bethea and MaeBelle Rich Sasser)*

In August 1944 *The Daily Sentinel* reported that two of the Rich's sons and one daughter were serving in the military and were all three were overseas at the same time. But Mae Belle tells us that all six boys were in the service: George, Frank and Robert in the Navy; Leonard, Steve and Jerold in the Army. Marjorie was in the Women's Army Corps (WAC). That's a hard record to match!

Frances was a real-estate broker in Grand Junction for 10 years. After Leonard's death she became assistant manager of the old Meeker Hotel in Meeker, Colorado. She was a very interesting and knowledgeable woman who played the piano and was an avid painter. She married and outlived two more husbands after Leonard.

Leonard died at age 76, at his home at Mack, 1 September 1956. Frances died at age 94, in Las Vegas, at the home of her daughter, Kay Frances, 27 May 1992. Two of the children, Stephen "Steve" Gerold and Kay Frances, are also deceased.

Following is a story written by Maxine Rich Bethea:

My family moved to Mack in the early fall of 1942 from Tierra Amarilla, New Mexico, where my youngest sister, Kay and I were born. I was six years old when we moved. My folks had made a trip to Colorado by bus before that to buy 160 acres from Saul Pacheco. We lived outside Tierra Amarilla, by ourselves, since no one could own land there because it was under a Spanish Land Grant.

My parents knew the boys would soon be drafted because of World War II, so they decided to move us to Mack, Colorado. I can remember being deathly sick for weeks after we got to Mack, but sick as I was, it was an exciting adventure to get there at last. My brother Jerry (Gerold) and I rode in the back of the truck to watch the chickens and all our possessions we brought to start our new life. We had a heavy tarp to cover the back, and it seemed like many days before we finally got to Mack. As hard as we tried, some of the chickens got out, and when we went through a big town — I can't remember the name of it — I was more concerned over the chickens flying out from under the tarp. Since we had never traveled before, I guess I was car-sick.

We could see our school house and the town, which seemed like a big city to me. There were even trains close by — something I had never seen close-up before. It was a busy place.

The Rich family after Leonard's funeral in September 1956. Back row, L-R: Beatrice Owens, Caroline Rich, Kay Beagley, Maxine Watts, Sharon Owens, Frances Rich mother), Jean Rich, Darlene and MaeBelle Sasser. Front: Jerold Rich, Art Beagley, Gene Watts, George Rich and Ralph Sasser. *(Photo courtesy of MaeBelle Rich Sasser)*

I met my first friend there, and over the years since then we have kept in touch by phone or letter. Her name was Marcia Davies.

We didn't haul any of the big animals with us — Steve and Papa drove the horses, mules and cows from Tierra Amarilla. They all got sore feet on the long journey overland. Papa put shoes on them; he put little "Burro" shoes on the cows. They got so sore-footed they'd lay down and refuse to walk. After George drove the truck with the family to Mack he made several trips back to haul the sore-footed ones who couldn't make it otherwise.

We really missed my Dad and brother, Steve — they didn't get to Mack until January, the beginning of 1943.

Leonard, my oldest brother, was already in the Army — he had enlisted while still in Tierra Ammarillo. What a great joy it was when Papa and Steve finally got there . Papa's whiskers

(Upper left) Pop and girls, 20 July 1956. L-R: Mae Belle, Leonard "Pops," Beatrice and Jean. *(Photo courtesy of Mae Belle Rich Sasser)* (Upper right) Mom and girls, 1987, at Mack. L-R: Frances (mother), Marjorie, Mae Belle, Maxine and Kay. (Above) Part of the Rich family, 1987, at Mack. L-R: Robert, George, Frank, Maxine and Leonard; Frances (mother) in front. *(Photo courtesy of Maxine Rich Bethea)*

were long, as he had not had time to shave on the way. Christmas came while they were near a little town in Colorado. A lady came to the wagon where they were getting ready to bed down for the night. She asked Steve if he believed in Santa Claus. He said "Yes, but he won't find us out here." She said, "I think he will, you hang up your stocking and we'll see." Sometime during the night she returned to fill his stocking with nuts and candy.

There were eleven children in our family. Between World War II and the Korean War — my brothers, all six of them, served in the military. Also one sister, Marjorie, served in the WACS. Those war years seemed so long. When we'd get a letter from one of the boys or Marjorie, we'd all share the news. Lots of people would come from Mack to our house to hear the news on the radio of our family members in the service.

Parents would bring their kids and we never did lack for fun. We'd skate on the pond in winter or go sledding down the hills.

In our community at Mack there were many socials at the school house. They'd put on plays, have dances and box-suppers. It was like church now except for the dances.

My fondest memories are of growing up at Mack. Soon I was the oldest at home and we always had horses to ride. We had a swimming hole to play in. All the kids from Mack would gather at our place to play with sleds on the hills in winter. We even made our own skis — even put bee's wax on the runners so they'd go faster. All the fun we had there! My parents would help us to have fun. Papa would let us take the water-sled he had made to haul water from the pond in winter. He'd hitch Jenny, our burro, to it and we'd have great fun on it in the winter.

We'd sleep out on the lawn in the summer and go riding at night after my parents were asleep. We were never afraid even though we had tramps who came through on the trains and would come to the house looking for hand-outs. But they never did any meanness, we never locked our doors.

We had many pets too. We had the goats we brought from New Mexico with us, as well as the dogs and cats. We also always had great fun herding cows.

All my brothers returned safely from the war, even though Leonard was wounded and he and Steve both had malaria.

My youngest brother, Bob, was born at the hospital in Fruita. Momma decided to have a doctor with him, but Dr. Orr (Sr.) was in a poker game, so his nurse, Thelma Bray, did the delivery.

On 3 September 1956 Papa died of cancer. That left Momma with Bobby to raise alone — he was eleven years old at the time. Then on 3 July 1958, Steve was on the way home for the 4th of July and was killed in his automobile near Whitewater, Colorado. He was employed in the mines at Uravan, Colorado. That was really hard on my mother then. She felt that since they had all came safely back from the war her trials were over. This devastated her for about three years after. I'd come up from Moab, where I was living then, and stay with her and Bobby a lot. Soon Vietnam came along and Bobby went into the Navy.

After 13 years in Moab, Utah, I moved back to Mack on 10 Road, part of the old place. Dick Bethea (my husband) and I lived there for 29 years. Momma moved in with us the last 10 years we were there. Then we moved to Midland , Texas, and soon after, she decided to live with us there.

My parents were true pioneers. Papa had a motto to live by: "There is no such word as 'Can't' — if it can be done, you too, can do it, maybe even better." They were good and moral people. And while we were poor by worldly standards, we were not only named "Rich," we had a rich heritage. I'm so thankful I had them for parents. They gave us all they had, which was themselves, and we were rich.

I especially miss my mother because I knew her longer than any of my family.

Besides their 11 children my parents also raised Fred Keeting. I never knew him — he was 13 when he came to live with my parents in Cheyenne Wells, Colorado. He lived with them until he joined the Navy. My parents then moved back to Missouri for awhile and they lost track of him. They think he was killed in World War II.

So, out of 11 children there were seven who served our country. There are now nine of us left. Kay, my youngest sister, was killed in an auto accident in 1991. My mother died on Memorial Day in 1990.

Roberts

The following came from an interview with Ruby, Chuck and Steve Roberts. Also obituaries and news items from *The Daily Sentinel* and the *Fruita Times*, and personal knowledge of the author.

Taylor Lee and Ruby Norene Hobbs Roberts, 1953
(Photo courtesy of Ruby Hobbs Roberts)

Caylor Lee Roberts was born 22 December 1914, at Nowata, Nowata, Oklahoma, the oldest of six children born to Arthur Lee "Al" Roberts and Bertha Taylor. When Taylor was about 10 years old his father and mother divorced and his father was remarried to Belle Elliot, who also bore six children. It's worth mentioning that the area where Taylor was born was also where Will Rogers grew up. Taylor's son, Chuck, says that Granddad Al told of trading horses with Will Rogers.

Taylor spent his childhood in Oklahoma, Utah and Colorado. When his parents divorced, the family was living in Glenwood Springs, Colorado. After the divorce his father moved to Grand Junction while his mother remained in Glenwood Springs and operated a cafe.

While living in Glenwood Springs, Taylor became acquainted with **Ruby Norene Hobbs,** who was born 28 February 1918 at Yukon, Texas County, Missouri. She was ninth of 11 children born to Arvel Hobbs and Amy Arizona Chambers. Ruby grew to womanhood in Missouri and became a school teacher, coming to Glenwood Springs, Colorado in 1940. She was working at the New Castle Hospital when she went to a dance in Glenwood Springs and met Taylor. They courted for about two years before being married in Grand Junction on 25 January 1942.

After marriage Taylor went to work at a building project for the Atomic Energy Commission at Pando, Colorado. Their honeymoon cottage was a tent.

In December 1942 Taylor enlisted in the Air Force and was stationed at St. Louis for a time. Soon he was assigned to the European Theatre, eventually serving in England, France and Germany. He left for overseas duty the day after their first child, **Charles "Chuck" Eugene** was born, 25 March 1943 at St. Louis. While Taylor was overseas Ruby lived with her mother and sister in the St Louis area. They didn't see Taylor again until in 1945 when Chuck was nearly three years old.

After Taylor was discharged from the Air Force he became an accomplished and respected farmer in the Grand Valley area. They lived at Orchard Mesa for a time before moving to the Bill Knapp farm on north 7th Street, near Grand Junction. While living there daughter **Donna Norene (Hooker)** was born 10 February 1947 in Grand Junction.

The Roberts moved to the Orval Herron farm north of Mack in 1948, about the time Chuck was ready to begin school. He attended Mack School through the fourth grade. Also while they were on the Herron place, **Steven "Steve" Lee** was born 15 February 1953 in Grand Junction.

They moved to the New Liberty community to operate the Bill Maluy's farm in 1953. After renting from Bill for a few years they made a deal to buy the place.

Chuck attended New Liberty School for the fifth and sixth grades, but went to seventh grade

Charles "Chuck" Eugene Roberts, 1957
(Photo courtesy of Ruby Hobbs Roberts)

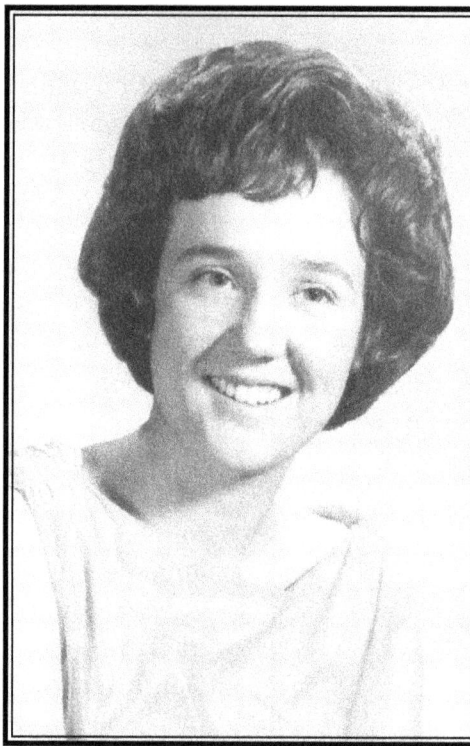

Donna Norene Roberts, 1963
(Photo courtesy of Ruby Hobbs Roberts)

Steven "Steve" Lee Roberts, 1963
(Photo courtesy of Ruby Hobbs Roberts)

in Fruita Junior High in the former Fruita Union High School building. Donna attended school at New Liberty, but Steve had to ride the bus to Loma after New Liberty was closed in 1959. All three graduated from Fruita Union High School.

Chuck tells the story of he and Reggie Berry being involved in a "test" with Don Weimer and Clem Maluy. It seems Don and Clem wanted to see how the boys would hold up under some very trying circumstances. They asked the boys to skin dead sheep for them at .50 cents per head. The boys were not told of some sheep that had been dead long enough that they had a chance to ripen quite a bit. But the boys were brave enough to keep their commitment! Chuck says they would skin awhile and gag awhile. But Don and Clem never did anything with the hides — just left them hanging on the fence! Chuck loves to chuckle over that experience now!

Chuck is remembered in another episode when he was about 12 years old. A carnival man had scheduled a one-man show at the New Liberty School one evening. Several people in the community were in attendance, including Chuck, who was the only member of his family to attend.

The man put on several demonstrations, including swallowing a sword and breaking a rock on the chest of Clem Maluy with a sledge hammer. Then he asked for a volunteer to be hypnotized and Chuck stepped forward. Chuck was soon under the influence of the hypnotist, who did some astounding feats with him. The most dramatic feat was to place Chuck's head on a chair and his feet on another with nothing in between. Then the hypnotist sat on his middle. Chuck was not aware of any of this happening until he was told about it after he was revived. Chuck went home and told his parents about it and they were very unhappy with him for submitting to such an experiment!

As Chuck and Steve became old enough to be involved in the farming, they, with their Dad, developed a large family operation. Eventually they bought the Bill Maluy, Bob Cox, Charles Cavendish and Clyde Likes farms, as well as part of the B. A. Harrison farm, making several hundred acres in all.

They raised a variety of crops, including hay and small grains, sugar beets, corn, tomatoes and beans (both pinto and white navy). They also raised purebred Angus cows and calves for several years.

Taylor farmed in the Mack and New Liberty areas for a total of 21 years before his death from heart failure, 12 July 1970. Since Taylor's departure, the farming has been done by Chuck and Steve, with some occasional hired help. The boys both built homes on the Robert Cox place. They have modern equipment to till the soil and harvest the crops; the irrigation system has been modernized to gated pipe, considerably reducing the time and labor required to water.

Chuck and Steve have also developed a hobby in addition to their farming operation; they restore and show antique John Deere tractors and currently (1994) have a collection of 41 of them.

Chuck was married 22 August 1969, in Grand Junction, to Caroline Sue Chamberlain. They have four children:

Julie Lyno
Amy Suzanne
Kurt Eugene
Kimberly Colleen

Donna was married 20 June 1970, in Fruita, to David Clyde Hooker. They have three children:

Lynelle Norene
Rebecca Ann
William Taylor

Steve was married 13 January 1979, in Fruita, to Debra Ann Vidmar. They have two children:

Trent Taylor
Shelby Irene

Ruby lived alone for years on the "home" place in the house that was originally built by George Bryan in 1925 for his bride, Lucy McCoy. The house was later remodeled by Bill Maluy, and still later, by the Roberts. Ruby died at her home 1 April 1996 and was buried in Elmwood Cemetery.

Robertson

The following comes from a history outline filled out by Donald Robertson and forwarded to us by Cecelia Anne Kiefer Schmalz. An item from *The Daily Sentinel* is also included.

Dewey "D.D." and Lovelia Robertson were employed at Dragon, Utah, by the Uintah Railway — they transferred to Mack in 1933 so the children could attend Fruita Union High School. According to Deyon Davidson Boughton, they lived on Red Mesa, north of Mack, for a time, but also spent some time in Mack.

Their children were:

Donald
Gordon
Ernest
Galen

A story in *The Daily Sentinel* 5 August 1945 told of D.D. Robertson being injured in an accident on Red Mesa. He was driving on the highway two miles north of Mack in his Ford coach when he ran into a tractor being backed out of a driveway by Milton Cox, age 16. It was reported that Robertson's injuries were quite painful, but not serious. His car suffered $100 worth of damage; the tractor was overturned and thrown into an irrigation ditch but not badly damaged. Captain James Cole, the highway patrolman who investigated the accident, found that the driveway from the Cox home was bordered with shrubbery, obstructing the view from the road.

Three of the Robertson boys were in the Navy during World War II. Donald was at Pearl Harbor at the time of the Japanese sneak attack, serving on the battleship Virginia. There was a time of anxiety in the Robertson family until they received word that Donald was safe. The boys all settled in California after the war and their parents joined them in 1948. Don and Galen and families still live in California. Gordon died in 1990 and Ernest in 1993.

Rowe

The following is from a letter and interview with Ben Henry Rowe. Also obituaries and news items from *The Daily Sentinel* were included.

Herman Carl and Edna Fickle Rowe
(Photo courtesy of Ben Henry Rowe)

Herman Carl Rowe was born 17 February 1892, at Cane Creek, Oklahoma, to Henry S. Rowe and Hannah Agnes Carpenter He came with his parents to the Grand Valley about 1904 where he lived for the rest of his life.

Herman was a pioneer in the livestock and ranching industry in the Grand Valley, homesteading in the Glade Park area many years ago.

He was married 20 October 1913, at Fruita, to **Edna S. Fickle.** Edna was born at Branson, Taney, Missouri, 20 January 1895. She attended schools in the Branson area before coming to Fruita with her parents, where she graduated from high school.

Herman and Edna lived for several years on the ranch at Glade Park; while there they became parents of three sons:

Carl LaVerne, born 10 June 1916

Jay Lamar, 12 December 1924
Ben Henry, 28 September 1926
All three were born at Fruita.

In the Mack items of *The Daily Sentinel* dated 5 October 1929 it was noted that Herman Rowe had purchased the Mack Cafe and Pool Hall from George Rittenhouse. At the same time he also purchased the Ray McBeth home in back of the cafe and moved his family there. But his son, Ben, said his mother was the one who owned and operated the cafe. It must have been around that time that Edna and Herman separated and were divorced.

Edna leased the cafe out and worked for several years as housekeeper for J. B. Deacon and sons. At the beginning of that time the two younger boys attended school at New Liberty. Later they attended Mack School because it was more convenient to catch the bus to ride into Mack. LaVerne graduated from the eighth grade at Fruita Central. Ben said he attended the first and second grades at New Liberty and then the third through the eighth grades at Mack. Jay also attended two years at New Liberty, then graduated from the eighth grade at Mack. All three graduated from Fruita Union High School.

After Herman and Edna were divorced, Herman continued to live in the Grand Junction/Fruita area. He married **Bernice Webb** at Rocky, Arkansas, 11 April 1930. Herman passed away in the Lower Valley Hospital at Fruita, 12 October 1968.

In 1950 Edna married **Elmer Bruce Packard** who had moved to Fruita from New Mexico. They lived in Fruita until 1960 then moved to Farmington, New Mexico, living there until 1973, when they moved back to Fruita. Edna died at Fruita, 26 March 1975 and Elmer on 17 April 1975. Both are buried at Elmwood Cemetery at Fruita.

LaVerne became a railroader, working 14 years for the Denver and Rio Grande as train dispatcher. He then transferred to the Western Pacific and worked there for 15 years, until retirement. He was married first to **Margaret Scott** on 6 March 1937, but they were divorced after about two years. On 11 September 1944, at Salt Lake City, LaVerne married **Martha Selby.**

Jay Lamar Rowe, 1942
(Photo courtesy of Delores Smith Likes)

Ben Henry Rowe, 1944
(Photo courtesy of Delores Smith Likes)

Wells, of Fruita, was a graduate from Fruita Union High School in 1945. Mr. Rowe, graduate of Fruita Union High School in 1944, was a football and basketball letterman. He served as signalman first class in the Navy, receiving his discharge in 1946.

The couple will make their home in Belleview, Idaho, where he and his brothers recently bought a large stock ranch.

A wedding dinner was served to 35 relatives and friends at the Wells home after the ceremony.

Ben went to work for the D&RGW Railroad in 1948 and eventually became a Signal Maintainer, retiring in October 1986. Ben and Mary Lou had one son and two daughters, and now live at Fruita.

They had two children, a boy and a girl. Laverne and Martha presently live at Roseville, California.

*J*ay worked as Colorado State Brand Inspector for a number of years and retired as State Brand Commissioner. Jay married **Lucille Bratton,** daughter of Mr. and Mrs. James Bratton of Fruita, 14 March 1947, at Fruita. They had two boys, and now live at Henderson, Colorado.

Jay and Ben tried their hand at ranching, forming a partnership on a spread in Haley County, Idaho, near Taylor. But they gave it up after a couple of years and sold out.

*B*en married **Mary Lou Wells** on 15 March 1947. Here's a story that appeared in *The Daily Sentinel* on Wednesday, 19 March 1947:

At the Catholic church rectory in Fruita Saturday morning at 11:30 o'clock, Miss **Mary Lou Wells** and **Ben Rowe,** both of Fruita, were married by Rev. Joseph Kane.

The bride chose a shell pink linen dress with white Irish lace trim and matching accessories. Her flowers were gardenias and cream roses. Her attendant, Miss Betty Gore, wore a deep rose street dress with black accessories and a corsage of pink roses. Mr. Rowe was attended by his cousin, Bob Johnson.

Mrs. Rowe, daughter of Mr. and Mrs. Ed

L-R: Carl LaVerne and Martha Selby Rowe, Lucille Bratton and Jay Lamar Rowe, and Mary Lou Wells and Ben Henry Rowe. *(Photo courtesy of Ben Henry Rowe)*

670

Family Biographies

S

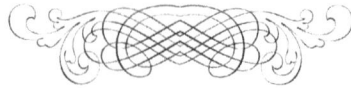

Sanders

Information from obituaries and news items in *The Daily Sentinel*. It is also from a history written by Helen Sanders Quain, daughter of Robert Wiley Sanders. Some items are from the author's personal knowledge.

Harry Maxwell Sanders II was born 7 February 1866, at Newport, Campbell, Kentucky. His parents were **Harry Maxwell Sanders** and **Sarah Rachel Williams**, English immigrants. Harry Maxwell II spent his childhood and early adulthood at Broughton, Clay, Kansas. He married **Flora Sylvia White** at Clay Center, Clay, Kansas, 4 April 1889.

They had five children:

> Stella S. (Rutherford)
> Flora Rachel (McCully)
> Harry Maxwell "Max" III
> Clifford William
> Robert Wylie "Bob"

The Sanders moved to western Colorado in 1912, settling in the area of Silt, near Glenwood Springs, Colorado. They spent some time at New Castle and Divide Creek before moving to Mesa County in December 1920. As a young man, Harry Maxwell II was engaged in farming, stock raising and marketing. He operated a dry-cleaning establishment when he first came to Grand Junction.

Harry Maxwell and May Belle Sanders
(Photo courtesy Virginia Thompson Hunter)

Harry "Max" Maxwell III was born 2 June 1896, at Broughton, Clay, Kansas. On 6 June 1920 he married **May Belle Porter** at Rifle. May was born 9 January 1898, at Divide Creek in Garfield County, Colorado, one of 10 children born to James Stephen Porter and Cora Wendell.

Max and May had a son whom they named **Harry Maxwell IV**. He was born in Grand Junction, 22 October 1923, but died 11 March 1927, at age 4, in Grand Junction, at the home of his grandparents. He had suffered from cancer of the liver since before Christmas of 1926.

In April of 1929 a boy named **Harold Floyd Carlson** came to live with Max and May. New Liberty items of 17 April 1929 tell us he enrolled in the seventh grade at New Liberty School at that time.

Max and May each lived a long time. Max passed away 7 June 1983, at the Lower Valley Hospital in Fruita, at 87 years of age. May died at Family Health West, 9 March 1987, at 89.

May was well known for her ability to compose verse; it seems fitting to remember her with at least one of her poems.

A HOUSE ON A HILL

When I was a bride, with life's road ahead
I lived in a valley, remote and still
But the days were happy with tasks of love
And through the nights under stars above
I dreamed of a house on a hill

The years sped swiftly along that road
The valley held me against my will
But songs made my tasks an easy rite
And kept my eyes on the distant site

Of my dream house high on a hill.

Now my days grow short, and the road is steep,
The valley floor is misty and chill,
My tasks are empty, my steps are slow,
I cannot see through sunset's glow
My dream house way up on a hill.
If my road should lead to your doorstep, Lord,
Could you, please, just one last wish fulfill,
For me no harp, or crown impearled,
Now my dream is to see your big wide world
From a house on a white cloud hill.

Robert Wylie Sanders Sr. was born at Broughton, Clay, Kansas, 17 February 1903. He lived at New Liberty from 1922 until 1964.

Let's pick up the story here as told by Helen Sanders Quain, daughter of Robert Wylie Sanders Sr. and Zella Hoover, published in *The Fruita Times*, 8 August 1991. There has been some editing.

The fear of winter blizzards and tornadoes in summer prompted my grandparents to find an area to live away from those elements. Floods or drought, chinch bugs and grasshopper swarms caused many a crop failure. In 1910, Grandpa and Grandma sold their farm in Kansas and bought another at Alamosa, Colorado, where a cousin lived. This proved to be a mistake as the black alkali, something they had never seen, surfaced when it rained and killed the crops. They went back to Kansas and a short time later Grandpa heard about land to be homesteaded in the Rifle, Colorado, area. He attended the drawing and acquired 160 acres. The irrigation ditch to water the newly-settled land failed, ending that venture too. Grandpa became acquainted with a Rifle store keeper who had come from Kansas. He put Grandpa in touch with a brother-in-law on East Divide Creek, south of Silt, who had a place to rent. An agreement was made, the searching was over; the Sanders family would soon live in Colorado.

Due to heavy snows in the winter of 1911-12, their departure from Kansas was delayed until June 1912. The household goods and livestock were loaded into railroad cars. The train came to Colorado Springs on the old Colorado Midland Railroad that came through Basalt to Glenwood Springs and on down the river to Silt, where they unloaded their belongings.

Because of the delay in getting to Colorado so late in the season, another person was operating the ranch on Divide Creek. This forced the family to rent the only place available in Silt, an old saloon building. To pay expenses, they opened an eating house in the front of the building and lived in the back part. The family moved to a rented ranch in February 1913 on East divide Creek and lived there until Grandpa sold that place in November 1920.

During the time the family spent on East and West Divide Creeks, Aunt Stella and Aunt Rachel married their Kansas sweethearts and left Colorado. Aunt Rachel and her husband, Harry McCully, returned to Divide Creek after he became terminally ill. He passed away in 1919. Not long after that Uncle Maxwell married May Porter, who lived west of them on Mamm Creek. They made their home on a farm near Bear Gulch until they moved to New Liberty.

The remaining family moved to Grand Junction in December 1920 and purchased the Ideal Cleaning Parlor. Aunt Stella and her husband, Jim Rutherford, and their daughter, Doris, came from Kansas City, Missouri, and entered the business too. The fumes from the cleaning fluid caused my dad, Bob, to temporarily lose his eyesight and he was forced to stay out of the business. He then returned to the Divide Creek area for one winter and fed cattle. The cleaning parlor was eventually turned over to Aunt Stella and Uncle Jim. Grandpa and Grandma went into other work and Aunt Rachel went to Denver to work. The three boys, Max, Bob and Clifford worked together farming in New Liberty.

Uncle Maxwell and Aunt May rented the Raver place when they first moved to New Liberty. Later, in January 1926, [April, according to *The Daily Sentinel*] they purchased part of the former William Hargraves homestead from Horine Neff.

Uncle Clifford rented the McCampbell place in New Liberty in 1922-23 and built a house on that place. In the spring of 1923, after school was out, he married Amy Ashley, a Kannah Creek girl who was teaching at the Rhone School.

In March of 1923 Dad (Bob) went from Divide Creek to the New Liberty community and rented the Sumnicht place for one year. That fall Bob and Clifford went to Kannah Creek to run the Elk Glen place for one year. Then Uncle Clifford worked as a salesman for a grocery supplier in Grand Junction and traveled all over the Western Slope for several years. In the mid-1940s, Uncle Clifford, and Aunt Amy and their son, Charles, moved to Napa, California, where Clifford worked for Coca Cola as a plant manager until his retirement. Uncle Clifford and Aunt Amy have both passed away.

Dad returned to New Liberty and lived with Max and May in the fall of 1924. He helped with the farming in the summer and ran horse and mule pack trains to supply winter sheep camps on the desert out of Cisco, Utah.

In 1925 Dad moved onto the Tom Gibbs place and bought it in 1926 as a proved-up homestead. That was part of the original homestead filed on in 1908 by William Hargraves. Through later years Bob added more land to the south of R Road, leveled and brought it into production.

On 2 July 1927 he married **Lula Mae Dean**, daughter of **Malcolm** and **Laura Dean**. Lula was born at Trinidad, Colorado, 18 August 1912. At the time of their marriage the Dean's were living on the William Price farm near the flume that crossed Badger Wash.

In the fall of 1927 Bob started working for the Mesa County Road Department, maintaining roads on the west end of the county, using teams on the grader much of the time. During periods of bad storms, he would work through the night to plow the road so the school bus could get through the next morning. Farm work and chores were incorporated with all other jobs.

Bob and Lula had two sons :

Robert Wylie Jr., born in 1929
Harry Lewis, 31 May 1930
Both were born in Grand Junction

In the summer of 1931, only a short time after Lewis was born, Lula suffered a ruptured appendix. Complications developed, and after nine weeks in St. Mary's Hospital and two operations, she died on 17 July 1931. She was only 19. After Lula's passing the boys went to stay with Aunt Stella and Uncle Jim in Grand Junction until the summer after my parents were married.

Dad married my mother, **Zella Jane Hoover**, 27 January 1934, at Fruita.

Zella was born 11 December 1894 at Macy, Miami, Indiana, and spent her childhood on a farm near Deedsville, Indiana.

Mother had come to Fruita, Colorado, in 1919 to help care for her Aunt Eliza Raber. She had previously quit high school in Indiana to care for her seriously ill mother and the younger children. She was encouraged by family and friends to finish high school and go on to college. She worked as a night telephone operator in Fruita and attended classes during the day until she received a diploma in 1925. Mother then worked her way through college, first at Western State at Gunnison, then at the University of Utah at Salt Lake City, where she earned her bachelor's degree and a teaching certificate.

Mother taught school in Utah and Colorado for several years. She was teaching school at Carbonera (where the Uintah Railway coal mine was) when she met dad in the fall of 1932. He was in the area hunting deer and attended a school program. Mother taught one more year and then became a farm wife and mother to Wylie and Lewis. I **(Helen)** was born in 1936, which completed the family.

In 1943 Mother became principal of the New Liberty School and taught the four upper grades. In later years she taught two years at Hunter and three years at Fruita before mandatory retirement at age 65.

Mother's cousin from Indiana, **Catherine Mowrer**, taught the upper four grades at New Liberty during Helen's first year of school in 1942-43. **Thelma Brenton** was the primary teacher that same year. They lived in the teacher's house by the school. Catherine and her husband, Dewey, located in the Paonia area and ran sheep, then cattle, for many years. After Dewey's death, Catherine moved from their ranch and now resides in Paonia. Thelma Brenton and her two children lived in the Grand Junction area for several years. Thelma passed away a few years ago. Catherine Mowrer passed away in November 1993.

Grandpa Sanders was superintendent for several years of the CCC[†] crews that worked in the New Liberty/Mack areas during the 1930s. Grandma had roomers/ boarders in her home as far back as I can remember until about 1950. Grandpa passed away on 17 November 1950, Grandma, on 15 November 1959. Aunt Rachel returned to Grand Junction from Denver in the early 1940s and worked for the Colorado Internal Revenue Service until retirement while living with Grandpa and Grandma. She never remarried and passed away in 1986.

A cousin, **Jim Sanders**, came to New Liberty from Divide Creek in the 1940s. He bought the place that Bob had purchased from Walter Weir, along Badger Wash and Highway 50. Bob helped Jim move a one-room cabin from the old Van Riper place onto a prepared location. That was Jim's home for all the years he lived at New Liberty. Jim married a widow lady from Castle Rock in the summer of 1956.

In about 1960 Jim sold his place and moved with his wife, **Nellie**, to a house in Clifton, where they lived until Jim's death. A short time after Jim's passing Nellie sold the place in Clifton and moved back to Castle Rock to be near her children. She is also deceased.

In 1947 my parents bought a ranch about seven miles from Aspen, Colorado. Dad, Lewis and I moved there in October with the milk cows and other livestock. Wylie stayed at the farm in New Liberty, as he wanted to finish his senior year at Fruita Union High School. Lewis had quit school the year before, partially because of an injury to his hand, making it so he couldn't write very well. He was interested mainly in farming, anyway.

Wylie, later that fall, went to stay with Jim and Mildred Cooper who lived on the old Diehl place. He graduated in 1948. After graduation, Wylie worked at Gay Johnson's station in Grand Junction. In July 1948, he and Ernest Paulson enlisted in the U. S. Marine Corps. In 1950 Wylie was sent to Korea and soon after was wounded. He spent many months in the Oakland Naval Hospital and was later sent to

Robert Wylie Jr., Helen and Harry Lewis Sanders, about 1991. The Sanders pictures were lost in storage. We decided to use this and the picture on two pages previous; feeling a poor picture is better than none at all. *(Photos used from the 8 August 1991 issue of the Fruita Times)*

the Veteran's Administration Hospital in Grand Junction. He had numerous bone grafts to repair the damage to his legs.

On 24 June 1951, Wylie married **Arliss Veatch**, a girl from the Pear Park area. They have three children: **Nancy, Donald** and **Cindy Lou**, and now have four grandchildren. Wylie worked at the AEC (Atomic Energy Commission) in Grand Junction for several years, then transferred to Rocky Flats, near Denver. He then was able to transfer to GSA Quality Control in the Denver area and later at Roy, Utah. In April of 1982, Wylie exercise the opportunity to early retirement from the government. He then worked several years with his son, Donald, who had a plumbing business. Wylie is presently working during the summer months at a gun range. He and Arliss live in Arvada, Colorado. Arthritis makes it difficult for Wylie to get around, so he hopes to retire fully within a year or so.

In the winter of 1949 Dad became critically ill. The doctors didn't expect him to live more than three months. The ranch near Aspen was sold and we moved back to the New Liberty farm in April. Lewis stayed in Aspen to finish out the school term, as he had returned to high school. Due to Dad's health, Lewis did not finish school, but stayed home to run the farm. Dad proved the doctors wrong in their predictions — 42 years wrong, to date. Dad is the only one of my grandparents' children still living (1991).

Lewis married **Wanda Black**, a Kannah Creek girl, 2 February 1951. Lewis and Wanda lived in the Jim Cooper house for about one-and-a-half years. He farmed with my folks until late fall of 1952, when he and Wanda moved to Garden Grove, California, where they still live.

[†] Civilian Conservation Corp.

Lewis has worked as a painter, serving as job foreman for many years. He is counting the months until he can retire next May (1992), as he has an injured back that makes it very painful to work certain jobs. Lewis helped paint former president Nixon's library complex and has painted many buildings at Disneyland. Lewis and Wanda have four children: **Harry**, **Steve**, **Amy** and **Tom**. Only Steve is married and they have no children to date.

$\mathcal{H}$elen (I) graduated from the eighth grade at New Liberty as Valedictorian in 1950, and from Fruita Union High School in 1954. That fall I went to Denver and went to school full time for a short period, then I worked days and attended night school. I married **John William "Bill" Quain**, 22 December 1955, at Fruita. We lived in Prescott, Arizona, where Bill was working until the summer of 1956. At that time we moved to New Liberty and farmed with my folks until Bill became disabled and could no longer walk or work. I worked at the Atomic Energy Commission compound for the service contractor as a secretary for about two years. I quit my job to care for Bill and have continued that ever since, as he is wheelchair-bound and needs assistance with many things. Bill and I moved to Hotchkiss in February 1964 where we still live on a small farm. We have two children, **Jim** and **Diana**, and six grandchildren, and are soon to have another.

Mother and Dad sold the farm at New Liberty in 1964 and moved to a second house on our place between Hotchkiss and Paonia. Their residence was there until Zella passed away 1 January 1979, after suffering many heart attacks over a five-year period. The folks spent the winters in Arizona, in later years, to get away from the cold and for mother's health. After Mother passed away, Dad lived in other areas for a period of time: Grand Junction, Craig and Fruita.

Lewis passed away at his home in Garden Grove, 14 May 1992, due to cancer.

Robert "Bob" Wylie Sr. died 1 September 1996 at the Community Care Center in Paonia, Colorado, at age 93. He was buried in the Masonic Cemetery at Grand Junction.

Saunders

Information from obituaries and news items in *The Daily Sentinel*, and Grand County, Utah marriage records and census records.

$\mathcal{R}$owland "Roe" Fowler Saunders was born 29 July 1890 at Alcester, Union, South Dakota. He came with his family to Palisade, Colorado, in 1903. As a young man, he engaged in the sheep and cattle business in eastern Utah and western Colorado.

He was married at Castleton, Utah, 10 July 1912, to **Lila M. Fish Ray**, daughter of Martin P. Fish and Alta Snavely of Castle Valley, Utah. (She was a grand daughter of Lewis C. Snavely).

Lila was previously married to Arthur Ray of Moab. She had one child, a daughter named Helen.

Roe and Lila had two children:

Alta Maude (Israel)
Martin
(Note they are named after Lila's parents).

Lila M. died of influenza in Fruita, 13 November 1918, and was buried in Elmwood Cemetery.

Their son, Martin, shows in the Mack School records of 1921/22. Their daughter, **Alta Maude**, was married 27 May 1939, to **Glen Israel**. Alta and Martin lived in the Grand Valley for many years. They both were mentioned occasionally in the Mack news items.

Roe was married at Moab, Utah, 15 November 1935, to **Lois Maurine Hollinger Collins**, daughter of **Edward Clayton Hollinger**. (See Collins and Hollinger stories).

Roe and Lois had one child: **Robert Hollinger Saunders**, born 14 December 1936.

Roe Saunders left an impressive record of public service to his credit. His career in public service began in 1935 when he was elected to the Mack School Board. Two years later he was elected to serve on the Fruita Union High School Board. He served on both boards, several times

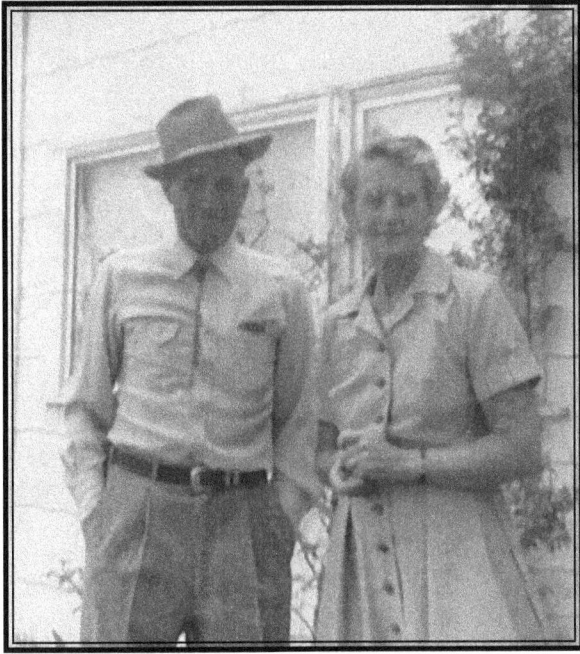

Rowland Fowler and Lois Maurine Hollinger   a s
Saunders *(Photo courtesy of Maurine Collins Reed)*

president, until the valley-wide District 51 was organized in 1951.

A stockman-farmer by vocation, Roe was active in a number of agricultural organizations in his early years. He has been a member of the 4-H Club's livestock committee for many years and was an honorary member of Fruita's Future Farmers of America.

In 1940 he began a 36-year career as a member of the Board of Directors of Grand Valley Rural Power Lines Inc.

In 1947 he became a member of the Mesa College Board of Directors. During his tenure in that office he was active in the founding of Rangley College, and served on the governing board during the decade the two institutions were associated in a single district. Construction of Mesa College's vocational school represented the fulfillment of a long - deferred goal to which he had given much effort. He served on that board for 24 years. The college's physical education building was named after him, reflecting his lifelong interest in sports, particularly football and baseball.

In 1952, he was elected to represent the lower valley as a Mesa County Commissioner, and served in that capacity until 1962. Completion of improvements to the Douglas

Pass road was the most significant of many county road projects he actively promoted during his period of service on the commission. He also served on the of the Colorado Association of County Commissioners, as both vice president and member of the legislative committee.

In 1956, the Saunders' sold their farm on Red Mesa, north of Mack, and moved to Fruita. He continued in public service and became Mayor of Fruita for a four-year term, and he was coordinator of Fruita's Neighborhood Center. He was a long-time member of Fruita's Chamber of Commerce and Rotary Club. Twice Roe was named outstanding citizen: in 1960 by Grand Junction's Chamber of Commerce and in 1966 by Fruita's Chamber of Commerce.

Roe's busy life began to change in 1971, when he retired from the Mesa College Board of Directors. One might say that he literally wore out his life in service to his family and neighbors. He died in the Lower Valley Hospital in Fruita 21 November 1977, at age 87, and was buried in Elmwood Cemetery.

Lois Maurine Hollinger spent her childhood in Bailey, Colorado, where she graduated from Bailey High School. She came with her family to Mack in 1918 and lived on the homestead on Mack Mesa with her parents. After her marriage to Emmett Collins, they established a home just east of her parents on part of that homestead. She raised all of her children while living on that farm.

Lois endured her share of sadness; she lost her first husband, Emmett Collins, her father and mother, her oldest daughter, Delores, her second husband, Roe Saunders, and her sister, Edna Smith.

But Lois lived a long time herself. She continued to live in Fruita after Roe's death, and had been a resident of Fruita for 33 years when she died 3 July 1989, at age 89.

Schunter

Information from a letter from Frances Schunter Yourdon, census records, obituaries and news items from *The Daily Sentinel.*

Hans **William Schunter** was born 30 August 1854, in Holstein Province, Germany. He came to the United States in 1873 and became a naturalized citizen in 1888. He was a meat cutter in Iowa before he came to Colorado. He married **Anna "Annie" May Harris**, 22 January 1900, at Erie, Weld, Colorado. Anna was born 15 October 1876, at Drybrook, England, and immigrated with her parents in 1881. She became a U.S. citizen in 1885. Her parents had settled at Erie, Colorado, where Anna spent her childhood. We have no other information on the parents of either William or Anna.

William and Anna had four children:

John Frederick, born 1 February 1901 at Erie, Colorado
William Edward, 13 November 1901, at Erie
Nellie May (Stotts), 21 October 1903, at Erie
Frances Margaret (Yourdon), 22 July 1908, at Lyons, Colorado
Information we have received from Frances alludes to John's being a stepson (note his and Bill's birth years), but we don't know any more than that.

Frances said that William Sr. and William Jr. (age 18) shipped their livestock, including horses, on the D&RGW Railroad from Lyons, Colorado, to Mack, arriving late in 1919. Mother Anna and the girls went to Pueblo to visit relatives before coming to Mack. They arrived on a cold day in November of 1919. The E. L. Shires family graciously offered to share their home with them until they could get settled on their own homestead. (It appears likely the Shires and Schunters were acquainted before they came to the west slope. See Shires history). Schunters established their home on Unit N of Sec. 10, originally filed on by Bryan J. Hayman. It was south west of Deacons' home.

Nellie and Anna Schunter
(Photo courtesy of Eugene Thomas)

School was already going when the Schunters arrived at New Liberty. Records show that Nellie was enrolled in the eighth grade and Frances in the sixth. Nellie probably graduated from the eighth grade in the spring of 1920, however, we don't know if they had any formal graduation ceremony. Frances graduated in the spring of 1922, with Ivan and Mabel Likes, Maudie Raver and Dan Pacheco. During that year she did the janitorial work in the school building. Before she graduated she was the champion speller for Mesa County and then went on to the state contest at Denver.

After the family arrived in the community they immediately became involved in the New Liberty Sunday School, with Anna serving as organist. Frances said that Margaret Morrow was her first Sunday School teacher. Frances earned a bible for perfect attendance.

Nellie Schunter Stotts, 1950,
on the Schunter farm.
(Photo courtesy of Eugene Thomas)

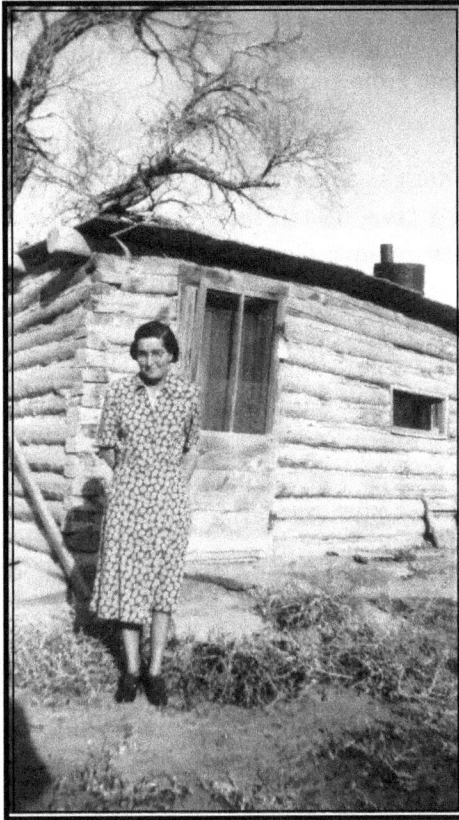

Nellie Schunter Stotts standing in front
of Schunter home.
(Photo courtesy of Mary Maluy)

Hans William died at the homestead, 21 October 1921, and was buried in the Orchard Mesa Cemetery.

John Frederick was married 2 April 1922, at Denver, to **Stella May Spaulding**. They lived in the Grand Valley area for several years, as evidenced by occasional mentions of them in Mack and New Liberty items in *The Daily Sentinel*. Eventually they moved to Fort Collins. John died there 13 October 1954. We don't know anything about their children.

William Edward "Bill" never married. He continued to live on the homestead for most of the rest of his life, with his mother, Anna, living with him for many years.

The Schunter homestead was only a 40-acre unit, due to a mix-up of section boundaries between two surveys. Bill worked much of the time for other farmers in the community, mostly for Deacons.

Bill was called up to serve in the armed forces during World War II. He evidently sold his farm to the Deacons sometime in the late 1960s.

He was found dead of a heart attack beside his car near Mack Mesa Reservoir on 21 January 1968. It appeared he had been in the process of putting chains on his car. He was buried in Elmwood Cemetery at Fruita.

Nellie married **Athol Lester Stotts**, 23 June 1923. Athol and Nellie lived on a homestead in Sec. 18, just south of his mother, Ella Stotts. Athol had filed on it in 1920. They bought the Howard Williams' homestead in the late 1920s. The record shows that transaction in Nellie's name. Not many years after that, they sold the Williams' farm to Claude Taylor, a stockman who needed a place to winter cattle and to comply with the requirement of grazing permits.

Following her mother-in-law, Ella B. Stotts, Nellie served as the New Liberty correspondent for *The Daily Sentinel* for several years. In October 1930, as she was making the rounds in the community gathering news items, she was one of the victims of what could have been a serious accident. As we look back on it now we can see some humor in the incident, but to Nellie it wasn't humorous.

Here is Nellie's account of the accident as it appeared in the New Liberty items of 7 October 1930.

While on the way home from school Monday evening, Darrell Maluy and Leonard Shires met with an accident. Darrell's horse was coming fast and he couldn't guide it, therefore it ran into Mrs. A. L. Stotts' buggy, and threw the boys to the ground. Darrell got bruised up quite badly and Leonard was knocked unconscious. We hope the school children will take more time when riding home from school and be more careful.

Darrell's memory of the accident is somewhat different. He says there were five of them, including himself, Leonard Shires, Clark Gerry, Edna Weir and one other (maybe Clyde Wright), racing on their horses, five abreast, between the school and Shires' corner. The situation was out of control by the time they met Nellie and her buggy. Nellie saw them coming and pulled over to the east side of the road, as close as she could get to the fence. Darrell's horse was on the left outside and ran into Nellie's left front buggy wheel, upsetting the buggy into the fence and throwing Nellie out. She was unhurt, but very upset. Leonard's arm was broken as he was thrown from his horse. This left Darrell with the responsibility of taking Leonard home and having Mrs. Shires curse him soundly as though it was all his fault.

Sometime in the fall of 1936 (we don't have all the story) Nellie was seriously burned in an accident on the farm. She reported in her New Liberty items in May of 1937 that she had recovered enough to be able to stand with some help. Gene Thomas says the story he remembers is that she was pouring gasoline into the carburetor of a car and it backfired, catching her in the flames.

Athol and Nellie sold out to Les Van Riper and, we assume, moved to Sage, Wyoming in the summer of 1937. At that time she turned *The Daily Sentinel* correspondence over to Margaret Morrow.

We do not have further information on Athol, but we know that Nellie died at La Barge, Wyoming, 5 September 1959. They had no children.

Frances married **Charlie Edward Yourdon** on 22 January 1926, at Grand Junction, a young man who lived in the Loma community and whom she had met at a birthday party. Edward and Frances had two girls and three boys.

They moved away from Grand Valley soon after they were married. Edward worked at the gilsonite mines at Dragon and Watson until they closed down. They lived for a time in California, near Truckee, where Edward was engaged in construction work. While there they lived in a tent in the woods. Later they moved to Ontario, Oregon, where they lived on a homestead, again living in a tent until they could build a house. Still later they moved to Idaho, where they have lived since. In 1992 Frances was living with a daughter at Wilder, Idaho. We received a letter from Frances and her daughter; from which we learned Frances is nearly blind. (In a recent (1996) phone conversation with Frances, we learned that the daughter she was living with had passed away.)

Mother Annie Schunter moved to Payette, Idaho, in July 1952, to live with Frances. She died there 19 October 1955, and was buried in the Riverside Cemetery at Payette.

Shires

Information from an interview with Laura Johnson Berry, a letter from Arthur Shires, census records, obituaries and news items from *The Daily Sentinel,* and personal knowledge of the author.

Edward Lincoln Shires was born 4 November 1863, in Wisconsin (1920 census says New York). We have no information about Edward's parents or childhood. On 7 October 1914, at Denver, he married **Anna Marie Larson Johnson.**

Anna Marie Larson was born in Gothenburg, Sweden, 10 April 1880. She accompanied her parents to Nebraska in 1885 and became a citizen in 1899. She was married in 1898 to **August Alfred Johnson,** at Lyons, Boulder, Colorado.

(Above) August Alfred and Anna Marie Larson Johnson, in 1900. (Upper right) Standing, L-R: Rudolph and Beda Marie Johnson. Sitting: Laura Lucille sitting on mother Anna's lap. (Below right) Leonard Burell and Arthur Edward Shires, 1923. *(Photo courtesy of Laura Johnson Berry)*

They had three children, all born at Lyons:
Rudolph, born 7 January 1900
Beda Marie (Tratos), 26 January 1901
Laura Lucille (Berry), 5 July 1907

Alfred Johnson died at Lyons in 1911.
In 1914, Anna married Edward Shires. Edward and Anna Shires had three children:

Adeline, who died soon after birth (we don't know her birth date or place).
Arthur "Art" Edward, born at Fruita, 26 August 1918 (the first new-born in the New Liberty community).
Leonard Burell, born 4 September 1921, at New Liberty

Sometime in 1983 we (the authors) interviewed Laura Johnson Berry and recorded a number of interesting stories she told us about events that led her family to the homestead in New Liberty.

In 1917, the family moved to Utah expecting to file on some land on the Ute Indian Reservation in the Vernal area. They established a temporary home near Price, Utah, while Edward Shires was trying to locate a permanent home for the family. The Ute Reservation didn't prove out, so he then turned his attention to the Grand Valley irrigation project.

Edward won the rights to a homestead in the drawing conducted by the Bureau of Reclamation in Grand Junction on 29 March 1918. The homestead consisted of 40 acres in the Southeast corner of Sec. 17 and 20 acres in the northeast corner of Sec. 20, referred to as farm unit "M." That place eventually became a point of reference in the community: "Shires' Corner."

After Edward filed on the homestead the family immediately prepared to move from Price to New Liberty. They had some cattle and horses they had brought from eastern Colorado. Rudolph, who was then 18 years of age, drove them across the desert from Price to the homestead all by himself. Since they had no place prepared to keep the cattle and horses, they kept them in the stockyards at Mack for a time.

The family all worked together to establish a home, living in a tent until they could build a house — a two room cabin that was to be their home for over 46 years. The house is still standing today (1997).

Anna had brought with her some "nice things" in a trunk that she planned to use when they built their "new home." Those nice things were never used, they were still in the trunk when she died.

Since there was no school yet at New Liberty in 1918, Laura had to miss a year. Laura told us that she begged to go to school at Mack that first year (1918-19) but her mother wouldn't hear of it; she was one of the students in the "new" New Liberty School when it opened in the fall of 1919. She graduated from the eighth grade in the spring of 1924 with Mr. Horn as her teacher. She went on to graduate from Fruita Union High School in 1928.

Following is a story written by Laura Johnson Berry when she was in the eighth grade, 12 February 1924. It was published in the *Fruita Times* 11 July 1991 (read more about Laura in the Berry story).

It was in March 1918 that we filed for the homestead. We came from Boulder, Colorado, to Price, Utah, and were there about a year. We did not like it in Utah so we came here. There were not very many people here for the first year we were here. We lived in a tent until we could get the corrals for the stock and the house built.

We began to do our farm work as soon as possible. First we had to clear off the ground before we could plow it. There was rabbit brush and weeds and some other brush which grew on the soil. We raised some vegetables, wheat, oats and sudan grass, which was used for hay.

We had 28 head of cattle, eight head of horses, five head of hogs, and of the fowls we had 36 chickens, six turkeys and three ducks that we brought here with us. The first year mother raised one turkey and a few chickens.

The second year we did a little better than we did the first year. Quite early in the year we put out 60 fruit trees which were of different varieties. There were apples, peaches, cherries, plums and pears. We also set out grape vines, raspberries, blackberries, and strawberries. We had a fine garden that year. We raised wheat, oats and alfalfa. Mother raised several turkeys and chickens and I raised one duck which ran with the chickens and when the duck would go into the water the chickens would run along the edge of the pond until the duck would come out.

We raised some little orphan lambs and that is where we got our start in sheep. When we first came out here there were a good many sheep and the herdsmen were glad to give the little orphans to anyone. We have 50 head of sheep now. We also raised some calves, pigs and colts.

The third year we did still better. We put some of the 20 acres into beets and the 40 acres had been put into hay, corn and wheat. We had a fine garden and raised some stock and flowers.

The fourth year we put the whole 60 acres into cultivation. We had beets, corn, wheat, oats and alfalfa. Mother and I had a small flower garden and a vegetable garden. We also put in a small lawn early in the spring. We raised quite a few turkeys and chickens. We had some strawberries and peaches to eat from the orchard.

The fifth year we made good off the homestead. Some of our fruit trees bore some fruit: the apples and peaches. We also had some grapes and strawberries. We had raised

(Above left) Edward Shires holding Leonard, 1922. (Upper right) Anna, Leonard, Arthur and Edward Shires about 1924. (Lower left) Arthur and Leonard Shires standing in front of Shires home about 1925. *(Photos courtesy of Laura Johnson Berry)* (Center) Laura Johnson Berry standing in front of the Shires house. (Bottom) Shires house as it looked in 1985. *(The last two pictures were taken by Phyllis Likes in 1985.)*

some turkeys, chickens and ducks and we sold them for $200. Besides what we made off the crops, we sold quite a few hogs, besides some other things. So we were quite proud of our homestead on the desert. It is Home Sweet Home to us.

We get our domestic water and irrigation water from the Colorado River. On the north side of our place is Mr. [Martin] Wells' place, on the south side is Mr. Pacheco, on the east is Mr. Roy Wells, and Mr. C. J. Phillips, and on the west is Mr. P. H. Maluy. The public road runs east and west between our 40 and 20 acres and a public road runs north and south on the east side.

Beda became acquainted with a young man by the name of **Mark Tratos** while the family lived at Price. They were married in Salt Lake City, 27 November 1922. After they had two children, Mark Tratos died and Beda then married his brother, **Michael Tratos**. They had five more children.

Beda spent the rest of her life in Utah, raising a family of six sons and one daughter. The Tratos family came to New Liberty occasionally for a visit. The children often spent the summer months with the Shires family. Beda died in Salt Lake City, 14 October 1983, at age 81.

In the early 1930s the Shires purchased the original Joseph Kiefer homestead (north and east of the New Liberty School) to enlarge their operation. Later, 40 acres in the northwest corner of that farm were sold to Clem Maluy. They also acquired some range land in the Bookcliff Mountains.

Tragedy struck the family on 8 May 1933. Edward Shires was riding a "skittish" young horse on an errand east of their home when the horse shied, throwing Edward off. He landed on his head and was found unconscious by family members some time later. He never regained consciousness. He was buried in the Elmwood Cemetery at Fruita. The family rallied and continued on with the farm operation.

Arthur and Leonard both graduated from the eighth grade at New Liberty. Arthur graduated from Fruita Union High School in 1937 and Leonard in 1939.

Leonard inherited the job of tending the sheep most of the time after graduating from high school. He would spend entire summers with them up in the Bookcliff mountains, seldom coming down to the valley until the sheep were brought down for the winter. Rudolph or Art would go up occasionally throughout the summer to take Leonard supplies and to check on him. (Leonard was an excellent camp cook, by the way).

Arthur served in the Army for four years (1942 to 1946) during World War II. While stationed in Oklahoma he met **Christine Moulder;** they were married at Mountain Park, Oklahoma, 29 September 1944.

During the time Art was in the Army, Rudolph and Leonard and their mother, Anna, handled the farming and sheep. Many will remember that Anna Shires didn't back away from work; a sturdy pioneer woman, she would dress and work like the men.

During World War II Rudolph was called up by the draft board for a physical, but was never inducted. Leonard was not called because of

Art, Anna, and Leonard in 1944
(Photo courtesy of Laura Johnson Berry)

The Art Shires family, 1994. Standing L-R: James, Arthur Edward Jr., Allen Lee Shires and Edna Maria Shires Riddle. Sitting: Arthur Edward, Christine Shires and Jean Marie Shires Kelleher. *(Photo courtesy Jean Shires Kelleher)*

physical problems.

While Art was away the sheep were sold and the operation changed to cattle. They had to change their grazing permits as well. That change gave them more time to raise feed crops for winter.

After the war, Art and Christine came back to the farm and lived there for many years. They had five children, all born in Fruita:

James, born 9 May 1947
Edna Maria (Riddle), 13 April 1949
Allen Lee, 27 August 1950
Jean Marie (Kelleher), 22 September 1957
Arthur Edward Jr., 7 August 1967

James has two children, Edna three, Jean two, and Arthur Jr. two.

At some point in time Art and Christine moved to Fruita, leaving Leonard in charge of the farm. But Leonard began to have problems and was eventually hospitalized and diagnosed with Alzheimer's. He spent several years in Family Health West and died 26 January 1991.

Art and Christine moved back to the farm during Leonard's illness. The farm was recently sold and Art and Christine are currently living in Fruita again. They celebrated their golden anniversary at Highline Lake State Park, north of Mack/Loma on Sunday, 25 September 1994. The gathering was hosted by their children.

Anna died 27 April 1964, at age 84; Rudolph died of an apparent heart attack, 31 October 1969; and Laura died 8 May 1985. All except Beda were buried in the Elmwood Cemetery at Fruita.

Simpson

Information from a history outline by Odis Simpson and obituaries and news items in *The Daily Sentinel*.

Clarence Paul "C. P." Simpson, was born 22 March 1873 at Springersville, Fayette, Indiana, to Henry Clay and Mary Simpson. He spent the early part of his life in Indiana, and his first marriage to Mary, whose last name is not known, occurred at Connersville, Indiana. One son, **Marion,** was born to that marriage. Marion was raised by Clarence's sister, Sidney Bibby. He spent his entire life in Indiana and died in about 1985.

Clarence moved to Loup City, Sherman, Nebraska, in 1900. In 1901 or 1902 he married **Ellen Mary Lofholm** at Loup City. She was born at Loup City, 2 November 1880, the second of four daughters of John Guthardt Lofholm and Marie, whose last name we don't have. They were immigrants from Sweden.

Clarence Simpson Family, 1917 at the Kilby place a quarter mile from Pear Park. Standing in the back are the parents: Ellen Mary Lofholm and Clarence P. Simpson. The children are lined up by their age, L-R: Palmer Clarence "Dinty," Henry Clay "Hank," Etta Mae, William "Bill" Howard, Odis Paul, John Stanley, and Francis Everett "Bud" Simpson. *(Photo courtesy of Odis Simpson)*

Clarence and Ellen had ten children:

Francis Everett "Bud", born 2 February 1904, at Loup City
John Stanley, 28 July 1905, Loup City
Odis Paul, 31 March 1907, Loup City
William Howard "Bill", 16 June 1909, Grand Junction
Etta Mae (Rector), 15 November 1910, Grand Junction
Henry Clay "Hank", 2 January 1913, Grand Junction
Palmer Clarence "Dinty", 8 November 1914, Grand Junction
Mary Ellen (Roche, Capson), 3 March 1917, Grand Junction
Alice Jodell (Suhr), 21 May 1919, Fruita
Warren (Nugent), 3 June 1922, Fruita

Left to Right: Bud, John, Odis, Bill, Etta Rector, Hank, Dinty, Mary Capson, and Warren. *(Photo courtesy of Odis Simpson)*

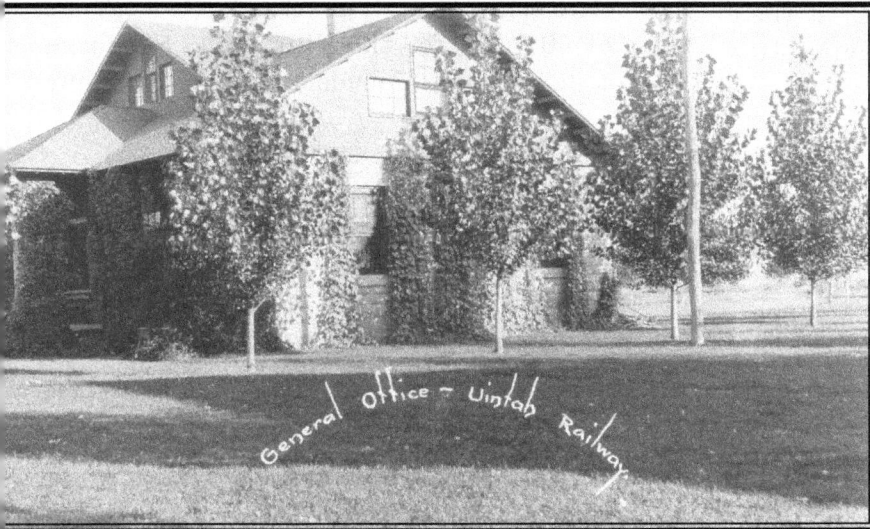

(Above left) Odis Simpson, telegrapher in Bond, Colorado, for the D&RGW Railroad, 1960. (Above right) John Simpson, engineer for the Southern Pacific Railroad. (Left) The general office of the Uintah Railway in Mack. (Below) Uintah Railway shop force at Atchee, Colorado, standing in front of the large #50 Mallet Engine. The engine was built especial for the Uintah Railway. The picture was taken 10 October 1928. Odis and John both worked for the Uintah Railway until it closed down in 1939. *(Photos courtesy of Odis Simpson)*

Clarence and Ellen Mary and the three oldest children, Francis, John and Odis, arrived in Colorado on 1 February 1908, settling first in the Pear Park district, east of Grand Junction. Clarence worked on various farms in the area, growing fruit for two years. Then he rented an orchard, growing apples and pears until he was starved out by association officials stealing most of the crops each year.

They moved to Mack on 29 January 1919, moving all their stuff on five wagons pulled by horses. The moving was done in one day from near Clifton. At Mack Clarence managed the large stock ranch owned by the Tawney Livestock Company. (At one time the original Kiefer place where Charlie Kiefer built the house which is still standing, was called the "Tawney Ranch." It is now owned by Country Jam USA)

Ellen Simpson died in Mack in 1922, at the birth of child number 10, Warren, leaving 10 children without a mother.

In 1923 the Simpsons moved to "down- town" Mack where Clarence managed the Uintah Railway Hotel for several years. He then purchased a restaurant which he ran until about 1939, when he retired and moved to Ely, Nevada.

On 10 August 1927, in Fruita, Clarence married **Effie Simmons Akin**. Effie was born in Arkansas, 19 January 1882, and in about 1903 came to Colorado, living for a short time in Fruita, then later in Grand Junction. She had two daughters, **Mrs. L. W. Haynes** and **Louise (Hyatt)**, and a son, **Harold**, by a former marriage. Her son, who excelled in athletics, died in September 1930 from injuries received while playing football at Colorado College in Colorado Springs. Daughter Louise lived with the Simpson family in Mack and attended Fruita Union High School. Effie died 7 December 1935, at St. Mary's Hospital.

We've learned that Clarence may have owned the Last Chance Service Station at some point in time — we don't know if he was the original owner.

According to his obituary ill health caused Clarence to move to the home of his son, John, at Bakersfield, California. He died there, 28 June 1944, at age 71, and was buried in the Elmwood Cemetery at Fruita.

Francis Everett "Bud" worked for his father until about 1923, then moved to Ely, Nevada. In June 1927, he went to work for the Nevada Railroad where he worked as a telegrapher until August 1931. He operated the Bank Club and the Hotel Nevada. He was very successful. He sold his businesses on 1 July 1962, but later opened the Mustang Club in the fall of 1967. Bud married Arline and they adopted two sons and a daughter: **James, Jerry**, and **Dorene**. Bud died 5 April 1968 in Salt Lake City.

John Stanley also worked for his father until 1923, and then he worked for the Uintah Railway. John married Georgia Belle Dunlap in Grand Junction in August 1930. They lived at Atchee until 1931. They had one son, **Jack**, who died at age 16. They moved to Los Angeles in 1932 where John worked for the Southern Pacific Railroad as a locomotive engineer until he retired. He worked a total of 50 years for the Uintah and Southern Pacific. John died at Palmdale, California, 8 July 1990.

Odis Paul worked for the Tawney Livestock Company until 1923. Then, beginning at age 15, he worked for the Uintah Railway until it was disbanded in 1939. He then went to work for the D&RGW RR, later going to school at Tyler, Texas, to learn Morse Telegraphy. On 16 February 1930, Odis married **Dorothy Gene Leighty** in Grand Junction. They had one son, **Odis "Kip" Leigh**, born 2 February 1939 at Grand Junction. Odis Sr. worked at the station at Bond, Colorado, for 30 years, until he retired 1 June 1972. He had worked 16 years for the Uintah and 34 years for the

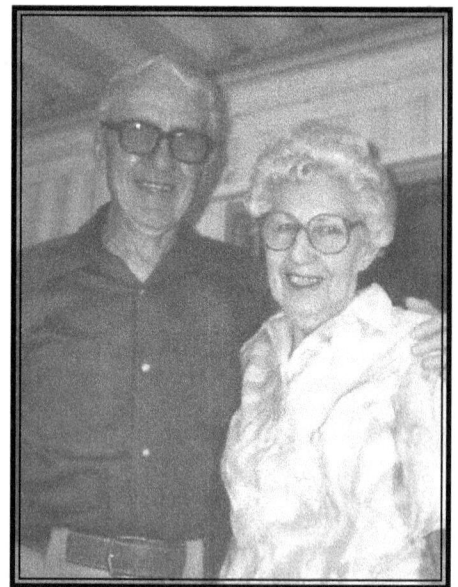

Odis Paul and Dorothy Gene Simpson, 1986. *(Photo courtesy of Odis Simpson)*

Alice Jodell, 8, and Etta Mae Simpson, 15.
(Photo courtesy Helen Overbye Peterson)

Mary Ellen Simpson, 15.
(Photo courtesy of Betty Booth Garber)

trains, telegraphy has become a lost art not required for station work.

Gene passed away in 1987 at Grand Junction. Odis married **Shirley Sowers (Kilmer),** 9 November 1991, at Bremerton, Washington. They live in Yuma, Arizona.

William Howard "Bill," after high school, went to work for the D&RGW RR at age 16 and learned Morse telegraphy. He worked at various stations between Denver and Ogden. He married **Elizabeth Christianson,** and they had a boy and a girl: **Dan** and **Billee Joyce.** In 1950 Bill and Elizabeth moved to Ely, Nevada, where he took over management of the Bank Club. In 1958 they moved to Stateline, Nevada, where he was employed at Harrah's Club at Tahoe Bill died 24 October 1965, at Stateline.

Etta Mae worked as a waitress at the Uintah Hotel and eventually married **Russell Rector.** They had two girls and a boy: **Russell, Mary Jo** and **Laurie.** They moved to Trona, California, in 1933. Russell died in 1989 and Etta Mae in 1996.

Henry Clay "Hank" moved to Ely, Nevada, after high school, where he worked until his death 29 June 1989.

Palmer Clarence "Dinty" worked in Utah after high school until joining the Air Corps at the beginning of World War II. After the war he worked in foreign countries as a manager of airports. After the Vietnam War he retired in Nevada. He married Mattie Green and they had one son, **David.** Mattie died in Cambodia and then he married Phu Trinh in Green River, Utah. Palmer "Dinty" died 19 October 1989.

Mary Ellen worked at the Uintah Hotel for two years after finishing high school. She

D&RGW RR. While living at Bond he acquired a small ranch at McCoy, Colorado. He kept the ranch until 1989, when he sold out and moved to Yuma, Arizona. (He spends the summers in Grand Junction). Odis informed us that since the railroads began using telephones for communications to move

Odis and Shirley Simpson, 1994. *(Photo courtesy of Odis Simpson)*

then moved to Ely, Nevada. She was married twice — first to a man named Roche, then to Capson. Both husbands are deceased. Mary lives in Las Vegas. She has a daughter, **Pat.**

Alice Jodell moved to California to live with her brother, John. She married a mining engineer named **Henry Suhr**. They lived in Chile for several years. They had one daughter, **Sylvia**, who died 5 November 1988. After moving back to California, Jodell died of cancer 20 August 1990.

Warren, whose mother died when he was born, was adopted by Arthur Nugent of Fruita when he was a very small child. He moved to Ely, Nevada, and worked as a casino manager, retiring in 1993. He married **Gloria Parodi** in Ely. They are now living in Reno, Nevada.

Sisler

Information from an interview with Fern Parsons Sisler and obituaries and news items in *The Daily Sentinel.*

John Edward "Ed" Sisler was born 2 December 1903, at Wellston, Lincoln, Oklahoma, and came to Colorado with his family when he was 12 years old. He attended schools in Grand Junction.

Fern Parsons was born 5 January 1906, at Hereford, Iowa, to Ray Parsons and Emma May Huntley. The family moved to Grand Junction in 1908 when Fern's father purchased an orchard south of town on Orchard Mesa. After a big freeze which destroyed many of the fruit trees, Fern's father gave that up and, for a time, operated a livery stable located behind the present-day public service building. Ray later went to work for the railroad and was a conductor on the west end from Grand Junction to Utah when he died of pneumonia at age 48; Fern was then 19 years old.

While Fern was going to high school, in the winter months she and others frequented a pond in Lincoln Park that would freeze over and provide a popular skating pond for the youngsters in the area. Fern would go over there to skate after school hours.

A boy by the name of Elmer, one of the skaters, wanted to date her, but Fern was not enthused about that. One Sunday evening Elmer showed up at her door accompanied by a big, tall, handsome boy named Ed Sisler, whom Elmer wanted Fern to find a date for. She made sure they didn't find a date for Ed — she took over.

Ed and Fern were married at Delta, Colorado, 23 November 1925. At the time Fern was employed as a telephone operator and her superiors would not let her take time off to get married. She then threatened to quit and they decided they could let her take enough time off to get married and then stay long enough to train someone to replace her. Therefore she did not get to live with Ed for the first two weeks of their married life. She continued to work part time for awhile.

At the time of their marriage Ed was working in a coal mine at Palisade. The honeymoon

Ray Eugene Sisler and Margaret "Margie" Floria , 1947.
(Photos courtesy of Fern Parsons Sisler)

cottage was a 10-foot by 10-foot shack near the mine.

They had two children:

Ray Eugene, born 2 May 1928
Margaret "Margie" Floria (Goodel), born 3 March 1934

(Upper left) Fern Parsons Sisler. (Upper center) Margaret "Margie" Floria Sisler ready to go to a prom, about 1950. (Upper right) Ray Parsons, Fern's father. (Lower left) Ed Sisler and granddaughter. (Lower right) Ed Sisler and granddaughter. *(Photos courtesy of Kimberly Goodell Bennett)*

Both were born at Grand Junction

After working at the mine for a while, Ed went to work for a railroad section crew as a fireman on a clamshell (a digging machine). Ed and Fern were sent to Woodside, Utah, for a time, and had to live in a crew-car on a siding. At the time, Fern was fascinated with the geyser at Woodside, which was later developed into a tourist attraction.

Ed was then sent to Pueblo while Fern stayed with a cousin at Palisade. Ed became homesick and quit his job to come home. He started working on a milk route for Charlie Witheron and then later for Clymer's Dairy.

While Ed was working on the Redlands pruning trees, a ditch-rider would drive by their house every day and one day Ed told him he didn't have a job. He was soon called to a job as ditch-rider on the Redlands where he worked for six years.

Ed worked for a time at the power plant (we assume it was the Redlands Project), when one day Wayne Chiesman, Superintendent of Grand Valley Water Users' Association, saw him at a barbershop. He asked Ed if he would like a job and it turned out to be as ditch-rider at Camp #7, north of Loma. Ed and Fern went out to look at the house and Fern didn't like it, so Ed didn't take the job and continued to work at the power plant.

Later a job opened up at Camp #8 at New Liberty and Ed was called to succeed William J. "Cap" Blamey. Since Fern felt she would be moving way out in the country, she told Ed she wouldn't live out there unless there were trees. They took the job but were not able to live out there for several months because Blamey was reluctant to give up the house. They stayed in a motel in Fruita.

They moved to New Liberty in 1941 and the children were enrolled at the New Liberty School. The family became a part of the community; Ed was well-liked as a ditch-rider. He and Fern were both involved in 4-H work in the community. After graduating from the eighth grade, each of the children attended Fruita Union High School.

Because of illness Ed was confined to the Morrison Nursing Home for about a year before he died, 11 March 1964.

Presently (1997) Fern lives in Fruita. She is blind from a degenerative disease that has now affected three generations. Fern has five grandchildren and eight great-grandchildren.

Ray Eugene enlisted in the Army, and while home on furlough, lost his life in a tragic accident in Mack. On 18 June 1948, at 1 a.m., for some reason not made clear, he was observed unconscious on the highway in Mack by a motorist who was traveling toward Utah. The motorist stopped and turned around to go back to offer assistance. To protect Ray from being ran over, the motorist tried to stop a Rio Grande Trailways bus that was approaching from the east. But the bus driver did not see Ray's body lying on the road until it was too late to avoid hitting him He tried to straddle the body but, in spite of that he ran over him, crushing his head.

Investigators determined that Ray may have suffered a heart attack and fell on the highway.

Margaret "Margie" Floria was married to Jim Goodell on 25 September 1955 in Fruita. They moved to Sand Springs, Oklahoma, in 1967. Jim and Margie were divorced in 1978.

They have five children:

Kimberly Dianne, born 16 July 1956, Fruita
Jamie Marie, 19 February 1959, Fruita
Gary Duane, 6 August 61, Tulsa, Tulsa, Oklahoma
Melanie Denise, 10 December 1962, Montrose, Montrose, Colorado
Tammie Dawn, 25 November 1967, Tulsa

Margie inherited a degenerative disease which has left her blind as she has gotten older. She received her Master's Degree in Applied Behavioral Sciences in 1991 and currently works for Ability Resources in Tulsa, Oklahoma, as an independent-living counselor. She is currently living in Tulsa and has 9 grandchildren.

Slaugh

Information from obituaries and news items in *The Daily Sentinel*, and letters from Ralph Slaugh and Erma Slaugh Armstrong.

Leonard Slaugh was born 1 September 1896, at Vernal, Uintah, Utah, the third of 13 children born to George Alfred Slaugh and Rachel Maria Goodrich. He spent his childhood in that area, attending schools in Vernal. His father was a farmer, so Leonard spent much of his early life sharing in the farm work. He developed a great love for the outdoors and later in life became a hunter and trapper.

On 24 November 1921 Leonard married Janke "Jennie" Postma at Vernal, 24 November 1921. The marriage was solemnized in the Salt Lake Temple on 25 November 1922.

Jennie was born 1 January 1904, in Amsterdam, Netherlands, to John Postma and Nellie Boelens. When she was about three years old her family immigrated to the United States. They settled for a time in the Salt Lake City area, then moved to the Uintah Basin near Vernal. Jennie's father was a musician, having been a band leader in Holland before coming to the United States. He taught his children the basics of music and Jennie was able to pick up from there, becoming an accomplished pianist and organist. She passed her talents on to her children and taught piano and organ to other children as well. The Slaugh family was well-known in later years for their musical talents.

There were six children:

Delbert George, born 5 June 1923
Calvin Emert, 31 January 1925
Ralph Welden, 12 April 1926
Erma Lenore (Armstrong), 2 December 1929
Vesta Joy (Tingey), 15 August 1931
Rachael "Rae" Elaine (Alderman), 18 November 1938

The Slaugh family in 1941. Back, L-R: Delbert George, Erma Lenore, Calvin Emert, Vesta Joy and Ralph Welden Slaugh. Front: Leonard, Rachael "Rae" Elaine and Janke "Jennie" Slaugh. *(Photo courtesy of Erma Slaugh Armstrong)*

All were born in Vernal except Rachael, who was born in Mack.

Ralph recalls that the family spent one winter at the town of Watson, Utah, the northern terminus of the Uintah Railway. Leonard was hired to trap some mountain lions for the stockmen in that area.

It was noted in *The Daily Sentinel* of 19 March 1945, that Leonard Slaugh placed fourth among the trappers employed by the state in number of predators trapped in the month of February.

Following are some memories written by Ralph Slaugh:

We left Vernal, Utah, in early June 1935 in a 1930 Model A Ford and a 1929 International truck, so you know the Model A was loaded. Mom hadn't driven very much before so the whole experience was pretty bad for her. My oldest brother, Delbert, stayed behind to work for grandfather (Slaugh?), which meant that Calvin, Ralph, Erma and Vesta were stuck in the two loads somewhere. Rachael was born after we moved to Mack.

We spent most of the summer at Trapper's Lake, east of Meeker, then moved to Mack just in time for the older ones to enroll in school. Dad had accepted a trapping job for the government and was assigned a large area bounded by the Bookcliffs on the north, Pinon Mesa and Glade Park on the south and the desert to the west. He had rented a "tent house" from Henry McCoy, who was residing at the time in the Mesa County jail for some "carvings" he did on some other man.

In a few months, Dad purchased the

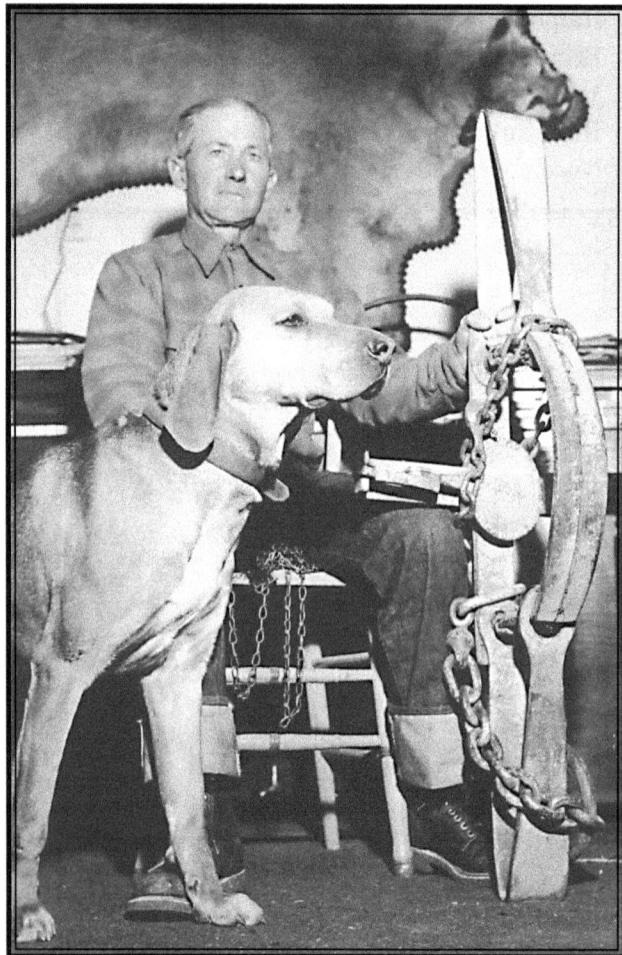

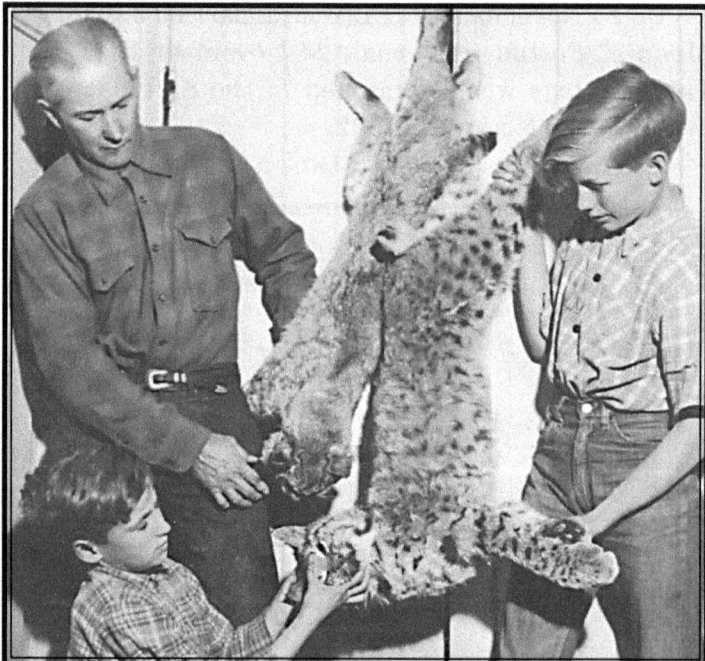

(Above) Leonard Slaugh, the Trapper, with one of his hounds and a big bear trap. (Above right) Leonard with foster children, Wayne and Jerald Jeffries, observing a couple of bobcats that he trapped. *(Photos courtesy of Erma Slaugh Armstrong)* (Below right) A live bobcat being observed by the family cat. *(Photo courtesy of JoAnn Bowen Montague)*

Johnny Wesner place just south of the tracks. It was a beautiful little place with nine acres, all green with many big cottonwood trees, a nice orchard and big vineyard. What more could we want? We thought we had died and gone to heaven; we'd never had an abundance of irrigation water like that before!

Mack was a thriving little community then, as the Uintah Railway and the D&RGW both had people there. The school had two class rooms and an all-purpose auditorium. There were four grades in each room, and one teacher per room. Erma was in the first grade, I was in the fourth, so we were in the same room. The teacher was Mildred Hogsett. Delbert and Calvin were in the "big room" with Walter Poirier as teacher.

At Mack School I was introduced to softball, for which I developed a life-long love. We had a good team and played New Liberty, Loma, Starr, Hunter, Fruita, Redlands and others. Occasionally it was big time, believe me!

Some of the names I remember at Mack were: Keffalos, Komatas, Booth, McCoy, Bowen, Eddings, Roy and Charlie Smith, Blank, Newell, Ray, Dalton, Cook, Robinson, Herron, Collins, Hollinger, Barr, Davidson, Simpson, Laird, Overbye, Davis, Kelly, Garber, Pappas and Velasquez. Of course I'll think of many others later.

The Uintah Railway had a "turn around" place for the engines in Mack. It was in the shape of a diamond (or triangle?). On one side was a big, old building, the ice house, where they stored ice from Lake McAndrews for the people to use in the summer. There was also a pump house and water tower where Mr.[Roy?] McCoy and Mr. [Odis?] Simpson fired a boiler and otherwise looked after things. The north leg of the "turn around" crossed the highway and ran up to the pump house. I don't know if they produced the power for Mack there or not.

Back in those days we were not burdened with TV and all those other entertainments — we entertained ourselves. The community affairs were very popular and well attended. I'll never forget the good fellowship at the dances and socials; most people just naturally participated. Since our family was musical, we had opportunity to furnish music for many community dances. It was great to associate with those super people who lived in and around Mack. (It is evident from the Mack news items the Slaugh family was integrated and well accepted into the Mack community - author)

When we moved to Mack there was a lumber yard, a mercantile store and quite a number of nice homes. Sarah Boyden was the Postmaster and Everett Bowen was the rural mail carrier. I have many happy memories of Mack in those days! It was truly a good place to grow up. The people were good, friendly, and willing to lend a helping hand.

Our next-door neighbors, the Bowens, had a good library, so by the time I left home I had read most of Zane Grey, Jack London, James Oliver Curwood, and William [McCleod] Raine. I've always felt sorry for people who never caught the vision and experienced the adventure of reading.

As a young man I worked for some of the farmers around the community, picking spuds, threshing beans and grain and stacking hay. Some of those farmers were Roe and Tom Saunders, Charlie Overbye, Charlie Kiefer, and later, Leo Kiefer, Arbuckles and Bill Baker. The farmers worked together and helped each other, so we would go around from farm to farm until all were taken care of. The ladies at every farm would feed the crew and boy! what feeds they put on! In the fall we would participate in the peach harvest at Palisade — anyone ever had any experience with peach fuzz?

The decision was made to disband the Uintah in 1939 and the town started to die. On 21 June 1940 our house burned to the ground and we lost about everything. Dad bought the Uintah office building and we lived there until about 1952 (That building also burned to the ground after the Slaugh's left).

Delbert graduated from Fruita Union High School in the spring of 1942. During their high school days he and **Delores Belle Collins** fell in love and were married at the home of her parents, 1 November 1942. Delores, who had graduated in 1941, was the daughter of Emmett Collins (deceased) and Lois Hollinger of Mack Mesa. Delbert and Delores had one child, **Gerald "Jerry,"** who currently resides in Fruita.

Delbert was inducted into the Army in August of 1944, and while serving with the 32nd Red Arrow infantry division on Luzon, in the Philippines, he died in battle on 4 May 1945. He was buried in a temporary military cemetery, but in 1949, his remains were shipped back to the states and buried in the family plot at Vernal.

Delbert George Slaugh
(Picture used from The Deseret News, *Salt Lake City, Utah, Friday, 1 June 1945:"Six Utah Men Casualties, Ten Released.")*

Calvin did not finish high school. During his early teen years he became interested in telegraphy and other goings-on of the railroads at Mack. With the help of **Red Davies**, station agent at Mack, and **Lester Caruthers**, section foreman, he became so well-learned in telegraphy that he was able to get a job with the D&RGW Railway as soon as he was 17 years old. He had worked at that trade for 42 years before he retired. His job with the railroad was interrupted when he began serving in the Navy in July 1944.

At present (1994) Calvin lives in North Salt Lake City. He married **Mary Garvene Garbe** in June 1966. They have two children.

Ralph graduated from Fruita Union High School in May 1944 and began serving in the Navy in June 1944. His boot training was interrupted when he had to be hospitalized and he had to start his training over.

He married **Dixie Eloise Vaughn** 25 December 1947. After three children they were divorced.

Ralph tells of an unusual courtship with his second wife, **Dorothy Brimhall**, who also had been married previously. Ralph knew her mother, a brother, and two sisters, who kept telling him about their younger sister who was divorced and needed a good husband. So one day Ralph drove way out in the boon docks to her farm, introduced himself, and they were married two weeks later. With Ralph's three children and her four and the three more girls they had together, they have quite a family! They have a common ancestor. Their great-grandfather, George Albert Goodrich, had three wives, two of whom were sisters. Ralph is descended from one sister and Dorothy from the other. Ralph and Dorothy currently live at Roosevelt, Utah. In addition to his talent with the violin (he tells us he still plays the violin almost daily) he also became interested in writing poetry and spends a lot of joyful hours composing stories in verse of happenings in the family. (Poetry will follow).

Erma **(Armstrong)**, who lives at Dallas, Oregon, is a professional pianist and former teacher of music education at many levels, including university. She has a Bachelor of Music degree from Colorado State University, a Masters of Music from Lewis and Clark, and a D.M.A. from the University of Oregon. She has also written a book about her father, "The Last Trapper, An American Saga," that is very interesting and well done.

Vesta **(Tingey)** lives at St. George, Utah, where she works for the St. George Planning Commission. She also teaches violin and performs often with the St. George Symphony and local chamber music groups.

Rachael **"Rae" (Alderman)**, who lives at Aloha, Oregon, works as an executive secretary. Rae also bought and managed a foster-care home for the elderly for a time, then sold that and bought a fourplex which she manages. She lives in one of the apartments. Each of the girls raised three children.

Rachael was the only one still at home when Leonard and Jennie moved to Fruita in 1952; the others were all married or had gone away to college or to work.

Leonard and Jennie remained in Fruita for

Jennie Slaugh in front of the old Fruita Hospital that she had converted into a nursing home. *(Photo courtesy of Erma Slaugh Armstrong)*

about 20 years operating a nursing home in the converted old Fruita Hospital. In 1972 they moved to Spring City, Utah, after living a short time at Dragerton, Utah (now East Carbon City). They moved to St. George, Utah, in 1985. Leonard died there 23 July 1989, at age 92. Jennie then moved to Dallas, Oregon, in 1990 and lived with daughter Erma until she passed away 16 September 1993, at age 89. Both she and Leonard are buried in the St. George City Cemetery. They left a sizable posterity: 23 grandchildren and 43 (or more) great-grandchildren.

Following are two of about 35 of Ralph's poems in our possession. We hope they will all be published some day.

Leonard Slaugh, The Lion Hunter

Rain, snow and mud get into your blood
On the trail of the mountain lion
It's there to stay, it's a fever they say
You can't shake it, just short of dying.

A saddle-sore butt, an empty gut
No sleep since can't remember
We'll get that cat. Wherever he's at
My dogs and I, the 15th of December

It's thirty below, three feet of new snow
I hear the dogs bayin'
That cat just leaped, off a ledge thirty feet
That's what the hounds are sayin'.

I help them down, too long to go around
Into the canyon they go flying
The going's rough, down off that bluff
We'll get him soon, or die trying.

We got that cat, don't know exactly where at
Could see the lights of Thompson
There's ten foot drifts, high in the Book Cliffs
If we get back, we'll be going some

Now that is a story, of a claim to glory
Of a famous Mountain Lion hunter
A bobcat he trailed, at twelve years he nailed
The hide on his Pa's barn door.

Most men would give, their arm to live
This story and hundreds more
That day seems past, too good to last
The old hunter and his era, gone before.

Pa's Temper

Pa had a frightful temper,
as bad as you will see
And if he ever lost it,
I can safely guarantee
You didn't want to be there,
'twould scare you half to death
For fear he'd have a heart attack,
and breathe his final breath.

But if you didn't rile him none,
was nice as nice could be
Polite and kind to everyone,
imparted generously
The ladies all thought he was swell,
so thoughtful he did seem
But when my Pa was mad as hell,
'twas like a nightmare dream.

We had a homemade tractor,
any job 'twould do it
To start it no real factor,
was really nothing to it
Just start the crank at bottom,
lightly pull it to the top
That motor would be running smooth,

without an errant pop.

Pa was working in the orchard,
the weather super hot
No bird, no mouse, no nothing stirred,
as shade and cool they sought
The tractor was performing well,
purring like a kitten
Pa was happy you could tell,
as on that seat he's sittin'

After while he took a break,
into the house he went
I strolled out for boredom's sake,
no other real intent
As I walked up the orchard rows
a plan began to form
I thought what if and just suppose,
and what would be the harm

I then looked back towards the
house, no sign of Pa as yet
Then to the tractor like a mouse,
as close as I could get
I opened the distributor,
and then removed the rotor
This part a prime contributor,
without it like no motor

I hid, waiting with impatience,
but soon Pa came out
He walked up oozing confidence,
it'd start he had no doubt
The thing had been so faithful,
it ran like one fine watch
But now a prank so hateful,
Would that reputation squash

Pa put the crank position down,
then pulled it up so neat
Then started nonchalantly round,
to his place upon the seat
He realized it didn't start,
when he was halfway there
He did the classic double-take,
then turned around to stare

He regarded that machine then,
like he'd never seen
Then slowly did a count to ten,
with time to spare between
When he was then for sure convinced,
that baby wasn't running
Back he went, no words he minced,
determined, I'm not funning
That process he repeated,
a dozen times at least

From this narrative deleted,
choice words whose flow increased
By now his rage was frightful,
in fury he did crank
Performance not delightful,
I now regret my prank

He checked the gas, he checked the oil,
he checked the water too
And all the while his wrath did boil,
he then did crank anew
His knuckles now were bloody skinned,
from times the crank had slipped
I was scared and, man, chagrined,
and limp like I'd been whipped

Of course the monster wouldn't start,
he couldn't rouse that motor
And me, I didn't have the heart
to tell him 'bout the rotor
In rage he raised the crank up high,
and swung with all his might
And struck the tractor on a tire, a
truly shameful sight

Yes, naturally the crank bounced back,
as you might know it would
And struck my Pa between the eyes,
man, he was out but good
I raced from my hiding place,
and put the rotor back
Then frantically I washed his face,
where he'd received the whack

By and by my Pa came to, man,
I feigned innocence
The spot between his eyes now blue,
my conduct pure pretense
I asked him did his heart give out,
or did he have a stroke
He never did explain that clout,
as how his nose got broke

I never ever told my Pa,
the truth about that day
And I don't think Pa told Ma,
I mean, what could he say?
It was plain he'd not discuss it,
made some lame excuse
How by a tree he did get hit,
a limb was hanging loose.

(Left) Alta Beatrice Davis and Charley Smith at the time of their wedding, in 1923. (Above left) Charlie Smith about 1918. (Above right) Alta Beatrice Davis about 1919. *(Photos courtesy of Delores Smith Likes)*

Smith

Much of the following information was furnished by Alta Smith and Delores Smith Likes; some information is from news articles and obituaries in *The Daily Sentinel.*

Charley Smith was born 8 August 1900, at Calloway, Custer, Nebraska, one of 14 children born to George Oscar and Lydia Smith. Charley spent the early part of his life in Nebraska. He married **Alta Beatrice Davis** at Garden City, Finney, Kansas, on 17 October 1923. Alta was born 17 August 1901, at Palmyra, Otoe, Nebraska, one of 10 children born to Elias Edger Davis and Beatrice Dulcimer Neel.

Alta was raised on a farm some distance north of Gothenburg, Nebraska. She attended high school at Gothenburg, making it necessary for her to live away from her family. She tended children to pay for her board and room. She went on to acquire a teaching certificate and taught for a few years at a country school, south of Gothenburg.

Charley and Alta had two children:

Delores Imogene (Likes), born 18 April 1925, Lakin, Kearney, Kansas
Richard "Dick" Layne, 31 July 1926, Garden City, Finney, Kansas
Since Charley was suffering from diabetes, and the excellent fruit region in western Colorado

Richard Layne and Delores Imogene Smith, about 1932.
(Photos courtesy of Delores Smith Likes)

made such an impression on him, he thought it would be beneficial to live in the drier climate. In the late summer of 1937 the family sent all their belongings in a truck to Mack. Charley, Alta, Delores and Richard rode in their old Model "A" Ford to Colorado. They sent the truck back to Nebraska loaded with peaches.

The family purchased the "Last Chance" service station, store and motel in Mack, with living quarters in the rear of the store. They were soon involved in community affairs. There was a very active community club with dances most Saturday nights. Charley played the fiddle for those dances with Alta chording on the piano.

Delores and Dick attended the nearby Mack School.

On 21 January 1939, they sold the "Last Chance" station to Reet and Ada Bush. In March Charley and Alta moved to Loma to operate the "Stranger" store. In early 1940 the Bushes turned the store back to them and Charley began driving the high school bus, hauling the New Liberty/Mack kids to Fruita.

On 17 August 1940, Alta was appointed Postmaster of the Mack Post Office and set up for business in a small building on the east side of the store. She kept the post office open six days a week and one hour on Sunday. Her salary the first year was about $550, based on the amount of stamps she sold.

On 26 November 1943, Charley became ill unexpectedly and was taken to the hospital in Grand Junction, where he died. This was a devastating blow to the family. Who would have expected such a seemingly robust young man as Charley to come to such an untimely end?

Alta sold the store in August 1944 to a family by the name Irvin. She then moved into a house a few yards northeast of the store and moved the post office over and joined it to the house, making

The Smith family in front of their newly purchased store in Mack, 1937. L-R: Delores, Charley, Dick and Alta Smith. *(Photo courtesy of Delores Smith Likes)*

it convenient by having living quarters and business all in the same building.

During World War II Alta faithfully wrote letters to all the New Liberty and Mack boys, whom she knew were serving overseas in the military. The author, Homer, was one of the beneficiaries of that kindly act — I will never forget those letters that arrived so regularly when

Alta Smith standing in front of her car that is parked in front of her home and post office, about 1945. *(Photo courtesy of Delores Smith Likes)*

699

I was so homesick.

In 1988, after 49 years in Mack, Alta moved to Independence Village in Fruita. She celebrated her 95th birthday on 17 August 1996. She is still going strong today in 1997.

Alta Beatrice Davis Smith, 1996.
(Photo used from the Fruita Times, August 1996 issue)

Delores graduated from Fruita Union High School in 1943 and married **Lewis Likes**, 17 June 1944, at the Likes farm in New Liberty. Lewis was serving in the Navy, so the newlyweds left shortly to live at Pensacola, Florida, where Lewis was stationed. They had three children:

Deana Lou, born 27 February 1945, Pensacola, Florida (Diana was born prematurely. She lived until 5 March 1945 and is buried at Pensacola).
James "Jim" Dean, 10 September 1946, Fruita
Janice Sue, 9 June 1950, Lincoln, Lancaster, Nebraska

After Lewis retired from the Navy in 1966, he and Delores came back to the Mack area to make their home. They lived for 22 years on the Serve farm, northeast of Mack. When Alta retired as Mack Postmaster in 1971, Delores was appointed to take her place. In 1984, while she was still postmaster, the Mack Post Office was relocated to a new building. She retired in 1987 after serving 16 years.

Delores and Lewis now live in Fruita. They have 10 grandchildren and one great-grandchild. (See more about Delores with the Likes story).

Dick graduated from Fruita Union High School in May 1944 and went into the Navy in July. He served on the D.D. McNair Destroyer for 14 months. Then he returned to the States and was assigned on a PGM 23 ship, a test craft. His job was to find out what damage an atomic bomb would cause to a warship. They placed several ships in the open sea and dropped a bomb called the Abel bomb, above a ship, and also placed a bomb beneath the ship, called Baker, and detonated those bombs. They would leave the area and go about nine miles away during the bombs detonation and then later return to measure the radiation and damage to the ships. In the process, their craft became radioactive and too hot to stay. They went to Pearl Harbor in an attempt to alleviate the danger. The Navy dry docked the ship and tried to sandblast out the radiation but was unsuccessful. As probably the only alternative, they took the ship out into the sea and sunk it. After that assignment, Dick went back to sea on a PC (Patrol Craft) used as a weather ship which sent weather balloons up every morning and also checked the currents. He then went to Guam and came home on the ship AKA. He was discharged 20 July, 1947.

Dick married **Thelma Lorene Fry** on 1 November 1948, in Fruita. Thelma was a Fruita girl who graduated from Fruita Union High School in 1947.

Dick and Thelma had three boys:

Martin Layne, born 19 March 1951, Salt Lake City, Salt Lake, Utah
Gary Allen, 21 September 1952, Salt Lake City
Stuart Lee, 10 January 1954, Glenwood Springs, Garfield, Colorado

(Above left) Delores standing in front of Mack School house, 1941, sweet 16. (Above right) Delores and Lewis Likes on their wedding day, 17 June 1944, at the Clyde Likes Sr. residence. (Center left) Delores Imogene Smith's high school graduation picture, 1943. (Center right) A new mother. Delores showing off her new son, James Dean Likes, in front of the Mack Post Office, September 1946. (Bottom left) The Lewis Likes family, about 1954. Delores and Lewis in back and Janice and Jim in front. (Bottom center) James Dean Likes age 17, 1963. (Bottom right) Janice Sue Likes, age nine, 1959. *(Photos courtesy of Delores Smith Likes and Homer Likes Collection)*

(Upper left) Delores and Dick Smith with the Mack Schoolhouse in the background, 1943. (Upper right) Dick in his Navy uniform in 1944. (Below) Thelma and Dick Smith, about 1948. (Lower left) Dick and Thelma on their wedding day, 1 November 1948 in Fruita. *(Photos courtesy of Delores Smith Likes)* (Lower right) The Dick Smith family, about 1965. Standing, L-R: Stuart Lee, Martin Layne and Gary Allen Smith. In front: Thelma and Dick Smith. *(Photo courtesy of Thelma Fry Smith)*

Dick worked as a signal maintainer for the D&RGW Railroad for 38 years; 15 of those years (1966-1981) were spent in Buena Vista, Colorado. He started in Salt Lake City and worked in Murray, Salina, and Price, Utah, and also Salida, Kremmling, Cañon City and then Buena Vista, Colorado. In 1981 he was transferred to Grand Junction, where he retired in 1986.

Thelma went to beauty school in Price and was certified in Utah. She and Dick then moved to Buena Vista and she earned a Beautician's Certificate for Colorado, but instead she went to work for Vista Supermarket as a bookkeeper and worked there for 15 years. In Fruita, she worked for the school food services at Shelledy School from 1982 to 1988.

Dick and Thelma have made their home in Fruita since 1981. They do a lot of traveling and fishing, and spend their winters in Yuma, Arizona.

Smith

The following information is from family information provided by Shirley Smith Gilbert and Blanche Hutchison, and obituaries and news items in *The Daily Sentinel.*

Roy Forrest Smith was born 10 February 1886, at Casey, Guthrie, Iowa, a son of Samuel and Almeda Smith. He moved with his family to Clifton, Colorado, in 1906, then to Mack in 1917. His daughter, Shirley, told us that Roy was a "mid-life child" whose sisters were married by the time he was born. Before marriage he worked as a ranch hand on Glade Park.

He was married first to **Amanda Shriver** of Clifton, Colorado. She died in 1917.

On 16 April 1922, he married **Edna Blanche Hollinger**, of Mack. Edna was born to Edward C. Hollinger and Blanche Fritz, 10 November 1897, in Salina, Mitchell, Kansas [see Hollinger story]. She spent her childhood in Salina and then moved with her parents to Bailey, Colorado, where they lived until 1909; they moved to the homestead at Mack in 1918.

Following is an account from *The Daily Sentinel* of Edna and Roy's wedding as written

Wednesday, 22 April 1922, by Mabel C. Kiefer, Fruita correspondent:

Sunday afternoon at 4 o'clock occurred the marriage of Miss Edna B. Hollinger and Roy Smith, at the home of the bride's parents, Mr. and Mrs. Hollinger, residing north of Mack. The bride was attired in a beautiful white satin dress, while her bridesmaid was attired in a lovely costume of pink organdie. The little MacTaggart twins, Josie and Jessie, acting as flower girls, wore cunning frocks of blue organdie. The groom, attired in the conventional black, was accompanied by Emmett Collins as best man. Reverend P. J. Tripp officiated at the ceremony, which was attended by about twenty guests. The bride and groom left on No. 4 for a short wedding trip and will be at home to their friends after their return at the home on the High Line.

Roy and Edna had three children. All attended schools at Mack and graduated from Fruita Union High School.

Blanche Almeda (Hutchison), born 19 February, Grand Junction
Wilbur Eugene, 16 August 1926, Grand Junction
Shirley Lucille (Gilbert), 4 December 1928, Grand Junction

Blanche Almeda, born 19 February 1924 at Grand Junction. She married **Donald Frances Hutchison** 10 September 1944 at the home of her parents on Mack Mesa. They had one daughter, **Donna Marie**, born 15 October 1946, in Grand Junction.

While they lived in Fruita for a few years Blanche was employed by Rio Grande Motorway and Don worked at Osborn's and possibly Moore's Hardware. He also edited the *Fruita Times* for awhile. Later they moved to Rifle for 15 years where Don worked as Assistant Administrator at the Clagett Hospital and Blanche worked for the Glenwood Springs Motorway. Don later quit the hospital and purchased a service station and worked at that until they moved back to Fruita in 1980. Don died at Fruita in 1981.

Wilbur Eugene married **Ada Ellen Efaw** in January 1949 to at Fruita.
They had three children:

Judy Ann, born January 1952, Grand Junction
Dale Allen, January 1955, Grand Junction
Terry Lee, 1957 at Casper, Wyoming
Wilbur died at Casper, 14 December 1987

Shirley Lucille was born 4 December 1928 at Grand Junction. She was married 12 January 1947 at her parents' home on Mack Mesa to **Delbert S. Gilbert**. They have lived in Grand Junction since then. They have two children:

Nancy, born 2 April 1951, Grand Junction
Darrell, 27 October 1954, Grand Junction

Snavely

The following history has been gleaned from obituaries and news items in *The Daily Sentinel*, census records and stories told by Louise Clow Likes.

Lewis Case Snavely was born 23 March 1849 at Union Mills, La Porte, Indiana. He was second of seven children born to Willis and Celeste Snavely. He spent his childhood in La Porte County and was married there in about 1869 to **Mary M. Irwin**. While still living in La Porte County, their oldest daughter, **Alta**, was born about 1870. In 1879 Lewis moved his young family to Butler County, Nebraska, where two more children joined the family. Another daughter, **Martha**, was born shortly after they arrived there, and then their son, **Lewis Vernon**, was born in August 1884.

The family came to Colorado in 1887 and located at Florisant, in the area near Cripple Creek mine. It's easy to assume that Lewis C. worked in the mines in that area. However, the 1900 census lists him as a farmer. Daughter Martha died there about 1895, and then wife Mary died in 1907.

In 1908 the Snaveley's moved to Utah. According to the 1910 census, Lewis C. and Lewis Vernon were employed at that time as farm hands by Joseph Burkholder in an area of Grand County called Mesa [Wilson Mesa?].

The same census record lists Lewis C.'s daughter, **Alta**, and husband, **Martin P. Fish**, whom she had married in Grainfield, Kansas. The record shows that Alta had given birth to four children, of whom only two were living. The Fish family was living near Castleton, in Castle Valley, upriver from Moab. Listed with them was a 14-year-old son, **Lewis C.**, and a daughter, **Lila M. Ray**, who, according to the census, was 24 years old and had been born in Kansas. Lila had a 2-year-old daughter named **Helen Ray**. We learned later that Lila had married Arthur Ray, 19 April 1906, in Moab.

We also learned that Lila M. was the first wife of Rowland "Roe" Saunders. She died during the flu epidemic in November 1918 in Fruita and is buried in the Elmwood Cemetery (see Roe Saunders' story).

Lewis Vernon "Vern" Snavely probably met **Selma Bertha Earp** in 1910/1911 (see the Earp history) when she was teaching at a little known school at Dewey Bridge, south of Cisco, Utah. They were married at Greenriver, Emery, Utah, 7 June 1911.

Some time in 1918 Vern and Selma moved to Fruita and purchased a home. (It was noted in the 1920 census that Vern, Selma and Lewis were living in Fruita). Louise Clow Likes, niece of Selma, tells an interesting story about that home. She said that Vern and Selma lived in the home in Fruita for awhile, and in 1920, after Vern purchased a relinquishment from James M. Morgan on a homestead in New Liberty, they dismantled the home and hauled it out to the homestead and reassembled it, piece by piece.

The Snavely's developed an attractive farmstead — the home itself was better by far than the average homestead shanty in New Liberty in the early days. They planted some poplar trees that provided ample shade for the home, and had an orchard and sizable garden area. Their corrals and out buildings were well arranged; they had a comfortable life.

It's likely that Lewis Case began to live with Vern and Selma not long after their marriage and continued to do so for the rest of his life. During his many years Lewis became a popular "old time fiddler," and it appears he won the hearts of people wherever he lived, especially the youngsters. He played for dances in the mining camps in Colorado and probably played for dances in the Moab/Castleton area. He was popular in Mesa County during the time he lived there also, and probably played for dances at New Liberty and Mack, though we have not been able to confirm that.

For several days in February 1926, *The Daily Sentinel* carried a glowing account of a Western Slope Championship Fiddling Contest that was held at the Avalon Theatre in Grand Junction. Lewis Snavely won the grand prize of $50 in gold in that contest. Prior to the final appearance on the night of February 27, numerous fiddlers had been eliminated in other phases of the contest. Lewis was the most popular choice among the audience for the final appearance. Sixteen hundred people were present to hear the fiddlers that night, the largest crowd ever assembled in that theatre. Many people were turned away, as there wasn't any seating or standing room available.

Here are some quotes from *The Daily Sentinel* article after the final contest:

Howls and shouts, the stamping of feet and clapping of hands of the vast audience greeted eight of the best fiddlers of the western slope as they stood on the stage and filled the house with the vibrant tones of the famed old tune, "Turkey in the Straw," as the concluding number of the eventful old fiddling contest. The theatre rocked on its foundation as it never rocked before.

And Mr. Snavely of Mack, aged 76, granddaddy of them all, was the star performer of the night and was accorded a thunderous ovation that drowned the other bursts of applause of the evening. He brought the house down when he played one of the ancient tunes while his son called off the square dance. Again, just before the final curtain brought an end to the event, while the eight star fiddlers played "Turkey in the Straw," he set the house into an uproar by dancing an old time jig in the old time way. His legs were stiff and wobbly after 76 years of hard usage, but it was a great jig.

Several months later, on 9 November 1926, Lewis Snavely died at the New Liberty farm home. As it was not uncommon in those days for family members to prepare the deceased for burial, Vern prepared the body and placed it in a homemade casket. A wake was held that night and the next day a funeral service was held in the home. Following that a funeral procession was led by a delivery van furnished by Chet Wright of Mack, bearing the casket to the Elmwood Cemetery at Fruita, where a grave-side service was held and the remains were laid to rest beside that of his granddaughter, Lila M. Fish Saunders.

The Daily Sentinel for 9 November 1926, carries notice of Lewis' death at age 88, but the age is erroneous, he was 77. The article also lauds his fame as "Mesa County's Champion Old Time Fiddler" and tells of his winning the fiddling championship at the Avalon Theater just a few months previous, in spite of his advanced years.

An obituary appeared in *The Daily Sentinel* of 14 November giving an account of his life and making it possible for us to add much to a good story about him. The article noted that "about 20of the New Liberty High School students attended the funeral, giving testimony of the esteem and respect they held for him."

Vern and Selma lived at New Liberty until February 1935, when they traded their farm to the Brisbin family in Hunter for the Brisbin store and 40-acre farm. Vern and Selma operated the store for several years. They then bought a home in Grand Junction where Selma died 26 February 1957. Vernon then moved to Glenwood Springs, Colorado, where he died 7 June 1975.

(Other families who lived on the Snavely farm after to the Snavelys were the **Merrits, McDaniels** and **Kessingers**)

June Spencer

Shirley Spencer

(Both photos courtesy of Delores Smith Likes)

Spencer

The Spencer story is compiled from a letter by June Spencer Alstatt Barnes.

Hearst and **Ruth Spencer** and two daughters, **June** and **Shirley**, moved to Mack in the summer of 1929. For a time, they operated the "Cities Service" gasoline station, which was probably what later became known as the "Last Chance" station with four little cabins out back that made it a "motel." Cities Service closed out later and it became a "Shell" station.

June remembers the "Gypsies" who camped in the vacant lot to the east of the station. They always provided lots of excitement and entertainment with their bonfire and dancing and singing far into the night. She says they were always gone when she awoke the next morning.

A son, **Roger**, was born while the family was living in Mack. He is now retired and lives in Florida.

Hearst was hired by the Uintah Railway and the family moved into one of the company houses. They lived there until the Uintah closed down in 1939. Mrs. J. L. Booth made mention in the Mack news items of the Spencer family moving to Grand Junction shortly after the demise of the Uintah.

The family lived in Grand Junction for about

two years, then Hearst was hired by the Rock Island Arsenal at Rock Island, Illinois. They worked there until both retired, then moved to Florida to be close to Shirley who had married by then and had three daughters.

June also worked at the arsenal until after the war when she and Amos Alstatt were married. (See more about June with the Alstatt story).

Stotts

Information is from news items and obituaries in *The Daily Sentinel.*

Willard Wilmot Stotts is one New Liberty homesteader that few, if any, of the people of the lower valley knew. We include a limited amount of information about the Stotts family. **Willard** and **Ella Boring Stotts** were mentioned earlier as having been the first citizens of the New Liberty community to marry (1920). They were probably married originally in Indiana around 1895. Boring may have been Ella's maiden surname. They resided for a time in Indiana and Ohio before moving to the Grand Valley in 1919.

Ella B. was born 9 July 1879 near Prattsfork, Ohio. She was the first news correspondent for the New Liberty community; her first news item appeared in *The Daily Sentinel,* 5 March 1926.

Willard and Ella had nine children:

Leon
Arley Allen
Athol Lester
Arthur W.
Sherley Everett
Willard James "Jim"
Harold S.
Helen
Elizabeth

We do not know their birth dates, birth places, nor their order of birth. Athol, Jim, Sherley, Elizabeth and Harold all lived at New

Liberty; Harold and Elizabeth attended New Liberty School.

Willard died at age 58 on 3 December 1929, at Big Piney, Wyoming. His obituary says he had been employed as a miner and had been living with his son, Arthur. His son, Athol, traveled to Big Piney and accompanied his father's body to Grand Junction for burial. The obituary says Willard's father, age 85, was still living in southern Ohio.

Ella's obituary said she went to Washington, D.C. in 1942 to live with Harold. She passed away there, 11 February 1943. Funeral services were held at Caledonia, Ohio, and she was buried there. That's probably near where she was born.

Arley Allen evidently was living with the family when they came to Grand Valley, before they moved to the homestead. He enlisted in the Navy in 1919 and served for 17 years before retiring because of ill health. He attained the rank of "Chief Aerographer" in 1926. He died 10 July 1939 at San Diego, California. His obituary says Arley was born in Pomeroy, Ohio, in 1901.

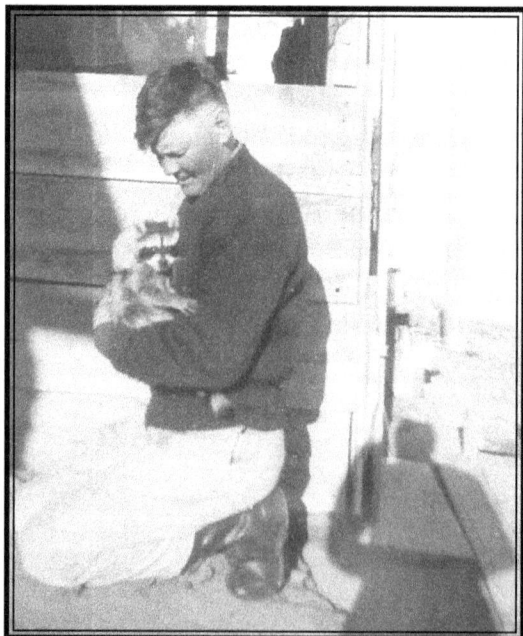

Athol Lester Stotts with his pet raccoon.
(Thomas/Morrow Collection)

Athol Lester was a veteran of World War I, having served in the Army in Germany. In 1923 he married **Nellie Schunter** of New Liberty. Nellie became New Liberty

Nellie and Athol Stotts in New Liberty.
(Mary Maluy Collection)

correspondent for *The Daily Sentinel* in September 1929, when her mother-in-law, Ella Stotts, left the community. We know little else about Athol and Nellie except that they moved to Sage, Wyoming. Both are deceased. (See Schunter history).

We should mention that for some time in the 1930s Athol and Nellie had a boy in their home named **Robert "Bob" Anderson**, who attended school at New Liberty. Many students of that time period will remember him. We don't know Bob's story, but it's apparent he had family who lived farther up the valley.

Willard James "Jim" lived in the community for several years. New Liberty news items in 1929 mentioned several times that Jim was employed at Watson, Utah. He may have been working in the gilsonite mines or for the Uintah Railway. He was married to **Ethel Brayton**, probably in 1930. A baby boy was born in January 1931, but only lived a short time. Jim and Ethel were later divorced.

Sherley lost the sight in one eye when he was nine years old, soon the other eye went blind in sympathy. A strange phenomenon! He attended a school for the blind in Colorado Springs, graduating in the spring of 1929. Shortly after he began further schooling at Mesa College in Grand Junction. He tuned pianos part time to help pay his way through college.

Sherley went on to acquire BA and MA degrees from Colorado University, majoring in psychology. The state furnished a person to read for him during his university years. That person read his course work for him while Sherley took notes in Braille.

He was able to accomplish many things in spite of his handicap. The following article appeared in *The Daily Sentinel* just before Christmas of 1934.:

Sherley Stotts of Mack, blind student at the University of Colorado famed for his overcoming his affliction, has added another to his list of accomplishments. He is the author of an article entitled, "What's in the Cosmopolitan Club," of which he is a member, appearing in the 1933–34 year book.

Among other of Stotts' accomplishments, he is a candidate for the degree of Master of Arts in Psychology at the June 11 commencement of the university. He received his bachelor of arts in the same subject in 1933. Before entering the university Stotts was a student at Grand Junction Junior college.

While a student, he has won the intramural wrestling championship in the 165-pound class. Recently he scaled the third Flat-iron, one of the most difficult rock climbs near Boulder, with the ease and skill of a veteran. Always he walks the campus and streets of Boulder with no guide or cane. He has worked his way through school by tuning pianos.

In an article in *The Daily Sentinel* dated 27 September 1934, it was noted that Sherley Stotts had been chosen to teach psychology courses in the adult education program. Another article in September 1937 noted that in August just past he had gone through a month of training and had acquired a "Seeing-Eye" dog named "Ranger."

Elizabeth married **William B. Price**, some time previous to 1929. He was a World War I veteran who had homesteaded on the east side of Badger Wash, just below the canal. William and Elizabeth had one child we know of; they named her **Ella Lucille**. After Bill's death Elizabeth married a man named **Lester Bayes**. We believe they lived on the Bill Price farm for a few years. Elizabeth's brother Arley's obituary locates her in Roswell, New Mexico in 1939.

The Stotts family, after homesteading in New Liberty in 1919, spent some winters in Grand Junction. Later, an item in *The Daily Sentinel* of 18 September 1929, said that Ella B., Sherley and Harold moved to Grand Junction. Another item on 17 June 1930 said Ella and Harold moved back to the farm at New Liberty, but Sherley went to the east slope where he tuned pianos. Harold graduated from Fruita Union High School in 1937. After that they moved to Boulder, Colorado. At the time of Arley's death, Ella B. and Harold were living in Boulder.

Harold attended New Liberty School but he may not have graduated from the eighth grade there. If you turn back to the New Liberty School History you will see that Harold was an outstanding student.

We don't know what kind of work Harold went into. Seems like there was a rumor that Harold was living in Las Vegas a few years ago.

Summers

Parts of the following stories were supplied by Evelyn Bush Welch, some by Ivan Leroy Likes, some from obituaries and news items from *The Daily Sentinel*.

Seaburn Simon Summers† was born 23 October 1870, in Madison County, Iowa, the youngest of eight children born to Eli Summers and Louisa T. Francis. He spent his early life in Kansas and Missouri.

† That's the best we can do with his name; the first name may have been spelled "Seabern" or "Seabran" or "Seaborn." His middle name, or perhaps his first name, could have been Silas. He was known variously as "S. S.," "Si" or "Seab."

(Above left) Seab and Ruperta Summers, 1905. (Above right) Seab and Ida Gregory Summers, 1906. (Lower left) Ida Gregory at age 19. (Lower right) Seab and family on 19 October 1906, at Frank Williams'. L-R: Seab, Ruperta and Ida Gregory Summers, and in front Marie Gregory. *(Photos courtesy of Leroy Likes)*

(Above right) Seab and Josephine Brayton Summers on their wedding day in 1923 in Missouri. *(Photo courtesy of Charlene Brayton Eldridge)* (Above left) 9 June 1919, Ida and Seab Summers sitting in front of the house they built in New Liberty, with the incubator and baby chicks. One flock is three weeks old and the second flock is one week old. (Center) A 1930s view of the house Seab built in New Liberty in 1919. (Below) A rear view of the Summers' New Liberty house when it was built in 1919. *(Photos courtesy of Leroy Likes)*

He was married in about 1893 to **Minnie Brown** and they had one daughter, **Ruperta (Steele)**, born 25 August 1894, at Richland, Missouri.

Minnie died in 1895, and on 18 March 1901, Seab married **Ida Gregory**. Ida was apparently a widow who had a daughter named Marie. They lived for awhile at Worland, Missouri. While living at Worland, Seab and his brother, William "Bill," owned and operated a shovel with which they dug coal. They would first dig off the overburden, then load the coal on wagons pulled by teams of horses. Later Seab and Bill bought a thresher and did custom threshing for farmers in the area.

Seab, Ida and Ruperta probably came to western Colorado in 1918. Seab and Ruperta filed on homesteads north and west of the corner of 6 and S Roads, in 1919 and 1920. Ida died in September 1921, probably at New Liberty; we have been unable to find any other information on her. She may have been buried in Kansas City. We do know that Seab and Ida were listed in New Liberty in the 1920 census.

Seab was a friendly fellow, well liked by his neighbors. He was forever helping someone in the neighborhood. He may have been the first farmer in the New Liberty community to use a tractor in his farm work — a Fordson. He was mechanically inclined, always looking for ways to improve farm equipment. He was an inventor and had patented several of his ideas.

Seab loved to associate with young people and would often host sleigh-rides and hay-rides. Once he was at the favorite community skating pond on the Daily farm, south of highway 6 and 50, when he saw an opportunity to add to the fun by driving his Model "T" onto the ice to tow those skating and sledding.

He owned a thresher and did threshing for his neighbors for many years. To power that thresher, he and Clyde Likes Sr. once bought a steam tractor at a saw mill on Glade Park. Clyde drove the tractor all that distance at about three miles per hour. That may have been the only steam tractor ever used in New Liberty.

Ruperta Summers Steele, Seab and Effie Wilsea Summers, taken on Seab's 78th birthday, 23 October 1948. *(Photo courtesy of Leroy Likes)*

Seab married **Josephine Brayton** in Missouri in 1923. After 13 stormy years they were divorced.

In about 1935 Seab sold his farm to Charles Brayton and moved to Fruita. Later Charles sold out and moved his family to Fruita. He and Seab were partners in an automotive repair shop in Fruita for some time.

Several years after he was divorced from Josie, Seab married **Effie Wilsea Biddick**, a widow who had lived around the valley for a long time. She was the mother of Charles Wilsea, a Grand Junction automobile dealer. After their marriage they lived for several years on her farm, north of Fruita, until she passed away in December 1950. In 1954 Seab moved to Grand Junction to live with his daughter, Ruperta.

Seab died 20 February 1962, in the Teller Arms Nursing home in Grand Junction at the age of 91 and was buried in Kansas City, Missouri.

Bill Summers sitting (center) on his combine, 1920s.
(Photo courtesy of Leroy Likes)

William Mason and Ruperta Summers Steele
(Photo courtesy of Leroy Likes)

Ruperta spent her childhood in Richland, Worland and Bates Counties, Missouri. She graduated from Hume High School at Hume, Missouri, in 1914. She married **William Mason Steele** 27 March 1921, in Kansas City, Missouri. There were no children. William Steele was accidentally electrocuted and died in Kansas City in October 1935.

Ruperta served as secretary to Harry S. Truman when he was county judge and during his first term as a United States Senator. She moved to Denver in 1939 where she was employed at the Colorado State Selective Service Appeals Board until that was terminated at the end of World War II. She then moved to Grand Junction in 1948, where she worked for the Atomic Energy Commission and the United States Postal Service, retiring in 1959. She never remarried.

Ruperta died 27 August 1988 at the Bethesda Nursing Home in Grand Junction, at age 94. She was buried in the Mount Moriah Cemetery in Kansas City, Missouri.

William "Bill" Henry Summers, an older brother of Seab, was born 1 May 1867, in Madison County, Iowa, and spent his early life there. Bill was a miner and prospector, as was one of his brothers, Matthew Reason Summers, the father of Ada Summers Bush. Bill came to the Grand Valley in about 1930 and spent quite a bit of time in the New Liberty community with his brother, Seab, and his niece, Ada Bush. He was quite attentive to the needs of his niece, Ada, doing whatever he could to help her.

Bill never married. He spent his last 16 years in Grand Junction where he died 29 July 1945.

Sumnicht

Most of the following history was supplied by Grace Eloise Arbuckle Gray, daughter of Tom and Mollie Arbuckle and granddaughter of August and Anna Sumnicht. Some information came from news items and obituaries from *The Daily Sentinel* and *The Deseret News* of Salt Lake City.

August Frederick Daniel Sumnicht was born at Alt Damero, Pomerania, Germany, 7

February 1854, a son of Frederick Wilhelm Sumnicht and Louisa Radke. August was the fifth child and the only boy in a family of eight. When he was 2 years old, August, with his parents and four older sisters, came to America, settling first at Watertown, Wisconsin, and later moving to Seymour, Wisconsin. He attended school in Wisconsin and received a good education. He was an avid reader, having a special interest in law and politics. Although he had no formal education in law, he continued to pursue an interest in law to add to his legal knowledge. He also learned the carpentry trade, a craft he continued to use throughout his life.

August married **Anna Eloise Nurnberg**, 6 June 1883, at Seymour, Outagamie, Wisconsin. Anna was the oldest of nine children. She born at Seymour, 17 September 1862, to Joachim Christian Nurnberg and Frances "Fannie" Harris. Her father was born in Germany and her mother in England.

Anna was a rather tall girl, about five feet eight inches. Her crowning glory was her thick, wavy, long, auburn hair. Being strong and healthy and the oldest in her family, she helped her father with the farm work. But she also helped care for the younger children. While she was growing up she became proficient in many kinds of needle work: tatting, knitting, crocheting, battenberg, dressmaking, millinery, embroidery, and quilting. These arts she later taught to her daughters, granddaughters and great-granddaughters.

She grew to adulthood in the Seymour area, graduated from high school and then became a teacher.

August and Anna had seven children, five girls and two boys:

Mollie Elsa (Arbuckle), 2 July 1884, Seymour, Wisconsin

The Sumnicht family in 1911 in Carbondale, Colorado. Back row, L-R: Lester Warren, William Ray, Mable "Mato" Alice, Jessa Eugenia and Freda Frances Sumnicht. Front row: Mollie Elsa, Anna Eloise, Florence Ena and August Frederick Daniel Sumnicht. *(Photo courtesy of Grace Arbuckle Gray)*

August Sumnicht as a rural mail carrier with his horse and cart in Carbondale, Colorado, in 1916. *(Photo courtesy of Grace Arbuckle Gray)*

Jessa Eugenia (Gibbs), born 27 June 1887, Seymour

Mable "Mato" Alice (Haifley), 11 May 1889, Carbondale, Colorado

William Ray, 24 April 1891, Carbondale

Freda Frances (Shadle), 11 April 1896, Carbondale

Lester Warren, 24 April 1901, Carbondale

Florence Ena (Brach), 22 June 1906, Carbondale

The first two children, Mollie and Jessa, were born at Seymour, Outagamie, Wisconsin. August and Anna and their two little daughters loaded the covered wagon and joined a caravan headed for Carbondale, Colorado, in 1887, where the other five children were born. Two of Anna's uncles and her parents had moved there in 1880 and 1882. August and Anna first lived in a small cottage, but as the family continued to grow August built a two-story, four-bedroom house. They lived on a small acreage where they had a garden and some fruit trees. They also had some pasture where they kept horses, cows, chickens and pigs.

August continued to pursue his carpentry trade; for a time he worked as foreman of a gang, building depots and section houses for the D&RGW Railroad. After the work for the railroad was completed, August went to work for the U.S. Postal Service as a rural mail carrier. He drove his route with a two-wheel cart pulled by one horse. During the winter when the snow was deep he rode a horse and used another to pack the mail.

The children attended grade school in Carbondale, but at first there was no high school. However, there was a high school at Aspen, Colorado. Since Anna's sister, Mable Nevitt, lived at Aspen, each of the three older girls went to live with Aunt Mable during school terms and graduated from Aspen High School.

Later, a high school was built at Carbondale and William Ray and Freda graduated there.

August and Anna and their two youngest children, Lester and Ena, moved to Fruita, Colorado, in the summer of 1918. By that time the older children had married and moved away. August and Anna traveled in wagons with all their household belongings, including Anna's piano. In Fruita they moved into a rented house and Lester enrolled in Fruita Union High School as a senior, Ena enrolled in the 8th grade.

Land records reveal the names of three of the Sumnicht family who filed on land in 1919 on the west side of the New Liberty community: Section 13 T 9S R 104W. They were **William R.**, **Lester W.** and **August**, as well as Mollie's husband, **Thomas B. Arbuckle.** None of that land was ever developed to farm except unit "M," the present (1995) home of Richard and Edith Young.

(Above) Anna Sumnicht quilting on the front porch of Mollie and Tom Arbuckles home in Fruita, Colorado. (Right) Anna and August Sumnicht in July 1929. (Below) The Sumnicht family in 1930. Back row, L-R: Lester Warren, Freda Frances (Shadle), Florence Ena (Brach) and William Ray Sumnicht. Front row: Jessa Eugenia (Gibbs), Anna Eloise, August Frederick Daniel, Mabel "Mato" Alice (Haifley) and Mollie Elsa (Arbuckle) Sumnicht. *(Photos courtesy of Grace Arbuckle Gray)*

Anna Sumnicht working in her garden in front of the"battenboard cabin" she and August built in 1919 at New Liberty. The tent they also lived in is visible in the background. *(Photo courtesy of Grace Arbuckle Gray)*

August built a two-room homestead shack and set about acquiring farm equipment and livestock. He planted some land on the hill; apparently about 50 acres was all that was ever developed on the homestead. The rest of the family moved to New Liberty in the summer of 1919, but there was not enough room in the cabin for Anna's piano so she gave it to her granddaughter, Grace Arbuckle. Years later, in 1945, that piano was crated and shipped to Grace at Palo Alto, California. Still later, in 1967, it was passed on to Grace's daughter who lives at Fair Oaks, California. In 1919 August built a more comfortable two-bedroom home on the farm and Anna bought another piano.

An interesting account involving Anna was found in the Fruita news items in *The Daily Sentinel* of 27 July 1920:

Mrs. A. Sumnicht, mother of Mrs. Tom Arbuckle, was hurt by a cow Thursday evening. She was badly bruised and one ankle was thrown out of place. Mrs. Sumnicht lives below Mack.

At some point in time there was another accident involving Anna that happened on "Weir's Hill." Ena was driving home from town with her mother and failed to get up enough speed to make the hill in "high." She had to shift gears just short of the top and killed the engine. The car began to roll back down the hill and Anna panicked and bailed out. The car ran over one of her ankles and broke it. She had to be rushed back to Fruita for medical attention.

August and Anna lived in New Liberty until August's health began to fail. Then he and Anna went to Fruita to stay with daughter Mollie. August died in Fruita at age 77, 30 September 1931. Afterward Anna divided her time between daughters Mollie and Ena. In 1954, at age 92, while living with Mollie and granddaughter Grace in Palo Alto, California, Anna fell and broke her hip. She died shortly after in a hospital in Palo Alto. August and Anna are both buried in Elmwood Cemetery at Fruita. They had 23 grandchildren; 17 of them were still living as of December 1995.

Mollie Elsa Sumnicht married **Thomas Bryant Arbuckle** 27 September 1908, at Carbondale, Colorado. Mollie was the oldest child of August and Anna. Many people of the Lower Valley knew Tom and Mollie. They operated a creamery and poultry/produce store in Fruita from 1919 to 1937. They had five children, all born in Fruita:

Florence, born 14 July 1909 (died in infancy)
Thomas Marvin, 5 June 1910
Grace Eloise (Gray), 10 January 1912
Ralph Willard, 29 May 1915
Edward Vernon, 11 March 1918

The children attended school in Fruita; all graduated from Fruita Union High School.

In 1937 Tom's health began to fail, so they leased the store. Mollie started working as a clerk in the Fruita Post Office; later she served as Acting Postmaster. She received her commission as Postmaster in 1939 and retired in 1947.

Tom and Mollie and mother Anna moved to Palo Alto, California, in December 1947. Thomas died there, 24 July 1952, and Mollie, 23 September 1968. Both are buried at Alta Mesa Cemetery at Palo Alto.

Lester Warren was born 24 April 1901, in Carbondale, Colorado. He graduated from Fruita Union High School in 1919. His obituary from *The Deseret News* (Salt Lake City) says he served in the military in World War I; if so he must have been very young, as he was only 17 when the war ended. His niece, Grace Arbuckle Gray, suggests there may have been an ROTC program, or something similar, that he was involved in.

Later, in June 1923, he graduated from Colorado Agricultural College at Fort Collins. After graduation he moved to Bingham Canyon, Utah, and joined his brother, William, at the Kennecott Copper mine.

On 20 August 1930, Lester married **Elizabeth "Beth" Clara Meade** in Midvale, Utah. As newlyweds they moved into a new home in Copperton, Utah. There they raised a daughter and son and lived there the remainder of their lives.

Lester was recognized as a great local baseball player. Injuries prevented him from playing professionally, but he did manage an industrial baseball team for many years. He retired in 1966.

Elizabeth died at Copperton, Utah, 25 October 1960, but Lester lived until 7 March 1992; he was nearing his 91st birthday.

Florence Ena Sumnicht was the youngest child. She was born 22 June 1906, at Carbondale, and was about 12 years old when the family moved to New Liberty. She went to school in Fruita, graduating from Fruita Union High School in 1924. She then went on to earn a teacher's certificate, graduating from Colorado University at Boulder, Colorado, 10 June 1924.

Ena taught school in Fruita several years before her marriage to **John Brach**, of Loma, 17 January 1931, at Provo, Utah. The first year they were married they lived on the Sumnicht homestead. The next year they bought a farm on 12 1/2 Road near Loma. In 1944 they bought the Mayne place to the south, also on 12 1/2 Road. In January 1946 Ena started teaching at Loma Elementary School, where she taught for 25 years.

Ena and John had a daughter and three sons:

Florence (Chandler)
John "Jack" W.
Tony Lee
James "Jimmy" Ray

Jimmy died at age 14; he was suffering from Bright's disease and had been receiving special treatment in a hospital at Compton, California. An article in *The Daily Sentinel* of 8 March 1954, told of his being flown by ambulance plane to Walker Field at Grand Junction, but he died en route; he was buried in Elmwood Cemetery at Fruita.

Florence now lives in Fruita; Jack and Tony at Loma.

Ena died of a heart attack 6 April 1971. She was buried in Elmwood Cemetery at Fruita. John still lives at Loma.

Sweitzer

The following is compiled from a letter sent to us by Oscar Sweitzer.

Oscar Sweitzer was born in Grand Junction, 13 June 1916, to **Oscar Sweitzer** and **Madge Herron**. Oscar Sr. deserted the family in 1919, so Madge raised the children alone. The 1920 census shows the mother, **Madge Sweitzer**, age 26, and her children, **Oscar**, age 3 1/2, and **Emily**, age 1 year and 7 months, living in Grand Junction at 824 North 7th St. Madge's occupation is given as, "Sales Lady for Curtis Publishing Co." Oscar and Emily never knew their father.

Oscar and Marcella Wells Sweitzer, in 1983
(Photo courtesy of Oscar Sweitzer)

Madge, daughter of John H. Herron and Jessie W. Herron, was born 7 November 1895, at Ainsworth, Brown, Nebraska. The Herron's came to Colorado about 1896. John H. Herron is listed in the 1920 census in the Grand Junction 7th Precinct as a "Stockman." (See Orval Herron history).

According to Oscar's time-line letter, the family moved to Loma in 1923, where Madge's father, John Herron, owned a grocery store. In 1924 they moved again to Montrose. In 1926 they came back to Loma and Madge took over operation of the Loma Hotel. A few years later they moved to a small dairy farm near Crawford, Colorado. After a few years there they moved to the Orval Herron farm on the Red Mesa north of Mack.

During World War II Madge Herron Sweitzer worked for the U. S. Navy on Treasure Island in San Francisco Bay. After the war she moved to Sacramento, where she died on 1 May 1981.

Oscar graduated from Fruita Union High School in 1933, and through that summer he worked for his mother's cousin, Robert M. Cox, on his farm in New Liberty. In 1934 and 1935 he worked for his uncle, Orval Herron. In the summer of 1936 he "punched cows" on West Douglas Creek for Ralph Wells, not far north of Douglas Pass.

In the summer of 1937 he went to work for the contractor who was building the Grand Valley Rural Power Lines throughout the lower valley. He worked for some time as a "hole digger" and "pole setter" and soon had an opportunity to learn how to climb poles to do "lineman's work." He then made a career of lineman, continuing with that until retirement.

After the job in Grand Valley was finished the company sent him to Nebraska, where he worked for a year. Then they moved back to Delta, Colorado, where he helped build the rural power lines there.

On 14 April 1939, at Fruita, Oscar married **Marcella Wells**, who was born at Messex, Colorado, 7 August 1919, to Edward Wells and Elizabeth "Libbie" Humbarger (see Wells story).

Oscar and Marcella had two children:

Nancy, born 16 May 1945, Renton, King, Washington
Edward, 15 May 1952, Kirkland, King, Washington
There are now four grandchildren.

In 1942 Oscar and Marcella went to Seattle for a visit and found there was a shortage of linemen. Oscar soon went to work for Puget Sound Power and Light Company. They lived at Renton, Washington, until 1951, when they moved to Kirkland, Washington. From that time Oscar worked in the office as a trouble shooter. In 1979 he retired after working for that company for almost 37 years.

Swyhart

From a history written by Frances Elizabeth Meyer Turner Miller. Information is also from obituaries and news items from *The Daily Sentinel,* and *Salt Lake Tribune..*

P. E. "Pete" Swyhart was born 14 April 1872, at Parsons, Labette, Kansas, one of a family of 18 children. He spent his childhood in Kansas. His second marriage was to **Della Irene Lane (Meyer)**, 22 June 1922, at Girard, Crawford, Kansas.

Pete and Della had two sons:

Richard
Oliver

Della was born 7 February 1894, at Stroud, Lincoln, Oklahoma, the youngest of 13 children of John Christopher Lane and Sarah Elizabeth Groves. Della was married first to **Joseph J. Meyer**, 3 June 1918, at Lamar, Barton, Kansas. They had two children:

Della Irene Lane and Joseph J. Meyer with Frances Elizabeth Meyer, 4 months old, 1919. *(Photo courtesy of Frances Meyer Miller)*

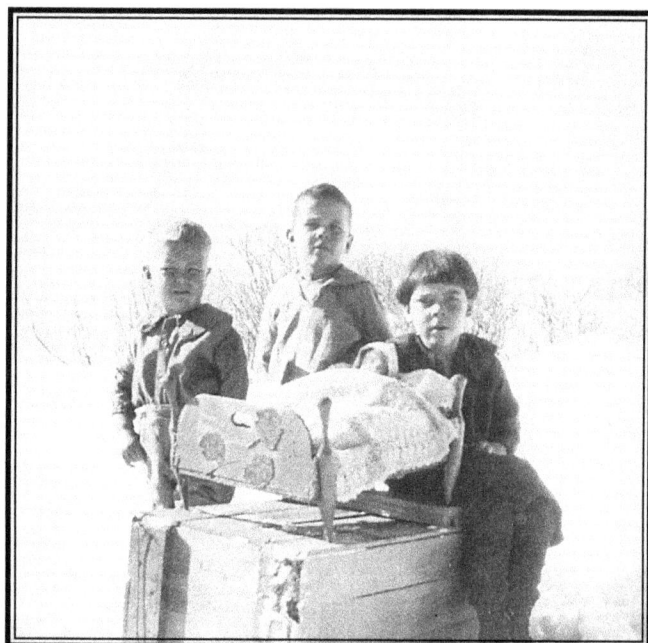

Richard Swyhart, age 3, Joseph Christopher Meyer, age 5, and Frances Elizabeth Meyer, age 6, in New Liberty. Della made the doll bed for Frances. *(Photo courtesy of Frances Meyer Miller)*

Frances Elizabeth Meyer (Turner, Miller), born 13 May 1919, Breezy Hill, Crawford, Kansas
Joseph Christopher Meyer, 27 September 1920, Breezy Hill

The Swyhart family moved from Kansas to Ridgway, Colorado in 1923. Frances said they traveled by covered wagon and horse and buggy. Pete drove the wagon with Della and the children following behind in a surrey. Frances was six years old then and was given the responsibility of Richard, age two months, while her mother drove the buggy. It took three months for the trip. Pete went to work at Ridgway as a coal miner. They moved to New Liberty in 1934.

The Swyharts established a crude home (a dugout) in the southwest corner of the community near Jim Sanders'. Later they built an adobe house. The boys, Joe, Richard and Oliver, all attended New Liberty School and Fruita Union High School.

When Pete and Della left New Liberty they moved to Mack and established a home in one of the old Uintah company houses. Pete passed away 31 July 1953, at age 81, in Pueblo, Colorado. Della lived alone in Mack for several years until she needed continuous care. She

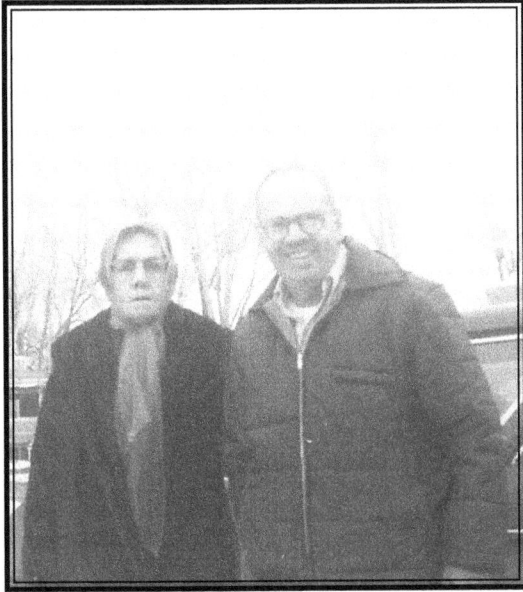

Della Swyhart and Joseph Christopher Meyer. *(Photo courtesy of Frances Meyer Miller)*

Della Swyhart and Frances Meyer Miller. *(Photo courtesy of Frances Meyer Miller)*

area for several years to be near her aging mother. At some point in time she married Darve Miller, but within a few years they were divorced. After her mother died she moved back to Salt Lake City and lived in an apartment complex in North Salt Lake City for about 23 years. She was active in the LDS Church and served a mission in West Virginia and then at the Salt Lake Temple Square. After she began to have health problems she went to live in a nursing home. She died 3 February 1997, in Salt Lake City, at age 77. She also was buried in Redwood Memorial Estates in Salt Lake City.

stayed in Lower Valley Nursing Home in Fruita until August 1980. At that time she was transferred to Evergreen Care Center at Montrose. Della passed away on her 87th birthday, 7 February 1981, at Montrose. She had been a resident of the Mack area for 49 years.

On 22 June 1934, **Frances Meyer** married **George Philander Turner**, son of **Bert** and **Rhoda Turner**, who lived on the Claude Taylor farm in New Liberty (see Turner story).

George and Frances had two boys and two girls:

Thomas
Herbert
Neva (Tanner)
Yvonne (Christensen)

George and Frances lived in the New Liberty community for several years while George helped construct the New Liberty School building during 193 5/36. Later he went to Clifton with the same contractor to build another school.

Then the family moved to Salt Lake City and George secured employment with the Union Pacific Railroad. George died in Salt Lake City, 16 December 1965, at age 56. He was buried at Redwood Memorial Estates.

Frances went back to live in the Mack/Fruita

Frances Miller, a missionary on Salt Lake Temple Square, 1989. *(Photo courtesy of Tom and Dixie Turner)*

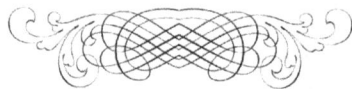

Thomas

Following is a history of the Thomas family, written by Eugene Thomas, Editor and Publisher of *The Fruita Times*. The history appeared in *The Fruita Times* 15 August 1991. There are some additions from the personal knowledge of the author.

Floyd Rush Thomas was born 29 August 1895, at Towner, Kiowa, Colorado, to **Leonard Thomas** and **Ida May Field**. His parents and older brother, Charles, and sister, Olive, had only recently moved to Towner from Merna, Nebraska (near Broken Bow). Leonard Thomas was born 4 April 1856, at Savanna, Illinois, on the Mississippi River. His parents were French-Canadians, living first at St. Albans, Vermont, after they came to the U.S. I've been told that Leonard's mother declined to learn to speak English and that Leonard spoke only French until he was six years old. I don't recall his speaking any French in the few years that I knew him before his death.

Ida died 29 August 1900 — my dad's fifth birthday. Grandpa Thomas apparently didn't keep in touch with her family, so we know virtually nothing about her.

Leonard farmed in the Towner area and for awhile was a partner in a store in Towner. He also served as a Kiowa County Colorado Commissioner. He would take the train (Missouri Pacific) to Eads to attend commissioner's meetings. He built two houses while in Towner. Leonard never remarried; and after Dad homesteaded in New Liberty, Leonard came to live with him. Some time after Dad and Mom were married, they built a one-room cabin for him separate from the family dwelling. Leonard lived there for several years; and I have many memories of visiting with him there. The cabin was located at the northwest corner of the original farm, several hundred feet from the main house.

At some point in time Grandpa decided to move to Grand Junction. He and John U. Daily (Ed's and Al's father) shared an apartment on Pitkin Avenue. for a time. Then Leonard's health began to fail. He was in the Fruita Hospital for awhile, then moved to Woodworth Rest Home at Appleton, Colorado. He died there 29 September 1940.

I believe Grandpa must have helped Dad with the farm and in other ways after he moved to New Liberty. From the time I remember him, he was crippled with arthritis and other infirmities of age, so was not able to do much. He was 84 when he died, and I was eight. (*New Liberty* news items relate that son Dave accompanied his father's body to the home town of Towner, where he was buried. — author)

Floyd attended Towner School through grade 11. It was not possible to graduate from high school at Towner, so he attended Holly High School at Holly, Colorado, for his senior year, graduating in June 1913. I remember Dad saying that even though he was born in Colorado, he never saw any mountains until he was 19 years old. I don't know what attracted him to Grand Valley, but he came here in 1914 and went to work for Art Swartzlander at Loma.

When Floyd came to the western slope in 1914, he was engaged in orchard and general farm work at Loma. He worked at the copper mine at Bingham Canyon, Utah, during the winter of 1916, then enlisted in the Army in 1917 and served for 29 months during World War I. He was a private 1st Class in the Cavalry. While he was in the Army he became afflicted with rheumatic fever, which left him with heart damage. He coped with the disability for many years; and up to the time of his death it was considered a service-connected disability, so in the last four years of his life he was permitted to stay at the Veteran's Hospital Nursing Home at Grand Junction.

In 1919, after the war, he returned to Loma and in 1920 worked for awhile for Guy Gerry.

The 1920 census shows Floyd with Gerrys. Gene who said that at the time of the Mack/New Liberty reunion, Julia Gerry Gosnel told him that Floyd stayed with the Gerry family in the Loma community at that time. She gave Gene a copy of a picture he had never seen before, showing Floyd with a motorcycle. — author

That year Floyd filed on a homestead in the New Liberty community, then moved onto the land in 1921 and began the "proving up" process by constructing the buildings, fences, ditches, etc. I've always been amazed that he was able to lay out an irrigation system that required very few changes later. He said he did it with a 2 x 4 and a level. The system also included several little wooden drops and some other wooden boxes in the ditches to control the water.

He and his dad built a small house to live in, did some landscaping, including some pine trees, one of which survived, and some poplars which are still surviving, and some plum, apricot and cherry trees. He built a shop, chicken house and barn out of some squared pieces of sandstone hauled in from nearby. He then roofed them with poles and straw. He gathered lots more rocks out of the fields to make the land easier to till.

The story was told that Floyd had his eye on Estellene for several years while he waited for her to become old enough for marriage. — author

Floyd married **Marjorie Estellene Morrow** 20 December 1930. After marriage Dad and Mom had a house hauled out from Mack (Herschel Shook told me in about 1960 that he built that house) and that is where we three children grew up:

Hubert Eugene, born 7 December 1931, in Grand Junction
Curtis Emerson, 27 March 1938, Fruita
Alice Kathleen, 30 June 1941, Fruita

Dad grew sugar beets in the early years but didn't like dealing with the necessary hired help involved, so had discontinued that before I was old enough to remember. He grew potatoes for awhile, but quit that also and concentrated on pinto beans, corn, barley and alfalfa. He sold alfalfa both for hay and for seed.

We usually had a milk cow and raised and butchered calves for our own use. When I was very young Dad raised pigs and calves to sell. We always had chickens and would often take eggs to the Fruita Co-op to apply on the grocery bill. We also occasionally took a little cream to Arbuckle's or Parish's Cream Station in Fruita.

Dad and Mom bought a piece of land adjacent to the original farm from neighbor Benjamin "Art" Harrison in about 1937, and that gave us more farm land. Dad put in many hours and days of work leveling that land over the next few years.

Dad never had much patience as a teacher, so there were some rather basic things, such as milking a cow, that I never learned because I didn't show much aptitude. I did help with a lot of things around the farm, however.

Dad did all the work with horses until he bought his first and only tractor about 1937. Before he bought it he did the heavier tasks with four horses. Then, after he bought the tractor, he sold two of the horses and continued to use the remaining two for a lot of work well into the 1940s. When I was old enough to ride the implements, he cut off the tongues and pulled them with the tractor. I remember riding and operating the bean and corn planter; the sprayer and the sulky rake. Dad had a pull plow he could control from the tractor, so he didn't need help with that. He later got a tractor-mounted mower he could also operate without help.

Dad tended toward a less labor-intensive operation as time went on. In the early years threshing involved hauling the bundles of grain or shocks of beans to a stationary threshing machine, which, in Dad's case, was probably Percy Blaser's. Then he, Max Bainter and John Morrow bought a combine which cut and threshed the grain in a single operation. With a pick-up attachment they were able to thresh the pinto beans out of the windrow. The co-op ownership didn't work out and Dad bought the others' shares of the machine and continued to use it as long as he operated the farm.

Haying took a lot of hand work in the early days, too. Later Dad got a Jayhawk stacker, which was attached to and pushed ahead of the tractor. He and I both got pretty good at driving it, but there were a few breaks before

(Above) Uncle Lawrence home on leave, 24 August 1941. L-R: Curtis Thomas, age three, Uncle Lawrence Morrow, age 20; and Eugene Thomas, age nine. (Upper right) L-R: Alice Kathleen, age nine months; Hubert Eugene, age 10; and Curtis Emerson , age four. (Upper center) The Thomas family in the 70s. L-R: Eugene, Estellene, Floyd, Kathleen and Curtis. (Below) The Floyd Thomas family in the late 1970s. Back row, L-R: Curtis Emerson Thomas, Estellene Morrow Thomas, Margaret Gibbs Morrow, Floyd Rush Thomas and Hubert Eugene Thomas. Front: Jay Pershing, Alice Kathleen Thomas Pershing and Pat Kresha Thomas. *(Photos courtesy of Eugene Thomas)*

we mastered it. [Actually this was the sweep-rake used to haul the hay to the Jayhawk stacker: See Crops and Machinery. — author]

During their many years at New Liberty Floyd and Estellene were very active in community affairs. Floyd served on the New Liberty School Board as well as the Fruita Union High School Board. Not everything on the farm nor in my parents' relationship was rosy. Mom always said she didn't want to live on a farm, and Dad had promised he would get away from it when they got married. Even so, she was active in a lot of things in the community and seemed to enjoy that and got a lot of satisfaction from it.

By the mid-'40s or so they talked a lot of selling, and I think they had the place on the market at one time. They did sell it in 1955 and purchased the Mulford place on 25 Road, northwest of Grand Junction. The place contained 15 acres and Dad took the tractor and some equipment to farm it.

Mom had done a little house-keeping and waitress work and had worked at the canning factory by about the time I was in high school. Aunt Elizabeth went to work at the State Home and Training School at Grand Junction in the early '50s. Mom went to work there too, as did my Dad. Mom was hurt on the job and was not able to go back to work after that. Dad continued to work there until he reached the mandatory retirement age, then went to work as custodian at the Mesa County Courthouse. He was in his 70s when he retired from that.

The house on 25 Road burned down in 1956, and my parents lost most of their furniture and personal belongings. They put up a temporary dwelling and stayed in that for about another year, then moved to Orchard Mesa; living first on Collum Lane, then Miriam St., and, since 1969, on Pine St.

After spending the last four years of his life in the VA Nursing home, Floyd passed away 8 December 1989, at age 94. Estellene continued to live in the home on Orchard Mesa, under the care of Eugene and his son, Joe. As she grew older she began to show symptoms of Alzheimer's disease and eventually, February 1992, she was placed in the care of Family Health West at Fruita, where she died 21 July 1992, at age 81. Both she and Floyd are buried in the Memorial Gardens Cemetery at Grand Junction.

About Eugene:

I, Eugene, was born 7 December 1931, at the Millard Gilbert residence at 6th and White Avenue in Grand Junction, in Aunt Sarah's apartment, where my Mom went for my birth.

The farm at New Liberty was my home during my growing-up years. I went to New Liberty School, starting in 1937 and graduating in 1946. It took me nine years instead of the usual eight because of an injury and illness in the spring of 1945. I'm not sure when it happened, but I cracked my left hip socket and the joint later disintegrated. Along with that injury, though probably unrelated, I had an infection that caused a fever of up to 106 degrees, and had not penicillin just become available for civilians, would probably have died.

A low grade fever persisted for several months, so my parents kept me in bed quite awhile, restricting my activities, so I didn't finish the eighth grade in 1945. The hip problem persisted, and in September of 1945, Dr. J. S. Orr sent me to Dr. Atha Thomas (no relation), an orthopedist in Denver, who put me in the Children's Hospital for a couple of months in a full length body cast and also put me on a diet to take off some of the fat that had accumulated through months of inactivity. They then put me in a shorter cast and, with crutches, let me go home. In 1946, I returned to New Liberty and, with the aid of crutches, finished the eighth grade. I was still on crutches during my freshman year in high school in 1946-47. I returned to Denver for periodic check-ups for several years.

The hip joint stabilized and, although the movement in it was limited, it functioned pretty well for about 20 years before I began having trouble and it gradually worsened until I had to have an artificial joint implanted in 1971. It now functions pretty well. In the meantime; my brother, Curt, had an artificial hip joint implanted also. Then Mom had fallen twice and broken each hip, so she had to have two artificial joints. I told my sister she'd better make an appointment to get hers done, but she wasn't amused.

My health problems through the years didn't cause too much trouble, but did keep me from learning to dance at a time when most of my classmates were learning. I never got around to learning later either, so that has been a social inconvenience. Nor did I get to play football in high school, which I probably would have tried and might have been so-so at it. I was a big kid when young and someone was always predicting I would play football some day. Actually I've never been able to figure out what is going on during typical football plays.

I thought when I started high school I would like to become a psychiatrist. Later I got somewhat interested in chemistry. In fact, Granddad Morrow told me I should become a chemist. In my sophomore year I started getting interested in graphic arts and newspapering and became more so in my junior year when at school. Butch Shaffer and I got the press going that had been given to us by Bob Walker. Later I worked a little for Karl Kagel at the *Fruita Times*.

Either Gene forgot or was too modest to mention one of his achievements recorded in *The Daily Sentinel* of 26 March 1947:

Fruita boy in Legion Oratorial Contest Today ... Eight boys and girls will vie this afternoon for the State American Legion Oratorical Championship and a chance to enter the regional contest April 7 at Colorado Springs. Eugene Thomas is representing the Western Slope...

When I got out of high school I went to Indiana for a course in operating a linotype. That fall I started college at Colorado University at Boulder, but dropped out after the first quarter. About that time Mr. Kagel sold the Fruita Times and the new owners began printing it at Palisade. As I look back now, I think I should have tried to buy it at that time, but I'm not sure I knew it was for sale until after it had already sold.

I ran a linotype for *The Daily Sentinel* part time for several months, then worked a year for *The Montrose Daily Press*. I went to Mesa College for two years and one year at Regis College in Denver. After that I went back to work for *The Daily Sentinel*, all of the above while living at home at New Liberty, except when I was in Denver or Montrose.

I married **Pat Kresha** of Osceola, Nebraska, in 1956. We moved to Denver while I went to medical school for a year; I didn't do well in that. Then I bought *The Fruita Times* in 1957; ran it until 1963. During those years three of our children were born: **Joe, Teri** and **Karen**. Then I bought *The Huerfano World* at Walsenburg and ran it for a little over a year. During that time we had another child: **Gloria**. We sold *The Huerfano World* and returned to

The Fruita Times in 1965, then sold it again in 1966.

I went back to Colorado University and completed a psychology major, graduating in 1967, and worked for a couple of years at *The Boulder Daily Camera*. We bought *The Pleasant Hill Times* in Missouri in 1969 and ran it until 1976. Then we returned to Colorado and bought *The Castle Rock, The Douglas County News* and *The Kiowa, Elbert County News*, and were running them when Pat died in 1977. I sold the papers shortly after and my brother, Curt, and I bought *The Breeze* at Johnston, Colorado. He was tired of the Nursing Home business at that time and thought he might like to be a newspaper man. He soon discovered that he didn't like it and went back to the nursing-home field. I sold the *Breeze* in 1980 and bought *The Nevada Iowa Journal,* a small daily paper, which I cut back to three times a week after about four years. I returned to Colorado in early 1989 and repurchased *The Fruita Times* on August 1.

I have never remarried; I know I need to get busy or I'm going to end up like Grandpa Thomas. I felt it important to keep Mom at home as long as possible, even though I wanted to move to Fruita (1991).

Curtis "Curt" Emerson Thomas was born at Maude George's Maternity Home at Fruita 27 March 1938. He grew up in New Liberty, attending school there and at Fruita Union High School. For awhile he worked at various jobs, some dealing with uranium mining. He then joined the Navy and later the Air Force, serving in such places as Guam, England and Germany. After leaving the Military he received training to become a Licensed Practical Nurse (LPN) at the Emily Griffith Opportunity School. He went on to become a nursing home administrator, working at nursing homes in the Denver and Grand Junction areas.

Eventually Curt developed a serious diabetic condition and spent the last days of his life in Family Health West, where he left this life 19 October 1992. He never married.

athleen was born at Fruita Community Hospital 30 June 1941, and spent most of her childhood at New Liberty. She graduated from Fruita Union High School in 1959 and stayed in Fruita with Pat and me part of the time in 1957, 1958 and 1959. She fed the press and helped in other ways around the paper during that time.

She was married to **Ben Schaffer** for a time and they lived at Moses Lake, Washington, for awhile, then moved to the Denver area. They were later divorced, but Kathy remained in the Denver area, and in 1974, was married to **Jay Pershing**. Jay works at Tandy Name Brands and Kathy is office manager for ATSI, a car transport firm.

Following letter was written by Curtis Thomas and published in the *Fruita Times*, 8 August 1991.

My memories are perhaps different from others. My first memory is picking up my sister Kathleen at the old Fruita hospital. That would have been in 1941. I remember that I was not allowed to go into the hospital, so I played around on the lawn until my Dad brought out Mom and Kathy.

I remember some birthday parties over the years, but my memory really begins when school started. I must have been about six years old. I remember Tom Berry, Charlene Ashburn, Dolores Cutler, Tiburcio Garcia, Kenneth Gaymon — all in my class. I also remember a lot of the kids who were older than I. There was Larry Paulson — I wasn't very good at sports and Larry was always looking out for me. I Also remember Maxine Cutler and Anna Jane Berry, both of whom I thought were very pretty. There were Billy, Bobby and Eddie Likes, Lemoyne Jones, Helen Sanders, the Denton kids, and I could go on forever. All of these kids were special to me when I was going to school at New Liberty. There were also Billy Likes and Basil Banning who met untimely deaths at an early age, and I still miss them.

Janie Berry Starr's recollections are terrific, but mine are from a slightly different viewpoint. For instance, I remember most of the teachers we had but can't say I loved them. There was one teacher she did not mention: Mrs. Cook. We guys used to chant: "Old Lady Cook is a dirty old crook."

Going to school was usually a 1 3/4 mile walk, but during bad weather Dad would take us in the old 1936 Ford. Or else Dora Tomlinson would pick us up at the mailbox and we could ride to school in the comfort of her DeSoto. There was the drainage ditch from the school for about a mile, we had trails and bridges in it to follow on the way home. We always hurried home to listen to the old radio programs such as "Superman," "The Lone Ranger," "Our Miss Brooks" and "Sgt. Preston of the Yukon."

There was the time of the old "Model T." The "T" provided me and my buddies a lot of pleasure. At one point we even wired an old car body onto the frame and drove it around as a sedan for awhile.

Getting enough gas for the old Model "T" was always a problem, although it would go quite a ways on a gallon. Dad was always a good provider, but that was never enough. Zella Sanders was always good for five gallons or so. We would drive up to her driveway and turn the ignition off, sometime producing a few loud pops and a cloud of smoke. Then we would tell her we were out of gas.

Walt and "Booze" Deacon would usually let us have ten gallons, which would fill the tank. My Granddad, John Morrow, was another good source; he always enjoyed kids.

John Morrow was a good carpenter and helped build or add onto many houses in New Liberty. He probably helped the Berrys add on their big new addition. I can remember what a large addition it was and how nice it was when completed. As I remember, the old part of the house was adobe. I could be wrong on that, though, as my memory plays tricks on me.

Margaret Morrow, my grandmother, was the first cook I remember after the new school lunch program was started. She liked bread and made her own at home. She would also make it for school. I remember her carrying a dishpan full of dough from her house to the school and then making it into buns for the kids. If she had to use bakery bread she always warmed it in the oven so the real butter would melt on it.

Jimmy Dick Tomlinson joined us in the seventh grade, I think. He and I had a kind of "off again - on again" relationship. But mostly we did things together, like riding our bikes. We had trails that had 2 x 4 bridges where we would take our bikes up into the hills south of New Liberty. We once found a "tree cactus" (Gene says it was Mesquite) on the edge of Ruby Canyon, the only one I've ever known of in this area. Over the years someone dug it up and it is no more. Jimmy and I had more adventures together, like the time we had been across the wash to visit Bobby Cotner and on the way back we antagonized a bunch of bees and Jimmy was wearing a T-shirt and got many bee stings, enough to make him pretty sick for a few days.

Then there was the eighth grade graduation at New Liberty School. There were others involved, but I remember that Dolores Cutler and I spent a lot of time running around the neighborhood collecting cat tails, etc., in my Granddad's old International pickup. We had a great time and in the end I think the stage at the schoolhouse looked pretty good.

As I got older I began to work for some of the farmers in the community, particularly harvesting the hay. By then almost everyone was baling their hay. They would pick up the bales with a tractor-drawn slip. We would then snag the bales as we went by them, drag them on board and stack them on the slip until we had a full load and take them to be stacked in whatever area the farmer wanted. The best part of this job was when I got to drive the tractor. I liked working for the Deacons best because we took our noon meal at Modine Cutler's house. Modine was one of the best cooks in New Liberty. I particularly remember giant platters of fried chicken, and mashed potatoes and gravy, along with other good things such as pie.

This letter is getting out of hand and I have only mentioned a few of my memories, but I can't stop without a few words about the rest of my family. There is Kathleen Thomas Pershing, who always wanted to tag along and usually did unless Mom forbade it. She and her husband have a four-acre spread near Elizabeth, Colorado, with a couple of horses to ride and a one-hour drive to work in Denver.

My brother, Gene, is owner and publisher of *The Fruita Times*. I didn't see much of him as a kid, as he was six years older than me. He now (1991) lives with Mom on Orchard Mesa and his son, Joe, takes care of Mom while Gene works. We usually get together on Wednesday evening for a cook-out and movie or to go somewhere, like the Willie Nelson concert. We try to stay together as a family as much as possible, even though Mom's mental capacity has failed considerably over the past three years.

Mom was always a hard worker and had a schedule for everything. As I remember, Monday was wash day and there had to be lots of hot water. She had a huge copper boiler that was filled and heated until it steamed. There was also a reservoir on the stove and various tea kettles to get enough hot water. She had an electric washing machine and twin rinse tubs. The washer had a pair of rollers to send the clothes through to wring out a lot of water and then they would be hung outside to dry, giving them a wonderfully clean smell. The whites went first, then the colored clothes, and last of all the jeans, Levi's etc.

She always raised a big garden and toward fall would begin to can vegetables and fruit. She canned almost everything, including beef cubes and gravy and baked beans.

My Dad, Floyd Thomas, was also a hard worker and tried to be easy on us kids. He would get up at 5 a.m. and do most of the chores and then come in and cook breakfast. One of his favorite breakfasts was a fresh side meat, fried eggs and pancakes. After breakfast he would head for the fields. He was one of the best farmers in the valley and if he had had better land he would probably have been the best. Our farm included a lot of area that could not be tilled due to small hills, etc. His irrigation techniques are well remembered by other farmers in the area. He maintained a large yard and lawn which became the talk of the community and we had many community picnics there. I may have a picture or two of those picnics. The whole yard was shaded by huge poplar trees and we never thought of air conditioning.

(Upper left) Joe Thompson standing beside his tractor in the alfalfa crop, 1953. (Upper right) Becky and Virginia Thompson, 1949. (Lower left) Ursula "Sue" McFarland Thompson standing in front of the teacherage. *(Photos courtesy of Virginia Thompson Hunter)*

They had two daughters:

Becky (Horn)
Virginia (Hunter)

The Thompsons came to Colorado from Wainwright, Oklahoma, in 1946. That same year, Sue became one of the teachers at New Liberty School and Joe, Sue and children lived in the teacherage at the school for the next five years.

Joe acquired the bottom land on the east bank of East Salt Creek that once belonged to Patrick Daily and Lee Foss (see Daily and Foss stories) and set up a farming operation. They built a home on that property and the family lived there for many years. In addition to his farming, Joe also worked on the side for various farmers in the neighborhood.

Sue continued teaching at New Liberty until the school was closed, then she transferred to Loma. She continued to teach there until her retirement in 1966.

After completing the eighth grade at New Liberty, the girls attended Fruita Union High School; Becky graduated in 1949 and Virginia in 1952.

Joe died at Lower Valley Hospital in Fruita, 24 July 1972, at age 75, after living in the Mack area for 26 years. Sue moved to a retirement center in Boulder, Colorado, in 1976, to be near Virginia. She still considers the Western Slope "home."

Sue and daughters attended the New Liberty/ Mack reunion in August 1991. Sue is still going strong at age 96 as of January 1997.

Thompson

Information from a letter from Virginia Thompson and obituaries and news items in *The Daily Sentinel.*

Joe Elliott Thompson was born 4 July 1897, at Peabody, Marion, Kansas. He spent his childhood in Kansas and Oklahoma. He married **Ursula "Sue" McFarland**, 22 June 1931, at Eufala, McIntosh, Oklahoma. Sue was born 24 November 1900.

Tomlinson

Information from a letter and family group sheet from Dora (Dode) Bailey Tomlinson Young. Also news items and obituary from *The Daily Sentinel.*

Alton E. "Dick" Tomlinson
(Photo courtesy of Dora Tomlinson Young)

Blanco, Colorado, 31 July 1918, to Silas Christopher Bailey and Bessie Rose Mobley. Dora spent her childhood in the Meeker area, going to schools at Piance Creek and Yellow Creek. She finished her grade school at Rangely and had two years of high school at Angora School, south of Meeker.

Dick and Dode were married 26 May 1937, in Fruita.

Dora L. "Dode" Bailey Tomlinson
(Photo courtesy of Dora Tomlinson Young)

Alton E. "Dick" Tomlinson was born at Green River, Emery, Utah, 6 February 1906, to Aldimer "Aultmer" "Mert" Tomlinson and Lillian Margarite Dahling. He spent his early life there and attended Green River Schools. In 1922, when his family moved to Fruita, Dick went to work on a cattle ranch in the Cisco area. Later, while he was working as a camp mover for a sheep ranch in the Meeker area, he came in with the herd and discovered a young lady who was cooking for the shearers; they began dating. Her name was **Dora L. "Dode" Bailey,** who was born at Meeker, Rio

They had three sons:

Jimmy Dick, born 13 May 1938, at Fruita
Terry Joe, 17 May 1944, Fruita (only lived two days)
Timmy Everett, 8 February 1951, Collbran

The family lived for a number of years on a ranch east of Cisco, where Dick was employed. Then, in 1948, when Jimmy was old enough to go to school, they bought the Percy Blasier farm (formerly the Daily farm) so Jimmy could go to

729

Jimmy Dick Tomlinson, 1957.   Timmy Everett Tomlinson, 1969.

(Both photos courtesy of Dora Tomlinson Young)

program at New Liberty, Loma and Fruita Elementary until 1972, when she resigned and married **William "Bill" John Young** at Vernal, Utah. They lived in Vernal for a year and then moved to Mack when Bill went into a painting business with his son. Dode went to beauty school and took teacher's training, then taught at American Beauty College for 17 years.

As of 1992 Bill and Dode were living at 1691 K Road, Fruita, Colorado.

school at New Liberty.

Dick would stay out on the ranch most of the time, and Dode and the boys would stay on the farm at New Liberty. All the family would work at the ranch in the summer. They made a practice of taking in boys from back east who had been in trouble. They would work with them and encourage them and help them become good citizens.

Jimmy graduated from the eighth grade at New Liberty, but the school was closed before Timmy reached graduation age; he had to finish grade school at Loma. Jimmy graduated from Fruita Union High School in 1957 and Timmy in 1969.

On 28 September 1969, as Dick and Jimmy were on the way home from the ranch to attend the funeral of one of Dode's aunts, Dick suffered a heart attack and died before they could get him to a hospital.

With the support of neighbors, Dode and the boys were able to suffer through that trying time. Dode said this about her neighbors: "The New Liberty people are a close-knit community."

Dode continued with the school lunch

Jimmy was married 11 December 1957, to **Dora K. Hughes**, daughter of Ed Hughes and Dora Baily. Dora was born 6 April 1939, in Fruita.

Following is a history written by Jimmy Dick and Dora Hughes Tomlinson:

Alton "Dick" and Dora Tomlinson bought what is now Jim and Dora Tomlinson's home at 1641 8 Road, Mack, Colorado, from a family named Fogg, who bought it from Harlin E. Bunch. Dick bought it in 1950. Several people had lived in the original house: such as Darrell and Beverly Maluy, who lived there for some time. Others who lived there were Dick and Toots Wright and Mrs. Ward, one of the New Liberty school teachers.

During high school Jim was active on the track team, and still holds a school track record, set in 1957, at Fruita Union High School. Jim always told people he learned to run fast chasing rabbits on his way to grade school at New Liberty, which was about a mile and half walk each way. He finally bought a second-hand bike from Wilma and Norma Maluy and learned to ride it to school, after a few skinned knees and elbows.

730

(Above left) Jimmy Dick and Timmy at the ranch, 1955. (Above right) L-R: Sonny, Timmy, Dick and Jimmy Dick. Sonny was a boy from new York who got into trouble and spent two summers with the Tomlinsons at the ranch. (Right) Timmy and Dora at one of the branding corrals. *(Photos courtesy of Dora Tomlinson Young)*

(Above) Bill and Dora L. Tomlinson Young, Christmas, 1979. (Right) Timmy's family. L-R: Patricia, Timmy Patrick, Jessie Marie and Timmy Sr. *(Photos courtesy of Dora Tomlinson Young)*

(Upper left) Jimmy Dick's family. L-R: Mikki, Jimmy Dick Jr., Jimmy Dick Sr., Dora K. and Debi Kathleen Tomlinson. *(Photo courtesy of Dora Tomlinson Young)* (Upper right) Jimmy Dick Jr.'s family. Back L-R: Jimmy Dick Jr., Bailie (4), Nancy holding Madison (2); Allan(7) Tomlinson in front. (Center left) Mikki's family. L-R: Mandi (10), Mikki, Scott and Tyler (6) Robertson. (Center right) Jimmy Dick Sr. and Dora Tomlinson in their home in New Liberty. (Lower left) Jimmy Dick St and Dora Tomlinson's home on 1641 8 Road in New Liberty, 1995 or 1996. *(Photos courtesy of Jimmy Dick Sr.*

Jim and Dora were married 11 December 1957, in Grand Junction, and made their first home on the family ranch in Main Canyon, south of Vernal, Utah.

They had four children:

Debi Kathleen, born 11 June 1958 (deceased)
Mikki Dora (Robertson), 5 December 1960
Jimmy Dick Jr., 17 September 1963
Kathy Louise (stillborn)
All were born in Grand Junction.

Dora and the children moved to New Liberty when Debi started going to school at Loma. Mikki and Jim Jr. also attended Loma, then Fruita Jr. High School and Fruita Monument High School. They would go back to Main Çanyon after school on Friday and on the days school was out for the summer. Jim would stay at the ranch year-around, visiting the family on week-ends, when they were not at the ranch.

The family moved its operation to 1641 8 Road after the larger portion of the ranch was sold in 1973. Jim and Dora still maintain their cattle on the south side of the Bookcliffs in the summer months. In the winter the cattle are kept at New Liberty.

Jim and Dora are actively ranching at this time (1997). Mikki married Scott Robertson, has two children, and lives on the family ranch, south of Rangely, Colorado. Jim Jr. and his wife, Nancy, and their three children, live on a ranch at Crawford, Colorado, and raise registered Angus cattle.

Dora drove a school bus for 14 years while the children were in school. She now works at the Fruita Co-op and the Valley Livestock Sales Barn. She also has served several years on the Colorado Cattle Women Executive Board, and is still active in the club.

Jim takes care of the cattle and family farm on 8 Road. He also works at the Valley Livestock Sales Barn as well as Buniger Construction Co. He helps both his children, with their extra ranch work.

Jim and Dora have remodeled the house they live in several times, and both do lawn and garden work. They usually grow enough garden vegetables for their children since Mikki and Jim Jr. both live in higher altitudes where gardens don't grow well.

Timmy married **Patricia Coppers** on 26 April 1980, and they have two children. Tim and Patricia live in Mack and he works at Family Health West in Fruita (1992).

Bert Brown and Rhoda Matilda Wilson Turner
(Photo courtesy of Jean Turner Brisbin)

Turner

Information from marriage record from San Juan County, Utah, and family information from Jean Turner Brisbin.

Bert Brown Turner was born 28 April 1882, at San Miguel, San Miguel, Colorado, to Adrian Elbinas Turner and Margaret Lilly. On 21 May 1901, at Monticello, San Juan, Utah, he married **Rhoda Matilda Wilson,** daughter of Nickolas Elijah Wilson and Phonetta Jane Crouse. Rhoda was born 23 December 1882, at Moab, Grand, Utah.

Rhoda's name is recorded on their marriage record as "Rhoda M. Carman," and that is also the way she signed it on the record.

Bert and Rhoda had ten children:

Albert Henry, born 23 September 1902, at Moab, Grand, Utah
Ernest Wilson, 30 October 1904, Monticello
Richard Quinton, 13 February 1907, Baggs, Carbon, Wyoming
George Philander, 21 May 1909, Moab
Effie Ouida (Hotz), 2 December 1911, Moab
Eva, 1913 (died at birth), Dewey, Utah
Paul Edward, 10 April 1915, Moab
Mildred Jean (Brisbin), 18 March 1920, Moab
Curtis Ray, 23 January 1923, Salt Lake City
Gordon L., 5 October 1928, Monticello

Jean Brisbin did not inform the author about all the families' activities for all the years, but you can tell from the birth places of the children that they moved around some. Jean indicated that her father, Bert, was a government trapper at some point in time.

The family moved to New Liberty from Ridgway, Colorado, in 1936 and lived for some time on the Claude Taylor farm (formerly the Howard Williams/Athol Stotts farm). Bert did some farming at that time. On the family group sheet Jean noted that at the time Eva was born, Bert was operating a ferry across the Colorado River at Dewey, Utah. A bridge was built at that place later.

While at New Liberty Jean went to Fruita Union High School and Ray went to New Liberty School. I (the author) don't recall any of the children living there except Albert, George, Jean and Ray — there could have been others. George married Francis Meyer and Jean married Bill Brisbin while the family lived there. (See Swyhart and Brisbin).

All the family are deceased except Jean and Gordon. Jean lives in St. George and Gordon, the youngest, lives in Salt Lake City, Utah.

Family Biographies

U

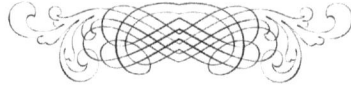

Underwood

Information from obituaries and news items in *The Daily Sentinel.*

George Underwood was born 19 June 1892, at Madrid, Perkins, Nebraska. He spent his early life there and moved to Model, Las Animas, Colorado, in 1917. He married **Anna "Ann" Mae Griffith** in Trinidad, Las Animas, Colorado, 14 March 1918. Anna was born 29 January 1900, at Hannibal, Marion, Missouri. She spent her childhood in California and attended schools at Trinidad, Colorado.

The couple moved to Glenwood Springs, Colorado in 1924, and to New Liberty in 1942.

While living in New Liberty they farmed the former McIntosh farm on the west end of the community on the west side of what is now called 6 Road, bordered on the north by R Road.

They had two children:

John O.
Carol Ann (Crider)

John served in the Army Field Artillery from 23 June 1943 until 20 January 1946, in the northern Solomon Islands and Luzon in the Philippines. On 7 June 1946 he married **Naomi Banning**, daughter of Ray and Nellie Banning. They had one daughter: **Darr Ann.**

Carol Ann attended school in New Liberty and graduated from Fruita Union High School in 1959.

In 1958 George retired from farming and moved to Fruita. He then began serving as custodian for at least two of the churches in Fruita. Ann went to work at the Lower Valley Nursing home in Fruita. George died in that nursing home 31 May 1981, and Ann died, 11 March 1982. Both were buried in the Memorial Gardens Cemetery at Grand Junction.

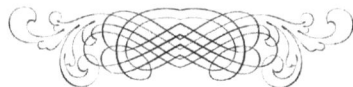
Wagaman

Most of the following was compiled by Dick Wagaman and Mae Wagaman Uhleman. We include information from obituaries and news items from *The Daily Sentinel*.

James Franklin "Frank" Wagaman was born 16 September 1880, in Carroll County, Missouri. He moved with his family to Barton County, Missouri, in the mid 1880s.

Frank married **Willa Mae Higgins**, 25 December 1904, in Barton County Missouri. Willa Mae was born 26 November 1887, at Flora, Dade, Missouri, to Lafayette Bryant Higgins and Louise L. Taylor. Willa Mae's sister, Eva Myrtle Higgins, married Edwin Wader Wagaman, Frank's brother.

Frank and Willa had seven children:

James Leroy "Roy," born 11 November 1905, at Lamar, Barton, Missouri
Paul Lafayette, 21 January 1907, Barton, Missouri
Orval Hugh, 19 October 1908, Barton, Missouri

Frank Wagaman family, 1 June 1928. Back row, L-R: Paul Lafayette, Hazel Emmaline, Orval Hugh. Middle row: James Franklin, Willa Mae and Ray Edwin and dog Shep in front. *(Photo courtesy of Dick Wagaman)*

Hazel Emmaline (Boardman), 19 April 1911, Lamar
Earle Bryant "Dick," 18 January 1913, Selma, Fresno, California
Ray Edwin, 12 September 1918, Mack
Willa Mae (Uhleman) 19 September 1920, Fruita

Frank developed severe asthma and arthritis and a doctor advised him to search for a dryer climate. They lived for a time in California, but eventually settled in Mack. While at Mack, Frank and his boys worked for the Uintah Railway, though Frank's poor health led to his early retirement. After living in Mack 16 years, Frank and Willa moved to Grand Junction, 20

The Wagaman Home in Mack, 1933.
(Photo courtesy of Dick Wagaman)

April 1934, and settled in a home on 10th Street, just off Grand Avenue. They ultimately purchased a rooming house near the D&RGW Railroad Depot in Grand Junction and provided rooms for trainmen laying over in Grand Junction between work runs.

Frank died 3 March 1941, and Willa died 10 December 1950. Both are buried near their son, Roy, in the Elmwood Cemetery at Fruita.

James Leroy "Roy" was born 11 November 1905, at Lamar, Barton, Missouri. He died at age 19 in a Uintah Railway accident near Atchee, Colorado, 19 August 1924. He was employed as fireman on an American ditcher (actually a steam-powered shovel) that had been dispatched to clear a slide on the track. The workmen had just moved the ditcher and blocked it up in a new position on freshly-moved earth. As the big machine raised the first scoop-full, the blocking sank into the soft earth and the ditcher turned over on it's side where Roy was working. Roy had no chance to save himself, he was crushed under the machine.

He had been honors student in his graduating class at Fruita Union High School the spring before. The entire graduating class attended the funeral.

Roy had been employed, off and on, by the Uintah for several years. It was noted in Mack items in *The Daily Sentinel* of 14 February 1923, that he had been driving the Fruita Union High School bus from Mack.

The Uintah Railway's new ditcher following its arrival in Mack
(Photo used from Uintah Railway *by permission of Henry E. Bender, Jr)*

Paul Lafayette was born 21 January 1907, in Barton County, Missouri. After the family left Missouri and eventually settled at Mack, Paul worked part time for the Uintah Railway Company while going to high school. After graduating he worked full time for the Uintah Railway.

He married **Deon Standifird** of Fruita, 11 May 1931. Deon was born at Moab, Utah, 30 April 1909, the daughter of George Standifird and Blanche Sperry.

As with many other companies across the nation, the Uintah Railway began to experience a business decline. Finally, because of lack of work, Paul left the Uintah Railway and worked at various odd jobs until he was able to get a job with the Union Pacific Railroad. During those difficult years, he and Deon moved their family to Salt Lake City, Ogden and Provo, Utah, and to Caliente and Las Vegas, Nevada, then back to Milford and Salt Lake City, Utah.

Orval Hugh was born 19 October 1908, in Barton County, Missouri. He graduated from Fruita Union High School in 1926. He was married in Grand Junction, 9 June 1928, to **Josie Maude Cox**, daughter of William H. Cox and Jennie Maude Jackson, who, at the time, were proprietors of the Mack Mercantile.

Mabel Kiefer, correspondent for *The Daily Sentinel* wrote the following on 11 June 1928, about their marriage:

> Fruita friends are interested in a wedding which took place Saturday evening in Grand Junction. The contracting parties were Miss Josie Cox and Orval Wagaman of Mack. The young people have been attending Fruita Union High School and are well-known by many here. They belong to old and respected families of the valley, the bride being the daughter of Mr. and Mrs. W. H. Cox of Mack and the groom is the son of Mr. and Mrs. Frank Wagaman of Mack. The ceremony was performed at the Baptist parsonage with the Reverend Franklin Fenner officiating, using the impressive ring service. Mr. and Mrs. Leonard Cox were witnesses. The bride and groom have made their homes in the valley during their entire childhood. Fruita friends

join with others in extending congratulations and best wishes. They will continue to live in Mack.

Orval and Josie had two sons:

James Leroy, who died as an infant
Charles Richard "Dick," who lives in Minneapolis, Minnesota.

Orval was stationed at Minneapolis during World War II where he was a master plumber and did shake-down cruises on ships. He remained in Minneapolis and had a plumbing shop there. He died of a heart attack while hunting deer in Minnesota in November 1976. Josie died in 1990 in Minneapolis.

Hazel Emmaline was born at Lamar, Barton, Missouri, 19 April 1911. She married **Merle Boardman**, 3 March 1935, at Palisade, Colorado. Merle was born at Crawford, Delta, Colorado, 12 November 1913, to Roy Boardman and Addie Collins. Hazel and Merle had one son: **James Leroy.**

Hazel and Merle lived most of their married life at Palisade, Colorado, where Merle worked in the coal industry, later becoming a movie projectionist. Hazel worked at the Palisade Drug. Later she worked for 11 years at the Grand Avenue Rexall Drug in Grand Junction. They also operated a small peach orchard southeast of Palisade for the last few years of Merle's life. He died in Grand Junction 1 May 1978.

Earle Bryant "Dick" was born 18 January 1913 at Selma, Fresno, California. He graduated from Fruita Union High School in 1931, where he was an outstanding athlete and earned nine varsity letters. He married **Mildred "Millie" Irene Hogge**, 15 January 1939. Dick and Millie had two children.

> **Richard Thomas**, born 11 June 1941, at Montrose, Montrose, Colorado. Richard works for Boeing Aircraft, in the unmanned plane division, at Washington D.C.
> **Linda Irene (Cates)**, 27 August 1946, Grand Junction. She is a retired school teacher and

lives in Denver.

After graduating from high school, Dick went directly into the grocery business and was involved in numerous Western Slope stores. He was with the large City Market chain in various capacities, such as manager of the Glenwood Springs and Grand Junction stores for many years. He ended his career in the Advertising Department when he retired in 1978.

Dick has been an active member of the First Congregational Church, BPOE #575 in Grand Junction and was awarded the Distinguished Service Award from the Redlands Lions Club of Grand Junction for the 1971-1972 year.

Ray Edwin was born at Mack, Mesa, Colorado, 12 September 1918. He attended school at Mack, Fruita and Grand Junction, Colorado, graduating from Grand Junction High School in 1935. On 15 July 1941, he married **Thelma Walker**, who was born 2 April 1919, at Fort Lupton, Weld, Colorado. Ray and Thelma had two children:

Janice Marie
Martha Lou

Ray served in the U.S. Army during World War II, attaining the rank of captain in the Corps of Engineers. He worked in various managerial positions for the J. C. Penney Co. for many years before and after his Army experience. While with J.C. Penney Co., he and Thelma lived in Colorado, Wyoming and Kansas. While in Boulder, Thelma worked several years for the University of Colorado. Both retired in 1980 while living in Boulder. They enjoy traveling, playing golf, and are active in their church and Elks and Kiwanis Clubs.

Ray, Hazel, Mae, and Dick Wagaman
(Photo courtesy of Dick Wagaman)

Willa **Mae** was born 19 September 1920, at Fruita, Mesa, Colorado. She married **Reinhold F. "Reine" Uhleman** at Salt Lake City, Utah, 19 May 1942. Reine was born at Sterling, Logan, Colorado, 15 June 1918, the son of Rudolph M. Uhleman, formerly of Frieburg, Germany, and Anna L. Binde, formerly of Wurttemberg, Germany. They met and married in Kansas City, Missouri. Rudolph was a sausage maker, having learned his trade in Germany.

Reine and Mae had three children:

Max Reinhold
Patricia Ann
Betty Ann

An item in *The Daily Sentinel,* 11 December 1945, says: "Corporal Reinhold Uhleman served from 16 May 1942 until 30 November 1945, in the U S Army." Following this, he worked as a butcher around Grand Junction, Colorado, for many years, ultimately becoming supervisor for the City Market grocery chain in Western Colorado. He died in the Veterans Hospital at Salt Lake City 21 September 1972.

Wallace

Information from obituaries and news items in *The Daily Sentinel.* Some information is from the personal knowledge of the author.

James "Jim" Withers Wallace was born 6 February 1886, at Prairie Grove, Washington, Arkansas, and spent his childhood there. In the early 1900s he joined his father and two brothers in proving on a claim near Hooker, Oklahoma. Later he attended business college and telegraph school in Topeka, Kansas. He worked in the oil fields, for the railroad, and had mining interests near Joplin, Missouri. Later, while still in his active years, Jim was employed by Schmidt Hardware in Grand Junction, Colorado, as an appliance man. Indeed he was a man with many talents.

On 27 June 1920, Jim married **Martha Carolyn Lamberton** in Harrison, Boone, Arkansas. Martha had spent her childhood at Harrison and graduated from high school at Little Rock, Arkansas. She attended the University of Arkansas at Fayetteville, then taught in Arkansas, before moving to Kansas City and later western Kansas.

The couple had three daughters:

Jean (Nelson)
Elizabeth (Hatch)
Georgia (Gilman)

The family moved to Mesa County in August 1937, first living on the Pat Maluy homestead in New Liberty. Jim had a truck and did some hauling in the community. He also worked as a farm hand for various farmers around the community. The children attended New Liberty School.

Martha's teaching career in Colorado began at kindergarten in Fruita. She then completed requirements for Colorado teaching credentials in 1942. She attended Mesa College and graduated from Adams State College with a bachelor's degree in 1952 at age 58.

She taught in Mesa County for 35 years, retiring in 1961, after teaching at Gateway, Pomona, Whitman and Nisley elementary schools. With her teaching experience in Arkansas and Kansas, she had taught for a combined total of 46 years.

During those years Martha, realizing the difficulties faced by non-English speaking students, initiated a bilingual kindergarten in Grand Junction. In April 1955, she received worldwide recognition for her effort at the Association for Childhood Education Convention in Kansas City. Martha was cited as the "Grandmother" of the free kindergarten movement and received a personal letter of commendation from Eleanor Roosevelt. The kindergarten program lasted 16 years until Grand Junction schools established free kindergartens. Martha estimated she had helped more than 600 students. Her 16-year bilingual kindergarten in Grand Junction was the forerunner of Operation Head Start.

Jim died in Grand Junction 7 February 1975, at age 88. Martha died 21 April 1983, at age 89. Both are buried in Memorial Gardens Cemetery at Grand Junction.

Wassenberg

Information from obituaries and news items in *The Daily Sentinel*, an interview with Mary Ellen Wassenberg Leeper and some information from Frank and Helen Overbye.

Theodore "Ted" Cornelius Joseph Wassenberg was born 7 September 1894, at Hay Springs, Sheridan, Nebraska, the youngest of 10 children born to Lawrence Frank Wassenberg and Mary Jane Heesacker. He grew to manhood in that area and became a bronco buster working in Nebraska, Montana, Idaho, Washington, Oregon and Wyoming. Ted joined the Army in the summer of 1918 during World War I, and subsequently served overseas for 21 months. His father drowned in the stock water tank on the family homestead, 30 July 1919. In 1920, after discharge from the military, he traveled to Colorado and bought a homestead from Jessie Paul Patten: farm unit "A" in Sec 16, just south of the Lofgren farm and north of Everett Bowen's. It was through his persuasion that his brother-in-law and sister, Tony and Cora Overbye, came to Colorado (see Overbye story).

Ted married **Goldie May Todd**, on 24 January 1921, at Gillette, Campbell, Wyoming. Goldie was born 4 May 1903, at Bowling Green, Wood, Ohio a daughter of William Todd and Mary Ellen Addy. They moved onto the homestead in New Liberty after their marriage.

Ted and Goldie had two daughters:

Mary Ellen (Leeper), born 6 November, 1924 at Mack
Patricia Ann (Rose), 28 January 1938, Gillette, Campbell, Wyoming

In about 1931 Ted and his family left the New Liberty homestead and moved into Mack. They built a house north of the Mack Mercantile. Ted worked for the Uintah Railway, transferring the sacks of gilsonite weighing an average of 235 pounds from the Uintah Railcars to the D&RGW Railroad cars. Mary Ellen says she can remember when he came home at night, after a days work, being covered with the black gilsonite dust. He wore goggles, and when he took them off his face would be all black with big white eyes.

Ted bought a motel in Gillette, Wyoming, in about 1932. Goldie and Mary Ellen went to Wyoming during the next three summers and ran the motel while Ted stayed in Mack and worked on the transfer gang. The motel was closed during the winter. In the spring of 1935 the family moved to Gillette. Ted, with the help of his nephew, Frank Overbye, spent the summer building 10 units onto the motel. They named the motel Gillette Cottage Park.

In 1950 they sold the motel and bought the Davis Gas and Supply Company on the Douglas Highway and called it Wassenberg Gas and Appliance. They delivered propane to people's home tanks, sold it privately at the store and also sold gas appliances. Their daughter, Mary Ellen

(Above left) Ted Wassenberg 12 years old and his sister, Lena Wassenberg,14 years old, in 1906 in Rushville, Nebraska. Lena died at age 24 from tuberculosis. (Above right) Ted the cowboy in about 1916. (Lower left) Ted Wassenberg family in 1938 in Gillette, Wyoming. L-R: Mary Ellen, Ted, Goldie and Patricia Ann. *(Photos courtesy of Helen Overbye Peterson)* (Lower right) Goldie sitting on the bird bath that she made from flatstone at her home in Fort Collins, 1990s. *(Photo courtesy of Mary Ellen Wassenberg Leeper)*

GILETTE COTTAGE PARK,   Gilette, Wyoming
On Highway 14 and 16   T. C. Wassenberg, Prop.

The motel that Ted Wassenberg bought in 1932. They built the 10 units onto it and moved to Gillette to run the motel in 1935. They lived in the unit on the far left. *(Photo courtesy of Mary Ellen Wassenberg Leeper)*

quietly died in his sleep from arrhythmia of the heart.

Goldie and girls sold the mobile park in 1975 and Goldie lived alone until her death on 1 November 1992 at 89 years of age.

Mary Ellen attended school in Mack from 1931 until the family moved to Gillette, Wyoming, in 1935. She finished school in Gillette. She married **Arnold "Bud" Leeper** on 10 March 1947, at Gillette, Wyoming. They never had any children. They worked for her parents at the Wassenberg Gas and Appliance store until they moved to Fort Collins in 1958 and bought a home. Her parents followed in 1959 and she formed a partnership with her parents and sister on a trailer park. After her father died in 1960, she and Bud finished remodeling the mobile park and ran it until it was sold in 1975. They traveled around for some time and eventually retired in Fort Collins. On 31 May 1993 they moved to Cottonwood, Arizona. Bud died there on 5 January 1997. Mary Ellen still lives there.

and her husband, Arnold, worked for them. Mary Ellen was the bookkeeper. Ted and Goldie sold the business in 1958 and traveled for awhile.

Then, in late 1959, they moved to Fort Collins, Colorado, and bought a home. They also bought a rundown trailer park in partnership with their two daughters, Mary Ellen and Patricia. They fully revamped the trailer park and made a mobile home and RV trailer park out of it, calling it XL Mobile Park. Ted had just finished a laundromat in the park and opened it for use on 24 March 1960, when he went in the house and laid down for a nap. He

The newly built laundromat in early February 1960. It was part of the facilities at the Wassenberg's XL Mobile Court in Fort Collins. L-R: Arnold "Bud" and Mary Ellen Leeper and Goldie and Ted Wassenberg. The Leeper's dog, Curly, is in front. *(Photo courtesy of Mary Ellen Wassenberg Leeper)*

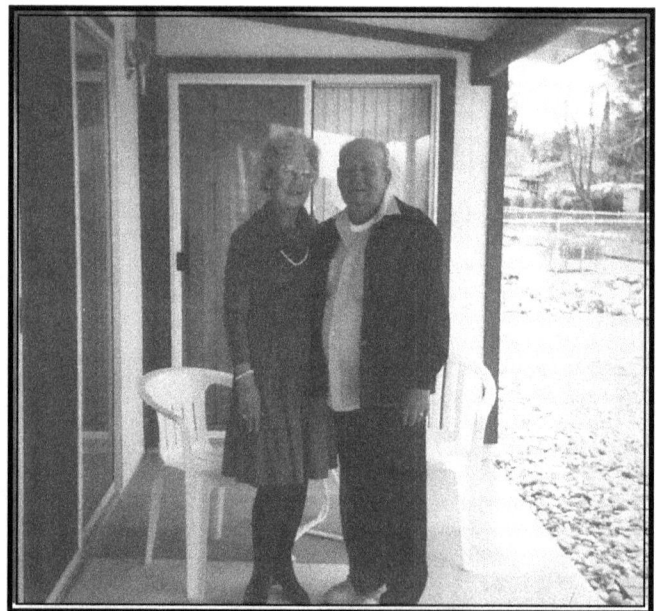

Mary Ellen Wassenberg and Arnold "Bud" Leeper, 10 March 1996. *(Photo courtesy of Mary Ellen Wassenberg Leeper)*

The Rose Family, 16 August 1979. Back row, L-R: Daniel Brian, Cynthia Ann, Lon and Christina DeAnn Rose. Front row: Patricia Ann and David Charles Rose. *(Photo courtesy of Mary Ellen Wassenberg Leeper)*

Patricia Ann was born and grew up in Gillette, Wyoming. She entered Colorado State University at Fort Collins in 1958 and graduated six years later with a master's degree in medical technology and bacteriology. She met her future husband, **Lon C. Rose,** at the university and they were married 2 July 1960 in Fort Collins. After they graduated, they moved to Colorado Springs. Lon and Patricia had four children:

> **Cynthia Ann (Flinger),** born 17 July 1961
> **Christina DeAnn (Ferguson),** 7 December 1962
> **Daniel Brian,** 12 April 1964
> **David Charles,** 17 March 1972
> All were born in Colorado Springs.

Lon sells commercial real estate, and he and Patricia still live in Colorado Springs.

Weimer

Information from obituaries and news items in *The Daily Sentinel.*

Ira Dominic "Don" Weimer was born 14 December 1895, near Frostburg, Garrett, Maryland, to Simon and Loretta McKenzie Weimer. He attended schools near Frostburg until moving to Mesa County with his family in about 1909, when he was 15 years of age. He was the only boy in a family of 11 children.

On 23 April 1921 he married **Jessie Catherine Lynch.** Jessie was born 10 January 1895, at Oro, near Leadville, Lake, Colorado, to Barton "Bart" and Maude Jessie Lynch. She moved with her family to Grand Junction in 1905, where she attended public schools. Her parents owned and operated a repair and sporting goods shop in Grand Junction for many years.

Jessie served as a secretary in the Surgeon General's office in Washington, D.C. during World War I.

Don and Jessie had no children. However,

Jessie Catherine Lynch and Ira Dominic "Don" Weimer
(Photo courtesy of the Maluy Collection)

they freely lavished their love on children belonging to other families. They were well-known and well-liked by their friends and neighbors, wherever they lived.

A news item in *The Daily Sentinel* of 5 August 1927, tells a story of Don and another man being severely burned in an explosion and fire on a well-drilling rig near Cisco. It took some time for Don to recover from that experience.

Don and Jessie homesteaded some land in Sulphur Canyon, north of Fruita, in 1928. It was called the "Uintah Ranch." In 1939 they moved to the New Liberty community after purchasing the former George Fisher homestead from Edward Dodge.

Don loved to work with livestock, always being involved with cattle, sheep, hogs and horses as long as he was able. For several years he participated in the rodeo at Cowpuncher's Reunion at Fruita.

The Weimers gave up the farm and livestock and moved to Fruita in 1968 and lived in a home at 157 S. Orchard St. until both required constant care. Don died 15 May 1985, at Family Health West in Fruita, at age 89. Jessie continued on for another year; she died also at Family Health West, on 3 May 1986, at age 91. Both were buried in the Elmwood Cemetery at Fruita.

Chariot Races at the Fruita fall rodeo. Passengers: Lute Shook and Frank Bremer. Don Weimer is the driver. If they won, they won with a big handicap. *(Photo used from the Fruita Times, 15 October 1959 issue)*

Weir

Information from stories written by Mildred Weir and Charlene Brayton Eldridge. Information is also from obituaries and news items from *The Daily Sentinel,* and some items are from the author's personal knowledge.

Laura Edna Crane and Walter Earnest Weir.
(Photo courtesy of Charlene Brayton Eldridge)

Walter Earnest Weir was born at Clay Center, Kansas, 23 April 1886, to Frank and Ada Tidyman Weir, one of three children. He spent his childhood there. On 11 February 1908, he married **Laura Edna Crane** at Randall, Jewell, Kansas. Laura was born 25 July 1886 at Randall, Kansas, where she spent her childhood. She was the oldest of nine children. We do not have the names of her parents.

Walter and Laura had four children:

William Henry, born 5 February 1909, Randall, Jewell, Kansas. He died 4 June 1914

Mildred Alice (Brayton, Tucker), born 20 June 1911, Randall

Loraine, born 28 February 1916, Randall — died 9 April 1916.

Edna Myrul (Bennett), born 24 May 1917, at Wakefield, Clay, Kansas

The Weirs farmed in Kansas for the first 11 years after marriage, then spent a year at Loveland, Colorado, before going to Idaho Falls, Idaho, to look into the possibility of living there. Laura had a cousin living there, but they opted to move to the Grand Valley because of the fruit.

The following was written by Charlene Brayton Eldridge, granddaughter of the Weirs. It was published in the *Fruita Times,* 11 December 1992.

In March of 1920, Walter went to New Liberty to pick out his 40-acre homestead. He picked a nice piece of land on top of a hill and built a small home on the east end of it with a beautiful view of the valley. [Land records show that Walter bought a relinquishment from Richard C. Horton in 1920; an addition was purchased through Grand Valley Water Users Association in 1925 — author].

There was a lot of work to be done; ditches to be dug, fences to be built. He built a cistern with a pump on it about halfway between the house and the barns. Water was carried from there to the stock and chickens and to the house. Walter and Laura planted grass, trees and flowers, so in a few years they had a pleasant yard. They also planted apple trees, cherry trees, apricot trees and all kinds of berries. They raised chickens and pigs, and always milked several cows. Walter had a big bull that the grandchildren were afraid of.

The girls, Mildred and Edna, both attended New Liberty School and later graduated from Fruita Union High School.

Mildred married **Charles Brayton** 7 October 1930. Within a few years George, Charlene and Charlotte came along. We loved to go to Grandfather and Grandmother Weir's. They had a wood-slat hammock to swing in. Grandmother would let us eat uncooked oatmeal with honey on it. She always had cheese and cake and cookies. Their ice-box was just right outside the kitchen door. It usually had food in it, too.

Walter farmed with a team of mules. He always drove a pickup. Laura could drive a team but she never learned to drive a car.

Walter's mother, sister and brother remained in Kansas, but his mother visited many times. She loved to come and dry fruit to take back.

Laura had several members of her family move to Colorado. Her younger sister, **Hazel**, and husband, **Allen Daily**, and children, homesteaded in 1921 west of Mack, moving to Grand Junction in 1939. (See Allen Daily story).

Her brother, **Jessie Crane**, and wife **Virginia**, farmed in the area in the 1940s, moving back to Jamestown, Kansas, in 1951.

(Above) Walter with his prize Holstein bull. (Below) Walter in front of his 1934/5 Chevrolet pickup. *(Photos courtesy of Charlene Brayton Eldridge)*

Jennie and George Blank
(Photo courtesy of Charlene Brayton Eldridge)

One of Laura's younger sisters, **Jennie**, married **George Blank**, and they and their two young sons farmed a year at New Liberty, moving back to Grand Junction on account of George's health. In 1938 they moved to Wichita, Kansas.

Edna, after graduating from high school, went to St. Joseph's Hospital School in Denver, graduating with a degree in nursing. She came back to Grand Junction and worked at St. Mary's hospital as a registered nurse. She married **Chuck Bennett** and they had a son named **Charles Michael "Mike."** After securing a divorce, Edna committed suicide 13 May 1944, in Fruita, Colorado. Walter and Laura took Mike, then age 3, to raise. [Mildred tells us that Mike has raised a family and now lives somewhere in Utah.]

Laura was a member of the New Liberty Sorosis Club. Walter and Laura were of the Baptist faith, but attended the New Liberty Sunday School, held each Sunday in the school building.

Laura sewed the family's clothes and mended socks. They resoled their shoes. Living there on the farm, they raised almost everything to eat. Walter eventually bought more land to farm. They sold the place in 1945, moving to Fruita. Walter passed away 8 July 1951, at age 65.

Laura continued to live in Fruita with Mike. She lived to see him graduate from college, get married and start a family. She died 24 June 1970, at age 84, just short of her 85th birthday.

Walter, Edna and Laura were all buried in Elmwood Cemetery at Fruita.

Mildred, Charlie holding Charlotte, and Charlene and George
in front, 1936, in New Liberty.
(Photo courtesy of Charlene Brayton Eldridge)

Edna Myrul and Charles Michael Bennett
(Photo courtesy of Charlene Brayton Eldridge)

Following is a history written by Mildred Weir Brayton and published in the *Fruita Times,* 30 May 1991.

In 1919 we were living on a farm five or six miles from Wakefield, Kansas. Dad (Walter) decided we should go to Colorado for mother's health. My sister was two years old and we had the flu. Mother didn't seem to get over it, so we had a sale and sold most everything we didn't want to keep. We had dishes and some household things shipped to Colorado by some of the relatives after we got settled.

Dad bought a Maxwell car and we drove to mother's folks at Randall, Kansas, and visited with them for awhile, then started on to Colorado. Dad's sister came with us to care for Edna. We would set up a tent at a campground at night, then go on the next day. Finally we got to Colorado. We were so thrilled when we saw the range of mountains but it was a long time before we got to them.

We rented an apartment and stayed in Loveland for awhile, then started to go on west over to the western slope. I don't remember the names of the passes we traveled over, but it was a scary trip crossing them. The road was so narrow in spots that there were wide planks for the wheels on the one side to go on. I don't think we ever met anyone. Dad drove really careful; it was a long way to the bottom of the canyon. I was 8 1/2 years old and I watched the road all the way. Later Dad's sister took the train back to Kansas to her home, then we came to Grand Junction. There was a nice park for camping, so Dad put up the tent and that was our home for awhile.

Mother had me go to school a few blocks away. I made it to school, but got lost on my way home. I asked a man on the street where the park was, he told me and I found the folks.

Dad got work on a farm in the Pear Park area. There was a house on it for us to live in. But we found a farm for sale a little ways down the road and bought it. It was real close to Pear Park School, so I went there to school. I was in the second grade. I had missed so much of the first grade in Kansas and had forgotten all I had learned, but the school had a good teacher and I learned to read and write. That farm where we lived had a pear orchard, so Dad farmed the place. We sure enjoyed the fresh fruit there.

I started in the third grade the next fall. Then Dad read in the paper about the sale of farm land in the Lower Valley that could be homesteaded.

My aunt and uncle came to visit us from Kansas. The men looked into the deal and both of them bought land in the New Liberty District. My uncle, Allen Daily, lived closer to Mack. He taught school and farmed his place. But both families had to build houses to live in. The two Daily boys were too young to go to school. I went to school at Pear Park until we moved to New Liberty in March, and I was doing real well. But after we moved I had so far to walk. I never got to go the rest of the year, but the teacher at Pear Park passed me to the fourth grade.

Starting to make a home on bare land was an awful job. Dad built the cistern real large so we had water for the house, cows and other animals. We had a pump on the cistern and it was my job to keep the tank full for the cows and horses. Everyone had to work real hard. Part of our place was on a hill and there was land below the hill too. All was real good soil and raised good crops. We were so thankful the house was built on a hill. Once it rained hard in the high country, and the wash ran so full it ran over on the land and the bridge went sailing down the stream. Our way to town was closed, but soon the county sent men to put in a new bridge. We never had a flood like that again.

In the fall of 1921 I started school at New Liberty. I was in the fourth grade and had to walk two miles. That year the Raver family moved in around the hill back of Guy Gerry's place.

Laura, Edna, Mildred and Walter Weir in front of the Weir home in New Liberty, 1921. *(Photo courtesy of Charlene Brayton Eldridge)*

(Above) Mildred Weir feeding a bum lamb in front of the Weir home and car, 1917 or 1918 Model "T" Ford, with Edna Weir and Warren Shriver looking on, about 1921. *(Photos courtesy of Charlene Brayton Eldridge)*

(Right) Walter Weir in the corral with his Holstein cows. His barn and haystack are in the background.

(Above) Mildred, Laura, Walter and Edna Weir, 1927.

(Right) Walter Weir, Charlie Brayton, Allen Daily and David Thomas with Edna Weir in front holding a puppy, 1927. A 1917 or 1918 Model "T" Ford is in the background. *(Photos courtesy of Charlene Brayton Eldridge)*

Maudie walked with me and showed me how to cut off some miles by cutting through the farmer's fields. She just went one year, then graduated from the eighth grade and went to high school, so I was alone again. I can't thank dear Maxwell Sanders enough, he gave me an old gentle black horse and I learned to ride him to school. In the fall of 1922 I was in the fifth grade, Mrs. Snavely was my teacher. (I still have my grade card). I went through the eighth grade at New Liberty then went to Fruita Union High School. I had to walk a mile and a half to catch the school bus.

The Sumnicht family lived a little over a mile from us. Ena was teaching school east of Fruita, so she and her mother rented a house a half mile or so from Fruita Union High School. They asked me to stay with them, and it wasn't far for me to walk to school. Ena drove to her job. When the weather got colder they decided to get a place closer to her school. They told me of an older couple they thought would let me stay with them, so I stayed across the street at the Tom Arbuckle home (Ena's sister). I stayed there most of the winter and went to school, catching the bus to ride to Shires' corner and walk home from there to spend weekends. I graduated in 1930.

The folks kept busy; all of us kept busy. I did take a few piano lessons. I had a good teacher in Fruita. Ena took some lessons too, but she didn't care for music like I did. I had to work in the fields all morning cutting weeds until it got too hot for me.

On October 4, 1930, Charlie Brayton and I were married. He had farmed the Summers place that year. We lived there after we were married. In the fall and winter he worked in the garage as a mechanic, then he decided to move to the Boyden place and farmed it one year.

On October 23 1931, George Kenneth was born in St. Mary's Hospital in Grand Junction. Charlene was born February 3 1934, then Charlotte was born March 15 1935. When the children were old enough they attended New Liberty School.

About 1945 we bought a place in the Pear Park area. We had a nice pear orchard and Charlie worked at the railroad yards. I canned 100 quarts of pears that year. It was a slow job. I would do one or two kettles a day. I always canned lots of fruit.

Charlotte went to Clifton Junior High School, then to Fruitvale High School. All three children graduated from Fruitvale High School. George Kenneth graduated from Mesa College. He clerked in a store when not in school, and cleaned the college yard in the evenings. When he got married he and his wife moved to Denver. There

he went to the Baptist Seminary, as he wanted to be a missionary in Africa. After he graduated he took a boat to France. He attended the Sorbonne University in Paris to learn the African language. I think his wife, Erma, went part time too. They have been in Africa 25 years. George and Erma had three children and there are four grandchildren. [The missionary work was completed a few years ago. George now has a church in north Denver.]

Charlene is married to a contractor. They had three children; one has passed away. There are three grandchildren. Now she is the greeter for the Newcomers Club in Grand Junction.

Charlotte went into office work and is secretary for a citrus broker at Lakeland, Florida. Her husband travels over many states. They have one daughter and two grandchildren. The daughter has a good job with a large fruit company. [Charlotte and husband are both deceased].

In 1956 Charlie and I were divorced. I moved to Fruita when I was well enough and worked in people's homes caring for children. One job was as companion for a very nice lady in Grand Junction whose husband was in the hospital with terminal cancer. Her son was a good friend of Elliot Roosevelt. I helped cook and serve their supper, and, one time he [her son] brought his wife and I met her too. The lady I worked for said she would fix the meat — I was to fix the rest of the meal for them.

I then took care of six children for an insurance man and his wife while they went to a meeting in Chicago for two weeks. They were a nice family to work for. I also worked in Gay Johnson's home. In fact, I had more jobs than I could do, working in the homes of women who worked, and I really enjoyed it. It seems the phone was ringing off the hook with people wanting me to work for them.

I wanted my children to have a better life than I had, and they have. I haven't lived with any of my children. I have always been able to make a home on my own and I intend to keep it that way.

Clifford Tucker's mother lived in Fruita across the street from my mother. He lived in Pueblo, but would come to visit his mother and I met him there.

Clifford and I were married 4 September 1963. We had a very nice wedding at the home of his sister, Bertha Dee, and her husband Harvey Buniger. Clifford rented a duplex apartment in Pueblo from a lady who was single and had taught school for years. It had three rooms, a bath and a big basement. He had the home all fixed nice for me with nice furnishings throughout: a bed room set, instant heat cook stove, refrigerator, table, chairs. The front room furnished with TV, record player, couch, chairs and everything. Then we purchased a piano. I never had a nicely furnished home before. Because the lady was pleased with the way we kept it up, our rent was very reasonable. The apartment was on the bus route so I could go downtown and most places. We had a very good life together. I liked Pueblo; it was such a good place to us. We lived there 17 years.

Clifford began to have problems with arthritis and soon had to have a hip replacement and it wasn't very long until he had to have the other one replaced. That was too much for his strength. He was in the hospital two months before he passed away 22 October 1980.

The lady we rented from so long wanted a couple in the apartment, so I had to move. I began to have health problems and one day when I went to walk out to my car to go to the grocery store, I blacked out and fell. When I came to nobody was home but an elderly couple. I heard the man come out of the house and called to him and asked him to call an ambulance. Charlene and Jim were called and arrived as quickly as possible. Charlene stayed for a week and advised me to move into the Villa. There I had a real nice apartment where I could cook for myself or eat in the dining room.

Later I had to be moved into the "Pavilion" at the Villa where we are served our meals. The Villa has 15 floors, two elevators, two big vans to take us places we want to go, and a car if only a few want to go some place.

(As far as we know, Mildred is still living in the Villa.)

Wells

John Edward and Elizabeth Wells did not live in the New Liberty/Mack communities, but their five youngest children figure in our history, so we have decided to include data on the whole family. Frank and Laurene's daughter, Kathy Wells Hurt, was kind enough to supply us with a family group sheet giving the family data.

John Edward Wells was born 7 August 1879 at New Cambria, Saline, Kansas, to John Wells and Elizabeth Slonaker Byers. On 16 May 1902, at Salina, Saline, Kansas, John married **Elizabeth "Libbie" Humbarger**. Elizabeth was born 1 June 1885, also at New Cambria, to Daniel Humbarger and Anna Giersch.

John and Elizabeth had 10 children:

Ann Elizabeth (Haines) born 11 July 1903, Salina, Saline, Kansas,
Daniel Edward, 17 March 1905, Salina
Andrew Solomon, 11 April 1907, Salina
Wealthy Josephine, 31 August 1909, Messex, Washington, Colorado
Leo Raymond, 12 March 1912, Messex
Paul Raphael, 12 August 1914, Messex
Ralph Joseph, 20 February 1917, Messex
Marcella (Sweitzer), 7 August 1919, Messex
Frank Allan, 4 March 1925, Messex
Mary Lou (Rowe), 28 July 1927, Messex

Paul married **Mildred Lucille Goddard**
Ralph married **Emily Jane Sweitzer**.
Marcella married **Oscar Sweitzer**.
Mary Lou, married **Ben Henry Rowe**.

Following is information from a family group sheet and history filled out by John Wells, son of Ralph and Emily Wells.

L-R: Ralph and Emily Wells with Madeline and Bud Rose. Madeline is Emily's half-sister. *(Photo courtesy of John Wells)*

Carole Lee, Patricia Anne, and John Ralph Wells
(Photo courtesy of John Wells

Ralph Joseph Wells was born at Messex, Washington, Colorado, 20 February 1917, to John Edward Wells and Elizabeth Humbarger. He spent his early years at Messex and came to the Loma, Colorado, area with his family in 1928 (see following Wells stories).

Ralph completed the eighth grade at Loma Elementary School and graduated from Fruita Union High School in 1934. During his school years he had five brothers whom son John says were involved in several "orderly disputes" with other boys. It's not hard to imagine that six boys could be a rather formidable force! Ralph was not easily intimidated. On one occasion, he had a run-in with one of the referees of an opposing basketball team. He was ejected from the game.

Numbered among Ralph's special friends were Leland Buniger and Carl Weaver.

Ralph always had a great love for horses and did some racing as well as Brahma bull riding in rodeos all over western Colorado. He belonged to a saddle club and also was involved in playing polo, a sort of "mayhem" on horse-back. Ralph still has a saddle horse in Washington, where they live now, even though he is now 80 years old.

Ralph married his high school sweetheart, **Emily Jane Sweitzer,** on 30 June 1935 at Fruita, Colorado. Emily was born 13 May 1918, in Grand Junction, to Oscar Sweitzer and Madge Herron. She attended schools in Fruita.

Ralph and Emily had two daughters and one son:

Patricia Anne (Farraro), born 2 March 1936
Carole Lee (Hoover), 10 April 1946
John Ralph, 11 February 1948
All three were born in Fruita.

Evidently Emily had trouble bearing children, as it appears she lost one or more between Patricia and Carole. John tells us that, when she gave birth to him, last rites were administered to her, as doctors had given up hope that she would survive. But she did survive, though she had to spend three months in the hospital. John said that he and the rest of the family will be forever indebted to "Granny Herron" (Emily's grandmother, Jessie Herron. See Herron story), who cared for John while his mother recovered.

Ralph and Emily lived on the Orval Herron farm for several years and were engaged in farming and raising livestock. They were involved in community activities. During 1947 Ralph served on the Mack School Board. Since parents and siblings of both Ralph and Emily lived nearby, there was lots of family togetherness. Their names are mentioned often in news items for the Mack and New Liberty communities.

In June 1949, Ralph and Emily became interested in an irrigation project in Washington, so they moved there and Ralph went to work in the construction part of the

Ralph Wells' 1932 Chevrolet truck used on the Orval Herron farm, north of Mack. The family dog is posing in front. *(Photo courtesy of John Wells)*

project. He was involved in building 1,500 miles of canals and laterals, as well as the highways and airports in an area north of Pasco. Before he retired, Ralph purchased some undeveloped land near Ephrata and Quincy and has spent some time developing that since retirement.

Emily worked as a nurse in hospitals in Olympia and Ephrata, Washington. Ralph and Emily are both retired and are living in Woodinville, Washington. They celebrated 62 years of married life in June of this year (1997). They have nine grandchildren.

Patty works for Holland American Lines (Cruise Ships) in Seattle as a private secretary. She is divorced.

Carole is a homemaker and works part time in a book store. Her husband is a manufacturer's representative for Boeing Aircraft Co.

John is head dispatcher for Puget Sound Truck Lines. The company has 500 trucks working throughout the Pacific Northwest. His wife is a part-time bookkeeper

Frank Allan and Naomi Laurene Conrad Wells, 1943. *(Photo courtesy of Laurene Wells)*

The following was written by Katherine Wells, daughter of Frank and Laurene Wells, as Frank and Laurene told the stories. We have done some editing.

Frank, the youngest boy of the family, continued farming after his father retired and most of the brothers had drifted away from farming. Frank farmed with two brothers: Ralph, who lived north of Mack on the Herron place, and Paul, who lived on the Bowen place.

Frank was married 15 August 1943, to **Naomi Laurene Conrad**, daughter of Willis Conrad and Bea Bancroft. She was born in Palisade, Colorado, 20 June 1925.

Frank recalls:

Farming has been in my family for many generations. My maternal grandfather, Daniel Humbarger, came to Kansas as a teenager with his family in 1857. Three years after that the state was opened for settlement. Daniel homesteaded a place next to his father's in the rich bottom lands of the Saline River where he raised wheat and grazed cattle.

My maternal grandmother, Anna Giersch, was born in France and came to America with her family when she was a small girl. They were among the first homesteaders in Kansas.

My paternal grandfather, John Wells, was born in Brooke County, Virginia, in 1827. His father and grandfather came from Wales. John Wells was a Civil War Veteran, who served in Company K 6th West Virginia Infantry. He participated in the Battle of Bull Run.

John Wells went to Kansas about 1872, where he married Elizabeth (Slonaker) Byers, a widow with one daughter named Sadie. Elizabeth "Lizzie" was Pennsylvania Dutch, born 23 October 1854, in Cambria County, Pennsylvania.

John and Elizabeth had seven children, including my father, John Edward. When Lizzie died at age 39, the children scattered to get work or to marry. After a tour of duty in the Army during the Spanish American War, John Edward returned to Kansas and found work on his future father-in-law's farm. He married Daniel Humbarger's youngest child, Elizabeth "Libbie," one month short of her 16th birthday, 16 May 1901.

In the early 1900s a land agency in northeast Colorado organized an area laid out in small acreages for growing sugar beets. My maternal grandmother, Anna Giersh Humbarger, decided to sell out at a public auction — house, furniture and farming equipment — and try this "get rich" way. Since her husband had died eight years earlier she was accompanied to Colorado in 1907 by two sons, two daughters and their families. One of those daughters was my mother, Elizabeth Humbarger, the wife of John Edward Wells. Elizabeth had asthma and the drier Colorado climate was beneficial.

John Edward and Elizabeth homesteaded at Messex, Colorado, which is located in the extreme north west corner of Washington County, southwest of Sterling. Seven of their 10 children were born there.

In 1928 we moved to the Loma, Colorado, area, trading farms with a man who wanted to return to the eastern slope. Some of the family came by train, some in automobiles. They must have felt at home in their new location when they found that sugar beets were being promoted by the Holly Sugar Company.

Although she was not raised on a farm, **Laurene's** family had a farming background.

Laurene recalls:

My father, Willis Conrad, came to the Appleton district of the Grand Valley when he was a boy. He and his brother were born in Barton County, Missouri. His parents were George Conrad, of German descent, and Nancy May Query of Scottish descent. They met and married in Barton County. There are still farms in that area owned by descendants of those families. George and Nancy and sons came to the Grand Valley in a covered wagon.

My mother, Bea Bancroft, and her family, came to Palisade in 1905 from Nodaway County, Missouri, where Bea was born. They came to join an uncle who was establishing a fruit orchard in the Fruita area for a nursery at Fairbury, Nebraska. That orchard was to become the Weckel place ,west of Fruita. My grandfather, W. T. Bancroft, had an orchard at Palisade and was town marshal.

One summer my grandfather Bancroft worked on the construction of the Highline Canal with his team of horses. During that time my grandmother and children went back to Missouri to visit maternal grandparents and other relatives.

My father, Willis Conrad, became a telegrapher for the D&RGW Railroad and was working at Palisade when he met my mother on a blind date. She was working in the telephone office. They were married in October 1917. My sister and I were born in Palisade. We moved to Eagle, Colorado, for a short time, then back west to Fruita, where my father was depot agent.

When Frank and I were married, we lived in a tiny house on the Herron place. Later Frank rented different places: we lived on the Scop Keffalos place on 12 Road, and at the Grover Stout place, also on 12 Road. While we were there we bought the Reese Arbuckle farm on 10 1/2 Road, north of the Davidson's.[†] This place had originally been homesteaded by the Bannister family of Grand Junction for rabbit hunting, but was not proved up on.[*] The Arbuckle house on the Red Mesa was a small, three-room house built on the ground; the floors were not very even. The water in the bucket sitting by the back door frequently froze overnight. The mice were a plague — we would turn off the lights at night and the mice would scurry. There was a modern barn on the place, and for awhile Frank had a herd of dairy cattle and sold milk to Carnation.[†]

† It was irrigated with pumped water.
* Remember Bannister Furniture?

754

(Above) Frank Wells with horses, Duke and Doc, raking hay at the Horse Farming Days in Silt, Colorado.

(Right) Wells Farms Belgians wagon in Fruita parade. Laurene Wells and granddaughter, Joanna Hurt, sitting in the wagon and Frank Wells on the driver's seat.

(Below left) Frank Wells with horses, Pete and Charlie, harrowing on the Berry place in New Liberty.

(Below right) The Frank Wells home before the addition was put on the back, 1965. Dale and John are on the sled. *(Photos courtesy of Laurene Wells)*

While we were living on the Arbuckle place, two of our five children were born. **Louise** was born 19 November 1946, at the old Fruita Hospital. On that occasion, when I sounded the alarm, we dashed out the door as Frank grabbed the chain to turn off the light, and the whole fixture came crashing down. We left it right there on the floor. We climbed into the Chevy coupe and Frank shivered all the way to Fruita. For some reason he kept commenting how cold it was.

Katherine "Kathy" was born in the old Fruita Hospital on 25 September 1949, at about noon. Frank was milking cows when we had to leave for the hospital, so the cows waited until mid-day to be milked. Frank was also in the middle of bean cutting.

We moved to New Liberty on Thanksgiving Day 1951. We bought the 120-acre place on R½ Road with the big frame house from Phillip Brayton. In addition to that place we were still farming the mesa farm on 10½ Road, north of Mack. My parents helped us move to our New Liberty home, which was located one-fourth mile east of the New Liberty School.

The house on the Brayton place was like a mansion to us. It was a two-story house built over a basement but was not completely finished. We moved the heating stove out of the living room and installed a furnace in the basement. In the process of finishing the upstairs there was a hole left in the ceiling for a light fixture, so the kids used to throw a ball through the hole. The bathroom was not finished, so an outdoor toilet was used for many years. We took candles upstairs for light until the electrical wiring was finished. We piled covers on in the winter time. When the bathroom was finished the basement stairs were moved and a large utility room was added on.

Martha Marie "Marty" was born at St. Mary's Hospital on 17 March 1953. After the birth a sister came in and asked what I was naming my beautiful daughter — I told her she was named Martha Marie and she said, 'She should be named Patricia for St. Patrick's Day.'

Dale was born 19 January 1955, at St. Mary's Hospital. I went to town with Frank to spend the day at my sister-in-law's, since I was having some contractions. Frank intended to be gone most of the day looking for winter work. When the time came to go to the hospital, Frank was not back, so my brother-in-law took me to the hospital. After

explaining two or three times to different nurses that he was not the father, he gave up and went along with them.

John was born in Fruita, 7 December 1964. We went to town on Monday afternoon for our children's religious education class. I had done a big laundry at the washeteria and went to Grandma Wells home to rest for awhile. I ended up in the hospital after it became apparent John was to arrive about one month earlier than calculated. The girls had to do the ironing.

When our children started school they walked to New Liberty School and complained about walking (¼ mile). Then when they could ride the bus to Junior and Senior High, they got tired of the bus.

New Liberty was a quaint country school housing eight grades, but later only six grades, when junior high began in Fruita. Louise and Kathy had Sue Thompson for first and second grades. Louise had Mary Lou Reeves for third grade, Helen Andrews for fourth grade, and Mabel Cooper for fifth and sixth grades. Kathy had Helen Turmon for fourth and fifth grades. Before the new room and indoor restrooms were added in 1957 or 58, one combination class was held either on the stage or in the gym. Tables were set up for the older children to eat lunch either on the stage or in the gym. The first and second grades ate in the kitchen with Mrs. Thompson. Before hot lunches, students brought their lard pails or sack lunches.

Children played kickball, softball, jacks, jump rope, high or broad jump. It was always a mad dash to get out there for a chance at two swings, or a chance at the teeter-totter or the merry-go-round, which accommodated quite a few. The boys chased the girls either to the old cistern lid for a safe base or to the girls' outdoor restroom. One teacher put a stop to that safe place after she nearly got ran over at the doorway!

Marty recalls playing house under the cottonwood trees on the playground; many rocks were gathered to outline the rooms. Many hours were spent with friends Becky, Neta and Fran Young, playing house. The smell of cottonwood trees can still elicit those memories.

The Christmas programs were memorable events. Louise was once an angel with clothes-hanger wings, and Kathy an elf in Santa's workshop.

Physical education teachers would come

† Most likely Meadow Gold.

Louise, Dale, Marty and Kathy Wells, 1958.
(Photo courtesy of Laurene Wells)

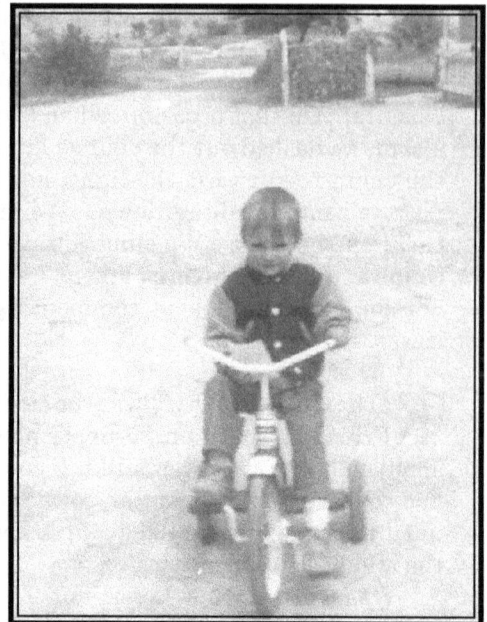

John Wells riding his tricycle.
(Photo courtesy of Laurene Wells)

out once or twice a month. Once the physical education men came out when it happened to be April 1st. They said the big building that housed the rock shop at Mack had burned. They had a hard time convincing the children that it was not an April Fool's joke. Mrs. Mary Heinz also came out to teach music with her pitch pipe. When the schools were consolidated about 1960, the New Liberty kids went to the Loma School.

All of the Wells family have fond memories of their friends and good times at school and community gatherings. They often recall the times they swam in the canals and ditches, including exciting and dangerous float trips through the flume at Camp #7.

The entire family was involved in Community Club activities, card parties, dances and 4-H demonstrations. Frank served as president of the Community Club one year. The Sorosis Club ladies purchased tin cups and plates for the club to serve sandwiches and coffee at the farm sales.

Louise was married in 1972 but it didn't last; she divorced and took her maiden name back. She has one daughter, born 14 September 1985, in Calcutta India; adopted when she was two months old.

Louise attended Colorado University Law School and got a master's degree in Estate Planning at University of Florida. She is now serving as an attorney at Lakewood, Colorado.

Kathy married **John Hurt**, 1 July 1968. They have two daughters, **Joanna Louise** and **Ginger Diane**. John was drafted into the Army after they were married only eight months; fortunately he didn't have to go to Vietnam. He did, however, go to Germany for awhile.

Kathy earned a degree in elementary education at Western State College. After the birth of two daughters, she completed a course in preschool administration at Colorado University. She is now doing private preschool and day-care in Fruita.

Back Row, L-R: Frank, Dale and John Wells. Front Row: Marty, Laurene, and Kathy Wells. *(Photo courtesy of Laurene Wells)*

757

arty married **Dennis Hardrick**, 27 March 1976. They have two boys and a girl: **Kelly Erin**, **Kevin Wade** and **Kaitlin Marie**.

Marty has a degree in elementary education from University of Northern Colorado at Greeley. She has taught first and second grades for 16 years at Shelledy Elementary at Fruita.

ale graduated from Fruita Union High School in 1973 and is involved in the farming operation with his dad, and does custom "big" baling on the side. Dale was married, but is now divorced. He has one son, **Curtis Franklin**.

ohn graduated from Fruita Union High School in 1983 and is also involved in the farming operation with his dad, and does custom combining on the side. He was married, but is now divorced.

When Everett Bowen retired from the mail carrier route in 1963, Laurene made the highest score on the letter-carrier's test. She started the half-day Mack route job in May 1963. Before long, when Tom Saunders retired, the Loma carrier's job was combined with Mack. So, in January 1964, Laurene began carrying the mail on both routes. When Bea Vanlandingham retired as Loma Postmaster, Laurene went to San Francisco and passed a test for that job. She held that position from November 1975 until her retirement in August 1985.

Frank has developed a very interesting and rewarding hobby. As a young man he used horses when he was farming with his father — he has retained a great love for horses. Once when he attended the Denver Livestock Show he became interested in draft horses. In 1982 he traveled to a small town southwest of Dodge City, Kansas, where he bought his first team, Pete and Charlie, Strawberry Roan Belgians. In the fall of that year he returned to the midwest to buy some Blond Sorrel Belgian colts. Now Barney is the stud, and Goldie's Donna and Babe are the mares.

In the spring of 1984, while Frank was on the way to Iowa to buy horses and equipment, Pete got out of the pasture one night and was badly injured on the road. On that trip, Frank purchased Doc and Duke, Blond Sorrel Belgians, to replace the other team. They had a Brownie Hayride first on their agenda.

The teams have been involved in several special events: Ground breaking for the Grand

Junction Hilton, Coors Trail Ride, Coors Wagon in the Rodeo Parade, Garfield County Draft Horse Show, Farming Days at Silt, Wells Farm Wagon at the Fruita Fall Festival Parade, and Hayrides for the Deaf.

Through the years the Wells family had many other interesting pets, such as bum lambs and bottle-fed calves. When Grandpa Conrad had to retire, Frank took his sheep to tend. Mary Ann, the lamb, thought she was a cow, since she had grazed with the cows so long. One day Mary Ann thought she should go to school and followed Louise onto the bus. How embarrassing for a teenager!

The family dog, Sandy, was protective of the children playing in the ditch. He would run back and forth along the bank barking, as if he was worried. He also knew when it was time for the school bus in the afternoon. He would sit on the drain-ditch bank, and when he saw the bus coming he would run to the corner to meet the kids.

The years of 1957 and 1958 were not very good on the farm. The sugar beets got a disease and in the fall the rains started and eventually most of the beets froze in the ground and were lost. Frank was given an opportunity to manage a wheat farm on the Oregon-Washington line, near Walla Walla, Washington. In March of 1959 he rented his farm out and went to Oregon to work. Laurene and the kids stayed until school was out in May, then went by train to join him.

Frank was not able to find good, steady laborers to work on the farm, plus there was 108° weather in the summer, so after a year, we decided this wasn't for us and that New Liberty looked pretty good. In the spring of 1960 we returned to the farm, happy for the experience, but glad to be home!

During the years we raised sugar beets, we had Navajos from Arizona to do the thinning and weeding. That was an experience for the kids. We would get the Indians from Grand Junction. Always there were all ages represented in the group; they lived in our little house on the mesa. The Navajo women dressed in several long velvet skirts and shirts with lots of turquoise jewelry and safety pins. The children and the babes in cradle-boards were an attraction too. We would take them in the back of the truck to Mack or Fruita to get groceries.

Frank and Laurene celebrated their 50th wedding anniversary 12 September 1993 with a reception at Highline Lake, north of Loma. The event was hosted by their children and grandchildren; an important milestone in the lives of any married couple.

Wells

Information is from obituaries and news items in *The Daily Sentinel,* plus some input from the author.

Lee Roy Wells was born in 1895 in Texas, but moved to Colorado with his parents, **Martin L.** and **Anna E. Wells.**

Lee Roy Wells and his parents are listed in the 1920 census (New Liberty/Mack area) with Lee Roy, age 24, as head of the family. The record shows Martin was born in Mississippi; he was then **69;** Anna, born in Tennessee, was **64.**

Lee Roy and his father both filed on homesteads in the New Liberty community. Lee Roy apparently bought a relinquishment from George Bryan some time prior to the drawing on 29 March 1918; it was unit "J" in the south west corner of Sec. 16. That was later purchased by Elva Gunst and eventually went to Oscar and Laura Berry. Martin bought a relinquishment from Walter Sarles in 1919 on unit "F" of Sec. 17, just south of Clyde Likes Sr. and west of New Liberty School. The names of Roy and M. L. Wells are on the list of voters when the New Liberty School District was organized. We know nothing further of the elder Wells.

Roy, young and single, began paying court to the new school teacher at New Liberty when school began in 1919. Her name was **Bonnie O'Bryan,** the first teacher in the New Liberty School. Bonnie was born 13 September 1896 at Berea, Iowa, and came to Fruita, Colorado, as a child with her parents, Mr. and Mrs. James O'Bryan. She spent her early life in Fruita and graduated from Fruita Union High School. We note with interest an item in the Fruita news in *The Daily Sentinel* of 14 January 1919: "Miss Bonnie O'Bryan is one of the latest students from Fruita to attend Hoel's Business College."

She taught one year at New Liberty, and also taught at Pear Park School at some point in time.

Roy and Bonnie were married at Fruita, 2 June 1921. They continued to live on the farm in New Liberty until May 1927, when they moved to Wellington, in the area of Fort Collins, Colorado.

They had 6 children:

Gale
Alice (Hansen)
May (Mitchell)
Clara
Elaine
Inez (Reed)

Roy died unexpectedly at age 59, 26 March 1953, at Fort Collins.

After that Bonnie and two of her daughters came back to Grand Junction for about four years. Then Bonnie moved to Denver. She and a daughter had been visiting with family in Clovis, New Mexico, when Bonnie died unexpectedly en route to Fort Collins on 11 July 1960. Both she and Roy were buried at Fort Collins.

Wesner

Following is a bit of Mack history provided by **Opal Wesner (Boss)** in the form of a letter to the editor of the *Fruita Times*, published 23 May 1991:

The article by the Kiefer Family was most informative and took much research. Later than Roy Wagaman's death in 1924 on the Uintah Railway, my uncle, **H. R. Kirksey**, was killed in July 1937 when he was foreman of the B&B gang. He was struck by a large timber and died soon after at St. Mary's Hospital. His son was drowned while serving under John F. Kennedy on a PT-109 during World War II.

My sister, **Gertrude**, and I were witnesses to the accident when Mr. Dean [Malcolm S. Dean] was struck by a D&RGW Railroad freight train as he crossed the tracks in front of the Independent Lumber Company. We were the only witnesses and were called to testify at the hearing.

Sheep shearing and shipping and all it entails clearly stand out in the memories of many of us. Shearing provided entertainment as we all perched on the rail around the shearing pens. There were no electric clippers then. Shipping season consisted of constant bleating and shifting of stock loading cars. To this day I cannot eat lamb!

My dad, **John Wesner**, a railroad telegrapher and station agent for both the Uintah Railway and D&RGW Railroad, missed many a meal during loading. No time out was given for meals unless 'nothing was coming,' and he asked out. Vacations were a luxury then and he worked seven years, seven days a week, with no time off.

With few phones in Mack and no radio until about 1930, urgent news came over the wire via Western Union in conjunction with the railroad. Also, without the luxury of automobiles and good roads, our family traveled by train to the doctor in Grand Junction, Mayo Brother's Clinic, and to visit relatives in the east and Washington, D. C. Railroading was a way of life.

Mr. Falvey, manager of the Uintah Railway, owned a car in Mack in 1915 or 16. I was given a ride around the loop in the big, black sedan. He picked me up in front of our home at that time, the Eberline house. This was later the

John Wesner, railroad telegrapher and station master at Mack is shown in front of the Mack Depot in an earlier day. The depot, and Wesner, served both the Uintah Railway and the D&RGW Railroad. *(Photo used from the Fruita Times, 23 May 1991 issue)*

Calderwood family residence. Mr. Calderwood was a worker on the gilsonite transfer gang and an avid baseball player.

My mother, **Clarinda**, was post-mistress during part of World War I, but later discontinued due to ill health. The post office was located south of the tracks, across from the pump house and west of Crew's grocery and Stables. Mail was handed out through the window, as there were no combination lock boxes at first. This entailed late hours for my mother, as she accommodated customers long after closing. Many were farmers who worked their fields until dark, and then came to town for their mail. Later my dad purchased and installed boxes as we know them now.

The Wesner family are listed in the 1920 census in Mack under the name "Wesley." John, age 35, was listed as "Telegraph Operator." The mother, Clarinda, was 37; and daughters were Opal, 8, and Gertrude, 5.

White

Information is from obituaries and news items in *The Daily Sentinel* and some input from personal knowledge of the author.

$\mathcal{E}$verett Herman White was born 3 July 1919, in Grand Junction. He attended schools in Colorado at Hunter, Campo, and Fruita Union High School. In Utah he attended schools at Enterprise, and Cisco. He also lived at one time in Montana.

Everett and **Mary Kovach** were married 7 October 1939, at Delta, Colorado.

They had four children:

> **Patricia Ann (Neff)**
> **Helen Marie (Jensen);**
> **Raymond**
> **Dale**

The White family lived in the New Liberty community during the 1940s and 50s on the Robert M. Cox farm. Everett and his brother, Gaylen, were partners in that operation. The children attended New Liberty School.

Everett had a keen interest in farming, and it showed. He also loved to hunt and fish. He received the Stockmen's Award in Collbran in 1983.

Everett died 4 March 1985 and was buried in Memorial Gardens Cemetery at Grand Junction.

Wilkinson

Information from letters and histories written by Lester, Alex, Rudy and Gene Wilkinson, plus obituaries and news items from *The Daily Sentinel.*

$\mathcal{C}$ecil R. Wilkinson was born 14 September 1897, in Indian Territory [presently Oklahoma] and was married to **Lora A. Brown**, 5 November 1926, in Oklahoma.

They had four sons:

Lester Cecil, born 16 June 1931, Beaver City, Beaver, Oklahoma
Alex D., 14 January 1933, Beaver City, Oklahoma
Rudy R., 10 December 1940, Mack, Colorado

Eugene B., 11 September 1944, at Fruita

Cecil, Lora, Lester and Alex moved from Allison, Texas, to Mack in 1938, driving a Model "A" Ford. They first moved into an old building located in the Uintah yards in Mack.

Cecil worked on the dismantling of the Uintah Railway, beginning in 1939. During that time he purchased a Uintah caboose which was still sitting on a spur near the ramp being used to load the scrap from the Uintah onto the Denver and Rio Grande. Before the tracks were all removed Cecil had the caboose moved over to the vicinity of the water tower and set on a foundation of railroad ties. The family lived in that for awhile. Then, in 1940, they moved to the Brewster farm, north of Mack (on Mack Mesa, across from Herron's). In 1943 they moved to a farm just west of Mack, then to the Claude Taylor place in New Liberty that fall.

During the time the family lived on the Taylor place, Lester and Alex finished grade school and Rudy started to school. Eugene "Gene" was born while they lived there. Cecil farmed during the summer months and worked in the coal mines in winter.

After they left the farm the family lived northeast of Fruita at a coal mine operated by members of the Patterson family of Fruita. Alex and Rudy attended school in Fruita while Cecil and Lester worked at the mine. After they left the coal mine they moved into a house west of the present Mack Post Office. While there Cecil began work at the Polar Mesa Uranium mine.

At some point in time (probably 1949/50) the family moved into a house south of the highway across from the old Kiefer log house (built in 1925 by Tony Overbye). That is where they were living when Cecil died. Lora continued to live there for some time and later married Dewey Porter. They moved to Fruita. Currently Lora is living at "The Oaks" in Fruita.

Sitting in back, L-R: Alex, Lora and Lester Wilkinson. Front: Eugene and Rudy Wilkinson, January 1997. *(Photo courtesy of Rudy Wilkinson)*

Lester graduated from New Liberty in 1946 and from Fruita Union High School in 1949. Later, in 1949, he married **Olive Bunch**. They had two daughters: **Leslie** and **Barbara**. Lester and Olive later divorced.

In 1964, Lester was married to **Mildred Nichols Harris**, who had previously been married and had four children: **Rita, Lorna, Gavin** and **Mark**. Later Lester and Mildred had a boy whom they named **Cecil**.

Lester worked for the D&RGW Railroad for 35 years; retiring in 1993.

Alex went to work at the uranium mine on Polar Mesa, where he worked until January 1951. Then he went to work for the D&RGW Railroad on a signal gang at Salt Lake City, Utah. At that time the signal gangs lived in outfit cars and were moved anywhere on the system they had work to do.

While working for the D&RGW, Alex met **Louise Tattershall**; they were married in June 1953. In April 1954, there first son, **Dennis**, was born in Grand Junction. In July 1955, Alex, Louise and young Dennis moved to Castro Valley, California, where Alex went to work for the Southern Pacific Railroad. In February 1956, their second son, **Wayne**, was born in Castro Valley.

Alex's job transferred him from Castro Valley to Suisun, California, in 1956. They lived in Valejo, California, and Alex commuted to Suisun.

In 1957, Alex was again transferred; to Oakland, California. While working there, the family lived in Hayward, California. They were living there at the time of Cecil R.'s death on 4 March 1961.

Alex, Louise and their two children came to Colorado for the funeral, and one week after Cecil's death, 11 March 1961, Louise was killed in a head-on collision with another car, a couple of miles east of Mack near the bridge over the Kiefer Canal. Alex and the two little boys, ages four and six, were seriously injured, but survived.

In June of 1962, Alex got a one year leave of absence from his job, and moved his family back to Colorado. Grandmother Tattershall watched Dennis and Wayne while Alex worked. While living there, Alex met **Mary Lee Covey** (the former Mary Lee Gerry), who had lost her husband to cancer. She had an eighteen-month old daughter, **Robin**. Alex and Mary were married in October 1962. They returned to California where Alex continued to work for Southern Pacific until he retired in 1991. After retirement they returned to Colorado, buying a place in Fruita where they live at the present time.

All three of their children are married and live in Colorado.

Dennis and his wife, **Patsy**, live north of Fruita with their two children, **Michalle** and **Keith**.

Wayne and his wife, **Etta,** live near Fruita.

Robin and her husband, **Arturo,** live in Delta, Colorado, with their two children, **Ivan** and **Jennifer.**

Rudy started grade school at New Liberty in 1946, Fruita Elementary in 1948, and Mack School in 1949. In 1953 the Mack School was closed and the students were bused either to New Liberty or Loma. Rudy had a choice of schools. He chose New Liberty and graduated from there in 1954. He graduated from Fruita Union High School in 1958.

On Christmas day in 1958, he married **Vivian Lee Peterson** of Loma; daughter of Harold and Winnie Peterson. They had two children: **Dwayne Ray,** born 2 February 1960 and **Janet Lee,** born 30 May 1963.

Rudy works as a salesman. They currently live at Fruita.

Gene says the family was living on a farm west of Mack when he was born. After that they moved to a house in Mack, "across the street from Della Swyhart." Next they moved to a home east of Mack, across from Kiefer's log house. The following is written by Gene.

I started school at Mack Elementary in September of 1950. I was in the last class to attend the school prior to its being closed and the students bused to New Liberty. Mack school was closed, I suppose, because of falling attendance. I went to New Liberty until 1956.

I attended Fruita Junior High School from September 1956 until 1959, when I entered Fruita Union High School. During my junior high years I was a paper carrier for *The Daily Sentinel* in the Mack area.

It was a great time in my life because all the people were so nice and gave me not only fond memories but treats and Christmas gifts as well.

Some of the names I remember are:
Mr. and Mrs. Guy Snook
Della Swyhart
Bill and Delores Archuleta[†]
Mr. and Mrs. Koch
Mr. and Mrs. Muth
Mr. and Mrs. John Garcia
Mr. and Mrs. Cecil Monger
Mr. and Mrs. Kelly
The Rich family
Joe and Jenny Brewster
Mr. and Mrs. Tony Garcia
Uncle Alex and Aunt Mary Wilkinson
The Vigil family
Mr. and Mrs. Marshall Eddings
Alta Smith

I started going to Fruita Union High School in 1959 and graduated in 1962. I worked at odd jobs for a year or so, then moved to Minturn, Colorado, where I lived with my oldest brother, Lester, and worked at the New Jersey Zinc mine. Later I moved to Climax and worked in the Molybdenum mine.

I enlisted in the Navy in 1964 and was stationed at San Diego, California, for my boot training. After that I was sent to a troop transport, the USS Whetstone LSD- 27. While on that we made three trips to Vietnam. I was awarded three medals on those tours. I later went to two Navy schools, and was then transferred to a nuclear submarine tender, the USS Proteus AS-19, on Guam, for an 18-month tour. I finished my tour in the Navy as an E-6 Electrician's Mate, stationed on a destroyer tender, the USS Prairie AD-14, in San Diego, California. I was in the Navy until 1968.

I met my first wife, **Carol Jean Sulzer,** while I was at Minturn; we were married 23 December 1965, in Glenwood Springs, Colorado. My oldest son was born at Denver, 19 February 1971; we named him **Russell Lynn Wilkinson.** Our second son, **Aaron Caly Wilkinson,** was born at Wheatridge, Colorado, 26 September 1973.

After I got out of the Navy in 1968 we moved to Denver, Colorado, where I went back to school. Then I opened my own air conditioning and heating company, R & A Maintenance Co. Later I opened a second company, Anatech Inc., and still later I opened Gene's Mechanical.

In 1990 I was separated from my first wife and in 1992 left Colorado to live in San Diego, California. On 30 October 1992 I married again to **Judy Benjamin** whom I chanced to meet while she was visiting from Australia. We moved to Tucson, Arizona, in 1994, purchased a home and set up residence in the desert

[†] He probably means Placito and Doris.

southwest.

Some of my memories of living in Mack will never and can never be replaced or forgotten, and here are a few I would like to share.

The time I was shooting sparrows on the railroad telegraph lines near our back yard, holding up trains in both directions for some time. Thanks to Mr. Kelly and his influence, nothing was done about it when he found out who had done it. But he sure put the fear in me not to do it again.

When I lost my dog, Danny. Those who were living in Mack at the time will remember Danny, a really ugly bulldog. But he was the best watch-dog in the area. We never knew for sure where he went, but we had some suspicions. It was a great loss to me and to my whole family.

The way all the neighbors would come to anyone's assistance when there was a need. Never asking what or why, just doing it.

The social times when the whole valley would come out for the school and community programs in New Liberty. All sharing, and good times were had by all.

The one thing that is and will always be in my heart and mind was the night I was at a birthday party in Loma and someone called, advising me that my Dad had been in a mine accident. He died the next day. That was the one thing that made all my memories seem so hard because my Dad was no longer there and the emptiness caused by his passing was hard to bear.

Then just a few days later my brother, Alex, and his wife, Louise, and my nephews, came from California for the funeral and they were hit by a drunken driver on the canal bridge east of Mack. Louise was killed instantly. This was the loss also of one of the people I loved most. I will never forget the pain and the hurt in that time of my life.

Over the years I have written poetry, but not until I moved to Tucson did I ever get really serious about it enough to consider having any published. I am now a published poet in several anthologies by various publishing companies. I recently received the "Editor's Choice Award" for one of my poems that was published in the National Library of Poetry Anthology. I'm in the process of putting a book of my poetry together to be published within the next year or so.

Gene was kind enough to send us some of his poems; we'll share two of them here.

Midnight Hour

As I sit here in this midnight hour
Amazed at the serenity it does hold
The power of the majestic night
Brings beauty that cannot be told
The silence, that darkness has
No words can or will come to mind
The peacefulness of the dark blue sky
To describe it, no thought can I find
I see its beauty, I feel it's vastness
Knowing time can never stand still
Yet hearing and seeing the shadows transcend
As though it cannot be for real
What makes the darkness seem so serene
How can the stars seem, oh so bright
The magic of all things around us
Seems so defined, in the stillness of the night
The daylight brings all things to color
And of course we need the blessed sun
But in the night the darkest night
The mind and soul seem to become as one

My Earth

Oh sweet earth, my eyes are wet
What are we doing to your beauty today
Take heed of my gift I give you
For I will never come this way again
I put my feet in your rivers to learn
It will never be the same water I touch
What great pain it gives me to see you
To feel you and yet not really know you
Can I give you new life as we know it
Do you accept our treatment as fools
Dear earth let my very soul be in you
So I too may know what pain you must feel
May I someday look back and see again
The beauty you hold for believers as I
Precious earth where my life starts and ends
Let not our destruction be your end
Teach us to give you only what you give us
Let us feel with our hearts and spirits
Oh precious earth of which we owe all
Lie peaceful in hopes of a better tomorrow

The following is from obituaries in *The Daily Sentinel.*

James Alexander "Alex" Wilkinson was born 29 December 1899, in Indian Territory (later Oklahoma). He spent his early life there. Alex and **Mary Ellen Tolle** were married at Lipscomb, Lipscomb, Texas, 26 December 1919. Mary Ellen was born 14 November 1902, in Dewey County, Oklahoma Territory. There were no children.

Alex and Mary Ellen lived in Oklahoma and Allison, Texas, for a time before they came to Mack in 1935. For several years Alex operated a garage in Mack, adjacent to the Last Chance Service Station. They lived for a time on a small farm immediately east and south of Mack, which was probably at one time part of the Charles Kiefer homestead. (Now it belongs to "Country Jam USA"). At one time Alex was employed as a blacksmith and welder in Fruita and Grand Junction. After World War II he worked in Mesa, Arizona, and as a miner at Polar Mesa, Utah. He retired in 1960.

Alex died of a heart attack in Grand Junction, 22 May 1972. Mary Ellen moved to Denver and lived there until her death, 13 December 1979. Both were buried in Elmwood Cemetery at Fruita.

Wing

The next three stories are taken from obituaries in *The Daily Sentinel.*

Reba Wing was born 19 September 1902 at Edgemont, Fall River, South Dakota, to James S. Wing and Mary Zeller. Reba moved with her family to Grand Junction in 1914 where she graduated from Grand Junction High School. Later she earned a bachelor of arts degree from Western State College at Gunnison, Colorado, and still later, a master's degree at University of Denver.

Reba became a teacher, and in addition to having taught with her sister, Wauneta, at New Liberty in 1930/31, she taught business courses at Grand Junction High School. Also during her career she taught at several other schools throughout School District #51.

Like her sister Wauneta, Reba never married. In retirement she enjoyed a wide variety of activities in the Methodist Church, Retired Teachers Association, Veterans Affairs Medical Center, Spanish American War Veterans Auxiliary and the Museum of Western Colorado. She loved traveling, hand work, sewing and music.

She died at age 90 in St. Mary's Hospital in Grand Junction, 22 November 1992.

Wauneta Wing was born 22 June 1906 at Edgemont, Fall River, South Dakota, to James S. Wing and Mary Zeller. Wauneta spent some of her childhood and received some schooling in South Dakota. She moved with her family to Grand Junction in 1914, where she graduated from high school. She graduated from Western State College in Gunnison, Colorado, with a teacher's degree.

Wauneta and her sister Reba were teachers at New Liberty School in 1930/31, with Wauneta taking responsibility of the lower grades. In addition to teaching at New Liberty she taught at Tope, Riverside and Pomona elementary schools. Teaching was her lifetime occupation.

She died at age 82 in La Villa Grande Nursing Home in Grand Junction, 24 August 1988.

Winkle

Information is from obituaries in *The Daily Sentinel*.

$\mathscr{E}$phraim "Eph" D. Winkle was born 16 October 1896, at Tate Springs, Tennessee, to Robert F. Winkle and Cora Elizabeth Harris. He spent his childhood in Tennessee, coming with his family to the Mack area in 1919. Eph was born with a handicap; his arms ended in short stumps extending a few inches from his elbows with barely distinguishable fingers. Yet, he was remarkably efficient in doing about as many different things as men with fully developed hands. He spent his lifetime doing farm and ranch work. He never let his handicap hinder him from working alongside other men.

He worked for many years at the Kirby ranch at Rangely and the Kelley ranch at Atchee.

He was married to **C. Aletha Cunningham** 16 October 1954, at Aztec, New Mexico. Aletha was born 13 January 1902, at Keystone, Oklahoma. She spent her childhood in Oklahoma and attended school there. She moved from Oklahoma to New Mexico, where she operated a coal company dining room with her mother. She also operated another coal company dining room at Sego, Utah. She came to Grand Junction in 1917 and operated the Lennox Rooming house, then worked for a time at a nursing home. She was married first to Jesse Good, who died in 1951.

After Ephraim and Aletha were married, they lived at Rangely until retirement, then moved to Appleton in 1959, and to Fruita in 1970.

Ephraim died at St. Mary's Hospital, 19 May 1980. Aletha died at Lower Valley Nursing home in Fruita, 6 November 1984. Both were buried in the Elmwood Cemetery at Fruita.

Wright

We express gratitude to Peggy Wright Murphy, daughter of Keith Wright, for the use of family records, and to members of Clyde's, Burke's, Billy's and Dixie's families for information on the Wright family; including Clyde Wright's autobiography. Information was also used from various obituaries; marriage, birth and church records in Grand County, Utah; 1880 Illinois Federal Census; 1885 Colorado State Census; 1900 Colorado Federal Census; and 1910 Utah Federal Census.

Chester Alfred Wright
(Photo courtesy of Kay Cook Wright)

$\mathscr{C}$hester Alfred "Chet" Wright was born 8 July 1888, at Buena Vista, Chaffee, Colorado, to James Franklin Wright and Mattie Belle Miller.

Chester was working on a ranch at Castleton, Utah, when he and **Vera Laura Bliss** were married, 27 September 1909, at Moab, Grand, Utah. Chester was 21 and Vera 17; Vera's mother signed consent for the marriage. Vera

Orley Dwight and Harriet Josephine Lee Bliss
(Photo courtesy of Peggy Wright Murphy)

Vera Laura Bliss Wright
(Photo courtesy of Kay Cook Wright)

was born at Wellington, Carbon, Utah, 26 February 1892, the 11th of 12 children born to Orley Dwight Bliss and Harriet Josephine Lee.

Some of you may be interested to know that Vera's mother, Harriet Josephine Lee, was a daughter of John Doyle Lee, who in Utah Mormon History became the scapegoat for the infamous "Mountain Meadows Massacre" which occurred in southern Utah in September 1857. John D. Lee was proven, to the satisfaction of the Territorial Courts, to have been the one white man who was most responsible in that incident. Even though there were others involved, only John was sacrificed for that terrible tragedy. After more than 20 years he was executed on the site by firing squad while seated on his casket. Was "justice" served? It seems that after his execution the furor over the massacre began to die down; perhaps some were satisfied that justice had been served. You may be the judge — it would do each of us well to study all that has been written on the subject and compare that with all the rumors circulated throughout the years.

Chester and Vera are listed in the 1910 census at Castleton, a little town with a post office several miles up the river from Moab. There were no children yet, but Chester's maternal grandfather was living with them and his occupation was given as "mail carrier." Chester was listed as "farmer."

Chester and Vera had 10 children:

Chester Edwin "Dick," born 16 July 1910, Moab, Grand, Utah
La Salle Bliss "Fritz," 7 December 1911, Castleton, Grand, Utah
Zona Maud (Goodell), 5 January 1914, Castleton
Keith Dwight, 21 December 1916, Moab
Clyde John, 22 February 1921, Moab
Burke Orley, 19 December 1924, Castleton
Billy Gene, 28 April 1927, Fruita, Mesa, Colorado
Dixie Rae (Dyer), 2 April 1929, Fruita
Donald Wayne, 27 August 1932, Mack
Mattie Barbara (Bittle, Narrans), 29 May 1936, Fruita
There was also one unnamed boy who was stillborn at Moab, between Zona and Keith.

Chet Wright family at Dick's funeral. L-R: Keith Goodell, Edna, Burke, Fritz Wright, Dixie Wright Dyer, Billie (Fritz' wife), Joe and Bert (Billie's sons), Billy Wright, Sharon Goodell (Zona's daughter), Vera Wright, Bonnie (Clyde's wife), Suzanne (Dick's), Barbara Wright Biddle, Clyde, Chester, Helen Marilee "Toots," Delbert Dyer, Donald, Keith, Elsie Wright, Zona Wright, and Elsa Goodell. *(Photo courtesy of Cherrie Wright Bauer)*

One can tell by the birth places of the children that the family lived in Grand County, Utah, until after Burke was born in 1924. At about that time they moved to Mack where Chester operated a store and garage for several years. After several owners, the store became known as the "Desert Gateway Store." The children attended school at Mack and Fruita.

In early 1931 the family moved to a farm in the New Liberty community which they had purchased from Leland Burkett. The farm had been originally filed on in 1911 by Frank Harrison, but he never developed it. Leland didn't do much with it either, so when Chester moved there he built a house and started to develop the land. The farm was designated unit "C" in the northwest corner of Sec. 19.

The family lived there for many years. Several of the children attended school at New Liberty; Clyde, Dixie, Burke and Billy all graduated from the eighth grade at New Liberty.

During the 1940s the older members of the family, including Chester and Vera, became interested in mining vanadium and later uranium and moved away. Chester and Vera, Dick, Fritz, Keith, Clyde, Burke and Billy all lived in the Moab area at one time or another during the uranium boom. In the 1950s some of them were operating a mine in the Naturita, Colorado, area (Paradox) where Dick lost his life on 30 March 1951, in a mine accident.

(Above left) Dick Wright working in the mine at Paradox, Colorado. (Above right) Clyde Wright running a Cat loader at one of the Wright mines, 1969. *(Photos courtesy of Cherrie Wright Bauer)*

(Above left) Dick and Toots Walker Wright. (Above center) Fritz L. B. Wright. (Above right) Keith Wright and son, Kenneth (Center left) 1955, L-R: Chester, Vera and Donald Wright. (Center) Burke Orley Wright. (Center right) Billy Gene Wright. (Below left) Barbara Wright. (Below right) L-R: Asa, Zona, Sharon and Keith Goodell, 1955. *(Photos courtesy of Kay Cook Wright)*

In 1959 a Golden wedding anniversary was held at Wright's New Liberty home for Chester and Vera. All of the children were there except Dick and Fritz. Several relatives from out of state were there to wish them well.

Chester died at Costa Mesa, California, 16 June 1971; Vera died 26 July 1974, also at Costa Mesa. The following is a letter to Sam Taylor, editor of *The Times Independent* of Moab, Utah:

The recent death of Chester A. Wright, who died in California at 83 years, reminded me that he is one of the last musicians who furnished music for the celebrations in Castleton. He played the mandolin and banjo and was usually accompanied on the violin by the late Lynn Pace. Chester also went to a drum school.

Chester Edwin "Dick" married **Helen Marilee (Toots) Walker**, 6 April 1933 at Moab. Their children are:

Darwin Dick, born 1 October 1934, Moab, Grand, Utah, died 4 December 1934
Sammy Edward, 2 August 1937, Moab. Died 1 April 1941
Suzanne (Mayberry), 25 May 1943, Moab. Suzanne married **Weldon L. Mayberry**, 15 November 1959
Dick died in a mine accident 30 March 1951.

LaSalle Bliss "Fritz" married **Wilma J. Kinkhead Peck**, 6 May 1941. There were no children. Fritz died 14 July 1978.

Zona married **Asa Goodell**. Her children were: **Keith, Shirley** and **Sharon**. Zona divorced Goodell, married **Randy Winbourne**, then remarried Asa Goodell. Zona died at Gallup, New Mexico, 17 February 1968.

Keith married **Elsie Evelynne Lampshire**, 5 August 1940. They had eight children

James Keith, born 15 May 1941 at Grand Junction, died 13 August 1944
Judy Lynn (Serve), 17 April 1943, Moab, Grand, Utah

Kathy Fern (Palmer), 11 April 1944, Grand

Keith Wright's children, 1960. Back row, L-R: Peggy Alma, Kathy Fern and Sally Gene Wright. Front row: Kenneth Dwight and Chester Dick Wright. Judy lynn is missing. *(Photo courtesy of Cherrie Wright Bauer)*

Junction
Sally Gene (Schaffer), 9 August 1945, Grand Junction
Peggy Alma (Murphy), 15 September 1947, Grand Junction
Kenneth Dwight, 25 February 1950, Price, Carbon, Utah. Married **Kathleen Barrett**. He died 23 October 1975
Chester Dick, 5 August 1953, Uravan, Montrose, Colorado. Married **Maureen Grimes**
Keith Breck, 16 August 1955, Dragerton, Carbon, Utah. Died 26 December 1956

Keith died 10 November 1990 at Las Vegas, Nevada.

Clyde enlisted in the Marines 23 September 1942, and served in the Pacific Theatre. He was involved in the terrible battle to retake Guadalcanal, spending 10 months there. He received a medical discharge from the Marines 13 July 1944. We have no personal account of his experiences on Guadalcanal, but, judging from reports of that battle, he must have gone through hell!

1988, Clyde Wright as Bishop in Fallon, Nevada *(Photo courtesy of Cherrie Wright Bauer)*

Quoting from an article in *The Daily Sentinel*.

On Sunday evening, 13 August 1944, a tragedy occurred involving Clyde and other members and relatives of the Wright family who were in and on a truck returning from a fishing outing at Roan Creek, above DeBeque. Clyde was driving, with Elsie Wright, wife of Keith, and her sister, Fern Lampshire, seated beside him in the cab. In the back, seated in the bed of the truck, were: Keith Wright, husband of Elsie; Billy; Mrs. William J. Lampshire and Loren Lampshire, mother and brother of Elsie; and Gregory Black of Blanding, Utah. Mrs. Lampshire was holding her little 3 year-old grandson, Jimmy Keith Wright, son of Keith and Elsie.

Clyde was not familiar with the road and, as the truck approached a sharp turn near Johnson's corner, northeast of Grand Junction, he was blinded by the lights of an on-coming car. The truck left the road and overturned, instantly killing little Jimmy Keith Wright. The rest of the party were bruised and shaken but survived.

Clyde, of course, was devastated. It was reported by others who were in the accident that Clyde picked up the body of the little boy and ran down the road screaming. He managed to flag down a passing car to take the little one to the hospital where it was determined he had died instantly. Clyde was troubled by that accident for the rest of his life, never wanting to discuss it with anyone. He brooded over his responsibility for the terrible tragedy for a long time, not really being able to forgive himself for it. He eventually came to terms with it and began to change his life-style. In Fallon, Nevada, where the family lived many years, he became active in the LDS church, serving in several leadership positions and was bishop of his ward at the time of his death.

Clyde married **LaVonne "Bonnie" Cockrum** 10 September 1945. They had three children:

Cherrie Bea (Bauer), 17 August 1946, Montrose, Montrose, Colorado. Married **David Bauer**
Clyde John Jr., 4 January 1948, Ouray, Ouray, Colorado. Married **Laura Matson**
Shirlee Jonetta, 13 October 1953, Uravan, Montrose, Colorado

Clyde's son-in-law, David Bauer, told us that Clyde carried much of the burden of the mining business for his brothers. It was he who secured the property and mining leases for he and his brothers.

Clyde was persuaded by his children to write his life's story. He never completed it, but what he did write is more than many of us do. We learn from his story that Clyde was a pretty resourceful boy.

Here it is, with some editing.

This Is My Life
As I Remember It

I was born on 22 February 1921, at Moab, Utah. My folks were then living on a ranch on Wilson Mesa, about 18 miles by road from Moab, on the west side of the La Sal Mountains. My parents said I was a healthy baby, but cried a lot.

I remember the house we lived in; it was a long log house with a porch on the west side. I can remember very well playing on that porch.

My dad was a part-time ranger, so they had a telephone wire strung from Moab, mostly through the tops of the trees, to our house. I

(Above left) 1983, La Vonne "Bonnie" and Clyde Wright. (Above right) Clyde and Bonnie's three children, L-R: Shirlee Jonetta, Clyde John Jr. and Cherrie Bea Wright (Bauer). (Center left) L-R: Clyde John Jr., Shirlee Jonetta and Cherrie Bea Wright. (Center right) David J. and Cherrie Wright Bauer's family. Back row, L-R: Cherrie, David J., David Clyde, Stephen and Timothy Bauer. Middle row: Frieda holding Elizabeth Bauer (Stephen's wife and child), Kimberlie Bauer Kehrer holding daughter, Sierra Kehrer. Front row: Cara (David C.'s wife), Catherine (Timothy's wife) and Robert Kehrer holding McKenzie Kehrer. (Bottom left) Clyde John Wright Jr. family: L-R in back: Tamaron Jyl Wright Leavitt, Laura Matsen Wright and Vareck Vaughn Wright. In front: Anthony Leavitt (grandchild) and Clyde John Wright Jr. (Insert) Grandchildren of Clyde John Jr. L-R: Tevin Wright, son of Vareck, and Brooke Leavitt, daughter of Tamaron. *(Photos courtesy of Kay Cook Wright and Cherrie Wright Bauer)*

772

remember when I was about four years old sitting on the porch one day with my Dad's hired hand, a man by the name of Ira Filmore. Ira was making a wooden whistle for me when lightning struck, shooting down the telephone line, striking Ira and knocking him out. It scared me and I remember my mother running out of the house screaming, as she thought I had been hit.

We used to go up the creek to an old bachelor's house to get raspberries in the summer. His name was Bob Deafendorf and he always had gum for us. He would store it in his hat and would pick it off for us. It didn't matter if it had been chewed once or twice.

One of my favorite spots was about four miles east of our house where there were many springs and lots of quaking aspen trees. We would go there on Sundays and picnic most of the day. Most of the family would go in the wagon, but the older boys would ride horses and a mule.

One time they put me on behind the saddle and as they started to run the horses I fell on my head in a pile of rocks. So you see, I have an excuse for being the way I am!

When I was four-and-a-half years old my folks bought a garage and store at Mack, Colorado. We didn't take much with us but a team and wagon and my Dad's Dodge Commercial delivery truck. It was a slow trip on 130 miles of dirt roads.

Our house in Mack was behind the garage. I used to play in the garage a lot. During the winter the swamp behind our house would freeze up and we would skate on it. I started to school in Mack.

Later my Dad bought an 80-acre ranch west of Mack, through which the Uintah Railway crossed. It (the railroad) was a narrow-gauge road about 50 miles long. The trains hauled gilsonite from a little mining town called Watson, Utah. The Uintah ran over Baxter Pass and was about the steepest, uncogged railroad in the United States.

My brother Fritz worked on that railway. They sure had a lot of wrecks on the pass; the tracks would get icy in the winter and they couldn't hold the train. The curves were so sharp the train wouldn't go very far before it would run off the track.

I remember the men who worked on the moving of the ore off the Uintah cars. They would man-handle the sacks that weighed 275 to 325 pounds. They would stack three or four sacks on a hand truck and wheel them onto the D&RGW Railroad box cars. We kids would play in the warehouse where they stored the sacks. We knew all the workers and they would always find time to play some kind of joke on us. But they would usually reward us afterwards.

One time they had us all line up for a race. They had a five-pound lard pail with a lot of jelly-beans and corn candy in it and the first one to get to the can would get to keep all he could pick up with his hands. That was one time I was glad I didn't win as we were all so excited about winning that we didn't see them switch buckets. A tall skinny kid by the name of Robertson rammed both hands in the bucket and it was filled with fresh cow-manure. But they *did* give us the candy later.

I liked to go hiking south of Mack in the high hills where there were lots of rims (ledges). The Colorado River was on the south side of those hills and we would hike over there and I would bring back Brigham Tea. I would sell it for 25 cents for a gunny-sack full. That doesn't sound like much, but I was the richest kid in town!

I always wanted to go fishing over those hills but my Mom wouldn't let me without someone with me because I was then only about seven years old. It was such a climb that none of the older kids would go.

I knew it was too far for my mother to go, but I fixed that. Once when I was going to go swimming in a canal I saw a big fish swimming by in the canal. It was hurt and so it was swimming on top of the water. I ran down the bank and jumped in and caught the fish. I took it home and told my Mom that I went fishing in Box Canyon over the hill on the river. She got so excited she forgot to reprimand me! After that we planned a trip, as she loved to fish. We took the wagon and went around those hills on a wagon road that was used for hauling cedar wood. We still had to walk about three miles down into the steep canyon. When we got there the water was so muddy we didn't catch any fish. Boy! I blew that one!

We went to school in a two-room school house. The first four grades were in one room and the next four grades in the other. We had an assembly hall in which we would have silent movies with Tom Mix or Charlie Chaplin shown to us by an old man by the name of Judge Kennedy. It cost us 10 cents each.

I liked to play baseball with our school team. Every Sunday in the spring and fall we would compete with all the schools in the area that had baseball teams. We also had track meets. I thought I was pretty good; I won several events.

We had stockyards at Mack and the sheepmen would bring their sheep there every spring on the railroad and ship them to the high country for the summer. The desert was so dry in the summer they couldn't live on it. They would ship them back in the fall to winter on the desert. Mack was the loading and unloading point.

We kids would go down to the stock yards during our spare time and help load or unload the sheep. They were always short-handed, so they would pay us a quarter apiece for about four hours work. Three of us worked almost all of one Saturday for a guy named Brown. He handed Doug Booth 35 cents for all three of us and told him not to spend it all in one place. Doug handed it back and said, "Fella, you probably need it worse than we do." That was during the depression and also during the drought. Times were pretty tough!

One time we were down at the stock yards playing when my older brother, Keith, Roach Robbins and Woody Booth were on the highway about a half-mile from the stock yards when they found some blasting caps under a bridge being built. Keith knew what they were and told the other kids to leave them alone. But Roach took one out of the box and was digging at it with a nail when it blew up, taking off four fingers and part of the thumb from one hand!

I was from a family of 10 children, three sisters and seven brothers; I was about in the middle. My oldest brother was Chester Edwin; we called him Dick. The next was LaSalle Bliss; we called him Fritz. Then came my sister Zona, then Keith and myself; and then Burke, Bill, Dixie, Don and Barbara.

When my Dad bought the 80-acre homestead five miles west of Mack my mother and the kids lived out there in the summer and moved back to Mack in the winter. My mother never learned to drive a car, so we didn't get around very much unless we drove the team and wagon, so we never got to church. My mother was LDS with a good testimony, so she taught us a lot about the church. All of the kids were baptized, except Keith and I. My Dad was an inactive Lutheran, but was later baptized in the LDS church when he was 65.

My Dad ran the garage and filling station at Mack for a few years, then after he went into trucking he moved out to the ranch. I was then about nine years old. He built a couple of railroad tie cabins, as we had only a little shack on the place. We boys slept in a tent-house with no heater, even in the winter when it was cold. But we had lots of covers.

My Dad traded for a sow pig and later she had 13 little ones and one was a runt that wasn't getting enough milk. We kids took her and fed her on a bottle and she slept with us when she was little. When winter came she had grown to about 50 pounds, so she had to sleep with her head on the pillow. You wouldn't want to cover her head, as she would bite you on the nose. Or you didn't want to let any smells or she would squeal and bite you. We liked to sleep with her, as she kept us warm, except when she went to the bathroom, which was down by the woodpile; she would come back with snow on her feet and jump on the bed and crawl under the covers and put her cold feet in the middle of our backs. She would follow us kids everywhere we went, if we let her.

The next summer she got so big and fat she became too lazy to keep up with us so Dad put her in with the rest of the pigs. That fall he had all the rest of the pigs butchered, but kept her for breeding purposes. She was a dandy — she would have 13 every litter and was a good mother. She grew to be about 500 pounds but was always a pet. Even when she had pigs you could get in the pen with the little ones right after they were born. My Dad kept her until she got too old to have any more pigs, then sold her, as we never could have butchered her.

I started school at New Liberty; a little country school about three miles east of our house. There were two rooms with two teachers; four grades were in each room. I started there when I was in the fourth grade and went through the eighth.

My brothers Burke, and later Billy, and myself, rode a horse to school — all on the same horse. I liked to race my horse and we would race about once a week with the other kids. We had a pretty fast mare and sometimes we won, so it was fun! The horse belonged to Keith, my older brother. My Dad had traded two of his pigs for her to a fellow by the name of Leland Burkett. Leland had a terrible temper and used to beat his horses. We kids thought he was crazy so we were scared of him. He had beat that mare so bad that she hated grown men, but she sure loved us kids.

We were racing a truck one time when a side board fell out of it in front of us and she tried to miss it and fell and turned a somersault with us kids on her. When she fell, her head was bent back under her. We pulled her head out and loved her and cried as we thought she had broken her neck. But as soon as she got her wind back she got up and walked right up to us. We were happy!

We liked to go fishing, but the only place to go was over a big hill by the Colorado River. We would go to a place called Ruby Canyon; it was the only place for several miles where we could get to the river. We had to walk the last two miles down into the canyon. It was really rocky and my mother had a hard time making it but she went every time, as it was about the only recreation we had. We had a team and wagon and we would take our bedding so we could stay all night. We would build a fire on the river bank and fish all night. We would catch a few catfish, some white salmon and a few suckers, but we kept them all and ate most of them. We would usually catch about half a sack of fish.

It would take about three hours to make the trip one way. We had to be back by dark ,as we usually had chores to do. My Dad didn't go with us except about once a year and that would be Easter. He would do the cooking and let my Mother fish, as she loved to fish. She would make her bed on the riverbank right next to the water, then wake every little while to check her line to see if there were any fish or to see if she had to renew the bate.

Above where we fished there was a steep box-canyon with rims several hundred feet high. I hiked up there with another kid and found where some pygmy cliff dwellers had built several houses in the cliffs. The handprints in the mud-mortar were like those of a little child about five or six years old. As far as I know nobody else knew of those houses even though cliff dwellings appear for several hundred miles along the length of the river. I suppose by now they have all been explored.

At the school in New Liberty the Mormons were made fun of. My family and a family by the name of Turner were the only LDS families in the community. We had to stand against the rest of the kids, except the Maluys and the Shires — they were our friends.

Ray Turner, Leonard Shires and Dale and Rex Maluy were my buddies. For a few years there was a family by the name of Pacheco who had a large family. They liked us and we were always friends.

During the 1930s there was a drought and depression and the range was so dry the desert west and south of my Dad's ranch was like a dust-bowl. Sometimes you could see 10 or 12 herds of sheep at a time being driven down the road to be shipped to the high country for the summer.

My Dad's ranch was on a mesa about 100 feet high and about six miles from the Utah state line. We were the last ranch on the Highline Canal, which furnished our irrigation water. We raised a huge garden and several acres of beans and potatoes and lots of berries and sold them to the town people in Mack. They would drive out to our ranch to buy our berries and garden vegetables.

One winter, when I was in the fifth grade, my mother moved to town (Mack) with the rest of the family, as Dad was running the garage and the truck there. I was selected to stay at the ranch with a bachelor by the name of Shorty Shrewsbury, who had a little herd of sheep he was pasturing on our lower field. He lived in one of the cabins and I stayed with him. Dad and Mom would come out every week or so to see how I was doing and bring me clean clothes.

I had to milk the cows and feed the pigs and chickens and horses. Shorty had to be with his sheep from daylight to dark. Once in awhile I would kill a rabbit and Shorty would make dumplings to go with it — that was pretty good!

I would get up in the mornings when Shorty did, as I had to get the chores done and ride three miles to school and be there by 9:00 a.m. I would come home at night and do the chores again. Shorty never helped me. Sometimes it would get down to 20 degrees below zero and I would wrap my feet with sacks and take them off just before I would get to school. I'd hide the sacks in some brush and pick them up again on the way home.

In the summer I would work for different farmers, helping them put up hay. We didn't bale it. We would bring it in from the field on hay slips that were just big sleds with wooden runners. We would put slings on the slips and pile the hay on the slings and take it to the derrick and hook pulleys to each end of the slings and hoist the load up and swing the derrick so the load would be over the stack. When the man on the stack got the load where he wanted it he would pull the trip-rope and the slings would separate in the middle and could be pulled out from under the load of hay. The slings would be placed back on the slip and away we'd go for another load. That was my job until I got bigger, then I would pitch shocks of hay on the slips or wagons. Sometimes we would use wagons; especially if we had a long haul.

When I got to be about 14½ the boys in the community made up a crew of about six boys to pick potatoes in the summer. We would contract for five cents per sack to pick up the potatoes, sort and sack them, as well as sew the sacks shut. Some times we were able to make $3 to $5 per day, we picked all we could as we could make more than anything else we could do — the going rate for farm labor was $1.25 to $ 1.75 per day.

About once a month the crew would go to Grand Junction, about 30 miles away, to a show and a dance; one of the older kids had a car.

We used to have dances at the school house two or three times a year. All the families would take their kids to those. There was a man by the name of Bob Cox who would be master of ceremonies. He would get up and crack funny jokes. He said one time that my Dad was running a race with the morning-glories (weeds) to see who could take over the valley first. My Dad had ten kids.

I sure looked forward to those shindigs, as everybody brought food of all kinds. We had several good musicians — my Dad played the banjo and mandolin.

My best friend's name was Leonard Shires, but I didn't get to see him during the summer months, as his brother, Rudolph, had a band of sheep and it was Leonard's job to herd them in the mountains every summer. He would get back just in time for school.

When I was about 14 years old I ran away from home with a 16 year old kid whose name was Bill Davis. We hopped a freight train at Grand Junction and went to Pueblo, Colorado, for our first stop. There was a transient camp there and we lined up for food, as neither of us had any money and were pretty hungry. It was during the depression and there were chow lines in every city to feed the hungry. A man in Pueblo took us to the Salvation Army and we stayed there two weeks and helped them in their drives for money. They gave us a bed and shower and fed us really good. They took good care of us — found us jobs, sometimes mowing lawns or doing other yard work. We could keep all our pay if we chose. The man who took us in told us the government was giving them $2 per week for our room and board. We saved enough to buy us a change of clothes, then left and went to Denver. The railroad bulls picked us up the first night we were there and put Bill in jail and me in a detention home and kept us there for about two weeks. The man then took us down to the railroad yards and told us to go back home the same way we got there or they would put us away for a long time. We took the advice gladly, as we were getting pretty

homesick. Our goal when we left home was to go to Pennsylvania — we didn't mind changing our plans. Not a bit!

We caught a slow freight that was going by way of Pueblo and stayed on that all the way to Grand Junction, about 36 hours. We never had anything to eat all that time! Bill had to walk about 14 miles and I about 29 miles to our homes. Dad was gone but my mother was there with Don and Barbara. Boy! Were they glad to see old dirty me — I was black as coal! Mom got a jar of jam and a loaf of bread and I ate the whole loaf!

Man! Was I ever glad to be home! I was ready to take my licking from Dad. But when he came home and saw that I was home safe he didn't know what to do. He really showed concern. Right then home was the neatest place on earth! It made a more humble kid of me. I had gotten out and seen what a rat race those cities were. And so much hunger and so much vice and corruption! We had some close calls on that trip! I went back to school and worked hard and graduated from the eighth grade that year.

About that time I met a trapper by the name of Albert Turner and he wanted me to go trapping with him the next winter. Of course, my parents wanted me to go back to school. I only went about six weeks of my freshman year then quit and went out on my own. I bought a Star car that had been in storage for about five years. It only had about 2,000 miles on it and those were town miles. I got the car for $20; it ran like new.

I started picking wool from dead sheep and would average about 10 cents per pound for all I could get. One day I picked 200 pounds. I made more money that day than my brothers would make in a week. When I would get several hundred pounds of wool a man from Ogden, Utah, would come to the ranch and buy it all. His name was Mr. Clemens — he sure treated me right. I picked wool until the snow came and I had to quit.

Then I went trapping for coyotes, bob cats and badgers. I did quite well until it got so cold in January that my traps froze. There weren't any good places to set traps on the desert around my Dad's ranch, so I came home and went to work for a sheep man named Tom Kelley at $30 per month. I took care of about 300 to 400 head of his poorer sheep that he had culled out of his other herds. In the spring we put them back in the other herds as they had fattened up by that time.

Tom took me to the summer range up Atchee Canyon. That's the canyon where the

Uintah Railway went. I herded the yearling sheep for a few months then went back to pulling wool.

Albert Turner, the trapper, talked me into going to the Arizona Strip, as they had lost herds of sheep the previous winter. He had a Model "A" Ford pickup. So we went down through the Navajo Reservation. They just had trails across the sand for miles. We had to let most of the air out of the tires to keep from getting stuck. Even so, we had to shovel out several times. Our first stop after we left Mexican Hat was at the trading post and filling station at Kayenta. We paid 35 cents per gallon for gas and thought we had been robbed. We had been used to paying 12 to 13 cents per gallon. As we were filling our car with gas we heard someone yelling, "Kill the old S O B! Kill him!" We went around the side of the building thinking we were about to see a devil, instead there were three old men playing marbles!

Through the years Clyde developed what is known among hard-rock miners as "Silicosis," caused from breathing too much rock dust. He fought the disease for many years but it finally got the best of him. He died in Fallon, Nevada, 26 April 1989, at age 68. His first wife, Lavonne "Bonnie," had died less than two years previous. They had lived in Fallon for 23 years. In Clyde's last year, he married **Coral Sorensen**.

Burke married **Edna Christensen** 24 August 1950, in Green River, Utah. They had five children:

> **Burke Edwin,** born 20 August 1951, Grand Junction
> **Brent Paul,** 25 February 1953, Dragerton, Carbon, Utah
> **Ronald William,** 11 November 1955, Fruita, Colorado
> **Adina,** 14 September 1957, Fruita, Colorado
> **Theresa Denise,** 29 October 1961, Moab, Grand, Utah

Burke died at age 38 on 29 November 1963, in the Veterans Hospital in Denver after two kidney transplants had failed. One of the kidneys had been donated by his sister, Barbara, and the other by a prisoner at Canon City. At that time Burke was a resident of Clifton. We can see from his obituary that the family was scattered all over the country: Fritz and Donald were living in Santa Ana, California; Clyde, Keith and Dixie were in Moab, Utah; Billy was in Silverton, Colorado; Zona in Grand Junction; Barbara in Fruita; and the parents, Chester and Vera, at Mack. The obituary also mentioned that Burke had served with the Army in Germany during World War II, and had been awarded the Bronze Star.

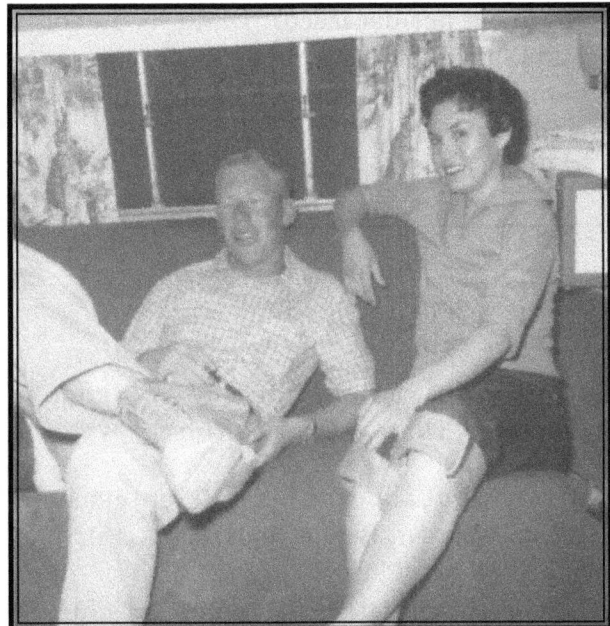

(Upper left) Donald and Eloidia Trujillo Wright. *(Photo courtesy of Kay Wright)* *(*Upper right) 1978, Dixie Wright Dyer's family. L-R: Mason Dee, Toni Fayette, Rodney Shane and Nila Burbridge Dyer, Donald Chris and Carrie Lynn Radabaugh Dyer, DeAnna Dyer and Jon H. Sundstrom, Delbert Eddie and Sophie Shes Dyer, and Dixie Wright and Delbert Escoe Dyer. *(Photo courtesy of DeAnna Dyer Sundstrom)* (Center left) Kay Jean Cook, William Gene, Billy Gene, Karen Kay Wright. *(Photo courtesy of Kay Wright)* (Center right) Dixie Wright Dyer in Fallon, Nevada, 1970s. (Lower right) Burke Wright's family. L-R: Brent, Edwin Burke, Burke holding Adina and Edna holding Ronald. Teresa is missing. *(The last two photos courtesy of Cherrie Wright Bauer)*

Billy married **Dorothy Johnson**; they were divorced. He then married **Kay Jean Cook**, 5 June 1954. They had two children:

William Gene, 2 October 1955, Grand Junction, Colorado
Karen Kay (Sabra), 26 July 1957, Belen, Valencia, New Mexico

Billy died 13 October 1976 in Denver.

Dixie married **Delbert Escoe Dyer**, 4 May 1946,.in Aztec, San Juan, New Mexico. They had six children.

Delbert Eddie, born 11 April 1947, Grand Junction. Married **Sophie Shes** in Germany. They had seven children. He is Under Sheriff in Mineral County, Nevada.
DeAnna Vee (Sundstrom), 7 October 1948, Grand Junction. Married **Jon H. Sundstrom** in 1965, they have four children and live in Emery, Utah.
Donald Chris, 18 March 1950, Grand Junction. Married **Carrie Lynn Radabaugh**. They have three children, and live in Vernal.
Toni Fayette, 27 October 1951. Has two children and lives in Reno, Nevada.
Rodney Shane, 15 September 1954, Sandpoint, Bonner, Idaho. Married **Nita Burbridge**. They have six children, and live in Hazen, Nevada.
Mason Dee, 13 April 1956. Telluride, San Miguel, Colorado. He also lives in Hazen.

Donald married **Eloidia Trujillo**. They had three children:

Maria Elizabeth, born 12 September 1957, Belen, Valencia, New Mexico
Donald William, Jr., 14 ;Ma;y 1959, Belen
Julia Ann, 9 October 1961, Belen

Barbara married **Donald Bittle** February 1952. They had three children:

Donna, born 2 January 1957, Helena, Lewis and Clark, Montana.
Darcy, 4 November 1955, Fruita
Kelly, 8 August 1958, Moab

She divorced Donald and married **Steven Narrans**. Barbara died in 1984.

As you can see, almost all of Chester and Vera's offspring are deceased. Dixie, of Reno, Nevada and Donald, of Costa Mesa, California, are the only ones left of the ten. Father Time has taken his toll.

Wynkoop

The following was provided by Wynkoop family members. There is some editing.

Rush Ivan Wynkoop was born 8 September 1894, at Lebanon, Boone, Indiana, to Harry Wynkoop and Maude Parrish.

On 12 November 1915, at Cement, Caddo, Oklahoma, he married **Lillie Mae Austell**, who was born at Waxahachie, Ellis, Texas, 26 May 1896, daughter of Robert Austell and Anne Belle Money.

They had 13 children:

Lovey Leora, born 2 November 1917 (died at 17 days)
Ivan Van Buren, 18 October 1918
Eddie Randall, 26 April 1920
Dorothy Evelyn (Roland), 2 February 1922
Lois Mae (Roofener), 1 May 1923
Virgie Anna (Brown), 20 August 1924
Paul Glenn, 22 May 1926
Joyce Hope (McPherson), 20 November 1927
Stanley Rush, 23 December 1928
Mary Nay (Young), 27 January 1930
Alva James "A.J.," 26 March 1931
Leatha Lillian (Kettle), 9 January 1933
Leona Belle (Justice), 13 October 1936
All were born at Cement, Oklahoma, except Lois and Virgie, who were born at Paonia, Colorado.

The family lived near Cement, Oklahoma, until 1936 when Rush went to Bisby, Arizona, and went to work in a copper mine. In 1939 Rush and oldest son, Ivan, rented a farm near Appleton, Colorado, where they stayed for one year. From there they went back to Oklahoma and farmed in the area of Eakley until they moved back to Colorado in 1943 and rented the

Bob Cox farm in the New Liberty community.

Leatha tells this story which was published in *The Fruita Times* in August 1991.

In the spring of 1943, my dad, Rush Wynkoop, rented the Cox place in the New Liberty area. He and son Paul moved down from Hotchkiss, leaving the rest of the family there while they did some remodeling and fixing in the house and began preparing the fields for planting.

Soon after this the rest of the family, including my mother, Lillie Wynkoop, Virgie, Joyce, Stanley, Mary, A.J. (Alva James), Leatha and Leona Belle, moved to the Cox farm. We children began attending New Liberty School and became acquainted with many of the families who made us feel so welcome.

I remember a Christmas program the young people put on for the community during the time we lived there. It was a very lovely and well-attended event. The youth also went all over the community on a hay-sled pulled by a tractor, singing Christmas Carols at many of the homes. I do not remember if we did this each Christmas we lived there. Mr. Likes was the Sunday School teacher for the young people and he also preached occasionally. Mrs. Wynkoop would lead the singing while Mrs. Banning played the piano.

The complete Wynkoop family, about 1938. Back row, L-R: Dorothy Evelyn, Lois Mae, Lillie Mae (mom) holding Leona Belle, Rush Ivan (dad) and Virgie Anna. Middle row: Joyce Hope, Mary Nay and Leatha Lillian. Front row: Eddie Randall, Paul Glenn, Stanley Rush, Alva James "A J" and Ivan Van Buren. *(Photo courtesy of Stanley Wynkoop)*

I remember skating parties, horseback riding, swimming in the canal, weddings, shivarees, picnics and many other fun events in the community.

Stanley, Mary, A.J., Leatha and Leona Belle attended school at New Liberty for two-and-a-half years. Virgie and Joyce worked in the school hot-lunch program for a few months. Mary and Stanley began high school in Fruita and Virgie began a job in Grand Junction.

The oldest son, Ivan, was in the service at the time and is the only member of the family who did not get to enjoy New Liberty. The oldest daughter, Dorothy, moved to the Weir place from California. She and her husband, Leonard Roland, farmed there for two-and-a-half years. Their son, Randy, was born in the old Fruita Hospital. They moved from there to Eakley, Oklahoma, and farmed there until Leonard's death. Dorothy still lives in Oklahoma. Also during that time, Vernie Austell, Lillie Mae Wynkoop's brother, lived near them on the Likes' farm.

Son Eddie was also in the service at the time the family moved to New Liberty, serving in the Philippines. The family was having breakfast when we heard on the radio that World War II had ended. The kids began to yell and throw biscuits at each other; it was one of the most joyous occasions of our

The Wynkoop family home at New Liberty; it was formerly the Bob Cox farm. It is now owned by Chuck and Steve Roberts. *(Photo used from the Fruita Times submitted by Leatha Wynkoop Kettle)*

(Above left) The Wynkoop children on a homemade horse-drawn cart in New Liberty. Looks like fun! (Above right) Those are potato[es]? They were grown on the Cox place by the Wynkoops. L-R: Rush Wynkoop, Dorothy, Randy (baby) and Leonard Roland, and Lil[lie] Wynkoop. (Center left) Wynkoop Children, 1945, L-R: Leatha, Stanley, Joyce, Paul, Virgie, and Mary. Leona Bell is in front. *(Pho[to] courtesy of Leatha Wynkoop Kettle)*

(Center right above) Taken at [a] family reunion about 1992. Ba[ck] row, L-R: A.J. Wynkoop, B[ob] McPherson, Ivan Wynkoo[p,] Stanley Wynkoop, Roy Young a[nd] Paul Wynkoop. Middle ro[w:] Delores Owens Wynkoop, Joy[ce] Wynkoop McPherson, Dor[is] Johnson Wynkoop, Doroth[y] Wynkoop Roland, Mary Wynkoo[p] Young and Aileen Byers Wynkoo[p.] Front row: Harry and Leath[a] Wynkoop Kettle, Margar[et] Henderson Wynkoop and Edd[ie] Wynkoop. *(Photo courtesy [of] Leatha Wynkoop Kettle)* (Lef[t)] The Wynkoop family on the Co[x] farm in New Liberty in 194[ ]. Leona Belle is in front. In bac[k,] L-R: A.J., Mary, Lillie (mom[),] Rush (dad), Leatha and Stanle[y.] *(Photo used from The Frui[t] Times, 8 August 1991 issue; pho[to] submitted by Leatha Wynkoo[p] Kettle)*

lives! We forgot all about eating and began to call friends and family members. We later took the old wagon and tractor, gathering up all the kids throughout the community, singing patriotic songs and yelling, **"The war is over!"** In due time the phone rang and it was Eddie telling us he was back in the States and would soon be home. He talked to each of us; how happy and thankful we were! He returned in very poor health, but was able to join in the farming operation and community life.

Paul had joined the Navy a short time before the war ended. He too, returned to the farm.

In 1946 my parents purchased a farm in the Fruita community on 16 Road. While living there, eight of their children married:

Ivan married **Doris Johnson**. They have two children and are retired and live in Fruita.

Eddie married **Margaret Henderson**. They have two daughters. They owned a farm in the Loma area for awhile, but they are now living in the Clifton, Arizona, area.

Virgie married **A. D. Brown** and had one son. They live at Henderson, Texas.

Paul married **Aileen Byers**. They have two sons and are living in Fruita.

Joyce married **Robert McPherson**. They have five children and live in Fruita.

Stanley married **Maxine Silvers**. They have three children and live on a farm in the Loma area.

Mary is married to **Roy Young**. They have three children and live at Garland, Texas.

G. J. married **Delores Owens**. They have three children and live at Littleton, Colorado.

Leatha married **Harry Kettle**. They have two children and live on a farm in the Fruita area.

Leona Belle married **Paul Justice**. They have three children and live at Helena, Montana.

Rush sold the farm on 16 Road to son Ivan and he and Lillie Mae moved to Cedaredge, Colorado, where Rush was pastor of a small church until Lillie Mae died in 1953. She was buried at Grand Junction Municipal Cemetery. Rush died 20 April 1985, at age 90, at Fort Cobb, Oklahoma. He was also buried at Grand Junction.

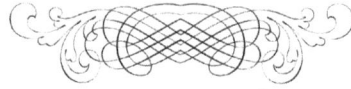

Young

The following history was compiled in part from excerpts of two family histories: "The Cowboy and The Saint," and "William L. Young, 1875-1929." These were graciously loaned to us by Neta Young Palfreyman, a granddaughter of Bill Young, and daughter of Dick and Edith Young.

William Richard Young
(Photo courtesy of Betty Jo Young Anderson)

illiam "Bill" Richard Young was born 2 December 1895, at Colonia Pacheco, Chihuahua, Mexico, to William "Will" Lorenzo Young and Annie Eliza Porter. Bill came from a long line of Youngs that date back to the early

days of this country: William Young who came from Europe and settled in Massachusetts in the 1600s and John Young who fought in the Revolutionary War under George Washington. His great-grandfather was Lorenzo Dow Young, a brother of Brigham Young; his grandfather was John R. Young, who played a large part in the settling of southern Utah and Arizona.

Bill's mother, Annie Eliza Porter, also came from a long line of early Americans from the New England states. Both Will and Annie came from polygamous families; Annie had 19 sisters and 10 brothers

Bill was the oldest of 12 children. He was called "Willie" at first because his grandfather, John R., didn't like for him to be called "Bill." He spent his early years at Pacheco. Because the family lived most of the time in isolation and made several moves during his growing-up years, Bill had little opportunity for education. That didn't deter him much, as he absorbed a lot of good "common sense" to make him a wise, gentle, kindly and charitable man who was always willing to go the extra mile to help some one in need. He never expected any praise nor anything else in return for his goodness. He was a hard worker who pulled more than his share of the load throughout his life.

When Bill was about four months old his parents went on a long trip from Pacheco to Fruitland, New Mexico, (in the area of Farmington) to visit his grandfather, John R. Young and family. They traveled by wagon to El Paso and then by train to Fruitland. The trip involved more time than they had anticipated, since they traveled by wagon from Fruitland to Huntington, Utah, and later, on over to Manti, Utah. Will and Annie's second child, May Theda, was born in June 1897, while on that journey. In the fall of 1897 they began the trip back to Mexico, arriving at Pacheco in the spring

William Lorenzo and Annie Elizabeth Porter Young's children in 1957 (L-R): Clyn, Darroll, Von, Bill, Loyd, Geraldine, Jack, Mildruff, Ray and Tamar. *(Photo used from The Cowboy and the Saint, page 53)*

of 1898. (It is not likely a young mother of today would undertake such a journey).

Some time in 1906 Will decided to move his family to Fruitland, New Mexico, where he began operating a sawmill. While living at Fruitland their home was near the Washburn family who had a little girl named Neta. It's not likely that Bill gave Neta much notice at that time, nor is it likely either of them realized that they would later spend many years together as husband and wife. Neta said years later that she met Bill on the road one day as she was going over to visit with his sister, May. Bill asked her, "Molly had her colt yet?" She said that everyone in both families knew that Molly, a mare belonging to the Washburn family, was expecting.

In 1908, because of favorable reports he'd heard about the area of Grayson, Utah (now called Blanding), Will decided they ought to investigate that part of the country. He and 13 year old Bill, each riding a horse and leading a

pack horse, traveled from Fruitland to Grayson and liked what they saw in San Juan County; invigorating climate, plenty of winter and summer grazing for cattle. The area had been partially settled in 1880 by people who had established a community at the present site of Bluff, several miles south of Blanding. That group of people and their settlement were known as the "San Juan Mission." They had many trying experiences in traveling to the area and became known as the "Hole In The Rock Pioneers" — but that's another story.

Will had sufficient savings to make a down payment on 100 head of cattle. So in the fall of 1908, Will, with his family of six children, and wife Annie, who was soon to give birth to another, left Fruitland with two wagons, several teams of horses and the 100 cattle. Bill, 13, his sister May, 11, and brothers Mildruff, 9, and Ray, 7, drove the cattle while other family members took care of the teams and wagons.

Now, if it seems too unusual for children

that young to have that much responsibility, we must tell of Will's experience of driving a herd of sheep from Snowflake, Arizona, to Pleasant Creek in southern Utah. Will spent most of a year on that drive, during which he turned 11.

Their destination, Grayson, had been established in 1905, and as in all new "Mormon" communities, a school was one of the first things to be established. True to that custom, when the Youngs arrived in Grayson on 8 October 1908, school was in session. Immediately four of the Young children: Bill, May, Mildruff and Ray, were enrolled, increasing the student body by 20 percent. That was one of the rare occasions when Bill was privileged to attend school. Classes were being held in two tents, pitched end to end. Later, in December, a heavy snowfall caved in the tents, putting the school out of business for a short time.

The winter of 1908-09 was severe and the cattle fared poorly. When spring finally came Will's horses and wagons were about the only assets he had left with which to support his family. He still owed some money on the 100 head of cattle, but there were not enough of them left to pay for themselves. He encouraged Bill and his younger brothers to hire out as cowboys and farm hands with the ranchers around the area, while he began a freighting business, hauling goods of all sorts to and from the railheads at Dolores, Colorado, a 100-mile trip, and Thompson, Utah, a 150-mile trip. Son Bill was soon to become an important part of that enterprise.

An incident worth telling about occurred in the spring of 1910. At Moab the Grande (Colorado) River had to be crossed on a ferry or by fording (wading or swimming. There was no bridge until years later) Will and his brother Ray and young Bill took three wagon outfits on a trip hauling wool to Thompson. While they were crossing with the second load the cable controlling the ferry broke, allowing the ferry to begin drifting down the stream. They had some anxious moments before Ray, who had already crossed, quickly rode a horse about a mile down stream and managed to throw a rope to Will, who fastened it to the runaway ferry so

Ray, with his horse, could pull it into the north bank.

For many years the San Juan people had to trail their livestock over the same route to the railroad at Thompson so they could be shipped to market. Bill told of driving not only cattle, but sheep and pigs as well, to the railroad over that route. There were incidents such as stampedes and bad weather that gave rise to many, many stories.

In 1917 Bill became anxious to do his share of defending his country in World War I. After talking it over with his parents, it was agreed that he should enlist before he was called by the draft. Will and Annie took him to Thompson where he boarded a train and traveled to Salt Lake City to enlist in the Army. It was not long until his younger brother, Mildruff, felt that he too should serve in the military. Soon both boys were in France.

Neta Washburn was born at Huntington, Emery, Utah, 18 November 1897, the fifth of 11 children of James Frederick Washburn and Lydia Spencer. When Neta was about four years old her family moved from Huntington, Utah, to Kirtland, New Mexico, not far from Fruitland.

In 1913, James Washburn moved his family to Grayson, Utah, so the Young and Washburn families were again in the same area. Neta was able to get in two years of high school at Blanding, which is all they had then. She was fortunate to be able to go to Provo, Utah, for another year.

Bill and Neta kept company for quite some time before he left for the Army. Neta tells of the excitement she felt when Bill returned from France in January 1919. They were married in the Salt Lake Temple, 19 July 1919. That involved a trip by automobile to Thompson, then by train to Salt Lake City.

It seems fitting at this point to retell a story told by Bill's brother, Loyd, who, at age 10, was pressed into service in July 1919 to drive a team on what may have been the final freight haul for Will Young and sons while brother Bill went to Salt Lake to get married.

Loyd tells of preparations beginning on 6 July 1919, when he and his father began repairing wagon wheels, re-shoeing horses, etc.

Neta Washburn Young
(Photo courtesy of Betty Jo Young Anderson)

They finally got under way in the afternoon of the 7th. He told in detail about the stops made and the general route they traveled, the process of taking the wagons up or down the steep hills, caring for the horses, crossing the river, unloading the freight at Thompson which they had brought from Blanding and Monticello, and loading more freight for the trip back.

They made it back to Blanding in the evening of 21 July, but still had to unload the next morning. Seems like that would have been an awesome experience for a 10 year old! But we have learned that in the Young Family, it was not so out of the ordinary.

It seems that Bill was preparing for a future as he had filed on 640 acres of land near Blanding soon after he returned from France in 1919. That was to be the beginning of a large cattle operation. At the time of the wedding, Bill's Grandpa Porter was about to complete a new house in Blanding for the newly-wed couple to move into. It was not quite ready for them when they returned from Salt Lake, so they had to move in with Bill's

family for a short time.

A big celebration dance was held a few nights after they were married and was well attended by friends who gathered from miles around. There were so many gifts they couldn't haul them all home that night, so a couple of Bill's brothers stood guard through the rest of the night and hauled the gifts home the next day.

In January of 1920 Bill went away from home to help his father, who had a contract to build a road in Colorado. Neta went along to help with the cooking. She said that the kitchen was a long tent with a coal/wood- burning range for cooking, a table for food preparation, and a long dining table. The tent was filled with hungry men three times a day.

In March Bill and Neta returned to Blanding; Bill to begin farming and Neta to prepare for their first baby. She was under the care of a mid-wife who helped her through the birth at home and then continued to care for her and the baby every morning during her ten days of confinement. She charged $25 for her services — modern childbirth is quite a different process, not to mention the difference in cost!

Bill and Neta had eight children and raised five:

> **Gene (Hacking)**, born 23 August 1920
> **Richard "Dick" Washburn**, 26 September 1922
> **Harold Francis**, 13 April 1925
> **William "L,"** 18 January 1927, died at birth
> **Neta Marie**, 23 March 1928, died 2 February 1929
> **Kendall Washburn**, 25 March 1930
> **Dorothy (Nowland)**, 13 November 1933
> **James Loyd**, 13 November 1942, died at birth

The first four living children were born at home in Blanding, the others were born in the hospital at Moab.

In 1921 Neta's mother died, leaving her father and three younger sisters very lonely and distraught. Neta spread herself a little thinner by going over to their house every day to help

Neta young and family, 1967, at the time of Bill's death. Back row, L-R: Harold Francis, Richard Washburn and Kendall Washburn. Front row: Gene (Hacking), Neta and Dorothy (Nowland). *(Photo courtesy of Edith Young)*

out. Then, to add to the sadness, in September of that year Neta's brother, Marion, accidentally shot himself while climbing through a fence and died a few days later. But that still wasn't enough; in November another brother, Francis, died when a wagon turned over on him.

Later, the father decided to go to St. George to work in the temple and the sisters moved in with Neta and Bill. By this time son Dick had arrived, so Neta had two children of her own to care for. Bill and Neta didn't have much room but, as one of the sisters commented: "Where there is love there is room." So Bill and Neta set up a bed for the sisters on the porch and Bill fastened a canvas around the bed to afford them some privacy and to help shield them from the cold.

In 1923 Bill was involved in the last Indian war in the United States. The Blanding community had been having problems with some renegade Utes who were stealing and killing cattle and sheep and creating other problems in the area. The two who had caused the most recent problem were tried in court in Blanding, and as they were being escorted to jail, they made a break for it and got away. A posse gave

chase and later Bill was invited to join in the roundup. The principal renegade character in that uprising and chase was known as "Posey." Many are the tales told of "Posey!"

At one point during the chase Bill and his companion discovered they were being set up for ambush. While Bill was trying to gain a vantage point he was shot at by the two escapees. He knew then that it was a matter of his life or theirs. Bill managed to get the drop on the two, killing one as the indian rode rapidly down the trail looking for Bill. The other was close behind. Bill had a bead on him, but when he saw the terror in the young Indian's face he let him ride away.

Bill was deeply troubled over that episode; it seemed at the time his entire life passed before him. He often visualized the dead Indian boy's family passing Bill's place on the way to town and recalled the pet names they had for the father and the son. He felt that the father would be his lifelong enemy for what had happened.

Bill later had a confrontation with the father as he was preparing something to eat over a campfire. He looked up and saw the older Indian sitting on his horse with a rifle across the saddle, watching him intently. Bill invited him to come have something to eat, but the old Indian just sat for a long time looking at Bill and off into the distance. Finally he dismounted and sat down to eat. From that time on Bill and Joe Bishop were good friends.

For the rest of his life Bill was reluctant to talk about that event in his life, but he did write his own full account from which the above condensed story is told.

As time passed Bill's father and brothers acquired more land and cattle around Blanding

Dick and Harold Young on the ranch.
(Photo courtesy of Richard Young)

until they became the principle cattle ranchers in the area. In 1925 Will and Bill were able to buy Camp Jackson, a delightful 40-acre plot in the National Forest on Blue Mountain, a place they had been coveting for years. Soon after, Bill built a new cabin on the place, made a cooler at the spring and put the following note on the door of the cabin: "Welcome! Come in and make yourself at home. There's flour in the bin, cool water, butter and bacon at the spring. Please wash your dishes and close the door when you leave — Bill." That was the kind of San Juan County Will and Bill had wanted for a long time.

In 1929 Bill's father died at only 53 years of age, increasing Bill's responsibility even more. His mother and brothers and sisters then looked to him as patriarch of the family. Bill's holdings kept on growing even though he had to spend much time taking care of his father's interests. As everyone will say who knew him, Bill was no

stranger to hard work.

His sons, Dick, Harold and Kendall grew up helping their father with the ranching business, which eventually became known as W. R. Young Cattle Company. Both Dick and Harold had attended elementary school in Blanding. Dick graduated from high school but Harold had to get on with his "cowboying" and only went to the 10th grade. Both boys served in the Marines during World War II. Harold left first in October 1943 and came home in January 1946. Dick left in February 1944 and returned in May 1946. Their paths never crossed even though both were in the Pacific Theatre. After their return both sons became partners in the cattle business.

In 1947 the U.S. Park Service purchased the Blue Mountain Ranch from them. Soon after that, the Youngs bought the Tom Kelley spread in Colorado, which included a large ranch in the Atchee area and farm land in the New Liberty community.

Gene, Kendall, and Dorothy never lived in New Liberty; however, they did come to visit occasionally. Kendall spent at least one summer working with his dad and brothers in Colorado. Daughter Gene graduated from high school in Blanding and went on to college at Brigham Young University at Provo. While in college she met LaVerle Hacking. They were married soon after. LaVerle served in the Air Force and while overseas was reported missing and wasn't heard from for about eight months. He eventually came home and they settled down at Cedar Fort, Utah. In October 1948 he died of meningitis, leaving Gene a widow with three children. She moved back to Blanding and is still living there; she never remarried.

Kendall graduated from high school in Blanding, then went to college at Brigham Young University. He served an LDS mission in France, then after his return he was drafted into the Army and soon was stationed at Paris, France. While attending the LDS meetings in Paris he met a girl named Gabriell "Gabby", whom he later married. They live in Salt Lake City at present.

Dorothy also finished high school in Blanding, then went to BYU. While in college she decided she wanted to become a nurse and went to Ogden

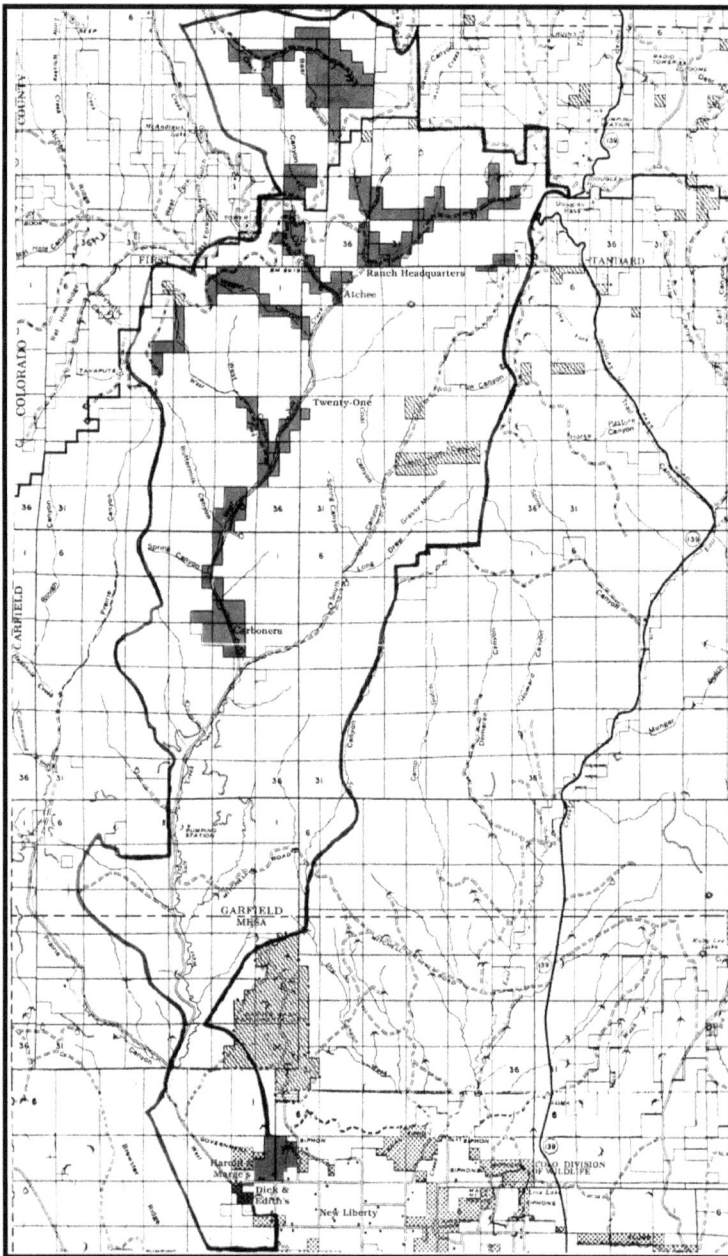

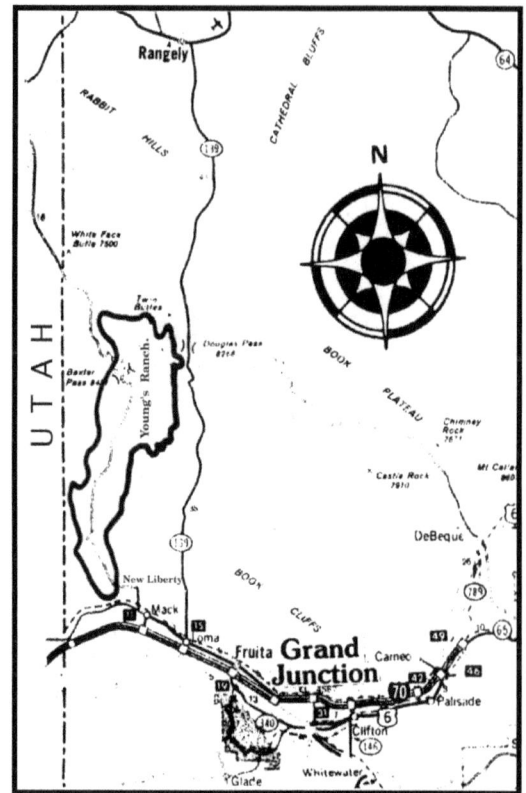

The large map on the left shows the ranch boundaries outlined in black; the black solid areas are the deeded areas and the rest is BLM land. New Liberty is where the farm homes were located. Harold and Marge's home was on the north farm and Dick and Edith's home on the south farm. There was a ranch at milepost 21 going toward Atchee and the summer ranch headquarters was located in Main Canyon, north of Atchee.

The small map on the right gives one a perspective of the size of the ranch. It covered an area including Mesa and Garfield Counties in Colorado and took in areas in New Liberty, Baxter Pass and Douglas Pass. *(Maps courtesy of Neta Young Palfreyman)*

(Left) A picture of ranch headquarters in Main Canyon, north of Atchee. The photo was taken from the mountain southwest of the buildings. The main house is upper left, then the branding corrals, outbuildings, tack shed and a house that was moved up from Twenty One. The calving barn was located in New Liberty across the road from Harold's house. *(Photo courtesy of BettyJo Young Anderson)*

William Young house in New Liberty. Bill standing in front of the house at the left. *(Photos courtesy of BettyJo Young Anderson)*

for nurses' training. After graduation she worked in the Dee Hospital at Ogden, and while there she met R. C. Nowland, a military man. They were married in October 1956 and lived in a lot of different places. They have six children and currently live in San Diego.

Not long after the Youngs arrived in New Liberty they went around to all residents of the community and invited them to a barbecue at the main ranch at Atchee. A good-sized beef was barbecued for that event, with salads and cooked vegetables to make a delicious meal. Not everyone showed up, but that sincere gesture of friendship did not go unnoticed.

Here is part of a tribute paid to Bill by one of his best friends, Frank Halls, with whom he rode the range and otherwise associated with for many years:

I am going to mention several of the good traits that were in his possession. He didn't use tobacco, never drank liquor or strong drink of any kind, never told dirty stories or used foul language, didn't knowingly make false statements, and was very careful to avoid taking the Lord's name in vain. I never heard him swear, even in mild terms. I never heard of him mistreating or being cruel to any kind of dumb animal.

I, Homer Likes, would like to add my thoughts regarding Bill Young: He was without a doubt one of the finest men I have ever met. I feel that my life was made better by having known and associated with him.

A little story about Neta should be included here. When I became acquainted with the Youngs, Neta already had several grandchildren. I observed at one time that she was sharing a photo album upon which were engraved the letters: S O G B B. When I asked what the letters stood for she explained — "Silly Old Grandmother's Brag Book."

Bill died 27 June 1966, and Neta died 25 January 1985. Both are buried in the Young family plot in the Blanding Cemetery.

More about the ranch enterprise will be included in Dick's and Harold's stories.

Following is a story written by Edith, wife of Richard Young.

In the small town of Blanding, in the southeast corner of Utah, lived a cowboy casanova by the name of **Richard Young**, but known by his family and friends as Dick.

Shortly after graduating from San Juan High School, Richard began a tour of duty in the Marine Corps. He spent a year in the South Pacific during his 2 1/2 years in the Marines. After his return he rejoined his father, William R. "Bill" and brother Harold in their farming and cattle operation.

Early in the year 1948 they purchased, in partnership with Cardon Jones, the Tom Kelley property in Colorado, which included approximately 100 acres of farm land adjacent to Badger Wash (the original William Price homestead). The main ranch consisted of several homesteads Kelley had purchased over the years, lying in the drainage of West Salt Creek from the mouth of South Canyon all the way to Main Canyon, which included the town of Atchee. There was also land in four other canyons, including Railroad, Wagon, West and Prairie. On the north side there was land in Cow Canyon and East Vac (Evacuation Creek). In all there was approximately 10,000 acres of deeded land, plus 102,000 acres of BLM grazing permits. This vast domain stretched all the way from the Bookcliffs on the north to

Richard and Edith Harvey Young, 1948.
(Photo courtesy of Neta Young Palfreyman)

Rabbit Valley on the south, almost to the Colorado River.

Shortly after the original purchase from Kelley, they bought the Dave Thomas farm, which was on the west side of the Badger Wash, west of the Kelley property.

In the first part of February, Richard and his father helped brother and sister-in-law, Harold and Marge, move into the adobe house formerly occupied by Dave Thomas. Cardon and Hattie Jones and children moved into the Kelley house.

While Harold and Marge were getting settled into life in Colorado, Richard began courting a high school senior, **Edith Harvey**, a daughter of Waldo Harvey and Maggie Hurst, who was born at Moab, Utah, 29 October 1930. Soon after they started dating, while working at their winter ranch called "Deckers," Dick's horse slipped on a frozen bank and fell, breaking Dick's leg. He had to do his courting for the next three months with his leg in a cast. Dick and Edith were married in the Salt Lake Temple, 1 September 1948.

During their first years of marriage, Dick managed the Utah property while Harold managed that in Colorado, with dad Bill keeping an eye on both.

Not long after the original purchase, father and sons added the Merton Arpke and Orlin Corn farms; both joined the land they already had. This made a large tract of about 420 acres of farm land lying north of S Road and between 5 1/2 and 6 1/2 Roads. Later they acquired 90 acres more from Claude Taylor and 100 acres from Lester Sumnicht.

Life was very pleasant and happy for Dick and Edith, living near their parents and families, with a close circle of friends.

Eventually four darling little girls came to bless their lives:

Naida Kay, born 1 June 1949
Neta, 2 November 1950
Rebecca "Becky," 7 June 1953
Kathryn "Kathy," 29 November 1954

In 1954 Cardon Jones felt it necessary to sell his interest to the Youngs, and he and Hattie and children moved back to Blanding.

Because of the many difficulties in running the two operations so far away from each other, when Uncle Earl Perkins offered Bill and sons a good business deal on the Utah property, they accepted his offer and moved all their interests to Colorado.

What a change occurred with the sale of the Utah property! Bill and Neta moved to the Orlin Corn property where Cardon and Hattie had been living. During the winter of 1955-56 Richard commuted to Colorado, staying two or three weeks at a time, coming home to Blanding only for a few days. This difficult operation helped Edith to prepare to leave family and friends. She found that being alone most of the time with four little girls was anything but ideal for the family.

As soon as school was out and Naida had finished the first grade, the family loaded their belongings into a truck, rented out the Blanding home, never to live in it again, and moved to Colorado.

That first summer they lived on the Thomas place in the adobe house. The Orlin Corn house became Harold and Marge's permanent home. A new little home was built below the brow of the hill for Bill and Neta.

After much consideration the decision was made to move the large room from the Kelley house and add it to the Arpke house as the new home for Richard's family. The adobe house would then be used for a hired man.

What a project that turned out to be! The beginning buildings were very ramshackle! Yount Cooper was hired to do the carpenter work. As soon as he had a room built, Edith would take over and do the papering and painting. Marge Young and Agnes Overbye helped with some of the papering. What a way to spend the first six months of a pregnancy!

Since a new concrete cistern had been poured at the Kelley property while the Jones' lived there, and since the cistern at the Arpke property was to become the septic tank for the plumbing system, the new cistern at the Kelley place was dug up and moved to the Arpke place. Everyone laughed at "moving a hole in the ground." That cistern was placed on the hill at the north side of the house so that gravity from that height would provide pressure for the water system. Despite the care taken in moving the cistern and setting it in it's new location, there were so many cracks in it that couldn't be sealed, it was abandoned and a new metal tank was purchased instead. Unfortunately, not enough thought had been given to purchasing the new metal tank, it had to be nearly empty before it would hold a full truck tank of water hauled from Fruita. It seemed we were always running out of water at the most inappropriate times. A load of water would last about a week. Edith always joked about having to measure water by the teaspoon. The water was expensive, so we had to conserve wherever possible. Several would bathe in the same water and the toilet wasn't flushed after every use.

The house was finally finished about two weeks before Christmas and the family moved in. What a winter that was! Lots of snow and cold weather! When it warmed up and the snow began to melt — such mud! A new road had been bulldozed to the house and there was no gravel on it, and that clay soil is something else! It was a good thing trips out weren't very frequent, for this is how the procedure went: the tractor was on hand to pull the car out of the mud holes several times before we could reach "S" road,

then on the return trip, the car would be left on the road and we would walk in on the grassy clumps and the rock-strewn gully along the west side of the road. On the next trip the procedure would be reversed. It seemed like winter lasted an eternity! When Edith's parents came to visit they were very concerned : "How are you going to get out when the baby comes?" But by 26 March 1957, warm sunshine had dried the mud and the trip to the hospital went very well.

A fifth little girl, **Helen**, joined the family on 26 March 1957. Everyone expressed concern that the baby wasn't a boy, but Richard and Edith felt no disappointment. Little baby Helen was so delightful, and with maturity, Edith remarked that it took five babies for them to learn to enjoy them. Richard especially enjoyed her, because he was so close, our home being right in the midst of his work. She was a small child and Richard began to call her "Nub," because she reminded him of a small ear of corn.

Two years later a baby boy was added! **Richard "Ricky" Harvey** arrived 20 February 1959, a husky 7 lb. 8 oz., a whole month early. Edith said that was the nicest thing that ever happened, to be spared that last month! Just 16 months later, Ricky received a new playmate, a little brother, **Scott "W,"** arrived 29 June 1960. What a perfect family: five little girls and two little boys.

During that time the cattle company prospered, usually employing two men. Richard used one to help him with the farming, and Harold used one to help with the cattle. Bill was the overseer. Then in the winter it took all the men to feed and care for the herd. At the peak of their operation, they ran 700 mother cows and with the bulls and replacement heifers, they had a total of about 1,400 head. With that many cattle to feed in the winter, additional feed had to be purchased. Many of the neighbors were thankful to have such a close-by market for their hay and corn. The corn was chopped for silage — the fragrance of ensilage — ugh!

As new haying equipment came on the market the Youngs tried several. The first was a baler that made haystacks that looked like loaves of bread. These had to be hauled to a stack-yard on low wagons pulled by tractors. Six strong men were required — three for each wagon, two to pick up the bales while a third placed them correctly on the wagon. A fourth person was needed to drive the tractor. When Neta and Becky were teenagers they became experts at driving the tractors. Many choice stories are told about their experiences. But the method was disappointing, as the stacks froze to the ground

(Above) The Dick Young family in 1961, at New Liberty. L-R: Kathy, Naida, Edith holding Helen, Becky, Dick holding Scott, Neta and Ricky. (Below) The Dick Young family in 1967. L-R in back: Kathy, Becky, Neta, Naida, Edith and Dick. In front: Scott, Ricky and Helen. *(Photos courtesy of Edith Harvey Young)*

in the winter and were difficult to pick up. Later that baler was traded for one that made large round bales and was quite well liked, as the bales could be picked up and transported easily.

A hearty noon meal was provided for the hay crew. Although it didn't take all summer to harvest the hay, it may have seemed like it, as there was so much to do in addition to caring for our large family. Most of the morning was spent preparing food and half the afternoon washing the dishes.

Richard and Edith belong to The Church of Jesus Christ of Latter-day Saints, commonly called 'Mormons.' It is very important to them that they and their children have all of the blessings offered them by their membership in the church. The distance of 15 miles they had to travel to Fruita to attend meetings and activities didn't stop them from doing their part in carrying on the work of sharing their belief. Richard and Edith both served in numerous callings in leadership as well as teaching. Richard served as a bishop's counselor for five years and as Stake High Councilman for nine years. Edith served as Relief Society President and counselor in the Primary and Young Women's programs. The church continues to be part of their lives today; recently they served a mission for 18 months in the Philippine Islands.

Young's car or station wagon had the reputation of being a 'Church Bus.' Edith would fill it with her own seven children, as well as many neighbor children, and attend the weekly children's religious training meeting that was called 'Primary.' She would help with the teaching as well as the chauffeuring. As the children turned 12 they began to attend the weekly MIA (Mutual Improvement Association) meetings one evening a week. Several of the neighbor girls were also offered rides to those meetings.

Early morning Seminary was another challenge. At first Granddad Bill Young took the responsibility to get the girls there, but as spring work began, the mothers took the early morning drive. The younger children would have to get themselves ready for school and down to the bus-stop. It was a great day when one of the girls was old enough to get a driver's license and could drive the others to seminary!

The family of nine bulged the walls of the first little home on the Arpke place. The Cattle Company had spent a considerable amount of money on the home on the Sumnicht property, which had such a nice location and rich sandy soil. This seemed an ideal place for a new home. Construction began as we added to the little

homestead house, which contained two bedrooms, a bath, kitchen and living room. Two large bedrooms and a very large living room, another bath, utility porch and storage were added. The original living room became a dining room, since the kitchen was small with an eating bar, but not large enough for a family meal. The family moved into that new home in March 1965.

About 15 years later, the kitchen, which had been a 'lean-to' began to 'lean-off.' Richard and Edith felt the need to have a family room, so the original kitchen and utility were removed and a large kitchen, family and utility and garage were added.

Due to heavy expenses, some of the land had to be sold. Prairie Canyon was sold to Dave Terrell. A tract of land on the north side was sold to our neighbors, the Kirbys. The land at the head of South Canyon, which had been purchased from Cleo Stanfield was sold to Billy Price from Tennessee.

In the fall of 1965 Granddad Bill became ill with cancer and died 27 June 1966. Neta stayed in her little home in Colorado for several years, then decided to return to her home in Blanding, where she lived until her demise in January 1985.

On Scott's birthday, 29 June 1967, a great tragedy struck our family. Ricky, Scott and cousin Eric Harvey went out to the pond without permission and Ricky drowned.

All of Richard and Edith's children attended the local schools. Naida, Neta, and Becky attended New Liberty. Becky was in the last class to begin her education there. It was a sad day when the school closed and then they had a 12-mile bus ride to go to the Loma School.

Naida didn't graduate from Fruita High School. After her sophomore year she visited her uncle and aunt in Richland, Washington, and graduated from Columbia High School there. Neta was in the last class to graduate from 'old' Fruita Union High School. All the children graduated from high school and had additional schooling at BYU, Ricks College or Mesa College. Naida received a degree in cosmetology from Hollywood Beauty School.

Hard times hit the New Liberty area. Among the many who met financial disaster were Richard and Harold Young. With great heartache they sold their big ranch at half its value in 1986. Richard kept his home and 100 acres (the Sumnicht place). Harold and Marge moved back to Blanding.

Although financial wealth is not their lot, in things that really matter, Richard and Edith consider themselves millionaires. At this time

Dick and Edith's home in New Liberty after they remodeled.
(Photo courtesy of Edith Harvey Young)

(1993) they are proud grandparents of 26 grandchildren: 13 boys and 13 girls. Their children are all married to wonderful individuals. Naida and her husband, Colonel John Westwood, are parents of four boys; Neta and her husband, Robert Palfreyman, followed her parents example and have four girls and two boys. To balance Naida's four boys, Becky and her husband, Devon Olson, have four girls. Kathy and her husband, Kent Roper, have two boys and two girls. Helen and her husband, Staff Sergeant Delwin Weeks, have three girls and two boys. Scott and his wife, Sheila, have two boys. The family doesn't get together very often because of the great distance, but those who live close do. There is a very close bond between all, regardless of how far or near. At family get-togethers a noisy but joyful time is had by all.

Dick and Edith sold their farm in the summer of 1995 and moved to Blanding.

Naida Kay married **John Samuel Westwood** on 1 November 1971, in Salt Lake City, Utah. They have four children: **Bret Harvey, Greg Samuel, Chad Joseph,** and **Kirk Richard.** John and Naida have lived in many areas of the United States and in Germany, as John has been in the Army for over 25

Dick and Edith Young, 1990s. *(Photo courtesy of Edith Harvey Young)*

years. They presently live in Virginia and John is working at the Pentagon.

*N*eta married **Robert Charles Palfreyman** on 9 July 1971 in Salt Lake City, Utah. They have seven children: **Kristie (Hansen), Sarah (Winward), Richard Lorus** (serving an LDS Mission in Brazil), **Morgan Robert, Lori, Emily,** and **Charles Young.** Robert has worked for American Express for 26 years, first in Phoenix, Arizona for eight years and for the last 18 years in Orem, Utah. The family lives in Orem.

*R*ebecca "Becky" married **Devon W. Olson** on 30 August 1978, in Salt Lake City, Utah. They have four daughters: **Maggie, Ashley, Mallory** and **Abby McKenzie.** Devon is an appraiser and the family lives in Salt Lake City.

*K*athryn married **Kent Walker Roper** on 24 March 1978, in Salt Lake City, Utah. They have four children: **Spence Richardson, Grant Young, Natalie Arla,** and **Edith Marie.** Kent works for the Shriver's Cheese Factory in Logan, Utah, and he and Kathy are distributors for AmWay. The family lives in Smithfield and has lived in the Cache Valley area for the last 19 years.

*H*elen married **Delwin Randahl Weeks** on 29 July 1978, in New Liberty, Colorado. They have five children: **Angela, Mark Delwin, Heidi, Aubrey,** and **Bradley Richard.** Delwin has been in Marines for the last 16 years, so they have lived in many places in the United States. They presently live in Ft. Leonard Wood, Missouri.

*S*cott "W" married **Shela Bacon** 22 August 1986, in Salt Lake City, Utah. They have two sons: **Nicholas Scott** and **William Richard.** Scott and Shela were later divorced. Scott got an associate's degree in electronics at Mesa College in Grand Junction and worked in Grand Junction and Arkansas. He presently lives in Blanding, Utah, with his folks and is getting a teaching degree.

The following is a tribute to Harold Young by his brother, Kendall:

*H*arold Francis Young was born 13 April 1925, at Blanding, Utah, the third of eight children born to William Richard Young and Neta Washburn.

From the beginning, it was plain that

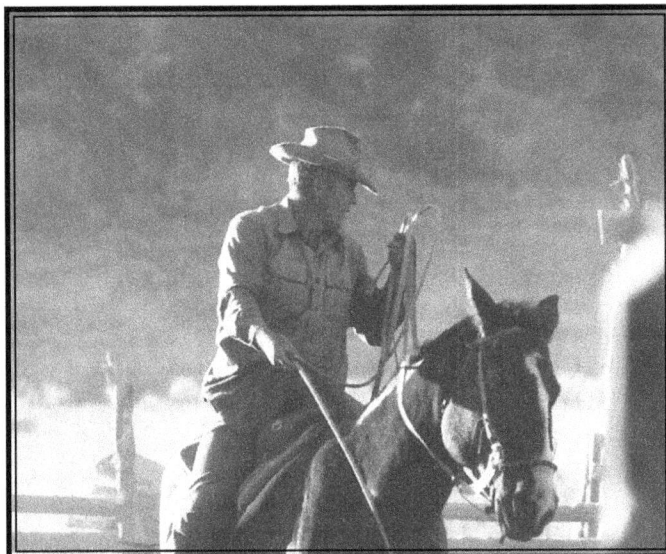
Harold Young the Cowboy at sunrise.
(Photo courtesy of BettyJo Young Anderson)

Harold was to be a cowboy. At the age of eight he began to drive horses to and from Blanding and Monticello, a distance of 20 miles. His brother Kendall stated that he worked like an adult, even as a child. He was always trying to do things two or three years before he was old enough to do them.

Even at that, he didn't miss out on childhood fun. His older sister, Gene, related that when she came home from a date, Harold would be hiding in the bushes to throw apples at her suitor.

Harold preferred being a cowboy to all else. In the 10th grade he and some of his friends were suspended from school for playing poker in shop class, and Harold headed into the hills to take up the cowboy's life, full time. He worked for the SS Cattle Company through the winter, then joined in the cattle business with his dad.

At age 18, in 1943, he joined the Marine Corps and fought in the Pacific Theatre during World War II. In the Marines he qualified as a marksman on the rifle range. He was an amphibious tank driver; a vehicle known as a DUK. He participated in the invasion of Saipan, Tinian, Okinawa, and in the occupation of Japan. His service record shows that he received the Good Conduct Medal on 20 October 1943, and as of his date of discharge, on 29 January 1946, he had no offense on his record. He enjoyed a lifelong friendship with many of his Marine buddies and enjoyed reunions with them throughout the years.

Harold met **Marjorie Merz** while in school and corresponded with her throughout his service abroad. In the last letter to her before arriving home he said, "Get your boots and spurs, we're going to Camp Jackson." That was a cow camp he and his father owned on the side of Blue Mountain near Blanding.

Harold and Marge were married on 28 May 1946, in the Manti Temple at Manti, Utah. Marge recalled the day after they were married they headed for Camp Jackson. When they arrived they found that the cows were in the wrong fields and they spent their honeymoon day chasing cows and fixing fence.

Harold and Marge, had five children in their 47 years of marriage:

Hallie Jean (Buniger), born 3 March 1947, Moab, Utah

Leslie Ann (Burrup), 10 June 1949, Fruita

Frances (Cronk, Hill), 10 December 1950, Monticello, Utah

BettyJo (Anderson), 11 August 1957, Fruita

John William, 4 November 1958, Fruita

They have 12 grandchildren at present (1993), with one grandchild and one great grandchild due in the summer.

In 1947 the U. S. Park Service purchased the Blue Mountain Ranch and the Youngs purchased the Kelley ranch in the Baxter Pass area northwest of Mack, Colorado. Harold, with his brother, Dick, and their father, Bill, developed "the best durned ranch in the whole world," as BettyJo described it.

On the ranch, he taught his children to ride, shoot, work cows, and love the earth that God created. He always said, "The land is the priority,

Marjorie Merz and Harold Francis Young, December 1989. *(Photo courtesy BettyJo Young Anderson)*

the cows are the by-product." He taught that if you take care of the land, it will take care of you.

The quaking aspen leaves in a summer breeze sounded like the Vienna Waltz to Harold, and he taught this love and appreciation for the outdoors to his children.

There were many times in the spring when Harold would drive into the yard after being out with the cows in the desert, load everyone in the pickup and take them back out to the desert to show them the first wild flowers in bloom, or to admire the carpet of fresh, green grass.

A favorite family outing on Sunday after church, was to drive for miles and miles to stand beside a corral fence and appreciate the "fine points of a good-looking horse."

Harold and his family were members of The Church of Jesus Christ of Latter-day Saints, and in the Fruita Ward he served in the bishopric, the Boy Scouts, the finance committee and various other callings throughout the 40 years he lived there. He filled his years with many helpful deeds to his neighbors. He often said, "If you are going to help someone, help those who really need it," and followed his words with actions to suit.

Harold and Marjorie spent 40 years on the ranch near Mack, then sold it and returned to Blanding where he worked for the White Mountain Ute Tribal Council, and later for Clisbee Lyman. He contracted prostate cancer and later passed away on 15 February 1993.

Harold's son-in-law, Jon D. Hill, who grew up on the Hill ranch next door to the Young ranch in the Bookcliff Mountains, paid this tribute to Harold:

I first remember seeing Harold when I

Harold Young Family, 1959. (L-R) Harold holding BettyJo, Frances, Hallie Jean, Marjorie holding John William, and Leslie Ann. *(Photo courtesy of BettyJo Young Anderson)*

was a small child. I had gone to town with my mother and grandmother and we got stuck on the desert, south of Baxter pass, with a railroad spike in a tire and a jack that wouldn't work. We were among the many he helped on the road over the years in one way or another. Some of those folks were taken to his home and fed, some staying on for many days until the mud dried up so they could go on. Most of them were strangers when they showed up, friends when they left.

Next, I remember him as one of the men who sat with my grandfather at the Bookcliff picnics and told stories about the great roundups and cowboys of the past, intriguing me for hours to the point where I didn't want to go off and play with the other kids unless he decided to join in the baseball games, as he often did. In the games he played, no one won or lost, because no one kept score, we just played.

Later on, as a rider on my own, I knew him as a man who knew livestock. I knew Harold as a cowboy and a cow man. He could ride and rope and hit the brush. He knew wild cattle, knew what they thought and knew how to catch them, but understood that cattle need to be handled in a manner to prevent them from becoming wild.

Harold was a man whose whole life revolved around water. When praying, he always thanked the Lord for the moisture received and sometimes asked for more. When we were together, whether it was in the Bookcliffs or in Blanding, he would say, "There is a spring right over here and it is the best water in the country."

Harold was a man who always had his fences fixed on time and tight. No one had to worry about their own cows if they crossed the fence, either. Harold would hold them as if they were his own, returning everything, branded or unbranded.

Later on I knew him as a family man who delighted in telling what each of his grandchildren were doing at home, church, or school. He followed his son John's progress towards his master's degree with as much interest as if he was directly involved.

He would spend hours discussing each new research project John was doing, the pros and cons, whether it would work on an open range-type ranch, and what could be accomplished by doing it.

After Harold moved to Blanding, he taught me about the land and plants there, what the land would produce, how to handle the cattle there, and the difference between Blanding's ecology and that of the Bookcliffs. I guess the best thing I can say about him is that he never stopped learning.

Above all else, Harold was a good husband, good father, as good a father-in-law as you could ever hope to find, and — a **friend**.

Kallie Jean married **William Harvey Buniger III**. They had a son named **William Harold** and a daughter named **Spring**. They are divorced.

Leslie Ann married **Dean Richard Burrup**. They have four children: **Jeanna Marie, Jay "D," James Cody** and **Libbie Ruth**.

Frances married **Thomas Allen Cronk** and they had two children: **Tim Duke** and **Jacob Wade**. They were divorced and Frances married **Jon D. Hill**. They have one son: **Logan "D."**

Betty Jo married **Dean Leslie Anderson**. They have three children: **Kirby Gene, Deana Marie** and **Joseph Francis**.

John William married **Angela Leslie Obert**. They have two children: **Brianna Marie** and **Frances Jo**.
All of Harold and Marge's children attended school at New Liberty and Fruita Union High School.

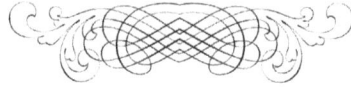

Zahnen

The following information was taken from Paul Zahnen and Myrtle Hamby's obituaries and the memories of Darrell Maluy and Phyllis Likes.

Paul Zahnen was born 27 February 1881 at St. Marks, Sedgwick, Kansas and spent his childhood there. He served in the army during World War I.

The first knowledge we have of Paul is when he came to New Liberty and went to work for Bill Maluy, in the spring of 1934. He lived on the Huckstep place, located east of Art Harrison and south of Don Weimer: Sec 21 Twp 9S R 103W.

Paul lived by himself and farmed 30 to 40 acres of land. He raised beans, hay and grain, and had about eight milk goats. He had a strong, German accent and was a very hard worker. He could shovel a ditch like no other — he would put his head down and shovel with great force and speed without looking up. He had one peculiarity; he always, winter and summer, wore a red, flannel lined denim jacket that came down below his hips. We never saw him without it, and seldom knew of him taking a bath.

He and Clem Maluy would trade off helping each other with the haying and harvesting. Darrell remembers one time when Clem had Darrell help Paul with the haying and Darrell had lunch with Paul. He served goat meat from an old male goat he had butchered and "blood cheese" for the meal. Darrell was unable to eat lunch because of the strong smelling meat, the nauseating blood cheese and the uncleanliness and stench of the house.

Mary Maluy, with daughters, Phyllis and Lee Ann, spent the winter of 1934–1935 in California with her sister, Claire, as Mary was recuperating from a serious case of ulcers.

Clem hired a woman by the name of Leatha to cook and keep house for himself and children, Darrell and Marilyn, and Gerald Coltharp, a boy that lived with the Maluys that year and went to school at New Liberty. Leatha had a little girl named Dorothy, about the same age as Marilyn. Darrell remembers Paul coming over to court Leatha (Paul called her Layta). Darrell and Gerald would hide and listen to him sweet talk to Leatha as he tried to get her favor, but he was not successful.

In the fall of 1939, Darrell and his friend, Leon Daily, went upon Douglas Pass to hunt deer. Paul asked Darrell if he would drive his car home for him, as he had left his 1929 Nash at the Van Riper homestead on Douglas Pass all summer and had no way to get it home. After he had finished hunting, Darrell started the car up and proceeded down the mountain. He soon realized that he had no brakes. He put the car in low gear, but it didn't do much good. He came flying down the mountain, speeding around the sharp curves; driving onto the bank of the mountain when possible trying to slow down. The road was on the opposite side of the mountain than it is today, and was steeper, curves sharper and had an underpass from one side to the other. By the time he got to the bottom, the car was almost out of oil as it had thrown the oil out from the high compression in low gear and going so fast. Darrell was on crutches, as he was recuperating from an injured knee while playing football, and couldn't go for help, so he slowly drove it on home.

In the winter of 1939 Paul moved to Palisade. He married **Myrtle Price Hamby** in January 1941 at Denver, Colorado. She was born 12 September 1894 at Bolivar, Polk, Missouri, and spent her childhood there. She was previously married to William Hamby who died in April 1939. She had three sons by that marriage; Lloyd, Ted and Dewey. Dewey married Edith Alstatt of New Liberty. Myrtle lived in Oklahoma until moving to Grand Junction in 1939.

Paul and Myrtle lived in Palisade and then on Texas Avenue in Grand Junction. Myrtle died in 1960 at age 64. She was struck by a car three years prior and had been in ill health since that time. After

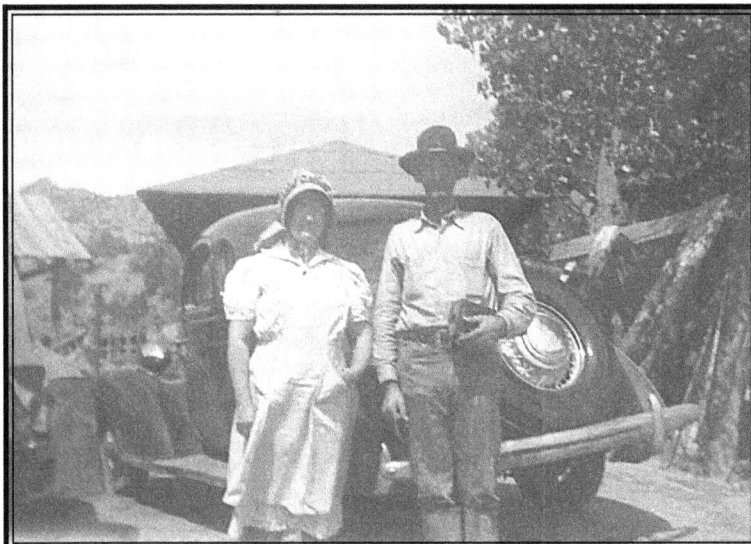

Myrtle and Paul Zahnen at Palisade, about 1941.
(Photo courtesy of Dorothy Hamby O'Brien)

Myrtle's death, Paul moved back to Palisade and was living at the Palisade Nursing Home when he died at St. Mary's Hospital in Grand Junction on 26 December 1974, at age 93. Paul's obituary states that a daughter, Theresa Trujillo, survives him, but we have no record of a former wife and children.

Myrtle Price Hamby and Paul Zahnen
(Photo courtesy of Dorothy Hamby O'Brien)

Addendum

The Three Maluys

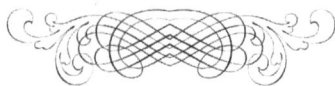

Taken from "The Three Maluys of New Liberty," written by Phyllis Likes and published in the *Fruita Times*, 15 August 1991

Patrick Henry Maluy was born 20 October 1861, at Sycamore, DeKalb, Illinois to William James Maluy and Catherine Bennett, who were Irish/English immigrants. In 1869 the family moved from Illinois to Hanover, Washington Co., Kansas, and settled on a homestead. On 24 April 1888, Patrick married his childhood sweetheart, **Mary Agnes Chloetilda Reel.** She was a lovely lass who was born at Galena, Jo Daviess Co., Illinois, to Irish immigrant parents, Patrick James Reel and Margaret Gertrude Burke. The Reels had homesteaded also at Hanover, Kansas, in 1879.

Patrick built a house for his bride on the family farm, and he and his father farmed together. He later purchased the farm from his father.

Patrick and Mary had six children:

Mary (Mae) Loretta
William (Bill) Benedict
Gertrude(Gertie) Kathryn
Adalyne (Addie) Margaret
Clement (Clem)
Thomas (Tom) Patrick

Patrick was an honest and charitable man who had to endure the loss of his wife Mary, who died soon after the birth of their sixth child; leaving him alone to raise children ranging in age from newborn to eight years. But with the help of Patrick's mother and sister, and later his daughters, he raised a happy and close-knit family.

In February 1917, Patrick sold his farm and auctioned off his equipment and livestock. By that time daughter Mae was married to Evan Charles Williams and living in California; Bill was single and living on the farm; Gertie was married to Oliver "Ollie" James and living on a homestead near Flagler, Colorado. Addie was single, living and working in Marysville, Kansas; Clem had married Mary Christine Darrow and was living on the farm. Tom was married to Cecil Worley and living at Rawlins, Wyoming.

Patrick, Bill, Clem and Mary all moved to Marysville after the auction. Patrick moved in with Addie, Mary went to work at the hotel, and Bill and Clem went into business selling "Puncture Proof", a sure cure for punctured tires. After they had a call-back because all four of the man's tires went flat, they decided it wasn't so "Puncture Proof" after all!

That summer (1917) Bill joined the Army and was soon sent to France. Clem and Mary moved to Rawlins, Wyoming where Clem went to work for the Union Pacific Railroad. Clem studied to be a fireman and brakeman, but they soon realized that this job would keep them separated for lengthy periods of time. Clem said: "We got married so we could be together"...so he quit. They went to Twin Falls, Idaho and found a job picking apples...a week later there came a freeze and ruined the rest of the apple crop. They then moved to Fowler, Idaho, and Clem got a job with a threshing crew and Mary did the cooking for the crew. After two months of this they went to Salt Lake City where both went to work for the railroad; Clem worked in the yard doing maintenance work and Mary cleaned passenger cars.

Early in the spring of 1918, Clem received a phone call from his sister, Addie, asking him to come home as their father was quite despondent. He was concerned because his money was dwindling away and nothing was coming in. So Clem and Mary went back to Marysville.

It was Patrick's desire to set up each of his three sons on a farm, and he had been looking for irrigated homestead possibilities. He had read about the Bureau of Reclamation Project

801

about to be opened up in the Grand Valley in Colorado, and was quite interested in it. Bill was serving in the Army in France and couldn't come home; Tom was working for the railroad in Wyoming and wasn't interested in farming. So Patrick and Clem went to Colorado to investigate.

They arrived in Grand Junction in time to join the auto tour that was being hosted 22 March 1918, by the Chamber of Commerce and the Bureau of Reclamation to give applicants an opportunity to see the new land being offered. They liked what they saw and each filed on a farm unit.

When the drawing came up on 29 March, Clem was successful but Patrick was not. However, the next day Patrick was allowed to file on a "free" unit that had not been included in the drawing. They were pleased to each have sixty acres of good level land and less than a mile apart.

Patrick and Clem did not go back to Kansas. Instead, they went right to work and purchased horses, equipment, and the necessary materials to build, and soon had built a 12 foot by 24 foot tar paper covered shack, a good sized barn and a chicken house. They had also prepared about twenty acres of ground on Clem's farm for planting.

Mary arrived at Mack by train on 7 June 1918; Clem met her with team and wagon. She was very excited to see their new home, but when they arrived at the homestead she could see it was no Garden of Eden! It was hot desert with no houses or trees in sight and "dust six inches deep." Her first thought was..."There is no place to hang my hammock."

The first summer was very hard with the three of them living in that tiny house with no shade, and a wood/coal burning cook stove adding to the heat. They hauled wood and coal from the Bookcliffs about 15 miles away. In order to start the fire in the cook stove, they soaked corn cobs in coal oil, lit them, added small kindling, wood, and then the coal.

They would open the windows to let air circulate, but they didn't have screens, so the flies were a big problem. The water supply was deplorable. All they had was ditch water that had sheep manure and many other kinds of debris in it. They would fill barrels with the water to let the mud settle to the bottom and the debris rise to the top. They would skim the stuff off the top and then put the water in canvas bags in hopes it would cool and be somewhat drinkable.

Because of the war, sugar was rationed and flour and butter were very scarce. They used what was called "war flour" which was made from barley and rye. It didn't make very good bread! They could get a little cornmeal so they had cornbread once in awhile. They had to buy everything.

Because there was no refrigeration they could not keep meat of any kind, except salty bacon and ham. They would have to boil it for a long time to get the salt out before it was edible. They could get beans, and so the combination of ham or bacon and beans became a regular staple. They had their own chickens to supply eggs and milk cows for their milk supply. They bought a couple of pigs to raise for meat. So, with five horses and two cows to feed they had to buy hay, which they had to haul from about ten miles away. It cost about $30 to $35 per ton and then it required almost a full day to haul a wagon load. On one occasion they were on the way home with a load of hay and it tipped over as they crossed the Uintah RR tracks. They were late in the night getting home after having to reload the hay.

The greatest challenge for Patrick and Clem was to learn to irrigate. The soil was silt loam and it washed away like sugar as the water ran through it. Yet it would become hard as brick after it dried out.

They raised a beautiful garden that first year...since it was new soil they didn't have much trouble with weeds. The cabbage grew so large they could only get a couple of heads in a bushel basket. Mary put up 28 gallons of sourkraut that first summer. She also canned some fruit, but because of the distance they had to travel to get it and the expense of the jars, etc., they were limited on the amount they could put up.

Winter presented a new challenge...The cook stove that added to the heat misery in the summer was not quite adequate to keep them warm in the winter. The stove wouldn't hold a fire overnight so when they got out of bed in the mornings their blankets were frosted from their breathing and frozen around their chins. The water would be frozen in the bucket on the cupboard. Since they had built a cistern in the fall, they had a good water supply. They met their challenges though, and as Mary said: "They were young and madly in love, so didn't resent it too much, and were happy".

After living with Clem and Mary for two or three years, Patrick built a house on his farm and moved in. Patrick became well known and respected by his friends and neighbors, who knew him as "Pat". He loved farming and felt that he had almost accomplished his dream by seeing two of his sons set up on irrigated farms.

During the winter of 1925 he went to California to visit daughter Mae. Since Mae's mother in law, Emily (Mully) Williams, was widowed, she and Patrick struck up a romance and were married that winter. He brought her back to Colorado to live in the spring of 1926. Bill purchased Patrick's farm in 1927, and he and his family moved in with Patrick and Mully. Patrick and Mully moved to California in 1928 but returned to Colorado in 1930. They were living in a room in the White House Hotel in Fruita when Mully died in October, only six weeks after they came back to Colorado.

Patrick then purchased the Piggly Wiggly store in Grand Junction across from Lincoln Park. He married Mrs. Stella Chappell, 1 June 1934, and they lived in Grand Junction. Patrick died in his sleep 29 July 1936.

Clement Maluy was born 3 October 1895, at Hanover, Washington Co., Kansas, and attended school there. He was married to **Mary Christine Darrow** 1 May 1916, at Salina, Saline Co., Kansas. Mary was born 3 April 1896 at Asherville, Mitchell Co., Kansas, to George Allen Darrow and Anna Lautrup. Mary spent her childhood years in the Asherville area but graduated from high school at Beloit. Clem came to Beloit to find work and stayed at the hotel owned by Mary's mother, so that is where Clem and Mary met.

Clem and Mary endured many trials during their first few years on the homestead, but because of the love they had for each other and their determination to make a go of it, they were able to tough it out until they could have a more comfortable life. Clem was a hard worker and became an outstanding farmer. They worked together for a good life that included going to dances and community gatherings for occasional entertainment.

Their first child, **Darrell Claire Maluy**, was born 15 December 1920, at New Liberty. This added extra laundry to Mary's already heavy burden. After hauling the water by bucket from the cistern or ditch, she had to heat it on the cook stove in pots and pans. She washed all the clothes, diapers and bedding on a scrub board in a #3 tub, then hung everything out on the line to dry in the sun and wind. Bill Bowen once had this to say: "Rain or shine, Darrell's pants are on the line."

Mary later acquired a hand powered washing machine. This was a metal tub with a long handle on it that one would rock back and forth to wash the clothes. Mary would rock it 200 times to wash the clothes and Darrell would rock it 50 times to rinse. Some years later she acquired a washer powered by a gasoline engine — a real luxury! She had raised turkeys to earn the money to buy it.

Their first daughter, **Marilyn May**, was born 5 October 1925. A red-head! Another red-headed daughter, **Phyllis Clemene** joined the family 29 January 1930. And then **Lee Ann "Bubbles"**, a blonde, came along 20 February 1933. All of the children attended New Liberty and Fruita Union High Schools.

Clem acquired more land and became one of the prominent farmers in the community. For many years he farmed over two hundred acres of good silt loam. In April 1929, he bought a John Deere Model "D" with a two-bottom two-way plow and ten foot tandem disc; while this was not the first tractor in the community, it was the first tractor purchased new. Clem's neighbor, Bob Cox, advised him that within a few years that tractor would be sitting against the fence with weeds growing up around it. Clem was undaunted. When there was plowing or discing to be done, neighbors would hear that tractor going from before sunrise until there was no longer enough light to see in the evening.

In later years Clem and Mary went quite heavily into livestock. From 1944 to 1949 they raised turkeys, in the last year they raised 3000. In 1947 they bought some sheep and kept an average of five to six hundred head for the remainder of their years on the farm. Clem acquired some wintering ground on the desert southeast of Mack and there he would spend his winters herding the sheep and batching in the camp wagon. It was like a vacation for him!

Clem was a friendly fellow - had no enemies. However, something happened to him one day because of his friendliness that deserves to be told. He always waved to people as he drove by. In this particular instance he waved to Bertie Dillbeck as he was driving through Mack. It so happened that Bertie was then keeping house for John and Frank Everetts. John saw that friendly wave and assumed Clem had a romantic interest in Bertie. As Clem parked in front of Desert Gateway Store at Mack, John followed very shortly and with a .45 pistol shoved against Clem's belly for emphasis told him not to flirt with Bertie anymore. Clem tried to apologize and convince John that he had no more than just a friendly interest in Bertie. It took a little while for John to cool off and put his pistol away.

Clem and Mary designed and built a lovely home on the farm, their "dream home". In the New Liberty items of October 1936 it was noted that construction was underway on the new home. It had running water, electricity and beautiful, shining hardwood floors. It seemed like a shining castle! The family anxiously awaited the arrival of electricity before moving into the new home. When they finally moved in 1937, they were in all new surroundings — what a change!. Nothing but their clothing had been brought over from the original homestead shack they had lived in for years. The old home was then used for storage.

Clem served eighteen years as a member of the New Liberty school board; nine years as a member of the Grand Valley Water Users Association Board of Directors, and six years as

a committee member for the AAA Farm Program. He was also an active member of the Wool-growers Association and the Farmers Union.

They sold the farm in 1964, expecting to spend their "golden" years in retirement. But, as Clem was finishing up the last of the hay baling, he received severe burns from an explosion as he was pouring gasoline into the baler engine. He died 21 days later, on 10 November 1964, at Fruita Hospital, and was buried in Memorial Gardens Cemetery.

Mary moved to Grand Junction and lived for some years in an apartment, eventually buying a home. She became an avid bowler and spent much time with her friends at the bowling alleys. She loved to travel and consequently toured most of the States, including three trips to Hawaii. She also toured some of Canada. She traveled to Europe on two occasions; also went on three Caribbean Cruises, the last one with her daughters and two of their spouses when she was 94. All of these interests were overshadowed by her devotion to her children and grandchildren. She had determined when she began to be older that she was not going to spend her last years in a rest home, and she made her children promise that they would not allow that to happen. She managed to live in her own home, with the help of a hired house keeper, until the very end. She died in her own home 17 January 1992 as she was nearing her 96th birthday. She had 11 grandchildren, 30 great grandchildren and two great great grandchildren.

As **Darrell** was growing up he had more than his share of accidents...Broke an arm on two occasions, had a broken nose and a broken leg. He was bit by a rabid dog and had to endure a painful series of shots to avoid the threat of rabies. In addition to that he had blood poisoning in one leg and for a time was under threat of having the leg amputated

He had a singular experience at age 12 years when his parents allowed him to ride alone on a horse to Rangely, some 40 miles away, to visit Gerald Coltharp. Today he relishes the memory of that experience...takes a little pride in having been resourceful enough and his parents trusting enough to allow him to make such a trip at a tender age.

He graduated from Fruita Union High School in 1938, taking a major interest in athletics during those years. Later he attended Colorado School of Mines at Golden.

On 26 December 1940, he and Homer Likes snuggled into the back of Leonard Appier's new Ford truck and rode to West Los Angeles, California where he worked at various jobs until he went north and secured a job in the ship yards at San Francisco. Later he worked at the shipyards at Long Beach and it was there he met **Beverly Busgen**, a welder. They were married 28 August 1943, during the lunch hour on the ship they were building; a minister who was part of their crew performed the ceremony. Their wedding ceremony captured nation-wide media attention for their patriotism in not taking any time off from work to get married. Later they did go on a brief honeymoon, and soon after that Darrell enlisted in the Army Air Corps and began training to be a navigator. After the end of World War II he returned to New Liberty to farm several years with his father. Later Darrell and family moved to Grand Junction, and Darrell pursued his desire to do some mining.

A couple of years after Clem's death, Darrell purchased the family farm from the man who had purchased it from Clem and farmed it for about three years and then resold. Darrell was involved for several years in uranium and coal mining in Utah, Wyoming and northern Colorado.

He and Beverly had five children:

Trudy Lee
Cindy Lou
Patty Sue
Nancy Gay
Dwight Darrell

Dwight Darrell lost his life at age three as a result of a tragic auto-pedestrian accident. There are now nine grandchildren.

Marilyn married **Charlie William Pacheco**, 11 October 1943, after she graduated from high school. (See Pacheco biography) Charlie was at that time serving in the U.S. Navy. Since their marriage they have lived virtually all over the USA, but returned to Fruita in 1991 to retire. They have three children:

Beau Allen
Kathi Mae
Darrell Alvin
There are now five grandchildren.

Phyllis Clemene married **Homer C. Likes**, 2 December 1946. They lived twelve years on the Likes homestead and then moved to Moab, and later Price and Orem, Utah. They have two children:

Dennis Wayne
Retta Marie

There are now 14 grandchildren living and twelve great grandchildren.

Lee Ann married **Buddy Raymond Blaney** of Grand Junction, 7 November 1954, in Grand Junction. They have lived in the same home since their marriage...but, due to numerous remodeling projects, the home looks but little like it did when they bought it. They have two children:

Brett Michael
Brook Sean.

There are two grandchildren.

William "Bill" Benedict Maluy was born 20 May 1890 at Hanover, Washington, Kansas. He lived with his father on the Maluy farm near Hanover until he was about age 20. and then went away from home to find work. He was in California in 1910, shortly after his sister Mae married and moved out there. He played a little professional baseball and worked in the grain harvest, following that into Montana and Canada. Somewhere along the line he learned to be a telephone lineman. After working for a time at that trade he enlisted in the Army in the summer of 1917 and was sent to Fort Sill, Oklahoma. After basic training he was assigned to serve with the 35th Division of the 128th Field Artillery, Battery E, and was shipped to France; to the Vosges mountains at Verdun. He took part in the battles of St. Michael and the Muese-Argonne. He did not return home until some time in 1919.

He went to Mexico soon after returning home, looking into an investment scheme which his father and brothers, Clem and Tom, and sister, Addie, became involved in. Some of the details of that venture just recently came to light when a letter was found that had been written by Patrick to his daughter Mae's husband, Evan Williams.

On 28 February 1921, Bill married **Clara Rosella Griffis**, at Atchison, Atchison Co., Kansas. Clara was born 6 October 1893 to Henry A. and Anna E. Griffis, at Washington, Washington Co., Kansas. Bill and Clara lived in that general area in Kansas for a number of years. Their first child, **Dale Clair**, was born 12 January 1923 at Marysville, Marshall Co., Kansas. **Rex Loren**, was born 3 January 1924 at Linn, Washington Co., Kansas.

In 1925 Bill and Clara and two boys went to California to work in the fruit harvest; living for awhile at Oakdale. They returned to Colorado late in 1925, and lived for a time in Grand Junction, where the third child, **Patty Jean (Huntley)**, was born 17 September 1926. During that time Bill was employed as a lineman for the Bell Telephone Company.

The following year (1927) Bill and Patrick struck a deal for Bill to buy his dad's homestead. So Bill and his family moved in with Patrick and Mully. Patrick and Mully left in 1928 and went back to California.

The fourth child, **Wilma Colleen (Walker)**, was born 23 February 1929, at Fruita, then **Norma Mae (Klapwyk)** arrived 10 October 1930, at Fruita.

During this period of time Bill was involved in the Mack baseball team and the IOOF at Fruita. Clara was involved in the Rebeccas.

Jackie Lee was born 30 April 1933, at Fruita, but he lived only until 5 June 1933, a victim of whooping cough. Then, Clara, again

pregnant, was stricken with pneumonia and died on 17 May 1934, leaving Bill alone with a family of five young children.

After Clara's death Bill moved with his children to Grand Junction and during the 1934/35 school year Dale, Rex and Patty attended Hawthorne School.

Through the next few years he hired several different women to keep house and help care for the children. One of those women was Agnes Lee, who married Ed Hiatt in October, 1937.

A woman whom Bill had known in Kansas years earlier, **Martha Potzner**, came to take over the housekeeping chores about 1939. Martha brought with her two children by a former marriage to Adam Potzner, **Audie** and **Joan Marie Potzner**, and they were integrated into Bill's family. Bill and Martha were married at Fruita 21 June 1941.

At that time Bill and Martha remodeled and modernized the former George Bryan home, making a comfortable home for the family. Quite a step up from the old Patrick Maluy homestead!

Within a short time after he started farming Bill began to have a desire to expand his farm operation...he wanted more land to farm than was available on his Dad's homestead. At various times he rented land from Bob Cox, Bob Phillips, Joe Owings, etc., using a McCormick Deering tractor he bought from Si Summers to do the heavy plowing and discing. In 1933 he bought the J. N. King farm on a tax sale, and in 1937 purchased the George Bryan farm and a new Model A John Deere tractor. By this time Dale and Rex were big enough to help with the farm work. Dale developed quite a reputation for making straight rows with that John Deere tractor...his half mile-long rows were straight as an arrow.

Bill was a successful farmer, but was known to gamble on unusual crops. It was he who began to grow red clover in lieu of alfalfa for hay; he raised seed from that crop as well. He did well with hay, potatoes and pinto beans, growing a large acreage of those crops. At one time he planted about 100 acres of radishes for seed. After harvesting the seed he bought about 200 pigs to root up the radishes. It worked, believe it or not! It was said by one of his neighbors that "Bill could fall in a toilet and come out smelling like a rose!" I have quite a memory of assisting several family members to herd one group of pigs from the stockyards in Mack...it created quite a sensation! The pigs made good conversation in the community.

The pigs were quite intelligent and became pets to the Maluy children...when they would hear and see the school bus coming around the hill at Thomas' about a mile away, they would start running toward the gate so they could meet the children as they got off the bus. It was a sad day when the trucks came and hauled the pigs away!

In 1953 Bill retired and rented the farm to Taylor Roberts. He and Martha lived in Fruita for about three years. Then they sold the farm to Taylor Roberts and moved to Grand Junction where they bought a home and lived comfortably the rest of their lives.

Bill was one who had a good understanding of the dangers of older people driving...when he realized that the time had come when he might be a danger to others, he simply quit driving.

Bill died in Grand Junction 28 March 1970, eight days after his 80th birthday. Beautiful tributes were paid to him by friends and family... a grandson, Rex Huntley, wrote the following, which was read at the funeral by Rex's brother Mark.

For Daddy Bill

And now the days will be shorter by one,
One whom we all loved and held dear.
A someone so close, warmer than any sun
One gentle, one fun, whose face is clear
And the earth he leaves, the wind takes his place
But in our hearts, he will forever live
And in our thoughts he'll walk without a trace
But in you, in me, he will still live
For of him we are all a part;
And even death cannot change it.

Dale graduated from Fruita Union High School in 1941 and enlisted in the Army Air Corps 6 January 1942. He was promoted to staff sergeant after he had completed training in the technical branch of the Air Corps. He became an air cadet in November 1942 and was trained to become a bomber pilot.

Dale went on to achieve fame in the Air Force as he flew B17 Bombers from England to Germany. An item in *The Daily Sentinel* of 3 September 1944 says that Lieutenant Dale Maluy was awarded the "Air Medal for 17 bombing missions over Germany." - then another article on 19 December 1944 tells that "Captain Dale Maluy, 21, veteran of 30 daylight bombing raids over Germany, was recently awarded the Distinguished Flying Cross."

He married **Mae Croitz** of Roswell, New Mexico, 10 November 1945. Dale was soon stationed at Salina, Kansas. They had one daughter: **Linda**, born at Salina, 20 July 1946. Dale and Mae were later divorced

Later, in the Korean War, he flew 59 bombing missions from Japan to Korea in B29 bombers. After that was over he was able to realize a secret ambition...he flew a B29 over the New Liberty community at very low altitude. In his words he flew low enough to "flush the toilets." That got the attention of the citizens in New Liberty! The following article found in *The Daily Sentinel* of 1 September 1947 refers to that incident:

> The Mack area was buzzed by a large unidentified aircraft which flew around the Mack/New Liberty area for over 1/2 hour. It was rumored to have crashed; but the story was later determined to be unfounded.

Dale retired from the Air Force with the rank of Lieutenant Colonel and has since lived in New Mexico. His interest in education continued and he has earned a Bachelor's Degree from New Mexico Highlands University and an Master's from University of New Mexico.

Rex also entered the Air Corps 25 November 1942 and trained to be a navigator at Harlingen Air Base at Harlingen, Texas. *The Daily Sentinel* article of 7 November 1944 said that "Lieutenant Rex Maluy was recently awarded the 3rd Oak Leaf Cluster. Then another article on 11 December said he received the Distinguished Flying Cross for extraordinary achievement in navigating Flying Fortresses for more than 35,000 miles during 8th Air force Bombing attacks on German military and industrial targets. He also has the Air Medal with Four Oak Leaf Clusters."

He flew 35 missions in B17s over Germany with the 96th Bomb Group, 8th Air Force.

He was discharged 11 October 1945 and on 16 June 1946 he married **Vernette Harker** at Fruita, Colorado.

Then in September 1946 it was discovered he had tuberculosis. He was sent to Fort Bayard Veterans Hospital in Silver City, New Mexico. During recovery he worked in Sporting Goods and Photography. Then in 1957 he went to work for New Mexico State highway Department; he was there for nine years. Then he worked for highway construction firms until retirement in 1986. Currently Rex and Vernette live in Santa Fe, New Mexico. They have one son: **Mike**, who has five children

Patty went to nursing school after graduating from high school, and became a Registered Nurse. She married **Grant Hugh Huntley** 8 February 1948 at Raton, New Mexico. They have six children; there are now two grandchildren. Grant died of cancer.

Wilma went to work as a telephone operator after graduating from high school, and stayed with that job for many years. She married **Louis Mac Walker** 27 December 1951 at Grand Junction. They have two children: **Norma Lou** and **Garrett**. There are now two grandchildren.

Norma worked also for many years as a telephone operator after graduating from high school. She was married to **George William Klapwyk** 14 February 1953 at Salt Lake City, Utah. They have three children:
There is one grand child.

Audie F. Potzner was born to Adam and Martha Potzner. Audie was born 31 January 1923. He graduated from Fruita Union High School in 1941 and afterward moved to Milwaukee, Wisconsin. After retirement he moved back to the home town of Hanover, Kansas, where he died of lung cancer on 22 July 1995.

Joan Marie Potzner graduated from Fruita Union High School in 1945. She was married to - - Tuttle. She is now deceased but we have no other information.

Index

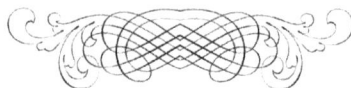

512
Barshaw 32, 332-333
Barshaw Shirley Cotner 32, 126-127, 332-333
Bartholomew, Bart 231, 337, 340, 428
Bartlett 386-388
Bartman, Connie 612-614
Barton 349, 383, 661, 719, 737-739, 744, 754
Barton, Christia Anne Currey 349-350
Barton, Golden 383
Bass, Esther 177
Bass, Velma 176
Basta, Mark 220
Basta, Mark, Jr. 220
Basta, Martha Joyce 220
Bates 263, 297
Battle of Bull Run 754
Bauer 768, 770-772
Bauer, Cherrie Bea Wright 768, 770-772, 778
Bauer, David Clyde 772
Bauer, David J. 771-772
Bauer, Elizabeth 772
Bauer, Frieda 772
Bauer, Timothy 772
Baughman 661
Baughman, Jessie 661
Baughman, Juanita (Rector) 661
Bauman, Mary Katherine 119, 564-565
Baumbauer 306
Baxter Pass 10, 12, 14-16, 19, 29, 200, 252, 254, 308, 319, 387, 399, 417, 455-456, 488, 534, 773, 789, 797-798
Bayes, Lester 708
Bayles, Mary Ella 593
Beagley 662-663
Beagley, Art 663
Beagley, Kay 662-665
Beahm, Bernice 48, 50
Bean Co-op Association 525
Bean Growers Association 206, 535-536, 639
Beard 545, 548
Beard, Casey Don 548
Beard, Kathi Pacheco (Wisdom) 545, 548
Beard, Lynn 548
Beard, Shauna Lynn 548
Beasley, Mamie Augusta 636-639
Beaslin Bill 177
Beaslin, Dorothy Marie (Russell) 179, 234-235
Beaslin, John 14
Becher 270, 290-291
Becher, Dee Elda 291
Becher, Leslie Ann 291
Becher, Ruth Marie Brisbin 269-270, 289-290
Becher, Thomas Arthur 290
Becher, Thomas Arthur, "Tommy," Jr. 291
Beck, Warren A. 615
Beede 361, 363-366
Beede, Joyce 365
Beede, Mary Catherine Daily 48, 50, 328, 361, 363-366
Beede, T. W. 365
Beede, Wayne Edward 365
Beeman, Mary 417
Beesley, Ina Mae 435
Beeson 175-176
Beeson, Harley 175-176
Beezer, Linda 305

Behrendt 460-461
Behrendt, Anna Burkschat 460
Behrendt, Gutley/Godlip 460
Behrendt, Helene 460-461, 463
Belside, M. P. 616
Beluchie, Thelma L. Cole 325
Beluchie, Thelma L. Cole 325
Belville, Linda Pacheco 619, 631-632
Bender 2, 16, 23, 25, 27, 738
Bender, Henry E., Jr. 2, 16, 23, 25, 27, 738
Benjamin, Judy 764
Bennedetti, Dale Paul 620-621
Bennedetti, John 619-620
Bennedetti, John Lee 620-621
Bennedetti, Virginia Pacheco (Rockvam) 180, 619, 621, 623
Bennett 329, 513, 690, 746-747
Bennett, Catherine (Maluy) 513
Bennett, Charles Michael 747
Bennett, Chuck 747
Bennett, Edna Myrul Weir 113-116, 145, 149-150, 180, 658, 679, 746-749
Bennett, Ila C. Corn 329
Bennett, Kimberly Goodell 690
Benny,Jack 346
Benson, Betty Pollock 120-121, 123, 180, 547, 640-642
Bentley 501
Bentley, Janice Sue Likes (Donovan) 501-502, 700-701
Benton 509, 513
Berg, Rita 134-135
Bergner, Merton 420
Berry 40, 99, 110, 120-122, 125, 127-130, 132-133, 136, 141-142, 149, 152, 156, 160-161, 179-180, 208-209, 211, 213, 235, 237-244, 316, 333, 401, 535, 553, 555-556, 560-561, 567, 639, 667, 679-683, 726, 755, 759
Berry, A. C. 209
Berry, Anna Jane (Starr) 125, 127-130, 136, 142, 179-180, 237-240, 242, 244, 556, 567, 726
Berry, Cynthia Lee 238
Berry, Edwin Marion 237, 121-122, 237-238, 243-244
Berry, Francis Lloyd 237
Berry, Frank Alfred 127, 129, 180, 189, 238, 553, 567
Berry, Gayle Marie Alstatt 181, 208-209, 613
Berry, Helen Viola (Hestand) 237
Berry, James Edwin 238
Berry, Laura Lucille Johnson 40, 99, 110, 113-114, 116, 120, 149, 156-157, 180, 237-239, 244, 555, 560-561, 567, 680, 679-683, 759
Berry, Lois 238
Berry, Nancy Jane Blanchard 237
Berry, Oscar Edwin 237, 639
Berry, Patricia 556
Berry, Raymond James 237-238
Berry, Reginald Ernest "Reg" 133, 136, 142, 180, 238, 316, 667
Berry, Susie 244
Berry, Thomas Carl "Tom" 127-130, 132, 136, 142, 152, 235, 238-239, 726
Berry, Tom, Jr. 244
Berry, Virginia Duncan 238
Bess, Kelly 384, 499
Bess, Venessa 384

Bessire, Fred 176
Bessire, George 176
Bessomette, Jane (Baird) 230
Bethea 662-665
Bethea, Dick 665
Bethea, Maxine Rich Lovern (Watts) 662-664
Bickel, Pearl 430
Biddick, Effie Wilsea (Summers) 711
Biggs 28, 343
Binde, Anna L. (Uhleman) 740
Bingham, Margaret 424
Bird, Betty 177
Bird, Margaret Lucina 387
Birka, Bill 503
Birka, Gary Lee 503
Birka, Randy Lynn 503
Birka, Virginia Likes (Sandifer, Haggerty) 117, 119-122, 152, 501
Birka, William Jack 503-504
Bischel, Pat 199
Bishop, Joe 788
Bittle 36, 767, 779
Bittle, Darcy 779
Bittle, Donald 779
Bittle, Donna 779
Bittle, Kelly 779
Bittle, Mattie Barbara Wright (Narrans) 124, 762, 768-769, 774, 776-777, 779 767
Bittle, Velda 36
Black 2, 40-41, 180, 199, 241, 248, 266, 270, 275, 278-279, 284, 313, 316-318, 323, 331, 370, 403, 419, 441, 491, 512, 555, 558, 560-561, 567, 640, 642, 670, 672, 674, 703, 741, 750, 760, 771, 776, 789
Black, Clint 199
Black, Dessie 180
Black, Gregory 771
Black, Wanda (Sanders) 674-675
Blackstone 509, 513
Blackstone, Alvin W. 509
Blackstone, Frank L. 513
Blackstone, Shirley Anita (Anderson) 509, 513
Blair, Jessie 510
Blair, Robert 511
Blamey, William J. Cap 691
Blanchard, C. J. 80
Blanchard, Nancy Jane (Berry) 237
Blaney 198, 513, 557-559, 565, 567-568
Blaney, Brett Michael 557-559
Blaney, Brook Sean 557-559
Blaney, Buddy Raymond 557, 558-559
Blaney, Jennie D. Hatch 557
Blaney, Lee Ann Maluy 124-126, 152, 180, 198, 227, 241, 298-299, 513, 520-522, 548, 556-559, 562, 564-565, 567, 799
Blaney, Meghan Lee Ann 559, 563, 568
Blaney, Raymond Bud 557-558
Blaney, Raymond John "Speck" 557, 568
Blaney, Sean Michael 557-559, 563, 568
Blaney, Shonna Martin 559
Blank, George 633, 747
Blasdel 120-121, 124, 180, 245-248, 535, 570, 647, 653, 656-657
Blasdel, Allie Mae Reece (Raver, Hiatt) 245-247, 429, 651-657
Blasdel, Danny Ray 247
Blasdel, David Eugene 247

Blasdel, Dennis Earl 247
Blasdel, Donald Eugene 245-248
Blasdel, Glen Harvey 121, 124, 245-247
Blasdel, Glenda 247
Blasdel, Gloria Mae 245
Blasdel, Harold 120-121, 124, 247
Blasdel, Harvey 245-246
Blasdel, Ira John 245
Blasdel, Ivel Lee Ehart 247
Blasdel, Jack 657
Blasdel, James Marlin "Jim" 245-248
Blasdel, Jimmy G. 247
Blasdel, John Harold 245-246
Blasdel, Lonnie 247
Blasdel, Mae Schultz 247
Blasdel, Marcella 247
Blasdel, Marsha (Barbee) 247
Blasdel, Noah Earl 179-180, 245-248
Blasdel, Noah Earle 245-248, 535, 653, 656
Blasdel, Roberta Schaffer 247
Blasdel, Sharon 247
Blasdel, Terry 247
Blasdel, Vanessa 247
Blasier 249, 364, 729
Blasier, Jennie 249
Blasier, Percy D. 249, 364, 722, 729
Blau, Harriet Cutler 119-122, 351, 351-354, 356-359, 644
Blau, Robert 358
Blazon 113, 616-617, 624
Blazon, Maria Lucia Pacheco 616
Blazon, Marie 113, 617, 624
Blendow 346
Bliss, Harriet Josephine Lee 767
Bliss, Orley Dwight 767
Bliss, Vera Laura (Wright) 766-768
BLM 199, 789, 791
Bloom 105, 280, 388, 797
Bloom, Lillian Frances 388
Bloomfield 651
Blue Mountain Ranch 788, 797
Blue, John W. 83
Blum, Ruth 465
Blumenshine, C. E. 183
Board of Directors of Grand Valley Rural Power Lines Inc 676
Boardman 737, 739
Boardman, Hazel Emmaline Wagaman 43-45, 57, 737, 739-740
Boardman, James Leroy 739
Boardman, Merle 739
Bocking, F. W. 109
Boelens, Nellie 692
Bookcliff Mountains 200, 258, 330, 379, 483, 683, 798
Bookcliffs 2, 82, 140, 196, 201, 330-331, 405, 452, 510, 520, 539, 656, 693, 733, 791, 798
Boone 616, 636, 740, 779
Booth 4, 14, 16, 20, 23, 25, 28, 32-34, 40, 42-47, 49, 59, 77, 81, 119, 165, 176, 181, 230, 249-253, 305, 387, 397, 411, 429, 688, 694, 706
Booth, Betty Louise (Garber) 16, 20, 23, 25, 28, 33-34, 42, 44-45, 47, 81, 176, 181, 249, 250-252, 327, 387, 688
Booth, Charlotte Jeanne (Cass) 250, 252-253, 255
Booth, Charlotte M. Shoults 32, 249, 253, 429
Booth, Douglas Alan 33, 46, 119, 176,

181, 249-255, 774
Booth, Gordon Everett 4, 46, 249-250, 252-254, 305
Booth, James Alan 249
Booth, James Edward 252, 254
Booth, James Harold 249, 253
Booth, James Leonard "J. L." 4, 14, 32, 40, 59, 249, 250, 251, 253
Booth, Mrs. J. L. 14, 230, 397, 429, 706
Booth, Patricia Louise 252, 254
Booth, Robert Douglas 252, 254
Booth, Sondra Jean 252, 245
Booth, Theresa 252
Booth, Woodrow Edward "Woody" 33, 46, 249-254, 774
Borland, Betty 565
Botkin 177, 326
Botkin, Mervin 177
Botkin, Raymond 176-177
Botkins, Barbara Gail Collins 326
Bottom, Lotus 591
Boughton 40, 47, 50, 53, 177, 367-369, 371-372, 420, 668
Boughton, David 371-372
Boughton, Jeri Leah 371
Boughton, Keith Lynn 371
Boughton, Lynn E. 371-372
Boughton, Reuben Byron 371
Boughton, Sarah Ann 177
Bourchard 432-433
Bourchard, Jean 432-433
Bowen 31-33, 35, 38-41, 57, 59, 112-119, 141, 144, 147, 150, 152, 157, 168, 171, 176, 180, 205-206, 219, 241, 250, 255-261, 305, 323, 362, 412, 429-430, 522, 535, 537, 693-694, 741, 753, 758
Bowen, Georgia Jo 31-32, 40, 144, 157, 255, 257
Bowen, JoAnn (Montague) 31-33, 35, 38-41, 57, 115, 117-119, 150, 152, 176, 180-181, 219, 235, 255-261, 693
Bowen, W. B. 255
Bowen, Walter 259
Bowen, William "Bill" L. 113-114, 143-144, 150, 256-258, 260, 305
Bowen, William Everett 32, 38-41, 59, 112-113, 115-116, 144, 147, 150, 157, 168, 171, 205-206, 250, 255-257, 259-261, 323, 362, 429, 535, 694, 741, 758
Bowers, LaJetta 194
Bowers, Terrell L. 30, 194
Boyce, Barbra 198
Boyden 31-32, 35, 38, 40-41, 56-58, 83, 85-86, 139, 216, 250, 253, 260-261, 265, 418, 420, 633, 694, 750
Boyden, Byron 38, 40-41, 56-58, 253, 260-262
Boyden, Donald 261
Boyden, F. 83, 261
Boyden, G. 31
Boyden, May F. 83, 85, 261, 420
Boyden, Sarah 31-32, 35, 57, 694
Boyer, Mary Margaret 662
Boyer, Rachel 366
Brach 157, 714-715, 717
Brach, Florence Ena Sumnicht 145, 157, 713-717
Brach, John "Jack" W. 717
Brach, Tony Lee 717
Braden, Unice / Unica Jane (Cox) 341
Brandon 181, 190, 262-263, 328, 339, 371, 461, 463, 465, 556

Brandon, Emma Joan Lander 465
Brandon, Emmett Russell 262, 328, 465
Brandon, Henry Vernon 181, 190, 262, 339, 371, 556
Brandon, James Henry 262-263, 465
Brandon, Roy V. "Bud" 263
Brandon, Russell, Jr. 263
Brandon, Sophronia 262
Brandow 135-136, 164, 494, 498-499, 549, 552
Brandow, Benteen Darrell 498, 552
Brandow, Beverly Rose 552
Brandow, Brian Patrick 552
Brandow, Kenneth William 498, 552
Brandow, Lance Edward 498-499, 528, 552
Brandow, Retta-Marie Likes (Clayburn) 135-136, 164, 494, 497-499, 549-550, 552
Brandow, Shauntai Marie 498, 552
Brandow, Warren Francis II 552
Brandow, Warren Francis III 498-499, 552
Brandow, Warren Francis IV "Butch" 552
Branson 669
Brassell 580
Brassell, Elizabeth 580
Brassell, Julia Helen 580
Bratton, Dorothy 179
Bratton, James 670
Bratton, Lucille 670
Bray, Jackie 266, 567, 570

Bray, Thelma 665
Brayton 40, 107, 116, 119, 124, 127-128, 138, 141-142, 145, 151, 153, 156, 180, 182, 213, 263-265, 267, 448, 485, 535-536, 563, 566, 591, 636-639, 707, 710-711, 745-750
Brayton, Bessie Mabel (Phillips) 180, 182, 263-264, 267, 637, 636-640
Brayton, Charlene Louise (Eldredge) 107, 116, 127, 145, 156, 263-265, 267, 536, 563, 636-638, 710, 745-749
Brayton, Charles Arnold 119, 142, 263, 566, 591, 711, 746, 749-750
Brayton, Charlotte Lois (Carlisle) 255, 265-266, 746-747, 750
Brayton, Erma 750
Brayton, Ethel Ellen (Stotts, Stacy) 263-264, 267, 639, 707
Brayton, George Kenneth 124, 151, 265-266, 750
Brayton, George Louke 263
Brayton, Jane 142, 153, 266
Brayton, JoElla 128, 142, 153, 267
Brayton, Josie Edna 263
Brayton, Lawson Wonnel 263-264
Brayton, Lillian 267
Brayton, Martha Josephine "Josie" Hess (Summers) 263-264
Brayton, Mildred Alice Wier (Tucker) 40, 113-116, 145, 149, 156-157, 263-265, 745, 748-749
Brayton, Phillip Walter 263, 267, 448, 485, 639, 756
Bremer, Frank 745
Brenneman 176, 349
Brenneman, James 176
Brenton 119, 549, 556, 566, 673-674
Brenton, Thelma 119, 673-674
Brewer, F. A. 26, 44, 51, 112, 343, 609

814

Colorado Bean Growers Association 535-536, 639
Colorado Farm Bureau 377
Colorado Midland Railroad 672
Colorado National Monument Park 131, 436, 613
Colorado State Brand Inspector 391, 670
Colorado State Line 171, 219, 539
Colorado State University 260, 322, 339, 372, 442, 641, 644, 695, 744
Colorado Sugar Manufacturing Company 100
Colorado Young Citizens League 50, 400, 404
Colorado, Lamar, Prowers 341, 343-344, 437, 459, 627
Colosanti 582-583
Colosanti, Jean McCoy 582-583
Coltharp 541-544
Coltharp, Ed 543
Coltharp, Gerald 121, 156, 224, 541-544, 799
Coltharp, Valry Webster 544
Coltharp, Venis Smuin 543-544
Coltharp, Vernon 543
Community Club 109, 154-155, 162-163, 165, 206, 262, 339, 352, 363, 369, 405, 454, 547, 556, 566, 637, 639, 699, 757
Community Hall 55, 159, 162, 359, 375, 545
Community Hospital 480, 485, 609, 726
Compton 249, 717
Connor 128-130, 132, 137, 176-177, 351, 354-355, 358, 443
Conrad, George 754
Conrad, Marjorie 176
Conrad, Naomi Laurene (Wells) 182, 753
Conrad, Willis 753-754
Consolidated Aircraft Co. 396
Consolidated Coal Company 533
Consolidated School Suburban Railway 170
Consolidated Shipyards 529
Cook 119, 162-163, 165, 181, 275, 286, 303-304, 312-313, 327-328, 362, 379, 423, 427-429, 449, 460, 476, 491, 518, 520, 533, 540, 560, 594-595, 606, 643-644, 683, 694, 726-727, 750-751, 766-767, 769, 778-779, 799
Cook, Alexander 303, 308
Cook, Alice B. (Alberts) 327-328
Cook, Beatrice (Hutton) 181, 327-328
Cook, Betty L. (Varney) 327-328
Cook, Dorothy L. (Harper) 327-328
Cook, Edna 118-119
Cook, Floyd Edward 181, 327-328
Cook, Frank 327
Cook, Helen Elizabeth Carroll 303-304
Cook, Icy Leona Cowan 327-328
Cook, Kay Jean 778-779
Cook, Nancy Joan (Wilkins) 327
Cook, Verna J. (Enz) 327-328
Cooley 58, 62
Cooley, John 58
Cooper 112, 119, 129-133, 159-160, 162-163, 233, 241, 243, 314-315, 329, 333, 373, 381, 404, 426, 674, 756, 792
Cooper, Ida Elaine Cotner 333
Cooper, J. Courtland 373
Cooper, James D. 329

Cooper, James Lewis 329, 381
Cooper, Jesse Ellen (Hawthorne) 329, 426
Cooper, Jim, Coach 129, 163, 426, 674
Cooper, Mabel Angela Lovejoy 119, 130-131, 133, 159-160, 162, 233, 243, 329, 426, 756
Cooper, Mildred 241, 674
Cooper, William Orlen 329, 426
Cooper, Yount 792
Copeco Dance Hall 397, 403
Copper, Robert 112
Coppers, Patricia 733
Cordova, Edward 115
Cordova, Frances 115
Cordova, Jesus 115
Cordova, Joe A. 535
Cordova, Josephita 411-413
Cordova, Lena 115
Cordova, M. A. 535
Cordova, Mary 115
Cordova, Victor 115
Cordova, Walter 115
Cordova. Valeria 412
Corn, Edna Mae Joyce 329-330
Corn, Graves Franklin 329-330, 417, 496
Corn, Ila C. (Bennett) 329
Corn, Jeanne 126-127, 129, 250, 252-253, 329, 548, 564-565
Corn, Orlene Mae (Sasser) 125-126, 180, 329, 564-565
Corn, Orlin H. 104, 185, 329-330, 332, 405, 791-792
Corn, Thelma Mock 329, 332
Cortez, Hernando 372
Cory, Homer 273
Cotner 32, 126, 128, 142, 152, 332-333, 611, 727
Cotner, Bobby 128, 142, 152, 727
Cotner, Carl Wayne 128, 332
Cotner, Ida Elaine (Cooper) 333
Cotner, Ira E. 332
Cotner, Ora Preston 32, 332, 611
Cotner, Robert "Bob" Eugene 332
Cotner, Shirley (Barshaw) 32, 126-127, 332-333
Cottier, Rich 196
Coulson, Cindy 244
Coulter, Elizabeth 645
Coulter, Sarah Annette 645
Country Jam USA 193, 198-199, 425, 452, 687, 765
Covey, Mary Lee (Gerry) 762
Covington, V. L. 16
Cowan, Icy Leona (Cook) 327-328
Cowden, Dixie 129, 142
Cowen 457-458
Cowen, John "Jack" 458
Cox 15, 28, 31-32, 40, 42, 44, 48, 50, 53, 59, 77-78, 86, 90, 96, 112-114, 120-122, 138, 146, 151, 153, 155, 157, 168, 180-183, 205, 218, 238, 245, 250, 295, 299, 305, 333-348, 351, 370, 378, 380, 425, 428, 454, 456, 475-476, 478, 480-481, 486, 502, 511, 523, 535, 546-547, 570, 652-653, 667-668, 718, 738-739, 761, 776, 780-781
Cox, Bessie Catherine (Brown) 31, 42-44, 182, 334-335, 338, 343, 348, 454
Cox, Careen 335
Cox, Catherine Ann 333
Cox, Clayton 335
Cox, Dorothy Margaret 119-122, 153,

180, 335-336, 351, 546-547
Cox, Earl Otis 42, 59, 342, 343-344
Cox, Edward E. 334-335
Cox, Eugene 342-344
Cox, Fern Margaret Walker 30, 40, 157, 194, 299, 335-336, 591, 689-691, 770-771
Cox, Freddie 335
Cox, Gail Marie 340
Cox, Gale 48, 151, 181, 338, 340, 370
Cox, Glenn 335
Cox, Gregory "Greg" 342, 348
Cox, Gregory Scott 340
Cox, Harrison 341
Cox, Hazel I. McCoy 341
Cox, Helen Scott 40, 53, 335, 337, 340
Cox, Ira B. 334
Cox, Ira W. 42, 78, 218, 334-337, 340
Cox, Jennie Maude Jackson 31, 341, 343-344, 349, 738, 747
Cox, Joan Lucille (Evans) 341-342, 344-347, 475, 480-482
Cox, John Wesley 341
Cox, Josie Maude (Wagaman) 42, 342-343, 348, 738-739
Cox, Jurah C. 333
Cox, Leala 340
Cox, Leonard Melvin 42, 343-345, 348, 475, 480-481, 486, 502, 739
Cox, Lucille Bessie 342-343, 345-346, 348
Cox, Mabel Dean Likes 113-114, 117, 149, 344, 346, 467-468, 481, 617, 652-653, 677
Cox, Mary Agnes "Mamie" Herron 42, 334-335
Cox, Mary Ethel 182, 334-335, 337, 509-510, 546
Cox, Maybelle Dean Likes 32, 467, 478, 481
Cox, Michael David 340
Cox, Micky Allen 340
Cox, Milton Scott 50, 151, 181, 333-340, 668
Cox, Naomi Maxine (Smith) 181, 342-343, 348
Cox, Robert Milton 44, 59, 77-78, 86, 90, 96, 112, 138, 153, 155, 168, 183, 205, 238, 295, 305, 334, 336, 380, 523, 547, 570, 667-668, 718, 761, 776, 780
Cox, Samuel Milton 333-334, 341
Cox, Sharie Lee 340
Cox, Unice (Unica) Jane Braden 341
Cox, W. H. 28, 250, 341, 343-344, 348, 456, 475, 739
Cox, William Gale 338, 340
Cox, William Henry 341-344, 738
Cox, William John 15, 59, 138, 146, 155, 250, 334-335, 337-339, 370, 378, 428, 511
Cox, Willie Paul 343-344
Cox, Zarna 335
Coyle 428
Coyle, Margaret Gaye Herron 428, 511
Craig, Laura 421
Craig, Orie 421
Crain 632
Crane 145, 245, 361, 745-746
Crane, Hazel Arminda (Daily) 361-364
Crane, Jesse 145, 245, 746
Crane, Laura Edna (Weir) 745-750
Crawford 324, 349, 372, 391, 394, 510-511, 624, 647, 718-719, 733, 739

Crevasse (Crevease) 6, 8, 19, 449
Crews, Betty Jean (Anderegg) 349
Crews, Luke J. 250, 348-349, 456
Crews, Matthew D. "Matt" 42, 45, 59
Crider 176-177, 735
Crider, Blanche 176
Crider, Floyd 176-177
Crisman, Jewel 177
Crockett, Mary 177
Crockett, Paul 176
Croitz, Mae 573
Croley, Farrie Veatch (Knapp) 389
Cronk 183, 797-798
Cronk, Stanley 183
Cronk, Thomas Allen 798
Cronk, Tim Duke 798
Cross Orchards Living History Site 54, 91, 92, 93, 102-103, 105-106
Crouse, Phonetta Jane (Wilson) 733
Crouser 576-577
Crouser, Lisa Ann Klapwyk 576-577
Crouser, Mitchell Steven 577
Crow Bottom 339, 374
Crow Canyon 455
Crowley 346, 543
Cuddy, Leola 177
Cunduff, Lydia Ann Eliza Tittus (Nelson) 593
Cunduff, Will 593
Cunningham, C. Aletha 766
Cupp 198
Cupp, Laddie D. "Rusty" 198
Currey 123, 180, 213, 349-351, 425
Currey, Christia Anne (Barton) 349-350
Currey, Donald Edmond 349-350
Currey, Dorothy Maxine 349
Currey, Edith Marie 123, 180, 213, 349
Currey, Frank Erwin 180, 349
Currey, Helen Martha (Sumner) 349
Currey, Hillary Slawson "Hux" 349-350
Currey, James Ervin 349
Currey, Jennie Beatrice (McKeel) 349-350
Currey, Lois Harris 46, 425
Currey, Mable Margaret (Moore) 180, 349-350
Currey, Nova Emma Slawson 349-350
Currey, Paul Emmett 349
Currey, Thomas Woodrow "Tom" 180, 349-350, 425
Curtis, Alta 311
Curtis, Betty 118, 389
Curtis, Grace Eleanor Chilson 40, 115, 139, 258, 324-325
Curtis, Leslie P. 324-325
Curtis, Richard 333
Curtis, William E. 83
Curwood, James Oliver 694
Cutler 40, 59, 84, 112-123, 125-130, 132, 137, 141-142, 150, 152, 156-157, 162, 170, 179-180, 213, 302, 351-359, 378, 391-392, 394, 401, 443, 557, 564, 590, 639, 643-644, 725-727
Cutler, Arthur Howard 59, 84, 112, 351-354
Cutler, Charles David 113-114, 116, 142, 352, 354, 590, 639
Cutler, Dolores (O'Connor) 128-130, 132, 241, 351, 354-355, 358, 392, 401, 726-727

Cutler, Edward 115, 117-121, 142, 150, 152, 180, 351, 356-357
Cutler, George Paul 356
Cutler, Harriett (Blau) 119-122, 180, 351, 351-354, 356-359, 644
Cutler, Harry 117, 119-123, 142, 180, 352-355, 357-259
Cutler, Hobart Arthur 112-114, 116, 170, 241, 352-355, 358, 391, 639
Cutler, Hobart Dale 126, 180, 355, 557, 564
Cutler, Janet 357
Cutler, Kevin 357
Cutler, Lee Edward 357
Cutler, Lynnae 359
Cutler, Mary Alice Russell 157, 162, 351-352, 355, 359, 392, 643
Cutler, Maxine Louise (Stutler) 125, 127-130, 142, 179-180, 443, 726
Cutler, Melvin Leroy 356
Cutler, Modine Jaynes (Deacon) 125, 156, 355, 378, 391, 727
Cutler, Paul Russell 115-116, 142, 150, 180, 352
Cutler, Robert Russell 356
Cutler, Rosemary Lois (Williams) 357
Cutler, Ruby Delores 180
Cutler, Vera Esther 352
CYCL 50, 400, 404

— D —

D&RGW Railway 19, 26, 59, 79-80, 101, 193, 220, 253, 305, 396-397, 399, 412, 447, 449, 452, 455, 461, 507, 534, 543, 548, 581, 606, 629, 633, 670, 677, 686-688, 694-695, 703, 714, 738, 741, 754, 760, 762, 773
D'Ambrosia, Norma Pacheco (Lohmeyer) 631-632
D-Day 189, 339
Dahling, Lillian Roberson 44
Daily 95, 112, 155, 176, 180, 367, 511, 721, 799
Daily, Al 40, 95, 112, 155, 361
Daily, Anita 364
Daily, Christopher "Chris" 366
Daily, Christopher Edmund 30, 363, 365-367
Daily, Corinne 46, 366, 372
Daily, Edmund 46, 57, 180, 361-367, 455
Daily, Hazel Crane 40, 361, 746
Daily, James Leon 46, 176, 180, 190, 250, 361, 363-364, 366, 799
Daily, Janice 364
Daily, John Uriah 361, 363, 366-367, 721
Daily, Joseph Edmund 361, 363, 365
Daily, Mary Catherine (Beede) 48, 50, 328, 361, 363-366
Daily, Mary Corinne 366
Daily, Patrick Allen "Al" 47, 95, 112, 155, 361-364, 366-367, 511, 535, 599, 639, 728, 746, 748-749
Daily, Paul Richard 366
Daily, Sharon 364
Dale, Clara Jane (Koch) 459
Dalebout, Thomas 438
Dalton, Henry 108

Dalton, John Richard 647
Dalton, Linda Louise Post 134-135, 181, 645, 647
Daniels, Esther 151
Daniels, Lois 229
Daniels, May 229
Daniels, Peter 315
Darr, Russell A. 354
Darrow, Anna Lautrup 517
Darrow, George 149
Darrow, George Allen 517
Darrow, Mary Christine (Maluy) 162, 515, 517-518, 525, 629, 803
Dauwalder, Kaye 437, 600
Dauwalder, Tina 600
Dauwalder, Tracy Lloyd 600
Davidson 40, 47, 50, 53, 90, 179, 181, 196, 262, 367-372, 378-379, 420, 535, 668, 694, 754
Davidson, Ansan Immanuel 372
Davidson, Clarence Fisher "Red" 262, 368-379, 535
Davidson, Deyon (Boughton) 40, 47, 50, 53, 179, 181, 262, 367-369, 371-372, 420, 668
Davidson, Emily Corinne 372
Davidson, Emma 53
Davidson, Erika Kathryn 372
Davidson, Garnet Hannah Rachel Hatcher 53, 262, 367-369
Davidson, James Charles 367-369, 372
Davidson, James F. 367-368
Davidson, Mary Deyon 369-370
Davidson, Samuel F. 367
Davies 50, 181, 194, 220, 372-374, 376, 400, 402, 412, 664, 695
Davies, Charles LeRoy "Chuck" 373-374
Davies, Frank Merritt "Red" 194, 372-373, 695
Davies, Frank Merritt, Jr. 50, 372, 376
Davies, Gladys 181, 220, 374-375
Davies, Gracia Elizabeth 181, 400, 373-376
Davies, Marcia Electa (Albert) 373-376, 400-402, 664
Davies, Shauna 375
Davis 42, 193-194, 349, 387-388, 426, 454, 456-457, 488, 504, 586, 694, 698, 700, 743, 776
Davis, Alice I. Ward (Hitner, Ferrell, Wilson) 30, 194, 375, 456, 488
Davis, Alta Beatrice (Smith) 35-39, 125, 220, 366, 398, 698-700, 704, 763
Davis, Bill 776
Davis, Elias Edger 698
Davis, George A. 194
Davis, Ida 42, 349, 457
Davis, Louis 586-587
Davis, Sarah Elizabeth 387
Davis, Senith Arvilla 504
Davis, Sue 426
Davis, W. C. 193-194
Davis, William George 387
Davison, Lela M. (Pacheco) 626
Davison, Phillip 626
Dawes 138, 249
Dawson 83, 366-367
Dawson, Corrine 363

821

Hoover, Carole Lee Wells 752-753
Hoover, Herbert 186
Hoover, Zella Jane (Sanders) 180, 182,
    672-673
Hope, Joyce 779-780
Horn 115-116, 201, 554, 581, 681, 728
Horn, Gertrude 115-116
Horr, Ella May 267
Horse Canyon 238-239, 630, 632
Horse Canyon Coal Mine 238-239, 630,
    632
Horse Thief Canyon Ranch 155, 343, 487,
    547, 645
Horton 83, 465, 746
Horton, Richard C. 83, 427, 746
Hosea 432
Hostler 468-469, 581, 661
Hotchkiss 325, 418, 426, 446, 545, 617,
    624-625, 675, 780
Hotel Circle 36
Houston 303, 420
Howes 162, 269-272, 274, 277-278, 280-
    284, 290-291
Howes, Frederick 281
Howes, Frederick V. 281
Howes, Freeman Milton 281
Howes, Freeman Wilson 271
Howes, Mabel Brisbin 121, 162, 269-270,
    272, 274, 277-278, 280, 282-284, 290-
    291
Howes, Monty Douglas 281
Howes, Ronald DeWayne 281
Howie, Howard 591
Howie, Jack 591
Howie, Madge 591
Howlet, W. J. 616
Howser 372-374, 376
Howser, Gladys Davies 372-374, 376
Howser, Lewis 376
Hudson, Linda 644
Huffman, Willie 44
Hughes 20, 26, 452, 457, 730
Hughes, Bernard 452
Hughes, Dora K. (Tomlinson, Young) 63,
    181, 243, 726, 729-733
Hughes, Ed 730
Hule, Joan 327-328
Hull, Charles Henry 645
Hull, Maymie Grace (Post) 151, 182, 321,
    645
Hulse, Dorothy 445
Humbarger 718, 751-754
Humbarger, Anna Giersch 751, 754
Humbarger, Daniel 751, 753-754
Humbarger, Elizabeth "Libbie" (Wells)
    718, 751-752, 754
Hume 263, 712
Hume High School 712
Humphries, Roy 390
Humphries, Sharon 390
Hunt 254, 311, 313, 475, 528, 542, 607,
    661, 761, 799
Hunt, Charles Alford "Charlie" 311, 313
Hunt, Mary Violet (Chaffin) 311, 313,
    321
Hunter School 42, 315
Hunter, Harriett "Hattie" 353
Hunter, Virginia Thompson 136, 180,
    671, 728
Huntington 308, 399, 783, 785

Huntington Canyon Coal Mine 399
Huntley 365, 513, 569, 571-572, 575,
    578, 689
Huntley, Emma May 689
Huntley, Grant Hugh 575, 578
Huntley, Patty Jean Maluy 34, 120, 123,
    125, 152, 180, 513, 538, 569-570,
    575, 572, 578, 644
Huntley, Rex 571
Hupmobile 288
Hurt, Ginger Diane 758
Hurt, Joanna Louise 755, 758
Hurt, John 758
Hurt, Kathy Wells 134-135, 751, 756-758
Hustlers 53-55, 159-161, 368-369, 511
Hutchison 49, 326, 371, 626, 703
Hutchison Brothers Appliance Shop 626
Hutchison, Blanche Smith 46, 49, 703
Hutchison, Dave 371
Hutchison, Donald Frances 703
Hutchison, Donna Marie 703
Hutchison, Kathleen Lois "Katy" 326
Hutchison, Lenn 326
Hutchison, Lois 326
Hutton 43-44, 327-328
Hutton, Beatrice Cook 327-328
Hutton, Irene 43-44
Hutton, Joe 43-44
Hutton, Nellie 43-44

— I —

Idaho 295-296, 323, 375-376, 384, 395-
    396, 417-418, 427, 488-489, 518, 529,
    670, 679, 741, 746, 779
Idaho Department of Law Enforcement
    488
Idaho Falls 395, 746
Ilk, Howard 177
Impact Promotional Products 548, 558-
    559
Independence Village 243, 700
Independent Lumber Company 28, 194,
    760
Independent Order of Odd Fellows (IOOF)
    308, 381, 570
Indians 12, 330, 453, 458, 615-616, 759
Ingelhart, John 176
Ingersoll 83
Ingleright 325
Innes 229-230
Innes, Joseph 229
Innes, Kate Blanche (Baird) 35, 229
International Harvestor Company 486
Interurban 473, 537
Irwin, Mary M. 704
Isley, Erma 266
Israel 675
Israel, Alta Maude Saunders 675
Israel, Glen 675
Ivie, Aloyes 549

— J —

Jackson, Jennie Maude (Cox) 341, 343-
    344, 349, 738, 747
Jackson, Marion Francis 341

James, Alva 779-780
James, F. R. 535
James, Floyd 235
James, Lola 515
James, Oscar M. 83
James, Virginia 570
Jaynes, Ed 355
Jaynes, Modine (Cutler, Deacon) 125,
    156, 355, 378, 391, 727
Jefferson, Melissa 199
Jefferson, Wayland 432
Jeffries, Jerild 134, 371, 693
Jeffries, Wayne 693
Jensen 761
Jerico Springs 384
Jerome, Delbert 119, 124, 176, 182, 211,
    622, 644
Jerome, Fae Miller 42-45, 119, 182, 358-
    359, 454, 622
Jerry Creek 68, 71
Jim Fuoco Motor Company 649
John Deere 490, 533, 555, 570, 609-610,
    668
John Deere Model A 319
John Deere Model G 319-320, 478, 523
John Martin Dam 627
Johnson 44, 110, 112-114, 116, 141, 149,
    156-157, 180, 214, 237-238, 244, 267-
    268, 293, 391, 427, 436, 459, 535,
    539, 571, 574, 583, 607, 639, 670,
    674, 679-683, 750, 771, 779, 781-782
Johnson, Alfred 679-680
Johnson, Anna Marie Larson (Shires) 40,
    150, 154, 157, 159-160, 162, 363,
    679-680, 684
Johnson, Arthur William 459
Johnson, August Alfred 679-680
Johnson, Autumn 214
Johnson, Beda Marie (Tratos) 680, 683-
    684
Johnson, Bob 670
Johnson, Doris (Wynkoop) 781
Johnson, Dorothy (Wright) 779
Johnson, Elizabeth 44
Johnson, Forrest 214
Johnson, Helen Mercedes (Koch) 151, 459
Johnson, Jessie B. Cody 293
Johnson, Josie Ellen Brewster 133, 181,
    267-268, 400
Johnson, Kurt 214
Johnson, Larry Dean 268
Johnson, Laura Lucille (Berry) 110, 113-
    114, 116, 149, 156-157, 180, 237-239,
    244, 680 237, 679-683
Johnson, Linda Thomas 214
Johnson, Meadow 214
Johnson, Rudolph 112, 436, 535, 639
Johnson, Shirley Mae Ebright 391
Johnson, Veronica 268
Johnson, Victoria Renee 268
Johnson, Virginia Ann 268
Johnston 725
Johnstown 618
Jones 42, 44, 129-133, 180, 242, 312,
    330, 397, 425, 441-443, 446, 565-566,
    606, 726, 791-792
Jones, Amon 44
Jones, Arlin 44
Jones, Betty Ann 129, 131-133, 441, 443,
    740
Jones, Cardon De 441, 443, 791-792

Koch, Andrew William 459
Koch, Clara Jane Dale 459
Koch, Cynthia "Cindy" Marie (Kribari) 459
Koch, Helen Johnson 151, 459
Koch, Roger Allen 151, 459
Koch, Sharyn Lorraine 134, 151, 459
Koch, Terrel Elayne 459
Koch, Terry 151
Koffer, Florence DeCrow 379
Koffer, Joe 379
Komatas 14, 48, 181, 412, 460-463, 694
Komatas, Christine 460
Komatas, Crystal Ann 48, 460-461
Komatas, Cynthia "Cindy" 463
Komatas, George, Jr. 14, 48, 181, 460
Komatas, George Spiros 460-461
Komatas, Kathleen Mary 129, 131-133, 142, 152-153, 181, 326, 364, 384, 585, 622, 722-723, 726-727, 730, 732, 770
Komatas, Kathryn G. (Prince) 48, 460-463
Komatas, Katrina Rose 461, 463
Komatas, Kaylene Rae 461, 463
Komatas, Wilda Barlow 461
Komatas, Pamela 461
Komatas, Patricia "Trish" 461
Komatas, Tony 623
Komorrow, Alla 134-135
Komorrow, Johnny 131
Kopf, Mary Frances "May" (Kiefer) 31, 449, 452, 456-457
Kopf, Simon 449, 451-452, 456
Korean War 416, 434, 573, 622, 635, 665
Kovach 179, 635, 761
Kovach, Helen 179
Kovach, Mary (White) 761
Kozal, Nick 603
Kramer, Walt 608
Kratz, Amanda Elizabeth 221
Kremmling 459, 703
Kreps, H. J. 245
Kresha, Karen 725
Kresha, Pat (Thomas) 725
Kribari 459
Kribari, Cynthis "Cindy" Marie Koch 459
Kriegies 287-288
Krohn, Guy 446
Kruse, Alice Wanetta 511
Kuner Empson Company 104
Kurtz Co. 28, 343
Kurtz, Walter 456

— L —

L'HommeDieu, Martha 432
La Sal Mountains 771
Labrum, Catherine Rose Hicks 594
Labrum, Rocco Jeffords "Rock" 594
Labrum, Virginia (Nelson) 195, 593-595
Lacey, Earl 394
Lacey, Jessie 42
Lafayette, Paul 737-738
Laird 57, 694
Lake McAndrews 16, 29, 252, 254, 694
Lamar, Frank 341
Lamberton, Martha Carolyn (Wallace) 740
Lampshire 770-771

Lampshire, Elsie Evelynne (Wright) 768, 770-771
Lampshire, Fern 771
Lampshire, Loren 771
Lampshire, William J. 771
Lancaster 293, 326, 466, 501, 580, 620, 700
Lander 185, 262, 465, 569
Lander, Emma Joan (Brandon) 465
Lander, Emma Johannah 262-263
Lander, Ethel Ellen 185, 465
Lander, Jane M. 465
Lander, Jane N. 262
Lander, John P. 262, 465
Lander, Minnie M. 465
Lander, Ola E. 185, 465
Landini 179, 233, 235
Landini, Carmel 179
Landini, Robert 235
Landis, Josephine 510
Landowners New Liberty 182
Lane, Andrew 485
Lane, Della Irene (Meyer) 719
Lane, Gordon 115
Lane, John Christopher 719
Lane, Wesley 115, 118
Larimer, Faris 175-176
Larson 95, 417, 548, 679-680
Larson, Anna Marie (Johnson, Shires) 40, 150, 154, 157, 159-160, 162, 363, 679-680, 684
Larson, Bud 95
Larson, Jeanne 548
Last Chance Service Station 30, 35, 193, 297-298, 366, 398, 459, 687, 699, 706, 765
Last Train Ride 12, 14, 224
Latham, Ella Virginia (Bainter) 231
Latham, John R. 231
Latham, Karen 201
Latham, Troy 201
Latham, Virginia (Bainter) 389, 629
Lautrup, Anna (Darrow) 517
Law, Arela "Della" Pacheco (Dickson) 625, 628
Law, Connie 628
Law, Dennis 628
Law, George 628
Lawler, J. E. 507
Layta (Leatha) 799
Layton, Lora Gallatin 380
LDS Church 322-324, 499, 507, 551, 720, 771, 774-775, 790, 796
Leach 115, 117-118, 126-128, 153, 155, 157, 196, 318, 465
Leach, Allene (Miller) 115, 155, 157
Leach, Amy 465
Leach, Betty 128, 153
Leach, Bill 126
Leach, Eula Mae 465
Leach, Guy 196, 315-318, 465-466
Leach, Harold Guy 465
Leach, Joe 115, 118
Leach, Sarah 117
Leavitt, Anthony 772
Leavitt, Brooke 772
Lee, Agnes Evelyn Shoults (Hiatt) 250, 429-430, 570
Lee, Harriet Josephine (Bliss) 767
Lee, Jennie 661
Lee, John Doyle 767

Lee, Vera (Wright) 156-157
Leeper 741-744
Leeper, Mary Ellen Wassenberg 34, 46, 741-744
LeGrand, Ida May 380
Lehman, George 14
Lehr, Millie (Keffalos) 445
Leighty, Dorothy Gene 687
Leighty, Gene 32, 687
Leischuck, Ronda 198
Leishman, Jennifer Lee Wiswell 399
Leiter, Joseph 6
Lemke, John 47
Lemmon, Tom 349
Lemon, Glen 115
Leonard, Bob 529
Letson, Otto 608
Levi, Eldon 175-176
Levi, Maude 4, 44, 250, 454
Levitt 339, 397, 399, 402
Levitt, Carrie 399, 402
Levitt, Carroll M. 399, 402
Levitt, Norma Lou Eddings 181, 397, 399, 575-576
Levitt, Todd 399, 402,
Lewin, Mabel Timartha Hunt (Driskell) 475
Liberty Bonds 62
Likes, Betty Alene (Smit) 296, 298, 482, 564
Likes, C. W.
Likes, Christina Louise 552
Likes, Clyde William 40, 59, 75, 81, 83, 141, 143, 183, 216, 258-259, 305, 307, 344, 384, 442, 466-467, 487-488, 501, 535, 549, 556, 658, 667
Likes, Clyde William, Jr. 93, 111, 113-114, 146, 384, 417, 468-475, 478, 482, 487-488, 493, 639, 648
Likes, Clyde William, Sr. 93, 101, 107, 112, 138, 140-141, 183, 205, 238, 353, 463, 468, 471-472, 478, 484, 493, 549, 564, 701, 711, 759
Likes, Deana Lou 501
Likes, Delores Imogene Smith 35-38, 125, 156, 181, 220, 232-233, 235, 482, 501-502, 623, 670, 698-702, 706
Likes, Denise Marie 498, 552
Likes, Dennis Wayne 133-134, 153, 161, 306, 494-495, 497-499, 526, 549-552
Likes, Diana Lou 700
Likes, Donald Fred 485-486
Likes, Dorothy Dove (Palmer) 484-485
Likes, Edward Lee "Eddie" 129-130, 383, 487-488, 726
Likes, Elmer Fred 112-114, 156, 208, 267, 353, 378, 390, 448, 467-468, 478, 486-487
Likes, Evelyn Leona Bush (Welch) 30, 42, 164, 167, 176-177, 296-299, 429, 447-448, 482-486, 556, 620, 708, 779-780
Likes, Homer Chilson 92-93, 114-115, 139-140, 142, 152, 154, 156, 209, 215-218, 223, 232, 247, 305-306, 355, 384, 390, 429, 466-467, 469, 472, 474, 478, 489-490, 491, 497-498, 526, 529, 549, 552, 568, 701, 790
Likes, Ivan Leroy 99, 180, 296, 299, 482-485, 708-712
Likes, Ivan Randle 92, 113-114, 156, 299, 467-468, 478 483-485

703
MacTaggart, Jody 241, 308, 562, 577
MacTaggart, Josie Helen (Simmons) 46, 181, 509-512, 703
MacTaggart, Kenneth Blair 509-510
MacTaggart, Mary Ethel (Burkitt) 42, 509-510
MacTaggart, Mary Melony 509
MacTaggart, Robert Edward "Bob" 46, 510-511
MacTaggart, Virgil Prescott 509, 513
Madison Rose Lane School 582
Maguire, Edith 456
Mahaney, Bert 419
Maile, Shirley 177
Main Canal Division 68
Main Canyon 730, 733, 789, 791
Main, Bud 609
Mair 396
Mair, Alice Lee Eddings 396
Maize 96, 338, 602
Malito, Janeva 44
Malito, Joe 44
Malito, Katherine 44
Malito, Louis 44
Mallet Engine 686
Malley 514
Mallory 796
Maltby, Mattie B. 193
Maluy 108, 213, 240, 339, 394, 513-514, 520, 543, 775, 799
Maluy, Adalyne Margaret "Addie" (Warner) 514-515, 518, 538, 568-569
Maluy, Beverly Bayne Busgen 119, 529-533, 564, 730
Maluy, Catherine Bennett 513
Maluy, Cecil Worley 515
Maluy, Cindy Lou 531-532, 674
Maluy, Clara 522, 538-539, 547, 567-569
Maluy, Clement "Clem" 83, 115, 119, 162, 513, 515, 517-518, 525, 535, 543, 552, 564, 629, 803
Maluy, Dale Clair 119-122, 152, 180, 538, 569, 572-573
Maluy, Darrell Claire 95, 101, 115, 117-120, 142, 150, 152, 156, 180, 193-194, 258, 490, 513, 520-523, 527, 529-531, 538, 541-542, 573, 678, 799
Maluy, Dwight Darrell "DD" 531-532
Maluy, Emily Josephine "Mully" Newell (Williams) 516-517, 570
Maluy, Gertrude Kathryn (Gertie) 44, 115-116, 233, 260, 372, 514-515, 523, 529, 577, 760
Maluy, Granny 517, 524
Maluy, Jackie Lee 570
Maluy, Laura Michelle 574
Maluy, Lee Ann "Bubbles" (Blaney) 124-126, 152, 180, 198, 227, 241, 298-299, 513, 520-522, 548, 556-559, 562, 564-565, 567, 799
Maluy, Linda 573
Maluy, Marilyn May (Pacheco) 118, 120-123, 153, 180, 513, 520-521, 522, 524, 544-546, 558, 546, 572, 625, 625, 628-630, 644
Maluy, Martha Gertrude (Rechtien, Potzner) 562, 571-572, 577
Maluy, Mary Agnes Chloetilda Reel 514
Maluy, Mary Christine Darrow 96, 108,

110, 123, 142, 144, 149, 152, 154-157, 159-161, 162-165, 299, 381, 513, 515-518, 525-526, 544, 547, 560, 566, 570, 629, 678, 707, 799
Maluy, Mary Loretta "Mae" (Williams) 514-515
Maluy, Melissa Ann 574
Maluy, Nancy Gay (Prosence) 181, 531-532
Maluy, Nellie Olivas 574
Maluy, Norma Mae (Klapwyk) 34, 124-125, 152, 180, 513, 562-563, 570, 572, 576, 578, 730
Maluy, Patrick Peter Henry 41, 84, 91, 96, 257, 513-517, 570, 740, 801
Maluy, Patty Jean (Huntley) 34, 120, 123, 125, 152, 180, 513, 538, 569-570, 572, 575, 578, 644
Maluy, Patty Sue (Miller, Christopher) 181, 531-532
Maluy, Phyllis Clemene (Likes) 53-54, 93, 124-125, 136, 148, 152, 156, 161, 164, 168, 171, 173, 179, 232, 247, 339, 379, 430, 494, 497-498, 513, 520-522, 533, 544, 548-550, 560, 623, 682, 799
Maluy, Rex Loren 119-122, 152, 163, 180, 190, 513, 569, 572-574, 775
Maluy, Rex Loren II 574
Maluy, Stella S. Chappell 517, 524
Maluy, Thomas Patrick 514-515
Maluy, Trudy Lee (Kareus) 131, 136, 531-532
Maluy, Vernette Mathews Harker 572, 574
Maluy, William Benedict 41, 241, 295, 430, 459, 513-515, 535, 568, 570-572, 577-578, 666-668, 799, 805
Maluy, William James 513-514
Maluy, Wilma Colleen (Walker) 34, 124-125, 152, 179-180, 241, 513, 547, 555, 560-562, 570, 572, 575-576, 578, 730
Mangan, James 322
Mangan, Maureen Ann (Chaffin) 310, 321-324, 770
Manice / Meniece, Josh 353-354, 542
Manning, Zella 277
Manor, Dixie Elaine 339-340
Manti Temple 797
Manzanares 112-113, 115-116, 475, 579, 615-617, 624
Manzanares, Adolpho 624
Manzanares, Agapito Eugenio "Peter" "Pete" 113, 617, 624
Manzanares, Charles 624
Manzanares, Carmela "Carmel" (Martinez) 113, 579, 624
Manzanares, Pedro "Peter" 624
Manzanares, Placida "Priscilla" (Pacheco) 615-618, 624
Manzanares, Raphael Franklin "Frank" 115-116,475, 615, 617, 624
Manzanares, Stella 624
Marciano 612, 614
Marciano, Chuck 614
Mardock 215-218, 232, 466-468
Mardock, John 467-468
Marez, Ernest 115
Marez, Fecundo 115
Marez, Juanita M. (Garcia) 413-414

Marez, Philip 115
Marez, Piedad 413, 416
Marine Corps 674, 791, 796
Marinelli, Albert 179
Marines 218, 458, 491, 531, 635, 771, 788, 791, 796
Markrud, Leo 175-176
Marques, Ascencion (Pacheco) 615-616
Marquette High School 203
Marshall, Bertha 42
Marshall, Charlene 220
Marshall, Kenneth 210-211
Marshall, Elsie Louise Alstatt 118, 120, 122-123, 125, 152, 180, 211, 547
Marshall, Lucille 42
Marshall, Margaret 509
Marshall, Marguerite 42
Marshall, Robert 210-211
Marshall, William H. 210
Martin, Patricia 580
Martin, Shonna (Blaney) 559
Martinez 115, 151, 180, 579, 615-616, 624
Martinez, Alda 580
Martinez, Antonio Jose, Father 615-616
Martinez, Carmela "Carmel" (Manzanares) 579, 624
Martinez, Cora 115
Martinez, Donald 579-580
Martinez, Ellen (Britt) 580
Martinez, Gary 580
Martinez, Glen C. 151, 180 579-580
Martinez, Harold 180, 579
Martinez, James 151, 579
Martinez, Jimmie 180
Martinez, Laurie (Ross) 580
Martinez, Lloyd 579
Martinez, Lucas 445-446, 449, 579
Martinez, Mary 115
Martinez, Priscilla 579-580
Martinez, Susan C. 580
Marysville Grade School 577
Marysville High School 577
Mason 557, 652, 656
Mason, Charlie 270-271, 280
Masonic Cemetery 231, 376, 466, 675
Massey 293, 475
Massey Ferguson 320
Massey, Eben B. 293
Massey, Mary Bryan 293
Massey, Phillip W. 293
Massey, Weston Thomas 293
Matheson 621
Matheson, Carole Ann Pacheco 621
Mathews, Kate Godwin 187
Mathis, J. H 64
Mathson, Edna 267
Matlock, Blanche 339
Matlock, William 382
May, Claude 42
Mayberry, Weldon L. 770
Maynard Steel 577
Maynard, Ernest 168
Maynard, G. E. 535
Maynard, Vera 149, 157
Mayne 53, 55, 176, 194, 528, 717
Mayne, Iona 53
Mayne, Orval 528
Mayne, Oscar 53, 55
Mayne, Rueben 176
Mayne, Willard 176

Palfreyman, Robert Charles 795-796
Palfreyman, Sara (Winward) 796
Palisade Cemetery 383
Palisade Nursing Home 640, 800
Palisade Town Park 380
Palmer 44, 47, 50, 258, 271, 346-347,
  454, 484-485, 685, 688, 770
Palmer Method 47, 50
Palmer, Dorothy Dove (Likes) 484-485
Palmer, Kathy Fern Wright 770
Palmer, Mel 271
Palmer, William 347
Palombo, Fillipi 83
Panama Canal 218, 491
Pappas 21, 32, 48, 230, 250, 454, 607,
  694
Pappas, Chris 21, 32, 230, 250, 454, 607
Pappas, George 48
Parish, Betty 176
Parish, Dale 179
Parish, Lee 177
Park, Reed 644
Parker, Lavantia A. 324
Parodi, Gloria 689
Parrish, Maude (Wynkoop) 779
Parry, Nellene 442
Parsons, Cora Belle Harris 425
Parsons, Fern (Sisler) 30, 194, 591, 689-
  690
Parsons, Ray 689-690
Partridge, Robert W. 83
Pasano, Charles 505
Patten, J. Paul 83
Patten, Jessie Paul 741
Patterson 207, 369, 454, 636, 761
Patterson, Edna Penfield 636
Patterson, George Owthit 636
Patterson, Lyda Mae 369
Paulson 125-126, 129, 180, 632-635, 674,
  726
Paulson, Ernest Edward 125, 180, 633-
  635, 674
Paulson, Eunice Sager 633
Paulson, Jim 634
Paulson, Lanny Duane 635
Paulson, Larry Wayne 126, 129, 180,
  632-635, 726
Paulson, Lawrence 632-633
Paulson, Linda Lucille (Kovach) 635
Paulson, Loren Wayne 635
Paulson, LuAnn Kay (Gauna) 635
Paulson, Martha Marie (Brown) 633, 635
Paulson, Martin 632
Paulson, Shawna Marie 635
Pavola, Fern E. 591
Pavola, Jennie 591
Pavola, John 591
Peach, Caroline 53
Pearce, Russ 196
Pearl Harbor 48, 188, 490, 500-501, 587,
  609, 668, 700
Pease 31, 42
Pease, Marian 31, 42
Pease, Marvin 42
Peck, Wilma J. Kinkhead 770
Pecos River Project 427
Peep, Miriam 176
Peggy Alma 770
Pellen, J. H 76
Penfield 42, 182, 635
Penfield, Edna (Patterson) 42, 182, 635-

636
Penfield, Edward 635
Penner, George Coach 175-176, 627
Pep Club 129, 179, 544, 546, 549, 575-
  576
Perez 615
Perkins 83, 735, 792
Perkins, Earl 792
Perkins, J. B. 83
Perry, Dave 558
Perry, Flora 44
Perry, Mary 44
Perry, Rose 44
Pershing, Alice Kathleen Thomas 129,
  131-133, 142, 152-153, 723, 727
Pershing, Jay 723, 726
Peters, Charley 603
Peters, John 603
Peterson 29, 34, 175, 432-439, 597-601,
  612, 618-619, 688, 742, 763
Peterson, Barbara Lucille 436
Peterson, Beatrice Pacheco 619
Peterson, Carolina Beatrice Pacheco 618
Peterson, Harold 763
Peterson, Helen Overbye (Wilkerson,
  Kendall) 29, 34, 47, 115-116, 175,
  597-601, 609, 612, 688, 741-742
Peterson, Lorenzo Stowell 436
Peterson, Roland 619
Peterson, Velma 437
Peterson, Virgial 600
Peterson, Vivian Lee (Wilkinson) 763
Peterson, Winnie 763
Pfaffenberger, Jewel 175
Philippine Islands 794
Phillipines Liberation Campaign 647
Phillips 4, 20, 35, 41, 59, 83, 115, 121,
  124-125, 151, 154, 180, 213, 219-220,
  256, 267, 316, 425-426, 535-536, 566,
  570, 622, 636-640, 683
Phillips, Bessie Mabel (Brayton) 154, 566
Phillips, Clifton Jackson 636
Phillips, Donna Rodwell 220
Phillips, Erin 219
Phillips, Francis Marion 636
Phillips, Harold K. 640
Phillips, Helen Margaret (Gore) 640
Phillips, Homer Marshall, Sr. 20, 640
Phillips, John 640
Phillips, Kris 219
Phillips, M. 4, 59, 83, 425, 535, 639
Phillips, Murray Hess 121, 124-125, 151,
  180, 263, 316, 622, 637-638
Phillips, Robert Marion"Bob" 59, 83, 267,
  425, 535-536, 570, 636-639
Phillips, Sarah Jane 636
Phillips, Shirley 115
Phipps, Charlotte Candace Cass, 252
Pierson 341
Pig-A-Sus Homestead Sanctuary 200
Pikes Peak Coast 19, 165, 168, 171
Piper Cub Aircraft 276
Pittman, Vonnie G. (Appier) 216
Pixler, Roy 58
Plateau Valley Nursing Home 479
Platt, Alta 44
Player, William 438
Pleasant Plains Friends Church 468-469
Poirier, Walter 47, 454, 694
Poley, Russell 119, 140
Pollock 40, 75, 78, 83-84, 119-124, 126-
  129, 132, 142, 151, 180, 182, 233,

242, 351, 383, 535, 547, 564-566,
  640-642, 644
Pollock Canyon 641, 644
Pollock, Agnes 644
Pollock, Betty (Benson) 120-121, 123,
  180, 547, 640-642
Pollock, Charles 180
Pollock, Elizabeth May 642
Pollock, Elmer Harley "Duke" 641-642
Pollock, Jack 179-180
Pollock, James William "Jimmie" 119-
  122, 180 642
Pollock, Lois Righdenour 40, 242, 642-
  644
Pollock, Mary Anne 640-641
Pollock, May Agnes Hay 641
Pollock, Norma (Gobbo) 127-129, 132,
  142, 642, 644
Pollock, Norma Lois (Gobbo) 242, 642
Pollock, Robert 124, 151, 180
Pollock, Veva 644
Pollock, Walter Henry "Walt" 126, 151,
  180,242, 564-566, 642
Pollock, William Ernest "Bill" "Willie"
  40, 84, 119, 182, 535, 640-642, 644
Pollock, William Hill, Sr. 640-644
Pollock, William Hill., Jr. 78, 83, 641-
  642, 644
Pollock, Wlater Henry "Walt" 642
Pollock,Jim 642
Pomona School 608
Pool, Ray 530
Poole, Ruth 44
Pork Barrel Cafe 193, 195, 200
Porter 40, 115, 119, 150, 176, 180, 182,
  232-233, 534, 537, 671-672, 761, 783-
  784, 786
Porter, Annie Elizabeth "Eliza" (Young)
  783-784
Porter, Clarence 115, 150, 176
Porter, Dewey 761
Porter, Dr. 534, 537
Porter, Eliza 783
Porter, Gertrude 233
Porter, Inez 40, 119, 150, 180, 182, 303,
  759
Porter, James Stephen 671
Porter, May 672
Porter, May Belle (Sanders) 40, 42, 44,
  112-113, 115, 155, 157, 159-161, 407,
  671
Porter, Vivian 180
Porton, Janet 371
Post, Charlie 645-646
Post, Clifford 645
Post, Linda Louise (Dalton) 134-135, 181,
  645, 647
Post, Mableann (Hawthorne) 131, 133-
  137, 151, 181, 209, 426, 596, 645
Post, Mamie 426
Post, Maymie Grace Hull 151, 321, 645
Post, Reva Sue (Terrell) 135-136, 596,
  645-647
Post, Vera Marie (Terrell) 181, 596, 645-
  647
Post, William Henry 645
Postma, Janke "Jennie" (Slaugh) 692
Postma, John 692
Postmaster 35-39, 57, 260, 262, 308, 448,
  694, 699-700, 716
Postmistress 32, 38, 229, 401, 758

833

Wynkoop, Leona Belle (Justice) 127, 129, 143, 779-782
Wynkoop, Lilie Mae Austell 779
Wynkoop, Lois Mae (Roofener) 779-780
Wynkoop, Lovey Leora 779
Wynkoop, Margaret Henderson 781-782
Wynkoop, Mary May (Young) 143, 781
Wynkoop, Maude Parrish 779
Wynkoop, Paul Glenn 143, 781, 779-780
Wynkoop, Rush Ivan 779-782
Wynkoop, Stanley Rush 126, 143, 779-782
Wynkoop, Virgie Anna (Brown) 143, 779-782
Wynonna 199

— Y —

Yates 40, 47, 115, 156, 246, 258, 433, 454, 651, 654-655, 657, 660
Yates, Billy Ray 654
Yates Eldon Lloyd 654-655
Yates, Claire 115
Yates, Connie 655
Yates, Debbie 655
Yates, Denise 655
Yates, Dennis 655
Yates, Diana 655
Yates, Dolores 655
Yates, Duayne 655
Yates, Edgar Lawrence 654
Yates, Eldon Levi 44, 175-176, 660
Yates, Eldon Lloyd 654-655
Yates, Faust M. 40, 47, 115
Yates, Judy 655
Yates, Kenneth Raverne 644-655
Yates, Lawrence 654-655, 657-658
Yates, Lorry 655, 660
Yates, Maudie Agnes Raver 113-114, 156, 245-247, 651-652, 660, 677
Yates, Richard Wesley 654
Yates, Shawn 655
Yates, Sheila 655
Yates, Steven 655
Yates, Tamara 655
Yates, Theresa 655
Yates, Wayne Ellsworth 754
Yeasley, Donna Jean Hamby 208
Young 50, 134-135, 175-177, 181, 235, 319, 323, 330, 427-428, 442, 446, 595, 714, 729-732, 738, 757, 779-798
Young, Annie Elizabeth "Eliza" Porter 783-784
Young, Bailey Tomlinson 729
Young, Betty Jo (Anderson) 181, 783, 786, 798, 789-790, 796-797
Young, Chad Joseph 796
Young, Charles 796
Young, Clyn 784
Young, Curt 323
Young, Dixie Lew 176-177
Young, Darroll 784
Young, Dorothy (Nowland) 786-788, 790
Young, Ed 643
Young, Edith 595, 714, 783, 787, 795
Young, Frances Jo 181, 757, 798
Young, Gabby Gabriell 790
Young, Gene (Hacking) 786
Young, Geraldine 784

Young, George 428
Young, Grant 796
Young, Hallie Jean 134-135, 797-798
Young, Harold Francis 596, 786-788, 795-797
Young, Helen (Weeks) 181, 792-793, 795-796
Young, Ida Maude 428-429
Young, Ivol 235
Young, Jack 784
Young, James Loyd 786
Young, John R. 783
Young, John William 181, 675, 730, 783, 797-798
Young, Kathryn "Kathy" (Roper) 181, 792-793, 795-796
Young, Kendall Washburn 786-788, 790, 796
Young, Leslie Ann 135, 181, 291, 797-798
Young, Lorenzo Dow 385, 783-784
Young, Lou 419
Young, Loyd 784, 786
Young, Marge 792
Young, Mary Wynkoop 143, 781
Young, May Theda 784
Young, Mildruff 784-785
Young, Naida Kay (Westwood) 135, 792-793, 795-796
Young, Neta (Palfreyman) 181, 792-793, 795-796
Young, Neta Marie 786
Young, Neta Washburn 783-787, 789, 791
Young, Nicholas Scott 796
Young, Rebecca "Becky" (Olson) 181, 792-793, 795-796
Young, Richard Harvey "Ricky" 792
Young, Richard Washburn "Dick" 783, 786-788, 791, 796
Young, Ray 759, 781-782
Young, Scott W. 181
Young, Tamar 784
Young, Virginia 175
Young, Von 784
Young, William "L" 786
Young, William Lorenzo 783-786, 790
Young, William Richard 796
Young, William Richard "Bill" 319, 427, 442, 596, 783-784, 791, 794
Yourdon 177, 677, 679
Yourdon, Charlie Edward 679
Yourdon, Floyd 177
Yourdon, Frances Schunter 677
Yourdon, Marvin 177

— Z —

Zahnen, Myrtle Price (Hamby) 799-800
Zahnen, Paul 799-800
Zaldain, Pete 46
Zeller, John Joseph 83
Zeller, Mary 765
Ziegler, Esther 119-120, 211, 644

841